Tuttle

Concise
Indonesian
Dictionary

Tuttle

Concise Indonesian Dictionary

Indonesian–English
English–Indonesian

A.L.N Kramer, Sr., Willie Koen

Completely revised and updated by
Katherine Davidsen

TUTTLE Publishing

Tokyo | Rutland, Vermont | Singapore

"Books to Span the East and West"

Tuttle Publishing was founded in 1832 in the small New England town of Rutland, Vermont [USA]. Our core values remain as strong today as they were then—to publish best-in-class books which bring people together one page at a time. In 1948, we established a publishing office in Japan—and Tuttle is now a leader in publishing English-language books about the arts, languages and cultures of Asia. The world has become a much smaller place today and Asia's economic and cultural influence has grown. Yet the need for meaningful dialogue and information about this diverse region has never been greater. Over the past seven decades, Tuttle has published thousands of books on subjects ranging from martial arts and paper crafts to language learning and literature—and our talented authors, illustrators, designers and photographers have won many prestigious awards. We welcome you to explore the wealth of information available on Asia at **www.tuttlepublishing.com**.

Published by Tuttle Publishing,
an imprint of Periplus Editions (HK) Ltd.

www.tuttlepublishing.com

Copyright @ 1993 Charles E. Tuttle
Publishing Co. Inc.
Copyright @ 2007, 2014 Periplus
Editions (HK) Ltd.

Library of Congress Control No:
2006930897
ISBN 978-0-8048-4477-2

26 25 24 23 22   7 6 5 4 3
2203TP   Printed in Singapore

Distributed by:

North America, Latin America & Europe
Tuttle Publishing, 364 Innovation Drive,
North Clarendon, VT 05759-9436 USA.
Tel: 1(802) 773-8930 | Fax: 1(802) 773-6993
info@tuttlepublishing.com
www.tuttlepublishing.com

Asia Pacific
Berkeley Books Pte. Ltd.
3 Kallang Sector #04-01,
Singapore 349278
Tel: (65) 6741-2178 | Fax: (65) 67414-2179
inquiries@periplus.com.sg
www.tuttlepublishing.com

Indonesia
PT Java Books Indonesia
Kawasan Industri Pulogadung
Jl. Rawa Gelam IV No. 9, Jakarta 13930
Tel: (62) 21 4682-1088 | Fax: (62) 21 461-0206
crm@periplus.co.id
www.periplus.com

Contents

Introduction To This Edition

A brief introduction to Indonesian

Indonesia is the world's fourth-largest nation with a population of over 200 million people. The national language is Indonesian, which in 1990 was spoken by an estimated 67% of people, and was the mother tongue to around 27 million. Indonesian acts as a unifying force among speakers of around 750 regional dialects across the archipelago. Indonesian is also understood in Singapore and Malaysia, as it is mutually intelligible with Malay, thus making it one of the major languages of Southeast Asia. Indonesian belongs to the Malayo-Polynesian subgroup of Austronesian languages, and is therefore distantly related to languages as diverse as Malagasy, Cham, Tagalog, Maori and Fijian. It is a very modern language, having been deliberately cultivated from the Riau variety of Malay by the Indonesian nationalist movement, as preparation for its role as the official language of the new Indonesian state in 1945. Its ability to absorb new influences yet repackage them in a typically Indonesian way makes it highly dynamic in its interaction with other languages, both local, foreign, dead and living, but also susceptible to regional variation and inclined to inconsistency, particularly in spellings of borrowed words. Regional languages such as Sundanese and Javanese, being the mother tongue of an even larger number of Indonesians, constantly influence Indonesian not only in terms of vocabulary borrowings, but also collocations, sentence structure and idioms. The similarity in structure and vocabulary of Indonesian and the regional languages enables both parties to exert influence on each other, adding a local flavor, or additional tone or register.

Indonesian is considered a relatively easy language to learn. It is almost completely free of irregularities. Adjectives follow the noun, as in French. Word order is flexible, although it generally follows a S V O (subject verb object) pattern. Indonesian is rich in verbs, with single words which translate into a complicated phrase in English (eg. *mengupil* = to pick your nose, *berjinjit-jinjit* = to walk on tiptoe). Words may also be left out if the context is clear, making the language succinct and snappy.

Pronunciation in Indonesian is similar to Spanish or Italian. Accents vary, but the standard pronunciation below is a guide.

Vowels:		Can be short or long.	
	a	long, as in *father*;	short, as in *cappuccino*
	e	most commonly as in *loosen* (swallowed "shwa" sound); occasionally as in *egg*. In older texts this is written as **é**	
	i	long, as in *marine*;	short, as in *sit*
	o	long, as in *open*;	short, as in *box*
	u	long, as in *blue*;	short, as in *push*

Diphthongs:	**ai**	as in *aisle*
	au	as in *sauerkraut*

Consonants:		as in English, except for:
	c	like **ch** in *child*
	g	always hard, as in *gum*, never soft as in *gem*
	kh	throaty sound as in *loch*
	ng	as in *thing*
	ngg	as in *finger* (ng+g)
	r	rolled, as in Spanish

Dictionaries of Indonesian

There currently exist a substantial number of dictionaries of Indonesian, both monolingual and bilingual, produced both overseas and locally. There is a variety of dictionaries from Indonesian into English, Dutch, German, French, Korean and most recently, Mandarin, while across the archipelago you can find dictionaries dealing with Indonesian and the larger regional languages, such as Javanese, Sundanese, Minangkabau and so on. Monolingual Indonesian dictionaries, which are almost all local publications, cover not only general meanings and usage, but also specific fields such as economics, engineering, law and other areas with specific jargon.

Indonesian dictionaries for English-speakers and those learning

English are numerous, but differ in terms of quality and date of publication. The most widely-used publication for both target groups would still have to be Echols and Shadily's *Kamus Indonesia Inggris* and *Kamus Inggris Indonesia*, with its wide range of lexis, much of which is still used today. However, these volumes were first published in the 1960s and '70s, and despite revisions, do not cover the development of Indonesian since the onset of political reform in 1998 and the wide-ranging influence of globalization and the Internet. Locally-published dictionaries often include such new entries and word forms, but lack accuracy and authenticity in their English translations. On the other hand, foreign publications tend to use rather archaic Indonesian terms, reflecting their authors' distance from the Indonesian heartbeat. A dictionary which reflects both modern Indonesian usage today as well as correct, authentic English is sorely needed. This revised and updated **Tuttle Concise Indonesian–English/English–Indonesian Dictionary** hopes to be a quality bilingual dictionary for both foreigners in Indonesia or those taking Indonesian studies, and the huge number of Indonesians learning English—in short, a useful and reliable resource for everyone who is interested in learning Indonesian or English.

This dictionary was originally published in 1993 by A.L.N. Kramer and Willie Koen, itself being a revision of *Van Goor's Indonesian Dictionary* of 1966. The present edition aims to move away from the emphasis on Dutch and Malay influences, as well as adding new terminology, improving accuracy and authenticity, including common collocations and phrases, identifying parts of speech and making the dictionary more useful for both speakers of English and Indonesian alike. Unlike most Indonesian dictionaries, this edition does not presume prior knowledge of Indonesian word structure, a necessity for negotiating most quality Indonesian dictionaries. For example, the word *melihat* is listed twice, under *melihat* as well as its base, *lihat*, whereas in most dictionaries the user would have to recognize the base *lihat* before looking for the word under L. By doing this, we hope to cater for the non-academic user as well as students of the language.

Selection of entries

No dictionary is ever "complete," ie. contains every single word of a language. This dictionary attempts to reflect general, everyday usage that will be understood throughout Indonesia and the English-speaking world. It includes many English words that are important to high school students and language learners. American spelling is used, but some British alternatives are included. Indonesian entries cover survival language for tourists, common everyday words, culture (dance, art, history, traditions etc.) and language both heard and seen on the street, thus targeting tourists and students alike. There is naturally some reflection of the editor's own linguistic background, as an Australian having lived 10 years in Java interacting with speakers of Jakarta dialect, Javanese and Sundanese. However, as Java is home to approximately half of Indonesia's population, as well as being the center of government, mass media and industry, the entries in this dictionary still represent spoken and written usage understood by a majority of Indonesians in their standard, national language.

There are differences between spoken (colloquial) and written forms in all languages, and Indonesian and English are no exceptions. Indonesian as heard on the street and informally tends to drop verb prefixes and suffixes, and minimalize repeating words if the context is clear. American English slang, in turn, has been popularized by Hollywood. A knowledge of what is slang or colloquial, and which words appear in written form, is essential for mastering a deeper knowledge of language and culture. This dictionary, while primarily aiming at foreigners learning Indonesian, also hopes to be of use to Indonesian students of English, and to explode the many myths, false friends and incorrect usage that abound in the current atmosphere, where learning English is a high priority not only at school, but at university, in the workplace and among the growing middle-class, which is becoming more and more widely-traveled.

Guide to using this dictionary

The dictionary is divided into two sections, Indonesian–English and English–Indonesian, followed by a list of quick reference for numbers, dates and time, and colors. Entries are listed alphabetically, in the following order:

menghalangi	entry (in bold, blue type)
halang: halangi	first word is not found (or commonly used) alone. Sub-entries (derived words) follow after semi-colon. Subsequent sub-entries are in the same bold font, but black.
v	word type (see list of dictionary symbols). This is not always given if there is no single word form in the other language: eg. **cas** charge (could be *n*, *v*)
child *n* **children**	irregular plurals are given after the noun symbol *n*
put *v* **put put**	irregular past tense forms (simple past and past perfect) are given after the verb symbol *v*
[nait]	Indonesian phonetic pronunciation of an irregularly-spelled word (see guide on page viii)
malam	meaning (in plain type)
session, meeting; hearing	Similar meanings are divided by commas, while different meanings are separated with a semi-colon
~ *tiri* stepmother; *anak* ~ mother and child	The preceding entry or sub-entry is indicated by ~ in common phrases, collocations or idioms (in italics). In the example on the left, ~ represents *ibu*.

out-of-date (of a joke) to (be able to) speak or use a language	Round brackets either contain additional information Or they may contain a possible additional meaning
baik ... maupun ... both ... and ...	... represents any word, in a set phrase
bersih, mem-bersihkan, pem-bersihan **nutty ← nut**	All entries are grouped, where possible, with sub-entries, generally in alphabetical order. Related entries which do not follow alpha-betically have a left-pointing arrow indicat-ing that they come from a base word.
abis → habis **went → go**	A right-pointing arrow shows an entry for further information or reference; or the base of an irregular past tense verb form.

General principles on selection and classification of entries

The following notes explain the process of selecting and classifying the entries:

SELECTION OF ENTRIES

- all base or root forms are listed. Entries with no meaning alone are referred directly to the derived forms. eg. **lamin → kelamin, pelaminan**
- only common or useful derived forms are included in this concise dictionary
- the selected entries and derived forms are those that appear in everyday life and conversation, simple texts and are of cultural value (food, arts, tourism etc.).

SPELLING

- The most common forms of spelling have been listed first (often after being checked on Google searches). Other, sub-standard, old or other spellings still visible are then listed. Common spelling variations may be listed as entries in the dictionary, but these will usually refer the reader to the most common, standard spelling.
- The accented **e** (**é**) has been used to indicate pronunciation *only* in the list of entries. Collocations and examples do not make use of **é**, as it is not standard in written Indonesian. If readers do need to check the pronunciation of a collocation for example, they could look up the component words.

PARTS OF SPEECH (*n v adj adv conj* etc.)

- entries which are difficult to categorize into parts of speech are *not* marked with *n v adj adv conj* etc. This is due to linguistic differences between Indonesian and English. The author has tried where possible to indicate how the word is used through examples or collocations, where there is no part of speech listed.

COLLOCATIONS (two or more words together)

- collocations beginning with the entry are listed first, followed by collocations where the entry is the second part, and lastly collocations or phrases of more than two words. Collocations chosen are common and useful ones: these may give information as to meaning. The author has also focused on including collocations which are not directly translatable.

SAMPLE SENTENCES

- In this dictionary, the author has only included these where they assist understanding of the word's meaning and use.

Dictionary symbols

The following list gives the symbols used in this dictionary:

abbrev	abbreviation	*interj*	interjection
adj	adjective	*Isl*	Islamic, Muslim
adv	adverb	*Jav*	Javanese
arch	archaic	*lit*	literary
art	article	*m*	male
aux	auxiliary (helping) verb	*mil*	military
		n	noun
Budd	Buddhist	*neg*	negative, or with a negative meaning
Cath	Catholic		
child	children's language	*pl*	plural
Chr	Christian	*pol*	polite
coll	colloquial	*pref*	prefix
conj	conjunction	*prep*	preposition
derog	derogatory, rude	*pron*	pronoun
eg	for example	*resp*	respectful
ejac	ejaculation	*s*	singular
esp	especially	*sl*	slang
etc	et cetera, and so on	*suf*	suffix
euph	euphemism	*Sum*	Sumatran usage
excl	exclamation	*tit*	title
f	female	*usu*	usually
form	formal	*v*	verb
gr	greeting	~	(base word +)
Hind	Hindu	→	comes from the base word
inf	informal		
interrog	interrogative, question word	←	see following entries

Acknowledgments

It has been both an honour and an enriching experience to update this dictionary. The editor would like to thank everyone involved in the project. In particular, thanks to Eric M. Oey of Periplus for his enthusiasm and support; Associate Professor Stuart O. Robson of Monash University for his thoughtful suggestions, proof-reading and constant encouragement; Nancy Goh of Periplus for her detailed editing, checking and helpful suggestions; Tony Mansanulu for his patient and thorough editing and explanations; Judo Suwidji and Kiki at Java Books in Jakarta; countless friends who cannot be named one by one but to whom I am forever grateful; *keluarga besar* Sumirat and *keluarga besar* Moch. Yunus, my family here in Indonesia, as is the household of Fauzi Bowo; my own family in Melbourne, always supportive, interested and curious; my students over the years, who show me how they learn language; and finally JS, always my first and last port of call for checks on usage, language and other inside information. I cannot thank you all enough.

References

Abdul Kadir Usman (2002). *Kamus Umum Bahasa Minangkabau Indonesia*. Anggrek Media, Padang.

Abdul Rahman bin Yusop (1975). *Collins Gem Malay Dictionary: Malay–English English–Malay*. HarperCollins.

Echols, John M. & Hassan Shadily (1994). *Kamus Indonesia–Inggris: an Indonesian–English Dictionary*. Direvisi & diedit oleh John U. Wolff & James T. Collins. PT Gramedia Pustaka Utama, Jakarta.

Echols, John M. & Hassan Shadily (1975). *Kamus Inggris–Indonesia: an English–Indonesian Dictionary*. PT Gramedia, Jakarta.

Hajek, John & Tilman, Alexandre Vital (2001). *East Timor Phrasebook*. Lonely Planet, Melbourne.

Hawkins, Joyce M. (1990). *The New Oxford School Dictionary*. Oxford University Press, Oxford.

Hornby, A.S. (1995). *Oxford Advanced Learner's Dictionary of Current English*. Editor: Jonathan Crowther. Fifth edition. Oxford University Press, Oxford.

Maman S. Mahayana, Nuradji & Totok Suhardiyanto (1997). *Kamus Ungkapan Bahasa Indonesia*. PT Grasindo/Gramedia Widiasarana Indonesia, Jakarta.

McGlynn, John H. (ed). (1998). *Language and Literature*. Indonesian Heritage Series, vol. 10. Archipelago Press, Singapore.

Menayang, Jan F. (2004). *Kamus Melayu Manado–Indonesia Indonesia–Melayu Manado*. IPCOS, Jakarta.

Panitia Kamus Lembaga Basa & Sastra Sunda (1994). *Kamus Umum Basa Sunda*. Penerbit Tarate Bandung.

Pusat Bahasa, Departemen Pendidikan Nasional (2002). *Kamus Besar Bahasa Indonesia*. Edisi Ketiga. Balai Pustaka, Jakarta.

Robson, Stuart (2004). *Welcome to Indonesian: a Beginner's Survey of the Language*. Tuttle, Singapore.

Robson, S. & Singgih Wibisono (2002). *Javanese English Dictionary*. Periplus, Hong Kong.

R.R. Hardjadibrata (2003). *Sundanese–English Dictionary*. Pustaka Jaya, Jakarta.

S. Prawiroatmodjo (1995). *Bausastra Jawa–Indonesia: Jilid I Abjad A–Ny*. Edisi ke-2. PT Toko Gunung Agung, Jakarta.

S. Prawiroatmodjo (1981). *Bausastra Jawa–Indonesia: Jilid II Abjad Ny–Z*. Edisi ke-2. Gunung Agung, Jakarta.

S. Wojowasito (2000). *Kamus Umum Belanda Indonesia*. IBVT/PT Ichtiar Baru van Hoeve, Jakarta.

Sahanaya, Wendy & Tan, Albert (2001). *Oxford Study Indonesian Dictionary*. Oxford University Press, Melbourne.

Sinclair, John (editor-in-chief) (1995). *Collins Cobuild English Dictionary*. Harper-Collins Publishers, London.

Simorangkir, J.C.T., Rudy T. Erwin & J.T. Prasetyo (1995). *Kamus Hukum*. Bumi Aksara, Jakarta.

Stevens, Alan M. & A. Ed. Schmidgall-Tellings (2004). *A Comprehensive Indonesian–English Dictionary*. Ohio University Press, Athens USA.

Susi Moeimam & Steinhauer, Hein (2005). *Kamus Belanda–Indonesia*. PT Gramedia Pustaka Utama, Jakarta.

Taniguchi, Goro (1995). *Kamus Standar Bahasa Jepang–Indonesia*. Edisi revisi. Dian Rakyat, Jakarta Timur.

Memperkenalkan bahasa Inggris

Bahasa Inggris yang berasal dari rumpun bahasa Germania dibawa oleh suku-suku Jerman yaitu orang Angle, Saxon dan Jute masuk ke kepulauan Britania sekitar abad kelima Masehi. Sejak orang Norman menduduki daerah tersebut pada tahun 1066, banyak kata yang berasal dari bahasa Perancis mulai masuk ke dalam bahasa Inggris. Selama masa kejayaan Kerajaan Inggris, bahasa Inggris disebarluas-kan melalui perdagangan dan penjajahan di Amerika Utara, Afrika bagian selatan, India, Australia dan Selandia Baru. Di setiap tempat baru, bahasa Inggris berkembang dengan cara tersendiri, terutama karena terpengaruh oleh pergaulan dengan para penduduk dan bahasa setempat. Daya serap bahasa Inggris yang tinggi terhadap kata-kata asing mengakibatkan sistem ejaan dan lafalnya menjadi tidak teratur. Sampai kini bahasa Inggris tetap merupakan bahasa yang penting dalam bidang perdagangan, teknologi dan perhubungan di seantero dunia, terutama setelah munculnya proses globalisasi dan jaringan internet yang amat populer. Sesungguhnya bahasa Inggris telah menjadi milik dunia, karena mayoritas penuturnya terdiri dari orang yang memakainya sebagai bahasa kedua.

Meskipun begitu, bahasa Inggris tidak mudah dikuasai. Tantangan untuk pelajar, antara lain, termasuk pemilihan bentuk kata kerja, penggunaan *a* dan *the*, serta bentuk jamak dan kata kerja yang tidak seragam namun harus dihafalkan. Memang banyaknya pilihan ben-tuk kata kerja dapat menghasilkan arti yang persis dan tepat dari segi waktu, juga seperti dalam bahasa Jepang. Susunan kalimat pada hakikatnya terdiri atas subyek, kata kerja dan obyek, meskipun beberapa kata sambung mengharuskan perubahan dalam susunan kalimat, seperti rumpun bahasa Germania pada umumnya. Satu hal yang berbeda dengan Bahasa Indonesia adalah kata sifat yang men-dahului kata benda dalam bahasa Inggris.

Berikut adalah pemandu cara pengucapan kata dalam bahasa Inggris, dengan memakai sistem fonetik Bahasa Indonesia. Namun, setiap kata di kamus ini yang tidak diucapkan sesuai dengan pedoman berikut, akan dijelaskan menurut ejaan Indonesia dalam kurung persegi setelah keterangan mengenai jenis kata.

huruf hidup dalam bahasa Inggris	panjang	pendek
a	**é** *(cake, late)*	diantara **a** & **e** *(cat, man)*
e	**i** *(cheese, theme)*	**é** *(pet, neck)*
i *y*	**ai** *(mine, light, fly, eye)*	**i** *(hit, thin, quickly, pyramid)*
o	**ou** *(hole, stone)*	**ok** (seperti bahasa Jawa) *(pot, dog)*
u	**u** *(rude, huge)*	**a** *(cup, hut)*

huruf hidup dalam bahasa Inggris	cara lafal	contoh kata
ai *ay (a panjang)*	**é**	*plain, aim, play, day*
au *aw*	**o** (pendek)	*cause, audio, paw, awful*
ee (e panjang) *ea ** *ei **	**i**	*green, see, leaf, ear, receive, either*
ea * *ei **	**é**	*bear, great, eight, neigh*
ei *	**ai**	*height*
ey	**é** **i**	*they, hey alley, key*
ie (i panjang)	**ai**	*pie, applied*
oa *ow * (o panjang)*	**ou**	*road, oar, show, own*
oi *oy*	**oi**	*coin, oil, boy, toy*
oo	**u**	*pool, cook*
ou *ow**	**au**	*mouse, out, how, owl*
ue *ew (u panjang)*	**u** **u**	*blue, clue, dew, ewe*

*terdapat di lebih dari satu baris, yaitu ada beberapa cara pengucapannya.

huruf mati dalam bahasa Inggris	cara lafal	contoh kata
c	• **s** sebelum huruf **e, i** • **k** sebelum huruf lain	*cent, acid* *cat, action*
ch	**c**	*child, match*
g	• **j** sebelum huruf **e, i** • **g** sebelum huruf lain	*general, gin* *gate, green, agree*
kn	**n**	*knee, knot*
ph	**f**	*phone, graph*
qu	**kw** diikuti dengan huruf hidup	*quick, queen*
r	• jelas terdengar (logat Amerika) • kurang terdengar; membuat huruf hidup didepannya lebih panjang (logat Inggris & Australia)	*car* [kar] *car* [ka]
sh	**sy**	*shell, ash*
th	• Tidak ada padanan dalam Bahasa Indonesia. Ada yang 'tebal'; • Ada pula yang 'tipis' (mirip huruf *dhal* dalam bahasa Arab): Bukan **t**	*thick, path* *thin, mother*
wh	**w**	*wheel, when*
x	**ks**	*xylophone, box*
z	**z** (bukan **j**)	*zoo, crazy*

Quick Reference Guide

Days of the week (Nama Hari)

Monday: *hari Senin*
Wednesday: *hari Rabu*
Friday: *hari Jumat*
Sunday: *hari Minggu*

Tuesday: *hari Selasa*
Thursday: *hari Kamis*
Saturday: *hari Sabtu*

Months of the year (Nama Bulan)

January: *bulan Januari*
March: *bulan Maret*
May: *bulan Mei*
July: *bulan Juli*
September: *bulan September*
November: *bulan November*

February: *bulan Februari*
April: *bulan April*
June: *bulan Juni*
August: *bulan Agustus*
October: *bulan Oktober*
December: *bulan Desember*

Colors (Nama Warna)

blue: *biru*
dark blue: *biru tua*
green: *hijau*
yellow: *kuning*
pink: *merah muda, merah jambu*
orange: *oranye, jingga*

light blue: *biru muda*
brown: *cokelat*
black: *hitam*
red: *merah*
white: *putih*
purple: *ungu*

Cardinal numbers (Bilangan Pokok)

one: *satu*
three: *tiga*
five: *lima*
seven: *tujuh*
nine: *sembilan*
eleven: *sebelas*
thirteen: *tiga belas*

two: *dua*
four: *empat*
six: *enam*
eight: *delapan*
ten: *sepuluh*
twelve: *dua belas*
fourteen: *empat belas*

fifteen: *lima belas*
twenty-one: *dua puluh satu*
forty: *empat puluh*
one hundred: *seratus*
one thousand: *seribu*

twenty: *dua puluh*
thirty: *tiga puluh*
fifty: *lima puluh*
two hundred: *dua ratus*
two thousand and six: *dua ribu enam*

five thousand: *lima ribu*
twenty thousand: *dua puluh ribu*
one hundred thousand: *seratus ribu*

ten thousand: *sepuluh ribu*
fifty thousand: *lima puluh ribu*
one million: *sejuta*

Times of the day (Pembagian Waktu)

morning (12 midnight to 12 noon)

afternoon (12 noon to 6 p.m.)

evening (6 p.m. to 12 midnight)

malam (jam 12–jam 4),
pagi (jam 4–10.30)
siang (jam 10.30–jam 3),
sore (jam 3–jam 6)
malam (jam 6–jam 12)

What time is it? (Jam berapa sekarang?)

one o'clock: *jam satu*
two o'clock: *jam dua*
five (minutes) past two (o'clock): *jam dua lewat lima (menit)*
a quarter past two: *jam dua (lewat) seperempat*
half past two: *jam setengah dua*
a quarter to three: *jam tiga kurang seperempat*
three o'clock: *jam tiga*
three forty: *jam tiga empat puluh*
four a.m., four o'clock in the morning: *jam empat pagi*
four p.m., four o'clock in the afternoon: *jam empat sore*
midday, noon: *jam dua belas siang*
midnight: *jam dua belas malam*
nine p.m.: *jam 21.00 (dua puluh satu)*
half an hour: *setengah jam*
five minutes: *lima menit*

Fractions and decimals (Pecahan dan angka desimal)

half   *setengah*
one third   *sepertiga*
two thirds   *dua pertiga*
one quarter   *seperempat*
one point six (1.6)   *satu koma enam (1,6)*

Ordinal numbers (Bilangan Urutan)

first   *pertama*
third   *ketiga*
fifth   *kelima*
seventh   *ketujuh*
ninth   *kesembilan*
eleventh   *kesebelas*
fifteenth   *kelima belas*
twentieth   *kedua puluh*
twenty-second   *kedua puluh dua*
thirtieth   *ketiga puluh*
fortieth   *keempat puluh*
one hundredth   *keseratus*

second   *kedua*
fourth   *keempat*
sixth   *keenam*
eighth   *kedelapan*
tenth   *kesepuluh*
twelfth   *kedua belas*
nineteenth   *kesembilan belas*
twenty-first   *kedua puluh satu*
twenty-third   *kedua puluh tiga*
thirty-first   *ketiga puluh satu*
fiftieth   *kelima puluh*

Personal pronouns (Kata ganti)

I—*saya; aku* (familiar); *gue, gua* (Jakarta slang)
you—*anda* (neutral, formal); *saudara* (neutral); *kamu* (familiar, to younger people); *engkau, kau* (less common) [name of person]
he (male), she (female), it (object)—*dia; beliau* (very respectful)
we—*kita* (including person addressed); *kami* (excluding person addressed)
you—*kalian; anda sekalian* (formal)
they—*mereka*

Indonesian–English

Indonesian–English

A

aba-aba *n* order, command (in army or at school)

abad *n* century; age, era; ~ *ke-emasan* golden age; **berabad-abad** *adv* for centuries

abadi eternal, everlasting; *cinta* ~ endless love; **mengabadikan** *v* to immortalize

abai *adj* neglectful; **mengabaikan** *v* to neglect, disregard, ignore; **terabaikan** *adj* neglected, ignored

abang *n, m, pron* elder brother; ~ *None* Mr and Miss Jakarta → **bang**

abang: abangan *adj* Javanese Muslim who follows local traditions rather than Islam (*cf.* **santri**)

abdi *n* servant, (in past) slave; ~ *dalem* court servant at a Javanese palace; **mengabdi** *v* to serve; **pengabdian** *n* service, servitude, devotion

abis *coll* → **habis**

abjad *n* alphabet; *menurut* ~ in alphabetical order, alphabetically

abon *n* shredded dry meat, eaten as a side-dish

abonemén *n* subscription, billing

aborsi, abortus *n* abortion; **mengaborsi** *v* to abort (a fetus); *melakukan* ~ to have an abortion

ABRI *abbrev Angkatan Bersenjata Republik Indonesia* Indonesian Armed Forces

absén *adj* not present; **mengabsén** *v* to call the roll

abu *n* ash; ~ *rokok* cigarette ash

abu-abu *adj* gray

AC *abbrev* [a sé] air-conditioner, air-conditioning

acak random, mixed; **mengacak** *v* to scramble, encode; **mengacak-acak** *v* to mess up

acap ~ *(kali)* often

acar *n* finely-cut pickled cucumber, shallot, carrot and chilli, eaten with fried rice, satay etc

acara agenda, program, event; ~ *hari ini* today's program; **pengacara** *n* lawyer, solicitor

acu: acuan *n* reference; ~ *silang* cross-reference; **mengacu** *v* to refer to, to use as a point of reference; ~ *pada hukum negara* following Indonesian law; **mengacukan** *v* to point, refer to; ~ *arah* indicate direction

acuh (don't) care; *tidak/tak* ~ indifferent, not care; ~ *tak* ~ to ignore, take no notice of

acung *v* raise; **acungan** *n* ~ *jempol* thumbs-up; **mengacungkan** *v* to raise, hold up; ~ *tangan* raise your hand

AD *abbrev Angkatan Darat* Army

ada *v* to be (present); to have, exist; ~ *Firman?* Is Firman here?; ~ *apa?* What's up?

What's wrong?; *tidak* ~ there isn't, there aren't, not here; **ketidakadaan** *n* absence, lack of; **ada-ada** ~ *saja* well, I never! Words fail me!; **adakala, adakalanya** *adv* sometimes; **adalah** *v* is, are (followed by a noun); *Rina* ~ *sepupu Dian* Rina is Dian's cousin; *yang menang* ~ *orang Madura* It was the Madurese who won; **adanya** *n* the existence of; *apa* ~ as it is, without any pretensions; **berada** *v* to be somewhere; to exist; *Ibu Menteri* ~ *di Padang* The Minister is in Padang; *adj* well-to-do, well-off; **keberadaan** *n* presence; **keadaan** *n* situation, condition; ~ *darurat* emergency situation; **mengada-ada** *v* to invent, make up; *sungguh* ~ to push your luck; **mengadakan** *v* to do, run, hold, create, organize, make available; ~ *kampanye* to run a campaign; **pengadaan** *n* supply, provision; **seadanya** *adj* what's there; *makan* ~ eat what's there

adab *n* culture, good manners, courtesy; **beradab** *adj* civilized, polite; **peradaban** *n* culture, civilization; ~ *Mesir kuno* ancient Egyptian civilization

adakala, adakalanya *adv* sometimes → **ada**

adalah *v* is, are (followed by a noun); *Rina* ~ *sepupu Dian* Rina is Dian's cousin; *yang menang* ~ *orang Madura* It

was the Madurese who won ← **ada**

adanya *n* the existence of; *apa* ~ as it is, without any pretensions ← **ada**

adat *n* tradition, custom, customary law, esp. of an ethnic group; ~ *istiadat* customs and traditions; ~ *Sunda* Sundanese traditions

adé *pron, coll* little one (used for the youngest or only child) ← **adik**

adegan *n* act, scene; ~ *panas* steamy scene

adi- *pref* higher; **adibusana** *n* haute couture; **adidaya, adikuasa** *negara* ~ superpower; **adikarya** *n* masterpiece; **adipura** *n* tidy town, cleanest town

adik *n* younger brother or sister; ~ *ipar* (younger) brother- or sister-in-law; ~ *laki-laki* (younger) brother; *kakak-ber* ~ siblings; ~ *kandung* (younger) blood brother or sister; ~ *sepupu* cousin (of lower status)

adikarya *n* masterpiece

adil *adj* just, righteous; *Ratu* ~ the Just Ruler, who is believed will save Indonesia (Java) one day; **keadilan** *n* justice; ~ *sosial* social justice; **mengadili** *v* to try someone, put someone on trial; **pengadilan** *n* court of justice or law, trial; ~ *negeri* district court

adipura *n* tidy town, cleanest town

adjéktiva, adjéktif *n* adjective

administrasi *n* administration, management; ~ *negara* public administration; **administrator, administratur** *n* administrator, manager

adon: mengadon *v* to knead; **adonan** *n* batter, dough, mixture

adu, beradu *v* to hit or fight; **mengadu** *v* to complain, report; ~ *domba* to play two parties against each other; **mengadukan** *v* to report someone/something, to make a complaint about; ~ *seseorang ke pengadilan* to sue, take to court; **pengaduan** *n* complaint; *surat* ~ letter of complaint

aduh *ejac* ouch! ow! (expression of pain); *excl* oh! (expression of sorrow); wow!; ~ *sakit!* Ow, that hurts!; ~ *berat sekali* Oh, how difficult!; ~ *cantiknya!* Isn't she beautiful?

aduhai *ejac, lit* oh! *adj* amazing, outstanding; ~ *negeriku* Oh, my beloved country; *pemain yang* ~ a fantastic player

aduk *campur* ~ mixed up; **mengaduk** *v* to stir, mix; ~ *semen* to mix cement

adzan → **azan**

Afganistan, Afghanistan *n* Afghanistan; *orang* ~ Afghan

afiat *sehat wal* ~ in good health

Afrika *n* Africa; *orang* ~ African; ~ *Selatan (Afsel)* South Africa

Aga *orang Bali* ~ the original (pre-Hindu) inhabitants of Bali

agak *adv* rather, somewhat; ~ *gemuk* rather fat; **agaknya** *adv* apparently, it seems

agama *n* religion; ~ *Budha* Buddhism; **beragama** *v* to have a religion; *Siti* ~ *Islam* Siti is Muslim; *adj* religious; **keagamaan** *adj* religious affairs

agar *conj* in order that/to; *Dia belajar keras* ~ *lulus ujian* He studied hard in order to pass the exam

agar, agar-agar *n* a kind of jelly made from seaweed

agén *n* agent, agency, distributor; ~ *koran* news agency; ~ *rahasia* secret agent; ~ *tunggal* sole distributor

agénda *n* agenda; appointment diary

agrowisata *n* agricultural tourism

agung great, high, supreme; *Jaksa* ~ Attorney-General; **keagungan** *n* greatness, majesty; **mengagungkan** *v* to glorify; **mengagung-agungkan** *v* to glorify, place on a pedestal

Agustus *n bulan* ~ August

ah *excl* oh (showing mild annoyance); *ke sana aja* ~! oh, let's just go there! (and stop wasting time)

Ahad → **Minggu**

ahli *n* expert, specialist; member; ~ *bahasa* linguist; ~ *bedah* surgeon; ~ *hukum* legal adviser; ~ *waris* heir; **keahlian** *n* expertise

aib *n* shame

air *n* water; juice; ~ *bah* flood; ~

jeruk orange juice; ~ *ledeng* reticulated water; ~ *liur* saliva; ~ *mata* tears; ~ *minum*, ~ *putih* drinking water; ~ *muka* facial expression; ~ *pasang* high tide, incoming tide; ~ *surut* low tide, outgoing tide; ~ *raksa* mercury; ~ *suci* holy water; ~ *tawar* fresh water; ~ *terjun* waterfall; *buang* ~ to go to the toilet; *cacar* ~ chicken pox; *mata* ~ spring; *pintu* ~ sluice; *tahan* ~ waterproof; *tanah* ~ native country, Indonesia; **berair** *v* juicy, containing water; **mengairi** *v* to irrigate; **pengairan** *n* to irrigation; **perairan** *n* territorial waters, waterworks

ajaib *adj* miraculous, strange; **keajaiban** *n* wonder, miracle; *Tujuh* ~ *Dunia* the Seven Wonders of the World

ajak, mengajak *v* to invite, ask out; to urge; ~ *jalan-jalan* to ask out; ~ *kawin*, ~ *nikah* to ask someone to marry you; **ajakan** *n, inf* invitation → **mengajak**

ajal *n* moment of death; *menemui* ~*nya, sampai* ~*nya* to die

ajar *kurang* ~ rude, badly brought-up; **ajaran** *n* teaching; ~ *agama* religious doctrine; *tahun* ~ academic year, school year; **belajar** *v* to learn, study; **belajar-mengajar** *kegiatan* ~ teaching and learning; **pembelajaran** *n* learning process; **mempelajari** *v* to study something in depth; **mengajar** *v* to teach; **mengajari** *v* to teach

someone; **mengajarkan** *v* to teach something; **pelajar** *n* pupil, student; **pelajaran** *n* lesson; *mata* ~ school subject; **terpelajar** *adj* educated; **pengajar** *n* teacher; **pengajaran** *n* teaching, tuition

aju: mengajukan *v* to forward, propose; to submit

akad *n* contract, agreement; ~ *nikah Isl* Muslim marriage contract, Muslim wedding ceremony

akadémi *n* academy, institute of higher education; ~ *Angkatan Bersenjata (Akabri)* Armed Forces Academy

akal *n* mind, intellect; ~ *budi*, ~ *sehat* intellect, common sense; *mencari* ~ find a way; *kehilangan* ~ to be at one's wits' end; *masuk* ~ make sense; **berakal** *adj* to be intelligent; **mengakali** *v* to find a way; to deceive, play a trick on; *Kita* ~ *saja* We'll find a way

akan *v, aux* will, going to (marks future time); *prep* about, concerning, regarding; *minggu yang* ~ *datang* next week; *sudah lupa* ~ has forgotten about; ~ *tetapi* however; **seakan-akan** *adv* as if, as though

akar *n* root; ~ *kuadrat* square root; *tingkat* ~ *rumput* grassroot level; **berakar** *adj* rooted; **mengakar** *v* to take root

akbar *adj* big, great; *Allahu* ~ Allah is great; *tablig* ~ big Islamic meeting

akhir *n* end; ~*nya* finally; ~-~ *ini*

recently; **akhiran** *n* ending, suffix; **berakhir** *v* to end; **mengakhiri** *v* to end, finish something; **terakhir** *adj* last, final, latest

akhirat *n* the hereafter

aki *n* vehicle battery; **mengisi** ~ to charge a car battery

akibat *n* result, consequence; *conj* due to, consequently; ~*nya* as a result; **berakibat** *v* to have consequences, implications; **mengakibatkan** *v* to result in

akil ~ *balig* of age, ready to take on religious obligations, etc

akrab *adj* close, intimate, friendly; **keakraban** *n* closeness, intimacy

aksara *n* letter, character, alphabet; ~ *Cina* Chinese characters

aksén *n* accent; **beraksén** *v* to have a touch of; *rumah* ~ *Jawa* a house with Javanese-inspired decor → **logat**

aksi *n* action, demonstration; ~ *militer* military action by the Dutch, 1945–50; ~ *sepihak* unilateral action; **beraksi** *v* to take action, do something

akta, akte *n* official document, certificate; ~ *lahir*, ~ *kelahiran* birth certificate; ~ *nikah*, ~ *pernikahan* marriage certificate

aktif *adj* activated, active, on, working; *HP saya masih belum* ~! My mobile phone still isn't working!; ~ *di kampus* involved in many university activities; **aktivitas** *n* activity; **beraktivitas** *v* to be doing something

aktual *adj* latest, up-to-date; *berita* ~ current affairs

aku *pron* I, me; **mengaku** *v* to admit, confess, acknowledge; to claim; ~ *salah* to admit guilt; **mengakui** *v* to admit something; to acknowledge, recognize; *Hak-hak TKW harus diakui* The rights of migrant workers must be recognized; **pengakuan** *n* confession, acknowledgment; ~ *dosa* confession (Catholic)

akuntan *n* accountant; **akuntansi** *n* accounting

akur *v* agree, agreed, get along; *Keluarga itu sangat* ~ That family gets along very well

AL *abbrev Angkatan Laut* Navy

a.l. *antara lain* among others

ala *adj* in the style of, à la

alah *ejac* (expression of exasperation) ~! *Lampunya rusak* Damn, the light's broken!

alaikum → **salam alaikum**

alam *n* nature, world; ~ *(ter)buka* open-air; ~ *semesta* the whole natural world; *dua* ~ two habitats; *ilmu pengetahuan* ~ *(IPA)* science; *sumber daya* ~ natural resources; **alami, alamiah** *adj* natural

alam: **mengalami** *v* to experience; **pengalaman** *n* experience; **berpengalaman** *adj* experienced, skilled

alamat *n* address; sign, omen; *salah* ~ wrong address or person; **beralamat** *v* to have an address; **mengalamatkan** *v* to address to; to indicate

alang → **halang**

alang-alang *n* tall, coarse grass

alangkah *adv* how ...! what a ...!; ~ *bagusnya!* how beautiful!

alas *n* foundation, basis, base; ~ *kaki,* footwear; **alasan** *n* cause, reason, motive; ~ *yang dicari-cari* pretext; **beralasan** *adj* with reason; *tidak* ~ without reason; **beralaskan** *v* based upon

alat *n* tool, instrument, means; ~ *kelamin* genitals; ~ *kontrasepsi,* ~ *KB* form of contraception; ~ *masak* kitchen utensils; ~ *pembayaran yang sah* legal currency; ~ *pendengaran* sense of hearing; ~ *bantu dengar* hearing aid; ~ *tulis* stationery; **memperalat** *v* to use or take advantage of someone; *Tina diperalat oleh kawannya* Tina was used by her friend; **peralatan** *n* equipment

Albania *n* Albania; *orang* ~, *bahasa* ~ Albanian

album *n* album; ~ *foto* photo album; *mengeluarkan* ~ *baru* to release a new album

alérgi allergy, allergic; **beralérgi** *v* to have an allergy; ~ *terhadap mangga* allergic to mangoes

Al-Fatihah *n* first chapter of the Koran; common prayer

algojo *n* hangman, executioner; *n, sl* butcher, murderer

alhamdulillah *ejac, Isl* thanks be to God; bless you! (when sneezing)

alhasil *conj* in the end, consequently

aliansi *n* alliance; **beraliansi** *v* to be allied with

alih *v* to shift, change position; ~ *bahasa* translation; ~ *profesi* change of career; ~ *teknologi* to upgrade technology; **alih-alih** *conj* instead of; **beralih** *v* to move, change, shift; **mengalih(kan)** *v* to shift something; ~ *perhatian* to shift attention, change the subject; **peralihan** *n* transition, change; *masa* ~ transition period

alim *adj, Isl* pious, religious

alinéa *n* paragraph

alir *flow* **aliran** *n* stream, current; ideology, school, sect; ~ *listrik* electric current; ~ *kepercayaan* unofficial religious movement; **beraliran** *v* to have an ideology; ~ *kiri* leftist; **mengalir** *v* to flow; **pengaliran** *n* flow (esp of money)

alis *n* eyebrow; *mengangkat* ~ to raise one's eyebrows

aljabar *n* algebra

Aljazair *n* Algeria; *orang* ~ Algerian

Alkitab *n* the Bible

alkohol *n* alcohol; **beralkohol** *v* to contain alcohol; *minuman* ~ alcoholic drink

Allah *n* God, Allah; ~ *subhanahu wa taala* Allah the Most High; ~*u Akbar* God is great; *demi* ~ by God, for God's sake; *firman* ~ the word of God

almanak *n* calendar; almanac →
kalénder

almarhum *adj, m, Isl* the late;
almarhumah *adj, f, Isl* the
late; ~ *Ibu* my late mother

almari → **lemari**

Almasih *n* the Messiah; *Kenaikan
Isa* ~ Assumption

alot *adj* tough (of meat); heavy-
going

alpukat, apokat, avokat *n* avocado; *jus* ~ avocado drink

Alqur'an, Al-quran, Alquran *n*
the Koran

AL(RI) *abbrev Angkatan Laut
(Republik Indonesia)* (Indonesian) Navy

alu *n* pestle; ~ *lumpang* mortar
and pestle

aluminium *n* aluminium; *atap* ~
aluminium roof

alun: mengalunkan *v* to put
something in motion, sing
something

alun-alun *n* town square

alur *n* groove, channel; ~ *cerita*
plot; **aluran** *n* channel

amal *n* charity; ~ *ibadah* service
to God; *badan* ~ charitable
institution; *konser* ~ charity
concert; **beramal** *v* to give to
charity; *adj* charitable; **mengamalkan** *v* to do something for
charity; to carry out

aman *adj* safe, in peace;
keamanan *n* safety, security;
Dewan ~ (UN) Security Council; **mengamankan** *v* to make
safe, restore order; place in
custody; **pengaman** *n* safety

device; **pengamanan** *n* securing, pacification

amanah, amanat *n* message,
instruction, mandate; *Partai
Amanat Nasional (PAN)*
National Mandate Party;
mengamanatkan *v* to entrust

amarah → **marah**

amat *adv* very, extremely;
kasihan ~! poor thing!;
teramat *sangat* extremely

amat: mengamati *v* to watch
closely, keep an eye on; **pengamat** *n* observer; ~ *politik* political observer; **pengamatan** *n*
observation, monitoring

ambang *n* threshold, doorstep,
verge; ~ *batas* threshold, limit;
~ *kebangkrutan* verge of bankruptcy; ~ *pintu* doorstep, verge

ambang *v* to float, be suspended
in water; **mengambang** *v* to
float

ambar *n* ambergris; *batu ambar*
amber

ambeien *n* hemorrhoids, piles

ambil *v* to take; to subtract; to
bring; ~ *saja* help yourself; ~
bagian to participate, take part
in → **ikut serta**; *Tiga* ~ *dua
sama dengan satu* Three
minus two is one; *Tolong* ~ *air*
Please bring some water;
mengambil *v* to take, get,
fetch; ~ *alih* to take over; ~
keputusan to make a decision;
mengambilkan *v* to get something for someone; **pengambilan** *n* act of taking, removal;
~ *gambar* photo shoot; ~

sumpah taking an oath

ambisi *n* ambition; **berambisi**, **ambisius** *adj* ambitious

ambruk *v* to collapse, break, crash; *jembatan ~* broken bridge

ambulans *n* ambulance

amén: (me)ngamén *v* to sing in the street for money, busk; **pengamén** *n* street singer, busker

Amérika *n* America; *~ Serikat* United States of America; *~ Latin* Latin America

amin *ejac* amen; **mengamini** to agree to, approve of

amis *adj* putrid, smelling fishy; *bau ~* fishy smell

amnésti *n* amnesty

ampas *n* dregs, grounds; *~ kopi* coffee grounds

ampela, empela *n* gizzard; *ati ~* liver and gizzards

amplop *n* envelope; *coll* bribe; *kasih ~* hand over a bribe

ampuh *adj* powerful, potent; *obat yang ~* powerful medicine

ampun *n* mercy, forgiveness, pardon; *ejac* Mercy! (expression of astonishment or disapproval); *minta ~* beg for mercy; *~ deh, macetnya!* I've never seen traffic like it!; **mengampuni** *v* to forgive; **pengampun** *n* *Tuhan Maha ~* God is all-forgiving; **pengampunan** *n* pardon, reprieve, amnesty

Amrik *n, sl* America

amuk amok; **mengamuk** *v* to run amok, go berserk

amunisi, munisi *n* ammunition, munitions; *~ kosong* blanks

anak *n* child; young (of an animal); member of a group; small part of a whole; *~ angkat* adopted child; *~ anjing* puppy; *~ ayam* chick; *~ buah* assistant, staff; *~ bungsu* youngest child; *~ cucu* descendants; *~ emas* favorite; *~ gedongan* rich kid; *~ haram* illegitimate child; *~ jalanan* street kid; *~ kalimat* sub-clause; *~ kapal* crew, sailor; *~ kembar* twins; *~ kolong, ~ tentara* soldier's child; *~ kos* boarder; *~ kucing* kitten; *~ kunci* key; *~ Medan* native of Medan; *~ panah* arrow; *~ perempuan* daughter; *~ perusahaan* subsidiary company; *~ sulung* eldest child; *~ sungai* tributary, creek; *~ tangga* rung of a ladder; *~ tiri* stepchild; **menganaktirikan** *v* to treat as a second-class citizen; *~ tunggal* an only child; *~ yatim* orphan; **anak-anak** *n, pl* children → **kanak-kanak**; **beranak** *v* (of animals) to give birth to, have offspring; *~ pinak* *v* to have descendants; **peranakan** *n* uterus; *adj* of mixed Chinese and Indonesian blood, Straits Chinese; *masakan ~* locally-influenced Chinese food

analisa, analisis *n* analysis; **menganalisa, menganalisir, menganalisis** *v* to analyze

ancam *v* to threaten; **ancaman** *n* threat; **mengancam** *v* to threaten, intimidate; **terancam** *adj* threatened; *harimau Jawa ~ punah* the Javan tiger is threatened with extinction

anda, Anda *pron* you (neutral, without status); *Untuk kenyamanan ~* for your comfort

andai, andaikan, andaikata, andainya, seandainya *conj* if, supposing that; **berandai-andai** *v* to speak hypothetically, imagine; **mengandaikan** *v* to suppose, assume

andal *adj* reliable; **andalan** *n* mainstay, security; **mengandalkan** *v* to rely on, trust

Andalas *n* Sumatra

andil *n* share, contribution

andong *n* four-wheeled horse-drawn carriage in Jogja and Solo

anéh *adj* strange, peculiar; **anéhnya** the strange thing is...; **keanéhan** *n* peculiarity, oddity

anéka *adj* all kinds of, various; *~ jenis* all sorts; *~ macam, ~ ragam* varied; *~ warna* various colors, multicolored; **beranéka ~ ragam** various; **keanékaragaman ~ hayati** biological diversity

angan-angan *n* idea, thought, fantasy; **berangan-angan** *v* to daydream, build castles in the air, fantasize

angdés *n* public minibus in rural areas ← **angkutan désa**

anggap *v* to consider; **anggapan** *n* point of view, opinion; **beranggapan** *v* to be of the

opinion; **menganggap** *v* to consider, regard; *~ enteng* take lightly; *sudah dianggap saudara* considered part of the family

anggar *n* fencing (sport)

anggar: anggaran *n* budget, estimate; *~ rumah tangga* by-laws, budgeted funds; **menganggarkan** *v* to budget

anggota *n* member; *~ badan* limb; *~ DPR* Member of Parliament; *~ kehormatan* honorary member; *~ keluarga* family member; **beranggota** *v* to have members; **beranggotakan** *v* to have a membership, have as members; *PKI dulu ~ jutaan orang* The PKI once had millions of members; **keanggotaan** *n* membership; *kartu ~* membership card

anggrék *n* orchid

angguk, mengangguk *v* to nod; **menganggukkan** *~ kepala* to nod your head

anggun *adj* elegant, stylish, graceful; **keanggunan** *n* grace, style

anggur *n* wine, grapes; *~ putih* white wine; *buah ~* grapes

anggur: menganggur *v* to be unemployed, idle; **pengangguran** *n* unemployment, unemployed person; *~ tersembunyi* hidden unemployment

angin *n* wind, breeze; *~ ribut, ~ topan* cyclone, typhoon; *masuk ~* to catch a cold, feel unwell; *mata ~* point of the compass;

tambah ~ to add air to a tire; **menganginkan** *v* to air (clothes, crackers)

angka *n* figure, numeral, digit; score, mark; ~ *kelahiran* birth rate; ~ *Romawi* Roman numeral

angkasa *n* space, sky; ~ *luar* outer space; *ruang* ~ space; **angkasawan** *n, m* **angkasawati** *n, f* astronaut

angkat *v* to lift; ~ *besi* weightlifting; ~ *tangan* give up; raise your hand; ~ *telepon* to pick up, answer the phone; *orang tua* ~ adoptive parents; **angkatan** *n* generation, year level (at school or university); force; ~ *darat (AD)* army; **berangkat** *v* to depart, leave; **keberangkatan** *n* departure; *pintu* ~ departure gate; **memberangkatkan** *v* to dispatch (a group); *Rombongan ke Medan sudah diberangkatkan* the party to Medan has departed; **mengangkat** *v* to lift or pick up, raise; appoint; to remove, amputate; *diangkat menjadi menteri* to be made a minister; ~ *payudara* to remove a breast; **pengangkatan** *n* appointment (to a position); **perangkat** *n* equipment, tool; **seperangkat** *n* set, suite

angker *adj* spooky, eerie, creepy

angkét *n* survey (form)

angklung *n* bamboo instrument, played in an orchestra

angkot *n, coll* public minibus ← **angkutan kota**

angkuh *adj* arrogant, proud, conceited; **keangkuhan** *n* arrogance, rudeness

angkut *v* to carry, lift, transport; **angkutan** *n* transport, transportation; ~ *darat* land transportation; ~ *kota (angkot)* city transportation; ~ *umum* public transport; **mengangkut** *n* to transport; **pengangkut** *n* carrier; *kapal* ~ *minyak* oil tanker

Angola *n* Angola; *orang* ~ Angolese

angpao, angpau *n* a red envelope containing money, given at Chinese New Year

angsa *n* goose

angsur *v* to pay in instalments; **angsuran** *n* instalment; **berangsur(-angsur)** *adv* gradually, little by little; **mengangsur** *v* to pay in instalments

angus → **hangus**

aniaya: menganiaya *v* to mistreat, oppress; **penganiayaan** *n* oppression, mistreatment; **teraniaya** *adj* oppressed, tyrannized

anjak, beranjak *v* to move, shift; ~ *dewasa* becoming a young adult

anjing *n* dog (also insult); ~ *herder* German shepherd; ~ *ras* pure-breed

anjlok *v* to derail, to fall drastically; *kereta api* ~ derailed train

anjung: anjungan *n* gallery, upper level, ship's bridge; ~ *tunai mandiri (ATM)* automated teller machine (ATM)

anjur: anjuran *n* suggestion; **menganjurkan** *v* to suggest, propose

anoa *n* dwarf buffalo of Sulawesi

antak: berantakan *adj* messy, in a mess

antar, anter *coll* take, escort; ~ *jemput* pick up and take home, door-to-door; **antaran** *n* things taken or carried; **mengantar** *v* to take, escort, accompany; **mengantarkan** *v* to take someone or something; **pengantar, kata** ~ preface

antar- *pref* between; **antarbangsa** *adj* international; **antarbudaya** *adj* cross-cultural; **antarpropinsi** *adj* interprovincial

antara *conj* between; ~ *lain* among others; *di* ~*nya* among them; **perantara** *n* broker, intermediary, go-between

antarbangsa *adj* international

antarbudaya *adj* cross-cultural

antarpropinsi *adj* inter-provincial

antem: berantem *v* to fight, scuffle ← **hantam**

anténa *n* antenna, aerial

antéro *n* whole, entire; **seantéro** ~ *dunia* across the entire world

anti- *pref, adj* against, resistant to; ~ *Barat* anti-Western; ~ *peluru* bullet-proof; ~ *perang* anti-war

antik *adj* quaint; *n* antique

anting *n* earring

antré, antri queue; **antréan** *n* queue; **mengantri** *v* to queue; **pengantri** *n* person who queues

antuk: mengantuk, terantuk-

antuk *adj* sleepy → **kantuk**

anu um, er; *n* so-and-so, what's-its-name; *si Anu* So-and-So

anugerah *n* gift, grace, blessing; **menganugerahi** *v* to confer upon; **penganugerahan** *n* presentation of an award

anut, menganut *v* to follow; **penganut** *n* follower, believer; ~ *agama Katolik* a Catholic

anyam, menganyam *v* to weave, plait, braid; **anyaman** *n* plait, braid; *kursi* ~ wicker chair

anyelir *n* carnation

anyir *adj* fishy-smelling, rancid

apa *interrog, n* what; ~ *lagi* what else; ~ *saja* anything; ~ *kabar?* how are you?; ~ *boleh buat* it can't be helped; *macam* ~? what sort?; **apa-apa** *n* something; *bukan* ~ nothing; *tidak* ~ it doesn't matter; **apabila** *conj* if, when; **berapa** *interrog* how many? what number?; *adj, coll* several ← **beberapa**; ~ *banyak?* how much? how many?; ~ *harganya?* how much is it?; *umur* ~? how old?; *nomor telepon Adi* ~? what's Adi's phone number?; **beberapa** *adj* several, a number of; **keberapa** *interrog, coll* which number? which one?; **mengapa** *interrog* why; *tak* ~ it doesn't matter; **ngapain** *sl* why, do what; **siapa** *interrog, n* who; ~ *saja* whoever; **siapa-siapa** *n* anybody; *bukan* ~ nobody

apakah, apa (question marker); ~ *Bapak ada di rumah?* Is your master in? ← **apa**

apal → **hafal**

apalagi *adv, conj* especially, moreover

aparat *n* government official

apartemén *n* apartment, flat

APBN *abbrev Anggaran Pendapatan dan Belanja Negara* National (Revenues and Expenditures) Budget

APDN *abbrev Akademi Pemerintahan Dalam Negeri* Academy of Public Administration, civil service academy

apek *adj* smelling musty, moldy

apel *n* apple; ~ *Malang* Malang apples

apél *n* call; assembly; ~ *besar* rally; ~ *nama* roll call; *v, coll* to visit your girlfriend's house

api *n* fire, flame; *gunung* ~ volcano; *kapal* ~ steamship; *kembang* ~ fireworks; *kereta* ~ train, railway; *korek* ~ match; **berapi** *v* to produce fire; **berapi-api** *adj* fiery, fervent; **perapian** *n* fireplace, oven

apik *adj* neat, tidy

apit, mengapit *v* to pinch, press, squeeze; to flank

apokat → **alpukat**

apoték, apotik *n* pharmacy, chemist (shop), dispensary; **apotéker** *n* pharmacist

April *bulan* ~ April

apung float; *batu* ~ pumice; **mengapung** *v* to float, be suspended; **pengapung** *n* buoy, float; **terapung** *adj* drifting, floating

Arab *bahasa* ~ Arabic; *Laut* ~ the Arabian Sea; *negeri* ~ Arabia; *orang* ~ an Arab

arah *n* direction; ~ *kiri* to the left; *berbelok* ~ to change direction; *satu* ~ one way; same direction; **mengarah** *v* to aim something towards; **mengarahkan** *v* to direct; **pengarah** *n* director; **pengarahan** *n* direction, guidance, briefing; **searah** *adj* the same direction; **terarah** *adj* directed

arak *n* rice wine

arak: arak-arakan *n* procession

arang *n* charcoal

arbéi *n, arch* strawberry

arca *n* statue

arén *n* areca palm; *gula* ~ palm sugar

Argéntina *n* Argentina; *orang* ~ Argentinian; *daging sapi* ~ Argentine or Argentinian beef

argo, argométér *n* taxi meter; ~ *kuda* taxi meter showing an inflated tariff

arguméntasi *n* reasoning, argument; **berarguméntasi** *v* to argue, reason

ari *kulit* ~ epidermis

ari-ari *n* placenta

arif *adj* wise, learned; **kearifan** *n* wisdom, learning

arisan *n* (monthly) social gathering involving a lottery

arit *n* sickle; *palu* ~ hammer and sickle

arloji *n, arch* watch; fob watch, watch and chain

arogan *adj* arrogant; **arogansi** *n* arrogance

arsip *n* archive, file; *gedung ~* archives (building); **kearsipan** archives, archival

arsiték *n* architect; *~ lanskap* landscape architect; **arsitéktur** *n* architecture

arti *n* meaning; *~nya* it means, that is to say; *dalam arti ~* in the sense of; **berarti** *v* to mean; *adj* meaningful; *tidak ~* meaningless; **mengartikan** *v* to define, interpret as; **pengartian** *n* understanding, interpretation → **erti**

artikel *n* article (in print media)

artis *n* celebrity; actor, actress or singer

arung *~ jeram* white water rafting; **mengarungi** *v* to cross water, wade, ford

arus *n* stream, current, flow; *~ bolak-balik* alternating current; *~ listrik* electric current; *melawan ~* go against the flow or tide

arwah *n* soul (of a dead person); *misa ~* Requiem Mass

AS *abbrev Amerika Serikat* the United States

asa *n* hope; *putus ~* lose hope, despair

asah sharpen; *~ otak* brain sharpener, brainteaser; **mengasah** *v* to sharpen, whet; **pengasah** *~ pensil* pencil sharpener

asal *n* origin; *~-muasal* *n* root; *~-usul* origins

asal-asalan *adv* carelessly, in any old way; **berasal** *v* to come from

asal, asalkan *conj* as long as, providing that

asam, asem sour, tamarind; acid; *~ belerang* sulphuric acid; *~ garam* hydrochloric acid; *~ manis* sweet and sour; *~ muka ~* sour look; *sayur asem* *n* sour vegetable soup

asap *n* smoke, exhaust, pollution; vapor; *~ rokok* cigarette smoke; *daging ~* smoked meat (usu beef); **berasap** *adj* smoky

asar *Isl, n* the afternoon prayer

asas, azas *n* foundation, principle, base; **berasas(kan)** *adj* based on; *~ Pancasila* based on Pancasila; **asasi, asazi** *adj* basic; *hak ~ manusia (HAM)* human rights

asbak *n* ashtray

asbés *n* asbestos

ASI *abbrev air susu ibu* breast milk

Asia *n* Asia; *bahasa-bahasa ~* Asian languages; *orang ~* Asian; *~ Tenggara* Southeast Asia

asin *adj* salty, salted; *ikan ~* salted fish; **asinan** *n* sour vegetable and fruit dish

asing *adj* strange, alien, foreign; *orang ~* stranger; foreigner; *bahasa ~* foreign language; **mengasingkan** *v* to exile; **pengasingan** *n* exile; *tempat ~* internment camp, exile

asistén *n* assistant; *~ pribadi (aspri)* personal assistant, PA

asli *adj* original, indigenous,

authentic, genuine; *orang* ~, *penduduk* ~ indigenous person, native; ~ *tapi palsu (aspal)* good imitation; **keaslian** *n* authenticity

asma *n* asthma

asmara *n* romantic love, passion

aso, mengaso *v* to take a rest, break

asong: asongan *n* street vendor; goods sold on the street (cigarettes, magazine, drinking water etc); *pedagang* ~ street vendor; **mengasong** *v* to sell on the street

aspal *n* asphalt; *Pulau* ~ Buton; **beraspal,** *jalan* ~ made or macadamized road; **mengaspal** *v* to asphalt

aspal *coll* (good) imitation, fake ← **asli tapi palsu**

aspék *n* aspect, point of view

aspérsé *n* asparagus

asrama *n* boarding house, dormitory, barracks (*mil*)

asri *adj* beautiful, scenic (of a view); **keasrian** *n* (natural) beauty

assalamualaikum, assalamualaikum salam alaikum *gr, Isl* peace be upon you

astaga, astaganaga *ejac* gosh, golly, gee whiz!

astagfirullah *ejac, Isl* God forbid

asuh care; *orang tua* ~ foster parents; **asuhan** *n* upbringing; column in print media; **mengasuh** *v* to care for; **pengasuh** *n* carer; ~ *anak* nursemaid, babysitter

asuransi *n* insurance; ~ *jiwa* life insurance; **mengasuransikan** *v* to insure

asut → **hasut**

asyik *adj* fun; *adv* absorbed, engrossed; eager; ~ *membaca* busy reading; **mengasyikkan** *n* fascinating, engrossing

atap *n* roof; ~ *genteng* tiled roof; **beratap** *v* to have a roof

atas *prep* up; *n* upper part; ~ *nama* on behalf of; *di* ~ on (top of), upon, above, over; upstairs; *terdiri* ~ to consist of; **atasan** *n* superior, boss; **mengatasi** *v* to overcome; **teratasi** *adj* can be overcome

atau *conj* or

atéis *adj* atheist; **atéisme** *n* atheism

ati ampela *n* liver and gizzards

atlét, atlit *n* athlete; **atlétik** *cabang* ~ athletics

atmosfér *n* atmosphere (around Earth)

atom *n* atom; *bom* ~ atomic bomb

atraksi *n* attraction, event

atur arrange; **aturan** *n* rule, regulation; ~ *main* rules of the game; **mengatur** *v* to arrange, organize, regulate; **pengatur** *n* regulator; **peraturan** *n* rule, regulation; **teratur** *adj* organized, (at) regular (intervals)

aula *n* hall (at school), auditorium

aum roar; **mengaum** *v* to roar, growl (of tigers)

AU(RI) *abbrev* Angkatan Udara *(Republik Indonesia)* (Indonesian) Air Force aus *adj* eroded, worn

Australia *n* Australia; *orang ~* Australian

Austria *n* Austria; *orang ~* Austrian

autis *adj* autistic; **autisme** *n* autism

avokad → **alpukat**

awak *n* person; *~ awak kabin, awak pesawat* cabin crew; **perawakan** *n* stature, build, figure; **berperawakan** *v* to have a build, stature

awal beginning, early; **awalan** *n* prefix; **berawal** *v* to begin with; **mengawali** *v* to start; to precede

awam *adj* common, lay; *orang ~* layman

awan *n* cloud; **berawan** *adj* cloudy, overcast

awang-awang *n* heavens, atmosphere

awas *ejac* be careful, beware; *~ ada anjing* beware of the dog; **mengawasi** *v* to supervise; **pengawas** *badan ~* supervisory board, trustees; **pengawasan** *n* supervision, control

awét *adj* durable, long-lasting; *~ muda* youthful; **mengawétkan** *v* to preserve (food); **pengawétan** *n* preservation

awur → **ngawur**

ayah, Ayah *n, pron* father; *~ bunda* parents

ayak, mengayak *v* to sieve, sift; **ayakan** *n* sieve

ayam *n* chicken, hen; *anak ~* chick; *~ betina* hen; *~ jago, ~ jantan* rooster, cock; *~ kampung* free-range chicken; *~ negeri* battery hen; *dada ~* chicken breast

ayan *n* epilepsy

ayat *n* verse (of a religious text)

ayo come on, let's go

ayom: mengayomi *v* to protect, care for, look after; **pengayom** *n* protector, carer

ayu *adj* beautiful; *pagar ~* girl attendants at a wedding reception

ayun, mengayun *v* to rock, swing, sway; **ayunan** *n* swings; *main ~* play on the swings; **mengayunkan** *v* to rock

azab *n* torture

azan, adzan *n* call to prayer

azas → **asas**

B

bab *n* chapter

babak *n* round (in sport); half (in football); stage, phase; *~ pertama* first half

babat *n* a kind of meat (from the stomach); *soto ~* a soup using this meat

babat *wingko ~* small coconut slice, a specialty of Semarang

babat: membabat *v* to cut or chop down, clear away; **pembabatan** *n* felling, chopping; *~ hutan* (unregulated) deforestation

babi *n* pig, boar (also as an insult); *~ hutan* wild boar;

daging ~ pork; **membabi** *v* ~ *buta* to act blindly and rashly

baca *v* to read; **bacaan** *n* reading material; **membaca** *v* to read; **membacakan** *v* to read something to someone; **pembaca** *n* reader; **pembacaan** *n* (act of) reading aloud

bacem *tempe* ~ sweet tempe

badai *n* hurricane, cyclone; storm; ~ *topan* typhoon

badak *n* rhino, rhinoceros; ~ *air* hippo, hippopotamus; ~ *bercula satu* one-horned rhino; *berkulit* ~ thick-skinned

badan *n* body; board, committee; *gerak* ~ physical exercise; ~ *pengawas* supervisory staff

Badui, Baduy *orang* ~ a Sundanese sub-ethnic group

badut *n* clown

bagai *conj* like, as; **berbagai** *adj* various, several; **sebagai** *conj* like, as; *dan* ~*nya* and so on

bagaimana *interrog, conj* how, in what way; **sebagaimana** *conj* in such a way that, in that way

bagasi *n* baggage; boot (of vehicle); hold (of ship or aircraft)

bagi *v* divide; **bagian** *n* part, share, section; *mengambil* ~ to take part, participate; **berbagi** *v* to share; **kebagian** *v* to get a share; **membagi** *v* to divide, distribute; ~ *rata* divide evenly; **membagi-bagi** *v* to split up; **pembagian** *n* distribution, division; **sebagian** *n* some, a section of

bagi *prep* for; ~ *saya* as for me

bagus *adj* good, fine, excellent (external qualities of concrete objects); *Buku ini* ~ *sekali* This is a very good book; ~*nya!* Isn't it lovely?

bah *n* flood; *air* ~ flood

bahagia *adj* happy, joyous; **berbahagia** *v* to be happy; *Selamat* ~ Congratulations (at a wedding); **kebahagiaan** *n* happiness; **membahagiakan** *v* to make happy

bahan *n* material, ingredients; cloth, fabric; ~ *bakar* fuel; ~ *peledak* explosive; ~ *pengajaran* teaching/study materials

bahari *adj* maritime; *Musium* ~ Maritime Museum

bahas *v* to discuss; **bahasan** *n* discussion, review; **membahas** *v* to discuss, debate; **pembahasan** *n* discussion, debate

bahasa *n* language; ~ *Indonesia* Indonesian; *juru* ~ interpreter (oral), translator (written); *ilmu* ~ linguistics; *tata* ~ grammar; **berbahasa** *v* to (be able to) speak or use a language; *Nenek hanya* ~ *Jawa* Grandma only speaks Javanese; **peribahasa** *n* proverb, idiom

bahasan *n* discussion, review ← **bahas**

bahaya *n* danger; *tanda* ~ warning signal, siren; **berbahaya** *v* to be dangerous; **membahayakan** *v* to endanger, jeopardize

bahkan *conj* moreover; on the contrary; indeed, even

bahu *n* shoulder; ~ *jalan* hard shoulder; ~-*mem*~ shoulder to shoulder, to help each other

bahwa *conj* that; *Saya tahu ~ itu tidak benar* I know that it's not true

baik *adj* good, fine, well, OK (ie. internal qualities of abstract objects); **baik-baik** *adj* fine; respectable; *Apa kabar?/~ saja* How are you?/Fine; ~ ... *maupun* ..., both ... and ...; ~ *hati* kind; **kebaikan** *n* goodness, kindness; **membaik** *v* to improve; **memperbaiki** *v* to repair, fix; **perbaikan** *n* repair, improvement; **sebaiknya** *adv* preferably, it's best if; **terbaik** *adj* the best

baja *n* steel

bajaj *n* three-wheeled motorized form of transport in Jakarta

bajak *v* to hijack; to copy illegally; ~ *pesawat* to hijack a plane; pirate; **bajakan** *adj* pirated; *CD ~* pirated CD; **membajak** *v* to plow; **pembajakan** *n* hijacking; piracy

bajigur *n* warm night drink containing coffee and coconut milk

bajing *n* squirrel; **bajingan** *n, sl, derog* bastard!

baju *n, inf* clothes; clothing for the upper body; ~ *dalam* singlet; underwear; ~ *pengantin* wedding dress; **berbaju** *v* to put on, wear clothes

bak *n* tub, basin, container; ~ *mandi* large tank in the bathroom from which water is taken

baka *adj* eternal, everlasting; *alam ~* the hereafter

bakal *adj* future, potential; *v, aux* will

bakar *v* to burn; *kayu ~* firewood; **kebakaran** *n* fire; ~ *hutan* forest fire, bushfire; *Ada ~!* Fire!; **membakar** *v* to burn; **pembakaran** *n* burning, combustion; **terbakar** *adj* burnt; *Kulit Bapak ~ oleh sinar matahari* Father was sunburnt

bakat *n* talent, gift; ~ *nyanyi* a talent for singing; **berbakat** *adj* talented, gifted

bakau *n* mangrove

baki *n* tray (for food)

bakmi, bami *n* Chinese noodles

bakpao *n* steamed white bread with filling of nuts or chicken

bakpia *n* sweet cake from Jogja with nutty filling

bakso, baso *n* meatball; meatball soup; ~ *tahu* meatballs and tofu (specialty of Bandung)

baktéri *n* bacteria

bakti *n* service, devotion; *kerja ~* volunteer work; **berbakti** *v* to serve, devote oneself to; **kebaktian** *n* (Protestant) service

baku *adj* standard; *harga ~* standard price

bakul *n* basket hung on a pole for selling goods; *f* vendor

bakwan *n* corn fritter, a specialty of Malang

bala *n, arch* army; ~ *Keselamatan* Salvation Army; ~ *tentara* army

balai *n* house, building, office; ~ *kota* town hall; **balai-balai** *n* traditional sofa, bamboo bed

balairung *n* (royal) reception room

balak: pembalakan *n* logging; ~ *liar* illegal logging

balap race; **balapan** *n* race; ~ *mobil* car race; **membalap** *v* to race

balas reply; ~ *dendam* take revenge; **balasan** reply, answer; **membalas** *v* to reply, respond

bale-bale *n* traditional sofa, bamboo bed → **balai**

balét *n* ballet; **pebalét** *n* ballet dancer, *f* ballerina

Bali *n pulau* ~ Bali; *bahasa* ~, *orang* ~ Balinese

balig, baligh *akil* ~ of age, ready to take on religious obligations, etc

balik *v* to return, reverse, retreat; ~ *nama* transfer of ownership; *n* back, flipside; return; **berbalik** to turn around, return; **membalik** *v* to return, reverse, turn over; **membalikkan** *v* to turn something over; **sebaliknya** *conj* on the contrary; **terbalik** *adj* overturned, upside-down, opposite

balok *n* beam, crossbeam (of a building)

balon *n* balloon

balur smear with oil; massage; **membalur** *v* to smear or massage with oil

balut *n* bandage; **membalut** *v* to bandage; **pembalut** *n* sanitary pad

bambu *n* bamboo

ban *n* tire; ~ *serep* spare tire; *coll* replacement person

banci *n* transvestite, cross-dressing male, often a prostitute; male homosexual (*derog*)

bandar *n* (sea) port; ~ *udara* → **bandara**

bandar *n* dealer (often in drugs), croupier

bandara *n* airport ← **bandar udara**

bandel *adj* naughty, disobedient (usually of children); **membandel** *v* to do something naughty, be disobedient

bandeng *ikan* ~ milkfish, a specialty of the north coast of Java

banding *tiada* ~, *tidak ada* ~ incomparable, the best there is; *naik* ~ to appeal against a decision; **dibandingkan** *v* to be compared with; **membandingkan** *v* to compare something; **perbandingan** *n* comparison, ratio

bandrék *n* ginger drink

bang *pron* older brother (in Jakarta or Malay areas) → **abang**

bang → **bank**

bangau *n* heron

banget *adj, sl* very, excessively; **kebangetan** *adj, coll* too much, excessive (of behavior or a situation)

bangga *adj* proud; **berbangga** *v* to be proud; **kebanggaan** *n* pride; something of which you are proud; **membanggakan** *v* to make proud, please

bangkai *n* carcass (usually of animals); *bunga* ~ the Rafflesia flower

bangkang: membangkang v to defy, resist, disobey; **pembangkang** n someone who defies; **pembangkangan** n act of defiance

bangkit, berbangkit v to rise, get up; **kebangkitan** n rise, awakening; *Partai ~ Bangsa (PKB)* Party of National Awakening; **membangkit** v to arouse, stimulate; **pembangkit** *~ listrik* power station; *~ listrik tenaga air (PLTA)* hydroelectric power station

bangkrut adj bankrupt; **kebangkrutan** n bankruptcy

bangku n bench (for sitting); stool; desk; *~ kelas* school bench

bangsa n people, nation, race; *~ Indonesia* the Indonesian people; *Perserikatan ~~* the United Nations; **berbangsa** v to have a nationality; **kebangsaan** adj national; *lagu ~* national anthem; **bangsawan** n aristocrat, member of royalty

bangsal n ward (in hospital), dormitory; shed

bangsat n flea; (term of abuse) scoundrel

bangsawan n aristocrat, member of royalty

bangun v get up, wake up; **membangunkan** v to (intentionally) wake someone up; **terbangun** adj woken up (of your own accord)

bangun: bangunan n building; **membangun** v to build or create; **pembangunan** n development

banjir n flood; *~ bandang* flash flood

bank n bank; *~ negara* state-owned bank; **perbankan** adj banking; *dunia ~* the banking world; **bankir** n banker

bantah, membantah v to deny, dispute

bantai, membantai v to slaughter, kill viciously; **pembantaian** n slaughter, mass killings

bantal cushion; pillow; *~ guling* bolster, Dutch wife (long cushion to hold when sleeping)

banteng n (Javan) ox

banting throw down, slam; *~ harga* cut prices; **membanting** v to throw down (with a bang); *~ pintu* slam the door; *~ tulang* to toil, work yourself to the bone

bantu v to help; **bantuan** n assistance, help, aid; *~ dana* financial assistance; **membantu** v to help (someone); **pembantu** n servant, maid; assistant; *kantor ~* (larger) branch office

banyak adj many, much; *orang ~* the public; **kebanyakan** n, adj too much; most; *~ orang tidak setuju* Most people don't agree; **memperbanyak** v to increase, multiply

banyol adj funny, silly; **banyolan** n joke, joking; **membanyol** v to joke

Bapa pron Father (title for own

father or respected older man), also **Bapak**; *Chr* God, Father, Lord

bapa *n* father; ~ *permandian* godfather

Bapak *pron* Father (title for own father or respected older man); ~ *Pembangunan* Father of Development (used by Soeharto)

bapak *n* father; ~ *angkat* adopted father; ~ *tiri* stepfather; *ibu* ~ parents; **kebapakan** *adj* fatherly; **bapakisme** *n* paternalism

Bappeda *Badan Perencanaan Pembangunan Daerah* Regional Development Planning Agency

Bappenas *Badan Perencanaan Pembangunan Nasional* National Development Planning Agency

baptis *adj* baptist; **membaptis** *v* to baptize, christen

bara *n* embers; *batu* ~ coal; **membara** *v* to glow with heat

barang *n* goods, things; ~ *bergerak* moveable property; *daftar* ~ inventory

barang *adj* some (indicating uncertainty); **barangkali** *conj* perhaps, maybe; **barangsiapa** *pron* whoever, whosoever

Barat *n* the West

barat *adj* west; ~ *daya* southwest; ~ *laut* northwest; *dunia* ~ the western world

Barelang *Batam, Rempang, Galang* group of islands in Riau Archipelago province

bareng *conj, sl* with; *v* to go together; *Dia* ~ *sama Dini* She's coming with Dini; **berbarengan** *adj* together, at the same time

barét *n* beret; ~ *merah* the Red Berets (nickname for Kopassus troops)

baring: berbaring *v* to lie down; **membaringkan** *v* to lay something down in rows

baris *n* line, row, rank; **barisan** *n* line; forces; ~ *depan* front-line; *Bukit* ~ mountain range in Sumatra; **berbaris** *v* to line up

barongsai *n* Chinese dragon for dance performances

baru *adj* new, recent; modern; just, only; ~~ *ini* just the other day; ~ *saja* just now; *orang* ~ newcomer; **memperbarui** *v* to renew, make new; **pembaruan** *n* renewal; **terbaru** *adj* latest, newest; **barusan** *adv, sl* just now

basa: basa-basi *n* good manners, politeness; platitudes

basah *adj* wet, moist, soaked; ~ *kuyup* soaking wet; *tisu* ~ wet towel, wipe; **membasahi** *v* to moisten, wet

basi *adj* off, rotten, inedible (of food); *sudah* ~ *sl* outdated, not funny any more

baskét *bola* ~ basketball

baskom *n* washbasin; large bowl for washing dishes, vegetables etc

basmi destroy; **membasmi** *v* to exterminate, destroy, wipe out; **pembasmi** ~ *rayap* termite exterminator; **pembasmian** n extermination, destruction, eradication

basuh, membasuh v to wash with water; ~ *wajah* to wash the face

bata *batu* ~ brick

bata-bata: terbata-bata *adv* brokenly, not fluently

batagor n fried tofu and meatballs, a specialty of Bandung ← **bakso tahu goréng**

Batak *adj* ethnic group of North Sumatra; *bahasa* ~, *orang* ~ Batak

batal *adj* cancelled; v not take place; break (a fast); **membatalkan** v to cancel, repeal; **pembatalan** n cancellation, annulment

batang n trunk, stem, stick (of a tree); shaft; handle; penis; counter for long cylindrical objects; *Minta rokok tiga* ~ I'd like three cigarettes; ~ *pohon* tree trunk; ~ *sungai* tributary; **sebatang** ~ *kara* all alone in the world

batas n limit, border; ~ *kota* city limits; **berbatas** v to have a boundary; *tak* ~ limitless; **berbatasan** v to be adjacent to; **membatasi** v to limit, restrict, curb something; **pembatas** n divider; ~ *buku* bookmark; **pembatasan** n restriction; **perbatasan** n border, frontier; **terbatas** *adj* limited; *perseroan* ~ proprietary limited; **keterbatasan** n limitation

baterai n battery

bathin → **batin**

batik n application of wax onto fabric to create a pattern after dyeing; fabric or clothes with designs produced in this manner; fabric or clothes resembling batik but with printed designs; ~ *cap* stamped batik; ~ *modern* batik produced with chemicals instead of wax; ~ *tulis* handmade batik; ~ *Yogya* Jogja-style batik; **membatik** n to apply wax onto fabric

batin, bathin *adj, n* inner, spiritual; soul, spirit; *Mohon maaf lahir* ~ I beg your complete forgiveness (greeting at Idul Fitri); **kebatinan** n mysticism

batok n shell, skull; ~ *kelapa* coconut shell; ~ *kepala* skull

batu n stone; ~ *apung* pumice; ~ *arang* charcoal; ~ *bara* coal; ~ *bata* brick; ~ *empedu* gallstones; ~ *pualam* marble; ~ *tulis* slate; inscription; *gula* ~ lump of sugar; *kepala* ~ obstinate, stubborn; **berbatu** *adj* rocky, stony; **membatu** v to freeze, become petrified, fossilized

batuk v cough

bau *n, v, adj* smell, smelly; ~ *amis* fishy smell; **berbau** v to smell, have connotations of

baur *campur* ~ mixed up; **berbaur, membaur** v to integrate, mix with others (of people); **pembauran** n integration, mixing of different ethnic groups

baut n bolt

bawa *v* to take, bring, carry; to conduct; ~ *diri* to conduct yourself; **bawaan** *adj* carried or inherited; *penyakit* ~ hereditary disease; **membawa** *v* to take, bring, carry; to conduct; **membawakan** *v* to bring or carry for someone; to sing; *Dia* ~ *lagu-lagu keroncong* She performed *keroncong* songs; **pembawa** *n* bearer, carrier; ~ *acara* host, MC; **pembawaan** *n* temperament, nature; **terbawa** *adj* (accidentally) taken away; ~ *arus* swept away in the current

bawah *prep* below; ~ *tangan* underhand, privately; ~ *umur* underage; *Yang bertanda tangan di ~ ini* the undersigned; *di* ~ below, under; **bawahan** *n orang* ~ inferior, assistant; **membawahi** *v* to head a section (with staff under you)

bawang *n* onion; ~ *bombai* (brown) onion; ~ *merah* red onion, shallot; ~ *putih* garlic; *anak* ~ a nobody; *daun* ~ spring onion

baya *n* age; *setengah* ~ middle-aged; **sebaya** *adj* the same age

bayam, bayem *n* spinach

bayang *n* shadow, image; **bayangan** *n* shadow; **membayangi** *v* to overshadow; **terbayang** *adj* imagined, conceivable

bayar *v* to pay; **bayaran** *adj* paid, hired; *pembunuh* ~ hired assassin; **membayar** *v* to pay; ~ *di muka* to pay in advance; **pembayaran** *n* payment; *tanda* ~ *yang sah* legal currency

bayi *n* baby; *toko* ~ shop selling baby needs

bayonét *n* bayonet; **membayonét** *v* to stab someone with a bayonet

béa *n* tax, duty, excise; ~ *cukai* customs; ~ *masuk* import duty

béasiswa *n* scholarship, bursary

beban *n* burden, load; responsibility; **membebani** *v* to burden someone with something; **membebankan** *v* to charge something to someone

bébas *adj* free; ~ *banjir* safe from floods; **kebébasan** *n* freedom; **membébaskan** *v* to exempt, liberate, free someone; **pembébasan** *n* liberation, release, exemption

bébék *n* duck; **membébék** *v* to quack; to follow blindly

bébér: **membébérkan** *v* to reveal, explain

beberapa *adj* several, a number of ← **apa, berapa**

bebuyutan *adj* ancestral; arch enemy; *musuh* ~ arch enemy ← **buyut**

bécak *n* pedicab, rickshaw tricycle; *tukang* ~ pedicab driver

bécék *adj* muddy, wet

béda *adj* different; ~*nya* ... the difference is, ...; **berbéda** *adj* different; **membédakan** *v* to discriminate, differentiate between, consider different; **pembédaan** *n* discrimination, differential treatment; **perbédaan** n difference

bedah n surgery; ~ *plastik* plastic or cosmetic surgery; *ahli* ~ surgeon; **membedah** v to operate; **pembedahan** n operation

bedak n powder

bedug, beduk n big drum, especially in a mosque; *menunggu* ~ to wait for the drum indicating the end of fasting at sunset

begadang v to stay up all night; to sleep late

begini *adv* like this, in this manner ← **ini**

begitu *adv* like that, in that manner; *adv* so; *conj* as soon as ← **itu**

bégo *excl, adj, sl* idiot; stupid

béha n bra

bejat *adj* depraved, filthy; *perbuatan* ~ sexual crime

bekal n provisions; something of future use; **berbekal** v to carry provisions (consisting of); **membekali** v to supply someone with provisions; **pembekalan** n supply

bekas *adj* used, old, former (for objects); ~ *pakai* used; *barang* ~ second-hand goods; **membekas** v to leave an impression

bekén *adj, sl* famous, well-known

bekerja v to work; ~ *sama* to co-operate, work together ← **kerja**

bekléding n upholstery (usu of seats in vehicles)

beku *adj* frozen; **membeku** v to freeze; **membekukan** v to freeze something; **pembekuan** n freezing; ~ *aset* freezing of assets

bekuk, membekuk v to arrest; **pembekukan** n arrest

bél n bell

béla v defend; ~ *diri* self-defense; **membéla** v to defend; **pembéla** n defender; ~ *Tanah Air* defender of the homeland; **pembélaan** n defense

belah n crack, fissure, divide, splinter; ~ *pecah* crockery, breakable household goods; *seperti pinang di~ dua* like two peas in a pod; **belahan** n half, side; ~ *bumi selatan* Southern Hemisphere; ~ *jiwa* other half (of a couple); **membelah** v to split in two; **sebelah** n on the left (side); ~ *mana* which side, where; *rumah* ~ next door; **bersebelahan** v to be next to

belai, membelai v to stroke, caress; **belaian** n stroke, caress

belajar v to learn, study; **belajar-mengajar** *kegiatan* ~ teaching and learning ← **ajar**

belaka *adj, neg* only, mere, pure

belakang *prep, n* behind; back, rear; *lampu* ~ tail-light; *tulang* ~ spine, backbone; **belakangan** *adv* recently, later (on), afterwards; after others; finally, at last; ~ *ini* recently; **membelakangi** v to turn your back on someone; **terbelakang, terkebelakang** *adj* backward, neglected; **keterbelakangan** n backwardness, neglect

belalang *n* grasshopper, locust; ~ *sembah* praying mantis

Belanda *n* the Netherlands, Holland; *bahasa* ~ Dutch (language); *orang* ~ Dutch (people)

belang *adj* striped; *lelaki hidung* ~ men who visit prostitutes

belanja *v* to go shopping; **belanjaan** *n* shopping; **berbelanja** *v* to go shopping; **membelanjakan** *v* to spend money; **pembelanjaan** *n* expenditure, spending, financing; **perbelanjaan** *n* expenditure; *pusat* ~ shopping center, mall

belantara *adj hutan* ~ forest, wilderness

belas: belas kasihan pity, compassion; **berbelas-kasihan** *v* to pity, feel compassion; **memelas** *adj* pitiful, pathetic

belas *n* number between 10–20, -teen; *lima* ~ fifteen; **belasan** *n* dozens; **sebelas** *n, adj* eleven; **kesebelasan** *n* team of eleven, soccer team

bélasungkawa *n* condolences; *Pak RT melayat ke rumah untuk menyampaikan* ~ The neighborhood leader went to the house to express his condolences

belatung *n* maggot

beledru, beludru *n* velvet

belenggu *n* handcuffs, shackles; **membelenggu** *v* to shackle, handcuff; **terbelenggu** *adj* in shackles, irons

belépotan *adj* smeared, stained; spotty ← **lépot**

belérang *n* sulfur; *asam* ~ sulfuric acid

Bélgia *n* Belgium; *orang* ~ Belgian

beli *v* to buy; *jual* ~ buying and selling, business, trade; **membeli** *v* to buy, purchase; **membelikan** *v* to buy something for someone; *Sinta* ~ *anak itu boneka;* Sinta bought the child a doll; **pembeli** *n* buyer, purchaser; **pembelian** *n* purchase

belia *adj* young

beliau *pron* he, she; him, her (respectful form of *dia*); *Bisa bertemu dengan Bapak?/ Maaf,* ~ *tidak boleh diganggu* May I see your master?/Sorry, but he mustn't be disturbed

belimbing, blimbing *n* starfruit

belit *n* coil, bend; **berbelit** *v* to wind, twist in and out; **berbelit-belit** *v* to wind around; to ramble, try to wriggle out of something; **membelit** *v* to twist; **terbelit** *adj* twisted, involved; ~ *hutang* debt-ridden

bélok bend, turn; **berbélok-bélok** windy, lots of bends and turns; **bélokan** *n* bend, turn in the road; **berbélok, membélok** *v* to bend, turn; **membélokkan** *v* to turn, divert something

beludak, bludak: membeludak *v* to burst out, spread everywhere, explode

beludru → **beledru**

belukar *semak* ~ bushland, scrub

belum *adv* **belon** *sl* not yet; no (not until now); ~ *pernah* until now, never (but possibly in the future); **sebelum** *adj* before; **sebelumnya** *adv* previously, before

belut *n* eel

bémo *n* motorized three-wheeled vehicle still operating in a few parts of Jakarta ← **bécak bermotor**

bémper *n* bumper bar

benak *n* brains, mind; *tidak terbayang di ~ saya* I couldn't imagine

benam: terbenam *adj* set, sunken; *matahari ~* sunset

benang *n* thread; *~ emas* gold thread; *~ gigi* dental floss; *~ merah* connecting thread (of a story or series of happenings)

benar, bener *adj* true, correct, right; **benar-benar** *adv* truly, really; **kebenaran** *n* truth; *Komisi ~ dan Rekonsiliasi* Truth and Reconciliation Commission; **membenarkan** *v* to confirm, verify; to justify; **sebenarnya** *adv* in fact, actually → **betul**

bencana *n* disaster, catastrophe; *~ alam* natural disaster, act of God

benci *v* to hate; **kebencian** *n* hatred; **membenci** *v* to hate

béncong *n, sl* transvestite; *m* homosexual

benda *n* thing, object; goods, valuables; *~ bergerak* moveable goods; *~ pos* postal items (postcards, stamps etc); *harta ~* worldly goods

bendahara *n* treasurer; bishop (in chess); **perbendaharaan** *n* treasury; *~ kata* vocabulary

bendéra *n* flag

béndi *n* two-wheeled horse-carriage

bendung: bendungan *n* dam; **membendungi** *v* to dam, stop a flow; **terbendung** *tak ~* unstoppable

bener → **benar**

bengis *adj* cruel, heartless; **kebengisan** *n* cruelty, harshness

bengkak *adj* swollen; **membengkak** *v* to swell up; **pembengkakan** *n* swelling, expanding

béngkél *n* garage; workshop; *~ las* welding workshop; *~ seni* artist's workshop, atelier, studio

béngkok *adj* bent, crooked; **membéngkokkan** *v* to bend something

bengkuang, bengkoang *n* kind of small fruit with brown skin and white flesh, used in salads and cosmetics

benih *n* seed, germ, sperm; **pembenihan** *~ buatan* artificial insemination

bening *adj* clear, transparent, clean (of glass, water etc)

bénjol, bénjolan *n* mole, lump, tumor

bénsin *n* petrol, gasoline

bentak shout; **bentakan** *n* shout; **membentak** *v* to shout, scold, snap

bentar → **sebentar**

bénténg *n* fort, fortress; castle

or rook (in chess)

bentrok *v* to clash head-on; **bentrokan** *n* clash, conflict

bentuk *n* shape, form; **berbentuk** *adj* shaped, with the shape of; **membentuk** *v* to form, set up something (eg. committee); **pembentukan** *n* formation, act of forming; **terbentuk** *adj* formed, shaped, created

bentur *v* to collide, bump; **membentur** *v* to hit, collide with; **terbentur** *adj* accidentally bumped; *Kepalanya ~ di atap* He banged his head on the roof

benua *n* continent; *~ Asia* Asia; *antar ~* intercontinental

béo *burung ~* mynah (bird); **membéo** *v* to parrot, imitate (superiors etc)

bepergian *v* to travel, be away ← **pergi**

berabad-abad *adv* for centuries ← **abad**

beracun *adj* poisonous, containing poison; *gas ~* poison gas ← **racun**

berada *v* to be somewhere; to exist; *adj* well-to-do, well-off; *Ibu Menteri ~ di Padang* the Minister is in Padang ← **ada**

beradab *adj* civilized, polite ← **adab**

beradu *v* to fight; *~ domba* to play two parties against each other ← **adu**

beragam *adj* various ← **ragam**

beragama *adj* religious; *v* to have a religion; *Siti ~ Islam* Siti is Muslim ← **agama**

berahi *n* lust, desire; heat (of animals); *~ tinggi* (*BT* or *bété*) sexually excited, horny; bad-tempered

berai *cerai-~* scattered, disordered

berair *v* to be juicy, containing water ← **air**

bérak *v* poo, defecate; *n* poo, feces

berakal *v* to be intelligent ← **akal**

berakar *adj* rooted ← **akar**

berakhir *v* to end ← **akhir**

berakibat *v* to have consequences, implications ← **akibat**

beraksén *v* to have a touch of; *rumah ~ Jawa* a house with Javanese-inspired decor ← **aksén**

beralamat *v* to have an address ← **alamat**

beralasan *adj* with reason; *tidak ~* without reason; **beralaskan** *v* based upon ← **alas**

beralérgi *v* to have an allergy; *~ terhadap mangga* allergic to mangoes ← **alérgi**

beraliansi *v* to be allied with ← **aliansi**

beralih *v* to move, change, shift ← **alih**

beraliran *v* to have an ideology; *~ kiri* leftist ← **alir**

beralkohol *v* to contain alcohol; *minuman ~* alcoholic drink ← **alkohol**

beramal *v* to give to charity; *adj* charitable ← **amal**

berambisi *adj* ambitious ← **ambisi**

berambut *adj* hairy; *v* to have hair; *~ coklat* dark-haired, *f* brunette; ~ *pirang*, *m* blond, *f* blonde ← **rambut**

beranak *v* (of animals) to give birth to, have offspring; ~ *pinak* to have descendants ← **anak**

beranda *n* veranda, balcony

berandai-andai *v* to speak hypothetically, imagine ← **andai**

beranéka ~ *ragam* various ← **anéka**

bérang *adj* furious, enraged

berangan-angan *v* to daydream, build castles in the air, fantasize ← **angan**

beranggapan *v* to be of the opinion ← **anggap**

beranggota *v* to have members; **beranggotakan** *v* to have a membership, have as members; *PKI dulu* ~ *jutaan orang* the PKI once had millions of members ← **anggota**

berangkat *v* to depart, leave; **keberangkatan** *n* departure; **diberangkatkan** *v* to depart; *Rombongan ke Medan sudah* ~ The party to Medan has departed; **pemberangkatan** *n* departure, sending off ← **angkat**

berangsur, berangsur-angsur *adv* gradually, little by little ← **angsur**

berangus *n* muzzle; **memberangus** *v* to muzzle, bridle; ~ *pers* to curb press freedom

berani *adj* brave, courageous; **keberanian** *n* bravery, courage; **memberanikan** ~ *diri* to dare, get up the courage; **pemberani**

n brave or courageous person, hero

beranjak *v* to move, shift; ~ *dewasa* becoming a young adult ← **anjak**

berantakan *adj* messy, in a mess ← **antak**

berantas, memberantas *v* to wipe out, fight against; ~ *korupsi* to wipe out corruption; **pemberantasan** *n* destruction, fight against

berantem *v* to fight, scuffle ← **antem, hantam**

berapa *interrog* how many? what number?; *adj, coll* several ← **beberapa**; ~ *banyak?* how much? how many?; ~ *harganya?* how much is it?; *umur* ~? how old?; *nomor telepon Adi* ~? what's Adi's phone number? **beberapa** *adj* several, a number of; **keberapa** *coll, interrog* which number?; **seberapa** *tidak* ~ not many; ~ *jauh* as far as ← **apa**

berapi *adj* burning, fire-producing (of volcanoes); **berapi-api** *adj* fiery, fervent ← **api**

berarguméntasi *v* to argue, reason ← **arguméntasi**

berarti *v* to mean; *adj* meaningful; *tidak* ~ meaningless ← **arti**

beras *n* rice (husked and uncooked, as sold in shops)

berasal *v* to come from ← **asal**

berasap *adj* smoky ← **asap**

berasas, berasaskan *adj* based on; ~ *Pancasila* based on Pancasila ← **asas**

beraspal *jalan* ~ made or macadamized road ← **aspal**

berat heavy, severe, difficult; weight; ~ *badan* body weight; ~ *bersih* net weight; ~ *hati* unwilling, reluctant; ~ *sebelah* unbalanced, tending to favor one side; *gaya* ~ gravity; **keberatan** *n* objection; **(ber)keberatan** *v* to object; **memberatkan** *v* to burden, make heavy; *adj* incriminating; *kesaksian yang* ~ incriminating evidence

beratap *v* to have a roof ← **atap**

beratus-ratus *adj* hundreds of ← **ratus**

berawal *v* to begin with ← **awal**

berawan *adj* cloudy, overcast ← **awan**

berbagai *adj* various, several ← **bagai**

berbagi *v* to share ← **bagi**

berbahagia *v* to be happy ← **bahagia**

berbahasa *v* to (be able to) speak or use a language; *Nenek hanya* ~ *Jawa* Grandma only speaks Javanese ← **bahasa**

berbahaya *v* to be dangerous ← **bahaya**

berbaju *v* to put on, wear clothes ← **baju**

berbakat *adj* talented, gifted ← **bakat**

berbakti *v* to serve, devote oneself to ← **bakti**

berbalik *v* to turn around, return; ← **balik**

berbangga *v* to be proud ← **bangga**

berbangkit *v* to rise, get up ← **bangkit**

berbangsa *v* to have a nationality ← **bangsa**

berbarengan *adj* together, at the same time ← **bareng**

berbaring *v* to lie down ← **baring**

berbaris *v* to line up ← **baris**

berbatas *v* to have a boundary; *tak* ~ limitless; **berbatasan** *v* to be adjacent to ← **batas**

berbatu *adj* rocky, stony ← **batu**

berbau *v* to smell, have connotations of ← **bau**

berbaur *v* to integrate, mix with others (of people) ← **baur**

berbéda *adj* different ← **béda**

berbekal *v* to carry provisions (consisting of) ← **bekal**

berbekas *v* to leave an impression ← **bekas**

berbelanja *v* to go shopping ← **belanja**

berbelas-kasihan *v* to pity, feel compassion ← **belas**

berbelit *v* to wind, twist in and out; **berbelit-belit** *v* to wind around; to ramble, try to wriggle out of something ← **belit**

berbentuk *adj* shaped, with the shape of ← **bentuk**

berbesar hati *adj* big-hearted accepting ← **besar**

berbicara *v* to speak; ~ *dalam bahasa Sunda* to speak in Sundanese ← **bicara**

berbincang, berbincang-bincang *v* to chat, discuss ← **bincang**

berbingkai *v* to have a frame, framed ← **bingkai**

berbintang *v* to have a star (sign); *jenderal ~ tiga* three-star general ← **bintang**

berbintik-bintik *adj* spotty, spotted ← **bintik**

berbisa *adj* poisonous; *ular ~* venomous snake ← **bisa**

berbisik *adj* whispering; *v* to whisper ← **bisik**

berbisnis *v* to do business ← **bisnis**

berbobot *adj* heavy, weighty; *bukunya ~* his book was heavy reading ← **bobot**

berbohong *v* to lie ← **bohong**

berbolak-balik *v* to go back and forth ← **bolak-balik**

berbolong-bolong *adj* full of holes ← **bolong**

berbondong-bondong *adv* in droves ← **bondong**

berbuah *v* to bear fruit, produce ← **buah**

berbuat *v* to do; *~ salah* to do wrong ← **buat**

berbudaya *n* to have a culture ← **budaya**

berbuih *adj* frothy, foaming ← **buih**

berbuka *~ puasa* to break the fast ← **buka**

berbukit *adj* hilly ← **bukit**

berbulu *adj* hairy; to have fur or feathers ← **bulu**

berbunga *v* to flower, blossom; to gain interest ← **bunga**

berbuntut *v* to go further, end; *ceritanya ~ sedih* the tale had a sad ending ← **buntut**

berbunyi *v* to sound, make a noise ← **bunyi**

berburu *v* to go hunting ← **buru**

berbusa *adj* foamy; *v* to have a layer of foam ← **busa**

berbusana *v* to wear ← **busana**

bercabang *v* to be split, branched ← **cabang**

bercahaya *v* to glow, shine ← **cahaya**

bercak *n* spot, blemish, pock (on body)

bercakap *v* to speak; **bercakap-cakap** *v* to chat ← **cakap**

bercampur *adj* mixed with ← **campur**

bercanda *v* to joke; *~ kok* just kidding ← **canda**

bercas-cis-cus *v* to speak a European language ← **cas-cis-cus**

bercawat *v* to wear a loincloth ← **cawat**

bercécéran *adj* scattered, dispersed ← **cécér**

bercékcok *v* to quarrel, have a fight ← **cékcok**

bercelana *v* to wear trousers, trousered ← **celana**

bercelotéh *v* to babble, gurgle ← **celotéh**

bercengkrama *v* to chat, hold a discussion ← **cengkrama**

bercerai *v* to be divorced ← **cerai**

berceramah *v* to give a lecture or talk ← **ceramah**

bercerita *v* to tell (a story) ← **cerita**

bercermin *v* to look in the mirror; to take as an example ← **cermin**

bercinta *v* to make love; to be in love ← **cinta**

bercita-cita, bercita-citakan *v* to dream of ← **cita-cita**

berciuman *v* to kiss each other ← **cium**

bercocok ~ *tanam* to work or till the soil ← **cocok**

bercorak *v* to have a design ← **corak**

bercucuran *v* to trickle down, drip, flow ← **cucur**

bercula *n* to have a horn; *badak* ~ *satu* one-horned rhino ← **cula**

bercumbu *v* to flirt, flatter ← **cumbu**

berdada *v* to have a chest ← **dada**

berdagang *v* to trade, do business ← **dagang**

berdahaga *adj* thirsty ← **dahaga**

berdahak *adj* containing phlegm or mucus; *batuk* ~ chesty cough ← **dahak**

berdalih *v* to pretend, give a pretext ← **dalih**

berdalil *adj* based on, grounded in ← **dalil**

berdamai *v* to make peace ← **damai**

berdampak *v* to have a (negative) effect ← **dampak**

berdampingan *adj* side by side ← **damping**

berdandan *v* to dress, put on make-up ← **dandan**

berdansa *v* to dance (Western-style) ← **dansa**

berdarah *v* to bleed ← **darah**

berdasar *adj* based; **berdasar-kan** *adj* based on; in accordance with, pursuant to ← **dasar**

berdasi *v* to wear a tie; *kaum* ~ white-collar workers ← **dasi**

berdatangan *v* to come (of many) ← **datang**

berdaulat *adj* sovereign; *negara yang* ~ sovereign state ← **daulat**

berdaya *v* to have power; ~ *guna* efficient; *tak* ~ powerless ← **daya**

berdayung *v* to go by boat or bicycle ← **dayung**

berdebar *v* to beat quickly; *hati* ~ a racing heart ← **debar**

berdebat *v* to have a debate or discussion ← **debat**

berdebu *adj* dusty ← **debu**

berdeham *v* to clear the throat, cough ← **deham**

berdekap-dekapan, berdekapan *v* to embrace each other ← **dekap**

berdekatan *adj* close (of two or more things) ← **dekat**

berdelapan *adj* a group of eight ← **delapan**

berdémo *v* to hold a protest ← **démo**

berdémpét *adj* stuck together ← **démpét**

berdendam *v* to be resentful, full of revenge ← **dendam**

berdéndang *v* to sing, chant ← **déndang**

berdengung *v* to drone, hum, shake with sound ← **dengung**

berdenyut *v* to throb, to beat ← **denyut**

berdérét-dérét *v* to line up ← **dérét**

berdering *v* to ring, tinkle ← **dering**

berdesah *v* to sigh, make a swishing noise ← **desah**

berdesakan *v* to push each other ← **desak**

berdesir *v* to hiss, rustle ← **desir**

berdiam *v* to reside; ~ *diri* to keep silent ← **diam**

berdiét *v* to diet, go on a diet ← **diét**

berdikir *v, Isl* to say additional prayers ← **dikir, zikir**

berdingin-dingin *v* to enjoy cold weather ← **dingin**

berdisiplin *adj* disciplined ← **disiplin**

berdoa *v* to pray, say a prayer; ~ *menurut keyakinan masing-masing* to pray according to your own religion ← **doa**

berdomisili *v* to be domiciled, reside ← **domisili**

berdosa *v* to sin, commit a sin ← **dosa**

berdua *adj* together, in pairs ← **dua**

berduka ~ *(cita)* to grieve, be in mourning ← **duka**

berdurasi *v* to last, have a duration of ← **durasi**

berduri *adj* thorny; *kawat* ~ barbed wire ← **duri**

berdusta *v* to lie ← **dusta**

beréaksi *v* to react ← **réaksi**

berebut *v* to fight for; **berebutan**

v to fight each other for ← **rebut**

berédar *v* to circulate ← **édar**

berékor *v* to have a tail; *bintang* ~ comet; *tulang* ~ coccyx ← **ékor**

berembuk *v* to confer, discuss ← **rembuk**

berembun *adj* moist, dewy ← **embun**

berembus *v* to blow ← **embus**

berémosi *adj* emotional ← **émosi**

berempat *adj* in a group of four ← **empat**

berenam *adj* in a group of six ← **enam**

berenang *v* to swim ← **renang**

berencana *v* to plan; *Keluarga* ~ *(KB)* family planning ← **rencana**

berénda *adj* lacy, lace ← **rénda**

berendam *v* to soak ← **rendam**

berénérgi *adj* energetic, containing energy ← **énérgi**

bérés finished, ready; ~, *bos!* Done, boss!; **membéréskan** *v* to clear up, make ready

beréstafét *adj* in stages ← **éstafét**

berétika *adj* ethical; to behave; ~ *baik* to behave well ← **étika**

berfaédah *adj* useful, worthwhile; *tidak* ~ useless ← **faédah**

berfasilitas *adj* with facilities ← **fasilitas**

berféderasi *v* to be federated ← **féderasi**

berfilsafat *v* to have a philosophy ← **filsafat**

berfirman *v* to utter, say; *Allah* ~ God said ← **firman**

berfokus *adj* focused ← **fokus**

berfoya-foya *v* to waste money, live frivolously ← **foya-foya**

berfungsi *v* to work, go; to act as ← **fungsi**

bergabung *v* to join together ← **gabung**

bergadang → **begadang**

bergairah *adj* lusty, passionate; enthusiastic ← **gairah**

bergambar *adj* illustrated ← **gambar**

bergandéng *v* to join or do together; **bergandéngan** *v* ~ *tangan* to link arms or hands ← **gandéng**

berganti *v* to change; **berganti-ganti, bergantian** in turns, repeatedly ← **ganti**

bergantung ~ *pada* to depend on ← **gantung**

bergaransi *adj* guaranteed ← **garansi**

bergaris *adj* lined ← **garis**

bergaul *v* to mix or associate with ← **gaul**

bergaung *v* to echo ← **gaung**

bergaya *adj* stylish, with style ← **gaya**

bergegas-gegas *v* to hurry ← **gegas**

bergejolak *v* to flare up, burst out ← **gejolak**

bergelantungan *v* to hang from (of several things) ← **gelantung**

bergelar *v* to have a title ← **gelar**

bergelimang *adj* smeared; ~ *lumpur* muddy, mud-stained ← **gelimang**

bergelimpang *adj* sprawled;

bergelimpangan *adj* sprawled all around; *mayat* ~ dead bodies lay everywhere

bergelombang *adj* wavy ← **gelombang**

bergelut *v* to wrestle; to romp ← **gelut**

bergema *v* to echo, reverberate ← **gema**

bergembira *v* to be happy, joyous ← **gembira**

bergeming *tak* ~ not bat an eyelid, make not the slightest reaction ← **geming**

bergenang *adj* flooded ← **genang**

bergéngsi *adj* prestigious ← **géngsi**

bergerak *v* to move; *aset* ~ movable assets ← **gerak**

bergerigi *adj* serrated, jagged ← **gerigi**

bergerilya *v* to wage guerrilla warfare ← **gerilya**

bergerombol *v* to gather in a group, amass ← **gerombol**

bergetar *v* to vibrate, tremble ← **getar**

bergilir, bergiliran *adj* in turns ← **gilir**

bergizi *adj* nutritious ← **gizi**

bergoncang *v* to rock, sway ← **goncang**

bergosip *v* to gossip ← **gosip**

bergoyang *v* to shake, sway; to dance ← **goyang**

bergulat *v* to wrestle, fight ← **gulat**

bergumam *v* to mumble ← **gumam**

bergumpal *v* to clot ← **gumpal**

bergumul *v* to wrestle ← **gumul**

berguna *adj* useful, worthwhile; *tidak* ~ useless ← **guna**

berguncang *v* to rock, sway ← **guncang**

bergundah ~ *hati* sad ← **gundah**

berhadapan *v* face to face; ~ *muka* face to face ← **hadap**

berhadiah *adj* with prizes ← **hadiah**

berhak *v* to have a right to, be entitled to ← **hak**

berhala *n* idol

berhalangan *v* to be prevented, unable ← **halang**

berhaluan ~ *kiri* leftist ← **halu**

berhamburan *adj* scattered about ← **hambur**

berharap *v* to hope ← **harap**

berharga *adj* precious, valuable ← **harga**

berhari-hari *adv* for days ← **hari**

berhasil *v* to succeed ← **hasil**

berhati *v* to have a heart; ~ *besar* open-hearted

berhati-hati *v* to be careful ← **hati**

berhawa *v* to have a climate; ~ *sejuk* cool climate ← **hawa**

berhémat *v* to be economical ← **hémat**

berhenti *v* to stop, cease ← **henti**

berhias *v* to dress up, put on make-up ← **hias**

berhimpun *v* to meet, assemble ← **himpun**

berhitung *v* to count

berhobi *v* to have as a hobby ← **hobi**

berhubung *conj* in connection

to, related with; ~ *dengan* in connection with; **berhubungan** *v, pl* to have a link or connection ← **hubung**

berhulu *v* to rise, have a source; *Sungai Mekong* ~ *di Cina* the source of the Mekong is in China ← **hulu**

beri *v* to give; ~ *semangat* give a cheer; ~ *tahu* inform, let know → **beritahu; memberi** *v* to give; **memberikan** *v* to give someone (as an act of kindness); to give something (for someone); **pemberi** *n* giver, donor; **pemberian** *n* present, gift, something given to someone

beriak *v* to ripple ← **riak**

beribadah *v* to worship, serve; *orang* ~ religious person ← **ibadah**

beribu ~ *bapak* to have parents ← **ibu**

beribu, beribu-ribu *adj* thousands of ← **ribu**

berijazah *adj* certified, qualified ← **ijazah**

beriklim *v* to have a climate; ~ *dingin* to have a cool climate ← **iklim**

berikrar *v* to promise, pledge ← **ikrar**

berikut *adj* following; ~ *itu* after that; *yang* ~, ~*nya* the next ← **ikut**

berilmu *adj* learned ← **ilmu**

beriman *adj* religious ← **iman**

berimbang *adj* balanced, proportional ← **imbang**

beringin *n* banyan; *pohon* ~

banyan tree; *Partai* ~ Golkar

berinisiatif *v* to take the initiative ← **inisiatif**

berintrospéksi *v* to be introspective ← **introspéksi**

berirama *adj* rhythmical ← **irama**

beriring-iringan *adv* in succession ← **iring**

berisi *v* to contain; *adj* full, filled out ← **isi**

berisik *adj* noisy, loud; to rustle ← **risik**

berisiko *v* to be risky ← **risiko**

beristeri, beristri *adj, m* married; *pria* ~ married man ← **isteri, istri**

beristirahat *v* to rest, take a break ← **istirahat**

berita *n* news, information; ~ *malam* evening news; **memberitakan** *v* to report

beritahu, beri tahu *v* to inform, let know; **memberitahu** *v* to advise, inform, tell; **pemberitahuan** *n* announcement, notice

berjabat, berjabatan ~ *tangan* to shake hands ← **jabat**

berjaga *v* to stand guard ← **jaga**

berjajar *adj* in a row ← **jajar**

berjalan *v* to walk, move; ~ *dengan baik* go well ← **jalan**

berjam-jam *adj* for hours and hours ← **jam**

berjamaah *adv, Isl* together, as a congregation ← **jamaah**

berjambul *v* to have a quiff or crest ← **jambul**

berjamur *adj* moldy; **berjamuran** *v* to pop up everywhere ← **jamur**

berjangka *adj* for a term; *deposito* ~ term deposit ← **jangka**

berjangkit *v* to spread, be infectious or contagious ← **jangkit**

berjanji *v* to promise ← **janji**

berjasa *adj* meritorious, deserving of reward; *v* to perform a service ← **jasa**

berjéjér, berjéjéran *adj* in a row, in a line ← **jéjér**

berjemur *v* to sunbathe, sun yourself ← **jemur**

berjénggot *adj* bearded ← **jénggot**

berjenis-jenis *adj* all kinds of, various ← **jenis**

berjeruji *adj* fitted with bars ← **jeruji**

berjihad *v* to conduct a war or crusade ← **jihad**

berjilbab *adj* in a veil, *v* to wear the veil ← **jilbab**

berjilid *adj* in volumes ← **jilid**

berjinjit-jinjit *v* to walk on tiptoe ← **jinjit**

berjiwa *adj* alive ← **jiwa**

berjogét *v* to dance ← **jogét**

berjongkok *v* to squat ← **jongkok**

berjual *v* to trade, sell ← **jual**

berjuang *v* to fight, struggle ← **juang**

berjubah *v* to wear a robe ← **jubah**

berjudi *v* to gamble ← **judi**

berjudul *adj* titled; *v* to have a title

berjumlah *v* to (have the) number ← **jumlah**

berjumpa *v* to meet ← **jumpa**

berjuntai *v* to dangle ← **juntai**

berjuta *v* to have millions of ← **juta**

berkabung *v* to mourn; *hari ~ nasional* day of national mourning ← **kabung**

berkaca-kaca *v* to fill with tears (of eyes) ← **kaca**

berkaitan *adj* related to ← **kait**

berkala *adj* regular; *secara ~* periodically ← **kala**

berkali-kali *adv* repeatedly, again and again ← **kali**

berkalung *adj* wearing a necklace ← **kalung**

berkampanye *v* to (hold a) campaign; to join a parade for a candidate ← **kampanye**

berkamuflase *v* to use camouflage ← **kamuflase**

berkantong *v* to have a pocket; *~ tebal* wealthy ← **kantong**

berkapasitas *v* with a capacity of ← **kapasitas**

berkarat *adj* rusty ← **karat**

berkas *n* bundle; file, dossier, brief

berkat *n* blessing; *conj* thanks to; *~ doamu, aku sudah sembuh* Thanks to your prayers, I am well again; **memberkati** *v* to bless; *Tuhan ~* God bless; **pemberkatan** *n* consecration, blessing

berkata *v* to say, speak ← **kata**

berkawan *v* to have or be friends with ← **kawan**

berkayuh paddle, row; pedal ← **kayuh**

berkeberatan *v* to object, have an objection ← **berat, keberatan**

berkecil *~ hati* to be disappointed ← **kecil**

berkecukupan *v* to have enough, get by ← **cukup**

berkedip *v* to blink (two eyes) or wink (one eye); **berkedip-kedip** *adj* blinking ← **kedip**

berkedok *v* to hide behind a mask, pretend ← **kedok**

berkehendak *v* to intend ← **hendak, kehendak**

berkejang *v* to have a cramp ← **kejang**

berkelahi *v* to quarrel, fight, fall out ← **kelahi**

berkelana *v* to roam, wander ← **kelana**

berkelas *adj* classy ← **kelas**

berkeliaran *v* to swarm or wander about ← **keliar**

berkeliling *v* to go around ← **keliling**

berkelip *v* to twinkle, flicker ← **kelip**

berkelompok *adj* in groups, group ← **kelompok**

berkeluarga *v* to have a family, be married ← **keluarga**

berkeluh *v* to complain ← **keluh**

berkémah *v* to camp, go camping ← **kémah**

berkemas-kemas *v* to tidy up, pack ← **kemas**

berkembang *v* to develop, expand; *~ biak* to breed, grow; *negara ~* developing nation ← **kembang**

berkenaan *~ dengan* in connection with, regarding ← **kena**

berkencan v to go on a date ← **kencan**

berkepala v to have a head ← **kepala**

berkepanjangan adj continuous, protracted ← **panjang**

berkepentingan v to have an interest in; yang ~ concerned party ← **penting**

berkepul v to smoke, billow ← **kepul**

berkeramas v to wash your hair ← **keramas**

berkeringat v to sweat ← **keringat**

berkeriput adj wrinkly, lined ← **keriput**

berkerja → **bekerja**

berkerudung adj veiled ← **kerudung**

berkerumun v to swarm, crowd ← **kerumun**

berkerut v to frown ← **kerut**

berkesan adj impressive ← **kesan**

berkesempatan v to have an opportunity ← **sempat**

berkesinambungan adj sustained, continuous; perkembangan yang ~ sustained development ← **sambung**

berketombé rambut ~ dry scalp, dandruff ← **ketombé**

berkeyakinan v to be convinced ← **yakin**

berkhasiat adj beneficial, therapeutic ← **khasiat**

berkhayal v to dream, imagine ← **khayal**

berkhianat v to betray ← **khianat**

berkibar v to wave, flutter ← **kibar**

berkiblat v to be oriented toward; ~ pada Amerika to look to America ← **kiblat**

berkilap v to shine, gleam ← **kilap**

berkilat v to shine, sparkle ← **kilat**

berkilau adj glittering, sparkling ← **kilau**

berkiprah v to move, dance, be active in ← **kiprah**

berkisah v to tell a story ← **kisah**

berkisar v to revolve, rotate, turn ← **kisar**

berkoalisi v to be in a coalition ← **koalisi**

berkobar v to blaze, burn ← **kobar**

berkokok v to crow; ayam ~ rooster's crow ← **kokok**

berkolaborasi v to collaborate, work together ← **kolaborasi**

berkoméntar v to (make a) comment ← **koméntar**

berkompromi v to compromise, reach a compromise ← **kompromi**

berkorban v to make sacrifices, do without ← **korban**

berkotéka adj wearing a penis sheath ← **kotéka**

berkuah adj with a soup or sauce ← **kuah**

berkuala v to have a mouth or confluence ← **kuala**

berkualitas adj quality ← **kualitas**

berkuasa *adj* powerful, mighty ← **kuasa**

berkubah *adj* domed ← **kubah**

berkubang *v* to wallow (in mud) ← **kubang**

berkuda *v* to ride a horse, go (horse-)riding ← **kuda**

berkuku *adj* having nails or claws; clawed ← **kuku**

berkulit to have skin, skinned; ~ *badak* thick-skinned ← **kulit**

berkuman *adj* full of germs, bacteria ← **kuman**

berkumandang *v* to echo ← **kumandang**

berkumpul *v* to assemble, meet ← **kumpul**

berkumur, berkumur-kumur *v* to gargle ← **kumur**

berkunjung *v* to visit, pay a visit to ← **kunjung**

berkurang *v* to decrease, diminish, subside; ~*nya* the fall in ← **kurang**

berkurban *v, Isl* to make a sacrifice, have a sacrifice slaughtered ← **kurban**

berkutat *v* to be busy or concerned with ← **kutat**

berkutik *v* to move slightly, budge ← **kutik**

berkutu *v* to have fleas or lice ← **kutu**

berlabuh *v* to anchor ← **labuh**

berladang *v* to cultivate the land ← **ladang**

berlagak *v* to act, pretend ← **lagak**

berlainan *adj* differing, different ← **lain**

berlaku *adj* effective, valid; *v* to behave ← **laku**

berlalu *v* to pass ← **lalu**

berlambang *v* to have a symbol ← **lambang**

berlandaskan *adj* based on ← **landas**

berlangganan *v* to subscribe to ← **langgan**

berlangsung *v* to take place ← **langsung**

berlanjut *v* to continue ← **lanjut**

berlantai *v* to have floors, stories ← **lantai**

berlari *v* to run ← **lari**

berlatarkan *v* to have as a background, be based on ← **latar**

berlawanan *v* to be opposed ← **lawan**

berlayar *v* to sail ← **layar**

berlebihan *adj* excessive ← **lebih**

berlendir *adj* mucous, slimy ← **lendir**

berlépotan → **belépotan**

berlian *n* diamond

berlibur *v* to go or be on holiday ← **libur**

berliku-liku *adj* twisted, complicated ← **liku**

berlima *adj* the five of them, a group of five ← **lima**

berlimpah-limpah *adj* overflowing, abundant ← **limpah**

berlinang *v* to trickle, drip; *air mata* ~ eyes filled with tears ← **linang**

berlindung *v* to (take) shelter ← **lindung**

berlipat ~ *ganda* many times over ← **lipat**

berliur *v* to drool, salivate ← **liur**

berlogat ~ *jawa* to have a Javanese accent ← **logat**

berlokasi *adj* located ← **lokasi**

berlomba *v* to compete, race ← **lomba**

berlumpur *adj* muddy ← **lumpur**

berlumuran *adj* smeared, stained ← **lumur**

berlutut to kneel (down) ← **lutut**

bermaaf-maafan *v, Isl* to beg forgiveness of each other (at Idul Fitri) ← **maaf**

bermacam-macam *adj* various ← **macam**

bermain *v* to play; ~ *api* to play with fire ← **main**

bermaksud *v* to intend ← **maksud**

bermalam *v* to spend or stay the night ← **malam**

bermalas-malas, bermalas-malasan *v* to lie or laze around, be lazy ← **malas**

bermandi *v* to bathe; ~ *keringat* to be soaked in sweat; **bermandikan** *adj* bathed in ← **mandi**

bermanfaat *adj* useful, of benefit ← **manfaat**

bermartabat *adj* dignified ← **martabat**

bermasalah *adj* problematic, troublesome ← **masalah**

bermérek *v* to have a label; *adj* branded ← **mérek**

bermigrasi *v* to migrate ← **migrasi**

bermimpi *v* to dream ← **mimpi**

berminat *v* to have an interest, be interested ← **minat**

berminggu-minggu *adv* for weeks ← **minggu**

berminyak *adj* oily, greasy ← **minyak**

bermodal *v* to have capital; ~ *dengkul* with only hard work ← **modal**

bermotif *v* to have a design ← **motif**

bermotivasikan *v* to be motivated by ← **motivasi**

bermuara *v* to have a mouth, empty into ← **muara**

bermuatan *v* to be laden with ← **muat**

bermuka *v* to have a face; ~ *dua* two-faced ← **muka**

bermukim *v* to reside, stay, live ← **mukim**

bermula *v* to start, begin ← **mula**

bermunculan *v* to show up (in large numbers) ← **muncul**

bermusuhan *v* to be enemies ← **musuh**

bermusyawarah *v* to reach an agreement ← **musyawarah**

bermutu *adj* quality; ~ *rendah* low quality ← **mutu**

bernada *v* to have a tone or edge; ~ *sinis* mockingly, sarcastically ← **nada**

bernafaskan, bernapaskan *v* with a breath of ← **nafas**

bernafsu *adj* passionate, lusty ← **nafsu**

bernama *adj* named ← **nama**

bernanah *v* to fester ← **nanah**

bernaung *v* to (take) shelter ← **naung**

berniat *v* to intend ← **niat**

bernostalgia *v* to reminisce, be nostalgic ← **nostalgia**

bernuansa *adj* with a touch of ← **nuansa**

bernyala *v* to burn, blaze ← **nyala**

bernyali *adj* brave ← **nyali**

bernyanyi *v* to sing ← **nyanyi**

bernyawa *adj* alive ← **nyawa**

berobat *v* to go to the doctor, seek medical advice ← **obat**

beroda *adj* wheeled ← **roda**

berolahraga *v* to do or play sport ← **olahraga**

berombak *adj* wavy; *rambut* ~ wavy hair ← **ombak**

beronani *v* to masturbate ← **onani**

berontak, memberontak *v* to rebel, revolt; **pemberontak** *n* rebel; **pemberontakan** *n* rebellion, revolt, mutiny

beroperasi *v* to operate, work, function ← **operasi**

berotot *adj* muscular ← **otot**

berpahala *adj* meritorious ← **pahala**

berpakaian *adj* dressed in ← **pakai**

berpaling *v* to turn away or from ← **paling**

berpamit *v* to take leave ← **pamit**

berpancar *v* to shine out ← **pancar**

berpandangan *v* to look at each other ← **pandang**

berpangkal *adj* based ← **pangkal**

berpangkat *v* to have the rank of ← **pangkat**

berpantang *v* to not be allowed, abstain from; *makan* ~ to be on a diet ← **pantang**

berpantulan *v* to reflect (of many things) ← **pantul**

berpantun *v* to recite or write a traditional poem ← **pantun**

berparas *v* to have a face or appearance ← **paras**

berpasang-pasangan *adv* in pairs ← **pasang**

berpedoman *v* to be guided by, based on ← **pedoman**

berpegang *v* to hold onto; ~ *teguh* to hold fast to ← **pegang**

berpeluang *v* to have an opportunity, a chance ← **luang**

berpeluh *v* to sweat, perspire ← **peluh**

berpencaran *v* to disperse (of many things) ← **pencar**

berpendapat *v* to have an opinion, believe ← **dapat**

berpendidikan *adj* educated, to have an education; ~ *SD* have a primary school education ← **didik**

berpendirian *v* to hold, be of an opinion ← **diri**

berpengalaman *adj* experienced, skilled ← **alam**

berpengaruh *adj* influential ← **pengaruh**

berperan *v* to play the role or part ← **peran**

berperang *v* to wage war, go to war ← **perang**

berperawakan *v* to have a build, stature ← **awak**

berperikemanusiaan *adj* humane ← **manusia**

berpésta v to (have a) party ← **pésta**

berpidato v to make a speech, give an address ← **pidato**

berpihak v to take sides ← **pihak**

berpijak v to stand on ← **pijak**

berpikir v to think ← **pikir**

berpiknik v to have a picnic ← **piknik**

berpindah v to move ← **pindah**

berpisah v to part, separate ← **pisah**

berpola v to have a pattern; adj patterned ← **pola**

berpolémik v to debate, argue over ← **polémik**

berpolitik v to play politics ← **politik**

berponi v to have a fringe or bangs ← **poni**

berpori adj porous, having pores; kulit ~ besar skin with large pores ← **pori**

berpose v to pose for a photograph ← **pose**

berposisi v to hold a position, be positioned ← **posisi**

berpotongan adj of a certain style or cut ← **potong**

berprédikat adj with the title of ← **prédikat**

berpréstasi adj prestigious; successful ← **préstasi**

berprinsip v to have principles; adj principled ← **prinsip**

berprofési v to have a profession, work as ← **profési**

berpuasa v to fast ← **puasa**

berpukul-pukulan v to hit each other ← **pukul**

berpulang v to pass away, die ← **pulang**

berpura-pura v to pretend, fake ← **pura-pura**

berpusar n to revolve, whirl ← **pusar**

berpusat ~ pada to focus or center on ← **pusat**

berputar v to rotate, turn ← **putar**

bersabar v to be patient ← **sabar**

bersabda v to say or speak; Sri Sultan ~ the Sultan expressed ← **sabda**

bersabun adj soapy ← **sabun**

bersahabat adj to be friends ← **sahabat**

bersahaja adj simple, natural ← **sahaja**

bersaing v to compete; harga ~ competitive price ← **saing**

bersaksi v to testify ← **saksi**

bersalah adj guilty ← **salah**

bersalam-salaman v, pl to shake hands with others ← **salam**

bersalin v to give birth; rumah sakit ~ maternity hospital ← **salin**

bersalju adj snowy, snow-covered ← **salju**

bersama adv together; jointly; kepentingan ~ common interest ← **sama**

bersambung adj in parts; to be continued; cerita ~ (cerber) serial ← **sambung**

bersambut gayung ~ receive a response ← **sambut**

bersampingan adj next to each other ← **samping**

bersampul *adj* in an envelope or folder; *diberi ~* to be given a protective jacket or wrapped in plastic (for a book) ← **sampul**

bersandar *v* to lean ← **sandar**

bersanding *v* to stand or sit next to; **bersandingan** *v* to stand or sit next to each other ← **sanding**

bersandiwara *v* to pretend ← **sandiwara**

bersanggama *v* to have sex ← **sanggama**

bersanggul *v* to wear a bun ← **sanggul**

bersangka *v* to suspect or think; *~ buruk* to think the worst ← **sangka**

bersangkutan *adj* concerned, involved; *yang ~ (ybs)* person concerned or involved ← **sangkut**

bersantai *v* to relax, take it easy ← **santai**

bersantan *adj* containing coconut milk ← **santan**

bersantap *v, pol* to eat, partake of; *~ pagi* breakfast ← **santap**

bersarang *v* to (make a) nest ← **sarang**

bersarung *adj* in a sarung; with a cover ← **sarung**

bersatu *v* to unite; *~ padu* to unite, integrate ← **satu**

bersaudara *v* to be related; to have brothers and sisters; *~ enam* to be one of six (children) ← **saudara**

bersayap *adj* winged; *vi* to have wings ← **sayap**

bersebelahan *conj* next to ← **belah**

berseberangan *adj* opposing, in disagreement ← **seberang**

bersedekah *v* to make a donation ← **sedekah**

bersedia *v* to be prepared or willing ← **sedia**

bersedih *v* to be or feel sad ← **sedih**

bersejarah *adj* historic, historical ← **sejarah**

bersekolah *v* to go to school ← **sekolah**

bersekongkol *v* to plot, conspire against ← **kongkol**

bersekutu *v* to be allies ← **sekutu**

berselancar *v* to surf, go surfing ← **lancar**

berselang *adj* with an interval of *~-seling* alternating ← **selang**

berseléra *v* to have a taste or appetite for ← **seléra**

berselimutkan *adj* blanketed in ← **selimut**

berselingkuh *v* to have an affair ← **selingkuh**

berselisih *v* to differ in opinion, have a different opinion, quarrel ← **selisih**

berselonjor *adj* with outstretched legs ← **selonjor**

berseloroh *v* to joke ← **seloroh**

berselubung *adj* veiled ← **selubung**

bersemangat *adj* spirited, enthusiastic ← **semangat**

bersembahyang *v* to pray, perform a prayer ← **sembahyang**

bersemboyan *adj* with the motto ← **semboyan**

bersembunyi *v* to hide (yourself) ← **sembunyi**

bersemedi *v* to meditate ← **semedi**

bersemi *v* to sprout buds ← **semi**

bersenandung *v* to hum, sing ← **senandung**

bersenang-senang *v* to enjoy yourself, have fun ← **senang**

bersenda ~ *gurau* to joke around ← **senda**

bersendawa *v* to burp, belch ← **sendawa**

bersénggolan *v, pl* to bump into each other ← **sénggol**

bersenjata *adj* armed ← **senjata**

bersentuh *v* to touch; **bersentuhan** *adv* touching each other ← **sentuh**

bersenyawa *v* to become a chemical compound ← **senyawa**

bersepatu *adj* in shoes ← **sepatu**

bersepéda *v* to ride a bicycle ← **sepéda**

bersérakan *adj* scattered everywhere ← **serak**

berserat *makanan* ~ high-fiber food ← **serat**

berseri *adj* beaming, glowing ← **seri**

bersértifikat *adj* with papers (of a house) ← **sértifikat**

berseru *v* to call, cry; ~ *kepada* to call on, appeal ← **seru**

berseteru *v* to be hostile, at odds with ← **seteru**

bersetubuh *v* to have sex ← **tubuh, setubuh**

bersetuju *v* to agree ← **tuju, setuju**

bersiaga *v* to be on the alert, on guard ← **siaga**

bersiap *v* to get ready; **bersiap-siap** *v* to make preparations ← **siap**

bersifat *v* to have the quality of ← **sifat**

bersih *adj* clean, neat; *berat* ~ net weight; **kebersihan** *n* cleanliness, hygiene; **membersihkan** *v* to clean; wipe out (eg. disease); **pembersih** *n* cleaning agent; **pembersihan** *n* cleaning, purification; purge

bersikap *v* to display an attitude ← **sikap**

bersikeras *v* to maintain, stick to, be obstinate ← **keras**

bersikukuh *v* to hold fast to ← **kukuh**

bersila *duduk* ~ to sit cross-legged ← **sila**

bersilang *adj* crossed ← **silang**

bersilaturahmi *v* to maintain good relations, visit or meet friends ← **silaturahmi**

bersimpang *v* to branch ← **simpang**

bersimpati *adj* sympathetic ← **simpati**

bersimpuh *v* to sit kneeling with feet to one side

bersin *v* to sneeze

bersinambung *adj* continuous ← **sambung**

bersinar *v* to shine, gleam ← **sinar**

bersisik *adj* scaly, rough ← **sisik**

bersitegang *v* to stand fast, persevere ← **tegang**

bersiul *v* to whistle ← **siul**

berskala *v* to be on a scale; ~ *besar* large-scale ← **skala**

bersobat *v* to be friends ← **sobat**

bersoda *adj* carbonated; *minuman* ~ carbonated drink ← **soda**

bersolék *v* to put on make-up, dress up ← **solék**

bersorak *v* to cheer, shout ← **sorak**

bersosok *v* to have a figure; ~ *tinggi* tall ← **sosok**

bersua *v* to meet ← **sua**

bersuami *adj, f* married; **bersuamikan** *v* to be married to ← **suami**

bersuap-suapan *v* to feed each other (in marriage rituals) ← **suap**

bersuara *v* to sound, have a voice ← **suara**

bersuhu *v* to have a temperature ← **suhu**

bersuit *v* to whistle using your fingers ← **suit**

bersujud *v* to prostrate yourself ← **sujud**

bersulang *v* to toast, drink to ← **sulang**

bersumpah *v* to swear ← **sumpah**

bersungguh-sungguh *v* to do your best ← **sungguh**

bersusah ~ *payah* to work hard ← **susah**

bersusila *v* to have good morals ← **susila**

bersyarat *adj* conditional ← **syarat**

bersyukur *adj* grateful ← **syukur**

bertabiat *v* to be of a character, be of a temperament ← **tabiat**

bertaburan *adj* scattered over ← **tabur**

bertahap *adj* in stages ← **tahap**

bertahun-tahun *adv* for years and years ← **tahun**

bertajuk *v* to have a topic ← **tajuk**

bertakhta *v* to reign ← **takhta**

bertakwa *n* pious ← **takwa**

bertamasya *v* to travel (for pleasure), go sightseeing ← **tamasya**

bertambah *v* to increase ← **tambah**

bertambal *adj* patched ← **tambal**

bertambat *adj* tied up, moored ← **tambat**

bertaméng *v* to hide behind, use as a shield or pretext ← **taméng**

bertanda *adj* marked ← **tanda**

bertandang *v* to (pay a) visit ← **tandang**

bertanding *v* to compete, play ← **tanding**

bertanggal *tak* ~ undated ← **tanggal**

bertanggung jawab *adj* responsible ← **tanggung jawab**

bertanya *v* to ask; **bertanya-tanya** *v* to wonder, ask yourself ← **tanya**

bertapa *v* to live as an ascetic or hermit, seclude oneself ← **tapa**

bertaraf *adj* of a certain standard ← **taraf**

bertaruh *v* to bet ← **taruh**

bertato *adj* tattooed ← **tato**

bertébaran *adj* scattered ← **tébar**

berteduh *v* to take shelter ← **teduh**

bertékad *v* to be determined ← **tékad**

bertekuk *v* to bend your knees ~ *lutut* to surrender, go down on your knees ← **tekuk**

bertekun *v* to work hard, be diligent ← **tekun**

bertelanjang *v* to be bare; ~ *dada* bare-chested ← **telanjang**

bertélé-télé *adj* long-winded ← **télé**

bertelur *v* to lay an egg ← **telur**

bertéma *v* to have as a theme ← **téma**

berteman *v* to be friends ← **teman**

bertempat *v* to take place or happen; ~ *tinggal* to live or reside ← **tempat**

bertempur *v* to fight ← **tempur**

bertemu *v* to meet; *sampai* ~ *lagi* see you later, so long ← **temu**

berténggér to perch, land ← **ténggér**

bertengkar *v* to quarrel ← **tengkar**

bertentangan *adj* contradictory, contrary, opposing ← **tentang**

bertenun *v* to weave ← **tenun**

bertepatan *adj* coinciding with, at the same time as ← **tepat**

bertepuk tangan *v* to applaud, clap ← **tepuk tangan**

berteriak *v* to scream or shout ← **teriak**

berterima kasih *v* to be grateful or thankful ← **terima kasih**

bertetangga *v* to have a neighbor or neighbors ← **tetangga**

bertiga *adj* in a three ← **tiga**

bertikai *v* to quarrel or disagree ← **tikai**

bertimbun-timbun *adv* in heaps, piled up ← **timbun**

bertindak *v* to act, take action ← **tindak**

bertingkah *v* to act, behave ← **tingkah**

bertingkat *adj* having different levels; *rumah* ~ two-storied house ← **tingkat**

bertinju *v* to box ← **tinju**

bertitel *v* to have the title ← **titel**

bertiup *v* to blow ← **tiup**

bertobat *v* to repent ← **tobat**

bertolak *v, form* to depart, leave ← **tolak**

bertongkat *adj* with a stick ← **tongkat**

bertransaksi *v* to make a transaction ← **transaksi**

bertuah *adj* lucky, having magic power ← **tuah**

bertubi-tubi *adv* repeatedly, without stopping, unceasing ← **tubi**

bertubuh *v* to have a body; ~ *gemuk* fat ← **tubuh; bersetubuh** *v* to have sex ← **tubuh**

bertujuan *adj* with a purpose of ← **tuju**

bertukar *v* to change ← **tukar**

bertumpu *v* to rest on ← **tumpu**

bertumpuk *v* to be in piles; **bertumpuk-tumpuk** *v* in piles ← **tumpuk**

berturut-turut *adj* consecutive, successive ← **turut**

bertutur *v* to speak or talk ← **tutur**

beruang *n* bear; ~ *putih* polar bear

berubah *v* to change ← **ubah**

beruban *v* to have gray hairs ← **uban**

berujar *v* to speak or say ← **ujar**

berulah *v* to behave ← **ulah**

berulang *v* to happen again, recur; **berulang-ulang** *adv* again and again, repeatedly ← **ulang**

berumah tangga *adj* married ← **rumah tangga**

berumur *adj* aged ← **umur**

berunding *v* to discuss ← **runding**

beruntun *adj* in a chain; *tabrakan* ~ pile-up ← **runtun**

beruntung *adj* lucky, fortunate ← **untung**

berupa *adj* in the shape or form of ← **rupa**

berupaya *v* to make an effort, try ← **upaya**

berurai *v* to hang down or loose ← **urai**

berurusan *v* to have dealings with, deal with ← **urus**

berurutan, berurut-urutan *adj* successive, consecutive, sequential ← **urut**

berusaha *v* to try, make an effort ← **usaha**

berusia *v* to be (aged) ← **usia**

berutang *v* to owe; ~ *budi* to have a debt of gratitude ← **utang**

berwajah *v* to have a face; ~ *muram* sour-faced ← **wajah**

berwajib *adj* responsible, competent ← **wajib**

berwarna *adj* colored ← **warna**

berwatak *v* to have a certain nature; ~ *keras* strict, stern, unyielding ← **watak**

berwawasan *v* to have an outlook; ~ *luas* broad or open mind ← **wawas**

berwenang *adj* competent, in charge ← **wenang**

berwibawa *adj* esteemed, respected, of good standing ← **wibawa**

berwisata *v* to travel or holiday ← **wisata**

berwudu *v* to wash before praying ← **wudu**

berwujud *v* in the form or shape of ← **wujud**

beryodium *garam* ~ iodized salt ← **yodium**

berziarah *v* to make a pilgrimage, visit a holy place ← **ziarah**

berzikir *v, Isl* to say additional prayers ← **zikir**

berzina *v* to commit adultery ← **zina**

bésan *n* relationship between two couples whose children have married; ~*nya orang tentara* His daughter's father-in-law is in the army

besar *adj* big, large, great; ~ *kepala* big-headed, arrogant; *hari* ~ (religious) holiday; **besar-besaran** *adj* large-scale; **berbesar** ~ *hati* big-hearted, accepting; **kebesaran** *n* greatness; *adj* too big; *Celana ini* ~! These pants are too big!; **membesar** *v* to get bigger, grow; **membesarkan** *v* to bring up, raise (children); **memperbesar** *v* to enlarge something; **pembesar** *n* big-shot, official; **pembesaran** *n* enlargement, expansion; **terbesar** *adj* largest, biggest

beserta *conj* along with, and ← **serta**

besi *n* iron; ~ *tua* scrap metal; ~ *tuang* cast iron; *tukang* ~ blacksmith

bésok *adv* tomorrow; *coll* in the future ← **ésok**

besuk *v* to visit someone in hospital; *jam* ~ visiting hours; **membesuk** *v* to visit someone in hospital

béta *lit, arch* I

betah *v* settle in, feel at home

betapa *adv* how (very); ~ *cantiknya!* How pretty she is!; *conj* ~*pun* however → **alangkah**

Betawi original inhabitants of Jakarta (since 1527); *orang* ~ the Betawi people

bété, BT *adj, sl* moody, bad-tempered ← **berahi tinggi**

beterbangan *v, pl* to fly about ← **terbang**

betina *adj* female (of animals);

anjing ~ bitch

betis *n* calf, lower part of leg

beton *n* concrete

betul *adj* true, correct, right; real; *adv* really, truly; **betul-betul** *adv* truly, completely; **kebetulan** *adv* by chance, accidentally; *n* coincidence; **membetulkan** *v* to correct, repair; **pembetulan** *n* correction, repair; **sebetulnya** *adv* in fact, actually

BI *abbrev Bank Indonesia* Bank Indonesia, the central reserve bank

bi *pron* Aunt; term of address for older housemaid ← **bibi**

biadab *adj* uncivilized, savage; **kebiadaban** *n* savagery

biak *berkembang* ~ to multiply, breed; **membiakkan** *v* to breed, cultivate; **pembiakan** *n* breeding, cultivation

biang *n* cause; ~ *keladi* source of the problem; ~ *keringat* prickly heat

bianglala *n* rainbow

biar let, no matter if; *conj* so that; ~*lah!* Never mind!; ~*pun* even if, although; **membiarkan** *v* to let, allow, permit; *biarkan!* let it be!; *biarin sl* who cares?

biara *n* abbey, monastery, convent; *kepala* ~ *m* abbot, *f* abbess; **biarawan** *n* monk; **biarawati** *n* nun

biasa *adj* normal, usual, common, ordinary; ~*nya* usually; *luar* ~ extraordinary; **kebiasaan** *n* habit, custom; **mem-**

biasakan *v* ~ *diri* to accustom yourself; **terbiasa** *adj* used to, accustomed

biawak *n* type of iguana, monitor lizard

biaya *n* cost, expense (for a service); ~ *hidup* cost of living; ~ *pengiriman* dispatch cost; **membiayai** *v* to finance someone or something; **pembiayaan** *n* financing

bibi *n, pron* aunt, sister of parent; mother's female cousin ← **bi**

bibir *n* lips; ~ *atas* upper lip

bibit *n* seedling; **pembibitan** *n* sowing, planting of seeds

bicara *v* speak; **berbicara** *v* to speak; ~ *dalam bahasa Sunda* to speak in Sundanese; **membicarakan** *v* to discuss; **pembicara** *n* speaker; **pembicaraan** *n* discussion

bidadari *n* fairy

bidan *n* midwife; **kebidanan** *n* midwifery

bidang *adj* spacious, wide; *n* area, field; *Sumitro adalah ahli dalam ~ ekonomi* Sumitro was an expert in the field of economics; *se~ tanah* piece of land

bidik aim; **membidik** *v* to take aim

bihalal *halal* ~ social gathering (especially after Idul Fitri)

bihun *n* vermicelli noodles

bijak *adj* wise; **kebijakan** *n* policy; **bijaksana** *adj* wise, prudent; **kebijaksanaan** *n* caution, prudence; policy

biji *n* seed, grain; counter for very small objects; *sl* counter; *Mau*

beli kancing berapa ~? How many buttons do you want to buy?; **biji-bijian** *n* seeds, grains

bijih *n* ore, tailings

bika Ambon *n* yellow cake like a crumpet, a specialty of Medan

bikin *v, coll* to make; ~ *marah* make angry; **bikinan** *n* product; ~ *Australia* product of Australia; **dibikin** *v* to be made → **buat**

biksu *n* Buddhist monk; **biksuni** *n* Buddhist nun

bila, bilamana *conj* if; when (usually in written form); ~ *kuingat* if I remember

bilah *n* chip; counter for long, narrow objects; **sebilah** *n* counter for long, narrow objects; *se ~ tombak* one spear, a spear

bilang *v, sl* say; *Jangan ~!* Don't tell anyone; **dibilang** *v* to be said

bilang: bilangan *n* number, figure, sum; **terbilang** *adj* counted; *tidak ~* countless; *Esa hilang, dua ~* One lost, two scored (epigraph at military cemeteries)

bilas, membilas *v* rinse; *Gosokkan pada rambut, lalu ~* Rub into the hair, then rinse

biliar, bilyar *n* billiards

biliun, bilyun *n* billion (1,000,000,000); **biliunér** *n* billionaire

Bimasakti *n* the Milky Way

bimbang *adj* nervous, doubtful; *hati yang ~* an uncertain heart

bimbing *v* to lead, guide; **bimbingan** *n* guidance; ~ *belajar* *(bimbel)* extra-curricular course to prepare for exams; **membimbing** *v* to lead, guide, coach; **pembimbing** *n* guide, coach, leader

BIN *abbrev Badan Intelijen Negara* State Intelligence Agency

bin *n, Isl* son of (father's name); **binti** *n, Isl* daughter of (father's name)

bina *v* build up; ~ *Graha* Presidential office during New Order; ~ *raga* body-building; **membina** *v* to build up, found; **pembina** *n* founder, patron; coach; **pembinaan** *n* development

binasa *adj* destroyed, ruined; **membinasakan** *v* to destroy, ruin

binatang *n* animal; ~ *melata* reptile

binatu *n* (commercial) laundry

bincang: berbincang(-bincang) *v* to chat, discuss; **perbincangan** *n* discussion

bingkai *n* frame; ~ *kacamata* glasses frames; **berbingkai** *v* to have a frame; *adj* framed; **membingkai** *v* to frame

bingkis: bingkisan *n* wrapped or free gift

bingung *adj* confused; **kebingungan** *n* confusion; **membingungkan** *adj* confusing

bini *sl* wife

binokular *n* binoculars

bintang *n* star; asterisk (*); ~ *berekor* comet; ~ *kejora* morning star (symbol of Papuan independence movement); ~ *ibukota* star from the capital; ~ *tamu* guest star; **berbintang** *v* to have a star (sign); *jenderal* ~ *tiga* three-star general; **membintangi** *v* to star in; *Dian Sastro* ~ *film Pasir Berbisik* Dian Sastro starred in *Pasir Berbisik*

binti *n, Isl* daughter of (father's name) ← **bin**

bintik *n* spot, stain, freckle; **berbintik-bintik** *adj* spotty, spotted

bintit(an), bintil *n* stye (swollen eyelid)

biodata *n* personal profile (name, address, date of birth, hobbies etc)

biola *n* violin, fiddle; *pemain* ~ violinist

biologi *n ilmu* ~ biology; **biologis** *adj* biological

bioskop *n* cinema, movie theater

bir *n* beer; ~ *niralkohol* non-alcoholic beer

biri-biri *n* sheep, goat

biro *n* office, center; ~ *perjalanan* travel agent; ~ *Pusat Statistik* Central Statistics Office

birokrasi *n* bureaucracy; red tape; **birokrat** *n* bureaucrat; **birokratis** *adj* bureaucratic

biru *adj* blue; ~ *lebam* black and blue; ~ *tua* dark blue; **kebiru-biruan** *adj* bluish; **membiru** *v* to turn blue

bis ~ *surat* letter box, mailbox (for posting)

bis, bus *n* bus; ~ *kota* city bus;

halte ~ bus stop

bisa *v, aux* can, be able; **bisa-bisa** *conj* it could happen that; ~ *kamu dipecat* You could get fired; **sebisanya, sebisa-bisanya** *adv* as well as you can, to the best of your ability

bisa *n* poison (of animals), venom; **berbisa** *adj* poisonous; *ular* ~ venomous snake

bisbol *n* baseball; *pemain* ~ baseball player

bisik whisper; **bisikan** *n* whisper; ~ *hati* conscience; **berbisik** *adj* whispering; *v* to whisper; **membisik** *v* to whisper; **pembisik** *n* whisperer

bising *adj* noisy; *n* static; **kebisingan** *n* noise, buzz

biskuit *n* biscuit, cracker

bismillah *ejac, Isl* in the name of God

bisnis *n* business, trade; **berbisnis** *v* to do business; **pebisnis** *n* businessman, businesswoman

bistik *n* steak; ~ *ayam* cut of barbecued chicken

bisu *adj* mute, dumb; ~ *tuli* deaf-mute; **kebisuan** *n* silence, lack of speech; **membisu** *v* to be silent, say nothing

bisul *n* abscess, boil, ulcer

bius *n* drug; *obat* ~ anesthetic; **membius** *v* to drug, anesthetize; **pembiusan** *n* anaesthesia

blak-blakan *adv* outspoken; *Adam selalu bicara secara* ~ Adam always speaks his mind

blangko *n* form

blangkon *n* traditional Javanese men's headwear

blasteran *adj* mixed, hybrid; *Sari* ~ *Sunda-Jerman* Sari is half-Sundanese, half-German

bléwah *n* kind of melon

blits *n* flash (of camera)

blok *n* block (in addresses); ~ *Timur* Eastern bloc

blokir, memblokir *v* to block; ~ *jalan* to block the road; *Begitu kecopetan, dia langsung* ~ *kartu kredit* After being robbed, he blocked his credit card

bloknot *n* writing pad

blong *adj, coll* loose, not taut; *Remnya* ~ the brakes failed

bloon *adj, coll* silly, naive, impressionable; *Mr Bean* ~ *tapi pinter* Mr Bean is naive but smart

bludak → **beludak**

blus *n* blouse

bobo, bobok *v, sl* to sleep (children's language)

bobol *v* to collapse; **membobol** *v* to break into; *Mesin ATM dibobol maling* Thieves broke into the ATM machine; **pembobolan** *n* breaking into, breach

bobot *n* weight; **berbobot** *adj* heavy, weighty; *Bukunya* ~ His book was substantial reading

bocah *n* young child

bocor *v* to leak; *Rahasia itu sudah* ~ *ke mana-mana* The secret has leaked out everywhere; **kebocoran** *n* leak; **membocorkan** *v* to leak something; **pembocoran** *n* leakage, divulging (of secrets)

bodoh *adj* **bodo** *coll* stupid; **kebodohan** *n* stupidity, ignorance; **membodohi** *v* to make someone stupid; **membodohkan** *v* to make stupid; **pembodohan** *n* tricking, duping; ~ *rakyat* fooling the people

boga *n* food, catering; *jasa* ~ catering

bohlam *n* light bulb

bohong lie; **berbohong** to lie; **kebohongan** *n* lie, deceit; **membohong** *v* to lie; **membohongi** *v* to lie to someone; **pembohong** *n* liar; **pemboikotan** *n* deception, lying

boikot *n* boycott; **memboikot** *v* to boycott something; **pemboikotan** *n* boycotting

bokong *n* buttocks, bottom

bokor *n* metal bowl (often for ceremonial use)

boks *n* playpen, bassinet; *mobil* ~ (closed) truck

bola *n* ball; football, soccer; ~ *basket* basketball; ~ *mata* eyeball; *main* ~ play football

bolak-balik *adv* back and forth, to and fro, there and back; **berbolak-balik, membolak-balik** to go back and forth

boléh may, can; allowed, permitted; okay; ~~~ *saja* sure you can; **keboléhan** *n* ability, what you can do; **memperboléhkan** *v* to allow, permit

boling *n* ten-pin bowling; *main* ~ to go bowling

bolong *adj* holey, perforated; *batu* ~ coastal rock form with a hole in it; **berbolong-bolong** *adj* full of holes; **membolongi** *v* to pierce

bolong *siang* ~ broad daylight

bolos, membolos *v* to skip, be absent, play truant, wag, skive; ~ *sekolah* to skip school; **pembolos** *n* truant, absentee; **pembolosan** *n* absenteeism, truancy

bolpoin *n* ballpoint pen, biro

bom *n* bomb; **mengebom** *v* to bomb something; **pengeboman** *n* bombing

bombai *bawang* ~ large onion

bon *n* bill, check, receipt; *minta* ~ to ask for the bill; *pakai* ~ to make out a receipt before paying (at another counter)

boncéng, memboncéng *v* to ride with someone else on a two-wheeled vehicle, dink; to sponge or cadge a lift; **boncéngan** *n* passenger

bondong: berbondong-bondong *adv* in droves

bonék *n* football fan or hooligan from Surabaya ← **bondo nékat**

bonéka *n* doll (like a person); soft toy (animal); puppet; *pemerintah* ~ puppet government

bongkah *n* counter for lumps; *se*~ *tanah* a clod of earth

bongkar, membongkar *v* to pull apart, dismantle; unpack; to unearth; **bongkaran** *n* component parts, unpacked goods;

pembongkaran *n* dismantling; exposure; ~ *usaha judi sudah lama dilakukan* There have long been efforts to expose gambling joints

bontot *n* youngest child in a family ← **buntut**

boong → **bohong**

boorwater, borwater *n* boric acid (as an eye salve)

bopong, membopong *v* to carry someone (bodily, or on the shoulders)

bor *n* drill; *mata* ~ drill bit

bordil *n* brothel, bordello; *rumah* ~ brothel

bordir *n* embroidery; **bordiran** *n* embroidery, lace edging; **membordir** *v* to embroider

borgol *n* handcuffs; **memborgol** *v* to handcuff

boro-boro *conj* what's the point of ...? It's not even worth ...; ~ *datang, telepon saja dia tidak mau* He won't even telephone, let alone come

borong, memborong *v* to buy up, buy in bulk; **borongan** *n* goods bought in bulk; *taksi* ~ un-metered taxi; **pemborong** *n* developer, contractor

boros *adj* wasteful; **memboroskan** *v* to waste something; **pemboros** *n* spendthrift; **pemborosan** *n* wastage

bos *pron, sl* boss, sir; *n* boss

bosan, bosen *adj* bored, fed up with, tired of; **membosankan** *adj* boring, tiresome

bot *sepatu* ~ boots

botak *adj* bald; **kebotakan** *n* baldness, hair loss; **membotak** *v* to go bald; **membotaki** *v* to shave, make bald

botok, bothok *n* Javanese side-dish of shredded coconut and fresh vegetables

botol *n* bottle; *teh* ~ bottled tea

Bouraq, borak *n* mythical winged creature with a woman's head and unicorn's body

boyong, memboyong *v* to take (someone) away; *Isteri barunya di~ ke Padang* He took his new bride with him to Padang

BNI *Bank Negara Indonesia* State Bank of Indonesia

BPKB *abbrev Buku Pemilik Kendaraan Bermotor* vehicle registration papers

BPPN *abbrev Badan Penyehatan Perbankan Nasional* Indonesian Bank Restructuring Agency (IBRA)

BPPT *abbrev Badan Pengkajian dan Penerapan Teknologi* Agency for the Research and Application of Technology

BPS *abbrev Biro Pusat Statistik* Central Statistics Bureau

brahmana, brahmin, brahma *n* highest Hindu caste in Bali

BRAj *Bendoro Raden Ajeng* Javanese title for unmarried female aristocracy

brankas, brangkas *n* safe

Brasil *n* Brazil; *orang* ~ Brazilian

BRAy *Bendoro Raden Ayu* Javanese title for married female aristocracy

brédel, membrédel v to muzzle, bridle, ban; *Majalah Tempo dibredel pada tahun 1994* Tempo magazine was closed down in 1994; **pembrédelan** n muzzling, being closed down

brem n a soft white biscuit made from fermented rice, a specialty of the Solo-Madiun area; alcoholic drink

bréndi n brandy

bréngsék *excl* blast! damn!; n bastard!; *adj* damn, bloody; ~ *lu!* You bastard!

bréwok, beréwok n beard, whiskers, sideburns; **bréwokan** *adj* whiskered, bearded

BRI *abbrev Bank Rakyat Indonesia* Indonesian People's Bank

Britania Raya n Great Britain

brokat n brocade

brokoli n broccoli

bros n brooch

brosur n brochure; ~ *wisata* travel brochure

bruder n Christian brother (Catholic); **bruderan** n Christian Brothers seminary

bruto *adj* gross; *pendapatan* ~ gross income

bu *pron* Mother (to respected older women); Mum(my), Mom(my); ~ *Haji* title for a woman who has completed the pilgrimage to Mecca

buah n fruit, result; piece, general counter for objects; ~ *hati* darling (child); ~ *nangka* jackfruit; ~ *tangan* souvenir, gift

brought home; **buah-buahan** n fruit(s); **berbuah** v to bear fruit, produce; **membuahkan** v to result in; **membuahi** v to impregnate, fertilize; **sebuah** *adj* a, one (generic counter); ~ *kursi* a chair

buai: membuai v to swing, rock, sway something

bual, membual v to foam; to froth at the mouth, talk rubbish; **bualan** n foaming; nonsense

buang v to throw (away); ~ *air* to urinate; ~ *muka* to look the other way; ~ *sampah* to throw rubbish away; **buangan** *adj* *orang* ~ exile; **membuang** v to throw out; waste; exile; ~ *ingus* blow your nose; ~ *kesempatan* to waste an opportunity; **terbuang** *adj* thrown out, wasted

buas *adj* fierce, wild; *binatang* ~ wild animal; **kebuasan** n ferocity

buat *prep* for; ~ *kamu* for you; v to do, make; *Apa boleh* ~ never mind; **buatan** n made in, product of; ~ *lokal* made locally; **berbuat** v to do; ~ *salah* to do wrong; **membuat** v to make; ~ *marah* to make angry; **membuat-buat** v to pretend; **pembuat** n producer; **pembuatan** n production, manufacture; **perbuatan** n act, deed

buaya n crocodile, alligator; ~ *darat* conman

bubar v to disperse, break up, spread out; **membubarkan** v to break something up; *Demo* *itu dibubarkan polisi* The demo was broken up by the police; **pembubaran** *n* dissolution, breaking up

bubuh: membubuhkan *v* to attach something; *~ tanda tangan*, attach your signature

bubuk *n* powder, dust; *Kayu sudah menjadi ~* The wood has rotted

bubur *n* porridge; *~ ayam* chicken porridge; *~ sumsum* porridge made from rice flour; *nasi telah menjadi ~* it's too late now

budak *n* slave; **perbudakan** *n* slavery

budaya *n* culture; **berbudaya** *n* to have a culture; **kebudayaan** *n* culture, civilization; **membudaya** *v* to spread, become entrenched; *Korupsi sudah ~* Corruption is part of the culture

Budha *agama ~* Buddhism; *orang ~* Buddhist

budi *n* goodness; intellect; *~ pekerti* ethics, good behavior

budidaya *n* cultivation; **membudidayakan** *v* to cultivate, grow; **pembudidayaan** *n* cultivation

bufét *n* buffet (meal)

bugar *adj* fit; *segar ~* fit and healthy; **kebugaran** *n* health; *pusat ~* gym, fitness centre

bugil *adj* naked, nude

Bugis ethnic group from South Sulawesi; *orang ~, bahasa ~* Buginese

bui *n* jail, prison

buih *n* foam, froth; **berbuih** *adj* frothy, foaming

bujang *adj* single, unmarried

(man); **bujangan** *n* bachelor; **membujang** *v* to remain unmarried

bujuk, membujuk *v* to coax; *~ rayu* to flatter; **bujukan** *n* enticement

bujur *n* longitude; vertical line down a sphere; crack in buttocks; *~ timur* east longitude

buka open; *~ baju* to take off clothes; **berbuka** *~ puasa* to break the fast; **membuka** *v* to open; *~ rahasia* to reveal a secret; **membukakan** *v* to open (for someone); **pembuka** *adj* opening; *kata ~* preface; **pembukaan** *n* opening; **terbuka** *adj* open; *sidang ~* public session; **keterbukaan** *n* openness

bukan no, not (of things, nouns); *~ apa-apa* nothing; *Fitri ~ adik saya* Fitri's not my sister; *Ini ~?* This one, isn't it?; *~ main* extraordinary, no kidding!; *~nya* isn't it ...?

buket *n* bouquet

buking, booking *n* booking; **membuking** *v* to book; **pembukingan** *n* bookings

bukit *n* hill; **berbukit** *adj* hilly; **perbukitan** *n* (range of) hills

bukti *n* proof, evidence; **membuktikan** *v* to prove; **terbukti** *adj* proven

buku *n* book; *~ harian* journal, diary; *~ pelajaran* textbook; *~ panduan* guide(book); *~ petunjuk* directory; **membukukan** *v* to enter into the accounts, books; **pembukuan**

n book-keeping

bulak-balik → **bolak-balik**

bulan *n* moon, month; ~ *Februari* February; ~ *madu* honey-moon; *ber~ madu* to go on a honeymoon; ~ *puasa* fasting month, Ramadan; ~ *purnama* full moon; ~ *datang* ~ menstru-ate, have your period; **bulan-bulanan** *n* laughing-stock, object of derision

bulat *adj* round; fat; *telanjang* ~ stark naked; *dengan suara* ~ unanimously; **bulatan** *n* circle; **membulatkan** *v* to round off; **pembulatan** *n* rounding-off

bulé *n, derog* white person, whitey, paleface; albino

bulu *n* feather; fur; body hair; ~ *ayam* feather; ~ *domba* wool; ~ *mata* eyelashes; ~ *tangkis* badminton; *tidak pandang* ~ to be objective, not discriminate; **berbulu** *adj* hairy; to have fur or feathers

buluh: **pembuluh** ~ *darah* blood vessel

bum boom!

bumbu *n* spice; **membumbui** *v* to season

bumerang *n* boomerang; *Itu sudah menjadi* ~ *bagi Hari* It's come back to haunt Hari

bumi *n* earth, ground; *ilmu* ~ geography; ~ *hangus* scorched earth; **membumihanguskan** *v* to scorch the earth, apply a scorched earth policy; **bumi-putera, pribumi** *n* native inhabitant, son of the soil

BUMN *abbrev Badan Usaha Milik Negara* state-owned corporation

buncis *n* string bean

buncit *adj* pot-bellied, fat; *sl* pregnant; *perut* ~ pot belly; pregnant

bundar *adj* **bunder** *coll* round; *meja* ~ round table; **bundaran** *n* roundabout

Bung *pron* brother; ~ *Karno* President Soekarno; *ayo* ~*!* Come on, mate!

bunga *n* flower, blossom; inter-est; ~ *mawar,* ~ *ros* rose; *karangan* ~ wreath, bouquet; *musim* ~ spring; ~ *hanya 3%* only 3% interest; **berbunga** *v* to flower, blossom; to gain interest

bungalo *n* bungalow, cottage, one-story house

bungkam *adj* quiet, silent; **membungkam** *v* to keep silent

bungker, bunker *n* (under-ground) bunker, hiding place

bungkuk, bongkok *adj* crooked, bent; **membungkuk** *v* to bow, be hunched; **membungkukkan** ~ *badan* to bow

bungkus *n* takeaway, pack; *nasi* ~ a takeaway rice meal; **mem-bungkus** *v* to wrap; ~ *kado* wrap a gift; **pembungkus** *n* wrapping, packing; **pem-bungkusan** *n* packaging

bunglon *n* chameleon

bungsu *n* youngest child in a family; *anak* ~, *si* ~ youngest child

bunting *adj* pregnant (of animals)

buntu *adj* one-way, useless; *jalan ~* dead-end; cul-de-sac, court

buntut *n* tail; *~nya* the consequence; *sop ~* oxtail soup; **berbuntut** *v* to go further, end; *Ceritanya ~ sedih* The tale had a sad ending; **membuntuti** *v* to follow someone

bunuh, membunuh *v* to kill; *~ diri* kill yourself, commit suicide; **pembunuh** *n* murderer, killer; *~ bayaran* hitman, hired killer; **pembunuhan** *n* murder, killing; **terbunuh** *adj* killed

bunyi *n* sound, noise; **berbunyi** *v* to sound, make a noise; **membunyikan** *v* to sound, ring something

bupati *n* regent; **kabupatén** *n* regency

buram *adj* cloudy, frosted, dull

buron *n* fugitive

bursa *n* exchange; *~ efek* stock exchange; *~ komputer* computer market

buru, memburu *v* to hunt, chase; **buruan, buron** *n* the hunted; **berburu** *v* to go hunting; **keburu** *sl* in time; too early; had already; *~ habis* already run out; **pemburu** *n* hunter; **pemburuan** *n* hunt, chase; **terburu-(buru)** *adj* in a hurry

buruh *n* laborer; *~ bangunan* construction worker; *Hari ~* Labor Day; *Partai ~* Labor Party; **perburuhan** *n* concerning labor

buruk *adj* bad (of a situation, weather); ugly; *kabar ~* bad news; **memburuk** *v* to worsen; **memperburuk** *v* to make even worse

burung *n* bird; *~ béo* parrot; *~ dara* pigeon, dove; *~ gereja* sparrow; *~ hantu* owl; *kabar ~* rumor, gossip

busa *n* foam, lather; **berbusa** *adj* foamy; *v* to have a layer of foam

busana *n* clothing, wear; *~ kantor* office wear; **berbusana** *v* to wear

busi *n* spark plug

busuk *adj* rotten; *bau ~* bad smell; *hati ~* evil, depraved; **membusuk** *v* to rot; **pembusukan** *n* (process of) decay

busung *adj* swollen, distended; *~ lapar* disease caused by starvation

busur *n* bow

buta *adj* blind; *~ huruf* illiterate; *pagi ~* very early in the morning, before sunrise

butik *n* boutique

butir *n* grain, counter for small oval objects; *se~ nasi* a grain of rice; *tiga ~ telur* three eggs

butuh *v* need; **kebutuhan** *n* need, necessity; **membutuhkan** *v* to need something

buyung *n* boy, lad; *~ upik* boy and girl, son and daughter

buyut *n* ancestor from your great-grandparents' generation; *nenek ~* great-grandmother; *musuh be~an* arch enemy

byarpet, byar pet *adj* on and

off; *Lampu masih* ~ The lights
still go out sometimes
byur splash, sound of an object
falling into water

C

C Celsius
ca → **cah**
cabai → **cabé**
cabang *n* branch; ~ *pohon*
tree branch; *kantor* ~ branch
(office); ~ *olahraga* a type of
sport; **bercabang** *v* to be split,
branched
cabé, cabai *n* chilli; ~ *rawit*
small, hot red chilli; small but
fiery (of a person)
cabik shred; **mencabik** *v* to
tear; **tercabik-cabik** *adj* torn,
to shreds
cabul *adj* obscene, indecent,
rude; *film* ~ pornographic film;
mencabuli *v* to rape, assault
someone
cabut *v* to pull out, remove; *sl*
to leave; **mencabut** *v* to pull
out, remove; ~ *gigi* to extract
a tooth; **pencabutan** *n* withdrawal, removal; **tercabut** *adj*
removed
cacah minced, chopped; *daging*
~ mincemeat; **mencacah** *v* to
mince, chop up
cacar *n* pock, pox; ~ *air* chicken
pox; *bekas* ~ pock; *penyakit* ~
smallpox; **cacaran** *v* to have

chicken pox
cacat *n* fault, defect, flaw; *adj*
disabled, handicapped, flawed;
~ *lahir* birth defect; *orang* ~,
penyandang ~ disabled or
handicapped person
caci ~ *maki* insults; **mencaci** ~
maki to insult, abuse
cacing *n* worm; ~ *tanah* earth-
worm; *obat* ~ worming tablets;
cacingan *adj* to have (intesti-
nal) worms
cadang *suku* ~ spare part;
cadangan *adj* spare, reserve;
stocks; ~ *minyak* oil reserves;
mencadangkan *v* to reserve,
set aside; to suggest something
cadel, cedal *adj* to have a speech
impediment
cagar *n* preserve; ~ *alam* nature
reserve; ~ *budaya* cultural
heritage area
cagub *n* candidate for governor;
gubernatorial candidate ←
calon gubernur
cah, ca *n* sauce in Chinese cooking; *daging sapi* ~ *cabai* beef
in spicy sauce
cahar: pencahar *n* laxative
cahaya *n* light, shine, glow; ~
bulan moonlight; *titik* ~ point
of light; **bercahaya** *v* to glow,
shine; **pencahayaan** *n* lighting
cair flow, melt; **cairan** *n* liquid;
mencair *v* to melt, turn into
liquid; **mencairkan** *v* to melt
something; to make (funds)
available
cakap, cakep *adj* handsome; *sl*
pretty

cakap *adj* able, capable;
kecakapan *n* ability

cakap: bercakap *v* to speak;
bercakap-cakap *v* to chat;
percakapan *n* conversation

cakar *n* claw; **cakaran** *n* scratch;
mencakar *v* to scratch;
dicakar kucing scratched by a
cat; **pencakar** ~ *langit*
skyscraper

cakram *n* disc; discus; *lempar*
~ discus (throw); *rem* ~ disc
brakes

cakrawala *n* horizon; sky

cakup: cakupan *n* scope; **mencakupi** *v* to include, cover;
pencakupan *n* coverage

cakwé *n* snack consisting of
fried strips of dough

calo *n* ticket scalper, profiteer;
percaloan *praktek* ~ profiteering

calon *adj* future; *n* candidate;
~ *suami* husband-to-be;
mencalonkan *v* to nominate
someone; **pencalonan** *n* nomination, candidacy

camar *burung* ~ seagull

camat *n* sub-district head; **kecamatan** *n* sub-district

cambuk *n* whip; **mencambuk** *v*
to whip; **mencambuki** *vt* to
whip repeatedly

camil, camilan → **cemil**

campak *n* measles; *penyakit* ~
measles

campur mix; ~ *baur* mix with
society; ~ *sari* a blend of traditional and modern Javanese
music; ~ *tangan* get involved,
interfere; *nasi* ~ rice with various side-dishes; ~ *aduk* all
mixed up; **mencampur-
adukkan** *v* to mix up, confuse;
campuran *n* mix, mixture;
anak ~ child of mixed descent;
bercampur *adj* mixed with;
mencampur *v* to mix, blend;
mencampuri *v* to mix into; to
meddle; **mencampurkan** *v* to
mix something to;
pencampuran *n* mixing;
percampuran *n* mixing, association

canai *roti* ~ kind of pancake

canda *n* joke; ~ *gurau* joking,
jokes; **bercanda** *v* to joke; ~
kok just kidding

candi *n* temple, ancient Hindu or
Buddhist temple or monument;
~ *Borobudur* Borobudur

candu *n* opium, drug; ~ *asmara*
intoxicating love; **kecanduan**
n addiction; *adj* addicted to; ~
obat drug addiction; **pecandu**
n addict

canggih *adj* sophisticated; *teknologi* ~ hi-tech; **kecanggihan**
n sophistication

canggung *adj* awkward, clumsy

cangkir *n* cup, mug; ~ *teh* teacup;
se~ kopi a cup of coffee

cangkok graft, transplant; ~ *ginjal* liver transplant; **mencangkokkan** *v* to graft (of plants),
transplant (of organs); **pencangkokan** *n* transplant operation, grafting

cangkul *n* hoe; **cangkulan** *n* card
game; **mencangkul** *v* to hoe

cantik *adj* beautiful, pretty; *nomor* ~ lucky (mobile phone) number; **kecantikan** *n* beauty; *ratu* ~ beauty queen; **mempercantik** ~ *diri* to make yourself beautiful

canting *n* tool to apply wax in making batik

cantum: mencantumkan *v* to attach; **tercantum** *adj* attached, included, inserted

cap *n* seal; brand, mark; ~ *jempol* thumbprint; ~ *pos* postmark; *batik* ~ stamped batik; **mengecap** *v* to brand

cap go méh *n* 15th day after the Chinese New Year

capai, mencapai *v* to reach, attain; **tercapai** *adj* achieved; *cita-cita tak* ~ unfulfilled dreams

capcay, cap cai *n* chop suey, Chinese vegetables in sauce

capék, capai *adj* tired; ~ *sekali* exhausted; **kecapékan** *adj* tired out; *n* exhaustion

capem *n* branch office ← **cabang pembantu**

caping *n* conical hat

caprés *n* presidential candidate ← **calon présidén**

capung *n* dragonfly

cara *n* way, means, style, method; **secara** *adv* in a way; used to form adverbs; ~ *besar-besaran* on a large scale

cari *v* to look for, search for, seek; **mencari** *v* to look or search for, seek; ~ *muka* get on; ~ *makan*, ~ *nafkah* to earn a living; ~ *tahu* to try to find

out; **mencari-cari** *v* to search repeatedly, everywhere; **mencarikan** *v* to look for something for someone; **pencarian** *n* search, hunt

carter charter; **carteran** *adj* chartered; *bis* ~ chartered or rented bus; **mencarter** *v* to hire, charter

cas charge; **mengecas** *v* to charge (electrical equipment)

cas-cis-cus European language (especially English); **bercas-cis-cus** *v* to speak a European language

cat *n* **cét** *coll* paint; ~ *air* watercolors; ~ *basah* wet paint; **mengecat** *v* to paint, dye; ~ *rambut* to dye, color your hair; **pengecatan** *n* painting, dyeing

catat, mencatat *v* to note; **catatan** *n* notes; ~ *kaki* footnotes; *buku* ~ notebook; *dengan* ~ on the condition or proviso; *kantor* ~ *sipil* civil registry office; **pencatatan** *n* registration; **tercatat** *adj* registered, noted; *surat* ~ registered mail

catur *n* chess; *buah* ~ chess piece; **pecatur** *n* chess player

catut *n* (carpenter's) pincers; *tukang* ~ ticket scalper, profiteer; **mencatut** ~ *nama* to use someone else's name illegally

cawat *n* loincloth; **bercawat** *v* to wear a loincloth

cc cubic centiliters, milliliters

CD compact disk

cébok to wash your bottom after using the toilet; **cébokan** *n* pail of water to wash your bottom

cébol *n* dwarf, midget

cébong → **kecébong**

cebur fall into water; **kecebur** *adj, coll* **tercebur** *adj* fallen into water; **menceburkan** *v* to push into water

cecak → **cicak**

cécér: bercécéran *adj* scattered, dispersed; **mencécérkan** *v* to scatter, disperse

cedera, cidera injured, injury; ~ *lutut* knee injury; **mencederai** *v* to damage, injure

cegah, mencegah *v* to prevent, fight against; **pencegahan** *n* prevention; ~ *AIDS* prevention of AIDS

cegat, mencegat *v* to hold up, bar; **pencegatan** *n* barring

ceguk, cekuk: cegukan *n* hiccups; *v* to have the hiccups

cék *n* cheque, check; ~ *kosong* blank cheque

cék, mengecék *v* to check, confirm; **pengecékan** *n* checking

cekal *kena* ~ not allowed to go abroad; **mencekal** *v* to prevent from leaving the country; **pencekalan** *n* ban on foreign travel ← **cegah dan tangkal**

cekam, cengkam: mencekam *adj* frightening, ominous; *situasi sudah* ~ things looked black

cekat: cekatan *adj* clever, good, adept

cékcok, bercékcok *v* to quarrel, have a fight; **percékcokan** *n* quarrel, dispute

cékér *n, sl* claw; ~ *ayam* chicken feet (dim sum)

cekik, mencekik *v* to strangle; **tercekik** *adj* strangled

cekikik: cekikikan *v* to giggle

ceking *adj* thin, gaunt, skin and bones; *si* ~ skinny

Céko *n* the Czech Republic; *bahasa* ~, *orang* ~ Czech; ~*slowakia* Czechoslovakia

cekung *adj* concave, sunken; *mata* ~ sunken eyes

cela *n* fault; **tercela** *adj* wrong; *perbuatan yang* ~ misdeed, wrong

celah *n* gap, crack, crevice; ~ *gigi* gap between teeth

celaka accident, bad luck, misfortune; **kecelakaan** *n* accident, disaster; ~ *pesawat* plane crash; **mencelakakan** *v* to bring misfortune on

celana *n* trousers; ~ *pendek* shorts; **bercelana** *v* to wear trousers, trousered

celémék *n* apron

céléng, céléngan *n* piggy bank, savings box

celetuk *v* **nyeletuk** *sl* to interrupt, call out, say suddenly

celotéh, bercelotéh *v* to babble, gurgle

celup, mencelup *v* to dye, dip; **celupan** *n* dip; **pencelupan** *n* dyeing process

celurit, clurit *n* crescent-shaped knife, sickle (traditionally carried by Madurese men)

cemar: mencemari *v* to dirty, pollute; **pencemar** *n* polluter;

pencemaran *n* pollution; ~ *udara* air pollution; **tercemar** *adj* polluted

cemara *n* casuarina (tree)

cemas *adj* worried, anxious; **kecemasan** *n* anxiety, concern; **mencemaskan** *adj* worrying, sobering

cemberut *adj* bad-tempered, in a bad mood

cemburu *adj* jealous; ~ *buta* blind jealousy; **kecemburuan** *n* jealousy; **pencemburu** *n* jealous person

cemerlang *adj* glittering, sparkling, brilliant; *ide* ~ brainwave; **kecemerlangan** *n* genius, brilliance

cemil, camil *v* to snack; **cemilan** *n* snack food

cemooh *n* mockery, scorn; **mencemoohkan** *v* to mock, ridicule

cempaka *n* a white kind of gardenia or magnolia

cempedak *n* fruit which is cut into slices and fried

cemplung plunge into water; **mencemplungkan** *vt* to plunge something into water; **kecemplung** *adj, sl*; **tercemplung** *adj* fallen into water

cendana *n kayu* ~ sandalwood; *Keluarga* ~ the Soeharto family (resident at Jl Cendana in Jakarta); *Pulau* ~ Timor

cendawan *n* fungi, toadstool, mushroom

cendekia: cendekiawan *n* intellectual; *Ikatan* ~ *Muslim seIndonesia* ICMI, Indonesian Association of Muslim Intellectuals

cenderung *v* to tend; **kecenderungan** *n* tendency, trend

céndol *n* sweet drink of green rice flour, molasses and coconut milk

cendramata, cinderamata *n* souvenir, keepsake

cengang: tercengang *adj* surprised, astonished

cengéng *adj* whiny, complaining

cengkam → **cekam**

cengkéh *n* cloves

cengkeram *v* to grip; **cengkeraman** *n* grip, squeeze; **mencengkeram** *v* to grip, squeeze

cengkrama, cengkerama: bercengkrama *v* to chat, hold a discussion

centil *adj* attention-seeking, coquettish

céntong ~ *nasi* spoon for serving rice

cepak *adj* shaven-headed; *rambut* ~ crew cut

cepat *adj* **cepet** *coll* fast, quick; *yang* ~, *dapat* first come, first served; ~ *marah* quicktempered; *kereta api* ~ express train; **cepatan** (*excl*) hurry up! **kecepatan** *n* speed; **mempercepat** *v* to speed up, accelerate, **secepat** *conj* as fast as; ~ *mungkin* **secepat(-cepat)nya** *adv* as fast as possible; **tercepat** *adj* fastest

cepék *n* Rp.100 (coin)

ceplas-ceplos *adv* forthright,

blunt, straight from the heart (of speech or behavior); **keceplosan** *n* directness

ceplok *telur ~* fried egg

ceprét → **jeprét**

cerah *adj* clear, sunny; *Di Banjarmasin ~, 33 derajat* Clear in Banjarmasin, 33 degrees; *wajah ~* happy face; **mencerahkan** *v* to enlighten, clear matters up; **pencerahan** *n* enlightenment, guidance; *Abad ~* the Enlightenment

cerai divorce; *~ mati* widowed; *~-berai adj* torn apart, dispersed; **mencerai-beraikan** *v* to tear apart, separate; **bercerai** *v* to be divorced; **mencerai(kan)** *v* to divorce someone; **perceraian** *n* divorce

ceramah *n* lecture, talk; *~ agama* sermon; **berceramah** *v* to give a lecture or talk; **penceramah** *n* speaker

cerber *n* short story ← **cerita bersambung**

cerdas *adj* intelligent, bright; **kecerdasan** *n* intelligence; **mencerdaskan** *v* to educate, sharpen your mind

cerdik *adj* clever, smart; cunning; **kecerdikan** *n* intelligence; shrewdness

cerét, crét *cerét berét* diarrhea; **mencrét** *v* to have diarrhea

ceréwét *adj* fussy, finicky, hard to please; talkative; **keceréwétan** *n* fussiness

céri *buah ~* cherry

ceria *adj* happy, in a good mood;

keceriaan *n* happiness, good mood; **menceriakan** *v* to liven up, make happy

cerita, ceritera story, tale; *~ bersambung* serial; *~ pendek* (**cerpen**) short story; *~ rakyat* folk tale; *habis ~* and that was it; *~nya panjang* it's a long story; **bercerita** *v* to tell (a story); **menceritakan** *v* to describe, relate

cermai, cermé *n* small, sour plum

cermat *adj* thorough, careful, accurate; **kecermatan** *n* precision, accuracy; **mencermati** *v* to observe closely

cermin mirror; **bercermin** *v* to look in the mirror; to take as an example; **mencerminkan** *v* to reflect; **tercermin** *adj* reflected

cerna, mencerna *v* to digest; **pencernaan** *n* digestion; *gangguan ~* digestive complaint

ceroboh *adj* careless; **kecerobohan** *n* carelessness

cerobong *n* chimney; *~ asap* smokestack

cerocos, mencerocos *v* **nyerocos** *coll* to talk too much, blather, chatter or rattle on → **nerocos**

cerpén *n* short story; **cerpénis** *n* short story writer ← **cerita péndék**

cerucut → **kerucut**

cerutu *n* cigar

cét → **cat**

cétak print; *~ biru* blueprint; *barang ~* printed material; *media ~* print media; **cétakan**

n mold; impression, printing; ~ *kedua* second edition; **mencétak** *v* to print; **pencétak** *n* printer; **percétakan** *n* printers, printing office; press

cetus: mencetus *v* to say something unexpected; **mencetuskan** *v* to spark off, provoke; **pencetus** *n* initiator, someone who creates ideas

céwék *n, coll* girl, young woman; *adj* female; ~ *matré* material girl; *Anaknya cowok atau ~?* Is the baby a boy or girl?

CGI Consultative Group on Indonesia

cicak, cecak *n* gecko, house lizard

cicil pay in instalments; **cicilan** *n* (payment by) instalments; **mencicil** *v* to pay by instalments

cicip taste; **mencicipi** *v* to try, taste something

cicit *n* great-grandchild

cidera → **cedera**

cidomo *n* horse-drawn cart in Lombok ← **cikar dokar mobil**

ciduk, cédok *n* dipper

ciduk: menciduk *v, coll* to arrest

Cik *pron* you, Sister (for Chinese women)

cikal ~ *bakal* origins

Cilé *n* Chile; *orang* ~ Chilean

cilik *adj* small, little; *penyanyi* ~ child singer

cilukba, ci luk ba *excl* peekaboo!

Cina *n* China; *derog* Chinese person; *bahasa* ~ Chinese (language); *orang* ~ Chinese (people); ~ *totok* full-blood Chinese (usu from China); **Pecinan** *n* Chinatown

cincang minced; *daging* ~ mincemeat; **mencincang** *v* to mince, chop up

cincau *n* jelly made from cinchona leaves, used in drinks; ~ *hijau* green cinchona jelly

cincin *n* ring; ~ *kawin* wedding ring

cinderamata, cendramata *n* souvenir, keepsake

cingur *rujak* ~ spicy food made from fruit and ox-snout

cinta love, like; ~ *monyet* puppy love; ~ *damai* peace-loving; **bercinta** *v* to make love; to be in love; **kecintaan** *n* love (for something); **mencintai** *v* to love someone; **pencinta, pecinta** *n* lover (of something); **tercinta** *adj* dear, beloved; *Hari yang* ~ Dear Hari

ciprat splash; **kecipratan** *adj* be splashed, sprayed accidentally

cipta idea, creativity; *daya* ~ creativity; **ciptaan** *n* creation; **mencipta** *v* to create; **menciptakan** *v* to create, make; **pencipta** *n* creator; ~ *lagu* songwriter; **tercipta** *adj* created

ciri *n* characteristic, identifying mark; ~ *khas* special feature

cita ~ *rasa* taste; *duka* ~ sorrow, grief; **cita-cita** *n* ideal, dream, ambition; **bercita-cita(kan)** *v* to dream of

citra *n* image; **mencitrakan** *v* to depict

cium kiss; smell; ~ *pipi* peck,

kiss on the cheek; ~ *tangan* kiss someone's hand (as a sign of respect); **ciuman** *n* kiss; sniff; **berciuman** *v* to kiss each other; **mencium** *v* to smell, to sniff; to kiss; **tercium** *adj* smelt; found out

ciut, menciut *v* to shrivel; **menciutkan** *v* to reduce

clurit → **celurit**

cm centimeter

coba *v, aux* try; please; *uji ~* experiment; **mengujicobakan** *v* to test something; **cobaan** *n* trial, ordeal; **mencoba** *v* to try, attempt; **percobaan** *n* experiment, test

cobék, coék *n* pestle for grinding chillies

coblos vote; pierce; *~ moncong putih!* vote for the white snout! (symbol of PDIP); **mencoblos** *v* to vote, pierce

cocok fit, match, suitable; **kecocokan** *n* suitability, compatibility; **mencocokkan** *v* to match

cocok: bercocok *v ~ tanam* to work or till the soil

cocol *v* dip into a liquid; *sambal ~* chilli sauce dip; **mencocol** *v* to dip into a liquid

coék → **cobék**

cokelat, coklat chocolate; *(warna) ~* brown; *rasa ~* chocolate-flavored; *sebatang ~* chocolate bar; *warna ~* brown; **kecoklatan** *adj* brownish

colék pinch; *sabun ~* cream soap for hand-washing clothes

colok, mencolok, menyolok *adj* glaring, standing out

colong, mencolong *v* to steal, nick, filch; **kecolongan** *adj* robbed; lost unjustly

comblang *mak ~* matchmaker

comro, combro *n* fried snack containing *oncom* ← **oncom di jero**

condong *v* lean, incline; *matahari ~ ke barat* the sun shifts to the west

congkél, mencongkél *n* to prise open

congklak *n* traditional game played with shells in a long wooden box

conték, menconték, menyonték *v* to copy, cheat; **contékan** *n* cram notes → **sonték**

contoh *n* example, model, sample; *~ baik* a good example; *~nya* for example; **mencontoh** *v* to copy, imitate; **mencontohi** *v* to give as an example; **percontohan** *adj* experimental; model

copét *n* pickpocket; **kecopétan** *adj* to be pickpocketed, robbed; *n* pickpocketing; **mencopét** *v* to pick someone's pocket

copot *v* to come off (accidentally); **mencopot** *vt* to pull (off); *coll* to sack, fire; **pencopotan** *n* removal

corak *n* design, pattern, motif, style; *~ Madura* Madurese style; **bercorak** *v* to have a design

corét scratch; **corét-corét** doodle, graffiti; **corétan** *n* scratch; **mencorét** *v* to scratch, cross out

corong *n* funnel, spout; ~ *radio* mike; *berbentuk* ~ funnel-shaped

coto *n* clear meat soup, specialty of Makassar

cowok *n, m, sl* boy, guy; boyfriend

cs *cum suis* and associates

CSIS Centre for Strategic and International Studies

cuaca *n* weather; *dinas* ~ meteorological or weather service; *ramalan* ~ weather forecast

cubit pinch; **mencubit** *v* to pinch; **secubit** *n* pinch; ~ *garam* a pinch of salt

cuci *v* to wash; ~ *darah* kidney dialysis; ~ *gudang* stocktake sale; ~ *mata* window-shopping; ~ *otak* brainwash; ~ *tangan* wash your hands; **cucian** *n* laundry; **mencuci** *v* to wash, clean; ~ *cetak* to develop photos (negatives and prints)

cucu *n* grandchild; *anak* ~ descendants

cucur flow, trickle; **cucuran** *n* flow; ~ *air mata* flow of tears; **bercucuran** *v* to trickle down, drip, flow

cuék *adj* uncaring, unfeeling, ignoring; independent; ~ *aja* who cares?

cuil *n* bit, speck; **secuil** *n* tiny bit; ~ *pun tidak* not one bit

cuka *n* vinegar

cukai *n* duty; *bea* ~ customs

cukong *n* wealthy businessman

cukup *adj* enough, sufficient; *adv* quite; ~ *sudah* enough; **berkecukupan** *v* to have

enough, get by; **mencukupi** *v* to satisfy, fulfill; **secukupnya** *adv* sufficient, adequate

cukur shave; *pisau* ~ razor; *tukang* ~ barber; **mencukur** *v* to shave

cula *n* horn; **bercula** *n* to have a horn; *badak* ~ *satu* one-horned rhino

culik, menculik *v* to kidnap; **penculik** *n* kidnapper; **penculikan** *n* kidnapping

cuma *adv* **cuman** *coll* but, only; **cuma-cuma** free, at no cost; **percuma** in vain

cumbu flattery; ~ *rayu* flirt; **bercumbu** *v* to flirt, flatter

cumi, cumi-cumi *n* squid

curah fall, pour; ~ *hujan* rainfall; **mencurahkan** *v* to pour out; ~ *tenaga* to spend energy

curam *adj* steep, sloping, precipitous

curang *adj* dishonest, cheating; **kecurangan** *n* cheating, dishonesty

curanmor *n* theft of motor vehicles ← **pencurian kendaraan bermotor**

curhat *v, coll* to pour out your heart ← **curah hati**

curi steal; **curi-curi** surreptitious, secret; **kecurian** *adj* to be robbed, burgled; **mencuri** *v* to steal; ~ *pandang* steal a look; **pencuri** *n* thief, burglar; **pencurian** *n* theft, burglary

curiga *adj* suspicious; **kecurigaan** *n* suspicion; **mencurigai** *v* to suspect someone; **mencuri-**

gakan *adj* suspicious, suspect

cuti leave; ~ *hamil* maternity leave; ~ *panjang* long service leave

CV curriculum vitae

D

D1 *Diploma Satu* 1-year diploma course

D2 *Diploma Dua* 2-year diploma course

D3 *Diploma Tiga* 3-year diploma course

da, dag, dah *gr* bye; **da-da** *gr* (children) bye-bye

d/a *dengan alamat* care of, c/-

dada *n* breast, chest, bosom; *buah* ~ *f* breast; *telanjang* ~ bare-chested; **berdada** *v* to have a chest

dadak: dadakan *adj* sudden; **mendadak** *adj* sudden; *secara* ~ suddenly

dadar *telur* ~ omelet

dadu *n* dice; *main* ~ to play games requiring dice

daérah *n* region, territory, area; provinces, country(side); ~ *Istimewa Yogyakarta (DIY)* Special Region of Jogjakarta; ~ *Khusus Ibukota (DKI)* Special Capital City Region; *bahasa* ~ regional language; *otonomi* ~ *(otda)* regional autonomy

daftar list, register, roll; ~ *barang* inventory, catalog; ~ *harga*

price list; ~ *hitam* blacklist; **mendaftar** *v* to register; **mendaftarkan** *v* to register something; **pendaftar** *n* applicant; **pendaftaran** *n* enrolment, registration; **terdaftar** *adj* registered, enrolled

dag → **da**

dagang trade; **dagangan** *v* to sell goods informally; *n* merchandise; **berdagang** *v* to trade, do business; **memperdagangkan** *v* to deal in; **pedagang** *n* merchant; **perdagangan** *n* commerce, trade; ~ *perempuan* trade in women

dag dig dug thump, thump, thump (of heartbeat)

daging *n* meat, flesh; ~ *babi* pork; ~ *sapi* beef; *tukang* ~ butcher; *mendarah* ~ to become second nature

dagu *n* chin

dah → **da**

dah → **sudah**

dahaga *n* thirst; **berdahaga** *adj* thirsty

dahak *n* phlegm, mucus; **berdahak** *adj* containing phlegm or mucus; *batuk* ~ chesty cough

dahan *n* branch

dahi *n* forehead

dahsyat *adj* terrible, dreadful, awesome; **kedahsyatan** *n* power

dahulu *adj* before, former(ly); first (more formal than **dulu**); ~ *kala* ancient times, the old days; *lebih* ~ first(ly); **mendahului** *v* to precede, overtake;

mendahulukan *v* to put before, give precedence to; **pendahulu** *n* predecessor; **pendahuluan** *n* introduction; *kata* ~ preface → **dulu**

da'i, dai *n* Islamic preacher

Dairi ethnic sub-group of the Batak people

daki: mendaki *v* to climb, ascend; ~ *gunung* (to go) mountaineering, bushwalking; **pendaki** ~ *gunung* mountaineer, bushwalker

daki *n* dirt, grime (of the skin)

daksa *tuna~* disabled, handicapped

daku *pron, lit* me; *Jangan tinggalkan* ~ don't leave me → **aku**

dakwa *n* charge, accusation; **dakwaan** *n* charge, accusation; **terdakwa** *n* the accused

dakwah *n* mission, religious proselytizing; **pendakwah** *n* preacher, missionary

dalam *pron* in, inside, into; *adj* deep, profound; inner; *n* inside ~ *negeri* national, domestic, internal; *Menteri* ~ *Negeri* (Mendagri) Minister of the Interior (or Home Affair), home secretary; *celana* ~ underpants; *di* ~ in, inside; *ke* ~ into; *Menteri* ~ *Negeri (Mendagri)* Minister of the Interior (or Home Affairs), home secretary; **kedalaman** *n* depth; **mendalam** *adj* deep; *duka cita yang* ~ deepest sympathy; **mendalami** *v* to delve into; **memperdalam** *v* to deepen; to

study in detail, broaden your knowledge; **pedalaman** *n* inland, hinterland

dalang *n* puppeteer (in shadow puppet plays); mastermind; **mendalangi** *v* to orchestrate (events)

dalih *n* excuse, pretext; reason; *Dia mundur, dengan* ~ *terlalu sibuk* He resigned, on the pretext that he was too busy; **berdalih** *v* to pretend, give a pretext

dalil *n* thesis, proposition, theorem; **berdalil** *adj* based on, grounded in

daluwarsa, kedaluwarsa, kadaluwarsa *n* expired, overdue; *tanggal* ~ expiry date, use by date (food)

damai peace; ~ *hati* inner peace; **berdamai** *v* to make peace; **kedamaian** *n* peace; **mendamaikan** *v* to reconcile, pacify; **perdamaian** *n* peace, reconciliation

damar *n* resin

damba *v* to long, yearn, wish for; **dambaan** *n* idol, dream; *cowok* ~ dream guy; **mendambakan** *v* to long or wish for; ~ *gadis mandiri, lulusan S1* Seeking an independent woman, university graduate

dampak *n* ill-effect; **berdampak** *v* to have a (negative) effect

dampar: terdampar *adj* beached, grounded, washed ashore; *Ada ikan paus* ~ *di pantai* A whale was beached on the sands

damping next to, close; **berdampingan** *adj* side by side; **mendampingi** *v* to accompany, flank; **pendamping** *n* companion; ~ *hidup* spouse; **pendampingan** *n* assistance

dan *conj* and; ~ *lain-lain (dll)* et cetera (etc); ~ *sebagainya (dsb)* and so on, and the like

dana *n* funds, money, grant; ~ *Moneter Internasional* International Monetary Fund (IMF); **mendanai** *v* to fund something; **pendanaan** *n* funding

danau *n* lake

dandan *v* to dress up, put on make-up; **dandanan** *n* dress, make-up; ~*nya norak* Her clothes are really tacky; **berdandan** *v* to dress, put on make-up; **mendandani** *v* to decorate, dress, adorn

dangdut *n* popular Indian-inspired music; *penyanyi* ~ *dangdut* singer; **dangdutan** *v* to go to a *dangdut* show; to dance to *dangdut* music

dangkal *adj* shallow, superficial; **kedangkalan** *n* shallow, (low) depth; ~ *laut* sea depth

dansa *n* Western-style dance; **berdansa** *v* to dance

dapat *v, aux* be able to, can; *v* find, get obtain; ~ *kesulitan* to have difficulties; **kedapatan** *adj* to be caught in the act; **mendapat** *v* to obtain, receive; ~ *kabar* to receive news; **mendapati** *v* to experience; **men-**

dapatkan *v* to obtain; discover; **pendapat** *n* opinion, point of view; *menurut* ~ *saya* in my opinion; **berpendapat** *v* to have an opinion, believe; **pendapatan** *n* income, revenue; **sedapatnya** *adv* what you can get

dapur *n* kitchen; ~ *rekaman* recording studio; *perkakas* ~ kitchen utensils

dara *n* (young) girl; *anak* ~ young girl; *selaput* ~ hymen

dara *burung* ~ pigeon, dove

darah *n* blood; ~ *tinggi* high blood pressure; *golongan* ~ blood group, type; *peredaran* ~ blood circulation; *pertumpahan* ~ spilling of blood, casualties; ~ *daging* flesh and blood; **mendarah daging** *v* to become second nature; **berdarah** *v* to bleed; **pendarahan** *n* bleeding

darat *n* land, shore; *angkatan* ~ army; *ke* ~ ashore; **daratan** *n* mainland; **mendarat** *v* to land; **pendaratan** *n* landing (of vessel); ~ *darurat* emergency landing

dari *prep* from, of; *conj* from the time; *selain* ~ except for; **sedari** *conj* since; **daripada** *conj* than

darma, dharma: darmawisata *n* excursion

darurat *adj* emergency, pressing; *keadaan* ~ (state of) emergency; *unit gawat* ~ *(UGD)* emergency ward

Darusalam, Darussalam *n* nation of peace, nation of

Islam; *Brunei* ~ Brunei

dasa *adj* ten; ~*lomba* decathlon; ~*sila* the Ten Commandments

dasar *n* base, basis, foundation; *sl* all because; ~ *maling!* that's thieves for you!; *pada* ~*nya* in principle; *undang-undang* ~ *(UUD)* constitution; **berdasar** *adj* based; **berdasarkan** *adj* based on; in accordance with, pursuant to; **mendasar** *adj* basic; **mendasarkan** *v* to base on something

dasbor *n* dashboard

dasi *n* necktie; **berdasi** *v* to wear a tie; *kaum* ~ white-collar workers

daster *n* house-coat, nightgown, nighty

data *n* data, information; ~ *pribadi* personal information; **mendatakan** *v* to record, document, collect data on; **pendataan** *n* documentation

datang *vi* to come, arrive; ~ *bulan* to menstruate, have your period; *minggu yang akan* ~ next week; **berdatangan** *v* to come (of many); **kedatangan** *n* arrival; **mendatang** *adj* coming, next; **mendatangkan** *v* to bring, import; **pendatang** *n* immigrant, migrant; newcomer

datar *adj* level, flat; **dataran** *n* plain; ~ *tinggi* plateau; **mendatarkan** *v* to make flat, level

DATI *Daerah Tingkat* administrative level

datuk *pron* (male) head of family; title in Malay areas

daulat *adj* sovereign, majesty; **berdaulat** *adj* sovereign; *negara yang* ~ sovereign state; **kedaulatan** *n* sovereignty; *Partai* ~ *Rakyat (PKR)* People's Sovereignty Party

daun *n* leaf; ~ *bawang* spring onion; ~ *bunga* petal; ~ *jendela* window pane; ~ *salam* bay leaf; ~ *telinga* ear; *hijau* ~ leaf green; **dedaunan** *n* leaves, foliage

daur *n* cycle; ~ *haid* menstrual cycle; ~ *ulang* recycling; **mendaur-ulang** *v* to recycle

dawai *n* string (of musical instrument); ~ *biola* violin string

dawet *n* sweet Javanese drink of green rice flour, pink syrup and coconut milk

daya *n* power, energy; ~ *beli* purchasing power; ~ *kuda (DK)* horsepower; ~ *upaya* efforts, means, resources; *barat* ~ southwest; **berdaya** *v* to have power; ~ *guna* efficient; *tak* ~ powerless; **memberdayakan** *v* to empower; **pemberdayaan** *n* empowerment; *Kementerian* ~ *Perempuan* Ministry for the Empowerment of Women

daya *tipu* ~ deceit, trick; **memperdaya** *v* to deceive, use, trick

Dayak generic name for indigenous (non-Malay) inhabitants of Kalimantan and Borneo; *orang* ~ Dayak; ~ *Iban* a Dayak of the Iban sub-group

dayung *n* oar; **berdayung** *v* to go by boat or bicycle; **men-**

dayung *v* to stroke (an oar), row; to pedal; **pendayung** *n* rower, oarsman, sculler

dé, dék *pron* little one (nickname for babies or youngest child in the family) ← **adé, adik**

debar pulse, beat; ~ *jantung* heart beat; **berdebar** *v* to beat quickly; *hati* ~ a racing heart; **mendebarkan** *adj* pulsating, throbbing

debat *n* debate; **berdebat** *v* to have a debate or discussion; **perdebatan** *n* debate, discussion

débet, débit *n* debit; **kedébet** *sl* to be wrongly debited (of a bank card); **mendébet** *v* to debit

débit ~ *air* rate of water flow

debu *n* dust; **berdebu** *adj* dusty

dedaunan *n* leaves, foliage ← **daun**

définisi *n* definition; **mendéfinisikan** *v* to define

deg: deg-degan *adj* anxious, worried

dégradasi *n* relegation (from a football league)

déh OK then, well; *Ayo, ~!* Come on, then!; *Saya nasi goreng* ~ I'll have fried rice then ← **sudah**

deham, dehem, berdeham, mendeham *v* to clear the throat, cough

dékan *n* (university) dean

dekap: dekapan *n* embrace; **berdekap-dekapan, berdekapan** *v* to embrace each other; **mendekap** *v* to hug, embrace

dékar: pendékar *n* (in martial arts) master, champion, leader

dekat *prep* close, near; *dalam waktu* ~ soon; **berdekatan** *adj* close (of two or more things); **kedekatan** *n* close relationship, closeness; **mendekati** *v* to approach; **mendekatkan** *v* to bring close; **pendekatan** *n* approach; getting to know; **terdekat** *adj* closest, nearest

dekil *adj* grimy, caked with dirt

déklamasi *n* declamation, reading poetry aloud; **mendéklamasikan** *v* to declaim

déklarasi *n* declaration; **mendéklarasikan** *v* to declare

delapan *adj* eight; ~ *belas* eighteen; ~ *puluh* eighty; *segi* ~ octagon; **berdelapan** *adj* a group of eight; **kedelapan** *adj* eighth

delima *n* pomegranate; *buah* ~ pomegranate

délman *n* two-wheeled horse-drawn carriage

demam *n* fever; ~ *berdarah* dengue fever; ~ *panggung* stage fright

demen, deman *v, coll* to like

demi *conj* for (the sake of); by; ~ *Allah* I swear to God; *seorang* ~ *seorang* one by one

demikian *adv* such, so, in this way, thus; *se~ rupa sehingga* in such a way that

démo, démonstrasi *n* demo, demonstration, protest; **berdémo** *v* to hold a protest; **mendémo** *v* to protest against

démokrasi *n* democracy; *pesta* ~ 'celebration of democracy' (general election); **démokrat** *n* democrat; *Partai* ~ Democrat Party; **démokratis** *adj* democratic

démonstrasi *n* demonstration, protest

démpét: berdémpét *adj* stuck together

dénah *n* plan, map, diagram; ~ *rumah* house plan

denda fine; *kena* ~ be fined; **mendenda** *v* to fine

dendam revenge; grudge; ~ *kesumat* long-standing grudge; **berdendam** *v* to be resentful, full of revenge

déndang *n* song, chant; **berdéndang** *v* to sing, chant

déndéng *n* dried meat, jerky; ~ *rusa* dried venison meat

dengan *conj* with; ~ *hormat* Dear Sir or Madam (in letter); ~ *sendirinya* by itself; *sesuai* ~ in accordance with

dengar *v* to hear; **dengar-dengar** *conj, coll* I've heard...; **kedengaran, terdengar** *adj* audible; **mendengar** *v* to hear; **mendengarkan** *v* to listen; ~ *lagu* listen to music; **memperdengarkan** *v* to play, broadcast; **pendengar** *n* listener; **pendengaran** *n* hearing; *indera* ~ sense of hearing

dengki spite, jealousy; **kedengkian** *n* spite

dengkul *n* knee

dengkur snore; **mendengkur** *v*

to snore; to purr (of a cat)

dengung *n* hum, buzz; **berdengung; mendengung** *v* to drone, hum, shake with sound

denyut pulse; throb; ~ *jantung* heartbeat; ~ *nadi* pulse; **berdenyut** *v* to throb, to beat

déodoran *n* deodorant

Dep. *Departemen* (government) department, ministry

Depag *Departemen Agama* Department of Religion

depak kick; **mendepak** *v* to kick something, kick out; *Haris didepak dari tim* Haris was kicked out of the team

depan *prep, n* front; *adj* next; *di* ~ front, in front of; *ke* ~ forward, to the front; *tahun* ~ next year

departemén *n* department, ministry; ~ *Luar Negeri* Department of Foreign Affairs; ~ *Tenaga Kerja* Department of Manpower

Depdagri *Departemen Dalam Negeri* department of Home Affairs, State Department, Ministry of the Interior

Depdikbud *Departemen Pendidikan dan Kebudayaan* Department of Education and Culture

Dephankam *Departemen Pertahanan dan Keamanan* Department of Defense and Security

Depkeh *Departemen Kehakiman* Department of Justice

Depkes *Departemen Kesehatan* Department of Health

Depkeu *Departemen Keuangan* Department of Finance

Depkimpraswil *Departemen Permukiman dan Prasarana Wilayah* Department of Regional Settlement and Infrastructure

Deplu *Departemen Luar Negeri* Department of Foreign Affairs

Depnaker *Departemen Tenaga Kerja* Department of Manpower

déposito *n* (bank) deposit

Depparpostel *Departemen Pariwisata, Pos dan Telekomunikasi* Department of Tourism, Post and Telecommunications

Depperindag *Departemen Perindustrian dan Perdagangan* Department of Industry and Trade

Deptamben *Departemen Pertambangan dan Energi* Department of Mining and Energy

derajat *n* degree, rank; *Balikpapan, hujan, tiga puluh ~* Balikpapan, rain, thirty degrees; *Tommy berubah pikiran 180 ~* Tommy did a 180-degree about-turn

derap *n* stamp, clap, hitting sound

deras *adj* swift; heavy; *hujan ~* heavy rain; *mengalir ~* to flow swiftly

dérék tow (a vehicle); *mobil ~* tow truck; **mendérék** *v* to tow; **pendérékan** *n* towing

dérét *n* row, line; **dérétan** *n* row; **berdérét-dérét** *v* to line up

dering ring, chime; **berdering, mendering** *v* to ring, tinkle

derita *n* suffering; **menderita** *v* to suffer, endure; **penderita** *n* sufferer; **penderitaan** *n* suffering

derma, darma *n* charity, donation; **dermawan** *n* donor, philanthropist; *adj* charitable

dermaga *n* pier, jetty

dermawan *n* donor, philanthropist; *adj* charitable ← **derma**

deru roar; **menderu** *v* to roar

désa *n* village; hometown; *gadis ~* village girl; **pedésaan** *n* country(side), rural areas; *angkutan ~* country minibus

desah *n* sigh, hiss, swish; **berdesah, mendesah** *v* to sigh, make a swishing noise

désain, disain *n* design; *juru-san ~* design major; **mendésain** *v* to design; **désainer** *n* designer

desak push; **desakan** *n* pressure, push; **berdesakan** *v* to push each other; **mendesak** *adj* pressing, urgent; *v* to press, urge, push

desas-desus *n* rumor

Désémber *bulan ~* December

désinféktan, disinféktan *n* disinfectant

desir hiss, rustle; **desiran** *n* hiss, rustle, swish; **berdesir, mendesir** *v* to hiss, rustle

destar *n, m* head cloth

desus: *desas-desus n* rumor

déterjén *n* detergent

detik *n* second

dévisa *n* foreign currency, foreign exchange; *cadangan* ~ exchange reserves

déwa *n, m* god; ~ *asmara* god of love; **mendéwakan** *v* to worship, idolize, put on a pedestal; **déwa-déwi, déwata** *n, pl, m & f* gods; **déwi** *n* goddess; ~ Sri Goddess of Rice

déwan *n* council, board; ~ *Keamanan (PBB)* (UN) Security Council; ~ *Perwakilan Rakyat (DPR)* Parliament, House of Representatives

déwasa adult; *orang* ~ adult, grown-up; *untuk* ~ adults only; **kedéwasaan** *n* maturity

déwata *n, pl, m & f* gods; *Pulau* ~ Island of the Gods (Bali) → **déwa**

déwi *n, f* goddess; ~ *fortuna* goddess of luck → **déwa**

dh *dahulu* formerly

DI *abbrev* Darul Islam

di *prep* at; on; in; ~ *atas* above, on top of; ~ *dalam* inside; ~ *samping* beside; *Saman tinggal* ~ *Cirebon* Saman lives in Cirebon; *Makanan ada* ~ *meja* The food is on the table; ~ *Amerika orang tidak begitu* People aren't like that in America

dia *pron* he, she, it; him, her (often replaced by **–nya** for possessive)

diabét, diabétés *n* diabetes; *penyakit* ~ diabetes

diagnosa *n* diagnosis; **mendiagnosa** *v* to diagnose

dialék *n* dialect; ~ *Surabaya*

Surabayan dialect

diam silent, not moving; **diam-diam** *adv* secretly; **berdiam** ~ *diri* to keep silent; **pendiam** *n* quiet, shy person; **terdiam** *v* to fall silent

diam: berdiam *v* to reside; **kediaman** *n* residence

dian *n* candle, lamp

diaré *n* diarrhea

dibandingkan *v* to be compared with ← **banding**

diberangkatkan *v* to depart, be sent off; *rombongan ke Medan sudah* ~ the party to Medan has departed ← **angkat**

dibikin *v, coll* to be made ← **bikin**

dibilang *v* to be said ← **bilang**

didih: mendidih *adj* boiling; **mendidihkan** *v* to boil water

didik educate; *anak* ~ pupil (of a teacher); **mendidik** *v* to educate, bring up, teach; **pendidik** *n* educator; **pendidikan** *n* education; *ilmu* ~ pedagogy; **berpendidikan** *adj* educated, to have an education; ~ *SD* to have a primary school education

diét *n* diet; **berdiét** *v* to diet, go on a diet

difaks *v* to be faxed ← **faks**

digips *v* be in or have a plaster cast ← **gips**

diinfus *v* to be put on a drip ← **infus**

dik *pron* you (used to a child, or young employee) ← **adik**

dikapling *v* to be divided up into blocks for development ← **kapling**

dikarenakan *v* caused by ← **karena**

dikau *pron, lit* you, thou

dikerjain *v, sl* to be tricked, taken for a ride ← **kerja**

dikir, dzikir, zikir *Isl* (recite) additional prayers; **berdikir** *v, Isl* to say additional prayers → **zikir**

diklakson *v* to be tooted at ← **klakson**

diklat *n* education and training for government workers ← **pendidikan dan latihan**

dikliring *v* to be cleared (in a bank) ← **kliring**

dikontrakkan *adj* for rent, lease ← **kontrak**

diktator *n* dictator

dikté *n* dictation; **mendikté** *v* to dictate (terms)

dilarang *v* to be prohibited; ~ *masuk* no entry, no admittance; ~ *merokok* no smoking ← **larang**

dilélang for auction, tender ← **lélang**

dilém *v* to be glued ← **lém**

dimaksud(kan) *v* to be meant or intended ← **maksud**

dimengerti *v* to be understood ← **erti, arti**

dinamit *n* dynamite

dinas (to work at a) government office; ~ *rahasia* secret service

dinding *n* (inner) wall; ~ *pembuluh darah* blood vessel wall

ding *coll* no, I mean (as correction); *Dia datang Sabtu. Eh, enggak ~, Jumat* He's coming on Saturday. No, I mean, Friday

dingin *n* cold, cool, chilly; **berdingin-dingin** *v* to enjoy cold weather; **kedinginan** *n* cold; feeling cold; **mendinginkan** *v* to chill, cool; **pendingin** ~ *ruangan* air conditioning, cooling

dingklik *n* low stool for sitting on (when washing clothes, grinding spices, etc)

dini *adj* very early, premature; ~ *hari* dawn, daybreak; *kelahiran* ~ premature birth; **sedini** ~ *mungkin* as early as possible

dinosaurus *n* dinosaur

diopname *v* to be admitted to hospital, be hospitalized ← **opname**

dipéhakakan *v* to lose your job, be fired ← **pé ha ka, PHK**

dipél *v* to be mopped, cleaned ← **pél**

diperban *v* to be bandaged ← **perban**

dipercaya *v* to be believed, trusted ← **percaya**

dipermak *v* to be altered, shortened ← **permak**

dipernis *v* to be varnished ← **pernis**

dipéstakan *v* to be celebrated with a party ← **pésta**

dipingit *v* to be secluded, kept at home

dipingpong *v* to be sent here and there, messed about ← **pingpong**

diplomasi *n* diplomacy; **diplomat** *n* diplomat

diplonco *v* to undergo an initiation at school or university ← **plonco**

diportal v to be blocked by a barrier, have a barrier lowered ← **portal**

diprételi v to be dismantled, taken apart or off ← **prételi**

diréksi n management, managing board; **diréktorat** n directorate; ~ *Jenderal Minyak dan Gas Bumi (Ditjen Migas)* Directorate-General of Oil and Gas; **diréktur** n director, manager; ~ *Jenderal (Dirjen)* Director-General

dirgahayu *ejac* long live!

dirgantara n sky, air; aerospace

diri n self; ~ *nya* he, she, it; himself, herself, itself; **berpendirian** v to hold, be of an opinion; **sendiri** adv alone; *pron* self; *salah* ~ it's your own fault; **degan** *~nya* automatic, by itself; **sendiri-sendiri** adv, pl alone, individually; **sendirian** adv alone, single-handedly; **tersendiri** adj its own; apart, separate; **terdiri** ~ *atas,* ~ *dari* to consist of, be based or founded on

dirigén n (music) conductor

dirjén n director-general ← **diréktor jénderal**

dironsen v to be x-rayed ← **ronsen**

diruilslag [dirélslag] v to be swapped, exchanged ← **ruilslag**

dirundung ~ *malang* to be cursed with or suffer bad luck ← **rundung**

dirut n (chief) director, director ← **diréktur utama**

disahkan v to be legalized ← **sah**

disain → **désain**

disanggul v to have your hair put into a bun ← **sanggul**

disantét v to have spells cast on you, be a victim of black magic ← **santét**

disaté v to be made into satay ← **saté**

disayangkan adj regrettable, unfortunate ← **sayang**

disebut-sebut v to be frequently mentioned ← **sebut**

disegani v to be respected ← **segan**

diselot v to be bolted ← **selot**

disemayamkan v to be laid out (of a dead body) ← **semayam**

diserut v to be sharpened ← **serut**

disérvis v to be serviced ← **sérvis**

disésar v to have a Cesarian ← **sésar**

disetrap v to be punished (at school) ← **setrap**

disholatkan v to be prayed for, have a prayer performed for you (after death) ← **sholat**

disinar v to have radiotherapy or chemotherapy ← **sinar**

disinféktan, désinféktan n disinfectant

disiplin discipline, disciplined; **berdisiplin** adj disciplined

diskét n diskette, disket

diskon n discount

diskors v to be suspended (from

school, work etc) ← **skors**

diskoték *n* disco, nightclub

diskriminasi *n* discrimination; ~ *rasial* racial discrimination; **mendiskriminasi(kan)** *v* to discriminate against

disomasi *v* to be summoned ← **somasi**

disoto *v* to be made into clear soup ← **soto**

distémpel *v* to be stamped ← **stémpel**

distribusi *n* distribution; **mendistribusikan** *v* to distribute

distrik *n* district

disun *v* to be kissed on the cheek ← **sun**

disunat *v* to be circumcised ← **sunat**

ditilang *v* to be fined ← **tilang**

ditim *v* to be steamed ← **tim**

ditipéks *v* to be whited-out, corrected ← **tipéks**

Ditjén *n* Directorate-General ← **Diréktorat Jénderal**

ditrap *v* to be layered (of hair) ← **trap**

ditumbuhi *adj* overgrown with ← **tumbuh**

divaksinasi, divaksin *v* to be vaccinated ← **vaksin**

divakum *v* to be vacuumed ← **vakum**

divalidasi *v* to be validated ← **validasi**

divérifikasi *v* to be verified ← **vérifikasi**

divisi *n* division (of a company)

divonis *v* to be sentenced ← **vonis**

DIY *abbrev Daerah Istimewa Yogyakarta* Special Region of Yogyakarta

DK *daya kuda* horsepower

DKI *abbrev Daerah Khusus Ibukota* Special Capital City Region

dkk *dan kawan-kawan* and friends

dll *dan lain-lain* et cetera

doa *n* prayer; ~ *restu* blessing; *membaca* ~ to pray, say a prayer; **berdoa** *v* to pray, say a prayer; ~ *menurut keyakinan masing-masing* to pray according to your own religion; **mendoakan** *v* to pray for

doang *adv, coll* only, just; *nasi* ~ just rice (no side-dishes)

dobel *adj* double, twice as much

dobrak, mendobrak *v* to break open, smash; ~ *pintu* to break down the door

dodol *n* soft, chewy sweet made from brown sugar or fruit; ~ *durian* durian sweet

doeloe *tempo* ~ the olden days, times past (old spelling of **témpo dulu**)

doi *pron, sl* he, she, boyfriend or girlfriend; *si* ~ your guy/girl

dok *pron* Doc, Doctor (used when addressing a doctor) ← **dokter**

dokar *n* (two-wheeled horse-drawn) buggy

dokter, dr *n* doctor, surgeon; ~ *gigi (drg)* dentist; ~ *hewan (drh)* vet; ~ *mata* oculist, optometrist; **kedokteran** *adj* medical; *fakultas* ~ School of Medicine

Doktor, Dr *pron* title for holder of a Ph.D.

Doktoranda, Dra *pron, f* graduate (Bachelor's degree); **Doktorandus, Drs** *pron, m* graduate (Bachelor's degree)

dokumén *n* document; **dokuméntasi** *n* documentation; **mendokuméntasi** *v* to document, file

dolar *n* dollar; ~ *Amerika* US dollar; *tukar* ~ to exchange dollars

DOM *abbrev Daerah Operasi Militer* region of military operations

domba *n* sheep; *adu* ~ play off against each other; **mengadu-dombakan** *v* to play people off against each other

doméstik *adj* domestic, internal, national; *penerbangan* ~ domestic flights

domisili *n* domicile; **berdomisili** *v* to be domiciled, reside

dompét *n* purse, wallet; ~ *saya hilang!* I've lost my wallet!

donat *n* donut, doughnut

dong, donk *sl* you should know that; *Jangan begitu* ~ Please don't do that

dongéng *n* tale, story, fable; *cerita* ~ tale; **mendongéng** *v* to tell a story

dongkol *adj* annoyed, resentful; **kedongkolan** *n* annoyance, resentment

dongkrak *n* (car) jack, lever; **mendongkrak** *v* to jack, lever,

raise; ~ *popularitas* to boost popularity

dor bang! (sound of gun, burst balloon, etc)

dorong *v* to push; **dorongan** *n* push, urge; ~ *hati* impulse; **mendorong** *v* to push, encourage; **terdorong** *adj* pushed, shoved

dosa *n* sin; ~ *asal Cath* original sin; *pengakuan* ~ *Cath* confession; **berdosa** *v* to sin, commit a sin

dosén *n* (university) lecturer

dosin → **lusin**

dosis *n* dose, dosage

dot *n* dummy; **mengedot** *v* to suck

doyan *v* to like, enjoy; ~ *kambing* enjoy eating goat or lamb

DPA *abbrev Dewan Pertimbangan Agung* Supreme Advisory Council

DPR *abbrev Dewan Perwakilan Rakyat* People's Representative Council

DPRD *abbrev Dewan Perwakilan Rakyat Daerah* Regional People's Representative Council

Dr *Doktor* holder of a Ph.D.

dr *dokter* doctor

dra *doktoranda* female holder of a Bachelor's degree

drainase *n* drainage

drastis *adj* drastic; *turun* ~ fall drastically

drg *dokter gigi* dentist

drh *dokter hewan* vet(erinary surgeon)

drs *doktorandus* male holder of

a Bachelor's degree

dsb *dan sebagainya* and so on

dua *adj* two; ~ *belas* twelve; ~ *kali* twice; ~ *puluh* twenty; *tiada ~nya* incomparable; **dua-duanya** *adj* both, the two of them; **berdua** *adj* together, in pairs; **kedua** *adj* second; **kedua(-dua)nya** *adj* both; **menduakan** ~ *Tuhan* to worship more than one god

dubes *n* ambassador; ~ *Australia* the Australian ambassador ← **duta besar**

dubur *n* anus; *liang* ~ anus

duda *n* widower; divorced man; ~ *cerai* divorced man; **menduda** *v* to become or live as a widower

duduk *v* to sit, be placed; *Silahkan* ~ Please sit down; ~ *perkara* facts of the case; **duduk-duduk** *v* to sit around; **kedudukan** *n* position; **menduduki** *v* to sit on something; to occupy; *Indonesia pernah diduduki Jepang* Indonesia was once occupied by Japan; **penduduk** *n* inhabitant, citizen, resident; **pendudukan** *n* occupation

duga, menduga *v* to suppose, suspect; **dugaan** *n* suspicion; **terduga** *tidak* ~ unexpected

dugem *n, sl* jetset, nightlife, underworld ← **dunia gemerlap**

duh → **aduh**

duit *n, sl* money, cash, dirt, dosh; *cari* ~ earn a living; *mata ~an* materialist, money-minded

duka *n* sorrow; ~ *cita* grief, sorrow; *suka* ~ good and bad, ups and downs; **berduka** ~ *(cita)* to grieve, be in mourning; **kedukaan** *n* grief, sorrow

duku *n* small sweet fruit with light brown skin, clear flesh and large dark seed

dukun *n* traditional or spiritual healer, shaman

dukung, mendukung *v* to support; **mendukung** *vt* to support; **dukungan** *n* support; ~ *moral* moral support; **pendukung** *n* supporter

dulang *n* serving tray; pan; **mendulang** *v* to pan (for gold); **pendulang** *n* prospector; **pendulangan** *n* panning, prospecting

dulu *adv* first, former, before; *kemarin* ~ the day before yesterday; *makan* ~ said when eating first before others; **duluan** *adv, coll* first, before others ← **dahulu**

dungu *adj* stupid, slow; *orang* ~ idiot

dunia *n* world; ~ *akhirat* the hereafter; *juara* ~ world champion; *keliling* ~ go around the world; **duniawi** *adj* earthly, secular

dupa *n* incense; **pedupaan** *n* stand for burning incense

durasi *n* duration; **berdurasi** *v* to last, have a duration of

durén → **durian**

durhaka *adj* treacherous, rebellious; *anak* ~ treacherous child

duri *n* thorn; **berduri** *adj* thorny; *kawat* ~ barbed wire; **durian** *n* durian, spiky yellow-skinned fruit with a strong smell

dus *conj, coll* so, then

dus, dos *n* cardboard box ← **kardus**

dusta *n* lie, fib; **berdusta** *v* to lie; **pendusta** *n* liar

dusun *n* hamlet, village

duta *n* envoy, messenger, representative; ~ *bangsa* representative of the nation; ~ *besar* ambassador; **kedutaan** ~ *(besar)* embassy

duyung *n* seacow; *putri* ~ mermaid

dwi- *pref* two; ~*bahasa* bilingual; ~*fungsi* dual function (of army); ~*mingguan adj* fortnightly; ~*warna* the red-and-white (Indonesian flag)

E

é *ejac* hey (showing recognition, disagreement)

é, éh *ejac* I mean; *Datang besok,* ~, *maksudnya lusa* Come tomorrow, no, I mean the day after

ébi *n* (dried) shrimp

écér: écéran *adj* retail; *harga* ~ retail price; **mengécér** *v* to retail, sell retail; **pengécér** *n* retailer

édar: édaran *n* circular; *surat* ~ memo; **berédar** *v* to circulate;

mengédarkan *v* to circulate something; **pengédar** *n* dealer; **pengédaran** *n* circulation; ~ *udara* air circulation

édisi *n* edition; **édit, mengédit** *v* to edit; **éditor** *n* editor

éféktif *adj* effective; **éféktivitas** *n* effectiveness, effect

éfisién *adj* efficient; *secara* ~ efficiently

égois *adj* egoist, egotistical

éh *ejac* I mean; *Datang besok,* ~, *maksudnya lusa* Come tomorrow, no, I mean the day after

éja: éjaan *n* spelling; ~ *yang disempurnakan* reformed spelling of 1972; **mengéja** *v* to spell; **pengéjaan** *n* spelling

éjakulasi *n* ejaculation (of semen)

ejan: mengejan *v* to strain, push the abdominal muscles (when defecating, giving birth)

éjék, mengéjék *v* to tease, mock, ridicule; **éjékan** *n* mockery, insult

ékonom *n* economist; **ékonomi** *n* economy; *ilmu* ~ economics; *kereta* ~ economy-class train; **perékonomian** *n* economic affairs; **ékonomis** *adj* economical, cheap

ékor *n* tail; counter for animals; ~ *kuda* pony tail; *tulang* ~ coccyx; *tiga* ~ *kucing* three cats; **berékor** *v* to have a tail; *bintang* ~ comet

ékosistém *n* ecosystem

éks- *pref* ex-, former → **mantan**

éksakta *ilmu* ~ exact sciences

(mathematics, physics etc)

éksékusi *n* execution; **mengéksékusi** *v* to execute (carry out the death penalty)

éksékutif executive; ~ *muda* young executive; *kereta* ~ exec-utive-class train

ékskul *n* extra-curricular activities, classes outside school; ~ *matematika* extra maths lessons ← **ékstra kurikulér**

ékspatriat *orang* ~ expatriate (esp. Caucasian)

ékspédisi *n* forwarding agent, freight service

éksplorasi *n* exploration (for mineral resources); *direktorat* ~ exploration directorate (of Pertamina)

ékspor export; **mengékspor** *v* to export; **pengékspor** *n* exporter; ~ *beras* exporter of rice

éksprés, ésprés *adj* express; *kereta api* ~ express train

ékstradisi *n* extradition; **mengékstradisi** *v* to extradite (someone)

élak, mengélakkan *v* to avoid, dodge, evade; **terélakkan** *tidak* ~ unavoidable, inevitable

elang *n* (*burung*) ~ eagle, hawk, falcon, bird of prey

éléktro *teknik* ~ electrical engineering; **éléktronik** *adj* electronic; *media* ~ electronic media; **éléktronika** *n* electronics

éliminasi *n* elimination; **teréliminasi** *adj* eliminated → **singkir**

élit, élite [élit] *n* elite; ~ *politik* political elite; *daerah* ~ elite

residential area

élok *adj* beautiful; **keélokan** *n* beauty

élpiji *n* liquid petroleum gas, LPG

ELS *abbrev Europese Lagere School* European Lower School, elementary school in colonial times

elu → **lu**

elus stroke, caress; **elusan** *n* stroke, caress; **mengelus** *v* to caress, stroke or pat (an animal)

émail *n* (tooth) enamel

émail → **imél**

emak, mak *n* mother

émang → **mémang**

emas, mas *n* gold; ~ *kawin* dowry; *kalung* ~ gold necklace; *kesempatan* ~ golden opportunity; *tukang* ~ goldsmith

emban: mengemban *v* to carry out, perform; **pengemban** *n* guardian, executor; ~ *tugas* worker responsible for performing a duty

embara: mengembara *v* to wander, roam; **pengembara** *n* wanderer, rover; **pengembaraan** *n* roaming, wandering

embék, embik bleat *coll* sheep or goat; **mengembék** *v* to bleat

émbél-émbél *n* details; extra decorations

émbér *n* bucket, pail

embun *n* dew; **berembun** *adj* moist, dewy; **pengembunan** *n* condensation

embus, hembus blow; **embusan** *n* blow; bellows; **berembus,**

mengembus *v* to blow

emis: **mengemis** *v* to beg;
pengemis *n* beggar

émisi *n* emission; ~ *kendaraan*
vehicle emissions

émosi, berémosi, émosional
adj emotional

empal *n* slice of beef

empang *n* dam, fish pond

empas, **mengempas** *v* to throw
down; **mengempaskan** ~ *diri*
to throw yourself down

empat *adj* four; ~ *belas* fourteen;
~ *puluh* forty; *segi* ~ square;
berempat *adj* in a group of
four; **keempat** *adj* fourth;
keempat(-empat)nya *n* all
four of them; **perempat** *n*
quarter; *tiga* ~ three-quarters,
¾; **perempatan, prapatan** *n*
crossroads, intersection;
seperempat *n* one quarter, ¼

empedu *n* gall, bile; *kandung* ~
gall bladder

empék-empék → **pémpék**

empela → **ampela**

émpér, émpéran *n* awning;
stall, booth

emping *n* chips made from the
melinjo bean

empu *n* creese-maker

empuk *adj* soft, tender; *kursi* ~
armchair

empunya *yang* ~, *si* ~ the owner
→ **punya**

emut, kemut, **mengemut** *v* to
suck on (sweets etc)

én *conj, sl* and

énak *adj* nice, tasty, delicious;
pleasant; ~*nya* the good thing

is, ...; ~ *saja,* ... ~ *aja* (sarcastically) that's nice! how dare
they!; *tidak* ~ *badan* not feeling well; **énakan** *adj, sl* better,
nicer, tastier; **keénakan** *adj* too
enjoyable or good; **seénaknya**
adv, neg just how you like, at
will

enam *adj* six; ~ *belas* sixteen;
~ *puluh* sixty; *segi* ~ hexagon;
berenam *adj* in a group of six;
keenam *adj* sixth; *indera* ~ sixth
sense; **keenam(-enam)nya** *n*
all six of them; **seperenam** *n*
one-sixth

éncér *adj* liquid, runny, watery;
mengéncér *v* to melt, become
liquid; **pengéncéran** *n* liquefaction, melting

éncik, cik *pron* form of address
to Chinese woman

encim *kebaya* ~ Chinese-style
traditional blouse

encok *n* rheumatism, arthritis

endap: **endapan** *n* precipitate,
sediment; **mengendap** *v* to
sink, silt up; **pengendapan** *n*
siltation

énérgi *n* energy; **berénérgi** *adj*
energetic, containing energy;
énérgik *adj* energetic →
tenaga

enga, engah: **terengah-engah**
adj gasping, puffing

enggak *coll* no, not ← **tidak**

enggan *adj* reluctant, unwilling;
~ *bicara* unwilling to speak;
keengganan *n* reluctance

enggang *n* hornbill

engkau, kau, dikau *pron* you;

Engkau *pron* You (when referring to God); ~ *yang punya langit dan bumi* both Earth and Heaven are Yours

engku *pron* title used for men in Malay areas

éngsél *n* hinge; joint

énsiklopédi, énsiklopédia *n* encyclopedia

entah who knows; ~ *ke mana* who knows where

entar soon ← **sebentar**

éntèng *adj* light; flippant; *menjawab* ~ to give a light, flippant answer

épiséntrum *n* epicenter

eram: mengeram *v* to sit on eggs, brood, hatch; **pengeraman** *n* brooding, hatching

erang groan; **erangan** *n* groan, moan; **mengerang** *v* to groan, moan

erat *adj* close, solid, strong; *hubungan* ~ close relations; **mempererat** *v* to strengthen, make closer

Éropa, Éropah *n* Europe; *orang* ~ European; *kebudayaan* ~ European civilization; *Uni* ~ European Union

érosi *n* erosion

érotis *adj* erotic; *penari* ~ erotic dancer

erti → **arti, mengerti**

és *n* ice; ~ *krim*, ~ *puter* ice cream; ~ *teler* sweet dessert with ice; *hujan* ~ hail; *lemari* ~ refrigerator

esa, ésa *n, lit* one, only; *Yang Maha* ~ the one and only

(God); **keesaan** *n* oneness; ~ *Tuhan* the oneness of God

ésai, éséi *n* essay; *lomba* ~ essay competition

Éslandia *n* Iceland; *bahasa* ~ Icelandic; *orang* ~ Icelander

ésok *adv* ~ *hari* tomorrow; **keésokan** ~ *harinya* the next day → **bésok**

ésprés → **éksprés**

éstafét *n* relay; *lari* ~ relay race; **beréstafét** *adj* in stages

étalase *n* shop window

étika *n* ethics, good manners; **berétika** *adj* ethical; to behave; ~ *baik* to behave well

étnik, étnis *n* ethnic group; ~ *Madura* the Madurese (ethnic group); *adj* ethnic, non-Western

étsa *n* etch; **mengétsa** *v* etch

évakuasi *n* evacuation → **ungsi**

EYD *abbrev Ejaan Yang Disempurnakan* reformed spelling, implemented in 1972

F

faédah *n* (insurance) benefit, use; **berfaédah** *adj* useful, worthwhile; *tidak* ~ useless

faham → **paham**

fajar *n* dawn, daybreak; ~ *menyingsing* crack of dawn

fakir ~ *miskin* poor person

faks, faksimili *n* fax, facsimile; *lewat* ~ by fax; *mesin* ~ fax machine; **difaks** *v* to be faxed

fakta *n* fact, the facts

faktor *n* factor

faktur *n* invoice, bill

fakultas *n* faculty; ~ *sastra* Arts faculty

fakultatif *adj* not fixed; optional; *hari libur* ~ optional holiday; *kereta* ~ train operated only at certain times

fals *adj* off-key, false (of music)

falsafah → **filsafat**

famili *adj* related, distant family

fana *adj* transitory, earthly; ~ *fana* on Earth

fanatik *n* fan; fanatic; *Kristen tapi tidak* ~ Christian but not fanatical

fans: ngefans *v, sl* to be a fan of; ~ *berat* a great fan of

fantasi *n* fantasy, imagination; *Dunia* ~ *(Dufan)* Fantasy World, an amusement park in Jakarta

farsi → **Parsi**

fase *n* phase

fasih *adj* fluent, eloquent; ~ *berbahasa Indonesia* to speak Indonesian fluently; **kefasihan** *n* ease, eloquence

fasilitas *n* facilities; ~ *sosial (fasos)* social facilities (eg. orphanage); ~ *umum (fasum)* public facilities; **berfasilitas** *adj* with facilities

fasis *adj* fascist; **fasisme** *n* fascism

fasos *n* social facilities (eg. orphanage) ← **fasilitas sosial**

fasum *n* public facilities (eg. reception hall, toilets) ← **fasilitas umum**

fatal *adj* very bad; fatal

Fatihah → **Al-Fatihah**

fatwa *n* fatwa, religious ruling

favorit *adj* favorite; *sekolah* ~ top school

FE *abbrev Fakultas Ekonomi* Faculty of Economics

Fébruari *bulan* ~ February

féderal *adj* federal; **féderasi** *n* federation; *Piala* ~ Federation Cup; **berféderasi** *v* to be federated

féng sui, hong sui *n* feng shui; *menurut* ~ according to feng shui

fénoména *n* phenomenon

féodal, féodalis *adj* feudal, feudalistic; **féodalisme** *n* feudalism

féri *n* ferry

FH *abbrev Fakultas Hukum* Faculty of Law

fikir → **pikir**

fiksi *n* fiction; **fiktif** *adj* fictitious, fictional

filatéli *n* philatelic sales; philately

Filipina *n* the Philippines; *orang* ~ Filipino, *f* Filipina

film *n* film; ~ *biru* blue film, pornographic film; *bintang* ~ film star

filsafat, falsafah *n* philosophy; **berfilsafat** *v* to have a philosophy

final *adj* final; *babak* ~ final (match); *semi-*~ semi-final; **finalis** *n* finalist

Finlandia *n* Finland; *bahasa* ~ Finnish; *orang* ~ Finn

firasat *n* presentiment, foreboding, bad feeling; ~ *buruk* bad feeling

Firaun *n* Pharaoh

firdaus *n* paradise

firman *n* word of God; **berfirman**
v to utter, say; *Allah* ~ God said

fisik *adj* physical; *bentrokan* ~
physical clash

fisika *n* physics; *ilmu* ~ physics

fisiotérapi *n* physiotherapy

FISIP *abbrev Fakultas Ilmu
Sosial dan Politik* Faculty of
Social Science and Politics

fiskal *n* departure payment (for
residents)

fitnah *n* slander, libel; **memfitnah**
v to slander

fitrah *zakat* ~ contribution to the
poor at Idul Fitri

fitri *adj* pure; *Idul* ~ feast after
the fasting month of Ramadan

FK *abbrev Fakultas Kedokteran*
Faculty of Medicine

FKG *abbrev Fakultas Kedokteran Gigi* Faculty of Dentistry

FKH *abbrev Fakultas Kedokteran Hewan* Faculty of Veterinary Science

flamboyan *pohon* ~ flame tree

flék *n* blemish, spot (on face)

flu *n* flu, influenza; ~ *burung*
bird flu; ~ *berat* bad or severe
flu

fokus *n* focus; ~ *pada* focus on;
berfokus *adj* focused; **memfokuskan** *v* to focus something; ~ *diri* to focus yourself

fondasi *n* foundation (of a building)

formal, formil *adj* formal

formulir *n* (blank) form

fosil *n* fossil

foto *n* photo, photograph;
~*model* (professional) model;
~ *udara* aerial photo; **berfoto**
v to take, pose for a photo;
fotokopi *n* photocopy; *difoto-
kopi* to be photocopied

foya: foya-foya, berfoya-foya
v to waste money, live
frivolously

fraksi *n* faction; ~ *Golkar* Golkar
faction

frambosen, frambozen *adj,
arch* raspberry-flavored

frustrasi *adj* frustrated

FS *abbrev Fakultas Sastra* Faculty of Letters, Arts Faculty

fungsi *n* function; *dwi*~ dual
function (of the army); **berfungsi** *v* to work, go; to act as;
fungsionaris *n* party functionary, official

fusi *n* fusion

fuyung hai, puyung hai *n*
sweet-and-sour omelet

G

G. *Gunung* Mt (name of mountain)

G30S (alleged) *Gerakan Tiga
Puluh September* 30th
September Movement

GA Garuda (Indonesia Airways)

gabah *n* unhusked rice

gabung connect, join; **gabungan**
adj joint; *tim* ~ team (comprising
various elements); **bergabung** *v*
to join together; **menggabungkan** *v* to connect, combine, fuse

gabus *n* cork

gadai *surat* ~ pawn ticket;
menggadaikan *v* to pawn
something; **pegadaian** *n*
pawnshop

gadang *rumah* ~ traditional
Minangkabau house

gadang → **begadang**

gading tusk, ivory (colored);
Pantai ~ Ivory Coast

gadis *n* girl, maiden, virgin,
unmarried woman; *sekolah* ~
girls' school; **kegadisan** *n*
virginity

gado-gado *n* cooked salad with
peanut sauce; *adj* mixed;
bahasa ~ mixture of Indonesian and another language

gaduh *adj* noisy; **kegaduhan** *n*
noise, uproar

gadungan *adj* fake, false

gaék *adj* old, veteran; *wartawan*
~ veteran reporter

gaét, gait, kait: menggaét *v* to
get (on board), snatch, hook →
gait, kait

gagah *adj* strong; ~ *perkasa*
heroic; handsome; **menggagahi** *v* to overpower, violate

gagak *burung* ~ crow, raven

gagal *v* to fail; **kegagalan** *n*
failure; **menggagalkan** *v* to
frustrate, make something fail

gagang *n* handle; ~ *telepon*
handset, telephone cradle

gagap stammer, stutter; ~ *teknologi (gaptek)* technophobe

gagas: gagasan *n* idea,
concept

gagu *adj* mute; *si* ~ deaf-mute

gaharu *kayu* ~ aloe wood, eagle-
wood

gaib *adj* mysterious, invisible;
kekuatan ~ unseen power,
magic

gairah *n* passion, lust; enthusiasm; **bergairah** *adj* lusty,
passionate; enthusiastic;
menggairahkan *adj* exciting,
stimulating

gait: menggait *v* to pull, hook
→ **gaét, kait**

gajah *n* elephant

gaji *n* (monthly) salary, pay; ~
bersih net salary, take-home
pay; *kenaikan* ~ pay rise;
menggaji *v* to pay, remunerate,
employ

gak *sl* no, not → **enggak, tidak**

galah *n* long pole, spear; *lompat*
~ pole vault

galak *adj* fierce, wild, vicious;
anjing ~ vicious dog; *guru
yang* ~ strict teacher

galang: galangan *n* dry dock;
menggalang *v* to support,
consolidate

galeri *n* gallery → **paméran**

gali *v* to dig; **galian** *n* excava-
tions, diggings; **menggali** *v* to
dig; **penggalian** *n* digging

Galungan *n* Balinese festival

gamang *adj* nervous, dizzy; ~
tinggi scared of heights

gambang *n* xylophone

gambar picture, drawing, illustration; **gambaran** *n* sketch,
idea; **bergambar** *adj* illustrated; **menggambar** *v* to draw,
depict; **menggambarkan** *v* to

describe, illustrate

gambir *n* gambier, spice used in chewing betel nut

gamblang *adj* clear, obvious, plain

gamelan *n* traditional orchestra

gamis *baju* ~ long Arab-style shirt

gampang *adj, coll* easy; ~~~ *susah* not as easy as it looks → **mudah**

gamping *n* limestone

ganas *adj* fierce, wild, ferocious; uncontrolled; *tumor* ~ malignant growth or lump; **keganasan** *n* ferocity

ganda double; -fold; over; ~ *putra* men's doubles; *berlipat* ~ many times; **menggandakan** *v* to duplicate, multiply

gandapura *n* tree with medicinal properties

gandéng link, join; *truk* ~ semitrailer; **bergandéng** *v* to join or do together; **bergandéngan** ~ *tangan* to link arms or hands; **menggandéng** *v* to include, involve, link with

gandol → **gandul**

gandrung: kegandrungan *adj, sl* to be absorbed or swept up in, madly in love

gandul *n* pendulum, clapper

gandum *n* wheat; *roti* ~ whole wheat bread

Ganésa, Ganésha, Ganéca *n* Hindu elephant god of wisdom

gang *n* alley, lane

Gangga *sungai* ~ the Ganges River

ganggang *n* pond weed, algae

ganggu, mengganggu *v* to bother, disturb; **gangguan** *n* disturbance, interference; problem; ~ *pendengaran* hearing problem; **terganggu** *adj* bothered, disrupted, disturbed

ganja *n* marijuana; *mengisap* ~ to smoke marijuana

ganjal *v* to wedge; to fill a gap; *Makan bakso yuk, buat* ~ Let's have some meatball soup, to fill us up

ganjil *adj* uneven, odd; *angka* ~ odd number; **keganjilan** *n* oddity, peculiarity

ganteng *adj, coll* handsome

ganti *silih* ~, **berganti-ganti, bergantian** *adv* in turns, repeatedly; **mengganti** *v* to change, substitute, replace; **menggantikan** *v* to substitute or replace someone/something; **pengganti** *n* replacement, substitute, successor; **penggantian** *n* substitution

gantolé *n* hang-glider, hanggliding; *main* ~ to go hanggliding

gantung hang; *jembatan* ~ suspension bridge; ~ *diri* hang yourself; **bergantung** ~ *pada* to depend on; **menggantung** *v* to hang, suspend; **tergantung** *adj* depending (on), it depends; **ketergantungan** *n* dependency; ~ *obat* drug dependency

ganyang *v* to crush, wipe out; ~ *Malaysia!* Crush Malaysia! (1960s political slogan)

gapai: menggapai *v* to strive

for, reach; ~ *cita-cita* to chase your dreams

gaplé *n* dominoes

gapték *n* technophobe ← **gagap téknologi**

gapura *n* (ornamental) gateway, entrance

gara-gara *adv, sl* all because of; *n* forest scene in shadow puppet play; fuss → **goro-goro**

garam *n* salt; *sudah makan ~* experienced, an old salt

garang *adj* fierce, savage, cruel

garansi *n* guarantee (on a product); **bergaransi** *adj* guaranteed

garap: garapan *adj* produced by, product; **menggarap** *v* to work on, produce; ~ *tanah* to till the land; **penggarapan** *n* production; ~ *film* film or movie production

garasi *n* carport, garage

gardu *n* post, station; ~ *listrik* transmission station

garebeg, garebek *n* one of the big Islamic festivals; ~ *Besar*, ~ *Haji* Idul Adha Feast of the Sacrifice; ~ *Maulud* Birthday of the Prophet; ~ *Puasa* Idul Fitri, post-fasting celebrations

Garéng *n* shadow puppet character

garing *adj* dry, crisp; *sudah ~ sl* stale, out-of-date (of a joke)

garis line, scratch; ~ *alas* baseline; ~ *peperangan* front, front line; ~ *tengah* diameter; ~ *tegak lurus* perpendicular (line); **bergaris** *adj* lined; **menggaris** *v* to draw a line;

menggarisbawahi to underline, emphasize; **penggaris** *n* ruler

garmén *pabrik ~* garment factory

garong *n* robber; **menggarong** *v* to rob, loot

garpu *n* fork; *sendok ~* spoon and fork

garuda *n* mythical bird of prey, national symbol of Indonesia

garuk, menggaruk *v* to scratch, scrape; ~ *kepala* to scratch your head

gas *n* gas; ~ *bumi* natural gas; *menancap ~* to step on the gas

gasing *n* (spinning) top; *main ~* to spin a top

gatal *adj* itchy; *sl* lustful; **gatal-gatal** *v* to have a rash

Gatotkaca, Gatutkaca *n* flying warrior in shadow puppet plays, son of Bima

gatra *n* phrase; aspect

gaul *v* to mix, associate; *adj, sl* trendy; *kafé ~* trendy café; **bergaul** *v* to mix or associate; **menggauli** *v* to have sexual intercourse with; **pergaulan** *n* mixing, social intercourse; association; ~ *bebas* promiscuity, permissiveness

gaun *n* (evening) gown; *f* evening dress; ~ *malam* evening gown

gaung *n* echo; **bergaung** *v* to echo

gawang *n* goal (in field sports); hurdle; *penjaga ~* goalkeeper; *lari ~* hurdles

gawat *adj* serious, very bad;

Unit ~ Darurat (UGD) emergency room, casualty ward

gaya energy, strength; style; ~ *berat*, ~ *bobot* gravity; *penuh* ~ stylish; **bergaya** *adj* stylish, with style

Gayo Acehnese sub-ethnic group

gayung *n* water dipper; stick; ~ *bersambut* to respond

Gd. *gedung* building

gebrak blow, bang, hit; **gebrakan** *n* bang, slam, blow; **menggebrak** *v* to hit or slam; ~ *meja* to hit the table

gebu: menggebu *v* to rage, bubble, froth over

gebuk hit, bash; **menggebuk** *v* to batter, bash

gebyar sparkle, glitter

gedé *adj, coll* big, large; ~ *banget* enormous, very big; ~ *rasa (GR)* stuck-up, full of yourself; **gedéan** *adj, sl* larger or bigger than

gedor: menggedor *v* to bang on repeatedly; ~ *pintu* to bang on the door

gedung *n* building, public hall; ~ *Arsip* State Archives

géér, gé ér, GR *adj* stuck-up, full of yourself ← **gedé rasa**

gegap ~ *gempita* noisy, thunderous

gegar shake, quiver; ~ *budaya* culture shock; ~ *otak* concussion

gegas: bergegas-gegas *v* to hurry

gégér noise, clamor

gejala *n* symptom, sign

gejolak *n* uprising, outburst, riot; **bergejolak** *v* to flare up, burst out

geladah → **geledah**

geladak *n* deck of a ship

geladi → **gladi**

gelagap: gelagapan confused; stammer, stutter

gelagat *n* mark, sign, omen

gelak laugh; ~ *tawa* burst or gale of laughter

gelandang *n* half-back

gelandang: gelandangan *n* tramp, homeless person

gelang *n* bracelet; **pergelangan** ~ *kaki* ankle; ~ *tangan* wrist

gelanggang *n* arena, stadium; ~ *dunia* world stage; ~ *olah raga (GOR, gelora)* sports complex

gelantung hang, suspend; **gelantungan** *adj* hanging from; **bergelantungan** *v* to hang from (of several things)

gelap *adj* dark; ~ *gulita* pitch black; *barang* ~ contraband, illegal goods; *imigran* ~ illegal immigrant; *pasar* ~ black market; **kegelapan** *n* darkness; **menggelapkan** *v* to embezzle, misappropriate; **penggelapan** *n* embezzlement

gelar *n* title; **bergelar** *adj* titled

gelar: menggelar, menggelarkan *v* to hold (an event)

gelatik *burung* ~ Java sparrow, Java finch

gelédah, geladah, menggelédah *v* to search; to ransack; **penggelédahan** *n* search, raid, operation

gelédék *n* lightning

gelembung *n* bubble

géléng: menggéléng, meng-géléngkan ~ *kepala* to shake your head

gelétak *v* to shudder; **tergelétak** *adj* sprawled

geli ticklish; uncomfortable; *merasa* ~ to feel uncomfortable; **menggelikan** *adj* funny, comic; off-putting

geliat ~ *geliut* wriggle, writhe; **menggeliat** *v* to stretch, twist

gelimang: bergelimang *adj* smeared; ~ *lumpur* muddy, mud-stained

gelimpang: bergelimpang, tergelimpang *adj* sprawled; **bergelimpangan** *adj* sprawled all around; *mayat* ~ dead bodies lay everywhere

gelincir: menggelincir *v* to slip, slide; **tergelincir** *adj* skidded, slipped; *pesawat* ~ the plane skidded

gelintir: segelintir *n* a small number

gelisah *adj* nervous, restless; **kegelisahan** *n* anxiety, nerves; **menggelisahkan** *v* to make nervous

gelitik, menggelitik *v* to tickle

geliut *geliat* ~ wriggle, writhe

gelombang *n* wave; (radio) frequency; **bergelombang** *adj* wavy

gelora *n* storm, surge, passion; ~ *asmara* passion; **menggelora** *v* to rage, storm, surge

gelut: bergelut *v* to wrestle; to romp; **menggeluti** *v* to be involved, deal with

gema *n* echo, reverberation; **bergema** *v* to echo, reverberate

gemar like, enjoy; **kegemaran** *n* hobby; **menggemari** *v* to like, enjoy; **penggemar** *n* fan, enthusiast

gemas, gemes *coll* cute, sweet (often said to children); annoyed; **menggemaskan** *adj* annoying

gembala, penggembala *n* shepherd; **menggembala** *v* to herd

gembira *adj* cheerful, happy, joyous; **bergembira** *v* to be happy, joyous; **kegembiraan** *n* joy, happiness; **menggembirakan** *adj* exciting, happy; *berita yang* ~ good news

gembok *n* padlock; **menggembok** *v* to padlock

gembos flat, deflated; **menggembos** *v* to deflate, go flat

gembul *adj* greedy; fat

gembung, kembung *adj* filled with air, inflated; bloated; *perut* ~ bloated belly → **kembung**

gemercik splash, spray, spatter

gemerlap shine, sparkle; **gemerlapan** *pl* shine, sparkle

gemes → **gemas**

gemetar shiver, tremble; **gemetaran** *adj* shivering, trembling

gemilang glitter, shine; brilliant

geming: bergeming *tak* ~ not bat an eyelid, make not the slightest reaction

gempa *n* quake, shudder; ~ *bumi* earthquake; **menggempakan** *v* to jolt, stir

gempar clamor, noise, uproar; **menggemparkan** *v* to cause a stir

gempita *gegap* ~ noisy, thunderous

gempur: menggempur *v* to attack, destroy

gemuk *adj* fat, plump, obese; *n* grease; *jalur* ~ busy route; **kegemukan** *n* fatness; *adj* overweight

gemulai *adj* supple, swaying

gemuruh *n* thunder → **guruh**

gén *n* gene; **génétik** *adj* genetic; **génétika** *n* genetics; *rekayasa* ~ genetic engineering

genang: genangan *n* puddle, flood; **bergenang** *adj* flooded; **menggenangi** *v* to flood something

genap *adj* even, complete, exact; *angka* ~ even number; **se-genap** *adj* each, all

gencat: gencatan ~ *senjata* ceasefire, truce, armistice

gendang *n* (kettle) drum; ~ *telinga* eardrum

géndong, menggéndong *v* to carry on the hip

gendut *adj* fat, pot-bellied

générasi *n* generation

génétik *adj* genetic; **génétika** *n* genetics; *rekayasa* ~ genetic engineering ← **gén**

géng, génk *n* gang

genggam fist; **genggaman** *n* grip, grasp; **menggenggam** *v* to grip, grasp; **segenggam** *n* handful

géngsi *n* prestige, face; ~ *dong* mustn't lose face!; **bergéngsi** *adj* prestigious

genit *adj* flirtatious

genjot, menggenjot *v* to push, pedal; ~ *sepeda* to pedal a bike

génsét *n* generator

gentar shiver, tremble; *tak* ~ unafraid

gentayangan *v* to wander, roam

genténg, genting *n* roof tile

genting *adj* critical; narrow; **gentingan** *n* isthmus; ~ *Kra* Isthmus of Kra

géografi *n* geography (school subject) → **ilmu bumi**

Georgia [Jorjia] *n* Georgia; *bahasa* ~, *orang* ~ Georgian

gépéng *adj* flat, concave, sunken

gerabah *n* earthenware pot

gerah *adj* sultry, muggy

geraham *gigi* ~ molar

gerak move; ~ *badan* (physical) exercises; ~ *gerik* movements, body language; ~ *jalan* long march; demonstration; **gerakan** *n* movement; ~ *Aceh Merdeka (GAM)* Free Aceh Movement; **bergerak** *v* to move; *aset* ~ movable assets; **menggerak-kan** *v* to move, shift something

geram *adj* very angry, furious; **menggeram** *v* to become very angry; to growl, roar

gerangan can it be?

gerayang: menggerayangi *v* to grope

gerbang *n* gate, gateway, door; ~ *tol* toll gate; *pintu* ~ main gate

gerbong *n* carriage; ~ *restorasi* restaurant car

gerebek, gerebeg: menggerebek *v* to raid, search; **penggerebekan** *n* raid, search

gereget: geregetan *adj* filled with pent-up emotion

geréja *n* church; ~ *Pantekosta* Pentecostal Church; *burung* ~ sparrow

gergaji *n* saw; *abu* ~ sawdust; **menggergaji** *v* to saw

gerhana *n* eclipse; ~ *bulan* lunar eclipse; ~ *matahari* solar eclipse

gerigi *n, pl* teeth, points; **bergerigi** *adj* serrated, jagged

gerilya *n* guerrilla; *perang* ~ guerrilla war; **bergerilya** *v* to wage guerrilla warfare

gerimis drizzle; *hujan* ~ drizzle

gerobak *n* cart; ~ *kaki lima* itinerant food vendor; ~ *sampah* rubbish cart

gerogot: menggerogoti *v* to eat into, erode, gnaw on; *digerogoti rayap* eaten by termites

gerombol: gerombolan *n* group, mass; **bergerombol, menggerombol** *v* to gather in a group, amass

gersang *adj* arid

gertak snarl, snap; **menggertak** *v* to snarl or snap at; to intimidate, threaten

gerutu: menggerutu *v* to grumble, complain, gripe

gesa: tergesa-gesa *adj* in a hurry or rush

gésék rub; **gésékan** *n* stroke, scrape; **menggésék** *v* to rub, scrape; ~ *biola* to play the violin; ~ *kartu* to swipe a card; **pergésékan** *n* friction

gésér, menggésér *v* to move aside or over; **pergéséran** *n* movement, shift

gesit *adj* nimble, adept, adroit; **kegesitan** *adj* agility, adroitness

géspér *n* (belt) clasp, buckle

Gestapu *n* (alleged) 30th September Movement (in 1965) ← **Gerakan Séptémber Tiga Puluh**

getah *n* sap, latex, gum

getah ~ *bening* lymph gland

getar shake, tremor; **getaran** *n* vibration, shake, tremor; **bergetar** *v* to vibrate, tremble

getol *adj, coll* hard-working, diligent

Gg *gang* lane, alley

Ghana *n* Ghana; *orang* ~ Ghanaian

GIA Garuda Indonesia Airways

giat *adj* active, busy; **kegiatan** *n* activity

gigi *n* tooth; ~ *palsu* false teeth; *dokter* ~ dentist; *menggosok gigi* ~ to brush your teeth; *pasta* ~ toothpaste; *sakit* ~ toothache; *sikat* ~ toothbrush; *tusuk* ~ toothpick

gigih *adj* persevering, tenacious; **kegigihan** *n* perseverance, tenacity

gigil: menggigil *v* to shiver

gigit: gigitan *n* bite; **menggigit** *v* to bite

gila *adj* crazy, mad, insane; **orang ~** lunatic; tramp; **kegilaan** *n* craze; **tergila-gila ~ dengan** crazy about

gilas, menggilas *v* to crush, pulverize

giling *daging ~* mincemeat; **gilingan** *n* mill, grinder; **menggiling** *v* to grind, mill; **penggilingan** *n* mill

gilir: giliran *n* turn; **bergilir, bergiliran** *adj* in turns

gimana *coll* how; **~ sih?** what about that? → **bagaimana**

gincu *n, arch* lipstick, lip gloss

ginékolog *n* gynecologist; **ginékologi** *n* gynecology → **kandungan**

gini *adv, coll* like this, in this way → **begini**

ginjal *n* kidney; *sakit ~* kidney disease

giok *n batu ~* jade

gips *n* plaster, plaster cast; **digips** *v* to be in or have a plaster cast

girang *adj* pleased, glad, happy; **kegirangan** *n* gladness, happiness

giring, menggiring *v* to herd, drive (cattle); **penggiring** *n* herder

giro *n* transfer, clearing (money)

gitar *n* guitar

gitu *adv, coll* like that, in that way → **begitu**

giur: menggiurkan *adj* tempting, mouth-watering; **tergiur** *adj* tempted

gizi *n* nutrient; *ahli ~* nutritionist; *penyakit kurang ~* malnutrition; **bergizi** *adj* nutritious

gk *gaya kuda* horsepower

gladi, geladi *~ resik, ~ bersih* dress-rehearsal

glétser *n* glacier

goa, gua *n* cave, tunnel; *~ Jepang* Japanese-built tunnel from World War II

goblok *derog* stupid, moron

gocéng *adj, sl* five thousand (rupiah)

goda tempt; **godaan** *n* temptation; **menggoda** *v* to tempt; **menggodai** *v* to tempt someone; **tergoda** *adj* tempted

godok boil; **menggodok** *v* to boil

gokar *n* go-kart

gol *n* goal; *~ bunuh diri* own goal; **mengegolkan** *v* to promote, campaign for someone

golak: pergolakan *n* disturbance, upheaval

golék *wayang ~* (performance using) three-dimensional wooden puppets from West Java

golf *n* golf; *lapangan ~, padang ~* golf course; **pegolf** *n* golfer

Golkar *n, arch* Functional Group (Soehartoist party, until 1998); *Partai ~* Golkar Party ← **Golongan Karya**

golok *n* machete, chopping knife; **menggolok** *v* to cut with a machete

golong: golongan *n* group, category; rank; *~ IV A* Rank IV A (in civil service); *~ Karya (Golkar)* Functional Group; *~ putih (golput)* 'white' group (abstainers in elections); **menggolongkan** *v* to group, classify; **penggolongan** *n* classification; **tergolong** *adj* to include, be part of or considered

gombal *adj* worthless; *rayuan* ~ sweet talk

goncang, guncang rock, sway; **goncangan** *n* shock wave, quake; **bergoncang** *v* to rock, sway; **menggoncangkan** *v* to rock or make something move

gondok *n* goitre

gondrong (excessively) long hair

gong *n* gong

gonggong woof, sound of dog barking; **menggonggong** *v* to bark; *anjing* ~ a dog barking

gono-gini *n* shared goods and chattels during a marriage, split up during divorce

gonta-ganti *v* to change constantly; ~ *pacar* to have had lots of boyfriends/girlfriends → **ganti**

GOR *abbrev Gelanggang Olah Raga* stadium, sports complex

gopék *n* five hundred (rupiah)

gordén, hordén *n* curtain(s)

goréng fry; *mie* ~ fried noodles; *nasi* ~ fried rice; **goréngan** *n* fried snacks (such as tofu, *tempe*); **menggoréng** *v* to fry; **penggoréngan** *n* wok, frying pan; process of frying

gorés line, scratch; **gorésan** *n* scratch, stroke; **menggorés** *v* to scratch, make a stroke; **tergorés** *adj* scratched

goro-goro *n* scene in shadow

puppet play → **gara-gara**

gosip gossip; *raja* ~ *(ragos)* gossip queen, gossip; **bergosip** *v* to gossip; **menggosipkan** *v* to gossip about something or someone

gosok rub; *minyak* ~ massage oil; **menggosok** *v* to rub, polish; ~ *sepatu* to polish, shine (shoes)

gosong *adj* burnt, singed, scorched; *bau* ~ burnt smell

got *n* roadside drain or ditch; *masuk* ~ fall in the drain; *tikus* ~ sewer rat

gotong carry; ~ *royong* mutual assistance; **menggotong** *v* to carry together

goyah *adj* unstable, wobbly; **tergoyahkan** *tak* ~ unshakable

goyang shake, wobble, unsteady; **bergoyang** *v* to shake, sway; to dance; **menggoyang** *v* to shake, rock; ~ *pinggul* to sway your hips; **menggoyangkan** *v* to shake or rock something

GR, gé ér *adj* stuck-up, full of yourself ← **gedé rasa**

grafik *n* graph; diagram; **grafis** *adj* graphic; *seni* ~ graphic design

graha, grha *n* building, house; *Bina* ~ presidential office

granat *n* grenade

grasi *n* pardon (from the President), clemency; *memberi* ~ to pardon someone (for a crime)

gratis *adj* free (of charge), gratis

greget, gereget: gregetan *adj* filled with pent-up emotion

grés *adj* newest, latest; *paling ~* most up-to-date

gringsing, geringsing *n* double-*ikat* cloth from Bali

griya *n* house

grogi *adj* nervous, groggy

grosir *n* wholesaler; **grosiran** *adj* wholesale

grup *n* group (esp business)

gua → goa

gua → gué

Guam *n* Guam; *orang ~* Guamanian

gubernur *n* governor; *calon ~* gubernatorial candidate

gubris: menggubris *v* to pay heed or attention to; *tidak digubris* ignored

gubuk *n* hut; *~ derita* my humble abode

guci *n* (earthenware) jar or pot

gudang *n* warehouse, shed, store; *cuci ~* stocktake sale

gudeg *n* sweet dish of cooked jackfruit, a specialty of Jogjakarta

gugat sue; **gugatan** *n* lawsuit, accusation; **menggugat** *v* to sue, accuse; **penggugat** *n* plaintiff

gugup *adj* nervous; **kegugupan** *n* nervousness, panic

gugur *v* to fall, be killed (in action) or eliminated; *musim ~* autumn, fall; **keguguran** *n* miscarriage; **menggugurkan** *v* to abort; **pengguguran** *n* abortion

gugus cluster; *~ bintang* constellation; **gugusan** *n* bunch, group, cluster; *~ pulau* chain of islands

gula *n* sugar; *~ batu* sugar lump; *~ Jawa* palm sugar; *kembang ~* fairy floss; *Ada ~ ada semut* if you have money, people will come

gulai, gulé *n* curry; *~ kambing* goat curry

gulat wrestling; **bergulat** *v* to wrestle, fight; **pergulatan** *n* wrestling, struggle, fight; **pegulat** *n* wrestler

guling *babi ~* suckling pig; *(bantal) ~* bolster, Dutch wife; **mengguling** *v* to roll; **menggulingkan** *v* to topple, roll something over

gulita *gelap ~* pitch-black

gulung: menggulung *v* to roll up

gumam, bergumam *v* to mumble; **menggumamkan** *v* to mumble or mutter something

gumpal *n* clot, lump; **gumpalan** *n* clot, lump; *~ darah* clot of blood; **bergumpal** *v* to clot

gumul, bergumul *v* to wrestle

guna use, benefit; for; *tepat ~* effective, appropriate; *tidak ada ~nya* there's no use; **berguna** *adj* useful, worthwhile; *tidak ~* useless; **kegunaan** *n* usefulness, use; **menggunakan** *v* to use; **pengguna** *n* user; **pengunaan** *n* usage, use

guna-guna *n* black magic

guncang, goncang rock, sway; **guncangan** *n* shock wave, quake; **berguncang** *v* to rock, sway; **mengguncangkan** *v* to rock or make something move

gundah *adj* depressed; **bergundah** ~ *hati* sad

gundik *n* mistress, concubine

gundul *adj* bald; **menggunduli** *v* to shave, denude, make bald; *bukit itu sudah digunduli* the hill has been deforested

gunting scissors, cut; ~ *kuku* nail clippers; **guntingan** *n* cutout; ~ *koran* newspaper clipping; **menggunting** *v* to cut (out)

guntur *n* thunder

gunung *n* mountain, mount; remote area; ~ *api* volcano; ~ *Bromo* Mount Bromo; *mendaki* ~ mountain-climbing, bushwalking; **gunungan** *n* symbolic mountain used in shadow-puppet plays; **pegunungan** *n* mountain range; ~ *Jayawijaya* the Jayawijaya range

gurah *n* rinsing, as an alternative medical treatment

guramé, guraméh, gurami *ikan* ~ large freshwater fish

gurat: guratan *n* scratch

gurau joke, jest; *bersenda* ~ to joke around

gurem *adj* tiny, insignificant; *partai* ~ minor parties (with very small vote)

gurih *adj ta*sty, delicious, mouthwatering

gurita *ikan* ~ octopus

gurita *n* cloth used by mothers after giving birth, to bind their stomach

guru *n* teacher; ~ *besar* professor; ~ *kepala* headmaster; **menggurui** *v* to lecture or talk

condescendingly to someone; **perguruan** ~ *tinggi* university

guruh *n* thunder

gurun *n* desert; ~ *Sahara* the Sahara Desert

Gus, Bagus *title, m, Isl* East Javanese title; ~ *Dur* common name for Abdurrahman Wahid

gusar *adj* angry, vexed; **kegusaran** *n* annoyance, anger

gusi *n* gums

gusti *n, pron, arch* lord; ~ *Allah* the Lord God; *kawula* ~ Javanese servant-patron relationship

gusur: menggusur *v* to evict, sweep aside, forcibly remove; **penggusuran** *n* eviction, forcible removal

H

H *hijriah* Islamic calendar

H. *Haji* title for man who has performed the major pilgrimage to Mecca

habis *adj* finished; empty; *adv* entirely; *coll* after; ~ *perkara* end of story; that was it; *stok sudah* ~ out of stock; ~ *mandi dia pergi* After washing, he went out; **habisnya** *adv* well, in any case; **kehabisan** *v* to run out of (water; food; stock); **menghabiskan** *v* to finish, use up, spend; ~ *uang jutaan rupiah* to spend millions of rupiah; **penghabisan** *n* end;

ujian ~ final examination;
sehabis *conj* after

hablur *n* crystal

hadap face; ~ *kiri* face left;
hadapan *n* front; facing; *di* ~
in front of; **berhadapan** *v* face
to face; ~ *muka* face to face;
menghadap *v* to face, appear
before; **menghadapi** *v* to face
someone or something; **terhadap** *conj* regarding; against;
with respect to

hadiah *n* present, gift; prize; ~
pertama first prize; **berhadiah**
adj with prizes; **menghadiahkan** *v* to give as a present or
prize; **menghadiahi** *v* to give
someone a present or prize

hadir present; available; *tidak* ~
absent; **hadirin** *n* audience;
kehadiran *n* presence; attendance; **menghadiri** *v* to attend;
menghadirkan *v* to present;
to bring forward; ~ *saksi baru*
bring forward a new witness

hadis, hadith *n, Isl* traditions of
the Prophet Muhammad

hafal, hapal know by heart;
hapalan *n* memorization;
menghafalkan *v* to learn by
heart

hai *sl* hi

haid *n* menstruation; *nyeri* ~
menstrual pain; *siklus* ~, *daur*
~ menstrual cycle

Haiti *n* Haiti; *orang* ~ Haitian

Haj, hajj → **haji**

hajat *n* want, need, wish; *buang*
~ to defecate; *punya* ~ to hold
a feast

haji *n, Isl* person who has made
the pilgrimage to Mecca; ~
kecil minor pilgrimage →
umroh; *Lebaran* ~ Idul Adha,
Feast of the Sacrifice (performed during the annual pilgrimage); *naik* ~ go on the
annual pilgrimage to Mecca;
ongkos naik ~ *(ONH)* cost of
making the pilgrimage; *Pak* ~
title for a man who has made
the pilgrimage to Mecca

hajjah *Isl, f* title for a woman
who has made the pilgrimage
to Mecca

hak *n* right; ~ *azasi manusia
(HAM)* human rights; ~
kekayaan intelektual (HAKI)
intellectual property rights; ~
milik ownership; ~ *pilih* right
to vote; suffrage; **berhak** *v* to
have a right to, be entitled to

hak *n* heel; *sepatu* ~ *tinggi* high
heels

HAKI *abbrev* Hak Kekayaan
Intelektual Intellectual Property
Rights

hakikat, hakékat *n* nature,
essence; *pada ~nya* basically,
essentially

hakim *n* judge; *dewan* ~ judicial
board; **kehakiman** *Departemen* ~ Department of Justice

hal *n* matter, case; ~-*ihwal* related matters; ~ *ini* this; *dalam* ~
itu in that case

halal *adj, Isl* permitted (to eat);
killed according to Islamic
practice; *pekerjaan yang* ~ a
decent job

halal bihalal *n* social gathering, usu after fasting month

halaman *n* yard, open area, page; ~ *rumah* yard; *lihat* ~ *sebelah (lhs)* please turn over (PTO)

halang: halangan *n* obstacle; hindrance; *kalau tidak ada* ~ if there are no problems; **berhalangan** *v* to be prevented; unable; *lagi* ~ have your period (said about a woman not fasting); **menghalangi** *v* to hinder, prevent; **terhalang** *adj* blocked; prevented

hal-ihwal *n* related matters; circumstances ← **hal**

halilintar *n* lightning bolt, thunderclap

halte *n* stop; ~ *bis* bus stop

haluan *n* bow (of a ship); prow, course, direction; **berhaluan** ~ *kiri* leftist

halus *adj* fine; soft; refined; *bahasa* ~ refined language; speech level in some regional languages; *makhluk* ~ spirit; **kehalusan** *n* delicacy; grace; **menghaluskan** *v* to refine; grind

HAM *abbrev* Hak Asasi Manusia Human Rights

hama *n* pest; plague; *suci*~ sterile

hamba *n, pron, arch* slave; me; your servant; ~ *Allah* mankind; anonymous (*lit* servant of God)

hambar *adj* flavorless; bland

hambat, menghambat *v* to obstruct, impede, hamper; **hambatan** *n* obstacle

hambur: berhamburan *adj* scattered about; **menghamburkan** *v* to scatter; throw about

hamil *adj* pregnant; ~ *muda* first trimester; ~ *tua* heavily pregnant; **kehamilan** *n* pregnancy; **menghamili** *v* to make someone pregnant

hampa *adj* empty; ~ *udara* vacuum

hampar: hamparan ~ *sungai* flood plain; **menghampar** *v* to spread out

hampir *adv* nearly, almost; **hampir-hampir** *adv* very nearly; **menghampiri** *v* to approach

hanacaraka *n* Sundanese and Javanese alphabet → **honocoroko**

hancur smashed, crushed; ~ *lebur* completely crushed, pulverized; **kehancuran** *n* destruction, ruin; **menghancurkan** *v* to smash, crush, destroy

handai ~ *tolan*, ~ *taulan* friends

handphone [hénpon; hénfon] *n* mobile phone, cell phone

handuk *n* towel

hangat *adj* warm, hot; *berita* ~ latest news; **kehangatan** *n* warmth, friendliness; **penghangat** heater

hanggar *n* (aircraft) hangar

hangus *adj* burnt, scorched; expired; *karcis itu sudah* ~ that ticket has expired; *bumi* ~ scorched earth; *membumi*~*kan* to conduct a scorched-earth policy; **menghanguskan** *v* to set fire to; burn down

Hanoman *n* white monkey from the Ramayana epic

hansip *n* local security guard; civil defense ← **pertahanan sipil**

hantam strike, blow; **menghantam** *v* to strike

hantar: menghantarkan *v* to conduct (electricity or heat); **penghantar** ~ *listrik* electrical conductor

hantu *n* ghost; *burung* ~ owl; *rumah* ~ haunted house; **menghantui** *v* to haunt

hanya *adv* only

hanyut drift, float; **terhanyut** *adj* drifting, floating; washed away

hapé, HP *n* mobile phone, cell phone ← **handphone**

hapermot → **havermut**

hapus, menghapus *v* to delete, erase, wipe; **menghapuskan** *vt* to wipe out, eliminate; **penghapus** *n* eraser; duster; **terhapus** *adj* disappeared; accidentally deleted

hara *huru-*~ riot, uproar; *polisi (anti) huru-*~ riot police

haram *adj, Isl* forbidden, not permitted; *anak* ~ illegitimate (child); *daging babi itu* ~ pork is forbidden

harap hope; please; ~ *maklum* please understand; **harapan** *n* hope, expectation; ~ *tipis* little hope; **berharap** *v* to hope; **mengharapkan** *v* to expect

hardik shout; scold; **menghardik** *v* to shout at; scold

harga *n* price; value; ~ *beli* buying price; ~ *diri* dignity; self-worth; ~ *mati* fixed price; last offer; *banting* ~ price cut; **berharga** *adj* precious; valuable; **menghargai** *v* to appreciate; **penghargaan** *n* appreciation; award; **seharga** *adj* of equal value; the same price

hari *n* day; ~ *besar* holiday; ~ *ini* today; ~ *kerja* weekday, working day; ~ *libur* holiday, day off; ~ *tua* old age; ~ *ulang tahun (HUT)* birthday, anniversary; *di kemudian* ~ in the future; *keesokan* ~*(nya)* the day after, the following day; *malam* ~ night-time; *sepanjang* ~ all day long; *siang* ~ daytime; **harian** *adj* daily; *buku* ~ diary; **berhari-hari** *adv* for days; **sehari-hari** *adv* every day, daily; **seharian** *adv, coll* all day

haribaan *n* lap ← **riba**

harimau *n* tiger

harpa *n* harp; *pemain* ~ harpist

hart *n* hearts (in cards)

harta *n* wealth, belongings; ~ *benda* property; goods and chattels; ~ *karun* hidden treasure; **hartawan** *n* wealthy person

haru emotion; touched; ~ *biru* black and blue; **mengharukan** *adj* moved, touched (emotionally); **terharu** *adj* moved, touched

harum *adj* fragrant; perfumed; ~ *namanya* well-known; **keharuman** *n* fragrance

harus *v* must, ought to, have to; **keharusan** *n* obligation, necessity, requirement; **mengharuskan** *v* to require; **seharusnya** should

hasil *n* product; result; ~ *panen* harvest; **berhasil** *v* to succeed; **keberhasilan** *n* success; **menghasilkan** *v* to produce; **penghasilan** *n* production; income; *pajak* ~ income tax

hasrat *n* desire; lust

hati *n* liver; heart; ~ *kecil* conscience; *di dalam* ~ in your heart; *buah* ~ darling; *kecil* ~ timid; offended, disappointed; *makan* ~ brood, dwell on, be upset; *sakit* ~ offended, hurt; upset

hati-hati take care; **berhati-hati** *v* to be careful; **berhati** *v* to have a heart; **memerhatikan** *v* to notice, pay attention to; **pemerhati** *n* observer; **perhatian** *n* attention; **sehati** *adj* of one mind

haul *n* annual commemoration of someone's death

haus *adj* thirsty; ~ *perhatian* longing for attention; **kehausan** *adj* to be thirsty; *n* thirst

havermut, hapermot *n* oatmeal porridge

Hawa *n, Chr* Eve; *Siti* ~ *Isl* Eve

hawa *n* air, atmosphere, climate; ~ *nafsu* passion; lust; **berhawa** *v* to have a climate; ~ *sejuk* cool climate

hayat *n* life; *sampai akhir* ~ until the end of your life; **hayati** *adj* biological; **menghayati** *v* to inspire, instill, vivify

HBS *abbrev* Hogere Burger School a high school in colonial times

hébat *adj* great; violent; terrific; **kehébatan** *n* force

héboh sensational; **kehébohan** *n* sensation, phenomenon; **menghébohkan** *v* to cause an uproar; *adj* sensational

héktar *n* hectare

héla, menghéla *v* to draw; drag; ~ *nafas* to sigh; draw a breath

helai *n* (counter) sheet; counter for thin fine objects; **sehelai** ~ *kertas* a piece of paper

hélat: perhélatan *n* celebration, feast

héli, hélikopter *n* helicopter

hélicak *n, arch* motorized rickshaw with passenger seat in front ← **hélikopter** + **bécak**

hélm *n* helmet

hémat *adj* economical, thrifty; ~ *air* to save water; **berhémat** *v* to be economical; **menghémat** *v* to save on or economize

hémat *n* judgment; opinion; *menurut* ~ *saya, pada* ~ *saya* in my opinion

hembus, embus blow, puff; **menghembus** *v* to blow

hendak *v, aux* to will, wish, intend; ~*nya* should; **berkehendak** *v* to have an intention; **kehendak** *n* will; ~ *rakyat* will of the people; **menghendaki** *vt* to want

héngkang *v* to flee, leave

hening clear; quiet; ~ *cipta* observe a moment's silence; **keheningan** *n* peace, quiet; clarity

hénpon, hénfon (HP) *n* mobile phone, cell phone → **télépon**

henti stop; **berhenti** *v* to stop, cease; **menghentikan** *v* to stop something; **memberhentikan** *v* to stop (a vehicle); to dismiss; *Oto diberhentikan* Otto was sacked; **perhentian** *n* stop, stopping place

hér resit a test or exam; *ujian* ~ make-up test or exam

héran *adj* astonished, amazed; **kehéranan** *n* astonishment; amazement; wonder; **menghérankan** *adj* astonishing, astounding

hérder *anjing* ~ German shepherd

héwan *n* animal, beast; ~ *piaraan* pet; *dokter* ~ vet, veterinarian

hias decorative; *ikan* ~ ornamental fish; **hiasan** *n* decoration; **berhias** *v* to dress up, put on make-up; **menghiasi** *v* to adorn; to decorate something; **perhiasan** *n* jewellery

hibah *n* donation, bequest, gift; **menghibahkan** *v* to donate, bequeath

hibur: hiburan *n* entertainment; **menghibur** *v* to entertain; to comfort, console; **penghibur** *wanita* ~ escort, prostitute

hidang: hidangan *n* dish, food served; **menghidangkan** *v* to serve up, offer

hidung *n* nose; ~ *belang* womanizer; ~ *mancung* straight nose; ~ *pesek* flat nose; ~ *tersumbat* blocked nose

hidup live; alive; lively; ~ *sederhana* live simply; ~ *Indonesia!* Long live Indonesia!; *bunga* ~ cut flowers; *riwayat* ~ biography; curriculum vitae; *sepanjang* ~ lifelong, all your life; **kehidupan** *n* life, existence; **menghidupkan** *v* to bring to life; to start or turn on (a device); ~ *kembali* to revive; ~ *mesin* to turn on the engine

higénis, higinis *adj* hygienic

hijau, hijo, héjo *adj* green; ~ *toska* turquoise green; ~ *tua* dark green; *jalur* ~ nature strip, median strip; **kehijau-hijauan** *adj* greenish; **menghijaukan** *v* to make green; **penghijauan** *n* greening (of an area)

hijrah evacuate, pack up and leave; move somewhere unexpected for a long time

hijriah, H *tahun* ~ the Islamic calendar; *Tahun 1415 H* 1997 AD (1415 in the Islamic calendar)

hikayat *n* tale, story; ~ *Hang Tuah* the tale of Hang Tuah

hikmah *n* wisdom, insight, moral; *ada* ~*nya* there's some good of it

hilang disappear; lost, missing; *orang* ~ missing person; **kehilangan** *n* (feeling of) loss; ~ *20 juta warga* to lose 20 million citizens; **menghilang** *v* to disappear, vanish; **menghilangkan** *v* to remove

hilir, ilir downstream; ~ *mudik* back and forth, up and down; *Sungai Mahakam* ~ the Lower Mahakam (River); **menghilir** *v* to go downstream

himpun: himpunan *n* association, gathering; **berhimpun** *v* to meet, assemble; **menghimpunkan** *v* to bring together, gather; **perhimpunan** *n* union, association, club; ~ *Mahasiswa Jambi* Jambi Students Assocation; **penghimpun** ~ *listrik* accumulator, storage cell, battery

hina low, insulting; humble; **hinaan** *n* insult; **menghinakan** *v* to humiliate, insult; **penghinaan** *n* insult, libel (written), slander (spoken); ~ *terhadap Presiden* insulting the President

hindar: menghindar *v* to steer clear, avoid; **menghindari** *v* to avoid something

Hindia *n* the Indies; ~ *Barat* the West Indies; ~ *Belanda* the Dutch East Indies; *Samudera* ~ the Indian Ocean

Hindu *agama* ~ Hinduism; *orang* ~ Hindu

hingar ~-*bingar* commotion, noise

hingga until; ~ *sekarang* up to now; **sehingga** *conj* to the point that, as far as, until, so that; **terhingga** *tidak* ~ unlimited, boundless

hinggap *v* to land, perch (of a bird)

hipoték *n* mortgage

hirau: menghiraukan *v* to take heed, to listen to advice; *tidak dihiraukan* ignored

hiruk ~-*pikuk*, ~-*piruk* clamor, confusion

hirup inhale; suck; *obat* ~ lozenge; **menghirup** *v* to breathe in; ~ *udara bebas* to breathe the air of freedom (be out of prison)

HIS *abbrev Hollands Inlandse School* Dutch lower school for natives in colonial times

hitam *adj* black; ~ *manis* dark and pretty; ~ *putih* black and white; *daftar* ~ blacklist; *orang* ~ black person, Negro; **menghitamkan** *v* to blacken, make black

hitung count; *ilmu* ~ arithmetic; **berhitung** *v* to count; **hitungan** *n* calculation, sum; **menghitung** *v* to count, calculate, reckon; **menghitungkan** *v* to count or calculate something; **perhitungan** *n* calculation; **penghitungan** *n* counting; **terhitung** *adj* counted, included

hiu, yu *ikan* ~ shark

Hj. *Hajjah* title for woman who has performed the major pilgrimage to Mecca

HKBP *abbrev Huria Kristen Batak Protestan* Batak Protestant church

HMI *abbrev Himpunan Mahasiswa Islam* Muslim Students Association

hobi *n* hobby; **berhobi** *v* to have as a hobby

hoki *n* good luck or fortune

homo *m, sl orang* ~ homosexual, gay

honai *n* round hut in Papua (Irian Jaya)

Hongaria *n* Hungary; *bahasa ~, orang ~* Hungarian

hong sui, féng sui *n* feng shui; *menurut ~* according to feng shui

honocoroko *n* Javanese alphabet → **hanacaraka**

honor, honorarium *n* fee (for a guest or part-time employee); **honorér** *adj* honorary

hordén, gordén *n* curtain(s); *tukang ~* itinerant curtain-rod seller

horé *ejac* hooray!

horisontal *adj* horizontal; at one level; *konflik ~* conflict within a group or level of society

hormat respect, honor; *~ saya* yours faithfully; *kurang ~* disrespectful; *memberi ~* to salute, pay respect; **kehormatan** *n* respect; *anggota ~* honorary member; **menghormat, menghormati** *v* to honor or respect; **penghormatan** *n* display of honor, sign of respect; **terhormat** *adj* respected; *yang ~* to; dear

horoskop *n* horoscope

hostés *n* hostess, bargirl

hot *adj, sl* sexy

hotél *n* hotel; *~ melati* cheap hotel; *~ (ber)bintang lima* five-star hotel; *~ prodeo* prison, jail; **perhotélan** *n* hotel studies; hospitality

hotmiks, hotmix *n* asphalt; *jalan sudah dihotmiks* the road has been macadamized

HP (hénpon, hénfon) *n* mobile phone, cell phone ← **hénpon**

HPH *abbrev Hak Penebangan Hutan* Forest Concession Rights

hubung: hubungan *n* link, connection, relationship; *~ masyarakat (humas)* public relations (PR); *~ saudara* family (relationship); **berhubung** *conj* in connection with, relating to; *~ dengan* in connection with; **berhubungan** *v, pl* to have a link or connection; **menghubungi** *v* to contact someone; **menghubungkan** *v* to connect, join, link different parts; **penghubung** *n* switch, connector; *kata ~* conjunction, connector; **perhubungan** *n* communications, connection; *~ udara* air route; *Menteri ~* Minister of Communications

hujan rain; *~ batu, ~ es* hail; *~ deras, ~ lebat* heavy rain, downpour; *~ rintik-rintik* drizzle; *curah ~* rainfall; *musim ~* rainy season, monsoon; **kehujanan** *adj* caught in the rain; **menghujani** *v* to pelt, rain down upon; **penghujan** *musim ~* rainy season; monsoon

hujat: hujatan *n* insult, blasphemy; **menghujat** *v* to swear, blaspheme

huk, hoek *n* street corner; *rumahnya di ~* her house is on the corner

hukum law; punish; ~ *fisika* laws of physics; ~ *perdata* civil code; ~ *pidana* criminal code; **hukuman** *n* punishment; ~ *mati* capital punishment, death penalty; ~ *penjara* imprisonment; **menghukum** *v* to punish, sentence, condemn

hulu *n* source, beginning; ~ *sungai* source, headwaters; **berhulu** *v* to rise, have a source; *Sungai Mekong ~ di Cina* the source of the Mekong is in China; **penghulu** *n, Isl* local chief who performs marriage ceremonies

huma *n* field, earth

humaniora *n* humanities

humas *n* PR, public relations ← **hubungan masyarakat**

huni: menghuni *v* to live in, occupy; **penghuni** *n* occupant, resident

hunus: menghunus *v* to unsheathe, take out; ~ *pedang* to pull out a sword

huru ~-*hara* riot, uproar; *polisi (anti)* ~-*hara* riot police

huruf *n* letter, character; ~ *besar* capital letters, upper case; ~ *bersambung* cursive; ~ *cetak* block letters, printing; ~ *Cina* Chinese characters; ~ *hidup* vowel; ~ *kecil* small letters, lower case; ~ *mati* consonant; ~ *miring* italics; *buta* ~ illiterate; *melek* ~ literate

HUT *abbrev* hari ulang tahun birthday, anniversary

hutan *n* forest, jungle, wood; ~ *kota* urban forest; ~ *rimba* jungle; **kehutanan** *n* forestry

I

ia *lit* he, she, it → **dia**

IAIN *abbrev* Institut Agama Islam Negeri State Institute for Islamic Studies

iba pity, compassion; *merasa* ~ to feel sorry for

ibadah *n* worship, religious devotion; **beribadah** *v* to worship, serve

ibarat *conj* like, as, example; **mengibaratkan** *v* to use figuratively, as an example

iblis *n* devil, Satan

Ibrani *bahasa* ~, *orang* ~ Hebrew

ibu *n, pron, f* mother; ~ *angkat* adopted mother; ~ *bapak* parents; ~ *jari* thumb; ~ *kos* concierge, house-mother; ~ *kota* capital (city); ~ *pertiwi* motherland; ~ *rumah tangga* housewife, homemaker; ~ *tiri* stepmother; *bahasa* ~ mother tongue; **ibu-ibu** *pl* ladies; *adj* of an age to be a mother; **beribu** ~ *bapak* to have parents; **keibuan** *adj* motherly; **seibu** *adj* having the same mother

ICMI *abbrev* Ikatan Cendekiawan Muslim se-Indonesia Indonesian Islamic Intellectuals Association

idam craving, longing; **idaman** *adj* dream, ideal; *rumah* ~ dream home; **ngidam** *coll* **mengidam** *v* to crave (esp of pregnant woman)

idap: mengidap *v* to suffer from; ~ *penyakit* to suffer from or have a disease; **pengidap** *n* sufferer; ~ *AIDS* AIDS sufferer

idé, ide *n* idea; ~ *gemilang* great idea

idéntik *adj* identical, same; ~ *dengan* just like, the same as

idéntitas *n* (proof of) identity; *kartu* ~ ID card → **jati diri**

IDI *abbrev* Ikatan Dokter Indonesia Indonesian Doctors' Association

idih *excl* yuck! (expressing disgust or revulsion); ~-~ ooh, that's disgusting

idola *n* idol, star; **mengidolakan** *v* to worship, idolize

idul, Ied ul *Isl* ~ *Adha* Feast of the Sacrifice; ~ *Fitri* end of fasting celebrations; *sholat Ied* mass prayer on the mornings of these holidays

iga *n* rib; ~ *bakar* barbecued ribs

igau: mengigau *v* to talk in one's sleep, be delirious

ihwal *hal*-~ related matters

ijab ~ *kabul Isl* marriage contract

ijazah *n* certificate, qualification; **berijazah** *adj* certified, qualified

ijin, izin permission; *minta* ~ ask permission; *surat* ~ *mengemudi (SIM)* driver's license; **mengijinkan** *v* to permit, allow

ikal *adj* curly; *rambut* ~ curly hair, wavy hair

ikan *n* fish; ~ *air tawar* freshwater fish; ~ *asin* salty fish; ~ *emas* goldfish; ~ *hiu* shark; ~ *laut* ocean fish; ~ *paus* whale; *pepes* ~ fish steamed in a banana leaf; ~ *teri* anchovy, small fry; **perikanan** *n* fisheries

ikat tie, knot; weaving, ikat; ~ *Lombok* Lombok weaving; ~ *pinggang* belt; **ikatan** *n* alliance, union; ~ *Dokter Indonesia (IDI)* Indonesian Doctors' Association; **mengikat** *v* to tie, fasten; **terikat** *adj* bound; **keterikatan** *n* bind, bond, commitment

ikhlas *adj* sincere; accepting; **keikhlasan** *n* sincerity

IKIP *abbrev, arch* Institut Keguruan Ilmu Pendidikan (former) teacher training college

ikke, ik *pron, coll* I, me

iklan *n* advertisement; *bintang* ~ advertising model; **mengiklankan** *v* to advertise

iklim *n* climate; ~ *tropis* tropical climate; **beriklim** *v* to have a climate; ~ *dingin* to have a cool climate

ikrar *n* promise, pledge, oath. **berikrar** *v* to promise, pledge

ikut *v* join in, go along with; ~ *Ibu* go with Mother; ~ *prihatin* feel concerned; ~ *serta* take part, participate; **keikutsertaan** *n* participation; **ikutan** *v, sl* to join in, go along with; **berikut** *adj* following; *yang* ~,

~*nya* the next; **mengikut** *v* to follow, accompany; **mengikuti** *v* to follow, join, participate in; ~ *kursus* to do a course; **pengikut** *n* participant; follower

ilahi *Isl* divine, godly

ilanun → **lanun**

iler drool, slobber; **mengiler** *v* to drool, slobber

ilir → **hilir**

ilmu *n* science, study; ~ *bumi* geography; ~ *falak* astronomy; ~ *filsafat* philosophy; ~ *fisika* physics; ~ *kimia* chemistry; ~ *pasti* the physical sciences, esp mathematics; ~ *sejarah* history; **berilmu** *adj* learned; **keilmuan, ilmiah** *adj* scientific; **ilmuwan** *n* scientist

ilusi *n* illusion

imam *n, Isl, m* prayer leader in the mosque

iman *n* faith, belief; *beda* ~ of a different religion; **beriman** *adj* religious

IMB *abbrev izin mendirikan bangunan* construction permit

imbal: imbalan *n* compensation, reward, repayment

imbang balanced; **berimbang** *adj* balanced, proportional; **mengimbangi** *v* to balance, offset; **perimbangan** *n* proportion; **seimbang** *adj* balanced, well-proportioned; **keseimbangan** *n* balance

imél *n* email; *alamat* ~ email address

imigrasi *n* immigration

iming: mengiming(-iming),

mengiming(-iming)kan *v* to tantalize, tempt

imitasi *n* fake

imla *n* dictation

Imlék *n* Chinese New Year; *Tahun Baru* ~ Chinese New Year

impas *n* impasse, balance

impi: impian *n* dream; **mengimpikan** *v* to dream of → **mimpi**

impor import; ~ *ekspor* import-export; **mengimpor** *v* to import; **pengimpor** *n* importer

imsak *n* time ten minutes before dawn, when those intending to fast should stop eating (around 5 a.m.)

inai *n* henna

inang *n* wet nurse

inap stay the night; *rawat* ~ stay in hospital, be hospitalized; **menginap** *v* to stay the night, stay over; **penginapan** *n* accommodation, hotel

incar: incaran *n* target, something aimed for; **mengincar** *v* to set your sights on, target

inci *n* inch

indah *adj* beautiful; *hari yang* ~ a lovely day; **keindahan** *n* beauty; **mengindahkan** *v* to take heed, pay attention to; **memperindah** *v* to beautify

indekos → **kos**

indera, indra *n* sense; ~ *keenam* sixth sense; ~ *penglihatan* sense of sight

India *n* India; *orang* ~ Indian

Indian *orang* ~ Native American, (South) American Indian

Indo *orang* ~ person of mixed

Western and Indonesian descent
Indonésia Indonesia; *Bahasa ~,
orang ~* Indonesian; **keindonésiaan** *n* sense of being Indonesian; **mengindonésiakan** *v* to
translate into or make Indonesian

induk mother (animal); *~ ayam*
mother hen; *~ semang* house-
mother, landlady; *kalimat ~*
main clause; *kapal ~* mother
ship; aircraft carrier

induksi *n* induction

indung mother, home; *~ telur*
ovary; *anak kucing dan ~nya* a
kitten and its mother

industri *n* industry; *desain ~*
industrial design; **perindustrian** *n* industry, industrial affairs;
*Departemen ~ dan Perdaga-
ngan (Depperindag)* Department of Industry and Trade

inféksi *n* infection; **terinféksi**
adj infected

inflasi *n* inflation

info, informasi *n* information, info;
menginformasikan *v* to inform

informatika *n* information technology (IT)

infus *n* (saline) drip; **diinfus** *v* to
be put on a drip

ingat remember; *daya ~* memory;
ingatan *n* memory; **mengingat**
v to remember, bear in mind;
mengingatkan *v* to remind
someone about something;
memperingati *v* to commemorate; **peringatan** *n* warning;
commemoration, remembrance

Inggris Britain; England, English;

~ Raya Great Britain; *bahasa ~*
English; *Kerajaan ~* the United
Kingdom; *orang ~* English;
British; *Sally orang ~* Sally's
British

ingin *v* to wish, desire; **keinginan**
n desire, wish; **menginginkan**
v to wish for, desire

ingkar *v* to break (a vow etc);
~ janji to break a promise;
mengingkari *v* to renege or go
back on

ingus *n* nasal mucus; *membuang
~* to blow your nose; **ingusan**
anak ~ toddler; still a child

ini *pron* this, these; *hari ~* today;
sekarang ~, belakangan ~
recently; **begini** *adv* like this

inisial initial, first letter of name

inisiatif, inisiatip *n* initiative,
enterprise; **berinisiatif** *v* to take
the initiative → **prakarsa**

injak *v* to tread, pedal; **menginjak** *v* to step, tread, or stamp
on; *~ gas* to accelerate, step on
the gas; **terinjak** *adj* stepped
upon; downtrodden

injil *n* gospel, Bible; *Kitab ~* Bible;
penginjil *n* preacher, evangelist

inna lillahi wa inna ilahi rojiun
excl, Isl we are truly God's, and
to Him we must return (said on
hearing of someone's death);
ashes to ashes, dust to dust

Inprés *n* Presidential Decree;
SD ~ primary school built
under a presidential instruction
← **Instruksi Présidén**

insaf, insyaf aware, conscious;
realize; **menginsafkan** *v* to

make conscious, raise awareness

insan *n* human, person; *setiap* ~ everyone; **insani** *adj* human

insang *n* gill

insidén *n* incident → **peristiwa**

insinyur, Ir *n* engineer; ~ *pertanian* agricultural engineer

inspéksi *n* inspection; **inspéktur** *n* inspector

instansi *n* agency, authority (esp state); ~ *terkait* related agencies

instruksi *n* instruction; ~ *Presiden (Inpres)* presidential decree → **petunjuk**; **instruktur** *n* instructor

insya Allah *Isl* God willing

intai: mengintai *v* to spy on or watch, conduct surveillance; **pengintai** *pesawat* ~ reconnaissance plane

intan *n* diamond

intél *n* secret agent, spy; **intélijén** *n* secret intelligence; *Badan ~ Negara (BIN)* State Intelligence Agency

intélék *n* brains, intellect; **intéléktual** *n* intellectual → **cendekiawan**

interlokal *adj* long-distance (dialing); *telepon* ~ long-distance call

intérn *adj* internal

internasional *adj* international

intérnis *n* specialist (doctor)

interpelasi *n* interpellation (in parliament)

interupsi *n* interruption (in parliament)

interviu, interpiu *n* interview; **menginterviu** *v* to interview

→ **wawancara**

inti *n* core, kernel, nucleus; ~*nya* basically; ~ *sari* essence

intim *adj* intimate, close; *hubungan* ~ sexual relations

intip, mengintip *v* to peep at, spy on

intisari *n* essence, extract

introspéksi *n* introspection, self-evaluation; **berintrospéksi** *v* to be introspective

IP *abbrev indeks prestasi* grade point average

IPA *abbrev ilmu pengetahuan alam* natural sciences

ipar in-law; *adik* ~ (younger) brother- or sister-in-law

IPB *abbrev Institut Pertanian Bogor* Bogor Agricultural University

IPS *abbrev ilmu pengetahuan sosial* social sciences

Ir *insinyur* title for holder of a degree in engineering or architecture

Irak *n* Iraq; *orang* ~ Iraqi

irama *n* rhythm; ~ *cepat* fast-paced, with a fast rhythm; **berirama** *adj* rhythmical

Iran *n* Iran; *orang* ~ Iranian

iri envy; ~ *(hati)* envious

Irian *n* (West) Papua, Irian; ~ *Jaya* Indonesian province between 1963 & 2000; *orang* ~ Irianese, Papuan

irigasi *n* irrigation; **mengirigasi** *v* to irrigate → **mengairi**

iring: iring-iringan *n* parade, convoy; **beriring-iringan** *adv* in succession; **mengiringi** *v* to accompany, escort; **pengiring** *n* escort, companion

ris slice thinly; **irisan** *n* slice; **mengiris** *v* to slice

rit economical; save money; *lebih* ~ cheaper, more economical; **mengirit** *v* to economize

rja *n* Irian Jaya, Papua ← **Irian Jaya**

rlandia *n* Ireland; *bahasa* ~ Irish (Gaelic); *orang* ~ Irish

sa *n* Jesus

sak sob; **mengisak(-isak)** *v* to sob; **terisak(-isak)** *adj* sobbing

sap *v* to suck on, to smoke; **isapan** ~ *jempol* lie, untruth; **mengisap** *v* to suck, to smoke; ~ *ganja* to smoke marijuana; ~ *cerutu* to smoke a cigar; **pengisap** ~ *darah* vampire; ~ *debu* vacuum cleaner

seng for fun, not serious; waste or kill time; ~ *aja* just for fun

si contents, volume, full; **berisi** *v* to contain; *adj* full, filled out; **mengisi** *v* to fill, load; ~ *bensin* to fill up with petrol; ~ *waktu* to fill in time; **pengisi** *n* filler; ~ *suara* dubber

slah *Isl* reconciliation; **mengadakan** ~ to come to a settlement

slam Islam; ~ *telu wektu* kind of Islam practiced in Lombok; *agama* ~ Islam; *masuk* ~ to become Muslim, convert to Islam; *orang* ~ Muslim; **mengislamkan** *v* to Islamize, make Islamic

solasi *n* isolation, insulation; adhesive tape; **terisolasi, ter-**

isolir *adj* isolated → **terpencil**

Isra Miraj *n, Isl* holiday commemorating Muhammad's ascent to Heaven

Israél Israel; *orang* ~ Israeli

istana *n* palace; ~ *presiden* presidential palace

isteri, istri *n* wife; ~ *kedua* second wife; ~ *muda* new or second wife; **beristeri, beristri** *adj, m* married; *pria* ~ married man

istiadat *adat* ~ customs and traditions

istilah *n* term, word; ~*nya* in other words, you could say; **mengistilahkan** *v* to define something

istiméwa *adj* special; **keistiméwaan** *n* special quality; **mengistiméwakan** *v* to treat as special

istiqlal *n* freedom; *Mesjid* ~ biggest mosque in Jakarta (& Southeast Asia)

istirahat rest, recreation, break; **beristirahat** *v* to rest, take a break; **peristirahatan** *n* place for rest or recreation; ~ *terakhir* final resting place

istri, isteri *n* wife; ~ *kedua* second wife; ~ *muda* new or second wife; **beristeri, beristri** *adj, m* married; *pria* ~ married man

isu *n* issue, controversy

isya night prayer (during the hours of darkness)

isyarat *n* signal, sign, gesture; *bahasa* ~ sign language; *memberi* ~ give a signal; **mengisyaratkan** *v* to give a sign, signal

Itali, Italia *n* Italy; *bahasa ~, orang ~* Italian

ITB *abbrev Institut Teknologi Bandung* Bandung Institute of Technology

itik *n* duck; *anak ~* duckling

itikad *n* faith, conviction; *dengan ~ baik* in good faith

itu *pron* that, those; *~ dia!* that's the problem!; **begitu** *adv* like that, in that manner; so; as soon as; *~ lah* that's how it is

IUD intra-uterine device, form of contraception

iuran *n* contribution, regular payment; *~ keanggotaan* membership fee

iya *coll* yes; *~ ya* it is, isn't it?; **mengiyakan** *v* to agree or assent to

izin, ijin permission; *minta ~* to ask permission; *surat ~ mengemudi (SIM)* driver's license; **mengizinkan** *v* to permit, allow

J

jabang *~ bayi* unborn child, fetus, embryo

Jabar *n* West Java ← **Jawa Barat**

jabat: jabatan *n* position, work; **berjabat(an)** *~ tangan* to shake hands; **menjabat** *v* to hold; to work as; *~ Menteri Keuangan* to be Minister of Finance; **pejabat** *n* (government) official; **penjabat** *n* official (esp temporary or acting)

Jabotabék *n* Greater Jakarta ← **Jakarta Bogor Tangerang Bekasi**

jadi *v* to become, happen; *conj* so; *~ orang* to succeed, make something of yourself; *~ tidak?* Is it going ahead or not?; *tidak ~* it didn't happen, it fell through; **kejadian** *n* event, happening; creation; **menjadi** *v* to be or become; *~ marah* to get angry; **menjadi-jadi** *v* to get worse; **menjadikan** *v* to create, make; **terjadi** *v* to happen, become

jadwal *n* timetable, schedule; *~ penerbangan* flight schedule; **menjadwalkan** *v* to timetable

jaga guard, nightwatchman; **berjaga** *v* to stand guard; **menjaga** *v* to guard, keep watch; *~ anak* to look after children, babysit; *~ jarak* to keep a distance; **penjaga** *n* guard; **terjaga** *adj* alert, on guard

jagad, jagat *n* world; *~ raya* universe, cosmos; **sejagat** *adj* worldwide

jagal *tukang ~* butcher; **pejagalan** *n* abattoir

jago *n* champion; cock, rooster; *~ bulu tangkis* good at badminton; *ayam ~* rooster; *si merah* fire; **jagoan** *n, sl* good at; **menjagokan** *v* to support

Jagorawi *jalan tol ~* Jakarta-Bogor-Ciawi toll road ← **Jakarta Bogor Ciawi**

jagung *n* corn, maize; *~ bakar*

roasted sweet corn

jahanam *n, Isl* hell

jahat *adj* bad, wicked, evil; **kejahatan** *n* crime; **penjahat** *n* criminal; ~ *perang* war criminal

jahé *n* ginger

jahil, jail *adj* mischievous, naughty

jahit *v* to sew; *mesin* ~ sewing machine; *tukang* ~ tailor; **jahitan** *n* stitches; sewing; **menjahit** *v* to sew; *tangan Pepi harus dijahit* Pepi's hand had to have stitches

jail → **jahil**

jaipong *tari* ~ modern Sundanese dance; **jaipongan** traditional dance; to dance the *jaipong*

jaja: **menjajakan** *v* to hawk, peddle; ~ *permen* to sell sweets, candy; **penjaja** *n* hawker, pedlar

jajah: **jajahan** *n* colony, territory; **menjajah** *v* to colonize, rule another country; **penjajah** *n* colonizer, ruler, colonial power; **penjajahan** *n* colonization

jajan buy cheap goods; *uang* ~ pocket money; **jajanan** *n* cheap snacks

jajar row, line, file; **jajaran** *n* level; **berjajar** *adj* in a row; **sejajar** *adj* parallel

Jakbar *n* West Jakarta ← **Jakarta Barat**

jakét *n* jacket; ~ *kulit* leather jacket

Jakpus *n* Central Jakarta ← **Jakarta Pusat**

jaksa *n* judge; ~ *Agung* Attorney-General; ~ *umum* public prosecutor; **kejaksaan** *n* district attorney's office

Jaksél *n* South Jakarta ← **Jakarta Selatan**

Jaktim *n* East Jakarta ← **Jakarta Timur**

jakun *n* Adam's apple

Jakut *n* North Jakarta ← **Jakarta Utara**

jala *n* fishing net; *roti* ~ kind of Malay pancake

jalak *n* starling, mynah

jalan street, road, way; walk; operate, go; ~ *besar* main road; ~ *keluar* exit, way out; ~ *masuk* entrance; ~ *raya* highway; ~ *terbaik* the best way; ~ *tikus* back street; *bahu* ~ hard shoulder; *rawat* ~ outpatient; **jalan-jalan** *v* to go for a walk; to go out (for fun); **jalanan** *n* streets, on the road; **berjalan** *v* to walk, move; ~ *dengan baik* to go well; **menjalani** *v* to undergo, do; ~ *hukuman penjara 3 tahun* to serve three years in jail; **menjalankan** *v* to operate, run, set in motion; **perjalanan** *n* journey, trip; *biro* ~, *agen* ~ travel agency

jalang *adj* wild, untamed; *perempuan* ~ street walker

jalar *adj* creeping; *ubi* ~ sweet potato; **menjalar** *v* to creep, climb; *tanaman* ~ climbing plant

jalin: **jalinan** *n* net, network; **menjalin** *v* to forge links, network; **terjalin** *adj* forged, involved

jalur lane, track; ~ *khusus* fast track; ~ *lambat* slow lane; ~ *sepeda* bicycle lane

jalusi *n* louvre, Venetian blinds

jam *n* hour; clock; ~ *berapa?* what time is it?; ~ *besuk* visiting hours; ~ *buka* opening hours; ~ *dinding* (wall) clock; ~ *karet* rubber time, unpunctuality; ~ *lima* five o'clock; ~ *malam* curfew; ~ *praktek* consulting hours; ~ *setengah sepuluh* half past nine, 9.30; ~ *tangan* (wrist)watch; **jam-jaman** *adj* hourly; **berjam-jam** *adj* for hours and hours

Jamaika *n* Jamaica; *orang* ~ Jamaican

jamak *adj* plural, more than one; *bentuk* ~ plural form

jaman, zaman *n* age, era, time, period; ~ *dahulu,* ~ *dulu* in the old days, times past; ~ *Belanda* the Dutch era; ~ *purbakala* prehistoric times; ~ *saya* in my day; *ketinggalan* ~ outdated

jambak *n* tuft; **menjambak** *v* to pull someone's hair

jambang, jambangan *n* vase, urn, pot

jamblang *nasi* ~ rice dish, specialty of the Cirebon area

jamboré *n* jamboree

jambrét snatch; **menjambrét** *v* to snatch

jambu *n* kind of fruit; ~ *air* rose-apple; ~ *batu,* ~ *biji* guava; *buah* ~ guava, rose-apple; *merah* ~ pink

jambul *n* quiff, cowlick; crest; **berjambul** *v* to have a quiff or crest

jamin, menjamin *v* to guarantee, promise; **jaminan** *n* guarantee; *surat* ~ (letter of) guarantee; **terjamin** *adj* guaranteed

jampi *n* magic formula or spell

jamrud, zamrud *n* emerald

Jamsosték *n* state social security system ← **Jaminan Sosial Tenaga Kerja**

jamu *n* traditional herbal medicine; ~ *kuat* aphrodiasiac; tonic

jamu: menjamu *v* to entertain guests, hold a feast; **perjamu-an** *n* feast, party; entertainment

jamur *n* mushroom, mold, fungus; ~ *kaki* athlete's foot; *pakai* ~ with mushrooms; **berjamur** *adj* moldy; **menjamur** *v* to spring up; **berjamuran** *v* to pop up everywhere

janda *n* widow; ~ *cerai* divorced woman, divorcée; ~ *muda* young (attractive) widow; **menjanda** *v* to be widowed, live as a widow

jangan *neg* don't, do not; ~ *begitu* don't do (or say) that; **jangan-jangan** *adv, neg* or else, otherwise, maybe even; **jangankan** *conj* let alone, not to mention

janggal *adj* odd, strange; **kejanggalan** *n* oddity, anomaly

janggut, jénggot *n* beard, goatee; **berjénggot** *adj* bearded

jangka *n* distance, term; ~ *panjang* long term; ~ *pendek* short term; **berjangka** *adj* for a term; *deposito* ~ term deposit

jangkar *n* anchor

jangkit: berjangkit, menjangkit
v to spread, be infectious or
contagious; **menjangkiti** *v* to
infect; **terjangkit** *adj* infected

jangkrik, jengkerik *n* cicada,
cricket

jangkung *adj, sl* tall, lanky

janin *n* fetus, embryo

janji promise; *ingkar* ~ break a
promise; *menepati* ~ to keep a
promise; *mengikat* ~ get married, exchange vows; **janjian** *v,
sl* to make a date, promise; **berjanji** *v* to promise; **menjanjikan**
v to promise something; **perjanjian** *n* agreement, contract

jantan male (animal), manly;
ayam ~ cock, rooster; **kejantanan** *n* masculinity

jantung *n* heart, core; ~ *kota*
city center, heart of the city;
serangan ~ heart attack;
jantungan *v, sl* to have a heart
attack; to be very scared

Januari *bulan* ~ January

janur *n* decoration woven from
coconut leaves, used at wed-
dings; ~ *kuning* wedding decoration; *memasang* ~ to put up
a *janur* decoration to indicate
the wedding location

jarah: jarahan *n* stolen or looted
goods; **menjarah** *v* to loot;
penjarah *n* looter; **penjarahan**
n looting

jarak *n* distance, space; ~ *pendek*
short-distance; *jaga* ~ keep a
distance; *sambungan langsung*

~ *jauh (SLJJ)* long-distance
direct dialing

jarak *minyak* ~ castor oil

jarang *adj, adv* seldom, rare,
rarely, hardly ever

jari *n* finger; ~ *kaki* toe; ~ *kelingking* little or baby finger; ~
manis ring finger; ~ *telunjuk*
forefinger, index finger; ~
tengah middle finger; *ibu* ~
thumb; *sidik* ~ fingerprint; **jari-
jari** *pl* spokes

jaring net, shoal; **jaringan** *n*
network; **menjaring** *v* to fish
with a net; to filter or sift

jarum *n* needle; hand; ~ *jam*
hand (of a clock or watch);
arah ~ *jam* clockwise; ~ *suntik*
(injection) needle; ~ *pentul* pin;
tusuk ~ acupuncture

jas *n* coat; ~ *hujan* raincoat;
pakai ~ *coll* wear a suit and tie

jasa *n* service, merit; ~ *boga*
catering service; **berjasa** *adj*
meritorious, deserving of
reward; *v* to perform a service

jasad *n* corpse, dead body

jasmani *adj* physical; *hubungan*
~ sexual relations

jatah *n* ration, serve; **menjatahkan** *v* to deal out, allocate

Jateng *n* Central Java ← **Jawa
Tengah**

jati *kayu* ~ teak

jati ~ *diri* identity; **sejati** *adj*
genuine, original, real

Jatim *n* East Java ← **Jawa
Timur**

jatuh fall; ~ *cinta,* ~ *hati* fall in
love; ~ *sakit* fall ill; *bintang* ~

shooting star; **kejatuhan** n fall; adj be struck by something falling; **menjatuhkan** v to fell, let drop; ~ hukuman to sentence, condemn; **terjatuh** adj (accidentally) fallen

jauh adj far; jarak ~ long-distance; ~ hari well in advance; **kejauhan** adj too far; **menjauh** v to move away; **menjauhi** v to avoid; **sejauh** conj how far; ~ mana to what point; **sejauh-jauhnya** adv as far away as possible

Jawa Java; ~ Barat (Jabar) West Java; bahasa ~, orang ~ Javanese; gula ~ palm sugar; pulau ~ Java

jawab answer, reply; tanggung ~ responsibility; **bertanggung jawab** adj responsible; tanya ~ question and answer; **jawaban** n answer, reply, response; **menjawab** v to answer, reply; **terjawab** adj answered

jawat: jawatan n office, division → jabat

jawi tulisan ~ Malay writing in Arabic script

jebak trap; **jebakan** n trap; **menjebak, menjebakkan** v to trap; **terjebak** adj trapped, caught; ~ macet caught in traffic

jeblos to push or stick through

jebol to collapse, fall apart, break through; **jebolan** n graduate

jeda n pause, break, ceasefire

jejak n footprint, track; ~ langkah footprint; **menjejaki** v to step on, trail, trace

jejaka n bachelor, young single man

jejamu → jamu

jéjér row, line; **berjéjér, berjéjéran** (stand) in a row, in a line; **menjéjérkan** v to place in rows

jelajah: menjelajahi v to travel through or explore a place; **penjelajah** n explorer

jelang: menjelang v to approach (usu time)

jelangkung n effigy used as spirit medium in seances

jelas adj clear, obvious; **kejelasan** n clarity; **menjelaskan** v to explain, clarify; **penjelasan** n explanation

jelata rakyat ~ common people, masses

jelék adj bad, ugly; ~nya the bad side is; **kejelékan** n badness, ugliness; **menjelékkan** v to criticize, say bad things about

jeli adj careful, cautious

jelita adj, f beautiful, charming

jelma: menjelma v to be incarnated, turn into, materialize; **menjelmakan** v to create or realize something; **penjelmaan** n incarnation

jemaah, jemaat n congregation, followers of a religion; **berjemaah** v, Isl together, as a congregation

jemari n finger; jari ~ fingers → jari

jembatan n bridge; ~ besi iron bridge; ~ gantung suspension bridge; **menjembatani** v to bridge (two things)

empol *n* thumb; *cap* ~ thumb-print; *acungan* ~ thumbs-up sign

emput pick up; *antar* ~ pick up and bring home, door to door; **jemputan** *n* vehicle which picks you up; **menjemput** *v* to pick up; ~ *bola* be proactive; **penjemputan** *n* act of picking up

emu *adj* sick or tired of, bored; **menjemukan** *adj* tedious, boring

emur dry (in the sun); **jemuran** *n* clothes or food drying in the sun; **berjemur** *v* to sunbathe, sun yourself; **menjemur** *v* to air, dry in the sun; ~ *baju cucian* to hang out the washing; ~ *krupuk* to air crackers before frying

enak: sejenak *adv* briefly, a moment

enaka *adj* funny, amusing, cute

enang *n* kind of fruit jelly; ~ *apel* apple-flavored jelly

enazah *n* dead body, corpse; *mobil* ~ hearse

endéla *n* window; *membuka* ~ *hati* to open your heart

énder *n* gender; *soal* ~ gender issue

jénderal *n* general; ~ *bintang empat* four-star general; *Brigadir-~ (Brigjen)* Brigadier-General; *Letnan-~ (Letjen)* Lieutenant-General; *Mayor-~ (Mayjen)* Major-General; ~ *(Polisi)* Police General

jénéwer *n* gin, genever

jénggot, janggut *n* beard;

kebakaran ~ lose your head, unable to cope; **berjénggot** *adj* bearded

jengkal: sejengkal *adj* handspan (between thumb and little finger)

jéngkél *adj* annoyed; **kejéngkélan** *n* annoyance, bad mood; **menjéngkélkan** *adj* annoying

jéngkol *n* pungent vegetable

jenis *n* kind, sort, type; species; ~ *kelamin* sex, gender; *lawan* ~ opposite sex; **berjenis-jenis** *adj* all kinds of, various; **sejenis** *adj* same type or species

jenjang *n* rank, stage, hierarchy

jentik ~ *nyamuk* mosquito larvae

jenuh *adj* fed up, bored; saturated; *lemak* ~ saturated fats; **kejenuhan** *n* saturation; boredom

Jepang *n* Japan; *bahasa* ~, *orang* ~ Japanese

jepit *n* tweezers; **jepitan** *n* clip; tweezers; ~ *rambut* hair clip; **menjepit** *v* to pinch, squeeze; **penjepit** *n* clip; **terjepit** *adj* pinched, caught in an uncomfortable situation

jeprét snap, click (like a camera); **jeprétan, penjeprét** *n* stapler; **menjeprét** *v* to snap, staple; ~ *foto* to take a photo

Jepun → **Jepang**

jera *adj* wary, deterred

jeram *arung* ~ white water rafting

jerami *n* straw; *beratap* ~ thatched roof

jerapah *n* giraffe

jerat snare, trap, noose; **menjerat** *v* to snare, trap; **terjerat** *adj* snared, trapped, caught

jerawat *n* pimple; **jerawatan** *adj* pimply

jérigén *n* jerrycan

jerih *adj* exhausted, tired; ~ *payah* toil, hard work

jerit scream, shriek; **jeritan** *n* scream, shriek; **menjerit** *v* to scream, shriek

Jerman *n* Germany; *bahasa ~, orang ~* German; *campak ~* rubella, German measles

jernih *adj* clear, transparent, pure; *air ~* clear water

jero: jeroan *n* innards

jeruji *n* trellis, iron bars; *di balik ~* behind bars; **berjeruji** *adj* fitted with bars

jeruk *buah ~* orange, mandarin; ~ *limau* lime; ~ *nipis* lemon; ~ *peras* orange; *rasa ~* orange (-flavored)

jerumus: menjerumuskan *v* to let drop, send down; **terjerumus** *adj* plunged into

jéwér: jewéran *n* pinch, reprimand; **menjéwér** *v* to pinch someone's ear, scold

Jibuti *n* Djibouti; *orang ~* Djiboutian

jidat *n* forehead

jihad *n, Isl* crusade, holy war; **berjihad** *v* to conduct a war or crusade

jijik *adj* disgusting, revolting, filthy; *rasa ~* disgust; **menjijikkan** *adj* disgusting, revolting, foul

jika, jikalau *conj* if, should

jilat lick; **jilatan** *n* lick; ~ *api* flames; **menjilat** *v* to lick; *sl* to suck up, flatter; **penjilat** *n* crawler, flatterer, lickspittle

jilbab *n, Isl* (full) veil; **berjilbab** *adj* in a veil; *v* to wear the veil

jilid *n* volume; **jilidan** *n* binding; **berjilid** *adj* in volumes; **menjilid** *v* to bind; **penjilid** *n* binder; **penjilidan** *n* binding (process)

jimat *n* lucky charm, talisman

jin *n* spirit; *dunia ~* spirit world

jinak *adj* tame, domesticated, friendly; **menjinakkan** *v* to tame

jingga *adj* orange (color)

jinjing *tas ~* carrybag; **jinjingan** *n* something carried by hand; **menjinjing** *v* to carry by hand

jinjit: berjinjit-jinjit *v* walk on tiptoe

jintan *n* cumin

jip *mobil ~* jeep

jiplak: jiplakan *n* copy, plagiarism; **menjiplak** *v* to copy, plagiarize; **penjiplak** *n* cheat; **penjiplakan** *n* plagiarism, cheating

jiran *n* neighbor; *negeri ~* neighboring country, usu Malaysia

jitu *adj* exact, accurate; *cara ~* exact method; *penembak ~* sniper

jiwa *n* life, soul; ~ *raga* body and soul; *asuransi ~* life insurance; *ilmu ~* psychology; *rumah sakit ~ (RSJ)* mental hospital; **berjiwa** *adj* alive; **kejiwaan** *adj* mental; **menjiwai** *v* to bring to life, inspire; **penjiwaan** *n* inspiration

JJS *jalan-jalan sore sl* going out in the afternoon

Jl *Jalan* street, road

jodoh *n* life partner, match; *m* Mr Right; **menjodohkan** *v* to set up, match

jogét, jogéd (spontaneous) dance; **berjogét** *v* to dance

joglo *rumah* ~ traditional Javanese house

jok *n* seat (in vehicle); ~ *belakang* back seat

joki *n* jockey; paid passenger (to avoid traffic restrictions)

joli: sejoli *dua* ~ a couple

jompo *adj* elderly; *panti* ~, *rumah* ~ old persons' home, senior citizens' home

jongkok, berjongkok *v* to squat

joran *n* fishing rod

jorok *adj* obscene, disgusting; sloppy; *cerita* ~ dirty story; *film* ~ pornographic film

jorok: menjorok *v* to stick out, protrude; **menjorokkan** *v* to poke something out

jotos fist; *adu* ~ fistfight

jréng *adj, sl* bright, lively

jua only; also, too; *tidak sedikit* ~ not a bit

jual *v* to sell; ~ *beli* business, buying and selling; *harga* ~ selling price; **jualan** *v* to sell informally; **berjual** *v* to trade, sell; **menjual** *v* to sell; **penjual** *n* seller, dealer; **penjualan** *n* sale, sales; **terjual** *adj* sold; *habis* ~ sold out

juang: berjuang *v* to fight, struggle; **memperjuangkan** *v* to fight for; **perjuangan** *n* battle, fight, struggle; *Partai Demokrasi Indonesia-~ (PDIP)* Indonesian Democratic Party of Struggle

juara *n* champion; ~ *satu* first place; **kejuaraan** *n* championship; **menjuarai** *v* to win (a competition)

jubah *n* gown, robe; **berjubah** *v* to wear a robe

judes *adj* mean, cruel, bitchy

judi *v* to gamble; *main* ~ to gamble; **berjudi** *v* to gamble; **penjudi** *n* gambler; **perjudian** *n* gambling

judul *n* title; **berjudul** *adj* titled; *v* to have a title

juga too, also; *hari itu* ~ that very day

jujur *adj* honest; **kejujuran** *n* honesty

julang: menjulang *v* to soar; *gedung* ~ *tinggi* skyscraper

Juli *bulan* ~ July

juling *adj* cross-eyed; *mata* ~ squint

Jumat, Jum'at *hari* ~ Friday; ~ *Agung* Good Friday; *sholat* ~ Friday prayers

jumlah *n* amount, total, sum, number; ~ *korban* total casualties; **berjumlah** *v* to (have the) number; **menjumlahkan** *v* to add (up)

jumpa meet; ~ *pers* press conference; *sampai* ~ see you later; **berjumpa** *v* to meet; **menjumpai** *v* to meet someone

jungkir ~ *balik* somersault

Juni *bulan* ~ June

junior, yunior *n* junior; student in a younger year level; co-worker of a lower rank

junjung: menjunjung ~ *tinggi* to honor

juntai: berjuntai, menjuntai *v* to dangle

junub *adj, Isl* state of impurity after having sex; *mandi* ~ to shower after sex

juragan *n* boss, master

jurang *n* ravine, gorge

juri *n* jury

jurnal *n* journal; **jurnalis** *n* journalist, reporter → **wartawan**

juru expert, skilled; ~ *bahasa* interpreter (spoken); translator (written); ~ *bicara* spokesperson; ~ *ketik* typist; ~ *masak* cook; ~ *mudi* helmsman; ~ *rawat* nurse; ~ *tulis* clerk; **kejuruan** *adj* technical; *sekolah* ~ technical or trade school

juru: penjuru *n* corner

jurus: jurusan *n* direction; major (at university); *bis* ~ *Palangkaraya* bus to Palangkaraya; ~ *sastra* arts major

jus *n* juice; ~ *alpukat* avocado juice

justru *adv* precisely, exactly

juta *n* million; *sepuluh* ~ ten million; **jutaan** *adj* millions; **berjuta** *v* to have millions of; **jutawan** *n* millionaire

K

K. *kali* creek, stream, river

KA *abbrev kereta api* train

Ka *Kepala* head of section

Kaabah, ka'abah *n* the black-covered shrine in the Great Mosque of Mecca

Kab. *Kabupaten* regency

kabag *n* head of section ← **kepala bagian**

kabar *n* news; ~ *nya* people say; ~ *angin*, ~ *burung* rumour; *apa* ~*?* how are you?; ~ *baik* good news; I'm well; ~*nya* people say; *surat* ~ newspaper; **mengabari** *v* to tell or inform someone; **mengabarkan** *v* to announce, report

kabé, ka bé, KB *n, coll* state family planning program ← **keluarga berencana**

kabel *n* cable; ~ *listrik* electrical cable

kabin *n* cabin (of a ship or aeroplane); *bagasi* ~ cabin luggage

kabinét *n* cabinet; ~ *Indonesia Bersatu* the United Indonesia cabinet; *rapat* ~ cabinet meeting

kabisat *tahun* ~ leap year

kabul: mengabulkan *v* to grant, approve, consent to; *semoga doanya dikabulkan* may your prayers be answered; **terkabul** *adj* granted

kabung: berkabung *v* to mourn; *hari* ~ *nasional* day of national mourning; **perkabungan** *n* mourning

kabupatén *n* regency; ~ *Bandung* Regency of Bandung ← **bupati**

kabur *adj* blurry, hazy; *mata sudah* ~ blurred vision

kabur *v* to disappear, vanish

kabut *n* fog, mist

kaca *n* glass; ~ *mata* glasses, spectacles; ~ *mata hitam* sunglasses, dark glasses; ~ *pembesar* magnifying glass; ~ *spion* rear-view mirror; *tukang* ~ glazier; **berkaca-kaca** *v* to fill with tears (of eyes)

kacang *n* bean, legume; ~ *kapri* snow pea; ~ *kedelai* soybean, soya bean; ~ *mede* cashew (nut); ~ *merah* kidney bean; ~ *panjang* kind of long bean; ~ *polong* (green) pea; ~ *tanah* peanut; ~ *lupa kulit* forget your origins; *selai* ~ peanut butter

kacapiring *n* gardenia

kacau *adj* disordered, confused, chaotic; ~ *balau* complete disorder; **kekacauan** *n* chaos; **mengacaukan** *v* to mix or mess up; **pengacau** *n* provocateur; **pengacauan** *n* disturbance

kadal *n* lizard

kadaluwarsa, kedaluwarsa *adj* expired; *tanggal* ~ expiry date, use-by date (food) ← **daluwarsa**

kadang, kadang-kadang, terkadang *adv* sometimes, occasionally

kadar *n* level, degree; *ala ~nya* the best you can; **sekadar** *adj* just; *~nya* as necessary

kade *n* quay, dock

kader *n* cadre, party member

kadét *n* cadet

Kadin *n* Indonesian Chamber of Commerce ← **Kamar Dagang Indonésia**

kafan *kain* ~ shroud, white cloth for wrapping a dead body

kafé *n* café, bar, pub, nightspot; ~ *gaul* popular café

kaféin *n* caffeine

kafilah *n* caravan

kafir *n, Isl* infidel, pagan

kagak *sl* no, not ← **tidak**

kagét *n* startled, surprised; *pasar* ~ temporary street market; *rasa* ~ surprise; **mengagétkan** *v* to surprise, startle

kagok *adj* stuck (in an awkward position)

kagum *adj* admiring; **kekaguman** *n* admiration; **mengagumi** *v* to admire; **pengagum** *n* admirer

-kah (suffix to make a question) *bisa~?* Can?; *tidak~* Isn't?

kaidah *n* law, rule; ~ *fisika* laws of physics

kail *n* fishing rod; **mengail** *v* to fish

kailan *n* Chinese broccoli, kailan

kain *n* cloth; ~ *kafan* shroud; ~ *kebaya* national dress for women; ~ *mori* white cotton for making batik

kais, mengais *v* to scratch; ~ *rejeki* to scratch a living

kaisar *n, pron* emperor; **kekaisaran** *n* empire; ~ *Roma* the Roman Empire

kait hook; **kaitan** *n* relationship,

link; *tidak ada ~nya* unrelated; **berkaitan** *adj* related to; **mengaitkan** *v* to link, connect, join; **pengait** *n* catch ← **gaét, gait**

kaji: **kajian** *n* studies; *~ Indonesia* Indonesian studies; **mengkaji** *v* to study, investigate

kaji: **mengaji, ngaji** *v* to recite or read the Koran; **pengajian** *n* Koranic recitation

kak *pron* term for older sibling or slightly older person; **kakak** *n pron* elder brother or sister; *~ kelas* someone in a class higher than you; *~ laki-laki* elder brother

kakap *ikan ~* large fish; *penjahat kelas ~* big-time criminal

kakas: **perkakas** *n* tool, implement; *~ dapur* kitchen utensils

kakatua *n burung ~* cockatoo

kakék *n, pron* grandfather; old man; **kakék-kakék** *adj, m* old and ailing

kaki *n* foot, leg; *~ langit* horizon; *~ lima* itinerant food vendor; *~ tangan* henchman, stooge; *jari ~* toe; *pergelangan ~, mata ~* ankle; *semata ~* to the ankle; *telapak ~* footprint, sole

kaktus *n* cactus

kaku *adj* stiff, frozen

kakus *n* toilet, outhouse

kala *n* time; *conj* when; *ada ~nya* sometimes; *dahulu ~* the old days; **berkala** *adj* regular; *secara ~* periodically

kalah lose, be defeated; *~ cepat* miss out, too slow; **kekalahan** *n* defeat, loss; **mengalahkan** *v* to conquer, defeat

kalajengking *n* scorpion

kalam *lit, Isl* pen, stylus

kalang *~ kabut* confused, mixed up

kalang: **kalangan** *n* circle, group; *untuk ~ sendiri* for believers or members only

kalau *conj* if; **kalau-kalau** *conj* in case; **kalaupun** *conj* even if

Kalbar *n* West Kalimantan ← **Kalimantan Barat**

kalbu, kaldéra *n* heart

kaldéra *n* caldera, crater

kaldu *n* broth; *~ sapi* beef stew

kalem *adj* calm, steady

kaléndar, kalénder *n* calendar *~ Masehi* Christian calendar

kaléng *n* tin, can; *ikan ~* tinned fish; *surat ~* anonymous letter

kali time, times; *satu ~, se~* once; *dua ~* twice; *enam ~* six times; *lima ~ delapan* five times eight; **berkali-kali** *adv* repeatedly, again and again; **mengalikan** *v* to multiply; **sekali** *adv* once; very; *~ besar* very large; **sekali-sekali, sesekali** *adv* every now and then, occasionally; **sekali-kali** *jangan ~* never (do this); **sekalian** *adv* all together, all at once; *adv, coll* at the same time; **sekaligus** *adv* all at once; **sekalipun** *conj* even though

kali *n* creek, stream, river; *~ Brantas* the River Brantas

kali *coll* maybe, perhaps ← **barangkali**

kalian *pron, pl* you; *anda se~* all of you

kaligrafi *n, Isl* Arabic calligraphy

Kalimantan *n* Kalimantan, Borneo; *~ Timur (Kaltim)* East Kalimantan; *~ Utara* Malaysian Borneo, North Borneo

kalimat *n* sentence; *pokok ~* subject; *menyusun ~* to make a sentence

kalium *n* potassium

kalk *n* limestone, chalk

kalkulator *n* calculator

kalkun *n* turkey

kalori *n* calorie; *~ rendah* low-calorie

Kalpataru *n* award presented for services to the environment

Kalsél *n* South Kalimantan ← **Kalimantan Selatan**

Kalteng *n* Central Kalimantan ← **Kalimantan Tengah**

Kaltim *n* East Kalimantan ← **Kalimantan Timur**

kalung *n* necklace; **berkalung** *adj* wearing a necklace; **mengalungkan** *v* to drape around someone's neck

kamar *n* room; *sl* bedroom; *~ belajar* study; *~ dagang* chamber of commerce; *~ kecil* toilet, lavatory; *~ makan* dining room; *~ mandi* bathroom; *~ pas* fitting room; *~ tamu* room for receiving guests, front room; living room; spare room; *~ tidur* bedroom

kambing *n* goat, sheep; *daging ~* goat; mutton, lamb; *kelas ~* cheapest class (on transport); *potong ~* sacrifice a goat; *~ hitam* scapegoat; **mengambing-hitamkan** *v* to make a scapegoat of someone

kamboja *bunga ~* frangipani

Kamboja *n* Cambodia; *bahasa ~* Khmer; *orang ~* Cambodian

kambuh relapse, chronic attack; *asmanya ~* have an asthma attack

kaméra *n* camera

kami *pron excl* we, us, our; (very polite) I; *~ punya* our, ours; *surat ~* my letter, our letter

Kamis *hari ~* Thursday; *~ Putih* Maundy Thursday

kamisol *n* camisole, strapless top

kampanye *n* campaign; **berkampanye** *v* to (hold a) campaign; to join a parade for a candidate

kamper *n* camphor, mothballs

kampung, kampong *n* village, hometown; *~ halaman* hometown; *~ Melayu* Malay quarter; *pulang ~* go home to the village; **kampungan** *adj* uneducated, backward, provincial

kampus *n* university, campus

kamu *pron, sing* you (to children and familiars); *~ punya* yours

kamuflase *n* camouflage; smokescreen; **berkamuflase** *v* to use camouflage

kamus *n* dictionary; *~ dwi-bahasa* bilingual dictionary; *~ Indonesia-Inggris* Indonesian-English dictionary; *~ saku* pocket dictionary

kan, 'kan you know; isn't it? ← **bukan**

Kanada *n* Canada; *orang ~* Canadian

kanak-kanak *taman ~ (TK)* kindergarten; **kekanak-kanakan** *adj* childish, infantile

kanan *adj* right; *~ kapal* starboard; *ke ~* to the right; *sebelah ~* on the right; *stir ~* right-hand drive; *tangan ~* right hand

kancil *n* mouse-deer; smart car used as a taxi ← **kendaraan angkutan niaga cilik irit dan lincah**

kancing *n* button, stud; *~ pencet* press-stud; *lubang ~* buttonhole; **mengancing** *v* to button

kandang *n* stable, pen; *coll* home ground; *~ anjing* kennel, doghouse; *~ ayam* chicken coop; *~ kuda* stable; *~ lawan* opponent's home ground

kandas *adj* stranded, aground; *v* to fail

kandidat *n* candidate → **calon**

kandung *n* uterus; bladder; *~ empedu* gall bladder; *~ kemih* bladder; **kandungan** *n* fetus, unborn child; contents; *~ merkuri* mercury content; **mengandung** *v* to contain, carry; to be pregnant

kangen *adj* long for, miss; *rasa ~* longing

kangguru, kanguru *n* kangaroo; *negeri ~* Australia

kangkung *n* water spinach; *~ tumis* stir-fried water spinach

kanibal *n* cannibal

kanker *n* cancer; *~ darah* leukaemia; *~ paru-paru* lung cancer; *~ payudara* breast cancer

kano *n* canoe

kans *n, coll* chance

kansel, kénsel, mengansel *v* to cancel → **batal**

kantin *n* canteen

kantong, kantung *n* pocket, pouch; **berkantong** *v* to have a pocket; *~ tebal* wealthy; **mengantongi** *v* to pocket

kantor *n* office; *~ cabang, ~ perwakilan* branch office; *~ pajak* tax office; *~ pos* post office; *~ pusat* head office; *pergi ke ~* go to work; *orang ~* someone from work; **kantoran** *adj coll* office; *orang ~* white-collar workers; **ngantor** *coll* to go to work; **perkantoran** *n* office block

kantuk *rasa ~* sleepiness; **mengantuk, ngantuk, terkantuk-kantuk** *adj* sleepy

kantung → **kantong**

kanwil *n* regional office ← **kantor wilayah**

kaos → **kaus**

kapak *n* ax; *~ merah* the Red Axes, a gang in Jakarta

kapal *n* ship, vessel; *~ api, ~ uap* steamer; *~ induk* aircraft carrier; *~ penumpang* passenger ship; *~ perang* warship; *~ selam* submarine; *~ tempur* fighter; *~ terbang* aeroplane, airplane; *anak buah ~ (ABK)* able seaman; *awak ~* crew; **perkapalan** *n* shipping

kapan *interrog* when; ~ *saja* whenever, any time; **kapan-kapan** *adv* one day, some time in the future

kapan → **kafan**

kapar: terkapar *adj* fallen, strewn

kapas *n* cotton, cotton wool; *seputih* ~ as white as snow

kapasitas *n* capacity; **ber-kapasitas** *v* with a capacity of

kapitalis capitalist; **kapitalisme** *n* capitalism

kapitan, kapitén *n* captain; ~ *Cina* leader of local Chinese in past times

kapling, kavling, kaveling, kav *n* block (in addresses); **dikapling** *v* to be divided up into blocks for development

Kapolda *n* Regional Chief of Police ← **Kepala Polisi Daérah**

Kapolrés *n* Local Chief of Police ← **Kepala Polisi Résort**

Kapolri *n* National Chief of Police ← **Kepala Polisi Republik Indonésia**

Kapolsék *n* Section Chief of Police ← **Kepala Polisi Séktor**

Kapolwil *n* District Chief of Police ← **Kepala Polisi Wilayah**

kapri *kacang* ~ snow pea

kapsul *n* capsule; *Kijang* ~ rounded model of Kijang car (post 1996)

kapuk, kapok *n* kapok

kapulaga *n* cardamom

kapur *n* lime(stone), chalk; *tanah* ~ limestone country; **mengapur** *v* to whitewash

karam *adj* shipwrecked; *v* to sink

karamba *n* large basket for catching fish

karambola, karambol *n* children's game

karamél *n* caramel pudding; *rasa* ~ caramel-flavored

karang *n* coral reef; *batu* ~ coral reef; *pulau* ~ coral island, atoll

karang: karangan *n* essay; ~ *bunga* bouquet, wreath; **mengarang** *v* to write, compose; *lomba* ~ essay competition; **ngarang** *v coll* to make something up (off the top of your head); **pengarang** *n* author, writer, composer; *hak* ~ copyright

karang: pekarangan *n* yard; ~ *sekolah* schoolyard

karantina *n* quarantine

karapan ~ *sapi* Madurese bull races

karat *n* rust; **karatan, berkarat** *adj* rusty

karat *n* carat; *emas delapan belas* ~ eighteen-carat gold

karawang → **kerawang**

karbol *n* carbolic acid, floor cleaner

karburétor, karburator *n* carburettor

karcis *n* ticket (of small value); ~ *bis* bus ticket; ~ *masuk* entrance ticket; ~ *kereta api* local train ticket; *loket* ~ ticket office; *penjual* ~ ticket seller

kardus *n* cardboard (box)

karé → **kari**

karédok *n* Sundanese fresh salad with peanut sauce

karena *conj* because, since;
dikarenakan *v* caused by

karét *n* rubber; rubber band; ~ *gelang* rubber band; *jam* ~ lack of punctuality; *kebun* ~ rubber plantation; *permen* ~ chewing gum, bubble gum

kargo *n* cargo, hold

kari, karé *n* curry; ~ *ayam* chicken curry

karib *adj* close, intimate

karikatur *n* caricature

karir *n* career; *wanita* ~ career woman

Karo sub-ethnic group of the Batak people, living around Brastagi in North Sumatra

karpét *n* carpet

kartika *n, lit* star

karton *n* cardboard

kartu *n* card; ~ *merah* red card (in soccer); ~ *nama* name card; ~ *pos* postcard; ~ *pelajar* student card; ~ *remi* playing cards; ~ *truf* trump card, trumps; *main* ~ play cards

kartun *n* cartoon, anime; **kartunis** *n* cartoonist

karuan, keruan *tidak* ~ very badly, in chaos

karun *harta* ~ hidden treasure

karung *n* sack; ~ *beras* sack of rice

karunia *n* blessing, grace; ~ *Allah* gift from God; **mengaruniai** *v* to bless

karya *n* works; *loka*~ workshop, seminar; **karyawan** *n* (salaried) employee; **karyawati** *n, f* (salaried) employee

kasa *kain* ~ gauze, muslin

Kasad *n* Army Chief of Staff ← **Kepala Staf Angkatan Darat**

kasar *adj* rough, rude, vulgar; *bahasa Jawa* ~ low Javanese; *sikap* ~ rudeness; **kekasaran** *n* coarseness, roughness

kasasi *n leg* appeal (to Supreme Court)

kasatmata *adj* clear, with the naked eye

kasét *n* cassette

kasih, kasi *v, coll* give; ~ *lihat* show; ~ *pinjam* lend; ~ *tahu* inform, tell; **dikasih** *v* to be given

kasih *n* affection, love; ~ *ibu* mother's love; ~ *sayang* love; *terima* ~ thank you; **kasihan** pity, feel sorry for; ~ *dia* poor thing!; **mengasihani** *v* to pity, feel sorry for; **kekasih** *n* darling, sweetheart, beloved; ~ *gelap* secret lover

kasir, kassa *n* cashier

kasmaran *adj* in love, smitten ← **asmara**

kasta *n* caste; ~ *sudra* lowest caste

kasuari *burung* ~ cassowary

kasur *n* mattress; ~ *per* spring bed

kasus *n* case

kata *n* word; ~ *nya*, ~ *orang* people say; ~ *benda* noun; ~ *kerja* verb; *lawan* ~ antonym; ~*nya*, ~ *orang* people say; ~ *pengantar* preface; ~ *sifat* adjective; *dengan* ~ *lain* in other words; *pendek* ~ in short, in a word; **berkata** *v* to say, speak; **mengatakan** *v* to say; **perkataan** *n* phrase, words

katai *n* pygmy, midget, dwarf

katak *n* frog, toad

katalog *n* catalog

katédral *n* cathedral; ~ *Santa Maria* St Mary's Cathedral

Katolik Catholic; *agama* ~ Catholicism; *gereja* ~ Catholic church; *orang* ~ Catholic

katrol *n* pulley

katulistiwa, khatulistiwa *n* the Equator

katun *n* cotton; *kain* ~ cotton fabric, cotton cloth

katup *n* valve

kau *pron, s* you (to equals or inferiors) ← **engkau**

kaum *n* people, community; ~ *buruh* labourers; ~ *intelektual* intellectuals; ~ *kolot* conservatives; ~ *wanita* women

kaus, kaos *n* stocking, sock; garment; ~ *kaki* sock; stocking; ~ *oblong* T-shirt; ~ *tangan* glove, mitten

kav, kavling, kaveling → **kapling**

kawah *n* crater

kawakan *adj* veteran, experienced; *wartawan* ~ veteran journalist

kawal guard; **kawalan** *n* escort, guard; **mengawal** *v* to guard, escort; **pengawal** *n* (body) guard, sentry

kawan *n* friend; ~ *baik* good friend; *setia* ~ loyal; **kesetiakawanan** *n* loyalty; **kawanan** *n* flock, swarm; **berkawan** *v* to have or be friends with; **sekawan** *tiga* ~ a trio of friends

kawas: kawasan *n* area, region; ~ *Asia-Pasifik Kawasan Asia* ~ (Asia-)Pacific region

kawat *n* wire; ~ *berduri* barbed wire; ~ *listrik* electrical wire

kawi *bahasa* ~ Old Javanese

kawin *v* marry, mate; ~ *lari* elope; ~ *muda* marry young; ~ *silang* cross-breed; ~ *siri* marry in secret; *emas* ~, *mas* ~ dowry; *musim* ~ on heat; **kawinan** *n coll* wedding ceremony or reception; **mengawini** *v* to marry someone; **mengawinkan** *v* to marry someone off; ~ *anak* to marry off a son or daughter; **perkawinan** *n* marriage, wedding; ~ *campuran* mixed marriage

kawula ~ *muda* youth, young people

kaya *adj* rich; ~ *raya* very rich; *orang* ~ *baru* new money, nouveau riche; **kekayaan** *n* wealth, riches; *pajak* ~ property tax; **pengayaan** *n* enrichment; ~ *uranium* uranium enrichment

kayak, kaya *conj, coll* like, as; **kayaknya** it seems, apparently

kayu *n* wood; ~ *bakar* firewood; ~ *cendana* sandalwood; ~ *jati* teak; ~ *mahoni* mahogany; ~ *manis* cinnamon; ~ *meranti* kind of reddish wood, morantee; *mata* ~ knot; *tukang* ~ carpenter

kayuh, berkayuh paddle, row; pedal; **mengayuh** *v* to paddle or pedal something; ~ *sepeda* to ride a bicycle

Kazakhstan *n* Kazakhstan; *bahasa* ~, *orang* ~ Kazakh

KB *abbrev* **kelompok bermain** playgroup

KB *abbrev* **Keluarga Berencana** Family Planning

KBRI *abbrev* **Kedutaan Besar Republik Indonesia** Embassy of the Republic of Indonesia

ke *prep* to, towards; ~ *atas* up, upwards; ~ *dalam* into; ~ *luar* out; ~ *muka* to the front; ~ *samping* to the side; ~ *tengah* to the middle

keadaan *n* situation, condition; ~ *darurat* emergency situation ← **ada**

keadilan *n* justice; ~ *sosial* social justice ← **adil**

keagamaan *adj* religious affairs ← **agama**

keagungan *n* greatness, majesty ← **agung**

keahlian *n* expertise ← **ahli**

keajaiban *n* wonder, miracle; *Tujuh* ~ *Dunia* the Seven Wonders of the World ← **ajaib**

keakraban *n* closeness, intimacy ← **akrab**

keamanan *n* safety, security; *Dewan* ~ *(UN)* Security Council ← **aman**

keanéhan *n* peculiarity, oddity ← **anéh**

keanékaragaman ~ *hayati* biological diversity ← **anéka ragam**

keanggotaan *n* membership; *kartu* ~ membership card ← **anggota**

keanggunan *n* grace, style ← **anggun**

keangkuhan *n* arrogance, rudeness ← **angkuh**

kearifan *n* wisdom, learning ← **arif**

kearsipan archives, archival ← **arsip**

keaslian *n* authenticity ← **asli**

keasrian *n* (natural) beauty ← **asri**

kebagian *v* to get a share

kebahagiaan *n* happiness ← **bahagia**

kebaikan *n* goodness, kindness ← **baik**

kebakaran *n* fire; ~ *hutan* forest fire, bushfire; *ada* ~! fire! ← **bakar**

kebaktian *n* (Protestant) service ← **bakti**

kebal *adj* resistant, immune; ~ *hukum* legal immunity; **kekebalan** *n* immunity

kebangetan *adj, coll* too much, excessive (of behavior or a situation) ← **banget**

kebanggaan *n* pride; something of which you are proud ← **bangga**

kebangkitan *n* rise, awakening; *Partai* ~ *Bangsa (PKB)* Party of National Awakening ← **bangkit**

kebangkrutan *n* bankruptcy ← **bangkrut**

kebangsaan *adj* national; *lagu* ~ national anthem ← **bangsa**

kebanyakan *n, adj* too much; most; ~ *orang tidak setuju* most people don't agree ← **banyak**

kebapakan *adj* fatherly ← **bapak**
kebatinan *n* mysticism ← **batin**
kebaya *n, f* women's blouse worn as national costume; ~ *encim* Chinese-style traditional blouse; ~ *Kartini* in the style as worn by female emancipist Kartini; *kain* ~ national dress for women
kebébasan *n* freedom ← **bébas**
kebelet *adj, coll* busting, desperate to go to the toilet ← **belet**
kebenaran *n* truth; *Komisi* ~ *dan Rekonsiliasi* Truth and Reconciliation Commission ← **benar**
kebencian *n* hatred ← **benci**
kebengisan *n* cruelty, harshness ← **bengis**
keberadaan *n* presence ← **ada**
keberangkatan *n* departure; *pintu* ~ departure gate ← **angkat, berangkat**
keberanian *n* bravery, courage ← **berani**
keberapa *interrog, coll* which number? which one? ← **apa, berapa**
keberatan *n* objection; *v* to object ← **berat**
keberhasilan *n* success ← **hasil**
kebersihan *n* cleanliness, hygiene ← **bersih**
kebesaran *n* greatness; *adj* too big; *celana ini* ~! these pants are too big! ← **besar**
kebetulan *adv* by chance, accidentally; *n* coincidence ← **betul**
kebiadaban *n* savagery ← **biadab**
kebiasaan *n* habit, custom ← **biasa**
kebidanan *n* midwifery ← **bidan**
kebijakan *n* policy ← **bijak**
kebijaksanaan *n* caution, prudence; policy ← **bijaksana**
kebingungan *n* confusion ← **bingung**
kebiri *adj* castrated, neutered; *kuda* ~ gelding; **mengebiri** *v* to castrate, neuter
kebiru-biruan *adj* bluish ← **biru**
kebisingan *n* noise, buzz ← **bising**
kebisuan *n* silence, lack of speech ← **bisu**
kebo *kumpul* ~ live together without being married
kebocoran *n* leak ← **bocor**
kebodohan *n* stupidity, ignorance ← **bodoh**
kebohongan *n* lie, deceit ← **bohong**
keboléhan *n* ability, what you can do ← **boléh**
kebotakan *n* baldness, hair loss ← **botak**
kebuasan *n* ferocity ← **buas**
kebudayaan *n* culture, civilization ← **budaya**
kebugaran *n* health; *pusat* ~ gym, fitness center ← **bugar**
kebuli *nasi* ~ lamb and rice dish of Middle Eastern origin
kebun, kebon *n* garden, plantation; ~ *apel* orchard; ~ *binatang* zoo; ~ *kopi* coffee plantation; ~ *raya* botanical garden; *tukang* ~ gardener; **berkebun** *v* to garden, do gar-

dening; **perkebunan** *n* plantation, estate; ~ *teh* tea plantation
keburu *adj, adv, coll* in time;
too early, had already; ~ *habis*
already run out ← **buru**
kebut *tukang* ~ speed merchant,
speedster; **kebut-kebutan** *n*
drag-racing; **mengebut** *v* to
speed
kebutuhan *n* need, necessity ←
butuh
kecakapan *n* ability ← **cakap**
kecam: mengecam *v* to criticize; **kecaman** *n* criticism
kecamatan *n* sub-district ←
camat
kecanduan *n* addiction; *adj*
addicted to; ~ *obat* drug addiction ← **candu**
kecanggihan *n* sophistication ←
canggih
kecantikan *n* beauty; *ratu* ~
beauty queen ← **cantik**
kecap sound of smacking lips;
mengecap *v* to taste
kécap *n* soy sauce; ~ *asin* soy
sauce; ~ *manis* sweet soy sauce
kecapékan *adj* tired out; *n*
exhaustion ← **capék**
kecapi *n* Sundanese zither
kecebur *adj, coll* fallen into water
← **cebur**
kecelakaan *n* accident, disaster;
~ *pesawat* plane crash ← **celaka**
kecemasan *n* anxiety, concern
← **cemas**
kecemburuan *n* jealousy ←
cemburu
kecemerlangan *n* genius, brilliance ← **cemerlang**

kecemplung *adj, sl* fallen into
water ← **cemplung**
kecenderungan *n* tendency,
trend ← **cenderung**
kecepatan *n* speed ← **cepat**
keceplosan *n* directness ←
ceplos
kecerdasan *n* intelligence ←
cerdas
kecerdikan *n* intelligence;
shrewdness ← **cerdik**
keceréwétan *n* fussiness ←
ceréwét
keceriaan *n* happiness, good
mood ← **ceria**
kecermatan *n* precision, accuracy
← **cermat**
kecerobohan *n* carelessness ←
ceroboh
kecéwa *adj* disappointed; **kekecéwaan** *n* disappointment;
mengecéwakan *v* to disappoint; *adj* disappointing
kecil *adj* small, little; young; ~
hati disappointed; timid;
offended; *nama* ~ everyday
name; *orang* ~ the little people,
the poor; *dari ~, sejak ~* since
youth; *berkecil ~ hati* to be disappointed; timid; **kekecilan**
adj too small; **mengecil** *v* to
shrink, become smaller;
mengecilkan *v* to make smaller, decrease
kecintaan *n* love (for something)
← **cinta**
kecipratan *adj* be splashed,
sprayed accidentally ← **ciprat**
kecocokan *n* suitability, compatibility ← **cocok**

kecoklatan *adj* brownish ← **coklat**

kecolongan *adj* to be robbed; to lose unjustly ← **colong**

kecopétan *adj* to be pickpocketed, robbed; *n* pickpocketing ← **copét**

kecrék, kecrékan *n* bottle-top rattle shaken by beggars

kecuali *conj* except; **ke-kecualian, pengecualian** *n* exception; **mengecualikan** *v* to except, make an exception; **terkecuali** *tidak ~, tanpa ~* without exception

kecubung *batu ~* ruby

kecup sound of a kiss; **kecupan** *n* peck; **mengecup** *v* to kiss lightly, peck

kecurangan *n* cheating, dishonesty ← **curang**

kecurian *adj* to be robbed, burgled ← **curi**

kecurigaan *n* suspicion ← **curiga**

kecut *adj* sour, acidic

kecut *adj* shrivelled; *hati ~* afraid; **pengecut** *n* coward

kedahsyatan *n* power ← **dahsyat**

kedai *n* stall, kiosk ~ *kopi* small coffee shop

kedalaman *n* depth ← **dalam**

kedaluwarsa, kadaluwarsa *adj* expired; *tanggal ~* expiry date, use-by date (food) ← **daluwarsa**

kedamaian *n* peace ← **damai**

kedangkalan *n* shallows, (low) depth; ~ *laut* sea depth ← **dangkal**

kedap *adj* free from; ~ *air* water-proof; ~ *suara* soundproof; ~ *udara* air-tight

kedapatan *adj* to be caught in the act ← **dapat**

kedatangan *n* arrival ← **datang**

kedaulatan *n* sovereignty; *Partai ~ Rakyat (PKR)* People's Sovereignty Party ← **daulat**

kedébet *sl* to be wrongly debited (of a bank card) ← **débet**

kedekatan *n* close relationship, closeness ← **dekat**

kedelai, kedelé soy; *kacang ~* soya bean, soybean; *susu kacang ~* soya milk, soymilk

kedelapan *adj* eighth ← **delapan**

kedengaran *adj* audible ← **dengar**

kedengkian *n* spite ← **dengki**

kedéwasaan *n* maturity ← **déwasa**

kediaman *n* residence ← **diam**

kedinginan cold; feeling cold ← **dingin**

kedip blink; wink; **berkedip** *v* to blink (two eyes) or wink (one eye); **berkedip-kedip** *adj* blinking; **mengedipkan** ~ *mata* to blink

kedok *n* mask; guise; **berkedok** *v* to hide behind a mask, to pretend

kedokteran *adj* medical; *fakultas ~* School of Medicine ← **dokter**

kedondong *buah ~* kind of fruit

kedongkolan *n* annoyance, resentment ← **dongkol**

kedua *adj* second; **kedua(-dua)-nya** *adj* both ← **dua**

kedudukan *n* position ← **duduk**

kedukaan *n* grief, sorrow ← **duka**

kedutaan *n* ~ *(besar)* embassy ← **duta**

keélokan *n* beauty ← **élok**

keempat *adj* fourth; **keempat-(-empat)nya** *n* all four of them ← **empat**

keénakan *adj* too enjoyable or good ← **énak**

keenam *adj* sixth; *indera* ~ sixth sense; **keenam(-enam)nya** *n* all six of them ← **enam**

keengganan *n* reluctance ← **enggan**

keesaan *n* oneness; ~ *Tuhan* the oneness of God ← **esa**

keésokan ~ *harinya* the next day ← **ésok, bésok**

kefasihan *n* ease, eloquence ← **fasih**

kegadisan *n* virginity ← **gadis**

kegaduhan *n* noise, uproar ← **gaduh**

kegagalan *n* failure ← **gagal**

keganasan *n* ferocity ← **ganas**

kegandrungan *adj, sl* to be absorbed or swept up in, madly in love ← **gandrung**

keganjilan *n* oddity, peculiarity ← **ganjil**

kegelapan *n* darkness ← **gelap**

kegelisahan *n* anxiety, nerves ← **gelisah**

kegemaran *n* hobby ← **gemar**

kegembiraan *n* joy, happiness ← **gembira**

kegemukan *n* fatness; *adj* overweight ← **gemuk**

kegesitan *adj* agility, adroitness ← **gesit**

kegiatan *n* activity ← **giat**

kegigihan *n* perseverance, tenacity ← **gigih**

kegilaan *n* craze ← **gila**

kegirangan *n* gladness, happiness ← **girang**

kegugupan *n* nervousness, panic ← **gugup**

keguguran miscarry, miscarriage ← **gugur**

kegunaan *n* usefulness, use ← **guna**

kegusaran *n* annoyance, anger ← **gusar**

kehabisan *v* to run out of (water, food, stock) ← **habis**

kehadiran *n* presence, attendance ← **hadir**

kehakiman *Departemen* ~ Department of Justice ← **hakim**

kehalusan *n* delicacy, grace ← **halus**

kehamilan *n* pregnancy ← **hamil**

kehancuran *n* destruction, ruin ← **hancur**

kehangatan *n* warmth, friendliness ← **hangat**

keharuman *n* fragrance ← **harum**

keharusan *n* obligation, necessity, requirement ← **harus**

kehausan to be thirsty; thirst ← **haus**

kehébatan *n* force ← **hébat**

kehébohan *n* sensation, phenomenon ← **héboh**

kehendak *n* will, wish; ~ *rakyat* will of the people; **berkehendak, mengehendaki** *v* to intend ← **hendak, kehendak**

keheningan *n* peace, quiet; clarity ← **hening**

kehéranan *n* astonishment, amazement, wonder ← **héran**

kehidupan *n* life, existence ← **hidup**

kehijau-hijauan *adj* greenish ← **hijau**

kehilangan (feeling of) loss; ~ *20 juta warga* to lose 20 million citizens ← **hilang**

kehormatan *n* respect; *anggota* ~ honorary member ← **hormat**

kehujanan *adj* caught in the rain ← **hujan**

kehutanan *n* forestry ← **hutan**

keibuan *adj* motherly ← **ibu**

keikhlasan *n* sincerity ← **ikhlas**

keikutsertaan *n* participation ← **ikut serta**

keilmuan *adj* scientific ← **ilmu**

keindahan *n* beauty ← **indah**

keindonésiaan *n* sense of being Indonesian ← **Indonésia**

keinginan *n* desire, wish ← **ingin**

keistiméwaan *n* special quality ← **istiméwa**

kejadian *n* event, happening; creation ← **jadi**

kejahatan *n* crime ← **jahat**

kejaksaan *n* district attorney's office ← **jaksa**

kejam *adj* cruel, merciless; **kekejaman** *n* cruelty

kejam: mengejamkan ~ *mata* to close your eyes

kejang *adj* stiff; **berkejang** *v* to have a cramp; **mengejang** *v* to cramp, seize up

kejanggalan *n* oddity, anomaly ← **janggal**

kejantanan *n* masculinity

kejap: sekejap *n* moment, flash, blink; *dalam* ~ *mata* in a moment, in the twinkling of an eye

kejar *v* chase; **kejar-kejaran** *v* chase each other; **mengejar** *v* to chase; ~ *waktu* to race against the clock

kejatuhan *n* fall; *adj* be struck by something falling ← **jatuh**

kejauhan *adj* too far ← **jauh**

kejawén *n* Javanese traditional mysticism

kejelasan *n* clarity ← **jelas**

kejelékan *n* badness, ugliness ← **jelék**

kejéngkélan *n* annoyance, bad mood ← **jéngkél**

kejenuhan *n* saturation; boredom ← **jenuh**

keji *adj* low, mean, despicable

kejiwaan *adj* mental ← **jiwa**

kejora *bintang* ~ morning star (symbol of Papuan independence movement), Venus

kéju *n* cheese

kejuaraan *n* championship ← **juara**

kejujuran *n* honesty ← **jujur**

kejurnas *n* national championship → **kejuaraan nasional**

kejuruan *adj* technical; *sekolah* ~ technical or trade school ← **juru**

kejut *adj* surprised, startled; **mengejutkan** *adj* surprising, startling; *v* to surprise or startle; **terkejut** *adj* surprised

kék whether it's this, or that; *sate ~, soto ~, saya mau* whether it's satay or soup, I'll have some

kekacauan *n* chaos ← **kacau**

kekaguman *n* admiration ← **kagum**

kekaisaran *n* empire; *~ Romawi* the Roman Empire ← **kaisar**

kekal *adj* everlasting, eternal; **kekekalan** *n* eternity

kekalahan *n* defeat, loss ← **kalah**

kekanak-kanakan *adj* childish, infantile ← **kanak**

kekang *n* bridle; *tali ~* rein

kekar *adj* solid, strong

kekasaran *n* coarseness, roughness ← **kasar**

kekasih *n* sweetheart, beloved, darling; *~ gelap* secret love ← **kasih**

kekayaan *n* wealth, riches; *pajak ~* property tax ← **kaya**

kekebalan *n* immunity ← **kebal**

kekecéwaan *n* disappointment ← **kecéwa**

kekecilan *adj* too small ← **kecil**

kekecualian *n* exception ← **kecuali**

kékéh: terkékéh-kékéh *v* to laugh

kekejaman *n* cruelty ← **kejam**

kekekalan *n* eternity ← **kekal**

kekeliruan *n* mistake, error ← **keliru**

kekentalan *n* thickness, viscosity ← **kental**

kekenyalan *n* elasticity ← **kenyal**

kéker *n* binoculars, field glasses

kekerabatan *n* kinship ← **kerabat**

kekerasan *n* violence; *~ dalam rumah tangga (KDRT), ~ domestik* domestic violence; *~ terhadap perempuan* violence against women ← **keras**

kekeringan *n* dryness, aridity ← **kering**

kekesalan *n* annoyance, bad mood ← **kesal**

kekhasan *n* special feature ← **khas**

kekompakan *n* solidarity ← **kompak**

kekosongan *n* emptiness ← **kosong**

kekuasaan *n* power; authority ← **kuasa**

kekuatan *n* strength, power ← **kuat**

kekuatiran *n* worry, fear ← **kuatir**

kekurangan *n* shortcoming (of a person), lack; flaw, mistake, defect ← **kurang**

kekurusan *adj* too thin ← **kurus**

kel. *keluarga* family

kelab, klab *n* club; *~ malam* nightclub

kelabu *adj* gray, cloudy; **mengelabui** *v* to trick, pull the wool over someone's eyes ← **abu**

keladi *biang ~* cause, root of the problem; mastermind; *tua-tua ~* the older, the more

kelahi: berkelahi *v* to quarrel, fight, fall out; **perkelahian** *n* fight, scuffle

kelahiran *n* birth; *adj* born; *hari ~* birthday; anniversary; *~*

Semarang born in Semarang ← **lahir**

kelainan *n* abnormality ← **lain**

kelak later, in the future

kelakuan *n* act, behavior ← **laku**

kelalaian *n* forgetfulness, negligence ← **lalai**

kelalawar → **kelelawar**

kelam *adj* dark, dull

kelamaan *adj* too long (a time) ← **lama**

kelambanan *n* lack of action, inertia ← **lamban**

kelambu *n* mosquito net

kelamin *alat* ~ sex organs, genitalia; *jenis* ~ gender, sex; *penyakit* ~ venereal disease, sexually transmitted disease (STD)

kelana: berkelana *v* to roam, wander

kelancangan *n* impudence, presumptiousness ← **lancang**

kelancaran *n* smoothness, good progress, fluency ← **lancar**

kelanggengan *n* eternity ← **langgeng**

kelanjutan *n* continuation, result ← **lanjut**

kelapa *n* coconut; ~ *muda* young coconut; ~ *sawit* oil-palm; *air* ~ coconut milk; coconut juice; *minyak* ~ coconut oil; *pohon* ~ coconut palm; *sabut* ~ coconut fiber

kelaparan *n* hunger, famine, starvation; *adj* very hungry ← **lapar**

kelar *adj, coll* finished, ready

kelas *n* class; ~ *kakap* big-time;

~ *kambing* cheapest class of seat; ~ *satu SD* grade 1 at primary or elementary school; **berkelas** *adj* classy

kelasi *n* sailor

kelautan *adj* maritime; *Departemen Perikanan dan* ~ Department of Fisheries and Marine Affairs ← **laut**

kelayakan *n* suitability; *studi* ~ feasibility study ← **layak**

kelebihan *n* extra, excess ← **lebih**

keledai *n* donkey

kelelahan *n* fatigue, weariness ← **lelah**

kelelap *adj* submerged, sunken into water

kelelawar, kelalawar *n* bat

keleluasaan *n* freedom (of choice) ← **leluasa**

kelemahan *n* weakness ← **lemah**

kelembaban *n* humidity ← **lembab**

kelembutan *n* softness ← **lembut**

keléngkéng *n buah* ~ small lychee ← **léngkéng**

kelenjar *n* gland; ~ *getah bening* lymph gland; ~ *gondok* thyroid; ~ *prostat* prostate

kelénténg, klénténg *n* Chinese or Confucian temple, pagoda

kelép → **klép**

keléréng *n* marble; *main* ~ play marbles

keléwat *adj, sl* too, unacceptably ← **léwat**

kelezatan *n* delicious taste ← **lezat**

keliar: berkeliaran *v* to swarm or wander about

kelicikan *n* trickery, cunning ← **licik**

kelihatan *adj* visible; ~*nya* apparently, it seems ← **lihat**

keliling around; edge, perimeter; ~ *dunia* go around the world; **berkeliling** *v* to go around; **mengelilingi** *v* to circle, go around

kelim *n* seam

kelimpahan *n* abundance, wealth ← **limpah**

kelincahan *n* agility ← **lincah**

kelinci *n* rabbit; ~ *percobaan* guinea-pig; *sate* ~ rabbit satay

kelingking *n* little or baby finger

kelip: berkelip *v* to twinkle, flicker

kelipatan *n* multiple ← **lipat**

keliru *adj* wrong, mistaken; **kekeliruan** *n* mistake, error

kélok *n* bend, curve; ~ *empat puluh empat* forty-four bends (on the descent to Lake Maninjau)

kelola: mengelola *v* to manage, run; **pengelola** *n* manager; **pengelolaan** *n* management

kelom, klompen *n* clogs; *kelom geulis* clogs made near Tasikmalaya, West Java

kelompok *n* group; ~ *bermain* playgroup; ~ *kerja* working group; **berkelompok** *adj* in groups, group; **mengelompokkan** *v* to group

kelonggaran *n* facility, dispensation ← **longgar**

kelontong *barang* ~ odds and ends, small wares; *pedagang* ~ pedlar, hawker; *toko* ~ shop selling cheap goods

kelop → **klop**

kelopak ~ *mata* eyelid

keluar go out; be issued; *prep* out, outside; **keluaran** *n* issue, edition, version; **mengeluarkan** *v* to issue, send out, release, publish ← **ke luar**

keluarga *n* family; ~ *berencana (KB)* state family planning program; ~ *besar* extended family; *anggota* ~ family members; *kartu* ~ family ID card; *kepala* ~ head of the family; *tunjangan* ~ family allowance; **berkeluarga** *v* to have a family, be married

kelucuan *n* cuteness ← **lucu**

keluh sigh; ~ *kesah* complain; **keluhan** *n* complaint; **berkeluh, mengeluh** *v* to complain

kelupaan *n* something forgotten ← **lupa**

kelupas, mengelupas *v* to peel, come off (of a skin)

kelurahan *n* administrative unit, village ← **lurah**

keluwesan *n* attractiveness, style ← **luwes**

kemacetan *n* jam; ~ *lalu lintas* traffic jam ← **macet**

kémah *n* tent; **berkémah** *v* to camp, go camping; **perkémahan** *n* camping, camp; *tempat* ~ camping ground, campsite

kemahalan *adj* too expensive ← **mahal**

kemahiran *n* skill ← **mahir**

kemajuan *n* progress, advance ← **maju**

kemakmuran *n* prosperity ← **makmur**

kemaksiatan *n* immorality, vice ← **maksiat**

kemalaman *adv* too late (at night); after dark ← **malam**

kemalangan *n* bad luck, misfortune ← **malang**

kemalasan *n* laziness ← **malas**

kemalingan *v* to be robbed ← **maling**

kemaluan *n* genital, sex organ ← **malu**

kemampuan *n* ability, capability ← **mampu**

kemandulan *n* infertility ← **mandul**

kemangi *n* Indonesian mint

kemanisan *adj* too sweet ← **manis**

kemantapan *n* stability ← **mantap**

kemarahan *n* anger ← **marah**

kemarau *musim* ~ dry season

kemari here, in this direction; *kesana* ~ here and there

kemarin *adv* yesterday; the other day; last; ~ *dulu* the day before yesterday; *minggu* ~ last week

kemas *peti* ~ freight container; **kemasan** *n* packaging; **berkemas-kemas** *v* to tidy up, pack; **mengemaskan** *v* to package

kemasukan *adj* possessed; accidentally got in ← **masuk**

kemasyarakatan *adj* social ← **masyarakat**

kematangan *n* maturity ← **matang**

kematian *n* death, passing ← **mati**

kemauan *n* want, will, desire ← **mau**

kembali back, return; again; ~ *ke Sang Pencipta* pass away; *(terima kasih)* ~ you're welcome; *tinjau* ~ review; *uang* ~ change; **kembalian** *n* small change; **kembalinya** *n* the return; **mengembalikan** *v* to give or send back, return; **pengembalian** *n* return, act of returning

kemban *n* cloth wrapped around a woman's chest

kembang *n* flower; ~ *api* fireworks, sparkler; ~ *kol* cauliflower; ~ *sepatu* hibiscus; **berkembang** *v* to develop, expand; ~ *biak* to breed, grow; *negara* ~ developing nation; **mengembangkan** *v* to develop something; **pengembang** *n* developer; **perkembangan** *n* development

kembar *n* twin; ~ *tiga* triplets; *saudara* ~ twin; **kembaran** *adj* dressed alike

kembara → **embara**

kembaran *adj* twin, matching ← **kembar**

kembung, gembung *adj* filled with air, inflated; bloated; *perut* ~ bloated belly

kemegahan *n* glory, luxury ← **megah**

keméja *n* Western-style shirt (with collar)

kemelaratan *n* poverty ← **melarat**

kemelék-hurufan n literacy ← **melék**

kemenakan → **keponakan**

kemenangan n victory ← **menang**

kementerian n ministry, department, office ← **menteri**

kemenyan n incense

kemérah-mérahan adj reddish ← **mérah**

kemerdékaan n freedom, independence, liberty ← **merdéka**

kemerosotan n descent, deterioration ← **merosot**

kemesraan n intimacy ← **mesra**

keméwahan n luxury ← **méwah**

kemih kandung ~ bladder; saluran ~ urinary tract

kemilau shiny, sheen

kemiri n candle nut

kemiringan n slope ← **miring**

Kemis → **Kamis**

kemis, emis: mengemis v to beg; **pengemis** n beggar

kemiskinan n poverty ← **miskin**

kemitraan n partnership ← **mitra**

kemocéng, kemucing n feather duster

kemolékan n beauty ← **molék**

kemontokan n plumpness ← **montok**

kempés, kempis adj deflated, flat; hollow; ban ~ flat tire; **mengempiskan** v to deflate

kemudahan n ease, facility ← **mudah**

kemudi n rudder, steering wheel; **mengemudikan** v to drive, steer; ~ mobil to drive a car; **pengemudi** n driver

kemudian conj then; ~ hari in the future, later on

kemuka: mengemukakan v to put forward, advance, nominate; **terkemuka** adj prominent ← **ke muka**

kemuliaan n honor, glory; ~ Tuhan the glory of God ← **mulia**

kemunafikan n hypocrisy ← **munafik**

kemunduran n deterioration, decline ← **mundur**

kemungkinan n possibility ← **mungkin**

kemurahan n cheapness ← **murah**

kemuraman n gloom ← **muram**

kemurkaan n anger, fury ← **murka**

kemurnian n purity ← **murni**

kemut, emut, mengemut v to suck on, chew

kena touch; ~ denda be fined; **kenapa** coll why, how come; what did you say?; **berkenaan** ~ dengan in connection with, regarding; **mengenai** conj about, concerning

kenaikan n rise, raise; ~ gaji pay rise ← **naik**

kenakalan n naughtiness ← **nakal**

kenal v to know, be acquainted with; **kenalan** n acquaintance; **mengenal** v to know, be acquainted with, recognize; **mengenali** v to identify; **memperkenalkan** v to introduce; **perkenalan** n introduction;

terkenal *adj* well-known

kenamaan *adj* famous, well-known ← **nama**

kenang recall; **kenangan** *n* memories; **kenang-kenangan** *n* souvenir, keepsake; **mengenang** *v* to commemorate, remember

kenanga *n* kind of flower, ylang-ylang

kenang-kenangan *n* souvenir, keepsake ← **kenang**

kenapa *interrog, coll* why, how come; what did you say? ← **kena apa**

kenari *burung* ~ canary

kencan *n* date; ~ *buta* blind date; *teman* ~ date; **berkencan** *v* to go on a date

kencang tight, taut; **mengencangkan** *v* to tighten

kencing urine; urinate; ~ *manis* diabetes; *saluran* ~ urinary tract

kencur *beras* ~ traditional Javanese drink

kendala *n* obstacle, problem, hindrance

kendali *n* reins; *lepas* ~ out of control; *peluru* ~ *(rudal)* guided missile; **mengendalikan** *v* to control; **pengendalian** *n* control; ~ *mutu* quality control; **terkendali** *adj* controlled

kendang *n* small drum → **gendang**

kendara: kendaraan *n* vehicle; ~ *bermotor* motor vehicle; ~ *umum* public transport; **me-**

ngendarai *v* to ride or drive (a vehicle); **pengendara** *n* rider; driver

kendati *conj* although, however

kendi *n* earthen water flask

kendor, kendur *adj* slack, loose

kenduri *n* feast, celebration

kenegaraan *adj* state (affairs) ← **negara**

kenék, kernét *n* assistant on a bus or truck

kenékatan *n* determination, resolve, recklessness ← **nékat**

kenikmatan *n* pleasure, enjoyment ← **nikmat**

kening *n* forehead, brow; **mengerutkan** ~ to frown

kénsel → **kansel**

kental *adj* thick, sticky, congealed; *logat* ~ thick accent; *susu* ~ condensed milk; **kekentalan** *n* thickness, viscosity; **mengental** *v* to congeal, thicken

kentang *n* potato; *coll* french fries; ~ *goreng* hot potato chips, french fries

kentara *adj* clear, evident, visible

kentut *n* fart, break wind; *gas* ~ methane

kenyal *adj* elastic, rubbery; **kekenyalan** *n* elasticity

kenyamanan *n* comfort ← **nyaman**

kenyang *adj* full, not hungry; ~ *pengalaman* have plenty of experience

kenyataan *n* fact ← **nyata**

keonaran *n* commotion, disturbance, sensation ← **onar**

kéong *n* snail

Kep. *kepulauan* archipelago, chain of islands

kepada *prep* to (someone); ~ *yang terhormat (kpd yth)* to (on letters)

kepagian *adj* too early ← **pagi**

kepahitan *n* bitterness ← **pahit**

kepahlawanan *n* heroism ← **pahlawan**

kepailitan *n* bankruptcy ← **pailit**

kepak: mengepakkan ~ *sayap* to flutter wings

kepal fist; **kepalan** *n* fist; **mengepal** *v* to form a fist

kepala *n* head, chief; ~ *batu* obstinate; ~ *kantor* boss; ~ *susu* cream; *sakit* ~, ~ *pusing* headache; **berkepala** *v* to have a head; **mengepalai** *v* to be head of

kepandaian *n* ability, intelligence ← **pandai**

kepanduan *n* scouting, Scouts; *n, f* guiding, Guides ← **pandu**

képang plait, weave

kepanjangan *adj* too long ← **panjang**

kepapaan *n* destitution, poverty ← **papa**

keparat *ejac, vulg* damn

kepariwisataan *n* tourist industry ← **wisata, pariwisata**

kepasrahan *n* submission ← **pasrah**

kepastian *n* certainty ← **pasti**

kepedasan *adj* too hot or spicy ← **pedas**

kepedihan *n* stinging ← **pedih**

kepedulian *n* concern ← **peduli**

kepegawaian *adj* staff, personnel ← **pegawai**

kepekatan *n* thickness, viscosity ← **pekat**

kepelését *adj, coll* slipped, skidded ← **pelését, lését**

kepemilikan *n* ownership ← **milik**

kepemimpinan *n* leadership (qualities) ← **pimpin**

kepencét *adj, coll* accidentally pressed ← **pencét**

kepéndékan *n* abbreviation ← **péndék**

kepéngén, kepingin *v, coll* really want to ← **péngén**

kepentingan *n* importance, interest ← **penting**

kepépét *adj, sl* in a fix, trapped; no time, rushed ← **pépét**

keperawanan *n* virginity ← **perawan**

kepercayaan *n* belief, faith; *menurut* ~ *masing-masing* each according to his/her own religion ← **percaya**

kepergian *n* departure ← **pergi**

kepergok *adj, coll* caught in the act, caught red-handed ← **pergok**

keperluan *n* needs, requirements; ~ *hidup* necessities of life ← **perlu**

kepiawaian *n* skill, expertise ← **piawai**

kepik *n* small bug, pest

kepikiran *adj* considered, thought of, sprang to mind ← **pikir**

kepincut *adj, coll* enchanted, taken with; attracted or drawn to ← **pincut**

keping *n* piece (counter for flat objects); splinter; ~ *kayu* woodchip; *album itu sudah terjual satu juta* ~ the album has already sold one million copies

kepingin → **kepéngén**

kepintaran *n* cleverness ← **pintar**

kepiting *n* crab

keplését *adj, coll* slipped, tripped, fell ← **plését**

kepodang, kepudang *burung* ~ oriole

kepolosan *n* simplicity, straightforwardness, lack of pretension ← **polos**

kepompong *n* cocoon

keponakan, kemenakan *n* niece or nephew; cousin; ~ *laki-laki* nephew; ~ *perempuan* niece; ~ *satu buyut* second cousin

kepongahan *n* arrogance ← **pongah**

kepprés *n* Presidential Decree ← **keputusan Présidén**

kepraktisan *n* practicality ← **praktis**

kepramukaan *adj* scouting ← **pramuka**

keprésidénan *adj* presidential ← **présidén**

Kepri *Kepulauan Riau* Riau Archipelago, a province in Sumatra

kepribadian *n* personality ← **pribadi**

keprihatinan *n* concern ← **prihatin**

kepul, kepulan *n* wisp, puff; **berkepul, mengepul** *v* to

smoke, billow

kepulauan *n* archipelago, chain; **Kepulauan Solomon** *n* the Solomon Islands; *orang dari* ~ Solomon Islander ← **pulau**

kepunahan *n* extinction ← **punah**

kepung, mengepung *v* to surround, encircle, besiege; **kepungan** *n* encirclement, surrounded area

kepunyaan *n* possession, belonging ← **punya**

kepustakaan *n* bibliography, list of references; literature ← **pustaka**

keputihan *n* thrush, vaginal itching (white discharge) ← **putih**

keputusan *n* decision, decree ← **putus**

kera *n* ape

kerabat *n* relative, family; **kekerabatan** *n* kinship

keracunan *adj* poisoned; ~ *makanan* food poisoning ← **racun**

keraguan, keragu-raguan *n* doubt, uncertainty ← **ragu**

kerah *n* collar; ~ *Cina* Chinese-style collar

kerah: mengerahkan *v* to mobilize

kerahasiaan *n* secrecy ← **rahasia**

kerajaan *n* kingdom; ~ *Inggris* the United Kingdom ← **raja**

kerajinan *n* crafts; ~ *tangan* handicrafts ← **rajin**

kerak *n* crust; ~ *bumi* the Earth's crust; ~ *telor* Betawi snack

kerakusan *n* greed ← **rakus**

kerakyatan *adj* populist; democratic ← **rakyat**

keram cramp

keramahan *n* friendliness ← **ramah**

keramaian *n* noise, din; lively atmosphere ← **ramai**

keramas, berkeramas to wash your hair

keramat *adj* holy, sacred; *tempat* ~ place sacred to locals; **mengeramatkan** *v* to consider or make sacred

keramik ceramic, earthenware

keran *n* tap, faucet; *buka* ~ turn on the tap

keranda *n* structure for carrying a coffin

kerang *n* shell; mollusc; *kulit* ~ seashell

kerangka *n* skeleton, framework

keranjang *n* basket; ~ *sampah* rubbish or garbage bin, trash can; *mata* ~ have a wandering eye

keranjingan *adj* addicted to, fanatic ← **ranjing**

kerap *adv* often; ~ *kali* often, frequently

keras *adj* hard, strong; severe, strict, violent; loud; ~ *kepala* stubborn; *minuman* ~ liquor, alcohol; *membaca dengan suara* ~ to read out loud; **bersikeras** *v* to maintain, stick to, be obstinate; **kekerasan** *n* violence; ~ *dalam rumah tangga (KDRT)*, ~ *domestik* domestic violence; ~ *terhadap perempuan* violence against women; **mengeras** *v* to get

louder, harder; **mengeraskan** *v* to make something harder, louder; **pengeras** ~ *suara* loudspeaker; **pengerasan** *n* hardening

kerasan *coll* settled, comfortable, feel at home ← **rasa**

kerasukan *adj* possessed ← **rasuk**

keraton, kraton *n* Javanese palace; *lingkungan* ~ palace circles

kerawang, karawang *n* filigree embroidery, esp from Menado

kerbau, kebo *n* buffalo

kerdil *n* dwarf

kérék *n* pulley; **mengérék** *v* to hoist, pull; ~ *bendera* to raise the flag

kerén *adj, coll* great, cool; trendy

kerendahan *n* lowness; ~ *hati* humility ← **rendah**

kerenggangan *n* rift, gulf, distance ← **renggang**

kerenyahan *n* crispness, crispiness ← **renyah**

keresahan *n* restlessness, nervous energy ← **resah**

keresak, keresek rustle, sound of rustling leaves

keréta *n* train; carriage; ~ *api* train; ~ *ekspres* express train; *gerbong* ~ (train) carriage, car; *naik* ~ go by train; ~ *kencana* royal (horse-drawn) carriage

keretakan *n* crack, fissure ← **retak**

keributan *n* disturbance; loud noise ← **ribut**

kericuhan *n* chaos ← **ricuh**

kerikil *n* gravel, pebble; small but annoying problem; *ada ~ di sepatu* there's a stone in my shoe

kerinduan *n* longing, craving ← **rindu**

kering *adj* dry; **kekeringan** *n* dryness, aridity; **mengering** *v* to become dry; **mengeringkan** *v* to dry something; *~ rambut* to dry your hair; **pengering** *~ rambut* hair dryer

keringat *n* sweat, perspiration; *~ dingin* cold sweat; *mandi ~* soaked in sweat; **keringatan** *adj* sweaty, sweating; **berkeringat** *v* to sweat

keripik, kripik *n* small chip or crisp; *~ kentang* potato chips; *~ singkong* cassava chips

keriput *n* wrinkle, line; **keriputan, berkeriput** *adj* wrinkly, lined

keris, kris *n* traditional dagger, creese; *pembuat ~* creese-maker

kerisauan *n* worry, anxiety ← **risau**

keriting curl, curly; clubs (in cards); **mengeriting** *~ rambut* to perm your hair

kerja work; job, occupation; *~ bakti* community work; *~ sama* co-operation; *kelompok ~ (pokja)* working group; *lapangan ~* employment opportunity; *mencari ~* to look for work; **kerjaan** *n* work, job, things to do; **kinerja** *n* performance; **bekerja** *v* to work; *~ sama* to co-operate, work together; **mengerjakan** *v* to do, carry out; *~ PR* to do your homework; **kerjain** *v, sl* to trick, take for a ride; **dikerjain** *v, sl* to be tricked, taken for a ride; **pekerja** *n* worker, laborer; **pekerjaan** *n* work, profession

kernét, kenék *n* assistant acting as conductor on a bus

kernyit: mengernyit *~ dahi, ~ kening* to frown

kerobohan *n* collapse ← **roboh**

kerok traditional treatment for minor illnesses by rubbing the back with a coin; *biang ~* agitator; **kerokan** *v* to be massaged in this way; **mengerok** *v* to rub someone's back with a coin

keroncong, kroncong *n* traditional songs and music of Portuguese origin

kerongkongan *n* throat

kerontokan *n* shedding; *~ rambut* hair loss ← **rontok**

keropos *adj* eroded, eaten away; *~ tulang* osteoporosis; **mengeropos** *v* to be eaten away, eroded; **pengeroposan** *n* (process of) erosion

keroyok, mengeroyok *v* to beat savagely in a mob; *dikeroyok massa* beaten up by a mob

kertas *n* paper; *~ kado* wrapping paper; *~ pasir* sandpaper; *~ tebal* cardboard; *uang ~* banknotes

keruan, karuan *tidak ~* very badly, unthinkably

kerucut, cerucut *n* cone

kerudung, kudungan *n, Isl* veil; **berkerudung** *adj* veiled

kerugian *n* loss; damage ← **rugi**

keruh *adj* turbid, cloudy

keruk dredge; *kapal* ~ dredger; **mengeruk** *v* to dredge, scrape out

kerumun: berkerumun *v* to swarm, crowd; **mengerumuni** *v* to mob, surround, crowd around someone

kerupuk, krupuk *n* large cracker, crisp, chip; ~ *ikan* fish-flavored cracker; ~ *kulit* cracker made from buffalo hide; ~ *udang* prawn cracker

kerusakan *n* damage ← **rusak**

kerusuhan *n* riot, disturbance ← **rusuh**

kerut *n* wrinkle; **berkerut** *v* to frown; **mengerut** *v* to shrink, shrivel, contract; **mengerutkan** ~ *kening* to frown

keruwetan *n* complexity ← **ruwet**

kesabaran *n* patience; *batas* ~ limit of your patience ← **sabar**

kesadaran *n* consciousness, awareness ← **sadar**

kesahajaan *n* simplicity ← **sahaja**

kesakitan *adj* in pain ← **sakit**

kesakralan *n* holy or sacred state ← **sakral**

kesaksian *n* evidence, testimony; *memberi* ~ to give evidence, bear witness; *surat* ~ testimonial, recommendation ← **saksi**

kesaktian *n* magic power ← **sakti**

kesal *adj* **kesel** *coll* annoyed, in a bad mood; **kekesalan** *n* annoyance, bad mood

kesalahan *n* mistake ← **salah**

kesampaian *adj* achieved, reached, realized ← **sampai**

kesamping: mengesamping-kan *v* to put to one side ← **ke samping**

kesan *n* impression; *memberi* ~ to give an impression; **berkesan, mengesankan** *adj* impressive; **terkesan** *adj* impressed; seemed

kesandung *adj, coll* to stumble on, trip (up) on ← **sandung**

kesanggupan *n* ability ← **sanggup**

kesasar *coll* to lose your way, (get) lost ← **sasar**

kesatria → **ksatria**

kesatu *adj, sl* first; **kesatuan** *n* unity; ~ *dan persatuan* national unity and integration ← **satu**

kesayangan *anak* ~ favorite, pe ← **sayang**

kesebelasan *n* team of eleven, soccer team ← **belas**

kesederhanaan *n* simplicity, modesty ← **sederhana**

kesediaan *n* readiness, willingness ← **sedia**

kesedihan *n* sadness, sorrow ← **sedih**

keseganan *n* reluctance, unwillingness ← **segan**

keséhatan *n* health; *dinas* ~ health service ← **séhat**

keseimbangan *n* balance ← **imbang**

kesejahteraan *n* welfare ← **sejahtera**

kesejukan *n* coolness ← **sejuk**

keseksamaan *n* thoroughness,

care ← **seksama**

kesel *coll* **kesal** *adj* annoyed, cheesed off

keselamatan *n* safety; salvation; *Bala ~* Salvation Army ← **selamat**

keselarasan *n* harmony ← **laras**

keselek, keselak *adj* choking (due to food or drink) ← **selak**

keseléo sprain; sprained; *kaki ~* sprained foot

keseluruhan *secara ~* totally, completely ← **seluruh**

kesemak, kesemek *n buah ~* persimmon, soft fruit with sweet orange flesh

kesempatan *n* opportunity; *~ dalam kesempitan* take an opportunity in difficult circumstances ← **sempat**

kesempitan *n* narrowness ← **sempit**

kesempurnaan *n* perfection ← **sempurna**

kesemrawutan *n* chaos ← **semrawut**

kesemutan *v* to have pins and needles ← **semut**

kesenangan *n* amusement, hobby ← **senang**

kesendirian *n* solitude ← **diri**

kesengajaan *n* deliberate or intentional act ← **sengaja**

kesengsaraan *n* torture, misery, suffering ← **sengsara**

kesengsem *adj, coll* engrossed in, absorbed with ← **sengsem**

kesenian *n* art (form); *~ tradisional* traditional art form ← **seni**

kesenjangan *n* gap, divide; *~ sosial* social imbalance ← **senjang**

kesenyapan *n* silence ← **senyap**

kesepakatan *n* agreement ← **pakat**

kesepian *n* loneliness, solitude ← **sepi**

keserakahan *n* greed, avarice ← **serakah**

keserasian *n* compatibility, suitability ← **rasi**

keseringan *n* frequency; *adv* too often ← **sering**

kesériusan *n* solemnity, seriousness ← **sérius**

kését *n* door mat

kesetiaan *n* allegiance, faithfulness ← **setia**

kesetiakawanan *n* solidarity ← **setia kawan**

kesetrum *v, coll* to receive an electric shock ← **setrum**

kesiagaan *n* readiness, preparedness ← **siaga**

kesiangan *adj* late, too late in the day ← **siang**

kesiapan *n* readiness, willingness ← **siap**

kesibukan *n* activity, fuss, bustle, business ← **sibuk**

kesigapan *n* efficiency, readiness ← **sigap**

kesilapan *n* mistake, error ← **silap**

kesima: *terkesima adj* amazed, astonished

kesimpulan *n* conclusion ← **simpul**

kesinambungan *n* continuity ←
sambung

kesohor *adj, coll* famous ←
sohor

kesoléhan *n* piety ← **soléh**

kesopanan *n* manners, politeness
← **sopan**

kesopan-santunan *n* manners,
etiquette ← **sopan santun**

kesoréan *adv* too late ← **soré**

kesuburan *n* fertility ← **subur**

kesucian *n* purity; virginity ←
suci

kesudahan *tidak ber~* endless,
infinite ← **sudah**

kesukaan *n* hobby; enjoyment
← **suka**

kesukaran *n* difficulty ← **sukar**

kesukuan *adj* ethnic, tribal ←
suku

kesulitan *n* difficulty, trouble
← **sulit**

kesuma → **kusuma**

kesumat *dendam ~* revenge

kesungguhan *n* earnestness,
sincerity, truth ← **sungguh**

kesunyian *n* quiet, still ← **sunyi**

kesurupan *v* to be possessed by
a spirit or ghost ← **surup**

kesusahan *n* trouble, difficulty
← **susah**

kesusasteraan, kesusastraan
n literature ← **sastra**

kesusilaan *n* modesty, decency,
ethics ← **susila**

ketabahan *n* strength of character
← **tabah**

ketabrak *adj, coll* to be hit; *~
mobil* hit by a car ← **tabrak**

ketagihan *adj* addicted to ← **tagih**

ketahanan *n* endurance ← **tahan**

ketahuan to be found out ←
tahu

ketajaman *n* sharpness ← **tajam**

ketakutan *adj* frightened, terrified, scared ← **takut**

ketamakan *n* greed ← **tamak**

ketampanan *n* good looks ←
tampan

ketan *n* sticky rice; *~ bakar*
grilled slabs of sticky rice;
bubur ~ hitam black sticky rice
porridge

ketangkap *adj, coll* to be
caught, arrested ← **tangkap**

ketangkasan *n* agility, dexterity;
menguji ~ to test your skill ←
tangkas

ketapél *n* catapult

ketat *adj* tight, strict; *baju ~*
tight clothes; *keamanan ~* high
security

ketawa *v, coll* to laugh; **mengetawakan** *v* to laugh at → **tawa**

ketebalan *n* thickness ← **tebal**

ketegangan *n* tension ← **tegang**

ketegaran *n* determination ←
tegar

ketegasan *n* resolve, determination ← **tegas**

kéték → **kétiak**

ketekunan *n* diligence, dedication ← **tekun**

kétél *n* boiler, kettle

ketéla *n* yam

ketelantaran *n* neglect ←
telantar

ketelatan *n* lateness ← **telat**

ketelaténan *n* patience, perseverance ← **telatén**

keteledoran *n* carelessness ← **teledor**

ketelitian *n* accuracy, care ← **teliti**

ketemu *v, coll* to meet ← **temu**

ketenangan *n* calm, peace ← **tenang**

ketenaran *n* popularity ← **tenar**

ketenteraman *n* peace ← **tenteram**

ketentuan *n* condition, stipulation ← **tentu**

ketepatan *n* precision, accuracy ← **tepat**

keterangan *n* explanation ← **terang**

keterbatasan *n* limitation ← **batas**

keterikatan *n* bind, bond, commitment ← **ikat, terikat**

keterlaluan *n* excess, too much ← **lalu**

keterlambatan *n* delay; *mengalami* ~ to be delayed ← **lambat**

keterlibatan *n* involvement, association ← **libat**

keterpaduan *n* integration ← **padu**

keterpaksaan *n* compulsion ← **paksa**

keterpurukan *n* depression, abyss ← **puruk**

ketertarikan *n* interest, attraction ← **tarik**

ketertiban *n* discipline, order; ~ *lalu lintas* traffic discipline, highway code; *Dinas Ketenteraman dan ~ (Tramtib)* city public order agency ← **tertib**

ketetapan *n* regulation; stipulation ← **tetap**

ketiadaan *n* absence, lack ← **tiada, tidak ada**

ketiak, keték *n* armpit

ketidakadaan *n* absence, lack of ← **tidak ada**

ketiduran *v* to fall asleep ← **tidur**

ketiga *adj* the third; ~*nya* all three ← **tiga**

ketik *v* type; *juru* ~ typist; *mesin* ~ typewriter; **ketikan** *n* typing; **mengetik** *v* to type

ketika *conj* when (in past); ~ *itu* at that time

ketilang → **kutilang**

ketimbang *conj, coll* than; instead of ← **timbang**

ketimpangan *n* inequality, imbalance; ~ *sosial* social inequality ← **timpang**

ketimun → **mentimun**

ketimuran *adj* Eastern, Oriental ← **timur**

ketinggalan *adj* left behind; ~ *kereta api* miss the train ← **tinggal**

ketinggian *n* altitude, height ← **tinggi**

ketinting *n* water taxi used on the rivers of Kalimantan

ketok *v* to knock; panel-beat; ~ *magic* 'magic' panel-beating

ketololan *n* stupidity ← **tolol**

ketombé *n* dandruff; *sampo anti* ~ anti-dandruff shampoo; **ketombéan** *v, coll* to have dandruff; **berketombé** *rambut* ~ dry scalp, dandruff

ketoprak *n* Betawi dish of vegetables in peanut sauce; folk play

ketrampilan *n* skill ← **trampil**

kéts *sepatu* ~ sports shoes, running shoes, sneakers

ketua *n* chief, chair, president, elder; ~ *RT* neighborhood leader; *wakil* ~ deputy chair; **mengetuai** *v* to preside over

ketuban *air* ~ amniotic fluid; *air* ~ *sudah pecah* the waters have broken

ketuhanan *n* divinity, deity; belief in God ← **tuhan**

ketuk, ketok knock; **mengetuk** *v* to knock; ~ *hati* to prick your conscience; ~ *pintu* knock on the door

ketularan *adj* infected, caught something ← **tular**

ketulusan ~ *hati* sincerity ← **tulus**

ketumbar *n* (ground) coriander; *daun* ~ (fresh) coriander

ketupat *n* coconut fronds woven into a diamond-shape for cooking rice, traditionally used at Idul Fitri; decorations in this shape

keturunan *n* descendant; ~ *WNI* Indonesian of Chinese descent ← **turun**

ketus *adj* sharp (of words)

keuangan *n* finance; *Menteri* ~ Minister of Finance, Chancellor of the Exchequer (UK) ← **uang**

keulungan *n* superiority ← **ulung**

keunggulan *n* superiority ← **unggul**

keunikan *n* unique thing, uniqueness ← **unik**

keuntungan *n* advantage, profit ← **untung**

keuskupan *n* diocese ← **uskup**

kewajaran *n* sense, logic ← **wajar**

kewajiban *n* obligation, duty ← **wajib**

kewalahan *adj* unable to cope, overcome

kewarasan *n* sanity, mental health ← **waras**

kewarganegaraan *n* citizenship ← **warga negara**

kewaspadaan *n* caution ← **waspada**

kewenangan *n* authority ← **wenang**

keyakinan *n* belief, conviction, faith ← **yakin**

kg kilogram

khalayak *n* public

khas *adj* special, specific; ~ *Ambon* Ambonese; *ciri* ~ characteristic; **kekhasan** *n* special feature

khasiat *n* benefit, special effect; **berkhasiat** *adj* beneficial, therapeutic

khatam finish reading or reciting the Koran

khatulistiwa, katulistiwa *n* the Equator

khawatir, kuatir *v* to worry, fear; *jangan* ~ don't worry; **kekuatiran** *n* worry, fear; **menguatirkan** *v* to worry about something

khayal *n* imagination; **khayalan** *n* dream, hallucination; **berkhayal** *v* to dream, imagine

khianat *n* treachery, betrayal;

disloyalty; **berkhianat** *v* to betray; **mengkhianati** *v* to betray someone; **pengkhianat** *n* traitor

khidmat *n* respect; **dengan ~** respectfully, solemnly

khilaf *v* to be wrong, make a mistake

khitan *n* circumcision; **khitanan** *n* feast held in honor of a circumcision; **mengkhitan(kan)** *v* to circumcise

khotbah *v* sermon; **pengkhotbah** *v* preacher

khusus *adj* special, particular; **~nya** in particular, especially; **mengkhususkan** *v* to give special treatment

khusyuk *adj* devout, religious, pious

ki, kiai, kyai *n, pron, Isl* religious leader; **~ Haji** title for leader who has completed the pilgrimage to Mecca

kiamat *hari* ~ day of judgment

kian *adv* such; increasingly, more and more; **sekian** *adv* so much, this much; **~ banyak** so many, so much; **~ dulu** that's all for now (used in speeches and letters)

kias *n* comparison, analogy, allusion; **kiasan** *n* figure of speech, metaphor

kiat *n* means, way, method

kibar: berkibar(-kibar) *v* to wave, flutter; **mengibarkan** *v* to wave, unfurl; **~ bendera** to fly a flag

kibas: mengibaskan *v* to wag (a tail)

kiblat, qiblat *n* direction of Mecca; **berkiblat** *v* to be oriented toward; **~ pada Amerika** to look to America

kibor *n* keyboard; **pemain ~** keyboardist

kibul *n, coll* bottom, bum; **mengibuli** *v* to fool someone

kidal *adj* left-handed

kidung *n* song, hymn

kijang *n* barking deer, kind of antelope; **Kijang** *n* large car produced by Toyota

kikir *adj* stingy, tight, miserly

kikis *adj* scraped; **kikisan** *n* scrapings, erosion; **mengikis** *v* to erode, eat away; **terkikis** *adj* eaten away, eroded

kikuk *adj* clumsy, awkward

kilang *n* refinery, mill; **~ minyak** oil refinery; **perkilangan** *n* refinery

kilap shine; **berkilap, mengkilap** *v* to shine, gleam

kilas ~ balik flashback; **sekilas** *n* flash, glance

kilat *n* lightning; **kursus ~** crash course; **penangkal ~** lightning rod; **berkilat** *v* to shine, sparkle

kilau: berkilau *adj* glittering, sparkling

kilir twist; **terkilir** *adj* twisted, sprained

kilo *n* kilo, kilogram; kilometer; **se~ pisang** a kilo of bananas; **60 ~ per jam** 60 kilometers per hour; **kiloan** *adv* by the kilogram, in kilograms

kimia *n* chemistry; **bahan ~** chemical; **ilmu ~** chemistry;

kimiawi *adj* chemical

kimono *n* kimono; dressing gown

KIM(S) *abbrev Kartu Izin Menetap [Sementara]* (temporary) residence permit for foreigners

kina *n* quinine; *pohon ~* cinchona tree

kincir *n* wheel; *~ air* waterwheel; *~ angin* windmill; *negeri ~ angin* the Netherlands

kinerja *n* performance ← **kerja**

kini *adv* now, nowadays (often when comparing with past); **terkini** *adj* the latest

kios *n* stall, kiosk; **kiostél, kiospon** *n* small phone agency, phone kiosk ← **kios télépon**

kipas *n* fan; *~ angin, ~ listrik* (electric) fan; **mengipasi** *v* to fan someone or something

kiper *n* (goal)keeper

kiprah *n* pace, progress; **berkiprah** *v* to move, dance, be active in

kir *n* inspection (for vehicles)

kira *v* to think, guess, estimate; **kira-kira** *adv* approximately, around, about; **kiranya** *adv* hopefully; **mengira** *v* to assume, think; **memperkirakan** *v* to estimate, calculate; **perkiraan** *n* estimate, guess; **sekiranya** *adv* if perhaps; **terkira** *tak ~* unsuspected, not thought of

kiri *adj* left; *~ kanan* left and right; *~ kapal* port, portside; *belok ~* turn left; *sayap ~* left-wing; *di sebelah ~* on the left

kirim *n* send; *~ salam* to send your best wishes; **kiriman** *n* parcel; **mengirim** *v* to send; **pengirim** *n* sender; **pengiriman** *n* dispatch, forwarding; *~ barang* goods dispatch; **terkirim** *adj* sent; *pesan ~* message sent

Kirgistan *n* Kyrgyzstan; *bahasa ~, orang ~* Kyrgyz

kisah *n* tale, story; *~ sejati* true story; **berkisah** *v* to tell a story; **mengisahkan** *v* to tell the story of

kisar: kisaran *n* rotation, revolution; **berkisar** *v* to revolve, rotate, turn

kismis *n* sultana, currant; *roti ~* sultana bread

kista *n* cyst

kita *pron* we, us, our (inclusive); *~ punya* our

kitab *n* holy book; *~ kuning* book of the traditions of the Prophet; *~ suci* holy book, the Koran

KITAP *abbrev Kartu Izin Tinggal Tetap* permanent residence permit for foreigners

kitar: sekitar *adv* around; near; *prep* around; **sekitarnya** *di ~* around (a place); *dan ~* and environs

KITAS *abbrev Kartu Izin Tinggal Sementara* temporary residence permit for foreigners

kiu *n* (billiards) cue

KK *abbrev kepala keluarga* head of family, household

KKN *abbrev korupsi, kolusi, nepotisme* corruption (collusion and nepotism)

KKN *abbrev kuliah kerja nyata*

practical work experience for graduating university students

klakson *n* horn; **diklakson** *v* to be tooted at

klarinét *n* clarinet

klasik *adj* classic, classical; *lagu* ~ classical music

klénténg, kelénténg *n* Chinese or Confucian temple, pagoda

klép, kelép *n* valve, catch

klién *n* client

klinik *n* clinic

kliping *n* news clipping

kliring: dikliring *v* to be cleared (in a bank)

klise *n* negatives

klisé *n* cliché

klop, kelop *adj* suitable, comfortable

klosét *n* cistern (of toilet)

kloter *n* departure group for the pilgrimage to Mecca ← **kelompok terbang**

klub *n* (sports) club; ~ *tenis* tennis club

KM *abbrev Kapal Motor* ship

km *kamar* room (in a hotel); kilometer

knalpot *n* exhaust pipe, muffler

KNIL *abbrev Koninklijk Nederlandsch-Indisch Leger* Royal Dutch-Indies Army, in colonial times

koalisi *n* coalition; **berkoalisi** *v* to be in a coalition

kobar: kobaran ~ *api* flame; **berkobar** *v* to blaze, burn

koboi *n* cowboy

kocék *n, sl* pocket (in clothes)

kocok *mie* ~ kind of noodles;

mengocok *v* to shake, shuffle; ~ *dadu* to roll the dice; ~ *kartu* to shuffle cards

Kodam *n* Regional Military Komando ← **Komando Daérah Militér**

kode *n* code; ~ *pos* postcode

kodok *n* frog; *gaya* ~ frogkick; *mobil* ~ Volkswagen VW, Beetle

kodrat *n* nature; ~ *wanita* female nature

Kodya *n* municipality, city ← **kotamadya**

koi *ikan* ~ Japanese carp

koin *n* coin

kok you know (emphasizing contrary argument); *tidak apa-apa* ~ really, it's OK; *interrog* how come, why; ~ *sakit?* How come you're sick?

koki *n* cook

kokoh, kukuh *adj* strong, robust

kokok *n* crowing; **berkokok** *v* to crow; *ayam* ~ rooster's crow

kokpit *n* cockpit

Kol. *kolonel* colonel

kol *n* cabbage; *kembang* ~ cauliflower

kolaborasi *n* collaboration; **berkolaborasi** *v* to collaborate, work together; **kolaborator** *n* collaborator

kolak *n* sweet fruit stew; ~ *pisang* banana *kolak*

kolam *n* pond; ~ *ikan* fish pond; ~ *renang* swimming pool

kolang-kaléng, kolang-kaling *n* sugar-palm fruit used in desserts and *kolak*

koléga *n* colleague

koléksi n collection

koléra n cholera

koli n package; counter for baggage; *Rp 3.000 per* ~ Rp. 3 000 per piece

kolintang n large wooden xylophone from Minahasa

Kolombia n Colombia; *orang* ~ Colombian

kolonél n, pron colonel; *letnan-~ (letkol)* lieutenant-colonel

kolong n space under a large object; ~ *meja* under the table; ~ *tempat tidur* under the bed; *anak* ~ army kid, child of a soldier

kolonial adj colonial; **kolonisasi** n colonization → **jajah**

kolor n drawstring shorts; *celana* ~ (boxer) shorts

kolot adj old-fashioned, out of date; conservative; *kaum* ~ conservatives

kolusi n collusion; *korupsi, ~ dan nepotisme (KKN)* corruption

koma n comma; *titik* ~ semicolon; n coma

komandan n commander

komando n command; ~ *Strategis Angkatan Darat (Kostrad)* Army Strategic Command

kombinasi n combination

Komdak abbrev *Komando Daerah Kepolisian* Regional Military Command, large police complex in south Jakarta

komédi n comedy

koméntar n comment; **berkoméntar** v to (make a) comment; **mengoméntari** v to comment on; **koméntator** n (sports) commentator

komidi ~ *putar* merry-go-round

komik *buku* ~ comic (book); **komikus** n comic book author or artist

komisaris n commissioner; ~ *polisi* superintendent of police; *dewan* ~ commission

komisi n committee, commission; ~ *Pemilihan Umum (KPU)* Electoral Commission

komité n committee → **panitia**

kompak adj close-knit, solid; **kekompakan** n solidarity

kompas n compass → **pedoman**

kompeténsi n competence, competency; *kurikulum berdasarkan* ~ competency-based curriculum

komplék, kompléks, kompléx n housing complex, compound

komplét, komplit adj complete; *nasi* ~ rice with various side-dishes

komplot: komplotan n plot against

komponis n composer

kompor n stove, cooker; ~ *gas* gas cooker

komprés n compress, pack; ~ *dingin* ice pack

kompromi n compromise; **berkompromi** v to compromise, reach a compromise

komputer n computer; **komputerisasi** n computerization

komunis adj n communist; *Partai* ~ *Indonesia (PKI)* Indonesian Communist Party;

komunisme *n* communism

konci → **kunci**

kondang *adj* famous, well-known

kondangan *v* be invited to an event

kondé *n, f* small bun worn with national costume; *tusuk ~* hair pin

kondéktur *n* conductor, guard (on a train or city bus)

kondisi *n* condition; *~ cuaca* weather conditions → **keadaan**

kondom *n* condom

kondusif *adj* conducive, allowing

konéksi *n* connections, contacts (at an institution)

konferénsi, konperénsi *n* conference; *~ Asia-Afrika* the Asian-African conference

konfrontasi *n* confrontation; Indonesian aggression towards Malaysia in the 1960s

Kong Hu Cu Confucius, Confucian; *agama ~* Confucianism

kongkol: sekongkol, berse-kongkol *v* to plot, work against; **persekongkolan** *n* plot, intrigue

konglomerat *n* wealthy financier

Kongo *n* (the) Congo; *Republik ~* Congo; *Republik Demokratik ~* Democratic Republic of the Congo (formerly Zaire); *orang ~* Congolese

kongrés *n* congress, convention

kongsi *n* commercial partnership

KONI *abbrev Komite Olahraga Nasional Indonesia* Indonesian National Sports Commission

konon it is said, allegedly

konperénsi → **konferénsi**

konsékuén *adj* consistent, logical

konséling *n* counselling; **kon-sélor** *n* counsellor

konsén, konséntrasi *adj* focused, concentrating

konsép *n* concept, draft

konsér *n* concert; *menonton ~* to go to a concert

konsési *n* concession → **hak guna**

konstruksi *n* construction, building → **bangunan**

konsul *n* consul; **konsulat** *n* consulate; *~ jenderal (konjen)* consulate-general

konsultan *n* adviser, consultant

konsumén *n* consumer

kontak contact; *stop ~* power point; **mengontak** *v* to contact someone → **hubung**

kontan *uang ~* cash

kontés *n* contest; *~ kecantikan, ~ mis-misan coll* beauty pageant

kontra *adj* against, opposing, anti

kontrak *n* contract; *~ kerja* employment contract; **kontrak-an** rented (house); **me-ngontrakkan** *v* to lease or rent out a house; **dikontrakkan** *adj* for rent, lease

kontrasépsi *alat ~* form of contraception, contraceptive device

kontrol *n* control; *lepas ~* out of control; **kontrolir** *n* supervisor, controller → **kendali**

konyol *adj* silly, foolish

konyong: sekonyong-konyong *adv* as if

kop *n* head; *~ surat* letterhead

Kopaja *n* medium-sized green and white bus in Jakarta ← **Kopérasi Angkutan Jakarta**

koper, kopor *n* suitcase, baggage

koperasi *n* co-operative, co-op

kopi *n* coffee; ~ *pahit* black coffee without sugar; ~ *susu* white or milk coffee; ~ *tubruk* ground coffee; **ngopi** *sl* to drink or have a coffee

kopi *n* copy; ~ *darat* meet face-to-face → **fotokopi**

kopiah *n, Isl* flat-topped cap, worn to the mosque; national headwear for men → **péci**

kopyor *n* very soft coconut flesh; *es* ~ sweet drink made from this coconut

koran *n* newspaper; *loper* ~ paper boy

korban *n* victim; ~ *jiwa* fatality; ~ *luka* injured; **berkorban** *v* to make sacrifices, do without; **mengorbankan** *v* to sacrifice; **pengorbanan** *n* (act of) sacrifice

Koréa *n* Korea; ~ *Selatan (Korsel)* South Korea; ~ *Utara* North Korea; *bahasa* ~, *orang* ~ Korean

korék ~ *api* matches; ~ *kuping* cotton bud; **mengorék** *v* to scrape, scratch

koréksi *n* correction; **mengoréksi** *v* to correct

koréspondén *n* correspondent; **koréspondénsi** *n* correspondence, letter-writing

korma, kurma *n* date; *pohon* ~ date palm

kornét, kornéd *n* (tinned) corned beef

Korsél *n* South Korea ← **Koréa Selatan**

korsi → **kursi**

kortsléting, korsléting *n* short-circuit

korup *adj* corrupt; **korupsi** *n* corruption; *adj* corrupt; ~ *kolusi dan nepotisme (KKN)* corruption; **mengorupsi** *v* to be corrupt; to corrupt; **koruptor** *n* corrupt person

Korut *n* North Korea ← **Koréa Utara**

kos board, lodging; ~ *putri* female boarding-house; *anak* ~ boarder; *terima* ~ boarder wanted; *uang* ~ board; **kos-kosan** *n* boarding-houses, rooms for board

kosa → **perkosa**

kosa ~ *kata* vocabulary

kosén → **kusén**

kos-kosan *n* boarding-houses, rooms for board ← **kos**

kosong *adj* empty, blank; hollow; zero; ~ *melompong* completely empty; *mata* ~ unseeing; *skornya dua* ~ it's two nil; **kekosongan** *n* emptiness; **mengosongkan** *v* to empty

Kostrad *n* Army Regional Strategic Command ← **Komando Stratégis Angkatan Darat**

kota *n* town, city; ~ *Hujan* Bogor, the Rainy City; ~ *Kembang* Bandung the Flower City; ~ *Pahlawan* Surabaya, the City of Heroes; *angkutan* ~ city transport; *balai* ~ town hall, city hall; *ibu* ~ capital (city); *wali* ~ mayor; **perkotaan** *n* metropolitan area; **kotamadya** *n* municipality

kotak *n* box; square; ~ *suara* ballot box; ~ *surat* letter box; *nasi* ~ box meal of rice and side-dishes; **kotak-kotak** *adj* check; *baju* ~ check shirt; **mengotak-ngotakkan** *v* to categorize, box, put in boxes

kotamadya *n* municipality ← **kota**

kotéka *n* penis sheath, worn in Papua; **berkotéka** *adj* wearing a penis sheath

Kotip, Kotif *n* administrative city, municipality ← **kota administratif**

kotor *adj* dirty, filthy; gross; *gaji* ~ gross salary; *penyakit* ~ venereal disease; *pikiran* ~ dirty thought, dirty mind; **kotoran** *n* excrement; dirt; **mengotori** *v* to (make) dirty, defile

kotrék *n* corkscrew

koyak *adj* torn; **terkoyak** *adj* torn

Kp. *kampung* village; densely-inhabited area in city

kpd *abbrev* *kepada* to (a person)

kran → **keran**

kraton, keraton *n* Javanese palace; *lingkungan* ~ palace circles

krédit *n* credit; ~ *rumah* home loan; *kartu* ~ credit card

kréték *rokok* ~ clove cigarette

kribo *rambut* ~ Afro

kriminal *adj* criminal; **kriminolog** *n* criminologist → **jahat**

kring *adj* active (of telephones); sound of telephone ringing

kripik, keripik *n* small chip or crisp; ~ *kentang* potato chips, ~ *singkong* cassava chips

krisis *n* crisis; ~ *monetér* *(krismon)* *n* financial crisis of 1997-8

kristal crystal

Kristen *adj* Christian, Protestant; *agama* ~ Christianity, Protestant church; *gereja* ~ Protestant church; *Gereja* ~ *Indonesia* Indonesian Protestant Church; *orang* ~ Christian, Protestant church; **mengkristenkan** *v* to convert someone to Christianity, Christianize; **kristenisasi** *n* Christianization

Kristus *Yesus* ~ Jesus Christ

Kroasia *n* Croatia; *bahasa* ~, *orang* ~ Croat

kroncong → **keroncong**

krupuk → **kerupuk**

ksatria, kesatria *n* knight, warrior; *adj* chivalrous; *kaum* ~ warrior class

KTP *abbrev* *Kartu Tanda Penduduk* national identity card

KTT *abbrev* *Konferensi Tingkat Tinggi* (international) high-level conference

ku, -ku *pron* I, my, mine; *akan* ~*cari* I'll look for it; *rumah*~ my home

KUA *abbrev, Isl* *Kantor Urusan Agama* Religious Affairs Office

kuaci *n* (sunflower, watermelon, pumpkin etc) seed

kuadrat *n* square

kuah *n* soup, sauce, gravy (accompanying a food); **berkuah** *adj* with a soup or sauce

kuak: terkuak *adj* to part, open; be revealed, exposed

kuala *n* mouth, confluence; **berkuala** *v* to have a mouth or confluence

kualat *adj* cursed; disastrous

kuali *n* wok, cooking pot

kualitas, kwalitas *n* quality; **berkualitas** *adj* quality → **mutu**

kuantitas, kwantitas *n* quantity; **kuantitatif** *adj* quantitative → **banyak**

kuap: menguap *v* to yawn

kuartal *n* quarter (of a year)

kuas *n* brush (for art or cosmetics); paintbrush

kuasa *n* power; ~ *hukum* legal counsel; *negara adi*~ superpower; *surat* ~ proxy letter, letter of authorization; power of attorney; **berkuasa** *adj* powerful, mighty; **kekuasaan** *n* power; authority; **menguasai** *v* to control, have power over; ~ *bahasa asing* to be able to speak a foreign language

kuat *adj* strong; *tidak* ~ *berdiri* unable to stand up; **kekuatan** *n* strength, power; **menguatkan** *v* to strengthen; **memperkuat** *v* to reinforce, make stronger; **terkuat** *adj* the strongest

kuatir, khawatir *v* to worry, fear; *jangan* ~ don't worry; **kekuatiran** *n* worry, fear; **menguatirkan** *v* to worry about something

Kuba *n* Cuba; *orang* ~ Cuban

kubah *n* dome; **berkubah** *adj* domed

kubang: berkubang *v* to wallow (in mud)

kubik *adj* cubic; *liter* ~ cubic liter

kubis *n* cabbage

kubu *n* block, faction; ~ *PKB* the PKB faction

kubur *n* grave, tomb; **kuburan** *n* cemetery, graveyard; ~ *Cina* Chinese cemetery; **menguburkan** *v* to bury; **terkubur** *adj* buried in an accident

kubus *n* cube; *berbentuk* ~ cube-shaped

kucil: mengucilkan *v* to ostracize, shun

kucing *n* cat; ~ *angora* Persian cat; ~ *belang* tabby cat; ~ *kampung* alley cat; ~ *Siam* Siamese cat; *malu-malu* ~ feign disinterest

kucur: kucuran *n* flow, torrent; ~ *dana* flow of funds; **mengucurkan** *v* to gush, pour

KUD *abbrev Koperasi Unit Desa* village co-operative

kuda *n* horse; ~ *hitam* dark horse; ~ *laut* seahorse; ~ *lumping* flat woven horse; Javanese performance using these toy horses; ~ *nil* hippo, hippopotamus; **kuda-kuda** *n* sawhorse; easel; roof beam; **berkuda** *v* to ride a horse, go (horse-)riding

kudéta *n* coup, *coup d'etat*; ~ *militer* military coup

kudis *n* scab; scabies

kuduk *bulu* ~ hairs on the back of your neck

kudung, kerudung *n* loose veil; **berkudung** *v* to wear a loose veil

kudus *adj, Chr* holy; *Roh* ~ the Holy Ghost

kué *n* cake, pastry; ~ *kering* biscuit; ~ *pasar* traditional cakes; *bahan pembuat* ~ cake ingredients

KUHAP *abbrev Kitab Undang-Undang Hukum Acara Pidana* criminal law statutes

kuil *n, Ch, Hind* temple

kuis *n* quiz

kuitansi → **kwitansi**

kuku *n* nail (of people), claw (of animals); *cat* ~ nail polish; *gunting* ~ nail clippers; *penyakit* ~ *mulut* foot and mouth disease; **berkuku** *adj* having nails or claws; clawed

kukuh, kokoh *adj* strong, robust; **bersikukuh** *v* to hold fast to; **mengukuhkan** *v* to strengthen; to ratify; **pengukuhan** *n* strengthening, reinforcement; ratification

kukuruyuk cock-a-doodle-doo

kukus steam; **mengukus** *v* to steam (food)

kulai: terkulai *adj* sprawled, splayed, fallen

kuli *n* laborer, coolie; ~ *bangunan* builder's laborer

kuliah *n* lecture; *v, coll* to study at university or college

kulit *n* skin, hide (of animals); leather; peel, rind (of fruit); ~ *asli* real or genuine leather; ~ *imitasi,* ~ *tiruan* imitation leather; ~ *jeruk* orange rind; ~ *telur* eggshell; *orang* ~ *putih* white person, Caucasian; *krupuk* ~ crackers made from cow hide; *kacang lupa* ~ forget your origins; *orang* ~ *putih* white person, Caucasian; **berkulit** to have skin, -skinned; ~ *badak* thick-skinned

kulkas *n* refrigerator, fridge

kultum *n, Isl* short TV sermon ← **kuliah tujuh menit**

kultus *n* cult; ~ *pribadi* personality cult

kulum: mengulum *v* to suck in the mouth

kumal *adj* dishevelled, dingy, grubby

kuman *n* germ, bacteria; *pembasmi* ~ kills germs; **berkuman** *adj* full of germs, bacteria

kumandang echo; **berkumandang** *v* to echo; **mengumandangkan** *v* to sing; to sound, reverberate

kumat, komat relapse

kumbang *n* beetle; bumblebee

kumis *n* mustache

kumpul *v* to get together, gather; ~ *kebo* to live together without marrying; **kumpulan** *n* collection; group; ~ *puisi,* ~ *cerita pendek* anthology; **berkumpul** *v* to assemble, meet;

mengumpulkan v to collect, gather; ~ *perangko* to collect stamps; **ngumpul** v, *sl* to get or come together; **perkumpulan** n association, club; assembly

kumuh *adj* dirty, slummy; *daerah* ~ slum

kumur *obat* ~ mouthwash; **berkumur(-kumur)** v to gargle

kunang-kunang n firefly

kunci key; lock; fastener; ~ *inggris* wrench; ~ *kombinasi* combination lock; ~ *mobil* car lock; ~ *slot* bolt; *anak* ~ key; *juru* ~ gatekeeper; *saksi* ~ key witness; **mengunci** v to lock (up)

kuncup n bud; ~ *bunga* flower bud

kuning *adj* yellow; *coll* light brown; n saffron, turmeric; ~ *telur* yolk; *kucing* ~ ginger cat; *sakit* ~ jaundice; **kuningan** n brass; **kuningisasi** n support for Golkar, in the form of the colour yellow

kunir → **kunyit**

kunjung *tak* ~ never

kunjung: kunjungan n visit, excursion; ~ *sekolah* school trip; **berkunjung** v to visit, pay a visit to; **mengunjungi** v to visit a place

kuno *adj* ancient, historic; old-fashioned, out-of-date, conservative; *barang* ~ antique; *bangunan* ~ colonial building

kuntilanak n ghost that preys on pregnant women

kuntum n ripening bud

kunyah: mengunyah v to chew

kunyit, kunir, kuning n saffron; turmeric

kupang n edible shellfish

kupas peel; **kupasan** n peeling; analysis; **mengupas** v to peel; to analyze

kuper *adj, sl* sheltered, inexperienced ← **kurang pergaulan**

kuping n ear; **menguping** v to eavesdrop, listen in

kupon n coupon

kupu: kupu-kupu n butterfly; ~ *malam* lady of the night, prostitute

kura: kura-kura n tortoise

kurang *adj, adv* less, lacking; ~ *ajar* rude, badly brought up; ~ *lebih* more or less, about; ~ *tahu* don't really know; *masih* ~ still not enough; **berkurang** v to decrease, diminish, subside; **kekurangan** n shortcoming (of a person), lack; flaw, mistake, defect; **mengurangi** v to take from, subtract, minus; *enam dikurangi dua sama dengan empat* six minus two is four; **mengurangkan** v to reduce, make smaller; **sekurang(-kurang)nya** *adv* at least

kuras, menguras v to clean out, drain; ~ *tenaga* to use up energy; **terkuras** *adj* drained

kurban, qurban n, *Isl* sacrifice, usu goats or cattle; **berkurban** v to make such a sacrifice, have a sacrifice slaughtered

kurcaci n gnome, dwarf; *Putri Salju dan Tujuh* ~ Snow White and the Seven Dwarfs

kurét *n* curette; **mengurét** *v* to scrape out, perform a curette

kurikulum *n* curriculum; ~ *baru* new curriculum

kurir *n* courier; *jasa* ~ courier service

kurma, korma *n* date; *pohon* ~ date palm

kurs *n* exchange rate; ~ *ambang* floating exchange rate

kursi *n* chair, seat; ~ *empuk* armchair; ~ *goyang* rocking chair; ~ *malas* easy chair; ~ *panjang* sofa; ~ *roda* wheelchair

kursus course; ~ *kilat* crash course; ~ *pengembangan diri* self-development course; **mengursuskan** *v* to send someone on a course

kurun time; ~ *waktu* period, length of time

kurung cage; **kurungan** *n* cage; *hukuman* ~ imprisonment; **mengurung** *v* to cage, put in a cage, lock up

kurus *adj* thin, skinny; ~ *kering,* ~ *kerempeng* as thin as a rake; **kekurusan** *adj* too thin

kusam *adj* dull

kusén, kosén *n* frame (of door or window)

kusir *n* coachman, driver

kuskus *n* cuscus

kusta *penyakit* ~ leprosy; *orang yang sakit* ~ leper

kusuma, kesuma *n, lit* flower

kusut *adj* tangled, tousled, unkempt; complicated

kutak, utak: mengutak-ngatik- **kan** *v* to work on or tinker with

kutang *n* bra, bodice

kutat: berkutat *v* to be busy or concerned with

kuték, kutéks *n, coll* nail polish

kutik: berkutik *v* to move slightly, budge; **mengutik** *v* to tinker with; to touch on

kutil *n* wart; **kutilan** *adj* to have warts

kutilang, ketilang *burung* ~ thrush

kutip, mengutip *v* to quote, cite an extract; **kutipan** *n* extract, quotation

kutu *n* louse, flea; ~ *buku* bookworm; ~ *busuk* bedbug; **berkutu** *v* to have fleas or lice

kutub *n* pole; ~ *selatan* the South Pole; ~ *utara* the North Pole; *beruang* ~ polar bear

kutuk curse; **kutukan** *n* curse; **mengutuk** *v* to curse; **terkutuk** *adj* cursed, accursed

Kuwait *n* Kuwait; *orang* ~ Kuwaiti

kuyup *basah* ~ soaking wet

kwaci → **kuaci**

kwalitas → **kualitas**

kwantitas → **kuantitas**

kwétiau, kwétiauw *n* large Chinese egg noodles; ~ *siram* boiled noodles

kwitansi, kuitansi *n* bill, receipt

kyai → **ki, kiai**

L

la → **lha**

laba *n* profit, gain; ~ *bersih* net profit; ~ *kotor* gross profit; *nir*~ non-profit

laba: laba-laba *n* spider; *rumah* ~, *sarang* ~ cobweb

labil *adj* unstable, unreliable; *tanah* ~ shaky ground

laboratorium, lab *n* laboratory

labu *n* gourd, pumpkin, squash

labuh: pelabuhan port, harbor; **berlabuh** *v* to anchor

lacak: melacak *v* to trace; **pelacak** *anjing* ~ sniffer dog

laci *n* drawer; chest of drawers, dresser

lacur immoral; *apa* ~ what can you do?; **melacurkan** ~ *diri* to sell your body, prostitute yourself; **pelacur** *n* prostitute; **pelacuran** *n* prostitution; *tempat* ~ red-light district

lada *n* pepper

ladang *n* field; area of opportunity; ~ *minyak* oilfield; ~ *padi* dry ricefield; **berladang** *v* to cultivate the land

ladén: meladéni *v* to serve someone

lafal *n* pronunciation; **melafalkan** *v* to pronounce

laga *n* fight; *film* ~ action film

lagak *n* manner, fashion, way; ~ *bahasa* way of speaking, accent; **berlagak** *v* to act, pretend

lagi *adv* again; more; *apa* ~ especially; *seminggu* ~ in a week; **lagipula** *n* furthermore, moreover; **selagi** *prep* during, as

lagi *sl* in the act of; ~ *makan* eating; ~ *pergi* out, not here ← **sedang**

lagipula *n* furthermore, moreover ← **lagi pula**

lagu *n* song, music; ~ *anak-anak* children's song; ~ *daerah* song or music from a certain region; ~ *kebangsaan* national anthem; ~ *lama* old song; *neg* familiar refrain; ~ *Natal* Christmas carol; ~ *wajib* song that must be learnt at school; *pencipta* ~ songwriter

laguna *n* lagoon

-lah added after a word to soften the message; *baik*~ OK then; *mari*~ let us go

lahan *n* ground, land, terrain; ~ *basah* area of financial opportunity; ~ *kosong* waste land

lahap gluttonous; **melahap** *v* to devor, gorge yourself on

lahar *n* lava

lahir born; external; ~*nya* the birth of; *maaf* ~ *batin* forgive all my sins (greeting at Idul Fitri); **kelahiran** *n* birth; *adj* born; *hari* ~ birthday, anniversary; ~ *Semarang* born in Semarang; **melahirkan** *v* to give birth to; to create; **terlahir** *adj* born

laik → **layak**

lain *adj* other, different; ~ *ibu* from a different mother (of siblings); ~ *lagi* different again; ~ *ikan* ~ *lubuk* each to their own;

dan ~-~ *(dll)* etc, et cetera; **berlainan** *adj* differing, different; **kelainan** *n* abnormality; **melainkan** *conj* rather, instead; **selain** except, apart from

lajang *adj* single, unmarried; *masih* ~ single; **melajang** *v* to live as a single

laju fast, rapid, quick; rate; ~ *inflasi* inflation rate; **melaju** *v* to proceed quickly; **pelaju** *n* commuter

lajur *n* lane (one of many); ~ *kiri* left lane → **jalur**

lakban *n* adhesive tape

laki *adj, sl* male; *n, sl* husband; ~ *bini* man and wife; **lelaki** *adj, n* male; **laki-laki** *adj, n* male; *adik* ~, *kakak* ~, *saudara* ~ brother; *anak* ~ son

laknat *n* curse; **melaknat** *v* to curse

lakon *n* play; act

laksa *n* Malay dish of vermicelli noodles with chicken in coconut sauce

laksa: selaksa *adj, lit* ten thousand

laksamana *n* admiral; ~ *muda* vice-admiral

laksana *conj* like, as; **melaksanakan** *v* to realize, execute, carry out; **pelaksana** *n* manager, producer, administrator; ~ *harian* acting manager; **pelaksanaan** *n* realization, execution

laku *adj* popular, in vogue; salable; ~ *keras* selling like hot cakes; *tingkah* ~ behavior, conduct; **berlaku** *adj* effective,

valid; *v* to behave; **kelakuan** *n* act, behavior; **melakukan** *v* to do, perform, carry out; **selaku** *adj* (acting) as, in the capacity of

lalai *adj* careless, negligent; **kelalaian** *n* forgetfulness, negligence

lalap, lalapan *n* raw vegetables, eaten as a side-dish

lalat, laler *n* fly

lalim → **zalim**

lalu *conj* then; *adj* last; ~ *lalang* to and fro; ~ *lintas* traffic; *bulan (yang)* ~ last month; *sambil* ~ in passing; *sepintas* ~ at a glance; **berlalu** *v* to pass; **melalui** *v* to pass through; *conj* through, via; **selalu** *adv* always; **terlalu** *adv* too; **keterlaluan** *adj* too much, overly, unacceptable

lama *adj* long; old, former; ~-*kelamaan* gradually, in the end; *teman* ~ old friend; **lama-lama** *adj* too long; *jangan* ~ don't be too long; **kelamaan** *adj* too long (a time); **melama-lamakan** *v* to make longer, draw something out; **selama** *conj* for, during, as long as; **selamanya** *adv* always, forever; **selama-lamanya** *adv* forever and ever

lamar, melamar *v* to apply; **lamaran** *n* application; proposal; *surat* ~ application letter; *upacara* ~ proposal ceremony

lambai: melambaikan *v* to wave something; ~ *tangan* to wave (goodbye)

lamban *adj* slow; **kelambanan** *n* lack of action, inertia

lambang *n* symbol; ~ *kebangsaan* national symbol; **berlambang** *v* to have a symbol; **melambangkan** *v* to symbolize, represent

lambat *adj* slow, late; ~ *laun* gradually; **melambatkan** *v* to slow down; **selambat-lambatnya** *adv* at the latest; **terlambat** *adj* (too) late, delayed; **keterlambatan** *n* delay; *mengalami* ~ to be delayed

lambung *n* stomach; ~ *kapal* hull

lambung: melambung *v* to bounce; **melambungkan** *v* to bounce something

lamin: pelaminan *n* bridal sofa where the couple greet guests; *naik ke* ~ get married

laminasi *n* laminating; **melaminasi** *v* to laminate

lampau past; *masa* ~ the past; **melampaui** *v* to surpass, outdo, overtake; **terlampau** *adj* too, extremely

lampias: melampiaskan *v* to release, indulge in; ~ *hawa nafsu* to release your sexual urges; **pelampiasan** *n* act of releasing, indulgence

lampion *n* paper lantern

lampir: lampiran *n* attachment, appendix; **melampirkan** *v* to attach, enclose; **terlampir** *adj* attached, enclosed

lampu *n* light, lamp; ~ *lalu lintas*, ~ *merah* traffic light; ~ *sen* indicator; ~ *senter* flash-light; ~ *sorot* searchlight

lampung: pelampung *n* floater; flotation device; *baju* ~ life-jacket

lamun: melamun *v* **ngelamun** *coll* to day-dream, fantasize

lancang *adj* impudent, impolite, shameless; **kelancangan** *n* impudence, presumptuousness

lancar *adj* smooth, fluent; ~ *berbahasa Indonesia* speak Indonesian fluently; **kelancaran** *n* smoothness, good progress, fluency; **memperlancar** *v* to ease, make easier; **selancar** *papan* ~ surfboard; **berselancar** *v* to surf, go surfing

lancip *adj* pointed, pointy

lancong: melancong *v* to go traveling, sightseeing; **pelancong** *n* tourist

landa: melanda *v* to engulf, attack, hit; *dilanda kelaparan* to be hit by starvation

landai *adj* sloping

landak *n* porcupine, echidna

landas *n* base, ground; *lepas* ~ take-off; **berlandaskan** *adj* based on; **melandasi** *v* to base something on

langgan: langganan *n* subscription; regular customer; *uang* ~ subscription; **berlangganan** *v* to subscribe to; **pelanggan** *n* subscriber, customer

langgar *n, Isl* small prayer house

langgar: melanggar *v* to disobey, offend; ~ *hukum* to break the law; **pelanggaran** *n* violation

langgeng *adj* everlasting, eternal; **kelanggengan** n eternity

langit n sky; *bagai bumi dan ~* as different as night is to day; **langit-langit** n palate, roof of your mouth; ceiling

langka adj rare

langkah n step; *~ tepat* the right move; *~ demi* step by step; **melangkah** v to step; **melangkahi** v to step across; to marry before an older sibling

langlang: melanglang *~ buana* to see the world, travel great distances

langsam slow

langsat *pohon ~* tree with yellow fruit; *kuning ~* creamy yellow skin

langsing adj slim, slender; **melangsingkan** *~ badan* to (go on a) diet

langsir: melangsir v to shunt

langsung adj direct, straight; *tayangan ~* live telecast; **berlangsung** v to take place

lanjur: terlanjur adv too late, already; *~ berangkat* already left

lanjut adj advanced, further; *~ usia* adj old, elderly; *manusia ~ usia (manula)* senior citizen; *stadium ~* advanced stage (of illness); **lanjutan** n continuation; *sekolah ~* secondary school; **berlanjut** v to continue; **kelanjutan** n continuation, result; **melanjutkan** v to continue something; **selanjutnya** adv then, after that

lansekap, lanskap n landscape

lansia adj elderly → **lanjut usia**

lanskap → **lansekap**

lantai n floor (of building), story (of house); *~ bawah* ground floor; **berlantai** v to have floors, stories

lantar: lantaran conj because, the reason being

lantar: terlantar, telantar adj neglected, abandoned; **ketelantaran** n neglect

lantas adv then, next

lantik, melantik v to install, inaugurate; **pelantikan** n inauguration

lanting *rumah ~* traditional house in Kalimantan

lantun: melantunkan *~ lagu* to sing (a song)

lanud n airfield ← **lapangan udara**

lanun, ilanun n pirate

Laos n Laos; *bahasa ~ Lao, orang ~* Lao, Laotian

laos n galingale → **lengkuas**

lap n rag, cloth; **mengelap** v to wipe, mop

lapang adj wide, spacious; *~ dada* openly, without reservation; **lapangan** n field; *~ kerja* job vacancy; *~ tenis* tennis court; *~ terbang, ~ udara (lanud)* airfield, airport

lapar adj hungry; *busung ~* disease caused by starvation; **kelaparan** n hunger, famine, starvation; adj very hungry

lapis layer, fold, lining; *kue ~* layer cake; *~ legit* kind of layer cake; **lapisan** n coat, layer;

berlapis *adj* layered; **melapis** *v* to layer, overlay; **melapisi** *v* to add a layer to

lapor, melapor *v* to report; **laporan** *n* report; ~ *tahunan* annual report; **melaporkan** *v* to report, inform

laptop *n* laptop computer, notebook

lapuk rotten, decayed; **melapuk** *v* to rot, decay

larang: melarang *v* to ban, prohibit, forbid; **dilarang** *v* prohibited; ~ *masuk* no entry, no admittance; ~ *merokok* no smoking; **larangan** *n* ban, prohibition; **terlarang** *adj* forbidden, banned; *buku* ~ banned book

laras *n* barrel; counter for rifles; *se*~ *bedil* a rifle

laras *n* pitch, key, scale; **selaras** *adj* harmonious; **keselarasan** *n* harmony

larat: melarat *adj* miserable, poor; poverty-stricken; *hidup* ~ live in poverty; **kemelaratan** *n* poverty

lari run; ~ *estafet* relay (race); ~ *gawang* hurdles; ~ *kawin* elope; *lomba* ~ (foot or running) race; **berlari** *v* to run; **melarikan** *v* to run off with, abduct, kidnap; ~ *diri* to run away, flee, escape; **pelari** *n* runner; **pelarian** *n* escape, solace; abduction, kidnapping

laris *adj* popular, in great demand; ~ *manis* very popular

laron *n* flying white ant

lars *sepatu* ~ boot

larut dissolve; ~ *malam* late at night; **larutan** *n* solution; **melarutkan** *v* to dissolve; **pelarut** *n* solute

las weld; ~ *karbit* oxy welding; ~ *listrik* electric welding; *bengkel* ~ workshop; *tukang* ~ welder; **mengelas** *v* to weld

laskar *n* army, troops; ~ *Jihad* volunteer Muslim soldiers; ~ *pemuda* youth army; ~ *rakyat* people's army

lata: melata *v* to crawl, creep; *binatang* ~ reptile

latah *v* to (unconsciously) imitate; to talk non-stop

latar *n* base; ~ *belakang* background; **berlatarkan** *v* to have as a background, be based on

latih, melatih *v* to train; **latihan** *n* training, practice, exercise; ~ *jasmani* physical exercise; **pelatih** *n* coach, trainer; **pelatihan** *n* training; *mengadakan* ~ to run a course

Latin *Amerika* ~ Latin America; *bahasa* ~ Latin; *lagu* ~ Spanish-language song

lauk *n* side-dish; ~ *pauk* side-dish

laun *lambat* ~ slowly, gradually

laut *n* sea; ~ *Tengah* the Mediterranean; *bajak* ~ pirate; *kapal* ~ ship; **lautan** *n* ocean; ~ *api* sea of flames; ~ *Hindia* the Indian Ocean; ~ *Teduh,* ~ *Pasifik* the Pacific Ocean; **kelautan** *adj* maritime; *Departemen Perikanan dan* ~ Department of Fisheries and Marine Affairs;

melaut *v* to go to sea; **pelaut** *n* sailor, seaman

lawak joke; **lawakan** *n* joke, jest; **melawak** *v* to joke, jest; **pelawak** *n* comedian, comic, clown

lawan *n* opponent, adversary; opposite; ~ *kata* opposite, antonym; **berlawanan** *v* to be opposed; **melawan** *v* to oppose, resist; ~ *arus* against the flow; **perlawanan** *n* opposition, resistance

lawat: lawatan, perlawatan *n* trip, visit; **melawat** *v* to visit, make a trip

layak, laik *adj* proper, suitable; ~ *jalan* roadworthy; **kelayakan** *n* suitability; *studi* ~ feasibility study; **selayaknya** *adv* properly, should

layan: layanan *n* service; **melayani** *v* to serve; **pelayan** *n* waiter, *m* waitress *f* attendant; **pelayanan** *n* service ~ *masyarakat* public services

layang: layang-layang kite; **melayang** *v* to float (in the air); *jiwa* ~ to die

layar sail; ~ *perak* small screen, television; **berlayar** *v* to sail; **pelayaran** *n* voyage; *perusahaan* ~ shipping company

layat: melayat *v* to visit a house in mourning, pay your respects; **pelayat** *n* person who pays their respects

layu wither, wilt

layuh paralysis; *lumpuh* ~ polio

lazim *adj* usual; *tidak* ~ unusual

LBH *abbrev Lembaga Bantuan Hukum* Legal Aid Agency

lebah *n* bee; *sarang* ~ beehive

lebam, lembam *biru* ~ black-and-blue; *gas* ~ inert or noble gas

lébar *adj* wide, broad; *panjang* ~ detailed, extensive; **lébarnya** *n* width; **melébarkan** *v* to widen; **pelébaran** *n* widening; ~ *jalan* widening the road, roadworks

lebar: Lebaran *n* Idul Fitri, first two days after the Ramadan fast; ~ *Haji* Idul Adha, Feast of the Sacrifice

lébarnya *n* width ← **lébar**

lebat *adj* thick, dense; *hujan* ~ heavy rain, downpour

lebih *adv* more; ~ *baik*, ~ *bagus* better; ~ *buruk*, ~ *jelek* worse; *kurang* ~ about; **berlebihan** *adj* excessive; **kelebihan** *n* extra, excess; ~ *bagasi* excess luggage; **melebihi** *v* to exceed, surpass; **selebihnya** *n* the rest or remainder; **terlebih** *adj* especially

lebur: melebur *v* to merge, fuse; **peleburan** *n* melting; merger

lécéh: melécéhkan *v* to insult; **pelécéhan** *n* contempt; ~ *seksual* sexual harassment

lécét sore, blister; *luka* ~ blister

léci *n* lychee

ledak: ledakan *n* explosion; **meledak** *v* to explode; **meledakkan** *v* to explode or detonate something; **peledak** *bahan* ~ explosive; **peledakan** *n* bombing

lédék, melédék v to tease, provoke

lédéng, léding air ~ plumbing, water pipes; tukang ~ plumber

lédré, lédri pisang ~ thinly sliced banana chips, a specialty of Malang

lega adj relieved; **melegakan** adj reassuring, consoling

légal adj legal; **légalisasi** n legalization; **melégalisasi, melégalisir** v to legalize

legam hitam ~ pitch-black, jet black

légénda n legend, myth; **légéndaris** adj legendary

legit lapis ~ kind of layer cake

légo v, coll to sell cheaply, get rid of, let go

légong tari ~ Balinese trance dance performed by young girls

léhér n neck

lejit: melejit v to shoot up, skyrocket; namanya ~ she suddenly became famous

lekas adj fast, quick, speedy; (semoga) ~ sembuh get well soon

lekat adj close; sticky, adhesive; **melekat** v to stick; **pelekat** bahan ~ adhesive

lekuk n hollow, cavity; concave; ~ mata eye socket

léla → **rajaléla**

lelah adj tired, weary; melepas ~ to take a rest; **kelelahan** n fatigue, weariness; **melelahkan** adj tiring

lelaki, laki-laki adj male; n man, male

lélang n auction; juru ~ auctioneer; **dilélang** for auction, tender

lelap adj sound, fast, completely; tidur ~ sound asleep

lélé ikan ~ catfish; pecel ~ catfish with rice and peanut sauce

léléh melt, run; **léléhan** n trickle; **meléléh** v to drip, run; **meléléhkan** v to melt something

leluasa adj free, unrestricted; dengan ~ freely; **keleluasaan** n freedom (of choice)

lelucon → **lucu**

leluhur n ancestor; tanah ~ ancestral home → **luhur**

lém n glue; ~ tikus sticky paper to catch rats; **dilém** v to be glued

lemah adj weak; ~ lembut gentle, tender; **kelemahan** n weakness

lemak n fat; grease; menimbun ~ to store fat

lemari, almari n cupboard, closet, shelf; ~ baju wardrobe

lemas, lemes adj weak, drained; mati ~ suffocated, drowned

lembab, lembap adj humid, damp, moist; cuaca ~ humid weather; **kelembaban** n humidity; **pelembab, pelembap** n moisturizer

lembaga n institute, foundation, board; ~ swadaya masyarakat (LSM) non-government organization (NGO); **melembagakan** v to make into an institution

lembah n valley

lembam, lebam adj slow, inert; gas ~ inert or noble gas

lembap → **lembab**

lembar n sheet (of paper), page;

membuka ~ baru to turn over a new leaf

lembék *adj* soft, weak, flimsy

lembing *n* javelin, spear; *lempar ~* javelin (throw)

lembu *n* cow

lembur *v* to work overtime, stay late

lembut *adj* soft, gentle; *lemah ~* gentle, tender; **kelembutan** *n* softness; **melembutkan** *v* to soften; **pelembut** *n* softener

lemes → **lemas**

Lemhanas *n* National Defense Agency ← **Lembaga Pertahanan Nasional**

Lemigas *n* Institute for Oil and Natural Gas ← **Lembaga Minyak dan Gas Bumi**

lémpar, melémpar *v* to throw; **lémparan** *n* throw; **melémpari** *v* to pelt, throw something at; *~ kereta api dengan batu* to throw rocks at a train; **melémparkan** *v* to throw something; **pelémparan** *n* (act of) throwing; **terlémpar** *adj* thrown, flung

lémpéng *n* large slightly curved shell; **lémpéngan** *~ bumi* tectonic plate

lemper *n* sweet cake of sticky rice with a meat filling

léna: terléna *adj* confused, bewildered

lencana *n* emblem, badge

léncéng: meléncéng *v* to deviate, go out of your way

lendir *n* mucus; **berlendir** *adj* mucous, slimy

léngah *adj* off-guard, careless

lengan *n* arm, sleeve; *baju ~ panjang* long-sleeved shirt

lengang *adj* deserted, quiet, empty

lénggang *adj* swaying; **melénggangkan** *~ tangan* to swing your arms while walking

lengkap *adj* complete; *adat ~* full ceremony; **melengkapi** *v* to furnish, supply; **pelengkap** *n* accessory; **perlengkapan** *n* outfit, equipment

léngkéng, keléngkéng *n buah ~* small lychee

léngkét *adj* sticky, close

lengking: melengking *v* to trill, soar (of a voice)

lengkuas *n* a kind of spice, galingale → **laos**

lengkung *adj* bent, convex; **melengkung** *v* to arch

léngsér *v* to abdicate, descend from power

lénong *n* Betawi folk play; *~ bocah* children's *lenong*

lénsa *n* lens; *~ kontak* contact lenses

lénso *tari ~* dance with a handkerchief

lentéra *n* lantern

lentur *adj* elastic, pliable

lenyap *adj* disappeared, gone, vanished

lepas loose, free; escape; *~ kendali* out of control; *penerjemah ~* freelance translator; **melepaskan** *v* to release, let free; *~ tembakan* to fire a shot; **pelepasan** *n* departure, farewell; *acara ~* goodbye (party); **selepas** *prep, conj* after

lépot → **belépotan**

léréng *n* slope; ~ *gunung* foothills

lés (to attend) a private class or course; ~ *bahasa* language class; ~ *piano* piano lesson; *guru* ~ private teacher

lésbi lesbian

lését: melését *v* to slip, skid; to miss the target; *jaman* ~ the Great Depression; **pelésétan** *n* parody; **terpelését** *adj* slipped

lestari *adj* eternal, everlasting; **melestarikan** *n* to preserve, maintain; ~ *hutan* to protect the forest; **pelestarian** *n* protection, preservation

lesu *adj* tired, weary; *letih* ~ dead tired, exhausted

lesung *n* dimple, hollow; ~ *pipi* dimple

letak place, location; **letaknya** *n* the location, position; **meletakkan** *v* to put in place, set down; ~ *jabatan* to resign; **terletak** *adj* situated, located

letih ~ *lesu* dead tired, exhausted

létnan *n* lieutenant; ~ *kolonel (letkol)* lieutenant-colonel

letus: letusan *n* eruption; **meletus** *v* to erupt

léver *n* liver → **hati**

léwat *prep* past; via; *jam empat* ~ *lima* five past four; **keléwat** *adj, sl* too, unacceptably; **meléwati** *v* to pass or go through; **meléwatkan** *v* to miss something

lezat *adj* delicious, tasty;

kelezatan *n* delicious taste

lha well (expression of mild surprise)

lho you know (used to emphasize a statement, often denying something); *ejac* well!; *gitu* ~ like that, you know

liang *n* hole, passage; ~ *dubur* anus; ~ *kubur* grave

liar *adj* wild, untamed; unregulated; *kucing* ~ wild cat; *pungutan* ~ *(pungli)* unofficial charge

liat *adj* tough; *tanah* ~ clay

Libanon *n* Lebanon; *orang* ~ Lebanese

libat: melibatkan *v* to involve, include; **terlibat** *adj* involved, implicated; **keterlibatan** *n* involvement, association

libur be free, on holiday (from school or work); ~ *panjang* long holiday; *hari* ~ holiday; **liburan** *n* holiday; ~ *sekolah* school holidays; **berlibur** *v* to go or be on holiday; **meliburkan** *v* to give a holiday to

lichtdruk *n, arch* duplicate, phototype

licik *adj* cunning, tricky; **kelicikan** *n* trickery, cunning

licin *adj* smooth; slippery; *kertas* ~ glossy paper

lidah *n* tongue

lidi *n* palm-leaf rib; *sapu* ~ small broom

liga *n* (football) league; ~ *Inggris* FA, English league

lihai *adj, neg* tricky, shrewd, cunning

lihat *v* to see; ~ *halaman sebelah*

(lhs) please turn over (PTO); **lihat-lihat** ~ *saja* just looking; **kelihatan** *adj* visible; *~nya* apparently, it seems; **melihat** *v* to see, look; **melihat-lihat** *v* to look around, have a look; **memperlihatkan** *v* to show, display; **penglihatan** *v* vision, sight

liku *n* turn, bend; **berliku-liku** *adj* twisted, complicated

lilin *n* candle; wax; *es* ~ icypole, iced lolly

liliput *adj* very small, mini

lilit turn, twist; **lilitan** *n* turn, twist; **melilit** *v* to wind, twist; **terlilit** *adj* caught up, twisted

lima *adj* five; ~ *belas* fifteen; ~ *puluh* fifty; *ke~* fifth; *kembar* ~ quintuplets; *simpang* ~ five-way intersection; **berlima** *adj* the five of them, a group of five; **seperlima** *n* one-fifth

limau *jeruk* ~ lime

limbah *n* waste; ~ *nuklir* nuclear waste; *pengolahan* ~ waste processing

limpa *n* spleen

limpah *adj* abundant, plenty; **berlimpah-limpah, melimpah** *adj* overflowing, abundant; **kelimpahan** *n* abundance, wealth; **melimpahkan** *v* to shower upon

linang: berlinang *v* to trickle, drip; *air mata* ~ eyes filled with tears

lincah *adj* nimble, deft, agile; **kelincahan** *n* agility

lindas: melindas *v* to run over, squash; **terlindas** *adj* run over

lindung: berlindung *v* to (take) shelter; **melindungi** *v* to protect, shelter; **pelindung** *n* protective device; **perlindungan** *n* protection

lingga *n* obelisk, traditional male symbol; ~ *yoni* obelisk in a square hole, traditional symbol of male and female sexuality

linggis *n* crowbar

lingkar *n* ring, circle, circumference; *jalan* ~ ring road; **lingkaran** *n* circle; **melingkar** *v* to go around, coil; **melingkari** *v* to circle or surround

lingkung: lingkungan *n* environment, surroundings, circle(s); *aktivis* ~ environmental activist

lingkup *n* scope, reach

linglung *adj* dazed, confused

lintah *n* leech; ~ *darat* loan shark

lintang across, latitude; **melintang** *adj* horizontal, across

lintas *lalu* ~ traffic; **lintasan** *n* path, route; **melintas** *v* to pass by

linu *pegal* ~ aches and pains, sore

liontin *n* pendant

lipat fold; *dua kali* ~ double, twice; **lipatan** *n* fold; **berlipat** ~ *ganda* many times over; **kelipatan** *n* multiple; **melipat** *v* to fold

LIPI *abbrev Lembaga Ilmu Pengetahuan Indonesia* Indonesian Institute of Sciences

lipstik *n* lipstick

lipur: pelipur ~ *hati* consolation

liput: liputan n coverage, reporting; **meliput** v to cover, report on; **meliputi** v to include, cover

lirih adj low-pitched, soft

lirik ~ lagu (song) lyrics

lirik: melirik v to steal a glance

lisan adj oral, verbal; secara ~ orally; ujian ~ oral examination

listrik electric, electricity; arus ~ electric current; pembangkit tenaga ~ power station

litbang n research and development (R & D) ← **penelitian dan pengembangan**

liter n liter, litre

litsus n special investigation ← **penelitian khusus**

liur air ~ saliva, spit; **berliur** v to drool, salivate

liwet nasi ~ rice cooked in coconut milk, a specialty of Solo

LN abbrev luar negeri overseas, foreign

lo → **lho**

lo → **lo mie**

loak second-hand; pasar ~ flea market

loba adj greedy

lobak n radish

lobang → **lubang**

lobi-lobi buah ~ kind of red fruit

lodéh sayur ~ vegetables in coconut milk

loe → **lu**

logam n metal; uang ~ coin, small change

logat n accent; ~ Batak a Batak accent; **berlogat** ~ Jawa to have a Javanese accent

logika n logic; **logis** adj logical

logistik n logistics

loh → **lho**

lohor Isl the midday prayer

lok, lokomotif n locomotive

lokakarya n seminar, workshop

lokal adj local; hujan ~ local showers; **lokalisasi** n red-light district

lokasi n location; **berlokasi** adj located

lokét n counter, desk, ticket window or office; ~ karcis ticket office

lokomotif, lok n locomotive

lolong howl; **melolong** v to howl (of dogs)

lolos v to escape; succeed, progress

lomba race, competition, contest; ~ lari (foot or running) race; **berlomba** v to compete, race; **perlombaan** n competition

lombok n chilli

lo mie n kind of Chinese noodles

lompat jump, leap; ~ jauh long jump; ~ tinggi high jump; **lompatan** n jump; **melompat** v to jump, leapfrog

lompong kosong ~ completely empty

loncat jump (over something); ~ indah diving; papan ~ springboard; **loncatan** n jump; **meloncat** v to spring, jump

loncéng n bell

londo n, coll white person; orang ~ white person ← **Belanda**

longgar adj loose, wide;

kelonggaran *n* facility, dispensation; **melonggarkan** *v* to loosen (restrictions)

longo: melongo *v* to gape or stare at

longsor slip; *tanah* ~ landslide

lonjak: lonjakan *n* surge, sudden rise; **melonjak** *v* to increase sharply, peak

lonjong *adj* oval; *bulat* ~ oval

lontar *daun* ~ palm leaf once used as writing material

lontar: lontaran *n* throw; ~ *martil* hammer throw; **melontarkan** *v* to throw; ~ *pertanyaan* to ask or pose a question

lontong *n* cooked, solid slab of rice

loper *n* delivery boy; ~ *koran* newspaper delivery boy

lopor → **pelopor**

loréng *adj* striped; *baju* ~ camouflage gear, cammo

lorong *n* path; lane, alley

Lorosae *Timor* ~ East Timor

lorot: melorot *v* to fall, drop, plummet

losin → **lusin**

losmén *n* guest house, accommodation, cheap hotel

loték *n* a dish of fresh vegetables with peanut sauce

loténg *n* attic, loft

loteré, lotré *n* lottery

lotot: melotot *v* to stare or gape at, with bulging eyes; **melototkan** ~ *mata* eyes bulging

lotré → **loteré**

lowong *adj* vacant; **lowongan** *adj* wanted, vacancy; ~ *kerja* work opportunities

loyang *n* cake tin, tray, mould

loyo *adj* very tired, exhausted

LP *abbrev lembaga pemasyarakatan* jail, prison

LSM *abbrev lembaga swadaya masyarakat* non-government organization, NGO

Lt. *lantai* floor, level

lu *sl* you; *gue* ~ on very close terms; [*derog*] you (bastard); *pergi* ~ get lost

luang *adj* free, empty; *waktu* ~ spare time; **meluangkan** ~ *waktu* to set aside time for; **peluang** *n* chance, opportunity; **berpeluang** *v* to have an opportunity, a chance

luap: luapan *n* wave, wash; **meluap** *v* to overflow, swell, wash

luar out, external; ~ *biasa* outstanding, extraordinary; ~ *negeri* overseas, abroad; *dunia* ~ outside world; *ke* ~ go out, outside; *orang* ~ outsider, stranger; foreigner; **keluar** go out; be issued; *prep* out, outside; **keluaran** *n* edition, version, issue; **mengeluarkan** *v* to issue, publish, send out, release

luas wide, broad; space; **luasnya** *n* width; area; **memperluas** *v* to widen, expand, enlarge

lubang, lobang *n* hole, passage; ~ *dubur* anus; ~ *hidung* nostril; ~ *di jalan* pothole; **melubangi** *v* to pierce, put a hole in

lubér leak, expand, seep out

lubuk *n* deep pool; ~ *hati* depth of your heart

lucu *adj* cute, sweet; funny; odd; **kelucuan** *n* cuteness; **melucu** *v* to make jokes, be funny

lucut: melucuti *v* to strip or pull off; ~ *senjata* to disarm; **perlucutan** ~ *senjata* disarmament

ludah *n* saliva, spit; **meludah** *v* to spit; **meludahi** *v* to spit at, on

ludes *adj* wiped out, finished off; ~ *dilahap api* completely gutted

ludruk *n* East Javanese folk play

lugas *adj* straightforward, to the point, direct

lugu *adj* naive, gullible

luhur *adj* lofty, noble, esteemed; **leluhur** *n* ancestor; *tanah* ~ ancestral home

luka wound; injured; ~ *bakar* burn; ~ *parah* badly wounded or injured; ~ *ringan* mild injury; ~ *tikam* stab wound; **melukai, melukakan** *v* to hurt or wound

lukis *v* to paint, draw; *seni* ~ (visual) art; **lukisan** *n* painting, picture, portrait (of a person); **melukis** *v* to paint, draw; **pelukis** *n* painter, artist

luks *adj* luxury

lulu → melulu

luluh ~ *lantak* crushed, pulverized

lulur *mandi* ~ traditional massage with body scrub; **luluran** *v, coll* to have such a traditional massage

lulus *v to* pass; ~ *ujian* pass an exam; *tidak* ~ fail; **lulusan** *n* graduate; **meluluskan** *v* to pass someone (in an exam or test)

lumas: pelumas *n* lubricant

lumayan *adv, adj* quite, not bad, fairly

lumba-lumba *n* dolphin, porpoise

lumbung ~ *padi* rice silo or barn

lumér leak, expand, seep out

lumpang *n* pestle, rice pounder; *alu* ~ mortar and pestle

lumpat → lompat

lumpia *n* spring rolls; ~ *basah* spring rolls eaten cold

lumping *kuda* ~ flat woven toy horse; East Javanese performance using a toy horse

lumpuh *adj* paralysed, lame; ~ *layuh* polio; **melumpuhkan** *v* to knock out, paralyse

lumpur *n* mud; **berlumpur** *adj* muddy

lumrah *adj* usual, accepted, common

lumur smear; **berlumuran** *adj* smeared, stained; **melumuri** *v* to smear, cover with

lumut *n* moss; *hijau* ~ moss green, bright green

lunak *adj* soft; *piranti* ~ software

lunas *adj* paid off, in full; **melunasi** *v* to pay off; ~ *hutang* to repay, pay off a debt

luncur: meluncurkan *v* to launch, set in motion; **peluncuran** *n* launch

luntur fade, lose color, run

lupa *v* to forget; **kelupaan** *n* something forgotten; **melupakan** *v* to forget something; **pelupa** *n* forgetful person; **terlupakan** *tak* ~ unforgettable

lupis *kue* ~ small round cakes made from palm sugar, pandan and desiccated coconut

lupus *penyakit* ~ a skin disease

luput *v* to escape, slip away

lurah *n* head of a kelurahan, village chief; **kelurahan** *n* administrative unit, village

lurik *kain* ~ striped Javanese cloth

lurus *adj* straight; *jalan yang* ~ the right path; **meluruskan** *v* to straighten; **pelurusan** *n* straightening

lusa *adv* the day after tomorrow; *besok* ~ tomorrow or the day after

lusin, losin, dosin *n* dozen, twelve; **selusin** *n* a dozen; *teh botol* ~ a dozen bottles of tea

lusuh *adj* old, faded (of clothes)

lutung, lotong *n* black monkey

lutut *n* knee; *tempurung* ~ kneecap; *bertekuk* ~ to surrender; *menekuk* ~ to go down on your knees; **berlutut** to kneel (down)

luwes *adj* attractive, well-presented; **keluwesan** *n* attractiveness, style

M

M *Masehi* Christian calendar

m meter

maaf sorry; *minta* ~ apologize, say you're sorry; *mohon* ~ *lahir (dan) batin* ask forgiveness for all sins (at Idul Fitri); *seribu* ~ a thousand apologies; *tidak ada* ~ no excuse, unforgivable; **bermaaf-maafan** *v, Isl* to beg forgiveness of each other (at Idul Fitri); **memaafkan** *v* to forgive, pardon; **pemaaf** *adj* forgiving

maag, mag *n, coll* stomach (disorder); *obat* ~ antacid; *sakit* ~ weak stomach, gastric pain

Mabad *n* Army Headquarters ← **Markas Besar Angkatan Darat**

mabes *n* headquarters; ~ *Polri* National Police Headquarters ← **markas besar**

mabrur *Isl haji* ~ pilgrim accepted by God

mabuk *adj* drunk; ill; motion sickness; ~ *jalan* carsick; ~ *laut* seasick; *orang* ~ drunk; **memabukkan** *adj* alcoholic; intoxicating

macam *n* kind, sort, model; *aneka* ~ all kinds, variety; *se~ itu* like that, of that type; **macam-macam** *adj, neg* all sorts; **bermacam-macam** *adj* various; **semacam** *adj* a kind or type of

macan *n* large spotted cat; *n, coll* tiger; ~ *kumbang* leopard, panther; ~ *tutul* cheetah

macet, macét jammed, blocked; traffic jam; ~ *total* gridlock; *kredit* ~ non-performing loans; **kemacetan** *n* jam; ~ *lalu lintas* traffic jam

Madagaskar *n* Madagascar, the

Malagasy Republic; *bahasa ~, orang ~* Malagasy

madani *adj* civil; *masyarakat ~* civil society

madat *n* opium; *v, coll* to do drugs; **pemadat** *n* (opium) addict

madrasah *n, Isl* school, college

madu *n* honey; co-spouse; *bulan ~* honeymoon; *berbulan ~* to (have your) honeymoon; **memadu** *v* to cheat on

madya *adj* medium, middle; *bahasa Jawa ~* middle level of Javanese; *kota~* municipality

mafhum *v* to understand, know

magang (do) work experience, apprentice

magister *n* Master's degree; *~ hukum* Master of Law

magnét → **maknit**

magrib, maghrib *n* sunset; sunset prayer

mah *coll* way of adding stress to phrases (often contrasting); *Tina tidak mau, tapi saya ~ oke saja* Tina doesn't want to, but as for me, that's fine

maha- *adj* great; *~bharata* Mahabharata, shadow puppet epic; *~siswa* university student; *Tuhan Yang ~ kuasa* Almighty God

mahal *adj* expensive, dear; *jual ~* have a high asking price; **kemahalan** *adj* too expensive; **memahalkan** *v* to raise the price, make more expensive

mahar *n, Isl* dowry, bride price

mahasiswa *n* (university or college) student; **mahasiswi** *n,* *f* (female) student

mahir *adj* expert, skilled; **kemahiran** *n* skill

mahkamah *n* court of law; *~ Agung* High Court; *~ Militer Luar Biasa (Mahmilub)* extraordinary court-martial

mahkota *n* crown, crest; *putra ~* crown prince

main *v* to play, do (a sport), to go ...ing; *~ golf* to play golf; *~ piano* to play the piano; *bukan ~* wow, extraordinary; **main-main** *v* to joke around, not be serious; **mainan** *n* toy; **bermain** *v* to play; *~ api* to play with fire; **memainkan** *v* to play something; *~ biola* to play the violin; **mempermainkan** *v* to ridicule, make a fool of; **pemain** *n* player, actor; *~ film* actor; *~ bola basket* basketballer; **permainan** *n* game, match

maizéna *n* corn; *tepung ~* cornflour

majalah *n* magazine; *~ bulanan* monthly (magazine)

majelis *n* assembly, council; *~ Permusyawaratan Rakyat (MPR)* People's Consultative Assembly (Parliament)

majemuk *adj* compound, complex; *kata ~* compound (word)

majikan *n* employer

maju go forward, advance, progress, improve; *~ mundur* back and forth; *~ tak gentar* ever onward; **kemajuan** *n* progress, advance; **memajukan** *v* to bring forward, propose

nak *pron* mother; ~ *comblang* matchmaker

naka *conj* therefore, so, then; **makanya** *conj* that's why, so

nakalah *n* paper, essay

nakam *n* grave; *Taman ~ Pahlawan* Heroes' Cemetery; **memakamkan** *v* to bury; **pemakaman** *n* funeral, burial

nakan *v* to eat; ~ *dulu* said when eating first before others; ~ *hati* brood, dwell on, be upset; ~ *malam* (eat or have) dinner; ~ *waktu* take (time); *kereta ~* restaurant car; *kurang ~* undernourished; *nafsu ~* appetite; *rumah ~* restaurant; **makanan** *n* food; **memakan** *v* to eat, consume, take; ~ *obat* to take a pill or capsule; *dimakan rayap* to be eaten by termites

nakanya *conj* that's why, so ← **maka**

nakar *v* to betray the government, be subversive

nakaroni *n* macaroni; ~ *skotel* kind of macaroni loaf

Makasar, Makassar *n* Macassar (formerly Ujung Pandang); *bahasa ~, orang ~* Macassarese

nakasi, makasih *coll* thanks → **terima kasih**

Makau *n* Macau; *orang ~* Macanese

Makédonia *n* Macedonia; former Yugoslav Republic of Macedonia (FYROM); *bahasa ~, orang ~* Macedonian

nakelar *n* broker

nakét *n* model

nakhluk, mahluk *n* creature

maki *caci ~* insult, abuse; **mencaci-maki** *v* to insult, abuse; **memaki, memaki-maki** *v* to insult, heap abuse on

makin *adv* increasingly; ~ *lama*, ~ *besar* the longer, the bigger; **semakin** *adv* even more

maklum *v* to know, be aware of; *agar ~* let it be known; **memaklumi** *v* to be aware of, accept; **maklumat** *n* announcement, proclamation, notice

makmur *adj* prosperous; **kemakmuran** *n* prosperity; **Persemakmuran** *n* (British) Commonwealth

makna *n* meaning

maknit, magnét *n* magnet

maksiat *n* immoral; *tempat ~* brothel; **kemaksiatan** *n* immorality, vice

maksimal maximal(ly); **maksimum** *n* maximum

maksud *n* purpose, intention, meaning; ~ *saya* I mean; **bermaksud** *v* to intend; **dimaksud(kan)** *v* to be meant or intended

mal, mol *n* shopping centre, mall

Maladéwa *Kepulauan ~* the Maldives

malagizi *n* malnutrition

malah, malahan instead, rather, on the other hand

malaikat *n* angel; ~ *maut* angel of death

Malaka, Melaka *n* Malacca; *Selat ~* Straits of Malacca

malam *n* night, evening; ~ *Jumat* Thursday night (when some believe ghosts are out); *Jumat* ~ Friday night; ~ *hari* at night; ~ *Natal* Christmas Eve; *larut* ~ late at night; *selamat* ~ good evening; *tadi* ~ last night; *tengah* ~ midnight; **malam-malam** *adv* late at night; **bermalam** *v* to spend or stay the night; **kemalaman** *adv* too late (at night); after dark; **semalam** *adv* last night; **semalaman** *adv* all night long

malang *adj* unlucky; ~ *melintang* lie across; **kemalangan** *n* bad luck, misfortune

malapetaka *n* disaster, calamity

malas *adj* lazy, can't be bothered; ~ *makan* not feel like eating; **bermalas-malas(an)** *v* to lie or laze around, be lazy; **kemalasan** *n* laziness; **pemalas** *n* lazy person, lazybones

Malaysia *n* Malaysia; *bahasa* ~, *orang* ~ Malaysian

maling *n* thief; **kemalingan** *v* to be robbed

Malta *n* Malta; *bahasa* ~, *orang* ~ Maltese

malu *adj* shy, ashamed, embarrassed; *jangan* ~ don't be shy; **malu-malu** *adj* shy; ~ *kucing* feign disinterest; **kemaluan** *n* genital, sex organ; **memalukan** *adj* embarrassing; **mempermalukan** *v* to embarrass, shame; **pemalu** shy (person)

mam, mam-mam *v, ch* eat

mamah, memamah *v* to chew, ruminate

mamalia *n* mammal

Mami, Mi *pron, coll* Mum, Mummy (in Westernized circles)

mampet *adj* stuck, blocked, jammed; *hidung* ~ blocked nose

mampir *v* to drop in, call on

mampu *adj* able, capable; *adj* well-off; *kurang* ~ poor, not well-off; **kemampuan** *n* ability, capability; **semampunya** *adv* as well as you can, to the best of your ability

mampus *sl* die, croak; *coll* in big trouble

mana *pron* where, which; ~ *mungkin* how could it be?; ~ *saja* whichever; *dari* ~ from where; *di* ~ where; *di* ~ *saja* wherever; *ke* ~ where; **mana-mana** *di* ~, *ke* ~ everywhere

manajemén *n* management → **pengelolaan**

manakala *conj* when, if

mana-mana *di* ~, *ke* ~ everywhere ← **mana**

manasik ~ *haji* preparations for the pilgrimage to Mecca

manca- *adj* many; ~*negara* international, overseas

mancing → **pancing**

mancung *adj* straight (of noses)

mancur *air* ~ fountain ← **pancur**

mandala *n* zone, circle

Mandar ethnic group in South Sulawesi; *bahasa* ~, *orang* ~ Mandarese

mandat *n* mandate

mandau *n* knife used in Kalimantan

mandek, mandeg stop, cease, get stuck, stagnate

mandi bathe, take a bath, wash (the body); ~ *lulur* traditional body scrub; **bermandi** v to bathe; ~ *keringat* to be soaked in sweat; **bermandikan** adj bathed in; **memandikan** v to wash someone; **mempermandikan** v to christen, baptize; **permandian** n bathing pool; christening, baptism; *bapak* ~ godfather

mandor n supervisor, overseer

mandul adj infertile, sterile, childless; **kemandulan** n infertility

manekin n dummy, mannequin

manfaat n benefit, use; **bermanfaat** adj useful, of benefit; **memanfaatkan** v to take advantage of, (draw) benefit from

mangga n mango

manggis n mangosteen

manggung v, coll to perform ← **panggung**

mangkal v, coll to use as a base, wait for work ← **pangkal**

mangkat v to pass away

mangkir v to not attend; be absent

mangkok, mangkuk n bowl

mangsa n prey

mangu: termangu-mangu adj confused, dazed; speechless

mani: air ~ sperm

manifés n passenger list (on an aircraft); cargo list

manik: manik-manik n beads

manikur n manicure

manis adj sweet; pretty; nice; ~nya the sweetness; jari ~ ring finger; kayu ~ cinnamon; duduk yang ~ sit nicely, sit properly; **manisan** n sweets, candy; sugared snacks; **kemanisan** adj too sweet; **pemanis** n sweetener; ~ buatan artificial sweetener

manja spoilt; anak ~ spoilt child; **memanjakan** v to spoil someone

manjur adj potent, effective; obat yang ~ strong medicine

mantan adj former (of people); ~ Presiden former President; ~ suami ex-husband

mantap adj stable, steady; **kemantapan** n stability; **memantapkan** v to stabilize or steady something

mantel n (long) coat, raincoat

mantu n son- or daughter-in-law; v to marry off a son or daughter → **menantu**

manula n old person, senior citizen → **manusia lanjut usia**

manusia n human (being); humanity; **berperikemanusiaan** adj human

manuver n maneuver

manyar: burung ~ weaverbird

map n folder

mapan adj settled, comfortable

marabahaya n great danger

marah adj angry; cepat ~, gampang ~ short-tempered, quick-tempered, hot-headed; **marah-marah** frequently angry; in a bad mood; **kemarahan** n anger; **memarahi** v to scold, be angry with; **pemarah** adj bad-tempered

marak, semarak shine, glow, bright; glittering, exciting

maraton *n* marathon

Maret *bulan ~* March; *Surat Perintah Sebelas Maret ~ (Supersemar)* Eleventh of March Instruction (enabling Suharto to take over power in 1966)

marga *n, lit* road; *Jasa ~* Roads Board; *Sapta ~* the Seven Paths (military motto)

marga *n* (Batak) family name

margarin *n* margarine

margasatwa *n* wild animals, fauna

marhaban *Isl* welcome, hello; *~ ya Ramadhan* happy fasting month

marhaén *arch kaum ~* proletariat

mari let's go, come on; please (said when someone begs leave); *~lah* let us

marinir *n* Marines; *Korps ~* Marine Corps

markas *n* office, headquarters; *~ besar (mabes)* headquarters

markisa *n* kind of passionfruit; *sirop ~* passionfruit cordial or syrup

marmer *n* marble

marmot, marmut *n* guinea pig, marmot

Maroko, Marokko *n* Morocco; *orang ~* Moroccan

mars *n* march; *lagu ~* march

martabak *n* large fried snack with filling; *~ keju* kind of cheese pancake; *~ manis* kind of sweet pancake; *~ telur* kind of omelet

martabat *n* dignity, rank; **bermartabat** *adj* dignified

martil *n* hammer; *lontar ~* hammer throw

Maryam *n, Isl* Mary

mas, emas *n* gold; *~ kawin* dowry; *~ putih* platinum, white gold; *anak ~* favorite, pet; *toko ~* jewelers; *tukang ~* goldsmith

Mas *pron, m* address for elder brother, male person slightly older than yourself, or worker in service industry

masa *n* time, period; *~ depan* future; *~ lalu* past; *sepanjang ~* forever

masa, masak no! I can't believe it! it's not possible (expression of disbelief)

masak cook; cooked; *juru ~* cook, chef; **masakan** *n* food, cooking, dish; *~ Cina* Chinese food, Chinese cuisine; **memasak** *v* to cook

masalah *n* problem; *~nya* the problem is; *tidak ~* no problem; **bermasalah** *adj* problem, troublesome; **mempermasalahkan** *v* to make a problem out of

masam, masem *adj* sour; acid; *bermuka ~* sour-faced

Maséhi *adj* Christian; *tahun ~* Christian calendar

masih *adv* still, yet

masin *adj* salty, brackish (of water)

masing: masing-masing *pron* each, respectively

masinis *n* train driver, engineer

masjid, mesjid *n* mosque

maskapai *n, arch* company; ~ *penerbangan* airline

maskara *n* mascara, eyeshadow

naskawin → **mas**

masker *n* surgical mask

massa *n* the masses, the public; *dikeroyok* ~ beaten up by a mob; **massal** *adj* mass; *perkawinan* ~ mass wedding

masuk *v* to come in, enter; ~ *akal* make sense, logical; ~ *angin* have or catch a cold; ~ *hitungan* included, considered; ~ *Islam* to become Muslim, convert to Islam; **kemasukan** *adj* possessed; **memasuki** *v* to enter (illicitly); **memasukkan** *v* to put in, insert, import, enter; **termasuk** *adj* including

masya Allah it is God's will, heavens above!

masyarakat *n* society; ~ *madani* civil society; **kemasyarakatan** *adj* social; **pemasyarakatan** *lembaga* ~ correctional centre, prison

masyhur *adj* famous, celebrated

mata *n* eye; ~ *air* spring, well; ~ *angin* direction, compass point; ~ *kaki* ankle; ~ *kayu* knot (in wood); ~ *keranjang* wandering eye; *telur* ~ *sapi* fried egg, sunny side up; ~ *uang* currency; *air* ~ tears; *bermain* ~ to flirt, ogle; *cindera* ~ souvenir; **mata-mata** *n* spy; **memata-matai** *v* to spy on; **semata-mata** *adv* only, entirely, solely

matahari *n* sun; *bunga* ~ sun-

flower; ~ *terbenam* sunset; ~ *terbit* sunrise

mata-mata *n* spy ← **mata**

matang *adj* ripe, cooked, mature; *setengah* ~ medium, half-cooked; **kematangan** *n* maturity

matématika *n* mathematics, maths

matéri *n* material; **matérial** *adj* material; **matérialis** *adj* materialist; **matérialisme** *n* materialism

mati die; go out, be extinguished; ~ *lampu* blackout; ~ *suri* coma; **mati-matian** *adv* as hard as possible, to the death; **kematian** *n* death, passing; **mematikan** *v* to kill, extinguish, put out; ~ *lampu* to turn off the light

matra *n* dimension

matras *n* mat (in gymnastics or martial arts)

matré *cewek* ~ material girl ← **matéri**

mau *v* to want, will; ~ *tidak* ~ whether you want to or not, there's no avoiding it; **kemauan** *n* want, will, desire; **semaunya** *adv* at will, as you like

Maulud, Mulud *n, Isl* the Prophet Muhammad's birthday

Mauritius *n* Mauritius; *orang* ~ Mauritian

maut *n* death; *malaikat* ~, *malaikatul* ~ angel of death

mawar *bunga* ~ rose

mawas ~ *diri* self-correction, introspection

maya *dunia* ~ cyberspace

mayang *n* palm blossom

mayat, mayit *n* corpse; **mem-buang** ~ to dispose of a body

mayor *pron* major; ~ *-Jenderal (Mayjen)* Major-General

Mbak *pron, f* address for elder sister, female person slightly older than yourself, or worker in service industry

mbok *coll* perhaps (softens message)

Mbok *pron, f* mother; address for female servants

MCK *abbrev mandi cuci kakus* toilet and bathing facilities

mébel, meubel *n* furniture; *toko* ~ furniture store

medali, médali *n* medal

médan *n* field, plain, square; ~ *perang* battlefield

médé, ménté, mété *kacang* ~ cashew (nut)

medok *adj* very thick (of an accent, esp Javanese)

méga *n* cloud; ~ *mendung* storm cloud

megah *adj* glorious, luxurious, grand; **kemegahan** *n* glory, luxury

Méi *bulan* ~ May

méja *n* table; ~ *hijau* court (of law); ~ *makan* dining table; ~ *tulis* desk

méjéng *sl* to hang out, be on display

Mekah, Mekkah *n* Mecca; *Serambi* ~ Aceh, the Gateway to Mecca

mékanik, mékanika *adj* mechanical

mekar *v* to blossom; **pemekaran** *n* expansion, development

Méksiko *n* Mexico; *orang* ~ Mexican

melacak *v* to trace ← **lacak**

melacurkan ~ *diri* to sell your body, prostitute yourself ← **lacur**

meladéni *v* to serve someone ← **ladén**

melafalkan *v* to pronounce ← **lafal**

melahap *v* to devour, gorge yourself on

melahirkan *v* to give birth to; to create ← **lahir**

melainkan *conj* rather, instead

melajang *v* to be single ← **lajang**

melaju *v* to proceed quickly ← **laju**

Melaka, Malaka *n* Malacca; *Selat* ~ Straits of Malacca

melaksanakan *v* to realize, execute, carry out ← **laksana**

melakukan *v* to do, perform, carry out ← **laku**

melalui *v* to pass through; *conj* through, via ← **lalu**

melama-lamakan *v* to take a long time, draw something out ← **lama**

melamar *v* to apply ← **lamar**

melambaikan *v* to wave something; ~ *tangan* to wave goodbye ← **lambai**

melambangkan *v* to symbolize, represent ← **lambang**

melambatkan *v* to slow down ← **lambat**

melambung *v* to bounce; **melambungkan** *v* to bounce

something ← **lambung**

nelaminasi v to laminate ← **laminasi**

nelampaui v to surpass, outdo, overtake ← **lampau**

nelampiaskan v to release, indulge in; ~ *hawa nafsu* to release your sexual urges ← **lampias**

nelampirkan v to attach, enclose

nelamun v to day-dream, fantasize ← **lamun**

nelancong v to go traveling, sightseeing ← **lancong**

nelanda v to engulf, attack, hit; *dilanda kelaparan* to be hit by starvation ← **landa**

nelandasi v to base something on ← **landas**

nelanggar v to disobey, offend; ~ *hukum* to break the law ← **langgar**

nelangkah v to step; **melangkahi** v to step across; to marry before an older sibling ← **langkah**

nelanglang ~ *buana* to see the world, travel great distances ← **langlang**

nelangsingkan ~ *badan* to (go on a) diet ← **langsing**

nelangsir v to shunt ← **langsir**

nelanjutkan v to continue something ← **lanjut**

mélankolis adj melancholic

nelantik v to install, inaugurate ← **lantik**

nelantunkan ~ *lagu* to sing (a song) ← **lantun**

nelapis v to layer, overlay;

melapisi v to add a layer to ← **lapis**

melapor v to report; **melaporkan** v to report, inform ← **lapor**

melapuk v to rot, decay ← **lapuk**

melar stretch, expand

melarang v to ban, prohibit, forbid ← **larang**

melarat adj miserable, poor, poverty-stricken; *hidup* ~ live in poverty; **kemelaratan** n poverty

melarikan v to run off with, abduct, kidnap; ~ *diri* to run away, flee, escape ← **lari**

melarutkan v to dissolve ← **larut**

melas: memelas adj pathetic, pitiful

melata v to crawl, creep; *binatang* ~ reptile ← **lata**

melati n jasmine

melatih v to train ← **latih**

melaut v to go to sea ← **laut**

melawak v to joke, jest ← **lawak**

melawan v to oppose, resist; ~ *arus* against the flow ← **lawan**

melawat v to visit, make a trip ← **lawat**

melayang v to float (in the air); *jiwa* ~ to die ← **layang**

melayani v to serve ← **layan**

melayat v to visit a house in mourning, to pay your respects ← **layat**

Melayu Malay; Indonesian; *bahasa ~, orang* ~ Malay; *Semenanjung* ~ Malaya, the Malay Peninsula; *spion* ~ local (ineffective) spy

melébarkan v to widen ← **lébar**

melebihi *v* to exceed, surpass ← **lebih**

melebur *v* to merge, fuse ← **lebur**

melécéhkan *v* to insult ← **lécéh**

meledak *v* to explode; **meledakkan** *v* to explode or detonate something ← **ledak**

melédék *v* to tease, provoke ← **lédék**

melegakan *adj* reassuring, consoling ← **lega**

melégalisasi, melégalisir *v* to legalize ← **légalisasi**

melejit *v* to shoot up, skyrocket; *namanya* ~ she suddenly became famous ← **lejit**

melék awake, eyes open; ~ *huruf* literate; **kemelék-hurufan** *n* literacy

melekat *v* to stick ← **lekat**

melelahkan *adj* tiring ← **lelah**

meléléh *v* to drip, run; **meléléhkan** *v* to melt something ← **léléh**

melembagakan *v* to make into an institution ← **lembaga**

melembutkan *v* to soften ← **lembut**

melémpar *v* to throw; **melémpari** *v* to pelt, throw something at; ~ *kereta api dengan batu* to throw rocks at a train; **melémparkan** *v* to throw something ← **lémpar**

meléncéng *v* to deviate, go out of your way ← **léncéng**

melénggangkan ~ *tangan* to swing your arms while walking ← **lénggang**

melengkapi *v* to furnish, supply ← **lengkap**

melengking *v* to trill, soar (of a voice) ← **lengking**

melengkung *v* to arch ← **lengkung**

melepaskan *v* to release, let free; ~ *tembakan* to fire a shot ← **lepas**

melését *v* to slip, skid; to miss the target; *jaman* ~ The Great Depression; **pelésétan, plésétan** *n* parody ← **lését**

melestarikan *n* to preserve, maintain; ~ *hutan* to protect the forest ← **lestari**

meletakkan *v* to put in place, set down; ~ *jabatan* to resign ← **letak**

meletus *v* to erupt ← **letus**

meléwati *v* to pass or go through; **meléwatkan** *v* to miss something ← **léwat**

melibatkan *v* to involve, include ← **libat**

meliburkan *v* to give a holiday to ← **libur**

melihat *v* to see, look; **melihat-lihat** *v* to look around, have a look; **memperlihatkan** *v* to show, display ← **lihat**

melilit *v* to wind, twist ← **lilit**

melimpah *adj* overflowing, abundant; **melimpahkan** *v* to shower upon ← **limpah**

melindas *v* to run over, squash ← **lindas**

melindungi *v* to protect, shelter ← **lindung**

melingkar *v* to go around, coil;

melingkari v to circle or surround ← **lingkar**

melinjo n buah ~, biji ~ seeds and nuts which are used for making *emping* chips

melintang adj horizontal, across ← **lintang**

melintas v to pass by ← **lintas**

melipat v to fold ← **lipat**

meliput v to cover, report on; **meliputi** v to include, cover ← **liput**

melirik v to steal a glance ← **lirik**

mélodi n melody

melolong v to howl (of dogs) ← **lolong**

melompat v to jump, leapfrog ← **lompat**

mélon n rockmelon, cantaloupe

meloncat v to spring, jump (over something) ← **loncat**

melonggarkan v to loosen (restrictions) ← **longgar**

melongo v to gape or stare at ← **longo**

melonjak v to increase sharply, peak ← **lonjak**

melontar, melontarkan v to throw; ~ pertanyaan to ask or pose a question ← **lontar**

melorot v to fall, drop, plummet ← **lorot**

melotot v to stare or gape at, with bulging eyes ← **lotot**

meluangkan ~ waktu to set aside time for ← **luang**

meluap v to overflow, swell, wash ← **luap**

melubangi v to pierce, put a hole in ← **lubang**

melucu v to make jokes, be funny ← **lucu**

melucuti v to strip or pull off; ~ senjata to disarm ← **lucut**

meludah v to spit; **meludahi** v to spit at, on ← **ludah**

melukai, melukakan v to hurt or wound ← **luka**

melukis v to paint, draw ← **lukis**

melulu adv always, all the time, continuously

meluluskan v to pass someone (in an exam or test) ← **lulus**

melumpuhkan v to knock out, paralyze ← **lumpuh**

melumuri v to smear, cover with ← **lumur**

melunasi v to pay off; ~ utang to repay, pay off a debt ← **lunas**

meluncurkan v to launch, set in motion ← **luncur**

melupakan v to forget something ← **lupa**

meluruskan v to straighten ← **lurus**

memaafkan v to forgive, pardon ← **maaf**

memabukkan adj alcoholic, intoxicating ← **maaf**

memacari v to date, go out with someone ← **pacar**

memacu v to spur on ← **pacu**

memadai adj enough, sufficient ← **pada**

memadamkan v to put out, extinguish ← **padam**

memadu v to cheat on ← **madu**

memadukan v to combine, unite ← **padu**

memagari v to fence (off) ← **pagar**

memahalkan *v* to raise the price, make more expensive ← **mahal**

memahami *v* to understand, comprehend ← **paham**

memahat *v* to sculpt, chisel ← **pahat**

memainkan *v* to play something; ~ *biola* to play the violin ← **main**

memajang *v* to display ← **pajang**

memajukan *v* to bring forward, propose ← **maju**

memakai *v* to wear; to use ~ *kacamata* to wear glasses ← **pakai**

memakamkan *v* to bury ← **makam**

memakan *v* to eat, consume, take; ~ *obat* to take a pill or capsule; *dimakan rayap* to be eaten by termites ← **makan**

memaki, memaki-maki *v* to insult, heap abuse on ← **maki**

memaklumi *v* to be aware of, accept ← **maklum**

memaksa *v* to force ← **paksa**

memaksudkan *v* to mean, intend ← **maksud**

memaku *v* to nail ← **paku**

memalak *v* to force (usu to pay money) ← **palak**

memalsukan *v* to falsify, forge ← **palsu**

memalu *v* to hammer, strike ← **palu**

memalukan *adj* embarrassing ← **malu**

memamah *v* to chew, ruminate ← **mamah**

memamérkan *v* to display, exhibit ← **pamér**

memanah *v* to shoot (with a bow) ← **panah**

memanas *v* to get hot, heat up; **memanaskan** *v* to heat (up) ← **panas**

memancang *v* to stake or drive in ← **pancang**

memancarkan *v* to broadcast ← **pancar**

memancing *v* to fish (with hook and line) ← **pancing**

memancung *v* to cut off, mutilate; ~ *kepala* to behead or decapitate ← **pancung**

memancur *v* to pour, gush, flow out ← **pancur**

memandang *v* to view, consider; ~ *rendah* to underestimate, disregard ← **pandang**

memandikan *v* to wash someone ← **mandi**

memandu *v* to guide ← **pandu**

memanfaatkan *v* to take advantage of, (draw) benefit from ← **manfaat**

mémang *conj*, **émang** *coll* indeed; ~*nya neg* do you think ...?

memanggang *v* to roast, bake, toast ← **panggang**

memanggil *v* to call ← **panggil**

memanggul *v* to carry on your hip ← **panggul**

memangkas *v* to cut, shear, trim ← **pangkas**

memangku *v* to take on (your lap); ~ *jabatan* to occupy a post ← **pangku**

memanjakan *v* to spoil someone ← **manja**

memanjang *v* to become long, lengthen; **memperpanjang** *v* to extend, make longer ← **panjang**

memanjat *v* to climb; **memanjatkan** *v* to send up; ~ *doa* to offer prayers ← **panjat**

memantapkan *v* to stabilize or steady something ← **mantap**

memantau *v* to observe, watch ← **pantau**

memantul *v* to rebound; **memantulkan** *v* to reflect something ← **pantul**

memapah *v* to support, prop up ← **papah**

memaparkan *v* to explain ← **papar**

memar *adj* bruised

memaraf *v* to initial, sign ← **paraf**

memarahi *v* to scold, be angry with ← **marah**

memarkir *v* to park ← **parkir**

memarut *v* to grate ← **parut**

memasak *v* to cook ← **masak**

memasak *v* to peg ← **pasak**

memasang *v* to put up, attach, fix; ~ *bendera* to hoist a flag; ~ *iklan* to advertise; ~ *lampu* to switch on a light ← **pasang**

memasarkan *v* to market ← **pasar**

memasok *v* to supply ← **pasok**

memastikan *v* to confirm, make sure, ascertain ← **pasti**

memasuki *v* to enter (illicitly); **memasukkan** *v* to put in, insert, import, enter ← **masuk**

mematahkan *v* to break ← **patah**

memata-matai *v* to spy on ← **mata-mata**

mematikan *v* to kill, extinguish, put out; ~ *lampu* to turn off the light ← **mati**

mematok *v* to fix, set; ~ *harga* to set a price ← **patok**

mematuhi *v* to obey ← **patuh**

mematuk *v* to peck, bite ← **patuk**

mematung *v* to freeze, not move, be as still as a statue ← **patung**

memayungi *v* to hold an umbrella over someone ← **payung**

membabat *v* to cut or chop down, clear away ← **babat**

membabi ~ *buta* to act blindly and rashly ← **babi**

membaca *v* to read; **membaca-kan** *v* to read something to someone ← **baca**

membagi *v* to divide, distribute; **membagi-bagi** *v* to split up ← **bagi**

membahagiakan *v* to make happy ← **bahagia**

membahas *v* to discuss, debate ← **bahas**

membaik *v* to improve ← **baik**

membajak *v* to hijack; to copy illegally; ~ *pesawat* to hijack a plane ← **bajak**

membajak *v* to plough ← **bajak**

membakar *v* to burn ← **bakar**

membalap *v* to race ← **balap**

membalas *v* to reply, respond ← **balas**

membalik *v* to return, reverse, turn over; **membalikkan** *v* to turn something over ← **balik**

membalur *v* to smear or massage with oil ← **balur**

membalut *v* to bandage ← **balut**

membandel *v* to do something naughty, be disobedient ← **bandel**

membandingkan *v* to compare something ← **banding**

membanggakan *v* to make proud, please ← **bangga**

membangkang *v* to defy, resist, disobey ← **bangkang**

membangkit *v* to arouse, stimulate ← **bangkit**

membangun *v* to build or create

membangunkan *v* to wake someone up ← **bangun**

membantah *v* to deny, dispute ← **bantah**

membantai *v* to slaughter, kill viciously ← **bantai**

membanting *v* to throw down (with a bang); ~ *pintu* to slam the door; ~ *tulang* to toil, work yourself to the bone ← **banting**

membantu *v* to help (someone) ← **bantu**

membanyol *v* to joke ← **banyol**

membaptis *v* to baptize, christen ← **baptis**

membara *v* to glow with heat ← **bara**

membaringkan *v* to lay something down in rows ← **baring**

membasahi *v* to moisten, wet ← basah

membasmi *v* to exterminate, destroy, wipe out ← **basmi**

membasuh *v* to wash with water; ~ *wajah* to wash the face ← **basuh**

membatalkan *v* to cancel, repeal ← **batal**

membatasi *v* to limit, restrict, curb someone ← **batas**

membatik *n* to apply wax onto fabric ← **batik**

membatu *v* to freeze, become petrified, fossilized ← **batu**

membaur *v* to integrate, mix with others (of people) ← **baur**

membawa *v* to take, bring, carry; conduct; **membawakan** *v* to bring or carry for someone; to sing; *dia ~ lagu-lagu keroncong* she performed *keroncong* songs ← **bawa**

membawahi *v* to head a section (with staff under you) ← **bawah**

membayangi *v* to overshadow ← **bayang**

membayar *v* to pay; ~ *dimuka* to pay in advance ← **bayar**

membayonét *v* to stab someone with a bayonet ← **bayonét**

membebani *v* to burden someone with something; **membebankan** *v* to charge something to someone ← **beban**

membébaskan *v* to exempt, liberate, free someone ← **bébas**

membébék *v* to quack; follow blindly ← **bébék**

membébérkan *v* to reveal, explain ← **bébér**

membedah *v* to operate ← **bedah**

membédakan v to discriminate, differentiate between, consider as different ← **béda**

membekali v to supply someone with provisions ← **bekal**

membekas v to leave an impression ← **bekas**

membeku v to freeze; **membekukan** v to freeze something ← **beku**

membekuk v to arrest ← **bekuk**

membéla v to defend ← **béla**

membelah v to split in two ← **belah**

membelakangi v to turn your back on someone ← **belakang**

membelanjakan v to spend money ← **belanja**

membelenggu v to shackle, handcuff ← **belenggu**

membeli v to buy, purchase; **membelikan** v to buy something for someone; *Sinta ~ anak itu boneka* Sinta bought the child a doll ← **beli**

membélok v to bend, turn; **membélokkan** v to turn, divert something ← **bélok**

membeludak v to burst out, spread everywhere, explode ← **beludak**

membenarkan v to confirm, verify; justify ← **benar**

membenci v to hate ← **benci**

membendungi v to dam, stop a flow ← **bendung**

membengkak v to swell up ← **bengkak**

membéngkokkan v to bend something ← **béngkok**

membentak v to shout, scold, snap ← **bentak**

membentuk v to form, set up something (eg. committee) ← **bentuk**

membentur v to hit, collide with ← **bentur**

membéo v to parrot, imitate (superiors etc) ← **béo**

memberangus v to muzzle, bridle; *~ pers* to curb press freedom ← **berangus**

memberanikan *~ diri* to dare, get up the courage ← **berani**

memberantas v to wipe out, fight against; *~ korupsi* to wipe out corruption ← **berantas**

memberatkan v to burden, make heavy; *adj* incriminating; *kesaksian yang ~* incriminating evidence ← **berat**

memberdayakan v to empower ← **daya**

membéréskan v to clear up, make ready ← **bérés**

memberhentikan v to stop (a vehicle); dismiss

memberi v to give; **memberikan** v to give someone (as an act of kindness); to give something (for someone) ← **beri**

memberitahu v to advise, inform, tell ← **beri tahu**

memberitakan v to report ← **berita**

memberkati v to bless; *Tuhan ~* God bless ← **berkat**

memberontak v to rebel, revolt ← **berontak**

membersihkan v to clean; wipe

out (eg disease) ← **bersih**

membesar v to get bigger, grow; **membesarkan** v to bring up, raise (children) ← **besar**

membesuk v to visit someone in hospital ← **besuk**

membetulkan v to correct, repair ← **betul**

membiakkan v to breed, cultivate ← **biak**

membiarkan v to let, allow, permit; *biarkan!* let it be! ← **biar**

membiasakan v ~ *diri* to accustom yourself ← **biasa**

membiayai v to finance someone or something ← **biaya**

membicarakan v to discuss ← **bicara**

membidik v to take aim ← **bidik**

membilas v to rinse; *gosokkan pada rambut, lalu* ~ rub into the hair, then rinse ← **bilas**

membimbing v to lead, guide, coach ← **bimbing**

membina v to build up, found ← **bina**

membinasakan v to destroy, ruin ← **binasa**

membingkai v to frame ← **bingkai**

membingungkan *adj* confusing ← **bingung**

membintangi v to star in; *Dian Sastro* ~ *film Pasir Berbisik* Dian Sastro starred in *Pasir Berbisik* ← **bintang**

membiru v to turn blue ← **biru**

membisik v to whisper ← **bisik**

membisu v to be silent, say nothing ← **bisu**

membius v to drug, anesthetize ← **bius**

memblokir v to block; ~ *jalan* to block the road; *begitu kecopetan, dia langsung* ~ *kartu kredit* after being robbed, he blocked his credit card ← **blokir**

membobol v to break into; *mesin ATM di*~ *maling* thieves broke into the ATM machine ← **bobol**

membocorkan v to leak something ← **bocor**

membodohi v to make someone stupid; **membodohkan** v to make stupid ← **bodoh**

membohong v to lie; **membohongi** v to lie to someone ← **bohong**

memboikot v to boycott something ← **boikot**

membolak-balik v to go back and forth ← **bolak-balik**

membolongi v to pierce ← **bolong**

membolos v skip, be absent, play truant, wag, skive; ~ *sekolah* to skip school ← **bolos**

memboncéng v to ride with someone else on a two-wheeled vehicle, dink; to sponge or cadge a lift ← **boncéng**

membongkar v to pull apart, dismantle; to unpack; to unearth ← **bongkar**

membopong v to carry someone (bodily, or on the shoulders) ← **bopong**

membordir *v* to embroider ← **bordir**

memborgol *v* to handcuff ← **borgol**

memborong *v* to buy up, buy in bulk ← **borong**

memboroskan *v* to waste something ← **boros**

membosankan *adj* boring, tiresome ← **bosan**

membotak *v* to go bald; **membotaki** *v* to shave, make bald ← **botak**

memboyong *v* to take (someone) away; *isteri barunya di~ ke Padang* he took his new bride with him to Padang ← **boyong**

membrédel *v* to muzzle, bridle, ban; *majalah Tempo di~ pada tahun 1994 Tempo* magazine was closed down in 1994 ← **brédel**

membuahkan *v* to result in; **membuahi** *v* to impregnate, fertilize ← **buah**

membuai *v* to swing, rock, sway something ← **buai**

membual *v* to foam; to froth at the mouth, talk rubbish ← **bual**

membuang *v* to throw out; to waste; to exile; *~ ingus* blow your nose; *~ kesempatan* waste an opportunity ← **buang**

membuat *v* to make; *~ marah* to make angry; **membuat-buat** *v* to pretend ← **buat**

membubarkan *v* to break something up; *demo itu dibubarkan polisi* the demo was broken up by the police ← **bubar**

membubuhkan *v* to attach something; *~ tanda tangan* to attach your signature ← **bubuh**

membudaya *v* to spread, become entrenched; *korupsi sudah ~* corruption is part of the culture ← **budaya**

membudidayakan *v* to cultivate, grow ← **budidaya**

membujang *v* to remain unmarried ← **bujang**

membujuk *v* to coax ← **bujuk**

membuka *v* to open; *~ rahasia* to reveal a secret; **membukakan** *v* to open (for someone) ← **buka**

membuking *v* to book ← **buking**

membuktikan *v* to prove ← **bukti**

membukukan *v* to enter into the accounts books ← **buku**

membulatkan *v* to round off ← **bulat**

membumbui *v* to season ← **bumbu**

membumihanguskan *v* to scorch the earth, apply a scorched earth policy ← **bumi hangus**

membungkam *v* to keep silent ← **bungkam**

membungkuk *v* to bow, be hunched; **membungkukkan** *~ badan* to bow ← **bungkuk**

membungkus *v* to wrap; *~ kado* wrap a gift ← **bungkus**

membuntuti *v* to follow someone ← **buntut**

membunuh *v* to kill; ~ *diri* to kill yourself, commit suicide ← **bunuh**

membunyikan *v* to sound, ring something ← **bunyi**

memburu *v* to hunt, chase ← **buru**

memburuk *v* to worsen ← **buruk**

membusuk *v* to rot ← **busuk**

membutuhkan *v* to need something ← **butuh**

memecah ~ *belah* to break into fragments, cause divisions; **memecahkan** *v* to break; to solve; ~ *soal* to solve a problem ← **pecah**

memecat *v* to fire, dismiss ← **pecat**

memecundangi *v* to swindle or trick; to beat or defeat ← **pecundang**

memedulikan *v* to care or be bothered about ← **peduli**

memegang *v* to hold, grasp ← **pegang**

memejamkan ~ *mata* to close your eyes ← **pejam**

memekakkan *adj* deafening, loud ← **pekak**

memekik *v* to scream or shriek ← **pekik**

memelankan *v* to slow something down ← **pelan**

memelantingkan *v* to throw everywhere ← **pelanting**

memelas *adj* pitiful, pathetic ← **belas**

memelésétkan *v* to up-end, send off-course ← **pelését**

memelihara *v* to take care of,

look after, cultivate ← **pelihara**

memelintir, memelintirkan *v* to twist ← **pelintir**

memelitur *v* to polish, varnish ← **pelitur**

memelopori *v* to pioneer, lead ← **pelopor**

memelotot *v* to stare, have bulging eyes; **memeloti** *v* to stare at someone; **memelototkan** ~ *mata* to stare ← **lotot**

memeluk *v* to hug or embrace; ~ *agama* to follow a religion ← **peluk**

memencét *v* to press (a button, key) ← **pencét**

meméndékkan *v* to shorten ← **péndék**

memengaruhi *v* to influence, affect ← **pengaruh**

memenggal *v* to cut off, amputate; ~ *kepala* to behead ← **penggal**

memenjara, memenjarakan *v* to put in prison, imprison ← **penjara**

meménsiunkan *v* to pension off ← **pénsiun**

mementaskan *v* to stage, present ← **pentas**

mementingkan *v* to make important, emphasize ← **penting**

memenuhi *v* to fulfill, meet requirements ← **penuh**

memeragakan *v* to display, show ← **peraga**

memérah *v* to blush ← **mérah**

memerah *v* to milk or squeeze ← **perah**

memerangi *v* to fight against ← **perang**

memerankan *v* to portray, play the role of ← **peran**

memeras *v* to squeeze, press; to blackmail, extort ← **peras**

memercayai *v* to trust someone; **mempercayakan** *v* to entrust with ← **percaya**

memerciki *v* to spatter something; **memercikkan** *v* to splash with something ← **percik**

memerhatikan *v* to notice, pay attention to ← **hati**

memeriahkan *v* to liven up, enliven ← **meriah**

memeriksa *v* to examine or investigate; ~ *ulang* to review ← **periksa**

memerintah *v* to rule, govern, reign; **memerintahkan** *v* to order or command something ← **perintah**

memerkosa *v* to rape ← **perkosa**

memerlahankan *v* to slow something ← **perlahan**

memerlukan *v* to need, require ← **perlu**

memerosokkan *v* to push something into ← **perosok**

memesan *v* to order ← **pesan**

memesona, memesonakan *adj* enthralling, enchanting ← **pesona**

memetik *v* to pick; to strum; ~ *gitar* to play or strum the guitar ← **petik**

memfitnah *v* to slander ← **fitnah**

memfokuskan *v* to focus something; ~ *diri* to focus yourself ← **fokus**

memicu *v* to trigger, set off ← **picu**

memihak *v* to take sides ← **pihak**

memijak *v* to tread or step on ← **pijak**

memijat *v* to massage ← **pijat**

memikat *adj* attractive, enticing ← **pikat**

memikirkan *vt* to think about ← **pikir**

memikul *v* to bear, carry on the shoulder ← **pikul**

memilih *v* to choose or select; to elect or vote (for) ← **pilih**

memiliki *v* to own, possess ← **milik**

memilukan *adj* moving, touching ← **pilu**

memimpikan *v* to dream of ← **mimpi**

memimpin *v* to lead ← **pimpin**

meminang *v* to propose, ask for a girl's hand in marriage ← **pinang**

memindah *coll* **memindahkan** *v* to move, transfer ← **pindah**

meminggir *v, coll* to move to the side, pull over; **meminggirkan** *v* to move to one side, cast aside ← **pinggir**

meminjam *v* to borrow; **meminjami** *v* to lend someone; **meminjamkan** *v* to lend something ← **pinjam**

meminta *v* to ask for, request; **meminta-minta** *v* to beg, ask for money ← **minta, pinta**

memintal *v* to spin (thread) ← **pintal**

memiringkan *v* to slant, tilt ←
miring

memisah *v* to separate; **me-misahkan** *v* to separate something ← **pisah**

mémoar *n* memoirs

memojokkan *v* to force into a corner ← **pojok**

memolés *v* to polish ← **polés**

memompa *v* to pump ← **pompa**

memonopoli *v* to monopolize ← **monopoli**

memorak-porandakan *v* to cause chaos, turn upside-down ← **porak-poranda**

mémori *n* (electronic) memory

memotivasi *v* to motivate ← **motivasi**

memotong *v* to cut, deduct; to slaughter, amputate; to interrupt ← **potong**

memotrét *v* to photograph ← **potrét**

mempan *adj* effective

mempelai *kedua* ~ bridal couple; ~ *pria* groom; ~ *wanita* bride

mempelajari *v* to study something in depth ← **ajar**

memperalat *v* to use or take advantage of someone; *Tina diperalat oleh kawannya* Tina was used by her friend ← **alat**

memperbaiki *v* to repair, fix ← **baik**

memperbanyak *v* to increase, multiply ← **banyak**

memperbarui *v* to renew, make new ← **baru**

memperbesar *v* to enlarge something ← **besar**

memperboléhkan *v* to allow, permit ← **boléh**

memperburuk *v* to make even worse ← **buruk**

mempercantik ~ *diri* to make yourself beautiful ← **cantik**

mempercepat *v* to speed up, accelerate ← **cepat**

memperdagangkan *v* to deal in ← **dagang**

memperdalam *v* to deepen; to study in detail, broaden your knowledge ← **dalam**

memperdaya *v* to deceive, use, trick ← **daya**

memperdengarkan *v* to play, broadcast ← **dengar**

memperebutkan *v* to seize, take by force ← **rebut**

mempererat *v* to strengthen, make closer ← **erat**

memperingati *v* to commemorate ← **ingat**

memperjuangkan *v* to fight for ← **juang**

memperkenalkan *v* to introduce ← **kenal**

memperkenankan *v* to approve, grant, allow ← **kenan**

memperkirakan *v* to estimate, calculate ← **kira**

memperkuat *v* to reinforce, make stronger ← **kuat**

memperlancar *v* to ease, make easier ← **lancar**

memperluas *v* to widen, expand, enlarge ← **luas**

mempermainkan *v* to ridicule, make a fool of ← **main**

mempermalukan *v* to embarrass, shame ← **malu**

mempermandikan *v* to christen, baptize ← **mandi**

mempermasalahkan *v* to make a problem out of ← **masalah**

mempermudah *v* to make easier ← **mudah**

memperoléh *v* to obtain, get ← **oléh**

memperolok *v* to tease, taunt ← **olok**

memperparah *v* to make worse, aggravate ← **parah**

memperpéndék *v* to shorten, make even shorter ← **péndék**

mempersalahkan *v* to blame ← **salah**

mempersatukan *v* to unite various things ← **satu**

mempersembahkan *v* to offer (up), present ← **sembah**

mempersenjatai *v* to arm someone ← **senjata**

mempersiapkan *v* to prepare something, get something ready ← **siap**

mempersilakan *v* to invite someone to do something ← **sila**

mempersingkat *v* to shorten ← **singkat**

mempersoalkan *v* to question, discuss ← **soal**

mempersunting *v* to marry (a woman) ← **sunting**

mempertahankan *v* to defend or maintain ← **tahan**

mempertajam *v* to sharpen, exacerbate ← **tajam**

mempertanggungjawabkan *v* to account for ← **tanggung jawab**

mempertanyakan *v* to query ← **tanya**

mempertaruhkan *v* to stake, risk, bet; ~ *nyawa* to risk your life ← **taruh**

mempertimbangkan *v* to consider ← **timbang**

mempertunjukkan *v* to display or perform ← **tunjuk**

memperuntukkan *v* to allocate or assign ← **untuk**

mempesona, mempesonakan *adj* enthralling, enchanting ← **pesona;** → **memesona**

mempraktékkan *v* to put into practice ← **prakték**

memprihatinkan *adj* worrying ← **prihatin**

memprioritaskan *v* to prioritize ← **prioritas**

memproduksi *v* to produce ← **produksi**

memproklamasikan *v* to proclaim (independence) ← **proklamasi**

mempromosikan *v* to promote ← **promosi**

memproséskan *v* to process ← **prosés**

memprotés *v* to (make a) protest ← **protés**

mempunyai *v* to have, own, possess ← **punya**

memuai *v* to expand, swell ← **muai**

memuakkan *adj* revolting, disgusting ← **muak**

memuaskan *adj* satisfactory ←
puas

memuat *v* to contain ← **muat**

memudar *v* to fade ← **pudar**

memugar *v* to restore, renovate
← **pugar**

memuja *v* to worship ← **puja**

memuji *v* to praise; **memuji-muji**
v to praise excessively ← **puji**

memukul *v* to hit, beat, strike
← **pukul**

memulai *v* to start or begin
something ← **mula, mulai**

memulangkan *v* to give back; to
send back, repatriate ← **pulang**

memuliakan *v* to honor, glorify
← **mulia**

memulihkan *v* to restore ←
pulih

memuluskan *v* to ease the way,
help ← **mulus**

memuncak *v* to culminate,
reach a peak ← **puncak**

memunculkan *v* to bring forward ← **muncul**

memundurkan *v* to retract,
bring back ← **mundur**

memunggungi *v* to turn your
back on ← **punggung**

memungkinkan *adj* conducive;
v to enable, make possible ←
mungkin

memungkiri *v* to deny ←
mungkir

memungut *v* to pick up, collect
← **pungut**

memuntahkan *v* to vomit or
bring up ← **muntah**

memupuskan *v* to wipe out,
destroy ← **pupus**

memusatkan *v* to focus; ~
perhatian to concentrate ←
pusat

memusingkan ~ *kepala* puzzling
← **pusing**

memusnahkan *v* to destroy ←
musnah; pemusnahan *n* act
of destruction ← **musnah**

memusuhi *v* to fight against,
antagonize, make an enemy of
← **musuh**

memutar *v* to wind; to rotate;
~ *balik* to turn around, do a
U-turn; **memutar-balikkan** *v*
to reverse, distort; **memutari** *v*
to go around, orbit; **perputaran**
n rotation ← **putar**

memutasi *v* to change someone's
status ← **mutasi**

memutihkan *v* to whiten, bleach
← **putih**

memutus *v* to break; ~ *hubungan*
to break or sever contact;
memutuskan *v* to terminate or
break; to decide ← **putus**

mena: semena-mena *(tidak)* ~
arbitrary, without reason, unjust

menaati *v* to obey or follow
something ← **taat**

menabrak *v* to collide with;
menabrakkan *v* to ram something into ← **tabrak**

menabuh *v* to beat (a drum) ←
tabuh

menabung *v* to save or deposit
money ← **tabung**

menabur *v* to scatter or sprinkle
← **tabur**

menafsirkan *v* to interpret
something ← **tafsir**

Ménag *n* Minister of Religious Affairs ← **Menteri Agama**

menagih *v* to ask for payment, bill ← **tagih**

menahan *v* to bear, endure; to detain; ~ *diri* to hold yourself back, restrain yourself ← **tahan**

menahbiskan *v* to consecrate, ordain ← **tahbis**

menahun *adj* chronic; *penyakit* ~ chronic illness ← **tahun**

menaiki *v* to ride, mount, get on; **menaikkan** *v* to raise, hoist ← **naik**

menakar *v* to measure ← **takar**

menakdirkan *v* to determine, to predestine ← **takdir**

menakjubkan *adj* astonishing, amazing ← **takjub**

menaklukkan *v* to defeat, conquer, subdue ← **takluk**

menaksir *v* to estimate, appraise, value; to like, find someone or something attractive ← **taksir**

menakut-nakuti *v* to frighten or intimidate (repeatedly); **menakutkan** *v, adv* frightening; to frighten or scare ← **takut**

menala *v* to tune ← **tala**

menamakan *v* to call, name ← **nama**

menamatkan *v* to end, finish, conclude ← **tamat**

menambah *v* to add to or increase; **menambahi** *v* to increase something; **menambahkan** *v* to add something to ← **tambah**

menambak *v* to dam (up) ← **tambak**

menambal *v* to mend, patch, darn; ~ *gigi* to fill a tooth, have a filling; ~ *jalan* to fill in a pothole ← **tambal**

menambang *v* to mine, dig for ← **tambang**

menambat, menambatkan *v* to fasten, tie up ← **tambat**

menampakkan *v* to show, make appear ← **tampak**

menampar *v* to slap ← **tampar**

menampi *v* to winnow ← **tampi**

menampik *v* to reject, refuse ← **tampik**

menampilkan *v* to present ← **tampil**

menampung *v* to collect, hold ← **tampung**

menanak ~ *nasi* to cook rice ← **tanak**

menanam *v* to plant or grow; to invest ← **tanam**

menandai *v* to mark ← **tanda**

menandaskan *v* to use up ← **tandas**

menandatangani *v* to sign something ← **tanda tangan**

menandu *v* to carry in a litter ← **tandu**

menang *v* to win; ~ *telak* to thrash, beat outright; ~ *tipis* narrowly defeat; **kemenangan** *n* victory; **pemenang** *n* winner, victor

menangani *v* to handle ← **tangan**

menanggalkan *v* to take off or remove; ~ *pakaian* to undress ← **tanggal**

menanggapi *v* to respond, reply ← **tanggap**

menangguhkan *v* to delay, postpone, put something off ← **tangguh**

menanggulangi *v* to deal or cope with ← **tanggulang**

menanggung *v* to guarantee, be responsible; ~ *beban* to bear ← **tanggung**

menangis *v* to cry; **menangisi** *v* to cry over, mourn ← **tangis**

menangkal *v* to ward off, repel ← **tangkal**

menangkap *v* to catch, capture ← **tangkap**

menangkis *v* to defend yourself, fend off, parry ← **tangkis**

menanjak *adj* rising, climbing, steep ← **tanjak**

menantang *v* to challenge; *adj* challenging ← **tantang**

menanti-nanti *v* to wait for a long time; **menantikan** *v* to wait for ← **nanti**

menantu *n* son- or daughter-in-law → **mantu**

menanyai *v* to question someone; **menanyakan** *v* to ask about ← **tanya**

menara *n* tower; minaret (of a mosque)

menari *v* to dance, perform a traditional dance; **menari-nari** *v* to dance about ← **tari**

menarik *v* to pull or draw; *adj* interesting, attractive; ~ *kesimpulan* to conclude, draw a conclusion; ~ *napas* to inhale ← **tarik**

menaruh *v* to put (away); ~ *dendam* to bear a grudge ← **taruh**

menasihati *v* to advise ← **nasihat**

menawan *v* to detain, take someone prisoner, intern; *adj* attractive, appealing ← **tawan**

menawar *v* to bargain; *tawar-~* bargaining; **menawarkan** *v* to offer or bid ← **tawar**

menayangkan *v* to telecast, show on TV ← **tayang**

mencabik *v* to tear ← **cabik**

mencabuli *v* to rape, assault someone ← **cabul**

mencabut *v* to pull out, remove; ~ *gigi* extract a tooth ← **cabut**

mencacah *v* to mince, chop up ← **cacah**

mencaci ~ *maki* to insult, abuse ← **caci**

mencadangkan *v* to reserve, set aside; suggest something ← **cadang**

mencair *v* to melt, turn into liquid; **mencairkan** *v* to melt something; to make (funds) available ← **cair**

mencakar *v* to scratch; *di~ kucing* scratched by a cat ← **cakar**

mencakupi *v* to include, cover ← **cakup**

mencalonkan *v* to nominate someone ← **calon**

mencambuk *v* to whip; **mencambuki** *vt* to whip repeatedly ← **cambuk**

mencampur *v* to mix, blend; ~ *baur* to mix with society; ~ *tangan* to get involved, interfere; **mencampuradukkan** *v* to mix up, confuse; **mencampuri** *v* to mix into; to meddle; **mencampurkan** *v* to mix something to ← **campur**

mencangkokkan *v* to graft (of plants), transplant (of organs) ← **cangkok**

mencantumkan *v* to attach ← **cantum**

mencapai *v* to reach, attain ← **capai**

mencari *v* look or search for, seek; **mencari-cari** *v* to search repeatedly, everywhere; **mencarikan** *v* to look for something for someone ← **cari**

mencarter *v* to hire, charter ← **carter**

mencatat *v* to note (down) ← **catat**

mencatut ~ *nama* to use someone else's name illegally ← **catut**

menceburkan *v* to push into water ← **cebur**

mencécérkan *v* to scatter, disperse ← **cécér**

mencederai *v* to damage, injure ← **cedera**

mencegah *v* to prevent, fight against ← **cegah**

mencegat *v* to hold up, bar ← **cegat**

mencekal *v* to prevent from leaving the country ← **cekal**

mencekam *adj* frightening, ominous; *situasi sudah* ~ things looked black ← **cekam**

mencekik *v* to strangle ← **cekik**

mencelakakan *v* to bring misfortune on ← **celaka**

mencelup *v* to dye, dip ← **celup**

mencemari *v* to dirty, pollute ← **cemar**

mencemaskan *adj* worrying, sobering ← **cemas**

mencemoohkan *v* to mock, ridicule ← **cemooh**

mencemplungkan *v* to plunge something into water ← **cemplung**

mencengkeram *v* to grip, squeeze ← **cengkeram**

mencerahkan *v* to enlighten, clear matters up ← **cerah**

mencerai, menceraikan *v* to divorce someone; **menceraiberaikan** *v* to tear apart, separate ← **cerai**

mencerdaskan *v* to educate, sharpen your mind ← **cerdas**

menceriakan *v* to liven up, make happy ← **ceria**

menceritakan *v* to describe, relate ← **cerita**

mencermati *v* to observe closely ← **cermat**

mencerminkan *v* to reflect ← **cermin**

mencerna *v* to digest ← **cerna**

mencerocos *v* **nyerocos** *coll* to talk too much, blather, chatter or rattle on ← **cerocos**

mencétak *v* to print ← **cétak**

mencetus *v* to scrape; to burst out; say something unexpected; **mencetuskan** *v* to spark off, provoke ← **cetus**

mencicil *v* to pay by instalments ← **cicil**

mencicipi *v* to try, taste something ← **cicip**

menciduk *v, coll* to arrest ← **ciduk**

mencincang *v* to mince, chop up ← **cincang**

mencintai *v* to love someone ← **cinta**

mencipta *v* to create; **menciptakan** *v* to create, make ← **cipta**

mencitrakan *v* to depict ← **citra**

mencium *v* to smell, to sniff; to kiss ← **cium**

menciut *v* to shrivel; **menciutkan** *v* to reduce ← **ciut**

mencoba *v* to try, attempt ← **coba**

mencoblos *v* to vote, pierce ← **coblos**

mencocokkan *v* to match ← **cocok**

mencocol *v* to dip into a liquid ← **cocol**

mencolok *adj* glaring, standing out ← **colok**

mencolong *v* to steal, nick, filch ← **colong**

méncong *adj* bent, skewed, not straight

mencongkél *n* to prise open ← **congkél**

menconték *v* to copy, cheat ← **conték, sonték**

mencontoh *v* to copy, imitate; **mencontohi** *v* to give as an example ← **contoh**

mencopét *v* to pick someone's pocket ← **copét**

mencopot *v* to come off; *coll* to pull (off); to sack, fire ← **copot**

mencorét *v* to scratch, cross out ← **corét**

méncrét *v* to have diarrhea

mencubit *v* to pinch ← **cubit**

mencuci *v* to wash, clean ← **cuci**

mencukupi *v* to satisfy, fulfill ← **cukup**

mencukur *v* to shave ← **cukur**

menculik *v* to kidnap ← **culik**

mencurahkan *v* to pour out; ~ *tenaga* to spend energy ← **curah**

mencuri *n* to steal ← **curi**

mencurigai *v* to suspect someone; **mencurigakan** *adj* suspicious, suspect ← **curiga**

mendaftar *v* to register; **mendaftarkan** *v* to register something ← **daftar**

Méndagri *n* Minister of the Interior, Minister of Home Affairs ← **Menteri Dalam Negeri**

mendahului *v* to precede, overtake; **mendahulukan** *v* to put before, give precedence to ← **dahulu**

mendaki *v* to climb, ascend; ~ *gunung* (to go) mountaineering, bushwalking ← **daki**

mendalam *adj* deep; *duka cita yang* ~ my deepest sympathy; **mendalami** *v* to delve into ← **dalam**

mendalangi *v* to orchestrate (events) ← **dalang**

mendamaikan *v* to reconcile, pacify ← **damai**

mendambakan *v* to long or wish for; ~ *gadis mandiri, lulusan*

S1 seeking an independent woman, university graduate ← **damba**

mendampingi v to accompany, flank ← **damping**

mendanai v to fund something ← **dana**

mendandani v to decorate, dress, adorn ← **dandan**

mendapat v to obtain, receive; ~ *kabar* to receive news; **mendapati** v to experience; **mendapatkan** v to obtain; discover ← **dapat**

mendarah daging v to become second nature ← **darah**

mendarat v to land ← **darat**

mendasar adj basic; **mendasarkan** v to base on something ← **dasar**

mendatakan v to record, document, collect data on ← **data**

mendatang adj coming, next; **mendatangkan** v to bring, import ← **datang**

mendatarkan v to make flat, level ← **datar**

mendayung v to stroke (an oar), row; to pedal ← **dayung**

méndé → **médé**

mendebarkan adj pulsating, throbbing ← **debar**

mendébet v to debit ← **débet**

mendéfinisikan v to define ← **définisi**

mendeham v to clear the throat, cough ← **deham**

mendekap v to hug, embrace ← **dekap**

mendekati v to approach;

mendekatkan v to bring close ← **dekat**

mendéklamasikan v to declaim ← **déklamasi**

mendeklarasikan v to declare ← **déklarasi**

mendémo v to protest against ← **démo**

mendenda v to fine ← **denda**

mendengar v to hear; **mendengarkan** v to listen; ~ *lagu* listen to music ← **dengar**

mendengkur v to snore; to purr (of a cat) ← **dengkur**

mendengung v to drone, hum, shake with sound ← **dengung**

mendepak v to kick something, kick out; *Haris didepak dari tim* Haris was kicked off the team ← **depak**

mendérék v to tow ← **dérék**

mendering v to ring, tinkle ← **dering**

menderita v to suffer, endure ← **derita**

menderu v to roar ← **deru**

mendesah v to sigh, make a swishing noise ← **desah**

mendésain v to design ← **désain**

mendesak adj pressing, urgent; v to press, urge, push ← **desak**

mendesir v to hiss, rustle ← **desir**

mendéwakan v to worship, idolize, put on a pedestal ← **déwa**

mendiagnosa v to diagnose ← **diagnosa**

mendiang adj the late

mendidih adj boiling; **mendidihkan** v to boil water ← **didih**

mendidik *v* to educate, bring up, teach ← **didik**

Méndiknas *n* Minister of National Education ← **Menteri Pendidikan Nasional**

mendikté *v* to dictate (terms) ← **dikté**

mending, mendingan *adj, coll* better, better off

mendinginkan *v* to chill, cool ← **dingin**

mendirikan *v* to build, establish, erect ← **diri**

mendiskriminasi, mendiskriminasikan *v* to discriminate against ← **diskriminasi**

mendistribusikan *v* to distribute ← **distribusi**

mendoakan *v* to pray for ← **doa**

mendobrak *v* to break open, smash; ~ *pintu* to break down the door ← **dobrak**

mendokuméntasi *v* to document, file ← **dokuméntasi**

mendongéng *v* to tell a story ← **dongéng**

mendongkrak *v* to jack, lever, raise; ~ *popularitas* to boost popularity ← **dongkrak**

mendorong *v* to push, encourage ← **dorong**

menduakan ~ *Tuhan* to worship more than one god ← **dua**

menduda *v* to become or live as a widower ← **duda**

menduduki *v* to sit on something; to occupy; *Indonesia pernah diduduki Jepang* Indonesia was once occupied by Japan ← **duduk**

mendukung *vt* to support

mendulang *v* to pan (for gold) ← **dulang**

mendung *adj* cloudy, overcast

menebak *v* to guess ← **tebak**

menebang *v* to fell, cut down ← **tebang**

menébarkan *v* to scatter; to cast (a net) ← **tébar**

menebus *v* to pay a ransom ~ *dosa* to atone for a sin ← **tebus**

menegakkan *v* to erect; to uphold or maintain ← **tegak**

menegangkan *adj* tense, stressful ← **tegang**

menegaskan *v* to clarify, point out, affirm ← **tegas**

meneguk *v* to gulp or guzzle ← **teguk**

menegur *v* to speak to, address; to warn, rebuke, tell off ← **tegur**

menekan *v* to press; **menekankan** *v* to stress, emphasize ← **tekan**

menéken *v* to sign, initial ← **téken**

menekuni *v* to apply yourself to ← **tekun**

menelaah *v* to analyze ← **telaah**

menelan *v* to swallow something ← **telan**

menelanjangi *v* to strip or denude ← **telanjang**

menélépon *v* to ring (up), call, (tele)phone ← **télépon**

meneliti *v* to investigate or research ← **teliti**

menelusuri *v* to follow, go along, trace ← **telusur**

menemani *v* to accompany ← **teman**

nenémbak *v* to shoot; **me-némbaki** *v* to shell ← **témbak**

nenembangkan *v* to sing something ← **tembang**

nenémbok, menémboki *v* to wall something up ← **témbok**

nenembus *v* to pierce, stab ← **tembus**

nenempa *v* to forge ← **tempa**

nenempati *v* to occupy, take a place; **menempatkan** *v* to place ← **tempat**

nenémpél *v* to stick or adhere to; **menémpélkan** *v* to stick, paste or glue something ← **témpél**

nenempuh *v* to endure, go through; to take on, take up; ~ *jalan* to go your way; ~ *ujian* to do an exam ← **tempuh**

nenemui *v* to meet up with, arrange to meet; ~ *ajal* to die; **menemukan** *v* to discover ← **temu**

nenenangkan *v* to calm someone (down) ← **tenang**

nenendang *v* to kick ← **tendang**

nenengadahi *v* to look up at ← **tengadah**

nenengah *adj* intermediate; *kelas* ~ middle class; *sekolah* ~ high school, secondary school ← **tengah**

nenenggelamkan *v* to sink or drown something ← **tenggelam**

nenéngok *v* to look or see; to look in on someone ← **téngok**

menentang *v* to oppose, resist ← **tentang**

menénténg *v* to carry dangling from the hand ← **ténténg**

menentukan *v* to decide, determine, stipulate ← **tentu**

menenun *v* to weave ← **tenun**

menepati *v* to fulfill; ~ *janji* to keep a promise ← **tepat**

menepi *v* to move to the side, move over ← **tepi**

menepis *v* ward off, deflect ← **tepis**

menepuk *v* to pat, slap ← **tepuk**

menerangi *v* to illuminate; **menerangkan** *v* to explain ← **terang**

menerapkan *v* to apply something ← **terap**

menerawang *v* to appear (through something translucent) ← **terawang**

menerbangkan *v* to fly something ← **terbang**

menerbitkan *v* to publish, issue ← **terbit**

meneriaki *v* to shout at someone; **meneriakkan** *v* to shout something ← **teriak**

menerima *v* to receive, accept ← **terima**

menerjang *v* to kick, attack, charge ← **terjang**

menerjemahkan *v* to translate (writing); to interpret (speaking) ← **terjemah**

menerjunkan *v* to drop something ← **terjun**

menerka *v* to guess ← **terka**

menerkam *v* to pounce, attack ← **terkam**

menernakkan *v* to breed ← **ternak**

menerobos *v* to break through ← **terobos**

menertawakan *v* to laugh at ← **tawa**

menertibkan *v* to keep order, discipline ← **tertib**

meneruskan *v* to continue, keep doing something ← **terus**

menetap *v* to stay; **menetapkan** *v* to appoint, fix, stipulate ← **tetap**

menetas *v* to hatch ← **tetas**

menéték *v* to suck, feed from the breast ← **téték**

menétéskan *v* to drip something, release something in drips ← **tétés**

menétralkan *v* to neutralize ← **nétral**

menéwaskan *v* to kill someone ← **téwas**

mengabadikan *v* to immortalize ← **abadi**

mengabaikan *v* to neglect, disregard, ignore ← **abai**

mengabari *v* to tell or inform someone; **mengabarkan** *v* to announce, report ← **kabar**

mengabdi *v* to serve ← **abdi**

mengaborsi *v* to abort (a fetus) ← **aborsi**

mengabsén *v* to call the roll ← **absén**

mengabulkan *v* to grant, approve, consent to; *semoga*

doanya dikabulkan may your prayers be answered ← **kabul**

mengacak *v* to scramble, encode; **mengacak-acak** *v* to mess up ← **acak**

mengacaukan *v* to mix or mess up ← **kacau**

mengacu *v* to refer to, to use as a point of reference; ~ *pada hukum negara* following Indonesian law; **mengacukan** *v* to point, refer to; ~ *arah* indicate direction ← **acu**

mengacungkan *v* to raise, hold up; ~ *tangan* to raise your hand ← **acung**

mengada-ada *v* to invent, make up; *sungguh* ~ to push your luck; **mengadakan** *v* to do, run, hold, create, organize, make available; ~ *kampanye* to run a campaign ← **ada**

mengadili *v* to try someone, put someone on trial; to punish ← **adil**

mengadu *v* to complain, report; **mengadukan** *v* to report someone/something, to make a complaint about; ~ *ke pengadilan* to sue, take to court; **mengadudombakan** *v* to play people off against each other ← **adu**

mengaduk *v* to stir, mix; ~ *semen* to mix cement ← **aduk**

mengagétkan *v* to surprise, startle ← **kagét**

mengagumi *v* to admire ← **kagum**

mengagungkan *v* to glorify;

mengagung-agungkan *v* to glorify, place on a pedestal ← **agung**

mengail *v* to fish ← **kail**

mengairi *v* to irrigate ← **air**

mengais *v* to scratch; ~ *rejeki* to scratch a living ← **kais**

mengaitkan *v* to link, connect, join ← **kait**

mengajak *v* to invite, ask out; to urge; ~ *jalan-jalan* to ask out; ~ *kawin,* ~ *nikah* to ask someone to marry you ← **ajak**

mengajar *v* to teach; **mengajari** *v* to teach someone; **mengajarkan** *v* to teach something ← **ajar**

mengaji *v* to recite or read the Koran ← **kaji**

mengajukan *v* to forward, propose; to submit ← **aju**

mengakali *v* to find a way; to deceive, play a trick on; *kita* ~ *saja* we'll find a way ← **akal**

mengakar *v* to take root ← **akar**

mengakhiri *v* to end, finish something ← **akhir**

mengakibatkan *v* to result in ← **akibat**

mengaku *v* to admit, confess, acknowledge; to claim; ~ *salah* to admit guilt; **mengakui** *v* to admit something; to acknowledge, recognize; *hak-hak TKW harus diakui* the rights of migrant workers must be recognized ← **aku**

mengalahkan *v* to conquer, defeat ← **kalah**

mengalamatkan *v* to address to; to indicate ← **alamat**

mengalami *v* to experience ← **alam**

mengalih(kan) *v* to shift something; ~ *perhatian* to shift attention, change the subject ← **alih**

mengalikan *v* to multiply ← **kali**

mengalir *v* to flow ← **alir**

mengalungkan *v* to drape around someone's neck ← **kalung**

mengalunkan *v* to put something in motion, sing something ← **alun**

mengamalkan *v* to do something for charity; to carry out ← **amal**

mengamanatkan *v* to entrust ← **amanat**

mengamankan *v* to make safe, restore order; to place in custody ← **aman**

mengamati *v* to watch closely, keep an eye on ← **amat**

mengambang *v* to float ← **ambang**

mengambil *v* to take, get, fetch; ~ *alih* to take over; ~ *keputusan* to make a decision; **mengambilkan** *v* to get something for someone ← **ambil**

mengambing-hitamkan *v* to make a scapegoat of someone ← **kambing hitam**

mengamén *v* **ngamén** *coll* to sing in the street for money, busk ← **amén**

mengamini *v* to agree to, approve of ← **amin**

mengampuni *v* to forgive ← **ampun**

mengamuk *v* to run amok, go berserk ← **amuk**

menganalisa, menganalisir, menganalisis *v* to analyze ← **analisa, analisis**

mengancam *v* to threaten, intimidate ← **ancam**

mengancing *v* to button ← **kancing**

mengandaikan *v* to suppose, assume ← **andai**

mengandalkan *v* to rely on, trust ← **andal**

mengandung *v* to contain, carry; to be pregnant ← **kandung**

menganga *v* to gape, be open (-mouthed) ← **nganga**

menganggap *v* to consider, regard; ~ *enteng* to take lightly; *sudah dianggap saudara* considered part of the family ← **anggap**

menganggarkan *v* to budget ← **anggar**

mengangguk *v* to nod; **menganggukkan** ~ *kepala* to nod your head ← **angguk**

menganggur *v* to be unemployed, idle ← **anggur**

menganginkan *v* to air (clothes, crackers) ← **angin**

mengangkat *v* to lift or pick up, raise; to appoint; to remove, amputate; *diangkat menjadi menteri* to be made a minister; ~ *payudara* to remove a breast ← **angkat**

mengangkut *v* to transport ← **angkut**

mengangsur *v* to pay in instalments ← **angsur**

menganiaya *v* to mistreat, oppress ← **aniaya**

menganjurkan *v* to suggest, propose ← **anjur**

mengansel *v* to cancel ← **kansel**

mengantar *v* to take, escort, accompany; **mengantarkan** *v* to take someone or something ← **antar**

mengantongi *v* to pocket ← **kantong**

mengantri *v* to queue ← **antré, antri**

mengantuk *adj* sleepy → **kantuk**

menganugerahi *v* to confer upon ← **anugerah**

menganut *v* to follow ← **anut**

menganyam *v* to weave, plait, braid ← **anyam**

mengapa why; *tak* ~ it doesn't matter ← **apa**

mengapit *v* to pinch, press, squeeze; to flank

mengapung *v* to float, be suspended ← **apung**

mengapur *v* to whitewash ← **kapur**

mengarah *v* to aim something towards; **mengarahkan** *v* to direct ← **arah**

mengarang *v* to write, compose; *lomba* ~ essay competition ← **karang**

mengartikan *v* to define, interpret as ← **arti**

mengarungi *v* to cross water, wade, ford ← **arung**

mengaruniai *v* to bless ← **karunia**

mengasah *v* to sharpen, whet ← **asah**

mengasihani *v* to pity, feel sorry for ← **kasihan**

mengasingkan *v* to exile ← **asing**

mengasong *v* to sell in the street ← **asong**

mengaspal *v* to asphalt ← **aspal**

mengasuh *v* to care for ← **asuh**

mengasuransikan *v* to insure ← **asuransi**

mengasyikkan *n* fascinating, engrossing ← **asyik**

mengatakan *v* to say ← **kata**

mengatasi *v* to overcome ← **atas**

mengatur *v* to arrange, organize, regulate ← **atur**

mengaum *v* to roar, growl (of tigers) ← **aum**

mengawal *v* to guard, escort ← **kawal**

mengawali *v* to start; to precede ← **awal**

mengawasi *v* to supervise ← **awas**

mengawétkan *v* to preserve (food) ← **awét**

mengawini *v* to marry someone; **mengawinkan** *v* to marry someone off; ~ *anak* to marry off a son or daughter ← **kawin**

mengayak *v* to sieve, sift ← **ayak**

mengayomi *v* to protect, care for, look after ← **ayom**

mengayuh *v* to paddle or pedal something; ~ *sepeda* to ride a bicycle ← **kayuh**

mengayun *v* to rock, swing, sway; **mengayunkan** *v* to rock ← **ayun**

mengebom *v* to bomb something ← **bom**

mengecap *v* to brand ← **cap**

mengecas *v* to charge (electrical equipment) ← **cas, charge**

mengecat *v* to paint, dye; ~ *rambut* to dye, color your hair ← **cat**

mengecék *v* to check, confirm ← **cék**

mengécér *v* to retail, sell retail ← **écér**

mengecéwakan *v* to disappoint; *adj* disappointing ← **kecéwa**

mengecil *v* to shrink, become smaller; **mengecilkan** *v* to make smaller, decrease ← **kecil**

mengecualikan *v* to except, make an exception ← **kecuali**

mengecup *v* to kiss lightly, peck ← **kecup**

mengédarkan *v* to circulate something ← **édar**

mengedipkan ~ *mata* to blink ← **kedip**

mengédit *v* to edit ← **édit**

mengedot *v* to suck ← **dot**

mengegolkan *v* to promote, campaign for someone ← **gol**

mengéja *v* to spell ← **éja**

mengejamkan ~ *mata* to close your eyes ← **kejam**

mengejan *v* to strain, push the abdominal muscles (when defecating, giving birth) ← **ejan**

mengejang *v* to cramp, seize up ← **kejang**

mengejar *v* to chase; ~ *waktu* to race against the clock ← **kejar**

mengéjék *v* to tease, mock, ridicule ← **éjék**

mengejutkan *adj* surprising, startling; *v* to surprise or startle ← **kejut**

mengéksékusi *v* to execute (carry out the death penalty) ← **éksékusi**

mengékspor *v* to export ← **ékspor**

mengékstradisi *v* to extradite (someone) ← **ékstradisi**

mengelabui *v* to trick, pull the wool over someone's eyes ← **kelabu, abu**

mengélakkan *v* to avoid, dodge, evade ← **élak**

mengelap *v* to wipe, mop ← **lap**

mengelas *v* to weld ← **las**

mengelilingi *v* to circle, go around ← **keliling**

mengelola *v* to manage, run ← **kelola**

mengelompokkan *v* to group ← **kelompok**

mengeluarkan *v* to issue, send out, release ← **keluar**

mengeluh *v* to complain ← **keluh**

mengelupas *v* to peel, come off (of a skin) ← **kelupas**

mengelus *v* to caress, stroke or pat (an animal) ← **elus**

mengemaskan *v* to package ← **kemas**

mengembalikan *v* to give or send back, return ← **kembali**

mengemban *v* to carry out, perform ← **emban**

mengembangkan *v* to develop something ← **kembang**

mengembara *v* to wander, roam ← **embara**

mengembék, mengembik *v* to bleat ← **embék**

mengembus *v* to blow ← **embus**

mengemis *v* to beg ← **emis, kemis**

mengempas *v* to throw down; **mengempaskan** ~ *diri* to throw yourself down ← **empas**

mengempiskan *v* to deflate ← **kempis**

mengemudikan *v* to drive, steer; ~ *mobil* to drive a car ← **kemudi**

mengemukakan *v* to put forward, advance, nominate ← **ke muka**

mengemut *v* to suck on (sweets etc) ← **emut, kemut**

mengenai *conj* about, over, on, concerning ← **kena**

mengenal *v* to know, be acquainted with, recognize; **mengenali** *v* to identify; **memperkenalkan** *v* to introduce ← **kenal**

mengenang *v* to commemorate, remember ← **kenang**

mengencangkan *v* to tighten ← **kencang**

mengéncér *v* to melt, become liquid ← **éncér**

mengendalikan *v* to control ← **kendali**

mengendap *v* to sink, silt up ← **endap**

mengendarai *v* to ride or drive (a vehicle) ← **kendara**

mengental *v* to congeal, thicken ← **kental**

mengepak *v* to pack ← **pak**

mengepakkan ~ *sayap* to flutter wings ← **kepak**

mengepal *v* to form a fist ← **kepal**

mengepalai *v* to be head of ← **kepala**

mengepél *v* to mop (up) ← **pél**

mengepul *v* to smoke, billow ← **kepul**

mengepung *v* to surround, encircle, besiege ← **kepung**

mengerahkan *v* to mobilize ← **kerah**

mengeram *v* to sit on eggs, brood, hatch ← **eram**

mengeramatkan *v* to consider or make sacred ← **keramat**

mengerang *v* to groan, moan ← **erang**

mengeras *v* to get louder, harder; **mengeraskan** *v* to make something harder, louder ← **keras**

mengérék *v* to hoist, pull; ~ *bendera* to raise the flag ← **kérék**

mengerém *v* to brake ← **rém**

mengerikan *adj* terrifying, horrifying ← **ngeri**

mengering *v* to become dry; **mengeringkan** *v* to dry something; ~ *rambut* to dry your hair ← **kering**

mengeriting ~ *rambut* to perm your hair ← **keriting**

mengerjakan *v* to do, carry out; ~ *PR* to do your homework ← **kerja**

mengernyit ~ *dahi*, ~ *kening* to frown ← **kernyit**

mengerok *v* to rub someone's back with a coin ← **kerok**

mengeropos *v* to be eaten away, eroded ← **keropos**

mengeroyok *v* to beat savagely in a mob; *dikeroyok massa* beaten up by a mob ← **keroyok**

mengerti *v* to understand; **dimengerti** *v* to be understood; **pengertian** *n* understanding ← **erti, arti**

mengeruk *v* to dredge, scrape out ← **keruk**

mengerumuni *v* to mob, surround, crowd around someone ← **kerumun**

mengerut *v* to shrink, shrivel, contract; **mengerutkan** ~ *kening* to frown ← **kerut**

mengesahkan *v* to validate, ratify, legitimize, legalize ← **sah**

mengesampingkan *v* to put to one side ← **ke samping**

mengesankan *adj* impressive ← **kesan**

mengetahui *v* to know something, have knowledge of ← **tahu**

mengetawakan *v* to laugh at ← **tawa**

mengetik *v* to type ← **ketik**

mengetuai *v* to preside over ← **ketua, tua**

mengetuk *v* to knock; ~ *hati* to prick your conscience; ~ *pintu* to knock on the door ← **ketuk**

menggabungkan *v* to connect, combine, fuse ← **gabung**

menggadaikan *v* to pawn something ← **gadai**

menggaét *v* to get (on board), snatch, hook ← **gaét, gait, kait**

menggagahi *v* to overpower, violate ← **gagah**

menggagalkan *v* to frustrate, make something fail ← **gagal**

menggairahkan *v* to excite, stimulate, enthuse ← **gairah**

menggait *v* to pull, hook ← **gait, gaét, kait**

menggaji *v* to pay, remunerate, employ ← **gaji**

menggalang *v* to support, consolidate ← **galang**

menggali *v* to dig ← **gali**

menggambar *v* to draw, depict; **menggambarkan** *v* to describe, illustrate ← **gambar**

menggandakan *v* to duplicate, multiply ← **ganda**

menggandéng *v* to include, involve, link with ← **gandéng**

mengganggu *v* to bother, disturb ← **ganggu**

mengganti *v* to change, substitute, replace; **menggantikan** *v* to substitute or replace someone/something ← **ganti**

menggantung *v* to hang, suspend ← **gantung**

menggarap *v* to work on, produce; ~ *tanah* to till the land ← **garap**

menggaris *v* to draw a line; ~ *bawahi* to underline, emphasize ← **garis**

menggarong *v* to rob, loot ← **garong**

menggaruk *v* to scratch, scrape; ~ *kepala* to scratch your head ← **garuk**

menggauli *v* to have sexual intercourse with ← **gaul**

menggebrak *v* to hit or slam; ~ *meja* to hit the table ← **gebrak**

menggebu *v* to rage, bubble, froth over ← **gebu**

menggebuk *v* to batter, bash ← **gebuk**

menggedor *v* to bang on repeatedly; ~ *pintu* *v* to bang on the door ← **gedor**

menggelapkan *v* to embezzle, misappropriate ← **gelap**

menggelar, menggelarkan *v* to hold (an event) ← **gelar**

menggelédah *v* to search; to ransack ← **gelédah**

menggéléng, menggéléngkan ~ *kepala* to shake your head ← **géléng**

menggeliat *v* to stretch, twist ← **geliat**

menggelikan *adj* funny, comic off-putting ← **geli**

menggelincir *v* to slip, slide ← **gelincir**

menggelitik *v* to tickle ← **gelitik**

menggelisahkan *v* to make nervous ← **gelisah**

menggelora *v* to rage, storm, surge ← **gelora**

menggeluti *v* to be involved, deal with ← **gelut**

menggemari *v* to like, enjoy ← **gemar**

menggemaskan *adj* annoying ← **gemas**

menggembala *v* to herd ← **gembala**

menggembirakan *adj* exciting, happy; *berita yang ~* good news ← **gembira**

menggembok *v* to padlock ← **gembok**

menggembos *v* to deflate, go flat ← **gembos**

menggempakan *v* to jolt, stir ← **gempa**

menggemparkan *v* to cause a stir ← **gempar**

menggempur *v* to attack, destroy ← **gempur**

menggenangi *v* to flood something ← **genang**

menggéndong *v* to carry on the hip ← **géndong**

menggenggam *v* to grip, grasp ← **genggam**

menggenjot *v* to push, pedal; *~ sepeda* to pedal a bike ← **genjot**

menggerakkan *v* to move, shift something ← **gerak**

menggeram *v* to become angry; to growl, roar ← **geram**

menggerayangi *v* to grope ← **gerayang**

menggerebek *v* to raid, search ← **gerebek**

menggergaji *v* to saw ← **gergaji**

menggerogoti *v* to eat into, erode, gnaw on; *digerogoti*

rayap eaten by termites ← **gerogot**

menggerombol *v* to gather in a group, amass ← **gerombol**

menggertak *v* to snarl or snap at; to intimidate, threaten ← **gertak**

menggerutu *v* to grumble, complain, gripe ← **gerutu**

menggésék *v* to rub, scrape; *~ biola* to play the violin; *~ kartu* to swipe a card ← **gésék**

menggésér *v* to move aside or over ← **gésér**

menggigil *v* to shiver ← **gigil**

menggigit *v* to bite ← **gigit**

menggilas *v* to crush, pulverize ← **gilas**

menggiling *v* to grind, mill ← **giling**

menggiring *v* to herd, drive (cattle) ← **giring**

menggiurkan *adj* tempting, mouth-watering ← **giur**

menggoda *v* to tempt; **menggodai** *v* to tempt someone ← **goda**

menggodok *v* to boil ← **godok**

menggolok *v* to cut with a machete ← **golok**

menggolongkan *v* to group, classify ← **golong**

menggoncangkan *v* to rock or make something move ← **goncang**

menggonggong *v* to bark ← **gonggong**

menggoréng *v* to fry ← **goréng**

menggorés *v* to scratch, make a stroke ← **gorés**

menggosipkan *v* to gossip about something or someone ← **gosip**

menggosok *v* to rub, polish; ~ *sepatu* to polish, shine (shoes) ← **gosok**

menggotong *v* to carry together ← **gotong**

menggoyang *v* to shake, rock ~ *pinggul* to sway your hips; **menggoyangkan** *v* to shake or rock something ← **goyang**

menggubris *v* to pay heed or attention to; *tidak digubris* ignored ← **gubris**

menggugat *v* to sue, accuse ← **gugat**

menggugurkan *v* to abort ← **gugur**

mengguling *v* to roll; **menggulingkan** *v* to topple, roll over ← **guling**

menggulung *v* to roll up ← **gulung**

menggumamkan *v* to mumble or mutter something ← **gumam**

menggunakan *v* to use ← **guna**

mengguncangkan *v* to rock or make something move ← **guncang**

menggunduli *v* to shave, denude, make bald; *bukit itu sudah digunduli* the hill has been deforested ← **gundul**

menggunting *v* to cut (out) ← **gunting**

menggurui *v* to lecture or talk ← **guru**

menggusur *v* to evict, sweep aside, forcibly remove ← **gusur**

menghabiskan *v* to finish, use up, spend; ~ *uang jutaan rupiah* to spend millions of rupiah ← **habis**

menghadap *v* to face, appear before; **menghadapi** *v* to face someone or something ← **hadap**

menghadiahkan *v* to give as a present or prize; **menghadiahi** *v* to give someone a present or prize ← **hadiah**

menghadiri *v* to attend; **menghadirkan** *v* to present, bring forward; ~ *saksi baru* bring forward a new witness ← **hadir**

menghafalkan *v* to learn by heart ← **hafal**

menghaluskan *v* to refine, grind ← **halus**

menghambat *v* to obstruct, impede, hamper ← **hambat**

menghamburkan *v* to scatter, throw about ← **hambur**

menghamili *v* to make someone pregnant ← **hamil**

menghampar *v* to spread out ← **hampar**

menghampiri *v* to approach ← **hampir**

menghancurkan *v* to smash, crush, destroy ← **hancur**

menghanguskan *v* to set fire to, burn down ← **hangus**

menghantam *v* to strike ← **hantam**

menghantarkan *v* to conduct (electricity or heat) ← **hantar**

menghantui *v* to haunt ← **hantu**

menghapus *v* to delete, erase, wipe; **menghapuskan** *v* to wipe out, eliminate

mengharapkan *v* to expect ← **harap**

menghardik *v* to shout at, scold ← **hardik**

menghargai *v* to appreciate ← **harga**

mengharukan *adj* moved, touched (emotionally) ← **haru**

mengharuskan *v* to require ← **harus**

menghasilkan *v* to produce ← **hasil**

menghayati *v* to inspire, instill, vivify ← **hayat**

menghébohkan *v* to cause an uproar; *adj* sensational ← **héboh**

menghéla *v* to draw, drag; ~ *nafas* to sigh, draw a breath ← **héla**

menghémat *v* to save on or economize ← **hémat**

menghembus *v* to blow ← **hembus**

menghendaki *v* to want ← **hendak**

menghentikan *v* to stop something ← **henti**

menghérankan *adj* astonishing, astounding ← **héran**

menghiasi *v* to adorn, decorate something ← **hias**

menghibahkan *v* to donate, bequeath ← **hibah**

menghibur *v* to entertain; to comfort, console ← **hibur**

menghidangkan *v* to serve up, offer ← **hidang**

menghidupkan *v* to bring to life, start or turn on (a device); ~ *kembali* to revive; ~ *mesin* to turn on the engine ← **hidup**

menghijaukan *v* to make green ← **hijau**

menghilang *v* to disappear, vanish; **menghilangkan** *v* to remove ← **hilang**

menghilir *v* to go downstream ← **hilir**

menghimpunkan *v* to bring together, gather ← **himpun**

menghinakan *v* to humiliate, insult ← **hina**

menghindar *v* to steer clear, avoid; **menghindari** *v* to avoid something ← **hindar**

menghiraukan *v* to take heed, listen to advice; *tidak dihiraukan* ignored ← **hirau**

menghirup *v* to breathe in ← **hirup**

menghitamkan *v* to blacken, make black ← **hitam**

menghitung *v* to count, calculate, reckon; **menghitungkan** *v* to count or calculate something ← **hitung**

menghormat, menghormati *v* to honor or respect

menghubungi *v* to contact someone; **menghubungkan** *v* to connect, join, link different parts ← **hubung**

menghujani *v* to pelt, rain down upon ← **hujan**

menghujat *v* to swear, blaspheme ← **hujat**

menghukum v to punish, sentence, condemn ← **hukum**

menghuni v to live in, occupy ← **huni**

menghunus v to unsheathe, take out; ~ *pedang* to pull out a sword ← **hunus**

mengibaratkan v to use figuratively, as an example ← **ibarat**

mengibarkan v to wave, unfurl; ~ *bendera* to fly a flag ← **kibar**

mengibaskan v to wag (a tail) ← **kibas**

mengibuli v to fool someone ← **kibul**

mengidam v to crave (esp of pregnant woman) ← **idam**

mengidap v to suffer from; ~ *penyakit* to suffer from or have a disease ← **idap**

mengidolakan v to worship, idolize ← **idola**

mengigau v to talk in one's sleep, be delirious ← **igau**

mengijinkan v to permit, allow ← **ijin, izin**

mengikat v to tie, fasten ← **ikat**

mengikis v to erode, eat away ← **kikis**

mengiklankan v to advertise ← **iklan**

mengikut v to follow, accompany; **mengikuti** v to follow, join, participate in; ~ *kursus* to do a course ← **ikut**

mengiler v to drool, slobber ← **iler**

mengimbangi v to balance, offset ← **imbang**

mengiming, mengiming-iming, mengimingkan, mengimingimingkan v to tantalize, tempt ← **iming**

mengimpikan v to dream of ← **impi**

mengimpor v to import ← **impor**

menginap v to stay the night, stay over ← **inap**

mengincar v to set your sights on, target ← **incar**

mengindahkan v to take heed, pay attention to; **memperindah** v to beautify ← **indah**

mengindonésiakan v to translate or make into Indonesian ← **Indonésia**

menginformasikan v to inform ← **informasi**

mengingat v to remember, bear in mind; **mengingatkan** v to remind someone about something ← **ingat**

menginginkan v to wish for, desire ← **ingin**

mengingkari v to renege or go back on ← **ingkar**

menginjak v to step, tread, or stamp on; ~ *gas* to accelerate, step on the gas ← **injak**

menginsafkan v to make conscious, raise awareness ← **insaf**

mengintai v to spy on or watch, conduct surveillance ← **intai**

menginterviu v to interview ← **interviu**

mengintip v to peep at, spy on ← **intip**

mengipasi *v* to fan someone or something ← **kipas**

mengira *v* to assume, think ← **kira**

mengirigasi *v* to irrigate ← **irigasi**

mengirim *v* to send ← **kirim**

mengiringi *v* to accompany, escort ← **iring**

mengiris *v* to slice ← **iris**

mengirit *v* to economize ← **irit**

mengisahkan *v* to tell the story of ← **kisah**

mengisak, mengisak-isak *v* to sob ← **isak**

mengisap *v* to suck on, to smoke; ~ *ganja* to smoke marijuana; ~ *cerutu* to smoke a cigar ← **isap**

mengisi *v* to fill, load; ~ *bensin* fill up with petrol; ~ *waktu* to fill in time ← **isi**

mengislamkan *v* to Islamize, make Islamic ← **Islam**

mengistilahkan *v* to define something ← **istilah**

mengistiméwakan *v* to treat as special ← **istiméwa**

mengisyaratkan *v* to give a sign, signal ← **isyarat**

mengiyakan *v* to agree or assent to ← **iya**

mengizinkan *v* to permit, allow ← **izin, ijin**

mengkaji *v* to study, investigate ← **kaji**

mengkhianati *v* to betray someone ← **khianat**

mengkhitan, mengkhitankan *v* to circumcise ← **khitan**

mengkhususkan *v* to give special treatment ← **khusus**

mengkilap *v* to shine, gleam ← **kilap**

mengkristenkan *v* to convert someone to Christianity, Christianize ← **kristen**

mengkudu *n* kind of root, used as a spice

mengobati *v* to treat, cure ← **obat**

mengobrak-abrik *v* to upset, turn upside-down ← **obrak-abrik**

mengobral *v* to put on sale ← **obral**

mengobras *v* to overlock ← **obras**

mengobrol *v* to chat ← **obrol**

mengobyék *v* to have a job on the side, moonlight ← **obyék**

mengocéh *v* to babble, talk nonsense ← **océh**

mengocok *v* to shake, shuffle; ~ *dadu* to roll the dice; ~ *kartu* to shuffle cards ← **kocok**

mengojék *v* to take passengers around on your motorbike ← **ojék**

mengolah *v* to process, treat ← **olah**

mengolés *v* to grease, spread, lubricate; **mengolési** *v* to grease something; **mengolés-kan** *v* to smear with something ← **olés**

mengomél *v* to complain, grumble, whinge, whine ← **omél**

mengoméntari *v* to comment on ← **koméntar**

mengompol *v* to wet your pants, the bed ← **ompol**

mengontak *v* to contact someone ← **kontak**

mengontrakkan *v* to lease or rent out a house ← **kontrak**

mengoper *v* to transfer, hand over; ~ *bola* to pass the ball ← **oper**

mengoplos *v* to mix in another liquid illegally ← **oplos**

mengorbankan *v* to sacrifice ← **korban**

mengorék *v* to scrape, scratch

mengoréksi *v* to correct ← **koréksi**

mengorupsi *v* to be corrupt; to corrupt ← **korupsi**

mengosongkan *v* to empty ← **kosong**

mengotak-ngotakkan *v* to categorize, box, put in boxes ← **kotak**

mengotori *v* to (make) dirty, defile ← **kotor**

menguap *v* to evaporate or steam; to yawn ← **kuap**

menguap *v* to evaporate or steam; to yawn ← **uap**

menguasai *v* to control, have power over; ~ *bahasa asing* to be able to speak a foreign language ← **kuasa**

menguatirkan *v* to worry about something ← **kuatir**

menguatkan *v* to strengthen; **memperkuat** *v* to reinforce, make stronger ← **kuat**

mengubah *v* to change or alter ← **ubah**

menguber *v, coll* to chase, go after ← **uber**

menguburkan *v* to bury ← **kubur**

mengucap, mengucapkan *v* to say or express something; ~ *terima kasih* to say thank you; to thank ← **ucap**

mengucilkan *v* to ostracize, shun ← **kucil**

mengucurkan *v* to gush, pour ← **kucur**

mengudarakan *v* to broadcast or air ← **udara**

menguji *v* to examine or test ← **uji**

mengujicobakan *v* to test something ← **uji coba**

mengukir *v* to carve or engrave ← **ukir**

mengukuhkan *v* to strengthen; to ratify ← **kukuh**

mengukur *v* to measure ← **ukur**

mengukus *v* to steam (food) ← **kukus**

mengulang *v* to repeat, do again; **mengulangi** *v* to repeat something ← **ulang**

mengulas *v* to comment, review, critique ← **ulas**

mengulek *v* to make fresh chilli sauce ← **ulek**

mengulum *v* to suck in the mouth ← **kulum**

mengulur-ulur *v* to spin out, take a long time; **mengulurkan** *v* to extend something ← **ulur**

mengumandangkan *v* to sing; to sound, reverberate ← **kumandang**

mengumpat *v* to curse, swear ← **umpat**

mengumpet *v* to hide or conceal yourself ← **umpet**

mengumpulkan *v* to collect, gather; ~ *perangko* to collect stamps ← **kumpul**

mengumumkan *v* to announce or declare ← **umum**

mengunci *v* to lock (up) ← **kunci**

mengundang *v* to invite (formally) ← **undang**

mengundi *v* to conduct a draw or lottery ← **undi**

mengundurkan *v* to postpone ← **undur**

mengungkap *v* to uncover; **mengungkapkan** *v* to express ← **ungkap**

mengungkit *v* to lever; to pry ← **ungkit**

mengungsi *v* to evacuate or flee; **mengungsikan** *v* to evacuate someone ← **ungsi**

mengunjungi *v* to visit a place ← **kunjung**

menguntai *v* to string, tie together ← **untai**

menguntungkan *v* to profit; *adj* profitable ← **untung**

mengunyah *v* to chew ← **kunyah**

mengupah *v* to employ, hire, pay someone (to do work) ← **upah**

mengupas *v* to peel; to analyze ← **kupas**

mengupayakan *v* to try to enable ← **upaya**

mengupil *v* to pick your nose ← **upil**

menguping *v* to eavesdrop, listen in ← **kuping**

menguraikan *v* to explain; to untangle ← **urai**

mengurangi *v* to take from, subtract, minus; *enam dikurangi dua sama dengan empat* six minus two is four; **mengurangkan** *v* to reduce, make smaller ← **kurang**

menguras *v* to clean out, drain; ~ *tenaga* to use up energy ← **kuras**

mengurét *v* to scrape out, perform a curette ← **kurét**

mengursuskan *v* to send someone on a course ← **kursus**

mengurung *v* to cage, put in a cage, lock up ← **kurung**

mengurus *v* to arrange, organize, manage ← **urus**

mengurut *v* to massage, rub ← **urut**

mengusahakan *v* to try, endeavor to ← **usaha**

mengusik *v* to tease, make fun of ← **usik**

mengusir *v* to drive away or out, chase away, expel ← **usir**

mengusulkan *v* to propose or suggest ← **usul**

mengusut *v* to investigate, sort out ← **usut**

mengutak-atik, mengutak-ngatikkan *v* to work on or tinker with ← **kutak, utak-atik**

mengutamakan *v* to give preference or priority to ← **utama**

mengutarakan *v* to put forward ← **utara**

mengutik *v* to tinker with; to touch on ← **kutik, utik**

mengutip *v* to quote, cite an extract ← **kutip**

mengutuk *v* to curse ← **kutuk**

mengutus *v* to send or delegate ← **utus**

Ménhankam *n* Minister for Defence and Security ← **Menteri Pertahanan dan Keamanan**

Ménhub *n* Minister of Transportation ← **Menteri Perhubungan**

meniadakan *v* to undo or cancel ← **tiada, tidak ada**

meniduri *v* to sleep with someone, have sex with someone; **menidurkan** *v* to put to sleep ← **tidur**

menikah *v* to marry, get married; **menikahi** *v* to marry someone; **menikahkan** *v* to marry off (a child) ← **nikah**

menikam *v* to stab ← **tikam**

menikmati *v* to enjoy ← **nikmat**

menikung *v* to bend, curve ← **tikung**

menilai *v* to evaluate, appraise

menimang-nimang *v* to rock (a child) ← **timang**

menimbang *v* to weigh (up) ← **timbang**

menimbulkan *v* to give rise, bring to the surface ← **timbul**

menimbun *v* to pile up, accumulate; to hoard; ~ *makanan* to hoard food ← **timbun**

menimpa *v* to fall upon, befall ← **timpa**

menindaklanjuti *v* to take a step or measure ← **tindak lanjut**

menindas *v* to oppress ← **tindas**

menindik *v* to pierce (ears) ← **tindik**

meninggal ~ *(dunia)* to die; **meninggalkan** *v* to leave (behind), abandon ← **tinggal**

meningkat *v* to rise, increase, improve; **meningkatkan** *v* to increase or raise the level of something ← **tingkat**

meninjau *v* to observe, view; ~ *kembali* to review ← **tinjau**

menipis *v* to become thin ← **tipis**

menipu *v* to trick, deceive ← **tipu**

meniru *v* to copy or imitate ← **tiru**

menit *n* minute

menitip *v* to leave in someone's care, entrust ← **titip**

meniup *v* to blow; ~ *lilin* to blow out a candle ← **tiup**

menjabat *v* to hold; to work as; ~ *Menteri Keuangan* to be Minister of Finance ← **jabat**

menjadi *v* to be or become; ~ *marah* to get angry; **menjadi-jadi** *v* to get worse; **menjadikan** *v* to create, make ← **jadi**

menjadwalkan *v* to timetable ← **jadwal**

menjaga *v* to guard, keep watch ← **jaga**

menjagokan *v* to support ← **jago**

menjahit *v* to sew ← **jahit**

menjajah *v* to colonize, rule another country ← **jajah**

menjajakan *v* to hawk, peddle; ~ *permen* to sell sweets, candy ← **jaja**

menjalani *v* to undergo, do; ~ *hukuman penjara 3 tahun* to serve three years in jail; **menjalankan** *v* to operate, run, set in motion ← **jalan**

menjalar *v* to creep, climb; *tanaman* ~ climbing plant ← **jalar**

menjalin *v* to forge links, network ← **jalin**

menjambak *v* to pull someone's hair ← **jambak**

menjambrét *v* to snatch ← **jambrét**

menjamin *v* to guarantee, promise ← **jamin**

menjamu *v* to entertain guests, hold a feast ← **jamu**

menjamur *v* to spring up ← **jamur**

menjanda *v* to be widowed, live as a widow ← **janda**

menjangan *n* deer

menjangkit *v* to spread, be infectious or contagious; **menjangkiti** *v* to infect ← **jangkit**

menjanjikan *v* to promise something ← **janji**

menjarah *v* to loot ← **jarah**

menjaring *v* to fish with a net; to filter or sift ← **jaring**

menjatahkan *v* to deal out, allocate ← **jatah**

menjatuhkan *v* to fell, let drop; ~ *hukuman* to sentence, condemn ← **jatuh**

menjauh *v* to move away; **menjauhi** *v* to avoid ← **jauh**

menjawab *v* to answer, reply ← **jawab**

menjebak, menjebakkan *v* to trap ← **jebak**

menjeblos *v* to break or fall through ← **jeblos**

menjejaki *v* to step on, trail, trace ← **jejak**

menjéjérkan *v* to place in rows ← **jéjér**

menjelajahi *v* to travel through or explore a place ← **jelajah**

menjelang *v* to approach (usu time) ← **jelang**

menjelaskan *adj* to explain, clarify ← **jelas**

menjelékkan *v* to criticize, say bad things about ← **jelék**

menjelma *v* to be incarnated, turn into, materialize; **menjelmakan** *v* to create or realize something ← **jelma**

menjembatani *v* to bridge (two things) ← **jembatan**

menjemput *v* to pick up; ~ *bola* to be proactive ← **jemput**

menjemukan *adj* tedious, boring ← **jemu**

menjemur *v* to air, dry in the sun; ~ *baju cucian* to hang out the washing; ~ *krupuk* to air crackers before frying ← **jemur**

menjéngkélkan *adj* annoying ← **jéngkél**

menjepit *v* to pinch, squeeze ← **jepit**

menjeprét *v* to snap, staple; ~ *foto* to take a photo ← **jeprét**

menjerat *v* to snare, trap ← **jerat**

menjerit *v* to scream, shriek ← **jerit**

menjerumuskan *v* to let drop, send down ← **jerumus**

menjéwér *v* to pinch someone's ear, scold ← **jéwér**

menjijikkan *adj* disgusting, revolting, foul ← **jijik**

menjilat *v* to lick; *sl* to suck up, flatter ← **jilat**

menjilid *v* to bind ← **jilid**

menjinakkan *v* to tame ← **jinak**

menjinjing *v* to carry by hand ← **jinjing**

menjiplak *v* to copy, plagiarize ← **jiplak**

menjiwai *v* to bring to life, inspire ← **jiwa**

menjodohkan *v* to set up, match ← **jodoh**

menjorok *v* to stick out, protrude; **menjorokkan** *v* to poke something out ← **jorok**

menjual *v* to sell ← **jual**

menjuarai *v* to win (a competition) ← **juara**

menjulang *v* to soar; *gedung ~ tinggi* skyscraper ← **julang**

menjumlahkan *v* to add (up) ← **jumlah**

menjumpai *v* to meet someone ← **jumpa**

menjunjung *~ tinggi* to honor ← **junjung**

menjuntai *v* to dangle ← **juntai**

Ménkéh HAM *n* Minister of Justice and Human Rights ← **Menteri Kehakiman dan Hak Azasi Manusia**

Ménkés *n* Minister of Health → **Menteri Keséhatan**

Ménkéu *n* Minister of Finance → **Menteri Keuangan**

Ménko *n* Co-ordinating Minister; *~ Kesra (Menteri Koordinasi Kesejahteraan Rakyat)* Co-ordinating Minister for Public Welfare → **Menteri Koordinasi**

Ménkop *n* Minister of Co-operatives → **Menteri Koperasi**

Ménlu *n* Foreign Minister → **Menteri Luar Negeri**

menobatkan *v* to install, crown ← **nobat**

menodai *v* to stain; to deflower (a girl) ← **noda**

menodong *v* to threaten or hold up at knifepoint ← **todong**

menolak *v* to refuse, reject ← **tolak**

menoléh *v* to look in a different direction, turn your head ← **toléh**

menolong *v* to help or assist ← **tolong**

menomersatukan *v* to put first, give priority ← **nomer satu**

menonaktifkan *v* to release from active service, non-activate ← **nonaktif**

menonjok *v* to punch, hit ← **tonjok**

menonjol *v* to stick out, protrude; *adj* prominent ← **tonjol**

menonton *v* to watch, look on ← **tonton**

menopang *v* to prop up, support ← **topang**

ménor *adj* gaudy, garish, trashy, tacky (of dress)

menoréh *v* to scratch, etch ← **toréh**

Ménpén *n* Minister of Information → **Menteri Penerangan**

Ménpora *n* Minister of Youth and Sports → **Menteri Pemuda dan Olahraga**

Ménristék *n* Minister of Research and Technology → **Menteri Risét dan Téknologi**

méns *coll* period; *lagi* ~ have your period; *sakit* ~ menstrual pain

mensablon *v* to screen-print ← **sablon**

mensabotase *v* to sabotage ← **sabotase**

mensangsikan *v* to doubt ← **sangsi**

mensénsor *v* to censor, cut out ← **sénsor**

mensinyalir *v* to signal, make a sign, point out ← **sinyalir**

mensortir *v* to sort, organize ← **sortir**

Ménsos *n* Minister of Social Affairs → **Menteri Sosial**

mensponsori *v* to sponsor ← **sponsor**

mensubsidi *v* to subsidize ← **subsidi**

mensukséskan *v* to make something succeed ← **suksés**

menswastakan *v* to privatize ← **swasta**

mensyukuri *v* to appreciate, be thankful ← **syukur**

mentah *adj* raw, uncooked, not ripe; *bahan* ~ raw material

méntal, méntalitas *n* way of thinking, mentality

Méntan *n* Minister of Agriculture → **Menteri Pertanian**

mentang: mentang-mentang just because

ménté → **médé**

mentéga *n* butter

mentéréng *adj* dressed up, fancy

menteri *n* minister; ~ *Dalam Negeri (Mendagri)* Minister of Home Affairs; ~ *Luar Negeri (Menlu)* Foreign Minister; *Perdana* ~ Prime Minister; **kementerian** *n* ministry, department, office

mentimun, timun *n* cucumber

mentraktir *v* to invite out, shout, treat, pay for another ← **traktir**

menuang, menuangkan *v* to pour something ← **tuang**

menuding *v* to accuse, point the finger ← **tuding**

menuduh *v* to accuse ← **tuduh**

menugaskan *v* to assign someone, give a task to ← **tugas**

menuju *v* to approach, go towards ← **tuju**

menukar *v* to change; **menukarkan** *v* to change something ← **tukar**

menukas *v* to counter, retort ← **tukas**

menular *v* to infect; *adj* contagious, infectious; *penyakit* ~ contagious disease ← **tular**

menulis *v* to write ← **tulis**

menumbangkan *v* to fall, cause something or someone to fall ← **tumbang**

menumbuk *v* to pound (rice), crush, grind ← **tumbuk**

menumpahkan *v* to spill something; ~ *darah* to shed blood ← **tumpah**

menumpang *v* **numpang** *coll* to make use of someone else's facilities; to get a lift or ride ← **tumpang**

menumpuk *v* to pile up ← **tumpuk**

menunaikan *v* to pay cash; to fulfill; ~ *ibadah puasa* to perform the Ramadan fast ← **tunai**

menunda *v* to delay, put off, postpone; **menundakan** *v* to delay or postpone something ← **tunda**

menunduk *v* to bow your head; **menundukkan** *v* to bow or lower something; to defeat ← **tunduk**

menung: termenung *adj* lost in thought

menunggak *v* to owe money ← **tunggak**

menunggang *v* to ride; ~ *kuda* to ride a horse ← **tunggang**

menunggu *v* to wait for something; **menunggu-nunggu** *v* to wait a long time for; **menunggui** *v* to wait for someone ← **tunggu**

menunjuk *v* to indicate, point out, refer to; **menunjukkan** *v* to show, point out; ~ *jalan* to give directions ← **tunjuk**

menuntaskan *v* to finish off, be done with, do thoroughly ← **tuntas**

menuntun *v* to guide, prop up ← **tuntun**

menuntut *v* to claim or demand ← **tuntut**

menurun *v* to fall, drop, decline; **menurunkan** *v* to lower or reduce ← **turun**

menurut *conj* according to; ~ *pendapat saya* in my opinion ← **turut**

menusuk *v* to stab, prick, pierce ← **tusuk**

menutup *v* to close or shut; **menutupi** *v* to cover (up) ← **tutup**

menuturkan *v* to tell ← **tutur**

menyabet *v* to snatch or grab; to whip ← **sabet**

menyabit *v* to cut with a sickle ← **sabit**

menyabuni *v* to soap or lather ← **sabun**

menyadap *v* to tap (rubber, telephones) ← **sadap**

menyadari *v* to realize, be aware of; **menyadarkan** *v* to make someone realize, raise someone's awareness ← **sadar**

menyaduh *v* to gild ← **sadur**

menyadur *v* to rewrite, adapt ← **sadur**

menyahut *v* to answer, reply, respond ← **sahut**

menyaingi *v* to compete with ← **saing**

menyajikan *v* to serve, present, offer ← **saji**

menyakiti *v* to hurt, treat badly; **menyakitkan** *adj* painful ← **sakit**

menyaksikan *v* to witness ← **saksi**

menyala *v* to burn, blaze; **menyalakan** *v* to light, set fire to ← **nyala**

menyalahi *v* to blame someone; **menyalahkan** *v* to blame ← **salah**

menyalami *v* to greet ← **salam**

menyalib *v* to crucify ← **salib**

menyalin *v* to copy ← **salin**

menyalip *v* overtake, slip past ← **salip**

menyalurkan *v* to channel ← **salur**

menyamai *v* to resemble, be like; **menyamakan** *v* to equate, consider the same ← **sama**

menyamar *v* to be in disguise; **menyamarkan** ~ *diri* to disguise yourself ← **samar**

menyamaratakan *v* to treat equally ← **sama rata**

menyambar *v* to pounce on, strike; *disambar petir* struck by lightning ← **sambar**

menyambung *v* to join, continue; **menyambungkan** *v* to connect to (something else) ← **sambung**

menyambut *v* to welcome or receive ← **sambut**

menyampaikan *v* to deliver, hand over, pass on ← **sampai**

menyamper *v, sl* to greet, acknowledge, say hello ← **samper**

menyampingi *v* to escort, accompany, flank ← **samping**

menyamun *v* to rob, plunder ← **samun**

menyandar *v* to lean ← **sandar**

menyandera *v* to take hostage ← **sandera**

menyangga *v* to hold up, support ← **sangga**

menyanggah *v* to object to, oppose, protest ← **sanggah**

menyangka *v* to suspect, suppose, presume; *tidak ~* never thought ← **sangka**

menyangkal *v* to deny ← **sangkal**

menyangkut *v* to involve, concern; *coll* to get caught, snagged; *conj* about

menyanjung *v* to flatter ← **sanjung**

menyanyi *v* to sing; **menyanyikan** *v* to sing something ← **nyanyi**

menyapa *v* to greet ← **sapa**

menyapih *v* to wean ← **sapih**

menyapu *v* to sweep or wipe ← **sapu**

menyaput *v* to cover, veil, shroud ← **saput**

menyarankan *v* to suggest ← **saran**

menyarap *v* to eat breakfast ← **sarap**

menyaring *v* to filter (through), screen, select ← **saring**

menyasak *~ rambut* to tease hair into a stiff position ← **sasak**

menyasar *v* to lose your way, get lost ← **sasar**

menyatakan *v* to declare, state, certify ← **nyata**

menyatroni *v* to clean out, go through (a house, by burglars) ← **satron**

menyatu *v* to become one; **menyatukan** *v* to unite various things ← **satu**

menyayangi *v* to love ← **sayang**

menyayat *v* to slice or cut off ← **sayat**

menyebabkan *v* to cause ← **sebab**

menyebalkan *adj* annoying, tiresome ← **sebal**

menyebar *v* to spread; **menyebarkan** *v* to spread something ← **sebar**

menyebarluaskan *v* to disseminate, spread something ← **sebar luas**

menyeberang *v* to cross; **menyeberangi** *v* to cross something ← **seberang**

menyebut *v* to mention, name, say ← **sebut**

menyedekahkan *v* to donate something to the poor ← **sedekah**

menyederhanakan *v* to simplify ← **sederhana**

menyediakan *v* to prepare, get ready ← **sedia**

menyedihkan *adj* depressing, sad ← **sedih**

menyedot *v* to suck (up) ← **sedot**

menyegarkan *adj* refreshing ← **segar**

menyégel *v* to seal (off), close up (a building) ← **ségel**

menyéhatkan *adj* healthy, with curing powers ← **séhat**

menyejukkan *adj* cooling, refreshing ← **sejuk**

menyéka *v* to wipe or rub off ← **séka**

menyekap *v* to lock up, detain ← **sekap**

menyekat *v* to partition, block off ← **sekat**

menyekolahkan *v* to send to school ← **sekolah**

menyela *v* to interrupt ← **sela**

menyelam *v* to dive; **menyelami** *v* to dive into; to study in depth ← **selam**

menyelamatkan *v* to save, rescue ← **selamat**

menyelenggarakan *v* to run, hold, organize ← **selenggara**

menyelesaikan *v* to finish, end, settle; ~ *masalah* to overcome a problem ← **selesai**

menyeléwéng *v* to deviate; to have an affair ← **seléwéng**

menyelidiki *v* to investigate ← **selidik**

menyelimuti *v* to (cover with a) blanket ← **selimut**

menyelinap *v* to sneak, move quietly ← **selinap**

menyelingi *v* to go between, intervene ← **seling**

menyelip *v* to slip; **menyelipkan** *v* to slip an object (into something) ← **selip**

menyelubungi *v* to veil or cover ← **selubung**

menyelundup *v* to sneak in illegally, infiltrate; **me-**

nyelundupkan *v* to smuggle (in) ← **selundup**

menyelusup *v* to penetrate, infiltrate ← **susup**

menyelusuri *v* to follow something, go along ← **selusur**

menyematkan *v* to pin, fasten with pins ← **semat**

menyembah *v* to pay homage to, worship ← **sembah**

menyembelih *v* to slaughter, butcher ← **sembelih**

menyembuhkan *v* to cure, heal ← **sembuh**

menyembunyikan *v* to hide or conceal something ← **sembunyi**

menyembur *v* to spurt out **menyemburkan** *v* to spit or spray something out ← **sembur**

menyemir *v* to polish ← **semir**

menyempatkan ~ *diri* to make time to ← **sempat**

menyempit *v* to (become) narrow ← **sempit**

menyemprot *v* to spray; **menyemprotkan** *v* to spray with something ← **semprot**

menyempurnakan *v* to perfect, complete; *Ejaan Yang Disempurnakan (EYD)* standardized spelling reform of 1972 ← **sempurna**

menyenangkan *adj* pleasing, agreeable ← **senang**

menyendiri *v* to go off by yourself ← **diri**

menyengat *v* to sting ← **sengat**

menyénggol *v* to bump, brush, tweak ← **sénggol**

menyengir *v* to smile nervously, grimace ← **sengir**

menyengsarakan *v* to torture, cause suffering ← **sengsara**

menyentak *v* to pull, jerk ← **sentak**

menyentil *v* to flick with your finger (often to rebuke a child) ← **sentil**

menyentuh *v* to touch ← **sentuh**

menyépak *v* to kick (out) ← **sépak**

menyepakati *v* to agree to ← **sepakat, pakat**

menyepélékan *v* to make light of, treat lightly ← **sepélé**

menyepi *v* to go away by yourself ← **sepi**

menyepuh *v* to plate or gild ← **sepuh**

menyerah *v* to surrender, give in, give up; **menyerahkan** *v* to hand over ← **serah**

menyeramkan *adj* creepy, frightening ← **seram**

menyerang *v* to attack ← **serang**

menyerap *v* to absorb, soak up ← **serap**

menyerbu *v* to attack (as a group), charge, invade ← **serbu**

menyerémpét *v* to scrape, scratch against ← **serémpét**

menyérét *v* to drag ← **sérét**

menyergap *v* to apprehend, ambush, catch ← **sergap**

menyerobot *v* to push in front ← **serobot**

menyertai *v* to accompany ← **serta**

menyerukan *v* to call or appeal for ← **seru**

menyerupai *v* to resemble, be similar to ← **rupa**

menyesal *v* to regret; **menyesalkan** *v* to feel bad about, regret (another's action) ← **sesal**

menyesatkan *adj* misleading, confusing ← **sesat**

menyesuaikan *v* to adapt, bring into line; ~ *diri* to adapt ← **sesuai**

menyetél *v* to tune, set, adjust; ~ *mesin mobil* to tune an engine ← **setél**

menyetir *v* to drive ← **setir**

menyetop *v* to stop (a vehicle) ← **setop**

menyetor *v* to pay in, deposit ← **setor**

menyetrika *v* to iron ← **setrika**

menyetubuhi *v* to have sex with ← **tubuh, setubuh**

menyetujui *v* to agree to, approve, ratify ← **tubuh, setubuh**

menyéwa *v* to rent, hire; **menyéwakan** *v* to let (a house), hire out, lease ← **séwa**

menyia-yiakan *v* to waste ← **sia-sia**

menyiapkan *v* to prepare something, get something ready ← **siap**

menyiarkan *v* to telecast, broadcast, disseminate ← **siar**

menyibukkan ~ *diri* to keep yourself busy, spend your time ← **sibuk**

menyidik *v* to investigate ← **sidik, selidik**

menyihir *v* to perform magic ← **sihir**

menyikat *v* to brush ← **sikat**

menyiksa *v* to torture ← **siksa**

menyilang *silang*-~ criss-cross ← **silang**

menyilét *v* to cut with a knife, slit ← **silét**

menyimak *v* to hear, monitor; *latihan* ~ listening practice ← **simak**

menyimpan *v* to keep, save up, store ← **simpan**

menyimpang *v* to deviate ← **simpang**

menyimpulkan *v* to conclude or summarize ← **simpul**

menyindir *v* to insinuate, allude ← **sindir**

menyinggahi *v* to stop over in ← **singgah**

menyinggung *v* to touch on; ~ *perasaan* to offend someone, hurt someone's feelings ← **singgung**

menyingkap *v* to open slightly, reveal; ~ *rahasia* to reveal a secret; **menyingkapkan** *v* to open something slightly ← **singkap**

menyingkatkan *v* to abbreviate, shorten ← **singkat**

menyingkir *v* to step or move aside; **menyingkirkan** *v* to remove, brush aside ← **singkir**

menyingsing *v* to lift, rise; ~ *lengan baju* to roll up your shirt sleeves, get to work; *fajar* ~ daybreak ← **singsing**

menyiram *v* to pour, water (plants); **menyirami** *v* to pour onto ← **siram**

menyisakan *v* to leave behind ← **sisa**

menyisihkan *v* to set aside ← **sisih**

menyisipkan *v* to insert ← **sisip**

menyisir *v* to comb, check thoroughly ← **sisir**

menyita *v* to confiscate ← **sita**

menyobék *v* to tear off; **menyobék-nyobék** *v* to rip up ← **sobék**

menyodét *v* to make an incision, cut a connecting channel ← **sodét**

menyodok *v* to poke ← **sodok**

menyodomi *v* to sodomize ← **sodomi**

menyodori *v* to hand to, offer; **menyodorkan** *v* to offer up, put forward ← **sodor**

menyogok *v* to bribe ← **sogok**

menyokong *v* to support, bolster ← **sokong**

menyolok *adj* glaring, standing out ← **colok**

menyombongkan ~ *diri* to show off, blow your own trumpet ← **sombong**

menyongsong *v* to welcome, greet ← **songsong**

menyonték *v* to copy, cheat ← **conték, sonték**

menyorong *v* to push, propose ← **sorong**

menyoroti *v* to light up, illuminate, focus on ← **sorot**

menyosialisasikan *v* to introduce to the public, disseminate ← **sosialisasi**

menyuap *v* to feed by hand; to bribe; **menyuapi** *v* to feed someone by hand; **menyuapkan** *v* to feed something by hand, to someone ← **suap**

menyuarakan *v* to voice ← **suara**

menyuburkan *v* to fertilize ← **subur**

menyucikan *v* to purify, cleanse ← **suci**

menyudahi *v* to end ← **sudah**

menyudutkan *v* to push into a corner, deflect ← **sudut**

menyuguhi *v* to offer (food), present (a performance) ← **suguh**

menyukai *v* to like ← **suka**

menyulam *v* to embroider ← **sulam**

menyulap *v* to conjure up; to make something vanish or change ← **sulap**

menyulih-suarakan *v* to dub ← **sulih**

menyuling *v* to distill ← **suling**

menyulitkan *v* to make difficult, complicate, cause problems ← **sulit**

menyuluh *v* to illuminate; to inform ← **suluh**

menyumbang *v* to contribute, make a donation ← **sumbang**

menyumbat *v* to plug, stop ← **sumbat**

menyumpahi *v* to swear at or curse someone ← **sumpah**

menyumpit *v* to use a blowpipe ← **sumpit**

menyunatkan *v* to have someone circumcised ← **sunat**

menyundul ~ *bola* to head the ball (in soccer) ← **sundul**

menyuntik *v* to inject or vaccinate ← **suntik**

menyunting *v* to edit ← **sunting**

menyupir *v* to drive ← **supir**

menyurati *v* to write a letter to ← **surat**

menyuruh *v* to command, order ← **suruh**

menyurut *v* to fall, subside ← **surut**

menyusahkan *v* to bother, make difficult ← **susah**

menyusu *v* to feed, suckle; **menyusui** *v* to feed; *binatang* ~ mammal ← **susu**

menyusul *v* to follow, go after ← **susul**

menyusun *v* to heap or pile; to arrange, organize, compile ← **susun**

menyusup *v* to penetrate, infiltrate ← **susup**

menyusut *v* to shrink, become smaller; **menyusutkan** *v* to reduce ← **susut**

menyutradarai *v* to direct ← **sutradara**

méong meow; *coll* puss, cat

mépét *adj* tight, squeezed

meraba *v* to feel or grope something; **meraba-raba** *v* to feel around or grope (in the dark) ← **raba**

meracik *v* to create a mix of ~ *obat* to mix up medicine ← **racik**

meracuni *v* to poison ← **racun**

meradang *v* to become inflamed; to become angry ← **radang**

meragukan *v* to doubt something ← **ragu**

mérah *adj* red; ~ *jambu* pink; ~ *tua* dark red, maroon; *lampu* ~ traffic light, red light; *Palang* ~ Red Cross; *Sang* ~ *Putih* the Red and White (Indonesian flag); **kemérah-mérah** *adj* reddish; **memérah** *v* to blush; **pemérah** ~ *pipi* rouge

merahasiakan *v* to keep secret ← **rahasia**

meraih *v* to reach for; to achieve ← **raih**

merajaléla *v* to be out of control, act violently ← **rajaléla**

merajam *v* to stone to death ← **rajam**

merajut *v* to knit; to crochet ← **rajut**

merak *n* peacock

merakit *v* to assemble ← **rakit**

merakyat *v* to become popular ← **rakyat**

meralat *v* to correct a mistake ← **ralat**

meramaikan *v* to liven up, enliven ← **ramai**

meramal *v* to tell fortunes; **meramalkan** *v* to predict, foretell ← **ramal**

merambah ~ *hutan* to clear away the forest, clear the land ← **rambah**

merampas *v* to take by force, rob, plunder ← **rampas**

merampok *v* to rob, hold up; ~ *bank* to rob or hold up a bank ← **rampok**

meramu v to gather, collect ← **ramu**

merana v to suffer, waste away; to live miserably, in poverty

merancang v to plan, design ← **rancang**

merang n rice-straw

merangkai v to bind together, combine ← **rangkai**

merangkak v to crawl ← **rangkak**

merangkap v to hold another position (temporarily) ← **rangkap**

merangkul v to hug, embrace; to get someone involved ← **rangkul**

merangkum v to carry in your arms ← **rangkum**

merangsang v to stimulate, excite ← **rangsang**

merantai v to chain up ← **rantai**

merantau v to sail away, seek your fortune, settle overseas ← **rantau**

meranti kayu ~ kind of reddish wood, morantee

merapat v to move closer ← **rapat**

merasa v to think, feel; **merasa- kan** v to feel something ← **rasa**

merasuk v to enter into, possess ← **rasuk**

meratakan v to level, flatten ← **rata**

meratap v to lament, wail ← **ratap**

meraung v to roar ← **raung**

meraup v to scoop up in your hands ← **raup**

merawat v to nurse, care for; to maintain, look after ← **rawat**

merayakan v to celebrate ← **raya**

merayap v to crawl, creep ← **rayap**

merayu v to tempt, flatter, seduce ← **rayu**

mercon n fireworks

mercu n top, summit; ~ suar lighthouse

Mércy n, coll Merc, Mercedes-Benz car ← **Mercédes-Benz**

merdéka adj free, independent; **kemerdékaan** n freedom, independence, liberty

merdu adj sweet, melodious, honeyed

merebah v to fall down, collapse ← **rebah**

meréboisasi v to reforest, replant trees ← **réboisasi**

merebus v to boil (in) water ← **rebus**

merebut v to snatch, capture; ~ kembali to recapture; **me- rebutkan** v to snatch some- thing ← **rebut**

mereda v to subside, abate; **meredakan** v to soothe; to calm something down ← **reda**

meredamkan v to muffle or stifle ← **redam**

mereguk v to gulp down, take a shot ← **reguk**

mérek n brand, make (vehicle), label (clothes); **bermérek** v to have a label; adj branded

meréka pron, pl they, them, their; ~ punya theirs

merekam v to record ← **rekam**

merékayasa *v* to engineer ← **rékayasa**

merékoméndasikan *v* to recommend ← **rékoméndasi**

merékonstruksi *v* to reconstruct ← **rékonstruksi**

merekrut *v* to recruit ← **rekrut**

merélakan *v* to approve, agree to ← **réla**

merem be asleep, eyes shut

meremajakan *v* to revitalize, refurbish, update ← **remaja**

meremas *v* to press, squeeze, knead ← **remas**

merembes *v* to seep in, leak, ooze ← **rembes**

meréméhkan *v* to belittle, treat as unimportant ← **réméh**

merencanakan *v* to plan ← **rencana**

merénda *v* to crochet ← **rénda**

merendahkan *v* to lower; to humiliate ← **rendah**

merendam *v* to soak something ← **rendam**

meréngék *v* to whimper, whine ← **réngék**

merenggut *v* to snatch, tug ← **renggut**

merengut *v* to grumble ← **rengut**

merénovasi *v* to renovate ← **rénovasi**

merentang *v* to span, stretch over; **merentangkan** *v* to extend, stretch out ← **rentang**

merenung *v* to daydream; **merenungi, merenungkan** *v* to think about, reflect on, muse ← **renung**

meréparasi *v* to repair ← **réparasi**

merépotkan *v* to make someone busy or go to some trouble ← **répot**

meresahkan *adj* disturbing, worrying ← **resah**

meresap *v* to be absorbed, penetrate, seep into ← **resap**

meresépkan *v* to write a prescription for a drug ← **resép**

meresmikan *v* to formalize, make official ← **resmi**

meréstorasi *v* to restore ← **réstorasi**

merestui *v* to agree to, give your blessing to ← **restu**

meretak *v* to crack ← **retak**

meriah *adj* merry, lively; **memeriahkan** *v* to liven up, enliven ← **riah**

meriak *v* to ripple ← **riak**

meriam *n* cannon

meriang feel unwell, sick

meributkan *v* to make a fuss about ← **ribut**

merica *n* pepper

merilis *v* to release, put out ← **rilis**

merinci *v* to specify, detail ← **rinci**

merinding *v* to have goosebumps or an eerie feeling, be spooked ← **rinding**

merindukan *v* to miss, long for ← **rindu**

meringankan *v* to ease, relieve, make easier ← **ringan**

meringkus *v* to catch (esp by the arm or leg), take into custody ← **ringkus**

merintih *v* to moan or groan ← **rintih**

merintis *v* to trace; to pioneer ← **rintis**

merisaukan *v* to worry about ← **risau**

merisihkan *v* to disturb, make you feel uncomfortable ← **risih**

mérk → **mérek**

merobék *v* to tear up, shred ← **robék**

merobohkan *v* to knock down, demolish ← **roboh**

merogoh *v* to grope around, search for (inside something else) ← **rogoh**

merokok *v* to smoke; *dilarang ~* no smoking ← **rokok**

merombak *v* to pull down, demolish; to reorganize ← **rombak**

merompak *v* to commit piracy ← **rompak**

merongrong *v* to gnaw at, undermine ← **rongrong**

meronta, meronta-ronta *v* to struggle, squirm to get loose ← **ronta**

merosot *v* fall down, descend, plummet; *celananya ~* his pants fell down; **kemerosotan** *n* descent, deterioration ← **rosot**

merpati *n* pigeon, dove

merta *serta-~* automatically, immediately

mertua *n* parents-in-law; *ibu ~* mother-in-law

merubah → **mengubah**

merugikan *v* to hurt, harm, injure ← **rugi**

merujuk *v* to refer to, use as a source ← **rujuk**

merumahkan *v* to be laid off (from work) ← **rumah**

merumuskan *v* to formulate ← **rumus**

meruncing *v* to become critical or sharp ← **runcing**

merundingkan *v* to discuss something, deliberate over ← **runding**

merungut *v* to grumble, complain ← **rungut**

meruntai *v* to hang loosely ← **untai**

meruntuhkan *v* to overthrow, destroy ← **runtuh**

merupakan *v* to be, form, constitute ← **rupa**

merusak *v* to spoil, damage; **merusakkan** *v* to destroy, break ← **rusak**

més *n* company accommodation or housing, boarding house

mésem smile

méses *n* chocolate sprinkles

mesin *n* machine, engine; *~ jahit* sewing machine; *~ pengisap debu* vacuum cleaner; *~ tik* typewriter; *teknik ~* mechanical engineering

Mesir *n* Egypt; *~ kuno* ancient Egypt; *orang ~* Egyptian

mesjid, masjid *n* mosque; *~ agung, ~ raya* great mosque

meski, meskipun *conj* although, even though

mesra *adj* intimate, close; **kemesraan** *n* intimacy

mesti, musti *v, aux* should; **semestinya** should have (been)

mesum *adj* dirty, immoral, sleazy; *tempat* ~ seedy place, red-light district

méter *n* meter; metre; **méteran** *n* tape measure

meterai, méterai *n* seal

méteran *n* tape measure ← **méter**

métode *n* method

Métromini *n* medium-sized orange and blue bus in Jakarta

mewabah *v* to spread (uncontrollably) ← **wabah**

méwah *n* luxurious; **keméwahan** *n* luxury

mewahyukan *v* to reveal something (in a vision) ← **wahyu**

mewajibkan *v* to enforce or make obligatory ← **wajib**

mewakili *v* to represent ← **wakil**

mewanti-wanti *v* to warn ← **wanti**

mewarisi *v* to inherit; **mewariskan** *v* to bequeath or leave something ← **waris**

mewarnai *v* to color (in) ← **warna**

mewaspadai *v* to watch out for, guard against ← **waspada**

mewawancarai *v* to interview ← **wawancara**

mewujudkan *v* to make something real, realize something ← **wujud**

meyakini *v* to believe (in), be convinced; **meyakinkan** *adj* convincing, believable ← **yakin**

mi, mie *n* noodles; ~ *ayam* chicken noodles; ~ *goreng* fried noodles; ~ *rebus* boiled noodles (in soup)

Mi, Mami *pron, coll* Mum, Mummy (in Westernized circles)

migrasi *n* migration; **bermigrasi** *v* to migrate; **migran** *n* migrant → **imigrasi, pendatang**

migrén *n* migraine; *sakit kepala* ~ migraine

mik, mikrofon *n* microphone, mike

mikrolét *n* small minibus converted for transport in Jakarta → **mikro oplét**

Mikronésia *n* Micronesia; *orang* ~ Micronesian

mikroskop *n* microscope

milénium *n* millenium

mili, miliméter *n* millimetre, millimeter

miliar, milyar *n* billion → **milyar**

milik *n* property, possession; ~ *negara* state-owned; *hak* ~ proprietary rights, ownership; **memiliki** *v* to own, possess; **pemilik** *n* owner; **kepemilikan** *n* ownership

milis *n* mail list

milisi *n* militia

militan *adj* militant; **militér** *n* military; *wajib* ~ military service

milyar, miliar *n* billion; **milyarder** *n* billionaire

mimbar *n* pulpit, platform, forum

mimisan nose bleed, blood nose

mimpi dream; ~ *buruk* nightmare, bad dream; ~ *indah* sweet dreams; **bermimpi** *v* to dream;

memimpikan *v* to dream of
→ **impi**

min → **minus**

minal aidin (wal faidzin) greeting
at Idul Fitri

Minang, Minangkabau ethnic
group of West Sumatra;
bahasa ~, orang ~ Minang,
Minangkabau; *ranah Minang*
the Minangkabau lands

minat *n* interest, attention;
berminat *v* to have an interest,
be interested; **peminat** *n* interested party

minder *coll* to lack confidence,
low self-esteem; to feel inferior

minggir *v, coll* move to one side,
pull over (on the road) →
pinggir

minggu *n* week; Sunday; *~
depan* next week; *~ ini* this
week; *~ yang lalu, ~ kemarin*
last week; *hari ~* Sunday;
malam ~ Saturday night;
berminggu-minggu *adv* for
weeks; **mingguan** *n* weekly
(publication); **seminggu** *adj*
a week; *tiga kali ~* three times
a week

miniatur *adj* miniature

minim, minimal, minimum
minimum, minimal(ly)

minoritas *n* minority

minta *v* to ask, beg, request; to
apply for; *~ ampun* to beg for
mercy; *~ uang* to ask or beg
for money; *~ doa restu* to
ask for prayers and blessings;
minta-minta *v* to beg (alms);
meminta *v* to ask for, request;

permintaan *n* request

minum drink; *air ~* drinking
water; *~ obat* to take (liquid)
medicine; **minum-minum** *v* to
go out drinking, drink (alcohol); **minuman** *n* drink; *~
hangat* hot drink, beverage; *~
keras* alcoholic drink, liquor;
peminum *n* drinker

minus, min *adj* minus; *berkaca-
mata ~* to be short-sighted

minyak *n* oil; *~ jarak* castor oil;
~ kelapa coconut palm oil; *~
mentah* crude oil; *~ rambut*
hair tonic or oil; *~ tanah* kerosene; *~ wangi* perfume; *~
zaitun* olive oil; *ladang ~* oil
field; *raja ~* oil baron, sheik;
*Perusahaan Pertambangan
~ dan Gas Bumi Negara
(Pertamina)* Pertamina, the
state-owned oil company;
berminyak *adj* oily, greasy;
perminyakan *n* oil and gas

miring *adj* sloping, slanting; not
straight; *berita ~* negative
story; *tulisan ~* italics; **kemiringan** *n* slope; **memiringkan** *v* to slant, tilt

misa *n, Cath* mass; *~ agung*
high mass

misal *n* example; **misalnya,
misalkan** for example, for
instance

misi *n* mission; *visi dan ~* mission
statement; **misionaris** *n* missionary

miskin *adj* poor, lacking in; *~
sumber daya alam* lacking
natural resources; *orang ~*

pauper; *pl* the poor; **ke-miskinan** *n* poverty

mistar *n* crossbar of goal; ruler

mistéri *n* mystery; **mistérius** *adj* mysterious

mistik, mistis *adj* mystical

mitos *n* myth

mitra *n* partner, friend; ~ *usaha* business partner; **kemitraan** *n* partnership

mobil *n* car; ~ *baja* armored car, tank; ~ *butut* old car, bomb; ~ *jenazah* hearse; ~ *kuno* classic or vintage car; ~ *mewah* luxury car

modal *n* capital, fund; *me-nanamkan* ~ to invest (capital); **bermodal** *v* to have capital; ~ *dengkul* with only hard work

mode *n* fashion, trend; **modiste** *n* dressmaker

modél *n* model; *foto~* model → **raga**

modérn *adj* modern

modiste *n* dressmaker

moga: moga-moga, semoga may, hopefully

mogok strike; break down; ~ *kerja* strike; ~ *makan* hunger strike; *mobil* ~ broken-down car

mohon *v* to request, ask, beg; please; ~ *diri* to take leave; ~ *perhatian* attention please; **pemohon** *n* applicant; **permohonan** *n* request, application → **pohon**

mol → **mal**

molék *adj* pretty, charming; *kecil* ~ delicate; **kemolékan** *n* beauty

molor stretch, become longer

momok *n* ghost, phantom

momong take care of a baby; **momongan** *n* baby, child

Monako *n* Monaco; *orang* ~ Monegasque

Monas *n* National Monument in Central Jakarta ← **Monumén Nasional**

moncong *n* muzzle, nose; ~ *putih* the white nose (symbol of PDIP)

mondar-mandir *v* to go back and forth, to and fro

mondok *v, coll* to board, stay; *uang* ~ board ← **pondok**

Mongolia *n* Mongolia; *bahasa* ~ Mongolian; *orang* ~ Mongol, Mongolian

monopoli *n* monopoly; **me-monopoli** *v* to monopolize

monorél *n* monorail

monoton *adj* monotonous

Montenégro *n* Montenegro; *bahasa* ~, *orang* ~ Montenegrin

montir *n* mechanic

montok *adj* plump, rounded, well filled-out; **kemontokan** *n* plumpness

monumén *n* monument; ~ *Nasional (Monas)* National Monument

monyét *n* monkey; *derog* term of abuse

monyong *adj* sticking out, protruding (of teeth), like a dog's muzzle

moral, moril moral; *dukungan* ~ moral support

moréng *coreng-~* streaked, smeared all over

nori *kain* ~ white cloth for
batik-making

nortir *n* mortar, shell

nosi *n* motion; ~ *tidak percaya*
vote of no confidence

Moskwa *n* Moscow; *orang* ~
Muscovite

notif *n* design, pattern, motif;
bermotif *v* to have a design

notif *n* motive; **motivasi** *n*
motivation; **bermotivasikan** *v*
to be motivated by; **me-
motivasi** *v* to motivate

noto *n* MSG, monosodium
glutamate; motto, chant ←
Ajinomoto

notor *n* motorcycle,
(motor)bike; *sepeda* ~ motorbike

noyang *nenek* ~ ancestors

Mozambik *n* Mozambique;
orang ~ Mozambican

MPP *abbrev Masa Persiapan
Pensiun* retirement preparation
period

MPR *abbrev Majelis Permusya-
warawatan Rakyat* People's
Consultative Council

MTQ *abbrev Musabaqah
Tilawatil Qur'an* Koranic
recitation competition

MU *abbrev Majelis Ulama*
Council of Islamic Scholars;
Muktamar Umum General
Congress

mu *pron, poss, s* your; *buku~*
your book → **kamu**

nua *n* eel

nuai: memuai *v* to expand,
swell; **pemuaian** *n* expansion

muak loathe; disgusted, fed up;
memuakkan *adj* revolting,
disgusting

mual *adj* nauseous, queasy, sick

mualaf *n, Isl* recent convert

Muang Thai *n* Thailand

muara *n* mouth (of a river);
bermuara *v* to have a mouth,
empty into

muasal *asal* ~ root, origin ←
asal

muat contain; *tidak* ~ it won't
fit; **muatan** *n* load, cargo;
bermuatan *v* to be laden with;
memuat *v* to contain

mubazir *adj* wasted, not used

muda *adj* young; *hijau* ~ light
green; *isteri* ~ new (younger)
wife; *merah* ~ pink;
Laksamana ~ Vice-Admiral;
pemuda *n* youth; young man;
pemudi *n* young woman

mudah *adj* easy; ~ *marah* easily
angry, quick-tempered;
mudah-mudahan *adv* hopefully, maybe; **kemudahan** *n*
ease, facility; **mempermudah**
v to make easier

mudi *juru* ~ helmsman

mudik *v* to go upstream, back to
the village; ~ *Lebaran* to return
to your hometown; *arus* ~ flow
of people going back to the
village (usu at Idul Fitri); *hilir*
~ to go up and down the river,
back and forth

mufakat *n* agreement, consensus;
permufakatan *n* discussion,
deliberation

MUI *abbrev Majelis Ulama*

Indonesia Indonesian Council of Islamic Scholars

mujur straight on; lucky

muka *n* face, front, surface; *air ~, raut ~* look, expression; *di ~* in front of; *ke ~* to the front, forward; **mengemukakan** *v* to put forward, advance, nominate; **terkemuka** *adj* prominent; **bermuka** *v* to have a face; *~ dua* two-faced; **permukaan** *n* surface; *~ air* water level; *di atas ~ laut* above sea level

mukenah *Isl* white prayer shawls

mukim: bermukim *v* to reside, stay; **permukiman** *n* housing, residential area

muktamar *Isl* congress, conference

mula beginning, start; **mula-mula** *adv* in the beginning, at first; **bermula** *v* to start, begin; **memulai** *v* to start or begin something; **pemula** *n* beginner; **permulaan** *n* beginning; **semula** *adj* original; *adv* originally

mulai *v* to begin, start; *~ tanggal 23 Desember* from December 23; **memulai** *v* to start or begin something ← **mula**

mula-mula *adv* in the beginning, at first ← **mula**

mules, mulas stomach upset, loose stomach

mulia *adj* honorable, noble; *logam ~* precious metal; *Paduka Yang ~* His/Her/Your Excellency; **kemuliaan** *n* honor, glory; *~ Tuhan* the glory of God; **memuliakan** *v* to honor, glorify

Mulo *n* secondary school in Dutch times ← **Meer Uitgebreid Lager Onderwijs**

Mulud → **Maulud**

mulus *adj* smooth, flawless; **memuluskan** *v* to ease the way, help

mulut *n* mouth; *~ kotor* filthy mouth; *tutup ~* to hold your tongue, keep silent

mumi *n* mummy

mumpung *v* to make the most of, capitalize on

munafik *adj* hypocrite; **kemunafikan** *n* hypocrisy

munas *n* national convention ← **musyawarah nasional**

muncrat *v* to spurt, spray

muncul *v* to appear, turn up; **bermunculan** *v* to show up (in large numbers); **memunculkan** *v* to bring forward

mundur *v* to go backwards, reverse, retreat; to resign; **kemunduran** *n* deterioration, decline; **memundurkan** *v* to retract, bring back → **undur**

mungil *adj* small, tiny, delicate; *rumah ~* small house

mungkin *conj* maybe, possibly; *tidak ~* impossible; **kemungkinan** *n* possibility; **memungkinkan** *adj* conducive; *v* to enable, make possible

mungkir, memungkiri *v* to deny

munisi → **amunisi**

munsyi *n* language teacher, linguist

muntabér *n* diarrhea and vomiting ← **muntah bérak**

muntah *v* to vomit, throw up; **memuntahkan** *v* to vomit or bring up

mur *n* nut; *baut dan* ~ nut and bolt

murah *adj* cheap; ~ *hati* generous; ~ *senyum* always smiling; **kemurahan** *n* cheapness; **termurah** *adj* the cheapest

murai *burung* ~ magpie

muram *adj* gloomy, sombre, mournful; **kemuraman** *n* gloom

murid *n* pupil, student

murka *adj* furious, wrathful; **kemurkaan** *n* anger, fury

murni *adj* pure; only; **kemurnian** *n* purity

murtad convert from Islam, apostate

murung *adj* gloomy, despondent

Musa *Nabi* ~ Moses

musafir *n, Isl* traveler

musang *n* civet cat

muséum → **musium**

mushola, musholla, mushala, mushalla, musola, musala *n, Isl* small prayer-house

musibah *n* disaster, calamity; *kena* ~ suffer a misfortune, disaster

musik *n* music; **pemusik, musikus, musisi** *n* musician

musim *n* season; ~ *bunga*, ~ *semi* spring; ~ *dingin* winter; ~ *gugur* autumn, fall; ~ *panas* summer; ~ *salju* snow season; **musiman** *adj* seasonal

musium, muséum *n* museum; ~ *Gajah* National Museum

muslihat *n* trick; *tipu* ~ (dirty) trick, deceit

Muslim *adj, Isl* Muslim; *baju* ~ Islamic dress; *orang* ~ Muslim; **Muslimah** *adj, Isl, f* Muslim (woman) → **Islam**

musnah *adj* destroyed; **memusnahkan** *v* to destroy; **pemusnahan** *v* act of destruction

mustahil *adj* impossible

musti → **mesti**

musuh *n* enemy; ~ *bebuyutan* arch-enemy; **bermusuhan** *v* to be enemies; **memusuhi** *v* to fight against, antagonize, make an enemy of; **permusuhan** *n* enmity, animosity, hostility

musyawarah *n* meeting, discussion (to reach an agreement); **bermusyawarah** *v* to reach an agreement

mutakhir *adj* modern, latest

mutasi *n* change (in status), mutation; **memutasi** *v* to change someone's status

mutiara *n* pearl; *ibu* ~ mother-of-pearl

mutlak *adj* absolute, unconditional

mutu *n* quality; **bermutu** *adj* quality; ~ *rendah* low quality

Myanmar *n* Myanmar, Burma; *bahasa* ~, *orang* ~ Burmese

N

naas *adj* unfortunate

nabati *adj* vegetable, plant; *lemak ~* vegetable fats

nabi *n, Isl, Chr* prophet; *~ Isa Isl* Jesus; *~ Nuh* Noah; *~ Yunus* Jonas

nada *n* note, tone, sound; *~ dering* ringtone; *~sela* call waiting; *tangga ~* scale; **bernada** *v* to have a tone or edge; *~ sinis* mockingly, sarcastically

nadi *n* pulse; *denyut ~* pulse, heartbeat; *pembuluh ~* artery

nafas, napas breath, breathe; *sesak ~* hard to breathe, asthmatic; *menarik ~* to take a breath; **bernafas** *v* to breathe; **bernafaskan** *v* with a breath of; **pernafasan** *n* breathing, respiration; *~ buatan* artificial respiration; *sistem ~* respiratory system

nafkah *n* means of livelihood; **menafkahi** *v* to pay for someone's daily needs

nafsu *n* desire; *~ makan* appetite; *hawa ~* passion, lust; **bernafsu** *adj* passionate, lusty

naga *n* dragon; *Tahun ~* Year of the Dragon

nagasari *kue ~* small coconut cake wrapped in a banana leaf

nah, na well, well then; look! *~ lu* well then, how about that?

Nahdlatul Ulama (NU) *n* Islamic social organization; **nahdlatin** *n* members of NU

naif *adj* naif → **lugu**

naik go up, climb, rise, ascend; go by; *~ gunung* climb a mountain; *~ haji* go on the pilgrimage to Mecca; *~ pesawat* board, boarding; fly; *~ pangkat* be promoted; *~ pitam* get angry; **kenaikan** *n* rise, raise; *~ gaji* pay rise; **menaiki** *v* to ride, mount, get on; **menaikkan** *v* to raise, hoist

najis *n* dirt, filth; excrement

nak *pron* child, son, lass → **anak**

nakal *adj* naughty; **kenakalan** *n* naughtiness

nakhoda *n* captain (of a ship)

naksir *v, coll* to like, find someone or something attractive ← **taksir**

nalar *n* reason, common sense

naluri *n* instinct; **naluriah** *adj* instinctive

nama *n* name; *~ depan* first name; *~ kecil* everyday name, nickname; *~ keluarga* family name, surname; *atas ~* for; **bernama** *adj* named; **kenamaan, ternama** *adj* famous, well-known; **menamakan** *v* to call, name

Namibia *n* Namibia; *orang ~* Namibian

nampak → **tampak**

nampan *n* tray

namun *conj* however, yet

nan *conj, lit* who, which

nanah *n* pus; **bernanah** *v* to fester

nanar *adj* confused, dazed

nanas, nenas *n* pineapple

nangka *n* jackfruit

nangkring *v, coll* to sit somewhere high up, perch → **tangkring**

nanti *adv* later; ~ *dulu* not now, later on; ~ *malam* tonight; ~ *sore* this afternoon; **menanti** *v* to wait; **menanti-nanti** *v* to wait for a long time; **menantikan** *v* to wait for

napas, nafas breath, breathe; *sesak* ~ hard to breathe, asthmatic; *menarik* ~ take a breath; **bernapas** *v* to breathe; **bernapaskan** *v* with a breath of; **pernapasan** *n* breathing, respiration; ~ *buatan* artificial respiration; *sistem* ~ respiratory system

napi *n* prisoner, inmate, criminal → **narapidana**

napsu → **nafsu**

Napza *abbrev narkotika, alkohol, psikotropika dan zat adiktif lainnya* narcotics, alcohol and other addictive drugs

nara: narapidana *n* prisoner, inmate, criminal; **narasumber** *n* source (person)

narik *v, coll* to work as a driver of public transport ← **tarik**

narkoba *n* (illegal) drugs, narcotics and other banned substances ← **narkotika, psikotropika dan obat terlarang**

narkotika *n* narcotics

nasabah *n* (bank) customer

Nasakom *n* nationalism, religion and communism, policy under Sukarno around 1959–1965 ← **nasionalisme, agama, komunisme**

naséhat → **nasihat**

nasi *n* (cooked) rice; ~ *goreng* fried rice; ~ *rames* rice with side-dishes; ~ *uduk* coconut rice with chicken, a specialty of Jakarta

nasib *n* fate, lot, destiny; **senasib** *adj* fellow sufferer

nasihat, naséhat *n* advice; **menasihati** *v* to advise; **penasihat** *n* adviser

nasional *n* national; *Partai* ~ *Indonesia (PNI)* Indonesian National Party; **nasionalis** *n* nationalist; **nasionalisme** *n* nationalism

naskah *n* manuscript, original (text); *penulis* ~ script writer

Nasrani *adj* Christian

Natal *Hari* ~ Christmas Day; *Malam* ~ Christmas Eve; **natalan** *v, coll* to celebrate Christmas

naung: naungan *n* shade, shelter; protection; *di bawah* ~ under the auspices of; **bernaung** *v* to (take) shelter

Nauru *n* Nauru; *bahasa* ~, *orang* ~ Nauruan

nb *abbrev nota bene* note (well)

ndak, nggak, enggak *coll* no, not ← **tidak**

nébéng *v, sl* to sponge, get a lift, use something without paying ← **tébéng**

nécis *adj* well-dressed

negara *n* state, country; ~ *berkembang* developing

nation; ~ *tetangga* neighbor; *antar* ~ international; *Ibu* ~ First Lady; *lambang* ~ national symbol; *milik* ~ *negara sekutu* state-owned; ~ *Kesatuan Republik Indonesia (NKRI)* the unitary state of the Republic of Indonesia; *warga*~ citizen; *kewarganegaraan* citizenship; **kenegaraan** *adj* state (affairs); **negarawan** *n* statesman

negeri *n* country, land; ~ *jiran* neighbor, Malaysia; *ayam* ~ battery hen; *dalam* ~ national, domestic, internal; *luar* ~ overseas, abroad

Nék *pron* term of address for a grandmother or elderly woman → **nénék**

nékad, nékat reckless; stubborn; *bondo* ~ *(bonek)* Surabaya soccer hooligans; **kenékatan** *n* determination, resolve, recklessness

Nékolim neo-colonialist; neo-colonialism, colonialism and imperialism, Sukarnoist slogan of the early 1960s ← **néokolonialisme, kolonialisme, impérialisme**

nelayan *n* fisherman

nenas → **nanas**

nénék *n, pron* grandmother; great-aunt; female relative of grandmother's generation; ~ *buyut* great-grandmother; ~ *moyang* ancestors → **Nék**

Néng *pron* term of address for girl or young woman in western Java

néngok → **téngok**

néon *n* neon; *lampu* ~ neon light

Népal *n* Nepal; *bahasa* ~ Nepali; *orang* ~ Nepalese

népotisme *n* nepotism; *korupsi, kolusi,* ~ *(KKN)* corruption (collusion and nepotism)

neraca *n* scales, balance

neraka *n* hell; *api* ~ flames of hell

nétral *adj* neutral; **menétralkan** *v* to neutralize

ngabén Balinese funeral ceremony

ngabuburit *v, sl* to fill in time waiting for the end of the fast at sunset

ngaco *v, sl* to shoot off your mouth, talk without thinking; to misbehave

ngaji *v, coll* to recite or read the Koran; *guru* ~ Arabic teacher ← **kaji**

ngambek *v, coll* to get angry ← **ambek**

nganga: menganga *v* to gape, be open(-mouthed); **ternganga** *adj* gaping, flabbergasted, wide open

ngantor *v, coll* to go to work ← **kantor**

ngantuk *adj, coll* sleepy ← **antuk**

ngarai *n, Sum* gorge, ravine, steep valley

ngarang *v, coll* to make something up (off the top of your head) ← **karang**

ngawur *v, coll* to talk nonsense

ngefans *v, sl* to be a fan of; ~ *berat* a great fan of ← **fans**

geri *adj* terrified; **mengerikan** *adj* terrifying, horrifying

gerumpi *v, sl* to (get together for a) chat or gossip ← **rumpi**

getém *v, coll* to wait for passengers (of public transport) ← **tém**

getop *v, sl* to be on top ← **top**

getrén, ngetrénd *adj, coll* trendy, fashionable ← **trénd**

ggak, enggak, ndak *coll* no, not → **tidak**

gilu *adj* painful (of teeth), smarting; *rasa* ~ pain

gobrol *v, coll* to chat ← **obrol**

gocéh *v, coll* to babble (of babies) ← **océh**

gomél *v, coll* to complain, grumble, whinge, whine ← **omél**

gomong *v, coll* to speak, talk; **ngomong-ngomong** *adv* by the way

gompol *v, coll* to wet your pants, the bed ← **ompol**

gopi *v, sl* to drink or have a coffee ← **kopi**

gorok *v, coll* to snore; to sleep

gos: ngos-ngosan *v* to puff, pant, gasp

gotot *v, coll* to be stubborn, refuse to back down → **otot**

gumpul *v, sl* to get or come together ← **kumpul**

guping *v, coll* to eavesdrop, listen in ← **kuping**

li *pron, f* term of address for Balinese woman

iaga *n* commerce; **perniagaan** *n* commerce, trade, business

niat *n* intention; **berniat** *v* to intend

NICA *abbrev* Netherlands Indies Civil Administration

nifas *n* childbirth; *masa* ~ *Isl* 40-day confinement after childbirth

Nigéria *n* Nigeria; *orang* ~ Nigerian

nih *pron, sl* this, these; here; *ini* ~ this one → **ini**

nihil *adj* nothing, nil

nikah *pol* marry; *akad* ~ *Isl* marriage contract; **menikah** *v* to marry, get married; **menikahi** *v* to marry someone; **menikahkan** *v* to marry off (a child); **pernikahan** *n* wedding; *pesta* ~ wedding reception

nikel *n* nickel

nikmat *adj* enjoyable, delicious; ~*nya* how enjoyable! isn't it good?; **kenikmatan** *n* pleasure, enjoyment; **menikmati** *v* to enjoy

Nil *kuda* ~ hippo(potamus); *sungai* ~ the (River) Nile

nila *n* indigo; *ikan* ~ a kind of freshwater fish

nilai *n* value, worth; mark, grade (at school); ~ *jual* selling price; ~ *tambah* added value; **menilai** *v* to evaluate, appraise; **penilaian** *n* evaluation; **ternilai** *tidak* ~ priceless, invaluable

NIM *abbrev Nomor Induk Mahasiswa* (university) student number

nimbrung *v, coll* to join in someone else's conversation, butt in

ninabobo lullaby; sing to sleep

ningrat *adj* aristocratic

NIP *abbrev Nomor Induk Pegawai* civil servant number

nipah *pohon* ~ kind of palm

nipis *jeruk* ~ lime

nir- *pref* without; **nirlaba** *adj* non-profit, not for profit; **nirmala** *adj* clean, pure; **Nirwana** *n* Nirvana

nisan *n* headstone, gravestone

niscaya *adv* surely, certainly, undoubtedly

NISP *abbrev Nederlands-Indies Spoorbank* Netherlands-Indies Railway Bank

nista *n* insult, abuse; stigma

NKRI *abbrev Negara Kesatuan Republik Indonesia* the unitary state of the Republic of Indonesia

Nn. *abbrev Nona* Miss, title for unmarried woman, especially a non-Indonesian

nobat: menobatkan *v* to install, crown

noda *n* stain; ~ *bandel* hard-to-remove stain; **menodai** *v* to stain; to deflower (a girl)

noktah *n* point, dot

nol *adj* zero, nil

nomor, nomer *n* number; event, match; ~ *urut* queue number; ~ *cantik* lucky mobile phone number; ~ *satu* number one, first; **menomersatukan** *v* to put first, give priority

nomplok *adj, coll* abundant, in large quantities; *rejeki* ~ windfall

non- *pref* not; non-; **nonaktif** *adj* not in active service; **menonaktifkan** *v* to release from active service, non-activate; **nonblok** *adj* Third World, neither Western nor Communist; **nonformal** *adj* irregular, informal; **nonpri(bumi)** *adj* ethnic Chinese, non-indigenous

Nona *pron* **Non** *coll* (Nn) Miss, title for unmarried woman

nonaktif *adj* not in active service

nonblok *adj* Third World, neither Western nor Communist

Noné *Abang* ~ Mr and Miss Jakarta contest

nonformal *adj* irregular, informal

nongkrong → **tongkrong**

nongol *v* to stick out

nonpri, nonpribumi *adj* ethnic Chinese, non-indigenous ← **pribumi**

nonton *v, coll* to watch, look on ← **tonton**

Nopémber → **November**

norak *adj, coll* tasteless, vulgar, tacky

norit *n* diarrhea tablets, made from black carbon

Norwégia *n* Norway; *bahasa* ~, *orang* ~ Norwegian

nostalgia, nostalgi *n* nostalgia; **bernostalgia** *v* to reminisce, be nostalgic

not *n* note (music)

nota *n* note, memo; bill, account

notaris *n* notary

Novémber, Nopémber *bulan* ~ November

NPWP *abbrev Nomor Pokok Wajib Pajak* tax file number

nr *abbrev nomor* number

ntar, entar *sl* just a minute, wait; ~ *malam* tonight → **sebentar**

NTB *abbrev Nusa Tenggara Barat* West Nusa Tenggara (the lesser Sunda islands)

NTT *abbrev Nusa Tenggara Timur* East Nusa Tenggara (the lesser Sunda islands)

NU *abbrev* Nahdlatul Ulama, Islamic organization based in East Java

nuansa *n* touch, nuance; **bernuansa** *adj* with a touch of

Nugini *Papua* ~ Papua New Guinea, PNG

Nuh *Nabi* ~ Noah

nujum *ahli* ~ astrologer

nuklir *adj* nuclear; *bom* ~ nuclear bomb; *limbah* ~ nuclear waste; *tenaga* ~ nuclear power; *pembangkit listrik tenaga* ~ *(PLTN)* nuclear power station

nun *lit* yonder, far away

nurani *adj* inner; *hati* ~ inner self, conscience

nuri *burung* ~ parrot

nusa *n* island; ~ *dan bangsa* Indonesia and its people; ~ *Tenggara* the Lesser Sunda Islands; **Nusantara** *n* Indonesia

NV *abbrev* Naamloze Vennootschap Pty Ltd

Ny. *abbrev Nyonya* Madam, title for married woman, especially a non-Indonesian

nya *suf, poss* added to words to indicate possession; the; *itu*

ibu~ that's her mother; *saya mau beli baju, tapi toko~ sudah tutup* I want to buy a shirt, but the shop's closed

nyahur *v, sl* to eat before dawn during fasting month ← **sahur**

nyai *pron* mistress (in colonial times)

nyala flame, blaze, burn; **bernyala, menyala** *v* to burn, blaze; **menyalakan** *v* to light, set fire to

nyalé annual fishing ceremony in southern Lombok; sea-worm

nyali *n* guts, bravery; **bernyali** *adj* brave

nyaman *adj* comfortable, pleasant; **kenyamanan** *n* comfort

nyamuk *n* mosquito; *obat* ~ mosquito repellent

nyantri, nyantrik *v, coll* to be a religious student or disciple ← **santri**

nyanyi sing; **nyanyian** *n* song; **bernyanyi, menyanyi** *v* to sing; **menyanyikan** *v* to sing something; **penyanyi** *n* singer, vocalist; ~ *latar* backing vocalist

nyaring *adj* clear, loud, shrill

nyaris *adv, neg* nearly, almost

nyata *adj* clear, obvious, plain; **kenyataan** *n* fact; **menyatakan** *v* to declare, state, certify; **pernyataan** *n* statement, declaration

nyawa *n* soul, life; *tiga puluh* ~ thirty lives; **bernyawa** *adj* alive; **senyawa** *n* (chemical) compound

nyekar *v, coll* to strew flower

petals on a grave; to visit a grave → **sekar**

nyeletuk v, sl to interrupt, call out, say suddenly ← **celetuk**

nyéntrik adj, coll eccentric, unusual

nyenyak adj sound asleep

Nyepi n Balinese Day of Seclusion

nyeri n pain; ~ haid menstrual pain or cramp

nyerocos v, coll to talk too much, blather, chatter or rattle on ← **cerocos**

nyiru n winnow

nyiur n coconut palm

nyokap n, sl Mum, Ma

nyonték → **conték**

nyonya pron, f term of address for a married woman, Madam; Mrs; ~ rumah the lady (mistress) of the house; untuk ~ for Madam; ~ Iskandar Mrs Iskandar

nyut throbbing pain

O

o excl oh; ~ ya oh yes, by the way

oase n oasis

obah → **ubah**

obat n medicine; ~ batuk cough medicine; ~ merah mercurochrome; ~ nyamuk mosquito repellent; makan ~, minum ~ to take medicine; narkotik, psiko-tropika dan ~ terlarang (narkoba) (illegal) drugs; ber-**obat** v to go to the doctor, seek medical advice; **mengobati** v to treat, cure; **pengobatan** n treatment

obéng n screwdriver; ~ kembang Phillips-head screwdriver

objék → **obyék**

obligasi n bond

oblong kaos ~, kaus ~ T-shirt

obor n torch

obrak-abrik: mengobrak-abrik v to upset, turn upside-down

obral n sale; **mengobral** v to put on sale

obras n overlocking, machine hemming; **mengobras** v to overlock

obrol: mengobrol v **ngobrol** coll to chat; **obrolan** n chat

obyék n object; ~ wisata tourist destination, sight; **obyéktif** adj objective

obyék: ngobyék v, coll to have a job on the side, moonlight

océ: océhan n babble; **mengocéh** v **ngocéh** coll babble, talk nonsense

OD abbrev overdose

ODHA abbrev orang dengan HIV-AIDS person infected with the HIV virus or AIDS

oditur n military prosecutor

odol n, arch toothpaste

ogah adj, sl unwilling, reluctant; Pak ~ man who directs traffic for payment

ojék, ojég n motorcycle taxi; pangkalan ~ place where motorcycle taxis wait; tukang ~ motorcycle taxi driver; **meng-**

ojék *v* to take passengers around on your motorbike; **pengojék** *n* motorcycle taxi driver

oké *sl* okay, OK

oknum *n, neg* individual (causing trouble in a group or company)

oksigén *n* oxygen

Oktober *bulan* ~ October

olah manner, process; *~raga* sport; **olahan** *adj* processed; **mengolah** *v* to process, treat; **pengolahan** *v* processing; **seolah-olah** *adv, conj* as if

olahraga *v* sport; ~ *bela diri* self-defense; *gelanggang ~ (GOR)* stadium; *lapangan ~* sports ground, athletic field; **berolahraga** *v* to do or play sport; **olahragawan** *n, m* sportsman; **olahragawati** *n, f* sportswoman

oléh *conj* by, through; ~ *karena* because of, due to; **oléh-oléh** *n* souvenir; **memperoléh** *v* to obtain, get; **peroléhan** *n* acquisition; ~ *suara* (number of) votes

oléng *adj* on a lean, leaning to one side; *gajah* ~ a batik design

olés: olésan *n* smear; **mengolés** *v* to grease, spread, lubricate; **mengolési** *v* to grease something; **mengoléskan** *v* to smear with something

oli, olie *n* (engine) oil; *ganti* ~ drain sump oil

Olimpiade *n* the Olympics, the Olympic Games

olok: memperolok *v* to tease, taunt

Om, Oom *pron* Uncle; term of address to extended family, parents' friends, friends' parents etc

Oma *pron* Grandma

ombak *n* wave; **berombak** *adj* wavy; *rambut* ~ wavy hair

ombang-ambing: terombang-ambing *v* to bob (up and down), float; to fluctuate

omél: mengomél *v* to complain, grumble, whinge, whine ← **omél**

omong chat, talk, speak; ~ *Sunda* (speak) Sundanese; ~ *kosong* nonsense; **omongan** *n* chat; gossip; **ngomong** *v, coll* to speak, talk; **ngomong-ngomong** by the way

ompol: mengompol *v* to wet the bed, wet your pants

ompong *adj* toothless

ompréng: ompréngan *n* truck converted into a passenger vehicle, unofficial taxi

omsét *n* turnover

onak *n* thorn

onani *n* masturbation; *melakukan* ~ to masturbate; **beronani** *v* to masturbate

onar *n* stir, commotion; *membuat* ~ to make a scene; **keonaran** *n* commotion, disturbance, sensation

oncom *n* fermented soybean cake

ondé: ondé-ondé *n* small round cakes made of green peanuts, covered in sesame seeds

ondél: ondél-ondél *n* giant figures used in Betawi celebrations

onderdil *n* (automotive) spare part

onderok *n* petticoat, slip

ongkos *n* cost (for a service), expense, charge; ~ *hidup* cost of living, living expenses; ~ *pengiriman* cost of freight or postage

ONH *abbrev ongkos naik haji* cost of the package covering the major pilgrimage to Mecca

ons ounce

onta → **unta**

oom → **om**

Opa *pron* Grandpa

opak *n* crisp or chip made from rice or cassava

opas *n* nightwatchman, attendant

oper, mengoper *v* to transfer, hand over; ~ *bola* to pass the ball

operasi *n* operation; **beroperasi** *v* to operate, work, function

opini *n* opinion → **pendapat**

oplah *n* circulation; print run

oplét *n, arch* old-fashioned minibus used in the 1960s, similar to the *bemo*

oplos: oplosan *adj* adulterated, mixed; **mengoplos** *v* to mix in another liquid illegally; **pengoplosan** *n* illegally adding another liquid

OPM *abbrev Organisasi Papua Merdeka* Free Papua Organisation, secessionist movement

opname go into hospital, hospitalization; **diopname** *v* to be admitted to hospital, be hospitalized

opor ~ *ayam* chicken in coconut sauce, traditionally eaten at Idul Fitri

oposan *n* opponent; **oposisi** *n* opposition

opsét *adj* off-side

opsi *n* option (in a referendum)

Opsus *n* special military operation ← **Operasi Khusus**

optik optician; optical

orak: orak-arik *n* scrambled egg with beans

oralit *n* powder mixed with water for rehydration after diarrhea

orang *n* person, human; ~ *asing* foreigner, stranger; ~ *awam* layman, public; ~ *banyak* public, people; ~ *Barat* Westerner; ~ *baru* newcomer; ~ *besar* person in power or authority; ~ *Cina,* ~ *Tionghoa* (ethnic) Chinese; ~ *Eropa* European; ~ *gila* tramp; mentally-ill person, lunatic; ~ *Indonesia* Indonesian; ~ *Islam* Muslim; ~ *jahat* criminal; ~ *kulit putih* white person; ~ *Kristen,* ~ *Nasrani* Christian; ~ *minta-minta* beggar; ~ *tua* parents; *kata* ~ people say; **orang-orangan** *n* doll, dummy; **perorangan** *adj* personal, individual; **seorang** a (person); counter for people; ~ *Arab* an Arab; ~ *diri* alone, single-handedly; **perseorangan** *adj* individual; **seseorang** *n* a certain person, somebody

orang *conj, coll* because; expression of surprise or defensiveness; ~ *saya baru pulang jam 12 malam* I only got home at midnight (so how would I know?)

oranye *adj* orange → **jingga**

Orba *n* New Order, Suharto's rule ← **Orde Baru**

orde *n* order; ~ *Lama (Orla)* Old Order

ordo *n* order

org *abbrev* orang person

organisasi *n* organization; *aktif dalam ~* active in a movement or group

orgel, organ *n* organ

orisinal, orisinil *adj* original → **asli**

orkés *n* orchestra; ~ *Melayu* Malay orchestra, traditional music group

Orla *n* Old Order, Sukarno's rule ← **Orde Lama**

ormas *n* social or people's organization ← **organisasi masyarakat**

orok *n* (newborn) baby

ortu *n, sl* parents, oldies → **orang tua**

oséng: oséng-oséng *n* stir-fried vegetables

OSIS *abbrev Organisasi Siswa Intrasekolah* high school students' organization, Student Council

ospék *n* O-week, (school) orientation → **oriéntasi studi dan pengenalan kampus**

otak *n* brain; ~ *udang derog* idiot; *gegar ~* concussion

otak: otak-otak *n* steamed fish cakes, baked in banana leaves

otak: otak-atik → **utak-atik**

otda *n* regional autonomy ← **otonomi daérah**

otobiografi *n* autobiography

otomatis *adj* automatic; *secara ~* automatically

otomotif *adj* automotive

otonomi *n* autonomy; ~ *daérah (otda)* regional autonomy

otopét *n* scooter

otorita, otoritas *n* authority; *Otorita Batam* Batam Authority

otoritér *adj* authoritarian

otot *n* muscle; *nyeri ~* cramp; **berotot** *adj* muscular; **ngotot** *v, coll* to be stubborn, refuse to back down

oven *n* oven, kiln; *cat ~* vehicle paint applied through heat

overdosis, OD overdose

oya, o ya oh yes, by the way

ozon *n* ozone; *lapisan ~* the ozone layer

P

P. *abbrev Pulau* Island

pabéan *n* customs (house) ← **béa**

pabrik factory

pacar *n* boyfriend, girlfriend; **pacaran** *v, coll* **berpacaran** *v* to be going out, go out, date; **memacari** *v* to date, go out with someone

pacar *n* henna, used to decorate the nails

pacé *n* kind of root, used as a

spice → **mengkudu**

paceklik *n* famine; *masa* ~ hard times before the harvest

pacu *n* spur; **pacuan** ~ *kuda* racecourse; **memacu** *v* to spur on

pacul *n* hoe

pada *prep* in, at, on (expressing time); to; ~ *hari itu* on that day

pada *coll, pl* pluralizing word; *sudah* ~ *pulang* everybody's going home

pada: memadai *v* enough, sufficient

padahal *conj* whereas, however

padam put out, extinguish; **memadamkan** *v* to put out, extinguish; **pemadam** *pasukan* ~ *kebakaran* fire brigade

padan: padanan *n* synonym; something that matches or fits; **sepadan** *adj* in keeping or proportion with

padang *n* field, plain; ~ *pasir* desert, sand dune

padat *adj* dense, full, crammed

padépokan *n* dormitory

padi *n* (unhusked) rice; *lumbung* ~ rice-producing area

padma *n* lotus

padu fused; *bersatu* ~ united; **memadukan** *v* to combine, unite; **perpaduan** *n* blend, synthesis; **terpadu** *adj* integrated; **keterpaduan** *n* integration

paduka *pron* title for rulers; ~ *Yang Mulia* His Excellency

pagar *n* fence; hedge; ~ *hidup* hedge; ~ *kawat berduri* barb-wire fence; **memagari** *v* to fence (off); **pemagaran** *n* fencing (off)

pagi *n* morning; ~ *buta* in the early hours of the morning; *kain* ~ *sore* reversible sarong worn during the war; *makan* ~ breakfast; *selamat* ~ good morning; *senam* ~ morning exercise; **pagi-pagi** *adv* (very) early; **kepagian** *adj* too early; **sepagi** ~ *mungkin* as early as possible

paguyuban *n* group, association

paha *n* thigh; ~ *ayam* chicken leg; *lipat* ~ groin; *pangkal* ~ hip

pahala *n* reward, merit; **ber-pahala** *adj* meritorious

paham, faham *v* to understand, know; **memahami** *v* to understand, comprehend; **sepaham** *adj* of the same opinion or belief

pahat chisel; *seni* ~ sculpture; **memahat** *v* to sculpt, chisel; **pemahat** *n* sculptor

pahit *adj* bitter; *kopi* ~ black coffee without sugar; **kepahitan** *n* bitterness

pahlawan *n* hero; *Taman Makam* ~ heroes' cemetery; **kepahlawanan** *n* heroism

pai *n* pie

pailit *adj* bankrupt; **kepailitan** *n* bankruptcy

pajak tax; ~ *Bumi Bangunan (PBB)* land tax, household rates; ~ *pendapatan*, ~ *penghasilan* income tax pajang: **pajangan** *n* display; **memajang** *v* to display

pak: **mengepak** *v* to pack

Pak, Bapak *pron* Father; term of address to older, respected men; ~ *Pos* the postman

pakai, paké wear; use; *bekas* ~ used; *siap* ~ ready to use (or wear); **pakaian** *n* clothes, dress; ~ *dalam* underwear; **berpakaian** *adj* dressed in; **memakai** *v* to wear; to use; ~ *kacamata* to wear glasses; **pemakai** *n* user; **pemakaian** *n* use, usage; **terpakai** *adj* used, in use

pakan *n* feed; ~ *ikan* fish food

pakansi → **vakansi**

pakar *n* expert, authority

pakat: **sepakat** *v* to agree; **kesepakatan** *n* agreement; **menyepakati** *v* to agree to

paké → **pakai**

pakem *n* mold, norm

pakét *n* packet, package, promotion; ~ *hemat (pahe)* cheap package

pakis *n* fern

Pakistan *n* Pakistan; *orang* ~ Pakistani

paksa force; *kerja* ~ forced labor; **memaksa** *v* to force; **pemaksaan** *n* force, pressure; **terpaksa** *adj* forced; *karena* ~ had or was forced to do it; **keterpaksaan** *n* compulsion

pakta *n* pact

paku *n* nail; **memaku** *v* to nail

paku *n* fern

pal *n, arch* milestone, post

pala *buah* ~ nutmeg; *bunga* ~ mace

palak: **memalak** *v* to force (usu to pay money); **pemalak** *n* extortionist, someone who demands payment

palang *n* barrier, bar, cross; ~ *Merah* Red Cross

palawija *n* secondary crop, planted in dry season

palem *n* palm

Palestina *n* Palestine; *orang* ~ Palestinian; *Organisasi Pembebasan* ~ Palestinian Liberation Front (PLO)

Pali *bahasa* ~ ancient language of Buddhist scriptures

paling *adv* most; at the most; ~ *baik* the best; ~ *jelek* the worst

paling: **berpaling** *v* to turn away or from

palsu *adj* false, forged; *identitas* ~ fake ID; *rambut* ~ wig; *sumpah* ~ perjury; *uang* ~ counterfeit money; **memalsukan** *v* to falsify, forge; **pemalsuan** *n* forgery

palu *n* hammer, gavel (in court); ~ *arit* hammer and sickle; **memalu** *v* to hammer, strike

palung *n* trough, riverbed; ~ *hati* the bottom of your heart

PAM *abbrev Perusahaan Air Minum* company providing reticulated water, water board

pamali *n* taboo

paman *n* uncle, male relative of parents' generation; ~ *Sam* Uncle Sam (America)

paméo *n* saying, proverb

pamér show off; **paméran** *n* exhibition; **memamérkan** *v* to display, exhibit

pamit, pamitan, berpamit *v* to take leave

pamong ~ *praja* civil service

pamor *n* prestige, lustre, glow

pamrih *n* reward; *tanpa* ~ altruistic, without expecting anything in return

pamungkas *adj* final, last

PAN *abbrev Partai Amanat Nasional* People's Mandate Party

pana: terpana *adj* struck, stunned

panah *n* bow; *anak* ~ arrow; **panahan** *n* archery; **memanah** *v* to shoot (with a bow); **pemanah** *n* archer

Panama *n* Panama; *orang* ~ Panamanian

panas *adj* hot, warm; ~ *badan* body temperature; *coll* high temperature; ~ *dingin* hot and cold; ~ *hati* angry; ~ *terik* hot and dry, dry heat; **kepanasan** *n* heat; *adj* too hot; **memanas** *v* to get hot, heat up; **memanaskan** *v* to heat (up); **terpanas** *adj* the hottest

panca *adj* five; **pancaindera** *n* the five senses; **pancalomba** *n* pentathlon; **Pancasila** *n* Indonesian state philosophy of five principles

pancang *n* pole, stake; **memancang** *v* to stake or drive in; **pemancangan** *n* planting, insertion

pancar: pancaran *n* emission; **berpancar** *v* to shine out; **memancarkan** *v* to broadcast; **pemancar** *n* transmitter

pancaroba *n* change of season; *musim* ~ transition between seasons

Pancasila *n* Indonesian state philosophy of five principles

panci *n* saucepan, pan

pancing *n* fishing rod or hook; **memancing** *v* to fish (with hook and line); **terpancing** *adj* hooked, caught up; involved

pancung: memancung *v* to cut off, mutilate; ~ *kepala* to behead or decapitate

pancur: pancuran, pancoran *n* fountain; shower; **memancur** *v* to pour, gush, flow out; **mancur** *air* ~ fountain

pandai *adj* clever; ~ *besi* smith; ~ *emas* goldsmith; **kepandaian** *n* ability, intelligence

pandan *daun* ~ pandanus leaf, used for green coloring in food

pandang see, gaze; *tak* ~ *bulu* not discriminate; **pandangan** *n* view, sight; **berpandangan** *v* to look at each other; **memandang** *v* to view, consider; ~ *rendah* to underestimate, disregard; **pemandangan** *n* view

pandu guide, scout, pilot; **kepanduan** *n* scouting, Scouts; *n, f* guiding, Guides; **memandu** *v* to guide

panekuk *n* pancake

panén *n* harvest, windfall

Pangab *n* Commander-in-Chief

of the Armed Forces ← **Panglima Angkatan Bersenjata**

pangan *n* food; *sandang ~* food and clothing

Pangdam *n* Regional Commander ← **Panglima Daérah Militér**

pangéran *n* prince

panggang *adj* roast baked, barbecued; *v* roast, bake, toast, barbecue; *ayam ~* barbecued chicken; *roti ~* toast; **memanggang** *v* to roast, bake, toast, barbecue; **pemanggang** *~ roti* toaster; **pemanggangan** *n* spit, barbecue

panggil call; **panggilan** *n* call, summons; *wanita ~* callgirl; **memanggil** *v* to call

panggul *n* hip; **memanggul** *v* to carry on your hip

panggung *n* stage; *demam ~* stage fright; **manggung** *v, coll* to perform

pangkal *n* base; **pangkalan** *n* terminal, base; *~ udara (lanud)* air base; **berpangkal** *adj* based; **mangkal** *v, coll* to use as a base, wait for work

pangkas cut; *~ rambut* barber; **memangkas** *v* to cut, shear, trim

pangkat *n* rank, class; to the power of; *~ dua* squared; *~ tiga* cubed; *naik ~* be promoted, get a promotion; **berpangkat** *v* to have the rank of

pangku lap; **pangkuan** *n* lap; **memangku** *v* to take on (your lap); *~ jabatan* to occupy a post; **pemangku** *n* functionary

panglima *n* commander; *~ besar* general for life; *~ tertinggi* commander-in-chief

pangling not recognize, unrecognizable

pangsa *n* segment; *~ jeruk* segment of orange; *~ pasar* market share

pangsit *n* wonton, dumpling

panik panic

panili → **vanili**

panitera *n* clerk, secretary; *~ pengadilan* registrar, clerk (of the court)

panitia *n* committee, board

panjang *adj* long; *~nya* length; *bulat ~* cylindrical; *~ ingatan* a long or good memory; *~ lebar* detailed; extensive *(empat) persegi ~* rectangle; *~ tangan* light-fingered, a thief; *~ umur* long life; *rumah ~* longhouse; **kepanjangan** *adj* too long; **berkepanjangan** *adj* continuous, protracted; **memanjang** *v* to become long, lengthen; **memperpanjang** *v* to extend, make longer; **sepanjang** *conj, adj* as long as; *~ hari* all day long; *~ jalan* the whole way; **terpanjang** *adj* the longest

panjat climb; *~ pinang* climbing a greased areca-nut palm, an Independence Day competition; *~ tebing* abseiling; **memanjat** *v* to climb; **memanjatkan** *v* to send up; *~ doa* to offer prayers

panser *n* tank, armored car

pansus *n* special committee (in Parliament) ← **panitia khusus**

pantai *n* beach, coast; ~ *batu* pebble beach; ~ *Gading* Ivory Coast; *(bola) voli* ~ beach volleyball

pantang forbidden, prohibited; ~ *menyerah* never give up, never say die; ~ *mundur* never look back; **berpantang** *v* to not be allowed, abstain from; *makan* ~ to be on a diet

pantas, pantes *adj* proper, decent, right; **pantesan** *sl* no wonder; **sepantasnya** *adv* proper, rightly

pantat *n* bottom, backside

pantau: pantauan *n* observation; **memantau** *v* to observe, watch; **pemantau** *n* observer, monitor; **pemantauan** *n* monitoring

Pantékosta *n* Pentecost, Whitsun; *Gereja* ~ Pentecostal Church

pantes *sl* no wonder ← **pantas**

panti *n* building; ~ *asuhan* orphanage; ~ *jompo* old people's home

panting: pontang-panting helter skelter

pantul: pantulan *n* reflection; **berpantulan** *v* to reflect (of many things); **memantul** *v* to rebound; **memantulkan** *v* to reflect something; **terpantul** *adj* reflected

pantun *n* traditional poem (of four lines); **berpantun** *v* to recite or write a traditional poem

panu *n* white spots caused by skin fungus; **panuan** *v, coll* to suffer from white spots

panut: panutan *n* leader, good example ← **anut**

papa *adj* destitute, poor; *kaum* ~ the destitute, the poor; **ke-papaan** *n* destitution, poverty

papah: memapah *v* to support, prop up

papan *n* plank, board, bench; ~ *catur* chessboard; ~ *tulis* blackboard, whiteboard; ~ *tuts* keyboard

papar: memaparkan *v* to explain; **pemaparan** *n* explanation

papaya → **pepaya**

Papi, Pi *pron* Papa, Daddy (in Westernized circles)

paprika *n* red or green pepper, paprika

Papua Nugini *n* Papua New Guinea, PNG; *orang* ~ Papuan

para pluralizes the following word; ~ *pembaca* readers; ~ *pemirsa* viewers; ~ *pendengar* listeners

parabola *n* satellite dish; parabola; *TV* ~ satellite TV

paraf *n* initials; **memaraf** *v* to initial, sign

paragraf *n* paragraph → **alinéa**

parah *adj* grave, serious, bad; *luka* ~ badly wounded; *sakit* ~ gravely ill; **memperparah** *v* to make worse, aggravate

parang *n* chopper, machete

paras *n* face, countenance; **berparas** *v* to have a face or appearance

parasit *n* parasite

parasut *n* parachute → **payung**

parau *adj* hoarse

paré, paria, peria *n* kind of bitter gourd or squash

parfum *n* perfume → **wangi**

pari *bintang* ~ Southern Cross; *ikan* ~ ray

paria → **paré**

paripurna *adj* complete; *sidang* ~ plenary session

parit *n* (roadside) ditch

pariwara *n* advertisement

pariwisata *n* tourism; *bis* ~ tourist bus; **kepariwisataan** *n* tourist industry

parkir park (a vehicle); *tempat* ~ car park, parking lot; *tukang* ~ parking attendant; **parkiran** *n, sl* car park; **memarkir** *v* to park

parkit *burung* ~ parakeet

parlemén *n* parliament

paro → **paruh**

parodi *n* parody

paroki *n, Cath* parish

parpol *n* (political) party ← **partai politik**

Parsi, Farsi *bahasa* ~ Farsi; *orang* ~ Persian, Iranian

partai *n* party; ~ *Amanat Nasional (PAN)* National Mandate Party; ~ *Demokrasi Indonesia – Perjuangan (PDIP)* Indonesian Democratic Party of Struggle; ~ *Demokrat* Democratic Party, Democrats; ~ *Kebangkitan Bangsa (PKB)* Party of National Awakening; ~ *Persatuan Pembangunan (PPP)* United Development Party; ~ *politik (parpol)* political party; *politik* ~ party politics

paru, paru-paru *n* lung; *radang* ~ pneumonia

paruh, paro *n* half, part; *kerja* ~ *waktu* work part-time; **separuh** *n* half; **separuh-separuh** *adj* half and half

paruh *n* bill, beak

parut grater; **memarut** *v* to grate

pas exact, just (as); fit; *kamar* ~ fitting room; ~ *dia buka pintu* just as he opened the door

pasak *n* peg, wooden nail; **memasak** *v* to peg

pasal *n, leg* paragraph, section; *conj* regarding, concerning

pasang *n* pair, couple; **pasangan** *n* pair; **berpasangan** *adv* in pairs; **sepasang** *n* a pair of

pasang, memasang *v* to put up, attach, fix; ~ *bendera* to hoist a flag; ~ *iklan* to advertise; ~ *lampu* to switch on a light, light a lamp; **pemasangan** *n* installation

pasang *air* ~ rising tide; ~ *surut* rise and fall, ebb and flow

pasar *n* market, bazaar; ~ *dunia* global market; ~ *gelap* black market; ~ *raya, pasaraya* supermarket; ~ *tenaga kerja* job market; **pasaran** *n* market (in abstract sense); **memasarkan** *v* to market; **pemasaran** *n* marketing

pasca [pasca, paska] *pref* after, post-; ~ *krismon* after the financial crisis; ~ *perang* postwar; **pascasarjana** *adj* postgraduate

pasfoto *n* passport (-sized) photo

pasién *n* patient

pasif *adj* passive; ~ *bahasa Inggris* passive English, can understand English

Pasifik *Kawasan Asia* ~ (Asia-) Pacific region; *Lautan* ~, *Lautan Teduh* the Pacific (Ocean)

pasir *n* sand; *kertas* ~ sandpaper; *gula* ~ (white) sugar

Paskah *n* Easter; *Hari* ~ Easter Sunday

Paskibraka, Pasibraka *n* select group of high-school students who unfurl and raise the flag on Independence Day ← **Pasukan Pengibar Bendéra Pusaka**

pasok: pasokan *n* supply; **memasok** *v* to supply; **pemasok** *n* supplier

Paspamprés *n* Presidential guards ← **pasukan pengamanan Présidén**

paspor *n* passport

pasrah *adj* accepting, fatalistic; **kepasrahan** *n* submission

pasta *n* paste; pasta, spaghetti; ~ *gigi* toothpaste

pastél *n* samosa, small pasty containing vegetables, egg and vermicelli noodles

pasti sure, certain, definite; *ilmu* ~ the physical sciences, mathematics; **kepastian** *n* certainty; **memastikan** to confirm, make sure, ascertain

pastor *n, Cath* priest

pasuk: pasukan *n* troops; ~ *berkuda* cavalry; ~ *khusus* elite troops, special troops

patah break, fracture (of bones); ~ *hati* broken-hearted; ~ *sema-*

ngat lose heart; ~ *tulang* break or fracture a bone; *se*~ *kata* a single word; **mematahkan** *v* to break

patas *bis* ~ bus with a passenger limit ← **penumpang terbatas**

pati *n* starch, essence

patina *n* sheen, patina (of polished metal)

patok: patokan *n* standard, peg; **mematok** *v* to fix, set; ~ *harga* to set a price

patri solder; *kaca* ~ stained glass

patroli *n* patrol

patron *n* (dressmaker's) pattern

patuh *adj* loyal, obedient; **mematuhi** *v* to obey

patuk: mematuk *v* to peck, bite

patung *n* statue, figurine; **mematung** *v* to freeze, not move, be as still as a statue; **pematung** *n* sculptor

patung: patungan *v* to pay together; to work together; *perusahaan* ~ joint venture

patut *adj* decent, proper, deserving; **sepatutnya** *adv* rightly, properly

pauk *lauk* ~ side dishes served with rice

paus *ikan* ~ whale

Paus *Sri* ~ the Pope; ~ *Benedictus XVI* Pope Benedict XVI; ~ *Johannes Paulus II* Pope John Paul II

pause, pauze *n* break, half-time (in sport); *adem* ~ break, breather

paut *sangkut* ~ to be connected with; **terpaut** *adj* fastened, bound; separated

paviliun *n* smaller house attached to a larger one, guest quarters in colonial times

pawai *n* procession, parade

pawang *n* tamer, animal trainer; *~ gajah* elephant trainer

payah *adj* difficult, serious; tired

payét *n* sequin

payudara *n, f* breast; *kanker ~* breast cancer

payung *n* umbrella; parachute; *terjun ~* parachuting; *menyediakan ~ sebelum hujan* to prepare for the worst; **memayungi** *v* to hold an umbrella over someone

PBB *abbrev Persatuan Bangsa-Bangsa* United Nations, UN

PBB *abbrev Pajak Bumi dan Bangunan* Land and Building Tax

PD *abbrev Partai Demokrat* Democrat Party

PD I *abbrev Perang Dunia Pertama* First World War

PD II *abbrev Perang Dunia Kedua* Second World War

PDAM *abbrev Perusahaan Daerah Air Minum* regional water board

PDI *abbrev Partai Demokrasi Indonesia* Indonesian Democratic Party

PDIP *abbrev Partai Demokrasi Indonesia Perjuangan* Indonesian Democratic Party of Struggle

Pdt. *abbrev Pendeta* (Protestant) minister, clergyman

pebisnis *n* businessman, businesswoman ← **bisnis**

Pébruari → **Fébruari**

pecah break, smash; curdled (of milk); *(barang) ~ belah* earthenware; *~nya perang* outbreak of war; **pecahan** *n* piece, fragment; fraction; **memecah ~ belah** to break into fragments, cause divisions; **memecahkan** *v* to break; to solve; *~ soal* to solve a problem; **pemecahan** *n* solution

pecandu *n* addict ← **candu**

pecat fired, sacked, dismissed; **memecat** *v* to fire, dismiss; **pemecatan** *n* sacking, dismissal

pecatur *n* chess player ← **catur**

pecel *~ lele* catfish with rice and side-dishes; *nasi ~* rice and salad with peanut sauce

péci *n* black, flat-topped cap worn by men, also with national dress

Pecinan *n* Chinatown ← **Cina**

pecinta *n* lover ← **cinta**

pecundang lose, be beaten; **memecundangi** *v* to swindle or trick; to beat or defeat

pedagang *n* merchant ← **dagang**

pedanda *n* Balinese priest

pedang *n* sword; **pedang-pedangan** *n* toy sword

pedas *adj* spicy, hot; **kepedasan** *adj* too hot or spicy

pedati *n* cart drawn by horse or ox

pédé, PD *sl* self-confidence; *kurang ~* lack self-confidence ← **percaya diri**

pedes → **pedas**

pedésaan *n* country(side), rural areas; *angkutan* ~ country minibus ← **désa**

pedih, perih smart, sting; *sampo anti* ~ shampoo that won't sting your eyes; **kepedihan** *n* stinging

pédikur *n* pedicure

pedoman *n* compass; guide; manual; **berpedoman** *v* to be guided by, based on

peduli *v* **perduli** *coll* to care, bother; *tidak* ~ not care; **kepedulian** *n* concern; **memedulikan** *v* to care or be bothered about

pedupaan *n* stand for burning incense ← **dupa**

Peg. *abbrev* Pegunungan (mountain) range

pegadaian *n* pawnshop ← **gadai**

pegal *adj* sore, cramped, stiff; ~ *linu* aches and pains

pégang, pegang hold, grip, grasp; **pegangan** *n* handle, grip; belief, principle; **berpegang** *v* to hold onto; ~ *teguh* to hold fast to; **memegang** *v* to hold, grasp; **pemegang** *n* keeper, holder

pegas *n* spring; *kasur* ~ spring bed

pegawai *n* official, employee; ~ *negeri* public or civil servant; **kepegawaian** *adj* staff, personnel

pegel → **pegal**

pegolf *n* golfer ← **golf**

pegulat *n* wrestler ← **gulat**

pegunungan *n* mountain range; ~ *Jayawijaya* the Jayawijaya range ← **gunung**

péhaka, PHK to lose your job, be unemployed; **dipéhakakan** *v* to lose your job, be fired ← **putus hubungan kerja**

pejabat *n* (government) official ← **jabat**

pejagalan *n* abattoir ← **jagal**

pejam: memejamkan ~ *mata* to close your eyes; **terpejam** *adj* closed

pék *sl, Ch* hundred; *go* ~ five hundred, Rp. 500 coin

pekak *adj* deaf; **memekakkan** *adj* deafening, loud

pekan *n* week; market; ~ *Olahraga Nasional (PON)* National Sports Week, national championships; *akhir* ~ weekend; **sepekan** *n* a week

pekarangan *n* yard; ~ *sekolah* schoolyard ← **karang**

pekat *adj* thick, strong, concentrated; *hitam* ~ pitch black; **kepekatan** *n* thickness, viscosity

pekerja *n* worker, laborer; **pekerjaan** *n* work, profession; ~ *rumah* (PR) homework; *lapangan* ~ employment opportunity ← **kerja**

pekerti *n* character, nature; *budi* ~ good conduct

pekik scream, yell; **pekikan** *n* scream, yell; **memekik** *v* to scream or shriek

pél *kain* ~ rag for mopping the floor; *obat* ~ floor disinfectant; **mengepél** *v* to mop (up); **dipél** *v* to be mopped, cleaned

pelabuhan port, harbor ← **labuh**

pelacak *anjing* ~ sniffer dog ← **lacak**

pelacur *n* prostitute; **pelacuran** *n* prostitution; *tempat* ~ red-light district ← **lacur**

pelajar *n* pupil, (school) student; schoolboy, schoolgirl; **pelajaran** *n* lesson; *mata* ~ (school) subject ← **ajar**

pelaju *n* commuter ← **laju**

pelaksana *n* manager, producer, administrator; ~ *harian* acting manager; **pelaksanaan** *n* realization, execution ← **laksana**

pelaminan *n* bridal sofa where the couple greet guests; *naik ke* ~ get married ← **lamin**

pelampiasan *n* act of releasing, indulgence ← **lampias**

pelampung *n* floater, flotation device; *baju* ~ lifejacket ← **lampung**

pelan, perlahan: pelan-pelan, perlahan-lahan *adv* slowly, softly; **memelankan** *v* to slow something down

pelana *n* saddle

pelancong *n* tourist ← **lancong**

pelanggan *n* subscriber, customer ← **langgan**

pelanggaran *n* violation ← **langgar**

pelangi *n* rainbow; *warna* ~ all the colours of the rainbow

pelan-pelan *adv* slowly, softly ← **pelan**

pelantikan *n* inauguration ← **lantik**

pelanting: memelantingkan *v* to throw everywhere; **terpelanting** *v* to fall heavily

pelari *n* runner; **pelarian** *n* escape, solace; abduction, kidnapping ← **lari**

pelarut *n* solute ← **larut**

pelat *n* plate; ~ *kuning* yellow number plate (for public transport & taxis); ~ *merah* government number plate; ~ *polisi* (vehicle) number plate, license plate

pelatih *n* coach, trainer; **pelatihan** *n* training; *mengadakan* ~ to run a course ← **latih**

Pelatnas *n* National Training squad ← **pelatihan nasional**

pelatuk *n* trigger (of a gun); woodpecker

pelaut *n* sailor, seaman ← **laut**

pelawak *n* comedian, comic, clown ← **lawak**

pelayan *n* waiter *m*, waitress *f*, attendant; **pelayanan** *n* service; ~ *masyarakat* public services ← **layan**

pelayaran *n* voyage; *perusahaan* ~ shipping company ← **layar**

pelayat *n* person who visits a house in mourning, pays his respects ← **layat**

pelbagai, berbagai *adj* all kinds or sorts of, various ← **bagai**

pelébaran *n* widening; ~ *jalan* widening the road, roadworks ← **lébar**

peleburan *n* melting; merger ← **lebur**

pelécéhan *n* contempt; ~ *seksual* sexual harassment ← **lécéh**

peledak *bahan* ~ explosive; **peledakan** *n* bombing ← **ledak**

pélek *n* rim of wheel ← **vélg**

pelekat *bahan* ~ adhesive ← **lekat**

pelembab, pelembap *n* moisturizer ← **lembab**

pelembut *n* softener ← **lembut**

pelémparan *n* (act of) throwing ← **lémpar**

pelengkap *n* accessory; **perlengkapan** *n* outfit, equipment ← **lengkap**

pelepasan *n* departure, farewell; *acara* ~ goodbye (party) ← **lepas**

pelesét: kepelését *adj, coll* **terpelését** *adj* slipped, skidded; tripped; **memelésétkan** *v* to up-end; to send off-course; **pelésétan, plésétan** *n* parody ← **lését**

pelesir: pelesiran *adj, arch* recreation, pleasure, amusement; *tempat* ~ place for recreation

pelestarian *n* protection, preservation ← **lestari**

pelihara take care of; **peliharaan** *hewan* ~ pet; **memelihara** *v* to take care of, look after; to cultivate; **pemeliharaan** *n* care, maintenance, cultivation; **terpelihara** *adj* well cared-for, well-maintained → **piara**

pelik *adj* complicated

pélikan *burung* ~ pelican

pelindung *n* protective device ← **lindung**

pelintat: pelintat-pelintut → **plintat-plintut**

pelintir: memelintir(kan) *v* to twist; **terpelintir** *adj* twisted

pelipis *n* temple (on head)

pelipur ~ *hati* consolation ← **lipur**

pelir *n* penis; *buah* ~ testicles

pelita *n, lit* (oil) lamp; light

Pelita *n* Five-Year Development; **Repelita** *n* Five-Year Plan ← **Pembangunan Lima Tahun**

pelitur polish; **memelitur** *v* to polish, varnish

Pélni *n* National Shipping Line, state passenger shipping service ← **Pelayaran Nasional Indonésia**

pelonco → **plonco**

pelor → **peluru**

pelosok *n* remote place

pelotot: melotot, memelotot *v* to stare, have bulging eyes; **memelototi** *v* to stare at someone; **memelototkan** ~ *mata* to stare ← **lotot**

peluang *n* opportunity; ~ *kerja* job opportunity; **berpeluang** *v* to have an opportunity, a chance ← **luang**

pelud *n, arch* airport ← **pelabuhan udara**

peluh *n* sweat, perspiration; **berpeluh** *v* to sweat, perspire

peluit, pluit *n* whistle

peluk hug; ~ *cium* hugs and kisses; **pelukan** n embrace; **memeluk** v to hug or embrace; ~ *agama* to follow a religion; **pemeluk** n follower, adherent

pelukis n painter, artist ← **lukis**

pelumas n lubricant ← **lumas**

peluncuran n launch ← **luncur**

peluntur n laxative ← **luntur**

pelupa n forgetful person ← **lupa**

peluru n bullet; ~ *kosong* blank (cartridge)

pelurusan n straightening ← **lurus**

pemaaf adj forgiving ← **maaf**

pemadam pasukan ~ kebakaran fire brigade ← **padam**

pemadat n (opium) addict ← **madat**

pemagaran n fencing (off) ← **pagar**

pemahat n sculptor ← **pahat**

pemain n player, actor; ~ *film* actor; ~ *bola basket* basket-baller ← **main**

pemakai n user; **pemakaian** n use, usage ← **pakai**

pemakaman n funeral, burial ← **makam**

pemaksaan n force, pressure ← **paksa**

pemalak n extortionist, someone who demands payment ← **palak**

pemalas n lazy person, lazy-bones ← **malas**

pemalsuan n forgery ← **palsu**

pemalu shy (person) ← **malu**

pemanah n archer ← **panah**

pemancangan n planting, insertion ← **pancang**

pemancar n transmitter ← **pancar**

pemandangan n view ← **pandang**

pemanggang ~ *roti* toaster; **pemanggangan** n spit ← **panggang**

pemangku n functionary ← **pangku**

pemanis n sweetener; ~ *buatan* artificial sweetener ← **manis**

pemantau n observer, monitor; **pemantauan** n monitoring ← **pantau**

pemaparan n explanation ← **papar**

pemarah adj bad-tempered ← **marah**

pemasangan n installation ← **pasang**

pemasaran n marketing ← **pasar**

pemasok n supplier ← **pasok**

pemasyarakatan lembaga ~ correctional centre, prison ← **masyarakat**

pematang n small dike (in a rice field)

pematung n sculptor ← **patung**

pembabatan n felling, chopping; ~ *hutan* (unregulated) deforestation ← **babat**

pembaca n reader; **pembacaan** n (act of) reading aloud ← **baca**

pembagian n distribution, division ← **bagi**

pembahasan n discussion, debate ← **bahas**

pembajakan n hijacking; piracy ← **bajak**

pembakaran *n* burning, combustion ← **bakar**

pembalakan *n* logging; ~ *liar* illegal logging ← **balak**

pembalut *n* sanitary pad ← **balut**

pembangkang *n* someone who defies; **pembangkangan** *n* act of defiance ← **bangkang**

pembangkit *n* ~ *listrik* power station; ~ *listrik tenaga air* hydroelectric power station ← **bangkit**

pembangunan *n* development ← **bangun**

pembantaian *n* slaughter, mass killings ← **bantai**

pembantu *n* servant, maid; assistant; *kantor* ~ (larger) branch office ← **bantu**

pembaruan *n* renewal ← **baru**

pembasmi ~ *rayap* termite exterminator; **pembasmian** *n* extermination, destruction, eradication ← **basmi**

pembatalan *n* cancellation, annulment ← **batal**

pembatas *n* divider; ~ *buku* bookmark; **pembatasan** *n* restriction ← **batas**

pembauran *n* integration, mixing of different ethnic groups ← **baur**

pembawa *n* bearer, carrier; ~ *acara* host, MC; **pembawaan** *n* temperament, nature ← **bawa**

pembayaran *n* payment; *tanda* ~ *yang sah* legal currency ← **bayar**

pembébasan *n* liberation, release, exemption ← **bébas**

pembédaan *n* discrimination, differential treatment ← **béda**

pembedahan *n* operation ← **bedah**

pembekalan *n* supply ← **bekal**

pembekuan *n* freezing; ~ *aset* freezing of assets ← **beku**

pembekukan *n* arrest ← **bekuk**

pembéla *n* defender; ~ *Tanah Air (Peta)* defender of the homeland; **pembélaan** *n* defense ← **béla**

pembelajaran *n* learning process ← **ajar, belajar**

pembelanjaan *n* expenditure, financing ← **belanja**

pembeli *n* buyer, purchaser; **pembelian** *n* purchase; purchasing ← **beli**

pembelian *n* purchase ← **beli**

pembengkakan *n* swelling, expanding ← **bengkak**

pembenihan ~ *buatan* artificial insemination ← **benih**

pembentukan *n* formation, act of forming ← **bentuk**

pemberangkatan *n* departure, sending off ← **berangkat**

pemberani *n* brave or courageous person, hero ← **berani**

pemberantasan *n* destruction, fight against ← **berantas**

pemberdayaan *n* empowerment; *Kementerian* ~ *Perempuan* Ministry for the Empowerment of Women ← **daya**

pemberi *n* giver, donor; **pemberian** *n* present, gift, something given to someone ← **beri** pemberitahuan *n* announcement, notice ← **beri tahu**

pemberkatan *n* consecration, blessing ← **berkat**

pemberontak *n* rebel; **pemberontakan** *n* rebellion, revolt, mutiny ← **berontak**

pembersih *n* cleaning agent; **pembersihan** *n* cleaning, purification; purge ← **bersih**

pembesar *n* big-shot, official; **pembesaran** *n* enlargement, expansion ← **besar**

pembetulan *n* correction, repair ← **betul**

pembiakan *n* breeding, cultivation ← **biak**

pembiayaan *n* financing ← **biaya**

pembibitan *n* sowing, planting of seeds, cultivation ← **bibit**

pembicara *n* speaker; **pembicaraan** *n* discussion ← **bicara**

pembimbing *n* guide, coach, leader ← **bimbing**

pembina *n* founder, patron; coach; **pembinaan** *n* development ← **bina**

pembisik *n* whisperer ← **bisik**

pembiusan *n* anesthesia ← **bius**

pembobolan *n* breaking into, breach ← **bobol**

pembocoran *n* leakage, divulging (of secrets) ← **bocor**

pembodohan *n* tricking, duping; ~ *rakyat* fooling the people ← **bodoh**

pembohong *n* liar; **pembohongan** *n* deception, lying ← **bohong**

pemboikotan *n* boycotting ← **boikot**

pembolos *n* truant, absentee; **pembolosan** *n* absenteeism, truancy ← **bolos**

pembongkaran *n* dismantling; exposure; ~ *usaha judi sudah lama dilakukan* there have long been efforts to expose gambling joints ← **bongkar**

pemborong *n* developer, contractor ← **borong**

pemboros *n* spendthrift; **pemborosan** *n* wastage ← **boros**

pembrédelan *n* muzzling, being closed down ← **brédel**

pembuat *n* producer, maker; **pembuatan** *n* production, manufacture ← **buat**

pembubaran *n* dissolution, breaking up ← **bubar**

pembudidayaan *n* cultivation ← **budidaya**

pembuka *adj* opening; *kata ~* preface; **pembukaan** *n* opening ← **buka**

pembukingan *n* bookings ← **buking**

pembukuan *n* book-keeping ← **buku**

pembulatan *n* rounding-off ← **bulat**

pembuluh ~ *darah* blood vessel, artery ← **buluh**

pembungkus *n* wrapping, packing; **pembungkusan** *n* packaging ← **bungkus**

pembunuh *n* murderer, killer; ~ *bayaran* hitman, hired killer; **pembunuhan** *n* murder, killing ← **bunuh**

pemburu *n* hunter; **pemburuan** *n* hunt, chase ← **buru**

pembusukan *n* (process of) decay ← **busuk**

Pémda *n* Regional Government → **Pemerintah Daérah**

pemecahan *n* solution ← **pecah**

pemecatan *n* sacking, dismissal ← **pecat**

pemegang *n* keeper, holder ← **pegang**

pemekaran *n* expansion, development ← **mekar**

pemeliharaan *n* care, maintenance, cultivation ← **pelihara**

pemeluk *n* follower, adherent ← **peluk**

pemenang *n* winner, victor ← **menang**

pementasan *n* staging, production ← **pentas**

pemérah ~ *pipi* rouge ← **mérah**

pemeran *n* actor, actress ← **peran**

pemerasan *n* blackmail, extortion ← **peras**

pemerhati *n* observer ← **hati**

pemeriksa *n* examiner; **pemeriksaan** *n* examination, investigation ← **periksa**

pemerintah *n* government; **pemerintahan** *n* administration, government ← **perintah**

pemerkosa *n* rapist; **pemerkosaan** *n* act of raping, rape ← **perkosa, kosa**

pemersatu *n* unifying agent, unifier ← **satu**

pemesanan *n* order, request ← **pesan**

pemetaan *n* mapping ← **peta**

pemetik *n* picker; ~ *daun teh* tea-picker ← **petik**

pemicu *n* trigger ← **picu**

pemikir *n* thinker; **pemikiran** *n* thinking, consideration ← **pikir**

pemilih *n* voter; **pemilihan** *n* election; ~ *umum (pemilu)* general election ← **pilih**

pemilik *n* owner; **kepemilikan** *n* ownership ← **milik**

pemilu *n* general election ← **pemilihan umum**

pemimpin *n* leader ← **pimpin**

peminat *n* interested party ← **minat**

pemindahan *n* transfer, shifting, removal ← **pindah**

peminjam *n* borrower; *kartu* ~ borrowing card; **peminjaman** *n* lending, borrowing ← **pinjam**

pemintal *n* spinning wheel; spinner ← **pintal**

peminum *n* drinker ← **minum**

pemirsa *n* television audience, viewer ← **pirsa**

pemisahan *n* separation ← **pisah**

pemohon *n* applicant; **permohonan** *n* request, application ← **mohon**

pémpék, mpék mpék *n* fried fish-cakes, a specialty of Palembang; ~ *kapal selam* large fish-cake containing an egg

pémprop, pemprov *n* provincial government ← **pemerintah propinsi**

pemprosésan *n* processing ← **prosés**

pemuaian, *n* expansion ← **muai**

pemuda, pemudi *n* youth; young man; **pemudi** *n* young woman ← **muda**

pemugaran *n* restoration, renovation ← **pugar**

pemuja *n* worshipper, fan ← **puja**

pemula *n* beginner ← **mula**

pemulangan *n* return, repatriation ← **pulang**

pemulihan *n* recovery, restoration; ~ *nama baik* rehabilitation ← **pulih**

pemungutan *n* collection; ~ *suara* vote ← **pungut**

pemusik *n* musician ← **musik**

pemusnahan *n* act of destruction ← **musnah**

pemutaran *n* screening; ~ *perdana* premiere, opening screening, opening night (of a film) ← **putar**

pemutih *n* bleach ← **putih**

pemutusan *n* termination, breaking-off; ~ *hubungan kerja (PHK)* to lose your job ← **putus**

péna *n* (fountain) pen, quill; *sahabat* ~ penfriend, penpal

penabung *n* depositor ← **tabung**

penabur *n* sower ← **tabur**

penahanan *n* detention, arrest ← **tahan**

penaksiran *n* evaluation ← **taksir**

penakut *n* coward ← **takut**

penambang *n* miner ← **tambang**

penampakan *n* apparition; visitation ← **tampak**

penampi *n* winnow ← **tampi**

penampilan *n* performance ← **tampil**

penampung *n* container; **penampungan** *n* reception, place that receives something ← **tampung**

penanaman ~ *modal* investment ← **tanam**

penanganan *n* handling ← **tangan**

penanggalan *n* calendar, dating ← **tanggal**

penangguhan *n* delay, postponement ← **tangguh**

penanggulangan *n* tackling, fight against ← **tanggulang**

penangkal ~ *petir* lightning rod; **penangkalan** *n* preventative measure ← **tangkal**

penangkapan *n* capture, arrest ← **tangkap**

penari *n* dancer ← **tari**

penasaran *adj* curious, inquisitive, impatient

penasihat *n* adviser ← **nasihat**

penat *adj* tired

penawar *n* antidote ← **tawar**

penawaran *n* offer, bid ← **tawar**

pencabutan *n* withdrawal, removal ← **cabut**

pencahar *n* laxative ← **cahar**

pencahayaan *n* lighting ← **cahaya**

pencak ~ *silat* traditional self-defense

pencakar ~ *langit* skyscraper ← **cakar**

pencakupan *n* coverage ← **cakup**

pencalonan *n* nomination, candidacy ← **calon**

pencampuran *n* mixing ← **campur**

pencangkokan *n* transplant operation, grafting ← **cangkok**

pencar: berpencaran *v* to disperse (of many things); **terpencar** *adj* dispersed

pencarian *n* search, hunt ← **cari**

pencatatan *n* registration ← **catat**

pencegahan *n* prevention; ~ *AIDS* prevention of AIDS ← **cegah**

pencegatan *n* barring ← **cegat**

pencekalan *n* ban on foreign travel ← **cekal, cegah tangkal**

pencelupan *n* dyeing process ← **celup**

pencemar *n* polluter; **pencemaran** *n* pollution; ~ *udara* air pollution ← **cemar**

pencemburu *n* jealous person ← **cemburu**

pencerahan *n* enlightenment, guidance ← **cerah**

penceramah *n* speaker ← **ceramah**

pencernaan *n* digestion; *gangguan* ~ digestive complaint ← **cerna**

pencét press; *kancing* ~ pressstud; **memencét** *v* to press (a button, key); **terpencét** *adj* **kepencét** *adj, coll* accidentally pressed

pencétak *n* printer ← **cétak**

pencetus *n* initiator, someone who creates ideas ← **cetus**

pencil: terpencil *adj* isolated, remote

pencinta *n* lover ← **cinta**

pencipta *n* creator; ~ *lagu* songwriter ← **cipta**

pencopotan *n* removal ← **copot**

penculik *n* kidnapper; **penculikan** *n* kidnapping ← **culik**

pencuri *n* thief, burglar; **pencurian** *n* theft, burglary ← **curi**

pendaftar *n* applicant; **pendaftaran** *n* enrollment, registration ← **daftar**

pendahulu *n* predecessor; **pendahuluan** *n* introduction; *kata* ~ preface ← **dahulu**

pendaki ~ *gunung* mountaineer, bushwalker ← **daki**

pendakwah *n, Isl* preacher, missionary ← **dakwah**

pendam: terpendam *adj* hidden, concealed

pendamping *n* companion; ~ *hidup* spouse; **pendampingan** *n* assistance ← **damping**

pendanaan *n* funding ← **dana**

pendapa → **pendopo**

pendapat *n* opinion, point of view; *menurut* ~ *saya* in my opinion; **pendapatan** *n* income, revenue ← **dapat**

pendarahan *n* bleeding ← **darah**

pendaratan *n* landing (of vessel); ~ *darurat* emergency landing ← **darat**

pendataan *n* documentation ← **data**

pendatang *n* immigrant, migrant; newcomer ← **datang**

pendayung n rower, oarsman, sculler ← **dayung**

péndék adj short; ~ kata in short; ~nya in a word; celana ~ shorts; cerita ~ (cerpen) short story; **kepéndékan** n abbreviation; **meméndékkan** v to shorten; **memperpéndék** v to shorten, make even shorter; **terpéndék** adj the shortest

pendékar n (in martial arts) master, champion, leader ← **dékar**

pendekatan n approach; getting to know ← **dekat**

pendengar n listener; **pendengaran** n hearing; indera ~ sense of hearing ← **dengar**

pendérékan n towing ← **dérék**

penderitaan n suffering ← **derita**

pendéta n, Chr minister, clergyman, vicar; Hind priest

pendiam n quiet, shy person ← **diam**

pendidik n educator; **pendidikan** n education; ilmu ~ pedagogy ← **didik**

pendingin ~ ruangan air conditioning, cooling ← **dingin**

pendiri n founder; **pendirian** n foundation; opinion, point of view ← **diri**

pendopo, pendapa n traditional large roofed verandah in front of an official residence

penduduk n supporter

pendukung v to need something ← **butuh**

pendulang n prospector; **pendulangan** n panning, prospecting ← **dulang**

pendusta n liar ← **dusta**

penebang n logger, woodcutter; **penebangan** n logging; ~ liar illegal logging ← **tebang**

penebus n redeemer; ransom; **penebusan** n redemption ← **tebus**

penegakan n upholding or maintenance; ~ hukum upholding the law ← **tegak**

penegasan n affirmation, reiteration ← **tegas**

peneliti n researcher; **penelitian** n research ← **teliti**

penémbak n marksman, gunman ← **témbak**

penemu n inventor, discoverer; **penemuan** n invention, discovery ← **temu**

penerangan n information; lighting, enlightenment ← **terang**

penerapan n application ← **terap**

penerbang n pilot, aviator; **penerbangan** n flight; aviation; perusahaan ~ airline ← **terbang**

penerbit n publisher ← **terbit**

penerimaan n receipt ← **terima**

penerjangan n attack, charge ← **terjang**

penerjemah n translator; ~ tersumpah sworn translator; **penerjemahan** n translation ← **terjemah**

penerjun, peterjun n ~ (payung) parachutist, sky diver ← **terjun**

penerus n successor; someone who continues another's work ← **terus**

penetapan *n* appointment ←
tetap

pengabdian *n* service, servitude,
devotion ← **abdi**

pengacara *n* lawyer, solicitor
← **acara**

pengacau *n* provocateur;
pengacauan *n* disturbance ←
kacau

pengadaan *n* supply, provision
← **ada**

pengadilan *n* court of justice
or law; trial; ~ *negeri* district
court ← **adil**

pengaduan *n* complaint; *surat* ~
letter of complaint ← **adu**

pengagum *n* admirer ← **kagum**

pengairan *n* irrigation ← **air**

pengait *n* catch ← **gaét, gait**

pengajar *n* teacher; **pengajaran**
n teaching, tuition ← **ajar**

pengakuan *n* confession,
acknowledgment; ~ *dosa*
confession (Catholic) ← **aku**

pengalaman *n* experience ←
alam

pengaliran *n* flow (esp of money)
← **alir**

pengaman *n* safety device;
pengamanan *n* securing, pacification; *satuan* ~ *(satpam)*
security guard ← **aman**

pengamat *n* observer; ~ *politik*
political observer; **pengamatan**
n observation, monitoring ←
amat

pengambilan *n* act of taking,
removal; ~ *gambar* photo
shoot; ~ *sumpah* taking an oath
← **ambil**

pengamén *n* street singer,
busker ← **amén**

pengampun *n Tuhan Maha* ~
God is all-forgiving; **pengampunan** *n* pardon, reprieve,
amnesty ← **ampun**

penganan *n* snack, food

pengangguran *n* unemployment, unemployed person; ~
tersembunyi hidden unemployment ← **anggur**

pengangkatan *n* appointment
(to a position) ← **angkat**

pengangkut *n* carrier; *kapal* ~
minyak oil tanker ← **angkut**

penganiayaan *n* oppression,
mistreatment ← **aniaya**

pengantar *kata* ~ preface, foreword
← **antar**

pengantin, pengantén *n, f*
bride; *n, m* (bride)groom;
marrying couple; ~ *baru*
newlyweds; *baju* ~, *busana* ~
wedding dress or costume; *kue*
~ wedding cake; *mobil* ~ bridal
car; ~ *pria* (bride)groom; ~
wanita bride

pengantri *n* person who queues
← **antré, antri**

penganugerahan *n* presentation
of an award ← **anugerah**

penganut *n* follower, believer;
~ *agama Katolik* Catholic ←
anut

pengap *adj* stuffy; stale, musty

pengapung *n* buoy, float ←
apung

pengarah *n* director; **pengarahan** *n* direction, guidance, briefing ← **arah**

pengarang *n* author, writer, composer; *hak* ~ copyright ← **karang**

pengartian *n* understanding, interpretation ← **arti**

pengaruh *n* influence; ~ *obat* effect of medicine or drugs; **berpengaruh** *adj* influential; **memengaruhi** *v* to influence, affect; **terpengaruh** *adj* affected or influenced

pengasah ~ *pensil* pencil sharpener ← **asah**

pengasingan *n* exile; *tempat* ~ internment camp, exile ← **asing**

pengasuh *n* carer; ~ *anak* nursemaid, babysitter ← **asuh**

pengatur *n* regulator; **peraturan** *n* rule, regulation ← **atur**

pengawal *n* (body)guard, sentry ← **kawal**

pengawas *badan* ~ supervisory board, trustees; **pengawasan** *n* supervision, control ← **awas**

pengawétan *n* preservation ← **awét**

pengayaan *n* enrichment; ~ *uranium* uranium enrichment ← **kaya**

pengayom *n* protector, carer ← **ayom**

pengeboman *n* bombing ← **bom**

pengecatan *n* painting, dyeing, coloring ← **cat**

pengecékan *n* checking ← **cék**

pengécér *n* retailer ← **écér**

pengecualian *n* exception ← **kecuali**

pengecut *n* coward ← **kecut**

pengédar *n* dealer; **pengédaran** *n* circulation; ~ *udara* air circulation ← **édar**

pengéjaan *n* spelling ← **éja**

pengékspor *n* exporter; ~ *beras* exporter of rice ← **pengékspor**

pengelola *n* manager; **pengelolaan** *n* management ← **kelola**

pengembalian *n* return, act of returning ← **kembali**

pengemban *n* guardian, executor; ~ *tugas* worker responsible for performing a duty ← **emban**

pengembang *n* developer ← **kembang**

pengembara *n* wanderer, rover; **pengembaraan** *n* roaming, wandering ← **embara**

pengembunan *n* condensation ← **embun**

pengemis *n* beggar ← **emis, kemis**

pengemudi *n* driver ← **kemudi**

péngén, pingin, kepéngén, kepingin *v, coll* to really want to

pengéncéran *n* liquefaction, melting ← **énccér**

pengendalian *n* control; ~ *mutu* quality control ← **kendali**

pengendapan *n* siltation ← **endap**

pengendara *n* rider; driver ← **kendara**

pengeraman *n* brooding, hatching ← **eram**

pengeras ~ *suara* loudspeaker; **pengerasan** *n* hardening ← **keras**

pengering ~ *rambut* hair dryer ← **kering**

pengeroposan *n* (process of) erosion; ~ *tulang* osteoporosis ← **keropos**

pengertian *n* understanding ← **erti, arti**

pengesahan *n* validation, legalization ← **sah**

pengetahuan *n* knowledge; *ilmu* ~ *alam (IPA)* science ← **tahu**

penggal: memenggal *v* to cut off, amputate; ~ *kepala* to behead

penggalian *n* digging ← **gali**

pengganti *n* replacement, substitute, successor; **penggantian** *n* substitution ← **ganti**

penggarapan *n* production; ~ *film* film or movie production ← **garap**

penggaris *n* ruler ← **garis**

penggelapan *n* embezzlement ← **gelap**

penggelédahan *n* search, raid, operation ← **geledah**

penggemar *n* fan, enthusiast ← **gemar**

penggembala *n* shepherd ← **gembala**

penggerebekan *n* raid, search ← **gerebek**

penggiring *n* herder ← **giring**

penggolongan *n* classification ← **golong**

penggoréngan *n* wok, frying pan; process of frying ← **goréng**

penggugat *n* plaintiff ← **gugat**

pengguguran *n* abortion ← **gugur**

pengguna *n* user; **penggunaan** *n* usage, use ← **guna**

penggusuran *n* eviction, forcible removal ← **gusur**

penghabisan *n* end; *ujian* ~ final examination ← **habis**

penghangat *n* heater ← **hangat**

penghantar ~ *listrik* electrical conductor ← **hantar**

penghapus *v* eraser, duster; **terhapus** *adj* disappeared; accidentally deleted

penghargaan *n* appreciation, award ← **harga**

penghasil *n* producer; **penghasilan** *n* production; income ← **hasil**

penghasilan *n* production; income; *pajak* ~ income tax ← **hasil**

penghibur *wanita* ~ escort, prostitute ← **hibur**

penghijauan *n* greening (of an area) ← **hijau**

penghimpun ~ *listrik* accumulator, storage cell, battery ← **himpun**

penghinaan *n* insult, libel (written), slander (spoken); ~ *terhadap Presiden* insulting the President ← **hina**

penghitungan *n* counting ← **hitung**

penghormatan *n* display of honor, sign of respect ← **hormat**

penghubung *n* switch, connector; *kata* ~ conjunction, connector ← **hubung**

penghujan *musim* ~ rainy season, monsoon ← **hujan**

penghulu *n, Isl* local chief who performs marriage ceremonies ← **hulu**

penghuni *n* occupant, resident ← **huni**

pengidap *n* sufferer; ~ *narkoba* drug addict ← **idap**

pengikut *n* participant; follower ← **ikut**

pengimpor *n* importer ← **impor**

penginapan *n* accommodation, hotel ← **inap**

penginjil *n* preacher, evangelist ← **injil**

pengintai *pesawat* ~ reconnaissance plane, spy plane ← **intai**

pengirim *n* sender; **pengiriman** *n* dispatch, forwarding; ~ *barang* goods dispatch ← **kirim**

pengiring *n* escort, companion ← **iring**

pengisap ~ *darah* vampire; ~ *debu* vacuum cleaner ← **isap**

pengisi *n* filler; ~ *suara* dubber ← **isi**

pengkhianat *n* traitor ← **khianat**

pengkhotbah *v* preacher ← **khotbah**

penglihatan *n* vision, sight ← **lihat**

pengobatan *n* treatment ← **obat**

pengojék *n* motorcycle taxi driver ← **ojék**

pengolahan *v* processing ← **olah**

pengoplosan *n* illegally adding another liquid ← **oplos**

pengorbanan *n* (act of) sacrifice ← **korban**

penguapan *n* evaporation ← **uap**

pengucapan *n* expression ← **ucap**

penguji *n* examiner ← **uji**

pengukuhan *n* strengthening, reinforcement; ratification ← **kukuh**

pengukuran *n* measuring, measurement ← **ukur**

pengumuman *n* notice, announcement ← **umur**

pengunduran *n* postponement, delay ← **undur**

pengungkit *n* lever ← **ungkit**

pengungsi *n* refugee, evacuee; **pengungsian** *n* evacuation ← **ungsi**

pengurus *n* manager, organizer; ~ *besar* board of directors, executive ← **urus**

pengusaha *n, m* businessman; *f* businesswoman ← **usaha**

penindasan *n* oppression ← **tindas**

pening *adj* dizzy; ~ *kepala* dizzy, light-headed

peninggalan *n* remains, remnants ← **tinggal**

peningkatan *n* rise, increase ← **tingkat**

peninjau *n* observer; **peninjauan** *n* observation, review ← **tinjau**

penipu *n* con man, trickster; **penipuan** *n* deception ← **tipu**

peniti *n* safety-pin; brooch

penitipan *n* care; *tempat* ~ *anak* child-minding center, creche ← **titip**

penjabat *n* official (esp temporary or acting) ← **jabat**

penjaga *n* guard ← **jaga**

penjahat *n* criminal ~ *perang* war criminal

penjaja *n* hawker, pedlar ← **jaja**

penjajah *n* colonizer, ruler, colonial power; **penjajahan** *n* colonization ← **jajah**

penjara *n* prison, jail; *hukuman* ~ imprisonment; **memenjara(kan)** *v* to put in prison, imprison

penjarah *n* looter; **penjarahan** *n* looting ← **jarah**

penjelajah *n* explorer ← **jelajah**

penjelasan *n* explanation ← **jelas**

penjelmaan *n* incarnation ← **jelma**

penjemputan *n* act of picking up ← **jemput**

penjepit *n* clip ← **jepit**

penjeprét *n* stapler ← **jeprét**

penjilat *n* crawler, flatterer, lickspittle ← **jilat**

penjilid *n* binder; **penjilidan** *n* binding (process) ← **jilid**

penjiplak *n* cheat; **penjiplakan** *n* plagiarism, cheating ← **jiplak**

penjiwaan *n* inspiration ← **jiwa**

penjual *n* seller, dealer; **penjualan** *n* sale, sales ← **jual**

penjudi *n* gambler ← **judi**

penjuru *n* corner; *seluruh* ~ *dunia* all parts of the world

penodong *n* attacker; **penodongan** *n* knife attack ← **todong**

penolakan *n* refusal, rejection ← **tolak**

penonton *n* spectator, audience; *para* ~ audience; ladies and gentlemen ← **tonton**

penopang *n* prop, support ← **topang**

pénsil *n* pencil; *rautan* ~ (pencil) sharpener

pénsiun pension, retired; ~ *dini* early pension; **pénsiunan** *n* pensioner **meménsiunkan** *v* to pension off

pentahbisan *n* consecration, ordination ← **tahbis**

pental: terpental *adj* flung, thrown down

pentas stage; **mementaskan** *v* to stage, present; **pementasan** *n* staging, production

péntil *n* valve; ~ *ban* tire valve

penting *adj* important; ~*nya* the importance; *urusan* ~ urgent business; **kepentingan** *n* importance, interest; **berkepentingan** *v* to have an interest in; *yang* ~ concerned party; **mementingkan** *v* to make important, emphasize

pentol: pentolan *n* boss, big shot

penugasan *n* assignment ← **tugas**

penuh *adj* full; ~ *sesak* crowded, chock-full; *sehari* ~ a full or whole day; **memenuhi** *v* to fulfill, meet requirements; **sepenuhnya** *adv* fully, completely; **terpenuhi** *adj* satisfied, fulfilled

penulis *n* author, writer; ~ *novel* novelist ← **tulis**

penumpang *n* passenger ← **tumpang**

penunjuk *n* guide, indicator; **penunjukan** *n* appointment ← **tunjuk**

penuntut *n* claimant, plaintiff, prosecuting party ← **tuntut**

penurunan *n* lowering ← **turun**

penurut *adj* obedient, meek ← **turut**

penutup *n* stopper, lid; end ← **tutup**

penutur *n* speaker; ~ *asli* native speaker ← **tutur**

penyabot *n* saboteur ← **sabot**

penyadap *n* tapper; **penyadap-an** *n* tapping ← **sadap**

penyair *n* poet ← **syair**

penyajian *n* presentation ← **saji**

penyakit *n* disease, illness, complaint; ~ *anjing gila* rabies; ~ *jiwa* mental problem; ~ *gula* diabetes; ~ *menular seksual (PMS)* sexually transmitted disease (STD), venereal disease ← **sakit**

penyaluran *n* channelling ← **salur**

penyambutan *n* welcoming, welcome ceremony ← **sambut**

penyampaian *n* handing over, presentation ← **sampai**

penyamun *n* robber, bandit ← **samun**

penyandera *n* hostage-taker; **penyanderaan** *n* taking of hostages ← **sandera**

penyangkalan *n* denial ← **sangkal**

penyanyi *n* singer, vocalist; ~ *latar* backing vocalist ← **nyanyi**

penyaringan *n* filtration, screening ← **saring**

penyebab *n* cause ← **sebab**

penyebar *n* carrier, infectious person; **penyebaran** *n* distribution ← **sebar**

penyeberangan *n* crossing ← **seberang**

penyedot *mesin* ~ *debu* vacuum cleaner ← **sedot**

penyegar *minuman* ~ tonic, energy drink ← **segar**

penyégélan *n* sealing (off), closure ← **ségél**

penyekapan *n* detention ← **sekap**

penyelam *n* diver ← **selam**

penyelamatan *n* rescue (operation) ← **selamat**

penyelenggara *n* organizer; *panitia* ~ organizing committee; **penyelenggaraan** *n* organization ← **selenggara**

penyelesaian *n* solution, settlement ← **selesai**

penyeléwéngan *n* affair, deviation ← **seléwéng**

penyelidik *n* investigator, detective; **penyelidikan** *n* investigation ← **selidik**

penyelundup *n* smuggler ← **selundup**

penyemat *n* pin ← **semat**

penyembelih *n* butcher, slaughterer; **penyembelihan** *n* slaughter ← **sembelih**

penyembuhan *n* cure, healing ← **sembuh**

penyendiri *n* loner ← **diri**

penyerahan *n* handing over, handover ← **serah**

penyerang *n* attacker; **penyerangan** *n* attack, aggression ← **serang**

penyerapan *n* absorption ← **serap**

penyerbuan *n* attack, charge, invasion ← **serbu**

penyesalan *n* repentance, remorse ← **sesal**

pényét *adj* flattened; *tempe ~* thin, fried slices of *tempe*

penyetélan *n* tuning ← **setél**

penyetor *n* depositor ← **setor**

penyiar *n* announcer ← **siar**

penyidik *n* investigator, detective; **penyidikan** *n* investigation ← **selidik, sidik**

penyihir *n* wizard, witch, sorcerer ← **sihir**

penyiksaan *n* torture, torment ← **siksa**

penyimpanan *n* storage ← **simpan**

penyimpangan *n* aberration, deviation ← **simpang**

penyinaran *n* radiation ← **sinar**

penyisiran *n* combing, checking ← **sisir**

penyitaan *n* confiscation, seizure ← **sita**

pényok, péyot, péot *adj* dented

penyu *n* turtle; *rumah ~* (tortoise) shell

penyulap *n* magician, conjurer ← **sulap**

penyulingan *n* distillation ← **suling**

penyuluh *n* scout; education worker; **penyuluhan** *n* education ← **suluh**

penyumbatan *n* blockage ← **sumbat**

penyunting *n* editor; **penyuntingan** *n* editing ← **sunting**

penyusun *n* compiler, author ← **susun**

penyusupan *n* infiltration ← **susup**

péot → **péyot**

pepatah *n* proverb, saying

pepaya, papaya *n* paw-paw, papaya

peperangan *n* battle ← **perang**

pépés method of cooking by steaming or roasting in banana leaves; *~ tahu* steamed tofu; *ikan ~* steamed fish; **pépésan** *n* food cooked in this way; *~ kosong* lies

pepet *n* shwa, unemphasized e in Indonesian

pépét: mépét *sl* tight; *waktunya sudah ~* time's running out; **kepépét** *adj, sl* in a fix, trapped; no time, rushed

Per. *abbrev Perusahaan* company

pér *n* spring

perabot *n* tools; *~ dapur* kitchen utensils; *~ rumah* furniture; **perabotan** *n* furnishings

peradaban *n* culture, civilization; *~ Mesir kuno* ancient Egyptian civilization ← **adab**

peraga *n* visual aid; **memeragakan** *v* to display, show; **peragawan** *n, m* male model; **peragawati** *n, f* model

perah *sapi ~* dairy cow; something valuable to milk dry; **memerah** *v* to milk or squeeze

perahu *n* (sail)boat; *~ layar* sailing boat; *naik ~* go on board, travel by boat

perairan *n* territorial waters; waterworks ← **air**

perajin *n* craftsman, artisan ← **rajin**

perak *n* silver; silver coin; *layar* ~ small screen; *medali* ~ silver medal; *perajin* ~ silversmith; *seratus* ~ *coll* one hundred rupiah

perakitan *n* assembly ← **rakit**

peralatan *n* equipment ← **alat**

peralihan *n* transition, change; *masa* ~ transition period ← **alih**

perampasan *n* hold-up, robbery ← **rampas**

perampok *n* robber; **perampokan** *n* robbery ← **rampok**

peran *n* part, role; **berperan** *v* to play the role or part; **memerankan** *v* to portray, play the role of; **pemeran** *n* actor, actress

peranakan *n* uterus; *adj* of mixed Chinese and Indonesian blood, Straits Chinese; *masakan* ~ locally-influenced Chinese food ← **anak**

perancang *n* designer, planner; ~ *busana* fashion designer ← **rancang**

Perancis, Prancis *n* France; *bahasa* ~, *orang* ~ French; *(negeri)* ~ France

perang *n* war; ~ *Dunia Kedua* World War II; ~ *mulut* war of words; ~ *gerilya* guerrilla war; **perang-perangan** *n* war games; paintball; **berperang** *v* to wage war, go to war; **memerangi** *v* to fight against; **peperangan** *n* battle

pérang → **pirang**

perangah: terperangah *adj* open-mouthed, astonished

perangai *n* character, nature

perangkap *n* trap; **memerangkap** *v* to trap, catch; **terperangkap** *adj* trapped, caught

perangkat *n* equipment, tool ← **angkat**

perangko, prangko *n* (postage) stamp; *mengumpulkan* ~ to collect stamps

perang-perangan *n* war games; paintball ← **perang**

perangsang *adj, n* stimulant; *obat* ~ aphrodisiac; **perangsangan** *n* stimulation; *fase* ~, *masa* ~ foreplay ← **rangsang**

peranjat: terperanjat *adj* startled, surprised

perantara *n* broker, intermediary, go-between ← **antara**

perantau *n* settler (in a foreign place); **perantauan** *n* abroad, in another place ← **rantau**

peranti, piranti *n* apparatus, equipment; ~ *lunak* software

perapatan *n* **prapatan**

perapian *n* fireplace, oven ← **api**

peras *jeruk* ~ orange (for juicing); **memeras** *v* to squeeze, press; to blackmail, extort; **pemerasan** *n* blackmail, extortion

perasa *n* sensitive person; **perasaan** *n* feeling ← **rasa**

perawakan *n* stature, build, figure ← **awak**

perawan *n* virgin; **keperawanan** *n* virginity

perawat *n* nurse, sister; **perawatan** treatment; maintenance, upkeep; *biaya* ~ cost of treatment, cost of upkeep ← **rawat**

perayaan *n* celebration ← **raya**

perbaikan *n* repair, improvement ← **baik**

perban *n* bandage, dressing; **diperban** *v* to be bandaged

Perbanas *n* private banking college in Jakarta ← **Perhimpunan Bank-Bank Nasional Swasta**

perbandingan *n* comparison, ratio ← **banding**

perbankan *adj* banking; *dunia* ~ the banking world ← **bank**

perbatasan *n* border, frontier ← **batas**

perbédaan *n* difference ← **béda**

perbelanjaan *n* expenditure, spending; *pusat* ~ shopping center, mall ← **belanja**

perbendaharaan *n* treasury; ~ *kata* vocabulary ← **bendahara**

perbincangan *n* discussion ← **bincang**

perboden, perboten → **verboten**

perbuatan *n* act, deed ← **buat**

perbudakan *n* slavery ← **budak**

perbukitan *n* (range of) hills ← **bukit**

perburuhan *n* concerning labor ← **buruh**

percakapan *n* conversation ← **cakap**

percaloan *praktek* ~ profiteering ← **calo**

percampuran *n* mixing, association ← **campur**

percaya trust, believe; ~ *akan* believe in; ~ *diri (PD)* self-confidence; **kepercayaan** *n* belief faith; *menurut* ~ *masing-masing* each according to their own religion; **memercayai** *v* to trust someone; **dipercaya** *v* to be believed, trusted; **memercayakan** *v* to entrust with; **terpercaya** *adj* trusted, reliable

percékcokan *n* quarrel, dispute ← **cékcok**

perceraian *n* divorce ← **cerai**

percétakan *n* printers, printing office; press ← **cétak**

percik *n* spot; **memerciki** *v* to spatter something; **memercikkan** *v* to splash with something

percobaan *n* experiment, test ← **coba**

percontohan *adj* experimental; model ← **contoh**

percuma in vain ← **cuma**

perdagangan *n* commerce, trade; ~ *perempuan* trade in women ← **dagang**

perdamaian *n* peace, reconciliation ← **damai**

perdana *adj* first, starter; ~ *Menteri* Prime Minister; *paket* ~ starter kit; *penerbangan* ~ inaugural flight

perdata *hukum* ~ civil law

perdebatan *n* debate, discussion ← **debat**

perdu *tanaman* ~ shrub, bush

perduli → **peduli**

peredam *n* device to muffle or reduce noise ← **redam**

perék *n, sl* slut ← **perempuan ékspérimén**

perekat *n* glue, adhesive → **rekat**

perékonomian *n* economic affairs ← **ékonomi**

peréli *n* rally driver ← **réli**

peremajaan *n* renewal, revitalization ← **remaja**

perempat *n* quarter; *tiga ~* three-quarters; **perempatan** *n* crossroads, intersection ← **empat**

perempuan *n* woman, female; *~ jalanan* street-walker; *hak ~* women's rights

perenang *n* swimmer ← **renang**

perencanaan *n* planning ← **rencana**

peresmian *n* formal ceremony, inauguration ← **resmi**

perétél → **prétél**

pergaulan *n* mixing, social intercourse; association; *~ bebas* promiscuity, permissiveness ← **gaul**

pergelangan *~ kaki* ankle; *~ tangan* wrist ← **gelang**

pergésékan *n* friction ← **gések**

pergéséran *n* movement, shift ← **gésér**

pergi go, leave; *~ jauh* travel far; *pulang ~* there and back, both ways; *sedang ~, lagi ~* out, not here; **bepergian** *v* to travel, be away; **kepergian** *n* departure

pergok: kepergok *adj, coll* **tepergok** *adj* caught in the act, caught red-handed

pergolakan *n* disturbance, upheaval ← **golak**

pergulatan *n* wrestling, struggle, fight ← **gulat**

perguruan *~ tinggi* university ← **guru**

perhatian *n* attention ← **hati**

perhélatan *n* celebration, feast ← **hélat**

perhentian *n* stop, stopping place ← **henti**

perhiasan *n* jewelery ← **hias**

perhimpunan *n* union, association, club; *~ Mahasiswa Jambi* Jambi Students Assocation ← **himpun**

perhitungan *n* calculation ← **hitung**

perhotélan *n* hotel studies, hospitality ← **hotél**

perhubungan *n* communications, connection; *~ udara* air route; *Menteri ~ (Menhub)* Minister of Communications ← **hubung**

peri- *pref* concerning; **perihal** *n* subject; *conj* about, concerning; **perikemanusiaan** *n* humanitarianism; **berperikemanusiaan** *adj* humane

peri *n* fairy; *ibu ~* fairy godmother

periang *n* cheerful person ← **riang**

perias *n* make-up artist ← **rias**

peribahasa *n* proverb, idiom

perigi *n* well, spring

perih, pedih smart, sting

perihal *n* subject; *conj* about, concerning

perikanan *n* fisheries ← **ikan**

perikemanusiaan *adj* humanitarianism ← **manusia**

periksa investigate, check; *ruang* ~ consultation room; **memeriksa** *v* to examine or investigate; ~ *ulang* to review; **pemeriksa** *n* examiner; **pemeriksaan** *n* examination, investigation

perimbangan *n* proportion ← **imbang**

perincian *n* details, detailed explanation ← **rinci**

perindustrian *n* industry, industrial affairs; *Departemen ~ dan Perdagangan (Depperindag)* Department of Industry and Trade ← **industri**

perintah order, command; *memberi* ~ to (give an) order or command; *menjalankan* ~ to carry out orders; **memerintah** *v* to rule, govern, reign; **memerintahkan** *v* to order or command something; **pemerintah** *n* government; **pemerintahan** *n* administration, government

perintis *n* pioneer ← **rintis**

période *n* period, time

perisai *n* shield

périskop *n* periscope

peristirahatan *n* place for rest or recreation; ~ *terakhir* final resting place ← **istirahat**

peristiwa *n* incident, occurrence, happening

periuk *n* cooking pot

perjaka *n* bachelor, young single man

perjalanan *n* journey, trip; *biro ~, agen* ~ travel agency ← **jalan**

perjamuan *n* feast, party; entertainment ← **jamu**

perjanjian *n* agreement, contract ← **janji**

perjuangan *n* battle, fight, struggle; *Partai Demokrasi Indonesia-~ (PDIP)* Indonesian Democratic Party of Struggle ← **juang**

perjudian *n* gambling ← **judi**

perkakas *n* tool, instrument; ~ *dapur* kitchen utensils

perkantoran *n* office block ← **kantor**

perkapalan *n* shipping ← **kapal**

perkara *n* matter, case, affair; *habis* ~ and that was the end of it, matter closed

perkasa *adj* powerful; manly, virile; *gagah* ~ brave, strong

perkataan *n* phrase, words ← **kata**

perkawinan *n* marriage, wedding; ~ *campuran* mixed marriage ← **kawin**

perkedél *n* (potato) patty, croquette; ~ *jagung* corn patty

perkelahian *n* fight, scuffle ← **kelahi**

perkémahan *n* camping, camp; *tempat* ~ camping ground, campsite ← **kémah**

perkembangan *n* development ← **kembang**

perkenalan *n* introduction ← **kenal**

perkici *burung* ~ rainbow lorikeet

perkilangan *n* refinery ← **kilang**

perkiraan *n* estimate, guess ← **kira**

perkosa: memerkosa *v* to rape, violate; **pemerkosa** *n* rapist; **pemerkosaan** *n* rape, raping; **perkosaan** *n* rape

perkotaan *n* metropolitan area ← **kota**

perkumpulan *n* association, club; assembly ← **kumpul**

perkusi *n* percussion

perkutut *burung* ~ turtledove

perlahan, pelan, perlahan-lahan, pelan-pelan *adv* slowly, softly; **memerlahankan** *v* to slow something down

perlawanan *n* opposition, resistance ← **lawan**

perlawatan *n* trip, visit ← **lawat**

perlengkapan *n* outfit, equipment ← **lengkap**

perlénté *adj* smartly dressed; *n* dandy

perlindungan *n* protection ← **lindung**

perlombaan *n* competition ← **lomba**

perlu need, necessary; **keperluan** *n* needs, requirements; ~ *hidup* necessities of life; **memerlukan** *v* to need, require

perlucutan ~ *senjata* disarmament ← **lucut**

permadani *n* carpet

permai *adj* beautiful, lovely

permainan *n* game, match ← **main**

permaisyuri, permaisuri *n* queen

permak, vermak alteration to clothes; **dipermak** *adj* altered, shortened

permandian *n* bathing pool; christening, baptism; *bapak* ~ godfather ← **mandi**

permata *n* jewel; ~ *hijau* emerald

permén *n* sweet, lolly, candy; ~ *karet* chewing gum, bubble gum

Permésta *n* 1950s secessionist movement in North Sumatra and Sulawesi ← **Perjuangan Semésta**

permintaan *n* request; *atas* ~ by request ← **minta**

perminyakan *n* oil and gas ← **minyak**

permisi excuse me; ~ *dulu* excuse me, excuse yourself

permohonan *n* request, application ← **mohon**

permufakatan *n* discussion, deliberation ← **mufakat**

permukaan *n* surface; ~ *air* water level; *di atas* ~ *laut* above sea level ← **muka**

permukiman *n* housing, residential area ← **mukim**

permulaan *n* beginning ← **mula**

permusuhan *n* enmity, animosity, hostility ← **musuh**

pernafasan, pernapasan *n* breathing, respiration; ~ *buatan* artificial respiration; *sistem* ~ respiratory system ← **nafas**

pernah *adv* ever; once; have + past perfect form of verb; *saya* ~ *ke Bali* I've been to Bali; ~ *makan bebek?* Have you ever eaten duck?; *Tidak* ~ Never

pernak: pernak-pernik *n* little things; small beads and trinkets

perniagaan *n* commerce, trade, business ← **niaga**

pernikahan *n* wedding; *pesta* ~ wedding reception ← **nikah**

penilaian *n* evaluation ← **nilai**

pernis *n* varnish; **dipernis** *v* to be varnished

pernyataan *n* statement, declaration ← **nyata**

peroléhan *n* acquisition; ~ *suara* (number of) votes ← **oléh**

perombakan *n* reorganization ← **rombak**

perompak *n* pirate; **perompakan** *n* piracy ← **rompak**

péron *n* platform; *karcis* ~ platform ticket

perona ~ *mata* eyeshadow; ~ *pipi* rouge ← **rona**

perosok: memerosokkan *v* to push something into; **terperosok** *adj* fallen, sunk, plunged

perosotan *n* (children's) slide ← **rosot**

perpaduan *n* blend, synthesis ← **padu**

perpeloncoan *n* practice of initiation ← **pelonco**

perpisahan *n* parting, farewell; *acara* ~, *pesta* ~ farewell (party) ← **pisah**

Perprés *n* Presidential Regulation ← **Peraturan Présidén**

perpustakaan *n* library ← **pustaka**

pérs *n* press, media; *jumpa* ~, *konperensi* ~ press conference

persahabatan *n* friendship; *pertandingan* ~ friendly (match) ← **sahabat**

persaingan *n* competition; ~ *ketat* intense competition ← **saing**

persalinan *n* childbirth ← **salin**

persamaan *n* similarity, likeness, resemblance; equation ← **sama**

persatuan *n* union, association ← **satu**

persaudaraan *n* brotherhood, fraternity; sisterhood; family ties ← **saudara**

persediaan *n* stock, supply ← **sedia**

persegi *adj* square; sided → **segi**

persekongkolan *n* plot, intrigue, conspiracy ← **kongkol**

persekutuan *n* alliance, partnership ← **sekutu**

perselingkuhan *n* affair ← **selingkuh**

perselisihan *n* dispute, difference of opinion ← **selisih**

Persemakmuran *n* (British) Commonwealth ← **makmur**

persembahan *n* offering; product or service ← **sembah**

persembunyian *n* hiding place, hideout ← **sembunyi**

persén *n* percent; *seratus* ~ one hundred percent; **persénan** *n* tip; **perséntase, proséntase** *n* percentage

persendian *n* joints ← **sendi**

persengkétaan *n* dispute ← **sengkéta**

persenyawaan *n* chemical compound ← **senyawa**

perseorangan *adj* individual ← **orang**

perserikatan *n* federation; ~ *Bangsa-Bangsa (PBB)* the United Nations (UN) ← **serikat**

perséro *adj* proprietary limited (Pty Ltd); **perséroan** *n* company; ~ *terbatas* proprietary limited ← **séro**

persétan *ejac* go to hell! ← **sétan**

perseteruan *n* feud ← **seteru**

persetubuhan *n* sexual intercourse ← **tubuh, setubuh**

persetujuan *n* agreement, approval ← **tuju, setuju**

persiapan *n* preparations ← **siap**

persidangan *n* meeting, assembly; (extended) court session ← **sidang**

persil *n* plot, block (of land)

persimpangan *n* intersection ← **simpang**

persinggahan *n* stopover ← **singgah**

persis *adv* exactly; ~ *ibunya* just like his mother

persnéling *n* gear(box); ~ *tiga* third gear

persoalan *n* problem, issue, matter ← **soal**

personalia, personél *adj* personnel, staff

pertahanan *n* defense; ~ *sipil* civil defense; *Menteri* ~ Minister for Defense ← **tahan**

pertalian *n* connection, relationship ← **tali**

pertama *adj* first; *hadiah* ~ first prize; **pertama-tama** *adv* first of all

pertamanan *adj* parks and gardens; *dinas* ~ parks service ← **taman**

pertambahan *n* increase ← **tambah**

pertambangan *n* mining ← **tambang**

Pertamina *n* state-run national oil and gas company ← **Perusahaan Pertambangan Minyak dan Gas Bumi Negara**

pertanda *n* sign, omen, indication ← **tanda**

pertandingan *n* contest, competition, match ← **tanding**

pertanggungan *n* insurance, responsibility ← **tanggung**

pertanian *n* agriculture; *sekolah* ~ agricultural college ← **tani**

pertanyaan *n* question; *mengajukan* ~ to ask questions ← **tanya**

pertapa *n* ascetic, hermit, recluse; **pertapaan** *n* hermitage, retreat ← **tapa**

pertempuran *n* battle ← **tempur**

pertemuan *n* meeting ← **temu**

pertengahan *n* middle; *Abad* ~ the Middle Ages ← **tengah**

pertengkaran *n* quarrel ← **tengkar**

pertentangan *n* conflict ← **tentang**

pertiga *dua* ~ two-thirds; **pertigaan** *n* T-junction ← **tiga**

pertikaian *n* quarrel, disagreement ← **tikai**

pertimbangan *n* consideration ← **timbang**

pertiwi *n* earth; *ibu* ~ motherland, native country

pertokoan *n* shopping center or complex, mall ← **toko**

pertolongan *n* help, assistance, aid; ~ *pertama* first aid ← **tolong**

pertukangan *n* repairs ← **tukang**

pertukaran *n* exchange; ~ *pikiran* exchange of ideas or views ← **tukar**

pertumbuhan *n* growth, development ← **tumbuh**

pertunangan *n* engagement ← **tunang**

pertunjukan *n* show, performance ← **tunjuk**

Péru *n* Peru; *orang* ~ Peruvian

perubahan *n* change, alteration ← **ubah**

perumahan *n* housing (complex) ← **rumah**

perumahtanggaan *n* household affairs ← **rumah tangga**

Perumnas National Housing → **Perumahan Nasional**

perumpamaan *n* parable, metaphor ← **umpama**

Perumtél *n, arch* telephone company (now Telkom)

perumusan *n* formulation ← **rumus**

perundingan *n* discussion; *meja* ~ discussion table ← **runding**

perunggu *n* bronze; *medali* ~ bronze medal

peruntungan *n* (good) fortune or luck ← **untung**

perupa *n* sculptor ← **rupa**

perusahaan *n* company ← **usaha**

perut *n* stomach, belly; ~ *buncit* fat belly; pregnant; ~ *kapal* hold; *sakit* ~ stomach ache, upset stomach

perwakilan *n* representation, delegation; *Dewan* ~ *Rakyat (DPR)* parliament, legislative assembly ← **wakil**

perwalian *n* guardianship, representation ← **wali**

perwira *n* officer; ~ *tinggi* general

pés *penyakit* ~ plague → **sampar**

pesan message, instruction, order; **pesanan** *n* order; *antar* ~ delivery; **memesan** *v* to order; **pemesanan** *n* order, request

pesangon *n* severance pay

pesantrén *n* Islamic boarding school → **santri**

pesat *adj* fast, rapid

pesawat *n* machine; ~ *televisi* television (set); ~ *telepon* telephone; ~ *terbang* aeroplane, airplane

pések *adj* flat-nosed

pésér *n, arch* half-cent; **sepésér** *tidak ada* ~ *pun* to have not even a cent

peserta *n* participant ← **serta**

pesiar *n* trip, cruise; *kapal* ~ cruise ship, pleasure craft

pésimis *adj* pessimistic

pesindén *n, f* singer accompanying a gamelan orchestra

pesing *bau* ~ stink of urine
pesisir *n* coast; *batik* ~ batik from the north coast of Java
pesona *n* magic; **memeso-na(kan)** *adj* enthralling, enchanting; **terpesona** *adj* enthralled, enchanted
pésta *n* party, celebration; ~ *perkawinan* wedding reception; **berpésta** *v* to (have a) party; **dipéstakan** *v* to be celebrated with a party
péstisida *n* pesticide
pesuling *n* flautist ← **suling**
pesuruh *n* messenger, errand boy; ~ *kantor* office boy ← **suruh**
pét *topi* ~ cap
peta *n* map, chart; ~ *dunia* world map; *buku* ~ atlas; *buku* ~ *jalan* road atlas, street directory; **pemetaan** *n* mapping
Péta *n* local paramilitary under the Japanese occupation ← **Pembéla Tanah Air**
petai → **peté**
petak *n* compartment, division; *rumah* ~ tenement, communal house
petang *adj, form* late afternoon to evening (from around 2.30 to sunset); *berita* ~ evening news
petani *n* farmer; ~ *cengkeh* clove farmer ← **tani**
petas: petasan *n* firecracker, fireworks
peté, petai *n* stinkbean; *nasi goreng* ~ fried rice with stinkbeans
peténis *n* tennis player ← **ténis**

peternak *n* (cattle) farmer; **peternakan** *n* cattle farm, ranch ← **ternak**
péterséli *n* parsley
peti *n* chest, case, box; ~ *es* ice-box; ~ *kemas* packing case, freight container; ~ *mati* coffin
petik pluck; **petikan** *n* extract, quotation; **memetik** *v* to pick; to strum; ~ *gitar* to play or strum the guitar; **pemetik** *n* picker; ~ *daun teh* tea-picker
petinju *n* boxer ← **tinju**
petir *n* thunder, lightning; *disambar* ~ to be struck by lightning
petis *tahu* ~ fried tofu with a spicy sauce
petisi *n* petition; ~ *Lima Puluh n* protest petition in the late 1970s against Suharto's rule
pétrokimia *adj* petrochemical
pétromaks *lampu* ~ kerosene lantern
Pétruk *n* clown figure in shadow-puppet plays
pétrus *n* mysterious killers (in the 1980s) ← **penémbak mistérius**
petunjuk *n* instruction, direction; *buku* ~ manual; *buku* ~ *jalan* street directory; *buku* ~ *telepon* telephone book ← **tunjuk**
pewarna *n* dye, stain ← **warna**
pewawancara *n* interviewer ← **wawancara**
péyot, péot, pényok *adj* dented
PGRI *abbrev* Persatuan Guru Republik Indonesia Indonesian Teachers' Association

phinisi → **pinisi**

PHK *abbrev, euph pemutusan hubungan kerja* unemployment

Pi → **Papi**

piagam *n* charter

piala *n* trophy, cup; ~ *Sudirman* Sudirman Cup (badminton)

piano *n* piano; *main* ~ to play the piano; **pianis** *n* pianist

piara, pelihara: piaraan *hewan* ~ pet

piatu *n* motherless child; *rumah* ~ orphanage; *yatim* ~ orphan

piawai *adj* expert, skilled; **kepiawaian** *n* skill, expertise

picik *adj* narrow; *berpikiran* ~ to be narrow-minded

picu *n* trigger; **memicu** *v* to trigger, set off; **pemicu** *n* trigger

pidana *hukum* ~ civil law; **terpidana** *n* the condemned

pidato *n* speech, address; ~ *pembukaan* opening speech; **berpidato** *v* to make a speech, give an address

pigi → **pergi**

pigméntasi *n* pigmentation

pigura *n* picture frame

pihak *n* party; side; ~ *ayah* paternal line, father's side; *di satu* ~ on the one side; **berpihak, memihak** *v* to take sides; **sepihak** *adj* unilateral

pijak: pijakan *n* foothold, something to stand on; ~ *kaki* pedal; **berpijak** *v* to stand on; **memijak** *v* to tread or step on

pijar *lampu* ~ light bulb

pijat, pijit massage; *panti* ~ massage parlor; *tukang* ~ masseur; **pijatan** *n* massage; **memijat** *v* to massage

pikat: memikat *adj* attractive, enticing; **terpikat** *adj* attracted, enchanted

pikét report for duty or be on stand-by outside work hours

pikir, fikir *v* to think; **pikiran** *n* thought, idea; ~ *kotor* dirty thought, dirty mind; **berpikir** *v* to think; **kepikiran** *v* considered, thought of, sprang to mind; **memikirkan** *v* to think about; **pemikir** *n* thinker; **pemikiran** *n* thinking, consideration

piknik *n* picnic; **berpiknik** *v* to have a picnic

pikul *n, arch* old measurement of weight; **memikul** *v* to bear, carry on the shoulder

pikun *adj* senile, dotty

pil *n* (contraceptive) pill, tablet

PIL *n, abbrev* lover, another man ← **pria idaman lain**

pilar *n* pillar

pilek sniffle, have a cold or runny nose

pilem → **film**

pilih choose; ~ *kasih* take sides; *hak* ~ right to vote; *salah* ~ make the wrong choice; **pilihan** *n* choice, selection; *adj* select; **memilih** *v* to choose or select; to elect or vote (for); **pemilih** *n* voter; **pemilihan** *n* election; ~ *umum (pemilu)* general election

pilkada *n* local or regional election ← **pemilihan kepala daérah**

pilu moved; **memilukan** *adj* moving, touching

pimpin *v* to lead; **pimpinan** *n* leadership, guidance; administration; **memimpin** *v* to lead; **pemimpin** *n* leader; **kepemimpinan** *n* leadership (qualities); **terpimpin** *adj* led, guided; *Demokrasi ~* Guided Democracy (under Sukarno)

pinak *anak ~* descendants, children and grandchildren; **beranak-pinak** *v* to have (many) descendants

pinang *n* areca nut; *seperti ~ dibelah dua* like two peas in a pod; **meminang** *v* to propose, ask for a girl's hand in marriage

pincang *adj* crippled, lame; *kaki ~* bad or gammy leg

pincut: **kepincut** *adj* enchanted, taken with; attracted or drawn to

pindah move; change; *~ agama* change religions; *~ rumah* move (house); *~ kewarganegaraan* change your nationality; **pindahan** *n* furniture etc to be moved; **berpindah** *v* to move; **memindahkan** *v* to move, transfer; **pemindahan** *n* transfer, shifting, removal

pindakas *n* peanut butter → **selai kacang**

pinggan *n* bowl, plate

pinggang *n* waist; *ikat ~* belt

pinggir *n* edge, border; **pinggiran** *n* edges, outskirts; *~ kota* city outskirts or limits; **meminggir** *v* **minggir** *v, coll* to move to the side, pull over; **meminggirkan** *v* to move to one side, cast aside; **terpinggirkan** *adj* cast aside, marginalized

pingit: **pingitan** *n* seclusion; **dipingit** *v* to be secluded, kept at home

pingpong *n* table tennis, ping-pong; **dipingpong** *v* to be sent here and there, messed about → **ténis méja**

pingsan faint, collapse; unconscious; *jatuh ~* to faint (away)

pinguin *n* penguin

pinisi, phinisi *kapal ~* Buginese cargo boat

pinjam borrow; **pinjaman** *n* loan; **meminjam** *v* to borrow; **meminjami** *v* to lend someone; **meminjamkan** *v* to lend something; **peminjam** *n* borrower; *kartu ~* borrowing card; **peminjaman** *n* lending, borrowing

pinsét *n* tweezers

pinta *n, arch* request; **(me)minta** *v* to request, ask for; **(me)minta-minta** *v* to beg, ask for money; **permintaan** *n* request; *atas ~* by request

pintal: **memintal** *v* to spin (thread); **pemintal** *n* spinning wheel; spinner

pintar *adj* **pinter** *coll* clever; **kepintaran** *n* cleverness

pintas *jalan ~* short cut; **sepintas** *~ lalu* at first glance

pintu *n* door, gate; *~ air* sluice, floodgates; *~ darurat* emergency exit; *~ geser* sliding door; *~ keluar* exit; *~ masuk* entrance;

mengetok ~ to knock at/on the door

pinus *pohon* ~ (European) pine (tree)

pipa *n* pipe, tube; ~ *karet* rubber tube; ~ *saluran* pipeline

pipi *n* cheek; *cium* ~ kiss on the cheek

pipih *adj* flat

pipis *n, ch* wee, pee, go to the toilet

piramida *n* pyramid; *berbentuk* ~ pyramid-shaped

pirang, pérang *adj,* fair-haired; *m* blond, *f* blonde,

piranti, peranti *n* apparatus, equipment; ~ *lunak* software

piring *n* plate, dish; *mencuci* ~ to wash the dishes; *sabun cuci* ~ dishwashing liquid; *tari* ~ dance from West Sumatra performed with plates; ~ *terbang* flying saucer; **piringan** *n* plate-shaped object; ~ *hitam* record, LP

pirsa: pemirsa *n* television audience, viewer

pisah separate, split; ~ *ranjang* separate *v* (of a couple); **berpisah** *v* to part, separate; **memisah** *v* to separate; **memisahkan** *v* to separate something; **pemisahan** *n* separation; **perpisahan** *n* parting, farewell; *acara* ~, *pesta* ~ farewell (party); **terpisah** *adj* separated

pisang *n* banana; ~ *goreng* (*pisgor*) fried banana

pisau *n* knife; ~ *bedah* scalpel

pispot *n* chamber pot, potty

pita *n* ribbon; ~ *suara* vocal cords; *cacing* ~ tapeworm

pitam *n* fit; *naik* ~ get angry

pités *n* psychotest, psychological test, IQ test

piton *n (ular)* ~ python

piutang *n* credit → **utang**

piyama *n* pyjamas, pajamas

Pjs. *abbrev Pejabat Sementara* acting official

PK *abbrev paardekracht* horsepower

PKB *abbrev Partai Kebangkitan Bangsa* Party of National Awakening

PKI *abbrev Partai Komunis Indonesia* Indonesian Communist Party

PKK *abbrev Pendidikan Kesejahteraan Keluarga* Family Welfare Education

PKS *abbrev Partai Keadilan Sejahtera* Justice and Prosperity Party

plafon *n* ceiling

plagiat *n* plagiarism; **plagiator** *n* someone who copies or commits plagiarism

plakat *n* placard, poster

plang *n* board, signpost; plank; barrier

planolog *n* town planner; **planologi** *n* town planning

plasma *petani* ~ farmer who supplies a commodity to a factory ← **pengembangan lahan dan sumber daya alam**

plastik *adj* plastic; *n* plastic bag, carrier bag

plat → **pelat**

platina *n* platinum

pléno *adj* plenary; *sidang ~* plenary session, full session

pléster *n* sticking plaster, bandaid

plin-plan, plintat-plintut *adj* swaying this way and that, bend with the wind

PLN *abbrev Perusahaan Listrik Negara* State Electricity Corporation

plonco, pelonco *n* new student or freshman awaiting initiation; **diplonco** *v* to undergo an initiation at school or university; **perpeloncoan** *n* practice of initiation

plong *adj* relieved

PLTA *abbrev Pembangkit Listrik Tenaga Air* hydro-electric power station

PLTPB *abbrev Pembangkit Listrik Tenaga Panas Bumi* geothermal power station

PLTU *abbrev Pembangkit Listrik Tenaga Uap* steam power station

pluit → **peluit**

plus *adj* plus, added; *kacamata ~* long-sighted glasses; *nilai ~* added bonus

PM *abbrev Perdana Menteri* Prime Minister

PMA *abbrev Penanaman Modal Asing* foreign investment

PMI *abbrev Palang Merah Indonesia* Indonesian Red Cross

PN *abbrev Perusahaan Negara* state corporation

PNG *abbrev Papua Nugini* Papua New Guinea

PNI *abbrev Partai Nasional Indonesia* Indonesian National Party

PNS *abbrev Pegawai Negeri Sipil* civil servant

poci *n* teapot; *teh ~* tea made in an earthenware pot, a specialty of the Tegal area

poco: poco-poco *n* line dance from North Sulawesi

pocong *n* ghost (wrapped in a shroud); *sumpah ~* oath taken while wrapped in a shroud

poco-poco *n* line dance from North Sulawesi

podéng *es ~* a kind of ice-cream snack ← **puding**

pohon *n* tree; *~ beringin* banyan (tree); *coll* Golkar; *~ cendana* sandalwood tree; *~ cemara* casuarina (tree); *~ jati* teak

pohon → **mohon**

poin *n* point, mark

pojok *n* corner; **pojokan** *n, sl* corner; **memojokkan** *v* to force into a corner; **terpojok(kan)** *adj* forced into a corner

pokok main; *~ kalimat* subject of a sentence; *~nya* basically, the main thing is; *~ pembicaraan* discussion topic; *gaji ~* base salary

pokrol *n* lawyer

pola *n* pattern; *~ baju* sewing pattern; **berpola** *v* to have a pattern; *adj* patterned

polan *si ~* so-and-so, whatshisname, whatshername

Polandia *n* Poland; *bahasa ~* Polish; *orang ~* Pole *pl* Polish

polantas *n* traffic police ← **polisi lalu lintas**

Polda *n* Regional Police; *~ Metro Jaya* Jakarta Metropolitan Police station ← **Polisi Daérah**

polémik *n* debate, polemic; **berpolémik** *v* to debate, argue over

polés polish; **memolés** *v* to polish

poligami *n* polygamy

poliklinik, poli *n* polyclinic, doctor's surgery; *~ gigi* dentist's surgery; *~ umum* GP's surgery, doctor's surgery

Polinésia *n* Polynesia; *orang ~* Polynesian; *~ Perancis* French Polynesia

polis *n* (insurance) policy

polisi *n* police; *~ militer* military police; *~ wanita (polwan)* policewoman; *kantor ~* police station

politik *n* politics; **berpolitik** *v* to play politics; **politikus** *n, sing* politician; **politisi** *n, pl* politicians; **politis** *adj* political

polong *kacang ~* (green) pea

polos *adj* plain, unpretentious; smooth; *baju ~* plain shirt; **kepolosan** *n* simplicity, straight-forwardness, lack of pretension

Polri *n* Indonesian police force; *Mabes ~* Indonesian federal police headquarters ← **Polisi Republik Indonésia**

polsék *n* local police station ← **polisi séktor**

polusi *n* pollution; *~ udara* air pollution; **polutan** *n* pollutant

Polwan *n* policewoman ← **polisi wanita**

pompa pump; *~ angin* air pump; *~ bensin* petrol station, gasoline pump, service station; **memompa** *v* to pump

PON *n* National Sports Week, national championships ← **Pekan Olahraga Nasional**

pon *n* pound; *~ sterling* pound sterling

ponco *n* poncho, cloak

pondok *n* hut, cottage; *~ pesantren (ponpes)* Islamic boarding school; **mondok** *v, coll* to board, lodge, stay

pong *tahu ~* tofu eaten with spicy sauce

pongah *adj* arrogant; **kepongahan** *n* arrogance

poni *n* fringe, bangs; **berponi** *v* to have a fringe or bangs

ponpés *n* Islamic boarding school ← **pondok pesantrén**

pontang: *pontang-panting* *adv* helter-skelter

pop *n* pop (music); *~ Bali* Balinese pop (music)

popok *n* napkin, diaper; *mengganti ~* to change a nappy; *ruam ~* nappy rash

populér *adj* popular; **popularitas** *n* popularity

porak-poranda *n* in a mess; **memorak-porandakan** *v* to cause chaos, turn upside-down

pori n pore; **berpori** adj porous, having pores; *kulit ~ besar* skin with large pores

porno adj pornographic; *film ~* porn(ographic) film; **pornoaksi** n pornographic actions; **pornografi** n pornography

poros n axis; *~ Setan* the Axis of Evil; *~ Tengah* coalition of Muslim parties in late 1990s

porselén n porcelain

porsi n serve, portion; *~ besar* large serve

portal n iron gateway into a building complex; barrier blocking access into a complex; **diportal** v to be blocked by a barrier, have a barrier lowered

porto n cost of freight or postage; *bebas ~* freepost

Portugal, Portugis n Portugal; *bahasa ~, orang ~* Portuguese

pos n post; *~ kilat* express mail; *~ penjagaan, ~ satpam* security post; *~ udara* airmail; *cap ~* postmark; *kantor ~* post office; *Pak ~, tukang ~* postman

pose n pose (for a photograph); **berpose** v to pose for a photograph

posisi n position; **berposisi** v to hold a position, be positioned

positif adj positive; *berpikir ~* to think positive

poskamling n neighborhood security post ← **pos keamanan lingkungan**

posko n post (for a political party or fund-raising effort) ← **pos koordinasi**

poswésél n (postal) money order

posyandu n all-in-one government administrative office ← **pos pelayanan terpadu**

pot n pot, vase; *~ bunga* vase (indoors), flowerpot (outdoors)

potong piece, cut; *~ kambing* slaughter a goat; *~ rambut* cut your hair, get your hair cut; hairdresser, barber (for men); **potongan** n discount, reduction; cut (of clothes); **berpotongan** adj of a certain style or cut; **memotong** v to cut, deduct; to slaughter, amputate; to interrupt; **terpotong** adj cut (off)

potrét n portrait; photograph of a person; *tukang ~* photographer; **memotrét** v to photograph

PP abbrev *pulang pergi* there and back, shown on public transport, to indicate that the vehicle also returns from its destination

PPLH abbrev *Pembinaan dan Pelestarian Lingkungan Hidup* Cultivation and Preservation of the Environment

PPN abbrev *Pajak Pendapatan Nasional* National Income Tax, a goods and services tax at restaurants and hotels

PPP (P3) abbrev *Partai Persatuan Pembangunan* United Development Party, a Muslim party

PR abbrev *pekerjaan rumah* homework

pra- pref pre-, before; *~karsa* initiative; *~nikah* pre-marital; *~sangka* prejudice

prada *n* coating, leaf; ~ *emas* gold-leaf

Praha *n* Prague

praja *pamong* ~ civil service

prajurit *n* soldier

prakarsa *n* initiative; *mengambil* ~ to take the initiative

prakiraan → **kira**

prakték, praktik *n* practice; practical; ~ *umum* general practitioner's; **mempraktékkan** *v* to put into practice; **praktis** *adj* practical; ~*nya* in practice; **kepraktisan** *n* practicality

pramugari *n, f* stewardess, air hostess; cabin crew; **pramugara** *n, m* steward; cabin crew

Pramuka *n* Scouts; **kepramukaan** *adj* scouting → **Praja Muda Karana**

Prancis → **Perancis**

prangko → **perangko**

prapatan, perapatan *n, coll* crossroads, intersection

prasangka *n* prejudice

prasasti *n* inscription, memorial plaque

prasmanan *adj* buffet-style

PRD *abbrev Partai Rakyat Demokratik* Democratic People's Party

prédikat *dengan* ~ with the title or designation; **berprédikat** *adj* with the title of

préféktur *n* prefecture (in Japan)

préman *n* thug

prémi *n* (insurance) premium

présdir *n* president-director ← **présidén diréktur**

préséntasi *n* (oral) presentation

présiden *n* president; *wakil* ~ *(wapres)* vice-president; **keprésidénan** *adj* presidential

préstasi *n* performance, achievement; **berpréstasi** *adj* prestigious; successful

prétéli, perétéli: diprétéli *v* to be dismantled, taken apart or off

pri → **pribumi**

pria *n* male, man; *pengantin* ~ (bride)groom

pribadi *n* self, individual, personality; *saya* ~ personally; *secara* ~ privately; **kepribadian** *n* personality

pribahasa → **peribahasa**

pribumi *n* **pri** *coll* native inhabitant, indigenous Indonesian; **non-pri** *coll* ethnic Chinese

prihatin concerned, worried; **keprihatinan** *n* concern; **memprihatinkan** *adj* worrying

prima *adj* outstanding, first-rate

primadona *n* primadonna

primata *hewan* ~ primate

primitif *adj* primitive

prinsip *n* principle; **berprinsip** *v* to have principles; *adj* principled

prioritas *n* priority; ~ *tinggi* high priority; **memprioritaskan** *v* to prioritize

prisma *n* prism

prit sound of a whistle

priyayi *n* upper class, esp in colonial era

problém, problim *n* problem

prodéo *n* without paying court costs, free

produk *n* product → **buatan;
produksi** *n* production; *rumah
~* production house; **memproduksi** *v* to produce

profési *n* profession; **berprofési**
v to have a profession, work as;
profésional *adj* professional

profésor *n* professor → **guru
besar**

profil *n* profile, outline

prokém *bahasa ~* Jakarta teen
slang

proklamasi *n* proclamation (of
independence); **memproklamasikan** *v* to proclaim (independence); **proklamator** *n*
proclaimer (of independence)

promosi *n* promotion; **mempromosikan** *v* to promote

propinsi *n* province; *~ Sumatera
Selatan* Province of South
Sumatra; *antar ~* interprovincial

proporsi *n* proportion; **proporsional** *adj* proportional, reasonable

prosa *n* prose

prosédur *n* procedure;
prosédural *adj* procedural

proséntase → **persén,
perséntase**

prosés *n* process; court case;
memproséskan *v* to process;
pemrosésan *n* processing

prospék *n* prospect, chance

protés protest; **memprotés** *v* to
(make a) protest

Protéstan *n* Protestant →
Kristen

protokol *jalan ~* main street (passed through by official visitors)

provinsi → **propinsi**

provokasi *n* provocation;
provokator *n* trouble-maker,
provocateur

proyék *n* project, scheme

PRRI/Permesta *abbrev Pemerintah Revolusioner Republik
Indonesia/Perjuangan Semesta*
Revolutionary Government of
the Republic of Indonesia/Total
Struggle, a secessionist movement in Sumatra and Sulawesi
in the 1950s

PRT *pembantu rumah tangga*
household servant

Ps. *pasar* market

psikiater [sikiater] *n* psychiatrist
→ **jiwa**

psikolog [sikolog] *n* psychologist;
psikologi *n* psychology → **jiwa**

psikotés [sikotés], **pités** *n*
psychotest, psychological test,
IQ test

psikotropika [sikotropika] *obat
~* prescription medicine (esp
when abused)

PT *abbrev Perseroan Terbatas*
Pty Ltd

PT KAI *abbrev PT Kereta Api
Indonesia* Indonesian Railways
Pty Ltd, formerly known as
*Perumka (Perusahaan Umum
Kereta Api)*

PU *abbrev Pekerjaan Umum*
Public Works

pualam *n* marble; *batu ~* marble

puas *adj* satisfied, content;
memuaskan *adj* satisfactory

puasa fast; *~ nasi* give up eating rice; *~ Senin Kamis* fast
on Mondays and Thursdays;

~ *setengah hari*, ~ *lohor* fast until the midday prayer; *buka* ~ break the fast, breaking of the fast; *bulan* ~ fasting month, Ramadan; *membatalkan* ~ to break your fast (intentionally); **berpuasa** *v* to fast

puber *n* puberty; *masa* ~ puberty

pucat *adj* pale; *adj, coll* scared

pucuk *n* shoot, sprout; counter for guns and letters; **sepucuk** ~ *surat* a letter

pudar faded, washed-out; **memudar** *v* to fade

pudel *anjing* ~ poodle

puding *n* pudding, dessert

Puerto Rico *n* Puerto Rico; *orang* ~ Puerto Rican

pugar: memugar *v* to restore, renovate; **pemugaran** *n* restoration, renovation

puing *n* ruins; rubble; *terima* ~ *bangunan* we buy building rubble

puisi *n* poetry (esp Western); **puitis** *adj* poetic

puja worship; **pujaan** *n* something worshipped or idolized; **memuja** *v* to worship; **pemuja** *n* worshipper, fan

Pujakesuma Sumatran-born Javanese → **putra Jawa kelahiran Sumatera**

pujangga *n, lit* poet; ~ *Baru* Malay-language literary group formed in the 1930s

pujaséra *n* food court, collection of food stalls ← **pusat jajan serba rasa**

puji praise; ~ *Tuhan Chr* thank God, Praise the Lord; **pujian** *n* praise; **memuji** *v* to praise; **memuji-muji** *v* to praise excessively; **terpuji** *adj* highly-praised

pukul strike; *form* hour; ~ *tiga belas* 1 pm; ~ *rata* in general; **pukul-memukul, berpukul-pukulan** *v* to hit each other; **pukulan** *n* strike, beat, hit; **memukul** *v* to hit, beat, strike; **terpukul** *adj* hard-hit

pul *n* (vehicle) pool

pula *adv* also, too; again; *lagi*~ moreover

pulang *v* to go home, return; ~ *hari* to return on the same day, not stay overnight; ~ *pergi (PP)* there and back, both ways; ~ *ke rahmat Allah*, ~ *ke rahmatullah Isl* to die, **berpulang** *v* to pass away, die; **memulangkan** *v* to give back; to send back, repatriate; **pemulangan** *n* return, repatriation

pulas *tidur* ~ sleep soundly

pulau *n* island; ~ *Dewata* Bali, Island of the Gods; ~ *karang* coral island, atoll; ~ *Seribu* the Thousand Islands; *antar* ~ between islands, inter-island; **kepulauan** *n* archipelago, chain

pulen *nasi* ~ delicious, well-cooked rice

pulih recovered; **memulihkan** *v* to restore; **pemulihan** *n* recovery, restoration; ~ *nama baik* rehabilitation

pulpén *n* fountain pen

pulsa *n* unit of credit (for a telephone); *hemat* ~ cheap rates

puluh *dua* ~ twenty; *tiga* ~ thirty; *empat* ~ forty; *lima* ~ fifty; **puluhan** *n* dozens; *tahun delapan* ~ the eighties; **sepuluh** *n* ten

pun emphasizing particle; too, also; even; then

punah *adj* extinct; **kepunahan** *n* extinction

punai *burung* ~ kind of green pigeon

puncak *n* peak, summit, top; ~ *es* tip of the iceberg; ~ *gunung* mountain-top, summit; ~ *kenikmatan* orgasm; ~ *popularitas* peak of popularity; *pimpinan* ~ top-level management; **memuncak** *v* to culminate, reach a peak

pundak *n* shoulder

pundi *n* piggybank, purse; ~ *amal* charitable fund

punggung *n* back; *tulang* ~ spine; **memunggungi** *v* to turn your back on

pungkas → **pamungkas**

pungli *n* unofficial charge ← **pungutan liar**

pungut pick up; *anak* ~ adopted child; **pungutan** *n* amount collected, levy; **memungut** *v* to pick up, collect; **pemungutan** *n* collection; ~ *suara* vote

puntung ~ *rokok* cigarette butt

punya have, own; *orang tidak* ~ the poor, the have-nots; *yang* ~ the owner; **kepunyaan** *n* possession, belonging; **mempunyai** *v* to have, own, possess

pup *sl* poo, pooh, empty the bowels

pupu: *sepupu n* cousin; *saudara* ~ cousin

pupuk *n* fertilizer; ~ *kandang* manure, dung

pupus wiped out, disappeared; **memupuskan** *v* to wipe out, destroy

pura *n* Balinese or Hindu temple

pura-pura pretend; **berpurapura** *v* to pretend, fake

purba *adj* ancient; *zaman* ~ ancient times; **purbakala** *n* ancient times

puri *n* palace, castle

purna- *pref* post-, after; **purnabakti** *adj* retirement; **purnajual** *adj* post-sales; **purnawirawan** *n* retired soldier

purnama *bulan* ~ full moon

purnawirawan *n* retired soldier

puruk: *terpuruk adj* hidden, buried, sunk; **keterpurukan** *n* depression, abyss

pus *n, coll* pussycat; **pus-pus-pus** puss-puss-puss, used to call a cat

pusaka *n* heirloom, inheritance

pusar *n* navel, belly button; ~ *kepala* crown; **pusaran** *n* vortex; ~ *air* eddy, whirlpool; ~ *angin* whirlwind; **berpusar** *v* to revolve, whirl

pusat *n* center; ~ *berat* center of gravity; *kantor* ~ head office; **berpusat** ~ *pada* to focus or center on; **memusatkan** *v* to focus; ~ *perhatian* to concentrate

pusing *adj* dizzy; ~ *tujuh keliling* completely confused; ~ *kepala* headache; **memusingkan** ~ *kepala* puzzling

puskésmas *n* clinic, public health center ← **pusat keséhatan masyarakat**

puspa *n, lit* flower

pustaka *n, lit* book; *daftar* ~ list of references; **kepustakaan** *n* bibliography, list of references; literature; **perpustakaan** *n* library; **pustakawan** *n* librarian

putar turn around, rotate; **putaran** *n* round, revolution; ~ *kedua Wimbledon* second round of Wimbledon; **berputar** *v* to rotate, turn; ~ *balik* to turn around, do a U-turn; **memutar** *v* to wind; to rotate; **memutarbalikkan** *v* to reverse, distort; **perputaran** rotation; **memutari** *v* to go around, orbit; **pemutaran** *n* screening; ~ *perdana* premiere, opening night (of a film); **seputar** *adj* around, about

puter *es* ~ homemade ice cream in a cup

putera → **putra**

puteri → **putri**

putih *adj* white; ~ *telur* albumen, egg white; *merah* ~ red and white; *orang kulit* ~ white person, Westerner; **keputihan** *n* thrush, vaginal itching (white discharge); **memutihkan** *v* to whiten, bleach; **pemutih** *n* bleach

puting *n* nipple; ~ *susu* nipple

putra, putera *n, pol* son; ~ *mahkota* crown prince; ~-*putri*

children, sons and daughters; *bumi*~ native or indigenous inhabitant

putri, puteri *n, pol* daughter; ~ *duyung* mermaid; ~ *Indonesia* Miss Indonesia; ~ *malu* a kind of shrub

putu *kue* ~ steamed pandan cake eaten with coconut and palm sugar

putus broken off; ~ *asa* give up hope; ~ *sekolah* leave or drop out of school (prematurely); **keputusan** *n* decision, decree; **memutus** *v* to break; ~ *hubungan* to break or sever contact; **memutuskan** *v* to terminate or break; to decide; **pemutusan** *n* termination, breaking-off; ~ *hubungan kerja (PHK)* to lose your job; **terputus** *adj* cut off; **terputus-putus** *v* to keep cutting out

puyeng *adj* dizzy, confused; with a headache

puyuh *angin* ~ whirlwind

puyuh *burung* ~ quail; *telur* ~ quail egg

puyung hai → **fuyung hai**

Q

qari, qori *n, m* **qariah, qoriah** *n, f* reciter of the Koran

Qatar *n* Qatar; *orang* ~ Qatari

qoriah *n, f* reciter of the Koran

Quran *al-*~ the Koran

R

R. *Raden* Javanese title for male nobility

RA, RAj *Raden Ajeng* Javanese title for unmarried female nobility

RA, RAy *Raden Ayu* Javanese title for married female nobility

raba: rabaan *n* caress, stroke; **meraba** *v* to feel or grope something; **meraba-raba** *v* to feel around or grope (in the dark)

rabat *n* rebate, (bulk) discount

Rabu, Rebo *hari* ~ Wednesday

rabun *adj* blurry; ~ *dekat* long-sighted; ~ *jauh* short-sighted

racik: racikan *n* blend, concoction; prescription; **meracik** *v* to create a mix of; ~ *obat* to mix up medicine

racun *n* poison (not from animals); ~ *tikus* rat poison; **beracun** *adj* poisonous, containing poison; *gas* ~ poison gas; **keracunan** *adj* poisoned; ~ *makanan* food poisoning; **meracuni** *v* to poison

rada *adv, coll* quite, rather

radang *adj* inflamed; ~ *paru-paru* pneumonia; **meradang** *v* to become inflamed; to become angry

radio *n* radio; ~ *Republik Indonesia (RRI)* Indonesian state radio; *acara* ~ radio program; *penyiar* ~ broadcaster, radio announcer; *penyiaran* ~ broadcast(ing)

rafia *tali* ~ plastic twine

raga *n* body; *bina* ~ body-building; *jiwa* ~ body and soul; *olah*~ sport; **peraga** *n* visual aid; **memeragakan** *v* to model, show; **peragawati** *n, f* model; **peragawan** *n, m* (male) model

ragam *n* manner, way; kind; **beragam** *adj* various; **seragam** *n* uniform

ragi *n* yeast

ragos *n, sl* gossip (queen) ← **raja gosip**

ragu doubt, doubtful; **ragu-ragu** *adj* doubtful, unsure; **keragu-(ragu)an** *n* doubt, uncertainty; **meragukan** *v* to doubt something

rahang *n* jaw; *tulang* ~ jawbone

rahasia *n* secret, mystery; ~ *umum* open secret; *membuka* ~ to reveal a secret; **kerahasiaan** *n* secrecy; **merahasiakan** *v* to keep secret

rahim *n* uterus, womb

raib vanished, disappeared

raih: meraih *v* to reach for; to achieve

raja *n* king; ~ *sehari* (bride)groom; ~ *singa* syphilis; ~ *Spanyol* the King of Spain; **kerajaan** *n* kingdom; ~ *Inggris* the United Kingdom

rajaléla: merajaléla *v* to be out of control; to act violently

rajam: merajam *v* to stone (to death)

rajawali *v* kind of hawk

rajin *adj* diligent, hard-working, industrious; ~ *belajar* study hard; **kerajinan** n crafts; ~ *tangan* handicrafts; **perajin** n craftsman, artisan

rajungan n kind of small edible crab

rajut: rajutan n knitting, crochet work; **merajut** v to knit; to crochet

rak n shelf; ~ *buku* bookshelf; ~ *piring* dish rack

raker n working meeting ← **rapat kerja; rakerda** n regional working meeting ← **rapat kerja daérah; rakernas** n national working meeting ← **rapat kerja nasional**

rakét n racquet, racket; ~ *bulu tangkis* badminton racquet

rakit n raft; ~ *penyelamat* life raft; **merakit** v to assemble; **perakitan** n assembly

raksa *air* ~ mercury, quicksilver

raksasa giant

rakus adj greedy; **kerakusan** n greed

rakyat n people; ~ *jelata* common people, proletariat; ~ *miskin* the poor; poor people; *Dewan Perwakilan* ~ *(DPR)* House of Representatives, parliament; **kerakyatan** adj populist; democratic; **merakyat** v to become popular

ralat n correction, errata; **meralat** v to correct a mistake

rama → **romo**

Ramadan Muslim fasting month

ramah adj friendly; ~ *tamah* informal get-together; **keramahan** n friendliness

ramai, ramé adj busy, lively;

crowded; *orang* ~ the public; **ramai-ramai** adv in a group, together; **keramaian** n noise, din; lively atmosphere; **meramaikan** v to liven up, enliven

ramal: ramalan n prediction, prophecy, forecast; ~ *cuaca* weather forecast; **meramal** v to tell fortunes; **meramalkan** v to predict, foretell

Ramayana n Hindu epic, performed in shadow-puppet plays and other traditional arts

rambah: merambah ~ *hutan* to clear away the forest, clear the land

rambut n hair; ~ *lurus* straight hair; ~ *ikal*, ~ *keriting* curly hair; **rambutan** n rambutan, fruit with hairy red skin; **berambut** adj hairy; v to have hair; ~ *coklat* dark-haired, f brunette; ~ *pirang* fair-haired, m blond f blonde

ramé → **ramai**

rames *nasi* ~ rice with a mix of side-dishes

rami n hemp, jute

rampas, merampas v to take by force, rob, plunder; **rampasan** n booty, plunder, loot; **perampasan** n hold-up, robbery

ramping adj slender

rampok, merampok v to rob, hold up; ~ *bank* to rob or hold up a bank; **perampok** n robber; **perampokan** n robbery

rampung adj finished; completed

ramu: ramuan n mixture; **meramu** v to gather, collect

rana: **merana** *v* to suffer, waste away; to live miserably

rancang: **rancangan** *n* plan, design; **merancang** *v* to plan, design; **perancang** *n* designer, planner; ~ *busana* fashion designer

rancu *adj* confused

randa → **janda**

Rangda *n* mythical Balinese witch

rangka *n* skeleton, framework; *dalam* ~ in connection with, in the context of ← **kerangka**

rangkai: **rangkaian** *n* combination, series; **merangkai** *v* to bind together, combine

rangkak: **merangkak** *v* to crawl

rangkap multiple; *tiga* ~ three copies, in triplicate; **merangkap** *v* to hold another position (temporarily)

rangkap → **perangkap**

rangking → **ranking**

rangkul, merangkul *v* to hug, embrace; to get someone involved; **rangkulan** *n* hug, embrace

rangkum, merangkum *v* to carry in your arms; **rangkuman** *n* armful

rangsang: **rangsangan** *n* stimulation; **merangsang** *v* to stimulate, excite; **perangsang** *n* stimulant; *obat* ~ aphrodisiac; **perangsangan** *n* stimulation; *fase* ~, *masa* ~ foreplay

ranjang *n* bed; *pisah* ~ separate (of a couple)

ranjau *n* mine; ~ *darat* land mine; *kapal penyapu* ~ minesweeper

ranjing: **keranjingan** *adj* addicted to, fanatic

ranking, rangking [réngking] *n* process of ranking marks in class

ransel *n* backpack; *turis* ~ backpacker

ransum *n* ration

rantai *n* chain; **merantai** *v* to chain up

rantang *n* stacked set of portable food containers

rantau *n* abroad, across the sea; **merantau** *v* to sail away, seek your fortune, settle overseas; **perantau** *n* settler (in a foreign place); **perantauan** *n* abroad, in another place

ranting *n* twig; small branch (of parties, banks)

ranum *adj* (very) ripe

rapat *adj* close to; tight; **merapat** *v* to move closer

rapat meeting, meet

RAPBD *abbrev Rencana Anggaran Pendapatan dan Belanja Daerah* Regional Income and Expenditure Budget Plan, regional (provincial) budget

RAPBN *abbrev Rencana Anggaran Pendapatan dan Belanja Negara* State Income and Expenditure Budget Plan, national budget

rapi *n* neat, tidy, organized

rapot, rapor *n* (school) report; *membagi* ~ to hand out reports

rapuh *adj* brittle, weak

ras *n* breed; pure-bred; *anjing* ~ pure-bred dog

rasa feel, feeling; sense; taste; ~*nya* it appears, it seems; ~ *malu* shame; ~ *pahit* bitterness, bitter taste; *saya* ~ I think, I feel; **kerasan** *coll* feel at home; **merasa** *v* to think, feel; **merasakan** *v* to feel something; **perasa** *n* sensitive person; **perasaan** *n* feeling; **terasa** *v* to be felt

rasé *n* civet cat

rasi *n* constellation; **serasi** *adj* suited, compatible; **keserasian** *n* compatibility, suitability

rasuk: merasuk *v* to enter into, possess; **kerasukan** *adj* possessed

rasul *n* prophet, messenger of God, apostle

rata *adj* flat, even, level; **rata-rata** *adv* equally; on average; **meratakan** *v* to level, flatten

ratap, meratap *v* to lament, wail; **ratapan** *n* lamentation

rata-rata *adv* equally; on average ← **rata**

ratib: ratiban *n* prayer recitation

ratu *n* queen; ~ *kecantikan* beauty queen

ratus *dua* ~ two hundred; **beratus-ratus** *adj* hundreds of; **seratus** *adj* one hundred, a hundred

raung: meraung *v* to roar

raup: meraup *v* to scoop up in your hands

raut ~ *muka* (facial) expression, look on your face; **rautan** *n* (pencil) sharpener

rawa *n* swamp, marsh

rawan *adj* vulnerable, troubled, unsafe

rawat *juru* ~ nurse; **merawat** *v* to nurse, care for; to maintain, look after; **perawat** *n* nurse, sister; **perawatan** treatment; maintenance, upkeep; *biaya* ~ cost of treatment, cost of upkeep

rawit *cabe* ~ small hot red chilli; *kecil-kecil cabe* ~ small but fiery

rawon *n* black meat soup from East Java

raya *adj* great, greater; *jalan* ~ highway, main road; *hari* ~ holiday, feast day; *Indonesia* ~ the national anthem; *Inggris* ~ Great Britain; *kaya* ~ wealthy; **merayakan** *v* to celebrate; **perayaan** *n* celebration

rayap *n* termite, white ant; *kena* ~*, dimakan* ~ eaten by termites; **merayap** *v* to crawl, creep

rayon *n* district, precinct, administrative unit

rayu: rayuan *n* flattery; ~ *gombal* sweet talk; **merayu** *v* to tempt, flatter, seduce

razia *n* raid, spot-check

RCTI *abbrev Rajawali Citra Televisi Indonesia* RCTI, a privately-owned television network

réaksi *n* reaction; ~ *berantai* chain reaction; ~ *kimia* chemical reaction; **beréaksi** *v* to react

réalitas *n* reality

rebab *n* two-stringed musical instrument

rebah, merebah v to fall down, collapse

rebana n tambourine

Rebo → Rabu

réboisasi n reforestation; meréboisasi v to reforest, replant trees

rebung n cooked young bamboo shoot

rebus v boil, boiled; mi ~ boiled noodles (with soup); merebus v to boil in water

rebut, merebut v to snatch, capture; ~ kembali to recapture; rebutan n something sought after by many people; v fighting for something; berebut v to fight for; berebutan v to fight each other for; merebutkan v to snatch something; memperebutkan v to seize, take by force

récéh, récéhan uang ~ small change

red. abbrev redaksi editor, (ed)

reda, mereda v to subside, abate; meredakan v to soothe; to calm something down

redaksi n editors, editorial staff; redaktur n editor

redam adj faint, muffled; meredamkan v to muffle or stifle; peredam n device to muffle or reduce noise

redup dim, go out

référénsi n reference; surat ~ reference (for a job)

réformasi n reform (esp after 1998); réformis adj reformist, pro-reform

regu n group, team

reguk: mereguk v to gulp down, take a shot

rejeki, rezeki, rizki n fortune, luck; livelihood, living; ~ nomplok windfall; mengais ~ to scrape a living

rekam: rekaman n recording; ~ video video recording; dapur ~ recording studio; merekam v to record

rekan n colleague, partner, associate; rekanan n regular service provider

rekat: perekat n glue, adhesive

rékayasa n engineering; ~ sosial social engineering; merékayasa v to engineer

rékening n (bank) account; ~ tabungan savings account

réklamasi n reclamation; tanah ~ reclaimed land

réklame n advertisement, banner

rékoméndasi n recommendation; merékoméndasikan v to recommend

rékonstruksi n reconstruction (of an incident); merékonstruksi v to reconstruct

rékor n record; ~ dunia world record

rékréasi n recreation, relaxing, fun

rekrut recruit; merekrut v to recruit

réktor n vice-chancellor, rector; réktorat n vice-chancellor's office

rél n rail; ~ kereta api railway line, railroad, train tracks

réla, réd(h)a, ridha, ridho willing; *secara sukarela ~* voluntarily; *relawan* volunteer; **merélakan** *v* to approve, agree to

rélaks → **rilék, riléks**

rélasi *n* customer, client

rélatif *adj* relative

réli *n* (vehicle) rally; **peréli** *n* rally driver

rém *n* brake; *~ tangan* hand brake; **mengerém** *v* to brake

remah *n* crumb

remaja *n* teen, adolescent, young single person, youth; *masa ~* youth; puberty; **meremajakan** *v* to revitalize, refurbish, update; **peremajaan** *n* renewal, revitalization

remang: remang-remang *n* shadows, darkness

remas, meremas *v* to press, squeeze, knead

rématik *n* rheumatism

rembes: rembesan *n* seepage, oozing liquid; **merembes** *v* to seep in, leak, ooze

rembuk, rembug: berembuk *v* to confer, discuss

rembulan *n, lit* moon ← **bulan**

réméh *adj* small, unimportant, trifling; **meréméhkan** *v* to belittle, treat as unimportant

rempah *n* spice; **rempah-rempah** *n* spices

rempak: serempak *adj* simultaneous, in unison

rempéyék, péyék *n* peanut crisps

renang swimming; *baju ~, pakaian ~* swimming costume, swimsuit; *kolam ~* swimming pool; **berenang** *v* to swim; **perenang** *n* swimmer

rencana *n* plan, program, draft; *~ lima tahun (Repelita)* five-year plan (under Suharto); *~ Undang-Undang (RUU)* draft act; **berencana** *v* to plan; *Keluarga ~ (KB)* family planning; **merencanakan** *v* to plan; **perencanaan** *n* planning; **terencana** *adj* planned

réncong *n* Acehnese dagger

rénda *n* lace; **berénda** *adj* lacy, lace; **merénda** *v* to crochet

rendah *adj* low, humble; *~ hati* humble; **kerendahan** *n* lowness; *~ hati* humility; **merendahkan** *v* to lower; to humiliate; **serendah-rendahnya** *adv* as low as possible; **terendah** *adj* lowest

rendam soak; *mandi ~* soak in a bath-tub; **berendam** *v* to soak; **merendam** *v* to soak something; **terendam** *adj* inundated, flooded, soaked

rendang *n* meat cooked in coconut milk

réngék: réngékan *n* whine, whimper; **meréngék** *v* to whimper, whine

renggang *adj* distant, apart; **kerenggangan** *n* rift, gulf, distance

renggut: merenggut *v* to snatch, tug

réngking → **ranking**

rengut, rungut: merengut *v* to grumble

rénovasi renovation; me-rénovasi *v* to renovate

renta *adj* worn; *tua* ~ worn with age, decrepit

rentak: serentak *adj* all at once, simultaneous, at the same time

rentan *adj* susceptible

rentang: rentangan *n* stretch, span; merentang *v* to span, stretch over; merentangkan *v* to extend, stretch out

réntét: réntétan *n* string, series

renung: renungan *n* reflection, musing, contemplation; merenung *v* to daydream; merenungi, merenungkan *v* to think about, reflect on, muse

renyah *adj* crisp, crispy; kere-nyahan *n* crispness, crispiness

réog *n* trance dance, most famously in Ponorogo, East Java

Rep. *Republik* Republic

réparasi *n* repair(s); meréparasi *v* to repair ← baik

répatriasi *n* repatriation

Repelita *n, arch* Five-Year Plan (under Suharto) ← Rencana Pembangunan Lima Tahun

réportase *n* reporting

répot very busy; bothered; répot-répot *v* to go to great trouble; merépotkan *v* to make someone busy or go to some trouble

réproduksi, répro *n* (art) repro-duction

républik *n* republic; ~ *Dominika* the Dominican Republic; ~

Indonesia the Republic of Indonesia

reruntuhan, runtuhan *n* ruins ← runtuh

resah *adj* restless; keresahan *n* restlessness, nervous energy; meresahkan *adj* disturbing, worrying

resap: resapan *n* absorption; meresap *v* to be absorbed; to penetrate, seep into

résé → risi

résénsi, risénsi *n* review; ~ *buku* book review

resép *n* recipe; prescription; meresépkan *v* to write a pre-scription for a drug

resépsi *n* reception; *meja* ~ reception desk; ~ *perkawinan*, ~ *pernikahan* wedding recep-tion; resépsionis *n* receptionist

resi *n* receipt; baggage check label

resérse *n* detective, forensic

résidivis *n* repeat offender

resik *adj* clean; *geladi* ~ dress-rehearsal

résimén *n* regiment

resmi *adj* official, formal; *kun-jungan* ~ state visit; *pakaian* ~ formal dress; *secara* ~ official-ly; meresmikan *v* to formal-ize, make official; peresmian *n* formal opening, inauguration

résolusi *n* resolution

resort *polisi* ~ *(polres)* local police, county police

réspon, réspons respond, response; réspondan *n* respondent

résto *n* up-market restaurant; **réstoran** *n* restaurant

réstorasi *gerbong ~, kereta ~* restaurant car

réstorasi *n* restoration; **meréstorasi** *v* to restore

restu *n* blessing; *doa ~* prayers and blessings; **merestui** *v* to agree to, give your blessing to

retak *adj* cracked; **retakan, keretakan** *n* crack, fissure; **meretak** *v* to crack

retrét *n, Chr* retreat, period of religious contemplation

rétribusi *n* fee to use a public facility; *uang ~* fee paid

rétur, retour *adj* return; *loket ~* return ticket counter

réuni *n* (school) reunion

révolusi *n* revolution; *zaman ~* the Indonesian Revolution, 1945-9; **révolusionér** *adj* revolutionary

réwél *adj* fussy, troublesome, difficult

rezeki, rizki → **rejeki**

RI *abbrev Republik Indonesia* Republic of Indonesia

ria *adj* merry, joyous, cheerful; *bergembira ~* to be happy, overjoyed

riak *n* ripples of water; **beriak, meriak** *v* to ripple

riak *n* phlegm

riam *n* (river) rapids

riang *adj* cheerful; **periang** *n* cheerful person

riang → **meriang**

rias *kamar ~* dressing room; *meja ~* dressing table; *tukang ~*

make-up artist; **riasan** *n* make-up; **perias** *n* make-up artist

riba, ribaan, haribaan *n* lap

riba *n* high interest on a loan, usury

ribu *n* thousand; *sepuluh ~* ten thousand; **beribu(-ribu)** *adj* thousands of; **seribu** *adj* one thousand, a thousand; *Pulau ~* the Thousand Islands

ribut noise; noisy; *angin ~* storm; **keributan** *n* disturbance; loud noise; **meributkan** *v* to make a fuss about

rica: *rica-rica adj* spicy Menadonese food; *ikan ~* spicy Menadonese-style fish

ricuh *adj* chaotic, out of control; **kericuhan** *n* chaos

rijstafel [réstafel] *n* colonial-style dinner of rice with small trays of side-dishes

rilék, riléks, rélaks relax, relaxed

rilis release (of an album or film); **merilis** *v* to release, put out

rim *n* ream of paper

rim *n* cream, skim (of milk) ← **kepala susu**

rimba *n* jungle, forest; *~ belantara, ~ raya* deep jungle; *tidak tentu ~nya* disappeared, lost without a trace

rinci detail; **rincian** *n* details; **merinci** *v* to specify, detail; **perincian** *n* details, detailed explanation

rindang *adj* leafy, shady

rinding: merinding *v* to have goose-bumps or an eerie feeling, be spooked

rindu longing; ~ **akan**, ~ **pada** long for, miss; **benci tapi** ~ love-hate relationship; **kerinduan** *n* longing, craving; **merindukan** *v* to miss, long for

ring *n* (boxing) ring

ringan *adj* light, easy; ~ **tangan** light-fingered; prone to violence; *kredit* ~ easy credit; *luka* ~ slight wound; **meringankan** *v* to ease, relieve, make easier

ringgit *n* ringgit, Malaysian currency (100 cents)

ringkas *adj* brief, short, concise; **ringkasan** *n* summary, synopsis

ringkus: meringkus *v* to catch (esp by the arm or leg), take into custody

rintang: rintangan *n* obstacle; barricade

rintih moan; **rintihan** *n* moan, groan; **merintih** *v* to moan or groan

rintik: rintik-rintik *hujan* ~ drizzle, light rain

rintis: merintis *v* to pioneer; **perintis** *n* pioneer

RIS *abbrev Republik Indonesia Serikat* United Republic of Indonesia, which existed from 1949–50

risalah, risalat *n* pamphlet, brochure, circular

risau *adj* uneasy, anxious; **kerisauan** *n* worry, anxiety; **merisaukan** *v* to worry about

risénsi → **résénsi**

risét *n* research; **riset dan teknologi (ristek)** research and technology; *mengadakan* ~ to do research

risih, risi, résé feel uncomfortable; **merisihkan** *v* to disturb, make you feel uncomfortable

risik: berisik *adj* noisy, loud; *v* to rustle

risiko *n* risk; **berisiko** *adj* risky

riskan *adj* risky

risték *n* research and technology ← **risét dan téknologi**

ritsléting *n* zip, zipper; ~ *celana* fly

riuh *n* noise, uproar

riwayat *n* story, tale; ~ *hidup* biography; curriculum vitae, CV

RM *abbrev Rumah Makan* restaurant, roadhouse

RMS *abbrev Republik Maluku Selatan* Republic of the South Moluccas/South Maluku, a separatist movement

robah, rubah → **ubah**

robék *adj* torn (of cloth), holey; *tangan* ~ grazed or cut arm; **merobék** *v* to tear up, shred

roboh, rubuh collapse; *pohon* ~ tree that has been blown down; **kerobohan** *n* collapse; **merobohkan** *v* to knock down, demolish

roda *n* wheel; ~ *gigi* cog; ~ *stir* steering wheel; *kendaraan* ~ *dua* two-wheeled vehicle; *kursi* ~ wheelchair; **beroda** *adj* wheeled

rodi *kerja* ~ forced labor

rogoh: merogoh *v* to grope around, search for (inside something else)

roh *n* spirit, ghost; ~ *Kudus* Holy Ghost; **rohani** *adj* spiritual, religious; *lagu* ~ *Chr* gospel or religious song

rok *n* skirt; dress; ~ *mini* miniskirt; ~ *pensil* straight skirt

rokok *n* cigarette; ~ *kretek* clove cigarette; *mengisap* ~ to smoke a cigarette; *uang* ~ tip; **merokok** *v* to smoke; *dilarang* ~ no smoking

rom, room → **rum**

Roma *n* Rome

roma *bulu* ~ body hair, hair on the back of your neck

roman *n* appearance, looks

roman *n* novel

Romania, Rumania *n* Romania, Rumania; *bahasa* ~, *orang* ~ Romanian, Rumanian

romansa *n* romance; **romantik** *adj* romantic

Romawi, Rumawi *adj* Roman; *bangsa* ~ the Romans; *huruf* ~ Roman letters, Latin alphabet; *kekaisaran* ~ *kuno* ancient Rome, the Roman Empire; *tiga* ~ III

rombak: merombak *v* to pull down, demolish; to reorganize; **perombakan** *n* reorganization

rombong: rombongan *n* group, party

romo, Romo *n, pron, Cath* (Catholic) priest, Father

rompak: merompak *v* to commit piracy; **perompak** *n* pirate; **perompakan** *n* piracy

rompi *n* waistcoat, vest

romusa, romusya *n* forced laborer under the Japanese occupation

rona *n* color, shade; **perona** ~ *mata* eyeshadow; ~ *pipi* rouge

ronda patrol; ~ *malam* night watch, night patrol

ronde *n* round (in sport)

rondé *wedang* ~ warm Javanese beverage

rongga *n* cavity, hollow, hole

ronggéng *n, f* dancer

rongkong → **kerongkongan**

rongrong: merongrong *v* to gnaw at, undermine

ronsen → **rontgen**

ronta: meronta(-ronta) *v* to struggle, squirm to get loose

rontak → **berontak**

rontgen [ronsen], **ronsen** *n* x-ray; *hasil* ~ x-ray (photograph); **dironsen** *v* to be x-rayed

rontok fall out, shed; *gigi* ~ tooth that has fallen out; *musim* ~ autumn, fall; **kerontokan** *n* shedding; ~ *rambut* hair loss

room, rom → **rum**

ros *bunga* ~ rose

rosario *n, Cath* rosary

rosot: merosot *v* to fall down, descend, plummet; *celananya* ~ his pants fell down; **kemerosotan** *n* descent, deterioration; **perosotan** *n* (children's) slide

rotan *n* rattan; *kursi* ~ wicker chair

roti *n* bread, bun; ~ *gandum* (brown or wholemeal) bread; ~ *kismis* currant bun; ~ *pang-*

gang toast; *remah* ~ bread
crumbs; *tempat* ~ bread basket,
bread bin; *toko* ~ bakery;
tukang ~ baker; bread-seller

royal *adj* extravagant, wasteful
(with money)

royong *gotong* ~ mutual
assistance

Rp. rupiah

RRC *abbrev Republik Rakyat
Cina* People's Republic of China

RRI *abbrev Radio Republik
Indonesia* Indonesian state
radio

RRT *abbrev Republik Rakyat
Tiongkok* People's Republic of
China

RS *abbrev rumah sakit* hospital

RSAB *abbrev Rumah Sakit
Anak dan Bunda* Mothers' and
Children's Hospital

RSAD *abbrev Rumah Sakit
Angkatan Darat* army hospital

RSAL *abbrev Rumah Sakit
Angkatan Laut* navy hospital

RSAU *abbrev Rumah Sakit
Angkatan Udara* air force
hospital

RSI *abbrev Rumah Sakit Islam*
Islamic hospital

RSJ *abbrev Rumah Sakit Jiwa*
mental hospital

RSU *abbrev Rumah Sakit
Umum* public hospital

RT/RW *abbrev Rukun Tetangga/
Rukun Warga* neighborhood
association/citizens' association: smallest administrative
unit, comprising one or more
neighborhood blocks

ruam *n* rash; ~ *popok* nappy
rash

ruang *n* space, room; ~ *angkasa*
outer space; ~ *kelas* classroom;
~ *makan* dining room; ~ *periksa*
consultation room; ~ *tunggu*
waiting room; **ruangan** *n*
room; hall; *sedang keluar* ~
not in the office

ruas *n* space between joints; ~
jari knucklebone, phalanx; ~
tulang punggung vertebrae

rubah *n* fox

rubrik *n* column, rubric

rubuh collapse, fall down ← **roboh**

rudal *n* guided missile ← **peluru
kendali**

rugi loss, lose out; *ganti* ~
compensation; *untung* ~ gains
and losses, pros and cons;
kerugian *n* loss; damage;
merugikan *v* to hurt, harm,
injure

ruh → **roh**

ruilslag [*rélslag*] *n* land swap;
diruilslag *v* to be swapped,
exchanged

rujak *n* fruit salad with spicy
sauce; ~ *cingur* fruit salad
with beef snout, specialty of
Surabaya

ruji *n* (bicycle) spoke; grill

rujuk reconciliation (after
separation)

rujuk: rujukan *n* reference;
merujuk *v* to refer to, use as a
source

rukan *n* office with a dwelling
upstairs, shophouse ← **rumah
kantor**

ruko *n* shophouse ← **rumah toko**

rukun *adj* harmonious; ~ *warga (RW)* citizens' association; ~ *tetangga (RT)* neighborhood association; *hidup* ~ live in harmony

rukun *n* pillar, principle; *lima* ~ *Islam* five pillars of Islam

rum, rhum, rom, room *n* cream

Rum → **Roma**

rumah *n* house; ~ *gadai* pawnshop; ~ *hantu* haunted house; ~ *jabatan* official residence; ~ *keong* snail's shell; ~ *lelang* auction house; ~ *makan* restaurant; ~ *panjang* (Dayak) longhouse; ~ *sakit* hospital; ~ *sakit jiwa* mental hospital, asylum; ~ *sewa* rented house; *di* ~ at home; *isi* ~ household, people in a house; *nyonya* ~ hostess, mistress; *perabot* ~ furniture; *tuan* ~ host, master; ~ *tangga* household, family; **berumah-tangga** *adj* married; **perumah-tanggaan** *n* household affairs; **merumahkan** *v* to lay off (from work); **perumahan** *n* housing (complex); **rumah-rumahan** dolls' house

Rumania, Romania *n* Rumania, Romania; *bahasa* ~, *orang* ~ Rumanian, Romanian

Rumawi → **Romawi**

rumbai *n* tassel

rumbia *n* sago palm; sago palm thatch; *beratap* ~ to have a thatched roof

rumpi: rumpian *n* chat, chatter, gossip; **ngerumpi** *v, sl* to (get together for a) chat or gossip

rumpun *n* clump, cluster; **serumpun** *adj* related, of one family; *bahasa* ~ languages related to Indonesian (such as Malagasy and Tagalog)

rumput *n* grass, lawn; ~ *kering* hay; *hewan pemakan* ~ ruminant

rumus *n* formula; **merumuskan** *v* to formulate; **perumusan** *n* formulation

runcing *adj* sharp, pointed; *bambu* ~ bamboo spear; **meruncing** *v* to become critical or sharp

runding: berunding *v* to discuss; **merundingkan** *v* to discuss something, deliberate over; **perundingan** *n* discussion; *meja* ~ discussion table

rundung: dirundung ~ *malang* to be cursed with or to suffer bad luck

rungut, rengut: merungut *v* to grumble, complain

runtai: meruntai *v* to hang loosely ← **untai**

runtuh fall down, collapse; **runtuhan, reruntuhan** *n* ruins; **meruntuhkan** *v* to overthrow, destroy

runtun: beruntun *adj* in a chain; *tabrakan* ~ pile-up

runyam be in difficulties, flounder

rupa shape, appearance, look; *Si Cantik dan si Buruk* ~ Beauty and the Beast; ~*nya* it seems, appears; **rupa-rupa** *adj* all kinds of; **berupa** *adj* in the shape or form of; **merupakan** *v* to be; to form, constitute; **perupa** *n* sculptor; **rupawan** good-looking (person); **serupa** *adj* similar

rupiah *n* rupiah, Indonesian currency

rusa *n* deer; ~ *betina* doe; ~ *jantan* buck; *sate* ~ deer satay

rusak *adj* broken, damaged, destroyed, spoilt; ~ *parah* badly damaged; **kerusakan** *n* damage; **merusak** *v* to spoil, damage; **merusakkan** *v* to destroy, break

Rusia *n* Russia; *bahasa* ~, *orang* ~ Russian

rusuh restless, disturbed, riotous; **kerusuhan** *n* riot, disturbance

rusuk *n* flank, side; *tulang* ~ rib

rusun *n* (government) flat, apartment, high-rise housing ← **rumah susun**

rutan *n* lock-up, detention center ← **rumah tahanan**

rute *n* route

rutin *adj* routine; **rutinitas** *n* routineness, boredom

ruwat purify, exorcise, clean; **ruwatan** *n* purification or exorcism ritual

ruwet *adj* complicated; **keruwetan** *n* complexity

RW *abbrev* er-we, rintek wuuk "fine hair" = (euph) dog meat, in North Sulawesi

Rwanda *n* Rwanda; *orang* ~ Rwandan

S

saat *n* moment, time; ~ *ini* at this moment

saban *adj* every, each; ~ *hari* every day

sabana *n* savannah

sabar *adj* patient; *tidak* ~ impatient; **bersabar** *v* to be patient; **kesabaran** *n* patience; *batas* ~ limit of your patience

sabda *n, pol* word; ~ *Tuhan* the word of God; **bersabda** *v* to say or speak; *Sri Sultan* ~ the Sultan spoke

sabet: menyabet *v* to snatch or grab; to whip

sabit *n* sickle; *bulan* ~ crescent moon; **menyabit** *v* to cut with a sickle

sablon *n* screen-printed cloth banner; screen-printing; **mensablon** *v* to screen-print

sabot: mensabotase, menyabot *v* to sabotage; **penyabot** *n* saboteur; **sabotase** *n* sabotage

Sabtu *hari* ~ Saturday

sabu-sabu → **shabu-shabu**

sabuk *n* belt, sash; ~ *hitam* black belt (in martial arts); ~ *pengaman* safety belt, seat beat

sabun *n* soap; ~ *colek* cream soap for scrubbing clothes; ~ *cuci piring* dishwashing liquid; *opera* ~ soap opera; **bersabun** *adj* soapy; **menyabuni** *v* to soap or lather

sabung ~ *ayam* cock fighting

sabut ~ *kelapa* coconut fiber

sadap: sadapan *n* something tapped; **menyadap** *v* to tap (rubber, telephones); **penyadap** *n* tapper; **penyadapan** *n* tapping

sadaqah, sadaqoh → **sedekah**

sadar conscious, aware; *tidak* ~ unconscious; **kesadaran** *n* consciousness, awareness; **menyadari** *v* to realize, be aware of; **menyadarkan** *v* to make someone realize, raise someone's awareness

sadel *n* saddle (on a bicycle)

sadis *adj* sadistic, cruel

sado *n* two-wheeled horse carriage

sadur, saduran *n* plating, coating; ~ *emas* gold-plated, gilt; **menyadur** *v* to gild

sadur: saduran *n* adaptation, rewrite; **menyadur** *v* to rewrite, adapt

safari *n* safari, tour; *baju* ~ safari suit

safir *batu* ~ sapphire

sagu *n* sago; *tepung* ~ sago flour

sah *adj* legal, legitimate, valid; *anak* ~ legitimate child; *tidak* ~ illegal, illegitimate; **mengesahkan** *v* to validate, ratify, legitimize, legalize; **disahkan** *v* to be legalized; **pengesahan** *n* validation, legalization

sahabat *n* friend; ~ *karib* close friend; ~ *pena* pen friend, penpal; ~ *sejati* real or true friend; **bersahabat** *adj* to be friends; **persahabatan** *n* friendship; *pertandingan* ~ friendly (match)

sahaja, bersahaja *adj* simple, natural; **kesahajaan** *n* simplicity ← **saja**

saham *n* share; *main* ~ play the share market

sahaya → **saya**

sahid → **syahid**

sahur, saur *n, Isl* meal before dawn during fasting month; **nyahur** *v, sl* to eat at this hour

sahut, menyahut *v* to answer, reply, respond

saing compete; **saingan** *n* competitor, the competition; **bersaing** *v* to compete; *harga* ~ competitive price; **menyaingi** *v* to compete with; **persaingan** *n* competition; ~ *ketat* intense competition

sains *n* science → **ilmu pengetahuan alam, IPA**

saja, aja *adv* only, just; *-ever*; *itu* ~ just that; *kapan* ~ whenever; *siapa* ~ whoever ← **sahaja**

sajadah, sejadah *n, Isl* prayer mat or rug

sajak *n* rhyme; poem

saji serve; *siap* ~ ready to serve, ready to eat; **sajian** *n* dish; offering; **sesajén** *n* ritual offering; **menyajikan** *v* to serve, present, offer; **penyajian** *n* presentation

Saka *Tahun* ~ Balinese calendar

sakelar *n* (electric) switch

sakinah *adj, Isl* peaceful, prosperous; *keluarga* ~ happy family

saking *conj, coll* all because of, due to, as a result of; ~ *marahnya* thanks to his anger

sakit sick, ill; pain, ache; ~ *gigi* toothache; ~ *hati* offended, hurt; upset; ~ *kepala* headache; ~ *keras* gravely ill; ~ *perut* stomach ache, upset stomach; *cuti* ~ sick leave; *rumah* ~ hospital; **sakit-sakitan** often ill, frequently unwell; **kesakitan** *adj* in pain; **menyakiti** *v* to hurt, treat badly; **menyakitkan** *adj* painful; **penyakit** *n* disease, illness, complaint; ~ *anjing gila* rabies; ~ *jiwa* mental problem; ~ *gula* diabetes; ~ *menular seksual (PMS)* sexually transmitted disease (STD), venereal disease

sakral *adj* holy, sacred; **kesakralan** *n* holy or sacred state

saksama → **seksama**

saksi witness; ~ *mata* eyewitness; **bersaksi** *v* to testify; **kesaksian** *n* evidence, testimony; *memberi* ~ to give evidence, bear witness; **menyaksikan** *v* to witness

saksofon *n* saxophone; **saksofonis** *n* saxophonist

sakti *adj* magically or supernaturally powerful; **kesaktian** *n* magic power

saku *n* pocket; *uang* ~ pocket money

Sala → **Solo**

salada → **selada**

salah *adj* wrong, mistaken, faulty; ~ *alamat* wrong address, wrong person; ~ *cetak* misprint; ~ *faham* misunderstanding; ~ *satu* one of; ~ *sambung* wrong number; ~ *urat* strained muscle; *apa ~nya* what's wrong; *kalau tidak* ~ if I'm not mistaken; **bersalah** *adj* guilty; **kesalahan** *n* mistake; **menyalahi** *v* to blame someone; **menyalahkan, mempersalahkan** *v* to blame

salak *buah* ~ fruit with a hard brown skin like a snake, snakefruit

salam peace; ~ *alaikum Isl* peace be upon you; *wa alaikum* ~ and upon you be peace (the response); ~ *hormat* respectfully yours, yours sincerely; ~ *saya* best wishes, regards; *kirim* ~ say hello, send best wishes to; **salaman** *v, coll* to say hello, greet; **bersalam-salaman** *v, pl* to shake hands with others; **menyalami** *v* to greet

salam *daun* ~ bay leaf

salat → **sholat**

salat → **selada**

saldo *n* balance; ~ *terakhir* current balance

saléh → **soléh**

salep *n* ointment, cream

salib *n* cross; **menyalib** *v* to crucify

salin copy, duplicate; *baju* ~ change of clothes, spare clothes; **salinan** *n* copy; **bersalin** *v* to give birth; *rumah sakit* ~ maternity hospital; **menyalin** *v* to copy; **persalinan** *n* childbirth

saling *pron* each other, mutual; ~ *mencintai* to love each other

salip, menyalip *v* overtake, slip past

salju *n* snow; *main* ~ play in the snow; *manusia* ~ snowman; *musim* ~ snow season, winter; *putri* ~ kind of biscuit with white icing sugar; **bersalju** *adj* snowy, snow-covered

salmon *(ikan)* ~ salmon

salon *n* beauty salon, hairdresser's

salto *n* somersault

salur: saluran *n* channel; ~ *pernafasan* windpipe, esophagus; *pipa* ~ pipeline; **menyalurkan** *v* to channel; **penyaluran** *n* channelling

salut *v, coll* to admire, salute

sama *adj, adv* same, both; ~ *sekali neg* completely; ~ *tingginya* of equal height, the same height (as each other); ~ *rata* equal, level; **menyamaratakan** *v* to treat equally; **sama-sama** you're welcome, think nothing of it (said in response to *terima kasih*); *adv* both, equally; **bersama** *adv* together; jointly; *kepentingan* ~ common interest; **menyamai** *v* to resemble, be like; **menyamakan** *v* to equate, consider the same; **persamaan** *n* similarity, likeness, resemblance; equation; **sesama** *adj* fellow, another; ~ *manusia* fellow human being

samar *adj* disguised, hidden; **samaran** *n* disguise, alias; *nama* ~ pseudonym, alias; **menyamar** *v* to be in disguise; **menyamarkan** ~ *diri* to disguise yourself

sama-sama you're welcome, think nothing of it (said in response to *terima kasih*; *adv* both, equally) ← **sama**

sambal, sambel *n* chilli sauce; ~ *ulek* fresh(ly ground) chilli sauce

sambar: sambaran *n* strike; ~ *petir* lightning bolt; **menyambar** *v* to pounce on, strike; *disambar petir* to be struck by lightning

sambel → **sambal**

sambil *v, aux* while, at the same time; ~ *lalu* in passing

sambung connect; *salah* ~ wrong number; **sambung-menyambung** *adj* continuously; **sambungan** *n* connection; ~ *langsung internasional (SLI)* international direct dialling (IDD); ~ *langsung jarak jauh (SLJJ)* long-distance direct dialling; **bersinambung** *adj* continuous; **kesinambungan** *n* continuity; **berkesinambungan** *adj* sustained, continuous; *perkembangan yang* ~ sustainable development; **bersambung** *adj* in parts; to be continued; *cerita* ~ *(cerber)* serial; **menyambung** *v* to join, continue; **menyambungkan** *v* to connect to (something else); **tersambung** *adj* connected

sambut welcome; **sambutan** *n* reception, welcome; **bersambut** *gayung* ~ receive a response; **menyambut** *v* to welcome or receive; **penyambutan** *n* welcoming, welcome ceremony

samenléven *v* to live together (outside marriage) → **kumpul kebo**

Samoa *n* Samoa; ~ *Barat* Western Samoa; *bahasa* ~, *orang* ~ Samoan

sampah *n* rubbish, garbage, trash, waste; *tempat* ~ rubbish bin, garbage can, trashcan; *tukang* ~ garbage man, garbage collector

sampai *conj* **sampé** *coll* arrive, reach; until; ~ *dengan* to, until, up to the point of, as far as; ~ *jumpa*, ~ *nanti* see you later; *kasih tak* ~ love that never was; **kesampaian** *adj* achieved, reached, realized; **menyampaikan** *v* to deliver, hand over, pass on; **penyampaian** *n* handing over, presentation

sampan *n* type of boat, sampan

sampanye *n* champagne

sampar *n* plague, pest

samper: menyamper *v, sl* to greet, acknowledge, say hello

sampéyan *pron, Jav, pol* you

samping *n* side; *dari* ~ *ke* ~ from side to side; *di* ~ next to, beside(s); **sampingan** *n* side-job, extra work; **bersampingan** *adj* next to each other; **menyampingi** *v* to escort, accompany, flank

sampo *n* shampoo; ~ *anti-ketombe* anti-dandruff shampoo

sampul *n* cover, folder, envelope; *gadis* ~ cover girl; **bersampul** *adj* in an envelope or folder; *diberi* ~ to be given a protective jacket or wrapped in plastic (for a book)

samudera, samudra *n* ocean; ~ *Atlantik* Atlantic Ocean; ~ *Hindia*, ~ *Indonesia* Indian Ocean

samun: menyamun *v* to rob, plunder; **penyamun** *n* robber, bandit

sana *adv* yonder, over there (far from speaker and listener); *di* ~ over there (far from both speaker and listener); ~-*sini* here and there

sanak ~ *saudara* relatives, family

sanatorium *n* sanatorium (esp for respiratory illnesses)

sanca *ular* ~ python

sandal *n* sandals (open-toed shoes); ~ *jepit* thongs, flip flops

sandang *n* clothing; ~ *pangan* food and clothing

sandar: sandaran *n* support, prop; ~ *kursi* chair back; **bersandar, menyandar** *v* to lean

sandera *n* hostage; **menyandera** *v* to take hostage; **penyandera** *n* hostage-taker; **penyanderaan** *n* taking of hostages

sandi *n* code, cipher; ~ *rahasia*, *nomor* ~ secret code

sanding: bersanding *v* to stand or sit next to; **bersandingan** *v* to stand or sit next to each other

sandiwara *n* drama, play; **bersandiwara** *v* to pretend

sandung: sandungan *batu* ~ stumbling block; **kesandung** *adj, coll* **tersandung** *adj* to stumble on, trip (up) on

sang *pref, pol* used to denote respect; ~ *Merah Putih* the Red and White (Indonesian flag); ~ *guru* respected teacher

sanga → **songo**

sangat *adv* very, extremely; *amat* ~ terribly

sangga: menyangga *v* to hold up, support

sanggah: menyanggah *v* to object to, oppose, protest

sanggama, senggama *n* sexual relations; **bersanggama** *v* to have sex

sanggar *n* workshop, studio

sanggul *n* bun (worn with women's national costume); **sanggulan** *v, coll* **bersanggul** *v* to wear a bun; **disanggul** *v* to have your hair put into a bun

sanggup *v, aux* to be able to, to be capable of; **kesanggupan** *n* ability

sangka *v* to guess, suspect; **sangkaan** *n* suspicion; **bersangka** *v* to suspect or think; ~ *buruk* to think the worst; **menyangka** *v* to suspect, suppose, presume; *tidak* ~ never thought; **tersangka** *n (yang)* ~ suspect; *tak* ~ unexpected

sangkal, menyangkal *v* to deny; **penyangkalan** *n* denial

sangkar *n* cage

sangkut ~ *paut* connection, link; **bersangkutan** *adj* concerned, involved; *yang* ~ *(ybs)* person concerned or involved; **menyangkut** *v* to involve, concern; *coll* to get

caught, snagged; *conj* about; **tersangkut** *adj* involved; caught, snagged

sangsi, sanksi *n* doubt; **mensangsikan** *v* to doubt

sanjung: menyanjung *v* to flatter; **tersanjung** *adj* flattered

sanksi *n* disciplinary action, sanction

Sansekerta, Sanskerta *bahasa* ~ Sanskrit

santa *tit, f, Chr* Saint; ~ *Ursula* Saint (St) Ursula; **santo** *tit, m, Chr* Saint; ~ *Petrus* St Peter

santai *adj* relaxed, easy-going, informal; **bersantai** *v* to relax, take it easy

santan *n* coconut milk (used in cooking); **bersantan** *adj* containing coconut milk

santap, bersantap *v, pol* to eat, partake of; ~ *pagi* breakfast; **santapan** *n* meal, dish, food

santer *adj* strong, rife; *isu yang* ~ hot topic

santét *n* black magic; *dukun* ~, *tukang* ~ witchdoctor, sorcerer; **disantét** *v* to have spells cast on you, be a victim of black magic

santo *tit, m, Chr* Saint; ~ *Petrus* St Peter

santri *n* student at a *pesantren* or Islamic school (esp a boarder); strict Muslim; **nyantri, nyantrik** *v, coll* to study at an Islamic boarding school; **pesantrén** *n* Islamic boarding school

santun *adj* polite, well-mannered; *sopan* ~ good manners;

kesopan-santunan *n* manners, etiquette; **santunan** *n* benefit, compensation (from insurance)

sanubari *hati* ~ innermost heart

saos → **saus**

sapa greet; *tegur* ~ greeting; **sapaan** *n* greeting; **menyapa** *v* to greet

sapi *n* cow; ~ *perah* dairy cow; endless source; *anak* ~ calf; *susu* ~ cow's milk; *telur mata* ~ fried egg, sunnyside up

sapih, **menyapih** *v* to wean

sapta *pref* seven; ~ *Marga* the seven guiding principles of the military

sapu broom; ~ *tangan* handkerchief, hanky; *tukang* ~ cleaner, sweeper, janitor; **menyapu** *v* to sweep or wipe

saput: **menyaput** *v* to cover, veil, shroud; **tersaput** *adj* covered, shrouded; ~ *awan* clouded over

SARA *adj* communal, sectarian; related to ethnicity, religion, race or socioeconomic group; *berbau* ~ potentially sensitive issue ← **suku agama ras antargolongan**

saraf *n* nerve; *penyakit* ~ nervous disorder; *perang* ~ war of nerves

saran *n* suggestion; ~ *saya* I suggest, my suggestion; **menyarankan** *v* to suggest

sarana *n* facility, means; ~ *umum* public amenity; *pra*~ infrastructure

sarang *n* nest; ~ *lebah* beehive; ~ *burung* bird's nest; **bersarang** *v* to (make a) nest

sarap: **sarapan** *n* breakfast; **menyarap** *v, coll* to eat breakfast

saraséhan *n* meeting, symposium

Saraswati *n, Hind* Hindu goddess of knowledge and the arts

sarat *adj* full of, laden with

sarat → **syarat**

sardin, sardén *ikan* ~ sardine

sari *n* essence, extract; flower; ~ *bunga* pollen; *inti* ~ essence; *taman* ~ garden

sariawan, seriawan (mouth) ulcer, have an ulcer

saring filter; **saringan** *n* filter, sieve; **menyaring** *v* to filter (through), screen, select; **penyaringan** *n* filtration, screening

sarjana *n* university graduate; ~ *ekonomi* economics graduate; ~ *hukum* law graduate; ~ *muda* undergraduate; *pasca* ~ postgraduate

sarung *n* sarong; cover, case; ~ *bantal* pillowcase, pillowslip; **bersarung** *adj* in a sarong; with a cover

Sasak ethnic group of Lombok; *bahasa* ~, *orang* ~ Sasak

sasak: **menyasak** ~ *rambut* to tease hair into a stiff position

sasana *n* boxing stadium

sasando *n* harp-like musical instrument from Timor

sasar: **sasaran** *n* target; **menyasar** *v*, **kesasar** *coll* to lose your way, (get) lost

sastra *n* literature; ~ *Indonesia* Indonesian literature; *Fakultas* ~ Arts Faculty; **kesusasteraan, kesusastraan** *n* literature; **sastrawan** *n* literary figure

Satal *n Sangihe dan Talaud* Sangihe and Talaud, archipelagos in North Sulawesi

sate, satai *n* satay, kebab, roasted pieces of meat on a skewer; ~ *ayam* chicken satay; ~ *kelinci* rabbit satay; ~ *kambing* goat satay; **disaté** *v* to be made into satay

satelit *kota* ~ satellite, dormitory town

satgas *n* security unit, task force (of a party) ← **satuan tugas**

satpam *n* security guard; *pos* ~ security post ← **satuan pengamanan**

satron: menyatroni *v* to clean out, go through (a house, by burglars)

satu *adj* one; ~ *sama lain* each other; *salah* ~ one of; ~ *per* ~ one by one; **satu-satu** *adv* one by one, individually; ~*nya* the only; **satuan** *n* unit; **bersatu** *v* to be united; ~ *padu* to unite, integrate; **kesatu** *adj, sl* first; **kesatuan** *n* unity; ~ *dan persatuan* national unity and integration; **menyatu** *v* to become one; **menyatukan, mempersatukan** *v* to unite various things; **pemersatu** *n* unifying agent, unifier; **persatuan** *n* union, association; ~ *Guru Republik Indonesia*

(PGRI) Indonesian Teachers' Association

satwa *n* animal, fauna

saudara *n* family (member); sibling, brother, sister; *pron* you; brother, sister; ~ *angkat* person considered family; ~ *perempuan* sister; ~ *sebangsa dan setanah air* fellow Indonesians; ~ *sepupu* cousin; *hubungan* ~ family (relationship); **bersaudara** *v* to be related; to have brothers and sisters; ~ *enam* to be one of six (children); **persaudaraan** *n* brotherhood, fraternity; sisterhood; family ties; **saudari** *pron, f* you, sister; *saudara-*~ brothers and sisters, fellow Indonesians

sauh *n* anchor; *membongkar* ~ to weigh anchor; *membuang* ~ to cast anchor

sauna *n* sauna; small steaming box in a salon

saung *n* open-air restaurant by a fish-pond, esp in West Java

saur → **sahur**

saus, saos *n* sauce, gravy; ~ *tomat* tomato sauce

saw. *salallahu alaihi wassalam* peace be upon Him, used after saying the name of the Prophet Muhammad

sawah *n* (irrigated or wet) rice paddy, ricefield

sawat → **pesawat**

sawér custom of audience throwing money to performers; custom in western Java of throwing rice, coins or sweets

(as part of a wedding ceremony)

sawi *n* bok choy, mustard greens; green leafy vegetable; ~ *putih* Chinese cabbage

sawit *kelapa* ~ oil palm

sawo *n* brown, sweet fruit; sapodilla; ~ *matang* brown-skinned

saya *pron* I, me, my; ~ *sendiri* I (myself); *diri* ~ myself; *kepada* ~ to me; *komputer* ~ my computer

sayang pity, regret; love; *pron* darling; ~*ku* my darling; ~ *se-kali* what a pity; *kasih* ~ love; **kesayangan** *anak* ~ favorite, pet; **menyayangi** *v* to love; **disayangkan** *adj* regrettable, unfortunate; **tersayang** *adj* dear, dearest; *yang* ~ *(yts)* beloved; dear (in letters)

sayap *n* wing; ~ *kiri* left-wing; ~ *roda* mudguard, fender; **bersayap** *adj* winged; *vi* to have wings

sayat, menyayat *v* to slice or cut off; **sayatan** *n* slice; ~ *daging* slice of meat

sayembara *n* contest, competition; ~ *menulis* writing competition

sayu *mata* ~ sloping, slanting or heavy eyes

sayup: sayup-sayup *adv* faintly; ~ *kedengaran* faintly audible

sayur *n* vegetable; ~ *asem* sour vegetable soup; ~ *hijau* greens, green vegetables; ~ *lodeh* vegetables in coconut milk; ~ *mayur* (all kinds of) vegetables; **sayur-sayuran** *n* vegetables

SBY *abbrev* (Susilo Bambang Yudhoyono) Indonesia's sixth President

SCTV *abbrev Surya Cipta Tele-visi* SCTV, a privately-owned television network

SD *abbrev Sekolah Dasar* primary/elementary school

SDM *abbrev sumber daya manusia* human resources

seadanya *adj* what's there; *makan* ~ eat what's there ← **ada**

seakan-akan *conj* as if, as though ← **akan**

seandainya *conj* supposing, if ← **andai**

seantéro ~ *dunia* across the entire world ← **antéro**

searah *adj* the same direction ← **arah**

sebab *n* reason, cause; *conj* because; ~*nya* the reason is, the reason being; *oleh* ~ *itu* therefore, consequently; **menyebabkan** *v* to cause; **penyebab** *n* cause

sebagai *conj* like, as; **sebagaimana** *conj* in such a way that, in that way; **sebagainya** *dan* ~ and so on ← **bagai**

sebagian *n* some, a section of ← **bagi**

sebaiknya *adv* preferably, it's best if ← **baik**

sebal *adj* fed up, annoyed, cheesed off; **menyebalkan** *adj* annoying, tiresome

sebaliknya *adv* on the contrary, on the other hand ← **balik**

sebar: menyebar *v* to spread; **menyebarluaskan** *v* to disseminate, spread something; **penyebarluasan** *n* dissemination; **menyebarkan** *v* to spread, distribute; **penyebar** *n* carrier, infectious person; **penyebaran** *n* distribution

sebatang ~*kara* all alone in the world ← **batang**

sebaya *adj* of the same age ← **baya**

sebelah *prep* next to; *n* half, side; ~ *mana* which side, where; *(di)* ~ *kanan* on the right (side); *rumah* ~ next door ← **belah**

sebelas *adj* eleven ← **belas**

sebelum *prep* before; **sebelumnya** *adj* previously, before-(hand); ~ *itu* before that; ~ *Masehi (SM)* BC, before Christ; ~ *waktunya* prematurely ← **belum**

sebenarnya *adv* in fact, actually ← **benar**

sebentar *n* **bentar** *coll* **entar** *coll* a moment, minute, while; ~ *lagi* in a few minutes, soon; *tunggu* ~ wait a minute

seberang *prep* other side, across; *negeri* ~ overseas, foreign country (usu neighboring); **berseberangan** *adj* opposing, in disagreement; **menyeberang** *v* to cross; **menyeberangi** *v* to cross something; **penyeberangan** *n* crossing

seberapa *tidak* ~ not much, not many; ~ *jauh* as far as ← **apa**

sebetulnya *adv* in fact, actually ← **betul**

sebilah *n* counter for long, narrow objects; ~ *tombak* one spear, a spear

sebisanya, sebisa-bisanya *adv* as well as you can, to the best of your ability ← **bisa**

sebuah *adj* a, one (generic counter); ~ *kursi* a chair ← **buah**

sebut mention; ~ *saja* take (for instance); **sebutan** *n* mention; **menyebut** *v* to mention, name, say; **disebut-sebut** *v* to be frequently mentioned; **tersebut** *adj* (afore)mentioned, said

secara *adv* in a way; used to form adverbs; ~ *besar-besaran* on a large scale; ~ *curang* dishonestly → **cara**

secepat *conj* as fast as; ~ *mungkin*, **secepat(-cepat)nya** *adv* as fast as possible ← **cepat**

secubit *n* pinch; ~ *garam* a pinch of salt ← **cubit**

secuil *n* tiny bit; ~ *pun tidak* not one bit ← **cuil**

secukupnya *adj* sufficient, adequate ← **cukup**

sedak: tersedak *adj* choking

sedan *sedu* ~ sobs; **tersedan-sedan** *adj* sobbing

sédan *(mobil)* ~ sedan, saloon

sedang *v, aux* while, -ing; ~ *pergi* out, not here; ~ *tidur* sleeping; **sedangkan** *conj* whereas, while

sedang *adj* medium, moderate; *ukuran* ~ medium-sized, M (of clothes)

sedangkan *conj* whereas, while ← **sedang**

sedap *adj* delicious, tasty

sedapatnya *adv* what you can get ← **dapat**

sedari *conj* since, from the time when

sedekah, sadaqah, sadaqoh *n* alms, charity, handout; **bersedekah** *v* to make a donation; **menyedekahkan** *v* to donate something to the poor

sedeng → **sedang**

sederhana *adj* simple, plain; *rumah sangat ~ (RSS)* basic housing; **kesederhanaan** *n* simplicity, modesty; **menyederhanakan** *v* to simplify

sedia ready, prepared; willing; **bersedia** *v* to be prepared or willing; **kesediaan** *n* readiness, willingness; **menyediakan** *v* to prepare, get ready; **persediaan** *n* stock, supply; **tersedia** *adj* available, prepared

sediakala *adj* of old, former; usual

sedih *adj* sad; **bersedih** *v* to be or feel sad; **kesedihan** *n* sadness, sorrow; **menyedihkan** *adj* depressing, sad

sedikit *adj* a little, a few, a bit; *~ banyak* at least, some; *~ demi ~* bit by bit, gradually; *~nya* lack, paucity ← **dikit**

sedini *~ mungkin* as early as possible ← **dini**

sedot suck; **sedotan** *n* straw; **menyedot** *v* to suck (up); **penyedot** *mesin ~ debu* vacuum cleaner

sedu sob; *~ sedan* sobs; **tersedu-sedu** *v* to sob, sniffle

seénaknya *adv, neg* just how you like, at will ← **énak**

segala *adj* all, every; *~ sesuatu* all (kinds of); **segala-galanya** *n* everything, the lot

segan *adj* reluctant, averse; **keseganan** *n* reluctance, unwillingness; **disegani** *v* to be respected

segar *adj* fresh; *~ bugar* fit and healthy; **menyegarkan** *adj* refreshing; **penyegar** *minuman ~* tonic, energy drink

ségel seal, stamp; **menyégel** *v* to seal (off), close (a building); **penyégelan** *n* blocking off, seizure

segelintir *n* a small number ← **gelintir**

segenap *adj* each, all ← **genap**

segenggam *n* handful ← **genggam**

segera *adv* immediately, directly; soon; *~ dibuka* opening soon; *dengan ~* express, immediately

segi *n* side, angle; point of view; *~ empat* square, rectangle; *~ tiga* triangle; *dari ~* from the point of view of; **persegi** *adj* square, rectangular; *~ empat* square, rectangle

segini → **ini**

segitu → **itu**

sehabis *conj* after ← **habis**

seharga *adj* of equal value, the same price ← **harga**

sehari-hari *adv* every day, daily; **seharian** *adv, coll* all day ← **hari**

seharusnya should ← **harus**

séhat *adj* healthy; ~ *sejahtera* healthy and prosperous; **keséhatan** *n* health; *dinas* ~ health service; **menyéhatkan** *adj* healthy, with curing powers

sehati *adj* of one mind ← **hati**

sehingga *conj* until, to the point that, as far as; so that ← **hingga**

seibu *adj* having the same mother ← **ibu**

seimbang *adj* balanced, well-proportioned ← **imbang**

sejadah → **sajadah**

sejagat *adj* worldwide ← **jagat**

sejahtera *adj* prosperous; **kesejahteraan** *n* welfare

sejajar *adj* parallel ← **jajar**

sejak, semenjak *conj* since, from the time when

sejarah *n* history; **bersejarah** *adj* historic, historical

sejati *adj* original, genuine, real ← **jati**

sejauh *conj* how far; ~ *mana* to what point; **sejauh-jauhnya** *adv* as far away as possible ← **jauh**

sejenak *adv* briefly, a moment ← **jenak**

sejengkal *adj* handspan (between thumb and little finger) ← **jengkal**

sejenis *adj* of the same type or species ← **jenis**

sejoli *dua* ~ a couple ← **joli**

sejuk *adj* cool; **kesejukan** *n* coolness; **menyejukkan** *adj* cooling, refreshing

séka, menyéka *v* to wipe or rub off

sekadar *adj* just; ~*nya* as necessary ← **kadar**

sekali *adv* very; *indah* ~ very beautiful

sekali *adv* once; ~ *waktu* once upon a time; *jangan* ~-*kali* never (do this); **sekali-sekali, sesekali** *adv* every now and then, occasionally

sekalian *adv* all together, all at once; *adv, coll* at the same time ← **kali**

sekaligus *adv* all at once ← **kali**

sekalipun *conj* even though ← **kali**

sekali-sekali *adv* every now and then, occasionally ← **kali**

sekap: menyekap *v* to lock up, detain; **penyekapan** *n* detention

sekarang *adv* now, at present; ~ *ini* nowadays; ~ *juga* immediately

sekarat *adj* dying

sekat bar, block, partition; **menyekat** *v* to partition, block off

Sekatén *n* folk festival in Jogjakarta celebrating the Prophet Muhammad's birthday

sekawan *tiga* ~ a trio (of friends) ← **kawan**

sekejap *n* moment, flash, blink; *dalam* ~ *mata* in a moment, in the twinkling of an eye ← **kejap**

séken *adj, coll* second-hand; *barang* ~ second-hand goods

sekian *adv* so much, this much; ~ *banyak* so many, so much; ~ *dulu* that's all for now (used in speeches and letters) ← **kian**

sekilas n flash, glance ← **kilas**
sekiranya adv if perhaps ← **kira**
sekitar prep around; adv around; near; **sekitarnya** di ~ around (a place); dan ~ and environs ← **kitar**
sékjén n secretary-general ← **sékretaris jénderal**
Séknég n Minister of the Interior ← **Sékretaris Negara**
sekoci n lifeboat; bobbin (of sewing machine)
sekolah n school; institute of learning; ~ Dasar (SD) primary school, elementary school; ~ kejuruan vocational school, technical college; ~ luar biasa special school; ~ menengah secondary school, high school; ~ menengah atas (SMA) senior high school; ~ menengah pertama (SMP) junior high school; ~ perawat nursing school; ~ tinggi college (of higher education); alat-alat ~ school supplies; kepala ~ principal; putus ~ drop out from or finish school (prematurely); tamat ~ to graduate from school; uang ~ school fees, tuition; ujian masuk ~ entrance test; **sekolahan** n, coll school (building); schooling; **bersekolah** v to go to school; **menyekolahkan** v to send to school
sekongkol, bersekongkol v to plot, conspire against; **persekongkolan** n plot, intrigue, conspiracy ← **kongkol**

sekonyong-konyong adv as if ← **konyong**
sekop, skop n spade, shovel; spades (in cards)
sekoteng, sekoténg n hot drink containing ginger
sékretariat n secretariat; **sékretaris** n secretary; ~ jenderal (sekjen) secretary-general
sekrup n screw
séks n sex; hubungan ~ sexual relations, sexual intercourse; **séksual** adj sexual; pelecehan ~ sexual harassment; **séksualitas** n sexuality
seksama, saksama adj careful, thorough, detailed; **keseksamaan** n thoroughness, care
séksi n section; kepala ~ head of section
séksi adj sexy ← **seks**
sékte n sect
séktor n sector
sekurangnya, sekurang-kurangnya adv at least ← **kurang**
sekuriti n security → **pengamanan**
sekutu n partner, ally; negara ~ the Allies; allied countries; **bersekutu** v to be allies; **persekutuan** n alliance, partnership
sékwilda n provincial secretary ← **sékretaris wilayah daérah**
sél n cell
sela n gap, pause; **menyela** v to interrupt
selada, salada, salat n salad; lettuce
selagi prep during, as ← **lagi**

selai *n* jam; ~ *jeruk* marmalade; ~ *kacang* peanut butter

selain *conj* except, besides, apart from ← **lain**

selaksa *adj, lit* ten thousand ← **laksa**

selaku *conj* as, in the capacity of ← **laku**

selalu *adv* always ← **lalu**

selam diving; *baju* ~ diving suit; *kapal* ~ submarine; **menyelam** *v* to dive; **menyelami** *v* to dive into; to study in depth; **penyelam** *n* diver

selama *conj* during, as long as; **selamanya** *adv* always, forever; **selama-lamanya** *adv* forever and ever ← **lama**

selamat safe; congratulations; ~ *berbahagia* congratulations (at a wedding); ~ *datang* welcome; ~ *jalan* goodbye; bon voyage, have a safe trip; ~ *malam* good evening; ~ *sore* good afternoon; ~ *tidur* good night; ~ *tinggal* goodbye; ~ *ulang tahun* happy birthday; happy anniversary; *dengan* ~ safely, safe and sound; *juru* ~ savior; *memberi* ~ to congratulate; **selamatan** *n* (thanksgiving) feast; **ke-selamatan** *n* safety; salvation; *Bala* ~ Salvation Army; **me-nyelamatkan** *v* to save, rescue; **penyelamatan** *n* rescue (operation)

selambat-lambatnya *adv* at the latest ← **lambat**

selancar ~ *angin* windsurfing; *papan* ~ surfboard; **berselancar** *v* to surf, go surfing ← **lancar**

Sélandia Baru *n* New Zealand; *keju* ~ New Zealand cheese; *orang* ~ New Zealander

selang *n* interval; ~ *sehari* every other day, every second day; **berselang** *adj* with an interval of; ~-*seling* alternating

selang *n* hose

selangkang, selangkangan *n* groin

selanjutnya *adv* then, after that ← **lanjut**

selaput *n* membrane; ~ *dara* hymen

selaras *adj* harmonious, in harmony; **keselarasan** *n* harmony ← **laras**

Selasa *hari* ~ Tuesday

selasar *n* verandah, balcony; gallery

selasih *biji* ~ sweet drink containing seeds

selat *n* strait; ~ *Inggris* the English Channel; ~ *Malaka* the Straits of Malacca

selatan *adj* south; *Amerika* ~ South America; *daerah* ~ southern region, the south

selayaknya *adv* properly, should ← **layak**

selebaran *n* leaflet, brochure, newsletter

selebihnya *n* the rest or remainder ← **lebih**

sélébritis, séléb *n* celebrity

selédri *n* celery

séléksi *n* selection; *lolos* ~ to be selected

seléndang, sléndang *n* shawl;

sash worn over the shoulder with women's national costume

selenggara: menyelenggarakan *v* to run, hold, organize; **penyelenggara** *n* organizer; *panitia* ~ organizing committee; **penyelenggaraan** *n* organization

seléo → **keseléo**

selepas *prep, conj* after ← **lepas**

seléra *n* appetite, taste; ~ *tinggi* good taste; expensive tastes; **berseléra** *v* to have a taste or appetite for

selesai finished, over; **menyelesaikan** *v* to finish, end, settle; ~ *masalah* to overcome a problem; **penyelesaian** *n* solution, settlement

selesma, selésma having a cold; cold

seléwéng: menyeléwéng *v* to deviate; to have an affair; **penyeléwéngan** *n* affair, deviation

selidik: menyelidiki *v* to investigate; **penyelidik** *n* investigator, detective; **penyelidikan** *n* investigation

selimut *n* blanket; **berselimutkan** *adj* blanketed in; **menyelimuti** *v* to (cover with a) blanket

selinap: menyelinap *v* to sneak, move quietly

seling *selang* ~ alternately; **selingan** *n* change, break; **menyelingi** *v* to go between, intervene

selingkuh, berselingkuh *v* to have an affair; **perselingkuhan** *n* affair

selip: menyelip *v* to slip; **menyelipkan** *v* to slip an object (into something); **terselip** *adj* fallen or slipped into

selir *n* concubine

selisih *n* difference; **berselisih** *v* to differ in opinion, have a different opinion, quarrel; **perselisihan** *n* dispute, difference of opinion

sélo *n* cello

selok: selokan *n* ditch, trench

seloki *n* small glass for drinking spirits

selonjor sit with legs sticking out in front; **berselonjor** *adj* with outstretched legs

selop *n* slipper

seloroh: berseloroh *v* to joke

selot *kunci* ~ bolt; **diselot** *v* to be bolted

sélotip *n* sellotape, adhesive or sticky tape

selubung: berselubung *adj* veiled; **menyelubungi** *v* to veil or cover; **terselubung** *adj* hidden, veiled

seluk ~ *beluk* ins and outs, details

sélulér *telepon* ~ *(ponsel)* mobile phone, handphone, cell phone

selundup: selundupan *barang* ~ contraband, smuggled goods; **menyelundup** *v* to sneak in illegally, infiltrate; **menyelundupkan** *v* to smuggle (in); **penyelundup** *n* smuggler

seluruh *adj* entire, whole; ~ *dunia* all over the world; **seluruhnya** *adv* completely; *adj* all; **keseluruhan** *secara* ~

totally, completely

selusin *n* a dozen; *teh botol ~* a dozen bottles of tea ← **lusin**

selusup: menyelusup *v* to penetrate, infiltrate ← **susup**

selusur: menyelusuri *v* to follow something, go along

semacam *adj* a kind or type of ← **macam**

semadi → **semedi**

semak shrub, bush; *~-belukar* scrub; **semak-semak** *n* bush(land), scrub

semakin *adv* even more ← **makin**

semak-semak *n* bush(land), scrub ← **semak**

semalam *adv* last night; **semalaman** *adv* all night long ← **malam**

semampai *tinggi ~* tall and slender

semampunya *adv* as well as you can, to the best of your ability ← **mampu**

semang *induk ~* house-mother, landlady

semangat *n* spirit, enthusiasm; *kurang ~* lacking enthusiasm; **bersemangat** *adj* spirited, enthusiastic

semanggi *n* clover leaf; *perempatan ~* clover-leaf intersection

semangka *n* watermelon

Semar *n* clown character in shadow-puppet plays

semarak *adj* glittering, exciting; shine, glow, bright

semat, menyematkan *v* to pin, fasten with pins; **penyemat** *n* pin

semata *adj* only, entirely, solely ← **mata**

semaunya *adv* at will, as you like ← **mau**

semayam: disemayamkan *v* to be laid out (of a dead body)

sembab, sembam *adj* swollen

sembah *n* homage, tribute, respect; **menyembah** *v* to pay homage to, worship; **mempersembahkan** *v* to offer (up), present; **persembahan** *n* offering; product or service

sembahyang pray, prayer; *~ subuh Isl* dawn prayer; **bersembahyang** *v* to pray, perform a prayer

sembako *n* nine daily necessities ← **sembilan bahan pokok**

sembarang *adj* any, whichever; **sembarangan** *adj* arbitrary, random

sembari *conj* while

sembelih: menyembelih *v* to slaughter, butcher; **penyembelih** *n* butcher, slaughterer; **penyembelihan** *n* slaughter

sembelit constipation, constipated

sembilan *adj* nine; *~ belas* nineteen; *~ puluh* ninety; *ke~* ninth

semboyan *n* motto, slogan; **bersemboyan** *adj* with the motto

sembrono *adj* thoughtless, reckless

sembuh recovered, better; *cepat ~, lekas ~* get well soon; **menyembuhkan** *v* to cure, heal; **penyembuhan** *n* cure, healing sembunyi hide, conceal; **sembunyi-sembunyi** *adv* secretly, in secret; **bersembunyi** *v* to hide (yourself); **menyembunyikan** *v* to hide or conceal something; **persembunyian** *n* hiding place, hideout

sembur: **semburan** *n* spout, fountain; outpouring; ~ *air panas* geyser; **menyembur** *v* to spurt out; **menyemburkan** *v* to spit or spray something out

semedi, semédi, semadi: bersemedi *v* to meditate

semén *n* (wet) cement

semena: **semena-mena** *(tidak)* ~ arbitrary, without reason, unjust ← **mena**

semenanjung *n* peninsula; ~ *Melayu* Malaya, the Malay Peninsula ← **tanjung**

semenjak, sejak *conj* since

sementara *conj* during; *adj* temporary; ~ *itu* in the meantime, meanwhile; *alamat* ~ temporary address; *buat* ~, *untuk* ~ for the time being

semésta *alam* ~ universe; *Perjuangan* ~ *(Permesta)* 1950s secessionist movement

semestinya should have (been) ← **mesti**

semi *musim* ~ spring; **bersemi** *v* to sprout buds

seminggu *adj* a week; *tiga kali* ~ three times a week ← **minggu**

semir polish; ~ *sepatu* shoe polish; *tukang* ~ shoeshine boy; **menyemir** *v* to polish

semoga may, hopefully ← **moga**

sempadan *n* border, boundary; ~ *jalan* right of way (ROW)

sempat chance, opportunity; *kalau* ~ when possible; *tidak* ~ not get the chance to; **kesempatan** *n* opportunity; ~ *dalam kesempitan* an opportunity in difficult circumstances; **berkesempatan** *v* to have an opportunity; **menyempatkan** ~ *diri* to make time to

sempit *adj* narrow; *berpikiran* ~ narrow-minded; *waktunya* ~ *sekali* there isn't much time; **kesempitan** *n* narrowness; **menyempit** *v* to (become) narrow

sempoa *n* abacus

semprong *kue* ~ tubular wafers shaped like brandy snaps

semprot squirt; spurt; *kena* ~ *coll* be shouted at or told off; **semprotan** *n* spray-gun; **menyemprot** *v* to spray; **menyemprotkan** *v* to spray with something

sempurna *adj* perfect, complete; **kesempurnaan** *n* perfection; **menyempurnakan** *v* to perfect, complete; *Ejaan Yang Disempurnakan (EYD)* reformed spelling of 1972

semrawut *adj* haphazard, uncontrolled; **kesemrawutan** *n* chaos

semu *adj* false, apparent

semua *adj* all; ~*nya* all, everyone

semula *adj* original; *adv* originally ← **mula**

semur *n* meat or tofu dish with soy sauce

semut *n* ant; ~ *api* small, stinging ant; ~ *putih* white ant, termite; **kesemutan** *v* to have pins and needles

sén cent

sén, séin *lampu* ~ indicator (on a vehicle)

senam *n* gymastics, aerobics; exercise; ~ *hamil* pre-natal exercises; ~ *pagi* morning exercise; *baju* ~ leotard

senandung hum; **bersenandung** *v* to hum, sing

senang *adj* happy, content; *v* to like; ~ *nonton TV* to like watching TV; **bersenang-senang** *v* to enjoy yourself, have fun; **kesenangan** *n* amusement, hobby; **menyenangkan** *adj* pleasing, agreeable

senantiasa *adv* always

senapan *n* rifle; ~ *mesin* machine gun

senar *n* (guitar) string

senasib *adj* fellow sufferer ← **nasib**

sénat *n* senate; ~ *mahasiswa* student council

senda ~ *gurau* joke; **bersenda** *v* ~ *gurau* to joke around

sendat: tersendat *adj* jammed, blocked

sendawa *n* saltpetre, saltpeter, potassium nitrate; gunpowder; *asam* ~ nitric acid; **bersendawa** *v* to burp, belch

sendi *n* joint; **persendian** *n* joints

sendiri *adv* alone; *pron* self; *salah* ~ it's your own fault; *dengan* ~*nya* automatic, by itself; **sendiri-sendiri** *adv, pl* alone, individually; **sendirian** *adv* alone, single-handedly; **kesendirian** *n* solitude; **menyendiri** *v* to go off by yourself; **penyendiri** *n* loner; **tersendiri** *adj* its own; apart, separate ← **diri**

séndok *n* spoon; ~ *bebek* ceramic spoon for eating Chinese soup dishes; ~ *makan* (dessert)spoon; ~ *teh* teaspoon; ~ *garpu* spoon and fork

séndratari *n* traditional performing arts, dance and drama ← **seni, drama, tari**

Sénégal *n* Senegal; *orang* ~ Senegalese

Senén → **Senin**

senéwen *adj* nervous, neurotic

séng *n* zinc

sengaja *adv* deliberately, on purpose; *tidak* ~ unintentionally; **kesengajaan** *n* deliberate or intentional act

sengat sting; **sengatan** *n* sting, bite; **menyengat** *v* to sting

sengau *adj* **nasal**

senggama → **sanggama**

senggang *adj* free, unoccupied; *waktu* ~ free time

sénggol brush, bump; *pasar* ~ crowded market; **bersénggol-an** *v pl* to bump into each other; **menyénggol** *v* to bump, brush, tweak; **tersénggol** *adj* bumped, brushed

sengir: menyengir v to smile nervously, grimace

sengkéta n dispute; *tanah* ~ disputed land; **persengkétaan** n dispute

sengsara misery; **kesengsaraan** n torture, misery, suffering; **menyengsarakan** v to torture, cause suffering

sengsem: kesengsem adj, coll engrossed in, absorbed with

seni n art; ~ *lukis* painting; ~ *pahat* sculpture; ~ *peran* drama; *nilai* ~ artistic value; **kesenian** n art (form); ~ *tradisional* traditional art form; **seniman** n, m **seniwati** n, f artist

seni *air* ~ urine

Senin, Senén *hari* ~ Monday

sénior n person in higher class or of higher position ← **kakak kelas**

senja n twilight, dusk

senjang: kesenjangan n gap, divide; ~ *sosial* social imbalance

senjata n weapon; ~ *api* firearm, gun; *gencatan* ~ ceasefire; **bersenjata** adj armed; **mempersenjatai** v to arm someone

senonoh adj fitting, decent; *tidak* ~ indecent, improper

sénsasi n sensation; **sénsasional** adj sensational

sénsor n censor; *kena* ~, *disensor* censored; **mensénsor** v to censor, cut out

sénsus n census

sentak: sentakan n jerk; **menyentak** v to pull, jerk; **tersentak** adj pulled, jerked

sénter n (*lampu*) ~ flashlight, torch

sénti n centimeter, centimetre; *berapa* ~ how many centimeters, how long ← **séntiméter**

sentil: sentilan n flick, nudge; **menyentil** v to flick with your finger (often to rebuke a child)

sentiméter, sénti n centimeter, centimetre; *berapa* ~ how many centimeters, how long

sentosa adj safe, peaceful

séntra n center, centre; ~ *elektronik* electronics center; **séntral** adj central; n center

sentuh touch; **sentuhan** n touch; ~ *eksotis* exotic touch; **bersentuh** v to touch; **bersentuhan** adv touching each other; **menyentuh** v to touch; **tersentuh** adj touched

senyap adj quiet, still; *sunyi* ~ completely still or quiet; **kesenyapan** n silence

senyawa n compound; **bersenyawa** v to become a chemical compound; **persenyawaan** n chemical compound

senyum smile; *murah* ~ quick to smile, always smiling; **senyuman** n smile; **tersenyum** v to smile

seolah-olah adv, conj as if ← **olah**

seorang a (person); counter for people; ~ *Arab* an Arab; ~ *diri* alone, single-handedly ← **orang**

sepadan adj in keeping or proportion with ← **padan**

sepagi ~ *mungkin* as early as possible ← **pagi**

sepaham *adj* of the same opinion or belief ← **paham**

sépak kick; ~ *bola* soccer, football; ~ *bola Amerika* gridiron; ~ *bola Australia* Australian rules (football); ~ *takraw* game played with a rattan ball; ~ *terjang* behavior, activity; **menyépak** *v* to kick (out)

sepakat *v* to agree; **kesepakatan** *n* agreement; **menyepakati** *v* to agree to ← **pakat**

sepan *rok* ~ (tight) skirt

sepanjang *conj, adj* as long as; ~*jalan* the whole way ← **panjang**

sepantasnya *adv* proper, rightly ← **pantas**

séparatis separatist; **séparatisme** *n* separatism

separo, separuh *n* half; **separuh-separuh** *adj* half and half ← **paruh**

sepasang *n* a pair of ← **pasang**

sepatbor *n* mudguard, fender

sepatu *n* shoe; ~ *hak tinggi* high heels; ~ *kets,* ~ *olahraga* running or sports shoes, sneakers; ~ *kuda* horseshoe; ~ *lars,* ~ *bot* boots; ~ *roda* rollerblades, rollerskates; ~ *sandal* sandals; *kembang* ~ hibiscus; *telapak* ~ sole; *tukang* ~ cobbler (for repairs), shoemaker; **bersepatu** *adj* in shoes

sepatutnya *adv* rightly, properly ← **patut**

sepéda *n* bicycle, (push)bike; ~ *motor* motor bike; *naik* ~ ride a bicycle; go by bicycle; **bersepéda** *v* to ride a bicycle

sepekan *adj* a week ← **pekan**

sepélé *adj* unimportant, trifling; *hal* ~ trifle; **menyepélékan** *v* to make light of, treat lightly

sepengetahuan *adj* with knowledge; ~ *saya* to my knowledge ← **tahu**

sepeninggal *conj* after someone's death ← **tinggal**

sepenuhnya *adv* fully, completely ← **penuh**

seperangkat *n* set, suite ← **angkat, perangkat**

seperempat *n* one quarter ← **empat**

seperenam *n* one-sixth ← **enam**

seperlima *n* one-fifth ← **lima**

seperti *conj* like; ~*nya* it seems

sepertiga *adj* one-third ← **tiga**

sepésér *tidak ada* ~ *pun* to have not even a cent ← **pésér**

sepi *adj* quiet, still, lonely; ~ *pengunjung* few visitors or customers; **kesepian** *n* loneliness, solitude; **menyepi** *v* to go away by yourself

sepihak *adj* unilateral ← **pihak**

sepintas ~ *lalu* at first glance ← **pintas**

sepoi: *sepoi-sepoi angin* ~ breeze, zephyr

seprei, seprai *n* (bed)sheet

Séptémber *bulan* ~ September

sepucuk ~ *surat* a letter ← **pucuk**

sepuh ~ *perak* silver plating; **sepuhan** *n* gilt; **menyepuh** *v* to plate or gild

sepuh *adj, coll* elderly

sepuluh *n* ten ← **puluh**

sepupu *n* cousin; *saudara ~* cousin ← **pupu**

sepur *n, coll* railway (line); rail; platform

seputar *adj* around, about ← **putar**

serabi *n* small, soft, crumpet-like cake

serabut *n* fiber, fibre; *~ kelapa* coconut fiber

seragam *n* uniform ← **ragam**

serah hand over, transfer; *~ terima* hand over to someone else; **seserahan** *n* gifts brought by the groom to the bride's house; **menyerah** *v* to surrender, give in, give up; **menyerahkan** *v* to hand over; **penyerahan** *n* handing over, handover; **terserah** *adj* it depends; up to you

serai, séréh *n* lemon grass, citronella

serak *adj* hoarse

sérak: bersérakan *adj* scattered everywhere

serakah *adj* greedy; **keserakahan** *n* greed, avarice

Séram *pulau ~* Seram, Ceram

seram *adj* weird, creepy; **menyeramkan** *adj* creepy, frightening

serambi *n* verandah; *~ Mekah* Aceh, Gateway to Mecca

serang attack; **serangan** *n* attack, raid; *~ fajar* dawn raid; **menyerang** *v* to attack; **penyerang** *n* attacker; **penyerangan** *n* attack, aggression

serangga *n* insect, bug

serap absorb; *daya ~* absorbency; **menyerap** *v* to absorb, soak up; **penyerapan** *n* absorption

serasi *adj* suited, compatible, harmonious ← **rasi**

serat *n* fiber, fibre; **berserat** *makanan ~* high-fiber food

seratus *adj* one hundred, a hundred ← **ratus**

Serawak *n* Sarawak

seraya *conj* while, during

serba *adj* all kinds of, various; *~-serbi* all kinds of; *~ salah* damned if you do, damned if you don't; wrong whatever you do; *toko ~ ada (toserba)* department store

serban, sorban *n* turban

serbét *n* serviette, table napkin

Sérbia *n* Serbia; *bahasa ~* Serbian; *orang ~* Serbian, a Serb

serbu: menyerbu *v* to attack (as a group), charge, invade; **penyerbuan** *n* attack, charge, invasion

serbuk *n* powder; *~ besi* iron filings; *~ bunga* pollen; *~ gergaji* sawdust

séréal *n* (breakfast) cereal

séréh, serai *n* lemon grass, citronella

serem → **seram**

serempak *adj* simultaneous, in unison

serémpét: menyerémpét *v* to scrape, scratch against; **terserémpét** *adj* scraped, scratched

serendah-rendahnya *adv* as low as possible ← **rendah**

serentak *adj* all at once, simultaneous, at the same time

sérep *adj* reserve, change; *ban* ~ spare tire

sérét, menyérét *v* to drag; **tersérét** *adj* dragged

sergap, menyergap *v* to apprehend, ambush, catch

seri *gigi* ~ incisor, eye tooth; **berseri** *adj* beaming, glowing

seri *n* draw, tie

séri *n* series; *film* ~ serial, series

seriawan → **sariawan**

seribu *adj* one thousand, a thousand; *Pulau* ~ the Thousand Islands ← **ribu**

serigala *n* wolf

serikat, sarékat, syarikat union, united; ~ *buruh* labor union; *Amerika* ~ the United States of America, USA; **perserikatan** *n* federation; ~ *Bangsa-Bangsa (PBB)* the United Nations (UN)

serikaya → **srikaya**

sering *adv* often, frequently; ~ *sakit* sickly; **keseringan** *n* frequency; *adv* too often

sériosa *n* semi-classical music

sérius *adj* serious; **kesériusan** *n* solemnity, seriousness

séro *n* share; **perséro** *adj* proprietary limited (Pty Ltd); **perséroan** *n* company; ~ *terbatas (PT)* proprietary limited (Pty Ltd)

serobot push in front; *main* ~ not queue; **menyerobot** *v* to push in front

seroja *(bunga)* ~ kind of lotus

sérong *adj* on an angle, oblique; *main* ~ to commit adultery

seronok *adj* tasteless, tarty, unpleasant

serpih, serpihan *n* shred, bit, piece; ~ *kayu* wood chip

sérsan *n* sergeant; ~ *mayor* sergeant-major

serta *conj* (together) with; ~-*merta* automatically, immediately; *ikut* ~, *turut* ~ take part, participate; **keikutsertaan** *n* participation; **beserta** *conj* along with, and; **menyertai** *v* to accompany; **peserta** *n* participant

sértifikat *n* certificate; **bersértifikat** *adj* with papers (of a house)

seru shout, call; *kata* ~ exclamation; *tanda* ~ exclamation mark; **seruan** *n* call, cry, exclamation; **berseru** *v* to call, cry; ~ *kepada* to call on, appeal; **menyerukan** *v* to call or appeal for

seru *adj* exciting, great

seruling, suling *n* flute

serumpun *adj* related, of one family; *bahasa* ~ languages related to Indonesian (such as Malagasy and Tagalog) ← **rumpun**

serundéng *n* fried desiccated coconut

seruni *(bunga)* ~ coastal flowering plant

serupa *adj* similar; **menyerupai** *v* to resemble, be similar to ← **rupa**

serut: serutan ~ *pensil* pencil shavings; **diserut** *v* to be sharpened

sérvis *n* repairs, service, maintenance; **disérvis** *v* to be serviced

sesajén *n* ritual offering ← **saji**

sesak *adj* close, dense, crowded; ~ *dada*, ~ *napas* short of breath; asthmatic; *penuh* ~ chock-a-block, chock-full

sesal regret; **menyesal** *v* to regret; **menyesalkan** *v* to feel bad about, regret (another's action); **penyesalan** *n* repentance, remorse

sesama *adj* fellow, another; ~ *manusia* fellow human being ← **sama**

sésar *operasi* ~ Cesarian (section); **disésar** *v* to have a Cesarian

sesar *n* fault, fault line

sesat lost; **menyesatkan** *adj* misleading, confusing; **tersesat** *adj* lost

sesekali *adv* every now and then, occasionally ← **kali**

seseorang *n* somebody, a certain person ← **orang**

seserahan *n* gifts brought by the groom to the bride's house ← **serah**

sesuai *adj* in accordance with, appropriate; **menyesuaikan** *v* to adapt, bring into line; ~ *diri* to adapt; **penyesuaian** *n* adaptation ← **suai**

sesuap *n* mouthful; ~ *nasi* a mouthful of rice; something to eat ← **suap**

sesuatu *n* something ← **suatu**

sesudah *prep* after; ~ *itu*, **sesudahnya** after that, then ← **sudah**

sesungguhnya *adv* actually, really ← **sungguh**

setahu *conj* as far as is known; ~ *saya* as far as I know ← **tahu**

sétan, syaitan *n* devil, demon; **persétan** *ejac* go to hell!

setang → **stang**

setara *adj* equal, equivalent ← **tara**

setaraf *adj* of the same standard ← **taraf**

setasiun, stasiun, setasion *n* (railway) station; *kepala* ~ stationmaster

seteguk *n a* gulp ← **teguk**

setél *n* set; **setélan** *n* set, suit

setél, menyétel *v* to tune, set, adjust; ~ *mesin mobil* to tune an engine; **penyetélan** *n* tuning

setelah *prep* after; ~ *itu* after that, then ← **telah**

setempat *adj* local ← **tempat**

setémpel → **stémpel**

setengah *adj* half; ~ *mati* half-dead; *adv* very hard; *jam* ~ *dua* half past one; **setengah-setengah** *adv* half-heartedly ← **tengah**

seterika → **setrika**

seteru: berseteru *v* to be hostile, at odds with; **perseteruan** *n* feud

seterusnya *adv* after that, henceforth ← **terus**

setia *adj* faithful; ~ *kawan* solidarity; loyal; **kesetiakawanan**

n solidarity; **kesetiaan** *n* allegiance, faithfulness; **setiawan** *adj* loyal, faithful

setiap *adj* each, every; ~ *saat* any time ← **tiap**

setidaknya, setidak-tidaknya *adv* at least ← **tidak**

setimbal *adj* equivalent, proportional, even ← **timbal**

setinggi *adj* as high as; **setinggi-tingginya** *adv* as high as possible ← **tinggi**

setingkat *adj* of the same level ← **tingkat**

setir wheel; handlebars; drive; ~ *kanan* right-hand drive; **menyetir** *v* to drive

Sétnég *n* State Secretariat, Ministry of the Interior ← **Sékrétariat Negara**

setop, menyetop *v* to stop (a vehicle); **setopan** *n, coll* traffic lights

setor: setoran (make a) deposit; *n* minimal amount taxi drivers must earn per day; **menyetor** *v* to pay in, deposit; **penyetor** *n* depositor

setrap: disetrap *v* to be punished (at school)

setrika, seterika iron; **setrikaan** *n* (clothes for) ironing; **menyetrika** *v* to iron

setrip, strip *n* (diagonal) slash; strip; section of a mobile phone battery symbol; *tinggal satu* ~ low battery

setrum *n* current; **kesetrum** *v, coll* to receive an electric shock

setubuh: bersetubuh *v* to have

sex; **menyetubuhi** *v* to have sex with; **persetubuhan** *n* sexual intercourse ← **tubuh**

setuju agree, agreed; **bersetuju** *v* to agree; **menyetujui** *v* to agree to, approve, ratify; **persetujuan** *n* agreement, approval ← **tuju**

seumpamanya *conj* for instance ← **umpama**

seumur *adj* the same age; lifelong; ~ *hidup* for life, lifelong ← **umur**

seutuhnya *adv* completely ← **utuh**

séwa hire, rent; ~ *VCD* VCD rental; *uang* ~ rent; **séwaan** *rumah* ~ rented house; **menyéwa** *v* to rent, hire; **menyéwakan** *v* to let (a house), hire out, lease

sewajarnya *adv* naturally ← **wajar**

sewaktu-waktu *adv* at any moment; every now and then ← **waktu**

sewenang-wenang *adv* tyrannically, arbitrarily ← **wenang**

sewindu *adj* eight years ← **windu**

séwot *adj* furious

Séychélles *n* Seychelles; *orang* ~ Seychellois, Seychellese

seyogianya *adv* properly, fittingly ← **yogia**

SH *abbrev Sarjana Hukum* legal graduate, LL.B

shabu-shabu *n, sl* heroin

shio *n* Chinese horoscope, based on year born

sholat, shalat, salat, solat *Isl* (perform) one of the five daily prayers; ~ *magrib* sunset prayer; ~ *isya* evening prayer; ~ *subuh* dawn prayer; ~ *lohor* midday prayer; ~ *asar* afternoon prayer; ~ *Jumat* Friday prayers; ~ *id* mass prayer at Idul Fitri or Idul Adha; **disholatkan** *v* to be prayed for, have a prayer performed for you (after death)

si *pref* used before the name of a familiar third party; ~ *Anu* so-and-so, whatshisname

sia: sia-sia *adj* pointless, useless; **menyia-yiakan** *v* to waste

siaga *adj* alert, on guard, ready; ~ *satu* red alert; **bersiaga** *v* to be on alert, on guard; **kesiagaan** *n* readiness, preparedness

sial unlucky; **sialan** *ejac* damn! hell!

siamang *n* gibbon

siang *n* day; late morning, early afternoon (usu between 10 am and 3 pm); ~ *ini* this morning, this afternoon; ~ *malam* day and night; ~ *bolong* broad daylight; *makan* ~ lunch; *masih* ~ it's still noon, it's only early afternoon; **kesiangan** *adj* late, too late in the day

sianida *n* cyanide

siap ready; ~ *pakai* ready-to-wear; *kurang* ~ under-prepared; **bersiap** *v* to get ready; **bersiap-siap** *v* to make preparations; **kesiapan** *n* readiness, willingness; **menyiapkan, mempersiapkan** *v* to prepare something, get something ready;

persiapan *n* preparations

siapa *interrog, pron* who; ~ *namanya* what's their name; ~ *lagi* who else; ~ *punya* whose is this; ~ *saja* anybody; *barang* ~ whosoever; **siapa-siapa** *pron, neg* nobody; *bukan* ~ nobody

siar *hak* ~ telecast or broadcast rights; **siaran** *n* telecast, broadcast; **menyiarkan** *v* to telecast, broadcast, disseminate; **penyiar** *n* announcer, (radio) broadcaster

siar: *pesiar* *n* trip, cruise; *kapal* ~ cruise ship; pleasure craft

siasat *n, neg* tactics, strategy

sia-sia *adj* pointless, useless; **menyia-yiakan** *v* to waste

sibuk *adj* busy; engaged (of phones); *nada* ~ busy tone; **kesibukan** *n* activity, fuss, bustle, business; **menyibukkan** ~ *diri* to keep yourself busy, spend your time

sidak *n* spot inspection ← **inspéksi mendadak**

sidang *n* session, meeting; hearing; ~ *istimewa* special assembly (of parliament); ~ *pengadilan* court hearing, court session; *Balai* ~ Jakarta Convention Centre; **persidangan** *n* meeting, assembly; (extended) court session

sidik ~ *jari* fingerprints; **menyidik** *v* to investigate; **penyidik** *n* investigator, detective; **penyidikan** *n* investigation ← **selidik**

sifat *n* quality, nature, character; **bersifat** *v* to have the quality of

sifon *n* chiffon; *kue ~* chiffon cake

sigap *adj* efficient, ready; **kesigapan** *n* efficiency, readiness

sih used as a filler; *saya ~ tidak keberatan* I myself have no objection; *kenapa kamu harus lari di dalam rumah ~* why are you running inside?

sihir *n* spells, witchcraft; *ilmu ~* black magic; **menyihir** *v* to perform magic; **penyihir** *n* wizard, witch, sorcerer

sikap *n* attitude; **bersikap** *v* to display an attitude

sikat brush; *~ gigi* toothbrush; *~ rambut* hairbrush; **menyikat** *v* to brush

siklon *n* cyclone ← **angin**

siklus *n* cycle; *~ kehidupan* life cycle

siksa torture; **siksaan, penyiksaan** *n* torture, torment; **menyiksa** *v* to torture; **tersiksa** *adj* tortured

siku *n* elbow; bracket; *~ segi tiga* right angle

sila *n* principle; *Panca~* Indonesian state philosophy, based on five principles

sila: bersila *duduk ~* to sit cross-legged

sila: silakan, silahkan please (when offering); *~ duduk* please sit down, please be seated; *~ masuk* please come in; **mempersilakan** *v* to invite someone to do something

silakan, silahkan please (when offering); *~ duduk* please sit down, please be seated; *~ masuk* please come in ← **sila**

silam *adj* past, ago; *beberapa tahun ~* several years ago

silang cross, across; *teka-teki ~ (TTS)* crossword puzzle; **bersilang** *adj* crossed; **menyilang** *silang-~* criss-cross

silap delusion; wrong; **kesilapan** *n* mistake, error

silat traditional self-defense; *pencak ~* Indonesian self-defense

silaturahmi *n* good relations, friendship; **bersilaturahmi** *v* to maintain good relations, visit or meet friends

silau *adj* blinded, dazzled

silét *n* razor, scalpel; **menyilét** *v* to cut with a knife, slit

silih *~ berganti* to take turns, replace

silika *n* silicon

silinder *n* (degree of) astigmatism

silsilah *n* family tree, pedigree (of an animal)

siluman *adj* invisible; *pesawat ~* spy plane

SIM *n* driver's license, driving license; *~ C* motorcycle license; *membuat ~* to get your driver's license ← **Surat Izin Mengemudi**

simak: menyimak *v* to hear, monitor; *latihan ~* listening practice

simalakama *buah ~* Catch-22 situation

simbah *pron, f* reference to an older servant

simpan *v* to keep, put; **simpanan** *n* something kept; *uang ~* savings, deposit; *wanita ~* kept woman, lover; **menyimpan** *v* to keep, save up, store; **penyimpanan** *n* storage

simpang cross; *~ empat* crossroads, intersection; *~ siur* confusing, disordered; *~ tiga* T-junction; **bersimpang** *v* to branch; **menyimpang** *v* to deviate; **penyimpangan** *n* aberration, deviation; **persimpangan** *n* intersection

simpati *n* sympathy; **bersimpati** *adj* sympathetic; **simpatik** *adj* amiable, likeable; **simpatisan** *n* follower, sympathizer (of a party)

simpuh: **bersimpuh** *v* to sit kneeling with feet to one side

simpul *n* knot; **kesimpulan** *n* conclusion; **menyimpulkan** *v* to conclude or summarize

simsalabim abracadabra

sinambung, **bersinambung** *adj* continuous; **kesinambungan** *n* continuity; **berkesinambungan** *adj* sustained, continuous; *perkembangan yang ~* sustainable development ← **sambung**

sinar *n* ray, beam; *~ matahari* sunbeam; *~-X* x-ray; **bersinar** *v* to shine, gleam; **disinar** *v* to have radiotherapy or chemotherapy; **penyinaran** *n* radiation

sindir, **menyindir** *v* to insinuate, allude; **sindiran** *n* allusion, insinuation

sindroma *n* syndrome; *~ Down* Down's syndrome

sinéas *n* cinematographer; **sinétron** *n* local TV comedy or drama ← **sinéma éléktronik**

singa *n* lion; *~ betina* lioness; *anak ~* lion cub; *negeri ~* Singapore

Singapura *n* Singapore; *orang ~* Singaporean

singgah *v* to drop by, call at, stop over; **menyinggahi** *v* to stop over in; **persinggahan** *n* stopover

singgung, **menyinggung** *v* to touch on; *~ perasaan* to offend someone, hurt someone's feelings; **tersinggung** *adj* offended, hurt; *mudah ~* touchy, over-sensitive

singkap: **menyingkap** *v* to open slightly, reveal; **menyingkapkan** *v* to open something slightly; *~ rahasia* to reveal a secret; **tersingkap** *adj* revealed

singkat *adj* short, brief, concise; *~nya* in brief; *~ kata, secara ~* in brief, briefly; **singkatan** *n* abbreviation; **menyingkatkan** *v* to abbreviate, shorten; **mempersingkat** *v* to shorten

singkir: **menyingkir** *v* to step or move aside; **menyingkirkan** *v* to remove, brush aside; **tersingkir** *adj* eliminated, swept aside

singkong *n* cassava; *daun ~* cassava leaves; *ubi ~* cassava

singsing: menyingsing *v* to lift, rise; ~ *lengan baju* to roll up your shirt sleeves, get to work; *fajar* ~ daybreak

sini *adv* here; *di* ~ here; *dari* ~ from here; *ke* ~ here ← **ini**

sinis *adj* cynical, sarcastic; *nada* ~ mocking tone

sinolog *n* specialist in Chinese studies, sinologist; **sinologi** *n* Chinese studies, sinology

sinsé, sin shé *n* Chinese doctor, practitioner of Chinese medicine or acupuncture

sintal *adj* well-fed, rounded; shapely

Sinterklas *n* Santa Claus

sintésa *n* synthesis

sinting *adj* silly, crazy

sinyal *n* signal; **sinyalir, menyinyalir** *v* to signal, make a sign, point out

siomay, sio may *n* fishcakes eaten with peanut sauce, a specialty of Bandung

sip, siip *adj, coll* great, fantastic

sipil *adj* civil; *keadaan darurat* ~ civil emergency; *pegawai negeri* ~ *(PNS)* civil servant

sipir *n* prison warden, jailer

sipit *adj* narrow, slanting (of eyes); *mata* ~ slanted eyes (esp of East Asians)

Siprus *n* Cyprus; *orang* ~ Cypriot

sipu: tersipu(-sipu) *adj* embarrassed, shy

siput *n* snail; *kulit* ~, *rumah* ~ snail shell

siram *v* to pour; *kwetiau* ~ boiled rice noodles; **siraman** *n* bathing ceremony before a wedding; **menyiram** *v* to pour, water (plants); **menyirami** *v* to pour onto

sirat: tersirat *adj* implied

siréne *n* siren

siri *n* humiliation in Macassarese culture

sirih *n* betel; *makan* ~ chew betel

sirik *adj* envious, jealous

sirip *n* fin; *sup* ~ *ikan hiu* shark fin soup

sirkuit *n* (racing) circuit, race track

sirkus *n* circus

sirna *adj* vanished, disappeared

sirop *n* syrup, cordial

sirsak *n* soursop, green-skinned fruit with white fleshy interior; *jus* ~ soursop juice

sisa *n* rest, remainder, remains; **menyisakan** *v* to leave behind; **tersisa** *adj* leftover

sisi *n* side; ~ *buruk* bad side, shortcoming

sisih: menyisihkan *v* to set aside

sisik *n* scale (of fish); **bersisik** *adj* scaly, rough

sisip: sisipan *n* infix; **menyisipkan** *v* to insert

sisir *n* comb; hand (of bananas); ~ *kuda* currycomb; *se~ pisang* a bunch of bananas; **sisiran** *v, sl* to comb your hair; **menyisir** *v* to comb, check thoroughly; **penyisiran** *n* combing, checking

siskamling *n* neighborhood

security system ← **sistém keamanan lingkungan**

sistém, sistim *n* system; **sistématis** *adj* systematic

siswa *n* pupil; ~ *-siswi* pupils; *Organisasi ~ Intra Sekolah (OSIS)* Student Council (secondary school); **siswi** *n, f* pupil

SIT *abbrev Surat Izin Terbit* publishing permit

sita confiscate, seize; *juru ~* bailiff; **sitaan** *barang ~* confiscated goods; **menyita** *v* to confiscate; **penyitaan** *n* confiscation, seizure

situ *di ~* there (close to listener); *dari ~* from there; *ke ~* there ← **itu**

situasi *n* situation

situs *n* site; ~ *internet* website; ~ *purbakala* archeological site

siul: siulan *n* whistling; **bersiul** *v* to whistle

siuman *v* to recover consciousness, come round

siung *n* clove (of garlic)

SIUPP *abbrev Surat Izin Usaha Penerbitan Pers* press publication permit

siur *simpang ~* in a mess, higgledy-piggledy

Siwa, Syiwa *n, Hind* Shiva, god of destruction

SK *abbrev Surat Keputusan* decree, binding decision

skala *n* scale; **berskala** *v* to be on a scale; ~ *besar* large-scale

skéma *n* diagram, sketch

skétsa *n* sketch

skop → **sekop**

skor *n* score

skors: diskors *v* to be suspended (from school or work); **skorsing** *n* suspension

Skotlandia *n* Scotland; *bahasa ~* Scots; Gaelic; *makanan ~* Scottish food; *orang ~* Scot; *wiski ~* Scotch whisky

SLI *abbrev Sambungan Langsung Internasional* international direct dialling

SLJJ *abbrev Sambungan Langsung Jarak Jauh* long-distance direct dialling

slof *n* carton of cigarettes

sloki → **seloki**

Slovakia *n* Slovakia; *Ceko~* Czechoslovakia; *bahasa ~, orang ~* Slovak

Slovénia *n* Slovenia; *bahasa ~* Slovenian; *orang ~* Slovenian, Slovene

SLTA *abbrev Sekolah Lanjutan Tingkat Atas* Senior High School

SLTP *abbrev Sekolah Lanjutan Tingkat Pertama* Junior High School

SM *abbrev sebelum Masehi* before Christ, BC

SMA *abbrev Sekolah Menengah Atas* Senior High School

SMEA *abbrev Sekolah Menengah Ekonomi Atas* Senior High School for Economics

SMP *abbrev Sekolah Menengah Pertama* Junior High School

SMU *abbrev Sekolah Menengah Umum* Senior High School

soal *n* question, issue, problem, matter; *conj* on the topic of;

~*nya* the problem is; ~ *kecil* small matter; ~ *ujian* exam question; *memecahkan* ~ to solve a problem; **mempersoalkan** *v* to question, discuss; **persoalan** *n* problem, issue, matter

sobat *n* friend, comrade; ~ *karib* close friend; **bersobat** *v* to be friends

sobék torn (esp of paper); **menyobék** *v* to tear; **menyobék-nyobék** *v* to rip up

SOBSI *abbrev Sentral Organisasi Buruh Seluruh Indonesia* All-Indonesian Federation of Labour Organisations

soda *air* ~ soda water; **bersoda** *adj* carbonated; *minuman* ~ carbonated drink

sodét, sudét: sudétan *n* diversion, canal; **menyodét** *v* to make an incision, cut a connecting channel

sodok: sodokan *n* shot (in billiards); **menyodok** *v* to poke

sodomi *n* sodomy; **menyodomi** *v* to sodomize

sodor: menyodori *v* to hand to, offer; **menyodorkan** *v* to offer up, put forward

sofbol *n* softball; *pemain* ~ softballer

soga *n* dark brown natural dye

sogok *uang* ~ bribe; **sogokan** *n* bribe; **menyogok** *v* to bribe

sohor: kesohor *adj, coll*; **tersohor** *adj* famous; **pesohor** *n* famous person, celebrity

sohun, so'un *n* vermicelli noodles

sok *coll* pretend; as if; ~ *tahu* be a know-all

sokong support; **sokongan** *n* support; **menyokong** *v* to support, bolster

sol ~ *sepatu* (shoe) sole

solar *n* diesel fuel

solat → **sholat**

soléh, saléh *adj* pious, religious; **kesoléhan** *n* piety

solék: bersolék *v* to put on make-up, dress up

solusi *n* solution

Somalia *n* Somalia; *bahasa* ~, *orang* ~ Somali

somasi *n* summons; **disomasi** *v* to be summoned → **panggil**

sombong *adj* arrogant, stuck-up; **menyombongkan** ~ *diri* to show off, blow your own trumpet

sonder *conj, coll* without

songkét *n (kain)* ~ woven cloth, often with gold thread

songkok *n* traditional velvet fez, esp in Malay areas

songo, sanga *Wali* ~ *Isl* nine holy men who spread Islam across Java

songsong: menyongsong *v* to welcome, greet

sono → **sana**

sonték → **conték**

sop *n* (western-style) soup; ~ *ayam* chicken broth

sopan *adj* polite, well-mannered; ~ *santun* good manners; **kesopanan** *n* manners, politeness; **kesopan-santunan** *n* manners, etiquette

sopir → **supir**

sorak cheer, shout; applause; **bersorak** v to cheer, shout

soré (late) afternoon, early evening; ~ *hari* late in the day; *nanti* ~ this evening; *selamat* ~ good afternoon; **soré-soré** adv late in the day; **kesoréan** adv too late

sorga → **surga**

sori sl sorry, pardon

sorong, menyorong v to push, propose

sorot n beam of light; *lampu* ~ spotlight; **sorotan** n focus; **menyoroti** v to light up, illuminate, focus on

sortir, mensortir v to sort, organize

sosial adj social; *Menteri* ~ Minister of Social Affairs; *visa* ~ *budaya (sosbud)* sociocultural visa; **sosialisasi** n socialization; **mensosialisasikan** v to introduce to the public, disseminate

sosialis n socialist; **sosialisme** n socialism

sosis n sausage

sosok n figure; **bersosok** v to have a figure; ~ *tinggi* tall

sospol sociopolitic, social studies and politics ← **sosial politik**

soto n clear soup; ~ *ayam* chicken soup; **disoto** v to be made into clear soup

sotong *ikan* ~ cuttlefish, squid

so'un → **sohun**

spanduk n large banner

Spanyol n Spain; *bahasa* ~ Spanish; *orang* ~ Spanish, a Spaniard

spasi n space, spacing; ~ *ganda* double spacing

SPBU abbrev *setasiun pompa bensin umum* petrol/fuel/gasoline station

spékkoek n, arch [spékuk] layer cake ← **lapis legit**

spérma n sperm

spésial adj special; **spésialis** n specialist

spidol n felt-tip marker or pen, texta; whiteboard marker

spidométer n speedometer

spion n spy; ~ *Melayu derog* (inept) local agent; *kaca* ~ rearview mirror; **spionase** n secret intelligence, espionage

spiral n IUD (intra-uterine device)

spiritus n spirits, alcohol

spons, spon n sponge

sponsor n sponsor; **mensponsori** v to sponsor

spontan adj spontaneous

sprei → **seprei**

SR abbrev *Sekolah Rakyat* People's School, forerunner of SD

sreg adj, coll comfortable, fitting

Sri *Dewi* ~ goddess of rice; ~ *Langka* Sri Lanka; *orang* ~ *Langka* Sri Lankan; ~ *Paduka* His Royal Highness, Her Royal Highness; ~ *Paus* the Pope, Holy Father

Srikandi n Arjuna's wife in shadow-puppet plays

srikaya, serikaya n custard-apple

SS abbrev Sarjana Sastra Bachelor of Arts, BA

ST abbrev Sarjana Teknik Bachelor of Engineering, BE

stabil adj stable

stabilo n highlighter, fluorescent marker

stadion n (sports) stadium

stadium n stage (of an illness); kanker ~ satu early cancer; ~ tiga advanced

stagén n corset-like belt worn with women's national costume

stang, setang n (on bicycles) bar, handlebar, stand

stasiun → **setasiun**

status n (marital) status

stémpel, setémpel n official stamp; **distémpel** v to be stamped

STh abbrev Sarjana Teologi Bachelor of Theology

STNK abbrev Surat Tanda Nomor Kendaraan motor vehicle license

stopkontak n power point, electricity socket

stoplés n glass jar for storing crackers & other loose food

Stovia n medical school in Dutch times, Native Doctors Training School ← **School tot Opleiding van Indische Artsen**

strata n level; ~ satu (S1) bachelor degree

stréng adj strict, harsh, disciplinarian

strés, setrés stress(ed)

strom, stroom → **setrum**

studi n studies; melanjutkan ~ ke Australia to continue your studies in Australia

stupa n stupa, bell-shaped dome covering a Buddha statue

sua: bersua v to meet

suai: sesuai adj in accordance or keeping with; **menyesuaikan** v to adapt; ~ diri dengan to adapt yourself to; **penyesuaian** n adaptation

suak adj weak (of batteries)

suaka n asylum; ~ politik political asylum; mencari ~ to seek asylum; pencari ~ asylum seeker

suami n husband; ~ isteri husband and wife, married couple; **bersuami** adj, f married; **bersuamikan** v to be married to

suap n mouthful; bribe; **suapan** n bribe; **bersuap-suapan** v to feed each other (in marriage rituals); **menyuap** v to feed by hand; to bribe; **menyuapi** v to feed someone by hand; **menyuapkan** v to feed something by hand, to someone; **sesuap** n mouthful; ~ nasi a mouthful of rice; something to eat

suar mercu ~ lighthouse

suara n voice; vote; ~ bulat unanimous; ~ terbanyak majority vote; kotak ~ ballot box; memberi ~ to (cast a) vote; memungut ~ to collect or get votes; pengeras ~ loudspeaker, megaphone; penghitungan ~ vote-counting; pita ~ vocal chords; **bersuara** v to sound, have a voice; **menyuarakan** v to voice

suasana n atmosphere; ~ politik political situation

suatu adj a (certain); ~ hari one day; **sesuatu** n something

subsidi n subsidy; **mensubsidi** v to subsidize

subuh n dawn; sholat ~ dawn prayer

subur adj fertile; **kesuburan** n fertility; **menyuburkan** v to fertilize

subyék n subject; **subyéktif** adj subjective

suci adj pure, holy; ~ hama sterile; air ~ holy water; kitab ~ holy book; **kesucian** n purity; **menyucikan** v to purify, cleanse

sudah aux **udah** coll already; indicates past time; **kesudahan** tidak ber~ endless, infinite; **menyudahi** v to end; **sesudah** prep after; ~ itu **sesudahnya** after that, then ← **sudah**

Sudan n (the) Sudan; orang ~ Sudanese

sudétan n diversion, canal → **sodét**

sudi adj willing; ~kah would you be willing to; please; tidak ~ unwilling

sudra n, Hind lowest caste, commoners

sudut n corner, angle, perspective, point of view; ~ 45 derajat 45 degree angle; **menyudutkan** v to push into a corner, deflect

suér sl I swear

sugésti n power of suggestion; **sugéstif** adj suggestive

suguh: suguhan n something offered or presented; **menyuguhi** v to offer (food), present (a performance)

suhu n temperature; ~ badan body temperature; ~ kamar room temperature; **bersuhu** v to have a temperature

suit whistling sound; **suitan** n whistle; **bersuit** v to whistle using your fingers

sujud touch your head to the floor during prayer, prostration; **bersujud** v to prostrate yourself

suka v to like; adv often; ~ cita happiness; ~ damai peace-loving; ~ duka good and bad times, happiness and sadness; ~rela voluntary; ~ menolong helpful, likes helping out; **kesukaan** n hobby; enjoyment; **menyukai** v to like

sukar adj difficult, hard; **kesukaran** n difficulty

sukaréla adj voluntary; **sukaré-lawan** n volunteer ← **réla**

sukma n spirit, soul

suksés n success; semoga ~ good luck, every success; tim ~ team working towards the election of a candidate; **mensukséskan** v to make something succeed

suku n tribe; part; ~ bangsa ethnic group; ~ kata syllable; **kesukuan** adj ethnic, tribal

sukun (buah) ~ breadfruit

sulam: sulaman *n* embroidery;
menyulam *v* to embroider

sulang: bersulang *v* to toast,
drink to

sulap magic, conjure; *bermain* ~
to do magic; **sulapan** *n* conjuring, magic; *tukang* ~ magician,
conjurer; **menyulap** *v* to conjure up; to make something
vanish or change; **penyulap** *n*
magician, conjurer

Sulawési, Sulawesi *pulau* ~
Sulawesi, Celebes; ~ *Selatan
(Sulsel)* South Sulawesi; ~
Tengah (Sulteng) Central
Sulawesi; ~ *Tenggara (Sultra)*
Southeast Sulawesi; ~ *Utara
(Sulut)* North Sulawesi

sulih substitute; ~ *suara* dubbing;
menyulih-suarakan *v* to dub;
penyulih ~ *suara* dubber;
penyulihan ~ *suara* dubbing

suling, seruling *n* flute; *pemain*
~ flautist; **pesuling** *n* flautist

suling: menyuling *v* to distill;
penyulingan *n* distillation

sulit *adj* difficult, complicated,
hard; ~ *bicara* find it hard to
speak; *masa* ~ hard times;
kesulitan *n* difficulty, trouble;
menyulitkan *v* to make difficult, complicate, cause problems; **tersulit** *adj* the hardest,
most difficult

Sulsel *n* South Sulawesi ←
Sulawési Selatan

Sulteng *n* Central Sulawesi ←
Sulawési Tengah

Sultra *n* Southeast Sulawesi ←
Sulawési Tenggara

suluh *n* torch; **menyuluh** *v* to
illuminate; to inform; **penyuluh** *n* scout; education
worker; **penyuluhan** *n*
education, explanation

sulung *anak* ~ eldest (child)

Sulut *n* North Sulawesi ←
Sulawési Utara

Sumatera, Sumatra *(pulau)* ~
Sumatra; ~ *Barat (Sumbar)*
West Sumatra; ~ *Selatan
(Sumsel)* South Sumatra; ~
Utara (Sumut) North Sumatra

sumbang *adj* false, out of tune;
suara ~ tuneless voice

sumbang: sumbangan *n*
contribution, donation; **menyumbang** *v* to contribute,
make a donation

Sumbar *n* West Sumatra ←
Sumatera Barat

sumbat plug; cork, stopper;
menyumbat *v* to plug, stop;
penyumbatan *n* blockage

sumber *n* source; well; ~
minyak oilwell; ~ *air* source; ~
terpercaya reliable source

sumbing *bibir* ~ harelip, cleft
palate

sumbu *n* fuse; wick (of a candle)

sumbu *n* axle

sumpah curse; oath; ~ *jabatan*
oath of office; *di bawah* ~
under oath; **bersumpah** *v* to
swear; **menyumpahi** *v* to
swear at or curse someone

sumpek *adj* crowded, stuffy

sumpit *n* chopsticks; **sumpitan**
n blowpipe; **menyumpit** *v* to
use a blowpipe

Sumsel *n* South Sumatra ← **Sumatera Selatan**

sumsum *n* bone marrow; *bubur* ~ rice-flour porridge

sumur *n* well; ~ *bor* artesian well

Sumut *n* North Sumatra ← **Sumatera Utara**

sun peck on the cheek, kiss; *memberi* ~ to kiss on the cheek; **disun** *v* to be kissed on the cheek

Sunan *pron, Isl* holy man, title used before the names of the Nine Holy Men (Wali Songo)

sunat: sunatan *n* circumcision (celebration); **disunat** *v* to be circumcised; **menyunatkan** *v* to have someone circumcised

Sunda *bahasa* ~, *orang* ~ Sundanese

sundul, menyundul ~ *bola* to head the ball (in soccer); **sundulan** *n* header

sungai *n* river; *anak* ~ tributary; ~ *Mahakam* the Mahakam (River)

sungguh *adj* real, true; **sungguh-sungguh** *adj* serious; **bersungguh-sungguh** *v* to do your best; **kesungguhan** *n* earnestness, sincerity, truth; **sesungguhnya** *adv* actually, really; **sungguhpun** *conj* although, even though

sungkawa *bela*~ condolences; **menyampaikan** *bela*~ to express your condolences or sympathy

sungsang *adj* upside down, reversed; *letak* ~ breech position (of a baby in the womb)

suntik *jarum* ~ (injecting) needle; **suntikan** *n* vaccination, injection; needle; **menyuntik** *v* to inject or vaccinate

sunting: menyunting *v* to edit; **penyunting** *n* editor; **penyuntingan** *n* editing

sunting: mempersunting *v* to marry (a woman)

suntuk *adj* late; *semalam* ~ all night long

sunyi *adj* lonely, still, quiet; **kesunyian** *n* quiet, still

sup *n* (Western-style) soup; ~ *ikan hiu* shark's fin soup

supaya *conj* in order that, so (used before nouns); *agar* ~ in order that

supel *adj* sociable, easy-going, flexible

supermi, supermie *n* (brand of) instant noodles ← **mi**

supir, sopir *n* driver, chauffeur; ~ *truk* truck driver; **menyupir** *v* to drive

surah *n* chapter of the Koran

suram *adj* gloomy, dark

surat *n* letter; certificate, card; ~ *cinta* love-letter; ~ *edaran* circular, memo; ~ *ijazah* diploma, certificate; ~ *kabar* newspaper; ~ *kawin*, ~ *nikah* marriage certificate; ~ *lahir* birth certificate; ~ *keterangan* written statement; ~ *kuasa* letter of authorization, proxy letter; power of attorney; ~ *rekomendasi* letter of recom-

mendation; ~ *perintah* warrant;
~ *wasiat* (last) will and testament; **surat-menyurat** *v* to
correspond with someone;
menyurati *v* to write a letter to
surau *n, Isl* small prayer-house
surga, syurga, sorga *n* heaven,
paradise; ~ *dunia* heaven on earth
suri *mati* ~ in a coma
suri *timun* ~ large cucumber,
often eaten at fast-breaking
suri *ibu* ~ the Queen Mother
Suriah *n* Syria; *orang* ~ Syrian
Suriname *n* Surinam; *orang* ~
Surinamese, a Surinamer
suruh order, ask; tell; **suruhan**
n messenger, errand-boy; **menyuruh** *v* to command, order;
pesuruh *n* messenger, errand
boy; ~ *kantor* office boy
surup: **kesurupan** *v* to be
possessed by a spirit or ghost
surut *v* to recede; *air* ~ low tide;
pasang ~ rise and fall; **menyurut** *v* to fall, subside
surya *sang* ~ the Sun; *tabir* ~
sunblock, sunscreen; *tenaga* ~
solar energy
sus *kue* ~ small sweet buns containing rum-flavored cream
susah difficult; trouble, sorrow;
~ *makan* won't eat; *ber~*
payah to work hard; **kesusahan** *n* trouble, difficulty;
menyusahkan *v* to bother,
make difficult
susastra, susastera → **sastra**
susila *adj* modest, polite; *tuna~*
immoral; *wanita tuna~ (WTS)*
prostitute; **bersusila** *v* to have

good morals; **kesusilaan** *n*
modesty, decency; ethics
suster *n* nurse(maid); *n, Cath* nun
susu *n* milk; *n, sl* breast; ~
bubuk powdered milk; ~ *formula* milk formula; *air* ~ *ibu*
(ASI) breast milk; ~ *kaleng*
condensed milk; *kepala* ~
cream; **menyusu** *v* to feed,
suckle; **menyusui** *v* to feed;
binatang ~ mammal
susuk *n* implant
susul: *susulan ujian* ~ make-up
exams; **menyusul** *v* to follow,
go after
susun heap, pile; *rumah* ~
(rusun) block of flats, apartment block; **susunan** *n*
arrangement, organization, system; ~ *kalimat* sentence structure; **menyusun** *v* to heap or
pile; to arrange, organize, compile; **penyusun** *n* compiler,
author
susup: **menyusup** *v* to penetrate, infiltrate; **penyusupan** *n*
infiltration
susut to shrink; **menyusut** *v* to
shrink, become smaller;
menyusutkan *v* to reduce
sutera, sutra *n* silk
sutradara *n* director; **menyutradarai** *v* to direct
swa- *pref* self-; ~*daya* self-
sufficient; ~*layan* self-serve;
supermarket; ~*sembada* self-
sufficient
swasta *adj* private; *bank* ~ private
bank; **menswastakan** *v* to
privatize

Swaziland *n* Swaziland; *bahasa ~*, *orang ~* Swazi

Swédia *n* Sweden; *bahasa ~* Swedish; *orang ~* Swede

swémpak *n*, *arch* swimming costume, swimsuit

Swis *n* Switzerland; *orang ~* Swiss

switer *n* jumper, pullover, sweater

swt. *abbrev subhanahu wa taala* the Almighty and Most Praiseworthy, said after saying the name of Allah

syahadat *n*, *Isl* profession of faith: I believe there is no God but God, and Muhammad is His Prophet

syahbandar *n* harbor master

syahdan *conj*, *lit* so it happened

syahdu *adj* calm, serene

syahid, sahid *Isl mati ~* martyr

syahwat *n* lust, desire

syair *n* poem; **penyair** *n* poet

syaitan → **sétan**

syal *n* shawl, scarf

syarat, sarat *n* condition, terms; *dengan ~* on condition; *memenuhi ~* to meet requirements; *tanpa ~* unconditional; **bersyarat** *adj* conditional

syariah *hukum ~* Islamic law

Syiwa → **Siwa**

syukur, sukur thanks, thanksgiving; thank goodness; *puji ~ Chr* thank God; **bersyukur** *adj* grateful; **mensyukuri** *v* to appreciate, be thankful

syur *adj* sexy, hot

syurga → **surga**

syuting *n* shooting (a film or TV program); *lokasi ~* on location

T

taat *adj* obedient; religious; **menaati** *v* to obey or follow something

tabah *adj* strong, resolute, brave; **ketabahan** *n* strength of character

tabel *n* table, chart

tabiat *n* character, nature, temperament; **bertabiat** *v* to be of a character

tabir *n* curtain, screen; *~ surya* sunscreen, sunblock

tabrak collide; *~ lari* hit and run; **tabrakan** *n* collision, accident; **menabrak** *v* to collide with; **menabrakkan** *v* to ram something into; **tertabrak** *adj* **ketabrak** *adj*, *coll* to be hit; *~ mobil* hit by a car

tabu taboo

tabuh *n* drum; drumstick; **menabuh** *v* to beat (a drum)

tabung *n* container, tube; *bayi ~* test-tube baby; **tabungan** *n* savings; *~ pos* postal savings account; *uang ~* savings; **menabung** *v* to save or deposit money; **penabung** *n* depositor

tabur scatter, sprinkle; *~ bunga* to scatter flowers on a grave; **taburan** *n* sprinkling; **bertaburan** *adj* scattered over; **menabur** *v* to scatter or sprinkle; **penabur** *n* sower

tadi *adv* just now; *~nya* originally, at first; *~ pagi* this morning; *~ malam* last night

tafsir *n, Isl* Koranic interpretation or commentary; **tafsiran** *n* interpretation; **menafsirkan** *v* to interpret something

tagih, menagih *v* to ask for payment, bill; **tagihan** *n* amount due, bill

tagih: ketagihan *adj* addicted to

tahan bear, stop, last; ~ *air* waterproof; ~ *lama* durable, lasting; *tidak* ~ can't bear; **tahanan** *n* prisoner, detainee; custody, detention; **ketahanan** *n* endurance; **menahan** *v* to bear, endure; to detain; ~ *diri* to hold yourself back, restrain yourself; **mempertahankan** *v* to defend or maintain; **penahanan** *n* detention, arrest; **pertahanan** *n* defence; ~ *sipil (hansip)* local security guard; civil defense; *Menteri* ~ Minister for Defense; **tertahan** *adj* held back, prevented; **tertahankan** *tak* ~ unbearable

tahap *n* stage, phase; **bertahap** *adj* in stages

tahayul, takhayul *n* superstition

tahbis: menahbiskan *v* to consecrate, ordain; **penahbisan** *n* consecration, ordination

tahi *n* shit, feces; ~ *lalat* mole

tahlil *n, Isl* declaration that there is no God but God (*la ilaha illa'llah*); **tahlilan** *n* recitation of this and other parts of the Koran

tahta → **takhta**

tahu [tau] *v* to know; ~ *diri* humble; *tidak* ~ *malu* shameless, without shame; **tahu-tahu**

adv suddenly, unexpectedly; **ketahuan** *v* to be found out; **mengetahui** *v* to know something, have knowledge of; **pengetahuan** *n* knowledge; *ilmu* ~ *alam (IPA)* science; **sepengetahuan** *adj* with knowledge; ~ *saya* to my knowledge; **setahu** *conj* as far as is known; ~ *saya* as far as I know

tahu *n* tofu; ~ *sutera* Japanese tofu; ~ *tempe* tofu and unprocessed soybean cake

tahun *n* year; ~ *anggaran* financial year; ~ *Baru* New Year; ~ *Baru Cina*, ~ *Baru Imlek* Chinese New Year; ~ *kabisat* leap year; ~ *Masehi* Christian calendar; **tahunan** *adj* annual, yearly; *buku* ~ yearbook; *laporan* ~ annual report; **bertahun-tahun** *adv* for years and years; **menahun** *adj* chronic; *penyakit* ~ chronic illness

tahu-tahu *adv* suddenly, unexpectedly ← **tahu**

taipan *n* magnate, wealthy financier

Taiwan *n* Taiwan; *orang* ~ Taiwanese

tajam *adj* sharp; *berotak* ~ to be sharp(-witted); **ketajaman** *n* sharpness; **mempertajam** *v* to sharpen, exacerbate

taji *n* spur (of a cock)

Tajikistan *n* Tajikistan; *bahasa* ~ Tajik; *orang* ~ Tajikistani (nationality)

tajuk *n* crown; editorial; ~ *rencana* editorial; **bertajuk** *v* to have a topic

tak no, not; ~ *terhingga* endless, infinite; ~ *kan*, ~*kan* will not, won't ← **tidak**

takar: takaran *n* measuring container or spoon; **menakar** *v* to measure

takbir *n, Isl* declaration that God is great *(Allah Akbar)*; **takbiran** *v* to reiterate that God is great; *malam* ~ eve of Idul Fitri when this statement is chanted

takdir *n* fate, predestination; **menakdirkan** *v* to determine, to predestine

takhayul, tahayul, takhyul *n* superstition

takhta, tahta *n* throne; ~ *Suci* the Holy See; *naik* ~ ascend to the throne; **bertakhta** *v* to reign

takjub *adj* astonished; **menakjubkan** *adj* astonishing, amazing

takkan will not, won't ← **tak kan**

takluk *v* to surrender, give in; ~ *pada* defer to; **menaklukkan** *v* to defeat, conquer, subdue

takraw *n* small rattan ball; *sepak* ~ game in which this ball is kicked without touching the ground

taksi *n* taxi; ~ *argo* metered taxi

taksir guess; **taksiran** *n* estimate, valuation, appraisal; **menaksir** *v* to estimate, appraise, value; to like, find someone or something attractive; **naksir** *v, coll* to like, find someone or something attractive; **penaksiran** *n* evaluation

takut *adj* scared, afraid; ~ *mati* scared of dying; ~ *Tuhan* God-fearing; *jangan* ~ don't be afraid; *rasa* ~ fear; **ketakutan** *adj* frightened, terrified, scared; **menakut-nakuti** *v* to frighten or intimidate (repeatedly); **menakutkan** *v, adv* frightening; to frighten or scare; **penakut** *n* coward

takwa *adj* piety; **bertakwa** *n* pious

tala *garpu* ~ tuning fork; **menala** *v* to tune

talak *n, Isl* repudiation; step towards divorce; ~ *pertama* first repudiation; ~ *ketiga*, ~ *terakhir* third and final repudiation, thus effecting a divorce

talang *n* (roof) gutter

talenan *n* chopping or cutting board

tali *n* rope, cord, tie; ~ *keluarga* family ties; ~ *pengikat* string; ~ *pusar* umbilical cord; ~ *sepatu* shoelace; **pertalian** *n* connection, relationship

talk *n* talc, talcum powder ← **bedak**

tamah *ramah*-~ informal get-together

tamak *adj* greedy; **ketamakan** *n* greed

taman *n* garden, park; ~ *bacaan*, ~ *pustaka* reading room, library; ~ *budaya* cultural center; ~ *kanak-kanak (TK)* kindergarten; **pertamanan** *adj* parks and gardens; *dinas* ~ parks service

tamasya view; spectacle; excursion; **bertamasya** v to travel (for pleasure), go sightseeing

tamat end, finish; ~ *sekolah* graduate; ~ *usia*, ~ *riwayatnya* die; **tamatan** n graduate; **menamatkan** v to end, finish, conclude

tambah add; **tambahan** n addition, increase; *biaya* ~ extra cost; **bertambah** v to increase; **menambah** v to add to or increase; **menambahi** v to increase something; **menambahkan** v to add something to; **pertambahan** n increase

tambak n dam, pond; dike, levee, embankment; ~ *udang* shrimp pond, shrimp farm; **menambak** v to dam (up)

tambal n patch; ~ *ban* tire repair; **tambalan** n patch, darn (on a sock); **bertambal** adj patched; **menambal** v to mend, patch, darn; ~ *jalan* to fill in a pothole

tambang n mine; ~ *batu bara* coal mine, colliery; ~ *emas* gold mine; **menambang** v to mine, dig for; **penambang** n miner; **pertambangan** n mining

tambang n thick rope, tow line; *tarik* ~ tug-of-war

tambat tie up, tether; **tambatan** n bollard; **bertambat** v to moor; **tertambat** adj tied up, moored; **menambat, menambatkan** v to fasten, tie up

tambun adj corpulent, fat

tambur n drum

taméng n shield; **bertaméng** v to hide behind, use as a shield or pretext

tampak visible, appear; ~*nya* it seems, apparently; **menampakkan** v to show, make appear; **penampakan** n apparition; visitation

tampal → **tambal**

tampan adj, m handsome; **ketampanan** n good looks

tampang n appearance; *coll* face; *jual* ~ succeed on looks alone; show off

tampar slap, smack; **tamparan** n slap; **menampar** v to slap

tampi: menampi v to winnow; **penampi** n winnow

tampik: menampik v to reject, refuse

tampil v to appear; **menampilkan** v to present; **penampilan** n performance

tampung: menampung v to collect, hold; **penampung** n container; **penampungan** n reception, place that receives something; **tertampung** adj contained

tamu n guest, visitor; ~ *negara* state guest; ~ *tak diundang* uninvited guest; *kamar* ~, *ruang* ~ front room, living room; room for receiving guests; spare room

tanah n earth, ground, land, soil; country; ~ *air* Indonesia, native country, homeland; ~ *leluhur* ancestral home; ~ *liat* clay; *minyak* ~ kerosene

tanak: menanak ~ *nasi* to cook rice

tanam *bercocok* ~ to till or work the soil; **tanaman** *n* plant; ~ *merambat* vine, climbing plant; **menanam** *v* to plant or grow; to invest; *penanaman* ~ *modal* investment

tancap *layar* ~ open-air makeshift cinema; **menancap** *v* ~ *gas* to step on the gas, accelerate

tanda *n* sign, mark, symbol; ~ *bayar* receipt; ~ *seru* exclamation mark; ~ *tanya* question mark; ~ *tangan* signature; **menandatangani** *v* to sign something; **bertanda** *adj* marked; **menandai** *v* to mark; **pertanda** *n* sign, omen, indication

tandan *n* hand (of bananas)

tandang: bertandang *v* to (pay a) visit

tandas *adj* finished, wiped out, desolated; **menandaskan** *v* to use up; to reiterate

tanding *n* match, equal; **bertanding** *v* to compete, play; **pertandingan** *n* contest, competition, match

tandu *n* litter; **menandu** *v* to carry in a litter

tanduk *n* horn; *(seperti telur)* *di ujung* ~ hanging in the balance

tandus *adj* infertile, barren

tang *n* pliers

tangan *n* hand, arm; sleeve; *kemeja* ~ *panjang* long-sleeved shirt; *di bawah* ~ secretly; underhand; *buah* ~ souvenir; *kaki* ~ accomplice; *kerajinan* ~ handicraft; *panjang* ~ light-fingered; a thief; *sapu* ~ handkerchief; *sarung* ~ gloves; *tanda* ~ signature; *telapak* ~ palm; **menangani** *v* to handle; **penanganan** *n* handling

tangga *n* ladder, stair(case); ~ *nada* musical scale; *rumah* ~ household, family; *sudah jatuh tertimpa* ~ kicked when you're down and out

tanggal *n* date; ~ *lahir* date of birth; ~ *muda* early in the month; ~ *tua* late in the month; **bertanggal** *tak* ~ undated; **penanggalan** *n* calendar, dating; **tertanggal** *adj* dated

tanggal: menanggalkan *v* to take off or remove; ~ *pakaian* to undress

tanggap: tanggapan *n* response, reaction; **menanggapi** *v* to respond, reply

tangguh *adj* strong, powerful

tangguh: menangguhkan *v* to delay, postpone, put something off; **penangguhan** *n* delay, postponement

tanggul *n* dike, levee, embankment

tanggulang: menanggulangi *v* to deal or cope with; **penanggulangan** *n* tackling, fight against

tanggung *adj* guaranteed; ~ *jawab* responsibility; *rasa* ~ *jawab* sense of responsibility; **bertanggung jawab** *v* to be responsible; **mempertanggungjawabkan** *v* to account for; **tanggungan** *n* dependent; responsibility; **menanggung** *v* to guarantee, be responsible; ~ *beban* to bear; **pertanggung-an** *n* responsibility; insurance

tangis *isak* ~ crying; **tangisan** *n* weeping, crying; **menangis** *v* to cry; **menangisi** *v* to cry over, mourn

tangkai *n* stem, stalk; ~ *bunga* flower stem

tangkal: **menangkal** *v* to ward off, repel; **penangkal** ~ *petir* lightning rod; **penangkalan** *n* preventative measure

tangkap, menangkap *v* to catch, capture; **ketangkap** *coll* (to be) caught, arrested; **penangkapan** *n* capture, arrest; **tertangkap** *adj* caught; ~ *basah* caught in the act

tangkas *adj* agile, adroit, deft; **ketangkasan** *n* agility, dexterity; *menguji* ~ to test your skill

tangki *n* tank

tangkis: **menangkis** *v* to defend yourself, fend off, parry

tangkring: **nangkring** *v, coll* to sit somewhere high up, perch

tani *n* farmer; *Pak* ~ farmer; **petani** *n* farmer; ~ *cengkeh* clove farmer; **pertanian** *n* agriculture; *sekolah* ~ agricultural college

tanjak: **tanjakan** *n* rise, ascent, climb; **menanjak** *adj* rising, climbing, steep

tanjidor *n* brass band found in Jakarta

tanjung *n* cape; ~ *Harapan* the

Cape of Good Hope; ~ *Verde* Cape Verde Islands; **seme-nanjung** *n* peninsula; ~ *Melayu* the Malay Peninsula

tanpa *prep, conj* without

tantang challenge; **tantangan** *n* challenge; **menantang** *v* to challenge; *adj* challenging

tante *pron* term of address to a familiar but unrelated woman, esp of mother's generation, in Westernized circles; ~ *genit*, ~ *girang* flirtatious older woman

tanya ask; ~ *jawab* question and answer session; *tanda* ~ question mark; **bertanya** *v* to ask; **bertanya-tanya** *v* to wonder, ask yourself; **menanyai** *v* to question someone; **menanyakan** *v* to ask about; **mempertanyakan** *v* to query; **pertanyaan** *n* question; *me-ngajukan* ~ to ask questions

Tanzania *n* Tanzania; *orang* ~ Tanzanian

taoco → **tauco**

taogé, taugé, togé *n* bean sprouts

tapa: **bertapa** *v* to live as an ascetic or hermit, seclude oneself; **pertapa** *n* ascetic, hermit, recluse; **pertapaan** *n* hermitage, retreat

tapai → **tapé**

tapak, telapak ~ *kaki* sole; footprint; ~ *tangan*, palm

tapal ~ *batas* border, frontier

tapal ~ *kuda* horseshoe

tapé, tapai *n* fermented rice; *air* ~ fermented rice wine

tapi → **tetapi**

taplak ~ *meja* tablecloth

tapol *n* political prisoner ← **tahanan politik**

tar, tart *kue* ~ (birthday) cake

tara *tiada* ~ unequalled, incomparable; **setara** *adj* equal, equivalent

taraf *n* standard, level; ~ *hidup* standard of living; **bertaraf** *adj* of a certain standard; **setaraf** *adj* of the same standard

tarawih, taraweh (to go to) evening prayers at the mosque during Ramadan

tari *n* (traditional) dance; ~ *lenso* dance with a handkerchief; **tarian** *n* (traditional) dance; ~-*tarian* traditional dancing; **menari** *v* to dance, perform a traditional dance; **menari-nari** *n* to dance about; **penari** *n* dancer

tarif, tarip *n* tariff, fare, rate

tarik pull; ~-*menarik* push and pull; ~ *tambang* tug-of-war; **menarik** *v* to pull or draw; *adj* interesting, attractive; ~ *kesimpulan* to conclude, draw a conclusion; ~ *napas* to inhale; **narik** *v, coll* to work as a driver of public transport; **tertarik** *adj* attracted, interested; **ketertarikan** *n* interest, attraction

taring *n* tusk; fang; *gigi* ~ fang, incisor, canine tooth

tarip → **tarif**

taruh *v* to place, put; **taruhan** bet, wager; **bertaruh** *v* to bet; **menaruh** *v* to put (away); ~ *dendam* to bear a grudge;

mempertaruhkan *v* to stake, risk, bet; ~ *nyawa* to risk your life

taruna, teruna *n* youth; cadet

tas *n* bag; ~ *pinggang* bum bag; ~ *tangan* handbag

tasbih, tasbeh *n, Isl* prayer beads

taskin *n* eradication of poverty ← **pengentasan kemiskinan**

tata *n* system, layout; ~ *acara* agenda, program; ~ *bahasa* grammar; ~ *negara* civics, state administration; ~ *rambut* hairstyle; ~ *usaha* administration

tatanan *n* arrangement, system; ~ *sosial* social structure

tatkala *conj* when, at the time

tato *n* tattoo; **bertato** *adj* tattooed

tau → **tahu**

taubat → **tobat**

tauco, taoco *n* brown sauce made from fermented soybeans

tauge, taoge, toge *n* bean sprouts

taulan, tolan *handai* ~ friends

Taurat *n* the Torah, the Old Testament

tawa laugh, laughter; **tawaan** *n* object of fun; **ketawa** *coll* **tertawa** *v* to laugh or smile; **menertawakan** *v* to laugh at

tawan: tawanan *n* prisoner of war (POW), detainee; **menawan** *v* to detain, take someone prisoner, intern; *adj* attractive, appealing

tawar bargain; **menawar** *v* to bargain; *tawar*-~ bargaining;

menawarkan *v* to offer or bid;
penawaran *n* offer, bid
tawar *adj* bland, plain, tasteless;
air ~ fresh water; **penawar** *n*
antidote
tawas *n* alum
tawon *n* bee
tawur: tawuran *n* gang or street
fight, often among schoolboys
tayang ~ *ulang* repeat, re-run;
kejar ~ continuous shooting
(of a TV series); **tayangan** *n*
program, telecast; ~ *langsung*
live telecast; ~ *tunda* delayed
telecast; **menayangkan** *v* to
telecast, show on TV
téater *n* theatre (building),
theater; drama group
tebak guess; **tebakan** *n* guess;
tebak-~ guessing game;
menebak *v* to guess
tebal *adj* thick; ~ *muka,* ~
telinga thick-skinned; *kertas*
~ card(board); **ketebalan** *n*
thickness
tebang fall, be cut down (of
trees); **menebang** *v* to fell,
cut down; **penebang** *n* logger,
woodcutter; **penebangan** *n*
logging; ~ *liar* illegal logging
tébar: bertébaran *adj* scattered;
menébarkan *v* to scatter; to
cast (a net)
tébéng → **nébéng**
tebing *n* cliff, gorge, steep bank;
panjat ~ rock-climbing, abseiling
tebu *n* sugarcane; *air* ~ sugarcane juice; *ladang* ~ cane fields
tebus: tebusan *n* ransom;
menebus *v* to pay a ransom;

~ *dosa* to atone for a sin;
penebus *n* redeemer; ransom;
penebusan *n* redemption
teduh *adj* shady; quiet, still;
Lautan ~ the Pacific Ocean;
berteduh *v* to take shelter
téga *v* to have the heart to, dare
to; ~*nya* how could you have
the heart
tegak *adj* upright, erect; ~ *lurus*
perpendicular, 90-degree angle;
menegakkan *v* to erect; to
uphold or maintain; **penegakan**
n upholding or maintenance; ~
hukum upholding the law
tegang *adj* tense, stressed,
strained; **bersitegang** *v* to
stand fast, persevere; **ketegangan** *n* tension; **menegangkan** *adj* tense, stressful
tegap *adj* strong, upright, sturdy
tegar *adj* stubborn, determined,
resolute; **ketegaran** *n* determination
tegas *adj* clear, distinct; **ketegasan** *n* resolve, determination; **menegaskan** *v* to clarify,
point out, affirm; **penegasan** *n*
affirmation, reiteration
tégel *n, arch* (floor) tile → **ubin**
tegor → **tegur**
teguh *adj* firm, fast, strong,
solid; ~ *hati* firm, resolute
teguk *n* gulp, swallow, draft;
tegukan *n* swallow, gulp;
meneguk *v* to gulp or guzzle;
seteguk *n* a gulp
tegun: tertegun *adj* taken aback
tegur speak; rebuke; ~ *sapa*
say hello; **teguran** *n* warning,

rebuke; greeting; **menegur** *v*
to speak to, address; to warn,
rebuke, tell off

téh *n* tea; ~ *botol* bottled tea; ~
melati jasmine tea; ~ *poci* tea
made in an earthenware pot,
specialty of the Tegal area; ~
tawar black tea no sugar; *kantong* ~ tea-bag

téhnik → téknik

teka: teka-teki *n* riddle, puzzle;
~ *silang (TTS)* crossword

tékad, tékat will, determination;
bertékad *v* to be determined

tekan press; **tekanan** *n* pressure,
stress; **menekan** *v* to press;
menekankan *v* to stress, emphasize; **tertekan** *adj* stressed,
pushed, pressured

teka-teki *n* riddle, puzzle; ~
silang (TTS) crossword

téken, menéken *v* to sign, initial

téknik, téhnik *n* engineering;
adj technical; ~ *mesin* civil
engineering

téknis *adj* technical; *bantuan* ~
technical assistance; **téknisi** *n*
technician

téknologi *n* technology; ~ *tinggi*
advanced technology

téko *n* kettle, teapot

tekor be short, not have enough

téks *n* text; subtitle

tékstil *n* textile

ték-ték *mi* ~ wandering noodle
sellers who tap on their carts

tekuk ~ *lutut* bend your knee;
bertekuk *v* to bend your knees;
~ *lutut* to surrender; **menekuk**
~ *lutut* to go down on your knees

tekukur *n* a kind of dove

tekun *adj* hard-working; **bertekun** *v* to work hard, be
diligent; **ketekunan** *n* diligence, dedication; **menekuni** *v*
to apply yourself to

telaah study, research; **menelaah**
v to analyze

teladan *n* example, model

telaga *n* lake

telah *adv* already; **setelah** *conj*
after

telak *menang* ~ win outright

telan *v* to swallow; **menelan** *v*
to swallow something; **tertelan**
v accidentally swallowed

telanjang *adj* naked, nude, bare;
~ *bulat* stark-naked; ~ *kaki*
barefoot; **bertelanjang** *v* to
be bare; ~ *dada* bare-chested;
menelanjangi *v* to strip or
denude

telanjur, terlanjur *adv* too late,
already; ~ *berangkat* already
left ← **lanjur**

telantar, terlantar *adj* neglected,
abandoned; **ketelantaran** *n*
neglect

telapak, tapak ~ *kaki* sole; footprint; ~ *tangan* palm

telat *adv, coll* (too) late; **ketelatan**
n lateness

telatén *adj* patient, persevering;
ketelaténan *n* patience, perseverance

télé: bertélé-télé *adj* long-winded

telédor *adj* careless; **ketelédoran**
n carelessness

téléfon → télepon

télékomunikasi *n* telecommuni-

cations; *warung ~ (wartel)*
small office where you can
make calls and send faxes

telekung *n* women's prayer shawl

telentang *adj* on your back,
prone ← **lentang**

télepon, télépon, téléfon telephone; *~ seluler (ponsel)*
mobile phone; *buku petunjuk
~* telephone directory, phone
book; **menélépon** *v* to ring
(up), call, (tele)phone

télér *adj* drunk, intoxicated;
exhausted

télér *es ~* iced fruit drink

télévisi, tévé, tivi *n* television,
TV; *menonton ~* to watch TV

telinga *n* ear; *daun ~* ear;
gendang ~ ear drum; *memasang ~* to listen carefully

teliti *adj* accurate, careful, metic-
ulous; **ketelitian** *n* accuracy,
care; **meneliti** *v* to investigate or
research; **peneliti** *n* researcher;
penelitian *n* research

Télkom *n* state telephone company; **Télkomsél** *n* state mobile
phone company

telor → **telur**

teluk *n* bay, gulf; *~ Bone* the Gulf
of Bone; *~ Jakarta* Jakarta Bay

telunjuk *jari ~* index finger, forefinger, pointer

telur, telor *n* egg; *~ ayam* egg;
~ dadar omelet; *~ ikan* roe (as
food), spawn; *~ mata sapi* fried
egg, sunnyside up; *~ puyuh* quail
egg; *indung ~* ovary; *kuning
~* yolk; *putih ~* albumen, egg
white; **bertelur** *v* to lay an egg

telusur: menelusuri *v* to follow,
go along, trace

tém: ngetém *v, coll* to wait for
passengers (of public transport)

téma *n* theme; **bertéma** *v* to
have as a theme

teman *n* friend; *~ sekantor*
friend from work, colleague;
berteman *v* to be friends;
menemani *v* to accompany

temaram *adj* dark

tembaga *n* copper; *~ kuning*
brass; *~ perunggu* bronze; *~
putih* pewter

témbak shoot, fire; *supir ~*
unregistered taxi driver;
témbakan *n* shot, shooting; **menémbak** *v* to shoot;
menémbaki *v* to shell;
penémbak *n* marksman,
gunman; **tertémbak** *adj* shot
(accidentally)

tembakau *n* tobacco

tembang *n* (esp Jav traditional)
song; *~ kenangan* old songs,
golden oldies; **menembang-
kan** *v* to sing something

tembikar *n* pottery, crockery,
ceramics

témbok *n* (concrete or outer)
wall; *~ Berlin* the Berlin Wall;
menémbok(i) *v* to wall something up

tembuni *n* placenta

tembus pierce, penetrate;
tembusan *n* copy; **menembus**
v to pierce, stab

temen → **teman**

tempa *besi ~* wrought iron;
menempa *v* to forge

tempat *n* place; ~ *istirahat* rest area; ~ *kerja* workplace; ~ *lahir* birthplace, place of birth; ~ *sabun* soap dish; ~ *tidur* bed; ~ *tinggal* home, residence; ~ *pemakaman umum (TPU)* public cemetery; *pada* ~*nya* proper; **bertempat** *v* to take place or happen; ~ *tinggal* to live or reside; **menempati** *v* to occupy, take a place; **menempatkan** *v* to place; **setempat** *adj* local

tempayan *n* water jar, pitcher

témpé *n* unrefined soybean curd; ~ *penyet* thin, fried slices of tempe

témpél stick to; *meterai* ~ adhesive seal; **témpélan** *adj* patch, sticker; **menémpél** *v* to stick or adhere to; **menémpélkan** *v* to stick, paste or glue something

tempéléng *v* to slap, box someone's ears

témpo *n* time, pace; ~ *dulu,* ~ *doeloe* the olden days, colonial times; ~ *hari* the other day, recently

tempuh: menempuh *v* to endure, go through; to take on, take up; ~ *jalan* to go your way; ~ *ujian* to do an exam

tempur fight, combat; *pesawat* ~ fighter (plane); **bertempur** *v* to fight; **pertempuran** *n* battle

tempurung *n* coconut shell; ~ *kepala* skull; ~ *lutut* kneecap, patella

temu find, locate; **temuan** *n* find, discovery; **bertemu** *v* to meet; *sampai* ~ *lagi* see you later, so long; **ketemu** *v, coll* to meet; **menemui** *v* to meet up with, arrange to meet; ~ *ajal* to die; **menemukan** *v* to discover; **penemu** *n* inventor, discoverer; **penemuan** *n* invention, discovery; **pertemuan** *n* meeting

temulawak *n* kind of root, curcuma

temurun *turun-*~ passed down through the generations

tenaga *n* energy, power; ~ *kerja* manpower, workforce; ~ *listrik* electricity; ~ *nuklir* nuclear energy

tenang *adj* calm, still, quiet; **ketenangan** *n* calm, peace; **menenangkan** *v* to calm someone (down)

tenar *adj* well-known, popular; **ketenaran** *n* popularity

ténda *n* tent

tendang kick; **tendangan** *n* kick; ~ *pertama* kick-off; **menendang** *v* to kick

tengadah face up; **menengadah** *v* to look up; **menengadahi** *v* to look up at

tengah middle, in the middle of, half; ~ *hari* midday, noon; ~ *malam* midnight; *garis* ~ diameter; **tengah-tengah** *prep* middle; **menengah** *adj* intermediate; *kelas* ~ middle class; *sekolah* ~ high school, secondary school; **pertengahan** *n* middle; *Abad* ~ the Middle Ages; **setengah** *adj* half; ~ *mati adv* half-dead; very

hard; *jam* ~ *dua* half past one;
setengah-setengah *adv* half-
heartedly

ténggang *n* period; ~ *waktu*
time frame

tenggara *adj* southeast; *Asia*
~ Southeast Asia; *Nusa* ~ the
Lesser Sunda islands

tenggelam sink, sunken; drown;
menenggelamkan *v* to sink or
drown something

Ténggér *bahasa* ~, *orang* ~
Tenggerese, a Hindu community of East Java

ténggér: berténggér *v* to perch,
land

tenggiling *n* anteater

tenggiri *ikan* ~ mackerel

tenggorok, tenggorokan *n*
throat; *sakit tenggorokan* sore
throat

tengkar: bertengkar *v* to quarrel;
pertengkaran *n* quarrel

tengkorak *n* skull

Tengku *pron, m* title for Malay
nobility

tengkuk *n* nape of the neck

tengkulak *n* agent, broker

tengkurap, tengkurup *adv* on
your front or face; *tidur* ~ sleep
on your stomach

téngok, menéngok *v* to look or
see; to look in on someone

ténis *n* tennis; *permainan* ~
tennis match; *pemain* ~ tennis
player; **peténis** *n* tennis player

ténsi *n* blood pressure

tentang *conj* about, concerning;
bertentangan *adj* contradictory, contrary, opposing; **me-**

nentang *v* to oppose, resist;
pertentangan *n* conflict

tentara *n* soldier; ~ *Nasional
Indonesia (TNI)* Indonesian
Army; ~ *payung* paratroops; ~
pelajar youth corps

ténténg, menénténg *v* to carry
dangling from the hand

tenteram, tentram *adj* peaceful,
calm; **ketenteraman** *n* peace

tentu *adj* certain, sure, definite;
~*nya,* ~ *saja* of course; **ketentuan** *n* condition, stipulation; **menentukan** *v* to decide,
determine, stipulate; **tertentu**
adj definite, fixed, certain

tenun *kain* ~ woven cloth;
tenunan *n* weaving, woven
fabric; **bertenun, menenun** *v*
to weave

téori *n* theory

tepat *adj* precise, exact; ~ *guna*
appropriate; effective;
bertepatan *adj* coinciding
with, at the same time as;
ketepatan *n* precision, accuracy; **menepati** *v* to fulfill; ~
janji to keep a promise

tepergok *adj* caught in the act,
caught red-handed ← **pergok**

tepi edge, side; ~ *jalan* side
of the road; ~ *laut* seaside;
menepi *v* to move to the side,
move over

tepis: menepis *v* ward off,
deflect

tepuk ~ *tangan* clap, applause;
bertepuk tangan *v* to applaud,
clap; **menepuk** *v* to pat, slap

tepung *n* flour; ~ *beras* rice

flour; ~ *maizena* wheat flour; ~ *terigu* flour

ter- *pref* (before adjectives) the most; **terbaik** *adj* the best; **tercantik** *adj* the most beautiful; **tertinggi** *adj* the highest

tér *n* tar

tera *n* official stamp, seal; **tertera** *adj* printed, stamped

terabaikan *adj* to be neglected, ignored ← **abai**

terakhir *adj* last, final, latest ← **akhir**

terali *n* trellis, lattice work

teramat ~ *sangat* extremely ← **amat**

terancam *adj* threatened; *harimau Jawa* ~ *punah* the Javan tiger is threatened with extinction ← **ancam**

terang *adj* clear; *terus* ~ direct, frank, straightforward; **terang-terangan** *adj* frank, open; **keterangan** *n* explanation; **menerangi** *v* to illuminate; **menerangkan** *v* to explain; **penerangan** *n* information; lighting, enlightenment

teraniaya *adj* oppressed, tyrannized ← **aniaya**

terap: terapan *adj* applied; *linguistik* ~ applied linguistics; **menerapkan** *v* to apply something; **penerapan** *n* application

térapi *n* therapy; *fisio~* physiotherapy

terapung *adj* drifting, floating ← **apung**

terarah *adj* directed ← **arah**

téras *n* balcony, terrace

terasa *v* to be felt ← **rasa**

terasi *n* shrimp paste

teratai *(bunga)* ~ lotus

teratasi *adj* can be overcome ← **atas**

teratur *adj* organized, (at) regular (intervals) ← **atur**

terawang: menerawang *v* to appear (through something translucent)

terbaik *adj* the best ← **baik**

terbakar *adj* burnt; *kulit Bapak* ~ *matahari* Father was sunburnt ← **bakar**

terbalik *adj* overturned, upside-down, opposite ← **balik**

terbang *v* fly; *kapal* ~, *pesawat* ~ aeroplane, airplane; *lapangan* ~ airfield; *piring* ~ flying saucer; **beterbangan** *v, pl* to fly about; **menerbangkan** *v* to fly something; **penerbang** *n* pilot, aviator; **penerbangan** *n* flight; aviation; *perusahaan* ~ airline

terbaru *adj* latest, newest ← **baru**

terbata-bata *adv* brokenly, not fluently ← **bata**

terbatas *adj* limited; *perseroan* ~ proprietary limited ← **batas**

terbawa *adj* (accidentally) taken away; ~ *arus* swept away in the current ← **bawa**

terbayang *adj* imagine, conceivable ← **bayang**

terbelakang *adj* backward, neglected; **keterbelakangan** *n* backwardness, neglect ← **belakang**

terbelenggu *adj* in shackles, irons ← **belenggu**

terbelit *adj* twisted, involved; ~ *hutang* debt-ridden ← **belit**

terbenam *adj* set, sunken; *matahari* ~ sunset ← **benam**

terbendung *tak* ~ unstoppable ← **bendung**

terbentuk *adj* formed, shaped, created ← **bentuk**

terbentur *adj* accidentally bumped; *kepalanya* ~ *di atap* he banged his head on the roof ← **bentur**

terbesar *adj* largest, biggest ← **besar**

terbilang *adj* counted; *tidak* ~, countless; *esa hilang, dua* ~ one lost, two scored (epigraph at military cemeteries) ← **bilang**

terbit *v* to rise, appear; *matahari* ~ sunrise; **terbitan** *n* publication, edition; **menerbitkan** *v* to publish, issue; **penerbit** *n* publisher

terbuang *adj* thrown out, wasted ← **buang**

terbuka *adj* open; *sidang* ~ public session ← **buka**

terbukti *adj* proven ← **bukti**

terbunuh *adj* killed ← **bunuh**

terburu-(buru) *adj* in a hurry ← **buru**

tercabik-cabik *adj* torn, to shreds ← **cabik**

tercabut *adj* removed ← **cabut**

tercantum *adj* attached, included, inserted ← **cantum**

tercapai *adj* achieved; *cita-cita tak* ~ unfulfilled dreams ← **capai**

tercatat *adj* registered, noted; *surat* ~ registered mail ← **catat**

tercebur *adj* fallen into water ← **cebur**

tercekik *adj* strangled ← **cekik**

tercela *adj* wrong; *perbuatan yang* ~ misdeed, wrong ← **cela**

tercemar *adj* polluted ← **cemar**

tercemplung *adj* fallen into water ← **cemplung**

tercengang *adj* surprised, astonished ← **cengang**

tercepat *adj* fastest ← **cepat**

tercermin *adj* reflected ← **cermin**

tercinta *adj* dear, beloved; *Hari yang* ~ dear Hari ← **cinta**

tercipta *adj* created ← **cipta**

tercium *adj* smelt; found out ← **cium**

terdaftar *adj* registered, enrolled ← **daftar**

terdakwa *n* the accused ← **dakwa**

terdampar *adj* beached, grounded, washed ashore; *ada ikan paus* ~ *di pantai* a whale was beached on the sands ← **dampar**

terdekat *adj* closest, nearest ← **dekat**

terdengar *adj* audible ← **dengar**

terdiam *v* to fall silent ← **diam**

terdiri ~ *atas,* ~ *dari* to consist of, be based or founded on ← **diri**

terdorong *adj* pushed, shoved ← **dorong**

terduga *tidak* ~ unexpected ← **duga**

terélakkan *tidak* ~ unavoidable, inevitable ← **élak**

teréliminasi *adj* eliminated ← **éliminasi**

terencana *adj* planned ← **rencana**

terendah *adj* lowest ← **rendah**

terendam *adj* inundated, flooded, soaked ← **rendam**

terengah-engah *adj* gasping, puffing ← **engah**

terganggu *adj* bothered, disrupted, disturbed ← **ganggu**

tergantung *adj* depending (on), it depends ← **gantung**

tergelétak *adj* sprawled ← **gelétak**

tergelimpang *adj* sprawled ← **gelimpang**

tergelincir *adj* skidded, slipped; *pesawat* ~ the plane skidded ← **gelincir**

tergesa-gesa *adj* in a hurry or rush ← **gesa**

tergiur *adj* tempted ← **giur**

tergoda *adj* tempted ← **goda**

tergolong *adj* to include, be part of or considered ← **golong**

tergorés *adj* scratched ← **gorés**

tergoyahkan *tak* ~ unshakable ← **goyah**

terhadap *conj* regarding, against, with respect to ← **hadap**

terhalang *adj* blocked, prevented; ← **halang**

terhanyut *adj* drifting, floating, washed away ← **hanyut**

terhapus *v* to delete, erase,

wipe; **menghapuskan** *vt* to wipe out, eliminate; **penghapus** *n* eraser; duster

terharu *adj* moved, touched ← **haru**

terhingga *tidak* ~ unlimited, boundless ← **hingga**

terhormat *adj* respected; *yang* ~ to, dear ← **hormat**

teri *ikan* ~ small fish, small fry

teriak scream, yell; **berteriak** *v* to scream or shout; **meneriaki** *v* to shout at someone; **meneriakkan** *v* to shout something

terigu *n* wheat; *tepung* ~ flour

terik *panas* ~ hot and dry, dry heat

terikat *n* bind, bond, commitment ← **ikat, keterikatan**

terima *tanda* ~ receipt; ~ *kasih* thank you; **menerima** *v* to receive, accept; **penerimaan** *n* receipt

terima kasih thank you, thanks; ~ *banyak* thank you very much; *mengucapkan* ~ to say thank you; **berterima kasih** *v* to be grateful or thankful

terinféksi *adj* infected ← **inféksi**

terinjak *adj* stepped upon; downtrodden ← **injak**

teripang, tripang *n* sea slug, sea cucumber, trepang

terisak, terisak-isak *adj* sobbing ← **isak**

terisolasi, terisolir *adj* isolated ← **isolasi, isolir**

terjadi *v* to happen, become ← **jadi**

terjaga *adj* alert, on guard ← **jaga**

terjal *adj* very steep, precipitous

terjamin *adj* guaranteed ← **jamin**

terjang kick, thrust; *sepak* ~ action, behavior; **menerjang** *v* to kick, attack, charge; **penerjangan** *n* attack, charge

terjangkit *adj* infected ← **jangkit**

terjatuh *adj* (accidentally) fallen ← **jatuh**

terjawab *adj* answered ← **jawab**

terjebak *adj* trapped, caught; ~ *macet* caught in traffic ← **jebak**

terjemah: terjemahan *n* translation; **menerjemahkan** *v* to translate (writing); to interpret (speaking); **penerjemah** *n* translator; ~ *tersumpah* sworn translator; **penerjemahan** *n* translation

terjepit *adj* pinched, caught in an uncomfortable situation ← **jepit**

terjerat *adj* snared, trapped, caught ← **jerat**

terjerumus *adj* plunged into ← **jerumus**

terjual *adj* sold; *habis* ~ sold out ← **jual**

terjun dive, fall; go down; ~ *payung* parachuting, sky diving; *air* ~ waterfall; **menerjunkan** *v* to drop something; **penerjun, peterjun** ~ *(payung)* parachutist, sky diver

terka: terkaan *n* guess; **menerka** *v* to guess

terkabul *adj* granted ← **kabul**

terkadang *adv* sometimes, occasionally ← **kadang**

terkam: menerkam *v* to pounce, attack

terkantuk-kantuk *adj* sleepy ← **kantuk**

terkapar *adj* fallen, strewn ← **kapar**

terkebelakang *adj* backward ← **belakang**

terkecuali *tidak* ~, *tanpa* ~ without exception ← **kecuali**

terkejut *adj* surprised ← **kejut**

terkékéh-kékéh *v* to laugh ← **kékéh**

terkemuka *adj* prominent ← **ke muka**

terkenal *adj* well-known ← **kenal**

terkendali *adj* controlled ← **kendali**

terkesan *adj* impressed; seemed ← **kesan**

terkesima *adj* amazed, astonished ← **kesima**

terkikis *adj* eaten away, eroded ← **kikis**

terkilir *adj* twisted, sprained ← **kilir**

terkini *adj* the latest ← **kini**

terkira *tak* ~ unsuspected, not thought of ← **kira**

terkirim *adj* sent; *pesan* ~ message sent ← **kirim**

terkoyak *adj* torn ← **koyak**

terkuak *adj* to part, open; be revealed, exposed ← **kuak**

terkuat *adj* the strongest ← **kuat**

terkubur *adj* buried in an accident ← **kubur**

terkulai *adj* sprawled, splayed, fallen ← **kulai**

terkuras *adj* drained ← **kuras**

terkutuk *adj* cursed, accursed ← **kutuk**

terlahir *adj* born ← **lahir**

terlalu *adv* too; **keterlaluan** *n* excess, too much ← **lalu**

terlambat *adj* (too) late, delayed ← **lambat**

terlampau *adj* too, extremely ← **lampau**

terlampir *adj* attached, enclosed ← **lampir**

terlanjur, telanjur *adj* too late, already; ~ *berangkat* already left ← **lanjur**

terlantar → **telantar**

terlarang *adj* forbidden, banned; *buku* ~ banned book ← **larang**

terlebih *adj* especially ← **lebih**

terlémpar *adj* thrown, flung ← **lémpar**

terléna *adj* confused, bewildered ← **léna**

terletak *adj* situated, located ← **letak**

terlibat *adj* involved, implicated ← **libat**

terlilit *adj* caught up, twisted ← **lilit**

terlindas *adj* run over ← **lindas**

terlupakan *tak* ~ unforgettable ← **lupa**

termangu-mangu *adj* confused, dazed; speechless ← **mangu**

termasuk *adj* including ← **masuk**

termenung *adj* lost in thought ← **menung**

términal *n* (bus) terminal, bus station

termurah *adj* the cheapest ← **murah**

ternak *n* cattle, livestock; *makanan* ~ fodder, cattle feed; **menernakkan** *v* to breed; **peternak** *n* (cattle) farmer; **peternakan** *n* cattle farm, ranch

ternama *adj* famous, well-known ← **nama**

ternganga *adj* gaping, flabbergasted, wide open ← **nganga**

ternilai *tidak* ~ priceless, invaluable ← **nilai**

terobos break through, pierce; **terobosan** *n* breakthrough; **menerobos** *v* to break through

terombang-ambing *v* to bob (up and down), float; to fluctuate ← **ombang-ambing**

terompét *n* trumpet; *pemain* ~ trumpet player, trumpeter

térong, térung, terung *n* eggplant, aubergine; small green eggplant eaten raw with salads; ~ *Belanda* tree tomato, tamarillo

teropong *n* telescope, binoculars

terowong: terowongan *n* tunnel, shaft

terpadu *adj* integrated ← **padu**

terpakai *adj* used, in use ← **pakai**

terpaksa *adj* forced; *karena* ~ had to do it, was forced to do it ← **paksa**

terpal *n* tarpaulin

terpana *adj* struck, stunned ← **pana**

terpanas *adj* the hottest ← **panas**

terpancing *adj* hooked, caught up; involved ← **pancing**

terpanjang *adj* the longest ← **panjang**

terpantul *adj* reflected ← **pantul**

terpaut *adj* fastened, bound; separated ← **paut**

terpejam *adj* closed ← **pejam**

terpelajar *adj* educated ← **ajar**

terpelanting *v* to fall heavily ← **pelanting**

terpelését *adj* slipped, skidded; tripped ← **pelését**

terpelihara *adj* well cared-for, well-maintained ← **pelihara**

terpelintir *adj* twisted ← **pelintir**

terpencar *adj* dispersed ← **pencar**

terpencét *adj* accidentally pressed ← **pencét**

terpencil *adj* isolated, remote ← **pencil**

terpendam *adj* hidden, concealed ← **pendam**

terpéndék *adj* the shortest ← **péndék**

terpengaruh *adj* affected or influenced ← **pengaruh**

terpental *adj* flung, thrown down ← **pental**

térpentin, térpéntin *n* turpentine, turps

terpenuhi *adj* satisfied, fulfilled ← **penuh**

terperangah *adj* open-mouthed, astonished ← **perangah**

terperangkap *adj* trapped, caught ← **perangkap**

terperanjat *adj* startled, surprised ← **peranjat**

terpercaya *adj* trusted, reliable ← **percaya**

terperosok *adj* fallen, sunk, plunged ← **perosok**

terpesona *adj* enthralled, enchanted ← **pesona**

terpidana *n* the condemned ← **pidana**

terpikat *adj* attracted, enchanted ← **pikat**

terpimpin *adj* led, guided; *Demokrasi* ~ Guided Democracy (under Sukarno) ← **pimpin**

terpisah *adj* separated ← **pisah**

terpojok, terpojokkan *adj* forced into a corner ← **pojok**

terpotong *adj* cut (off) ← **potong**

terpuji *adj* highly-praised ← **puji**

terpukul *adj* hard-hit ← **pukul**

terpuruk *adj* hidden, buried, sunk ← **puruk**

terputus *adj* cut off; **terputus-putus** *v* to keep cutting out ← **putus**

tersambung *adj* connected ← **sambung**

tersandung *adj* to stumble on, trip (up) on ← **sandung**

tersangka *n (yang)* ~ suspect; *tak* ~ unexpected ← **sangka**

tersangkut *adj* involved; caught, snagged ← **sangkut**

tersanjung *adj* flattered ← **sanjung**

tersaput *adj* covered, shrouded; ~ *awan* clouded over ← **saput**

tersayang *adj* dear, dearest; *yang* ~ *(yts)* dear (in letters) ← **sayang**

tersebut *adj* (afore)mentioned, said ← **sebut**

tersedak *adj* choking ← **sedak**

tersedan-sedan *adj* sobbing ← **sedan**

tersedia *adj* available, prepared ← **sedia**

tersedu-sedu *v* to sob, sniffle ← **sedu**

terselip *adj* fallen or slipped into ← **selip**

terselubung *adj* hidden, veiled ← **selubung**

tersendat *adj* jammed, blocked ← **sendat**

tersendiri *adj* its own; apart, separate ← **diri, sendiri**

tersénggol *adj* bumped, brushed ← **sénggol**

tersentak *adj* pulled, jerked ← **sentak**

tersentuh *adj* touched ← **sentuh**

tersenyum *v* to smile ← **senyum**

terserah *adj* it depends; up to you ← **serah**

terserémpét *adj* scraped, scratched ← **serémpét**

tersérét *adj* dragged ← **sérét**

tersesat *adj* lost ← **sesat**

tersiksa *adj* tortured ← **siksa**

tersinggung *adj* offended, hurt; *mudah* ~ touchy, over-sensitive ← **singgung**

tersingkap *adj* revealed ← **singkap**

tersingkir, tersingkirkan *adj* eliminated, swept aside ← **singkir**

tersipu, tersipu-sipu *adj* embarrassed, shy ← **sipu**

tersirat *adj* implied ← **sirat**

tersisa *adj* leftover ← **sisa**

tersohor *adj* famous ← **sohor**

tersulit *adj* the hardest, most difficult ← **sulit**

tertabrak *adj* hit; ~ *mobil* hit by a car ← **tabrak**

tertahan *adj* held back, prevented; **tertahankan** *tak* ~ unbearable ← **tahan**

tertambat *adj* tied up, moored ← **tambat**

tertampung *adj* contained ← **tampung**

tertanggal *adj* dated ← **tanggal**

tertangkap *adj* caught; ~ *basah* caught in the act ← **tangkap**

tertarik *adj* attracted, interested ← **tarik**

tertawa *v* to laugh; **menertawakan** *v* to laugh at ← **tawa**

tertegun *adj* taken aback ← **tegun**

tertekan *adj* stressed, pushed, pressured ← **tekan**

tertelan *adj* accidentally swallowed ← **telan**

tertémbak *adj* shot (accidentally) ← **témbak**

tertentu *adj* definite, fixed, certain ← **tentu**

tertera *adj* printed, stamped ← **tera**

tertib *adj* orderly, organized, disciplined; *tata* ~ rules and regulations; **ketertiban** *n* discipline, order; ~ *lalu lintas* traffic discipline, highway code; *Dinas Ketenteraman dan* ~ *(Tramtib)* city public order agency; **menertibkan** *v* to keep order, discipline

tertidur *adj* fallen asleep ← **tidur**

tertimpa *adj* hit or struck by; to suffer; ~ *musibah* struck by disaster ← **timpa**

tertiup *adj* blown ← **tiup**

tertolong *adj* saved, rescued; *tidak* ~ beyond help ← **tolong**

tertuduh *n* the accused ← **tuduh**

tertukar *adj* changed by accident ← **tukar**

tertulis *adj* written; *ujian* ~ written examination ← **tulis**

tertumpah *adj* spilt ← **tumpah**

tertunda *adj* delayed, postponed ← **tunda**

tertusuk *adj* pricked, jabbed; ~ *hati* hurt, offended ← **tusuk**

tertutup *adj* closed ← **tutup**

teruji *adj* tested ← **uji**

terulang *adj* repeated ← **ulang**

terumbu *n* coral; ~ *karang* coral reef

teruna → **taruna**

terung, térung → **térong**

terungkap *adj* expressed, revealed ← **ungkap**

teruntai *adj* dangling, strung up ← **untai**

terurai *adj* hanging loose ← **urai**

terus *adv* straight on; continuous, constant; ~ *menerus* constantly, continually; ~ *terang* direct, frank, straightforward; **terus-menerus** constantly, continually; **terus-terusan** *adv* constantly, continuously; **terusan** *n* extension; canal; ~ *Panama* the Panama canal;

meneruskan *v* to continue, keep doing something; **penerus** *n* successor; someone who continues another's work; **seterusnya** *adv* after that, henceforth

terutama *adv* especially, particularly ← **utama**

tetangga *n* neighbor; *negara* ~ neighbor, neighboring country; *rukun* ~ *(RT)* neighborhood association; **bertetangga** *v* to have neighbors

tetap *adj* fixed, definite, constant; *adv* still; *penduduk* ~ permanent resident; **ketetapan** *n* regulation; stipulation; **menetap** *v* to stay; **menetapkan** *v* to appoint, fix, stipulate; **penetapan** *n* appointment

tetapi, tapi *conj* but; *akan* ~ however

tetas: menetas *v* to hatch

téték *n, sl* breast; **menéték** *v* to suck, feed from the breast

tétés drip, drop; **tétésan** *n* drip, drop, droplet; **menétéskan** *v* to drip something; to release something in drips

Tétum, Tétun *bahasa* ~ Tetum, language of East Timor

tetumbuhan → **tumbuh**

tévé, tivi *n* TV; *nonton* ~ watch TV ← **télévisi**

téwas *v* to be killed, die; killed in action; **menéwaskan** *v* to kill someone

Thai *bahasa* ~, *orang* ~ Thai; *Muang* ~ Thailand; **Thailand** *n* Thailand

THR *abbrev Taman Hiburan Rakyat* amusement park

THR *abbrev Tunjangan Hari Raya* holiday bonus, paid at Idul Fitri or Christmas

THT *abbrev telinga, hidung, tenggorokan* ear, nose and throat

tiada no; there isn't any, there aren't any; ~ *lagi* there is no other; no more; **ketiadaan** *n* absence, lack; **meniadakan** *v* to undo or cancel ← **tidak ada**

tiang *n* pillar, pole, mast; ~ *bendera* flagpole

tiap, setiap *adj* each, every; ~ *saat* any time

tiarap lie face down (on the floor)

tiba *v* to arrive or come; **tiba-tiba** *adv* suddenly

tidak, tak, ndak, nggak, enggak no, not; ~ *beralasan* ungrounded, unfounded; ~ *hadir* absent; ~ *sah* illegal, not recognized; **ketidakhadiran** *n* absence; ~ *pasti* uncertain; **ketidakpastian** *n* uncertainty; **setidak(-tidak)nya** *adv* at least

tidur sleep; asleep; ~ *pulas*, ~ *nyenyak* sleep heavily, sleep well; *kamar* ~ bedroom; *kurang* ~ not enough sleep; *obat* ~ sleeping tablet; *tempat* ~ bed; **tidur-tiduran, tiduran** *v* to lie down, rest; **ketiduran** *v* to fall asleep; **meniduri** *v* to sleep with someone, have sex with someone; **menidurkan** *v* to put to sleep; **tertidur** *adj* fallen asleep

tifa *n* large drum from Papua

tifus, tipus *n* typhoid (fever); *kena* ~ have typhoid

tiga *adj* three; ~ *belas* thirteen; ~ *puluh* thirty; ~ *kali* three times; *kembar* ~ triplets; **bertiga** *adj* in threes; **ketiga** *adj* the third; ~*nya* all three; **pertiga** *dua* ~ two-thirds; **sepertiga** *adj* one-third; **pertigaan** *n* T-junction

tikai: bertikai *v* to quarrel or disagree; **pertikaian** *n* quarrel, disagreement

tikam stab; *luka* ~ stab wound; **tikaman** *n* stab; **menikam** *v* to stab

tikar *n* mat; *gulung* ~ close down, close shop; go bankrupt

tikét *n* (relatively expensive) ticket; ~ *kereta api* (long-distance) train ticket; ~ *pesawat* plane ticket

tikung: tikungan *n* bend, curve; **menikung** *v* to bend, curve

tikus *n* (small) mouse, (large) rat; ~ *besar* rat; ~ *got* sewer rat; *jalan* ~ back road, side-street; *lem* ~ adhesive tape for trapping rats

tilang *n* traffic fine; **ditilang** *v* to be fined ← **bukti pelanggaran**

tilas *napak* ~ retrace your steps, make a journey again

tilpon → **télépon**

TIM *abbrev Taman Ismail Marzuki* arts and theater complex in Jakarta

tim *n* team

tim *nasi* ~ steamed rice; **ditim** *v* to be steamed

timah *n* tin; ~ *campuran* pewter; ~ *hitam* lead; ~ *putih* tin; *tambang* ~ tin mine

timang: menimang-nimang *v* to rock (a child)

timbal ~ *balik* mutual, reciprocal; **setimbal** *adj* equivalent, proportional, even

timbang ~ *rasa* consider another person's feelings; *jembatan* ~ weighbridge; **timbangan** *n* scales; **ketimbang** *conj, coll* compared with; **menimbang** *v* to weigh (up); **mempertimbangkan** *v* to consider; **pertimbangan** *n* consideration

timbel, timbal *n* lead; *tanpa* ~ *(TT)* lead-free (fuel)

timbrung → **nimbrung**

timbul emerge; **menimbulkan** *v* to give rise, bring to the surface

timbun *n* pile, heap; **bertimbun-timbun** *adv* in heaps, piled up; **menimbun** *v* to pile up, accumulate; to hoard; ~ *makanan* to hoard food

timnas *n* national team ← **tim nasional**

Timor *n* ~ *Lorosae* Timor Lorosae, East Timor; ~ *Barat* West Timor; ~ *Timur (Timtim) arch* East Timor; *pulau* ~ Timor

timpa: menimpa *v* to fall upon, befall; **tertimpa** *adj* hit or struck by; to suffer; ~ *musibah* to be struck by disaster

timpang: ketimpangan *n* inequality, imbalance; ~ *sosial* social inequality

Timteng *n* the Middle East ← **Timur Tengah**

Timtim *n, arch* East Timor, Timor Loro Sae ← **East Timor**

timun, mentimun *n* cucumber; ~ *laut* sea cucumber, trepang; ~ *suri* large cucumber, often eaten at fast-breaking ← **mentimun**

timur *adj* east; ~ *laut* northeast; ~ *Tengah (Timteng)* Middle East; *bintang* ~ morning star; *di* ~ *Jakarta* east of Jakarta; **ketimuran** *adj* Eastern, Oriental

tindak act, deed; ~ *lanjut* follow-up; ~ *pidana* criminal act; **menindaklanjuti** *v* to take a step or measure; **tindakan** *n* action, measure, step; ~ *pencegahan* preventative measure; *mengambil* ~ to act, take action or measures; **bertindak** *v* to act, take action

tindas: menindas *v* to oppress; **penindasan** *n* oppression

tindih *bertumpang* ~ to overlap

tindik ~ *telinga* pierced ears; **menindik** *v* to pierce (ears)

tinggal *v* to live, stay, remain; ~ *dua ribu rupiah* there's only Rp. 2000 left; *rumah* ~, *tempat* ~ dwelling; *selamat* ~ goodbye (to someone who is staying); **ketinggalan** *adj* left behind; ~ *kereta api* to miss a train; **meninggal** *v (dunia)* to die; **meninggalkan** *v* to leave (behind), abandon; **peninggalan** *n* remains, remnants; **sepeninggal** *conj* after someone's death

tinggi *adj* high, tall; ~*nya* height; **menjunjung** ~ to respect, hold in great esteem; *pejabat* ~ high-ranking official; *sekolah* ~ college; **ketinggian** *n* altitude, height; **setinggi** *adj* as high as; **setinggi-tingginya** *adv* as high as possible

tingkah action; ~ *laku* behavior, actions; **bertingkah** *v* to act, behave

tingkat *n* level, floor, story, grade; ~ *pemula* beginner; **tingkatan** *n* grade, degree, level; **bertingkat** *adj* having different levels; *rumah* ~ multi-story house; **meningkat** *v* to rise, increase, improve; **meningkatkan** *v* to increase or raise the level of something; **peningkatan** *n* rise, increase; **setingkat** *adj* of the same level

tinja *n* excrement, feces, sewage

tinjau: tinjauan *n* review; **meninjau** *v* to observe, view; ~ *kembali* to review; **peninjau** *n* observer; **peninjauan** *n* observation; ~ *kembali* review

tinju *n* boxing; fist; **bertinju** *v* to box; **petinju** *n* boxer

tinta *n* ink; *habis* ~ out of ink

Tionghoa *adj, pol* Chinese; *orang* ~ Chinese; **Tiongkok** *n, arch* China

tipe *n* type, sort

tipék, tipéks *n* correction fluid, white-out, Tipp-Ex; **ditipéks** *v* to white-out, be corrected

tipis *adj* thin; *kemungkinan* ~ slim chance; *rambut* ~ fine

hair; **menipis** *v* to become thin

tipu trick, cheat; ~ *daya* scam, con; ~ *muslihat* (dirty) trick, deceit; **menipu** *v* to trick, deceive; **penipu** *n* con man, trickster; **penipuan** *n* deception

tipus, tifus *n* typhoid (fever); *kena* ~ have typhoid

tirai *n* curtain; ~ *besi* iron curtain; *negeri* ~ *bambu* China

tiram *n* oyster; *saus* ~ oyster sauce

tiras *n* circulation

tiri *adj* step-; *adik* ~, *kakak* ~ stepbrother or stepsister; *ibu* ~ stepmother

tirta *n, lit* water

tiru, meniru *v* to copy or imitate; **tiruan** *n* imitation, fake

tisu *n* tissue; ~ *basah* wet towel, wipe; *tempat* ~ tissue box

titah *n* royal order, command

titel *n* title (of a person); **bertitel** *v* to have the title → **gelar**

titik *n* dot, point; full stop, period; ~ *didih* boiling point; ~ *dua* colon; ~ *koma* semicolon

titip, menitip *v* to leave in someone's care, entrust; ~ *beli gula* please buy some sugar; **titipan** *n* parcel, something sent with another person; **penitipan** *n* care; *tempat* ~ *anak* child-minding center, creche

titis: titisan *n* reincarnation

tiup blow; **bertiup** *v* to blow; **meniup** *v* to blow; ~ *lilin* blow out the candles; **tertiup** *adj* blown

tivi, tévé *n* TV; *nonton* ~ to watch TV ← **télévisi**

TK *abbrev Taman Kanak-kanak* kindergarten, preschool

TKI *abbrev Tenaga Kerja Indonesia* Indonesian worker abroad

TKW *abbrev Tenaga Kerja Wanita* Indonesian female worker abroad

Tn. *Tuan m* master, sir (esp for foreigners); Mr (with surname)

TNI *abbrev Tentara Nasional Indonesia* Indonesian National Army/Armed Forces

toalét, toilét *n* toilet, washroom

tobat, taubat *n* repentance; **bertobat** *v* to repent

todong, menodong *v* to threaten or hold up at knife-point; **penodong** *n* attacker; **penodongan** *n* knife attack

togél *n* illegal small-scale gambling, lottery or bingo game ← **toto gelap**

Togo *n* Togo; *orang ~* Togolese

toh *adv, coll* still, after all

toilét, toalét *n* toilet, washroom

tokcér *adj, coll* work, spring to life, effective

tokék *n* large gray house gecko

toko *n* shop, store; *~ mas, ~ emas* jewelery shop; *~ roti* bakery; *~ serba ada (toserba)* general store; department store; *~ swalayan* supermarket; **pertokoan** *n* shopping center or complex, mall

tokoh *n* figure, character; *~ dunia* world figure; *~ utama* main character

toksoplasmosis, tokso *n* toxo-

plasmosis, parasitic disease from cats which can affect pregnant women

tol *n* toll; *jalan ~* toll road; *gerbang ~, pintu ~* tollbooth, tollgate

tolak *v* to refuse, reject; *~ korupsi* down with corruption; **bertolak** *v, form* to depart, leave; **menolak** *v* to refuse, reject; **penolakan** *n* refusal, rejection

tolan, taulan *handai ~* friends

toléh: menoléh *v* to look in a different direction, turn your head

tolol *adj* stupid; **ketololan** *n* stupidity

tolong help; please; *minta ~* to ask for help; *~ dibuka* please open it; **menolong** *v* to help or assist; **pertolongan** *n* help, assistance, aid; *~ pertama* first aid; **tertolong** *adj* saved, rescued; *tidak ~* beyond help

tomat *n* tomato; *sup ~* tomato soup

tombak *n* spear; *ujung ~* spearhead, striker (in soccer)

tombok → **nombok**

tombol *n* knob, button; *tekan ~* push the button

tong *n* drum, barrel, bin; *~ sampah* rubbish bin, garbage bin

Tonga *n* Tonga; *bahasa ~, orang ~* Tongan

tongkang *n* barge

tongkat *n* stick, cane; *pakai ~* use a cane; **bertongkat** *adj* with a stick

tongkol *ikan ~* tuna (fish)

ongkrong → **nongkrong**

ongséng *n* goat and cabbage curry

onjok, menonjok *v* to punch, hit

onjol: menonjol *v* to stick out, protrude; *adj* prominent

onton: tontonan *n* show, performance; **menonton, nonton** *v* to watch, look on; **penonton** *n* spectator, audience; *para* ~ audience; ladies and gentlemen

op *adj, sl* great, wonderful, top; **ngetop** *v, sl* to be on top

opan *(angin)* ~ typhoon, hurricane

opang: menopang *v* to prop up, support; **penopang** *n* prop, support

opéng *n* mask; *tari* ~ masked dance

opi *n* hat; ~ *pet* cap

oplés → **stoplés**

opografi *n* topography

oraja Toraja, ethnic group of central Sulawesi; *bahasa* ~, *orang* ~ Toraja

oréh: menoréh *v* to scratch, etch

ortor *n* traditional Batak dance

osérba *n* general store; department store ← **toko sérba ada**

otok *adj* full-blood; *Cina* ~ 100% or overseas Chinese

PI *abbrev Televisi Pendidikan Indonesia* privately-owned television network

PA *abbrev tempat pembuangan akhir* tip, rubbish dump

PS *abbrev tempat pemilihan suara* polling booth

tradisi *adj* tradition (not *adat*); **tradisional, tradisionil** *adj* traditional

trafo, travo *n* transformer, adapter

trah *n* lineage, descent; *anjing* ~ pure-breed dog

traktir, mentraktir *v* to invite out, shout, treat, pay for another

traktor *n* tractor

tralis → **terali**

trampil *adj* skilled; **ketrampilan** *n* skill

transaksi *n* (bank) transaction; **bertransaksi** *v* to make a transaction

transformator *n* transformer

transisi *n* transition; *masa* ~ transition period

transmigrasi *n* transmigration (from Java to other islands); **transmigran** *n* migrant who has joined the internal transmigration program

trap: ditrap *v* to be layered (of hair)

trapésium *n* trapezium

travo → **trafo**

trayék *n* route (of public transport)

trém *n* tram, streetcar

trén, trénd *n* trend, fashion; **ngetrén** *adj, coll* trendy, fashionable

tribune *n* [tribun] stand, open area in a stadium or concert hall

Trinidad dan Tobago *n* Trinidad and Tobago; *orang* ~ Trinidadian, Tobagonian

tripang → **teripang**

triplék, tripléks *n* plywood, used for ceilings

trisula *n* trident

triwulan *n* quarter (of a year); trimester; term (when four terms in a year)

tromol ~ *pos* road mail box (RMB)

trompét *n* trumpet; *pemain* ~ trumpeter

tropis *adj* tropical

trotoar *n* pavement, sidewalk

truk *n* truck; ~ *barang* goods truck; ~ *tronton* semi-trailer

tsb. *tersebut* the aforementioned

tt(d) *tertanda* signed

ttg *tentang* about, re

TTS *abbrev teka-teki silang* crossword

tua *adj* old; dark (of colors); ~ *renta* very old, senile; *biru* ~ dark blue; *orang* ~ parents; **ketua** *n* chair(person); chief

tuah: bertuah *adj* lucky, having magic power

tuak *n* palm wine

tuan (Tn) *m, pron* master, sir (esp for foreigners); Mr (with surname); ~ *rumah* host; **tuan-tuan** *pron* gentlemen

tuang *v* to pour; **menuang, menuangkan** *v* to pour something

tuan-tuan *pron* gentlemen ← **tuan**

tubi: bertubi-tubi *adv* repeatedly, without stopping, unceasingly

tubruk *kopi* ~ ground coffee

tubuh *n* body; **bertubuh** *v* to have a body; ~ *gemuk* fat;

bersetubuh *v* to have sex; **menyetubuhi** *v* to have sex with; **persetubuhan** *n* sexual intercourse

tuding: tudingan *n* accusation; **menuding** *v* to accuse, point the finger

tuduh: tuduhan *n* charge, accusation; **menuduh** *v* to accuse; **tertuduh** *n* the accused

tudung *n* head scarf

tugas *n* task, duty, function; **menugaskan** *v* to assign someone, give a task to; **penugasan** *n* assignment

tugu *n* monument, column

tuh *pron, coll* that; *itu* ~ that one ← **itu**

Tuhan *n, pron* God, Allah; **tuhan** *n* god; **ketuhanan** *n* divinity, deity; belief in God

tuju: tujuan *n* direction, destination; aim, goal; **bertujuan** *adj* with a purpose of; **menuju** *v* to approach, go towards; **setuju** agree, agreed; **bersetuju** *v* to agree; **menyetujui** *v* to agree to, approve, ratify; **persetujuan** *n* agreement, approval

tujuh *adj* seven; ~ *belas* seventeen; ~ *puluh* seventy

tukang *n* (unskilled) worker; handyman; ~ *becak* pedicab driver; ~ *cat* painter; ~ *cukur* barber; ~ *kayu* carpenter; ~ *roti* itinerant bread-seller; ~ *sepatu* cobbler; **pertukangan** *n* repair

tukar *v* to exchange; ~~*menukar* barter; ~ *tambah* trade in; **bertukar** *v* to change; **menukar** *v* to change; **menukarkan** *v* to change something; **pertukaran** *n* exchange; ~ *pikiran* exchange of ideas or views; **tertukar** *adj* changed by accident

ukas, **menukas** *v* to counter, retort

ulalit *adj* sound of telephone fault or misconnection; not connect or make sense

ulang *n* bone; ~ *belakang* spine; *sumsum* ~ bone marrow; *membanting* ~ to work yourself to the bone; *tinggal* ~ *dan kulit* nothing but skin and bones

ular: ketularan *adj* infected, caught something; **menular** *v* to infect; *adj* contagious, infectious; *penyakit* ~ contagious disease

ulén *adj* real, pure, genuine

uli *adj* deaf; *bisu* ~ deaf and dumb, deaf-mute

ulip, **tulpen** *n* tulip

ulis *v* to write; *batu* ~ slate; stone tablet or inscription; *buku* ~ notebook, exercise book; *juru* ~ clerk; *meja* ~ writing table; *papan* ~ blackboard, whiteboard; **tulisan** *n* writing, script; ~ *halus* calligraphy; **menulis** *v* to write; **penulis** *n* author, writer; ~ *novel* novelist; **tertulis** *adj* written; *ujian* ~ written examination

ulus *adj* sincere; *ketulusan* ~ *hati* sincerity

umbang fall, fallen; ~*nya* the fall of; **menumbangkan** *v* to fell, cause something or someone to fall

tumbén *adj, coll* unusual, never before, rare

tumbuh *v* to grow; **tetumbuhan, tumbuh-tumbuhan** *n* plants; **tumbuhan** *n* a growth; plant; **ditumbuhi** *adj* overgrown with; **pertumbuhan** *n* growth, development

tumbuk, **menumbuk** *v* to pound (rice), crush, grind

tumis *v* to stir-fry, sautée; ~ *sayur* stir-fried vegetables

tumit *n* heel (of foot)

tumpah spill, spilt; **menumpahkan** *v* to spill something; ~ *darah* to shed blood; **tertumpah** *adj* spilt

tumpang: menumpang *v* to make use of someone else's facilities; to get a lift or ride; **penumpang** *n* passenger

tumpeng *nasi* ~ rice shaped in a tall cone, made on special occasions

tumpu: bertumpu *v* to rest on

tumpuk *n* heap, pile; **bertumpuk** *v* to be in piles; **bertumpuk-tumpuk** *adv* in piles; **menumpuk** *v* to pile up

tumpul *adj* blunt

tuna- *pref* without; ~*daksa* disabled, physically handicapped; ~*grahita* mentally handicapped; ~*netra* blind; ~*wisma* homeless

tunai *n* cash; **menunaikan** *v* to pay cash; to fulfill; ~ *ibadah puasa* to perform the Ramadan fast

tunang: tunangan *n, f* fiancée; *n, m* fiancé; *v, coll* to be engaged; **bertunangan** *v* to be engaged; **pertunangan** *n* engagement

tunas *n* shoot, sprout

tunda delay; *tayangan* ~ delayed telecast; **menunda** *v* to delay, put off, postpone; **menundakan** *v* to delay or postpone something; **tertunda** *adj* delayed, postponed

tunduk *v* to bow to, submit, obey; **menunduk** *v* to bow your head; **menundukkan** *v* to bow or lower something; to defeat

tungau *n* dust mite

tunggak: tunggakan *n* debt; ~ *sewa* back rent; **menunggak** *v* to owe money

tunggal *adj* single, sole; *anak* ~ only child; *orang tua* ~ single parent; *Bhinneka* ~ *Ika* Unity in Diversity

tunggang: menunggang *v* to ride; ~ *kuda* to ride a horse

tunggu *v* to wait; ~ *dulu* wait a minute; *ruang* ~ waiting room; **menunggu** *v* to wait for something; **menunggu-nunggu** *v* to wait a long time for; **menunggui** *v* to wait by or look after someone

tungku *v* furnace, oven

Tunisia *n* Tunisia; *orang* ~ Tunisian

tunjang: tunjangan *n* allowance, bonus; ~ *Hari Raya* one month's extra pay, awarded on a religious holiday

tunjuk, menunjuk *v* to indicate, point out, refer to; **menunjukkan** *v* to show, point out; ~ *jalan* to give directions; **mempertunjukkan** *v* to display or perform; **penunjuk** *n* guide, indicator; **penunjukan** *n* appointment; **pertunjukan** *n* show, performance; **petunjuk** *n* instruction, direction; *buku* ~ manual, guide; *buku* ~ *jalan* street directory; *buku* ~ *telepon* telephone directory; *coll* phone book

tuntas *adj* complete, total; **menuntaskan** *v* to finish off, be done with, do thoroughly

tuntun, menuntun *v* to guide, prop up

tuntut claim; **tuntutan** *n* claim, charge; **menuntut** *v* to claim or demand; **penuntut** *n* claimant, plaintiff, prosecuting party

tupai *n* squirrel

tur *n* tour; *pemimpin* ~ tour leader

turangga *n, lit* horse

turbin *n* turbine

turis *n* tourist; ~ *asing* foreign tourist; ~ *lokal* domestic tourist

Turki *n* Turkey; *bahasa* ~ Turkish; *orang* ~ Turkish, Turk

Turkménistan *n* Turkmenistan; *bahasa* ~, *orang* ~ Turkmen

turun *v* to descend, fall, come down; ~-*temurun* from generation to generation, hereditary; ~ *ke lapangan* go out into the field; **keturunan** *n* descendant; *WNI* ~ Indonesian of Chinese descent; **menurun** *v* to fall, drop, decline; **menurunkan** *v* to lower or reduce; **penurunan** *n* lowering

turut *v* to take part, join; ~ *serta* participate, take part; ~ *berduka cita* express your condolences; **berturut-turut** *adj* consecutive, successive; **menurut** *conj* according to; ~ *pendapat saya* in my opinion; **penurut** *adj* obedient, meek

tuslah *n* surcharge; ~ *Lebaran* surcharge on transport at Idul Fitri

tustél *n, arch* camera

tusuk skewer, needle; poke; ~ *jarum* acupuncture; ~ *sate* satay stick; **tusukan** *n* stab wound; **menusuk** *v* to stab, prick, pierce; **tertusuk** *adj* pricked, jabbed; ~ *hati* hurt, offended

tuts *n* key, button; ~ *piano* piano keys

tutul *adj* spotted; *macan* ~ leopard

tutup lid, cover; closed, shut; ~ *botol* bottle-cap; ~ *mulut* keep your mouth shut; **menutup** *v* to close or shut; **menutupi** *v* to cover (up); **penutup** *n* stopper, lid; end; **tertutup** *adj* closed

tutur speak; **bertutur** *v* to speak or talk; **menuturkan** *v* to tell; **penutur** *n* speaker; ~ *asli* native speaker

TV *abbrev* te-ve, ti-vi, televisi television

TVRI *abbrev Televisi Republik Indonesia* Indonesian state-owned television

U

uang *n* money; ~ *kembali* change; ~ *muka* down payment; ~ *receh(an)* small change; ~ *saku* pocket money; ~ *sekolah* school fees, tuition; ~ *tunai* cash; *mata* ~ currency; *setali tiga* ~ six of one, half a dozen of the other; it's all the same; **keuangan** *n* finance; *Menteri* ~ Minister of Finance, Chancellor of the Exchequer (UK)

uap *n* steam, vapor; *kapal* ~ steamer, steamship; **menguap** *v* to evaporate or steam; to yawn; **penguapan** *n* evaporation

ubah change; **berubah** *v* to change; **mengubah, merubah** *v* to change or alter; **perubahan** *n* change, alteration

uban *n* (strand of) gray or white hair; **beruban** *v* to have gray hairs

uber, menguber *v, coll* to chase, go after

ubi *n* edible tuber or root; sweet potato, yam; ~ *kayu* cassava

ubin *n* (floor) tile

ubun-ubun *n* crown, fontanel

ubur-ubur *n* jellyfish

ucap say; **ucapan** *n* greetings; ~ *selamat* congratulations; **mengucap, mengucapkan** *v* to say or express something; ~ *terima kasih* to say thank you; to thank; **pengucapan** *n* expression

udah → **sudah**

udang *n* shrimp; *ada ~ di balik batu* there's something going on here, there's something behind it

udara *n* air, atmosphere; *angkatan ~* air force; *pesawat ~* aeroplane, airplane; *pos ~* air mail; *tekanan ~* air pressure, atmospheric pressure; **mengudarakan** *v* to broadcast or air

udik → **mudik**

udur, udzur → **uzur**

ufuk *n* horizon

ugal: ugal-ugalan *adj* reckless

Uganda *n* Uganda; *orang ~* Ugandan

UGM *abbrev Universitas Gadjah Mada* Gadjah Mada University, in Yogyakarta

UI *abbrev Universitas Indonesia* University of Indonesia, in Jakarta

UII *abbrev Universitas Islam Indonesia* Indonesian Islamic University, in Yogyakarta

ujar speak, say; *~nya* says, said; **berujar** *v* to speak or say

uji test; *~ coba* experiment, trial; **ujian** *n* test, exam(ination); *~ lisan* oral test; *~ masuk* entrance test; *~ tertulis* written exam or test; *menempuh ~* to sit for or do an exam; *lulus ~* pass an exam; *tidak lulus ~* fail an exam; **menguji** *v* to examine or test; **penguji** *n* examiner; **teruji** *adj* tested

ujung *n* point, end; *~ jari* fingertip; *~ dunia* ends of the earth;

~ Pandang former name for Makassar

UKI *abbrev Universitas Kristen Indonesia* Indonesian Christian University, in Jakarta

ukir, mengukir *v* to carve or engrave; **ukiran** *v* carving

Ukraina *n* (the) Ukraine; *bahasa ~, orang ~* Ukrainian

Ukrida *Universitas Kristen Djaya* Christian university in Jakarta

ukur measure; **ukuran** *n* size, measurement; *~ sedang* medium size; **mengukur** *v* to measure; **pengukuran** *v* measuring, measurement

ulah *n* behavior, manners; **berulah** *v* to behave

ulama *n, Isl* religious leader(s)

ulang repeat; *~ alik* back and forth, both ways; *pesawat ~* shuttle; *~ tahun* birthday, anniversary; *tayangan ~* re-run, repeat; **ulangan** *n* test; **berulang** *v* to happen again, recur; **berulang-ulang** *adv* again and again, repeatedly; **mengulang** *v* to repeat, do again; **mengulangi** *v* to repeat something; **terulang** *adj* repeated

ular *n* snake

ulas: ulasan *n* comment, review; **mengulas** *v* to comment, review, critique

ulat *n* worm, caterpillar; *~ sutera* silkworm

ulek, uleg *sambal ~* ground chilli sauce; **mengulek** *v* to make fresh chilli sauce

uler → **ular**

ulet *adj* diligent, hard-working

uli *n* sticky rice mixed with shredded coconut

ulin *kayu* ~ very hard wood

ulos *n* woven cloth used in Batak ceremonies

ultah *n* birthday, anniversary ← **ulang tahun**

ulu ~ *hati* solar plexus

ulung *adj* excellent, first-rate, superior; **keulungan** *n* superiority

ulur: **uluran** *n* assistance, help; ~ *tangan* helping hand; **mengulur-ulur** *v* to spin out, take a long time; **mengulurkan** *v* to extend something

umat *n* people (of one faith); ~ *Islam* the Muslim community

umbai, rumbai *n* tassel

umbi *n* tuber; **umbi-umbian** *n* tubers

umbul: **umbul-umbul** *n* pennants, small flags, banner

umpama *n* example; ~*nya* for example; **perumpamaan** *n* parable, metaphor; **seumpamanya** *conj* for instance

umpan *n* bait

umpat, mengumpat *v* to curse swear; **umpatan** *n* oath, swear word

umpat, umpet: **umpet-umpetan** *n, coll* hide and seek; **mengumpet** *v* to hide or conceal yourself

umroh, umrah *n* minor pilgrimage to Mecca

umum *adj* general, public, com-

mon; *(pada)* ~*nya* generally, in general; *kepentingan* ~ public or common interest; **meng-umumkan** *v* to announce or declare; **pengumuman** *n* notice, announcement

umur *n* age; ~ *berapa?* how old?; *di bawah* ~ underage; **berumur** *adj* aged; **seumur** *adj* the same age; lifelong; ~ *hidup* for life, lifelong

Unair *n* Airlangga University (in Surabaya) ← **Univérsitas Airlangga**

Unas *Universitas Nasional* National University, in Jakarta

undang, mengundang *v* to invite (formally); **undangan** *n* invitation; formal event

undang: **undang-undang** *n* law, act; ~ *Dasar* constitution; *Kitab* ~ *Hukum Perdata* civil code

undi *n* lot; **undian** *n* lottery; **mengundi** *v* to conduct a draw or lottery

undur, mundur *v* to reverse, go back; **mengundurkan** *v* to postpone; **pengunduran** *n* postponement, delay

uneg, unek: **uneg-uneg, unek-unek** *n* grudges

unggas *n* poultry, bird

unggul *adj* superior; **ke-unggulan** *n* superiority

unggun *api* ~ (camp) fire

ungkap *v* to express, reveal; **ungkapan** *n* expression; **mengungkap** *v* to uncover; **mengungkapkan** *v* to express;

terungkap *adj* expressed, revealed

ungkit: mengungkit *v* to lever; to pry; **pengungkit** *n* lever

ungsi: mengungsi *v* to evacuate or flee; **mengungsikan** *v* to evacuate someone; **pengungsi** *n* refugee, evacuee; **pengungsian** *n* evacuation

ungu *adj* purple; ~ *muda* violet

Unhas *n* Hasanuddin University (in Makassar) ← **Univérsitas Hasanuddin**

uni *n* union; ~ *Arab Emirat* United Arab Emirates; ~ *Eropa (UE)* European Union (EU); ~ *Sovyet*, ~ *Soviet* Soviet Union

Unibraw *n* Brawijaya University (in Malang) ← **Univérsitas Brawijaya**

unik *adj* unique; **keunikan** *n* unique thing, uniqueness

Unisba *Universitas Islam Bandung* Bandung Islamic University

univérsitas *n* university

unjuk ~ *gigi* show your teeth; ~ *rasa* demonstration

Unpad *n* Padjadjaran University (in Bandung) ← **Univérsitas Padjadjaran**

Unpar *Universitas Parahyangan* Parahyangan University, in Bandung

UNS *abbrev Universitas Negeri Sebelas Maret* Eleventh of March State University, in Solo

unsur *n* element

unta, onta *n* camel; *burung* ~ ostrich

untai string; counter for string-like objects; **untaian** *n* string, chain; **menguntai** *v* to string, tie together; **teruntai** *adj* dangling, strung up

Untar *Universitas Tarumanagara* Tarumanagara University, in Jakarta

untuk *prep* for; **memperuntuk-kan** *v* to allocate or assign

untung advantage, gain, profit; luck; ~*nya* the good thing was; **beruntung** *adj* lucky, fortunate; **keuntungan** *n* advantage, profit; **menguntungkan** *v* to profit; *adj* profitable; **peruntungan** *n* (good) fortune or luck

Unud *n* Udayana University (in Denpasar) ← **Univérsitas Udayana**

upaboga *n* cuisine, gastronomy

upacara *n* ceremony; ~ *pemakaman* funeral; ~ *pernikahan*, ~ *perkawinan* wedding ceremony

upah *n* wage, wages; **mengupah** *v* to employ, hire, pay someone (to do work)

upaya *n* effort; **berupaya** *v* to make an effort, try; **mengupayakan** *v* to try to enable

upeti *n* tribute; bribe

upik *n* nickname for a girl, esp in Sumatra; *buyung* ~ boy and girl, son and daughter

upil *n* snot, bogey, nasal mucus; **mengupil** *v* to pick your nose

urai: uraian *n* explanation, analysis; **berurai** *v* to hang down or loose; **menguraikan** *v* to explain; to untangle; **terurai** *adj* hanging loose

urak: urakan *adj* eccentric; bad-mannered

urang-aring *n* kind of medicinal plant

urap *n* vegetable salad with grated coconut

urat *n* tendon, vein; muscle; ~ *saraf* nerve; *salah* ~ strained or pulled muscle

uréa *pupuk* ~ kind of fertilizer

uri *n* placenta, afterbirth

URSS *abbrev Uni Republik Sovyet Sosialis* Union of Soviet Socialist Republics, USSR

Uruguay *n* Uruguay; *orang* ~ Uruguayan

urus organize, arrange; **urusan** *n* arrangement, dealing, affair; *bukan* ~ *saya* none of my business; **berurusan** *v* to have dealings with, deal with; **mengurus** *v* to arrange, organize, manage; **pengurus** *n* manager, organizer; ~ *besar* board of directors, executive

urut order in a series; *nomor* ~ number; **urutan** *n* order, sequence; **berurut(-urutan)** *adj* successive, consecutive, sequential

urut massage, rub; *tukang* ~ mas-seur; **mengurut** *v* to massage

urutan *n* order, sequence ← **urut**

US *abbrev Uni Sovyet* Soviet Union

usah *tidak* ~ not necessary; **usahkan** let alone, not to mention

usaha *n* effort; *dunia* ~ business world; *tata* ~ administration; **berusaha** *v* to try, make an effort; **mengusahakan** *v* to try, endeavor to; **pengusaha** *n, m* businessman; *n, f* business-woman; **perusahaan** *n* company

usahkan let alone, not to mention ← **usah**

usai *adj* over, finished; ~ *perang* after the war, post-war

usang *adj* worn out, old, out-of-date

USG ultrasonogram

usia *n, pol* age; ~ *lanjut n* old age; ~ *lanjut adj* old; **berusia** *v* to be (aged)

usik: mengusik *v* to tease, disturb

usil *adj* annoying, cheeky

usir, mengusir *v* to drive away or out, chase away, expel

uskup *n* bishop; ~ *agung* arch-bishop; **keuskupan** *n* diocese

ustad, ustadz *n, Isl* term of address for a religious leader or teacher

USU *abbrev Universitas Suma-tera Utara* University of North Sumatra, in Medan

usul *n* origin; *asal* ~ origin(s), background

usul propose, suggest; motion; *atas* ~ on the suggestion of; **mengusulkan** *v* to propose or suggest usus *n* intestine; ~ *besar* large intestine; ~ *buntu* appendix

usut: mengusut *v* to investigate, sort out

UT *abbrev Universitas Terbuka* Open University

utak ~-*atik* fiddle or tinker with ← **kutak-katik**

utama *adj* main; **mengutamakan** *v* to give preference or priority to; **terutama** *adv* especially, particularly

utang, hutang *n* debt; ~ *piutang* debits and credits; *surat* ~ IOU (I owe you); **berutang** *v* to owe; ~ *budi* debt of gratitude

utara *adj* north; *Korea* ~ *(Korut)* North Korea; **mengutarakan** *v* to put forward

utas *n* string (of beads); counter for ropes etc; *se*~ *tali* a length of string

utuh *adj* whole, complete, untouched; **seutuhnya** *adv* completely

utus, mengutus *v* to send or delegate; **utusan** *n* delegate, deputy; mission

UU *abbrev Undang-Undang* legal statutes

UUD *abbrev Undang-Undang Dasar* constitution

Uzbék *bahasa* ~ Uzbek; **Uzbékistan** *n* Uzbekistan; *orang* ~ Uzbekistani

uzur, udur, udzur *adj* old and infirm

V

vakansi, pakansi vacation, on holiday

vaksin *n* vaccine; **vaksinasi** *n* vaccination; **divaksinasi** *v* to be vaccinated

vakum *n* vacuum; **divakum** *v* to be vacuumed

valas *n* foreign currency ← **valuta asing**

validasi *n* validation; **divalidasi** *v* to be validated

validitas *n* validity

valuta *n* currency; ~ *asing (valas)* foreign currency

vampir *n* vampire

vanili *n* vanilla; *rasa* ~ vanilla-(-flavored)

varia *n* variety; **variasi** *n* accessories (esp vehicle), variation

varisés *n* varicose veins

vas *n* vase

Vatikan Vatican; *Kota* ~ Vatican City

végétarian, végétaris *adj* vegetarian

vélg, véleg, pélek *n* wheel rim

vélodrom *n* velodrome, cycling track

Vénésia *n* Venice

Vénézuéla *n* Venezuela; *orang* ~ Venezuelan

véntilasi *n* ventilation

vérba *n* verb

verboden, perboden no entry

vérifikasi *n* verification; **divérifikasi** *v* to be verified vermak → **permak**

vernis → **pernis**

vérsi *n* version

versnéling → **persnéling**

véspa *n* moped, motor scooter

vétsin *n* MSG (monosodium glutamate)

viaduk *n* viaduct

vidéo video; *kamera ~* video camera

Viétnam *n* Vietnam; *bahasa ~, orang ~* Vietnamese

vihara, wihara *n* Buddhist temple or monastery

vila *n* villa, holiday house, summer cottage

visa *n* visa; *~ sosial budaya (sosbud)* sociocultural visa

visi *~ dan misi* mission statement

Visnu, Vishnu → **Wisnu**

visum *~et repertum* autopsy (official report)

vital *adj* vital; *alat ~* vital organs; genitals

VJ *abbrev* video jockey

vlék → **flék**

VOC *abbrev Vereinigde Oost-Indische Compagnie* United East India Company, in colonial times

vocer, voucer *n* credit voucher (for mobile phones)

vokal *adj* vocal, outspoken; *huruf ~* vowel; **vokalis** *n* vocalist

voli *bola ~* volleyball; *(bola) ~ pantai* beach volleyball; *pemain ~* volleyball player

volt *n* volt; **voltase** *n* voltage

volume *n* volume, size, bulk

vonis *n* ruling; sentence; *~ mati* death sentence; **divonis** *v* to be sentenced

voucer → **vocer**

W

wabah *n* epidemic, plague; *~ belalang* locust plague; *~ flu burung* bird flu epidemic; **mewabah** *v* to spread (uncontrollably)

wadah *n* pot, container, place to put something

waduk *n* reservoir; dam

wafat *v, pol* to pass away or die; *~nya* his/her death; *~ 1970* died 1970

wagub *n* deputy governor ← **wakil gubernur**

wah *excl* wow! oh! *adj* amazing, outstanding; fantastic, wonderful

wahai *lit* oh, o

wahana *n* vehicle, means; *~ Lingkungan Hidup Indonesia (Walhi)* Indonesian environmental group

wahid *adj* one, single; *nomor ~* best, number one

wahyu *n* revelation, vision, inspiration; **mewahyukan** *v* to reveal something (in a vision)

Waisak, Wésak *n* Buddhist New Year

wajah *n, pol* face; **berwajah** *v* to have a face; *~ muram* sour-faced

wajan *n* wok

wajar *adj* natural; **kewajaran** *n* sense, logic; **sewajarnya** *adv* naturally

wajib compulsory; must, obliged; ~ *militér* military service; *lagu* ~ song learnt at school, compulsory song; **berwajib** *adj* responsible, competent; **kewajiban** *n* obligation, duty; **mewajibkan** *v* to enforce or make obligatory

wajik *n* diamonds (card suit); diamond-shaped cake of sticky rice

wakaf *Isl tanah* ~ land donated to the local Muslim community

wakil *n* representative, substitute; *adj* vice; ~ *presiden* vice-president; **mewakili** *v* to represent; **perwakilan** *n* representation, delegation; *Dewan* ~ *Rakyat (DPR)* parliament, legislative assembly

waktu *n* time, hours; *conj* when; *membuang* ~ to waste time; *pada ~nya* in due time, at the right time; *sebelum ~nya* prematurely; **sewaktu-waktu** *adv* at any moment; every now and then

walaah *excl* oh no; come on! you must be joking (in disbelief)

walafiat *sehat* ~ healthy, hale and hearty, in good health

walaikum *Isl* ~ *salam (warahmatullahi wabarakatuh)* and upon you be peace (said in response to *salam alaikum*)

walau, walaupun *conj* although

walét *burung* ~ swift; *rumah* ~ building where swiftlet nests are cultivated

walhasil *conj* with the result that ← **alhasil**

Walhi *n* Indonesian environmental group ← **Wahana Lingkungan Hidup Indonésia**

wali *n* guardian; saint; ~ *kelas* form or homeroom teacher, tutor; ~ *kota* mayor; **perwalian** *n* guardianship, representation

wallahualam *Isl* only God knows

wals, walsa *n* waltz

-wan *suf, m* -man, one who does something; *negara~* statesman; *olahraga~* sportsman

wana- *pref* forest

wangi fragrant; perfume; *minyak* ~ perfume; **wangi-wangian, wewangian** *n* scents, perfumes

wangsit *n* divine inspiration or revelation

wanita *n* woman; *polisi* ~ *(polwan)* policewoman; *kaum* ~ women, the fair sex

wanti: wanti-wanti *n* reminder, warning; **mewanti-wanti** *v* to warn

waprés *n* vice-president; *calon* ~ *(cawapres)* vice-presidential candidate ← **wakil présidén**

wara: wara-wiri, wira-wiri *adj* back and forth

waralaba *n* franchise

waras *adj* sane, healthy; **kewarasan** *n* sanity, mental health

warga *n* citizen; **warganegara** *n* citizen, national; ~ *Indonesia (WNI)* Indonesian citizen; **kewarganegaraan** *n* citizenship

waris *ahli* ~ *m* heir *f* heiress; **warisan** *n* inheritance; **mewarisi** *v* to inherit; **mewariskan** *v* to bequeath or leave something

warkat *n* letter

warna *n* color; ~ *putih* white; ~-*warni* colorful, multicolored; **berwarna** *adj* colored; **mewarnai** *v* to color (in); **pewarna** *n* dye, stain

warnét *n* internet café ← **warung internét**

warok *n* male leader of East Javanese *reog* performance

warpostél *n* office where you can make calls, and send post and faxes ← **warung pos dan télékomunikasi**

Warsawa *n* Warsaw

warta *n* news; ~ *berita* news (items); **wartawan** *m*; **wartawati** *f* journalist, reporter

warteg *n* small, cheap food stall ← **warung Tegal**

wartél *n* small office where you can make calls and send faxes ← **warung télékomunikasi**

waru *pohon* ~ kind of hibiscus tree

waruga *n* stone sarcophagus, found in North Sulawesi

warung *n* stall, small local shop; ~ *kopi* coffee stall

waserai *n* (commercial) laundry

wasiat *n* will; *surat* ~ will, testament

wasir *n* hemorrhoids

wasit *n* umpire, referee

waslap *n* washcloth, flannel

waspada *adj* on guard, careful, cautious; **kewaspadaan** *n* caution; **mewaspadai** *v* to watch out for, guard against

wassalam *Isl* upon you be peace, best regards (in closing letters); ~ *alaikum warahmatullahi wabarakatuh (wr wb)* and upon you be peace, mercy and the blessing of God (used as response to *assalamualaikum wr wb*)

wastafel *n* basin, sink (in bathroom)

waswas *adj* worried, anxious, nervous

watak *n* nature, character; **berwatak** *v* to have a certain nature; ~ *keras* strict, stern, unyielding

-wati *suf, f* -woman, one who does something; *peraga*~ model

wawancara *n* interview; ~ *kerja* job interview; **mewawancarai** *v* to interview; **pewawancara** *n* interviewer

wawas: wawasan *n* outlook, view, concept; **berwawasan** *v* to have an outlook; ~ *luas* broad or open mind

wayang *n* puppet; ~ *golek* wooden, three-dimensional puppet; ~ *kulit* shadow puppet (performance); ~ *orang* traditional performance with actors;

pertunjukan ~ (shadow) puppet play or performance

WC [wé sé] *n* toilet, bathroom, lavatory

wédang *n* warm Javanese beverage; ~ *jahe* warm ginger drink; ~ *kopi* hot coffee

wéker *n* alarm; *jam* ~ alarm clock; *memasang* ~ to set the alarm

wektu ~ *telu Isl* community in Lombok which prays three times a day, not five

wenang: *berwenang adj* competent, in charge; **kewenangan, wewenang** *n* authority; **sewenang-wenang** *adv* tyrannically, arbitrarily

wésel *n* money order; *pos* ~ postal money order

wewangian → **wangi**

wewenang *n* authority ← **wenang**

WIB *abbrev Waktu Indonesia Barat* Western Indonesian time

wibawa *n* authority, esteem; **berwibawa** *adj* esteemed, respected, of good standing

wihara, vihara *n* Buddhist temple or monastery

wijén *n* sesame seed

WIL *n, f* dream woman; lover ← **wanita idaman lain**

wilayah *n* area, territory; *kantor* ~ *(kanwil)* regional office

Wina *n* Vienna

windu *n* eight-year cycle; **sewindu** *adj* eight years

wira-: **wiraswasta** *n, m* businessman *f* businesswoman; **wirausaha** *n* business

wira: **wira-wiri, wara-wiri** *adv* back and forth

wiraswasta *n, m* businessman *f* businesswoman

wirausaha *n* business

wisata *n* tourism, travel; *biro* ~ travel agent; *pari*~ tourism; **berwisata** *v* to travel or holiday; **wisatawan** *n* tourist; ~ *mancanegara (wisman)* foreign tourist; ~ *Nusantara (wisnu)* domestic or local tourist

wiski *n* whisky, whiskey

wisma *n* house, building; *tuna*~ homeless

wisman *n* foreign tourist ← **wisatawan mancanegara**

wisnu *n* domestic or local tourist ← **wisatawan Nusantara**

wisuda graduate; *upacara* ~ (university) graduation ceremony; **wisudawan** *n, m* graduate; **wisudawati** *n, f* graduate

WIT *abbrev Waktu Indonesia Timur* Eastern Indonesian time

WITA *abbrev Waktu Indonesia Tengah* Central Indonesian time

WNA *abbrev warga negara asing* foreign national

WNI *abbrev warga negara Indonesia* Indonesian national; ~ *keturunan* Indonesian of Chinese descent

wol *n* wool

wong *conj, coll* because; what do you mean?

wortel *n* carrot

Wr Wb. *warahmatullahi wabarakatuh* may God's blessing and mercy be upon you, used to close speeches

WTS *abbrev wanita tuna susila* immoral woman = *euph* prostitute

wudu, wudhu, wudlu *n, Isl* ritual ablutions before praying; *mengambil ~* to wash before praying; *tempat ~* tap used for washing before praying; **berwudu** *v* to wash before praying

wujud *n* existence; **berwujud** *v* in the form or shape of; **mewujudkan** *v* to make something real, realize something

wulan *catur ~* trimester, term; *~ (cawu) ketiga* third term

X

X *sinar ~* X-ray

Y

ya, iya yes

ya *ejac* oh, O; *~ Allah* oh God!

yad. *yang akan datang* future

yah yes, well ...

yahud *adj* great, number one

Yahudi *adj* Jewish; *agama ~* Judaism; *bahasa ~* Yiddish; *orang ~* Jewish, Jew

yaitu *conj* namely, that is

yakin *adj* sure, convinced; **keyakinan** *n* belief, conviction, faith; **berkeyakinan** *v* to be convinced; **meyakini** *v* to believe (in), be convinced; **meyakinkan** *adj* convincing, believable

yakni *conj* namely

Yaman *n* Yemen; *orang ~* Yemeni

yang *conj* that, which, who; *~ biru* the blue one; *~ lalu (yl)* in the past; *~ akan datang (yad)* in the future

Yasin *Isl surat ~* chapter of the Koran, recited for the dead

yatim *n* orphan, fatherless child; *~ piatu* orphan; *rumah ~* orphanage

yayasan *n* foundation (not for profit)

yél *n* chant, war-cry, shout

yl. *yang lalu* in the past

YME *abbrev Yang Maha Esa* the One and Only, when referring to God

yodium *n* iodine; **beryodium** *garam ~* iodized salt

yogia, yogya: seyogianya *adv* properly, fittingly

yoni *n* square hole, traditional female symbol; *lingga ~* obelisk in a square hole, traditional symbol of male and female sexuality

Yordania *n* Jordan; *orang ~* Jordanian

yth. *yang terhormat* the respected, used when addressing letters

yts. *yang tersayang* beloved, used when addressing letters to family or friends

yu → **hiu**

Yugo, Yugoslavia *n* Yugoslavia; *orang ~* Yugoslav

yuk → **ayo**

Yunani *n* Greece; *bahasa ~, orang ~* Greek

yunior junior (at work or school)

yuridis *adj* jurisdictive, legal

Z

zaitun *n* olive; *minyak ~* olive oil

Zaire → **Kongo**

zakar *n* penis; *buah ~* testicles

zakat, jakat *n* alms; *~ fitrah* alms paid before Idul Fitri

zaman, jaman *n* age, era, time, period; *~ dahulu, ~ dulu* in the old days, times past; *~ Batu* Stone Age; *~ Belanda* the Dutch era; *~ saya* in my day; *ketinggalan ~* outdated

Zambia *n* Zambia; *orang ~* Zambian

zamrud, jamrud *n* emerald; *~ khatulistiwa* emeralds of the Equator (ie. Indonesia)

zat, jat *n* element, substance; *~ air* hydrogen; *~ besi* iron (as a vitamin); *~ pewarna* dye

zébra *n* zebra

ziarah *n* pilgrimage, visit to a holy place or cemetery; **ber- ziarah** *v* to make a pilgrimage, visit a holy place

zikir, dikir, dzikir *Isl* (recite) additional prayers; **berzikir** *v, Isl* to say additional prayers

Zimbabwé *n* Zimbabwe; *orang ~* Zimbabwean

zina, zinah *n* adultery; sex outside marriage; **berzina** *v* to commit adultery

zohor → **lohor**

zona *n* zone

zuhur → **lohor**

zus → **sus**

zuster → **suster**

English–Indonesian

English–Indonesian

A

& co *and Company* cs (cum suis)

a *art* (sebelum huruf mati) satu, suatu, sebuah; per, tiap; ~ *blade of grass* sebilah rumput; ~ *cigarette* sebatang rokok; ~ *dog* seekor anjing; ~ *house* sebuah rumah; ~ *letter* sepucuk surat; ~ *man* seorang lelaki; ~ *month* sebulan; ~ *piece (of paper)* sehelai (kertas)

abacus *n* sempoa

abandon *v* mengabaikan, menelantarkan; **abandoned** *v, adj* terabaikan, telantar

abattoir *n* [abatuar] pejagalan

abbess *n, f* kepala biarawati; **abbey** *n* biara; **abbot** *n, m* kepala biarawan

abbreviate *v* menyingkatkan, memendekkan; **abbreviation** *n* singkatan, kependekan

ABC *abbrev* American Broadcasting Corporation, Australian Broadcasting Corporation ABC

abdicate *v* lengser, turun takhta

abdomen *n* perut; **abdominal** ~ *pain* rasa sakit di daerah perut

abduct *v* menculik; **abduction** *n* penculikan; **abductor** *n* penculik

abhor *v* membenci

ability *n* [abiliti] kemampuan, kesanggupan, kepandaian ← **able**

ablaze *adj* menyala, terbakar ← **blaze**

able *adj* [ébel] bisa, mampu, sanggup; *She wasn't ~ to come* Dia tidak bisa datang (waktu itu)

abnormal *adj* tidak normal, tidak biasa; **abnormality** *n* cacat

aboard *adj* di atas kendaraan; *to go ~* naik kapal

abolish *v* menghapus, meniadakan; **abolition** *n* penghapusan, pencabutan

abominable *adj* mengerikan, menjijikkan; *the ~ Snowman* yeti; **abomination** *n* tindakan yang jahat

Aborigine *n* [Aborijini] orang Aborijin, penduduk asli Australia; **aboriginal** *adj, n* orang Aborijin

abort *v* menggugurkan; **abortion** *n* pengguguran, aborsi; **abortive** *adj* gagal

abound *v* berlimpah (ruah)

about *prep* tentang, mengenai, seputar (sebuah topik); *Stewart knows all ~ it* Stewart yang tahu tentang itu; sekitar, keliling (sebuah tempat); *they know their way ~ town* mereka tahu jalan di kota; kurang lebih, kira-kira (jumlah); ~ *to* segera akan; **about-face** putar balik

above *prep* [abav] (di) atas; lebih daripada; ~ *all* terutama,

ENGLISH–INDONESIAN

yang paling penting; ~-*board* legal, resmi; *heavens ~!* ya Allah!; ~-*mentioned* yang tersebut di atas

abrasion *n* luka ringan, goresan pada kulit; **abrasive** *adj* (bersifat) kasar

abridged *adj* singkat; ~ *dictionary* kamus singkat

abroad *adj* luar negeri, negeri orang; *Liz has gone ~* Liz sudah pergi ke luar negeri

abrupt *adj* tiba-tiba; kasar, kurang sopan

abscess *n* abses

absence *n* ketidakhadiran; **absent** *adj* tidak hadir; ~-*minded* sering lupa; **absentee** *n* orang yang tidak hadir

absolute *adj* mutlak, total; **absolutely** *adv* secara mutlak, betul

absorb *v* menyerap; ~*ed in* asyik; ~*ed in thought* termenung; **absorbent** *adj* menyerap; **absorption** *n* penyerapan, serapan, absorpsi

abstain *v* tidak ikut (memilih dalam pemilihan suara), menjadi netral; berpantang; ~ *from drinking alcohol* tidak minum alkohol; **abstainer** *n* orang yang tidak melakukan sesuatu; **abstinence** *n* pantang

abstract *adj* abstrak; ~ *art* seni abstrak, aliran abstrak; tidak konkret; *n* ringkasan

absurd *adj* gila, tidak masuk akal

abundance *n* kelimpahan;

abundant *adj* berlimpah (ruah)

abuse *n* [abyus] penganiayaan, penyalahgunaan; kekerasan; *child ~* kekerasan terhadap anak-anak; *v* [abyuz] menganiaya, menyalahgunakan, memperlakukan dengan kasar; **abusive** *adj* kasar; ~ *language* makian, kata-kata kasar atau jorok

abyss *n* jurang; **abysmal** *adj* sangat jelek

academic *adj* akademis; ~ *record* hasil rapot atau nilai; *n* akademisi; **academy** *n* akademi, sekolah tinggi

accelerate *v* mempercepat; menginjak gas (di mobil); **acceleration** *n* percepatan; **accelerator** *n* (pedal) gas

accent [aksént] *n* logat, aksen, nuansa; **accentuate** *v* menekankan

accept *v* menerima; **acceptable** *adj* layak, dapat diterima; **acceptance** *n* penerimaan

access *n* akses; *v* mendapat, memakai; **accessible** *adj* terjangkau, dekat

accessory: accessories *n, pl* aksesoris, variasi (pada mobil), perlengkapan

accident *n* [aksident] kecelakaan; *it was an ~* tidak sengaja; **accidental** *adj* kebetulan, tidak disengaja

accommodate *v* menampung, menyesuaikan; **accommodation** *n* penginapan, akomodasi

accompaniment *n* [akampaniment] pengiringan; **accompany** v menemani, mengantarkan, mengiringi

accomplice n [akamplis] kaki tangan, antek

accomplish v melaksanakan; **accomplished** adj ulung; **accomplishment** n prestasi

accord n kesepakatan, persetujuan; of its own ~ dengan sendirinya, secara otomatis; **accordance** in ~ with sesuai dengan; **according** ~ to menurut; **accordingly** adv oleh karena itu, maka

account n rekening (bank); pertanggung jawab; laporan, cerita; on ~ of karena, lantaran; of no ~ tidak penting; on no ~ sekali-kali tidak; v ~ for mempertanggungjawabkan; **accountable** adj bertanggung jawab; **accountancy** n akuntansi; **accountant** n akuntan

accumulate v bertumpuk; menghimpun; **accumulation** n timbunan, akumulasi; **accumulator** n aki

accuracy n [akurasi] ketelitian, ketepatan; **accurate** adj teliti, cermat, tepat

accusation n tuduhan; **accusative** adj akusatif, penderita; **accuse** v menuduh, menuding; **accused** the ~ tertuduh, tergugat; **accusingly** adv secara menuduh

accustom v ~ yourself membiasakan diri; **accustomed** adj terbiasa

ace n (kartu) as; pukulan awal yang langsung memenangkan poin; adj, coll mahir, hebat

acetylene n [asétilin] gas karbit

ache n [ék] sakit, pegal; head~ sakit kepala, pusing kepala; tooth~ gigi ngilu; v sakit; rindu

achieve v mencapai, meraih; **achievement** n prestasi; **achiever** high ~ orang yang banyak berprestasi

acid n asam; nitric ~ asam nitrat; adj pahit; **acidity** n keasaman, kadar asam

acknowledge v [aknolej] mengakui; menyebut (sebagai ucapan terima kasih); **acknowledgment** n pengakuan; ucapan terima kasih; referensi (dalam karangan)

acne n, pl [akni] jerawat (terutama yang besar dan sulit sembuh)

acorn n biji pohon ek

acoustic [akustik] ~ guitar gitar (klasik); **acoustics** n keadaan suara atau musik berbunyi di dalam ruangan, akustik

acquaint v ~ yourself memperkenalkan diri, membiasakan diri; well-~ed with tahu banyak tentang; **acquaintance** n kenalan; to make your ~ with memperkenalkan diri kepada, berkenalan dengan

acquire v memperoleh; **acquisition** n perolehan, barang yang diperoleh

acquit v membebaskan dari tuduhan, menyatakan tidak bersalah; ~ yourself well mulai dengan baik; **acquittal** *n* pembebasan

acre *n, arch* [éker] ukuran tanah (0,46 hektar)

acrid ~ *smell* bau hangus, bau tajam

acrobat *n* akrobat, pesenam; **acrobatics** *n* gerakan pesawat di udara yang berliku-liku

across *prep* (di) seberang, melintang, lintas; mendatar; *two* ~ dua mendatar (dalam teka-teki silang)

act *n* perbuatan; babak, lakon (dalam pertunjukan); undang-undang; *Marriage* ~ *of 1974* Undang-Undang Perkawinan tahun 1974; *caught in the* ~ tertangkap basah; *in the* ~ *of* sedang; *v* berbuat, bertindak, memerankan; ~*ing* pemangku jabatan; **action** *n* perbuatan, aksi; proses; ~ *film* film laga; *killed in* ~ gugur; *to take* ~ bertindak; **activate** *v* menghidupkan, menggerakkan; **active** *adj* giat, rajin, sibuk, aktif; hidup (telepon genggam); **activist** *n* aktivis; **activity** *n* kegiatan, kesibukan; **actor** *n, m* aktor, pemain (film); **actress** *n, f* aktris, pemain (film); **actual** *adj* **actually** *adv* sebenarnya

acupuncture *n* [akupanktyur] tusuk jarum; **acupuncturist** *n* ahli tusuk jarum

acute *adj* parah, akut; ~ *attack* serangan mendadak (penyakit); ~ *angle* sudut lancip

AD *abbrev Anno Domini* M (Masehi)

adage *n* [adij] pepatah, peribahasa

adapt *v* menyesuaikan; menyadur; **adaptable** *adj* mudah menyesuaikan diri, supel; **adaptation** *n* penyesuaian; saduran

add *v* bertambah, menambah, menambahkan

adder *n* semacam ular; ular biludak

addict *n* pecandu; ~*ed to heroin* ketagihan shabu-shabu; **addiction** *n* ketagihan, shabu-shabu

addition *n* tambahan, penambahan, jumlah; *in* ~ ditambah pula, lagipula; **additional** *adj* tambahan, ekstra ← **add**

address *n* alamat, adres; pidato; *v* mengalamatkan (surat); berpidato; menegur, menyapa; **addressee** *n* si alamat

adequate *adj* cukup, memadai

adhere *v* melekat, lengket; menganut; **adherent** *n* penganut (agama atau aliran); **adhesion** *n* adhesi

adjacent *adj* berdekatan, berdampingan, bersebelahan

adjoin *v* **adjoining** *adj* berdampingan

adjourn *v* [ajérn] menunda, menangguhkan, mengundurkan; **adjournment** *n* penundaan, penangguhan, pengunduran

adjudicate *v* memutuskan, menilai

adjust *v* menyetel, mencocokkan, mengatur, menyesuaikan;

adjustment *n* penyetelan, pengaturan, penyesuaian

adjutant *n* ajudan

administer *v* [administer] memerintah, mengelola, mengurus; melaksanakan; memberikan; ~ *justice* mengadili; ~ *medicine* memberi obat; ~ *an oath* mengambil sumpah; **administration** *n* pemerintahan; pemerintah; pelaksanaan, pemberian; **administrative** *adj* pengelolaan, pemerintahan; **administrator** *n* pemerintah, pelaksana, pengurus

admirable *adj* [admirabel] mengagumkan, patut dikagumi ← **admire**

admiral *n* [admiral] laksamana; *vice-~* laksamana muda

admiration *n* [admirésyen] kekaguman; **admire** *v* mengagumi; **admirer** *n* pengagum

admissible *adj* dapat diterima; **admission** *n* penerimaan, izin masuk; pengakuan; **admit** *v* menerima, mengizinkan masuk; mengakui; **admittance** *no ~* dilarang masuk

admonish *v* menegur

ado *n* [adu] kegaduhan; *without further* ~ sekarang juga

adolescence *n* masa remaja, pubertas; **adolescent** *n* remaja, anak puber

adopt *v* mengangkat atau memungut anak; mengambil; **adoption** *n* adopsi; penerimaan, pemakaian; **adoptive** *adj* ~ *child* anak angkat, anak pungut

adorable *adj* lucu, menggemaskan, manis, jelita; **adoration** *n* penyembahan, pemujaan; **adore** *v* menyembah, memuja; sangat mencintai, gila akan

adorn *v* menghiasi, mendandani; ~*ed with roses* dihiasi dengan bunga mawar

adrift *adj* terapung, terkatung-katung ← **drift**

adroit *adj* gesit, cekatan

adulation *n* pemujaan ← **adore**

adult *adj* dewasa; *n* orang dewasa; **adulthood** *n* masa dewasa

adulterate *v* mencampurkan sesuatu ke dalam, mengganggu

adulterer *n* orang yang berbuat zinah; **adultery** *n* zinah

advance *n* kemajuan; uang muka; *in* ~ di muka, terlebih dahulu, sebelumnya; *v* maju; memajukan, mempercepat; **advancement** *n* kemajuan

advantage *n* untung, keuntungan; **advantageous** *adj* [advantéjus] menguntungkan, berguna

advent *n* kedatangan; (masa) adven; ~ *calendar* kalender adren; untuk bulan Desember yang menyambut datangnya Natal; *before the* ~ *of computers* sebelum munculnya zaman komputer; **adventist** *Seventh-Day* ~ *Church* Gereja Advent Hari Ketujuh

adventure *n* petualangan; **adventurous** *adj* berani, suka berpetualangan

adverb *n* kata keterangan (pada kata kerja)

adversary *n* lawan, musuh;
adverse *adj* bermusuhan; tidak
ramah; ~ *weather* cuaca buruk;
adversity *n* malang, sial
advertise *v* mengiklankan,
memasang iklan; **advertiser** *n*
pihak yang memasang iklan;
advertisement *n* iklan, pariwara, reklame
advice *n* [advais] nasihat, saran;
advisable *adj* sebaiknya,
dianjurkan; **advise** *v* [advaiz]
menasihati; **advisor** *n* penasihat; **advisory** *adj* penasihat
advocate *n* [advokat] orang
yang memperjuangkan; pengacara, pembela; *v* [advokét]
menyeru agar
aerial *n* [érial] antena; *adj*
angkasa, udara; ~ *acrobatics*
jungkir-balik di udara
aeronautical *adj, n* aeronautika,
ilmu penerbangan; ~ *engineering* teknik penerbangan;
aerospace *n* bidang angkasa
dan penerbangan
aeroplane → **airplane**
afar *from* ~ dari jauh
affable *adj* ramah
affair *n* perkara, hal, soal, urusan;
perselingkuhan, cerita cinta
affect *v* mempengaruhi; **affection** *n* rasa kasih sayang; **affec-
tionate** *adj* memperlihatkan
kasih sayang
affiliate: affiliated *v, adj* berafil-
iasi dengan; **affiliation** *n* afil-
iasi, penggabungan
affinity *n* daya tarik, rasa dekat
atau pengertian

affirm *v* menguatkan, membenarkan, menegaskan, mengiyakan;
affirmation *n* pembenaran,
penegasan; **affirmative** *n* ya
affix *n* (kata) imbuhan; *v* membubuhi, mencantumkan, menempelkan
afflict *v* melanda; ~*ed by* terkena
menderita; **affliction** *n* penderitaan
affluence *n* kekayaan; **affluent**
adj kaya, berada, mampu
afford *v* mampu (membayar dll)
I can't ~ *it* saya tidak mampu
(membayar atau membeli);
affordable *adj* terjangkau
(harganya)
affront *v* menghina; *n* penghinaan
Afghan *adj* berasal dari Afganistan; **Afghani** *n* orang Afganistan; **Afghanistan** *n*
Afganistan
afloat *adj* hanyut, terapung-apung
← **float**
aforementioned, aforesaid *adj*
tersebut (di muka), tadi
afraid *adj* takut
afresh *adj* baru, sekali lagi ←
fresh
Africa *n* Afrika; **African** *adj* berasal
dari Afrika; *n* orang Africa
Afrikaans *n* bahasa Afrikaans
(yang dipakai di Afrika Selatan
Afrikaner *n* orang Afrikaans,
orang kulit putih keturunan
Belanda di Afrika Selatan
Afro-American *n* orang Amerika
berkulit hitam (keturunan
Afrika); orang Negro
after *prep, conj, adv* kemudian;

prep setelah, sesudah; ~ *all* lagipula; meskipun demikian; *to be* ~ mendesak, mengejar; **afternoon** *n* sore, petang; sesudah jam 12 siang sampai dengan matahari terbenam; ~ *tea* makan sore; *good* ~ selamat siang (jam 12–15); selamat sore (jam 3–7); **afterpains** *n* royan; **afterwards** *prep* sesudahnya, kemudian

again *adv* (sekali) lagi; ~ *and* ~ berulang kali, berkali-kali; *then* ~ tapi

against *prep* terhadap; berlawanan, bertentangan; ~ *all odds* meskipun kemungkinan sangat kecil

agate *n* [aget] batu akik

age *n* umur, usia; *thirty years of* ~ berusia tiga puluh tahun; abad; *the Middle* ~s Abad Pertengahan; *of* ~ dewasa, akil balig, sampai umur; *under*~ di bawah umur; **aged** *adj* sepuh, tua, lanjut usia; berumur

agency *n* agen, perwakilan; *news*~ kantor berita ← **agent**

agenda *n* agenda, acara; rencana; *on the* ~ direncanakan, masuk agenda

agent *n* agen, wakil

aggravate *v* memperparah, mengganggu

aggregate *n, adj* jumlah, total

aggression *n* penyerangan, serangan, agresi; **aggressive** *adj* galak, bersifat menyerang, agresif; **aggressor** *n* penyerang, agresor

aggrieve: aggrieved *adj* sakit hati, dirugikan

aghast *adj* [agast] tercengang, terperanjat, terheran-heran

agile *adj* gesit; **agility** *n* [ajiliti] ketangkasan, kecerdasan, kegesitan

agitate *v* mengganggu, mengguncangkan, menghasut; **agitation** *n* kekacauan, penghasutan; **agitator** *n* pengacau, penghasut; pengaduk

AGM *abbrev Annual General Meeting* rapat tahunan

ago *adv* (yang) lalu, lampau, silam; *three days* ~ tiga hari yang lalu

agonize *v* sangat kuatir; tidak bisa mengambil keputusan; **agony** *n* (ageni) kesakitan, penderitaan; sakratulmaut, azab

agrarian *adj* berkaitan dengan tanah

agree *v* setuju, bersepakat; menyetujui, mengiyakan; ~ *to* menyetujui, mengabulkan; **agreeable** *adj* setuju, sepakat; **agreement** *n* persetujuan, kesepakatan, perjanjian

agricultural *adj* berkaitan dengan pertanian; ~ *science* ilmu pertanian; **agriculture** *n* pertanian

agronomics *n* agronomi

aground *adj* kandas, terdampar; *the ship ran* ~ kapalnya terdampar

AH *abbrev after hours* r, rmh (rumah)

ahead *adv* [ahéd] di depan, di muka, terlebih dahulu ← **head**

aid *n* bantuan, pertolongan; *first ~* pertolongan pertama; *v* membantu, menolong

AIDS (Acquired Immune Deficiency Syndrome) *n* AIDS; *~ patient* orang dengan HIV/AIDS (ODHA)

ail *v* sakit; **ailing** *adj* sering sakit, sakit-sakitan; **ailment** *n* penyakit

aim *n* sasaran, maksud, tujuan; *v* membidik, mengincar, menuju; **aimless** *adj* tanpa tujuan

ain't *sl* tak, tidak ← **is not**

air *n* udara; angin; *~ conditioner, ~ conditioning* AC; *hot-~ balloon* balon udara; *~ mail* pos udara; *~ pump* n pompa angin; *~ pressure, atmospheric pressure* tekanan udara; *~s and graces* sikap sombong; *by ~* dengan pesawat terbang; *on ~* mengudara; *v* menjemur, menganginkan; **aircraft** *n* pesawat terbang, kapal terbang; *~ carrier* kapal induk; **air crew** *n* awak kabin; **airfield** *n* lapangan terbang; **air force** *n* angkatan udara; **air hostess** *n*, *arch* pramugari; **airer** *n* jemuran; **airline** *n* perusahaan penerbangan, maskapai penerbangan; **airliner** pesawat (terbang) penumpang; **airman** *n* penerbang, pilot; **airplane, aeroplane** *n* pesawat terbang; **airport** *n* bandara, bandar udara; **air raid** *n* serangan udara; **airship** *n* kapal udara; **airsick** *adj* mabuk (udara); **airtight** *adj* kedap udara; **airway** *n* kerongkongan; **airy** *adj* berangin

aisle *n* [ail] lorong; *to go down the ~* menikah

ajar *adj* (pintu) terbuka sedikit

alarm *n* weker; tanda bahaya; rasa kaget; *v* membuat kaget, mengagetkan

alas *ejac* aduh, wahai

Albania *n* [Albénia] Albania; **Albanian** *n* bahasa Albania, orang Albania; *adj* berasal dari Albania

albatross *n* elang laut

albumen *n* (zat) putih telur

alcohol *n* alkohol, minumam keras; **alcoholic** *n* peminum berat, pemabuk; *adj* beralkohol

ale *n* bir

alert *n* tanda (bahaya); *red ~* siaga satu; *on the ~* berjaga-jaga; *v* memperingatkan; *adj* siaga, waspada

algebra *n* aljabar

Algeria *n* Aljazair; **Algerian** *n* orang Aljazair; *adj* berasal dari Aljazair

alien *n* [élien] makhluk asing, orang asing; *illegal ~* orang yang berada di negeri asing tanpa izin; *adj* asing; **alienate** *v* mengasingkan, menjauhkan; **alienation** *n* pengasingan, penyingkiran

alight *v* [alait] turun (dari angkutan umum); hinggap

alight *adj* menyala; bercahaya

align *v* [alain] menyejajarkan; *Non-~ed Movement* Gerakan

Non-Blok; **alignment** n kesejajaran

like adj serupa, mirip ← **like**

live adj (dalam keadaan) hidup ← **live**

all adj [ol] semua, seantero; sekalian, seluruh; ~ in ~ sesudah dipertimbangkan matang-matang; ~ but hampir-hampir; semua kecuali; ~ day sepanjang hari, seharian; ~ over habis; di mana-mana; ~ right baiklah; ~ of us kita semua; not at ~ sama sekali tidak; **all-round** adj berbakat di lebih dari satu bidang; umum; **all-rounder** n olahragawan yang berbakat di lebih dari satu bidang

allegation n tuduhan, tudingan; pengakuan, pernyataan; **allege** v [aléj] menuduh, menuding; mengaku, menyatakan; **allegiance** n [alijens] kesetiaan

allegory n ibarat

allergic adj mempunyai alergi; ~ to cheese ada alergi keju; **allergy** n alergi

alleviate v meringankan, mengurangi; **alleviation** n pengurangan

alley n [ali] lorong, gang; ~ cat kucing kampung; blind ~ gang buntu, jalan buntu

alliance n [alaiens] perserikatan, persekutuan, gabungan; **allied** adj serikat, sekutu, gabungan ← **ally**

alligator n [aligétor] buaya (bermoncong pendek)

allocate v mengalokasikan, memperuntukkan; **allocation** n alokasi, peruntukan

allot v memperuntukkan, menjatahkan; **allotment** n jatah, bagian; vacant ~ tanah atau kapling kosong

allow v mengizinkan, memperbolehkan, memperkenankan; **allowance** n tunjangan, uang harian, uang saku

alloy n logam campuran

allude v menyindir, menyinggung; he ~d to my money dia menyindir soal uang saya

allure n daya pikat; **alluring** adj memikat, mempesona

allusion n sindiran ← **allude**

ally [alai] n sekutu; v bersekutu; Spain allied itself with Portugal Spanyol bersekutu dengan Portugal

almanac n, arch almanak, kalender, penanggalan

almighty adj [olmaiti] maha kuasa

almond n [amond] kacang almond, buah badam

almost adv [olmost] hampir, nyaris

alms n, pl [ams] sedakah

aloft adv di atas, ke atas; di udara

alone adj, adv sendiri, seorang diri; hanya, saja

along prep sepanjang; adj ~ (with) bersama (dengan); all ~ selama ini; **alongside** adj di sisi, di tepi

aloof adj sombong; menjauh;

aloofness n kedinginan, kesombongan

aloud adj dengan suara keras, dengan suara nyaring

ALP abbrev Australian Labor Party Partai Buruh Australia

alphabet n abjad, aksara, alfabet; the Latin ~ huruf Rumawi

alpine adj gunung

already adv [olrédi] sudah, telah

also adv [olso] juga, pula, pun

altar n [oltar] altar; going to the ~ menikah

alter v [olter] mengubah; memperbaiki; **alteration** n perubahan; perbaikan

altercation n pertikaian, pertengkaran

alternate v berselang-seling, menyelang-nyeling; adj berselang-seling; **alternating** ~ current arus bolak-balik; **alternative** n pilihan lain, alternatif; adj lain, alternatif; ~ music musik alternatif; musik yang di luar aliran umum

although conj [oltho] meskipun, walaupun

altitude n ketinggian, tinggi

altogether adj [oltogéther] semuanya, secara keseluruhan; neg sama sekali

alum n tawas

aluminium, aluminum n aluminium; ~ foil kertas perak

alumni [alamnai] n, pl **alumnus** s lulusan universitas tertentu

always adv selalu, senantiasa

am abbrev ante meridiem pagi, siang (jam 0.00–12.00)

amalgamate v mempersatukan, menggabungkan, melebur; **amalgamation** n penggabungan

amateur adj, n [amater] amatir; tidak profesional

amaze v mengherankan, menakjubkan, mengagumkan; **amazement** n rasa heran, rasa kagum

ambassador n duta besar

amber n ambar

ambiguity n [ambiguiti] hal yang kurang jelas, ambiguitas; **ambiguous** adj ambigu, kurang jelas

ambition n ambisi, cita-cita; **ambitious** adj berambisi, mempunyai cita-cita tinggi

ambulance n ambulans

ambush n serangan mendadak, penyergapan; v menyerang secara mendadak, menyergap

amen ejac amin

amenable adj setuju

amend v membetulkan, memperbaiki; to make ~s meminta maaf, mengganti kerugian; **amendment** n pembetulan; amandemen

amenities n, pl fasilitas, sarana

America n Amerika (Serikat); North ~ Amerika Utara; the ~s Amerika Utara dan Selatan; **American** n orang America; adj berasal dari Amerika

Amerindian n, adj orang Indian di Amerika

amethyst n batu kecubung

amiable adj [émiabel] ramah, baik hati

amicable *adj* [amikabel] ramah, baik-baik; **amicably** *adv* secara baik-baik

amid, amidst *prep* di tengah, di antara

ammonia *n* amonia

ammunition *n* amunisi

amnesty *n* grasi, amnesti, pengampunan

among [amang], amongst *prep* di tengah, di antara

amorous *adj* [ameres] bernafsu

amount *n* jumlah, banyaknya; *v* berjumlah, menjadi; *he won't ever ~ to much* dia tidak akan pernah berhasil

amphibian *n* binatang yang tinggal di dua dunia, seperti katak

ample *adj* banyak, besar, luas; **amplifier** *n* pengeras; **amplify** *v* memperbesar

amplitude *n* amplitudo, luas ayunan

amputate *v* memotong anggota badan, mengamputasi; **amputation** *n* amputasi; **amputee** *n* orang cacat yang kehilangan anggota badan

amulet *n* jimat

amuse *v* menghibur; **amused** *adj* terhibur, tertawa; **amusement** *n* hiburan, kesenangan; *~ park* taman hiburan; *to my ~* yang menggelikan bagi saya; **amusing** *adj* lucu, menyenangkan

an *art* (sebelum huruf vokal) satu, suatu; per, tiap; *~ apple* sebuah apel; *~ egg* sebutir

telur; *~ envelope* sehelai amplop; *~ owl* seekor burung hantu

anaemia → **anemia**

anaesthesia → **anesthesia**

anal *adj* melalui dubur; *~ retentive* orang yang banyak menguatirkan hal-hal sepele; *~ sex* sodomi ← **anus**

analogy *n* analogi, persamaan

analysis *n* analisa, analisis, uraian; *in ~* sedang menjalankan terapi dengan psikiater; **analyze** *v* menganalisa, meneliti

anatomy *n* anatomi, ilmu urai tubuh; **anatomically** *adj* sesuai dengan anatomi

ancestor *n* leluhur, nenek moyang; **ancestral** *adj* berasal dari nenek moyang, turun-temurun; **ancestry** *n* silsilah, nenek moyang

anchor *n* [anker] sauh, jangkar; *v* membuang sauh, berlabuh; *to weigh ~* mengangkat sauh; **anchorage** *n* pelabuhan

ancient *adj* [énsyent] kuno, zaman purbakala; *~ Egypt* Mesir Kuno

& co *and company* cs (cum suis)

and *conj* dan, serta, bersama; *~ so on* dan lain sebagainya

anecdote *n* lelucon, cerita, anekdot

anemia *n* [animia] kurang darah, anemia; **anemic** *adj* kurang darah

anesthesia *n* [anesthisya] pembiusan, anestesi; **anesthetic** *n* obat bius; *general* ~ bius total; *local* ~ bius lokal; **anesthetize** *v* [anisthetaiz] membius; **anesthetist** *n* ahli obat bius

anew *adj* sekali lagi, baru ← **new**

angel *n* [énjel] malaikat; *the ~ of death* malaikatul maut; **angelic** *adj* [anjélik] seperti malaikat, tanpa dosa

anger *n* [angger] kemarahan, murka; *v* membuat marah

angle *n* [anggel] sudut; *right ~* tegak lurus

angle: angling *n* memancing; ~ *rod* joran; **angler** *n* pemancing

Anglo- *adj* [anglo] Inggris; ~*centric* hanya melihat dari segi Inggris; ~*Saxon* berdarah Inggris (bukan Wales, Skotlandia atau Irlandia)

Angola *n* Angola; **Angolan** *n* orang Angola; *adj* berasal dari Angola

angry *adj* marah, murka ← **anger**

angular *adj* bersiku-siku; kaku; *an ~ figure* berbadan kurus ← **angle**

animal *n* binatang, hewan, satwa; *adj* hewani, biadab

animate *v* menghidupkan; **animated** *adj* bersemangat, hidup; **animation** *n* semangat; kartun animasi, anime

animosity *n* dendam, permusuhan

aniseed, anise *n* adas

ankle *n* [angkel] pergelangan kaki

annals *n, pl* babad, sejarah; *the Malay ~* Sejarah Melayu

annexe, annex *n* pavilyun; *v* mencaplok, menggabungkan; **annexation** *n* penggabungan

annihilate *v* [anaihilét] membinasakan, membasmi, memusnahkan; **annihilation** *n* pembinasaan, pembasmian, pemusnahan; kemenangan besar

anniversary *n* (hari) ulang tahun, hari jadi, hari peringatan (tidak digunakan untuk makhluk hidup); *wedding* ~ hari ulang tahun perkawinan

annotate *v* membubuhi catatan; **annotation** *n* catatan

announce *v* mengumumkan, memberitahukan; **announcer** *n* penyiar; **announcement** *n* pengumuman, maklumat

annoy *v* mengganggu, mengusik; **annoyance** *n* gangguan; **annoying** *adj* mengganggu, menjengkelkan

annual *n* edisi tahunan; *adj* tahunan; ~ *general meeting* rapat tahunan; **annually** *adv* setiap tahun

annuity *n* tunjangan hari tua

annul *v* membatalkan, mencabut; **annulment** *n* pembatalan

anomaly *n* kelainan, keganjilan, penyimpangan; **anomalous** *adj* aneh, ganjil

anonymous *adj* tanpa nama, anonim; ~ *letter* surat kaleng

another *n, adj* [anather] satu lagi, yang lain

answer *n* [anser] jawaban, jalan keluar (dari masalah); *v* menjawab, membalas (surat)

ant *n* semut; *flying ~* laron; *white ~* rayap

antagonist *n* lawan; **antagonistic** *adj* bersikap melawan

Antarctic *adj* berasal dari Antartika; *the ~* Kutub Selatan; **Antarctica** *n* Antartika, Kutub Selatan

antenna *n* antena

anterior *n* yang mendahului, bagian depan

anthem *n* lagu wajib; *national ~* lagu kebangsaan

anthill *n* [ant hil] sarang semut ← **ant**

anthology *n* kumpulan, antologi, bunga rampai

anthropological *adj* berkaitan dengan antropologi; **anthropologist** *n* antropolog; **anthropology** *n* ilmu antropologi

anti- *adj* anti-, anti, bersifat melawan; **anticlimax** *n* [antiklaimaks] kekecewaan, hasil yang berbeda dengan harapan; **antidote** *n* penawar; **antipathy** *n* antipati, perasaan tidak suka, perasaan benci; **antiseptic** *n* obat anti-kuman

antics *n, pl* tingkah lucu, kelucuan

anticipate *v* mengantisipasi, mengharapkan, menanti-nanti; **anticipation** *n* harapan; *thanking you in ~ of your reply* terima kasih sebelumnya (dalam surat)

anticlimax *n* kekecewaan, hasil yang berbeda dengan harapan

antidote *n* penawar

Antigua *n* Antigua; **Antiguan** *n* orang Antigua; *adj* berasal dari Antigua

antipathy *n* antipati, perasaan tidak suka, perasaan benci

antique *n* [antik] barang kuno, barang antik; *adj* kuno, antik; **antiquity** *n* [antikuiti] (barang dari) zaman purbakala

antlers *n, pl* tanduk rusa

antonym *n* lawan kata

anus *n* [énus] dubur

anvil *n* landasan, paron

anxiety *n* [angzayeti] kecemasan, kegelisahan, kekuatiran; **anxious** *adj* [angsyes] gelisah, cemas

any *adj* [éni] sesuatu, beberapa, sembarang; *neg* sedikit pun; *~one* mana saja; *do you have ~ food?* apakah ada makanan?; *~ color is fine* warna apa saja boleh; **anybody, anyone** *n* [éniwan] siapa pun, siapa saja; **anyhow** *adv* bagaimanapun; **anything** *n* apa saja, apa pun; **anywhere** *n* [éniwér] di mana saja, ke mana saja

apart *adv* terpisah; *~ from* selain, kecuali

apartheid *n* [apart hét] apartheid, kebijakan pemisahan antar-golongan di Afrika Selatan dari 1948–1994

apartment *n* apartemen, rumah susun

apathetic *adj* [apathétik] apatis, acuh tidak acuh; **apathy** *n* [apethi] apati, sikap acuk tak acuh

ape *n* kera, siamang; *v* meniru

APEC *abbrev Asia-Pacific Economic Cooperation* APEC, Kerjasama Ekonomi Asia Pasifik

aperture *n* [apertyur] lubang, bukaan

apologize *v* minta maaf; **apology** *n* permintaan maaf

apostle *n* [aposel] rasul; **apostolic** *adj* kerasulan

appall *v* [epol] membuat ngeri, mengerikan; **appalled** *adj* ngeri, heran; **appalling** *adj* mengerikan, sangat buruk

apparatus *n* perkakas, aparat, alat

apparent *adj* nyata, jelas, kentara; **apparently** *adv* tampaknya, ternyata ← **appear**

apparition *n* [aparisyen] hantu, penampakan ← **appear**

appeal *n* permohonan, permintaan, seruan; banding; *v* naik banding; **appealing** *adj* menarik, menawan

appear *v* tampak, muncul, timbul, menghadap; **appearance** *n* tampang, penampilan

appease *n* menenteramkan, menenangkan; **appeasement** *n* kebijakan membiarkan kejadian buruk terjadi tanpa ditindak

append *v* menambahkan, membubuhkan, melampirkan; **appendicitis** *n* [apéndisaitis] radang usus buntu; **appendix** *n* lampiran; usus buntu

appetite *n* selera, nafsu makan; *Sue has lost her ~* Sue tidak ada selera makan

applaud *v* bertepuk tangan,

memuji; **applause** *n* tepuk tangan

apple *n* buah apel

appliance *n* [aplayans] peranti, pesawat, alat

applicable *adj* [aplikabel] berlaku, dapat diterapkan ← **apply**

applicant *n* [aplikant] pelamar, pemohon; **application** *n* (surat) lamaran; penerapan, pemakai; *~ form* formulir (pendaftaran); **apply** *v* [aplai] berlaku; menerapkan, menggunakan; *~ for a job* melamar untuk pekerjaan

appoint *v* menunjuk, menetapkan, mengangkat; **appointed** *adj* yang ditentukan

appraisal *n* taksiran, penilaian; **appraise** *v* menaksir nilai, menilai

appreciate *v* [aprisyiét] berterima kasih; menghargai, menaksir harga, menilai; mengerti; *fin* bertambah nilai; **appreciation** *n* penghargaan; pengertian; taksiran; *fin* apresiasi

apprehend *v* menangkap; **apprehension** *n* rasa gelisah, kekuatiran; **apprehensive** *adj* kuatir, gelisah

apprentice *n* [apréntis] murid; *to be ~d to a welder* magang di bengkel las; **apprenticeship** *n* masa magang

approach *n* pendekatan; *v* mendekati, menuju (tempat); menjelang (waktu); **approachable** *adj* ramah, dapat didekati

appropriate *adj* patut, layak, pantas, sesuai

approval *n* [apruval] izin, persetujuan; **approve** *v* memperkenankan, mengizinkan, menyetujui

approximate *v* menaksir, menebak; *adj* kira-kira, kurang lebih; **approximately** *adv* kira-kira, kurang lebih

apricot *n* [éprikot] aprikot

April *n* [Épril] bulan April

apt *adj* layak, patut; cenderung; *children are ~ to tire easily* anak-anak cenderung cepat capek; **aptitude** *n* kecakapan, bakat

aqua *adj* biru toska

aquamarine *adj* [akuamarin] sejenis warna biru terang

aquarium *n* akuarium, kolam ikan

aquatic *adj* [akuotik] berhubungan dengan air atau laut; *~ center* kompleks kolam renang

aqueduct *n* jalan air (di atas tanah)

aqueous *adj* [akwius] berair

Arab *n* orang Arab; *adj* berasal dari daerah Arab; **United Arab Emirates (UAE)** Uni Emirat ~ (UEA); **Arabia** *n* [Arébia] (daerah) Arab; *Saudi ~* Arab Saudi; **Arabian** *adj* berasal dari Arab; **Arabic** *n* [Arabik] bahasa Arab; *~ script* huruf Arab

arable *adj* [arebel] dapat ditanami

arbitrary *adj* tanpa aturan, secara acak

arbitration *n* arbitrase, perantaraan

arc *n* garis lengkung

arcade *n* lorong atau gang beratap; *~ game* mesin permainan di tempat umum

arch *n* garis lengkung; busur; *v* melengkungkan; *~ enemy* musuh bebuyutan; **archer** *n* pemanah; **archery** *n* panahan

archeological *adj* purbakala; **archeologist** *n* ahli purbakala, arkeolog; **archeology** *n* ilmu purbakala, arkeologi

archipelago *n* [arkipélago] kepulauan, pulau gugusan; *the Malay ~* Nusantara

architect *n* [arkitekt] arsitek; *landscape ~* arsiték lanskap; **architecture** *n* arsitektur; **architectural** *adj* **architecturally** *adv* dari segi arsitektur

archive *n* [arkaiv] arsip; *the State Archives* kearsipan negara

Arctic *adj* Arktik, Artik, berasal dari kawasan Kutub Utara; *sub-~ temperatures* suhu yang sangat dingin; *the ~ (Circle)* daerah (lingkaran) Arktik

ardent *adj* bersemangat, bergairah; **ardor** *n* semangat, gairah, hasrat

are *v, pl →* **be**

area *n* [éria] daerah, wilayah, kawasan

Argentina *n* [Arjentina] Argentina; **Argentine** *n, arch* orang Argentina; *the ~* Argentina; *adj* berasal dari Argentina; **Argentinian** *n* orang Argentina; *adj* berasal dari Argentina argue *v* [argyu] berdebat, bertengkar; memperdebatkan, membantah; **argument** *n* beda pendapat, pertengkaran; alasan, dalih; **argumentative** *adj* suka bertengkar

arid *adj* gersang, kering; *semi-~* kering; **aridity** *n* ketidaksuburan, kekeringan

arise *v* arose, arisen bangkit, bangun, timbul ← **rise**

aristocracy *n* kaum ningrat; **aristocrat** *n* orang ningrat, bangsawan; **aristocratic** *adj* bersifat ningrat atau bangsawan

arithmetic *n* ilmu berhitung

ark *n* bahtera; *Noah's ~* bahtera Nabi Nuh

arm *n* lengan, tangan (baju)

arm *n* senjata; *v* mempersenjatai; *call to ~s* seruan untuk berjuang; *up in ~* marah sekali, kacau-balau; **armament** *n* persenjataan

armchair *n* kursi sofa, kursi tamu

Armenia *n* [Arminia] Armenia; **Armenian** *n* bahasa Armenia; orang Armenia; *adj* berasal dari Armenia

armistice *n* [armistis] gencatan senjata

armor *n* baju baja; *~ed car* mobil lapis baja

armpit *n* ketiak

army *n* tentara, bala tentara; angkatan darat

aroma *n* bau harum, aroma; **aromatic** *n* berbau harum; **aromatherapy** *n* aromaterapi, pengobatan atau relaksasi dengan wewangian

around *prep* [araund] sekeliling, sekitar, seputar; dekat; *adj* kira-kira, sekitar

arrange *v* [arénj] mengurus, menata, mengatur; mengaransemen (lagu); *~d marriage* penjodohan; **arrangement** *n* penataan, pengaturan, perjanjian; aransemen

arrest *n* penahanan, penangkapan; *cardiac ~* serangan jantung; *under ~* ditahan; *v* menahan, menangkap

arrival *n* kedatangan; **arrive** *v* datang, tiba

arrogance *n* kesombongan, keangkuhan; **arrogant** *adj* sombong, angkuh

arrow *n* (anak) panah; *red ~* tanda belok yang merah (di lampu merah)

arsenic *n* arsenikum, arsenik

arson *n* pembakaran yang disengaja; **arsonist** *n* orang yang dengan sengaja menyebabkan kebakaran

art *n* seni lukis; kesenian; *abstract ~* seni abstrak; **arts** *n* kesenian; sastra (jurusan); **arty** *adj, coll* (sok) artistik

arterial *adj* [artirial] berkaitan dengan pembuluh nadi atau arteri; *~ road* jalan arteri; **artery** *n* pembuluh nadi, arteri

arthritic *adj* [arthritik] berkaitan dengan radang sendi; **arthritis** *n* [arthraitis] encok, radang sendi

article *n* barang, benda; pasal,

bab (hukum); kata sandang; ~ *of clothing* sepotong baju

articulate *v* menyuarakan pikiran dengan lancar; *adj* menguasai bahasa, pandai menyuarakan pikiran

artifact *n* benda atau barang bersejarah

artificial *adj* buatan, palsu; ~ *insemination* pembuahan buatan

artillery *n* artileri; *heavy* ~ senjata berat, meriam

artist *n* seniman, seniwati; artis (seni peran); **artistic** *adj* artistik, indah; **artistry** *n* seni ← **art**

as *adv, conj* sama, se-; seperti; karena, sebab; ~ *well (as)* juga; ~ *if* seolah-olah; ~ *for me* kalau saya; ~ *big* ~ *a house* sebesar rumah; *Rob can't come* ~ *it's raining* Rob tidak bisa datang karena hujan

asbestos *n* asbes

ascend *v* naik, mendaki, memanjat; **ascendancy** *n* keunggulan, kekuasaan; **ascension** *n* kenaikan (ke surga); *Isl* Miraj; **ascent** *n* kenaikan; tanjakan

ascertain *v* [asértén] memastikan, mengetahui dengan pasti, mengecek

ASEAN *abbrev Association of South East Asian Nations* ASEAN, Asosiasi Negara-Negara Asia Tenggara

ash *n* abu; ~ *Wednesday* Rabu Abu

ashamed *adj* malu

ashen *adj* putih, pucat ← **ash**

ashore *adj* di darat; *go* ~ naik ke darat ← **shore**

ashtray *n* asbak

Asia *n* [Ésya] Asia; *Southeast* ~ Asia Tenggara; **Asian** *n* orang Asia; *adj* berhubungan dengan Asia; ~ *Development Bank (ADB)* Bank Pembangunan Asia

aside *adv* di sebelah; ~ *from* selain dari; *cast* ~ dibuang ← **side**

ASIO *abbrev Australian Security Intelligence Organisation* Organisasi Intelijen Keamanan Australia

ask *v* bertanya, minta, memohon; ~ *after* bertanya mengenai (orang); ~ *out* mengajak berkencan; ~*ing rate* harga jual; *a big* ~ tantangan besar

asleep *adj* sedang tidur; *to fall* ~ tertidur

asp *n* sejenis ular kecil

asparagus *n* asperse

aspect *n* segi pandangan, sudut pandangan, aspek

asphalt *n* [asyfalt] aspal

aspiration *n* cita-cita, harapan, aspirasi; **aspire** *v* berharap, mencita-citakan; *Stewart* ~*s to be an artist* Stewart bercita-cita menjadi seniman

ass *n* keledai; *sl* pantat; orang bodoh

assailant *n* penyerang, penyerbu ← **assault**

assassin *n* pembunuh (tokoh terkenal); **assassinate** *v* membunuh tokoh terkenal; **assassi-**

nation *n* pembunuhan tokoh terkenal

assault *n* serangan, serbuan; *v* menyerang, menyerbu

assemble *v* berkumpul, berhimpun, bersidang; mengumpulkan; merakit; **assembly** *n* perkumpulan, perhimpunan, sidang; perakitan; apel (di sekolah)

assent *v* memperkenankan, mengizinkan, menyetujui

assert *v* menyatakan dengan tegas; **assertion** *n* pernyataan, penegasan; **assertive** *adj* berani

assess *v* menaksir, menilai; **assessment** *n* taksiran, penilaian; **assessor** *n* penguji, orang yang menilai

asset *n* aset, modal; *fin* aktiva; *he is an ~ to the school* sekolah itu bangga padanya

assiduous *adj* rajin

assign *v* [asain] menugaskan, menetapkan, memperuntukkan; **assignation** *n* [asignésyen] penugasan; **assignment** *n* tugas

assimilate *v* membaur; **assimilation** *n* pembauran, asimilasi

assist *v* menolong, membantu; **assistance** *n* pertolongan, bantuan; *may I be of ~?* bisakah saya bantu?; **assistant** *n* pembantu, asisten

associate *n* kawan, mitra, rekan; *v* bergaul; mengaitkan, menghubungkan; **association** *n* gabungan, persatuan, asosiasi

assorted *adj* bermacam jenis; **assortment** *n* campuran, persediaan yang bermacam jenis

assume *v* menganggap; menjabat; *~ed name* alias, nama samaran; **assumption** *n* asumsi, prasangka

assurance *n* kepastian, jaminan, janji; **assure** *v* memastikan, menjamin; *~d of* dijamin akan

asterisk *n* tanda bintang

astern *adv* di bagian belakang kapal, di buritan ← **stern**

asthma *n* (penyakit) asma, sesak dada; **asthmatic** *adj* berpenyakit asma

astonish *v* mengherankan, menakjubkan; **astonished** *adj* heran; **astonishment** *n* keheranan

astound *v* **astounding** *adj* mengejutkan, mengherankan

astray *adj* sesat, tersesat; *to lead ~* menyestkan

astride *adv* mengangkang (naik kuda, sepeda dsb)

astrologer *n* [astrolojer] peramal; **astrology** *n* nasib menurut bintang, astrologi

astronomer *n* astronom, ahli bintang; **astronomy** *n* (ilmu) astronomi, ilmu bintang

astute *adj* cerdik, berakal

asylum *n* [asailum] suaka, tempat perlindungan; *~-seeker* pencari suaka; *mental ~* rumah sakit jiwa; *political ~* suaka politik

asymmetrical *adj* tidak berimbang, asimetris

at *prep* di; pada; ~ *all* sama sekali; pernah (dalam pertanyaan); ~ *home* di rumah; betah; ~ *last* akhirnya; ~ *least* paling tidak; ~ *once* sekarang juga; ~ *times* kadang-kadang; ~ *seven o'clock* pada jam tujuh

atheism *n* [éthiizem] ateisme; **atheist** *n* ateis

athlete *n* [athlit] atlet, olahragawan; pelari; **athletic** *adj* [athlétik] kuat, berotot, fit; **athletics** *n* cabang atletik, lari

Atlantic *n* the ~ *(Ocean)* Laut Atlantik; *the South* ~ Laut Atlantik Selatan; *North* ~ *Treaty Organisation (NATO)* Organisasi Pakta Pertahanan Atlantik Utara

atlas *n* atlas, buku peta; *road* ~ buku peta jalan

ATM *abbrev automated teller machine* ATM (anjingan tunai mandiri)

atmosphere *n* suasana; hawa, udara; angkasa, atmosfer; **atmospheric** *adj* [atmosférik] bersuasana khas; ~ *pressure* tekanan udara

atoll *n* pulau karang, atol

atom *n* atom; ~ *bomb* bom nuklir, bom atom; **atomic** *adj* berkaitan dengan atom, nuklir; ~ *energy* tenaga nuklir; ~ *power station* pembangkit listrik tenaga nuklir (PLTN)

atone *v* bertobat, menebus (dosa); **atonement** *n* penebusan dosa; *the Day of* ~ Hari Penebusan (Dosa)

atrocious *adj* [atrosyus] buruk; kejam, bengis; **atrocity** *n* kekejian, kekejaman, kebengisan

attach *v* menambat, melekatkan, mengaitkan, melampirkan; **attaché** *n* [atasyé] atase; **attached** *adj* terlampir; berpasangan; sayang; **attachment** *n* lampiran; rasa sayang

attack *n* serangan; *v* menyerang

attempt *n* usaha, percobaan; *v* mencoba, berusaha; ~ed *murder* upaya pembunuhan

attend *v* hadir; menghadiri; ~ *to* melayani; merawat; **attendance** *n* kehadiran; **attendant** *n* pelayan; *flight* ~ pramugari, pramugara

attention *n* perhatian; **attentive** *adj* penuh perhatian

attic *n* loteng

attire *n* busana, pakaian; *suitably* ~d berbusana yang pantas

attitude *n* [atityud] sikap, pendirian; *sl* keberanian

attorney *n* [atérni] pengacara; ~-*General* Jaksa Agung; *power of* ~ surat kuasa

attract *v* menarik atau memikat (hati); **attraction** *n* daya tarik, daya pikat; atraksi; *tourist* ~ obyek wisata; **attractive** *adj* menawan

attribute *v* menghubungkan, mengaitkan, *n* sifat, ciri, lambang; *v* ~ *to* dihubungkan dengan, dikaitkan; *the fire was* ~d *to a short circuit* kebakaran diperkirakan diakibatkan kortsleting auction *n* lelang; ~ *house* rumah lelang; *v* melelangkan; **auctioneer** *n* juru lelang

audacious *adj* [odésyus] berani sekali; **audacity** *n* [odasiti] keberanian

audible *adj* [odibel] kedengaran, terdengar

audience *n* [odiéns] para penonton, tamu, hadirin; *to have an* ~ *with* beraudiensi dengan

audit *n* pemeriksaan keuangan; *v* memeriksa keuangan, mengaudit; **auditor** *n* akuntan

audition *n* audisi; *v* mengikuti audisi

August *n* bulan Agustus

aunt *n* [ant] **aunty, auntie** *sl* bibi, tante; **great-~** saudara perempuan dari kakek atau nenek

aura *n* [ora] pancaran, suasana

auspice [ospes] *under the* ~s *of* di bawah pengawasan

Australia *n* [Ostrélia] Australia; *Western* ~ Australia Barat; **Australian** *n* orang Australia; *adj* berasal dari Australia

Austria *n* Austria; **Austrian** *n* orang Austria; *adj* berasal dari Austria

authentic *adj* asli, otentik

author *n* pengarang, penulis

authoritative *adj* berkuasa, berwenang, berotoritas; dapat dipercaya; **authority** *n* otoritas, kekuasaan; yang berwajib, instansi; ahli, pakar; **authorization** *n* kewenangan; **authorize** *v* mengizinkan

autism *n* [otizem] autisme; **autistic** *adj* autis

autobiographical *adj* [otobayografikal] yang berkaitan dengan pengalaman sendiri; **autobiography** *n* otobiografi

automatic *adj* otomatis, dengan sendirinya

autonomous *n* otonom; **autonomy** *n* otonomi; *regional* ~ otonomi daerah (otda)

autopsy *n* otopsi, bedah mayat

autumn *n* [otum] musim gugur

auxiliary *n* [oksiliari] alat pembantu; *adj* bantu, pembantu; ~ *verb* kata kerja bantu

Av, Ave *Avenue* Jl (Jalan)

avail *to no* ~ sia-sia

available *adj* tersedia

avarice *n* [avaris] ketamakan

avenge *v* membalas dendam (terutama atas kematian); **avenger** *n* orang yang membalas dendam

avenue *n* [avenyu] jalan (terutama yang di antara dua deretan pohon)

average *n, adj* [averej] rata-rata; *on* ~ rata-rata

averse *adj* enggan, segan; **aversion** *n* keengganan, ketidaksukaan; **avert** *v* menghindari, menjauhkan; ~ *your gaze* menghindari pandangan

aviary *n* [éviari] kandang burung yang besar

avid *adj* gemar sekali

avocado *n* alpukat

await *v* menantikan ← **wait**

awake *v* **awoke awoken** bangun; *adj* dalam keadaan bangun; **awaken** *v* bangun; **awakening** *n* kesadaran; awal ← **wake**

award *n* penghargaan; *v* memberi penghargaan

aware *adj* sadar akan, menyadari; **awareness** *n* kesadaran

away *adj* tidak di sini, tidak ada; dari tempat itu; *go away!* pergilah!; *he's ~ today* dia tidak masuk hari ini

awe *n* [oa] perasaan kagum; **awful** *adj* dahsyat, mengerikan

awkward *adj* kikuk, canggung; **awkwardness** *n* kecanggungan

ax, axe *n* kapak

axiom *n* aksioma

axis *n* [aksis] poros, sumbu; *the ~ of Evil* Poros Kejahatan

axle *n* [aksel] as roda

aye *n* [ai] ya, setuju

Azerbaijan *n* Azerbaijan; **Azerbaijani** *n* bahasa Azerbaijan; orang Azerbaijan; *adj* berasal dari Azerbaijan; **Azeri** *n* bahasa Azerbaijan, bahasa Azeri

azure *adj* biru muda

B

B & B *abbrev bed and breakfast* losmen, penginapan murah yang termasuk sarapan

BA *abbrev Bachelor of Arts* SS (Sarjana Sastra)

babble *v* berceloteh, mengoceh; bicara tanpa kendali

babe *n, arch* [béb] bayi; *a ~ in arms* bayi, orok; *sl* cewek; **baby** *n* bayi; *adj* anak; *a ~ elephant* anak gajah; *~face* wajah imut-imut; **babysit** *v* **babysat**, **babysat** *v* menjaga anak; **babysitter** *n* penjaga anak

baboon *n* babon; *sl* orang tolol

bachelor *n* bujangan, jejaka; *~'s degree* S1 (Strata Satu); *~ of Arts (BA)* Sarjana Sastra (SS); *~ flat* apartemen sederhana, seperti untuk kaum bujangan

back *n* belakang, punggung, balik; *at the ~ of* di belakang; *behind his ~* dari belakang, tidak terus terang; *~s to the wall* membelakangi tembok, dalam keadaan terjebak; *adj, adv* ke belakang, mundur; *~ and forth* mondar-mandir, bolak-balik; *~ seat* jok belakang; kurang penting; *v* mendukung, mendanai; *~ down* akhirnya menyerah; *~ up* bertumpuk, menjadi antrean panjang; membela; memundurkan; **backbone** *n* tulang belakang; **backdrop** *n* latar belakang (di panggung); **backfire** *v* senjata makan tuan; **background** *n* latar belakang; **backing** *n* sokongan, dukungan; **backroom** *~ boys* orang di balik tokoh; **backside** *n, sl* pantat; **backstab** *v* memfitnah, menikam dari belakang; **backstreet** *adj, sl* tidak resmi, lewat pintu belakang; **backstroke** *n* gaya punggung; **backward, backwards** *adj, adv* ke belakang, mundur

bacon *n* irisan daging babi asap; *beef* ~ daging sapi yang diasap seperti *bacon*; *save my* ~ menyelamatkan saya

bacteria *n, pl* bakteri, kuman

bad *adj* jelek, buruk, kurang baik; ~ *dream* mimpi buruk; ~*-mannered* tidak sopan

badge *n* lencana, pin

badger *n* sejenis binatang hutan di Eropa, luak

badness *n* keburukan ← **bad**

baffle *v* **baffling** *adj* membingungkan; **baffled** *adj* bingung

bag *n* tas, karung; *bum* ~ tas pinggang; *carry*~ tas tenteng, keresek; *hand*~ tas tangan; *old* ~ *sl* nenek-nenek; *plastic* ~ keresek, plastik; *it's in the* ~ sudah pasti; *v, sl* memesan tempat

baggage *n* [bagej] bagasi, koper, tas; *emotional* ~ beban mental; *left* ~ penitipan tas

baggy *adj* [bagi] kendor, kebesaran

Bahamas *the* ~ Bahama; **Bahamian** *n* orang Bahama; *adj* berasal dari Bahama

Bahrain *n* Bahrain; **Bahraini** *n* orang Bahrain; *adj* berasal dari Bahrain

bail *n* uang jaminan; *released on* ~ dibebaskan dengan jaminan; *v* menimba air dari kapal; *sl* cabut; ~ *out* menyelamatkan

bait *n* umpan; *v* menggoda, mengumpani

bake *v* membakar; **baker** *n* tukang memasak roti; ~*'s dozen* tiga belas; **bakery** *n* toko roti

balance *n* keseimbangan; neraca, timbangan; *fin* saldo; *v* menimbang; ~ *sheet* neraca; **balanced** *adj* berimbang

balcony *n* balkon, teras, beranda

bald *adj* [bold] botak, gundul, plontos

bale *n* bungkus atau bal (jerami)

baleful *adj* tidak ramah, tidak senang

ball *n* [bol] bola; ~*boy*, ~*girl* orang yang mengambilkan bola selama pertandingan tenis; *n* pesta berdansa; *I had a* ~ saya sangat menikmatinya; *on the* ~ cerdas, sadar; *to start the* ~ *rolling* memulai

ballast *n* pemberat

ballerina *n* p pebalet; **ballet** *n* [balé] balet; ~ *dancer* pebalet

balloon *n* balon; *hot-air* ~ balon udara

ballot *n* [balet] pemilihan suara, pengambilan undi; ~ *box* kotak suara

bamboo *n* bambu

ban *n* larangan; *v* melarang; **banned** *adj* dilarang

banana *n* pisang

band *n* gerombolan, geng, kawanan; band, grup musik; gelang; *v* ~ *together* bersatu, bekerja sama

bandage *n* [bandej] perban; *v* memerban, membalut

bandanna *n* ikat kepala

bandit *n* bandit, penyamun

bang *ejac* dor!, suara keras; *v* berdentang; membanting

Bangladesh *n* Bangladesh; **Bangladeshi** *n* orang Bangladesh; *adj* berasal dari Bangladesh

banish *v* membuang; **banishment** *n* pembuangan

bank *n* bank; tepi, sisi (sungai); *v* menjadi nasabah; membelok (pesawat terbang); **banker** *n* bankir; **banknote** *n* uang kertas; **bankrupt** *adj* bangkrut, pailit; **bankruptcy** *n* kepailitan

banner *n* spanduk

banquet *n* [bankuet] perjamuan lengkap

banter *n* senda gurau; *v* bersenda gurau

baptism *n* permandian; ~ *of fire* awal yang mengerikan; **baptist** *n* pembaptis; *John the* ~ *Cath* Yohanes Pembaptis; *Chr* Yahya; **baptize** *v* mempermandikan, membaptis

bar *n* palang pintu, batang, halangan, rintangan; tempat minum, kafe; *v* memalang, menghalangi, merintangi; melarang

barb *n* duri; *sl* kata sindiran; ~*ed wire* kawat berduri

Barbadian *n* orang Barbados; *adj* berasal dari Barbados; **Barbados** *n* [Barbédos] Barbados

barbarian *n* [barbérian] barbar, orang biadab; **barbarity** *n* kebengisan, kebiadaban;

barbarous, barbaric *adj* bengis, biadab, barbar

barbecue, barbeque, BBQ *n* acara memanggang daging di luar rumah; *v* memanggang daging

barber *n* tukang cukur

bare *adj* telanjang, polos; hanya; *v* menelanjangi, memamerkan; **barefoot** *adj* dengan kaki telanjang; **bareheaded** *adj* tanpa tutup kepala; **barely** *adj* hampir tidak

bargain *n* [bargen] pembelian yang murah; *v* tawar-menawar, menawar

barge *n* tongkang; *v* menyerobot masuk

bark *n* kulit kayu; gonggongan anjing; *v* menggonggong

barn *n* gudang (tempat menyimpan jerami, rumput kering dsb)

baron *n* baron (gelar bangsawan)

barracks *n* barak, tangsi, asrama

barrage *n* [baraj] aliran yang deras; *a* ~ *of questions* banyak ditanya secara terus-menerus

barrel *n* tong; laras bedil; *a* ~ *of laughs* lucu sekali, jenaka

barren *adj* tandus, gersang; tidak subur, mandul

barricade *n* [barikéd] rintangan, barikade; *v* memblokir, merintangi

barrier *n* palang, penghalang, rintangan

barrister *n* advokat, pengacara (yang tampil di pengadilan)

barrow *n* gerobak

bartender *n* pelayan yang

menyediakan minuman di bar atau kafe ← **bar**

barter n niaga tukar-menukar barang, barter; v tukar-menukar barang, barter

base n markas, dasar; v berdasar, mendasarkan

bashful adj malu, tersipu-sipu

basic adj asasi, pokok; the ~s prinsip-prinsip dasar ← **base**

basil n [bazil] sejenis kemangi

basin n baskom, wastafel; lembah, daerah aliran sungai (DAS)

bask v berjemur (di bawah sinar matahari); menikmati

basket n keranjang, bakul, basket; ~ball bola basket; ~ case tidak ada harapan

bass n [bés] bas

bastard n anak haram, anak yang lahir di luar nikah; sl brengsek, bajingan

bat n alat pemukul (dalam olahraga); v memukul bola (dalam kriket, bisbol dsb)

bat n kelelawar, kampret, kalong

batch n sejumlah; seri (keluaran barang)

bath n (bak) mandi; to take a ~, have a ~ mandi; ~robe kimono; ~tub bak untuk mandi rendam; **bathe** v [béth] mandi; memandikan; **bather** n orang yang mandi; **bathroom** n kamar mandi; may I use your ~? boleh saya ke WC?

baton n tongkat kecil

battalion n batalyon

batter n adonan kue; pemukul bola; v memukul-mukul; ~ed wife isteri yang sering dipukuli

battery n [bateri] baterai

battle n pertempuran, peperangan; perjuangan; v bertempur, berjuang; **battleground** n medan peperangan; **battler** n pejuang, orang kecil; **battleship** n kapal perang, kapal tempur

bawl v berteriak; menangis keras-keras

bay n teluk; ~ leaf daun salam

bayonet n [béyonét] sangkur, bayonet

bazaar n [bezar] pasar kaget

BBC abbrev British Broadcasting Corporation penyiar nasional Inggris

BC abbrev before Christ SM (sebelum Masehi)

BE abbrev Bachelor of Economics SE (Sarjana Ekonomi)

be v **was been** menjadi, adalah, merupakan

beach n pantai, pesisir; v mendamparkan diri; **beached** adj terdampar

beacon n rambu

bead n manik-manik; tetesan; **beady** little ~ eyes bola mata yang kecil dan bulat

beam n balok; sinar (cahaya); v bersinar, tersenyum lebar

bean n buncis, kacang; kidney ~ kacang merah; string ~ kacang panjang; spill the ~s menceritakan semua

bear n [bér] beruang; polar ~ beruang putih

bear *v* [bér] **bore born** memikul, menahan; bersalin, melahirkan

beard *n* [bird] jenggot; **bearded** *adj* berjenggot

bearer *n* [bérer] pembawa ← **bear**

bearing *n* [béring] sikap; arah, tujuan, pengaruh ← **bear**

beast *n* binatang; orang yang bengis; ~ *of burden* hewan pekerja; **beastly** *adj* seperti binatang, bengis

beat *n* pukulan; irama, ritme; *v* **beat beaten** memukul; mengalahkan; ~ *it* pergi lu; *it ~s me* tidak masuk akal

beautiful *adj* [byutiful] cantik (perempuan), asri (pemandangan), bagus, indah; **beauty** *n* kecantikan, keindahan; wanita cantik

beaver *n* sejenis berang-berang

became *v, pf* → **become**

because *conj* [bikoz] (oleh) karena, sebab; ~ *of* karena, lantaran

become *v* [bikam] **became become** menjadi; **becoming** *adj* cocok, menarik

bed *n* tempat tidur, ranjang; *v, sl* meniduri, tidur bersama; ~ *and breakfast (B & B)* hotel kecil; **bedroom** *n* kamar (tidur); **bedspread, bedcover** *n* selimut

bee *n* lebah, tawon, kumbang

beef *n* daging sapi; **beefy** *adj* gemuk, berotot

beehive *n* sarang lebah ← **bee**

been *v, pf* → **be**

beer *n* bir

beeswax *n* lilin; *mind your own* ~ *sl* bukan urusanmu

beetle *n* kumbang

before *prep* di muka, depan; sebelum; *adv* sebelum; **beforehand** *adj* terlebih dahulu

beg *v* meminta-minta, mengemis, memohon; ~ *your pardon* maaf; *I ~ to inform you* dengan hormat saya memberitahu Anda; **beggar** *n* pengemis

begin *v* [begin] **began begun** mulai, memulai; **beginning** *n* awal, permulaan

behalf *on ~ of* atas nama, demi

behave *v* berkelakuan (baik); ~ *yourself* berkelakuan baik, sopan; **behavior** *n* perilaku

behead *v* memenggal, memancung (kepala)

behind *n* [behaind] belakang; *sl* pantat; *prep* di belakang, ke belakang; *adv* tertinggal, ketinggalan

being *n* makhluk; keadaan → **be**

Belarus *n* Belarus

Belgian *n* [Béljen] orang Belgia; *adj* berasal dari Belgia; **Belgium** *n* [Béljum] Belgia

belief *n* [belif] **beliefs** pendapat, kepercayaan, iman, agama; *beyond* ~ mustahil; **believe** *v* percaya, berpendapat; **believer** *n* orang beriman

belittle *v* meremehkan

bell *n* bel, lonceng, genta; *saved by the* ~ nyaris tidak selamat

belligerent *adj* [belijerent] galak, suka berkelahi

bellow *v* berteriak, meneriakkan

belly *n* (bagian bawah) perut; ~*ache* sakit perut; ~ *button* pusar

belong *v* milik, termasuk kepunyaan; **belonging** *n* rasa betah, rasa diterima; **belongings** *n* barang milik

Belorussia *n, arch* Belarus; **Belorussian** *n* orang Belarus; *adj* berasal dari Belarus ← **Belarus**

beloved *n* [belovéd] *adj* yang dicintai, yang dikasihi, yang disayangi

below *prep* di bawah, ke bawah; ~ *the belt* di luar aturan, curang

belt *n* ikat pinggang, sabuk; *seat* ~ sabuk pengaman; *v, sl* mencambuk; ~ *up!* diam!

bemused *adj* bingung

bench *n* bangku, tempat duduk

bend *n* belokan; *v* **bent bent** membelok, melengkung; *it's driving me round the* ~ itu membuat saya gila

beneath *prep* di bawah; ~ *your dignity* merendahkan, menghinakan

benediction *n* doa, ucapan syukur

beneficial *adj* [bénefisyel] menguntungkan, bermanfaat; **benefit** *n* manfaat, untung; ~ *concert* konser amal; *for the* ~ *of* demi; *v* menguntungkan

benevolence *n* kemurahan hati, kebaikan, perbuatan baik; **benevolent** *adj* baik

BEng *abbrev* Bachelor of Engineering ST (Sarjana Teknik), Ir (insinyur)

benign *adj* [benain] baik; ~ *tumor* tumor jinak

bent *v, pf* → **bend**; *adj* bengkok, tidak lurus; *sl* homoseksual; *hell-*~ *on* nekat

bequeath *v* mewarisan; **bequest** *n* warisan

beret *n* [béré] baret, pici; *the Blue* ~*s (UN peacekeepers)* pasukan Baret Biru

Bermuda *n* Bermuda; ~ *shorts* sejenis celana pendek

berth *n* kamar, bilik kapal; tempat

beside *prep* di sisi, di dekat; kecuali, di luar, selain dari; *he was* ~ *himself* dia sudah tidak waras lagi; **besides** *adv* lagipula, ditambah lagi

besiege *v* [besij] mengepung

best *adj* paling bagus, paling baik, terbaik; ~ *man* pendamping pengantin pria; ~*seller* laris terjual; *the* ~ *part of* bagian terbesar; *to give it your* ~ *shot* berusaha sebisa-bisanya; *it's (all) for the* ~ lebih baik begitu

bestial *adj* seperti binatang, hewani

bestow *v* menganugerahi

bet *n* taruhan; *a safe* ~ kemungkinan besar; *v* **bet bet** bertaruh; *I* ~ *my bottom dollar* saya yakin

betray *v* mengkhianati; **betrayal** *n* pengkhianatan

betrothed *n* tunangan; *adj* bertunangan

better *adj* lebih baik; sembuh; ~

not lebih baik jangan; *your ~s* orang di atas, orang tua; *v* memperbaiki, mengungguli

between *prep* (di) antara, di tengah; ~ *girlfriends* sedang sendiri, tanpa pacar

beverage *n* [béverej] minuman (terutama yang panas)

beware *adj* [bewér] awas, berhati-hati; ~ *of the dog* awas anjing

bewilder *v* membingungkan; **bewildered** *adj* bingung; **bewildering** *adj* membingungkan; **bewilderment** *n* kebingungan

bewitched *adj* tersihir

beyond *prep* (di) sebelah, lebih (jauh), melampaui, melebihi

BH *abbrev business hours* k, ktr (kantor)

Bhutan *n* Bhutan; **Bhutanese** *adj* berasal dari Bhutan

bias *n* [bayas] kecenderungan; **biased** *adj* tidak berimbang

Bible *n* [Baibel] Injil, Alkitab; ~-*basher* orang Kristen yang fanatik; **biblical** *adj* [biblikal] berasal dari Alkitab

bicycle *n* [baisikel] sepeda; ~ *path* jalur sepeda; *v, arch* bersepeda

bid *n* tawaran, usaha; *v* **bid bidden** menawar; **bidder** *n* orang yang menawar; **bidding** *n* penawaran

bide ~ *your* time menanti, menunggu

biennial *n* [bayénial] acara dua tahun sekali; *adj* terjadi dua tahun sekali

big *adj* besar, gemuk; raksasa; ~-*headed* sombong, egois; ~ *brother* bang, kakak (laki-laki); ~ *shot* tokoh penting, orang besar; ~ *toe* jempol kaki; *think* ~ berpikir pada skala besar; ~ *Brother is watching* pemerintah atau dinas rahasia sedang mengintai

bigamist *n* [bigamist] orang dengan lebih dari satu suami atau isteri; **bigamy** *n* hal beristeri atau bersuami dua

bight *n* [bait] teluk

bike *n* sepeda (motor); *v* naik sepeda; *trail* ~ sepeda motor gunung; **biker** *n* penggemar sepeda motor

bile *n* empedu

bilingual *adj* [bailingguel] dwibahasa; **bilingualism** *n* kedwibahasaan berbahasa lebih dari satu

bill *n* bon, rekening, nota; wesel, daftar; rancangan undang-undang (RUU); paruh (pada burung); ~ *of lading* surat muatan kapal; *v* menagih

billet *n* penginapan; *to be ~ed* dikirim ke penginapan yang berbeda-beda

billiards *n, pl* bilyar

billion *n* satu milyar (1.000.000.000); **billionaire** *n* milyarder

bin *n* tempat sampah, tong; *dust~*, *rubbish* ~ tempat sampah; *v* membuang

bind *n* [baind] *in a* ~ terkekang; *v* **bound bound** mengikat, menghubungkan; mewajibkan; *the law is ~ing* terikat hukum

bind *v* [baind] menjilid; **binder** *n* map; **binding** *n* penjilidan

binoculars *n, pl* teropong, binokular

biographer *n* [bayografer] penulis biografi; **biographical** *adj* terkait dengan pengalaman sendiri; **biography** *n* biografi, riwayat hidup

biologist *n* [bayalojist] ahli biologi; **biology** *n* ilmu biologi

biplane *n* [baiplén] pesawat terbang bersayap dua lapis

bird *n* burung; *~ brain* bodoh; *~ cage* sangkar burung; *~ flu* flu burung; *~'s eye view* pandangan dari atas; *a little ~ told me* kabar burung

birth *n* kelahiran; *~day* hari ulang tahun, hari jadi; *~mark* tahi lalat; *~ mother* ibu kandung; *home ~* melahirkan di rumah

biscuit *n* [bisket] biskuit, kue kering

bisexual *adj* [baiséksyual] biseks

bishop *n* uskup

bit *n* sedikit, sepotong; *not a ~* sedikit pun tidak, sama sekali tidak; *v, pf* → **bite**

bitch *n* anjing betina; perempuan jelek; *v, sl* mengeluh, mengadu

bite *n* gigitan; *v* **bit bitten** menggigit

bitter *adj* pahit; **bitterness** *n* kepahitan, rasa pahit

bizarre *adj* [bizar] luar biasa aneh

blab *v* membocorkan rahasia; **blabber** *v* berbicara tanpa

berpikir lebih dahulu; **blabbermouth** *n* orang yang membocorkan rahasia

black *adj* hitam, gelap; *~board* papan tulis; *~ market* pasar gelap, tidak resmi; *~out* mati lampu; *~smith* pandai besi; *~ and blue* biru lebam; *in ~ and white* di atas kertas, hitam di atas putih; *in the ~* sedang menguntungkan; *v ~ out* pingsan; **blacken** *v* menghitamkan; **blackmail** *n* pemerasan; *v* memeras

bladder *n* kandung kemih; *~ infection* infeksi saluran kemih

blade *n* mata pisau; *a ~ of grass* sebilah rumput

blame *n* kesalahan; *v* menyalahkan, menyalahi (orang); *nobody's to ~* tidak ada yang bersalah; **blameless** *adj* tidak tercela, sempurna

blank *n* tempat kosong; peluru kosong; *mental ~* tiba-tiba lupa; *adj* kosong, hampa

blanket *n* selimut; *v* menyelimuti

blaspheme *v* [blasfim] menggunakan kata yang menghina Tuhan atau agama, memaki, mengumpat; **blasphemous** *adj* [blasfemus] yang menghina Tuhan; **blasphemy** *n* penghinaan terhadap Tuhan, cacian, makian

blast *n* angin kencang, letupan, tiupan; *sl it was a ~* sangat asyik; *ejac* keparat

blaze *n* kebakaran; *v* menyala; **blazing** *adj* menyala

blazer *n* jas (setengah resmi)
bleach *n* pemutih; *v* memutihkan (baju)
bleak *adj* suram, gelap
bleat *n* embikan; *v* mengembik
bleed *nose~* mimisan; *v* **bled bled** berdarah; **bleeding** *adj* berdarah; *sl* sialan
blemish *n* [blémisy] noda, cacat
blend *n* campuran; *v* berbaur; mencampur
bless *v* memberkati; ~ *you Isl* alhamdulillah (sesudah bersin); *God* ~ *you Chr* Tuhan memberkati; **blessed** *adj* yang diberkati; *sl* gila; **blessing** *n* pemberkatan; doa restu
blew *v, pf* → **blow**
blind *n* [blaind] horden, penutup jendela, kerai; *v* menyilaukan, membutakan; ~ed silau; *adj* buta; ~ *in one eye* buta sebelah mata; **blindfold** *n* kain penutup mata; *v* menutup mata dengan kain; **blindly** *adj* membabi buta, tanpa melihat atau berpikir; **blindness** *n* kebutaan
blink *n* kedipan mata, kejapan mata; *v* mengedip, mengejapkan mata; **blinking** *adj* berkedip-kedip; *sl* gila
bliss *n* kebahagiaan; *wedded* ~ perkawinan yang membahagiakan; **blissful** *adj* bahagia, berbahagia
blister *n* lecet, lepuh; *v* menjadi lecet, melepuhkan
blitz *n* serangan kilat; *The* ~ serangan udara terhadap kota London oleh angkatan udara Jerman pada tahun 1940
bloat *v* membengkak, mengembung; ~ed bengkak, kembung
block *n* balok; blok; *v* merintangi, membatasi, menghambati; ~ed tersumbat, mampet; **block-ade** *n* [blokéd] blokade, pemblokiran; *v* memblokir; **blockhead** *n* orang bodoh
blood *n* [blad] darah; ~ *nose* mimisan; ~ *relation* saudara kandung, hubungan darah; ~ *vessel* pembuluh darah; **blood-stain** *n* bekas darah; **blood-thirsty** *adj* ganas, haus darah; **bloody** *adj* berdarah; *sl* gila, persetan; ~ *hell* persetan
blossom *n* bunga; *cherry* ~ sakura; *v* berbunga
blot *n* noda (tinta); *v* menodai, mencemari; ~*ting paper* kertas isap
blouse *n* [blauz] blus
blow *n* pukulan, tamparan; tiupan; *v* **blew blown** bertiup; meniup; ~ *your nose* membuang ingus, bersin; **blowpipe** *n* sumpitan
blubber *n* lapisan lemak (ikan paus); *v* menangis dengan keras
bludge *v, sl* tidak bekerja, bermalas-malas; **bludger** *n* pemalas; *dole-*~ orang yang hidup dari tunjangan tunakarya
blue *adj* [blu] biru; ~ *blood* bangsawan, darah biru; ~-*collar* pekerja berpenghasilan rendah; ~ *film* film porno; ~*print* cetakan biru; ~ *ribbon* mutu tertinggi; hadiah pertama;

black and ~ biru lebam; *to feel* ~ bersedih; *once in a* ~ *moon* jarang sekali; *out of the* ~ tiba-tiba

bluff *n* pura-pura; jurang tebing; *v* berpura-pura, berlagak

blunder *n* [blander] kesalahan besar; *v* berbuat salah

blunt *adj* tumpul

blur *n* kabur; *v* mengaburkan; **blurred, blurry** *adj* kabur, kurang jelas

blurb *n* paragraf mengenai isi buku di sampul belakang

blush *v* memerah (muka); **blusher** *n* pemerah pipi, perona pipi

bluster *n* omong banyak, bicara dengan keras; *v* omong banyak

Blvd *Boulevard* Bulevar, Adimarga, Jalan

BM *abbrev Bachelor of Medicine* SK (Sarjana Kedokteran)

BO *abbrev body odor* bau badan

boar *n* babi jantan

board *n* papan; karton, kertas tebal, kardus

board *on* ~ di kapal, di pesawat; bersama; **boarding** naik pesawat; ~ *pass n* pas naik pesawat

board *v* mondok, kos; ~ *and lodging* kos (termasuk makanan); **boarder** *n* anak kos; **boarding** ~ *house* rumah kos, asrama (sekolah); ~ *school* sekolah dengan asrama

board *n* dewan; ~ *of governors* dewan pengurus

boast *n* bualan; *v* membual; **boastful** *adj* sombong, sok hebat

boat *n* kapal, perahu; *all in the same* ~ dalam keadaan yang sama

bob *n* potongan rambut pendek untuk wanita; *v* membungkuk; turun naik

bobbin *n* bobin, kumparan, gulungan

bobby *n, sl* Ing polisi; ~*-socks adj* kaus kaki pendek yang berwarna menyolok

bodice *n* [bodis] korset

body *n* badan, tubuh; organisasi, himpunan; **bodyguard** *n* pengawal pribadi; **bodysurfing** *n* berselancar tanpa papan

bog *n* rawa, payau; *v* terhenti (kendaraan)

bohemian *adj* gaya bebas, seperti seniman

boil *n* bisul; *on the* ~ sedang memanas; *v* mendidih; merebus; **boiler** *n* ketel (kukus); *sl old* ~ perempuan tua yang jelek

boisterous *adj* ribut, ramai, riuh

bold *adj* berani; ~ *type* huruf tebal

Bolivia *n* Bolivia; **Bolivian** *n* orang Bolivia; *adj* berasal dari Bolivia

bolt *n* baut, slot; ~ *of lightning* halilintar, petir; *v* mengunci; kabur

bomb *n* [bom] bom; *v* mengebom; **bomber** *n* pesawat pengebom; **bombing** *n* pengeboman

bombard *v* [bombard] mengebom; **bombardment** *n* pemboman, pengeboman

bond *n* pengikat; ikatan; kewajiban; obligasi

bone *n* tulang; gading; *jaw~* tulang rahang; *adj* gading

bonfire *n* api unggun

bonnet *n* topi (untuk bayi atau perempuan)

book *n* buku, kitab, novel; *v* memesan; *~-binding* penjilidan buku; *~ shelf, ~ shelf* lemari buku; **booking** *n* pemesanan, buking; **bookkeeper** *n* akuntan; bandar taruhan; **book-keeping** *n* pembukuan; **booklet** buku kecil, buklet; **bookseller** penjual buku, toko buku; **bookshop** *n* toko buku; **bookworm** *n* kutu buku

boom *n* ledakan; *v* meledak; *ejac* dor!; **booming** *adj* laris

boost *n* dorongan, kemajuan; *v* menaikkan; **booster** *n* tambahan

boot *n* sepatu (bot), sepatu lars; *~ camp* latihan militer; *v* menghidupkan (komputer); *re~* menghidupkan (komputer) kembali; *~ out* mendepak, mengusir; *~ polish* semir sepatu

booth *n* loket, gerai

bootie, bootee *n* kaus kaki atau sepatu bayi yang empuk

bootlace *n* tali sepatu (bot) ← **boot**

booty *n* (hasil) rampasan

booze *sl, n* minuman keras; *v* banyak minum alkohol; **boozer** *n* peminum berat

border *n* tepi, sisi; perbatasan, tapal batas; *v* berbatasan dengan; membatasi; **borderline** *n* batas; *adj* hampir, nyaris

bore *n* orang atau kegiatan yang membosankan; *v* membosankan, menjemukan; mengebor; **boredom** *n* kebosanan, kejenuhan, rasa bosan atau jenuh; **boring** *adj* membosankan, menjemukan

bore *v, pf* → **bear**

born *v, pf* dilahirkan, lahir, terlahir → **bear**

borne *v, pf* → **bear**

borrow *v* pinjam, meminjam; *~er* orang yang meminjam

Bosnia *n* Bosnia (and Herzegovina); **Bosnian** *n* orang Bosnia; *adj* berasal dari Bosnia

boss *n* pemimpin, bos; **bossy** *adj* suka menyuruh

botanist *n* ahli tumbuh-tumbuhan, ahli botani; **botany** *n* ahli tumbuh-tumbuhan

both *adj* kedua, kedua(-kedua)nya; *both … and …* baik … maupun …

bother *n* repot, kesusahan; *v* merepotkan, menyusahkan; mengganggu; *ejac* sialan!

Botswana *n* Botswana; **Botswanan** *n* orang Botswana; *adj* berasal dari Botswana

bottle *n* botol; *to lose your ~* tiba-tiba kehilangan keberanian; *v* membotolkan

bottom *n* bawah, pantat, alas; *adj* bawah; *at the ~ of* di bawahnya, di tempat bawah; *~less* tidak berdasar, dalam sekali

bough [bau] cabang (pohon)

bought *v, pf* [bot] → **buy**

bounce n lambungan; semangat; v melambung, memantul; *the check ~d* cek pembayaran tidak diterima oleh bank; **bouncy** adj bersifat melambung

bound v melompat, berlari-lari; *~ for* menuju; v, pf → **bind**

bounds *out of ~* di luar daerah yang diizinkan; **boundary** n (tapal) batas; **boundless** adj tanpa batas

bounty n hadiah uang; *~ hunter* pemburu buronan demi hadiah

bouquet [buké] karangan bunga, buket

bow [bau] n tundukan; haluan; v membungkukkan badan, menunduk; menyerah

bow [bo] n busur; penggesek (alat musik); **bow-legged** adj kaki O

bowels n [bauls] usus; *to move your ~* membuang air besar; *small bowel* usus kecil

bowl n [bol] mangkuk, pinggan; lemparan (bola); v melempar (bola)

bowling n boling ← **bowl**

box n kotak, dus, peti; tinju; v bertinju; meninju; *~ someone's ears* menempeleng orang; **boxer** n petinju; **boxing** n tinju; *~ Day* tanggal 26 Desember

boy n anak lelaki; *~ scout* pramuka, pandu

boycott n boikot; v memboikot

boyfriend n, m [boifrénd] pacar

boyhood n, m masa kanak-kanak ← **boy**

boyish adj seperti anak lelaki ← **boy**

brace n penahan; *~ yourself* mempersiapkan diri; *~s* kawat gigi

bracelet n [bréslét] gelang (berantai)

bracken n tumbuhan paku

bracket n tanda kurung; penyangga

brackish adj payau, masin (air)

brag v membual, menyombong

braid n kepang

brain n otak, benak; *sl* orang yang pinter; *~s* akal sehat; otak (makanan); **brainpower** n daya pikir; **brainwash** v mencuci otak; **brainwave** n ide gemilang; **brainy** adj pandai, pinter

brake n rem; *hand~* rem tangan; v mengerem

bran n sejenis sereal, kulit gandum

branch n cabang; bagian; *~ office* kantor cabang; v bercabang

brand n cap, merek; v mengecap; *~-new* sama sekali baru

brandy n brendi; *~ snap* semacam kue semprong

brass n kuningan; **brassy** adj, sl menyolok, norak

brat n anak nakal, anak manja

brave adj berani; **bravery** n keberanian

brawl n tawuran, pertikaian; v tinju, bergumul

brawn n kekuatan; *more ~ than brain* lebih banyak otot daripada otak; **brawny** adj berotot, tegap bray *v* meringkik (binatang)

brazen *adj* terang-terangan

Brazil *n* Brasil; ~ *nut* kacang Brazil; **Brazilian** *n* orang Brasil; *adj* berasal dari Brasil; ~ *wax* pencabutan bulu kemaluan dengan lilin

breach *in the* ~ kekecualian

bread *n* [bréd] roti; ~ *crumbs* remah-remah roti; *short*~ semacam biskuit

breadth *n* [brédth] lebar

break *n* [brék] istirahat, rehat, jeda; patah, putus; *v* **broke broken** memecahkan, mematahkan; ~ *and enter* memasuki dengan maksud mencuri; ~ *down* gagal; memecahkan menjadi lebih kecil; **breakdown** *n* perincian; kegagalan, kerusakan; *nervous* ~ masalah mental; **breaker** *n* ombak besar; **breakfast** [brékfast] *n*, *v* sarapan, makan pagi

breakwater *n* [brékwoter] tembok laut

breast *n* [brést] dada, payudara; *sl* susu, tetek; ~ *cancer* kanker payudara; ~ *milk* ASI (air susu ibu)

breath *n* [bréth] nafas, napas; **breathe** *v* [brith] bernafas, menarik nafas; **breather** *n* waktu istirahat

breech ~ *birth* kelahiran sungsang; **breeches** *n*, *pl* celana pendek

breed *n* ras; *v* **bred bred** mengembangbiakkan; mendidik; **breeder** *n* peternak;

breeding *n* trah, nenek moyang; sopan santun

breeze *n* angin sepoi-sepoi; *v* masuk dengan enteng

brethren *n, pl, arch* saudara-saudara ← **brother**

brevity *n* [bréviti] keringkasan; ~ *is the soul of wit* semakin singkat, semakin lucu

brew *n* minuman panas; *v* membuat minuman (terutama bir); **brewer** *n* orang atau perusahaan yang membuat bir; **brewery** *n* tempat pembuatan bir

bribe *n* uang sogok, uang suap; *v* menyogok, menyuap; **bribery** *n* suapan, sogokan; ~ *and corruption* KKN (korupsi, kolusi, nepotisme)

brick *n* batu bata; ~ *kiln* oven pembakaran keramik; **bricklayer** *n* tukang batu

bridal *adj* berkaitan dengan acara pernikahan; **bride** *n* pengantin wanita, mempelai wanita; **bridegroom** *n* pengantin pria

bridge *n* jembatan; *foot*~ jembatan kaki; *suspension* ~ jembatan gantung; *v* menjembatani, mempertemukan

bridle *n* [braidel] tali kekang, kendali; *v* mengekang, mengendalikan; membredel

brief *adj* pendek, ringkas, singkat; *v* memberi informasi secara singkat; **briefing** *n* rapat pendek, penyebaran informasi

brigade *n* [brigéd] regu, pasukan; *fire* ~ pasukan

pemadam kebakaran; **brigadier** *n* brigjen (brigadir-jenderal)

bright *n* [brait] terang, gemilang; cerdik, cemerlang, pandai; ~*ly* dengan gembira; **brighten** *v* menerangkan; menggembirakan; **brightness** *n* kecerahan

brilliant *adj* gemilang, berseri

brim *n* tepi, pinggir (topi); *to the* ~ hampir penuh

bring *v* **brought brought** [brot] membawa; ~ *about* menghasilkan, mengakibatkan; ~ *on* menyebabkan, mendatangkan; ~ *up* membesarkan; memuntahkan

brink *n* sisi, tepi, pinggir

brisk *adj* cepat; segar, dingin

Britain *n* [Briten] Britania *coll* Inggris; *Great* ~ Inggris Raya; **British** *adj* orang berkewarganegaraan Inggris/Britania; **Briton** *n* [Briton] orang yang berasal dari Inggris, Wales, Skotlandia atau Irlandia Utara

brittle *adj* rapuh

broad *adj* lebar, luas; ~*-minded* berwawasan luas

broadcast *n* siaran; *v* **broadcast broadcast** menyiarkan; **broadcaster** *n* (stasiun) penyiar

broaden *v* melebarkan, meluaskan ← **broad**

brocade *n* [brokéd] kain brokat

broccoli *n* brokoli

broil *v* memanggang

broke, broken *v, pf* ← **break** *adj* rusak

broker *n* makelar, calo, perantara

bronze *n* perunggu; ~*d* berkulit warna perunggu atau gelap

brooch *n* [broc] bros

brood *n* anak-anak; *v* merenungkan; mengeram; **brooding** *adj* banyak merenung, cepat marah

brook *n* kali, anak sungai

broom *n* sapu

Bros *abbrev* **brothers** bersaudara

broth *n* kaldu

brothel *n* tempat pelacuran, bordil

brother *n* [brather] kakak atau adik lelaki; saudara; ~*-in-law* (adik atau kakak) ipar; **brotherhood** *n* persaudaraan

brought *v, pf* → **bring**

brow *n* kening, dahi; *eye*~ alis

brown *n* (warna) coklat; ~*-skinned* berkulit sawo matang

brownies *n, pl* [brauniz] kue coklat; **Brownies** kegiatan kepanduan untuk anak perempuan

bruise *n* [bruz] memar; *v* memukul sehingga timbul memar; **bruised** *adj* memar, bengkak

Brunei *n* Brunei; **Bruneian** *n* orang Brunei; *adj* berasal dari Brunei

brunette *n, f* [brunét] wanita yang berambut coklat

brush *n* sikat, kuas (alat seni); *v* menyikat

brutal *adj* brutal, bengis, kasar; **brutality** *n* kebrutalan, kebengisan, kekasaran; **brute** *n* orang yang brutal atau kasar; **brutish** *adj* seperti orang kasar

BSc *abbrev Bachelor of Science* SSi (Sarjana Sains)

bubble *n* gelembung; *v* membual; menggelembung; **bubbly** *adj* bersoda; ceria

buck *n* rusa jantan; *sl* dolar; *to pass the ~* mengelakkan tanggung jawab

bucket *n* ember; *~ down* hujan deras

buckle *n* [bakel] gesper; *v ~ down* bekerja keras

bud *n* kuntum; *v* berkuntum, bersemi; **budding** *adj* calon, yang diharapkan

Buddha *n* Budha; **Buddhism** *n* agama Budha; **Buddhist** *n* orang Budha; *adj* berkaitan dengan agama Budha

budge *v* bergerak sedikit

budgerigar, budgie *n* sejenis burung bayan kecil

budget *n* [bajét] anggaran; *v* menganggarkan

buff *n* penggemar; *in the ~* telanjang

buffalo *n* kerbau

buffer *n* penyangga; *~ zone* daerah penyangga

buffet *n* [bafé] bufet, prasmanan

bug *n* serangga, kumbang, kutu; *v* mengganggu

bugger *n* orang yang berhubungan badan dengan binatang; *ejac* sialan; *~ off* pergi!

buggy *n* kereta atau kendaraan kecil

build *v* [bild] **built built** mendirikan, membangun, membina; **builder** *n* pemborong; **build-**

ing *n* gedung, bangunan

bulb *n* lampu pijar, bola lampu, bohlam; ubi-ubian (tanaman)

Bulgaria *n* [Balgéria] Bulgaria; **Bulgarian** *n* bahasa Bulgaria; *adj* berasal dari Bulgaria

bulge *n* benjolan, tumpukan, tonjolan; *v* membengkak, menonjol

bulk *n* tumpukan, timbunan; *~-billing* disubsidi pemerintah; *to buy in ~* belanja secara grosir; **bulky** *adj* besar, bertumpuk

bull *n* [bul] sapi jantan; *~-fighter* matador; *~-fighting* pertandingan antara manusia dan banteng; *~'s eye* sasaran

bullet *n* [bulet] peluru; *~-train* shinkansen

bulletin *n* [buletin] selebaran, berita kilat; *~ board* papan untuk menempelkan kertas-kertas

bully *n* [buli] orang yang menakut-nakuti atau mengejek orang lain; *v* menakut-nakuti orang lain

bum *n, sl* pantat, kibul; gelandangan

bump *n* pukulan, tonjokan; *v* menabrak; **bumpy** *adj* tidak rata, bergelombang

bumper *n ~ (bar)* bemper (mobil)

bun *n* sanggul, konde; roti berbentuk bola, biasanya manis; *Boston ~* semacam roti dengan kismis dan kayu manis

bunch *n* tandan, gugus, segenggam; segerombolan

bundle n [bandel] berkas, paket; v membungkus

bungle v [banggel] mengerjakan dengan serampangan, mengerjakan dengan salah

bunk n ranjang yang sempit; ~ bed ranjang yang bertingkat

bunker n [bangker] ruang bawah tanah, bungker

bunny n, sl kelinci; the Easter ~ kelinci yang membawa anak-anak telur cokelat pada saat Paskah

buoy n [boi] pelampung; ~ed by disemangati; **buoyancy** n sifat mengapung; kegembiraan; **buoyant** adj terapung; gembira

burden n beban; muatan, tanggungan; v membebani, memberatkan

bureau n [byuro] kantor, biro; meja tulis; **bureaucracy** n [byurokrasi] birokrasi; **bureaucrat** n birokrat; **bureaucratic** n birokratis

burglar n maling; cat ~ maling yang masuk dari atas bangunan; **burglary** n kemalingan; **burgle** v mencuri dari rumah atau gedung

burial n [bérial] pemakaman; ~ ground kuburan → **bury**

Burkina Faso n Burkina Faso, arch Volta Hulu; **Burkinabe** n orang Burkina Faso; adj berasal dari Burkina Faso

burn n luka terkena panas, luka bakar; v **burned burnt** menyala; membakar; **burner** n sumbu

burp n sendawa; v bersendawa

burrow n liang (binatang); v menggali liang

burst n **burst burst** letusan, ledakan; semburan; v meletus; menyembur

bury v [béri] mengubur, menanam

bus n bis; ~ shelter, ~ stop halte bis

bush n [busy] semak belukar; ~ tucker makanan dari semak belukar; **Bushman** n penduduk asli gurun Kalahari

busily adv [bizili] dengan sibuk ← **busy**

business n pekerjaan; perkara, urusan; perdagangan, perniagaan; bisnis; perusahaan; ~-like profesional; monkey ~ kenakalan; not your ~ bukan urusan anda; **businessman** n, m pengusaha, wiraswasta; **businesswoman** n, f pengusaha, wiraswasta

bustle n [basel] kesibukan, keramaian; v bergegas-gegas, buru-buru

busy adj [bizi] sibuk; **busybody** n orang yang suka ikut campur, raja gosip

but conj tetapi, tapi, namun; kecuali

butcher n [bucer] jagal, tukang potong, tukang daging, pembantai; toko daging

butt n puntung (rokok); sasaran; the ~ of many jokes sering menjadi korban lelucon

butter n mentega; ~ up merayu

butterfly n [baterflai] kupu-

kupu; gaya kupu-kupu

button *n* kancing; ~ *up*
mengancing; ~hole lubang
kancing

buy *n* [bai] pembelian; *v* **bought
bought** [bot] membeli; **buyer**
n pembeli

buzz *n* dengung, deru; *v* mendengung, menderu

by *prep* oleh, dengan; ~ *yourself*
sendiri; ~ *the* ~, ~ *the way*
ngomong-ngomong; ~ *God*
demi Allah; **bystander** *n* orang
di jalan, penonton

bye *ejac* selamat jalan, selamat
tinggal; ~~~ *child* selamat jalan,
selamat tinggal; *n* giliran tidak
bertanding; ~ *laws* peraturan
kota

BYO *abbrev* bring your own
bawa sendiri (minuman
beralkohol)

C

C *abbrev Celsius* Celsius

c *cent* sen

cab *n* bagian depan truk; ~ *driver*
supir taksi

cabbage *n* [kabej] kol, engkol,
kubis

cabbie, cabby *n, sl* supir taksi

cabin *n* bagian depan truk; ~
crew awak kabin; ~ *luggage*
bagasi kabin; *log* ~ pondok
(dibuat dari balok kayu)

cabinet *n* kabinet; lemari

cable *n* [kébel] kabel; *arch* kawat,
telegram; ~ *TV* TV kabel; *v,
arch* mengirim telegram

cacao *n* kakao, buah coklat

cackle *v* [kakel] berkekek,
berkotek *(of hens)*

cactus *n* **cacti** kaktus

cadet *n* kadet; semacam pramuka

caddy *n* kedi

cadre *n* [kader] kader

Caesarian → **Cesarian**

café, cafe *n* kafe, warung kopi

cage *n* sangkar, kurungan; *v*
mengurung

cajole *v* [kejol] membujuk

cake *n* kue; ~ *mix* adonan kue; *a
~ of soap* (sepotong) sabun

calamity *n* [kalamiti] bencana,
malapetaka; **calamitous** *adj*
sangat buruk

calcium *n* kalsium, zat kapur

calculate *v* menghitung-hitung,
memperhitungkan, menaksir;
calculation *n* perhitungan,
kalkulasi; **calculator** *n*
kalkulator

calendar *n* kalender, almanak;
penanggalan; *Islamic* ~ tahun
hijriah

calf *n* [kaf] betis

calf *n* [kaf] anak sapi; *v* **calved
calved** beranak (sapi)

caliber *n* [kaliber] kaliber, mutu

calico *n* [kaliko] belacu, kain
mori; ~ *cat* kucing yang
bulunya berwarna putih, hitam
dan coklat

call *n* [kol] panggilan, seruan;
percakapan telepon; kunjungan;
v memanggil; menelepon; ~ *at*

mampir di; ~ *on* berkunjung ke, mengunjungi; ~ *out* berteriak; ~ *box* telepon umum; ~ *center* pusat pelayanan melalui telepon; ~*girl* wanita panggilan, pelacur; **caller** *n* penelepon; tamu

calligrapher *n* [kaligrafer] orang yang bisa membuat tulisan tangan indah; **calligraphy** *n* tulisan tangan yang indah; *Arabic* ~ kaligrafi

callous *n* [kales] kapal (di kaki); *adj* tidak berperasaan

calm *n* [kam] ketenangan, keteduhan; *v* menenangkan, menenteramkan; *adj* tenang, teduh

calorie *n* kalori

Cambodia *n* Kamboja; **Cambodian** *n* orang Kamboja; *adj* berasal dari Kamboja

came *v, pf →* **come**

camel *n* [kamel] unta; *adj* warna coklat atau abu-abu muda

camera *n* kamera

Cameroon *n* Kamerun; *the* ~*s arch* Kamerun; **Cameroonian** *n* orang Kamerun; *adj* berasal dari Kamerun

camouflage *n* [kamuflasy] kamuflase, penyamaran; *in* ~ memakai baju loreng; *v* menyamar

camp *n* perkemahan, kamp; *v* berkemah; *adj, sl* (pria yang) tampak seperti wanita

camphor *n* [kamfer] kamper, kapur barus

campus *n* lokasi universitas, kampus

can *n* kaleng; *v* mengalengkan; ~ *it! sl* hentikan!

can *aux, v* **could/was able, been able** dapat, bisa

Canada *n* Kanada; **Canadian** *n* [Kanédian] orang Kanada; *adj* berasal dari Kanada

canal *n* [kanal] terusan; kali; *the Suez* ~ Terusan Suez

canary *n* [kanéri] burung kenari; ~*-colored* berwarna kuning muda

cancel *v* membatalkan, mencoret, menghapus; **cancellation** *n* pembatalan

cancer *n* kanker; **cancerous** *adj* ganas

candid *adj* terus terang, terbuka ← **candor**

candidacy *n* pencalonan; **candidate** *n* calon, kandidat

candle *n* lilin; **candlestick** *n* tempat lilin

candor *n* keterbukaan

candy *n* permen, kembang gula

cane ~ *toad* katak ladang tebu; *sugar* ~ tebu

cane *n* tongkat

canine *n* anjing; *adj* berhubungan dengan anjing; ~ *tooth* gigi taring

cannibal *n* [kanibol] kanibal, pemakan sejenis; **cannibalism** *n* kebiasaan makan sesama manusia; **cannibalistic** *adj* bersifat makan sejenis

cannon *n* meriam, kanon; ~ *into* menabrak, menghantam

canoe *n* [kanu] kano

canopy *n* [kanopi] lapisan atas

cantaloupe *n* [kantalop] melon, blewah

canteen *n* kantin

canvas *n* kanvas; kain terpal

canvass *v* mencari dukungan untuk calon tertentu; **canvasser** *n* orang yang mencari dukungan

canyon *n* ngarai

cap *n* topi pet; tutup; ~ *off* mengakhiri

capability *n* kesanggupan, kemampuan; **capable** *adj* bisa, mampu, dapat

capacity *n* daya tampung, kapasitas

cape *n* tanjung; *the* ~ *of Good Hope* Tanjung Harapan

capital *n* modal; huruf besar; ~ *(city)* ibukota; ~ *punishment* hukuman mati; **capitalist** *n* kapitalis; **capitalism** *n* kapitalisme

capitol *n* ibukota

capitulate *v* menyerah (kalah); **capitulation** *n* penyerahan

capsize *v* terbalik (kapal atau perahu)

capsule *n* kapsul

captain *n* kapten, nahkoda; kapitan

caption *n* [kapsyen] tulisan di bawah gambar

captive *n* [kaptiv] tawanan; **captivity** *n* penawanan, tahanan; *animals in* ~ satwa di kebun binatang; **capture** *n* penangkapan; *v* menangkap

car *n* mobil; gerbong; ~-*jacking* perampasan mobil; ~ *park* tem-

pat parkir; ~ *wash* cuci mobil; *dining* ~ (gerbong) restorasi

caramel *n* gula bakar, permen rasa karamel; *adj* rasa karamel

carat *n* karat

caravan *n* kafilah; karavan

carbohydrate *n* [karbohaidrét] karbohidrat

carbolic ~ *acid* karbol

carbon *n* karbon, zat arang; ~ *dioxide* karbon dioksida; **carbonated** ~ *drink* minuman bersoda

carburettor *n* karburator

carcass *n* bangkai (binatang)

card *n* kartu; kardus; ~ *shark* pemain kartu jagoan; *credit* ~ kartu kredit; *playing* ~s kartu remi; *to play* ~s main kartu

cardboard *n* karton, kertas tebal

cardinal *n* kardinal; *adj* utama, pokok

care *n* pemeliharaan, perawatan; ~ *of (c/-)* dengan alamat (d/a); *v* peduli, memedulikan; ~ *for* merawat; suka pada; *child* ~ penitipan anak-anak; *to take* ~ berhati-hati, jaga diri; *to take* ~ *of* memelihara, mengurus

career *n* karir; ~ *woman* wanita karir

carefree *adj* tanpa beban, riang; **careful** *adj* hati-hati; **careless** *adj* teledor, lalai ← **care**

carer *n* perawat, penjaga anak ← **care**

caress *n* [kerés] belaian; *v* membelai

caretaker *n* penjaga ← **care**

cargo *n* muatan kapal; ~ *boat* kapal barang

Caribbean *adj* berasal dari kawasan Laut Karibia; the ~ (Sea) Laut Karibia

caricature *n* karikatur

carnation *n* anyelir

carnival *n* pesta, pasar malam

carnivore *n* pemakan daging; **carnivorous** *adj* yang makan daging

carol *n* lagu Natal; *v* bernyanyi, berkicau

carp *n* ikan gurame; *Japanese ~* ikan koi

carpenter *n* tukang kayu; **carpentry** *n* pekerjaan kayu

carpet *n* permadani, karpet

carport *n* garasi, atap untuk perlindungan mobil

carriage *n* [karij] kereta; gerbong ← **carry**

carrier *n* [karier] pembawa (penyakit dsb); ~ *bag* plastik, keresek; ~ *pigeon* merpati pos; *aircraft ~* kapal induk ← **carry**

carrot *n* wortel; insentif

carry *v* mengangkut, membawa; ~ *on* meneruskan; ~ *out* menjalankan, melakukan, melaksanakan

cart *n* kereta, pedati, gerobak; *horse and ~* kereta kuda

cartographer *n* orang yang membuat peta; **cartography** *n* pembuatan peta, pemetaan, kartografi

cartoon *n* (film) kartun; komik

cartridge *n* [kartrij] pelor, peluru; isi pulpen

carve *v* mengukir; memotong daging dari tulang

cascade *n* air terjun

case *n* peti, koper; kasus, perkara, hal, perihal; *in ~* jika, kalau

cash *n* uang kontan, uang tunai; ~ *crop* hasil pertanian yang akan dijual; ~ *and carry* toko yang membeli barang bekas

cashew *n* kacang mede

cashier *n* [kasyir] kasir, kassa ← **cash**

casino *n* tempat berjudi, kasino

casserole *n* [kaserol] masakan yang berkuah, biasanya mengandung daging; ~ *dish* tempat masakan yang terbuat dari kaca

cassette *n* kaset; ~ *player* radio kaset, tape

cassowary *n* burung kasuari

cast *n* lemparan; tuangan; pemain-pemain sandiwara; *v* **cast cast** melempar, melontar; menuangkan; memilih untuk peran; ~ *iron* besi tuang; ~ *off* menyelesaikan rajutan; ~ *on* memulai rajutan

castaway *n* orang yang telantar di pulau

caste *n* [kast] kasta

castle *n* [kasel] puri, benteng, istana; ~s *in the air* mimpi belaka

castor ~ *oil* minyak jarak, kastroli

casual *adj* [kasyuel] santai; ~ *labor* pekerja yang tidak terikat kontrak

casualty *n* [kasyuelti] korban kecelakaan; Unit Gawat Darurat (UGD)

cat *n* kucing; ~ *nap* tidur sebentar; *alley* ~ kucing kampung

catalog *n* katalog, daftar; *v* mendokumentasi

catastrophe *n* [katastrofi] bencana, malapetaka; **catastrophic** *adj* yang berkait dengan bencana

catch *n* angkapan, hasil; jepitan, gesper; *v* **caught caught** [kot] menangkap; terkena, terjangkit (penyakit); ~ *22 situation* buah simalakama; ~ *cold* masuk angin; ~ *up* mengejar; mengobrol setelah lama tidak bertemu; **catchphrase** *n* semboyan; **catchy** *adj* mudah diingat

category *n* kategori, golongan

cater *v* melayani; menyediakan makanan; **caterer** *n* perusahaan jasa boga; **catering** *n* jasa boga

caterpillar *n* [katerpilar] ulat

cathedral *n* [kathidral] katedral

Catholic *n* orang Katolik; *adj* Catholic; *Roman* ~ Katolik

cattle *n* sapi, ternak

Caucasian *n* [Kokésyan] orang kulit putih; *adj* berkulit putih; **Caucasus** *n* [kokesus] *the* ~ Kaukasus

caught *v, pf* ← **catch**

cauldron *n* ketel, kawah

cauliflower *n* [koliflauer] kembang kol

cause *n* [coz] sebab; *v* menyebabkan, mengakibatkan

caution *n* sikap hati-hati, kewaspadaan; *v* mengingatkan; **cautious** *adj* hati-hati

cavalry *n* pasukan kuda

cave *n* gua; **cavern** *n* [kavern] gua (besar); **cavernous** *adj* seperti gua besar

caviar *n* telur terubuk (ikan)

cavity *n* rongga, lubang (gigi)

cayman *n* buaya

cc *cubic centimeter* cc (sentimeter kubik)

CD *abbrev compact disk* CD

CD *abbrev Corps Diplomatique* kedutaan

cease *v* [siis] menghentikan; ~-*fire* gencatan senjata

cedar *n* sejenis pohon

cede *v* menyerahkan

ceiling *n* [siling] langit-langit, plafon; *glass* ~ tingkat paling atas yang tercapai oleh seorang wanita karir karena diskriminasi

celebrate *v* [sélebrét] merayakan; **celebrated** *adj* ternama, mashur, termasyhur; **celebration** *n* perayaan

celebrity *n* selebriti

celery *n* seledri

celibacy *n* [sélibesi] keadaan selibat, hidup melajang; **celibate** *adj* selibat, tidak melakukan hubungan seks

cell *n* sel; bilik penjara; ~ *phone* telepon seluler (ponsel), telepon genggam

cellar *n* besmen, ruang bawah tanah

cellophane *n* [sélofén] kertas kaca

cement *n* semen, beton; perekat; *v* menyemen; merekat

cemetery *n* [sémeteri] kuburan, tempat peristirahatan akhir (TPA)

censor *n* sensor; *v* mensensor; **censorship** *n* pensensoran

census *n* sensus; *~-taker* petugas pelaksana sensus

centenary, centennial *n* peringatan seratus tahun; **centenarian** *n* orang yang berusia seratus tahun

center *n* pusat; *~ of attention* pusat perhatian; *~ of gravity* titik berat; *shopping ~* pusat perbelanjaan, mal; **central** *adj* pusat, tengah, pokok; *~ African Republic* Afrika Tengah; *~ Jakarta* Jakarta Pusat (Jakpus); *~ Java* Jawa Tengah (Jateng); **centralize** *v* memusatkan

centimeter *n* senti, sentimeter

centipede *n* [sentipid] kaki seribu, lipan

century *n* abad; seratus poin (dalam pertandingan kriket)

cereal *n* [sirial] sereal

ceremonial *adj* berkaitan dengan upacara, seremonial; **ceremony** *n* upacara

certain *adj* [serten] tentu, pasti, yakin; **certainly** *adj* tentu saja; **certainty** *n* kepastian

certificate *n* sertifikat, ijazah, surat; **certified** *adj* berijazah; **certify** *v* mengesahkan

cervical *adj* berhubungan dengan leher atau leher rahim; **cervix** *n* leher rahim

Cesarian, Caesarian *n* [Sisérian] disesar; *to have a ~, by ~ section* disesar

cessation *n* pemberhentian

Ceylon *n, arch* Sri Langka, Sailan; **Ceylonese** *n* orang Sri Langka; *adj* berasal dari Sri Langka

cf *compare* dibandingkan

chain *n* rantai; kalung; serangkaian; *~ letter* surat berantai; *~-smoke* merokok terus-menerus; *~ of events* rangkaian peristiwa; *in ~s* dibelenggu; *v* merantai

chair *n* [cér] kursi; ketua; **chairman** *n, m* **chairperson** *n* ketua

chalet *n* [syalé] vila di gunung

chalk *n* [cok] kapur

challenge *n* tantangan; *v* menantang; **challenging** *adj* menantang

chamber *n* [cémber] kamar; *~ of commerce* kamar dagang

chameleon *n* [kamilion] bunglon

champagne *n* [syampéin] sampanye; *adj* warna kuning muda

champion *n* juara; **championship** *n* kejuaraan

chance *n* kesempatan, peluang; *by ~* secara kebetulan; *to take a ~* mengambil risiko

chancellor *n* kanselir; *vice-~* pembantu rektor

change *n* [cénj] perubahan; uang kembali; *v* ganti; menukar, mengubah; *~ trains at Cardiff* turun di Cardiff; *~ your clothes* ganti pakaian; *~ your mind* berubah pikiran; **changeable** *adj* [cénjabel] dapat berubah, tidak tetap

channel *n* saluran, selat; *v* menyalurkan

chant *n* lagu yang dinyanyikan atau diucapkan; *v* bernyanyi;

menyanyikan (berulang-ulang)

chaos n [kéos] kekacauan; **chaotic** adj kacau balau

chap n, sl, m orang, lelaki

chapel n [capel] kapel, gereja kecil; **chaplain** n pastor atau pendeta di lingkungan tertentu

chaperone n [syaperon] pendamping, pengantar

chapter n bab, pasal

character n [karakter] sifat; peran; huruf; **characteristic** n ciri; adj khas; **characterize** v menjiwai, memerankan; menggambarkan

charade n [syerad] adegan, sandiwara

charcoal n arang

charge n [carj] muatan; ongkos, harga; serangan, serbuan; tuduhan; in ~ berkuasa, berwenang; free of ~, no ~ gratis, cuma-cuma; v menyerang; meminta bayaran, menagih; (me)ngecas

charisma n karisma, pesona; **charismatic** adj memesona

charitable adj amal, murah hati; **charity** n [cariti] amal

charm n pesona; sihir; gantungan gelang; v memesonakan, menarik hati; menyihir; **charming** adj jelita, juwita, memesonakan

chart n grafik; peta; v memetakan

charter n piagam; v mencarter; **chartered** adj carteran

chase n pengejaran; v mengejar

chasm n [kazem] ngarai, jurang

chaste adj [céist] suci; **chastity** n [castiti] kesucian; ~ belt alat anti-perkosaan

chat n percakapan; v mengobrol, bercakap-cakap; chit-~ obrolan ringan; **chatter** n celotehan, obrolan; v berceloteh, mengobrol; **chatterbox** n orang yang sering cerocos; **chatting** n kegiatan berkomunikasi lewat internet

chauffeur n [syofer] supir, sopir

cheap adj murah; on the ~ dengan murah; **cheapen** v menurunkan harga, merendahkan; **cheapskate** n orang pelit

cheat n penipu; v menipu; curang; **cheating** n curang, kecurangan

check n motif kotak-kotak; ~ shirt kemeja bermotif kotak-kotak

check, cheque n cek

check n pemeriksaan, uji, cek; v memeriksa, menguji, mengecek; ~ in melapor (di hotel), cek in; ~ out membayar lalu meninggalkan hotel

checkmate ejac skakmat

checkout n kasir, kassa (terutama di swalayan); ~ chick (sl) gadis kasir

cheek n pipi; keberanian; what a ~ enak saja; **cheeky** adj berani, nakal

cheer n kegembiraan; sorak; v memberi semangat, bersorak; mendukung; **cheerful** adj gembira, senang hati; **cheerleader** n pemandu sorak

cheese n keju

chef *n* [syéf] juru masak

chemical *n* [kémikel] bahan kimia; *adj* kimiawi; ~ *reaction* reaksi kimiawi; **chemist** *n* ahli kimia; apoteker; **chemistry** *n* ilmu kimia; *the ~ between the two of them was great* interaksi di antara mereka berdua sangat baik

cheque → **check**

cherish *v* menyayangi, menghargai; ~*ed* tersayang

cherry *n* buah ceri

chess *n* catur; ~ *piece* buah catur; **chessboard** *n* papan catur

chest *n* dada; peti, kopor; *a ~ of drawers* (susunan) laci

chew *v* mengunyah; ~*ing gum* permen karet

chic *adj* [syik] anggun, bergaya, modis

chicken *n* (rasa) ayam; *adj, sl* takut, penakut; ~ *pox* cacar air

chief *n* **chiefs** kepala (suku), pemimpin; *commander in ~* panglima tertinggi; *editor-in-~* pemimpin redaksi; *adj* utama, pokok; **chiefly** *adv* terutama, pertama-tama

child *n* [caild] **children** [cildren] anak, putra; **childhood** *n* [caildhud] masa kanak-kanak, masa kecil; **childish** *adj* kekanak-kanakan; **childless** *adj* tanpa anak

Chile *n* [Cili] Cile; **Chilean** *n* orang Cile; *adj* berasal dari Cile

chili → **chilli**

chill *n* udara dingin; *to have a ~* masuk angin

chilli *n* cabe; ~ *sauce* (saus) sambal

chilly *adj* sejuk, dingin ← **chill**

chimney *n* **chimneys** cerobong asap

chimpanzee *n* simpanse

chin *n* dagu; **chinwag** *n, sl* obrolan

China *n* [Caina] (negeri) Cina, Tiongkok; **china** *n, adj* porselen; **Chinatown** *n* Pecinan; **Chinese** *n* orang Cina, orang Tionghoa; *adj* Cina, Tionghoa

chink *n* celah

chip *n* keping; keripik; *hot ~s* kentang goreng; *v* pecah, mengelupas

chipmunk *n* tupai atau bajing tanah dengan gigi besar

chiropractor *n* [kairopraktor] ahli pengobat tulang punggung

chisel *n* [cizel] pahat; *v* memaha

chivalrous *adj* [syivelres] bersifat kesatria; **chivalry** *n* kekesatriaan

chives *n, pl* lokio

chlorine *n* klorin; **chlorinated** *adj* berklorin

chloroform *n* kloroform, obat bius

chock ~-*a-block*, ~-*full* penuh sesak

chocolate *n, adj* coklat; ~*s* kotak berisi coklat (yang masing-masing dibungkus)

choice *n* pilihan, terpilih ← **choose**

choir *n* [kuaier] koor

choke *v* mencekik

cholera *n* (penyakit) kolera

cholesterol *n* kolesterol; *high ~* kolesterol tinggi

choose *v* **chose chosen** memilih; **choosy** *adj* suka memilih-milih, rewel

chop *n* potong; steik yang bertulang; *v* memotong, mencincang; **chopper** *n* parang; helikopter; **choppy** *adj* berombak (laut)

chopsticks *n, pl* sumpit

choral *adj* [koral] berhubungan dengan koor atau bernyanyi ← **choir**

chore *n* tugas (rumah)

choreographer *n* pencipta tarian, koreografer; **choreography** *n* koreografi

chose, chosen *v, pf* ← **choose**

Christ *n* [Kraist] (Yesus) Kristus; **christen** *v* [krisen] mempermandikan, membaptis; memberi nama; **christening** *n* permandian; **Christian** *n* orang Kristen atau Katolik; *adj* Kristiani, Nasrani, Masehi; **Christmas** *n* (hari) Natal; *~ card* kartu Natal; *~ Eve* malam Natal

chrome *n, adj* krom; **chromium** *n* krom

chronic *adj* kronis, menahun; **chronicle** *n* sejarah

chronological *adj* menurut tanggal; **chronology** *n* kronologi, sejarah

chubby *adj* gemuk, berlebihan berat badan

chuck *v, sl* membuang

chum *n, sl* kawan, sobat; **chummy** *adj* bersahabat

chunk *n* gumpal, bongkah; **chunky** *adj* berisi, berat

church *n* gereja; *to go to ~* pergi ke gereja; **churchyard** *n* kuburan dekat gereja

CIA *abbrev Central Intelligence Agency* Badan Intelijen Pusat (Amerika Serikat)

cicada *n* sejenis jangkrik

CID *abbrev Criminal Investigation Department* Bagian Penyelidikan Kriminal

cider *n* sari buah (terutama apel)

cigar *n* [sigar] cerutu; *~ case* tempat cerutu; **cigarette** *n* [sigarét] rokok; *clove ~* (rokok) kretek

cinder *n* kerak, sisa bara api

cinema *n* [sinema] (gedung) bioskop

cinnamon *n* kayu manis

circle *n* [serkel] lingkaran, bulatan; kawasan, lingkungan; *v* melingkari; mengedari

circuit *n* [serket] sirkuit; peredaran; **circuitous** *adj* [serkyuitus] memutar

circular *n* [serkyuler] surat edaran; *adj* bulat, bundar; **circulate** *v* beredar; mengedarkan; **circulation** *n* peredaran, sirkulasi

circumcise *v* menyunat; *~d* disunat; **circumcision** *n* [sirkumsisyen] sunatan

circumstances *n, pl* keadaan

circus *n* sirkus

citadel *n* [sitadél] benteng

citation *n* [saitésyen] kutipan; **cite** *v* mengutip, menyebutkan

citizen *n* [sitizen] warganegara; **citizenship** *n* kewarganegaraan

city *n* [siti] kota; ~ *hall* balaikota; *capital* ~ ibukota

civil *adj* sipil; sopan; ~ *law* hukum perdata; *American* ~ *War* Perang Sipil Amerika; **civilian** *n* orang sipil; **civility** *n* kesopanan; **civilization** *n* [sivilaizésyen] peradaban; **civilized** *adj* beradab

Ck *creek* K. (kali)

claim *n* tuntutan; tagihan; pengakuan; *v* menuntut; menagih; mengaku; meminta

clam *n* kerang; **clammy** *adj* lembab, basah

clamber *v* memanjat, naik

clamor *n* keriuhan, keramaian, kegaduhan; **clamorous** *adj* riuh, ramai, gaduh

clan *n* suku bangsa, kaum, marga; **clannish** *adj* hanya bergaul dengan kaum sendiri

clandestine *adj* [klandéstin] gelap, diam-diam, sembunyi-sembunyi, rahasia

clap *n* tepuk; *a* ~ *of thunder* sambaran petir; *v* bertepuk tangan; **clapper** *n* anak lonceng

clarify *v* [klarifai] menjelaskan, menerangkan; **clarification** *n* [klarifikésyen] penjelasan, penerangan ← **clear**

clarinet *n* klarinet

clarity *n* kejernihan ← **clear**

clash *n* bentrokan; *v* bentrok; *those colors* ~ dua warna itu ramai

clasp *n* jepitan, gesper; pelukan; *v* menjepit, memegang

class *n* kelas; pelajaran; golongan; *first* ~ terbaik; *science* ~ kelas IPA; **classify** *v* menggolongkan; **classmate** *n* teman sekelas; **classroom** *n* ruang kelas

class *n* mutu, kualitas (tinggi); **classic** *n* sesuatu yang terkenal; *adj* klasik; **classical** ~ *music* musik klasik; **classy** *adj* bermutu

clatter *n* gemertak; *v* bergerak dengan bunyi ramai

clause *n* ayat, klausa; syarat; anak kalimat

claw *n* cakar, jepit; *v* mencakar

clay *n* tanah liat

clean *adj* bersih; *v* membersihkan; *to come* ~ mengaku; **cleaning** *n* pembersihan; **cleanliness** *n* [klénlines] kebersihan; **cleanse** *v* membersihkan, mencuci; **cleanser** *n* pembersih

clear *adj* terang, jernih, jelas, nyaring, nyata; ~ *skies* langit biru, cuaca cerah; *to keep* ~ menghindari, mengelakkan; *in the* ~ bebas; *v* membereskan; **clearance** *n* izin; ~ *sale* cuci gudang; **clearing** *n* tanah terbuka di tengah hutan; *fin* kliring

cleave *v* clove/cleaved cleft/cloven membelah; **cleavage** *n* belahan dada

clench *v* menggenggam; ~*ed fist* kepalan tangan

clergy *n* [klerji] kaum pastor atau pendeta; **clergyman** *n* pendeta, pastor

clerk *n* [klark] juru tulis

clever *adj* [klever] pandai, cerdas, pintar; **cleverness** *n* kepandaian, kepintaran

cliché *n* klise

client *n* [klaient] nasabah, pelanggan, tamu, klien; **clien-tele** *n*, *pl* [klaientél] para nasabah, pelanggan, klien

cliff *n* tebing; ~*hanger* sangat menegangkan; ~*-top* di atas tebing

climate *n* [klaimet] iklim

climax *n* [klaimaks] puncak, klimaks, orgasme

climb *n* [klaim] perjalanan naik; *v* memanjat; menaiki; ~*ing plant* tanaman merambat; **climber** *n* pemanjat

cling *v* **clung clung** melekat; ~ *wrap* plastik pembungkus makanan

clinic *n* klinik, pusat kesehatan masyarakat (puskesmas)

clink *v* berbunyi (gelas)

clip *n* jepitan; *v* menjepit, menggunting, memotong; **clippers** *n* gunting; **clipping** *newspaper* ~ guntingan koran, kliping

clique *n* [klik] geng, kelompok

clitoris *n* kelentit, klitoris

cloak *n* mantel; **cloakroom** *n* tempat gantung jas dan mantel

clock *n* jam; *like* ~*work* seperti mesin jam, sangat teratur;

alarm ~ weker; *three o'*~ jam tiga; *v* mencatat waktu

clod *n* gumpal, bungkah

clog *n* kelom, bakiak

close *v* [kloz] menutup; ~*d* tutup

close *adj* [klos] dekat, akrab; ~*-fisted* pelit, kikir; ~ *quarters* dari dekat; ~ *shave* nyaris celaka; ~ *up* dari dekat; gambar yang diperbesar

closet *n* [klozet] lemari baju; *to come out of the* ~ mengaku sebagai orang homo

closure *n* [klosyer] penutupan ← **close**

clot *n* gumpal; *blood* ~ gumpalan darah beku; *v* bergumpal

cloth *n* kain, bahan; *table*~ taplak meja; **clothe** *v* memberi baju; **clothes** *n* pakaian, baju; ~ *dryer* mesin pengering baju; ~ *horse* jemuran pakaian

cloud *n* awan; *v* memperkeruh; ~ *over* menjadi berawan, tertutup awan; **cloudy** *adj* berawan

clove *n* cengkeh; ~ *cigarette* rokok kretek

clove, cloven *v*, *pf* → **cleave**

clover *n* semanggi; ~*-leaf inter-change* simpangan susun semanggi

clown *n* badut, pelawak; *v* melucu

club *n* perhimpunan, klub, kelab; ~ *sandwich* roti dengan isi dag-ing dan selada; *night*~ kelab malam, diskotek; *v* ~ *together* bersatu, bekerja sama (untuk membeli sesuatu); **clubbing** *n* pergi ke diskotek clue *n* tanda, petunjuk

clumsy *adj* canggung, kikuk; **clumsiness** *n* kecanggungan

clung *v, pf* → **cling**

cluster *n* gugus, tandan; *v* berkerumun

clutch *n* genggam; kopling; ~ *bag* tas tangan tanpa pegangan; *v* menggenggam

cm *centimeter* cm (sentimeter)

coach *n* pelatih; bis pariwisata; kereta kencana; *v* melatih

coagulate *v* [koagulét] bergumpal, membeku (darah)

coal *n* batu bara; ~ *mine* tambang batu bara; ~ *miner* pekerja tambang batu bara

coalition *n* koalisi

coarse *adj* [kors] kasar

coast *n* pantai, pesisir; **coastal** *adj* berkaitan dengan pantai

coast *v* meluncur, jalan bebas (karena gaya berat)

coaster *n* alas gelas

coastline *n* garis pantai ← **coast**

coat *n* mantel, jas; lapisan; kulit atau bulu binatang; ~ *of paint* lapisan cat; ~ *of arms* lambang (kerajaan, kenegaraan dsb); *v* melapisi

coax *v* membujuk

cobble ~*stone* batu trotoar; **cobbler** *n* tukang reparasi sepatu; toko reparasi sepatu

cobra *n* kobra, ular sendok

cobweb *n* sarang laba-laba

cocaine *n* [kokéin] kokain

cock *n* ayam jantan; ~ *fighting* sabung ayam; **cocky** *adj* arogan

cockatoo *n* [kokatu] burung kakatua

cockpit *n* kokpit

cockroach *n* kecoa

cocktail *n* sejenis minuman keras, koktil

cocoa *n* [koko] (biji) coklat

coconut *n* (buah) kelapa; ~ *palm* pohon kelapa, pohon nyiur; *desiccated* ~ kelapa parut kering

cocoon *n* [kekun] kepompong

COD *abbrev cash on delivery* membayar saat diantarkan

code *n* sandi, kode; undang-undang, peraturan; *the highway* ~ undang-undang lalu lintas

co-educational ~ *school* sekolah untuk murid laki-laki dan perempuan

coerce *v* [koérs] memaksa; **coercion** *n* [koérsyen] paksaan, pemaksaan

coffee *n* kopi; *white* ~, *milk* ~ kopi susu

coffin *n* peti mati

cog *n* roda gigi

coherence *n* pertalian, perhubungan; **coherent** *adj* jelas; masuk akal

cohesion *n* kepaduan; **cohesive** *adj* bersatu, berpadu

coil *n* gulungan, gulung; *v* bergelung

coin *n* uang logam, koin

coincide *v* [koinsaid] bertepatan; **coincidence** *n* [koinsidens] kebetulan

coke → **cocaine**

cold *n* masuk angin, pilek; rasa

dingin; *to feel the* ~ sering kedinginan; *adj* dingin; ~-*box* kotak pendingin; ~ *comfort* tidak menghibur; *to give the* ~ *shoulder* menghindari

collaborate *v* bekerja sama; **collaboration** *n* kerjasama; **collaborator** *n* orang yang bekerja sama

collapse *n* keruntuhan, kerobohan; *v* runtuh, ambruk, roboh; **collapsible** *adj* dapat dibongkar atau dilipat

collar *n* kerah, leher baju; **collarbone** *n* tulang selangka

collateral *n* jaminan; *adj* tambahan; ~ *damage* kerusakan sampingan

colleague *n* [kolig] rekan, kolega, teman kantor

collect *v* mengumpulkan, memungut; **collection** *n* kumpulan, koleksi; **collective** *n* koperasi, usaha kolektif; *adj* bersama, kolektif; **collector** *n* kolektor

college *n* [kolej] sekolah, kolese; perguruan tinggi, universitas; ~ *student* mahasiswa; *to go to* ~ (sudah) kuliah

collide *v* bertabrakan, menabrak; **collision** *n* [kolisyen] tabrakan; ~ *course* arah yang akan mengakibatkan tabrakan

colloquial *adj* percakapan, sehari-hari; **colloquialism** *n* ucapan sehari-hari

Colombia *n* Kolombia; **Colombian** *n* orang Kolombia; *adj* berasal dari Kolombia

colon *n* titik dua; usus besar; **colonoscopy** *n* pemeriksaan usus besar

colonel *n* [kernel] kolonel; *lieutenant-*~ letkol (letnan kolonel)

colonial *adj* kolonial, penjajah; ~ *house* rumah Belanda; **colonization** *n* penjajahan; **colonize** *v* menjajah, menduduki; **colonist** *n* penduduk baru; **colony** *n* jajahan

color *n* [kaler] warna; *v* mewarnai; ~*blind* buta warna; **colorful** *adj* berwarna-warni

colossal *adj* sangat besar, raksasa

colt *n* kuda jantan yang muda

column *n* tiang; barisan; kolom; *fifth* ~ pihak rahasia; **columnist** *n* pengasuh rubrik

coma *n* koma, mati suri; **comatose** *adj* mati suri, di dalam koma

comb *n* [koom] sisir; *v* menyisir

combat *n* peperangan, pertempuran; *v* memerangi

combination *n* gabungan, kombinasi; ~ *lock* kunci kombinasi; **combine** *v* menggabungkan, mengombinasikan, memadukan

come *v* [kam] **came come** datang, tiba, sampai; ~ *clean* mengaku; ~ *a cropper* kapok; ~ *what may* bagaimanapun; ~ *forward* tampil, maju; ~ *from* berasal dari, datang dari; ~ *in* masuk; ~ *out* keluar; ~ *through* lewat, menempuh; **comeback** *n* kembali

comedian *n* [komidien]

pelawak, komik; **comedy** n lawak, komedi

comet n bintang berekor

comfort n [kamfert] kenyaman; hikmah, hiburan; v menghibur; **comfortable, comfy** adj nyaman

comic n pelawak; adj lucu; **comical** adj lucu, kocak → **comedy**

coming n [kaming] kedatangan; the Second ~ kembalinya Almasih; adj mendatang ← **come**

comma n koma

command n perintah; komando; v memimpin; **commandant, commander** n komandan; **commando** n komando, prajurit penyerang

commemorate v memperingati, merayakan; **commemoration** n peringatan, perayaan; **commemorative** adj dalam rangka memperingati

commence v mulai, memulai; **commencement** n awal, permulaan

commend v memuji, merekomendasikan; **commendable** adj terpuji; **commendation** n penghargaan

comment n komentar; no ~ tidak ada keterangan; v berkomentar, memberi komentar; mengomentari; **commentary** n tafsir; **commentator** n komentator

commerce n perdagangan, perniagaan; chamber of ~ kamar dagang (kadin); **commercial** n

[komérsyal] iklan; adj dagang, perniagaan; komersial

commission n pesan; komisi; v memesan, memerintahkan; **commissioner** n komisaris

commit v berjanji; melakukan, menjalankan; **commitment** n janji, tanggung jawab, ikatan

committee n [komiti] panitia, komite

commodity n barang dagangan, komoditi; basic ~ bahan pokok

common adj biasa, umum; bersama; rendah; to have something in ~ memiliki persamaan; **commoner** n orang kebanyakan, rakyat biasa; **commonly** adv biasanya; **Commonwealth** n Persemakmuran

commotion n kegemparan, kegaduhan, huru-hara

commune n komunitas yang hidup bersama

communicate v berkomunikasi; memberitahu, menghubungi; **communication** n komunikasi, perhubungan

communion n perjamuan

communiqué n komunike ← **communicate**

communism n komunisme; **communist** n orang komunis; adj komunis; Indonesian ~ Party Partai Komunis Indonesia (PKI)

community n masyarakat, umat, komunitas ← **commune**

commute v pergi berulang alik, wira-wiri; **commuter** n pelaju

Comoros the ~ Kepulauan

Komoro, Kepulauan Comoros

compact *n* tempat bedak; *v* memadatkan; *adj* kompak, padat

companion *n* kawan, teman; *longtime* ~ pasangan hidup; **company** *n* [kam peni] kawan-kawan; perusahaan, maskapai (penerbangan)

comparative *adj* perbandingan, komparatif; **compare** *v* membandingkan; **comparison** *n* perbandingan

compartment *n* ruang (kereta)

compass *n* [kampas] pedoman, kompas; **compasses** *a pair of* ~ jangka

compassion *n* rasa (belas) kasih, pengertian; **compassionate** *adj* mengasihani, berbelas kasih

compatriot *n* orang dari negeri yang sama

compel *v* memaksa; **compelling** *adj* sangat menarik

compensate *v* mengganti (rugi); **compensation** *n* ganti rugi, kompensasi

compete *v* [kompit] bersaing, bertanding

competence *n* kemampuan, kompetensi; *~-based curriculum* kurikulum berbasis kompetensi; **competent** *adj* mampu, kompeten

competition *n* persaingan; pertandingan; **competitive** *adj* (suka) bersaing; **competitor** *n* saingan ← **compete**

compilation *n* antologi, koleksi, susunan, kompilasi, bunga rampai; **compile** *v* menyusun

complacent *adj* [kompléisent] (mudah) puas, tidak ambisius; **complacency** *n* rasa mudah puas

complain *v* mengadu, mengeluh; **complaint** *n* pengaduan, keluhan

complete *adj* lengkap, komplit; *v* menyelesaikan; **completely** *adj* sama sekali; **completion** *n* selesainya, penyelesaian

complex *n* kompleks; *adj* rumit, ruwet; **complexion** *n* [kompléksyen] kulit wajah, kulit muka

compliant *adj* [komplaient] sesuai dengan ← **comply**

complicate *v* mempersulit; *~d* rumit, kompleks, berbelit-belit; **complication** *n* kesulitan; komplikasi (penyakit)

complicit *adj* terlibat; **complicity** *n* keterlibatan

compliment *n* pujian; *a back-handed* ~ pujian yang mengandung unsur kritik; *v* memuji; **complimentary** *adj* memuji; cuma-cuma, gratis

comply *v* [komplai] mengikuti, memenuhi

component *n* unsur, komponen, suku cadang

compose *v* menyusun, membentuk, mengarang; **composer** *n* komponis; **composite** *adj* majemuk; **composition** *n* karangan; susunan

compose *~d* tenang, tidak mudah tergoncang; ~ *yourself* kendalikan diri sendiri; **com-posure** n ketenangan

compost n kompos

compound n kompleks (perumahan); gabungan; senyawa

comprehend v mengerti, memahami; **comprehensible** adj dapat dipahami; **comprehension** n pengertian, pemahaman

compress n kompres; v memampatkan, memadatkan; ~ed padat

comprise v meliputi, mencakup; ~d of terdiri dari, terdiri atas

compromise n [kompromaiz] kompromi; v mencari jalan tengah, berkompromi; mengorbankan

compulsion n paksaan; **compulsive** adj terdorong untuk melakukan; ~ shopper sangat gemar berbelanja; **compulsory** adj paksa, wajib

computation n perhitungan, kalkulasi; **computer** n komputer; **computerization** n komputerisasi

comrade n [komrad] kawan, teman; kamerad

concave adj cekung

conceal v menyembunyikan; ~ed tersembunyi; **concealment** n persembunyian

concede v [konsid] mengaku, menerima

conceit n [konsit] kesombongan, keangkuhan; **conceited** adj sombong, angkuh

conceive v [konsiv] mengerti; membayangkan; menjadi hamil

concentrate v memusatkan (perhatian), konsen; **concentration** n pemusatan, konsentrasi

conception n pengertian, konsepsi; pembuahan ← **conceive**

concern n perkara, hal; perhatian; perusahaan; ~ed prihatin; tersangkut; to be ~ed about memperhatikan, prihatin, memedulikan; menaruh minat; ~ing tentang, mengenai

concert n konser

concession n izin, kelonggaran; konsesi ← **concede**

conciliation n tindakan mendamaikan; **conciliatory** adj bersifat mendamaikan

concise adj pendek, ringkas, singkat

conclude v menyimpulkan; memutuskan; **conclusion** n kesimpulan; akhir; in ~ sebagai kata akhir; **conclusive** adj meyakinkan, menentukan

concourse n tempat terbuka

concrete n [konkrit] semen, beton; v menggunakan semen; adj nyata

concubine n selir

concur v setuju, sependapat

concussed adj gegar otak; **concussion** gegar otak

condemn v [kondém] menghukum; menghakimi; mengutuk; **condemnation** n kritikan, hujatan

condensation n pengembunan, kondensasi; **condense** v mengembun; menyingkat

condescend v merendahkan

diri; ~*ing* sombong; **condescension** *n* sikap sombong

condition *n* keadaan, kondisi; syarat; *v* memelihara, membiasakan; **conditional** *adj* dengan syarat; ~ *tense* bentuk pengandaian

condolences *n, pl* belasungkawa; *our* ~ kami ikut berduka cita, kami ucapkan belasungkawa

condom *n* kondom

condone *v* tidak menilai sebagai salah, menerima

conduct *n* kelakuan, cara; **conductor** *n* dirigen (musik); kondektur (angkutan umum); penghantar

cone *n* kerucut; marka jalan; *pine* ~ buah cemara

confectioner *n* pembuat permen; **confectionery** *n* permen, gula-gula

confederate *adj* sekutu; bersekutu; ~ *Army* Tentara Konfederasi (wilayah selatan selama Perang Saudara Amerika); **confederation** *n* persekutuan

confer *v* bermusyawarah, berembuk; **conference** *n* konferensi, konperensi, permusyawaratan

confess *v* mengaku; **confession** *n* pengakuan

confetti *n* guntingan kertas yang dilempar saat berpesta, hujan kertas

confidant *n* orang kepercayaan; **confidante** *n, f* [konfidant] orang kepercayaan; **confide** *v* memercayai, membuka rahasia;

confidence *n* kepercayaan; *in* ~ rahasia; *self-*~ percaya diri (PD); **confident** *adj* berani, percaya diri; **confidential** *adj* [konfidénsyel] rahasia

confine *v* membatasi, mengurung; memingit; **confinement** *n* masa sakit atau hamil; pingitan

confirm *v* menegaskan, memastikan; **confirmation** *n* kepastian, penegasan, konfirmasi

confiscate *v* menyita; **confiscation** *n* penyitaan

conflict *n* perselisihan, pertikaian, percekcokan, konflik; perang; ~*ing* bertentangan; *v* bertentangan

confluence *n* pertemuan dua sungai

conform *v* menurut, sesuai dengan; mengikuti orang kebanyakan

confound *v* mengherankan, membingungkan; ~*ed* bingung; persetan

confront *v* **confronting** *adj* menghadapi; menentang, melawan; **confrontation** *n* konfrontasi

confuse *v* membingungkan; ~*d* bingung

congeal *v* [konjil] membeku (darah)

congenital *adj* [kongénital] ~ *disease* penyakit turunan, penyakit bawaan

congested *adj* macet, sesak; **congestion** *n* kesesakan, kemacetan

conglomeration *n* konglomerasi

Congo *n* (the) Kongo; ~ *(formerly Zaire)* Kongo Kinshasa; *the* ~ *Democratic Republic* Kongo Brazzaville; **Congolese** *n* orang Kongo; *adj* berasal dari Kongo

congratulate *v* mengucapkan selamat; **congratulations** *n, pl* ucapan selamat; *ejac* selamat

congregate *v* berkumpul; **congregation** *n* jemaah (gereja)

congress *n* kongres, muktamar; **Congress** *n* Perwakilan Rakyat Amerika (Senat dan Dewan Perwakilan Rakyat); **congressional** *adj* berhubungan dengan Perwakilan Rakyat Amerika

conical *adj* kerucut, mengerucut ← **cone**

conjunction *n* kata sambung, kata penghubung; *in* ~ *with* bersama

conjure *v* [konjer] menyulap, menyikir; **conjurer** *n* tukang sulap, penyulap

connect *v* menghubungkan, menyambung; **connection** *n* hubungan, sambungan; koneksi

connive *v* berkomplot

connoisseur *n* [konesur] penggemar; ahli, pakar

conquer *v* [konker] mengalahkan, menaklukkan, merebut; **conquest** *n* penaklukan

conscience *n* [konsyens] hati nurani; **conscientious** *adj* rajin

conscious *adj* [konsyus] sadar; **consciousness** *n* kesadaran

conscript *n* wajib militer; **conscription** *n* wajib militer

consecrate *v* menahbiskan; mengabdikan; **consecration** *n* konsekrasi

consecutive *adj* berturut-turut

consensus *n* mufakat; **consent** *v* menyetujui; *adj* izin; *~ing adults* orang dewasa yang suka sama suka (dalam hal bersanggama)

consequence *n* akibat, dampak; **consequent** *adj* yang berikut; **consequently** *adv* oleh karena itu, maka

conservation *n* perlindungan, pemeliharaan, konservasi; **conservative** *adj* kolot, konservatif; ~ *Party* Partai Konservatif (di Inggris); **conservatory** *n* sekolah musik; ruang berkaca (untuk menangkap cahaya matahari); **conserve** *n* selai; *v* menghemat

consider *v* menganggap, mengindahkan; mempertimbangkan; **considerable** *adj* cukup banyak; **consideration** *n* pertimbangan; **considering** *conj* mengingat

consign *v* [konsain] menyerahkan; mengirimkan; **consignment** *n* kiriman

consist *v* terdiri atas, terdiri dari

consistent *adj* konsekuen, tetap; **consistently** *adv* terus-menerus

consolation *n* hiburan; ~ *prize* juara harapan; **console** *n* meja atau papan (untuk peralatan); *v* menghibur

consolidate *v* memperkuat, mengukuhkan; ~d gabungan; **consolidation** *n* penguatan, pengukuhan

consonant *n* huruf mati, konsonan

consort *n* kawan; pasangan raja atau ratu; *v* bergaul

conspicuous *adj* menonjol, jelas

conspiracy *n* [konspirasi] komplotan, persekongkolan; **conspirator** *n* sekongkol, komplot; **conspire** *v* bersekongkol, berkomplot

constable *n* [kanstabel] polisi

constant *adj* tetap, selalu; **constantly** *adv* selalu, terus-menerus

constellation *n* gugus bintang, konstelasi

constipated *adj* sembelit

constitute *v* merupakan; terdiri dari; **constitution** *n* undang-undang dasar (UUD), konstitusi; keadaan tubuh; **constitutional** *adj* menurut undang-undang dasar

constrain *v* membatasi; **constraint** *n* batasan, kendala, hambatan

construct *v* membangun, membuat, membentuk; **construction** *n* bangunan, pembangunan (gedung), konstruksi; ~ *site* proyek

consul *n* konsul, wakil; **consular** *adj* berhubungan dengan konsul; **consulate** *n* konsulat; ~-*General* konjen (konsulat-jenderal)

consult *v* menanyakan, mencari pendapat, berkonsultasi; ~*ing room* *n* kamar periksa; **consultation** *n* perundingan, konsultasi; **consultative** *adj* bersifat memberi nasihat

consume *v* memakan, menghabiskan; memakai, menggunakan; **consumer** *n* pengguna, pemakai, konsumen; **consumption** *n* pemakaian; *arch* sakit paru-paru

contact *n* hubungan, kontak; ~ *lenses* lensa kontak; *v* menghubungi, mengontak

contagious *adj* menular, menjangkit

contain *v* berisi, memuat, mengandung; **container** *n* tempat; ~ *ship* kapal barang

contaminate *v* mencemari; **contamination** *n* kontaminasi

contemplate *v* merenungkan; **contemplation** *n* renungan

contemporary *n* teman seangkatan; *adj* modern, kini, kontemporer

contempt *n* penghinaan; **contemptible** *adj* hina

contend *v* berpendapat; ~ *with* menghadapi; **contender** *n* pesaing, peserta, calon juara

content *n* [kentént] kepuasan; *to your heart's* ~ sepuas-puasnya; ~*(ed)* puas, senang

content *n* [kontént] isi, bahan; **contents** *n, pl* isi, muatan; *table of* ~ daftar isi

contention *n* anggapan, pendapat; **contentious** *adj* kontroversial, dapat diperdebatkan ← **contend**

contest n pertandingan, lomba; *beauty* ~ kontes kecantikan; v bertanding; memperjuangkan; **contestant** n peserta

context n hubungan, kaitan; konteks

contiguous *adj* [kontigyues] bersebelahan, berdampingan

continent n benua; **continental** *adj* berhubungan dengan benua (Eropa); ~ *breakfast* sarapan ala Eropa

contingency ~ *plan* rencana alternatif

continual *adj* selalu, terus-menerus; **continuation** n terusan, lanjutan, sambungan; **continue** v terus; melanjutkan, meneruskan; *to be* ~d bersambung; **continuous** *adj* terus-menerus

contour n garis bentuk; ~ *map* peta kontur

contraband n, *adj* barang selundupan

contraceptive n, *adj* kontrasepsi; ~ *pill* pil KB

contract n kontrak, surat perjanjian; v mengecil; mengidap (penyakit); memborong; mengontrak; **contraction** n kontraksi; **contractor** n kontraktor, pemborong; **contractual** *adj* menurut kontrak

contradict v membantah, menyanggah; **contradiction** n pertentangan, kontradiksi; **contradictory** *adj* bertentangan, berlawanan

contrary *adj* [kontrari] berlawanan; sulit patuh; *on the* ~ sebaliknya

contrast n perbedaan, kontras; v berbeda; membandingkan; ~*ing* berbeda, berlawanan

contravene v [kontravin] melanggar; **contravention** n pelanggaran

contribute v menyumbang, memberikan; **contribution** n sumbangan, kontribusi

contrite *adj* bersikap menyesal

contrive v membuat-buat, merekayasa

control n kendali, kontrol; *in* ~ *of* mengendalikan; v mengendalikan; ~ *tower* menara pengawas

controversial *adj* kontroversial; **controversy** n isu, kontroversi

convalescence n masa pulih; masa istirahat; **convalescent** n orang yang sedang sembuh dari sakit

convene v [konvin] bersidang

convenience n kesempatan; kemudahan; *at your* ~ sesempat anda; **convenient** *adj* enak; dekat

convent n biara (untuk biarawati)

convention n seminar, rapat, konvensi; kebiasaan; **conventional** *adj* biasa ← **convene**

conversant *adj* kenal, berpengalaman

conversation n percakapan, pembicaraan; **converse** v berbincang, bercakap-cakap; **conversely** *adj* sebaliknya conversion *n* perubahan; **convert** *n* orang yang telah masuk agama lain; *Isl* mualaf; *v* masuk agama baru; mengubah; **convertible** *n* mobil yang atapnya bisa dibuka; *adj* dapat disesuaikan

convex *adj* cembung

convey *v* [konvé] membawa, mengangkut; menyampaikan; **conveyance** *n* kendaraan

convict *n* narapidana; *v* menghukum

conviction *n* keyakinan, kepercayaan

convince *v* meyakinkan; ~*d* yakin; ~*ing* meyakinkan

convoy *n* iring-iringan, konvoi

convulse ~*d with laughter* tertawa berbahak-bahak; **convulsion** *n* kejang-kejang

cook *n* juru masak, koki; *v* memasak; ~*book* buku resep; ~*ing* masakan; **cookery** *n* cara memasak; **cookie** *n* kue kering yang keras

cool *adj* sejuk, dingin; *sl* gaya; *v* menyejukkan, mendinginkan; **cooler** *n* (ruang) pendingin

coolie *n* kuli

co-operate, cooperate *v* bekerja sama; **co-operation** *n* kerja sama; **co-operative** *n* (toko) koperasi

cop *n, sl* polisi

cope *v* menghadapi, hidup dengan (kesulitan)

copper *n* tembaga; *adj* warna tembaga

copy *n* salinan, kopi; *v* menyalin, meniru; memfotokopi; **copyright** *n* hak cipta

coral *n* karang

cord *n* tali

cordial *n* sirop; *adj* ramah, sopan

corduroy *n* beledru, korduroi

core *n* inti, hati; *the Earth's* ~ inti bumi

coriander *n* ketumbar

cork *n* gabus; sumbat; **corkscrew** *n* pembuka botol, kotrek

corn *n* jagung; katimumul

corned ~ *beef* kornet

corner *n* sudut, penjuru; *v* memojokkan

cornet *n* semacam terompet

cornflour *n* tepung maizena ← **corn**

corny *adj* kuno, sudah basi (lelucon)

coronary ~ *(attack)* serangan jantung

coronation *n* upacara penobatan

coroner *n* petugas pemeriksa mayat

corporal *n* kopral

corporate *adj* berkaitan dengan perusahaan; **corporation** *n* perusahaan, perkumpulan, persekutuan, grup

corps *n* [kor] korps; pasukan

corpse *n* [korps] mayat (manusia)

correct *adj* benar, betul; *v* membetulkan, memperbaiki; **correction** *n* pembetulan, perbaikan

correspond *v* surat-menyurat; sesuai dengan; **correspondence** *n* surat-menyurat, korespondensi; **correspondent** *n*

orang yang menulis surat atau
artikel; wartawan

corridor *n* lorong

corrode *v* berkarat, karatan;
corrosive *adj* keras; merusak

corrugate ~*d* berombak,
bergelombang

corrupt *adj* korup, dapat disuap;
v menyuap; merusak; **corruption** *n* korupsi, suap

cosmetic *adj* berkaitan dengan
kecantikan; ~ *surgery* bedah
plastik; **cosmetics** *n, pl* alat-
alat kecantikan (seperti lipstik,
perona pipi dsb)

cosmic *adj* berasal dari kosmos;
cosmonaut *n* antariksawan,
astronot (dari Uni Soviet);
cosmos *n* kosmos, jagat raya;
cosmopolitan *adj* internasional, kosmopolitan

cost *n* **cost cost** harga (barang),
ongkos (perjalanan), biaya
(jasa); *v* berharga; **costly** *adj*
mahal

Costa Rica *n* Kosta Rika; **Costa
Rican** *n* orang Kosta Rika; *adj*
berasal dari Kosta Rika

costume *n* pakaian, busana,
kostum

cosy, cozy *adj* enak, mungil

Cote d'Ivoire *n* Pantai Gading
→ **Ivory Coast**

cottage *n* pondok, bungalo; ~
cheese keju putih untuk
mengisi makanan

cotton *n, adj* kapas, katun; ~ *field*
kebun kapas; ~ *wool* kapas

cough *n, v* [kof] batuk; *whooping* ~ batuk rejan

could *v* [kud] bisa, dapat,
mampu; *pf* → **can**

council *n* dewan; pemerintah
setempat (seperti kecamatan);
councillor *n* anggota dewan

counsel *n* pengacara; nasihat; *v*
menasihati, memberi nasihat;
counsellor *n* konselor,
penasihat

count *n* penghitungan; *v* berhitung; menghitung; **countdown**
n penghitungan dari nomor
besar sampai zero

count *n, m* gelar bangsawan

counter *n* loket; *v* melawan,
menangkis

counterfeit *adj* [kaunterfét] palsu

counterpart *n* teman, rekan,
pasangan

countersign *v* [kauntersain] ikut
menandatangani

countess *n, f* gelar bangsawan
← **count**

countless *adj* tak terhitung ←
count

country *n* [kantri] negeri,
negara; tanah air; *in the* ~ di
pedesaan, di pedalaman;
countryman *n* orang setanah
air; **countryside** *n* pedesaan,
pedalaman

county *n* kabupaten, wilayah
tingkat bawah; ~ *court* pengadilan negeri

coup *n* [ku] kudeta

couple *n* [kapel] pasang, pasangan

couplet *n* [kaplet] ayat, bait

coupon *n* kupon

courage *n* [karej] keberanian;
Dutch ~ minuman keras;

courageous *adj* [karéjus] berani

courier *n* kurir; ~ *service* jasa pengiriman barang

course *n* [kors] kursus; jalan, arah; *~work* bahan pelajaran; *golf* ~ padang golf; *of* ~ tentu saja, memang, pasti; *three-~ meal* santapan dengan tiga tahap; *in due* ~ pada waktunya

court *n* [kort] pengadilan; *~-martial* pengadilan tentara; *the High* ~ Pengadilan Tinggi

court *n* [kort] jalan buntu; taman; lapangan main; *basketball* ~ lapangan basket

court *n* [kort] istana; *at* ~ di istana

court *v* [kort] berpacaran dengan, mengencani, memacari; *~ing* berpacaran

courteous *adj* [kertiyes] sopan; **courtesy** *n* kesopanan, sopan-santun

courtier *n* anggota istana

courtship *n* [kortsyip] masa cumbuan, masa pacaran ← **court**

cousin *n* [kazen] (saudara) sepupu; *distant* ~ sepupu jauh; *first* ~ saudara sepupu

cove *n* teluk kecil

cover *n* [kaver] tutup, penutup; sampul (buku); sarung (bantal); perlindungan; *v* menutup; meliputi

cow *n* sapi, lembu; *~'s milk* susu sapi; *dairy* ~ sapi susu; *milk* ~ sapi susu, sapi perah

coward *n* pengecut, penakut;

cowardice *n* [kauerdis] rasa takut, ketidakberanian; **cowardly** *adj* penakut, pengecut

cower *v* tunduk

coyote *n* [koyoti] sejenis anjing liar

crab *n* kepiting, rajingan; **crabby** *adj* marah-marah, rewel

crack *n* retak; bunyi; *sl* kokain; *~ed* retak; gila; *a ~ing pace* sangat cepat; *v* retak, pecah dengan bunyi gemeretak; ~ *up* menjadi gila; **cracker** *n* petasan; biskuit kering

cradle *n* [krédel] buaian, ayunan

craft *n* kerajinan tangan; ketrampilan; **craftsman** *n* perajin, tukang

crafty *adj* licik

cram *n* keadaan penuh sesak, macet; *v* menjejalkan, memasukkan dengan paksa; belajar mati-matian sebelum ujian; ~ *school* bimbingan belajar; *~med in* penuh sesak

cramp *n* kejang; *don't ~ my style* jangan mencoreng citraku, jangan mengganggu gayaku

cranium *n* [kréniem] tengkorak, batok kepala

crank *n* engkol; orang yang aneh; **cranky** *adj* marah-marah, rewel

crash *n* tabrakan, ambruknya; ~ *course* kursus kilat; *plane* ~ kecelakaan pesawat, pesawat jatuh; *v* bertabrakan, menubruk; jatuh (pesawat terbang)

crate *n* peti kayu

crater *n* kawah

cravat *n* semacam dasi

crave *v* mengidamkan, merindukan; **craving** *n* idaman

crawl *n (front)* ~ gaya bebas; *back* ~ gaya punggung; *v* merangkak, merayap

crayon *n* krayon, kapur tulis lilin

craze *n* tren, kegemaran; **crazy** *adj* gila

creak *v* **creaky** *adj* berbunyi karena diinjak

cream *n* krim, kepala susu; *the* ~ *of the crop* yang terbaik; *adj* (warna) krem

crease *n* lipatan, wiron; *v* membuat lipatan

create *v* [kriét] menciptakan, membuat; **creation** *n* ciptaan, kreasi; Kejadian; **creator** *n* pencipta; **creature** *n* makhluk

credible *adj* dapat dipercaya

credit *n* penghargaan; kredit; ~ *card* kartu kredit

creek *n* kali, sungai kecil

creep *n, sl* orang yang menjijikkan atau mengerikan; *v* merangkak, merayap, menjalar; *it made my flesh* ~ bulu roma saya berdiri; **creepy** *adj* angker, mengerikan

cremate *v* membakar mayat, memperabukan; **cremation** *n* kremasi, pembakaran mayat

crescent *n* jalan yang melingkar; ~ *(moon)* bulan sabit; *the Red* ~ Sabit Merah

crest *n* jambul

crevice *n* [krévis] celah

crew *n* awak kapal; regu, kru; ~ *cut* rambut cepak; *cabin* ~ awak kabin

cricket *n* jangkrik, belalang; semacam olahraga seperti kasti

crier *arch* [kraier] *town* ~ petugas yang mengumumkan berita di tempat umum

crime *n* kejahatan; **criminal** *n* penjahat; *adj* jahat

crimson *adj* merah tua

cringe *v* [krinj] ngeri

cripple *n* timpang, pincang; *v* melumpuhkan, membuat pincang; **crippling** *adj* melumpuhkan, berat

crisis *n* [kraisis] krisis

crisp *n* (kripik) kentang; *adj* garing; segar

criteria *n, pl* syarat; patokan, norma; **criterion** *n* syarat; patokan, norma

critic *n* pemerhati; **critical** *adj* kritis, genting; **criticism** *n* kritik; **criticize** *v* mengritik

croak *n* suara kodok; *v* menguak

Croat *n* [Kroat] orang Kroasia; *Serbo-*~ *arch* bahasa Serbia dan Kroasia; **Croatia** *n* [Kroésya] Kroasia; **Croatian** *n* bahasa Kroasia; *adj* berasal dari Kroasia

crochet *n* [krosyé] rajutan; *v* merajut

crockery *n* tembikar

crocodile *n* buaya; ~ *tears* air mata yang dibuat-buat

crony *n* kawan seperkongkolan, konco

crook *n, sl* penipu; **crooked** *adj* bengkok

crop *n* panen; *v* memotong;

close-~ped hair rambut cepak

croquet *n* [kroké] semacam permainan seperti mini-golf

cross *n* silang; salib; persimpangan, persilangan; *v* melintasi, menyeberangi; *~-country* lari lintas alam; *~-eyed* juling; *~-section* potong melintang; **crossing** *n* penyeberangan; **crossroads** *n* simpang, perempatan; **crossword** *n* teka-teki silang (TTS)

crouch *v* berjongkok

crow *n* [kro] burung gagak; *v* berkokok; membual

crowbar *n* [krobar] linggis

crowd *n* orang banyak, gerombolan orang, kerumunan orang; *v* berkerumunan, mengerumuni; *~ed* penuh sesak, ramai

crown *n* mahkota; ubun-ubun; *v* menobatkan sebagai raja atau ratu

crucial *adj* [krusyel] utama, pokok; penting

crucifixion *n* penyaliban; **crucify** *v* menyalibkan

crude *adj* kasar, mentah; primitif; *~ oil* minyak mentah

cruel *adj* bengis, kejam; **cruelty** *n* kebengisan, kekejaman

cruise *n* [kruz] pelayaran pesiar; *~ ship* kapal pesiar; *v* menjelajah; **cruiser** *n* kapal jelajah

crumb *n* [kram] remah; *~s!* ampun!; **crumble** *v* merepih, ambruk, merapuh; **crumbly** *adj* repih

crumpet *n* sejenis roti panggang

crumple *v* rebah; menggumpalkan

crunch *n* saat yang menentukan; *v* mengerkah, menimbulkan bunyi berderak; **crunchy** *adj* garing

crusade *n* perjuangan; perang salib; *v* melawan; **crusader** *n* orang yang memperjuangkan sesuatu

crush *n, sl* cinta monyet; *v* menghancurkan; menekan

crust *n* kerak, kulit; *the Earth's ~* kerak bumi

crustacean *n* [krastésyen] keluarga kerang-kerangan

crutch *n*; **crutches** *pl* kruk

cry *n* [krai] teriak, pekik; tangis; *v* berteriak, memekik; menangis

cryptic *adj* tidak jelas, samar

crystal *n, adj* hablur, kristal

Ct *Court* jalan buntu

Cuba *n* Kuba; **Cuban** *n* orang Kuba; *adj* berasal dari Kuba

cubby-house *n* rumah bermain untuk anak-anak

cube *n* kubus; **cubic** *~ meter* (cm³) meter kubik

cubicle *n* bilik

cucumber *n* [kyukamber] timun, ketimun, mentimun

cuddle *n* [kadel] pelukan; *v* memeluk, mengemong; **cuddly** *adj* enak diemong atau dipeluk

cue *n* petunjuk, isyarat; kiu (bilyar); *v* memberi isyarat, mengisyaratkan; mempersiapkan (kaset)

cuff *n* ujung tangan, manset

cuisine *n* [kuisin] santapan, masakan

culminate *v* memuncak, berakhir;

culmination *n* puncak

culprit *n* pelaku, yang bersalah

cult *n* kultus; *personality* ~ kultus individu

cultivate *v* memelihara, menanam; mengolah; ~*d* sopan, beradab, berpendidikan; **cultivation** *n* pemeliharaan, penanaman

cultural *adj* **culture** *n* kebudayaan, budaya; ~ *shock* gegar budaya

cunning *n, adj* cerdik, licik

cup *n* cangkir, cawan; piala; **cupboard** *n* [kaberd] lemari; **cupcake** *n* kue kecil (seperti kue bolu)

cupola *n* [kyupola] kubah

curator *n* kepala musium, kurator

curb *n* pinggiran jalan; penahan; *v* mengekang, membatasi

cure *n* obat, pengobatan; *v* mengobati (sampai sembuh)

curfew *n* jam malam

curiosity *n* penasaran, keingintahuan; keajaiban; **curious** *adj* penasaran, ingin tahu; aneh

curl *n, v* keriting; **curly** *adj* ikal, keriting; *a* ~ *question* pertanyaan yang susah

currant *n* kismis (kecil, berwarna hitam); ~ *bun* roti kismis

currency *n* mata uang; *foreign* ~ mata uang asing

current *n* arus; *alternating* ~ *(AC)* arus bolak-balik; *direct* ~ *(DC)* arus searah; *adj* kini; berlaku; ~ *affairs* berita kini

curricular *adj* berhubungan dengan kurikulum; *extra-*~ ekskul; **curriculum** *n* kuriku-

lum; *competency-based* ~ kurikulum berbasis kompetensi

curry *n* kari, gulai

curse *n* kutukan; umpatan, makian; *v* mengutuk; mengumpat, memaki

cursive *n* tulisan miring, tulisan bersambung

curtain *n* [kerten] horden, gorden, tirai; *the Iron* ~ Tirai Besi

curtsey *v, f* [kertsi] membungkukkan badan di depan anggota kerajaan

curve *n* lengkung; *v* melengkung; **curvy** *adj* sintal, montok

cushion *n* [kusyen] bantal; *v* melindungi dengan bantalan

custard *n* sejenis puding

custodian *n* pemegang kunci, pemilik; **custody** *n* tahanan, kurungan

custom *n* adat, kebiasaan; langganan; **customary** *adj* biasa, lazim; **customer** *n* langganan, nasabah (bank)

customs *n* bea cukai, pabean; ~ *house* kantor, pabean; ~ *officer* petugas bea cukai

cut *n* **cut cut** potongan; *final* ~ versi terakhir; *short* ~ jalan pintas; *v* memotong, menggunting; ~ *back* mengurangi; ~ *down* menebang; mengurangi; ~ *off* memutuskan

cute *adj* lucu; mungil, manis

cuticle *n* [kyutikel] kulit tipis di sekitar kuku

cutlet *n* potongan daging

cuttlefish *n* ikan sotong

CV *abbrev curriculum vitae* CV, riwayat kerja

cyberspace *n* [saiberspés] dunia maya

cycle *n* [saikel] daur, siklus; *v* bersepeda, naik sepeda; **cyclist** *n* pengendara sepeda; *(professional)* ~ pembalap sepeda

cyclone *n* [saiklon] angin topan, siklon

cylinder *n* silinder; **cylindrical** *adj* berbentuk silinder, bulat panjang

cynic *n* orang yang suka mengejek; **cynical** *adj* suka mengejek; **cynicism** *n* sifat mau mengejek atau memperolok

cypress *n* [saipres] pohon eru

Cypriot *n* [Sipriet] orang Siprus; *adj* berasal dari Siprus; **Cyprus** *n* [Saiprus] Siprus

Czech *n* [Cék] bahasa Ceko, orang Ceko; *adj* Ceko; ~*slovakia* Czechoslovakia; *the* ~ *Republic* Republik Ceko

D

DA *abbrev District Attorney* jaksa wilayah

dab *v* mengoles, mencolek; *a* ~ *hand* pandai

dabble *v* mencoba-coba

Dad *n, sl* Pak; *my* ~ ayahku; **Daddy** *n, sl, child* Papa; ~-*long-legs* sejenis laba-laba

daft *adj* gila, sinting

dagger *n* keris

daily *n* harian; ~ *(newspaper)* (koran) harian; *adv* tiap hari, setiap hari, sehari-hari

dainty *adj* manis, cantik

dairy *n* perusahaan susu; *adj* susu; ~ *products* produk olahan susu

daisy *n* bunga aster

dam *n* bendungan; *v* membendung

damage *n* [damej] kerusakan; rugi, kerugian; *v* merugikan, merusak

dame *n, f* gelar bangsawan

dammit *ejac* persetan! ← **damn it**

damn *v* mengutuk; *adj* terkutuk; *ejac* persetan; ~ *it* persetan; ~*ed* terkutuk

damp *n* kelembaban, iklim lembab; *adj* lembab; **dampen** *v* melembabkan

dance *n* tari, tari-tarian; dansa; *v* menari; berdansa; **dancer** *n* penari; **dancing** *n* tari-tarian, seni tari

dandruff *n* ketombe; *anti-~ shampoo* sampo anti ketombe

Dane *n* orang Denmark; *Great* ~ sejenis anjing

danger *n* [dénjer] bahaya; **dangerous** *adj* berbahaya

dangle *v* [danggel] menjuntai; menguntai; **dangling** *adj* terjuntai

Danish *n* bahasa Denmark; *adj* berasal dari Denmark; ~ *pastry* semacam roti dengan buah

Danube [Danyub] *the (River)* ~ sungai Donau

dare *n* tantangan; *v* menantang; *adj* berani; *I ~ say* berani saya katakan; **daredevil** *n* pemberani, orang yang berani mati; **daring** *n* keberanian; *adj* berani

dark *n* gelap, kegelapan; *adj* gelap; *~ glasses* kacamata hitam; *~ green* hijau tua; *~-skinned* berkulit gelap; **darken** *v* menjadi gelap; menggelapkan; **darkness** *n* kegelapan; **darkroom** *n* kamar gelap

darling *n* sayang, buah hati; *adj* tersayang

darn *v* menambal, menjerumat; *ejac* sialan; *~ed* sialan; *~ing needle* jarum tisik

dash *n* garis datar; lari cepat; *the 100 m ~* lomba lari seratus meter; *v* berlari

dashboard *n* dasbor, panel peralatan

data *n* data; **database** *n* bank data

date *n* korma; *~ palm* pohon korma

date *n* tanggal; kencan; *best before ~, use-by ~* tanggal kedaluwarsa; *out of ~* kolot, kuno; *up to ~* modern, mutakhir; *v* mengencani, memacari; *~ from* sejak; *~d* tertanggal; ketinggalan jaman, kuno; **dating** *~ agency* biro perjodohan

daughter *n, f* [doter] anak perempuan, putri; *god-~* putri anak baptis; *grand~* cucu; *~-in-law* menantu

daunt *~ed* takut, segan; **daunt-**

ing *adj* menakutkan, berat; **dauntless** *adj* tidak takut, berani

dawdle *v* berjalan perlahan-lahan sambil membuang waktu

dawn *n* dini hari, fajar; permulaan; *at ~* waktu fajar menyingsing; *the ~ prayer* sholat subuh; *v* menyingsing; *~ upon* disadari

day *n* hari; siang; *~ school* sekolah yang tidak memiliki asrama; *~ student* pelajar yang tidak tinggal di asrama; *all ~* sepanjang hari; *one ~* sekali waktu; *the good old ~s* tempo dulu; *the other ~* baru-baru ini; *twice a ~* sehari dua kali; *~ of Judgment* hari kiamat; *during the ~* siang hari; **daybreak** *n* dini hari, fajar; **daydream** *n* lamunan, khayalan; **daylight** *n* siang, sinar matahari; *~ saving* kebijakan memajukan jam selama musim panas; *in broad ~* siang bolong; **daytime** *n, adj* siang hari; *in the ~* siang hari

daze *n* keadaan pusing; *~d* linglung, pusing

dazzle *v* menyilaukan, memesonakan; **dazzling** *adj* memesonakan, menyilaukan

dead *adj* [déd] mati; sunyi senyap; *~ end* jalan buntu; *~ heat* seri (dalam perlombaan); **deaden** *v* mematikan; **deadline** *n* batas waktu; **deadlock** *n* jalan buntu; **deadly** *adj* mematikan; sungguh-sungguh → **die**

deaf *adj* [déf] tuli; *~-mute* bisu tuli; *stone-~* tuli; *tone-~* tidak bisa mendengar nada lagu; **deafen** v merusak telinga

deal n persetujuan; *a great ~, a good ~* sebagian besar; cukup banyak; *it's a ~* setuju; v **dealt dealt** [délt] membagi (kartu); *~ in* jual-beli; *~ with* memperlakukan, menghadapi; **dealer** n pedagang; **dealings** n, pl urusan, transaksi

dear n yang baik, yang terhormat (in letters); *my ~* sayangku; *adj* mahal

death n [déth] kematian; *~ penalty* hukuman mati; *~ rate* angka kematian; **deathly** *adj* seperti kematian

debate n perdebatan; v berdebat; memperdebatkan; **debatable** *adj* dapat diperdebatkan; **debating** n kegiatan berdebat

debit n debit; v mendebitkan, membebankan

debrief v **debriefing** n tanya jawab sepulang dari tugas

debris n [debri] reruntuhan, puing

debt n [dét] hutang; *~-collector* petugas penagih hutang; *in ~* berhutang; **debtor** n orang yang berhutang

debut n [débyu] penampilan pertama; v tampil untuk pertama kali

decadence n kemerosotan, dekadensi; **decadent** *adj* merosot

decaffeinated *~ coffee (decaf)* kopi tanpa kafein

decapitate v memenggal kepala;

decapitation n pemenggalan kepala

decathlete n atlet dasalomba; **decathlon** n dasalomba

decay n kerusakan, kebusukan; *in ~* dalam keadaan tidak terawat; *tooth ~* karis; v melapuk, membusuk

deceased *n the ~* orang yang meninggal; *adj* telah meninggal, mangkat, wafat; *~ estate* bangunan dan tanah milik orang yang meninggal

deceit n [disit] tipu daya; **deceitful** *adj* penuh tipu daya, bersifat menipu; **deceive** v menipu; *~d* tertipu; **deceiver** n penipu

December n bulan Desember

decency n kesopanan; **decent** *adj* sopan, patut, layak

decentralization v desentralisasi; **decentralize** v mendesentralisasi

deception penipuan ← **deceit**

decide v memutuskan, menentukan, menetapkan; **decider** n tahap atau babak yang menentukan

decimal n persepuluhan, desimal; *~ point* koma (desimal); *Dewey ~ System* sistem klasifikasi Dewey

deciduous *adj* berganti daun

decision n keputusan; **decisive** *adj* menentukan ← **decide**

deck n geladak, dek; *~ chair* kursi pantai, kursi malas; *~ of cards* kartu remi

declaration n pernyataan, pengumuman, maklumat, deklarasi;

declare v menyatakan, mengumumkan

decline n kemunduran, kemerosotan; v mundur, menjadi kurang; menolak

decode v membaca atau memecahkan sandi

decompose v membusuk; ~d busuk

décor n dekor, hiasan

decorate v menghiasi; **decoration** n hiasan, perhiasan; tanda kehormatan

decorous adj [dekorus] sopan (santun); **decorum** n kesopanan

decoy n, adj umpan, pemikat

decrease n pengurangan, penurunan; v berkurang; mengurangi, menurunkan

decree n keputusan, dekrit, penetapan; v memutuskan, menetapkan

dedicate v mempersembahkan, mengabdikan; **dedication** n pengabdian, persembahan, dedikasi

deduct v memotong, mengurangi; **deduction** n potongan, pengurangan

deduction n kesimpulan ← **deduce**

deed n perbuatan ← **do**

deem v menganggap, menyatakan

deep adj dalam; a ~ sleep tidur pulas; ~ freeze lemari es; ~-rooted berurat-berakar; ~-seated yang mendalam; **deepen** v mendalam; memperdalam; **deeply** adv dalam

deer n rusa, menjangan

deface v merusak; mengotori, mencoret-moret

defamation n **defamatory** adj fitnah; **defame** v memfitnah

default v gagal; lalai membayar; by ~ dengan tak hadir; secara otomatis; v gagl; lalai membayar

defeat n kekalahan; v mengalahkan, menggagalkan; ~ed terkalahkan, kalah

defecate v buang air besar, berak

defect n [difékt] cacat, cela, kerusakan

defect v [defékt] durhaka, menyeberang ke pihak lain

defective adj rusak, cacat ← **defect**

defend v membela, mempertahankan; **defendant** n tergugat; **defender** n pembela; bek; **defense** n pertahanan, pembelaan, perlawanan; **defenseless** adj tidak dapat melawan, tak berdaya; **defensive** adj bersikap bertahan, defensif

defer v menunda, menangguhkan; ~ to tunduk pada; **deference** n sikap tunduk, hormat

defiance n [defaiens] pemberontakan; **defiant** adj bersifat menentang, bersifat melawan

deficiency n [defisyensi] kekurangan; **deficient** adj kurang

deficit n kekurangan (uang), defisit

defile v mencemarkan, memerkosa

define v menentukan, menetapkan, mengartikan; **definite** adj tertentu, pasti; **definitely** *adv* tentu; **definition** *n* definisi

deflate *v* kempes; mengempeskan; ~d kempes

deflect *v* menangkis, membelokkan; **deflection** *n* pembelokan, defleksi

deforestation *n* deforestasi, penebangan hutan

deformed *adj* **deformity** *n* cacat

defraud *v* menipu ← **fraud**

degenerate *v* memburuk, merosot; **degeneration** *n* kemerosotan, degenerasi

degradation *n* penurunan pangkat; pelecehan; **degrading** *adj* hina, melecehkan

degree *n* (suhu) derajat; gelar sarjana; *Bachelor's* ~ S1; *Master's* ~ S2

dehydrated *adj* [dihaidréted] dehidrasi, kurang minum

deign *v* [déin] sudi, berkenan

deity *n* [déiti] tuhan, dewa

dejected *adj* murung, tanpa semangat

delay *n* keterlambatan, penundaan; *v* menunda, memperlambat

delegate *n* wakil, utusan; *v* menyerahkan; mengutus; **delegation** *n* delegasi, perwakilan

delete *v* menghapus, mencoret; **deletion** *n* penghapusan, pencoretan

deliberate *v* menimbang-nimbang; berembuk; *adj* (dengan) sengaja; **deliberation** *n* pertimbangan, perundingan

delicacy *n* [délikasi] makanan istimewa; kehalusan; **delicate**

adj halus; sering sakit; **delicatessen** *n* toko makanan kering (seperti daging, keju)

delicious *adj* [delisyus] enak, sedap, lezat

delight *n* [delait] kesenangan, kegembiraan; *Turkish* ~ sejenis agar yang ditaburi tepung gula; **delightful** *adj* menyenangkan, membahagiakan

delinquent *n* anak nakal; *adj* nakal

delirious *adj* mengigau, berdemam tinggi; **delirium** *n* keadaan mengigau

deliver *v* mengirim, menghantarkan, memberi; membidani; melahirkan; ~ *a speech* berpidato; **delivery** *n* penyerahan, pengiriman; ~ *boy* kurir

delude ~d hidup berkhayal; **delusion** *n* khayal, angan-angan

demand *n* tuntutan; *in* ~ laku; *supply and* ~ persediaan dan permintaan; *v* menuntut, minta; ~*ing* banyak meminta atau menuntut

democracy *n* demokrasi, kerakyatan; **democrat** *n* demokrat; **democratic** *adj* demokratis

demolish *v* membongkar, merobohkan; **demolition** *n* pembongkaran

demon *n* [dimon] jin, iblis, setan; **demonic** *adj* jahat, seperti jin

demonstrate *v* berunjuk rasa; menunjukkan, memperlihatkan, membuktikan; **demonstration** *n* pertunjukan; demonstrasi, demo, unjuk rasa

demoralize v **demoralizing** adj merusak semangat

den n sarang, liang; ruang santai

dengue [déngi] ~ *fever* demam berdarah

denial n [denayal] penyangkalan ← **deny**

denim n (bahan) jins

Denmark n Denmark

denomination n satuan; pecahan, lembaran (uang); aliran (gereja); **denominator** n angka sebutan

dense adj padat, rapat, lebat; sl bodoh; **density** n kepadatan

dent n peot, peyok; v melekukkan

dental adj berhubungan dengan gigi; **dentist** n dokter gigi; **dentistry** n (ilmu) kedokteran gigi; **denture** n [déntyur] gigi palsu

deny v [denai] menyangkal, memungkiri, menolak

depart v berangkat, pergi; the ~ed almarhum, mendiang

department n departemen; bagian; ~ of Agriculture Departemen Pertanian; ~ store toko serba ada (toserba); **departmental** adj berhubungan dengan departmen

departure n [departyur] keberangkatan ← **depart**

depend v bergantung, tergantung; **dependant** n orang tanggungan; **dependency** n daerah jajahan; **dependent** adj tergantung pada; tanggungan

depict v menggambarkan; **depiction** n menggambarkan

deplete v menghabiskan,

mengurangi; **depletion** n kehabisan, penipisan

deplorable adj tercela, patut disesalkan; **deplore** v menyesali, mengecam

deport v mendeportasi, membuang; **deportation** n deportasi, pembuangan

deposit n deposito, simpanan; endapan; term ~ deposito berjangka; v menaruh, menyimpan

depot n [dépo] depot, depo, gudang

depreciate v [deprisyét] turun nilai; **depreciation** n penurunan nilai, depresiasi

depress v menekan, menyusahkan hati; ~ed tanpa semangat, murung; ~ing menyedihkan; **depression** n bagian yang rendah; depresi, jaman meleset; kehilangan gairah hidup

deprivation n [déprivésyen] kehilangan; sleep ~ kurang tidur; **deprive** v [depraiv] mengambil, merampas

Dept Department Dep (Departemen)

deputy n wakil; ~ head wakil kepala (waka)

derail v anjlok, keluar dari rel; **derailment** n kejadian anjlok

derelict n orang gila, gembel, gelandangan; adj tertinggal, tidak terpelihara

derivation n asal; **derive** v berasal

derrick n kerekan, derek, menara pengeboran minyak

descend v turun; ~ed from keturunan; ~ing order dari atas ke bawah; **descendant** *n* keturunan, anak cucu; **descent** *n* jalan turun

describe *v* melukiskan, menggambarkan; **description** *n* penggambaran, deskripsi; **descriptive** *adj* yang menggambarkan, deskriptif

desert *n* [désert] gurun, padang pasir; ~ *island* pulau tak terhuni

desert *v* [desert] meninggalkan, membelot; desersi; **deserted** *adj* sunyi (senyap); **deserter** *n* pembelot

deserve *v* berhak mendapat, patut (menerima); **deservedly** *adv* sepantasnya, seharusnya; **deserving** *adj* patut terima

design *n* rancangan, contoh, gambar, desain; *by* ~ dengan sengaja; *graphic* ~ desain grafik; *v* merancang, mendesain

designate *v* [désignét] menandai, memperuntukkan; ~d tertandai

designer *n* perancang, desainer; *fashion* ~ perancang busana; *adj* bermerek ← **design**

desirable *adj* yang diinginkan; **desire** *n* keinginan, nafsu, hasrat; *v* ingin, menginginkan, mendambakan

desk *n* meja (tulis); bangku (di sekolah)

desolate *adj* [désolet] sepi, sunyi; gersang; **desolation** *n* kesunyian, kesepian

despair *n* keputusasaan; *v* putus asa; **desperate** *adj* sudah putus asa

despicable *adj* [despikabel] dibenci; **despise** *v* membenci

despite *conj* meskipun, kendati

despondent *adj* sedih (hati)

dessert *n* [desert] pencuci mulut, puding

destination *n* tujuan, jurusan

destined *adj* [déstind] ditakdirkan; **destiny** *n* nasib, takdir

destitute *adj* miskin, papa; **destitution** *n* kepapaan, kemiskinan

destroy *v* menghancurkan, memusnahkan, membinasakan; **destroyer** *n* (kapal) perusak; **destruction** *n* kerusakan, kehancuran, pemusnahan, pembinasaan; **destructive** *adj* merusak, membinasakan

detach *v* melepaskan; **detach-ment** *n* obyektivitas, hati dingin

detail *n* rinci, perincian, seluk-beluk; *in* ~ secara terinci; *v* merincikan; ~ed terinci

detain *v* menahan; ~ed at Her Majesty's pleasure dipenjara; **detainee** *n* tahanan

detect *v* menemukan, mendapat-kan, mendeteksi; **detection** *n* penemuan, deteksi; **detective** *n* reserse, detektif

detention *n* penahanan, penawanan; *in* ~ disetrap ← **detain**

deter *v* [detér] menghalangi

detergent *n* sabun, obat, deterjen

deteriorate *v* [detiriorét] mem-buruk, merosot; **deterioration** *n* kemerosotan

determination *n* tekad bulat; **determine** *v* menetapkan, menentukan, memutuskan; ~*d* bertekad, bersikeras

deterrent *n* pencegah ← **deter**

detest *v* membenci

detract ~ *from* mengurangi, menurunkan nilai, mengecilkan nilai; **detractor** *n* kritik

detrimental *adj* merugikan

deuce *adj* [dyus] jus, skor 40-40 (dalam pertandingan tenis)

devastate *v* menghancurkan; **devastating** *adj* menghancurkan; ~ *looks* sangat rupawan; **devastation** *n* penghancuran

develop *v* mengembangkan, membangun, membina; mencuci (film); **developer** *n* pengembang, pemborong; **development** *n* pembangunan, perkembangan; pengembangan, pembinaan

deviate *v* [diviét] menyimpang, melenceng; **deviation** *n* penyimpangan; jalan alternatif

device *n* alat; *left to your own* ~*s* telantar, dibiarkan

devil *n* setan, iblis; **devilish** *adj* seperti setan

devious *adj* [divius] berbelit-belit, culas

devise *v* memikirkan, merencanakan

devolve *v* menyerahkan; **devolution** *n* devolusi; ~ *to the provinces* otonomi daerah (otda)

devote *v* mengabdikan, menyediakan; **devoted** *adj* tekun; **devotee** *n* penggemar; **devotion** *n* ketaatan, kebaktian; rasa sayang

devour *v* melahap

devout *adj* soleh, beriman ← **devote**

dew *n* embun; **dewy** *adj* berembun

dexterity *n* ketangkasan; **dextrous** *adj* tangkas, gesit

diabetes *n* [daiabitis] penyakit gula, kencing manis; **diabetic** *n* [daiabétik] penderita kencing manis

diagnose *v* mendiagnosa, menentukan; **diagnosis** *n* diagnosa

diagonal *n* garis sudut-menyudut, diagonal; *adj* sudut-menyudut, diagonal

diagram *n* denah, bagan

dial *n* [daial] piringan, muka jam; *v* memencet (nomor telepon)

dialect *n* dialek

dialogue *adj* percakapan, dialog

diameter *n* garis tengah, diameter

diamond *n* berlian, intan

diaper *n* popok; *disposable* ~ pamper

diarrhoea, diarrhea *n* [daiaria] mencret, sakit perut, diare

diary *n* [daiari] buku harian; *to keep a* ~ menulis buku harian

dice *n, pl* dadu → **die**

dictate *v* mendikte; **dictation** *n* dikte, imla

dictator *n* diktator

dictionary *n* kamus; *abridged* ~ kamus singkat; *bilingual* ~ kamus dwibahasa

did *v, pf* → **do**

die *v* [dai] **died died** mati, meninggal, pol wafat; gugur (dalam perang); ~ *out* menjadi punah; padam

die *n, s* [dai] **dice** dadu

diesel *n* [disel] minyak solar; mesin disel

diet *n* [daiet] diet; makanan; *on a ~* (mengikuti) diet; *v* mengikuti diet, membatasi makan; **dietary** *adj* berhubungan dengan pola makan; **dietician** *n* ahli diet

differ *v* berbeda; **difference** *n* beda, perbedaan; **different** *adj* beda, lain, berbeda; **differentiate** *v* membedakan; **differentiation** *n* pembedaan

difficult *adj* susah, sulit, sukar; **difficulty** *n* kesulitan, kesusahan

dig *v* **dug dug** menggali; **diggings** *n* penggalian

digest *v* mencerna; **digestion** *n* pencernaan

digit *n* [dijit] angka; jari; **digital** *adj* digital

dignified *adj* [dignifaid] bermartabat, mulia; **dignitary** *n* pejabat; **dignity** *n* martabat

digress *v* [daigrés] menyimpang; **digression** *n* penyimpangan

dike *n* pematang, bendung, tanggual

dilapidated *adj* [dilapidéted] telantar, bobrok, buruk

dilate *v* membesar; *~d pupils* pupil mata membesar

dilemma *n* pilihan sulit, dilema

diligence *n* kerajinan, ketekunan; **diligent** *adj* rajin, telaten

dilute *v* meredup; mengencerkan; *adj* encer; *~d* encer

dim *v* meredup; meredupkan; *adj* redup, suram; *sl* kurang cemer-lang otaknya

dime *n* sepuluh sen (Amerika); *a ~ a dozen* banyak, mudah didapat

dimension *n* matra, dimensi; **dimensional** *three-~* tiga dimensi

diminish *v* mengurangi; **diminutive** *n* nama kecil; kata pengecil

dimple *n* lesung pipi

dimwit *n* orang bodoh; *~ted* bodoh

din *n* gempar, gaduh, riuh

dine *v* bersantap (malam); **diner** *n* rumah makan kecil

dingy *adj* [dinji] kotor, suram

dining *n* santapan; *~ car* restorasi, gerbong makan; *~ room* ruang makan ← **dine**

dinner *n* makan malam; makan siang; *~ party* acara makan malam; *school ~* makan siang yang tersedia di sekolah

dinosaur *n* [dainosor] dinosaurus

dip *n* bagian yang turun; pence-lupan, mandi sebentar; *v* mencelupkan

diphthong *n* [difthong] bunyi rangkap, diftong

diploma *n* ijazah, diploma

diplomacy *n* diplomasi; **diplomat** *n* pegawai kedutaan, diplomat; **diplomatic** *adj* diplomatik, berkaitan dengan kedutaan

dipper *n* gayung ← **dip**

direct *adj* langsung; serta merta; terus terang; *~ current* arus searah; *v* memimpin, mengarahkan, memerintahkan,

menunjukkan; menyutradarai;
direction *n* arah, petunjuk;
directive *n* petunjuk, pedoman,
pengarahan; **directly** *adv*
secara langsung, serta merta,
segera; **director** *n* direktur,
pemimpin; sutradara; **directorate** *n* direktorat

directory *n* buku alamat, buku
daftar

dirt *n* kotoran, debu; tanah;
~-*cheap* murah sekali; ~-*poor*
miskin sekali; ~ *road* jalan
tanah; **dirty** *adj* kotor, dekil; ~
word kata jorok

disability *n* cacat; **disable** *v*
[disébel] mematikan, menonaktifkan; ~*d* cacat; orang cacat

disadvantage *n* rugi, kerugian;
~*d* dirugikan, merugi; **disad-
vantageous** *adj* merugikan

disagree *v* tidak setuju;
disagreeable *adj* tidak enak,
marah-marah; **disagreement**
n percekcokan, perbedaan
pendapat

disappear *v* hilang, lenyap; **dis-
appearance** *n* hilangnya,
lenyapnya

disappoint *v* **disappointing**
adj mengecewakan; **disappointment** *n* kekecewaan, rasa
kecewa

disapproval *n* sikap tidak setuju
atau suka; **disapprove** *v* tidak
menyetujui, tidak suka, menolak; **disapproving** *adj* bersikap
tidak suka

disarm *v* melucuti senjata; **disarmament** *n* perlucutan senjata

disaster *n* musibah, malapetaka,
bencana; *natural* ~ bencana
alam; **disastrous** *adj* malang,
celaka

disband *v* bubar, membubarkan

disbelief *n* ketidakpercayaan,
rasa tidak percaya; **disbelieve**
v tidak percaya

disc, disk *n* cakram; *compact* ~
(CD) CD; *floppy* ~ disket

discard *v* membuang

discharge *n* pemecatan, pemberhentian; cairan yang keluar,
keputihan; *honorable* ~ pemberhentian dengan hormat; *v*
memecat, melepaskan

disciple *n* [disaipel] murid; *the
Twelve* ~*s* dua belas murid
Yesus

discipline *n* disiplin, tata tertib,
ketertiban

disclose *v* membuka, menyatakan, menyingkap; **disclosure**
n pernyataan

discolored *v* luntur, berubah warna

discomfort *n* rasa tidak nyaman,
kesusahan

disconcert *v* [diskonsért]
membingungkan; ~*ed* bingung

disconnect *v* mencabut, memutuskan; ~*ed* terputus(-putus)

disconsolate *adj* [diskonsolet]
putus asa, tidak dapat terhibur

discontent *n* rasa kurang
senang, rasa tidak puas; ~*ed*
kurang senang atau puas

discontinue *v* memberhentikan

discord *n* perselisihan, bunyi
sumbang; **discordant** *adj* tak
selaras, sumbang

discount *n* potongan (harga), diskon, korting; *v* memotong harga, mendiskon

discourage *v* [diskarej] tidak menganjurkan; mengecilkan hati; ~d kecil hati, kehilangan semangat

discourse *n* pembicaraan, percakapan

discover *v* menemukan, mendapati; **discovery** *n* penemuan

discredit *v* tidak percaya; mencoreng nama; ~ed rusak namanya, tidak dipercaya

discreet *adj* sopan, bijaksana, berhati-hati (dalam keadaan yang sulit)

discrepancy *n* [diskrépansi] selisih, ketidaksesuaian, perbedaan

discretion *n* [diskrésyen] kebijaksanaan; *at your* ~ tergantung anda ← **discreet**

discriminate *v* membedakan, mendiskriminasikan; **discrimination** *n* pembedaan, diskriminasi; *racial* ~ diskriminasi berdasarkan warna kulit atau ras

discus *n* (lempar) cakram; ~ *throw* lempar cakram

discuss *v* [diskas] berembuk; membicarakan; **discussion** *n* pembicaraan, diskusi

disdain *n* hina, penghinaan; *v* menghina; **disdainful** *adj* penuh penghinaan

disease *n* penyakit

disembark *v* mendarat, turun dari kapal; **disembarkation** *n* pendaratan

disengage *v* melepaskan, membebaskan; **disengagement** *n* pelepasan, pembebasan

disentangle *v* menguraikan

disgrace *n* aib, malu; *in* ~ kena aib; *v* mencoreng muka, memalukan; **disgraceful** *adj* memalukan

disguise *n* [disgaiz] samaran; *in* ~ menyamar; *v* menyamar, menyembunyikan

disgust *n* rasa muak; *v* menjijikkan, memuakkan; ~ed muak

dish *n* piring, pinggan; sajian, hidangan; ~*cloth* lap piring

disheartened *adj* kehilangan semangat; **disheartening** *adj* mengecewakan

dishonest *adj* [disonest] tidak jujur, suka bohong; **dishonesty** *n* ketidakjujuran

dishonor *n* [disonor] aib, malu; *v* memalukan

dishwasher *n* mesin pencuci piring; **dishwater** *n* air bekas cuci piring ← **dish**

disillusion *v* mengecewakan; ~ed kecewa, tidak percaya lagi

disinclined *adj* enggan, segan

disinfect *v* membasmi kuman; **disinfection** *n* pembasmian kuman

disinherit *v* mencabut hak warisan; ~ed tercabut hak warisannya

disinterested *adj* tidak memihak, obyektif

disjointed *adj* terpotong-potong, terputus-putus

disk → **disc**; **diskette** *n* disket

dislike n ketidaksukaan; v tidak suka

dislocate v keluar dari tempat-nya, tergelincir; **dislocation** n dislokasi

dislodge v mengeluarkan, mencabut

disloyal adj tidak setia; **disloyalty** n ketidaksetiaan

dismantle v membongkar

dismay n kecemasan; v mencemaskan; ~ed cemas

dismiss v menolak; membubarkan, memecat; **dismissal** n pembubaran, pemecatan; **dismissive** adj tidak mau mendengar

dismount v turun (dari kuda)

disobedience n ketidakpatuhan; **disobedient** adj tidak patuh, nakal; **disobey** v melawan, tidak mematuhi

disorder n kekacauan; penyakit; **disorderly** adj kacau

disown v tidak mengakui

disparate adj [disparat] tidak sama; **disparity** n selisih, ketidaksamaan, perbedaan

dispassionate adj tidak berpihak

dispatch n pengiriman; v mengirimkan

dispensary n apotik

dispensation n kelonggaran, dispensasi

dispenser n alat atau mesin dengan persediaan; water ~ tempat akua

dispersal n berhamburnya; **disperse** v berhamburan; bubar, menghamburkan, membubarkan

dispirited adj kecil hati

displace v menggantikan; ~d person pengungsi

display n pameran, pertunjukan; v memperlihatkan, mempertunjukkan, memamerkan

displease v membuat tidak senang atau sakit hati; ~d sakit hati; **displeasing** tidak menyenangkan; **displeasure** n ketidaksenangan

disposal n persediaan; pembuangan; **dispose** ~ of membuang; menjual

disposed adj cenderung; **disposition** n kepribadian, kecenderungan

dispossess v menyita, mencabut hak milik

disproportionate adj [disproporsyionet] tidak sebanding

disprove v [dispruv] membantah, menyangkal; membuktikan salah

dispute n perselisihan, percekcokan; v membantah; mempermasalahkan

disqualified adj dinyatakan tidak berhak atau keluar, dibatalkan

disregard n sikap acuh, pengabaian; v tidak mengindahkan, mengabaikan

disreputable adj bernama buruk; **disrepute** n nama buruk

disrespect n sikap tidak hormat; **disrespectful** adj tidak hormat

dissatisfaction n ketidakpuasan, kekecewaan; **dissatisfy** v membuat tidak puas, mengecewakan

dissect *v* [daisékt] membedah, membelah; **dissection** *n* pembedahan

dissent *n* ketidaksetujuan, perbedaan pendapat; **dissenter** *n* orang yang berbeda pendapat

dissident *n* orang yang melawan kekuasaan

dissimilar *adj* tidak sama, berbeda

dissolve *v* larut; melarutkan

dissuade *v* meminta agar jangan

distance *n* jarak, kejauhan; *in the ~* dari kejauhan; **distant** *adj* jauh

distaste *n* rasa tidak suka; **distasteful** *adj* memuakkan

distill *v* menyuling; **distillation** *n* penyulingan, distilasi

distinct *adj* jelas, kentara; **distinction** *n* perbedaan; nilai unggul; **distinctly** *adv* secara jelas

distinguish *v* membedakan; ~*ed* terhormat, ternama

distorted *adj* berubah; diubah; **distortion** *n* distorsi

distract *v* mengalihkan perhatian; menyesatkan; ~*ed* tersesat, bingung; **distraction** *n* selingan; gangguan, kesesatan

distress *n* kesulitan, kesusahan; ~*ed* menderita

distribute *v* menyebarluaskan, menyiarkan, membagikan, mendistribusikan; **distribution** *n* penyebarluasan, pendistribusian; penyiaran; pembagian; penyaluran, distribusi; **distributor** *n* penyalur, pengecer

district *n, adj* distrik, daerah; ~ *court* pengadilan wilayah, pengadilan negeri

disturb *v* mengganggu; **disturbance** *n* kekacauan, kegaduhan, gangguan

disunited *adj* tidak bersatu, tercerai-berai; **disunity** *n* keadaan tidak bersatu

ditch *n* selokan, parit; *v, sl* membuang, meninggalkan

ditto *adj* sama

divan *n* dipan, ranjang

dive *v* menyelam, terjun; ~ *bomber* pesawat pengebom; **diver** *n* penyelam; *sky~* penerjun payung; **diving** *n* selam; loncat indah; ~ *board* papan loncat; *sky~* terjun payung

diverge *v* menyimpang; **divergence** *n* penyimpangan, perbedaan; **divergent** *adj* menyimpang, berbeda

diverse *adj* berbagai (macam), aneka, pelbagai; **diversion** *n* sesuatu yang mengalihkan perhatian; hiburan; **diversity** *n* keanekaragaman; **divert** *v* menangkis, mengalihkan perhatian; menghibur

divide *n* jurang, kesenjangan; *v* membagi; **divisive** *adj* bersifat memecah-belahkan

divine *adj* ilahi; hebat; **divinity** *n* ketuhanan

division *n* pembagian; bagian; divisi

divorce *n* perceraian; *v* bercerai; **divorced** *adj* cerai; **divorcée** *n* janda

divulge *v* membuka rahasia

DIY *abbrev do it yourself* barang

yang dirakit atau dikerjakan sendiri

dizziness *n* rasa pusing; **dizzy** *adj* pusing (kepala), pening, bingung

DJ *abbrev disc jockey* DJ

Djibouti *n* [Jibuti] Djibouti; **Djiboutian** *n* orang Djibouti

do *v* [du] **did done** [dan] berbuat, bikin; membuat, melakukan, mengerjakan; ~ *up* memperbaiki, mempercantik; ~ *without* jalan tanpa; *how do you* ~ apa kabar; ~ *your best* kerjakan sebaik-baiknya

docile *adj* jinak, mudah diajar

dock *n* galangan, dok; **docker** *n* buruh pelabuhan; **dockyard** *n* galangan

doctor *n* dokter; doktor (S3); **doctorate** *n* gelar S3

doctrine *n* ajaran, doktrin

document *n* surat, dokumen; *v* mendokumentasi; **documentary** *n* film dokumenter; **documentation** *n* catatan, dokumentasi

dodge *v* mengelakkan, menghindar

dodgem ~ *car* bom-bom car

doe *n* [do] rusa betina; ~-*eyed* bermata besar

dog *n* anjing; ~-*eared* kertas yang sudutnya terlipat; ~ *paddle* berenang seperti anjing; ~-*tired* capek sekali; *in the* ~*house* sedang diacuhkan

dog *v* membuntuti, selalu menjadi masalah; **dogged** *adj* [doged] berkeras kepala, nekat

dogma *n* dogma, kepercayaan agama; **dogmatic** *adj* fanatik mengikuti ajaran

doing *n* perbuatan; *v what are you* ~? sedang apa? → **do**

dole *n* tunjangan pengangguran; *on the* ~ sedang menganggur

doleful *adj* murung

doll *n* boneka; ~'s *house* rumah boneka; **dolly** *n, child* boneka

dollar *n* dolar; *US* ~ dolar AS

dolphin *n* [dolfin] lumba-lumba

domain *n* daerah, wilayah

dome *n* kubah

domestic *adj* dalam negeri, domestik; ~ *servant* pembantu (rumah tangga, PRT), pramuwisma; **domesticate** *v* menjinakkan

dominant *adj* berkuasa, berpengaruh, dominan; **dominance** *n* kekuasaan; **dominate** *v* menguasai, mendominasi; **domination** *n* penguasaan, dominasi

Dominica *n* Dominika; **Dominican** *n* orang Dominika; ~ *Republic* Republik Dominika

domino *n* gaplek, domino; ~ *effect* efek domino

donate *v* menyumbangkan; **donation** *n* sumbangan

done *v, pf* [dan] → **do**

donkey *n* keledai

donor *n* pemberi, donor; *blood* ~ donor darah ← **donate**

donut *n* donat

don't *v* jangan ← **do**

doodle *n* coretan, lukisan iseng; *v* mencoret-coret

doom *n* malapetaka, ajal; ~*ed* bernasib sial

door *n* pintu; ~*bell* bel (pintu); ~*man* petugas pembuka pintu; ~*mat* keset; ~*step* ambang pintu; ~*way* pintu; *trap*~ pintu di lantai atau langit-langit

dope *n, sl* obat-obatan, obat bius, ganja; orang bodoh; ~ *fiend* pecandu obat; *v* membius, madat; ~ *test* tes darah untuk mengetahui adanya obat-obat terlarang; **dopey** *adj* pusing; tolol; **doping** *n* praktek memakai obat-obat terlarang oleh atlet

dorm, dormitory *n* asrama; ~ *suburb* daerah perumahan yang cukup jauh dari kota

dosage *n* takaran, dosis; **dose** *n* dosis

dot *n* titik, noktah, percik; *join the* ~*s* menyambung titik; *on the* ~ tepat, pas pada waktunya; *polka* ~ bercorak bulatan besar; **dotty** *adj* pikun

double *adj* [dabel] ganda; kembaran; *v* melipatgandakan; ~ *agent* mata-mata yang bekerja untuk dua pihak; ~ *bed* tempat tidur untuk dua orang; ~*-cross* mengkhianati; ~*-decker (bus)* bis tingkat; *on the* ~ segera

doubt *n* [daut] ragu, keraguan; *v* menyangsikan, meragukan; **doubtful** *adj* sangsi, ragu-ragu; **doubtless** *adj* tidak ragu-ragu, pasti

dough *n* [do] adonan; **doughnut** → **donut**

dove *n* [dav] burung merpati

dowdy *adj* berbaju kuno, tidak menarik

down *n* bulu halus (burung); *adv* di bawah, ke bawah; ~*-hearted* *adj* kecil hati; ~ *and out* melarat, sengsara; ~*-to-earth* sederhana, bersahaja; **down-cast** *adj* murung, sedih; **down-fall** *n* jatuhnya; **downpour** *n* hujan lebat; **downright** *adj* terus terang; **downstairs** *adv* di lantai bawah; **downtown** *adv* di pusat kota; **downward, downwards** *adv* ke bawah

dowry *n* [dauri] mas kawin, mahar

doze *n* tidur sebentar, tidur ayam

dozen *n* [dazen] lusin; ~*s* berpuluh-puluh, puluhan

Dr *Doctor* dr (dokter)

draft *n* rancangan; wajib militer; *bank* ~ wesel; *v* merancang; memanggil untuk wajib militer; *Ian didn't get* ~*ed* Ian tidak dipanggil untuk wajib militer

drag *n* gaya tolak; *v* menyeret, menarik

dragon *n* naga

dragonfly *n* capung

drain *n* saluran, parit, got; kali; aliran; *v* menguras, mengalirkan, mengeringkan; ~*ed* capek, lemas; **drainage** *n* saluran, drainase; **drainer** *n* rak piring

drama *n* seni peran, drama, sandiwara; **dramatic** *adj* mengesankan, dramatis; **dramatically** *adv* secara mengesankan

drank *v, pf* → **drink**

drastic *adj* drastis, radikal; **drastically** *adv* secara drastis

draught *n* [draft] angin (di dalam bangunan); sejenis bir; ~ *horse* kuda pedati; **draughtsman** *n* juru gambar, perancang; **draughty** *adj* berangin

draw *v* **drew drawn** menggambar; menarik; **drawback** *n* kekurangan, sisi buruk; **drawer** *n* laci; *chest of* ~s (lemari) laci; **drawing** *n* lukisan, gambar; ~ *room arch* kamar penerima tamu

dread *n* [dréd] ketakutan, rasa takut; *v* takut; **dreadful** *adj* menakutkan, dahsyat

dream *n* mimpi, impian; *v* mimpi; bermimpi, mengimpikan; **dreamer** *n* pemimpi; orang yang melamun

dreary *adj* berawan; suram, redup

dredge *n* kapal keruk; *v* mengeruk

dregs *n, pl* sisa (minyak, kopi)

drench *v* membasahi; ~*ed* basah kuyup

dress *n* rok; pakaian, baju, kostum; *v* berpakaian, mengenakan pakaian; menghiasi; ~ *pattern* pola pakaian, patron; ~ *rehearsal* gladi resik, gladi bersih; ~ *up* berdandan, berpakaian formal; **dressing** *n* perban; saus (untuk salada); ~ *gown* kimono; **dressmaker** *n* tukang jahit; **dressy** *adj* bergaya formal

drew *v, pf* → **draw**

drift *n* arus, aliran, arah; *v* terbawa arus, terhanyut; **drifter** *n* orang tanpa pekerjaan atau rumah tetap, gelandangan; **driftwood** *n* kayu yang terbawa arus

drill *n* bor; latihan; *v* mengebor; melatih

drink *n* **drank drunk** minuman; *v* minum, meminum; **drinker** *n* peminum; *heavy* ~ peminum berat

drip *n* tetes, tetesan; *v* menetes; ~-*dry* tidak perlu disetrika

drive *n* **drove driven** [drivven] semangat, dorongan; *v* menjalankan atau membawa (mobil), mengemudikan, menyupir; **driver** *n* supir, sopir, pengemudi, pengendara (mobil); kusir, sais (kendaraan berkuda); ~'s *license* surat izin mengemudi (SIM); *engine* ~, *train* ~ masinis; **driveway** *n* jalanan masuk halaman untuk mobil; **driving** *adj* mendorong; ~ *lesson* les mengemudi; ~ *rain* hujan deras

drizzle *n, v* hujan rintik-rintik

droll *adj* lucu, ironis

drone *n* dengung; lebah jantan yang pekerja; *v* berdengung, mendengung

droop *v* merana, lemas; **droopy** *adj* berjuntai

drop *n* titik, tetes; *cough* ~ permen obat batuk; *v* jatuh, turun, terjun; menjatuhkan, menurunkan; ~ *a hint* mengingatkan; ~ *a line* mengirim surat; ~ *by,* ~ *in* mampir

drought *n* [draut] masa kering tanpa hujan

drove *v, pf* → **drive**

drover *n* gembala

drown *v* tenggelam; menenggelamkan; *Andy nearly ~ed* Andy nyaris mati tenggelam

drowsy *adj* mengantuk

drudge *v* tugas yang melelahkan

drug *n* obat (bius), obat-obatan; *v* membius; *~store* toko kecil; apotik

drum *n* gendang, tambur; *ear~* gendang telinga; *v* mengetuk; **drummer** *n* penabuh

drunk *n* mabuk; *v, pf →* **drink**; **drunkard** *n* peminum, pemabuk

dry *adj* kering, haus; membosankan; *v* menjemur, mengeringkan; *~-cleaning* binatu, waserai; *~ season* musim kemarau; **dryer** *n* alat atau mesin pengering; *clothes ~* mesin pengering baju; *hair ~* pengering rambut

dual *adj* dwi, (rangkap) dua

dub *v* menyulih-suarakan; **dubbing** *n* sulih suara

dubious *adj* ragu-ragu, meragukan

duck *n* itik, bebek; *v* berjongkok menghindari; **duckling** *n* anak itik

due *adj* jatuh tempo; perlu, wajib; *in ~ time* pada waktunya; *the train is ~ at 12* kereta api dijadwalkan masuk jam 12; **dues** *n, pl* bea, cukai

dug *v, pf →* **dig**; **dugout** *n* bungker; *~ canoe* kano yang terukir dari sepotong kayu

dull *adj* dof; bodoh, dungu

dumb *adj* bisu; bodoh; *~-bell* halter; **dumbfound** *v* membuat

tercengang; *~ed* tercengang

dummy *n* manekin, orang-orangan; *n, adj* tiruan

dump *n* (*rubbish*) *~* tempat pembuangan sampah, tempat pembuangan akhir (TPA); *~ truck* truk sampah; *v* membuang; **dumpster** *n* tong sampah yang besar

dumpling *n* pangsit

dunce *n* orang bodoh; *~'s cap arch* topi kertas dikenakan pada murid yang menjawab salah

dune *n* bukit pasir

dung *n* tahi, pupuk; *~ beetle* semacam kumbang tahi; **dunghill** *n* timbunan tahi

dungeon *n* [danjen] sel bawah tanah

dupe *v* menipu, mengibuli

duplicate *n* rangkap kedua, salinan, kopi, duplikat; *v* membuat kopi atau rangkap

durability *n* keawetan, daya tahan; **durable** *adj* awet

duration *n* lamanya

during *conj, prep* selama, sementara

dusk *n* senja

dust *n* abu, debu; *v* membersihkan, menghilangkan debu; *~ jacket* sampul buku; **dustbin** *n* tempat sampah; **duster** *n* lap debu, penyapu; **dusty** *adj* berdebu

Dutch *n* bahasa Belanda; *adj* berasal dari Belanda; *double-~* kata-kata yang tidak bisa dimengerti; *to go ~* membayar masing-masing; **Dutchman** *n, m*

lelaki Belanda; **Dutchwoman**
n, f wanita Belanda

dutiful *adj* patuh, menurut; **duty**
n kewajiban; pekerjaan, tugas;
bea; ~ *free* bebas bea cukai

dwarf *n* katai, cebol; *v* tampak
jauh lebih besar daripada

dwell *v* berdiam, tinggal;
dwelling *n* tempat tinggal

dwindle *v* berangsur-angsur
berkurang, surut, susut

dye *n* zat pewarna; *natural* ~ zat
pewarna alam; *v* mencelupkan,
mengecat (rambut)

dyke *n, sl* lesbi, orang lesbian

dynamic *adj* dinamis, hidup

dynamite *n* dinamit, bahan
peledak

dynamo *n* dinamo

dynasty *n* keluarga, dinasti

dysentery *n* disentri

E

each *adj* masing-masing; tiap-
tiap, saban; ~ *other* saling, satu
sama lain

eager *adj* ingin sekali, pengen;
eagerness *n* keinginan yang
besar

eagle *n* burung rajawali; ~-*eyed*
bermata tajam

ear *n* telinga, kuping; **eardrum** *n*
gendang telinga

early *adj* [érli] pagi-pagi, dini; ~
next month awal bulan depan;
~ *bird* orang yang bangun pagi

atau cepat datang

earn *v* [érn] mendapat gaji,
memperoleh

earnest *adj* [érnest] sungguh-
sungguh; *in* ~ sungguh-sungguh

earnings *n, pl* pendapatan, gaji,
upah ← **earn**

earplug *n* penyumbat telinga

earring *n* anting ← **ear**

earth *n* [érth] bumi, dunia; tanah,
debu; *on* ~ di dunia; *planet* ~
Bumi; *down to* ~ sederhana,
bersahaja; **earthenware** *n*
tembikar; **earthquake** *n* gempa
bumi

ease *n* kemudahan, kesenangan;
at ~ tenang, santai; *v* mempermudah, meringankan

easel *n* kuda-kuda

east *adj* timur; *the Far* ~ Asia;
the Middle ~ Timur Tengah
(Timteng); ~ *Timor* Timor Loro
Sae; *arch* Timor Timur (Timtim)

Easter *n* Paskah; ~ *Monday* hari
Senin sesudah Paskah; *the* ~
Bunny kelinci yang mem-
bagikan telur coklat kepada
anak-anak

easterly ~ *(wind)* angin dari arah
timur; **eastern** *adj* (daerah)
timur; **eastward** *adv* ke (arah)
timur ← **east**

easy *adj* mudah, gampang; ~
chair kursi malas; ~-*going*
bersikap santai; *take it* ~ tenang
← **ease**

eat *v* **ate eaten** makan

eaves *n, pl* ujung bawah atap;
eavesdrop *v* menguping;

eavesdropper *n* orang yang suka menguping

ebb *v* surut; ~ *tide* air surut; ~ *and flow* pasang surut

ebony *n* kayu eboni

eccentric *adj* [éksentrik] aneh, antik

echo *n* [éko] gema, gaung, kumandang; *v* bergema, bergaung, berkumandang

éclair *n* semacam kue berisi krim

eclipse *n* gerhana; *lunar* ~ gerhana bulan; *solar* ~ gerhana matahari

ecological *adj* berkaitan dengan ekologi; **ecology** *n* ekologi

economic *adj* berkaitan dengan ekonomi; **economical** *adj* hemat, ekonomis; **economics** *n* ilmu ekonomi; **economist** *n* ekonom; **economize** *v* menghemat; **economy** *n* ekonomi, dunia usaha; kehematan; *planned* ~ ekonomi berencana

ecstasy *n* kegembiraan, kebahagiaan; ekstasi; **ecstatic** *adj* sangat gembira atau bahagia

Ecuador *n* Ekuador; **Ecuadorian** *n* orang Ekuador; *adj* berasal dari Ekuador

eczema *n* eksema

ed. *editor, edition* red. (redaksi); edisi, cetakan

eddy *n* pusaran air

edge *n* [éj] pinggir, sisi, tepi; mata (pisau); *on* ~ tegang; **edgy** *adj* tegang, suka marah

edible *adj* dapat dimakan;

edibles *n, pl* makanan

edit *v* menyunting, mengedit; **edition** *n* terbitan, keluaran, edisi, cetakan; **editor** *n* redaktur, penyunting, editor; ~-*in-chief* pemimpin redaksi; **editorial** *n* tajuk rencana; ~ *board* dewan redaksi

educate *v* mendidik; **education** *n* pendidikan; *primary* ~ sekolah dasar; **educational** *adj* mendidik, edukatif; **educator** *n* pendidik, pengajar, guru

EEC *abbrev European Economic Community* MEE (Masyarakat Ekonomi Eropa)

eel *n* [iel] belut, lindung

eerie *adj* ngeri

effect *n* pengaruh, efek; akibat, hasil; **effects** *n, pl* barang-barang, harta milik; *v* mengerjakan, mengadakan; **effective** *adj* berhasil, efektif

effeminate *adj* seperti perempuan

efficiency *n* daya guna, efisiensi; **efficient** *adj* berdaya guna, tepat guna, efisien; **efficiently** *adv* secara efisien

effort *n* usaha, upaya; **effortless** *adj* dengan mudah

eg *exempli gratia = for example* mis., (seperti) misalnya

egalitarian *adj* egaliter, percaya bahwa semua orang sederajat

egg *n* telur; ~ *cup* tempat telur rebus; ~ *white* putih telur; *quail's* ~ telur puyuh; **eggplant** *n* terong; **eggshell** *n* kulit telur

ego *n* [igo] ego; **egoism** *n* egoisme; **egoist** *adj* egois; **egotis-**

tic, egotistical *adj* egois, suka mementingkan diri sendiri

Egypt *n* [Ijipt] Mesir; *ancient ~* Mesir Kuno; **Egyptian** *n* orang Mesir; *adj* berasal dari Mesir

eight *adj, n* [éit] delapan; **eighteen** *adj, n* delapan belas; **eighteenth** *adj* kedelapan belas; **eighth** *adj* kedelapan; **eighty** *adj, n* delapan puluh

either *adj* [ither, aither] salah satu; ~ ... or ... ... atau...; *I don't like ~* dua-duanya saya tidak suka

ejaculate *v* berseru; **ejaculation** *n* ejakulasi

eject *v* mengeluarkan, mengusir

elaborate *v* menguraikan, menjelaskan secara panjang lebar; *adj* rumit, panjang lebar, teliti; **elaboration** *n* penjelasan, perincian

elapse *v* lewat, berlalu

elastic *n* karet; *adj* karet, kenyal, elastis

elated *adj* bahagia; **elation** *n* kegembiraan

elbow *n* siku; *v* menyikut; ~ *grease* bekerja keras

elder *n* yang lebih tua; sesepuh; *adj* kakak; ~ *brother* kakak (laki-laki); **elderly** *adj* sepuh, sudah tua; **eldest** *n* anak sulung; *adj* paling tua, sulung

elect *v* memilih; **election** *n* pemilihan; *general ~* pemilihan umum (pemilu); **elective** *n* mata pelajaran pilihan; **elector** *n* pemilih; **electoral** ~ *roll* daftar pemilih

electric *adj* listrik; *the ~ chair* kursi listrik; **electrical** *adj* (berkaitan dengan) listrik; ~ *engineering* teknik elektro; **electrician** *n* tukang listrik; **electricity** *n* listrik; **electrocute** *v* menyetrum

electron *n* elektron; **electronic** *adj* elektronik; **electronics** *n, pl* barang elektronik, elektronika

elegance *n* keanggunan; **elegant** *adj* anggun, elok

element *n* unsur, bagian, bahan, elemen; *(periodic) table of ~s* tabel periodik; **elementary** *adj* dasar; ~ *school* sekolah dasar (SD)

elephant *n* [élefant] gajah; *white ~* barang tidak berguna

elevate *v* menaikkan, mengangkat; **elevation** *n* ketinggian; **elevator** *n* lift

eleven *adj, n* sebelas; **eleventh** *adj* kesebelas; *at the ~ hour* pada saat terakhir

elf *n* **elves** peri; **elfin** *adj* mungil, seperti peri

elicit *v* memperoleh (arti), mengeluarkan

eligibility *n* memenuhi syarat; kepantasan; **eligible** *adj* memenuhi syarat, dapat dipilih

eliminate *v* menyisihkan, menyingkirkan; **elimination** *n* penyisihan, eliminasi; ~ *round* babak penyisihan

elite *the ~* para elit, kaum atas; *adj* elit

ellipse *n* bulat panjang, elips

elope *v* kawin lari

eloquence *n* kefasihan, kepandaian bicara; **eloquent** *adj* fasih, pandai bicara

El Salvador *n* El Salvador; **Salvadorean** *n* orang El Salvador; *adj* berasal dari El Salvador

else *adv* lain; *or* ~ jika tidak; *someone* ~ orang lain; *what* ~ apa lagi; **elsewhere** *adv* di lain tempat

elucidate *v* menjelaskan, menerangkan; **elucidation** *n* penjelasan, keterangan

elude *v* menghindar dari, menghindari, mengelak

emaciated *adj* sangat kurus, ceking

emanate *v* berasal atau keluar dari

emancipate *v* memerdekakan, membebaskan; **emancipation** *n* kemerdekaan, pembebasan

embalm *v* membalsem; **embalming** *n* pembalseman

embankment *n* tepi

embark *v* naik (kendaraan); **embarkation** *n* naiknya, embarkasi

embarrass *v* memalukan, mempermalukan; **embarrassment** *n* keadaan yang membuat malu, rasa malu

embassy *n* kedutaan

embellish *v* menghiasi, membesar-besarkan, membumbui; **embellishment** *n* perhiasan

embers *n, pl* bara

embezzle *v* menggelapkan; **embezzlement** *n* korupsi, penggelapan uang

embittered *adj* dendam, sakit hati

emblem *n* lambang, tanda

embrace *n* pelukan; *v* memeluk

embroider *v* menyulam, membordir; membesar-besarkan; **embroidery** *n* sulaman, bordiran

embryo *n* [émbrio] janin; **embryonic** *adj* masih sangat kecil

emerald *n* zamrud; *adj* hijau

emerge *v* [emérj] timbul, muncul; **emergence** *n* timbulnya, munculnya

emergency *n* [emérjénsi] keadaaan darurat; ~ *brake* rem bahaya; ~ *exit* pintu darurat

emergent *adj* [emérjent] sedang muncul, naik daun ← **emerge**

emery [émeri] ~ *board* kertas ampelas, amril

emigrant *n* emigran; **emigrate** *v* pindah, beremigrasi; **emigration** *n* emigrasi

eminent *adj* [éminent] ternama, terpandang, unggul

emission *n* pancaran, buangan, emisi; **emit** *v* memancarkan, mengeluarkan

emotion *n* perasaan, emosi; **emotional** *adj* emosi

emperor *n* kaisar ← **empire**

emphasis *n* [émfasis] tekanan; **emphasize** *v* menekankan, menitikberatkan; **emphatic** *adj* tegas, kuat

empire *n* kekaisaran, kerajaan; *the British* ~ kerajaan Inggris

employ *v* mempekerjakan;

menggunakan, memakai;
employee *n* pegawai, buruh,
pekerja, karyawan, karyawati;
employer *n* majikan; **employment** *n* pekerjaan

empower *v* memperdayakan;
empowerment *n* pemberdayaan; ~ *of women* pemberdayaan perempuan

empress *n, f* kaisar wanita ←
empire

emptiness *n* kekosongan,
kehampaan; **empty** *adj* kosong,
hampa; *v* mengosongkan;
~-*headed* bodoh

emulate *v* berusaha menyaingi
atau melebihi

enable *v* [enébel] memungkinkan

enamel *n* glasir, cat halus; email;
nail ~ cat kuku, kutek

enact *v* menjadikan

encephalitis *n* radang otak

enchant *v* memesonakan,
memikat, menyihir; **enchant-
ment** *n* sihir

encircle *v* mengepung, mengelilingi, melingkari

enclave *n* daerah kantung

enclose *v* memagari; melampirkan, menyertakan; **enclo-
sure** *n* kandang

encounter *n* pertemuan; *v* bertemu, berjumpa

encourage *v* [énkarej] mendorong, mendukung, memberi
semangat, membesarkan hati;
encouraging *adj* menggembirakan; **encouragement** *n*
dorongan, desakan

encumber *v* membebani;
encumbrance *n* beban

encyclopedia *n* ensiklopedi

end *n* akhir, ujung; *loose ~s*
urusan yang belum selesai; *The
~ tamat*; *at a loose ~* bosan,
tanpa kegiatan; *in the ~*
akhirnya; *v* berakhir; menyudahi; mengakhiri

endanger *v* [endéinjer] membahayakan, mengancam; *~ed
species* binatang yang terancam
punah

endear *~ yourself* membuat dirinya disayangi; **endearing** *adj*
manis, lucu

endeavor *n* [endévor] usaha; *v*
berusaha, mencoba

endless *adj* tanpa ujung, tiada
hentinya, tidak ada akhirnya,
tak terhingga, tidak berkeputusan ← **end**

endorse *v* menyokong, mendukung; **endorsement** *n*
dukungan

endowed *adj* diberkati, dianuge-
rahi; **endowment** *n* tunjangan

endurance *n* daya tahan;
endure *v* bertahan; menahan,
menderita, menempuh

enema *n* obat urus-urus, obat
pencahar

enemy *n* musuh, seteru; *arch ~*
musuh bebuyutan

energetic *adj* [énerjétik] energik,
bersemangat; **energy** *n* tenaga,
usaha; *geothermal ~* tenaga
panas bumi; *hydro-electric ~*
tenaga air; *nuclear ~* tenaga
nuklir

enforce *v* menjalankan, melaksanakan; menegakkan; **enforcement** *n* penegakan; *law* ~ penegakan hukum

engage *v* memasang; ~d bertunangan; **engagement** *n* janji; pertunangan; *to have a prior* ~ terlanjur janji

engender *v* melahirkan, menimbulkan

engine *n* [énjin] mesin; ~ *driver* masinis; *train* ~ lokomotif, lok; **engineer** *n* insinyur; masinis; *v* merekayasa; **engineering** *n* ilmu teknik, rekayasa; *civil* ~ teknik mesin; *electrical* ~ teknik elektro; *genetic* ~ rekayasa genetik

England *n* [Ingland] Inggris; **English** *n* bahasa Inggris; *adj* berasal dari Inggris; **Englishman** *n, m* lelaki Inggris; **Englishwoman** *n, f* perempuan Inggris

engrave *v* mengukir atau melukis pada batu atau logam; menggoreskan; **engraver** *n* pengukir, pelukis; **engraving** *n* etsa

enhance *v* meningkatkan; ~d lebih jelas; **enhancement** *n* peningkatan, perbaikan

enigma *n* teka-teki; **enigmatic** *adj* misterius

enjoy *v* menikmati; ~ *yourself* bersenang-senang; **enjoyable** *adj* menyenangkan; **enjoyment** *n* kenikmatan, kesenangan

enlarge *v* membesarkan, memperbesar, memperluas;

enlargement *n* pembesaran

enlighten *v* [énlaiten] memperjelas, memberi keterangan; **enlightenment** *the* ~ Masa Pencerahan

enlist *v* mendaftarkan; **enlistment** *n* pendaftaran

enormous *adj* sangat besar; **enormity** *n* besarnya

enough *adj* [enaf] cukup, sudah

enrage *v* menimbulkan atau membuat marah; ~d marah, berang

enrich *v* memperkaya; **enrichment** *n* pengayaan; *uranium* ~ pengayaan uranium

enroll *v* mendaftarkan; **enrolled** *adj* terdaftar; **enrollment** *n* pendaftaran

ensign *n* [ensain] bendera

ensue *v* [énsiu] terjadi

ensure *v* memastikan, menjamin

enter *v* masuk; memasuki, memasukkan

enterprise *n* perusahaan, usaha; **enterprising** *adj* yang mengambil inisiatif, yang berusaha

entertain *v* menghibur; **entertainer** *n* artis, penghibur; **entertainment** *n* hiburan

enthusiasm *n* semangat, gairah, antusiasme, gelora; kegemaran, hobi; **enthusiastic** *adj* antusias, bersemangat

entice *v* membujuk; **enticement** *n* tawaran, bujukan

entire *adj* seluruh, seantero; **entirely** *adv* benar-benar

entitled *adj* berhak

entourage *n* [onturaj] rombongan,

para pengiring

entrails *n, pl* isi perut, jeroan

entrance *n* pintu masuk ← **enter**

entrepreneur *n* [ontreprenur] pengusaha, wiraswasta; **entrepreneurial** *adj* berjiwa pengusaha, berjiwa pedagang

entrust *v* memercayakan kepada

entry *n* jalan masuk, pintu masuk; pembukuan; masukan, kata kepala ← **enter**

enunciate *v* melafalkan, mengucapkan; **enunciation** *n* lafal, pengucapan

envelop *v* menyelubungi, menyampuli; **envelope** *n* amplop

envious *adj* iri ← **envy**

environs *in the* ~ sekitar, sekeliling, dekat; **environment** *n* lingkungan; **environmental** *adj* berkaitan dengan lingkungan; ~*ly friendly* ramah lingkungan; **environmentalist** *n* aktivis lingkungan

envoy *n* utusan

envy *n* (rasa) iri

epic *n* cerita panjang, epik; *adj* hebat, patut dikenang

epicenter *n* titik pusat gempa bumi, episentrum

epidemic *n* wabah

epilepsy *n* penyakit ayan, epilepsi, sawan; **epileptic** *n* penderita penyakit ayan

epilogue *n* kata penutup, epilog

episode *n* bagian (waktu), episode

equal *n* [ikuel] bandingan; *v* menyamai, menyamakan; *adj* sama, setara; **equality** *n* kesamaan; **equalize** *v* menyamakan; **equation** *n* persamaan; *chemical* ~ persamaan kimia

equator *n* katulistiwa; **equatorial** *adj* berhubungan dengan katulistiwa; ~ *Guinea* Guinea Katulistiwa

equestrian *n* atlet penunggang kuda; *adj* berkaitan dengan penunggangan kuda

equilateral *adj* sama sisi; ~ *triangle* segi tiga sama sisi

equilibrium *n* keseimbangan

equine *adj* berkaitan dengan kuda

equinox *n* saat malam dan siang sama panjangnya

equip *v* melengkapi; **equipment** *n* perlengkapan; *play* ~ tempat bermain anak-anak, ayunan

equitable *adj* adil; **equity** *n* keadilan

equivalent *n* yang sama atau setara; *adj* sama harga atau nilainya

equivocal *adj* ambivalen, tidak berpihak

era *n* [ira] masa, zaman, era

eradicate *v* membasmi; **eradication** *n* pembasmian

erase *v* menghapus; **eraser** *n* penghapus; *board* ~ penghapus papan

erect *v* mendirikan, membangun; *adj* tegak, tegang; **erection** *n* pembangunan; ereksi

Eritrea *n* Eritrea; **Eritrean** *n* orang Eritrea; *adj* berasal dari Eritrea

erode *v* mengikis; **erosion** *n* kikisan, erosi

erotic *adj* erotis, merangsang

err *v* berbuat salah

errand *n* urusan, pesan

erratic *adj* tidak menentu, tidak teratur

error *n* salah, kesalahan ← **err**

erupt *v* meletus; **eruption** *n* letusan, erupsi

escalate *v* naik, tambah; meningkatkan; **escalator** *n* tangga berjalan, eskalator

escape *n* pelarian; *v* melarikan diri, kabur, menghindari; **escapee** *n* buronan

escort *n* pendamping, rombongan; *v* mendampingi, mengiringi; ~ *agency* jasa wanita penghibur

ESP *abbrev* extra-sensory perception indera keenam

especially *adv* khususnya, terutama ← **special**

Esperanto *n* bahasa Esperanto

espionage *n* [éspionaj] pengintaian, spionase

essay *n* karangan; *to write an* ~ membuat karangan

essence *n* inti, sari, esensi; **essential** *adj* mutlak; ~ *oil* minyak esensial

establish *v* mendirikan, mengadakan; menentukan, menetapkan; **establishment** *n* pendirian, penentuan, penetapan; pembangunan

estate *n* tanah milik; kebun, perkebunan

esteem *n* hormat, kehormatan; *held in high* ~ dipandang dengan hormat; ~*ed* terhormat

estimate *n* taksiran, anggaran, perkiraan; pendapat; *v* menaksir, memperkirakan; ~*d time of arrival (ETA)* perkiraan waktu kedatangan

Estonia *n* Estonia; **Estonian** *n* bahasa Estonia; *adj* orang Estonia

estranged *adj* [estrénjd] terpisah, menjadi asing

estuary *n* muara, kuala

ETA *abbrev* estimated time of arrival perkiraan waktu kedatangan

etc *et cetera* dll (dan lain-lain), dsb (dan sebagainya)

eternal *adj* abadi, kekal; **eternity** *n* keabadian, kekekalan

ethical *adj* etis; ~ *Policy* Politik Etis; **ethics** *n, pl* etika

Ethiopia *n* Etiopia; **Ethiopian** *n* orang Etiopia; *adj* berasal dari Etiopia

ethnic *adj* etnis, kesukuan; tradisional; ~ *group* suku (bangsa), kelompok etnis; **ethnicity** *n* kesukuan, asal-usul

etiquette *n* tata cara, sopan santun, etiket

EU *abbrev* European Union UE (Uni Eropa)

eulogy *n* [yuloji] pujian

euphemism *n* kata pengganti yang lebih sopan atau lembut; **euphemistic** *adj* yang memakai kata lebih sopan

euthanasia *n* [yutanésia] mencabut jiwa karena belas kasihan, eutanasia, mati tenang

Europe *n* [Yurop] Eropa; *Eastern* ~ Eropa Timur; **European** *n*

orang Eropa; *adj* berasal dari Eropa; ~ *Economic Community* Masyarakat Ekonomi Eropa; ~ *Union* Uni Eropa

evacuate *v* mengungsi; mengungsikan; **evacuation** *n* pengungsian, evakuasi; **evacuee** *n* pengungsi

evade *v* mengelakkan

evaluate *v* menilai; **evaluation** *n* evaluasi, penilaian

evangelical *adj* yang menyebarkan agama Kristen; **evangelist** *n* penyebar agama Kristen

evaporate *v* menguap; evaporation; *n* penguapan

evasion *n* [ivéisyon] pengelakan; penghindaran; *tax* ~ tidak membayar pajak; **evasive** *adj* mengelak ← **evade**

eve *n* [iv] malam (sebelumnya); *Christmas* ~ malam Natal; *New Year's* ~ Malam Tahun Baru; *on the* ~ *of* malam sebelum; **Eve** *n* Hawa; *Isl* Siti Hawa

even *adj* rata; genap; pun; *prep* bahkan; ~ *if* kalaupun; ~ *though* meskipun; *to get* ~ membalas dendam

evening *n* sore, petang; malam; *good* ~ selamat malam; *this* ~ nanti malam; *yesterday* ~ tadi malam, kemarin malam

event *n* peristiwa, kejadian, acara; ~ *organizer* penyelenggara (acara); *200m freestyle* ~ lomba 200 meter gaya bebas; **eventful** *adj* penuh kejadian; **eventual** *adj* akhir, **eventually** *adv* akhirnya

ever *adj* [éver] pernah; ~ *since* (mulai) sejak; *for* ~ *more* untuk selamanya; *have you* ~? pernahkah?; selalu, senantiasa; *thank you* ~ *so much* terima kasih banyak; **evergreen** *adj* yang tetap hijau dan tidak rontok; **everlasting** *adj* kekal, abadi

every *adj* [évri] setiap, tiap; ~ *day* setiap hari, saban hari; ~ *other day* selang hari; **everybody, everyone** *adj* semua orang, setiap orang; **everyday** *adj* sehari-hari; **everything** *n* semua; **everywhere** *adj* di mana-mana

evict *v* mengusir, menggusurkan; **eviction** *n* pengusiran, penggusuran

evidence *n* bukti; *to give* ~ menjadi saksi; **evident** *adj* jelas, nyata, terang; **evidently** *adv* jelas

evil *n* [ivel] kejahatan; *adj* jahat; *axis of* ~ poros kejahatan

evolution *n* evolusi; **evolve** *v* berkembang

ewe *n* [yu] domba betina

exacerbate *v* [égzaserbét] memperparah, membuat lebih buruk

exact *adj* tepat, persis; betul; **exactly** *adv* persis; **exactness** *n* ketelitian

exaggerate *v* [egzajerét] membesar-besarkan; **exaggeration** *n* pernyataan yang berlebihan

exam, examination *n* ujian; **examine** *v* menguji, memeriksa; **examiner** *n* penguji, pemeriksa

example *n* contoh, teladan; *for ~* (seperti) misalnya, seumpamanya

exasperate *v* menjengkelkan, membuat kesal; **exasperation** *n* kejengkelan, kekesalan

excavate *v* menggali; **excavation** *n* penggalian; **excavator** *n* mesin gali

exceed *v* melebihi, melampaui; **exceedingly** *adv* teramat, sangat

excel *v* unggul; **excellency** *Your ~* Yang Mulia; **excellent** *adj* bagus sekali, hebat

except *prep* kecuali; *v* mengecualikan; *~ing* terkecuali; **exception** *n* kekecualian, pengecualian, eksepsi; **exceptional** *adj* luar biasa, istimewa

excerpt *n* kutipan

excess *n* kelebihan; **excessive** *adj* berlebihan, melampaui batas

exchange *n* pertukaran, penukaran; kurs; kantor telepon; *foreign ~* devisa, mata uang asing; *v* menukar

exchequer [ékséker] *Chancellor of the ~* Menteri Keuangan (Inggris)

excise *n* [éksais] cukai

excite *v* merangsang, membangkitkan; *~d* gembira; **excitement** *n* kegembiraan

exclaim *v* berseru; **exclamation** *n* seruan; *~ mark* tanda seru

exclude *v* mengecualikan; **excluding** *v* tidak termasuk; **exclusion** *n* pengecualian; **exclusive** *adj* eksklusif, elit; *~ to* hanya di; **exclusively** *adv* secara eksklusif; terus-menerus

excrete *v* mengeluarkan cairan; buang air; **excretion** *n* hal buang air

excruciating *adj* sangat menyiksa atau menyakitkan

excursion *n* kunjungan

excuse *n* [ékskyus] alasan, dalih; *v* [ékskyuz] memaafkan; *~ me* permisi

execute *v* melakukan, melaksanakan, mengerjakan; menjalankan keputusan; melakukan hukuman mati; **execution** *n* pelaksanaan (hukuman mati); **executioner** *n* algojo; **executive** *n* pemimpin (harian), eksekutif; *adj* eksekutif

exempt *adj* bebas dari; *v* membebaskan; **exemption** *n* pembebasan, pengecualian

exercise *n* olahraga; latihan, pelajaran; *v* berlatih; melakukan; *~ bike* sepeda stasioner; *~ book* buku tulis

exert *~ yourself* membanting tulang; **exertion** *n* usaha keras

exhale *v* mengeluarkan napas

exhaust *n* [ékshost] asap kendaraan; menyelesaikan sampai tuntas; menguras tenaga; **exhaustion** *n* kecapekan yang luar biasa

exhibit *n* [éksibit] barang yang dipamerkan; *v* mempertunjukkan, memperlihatkan; **exhibition** *n* pameran

exhilarate *v* menyegarkan, menggembirakan; **exhilaration** *n* rasa gembira

exhorbitant *adj* sangat mahal

exile *n* buangan; pembuangan; *v* membuang

exist *v* ada; *it doesn't* ~ tidak ada; **existence** *n* keberadaan; **existent** *adj* yang ada

exit *n* pintu atau jalan keluar; kepergian; *v* pergi keluar

exodus *n* kepergian, eksodus

exonerate *v* membebaskan dari hukuman

exorcise *v* mengusir setan; **exorcist** *n* pengusir setan

exotic *adj* eksotik, dari negeri asing

expand *v* memperluas, mengembangkan; memuai; **expandable** *adj* dapat diperluas; **expanse** *n* luas; **expansion** *n* perluasan, pengembangan

expat, expatriate *n* orang asing, orang yang tinggal di luar negeri, ekspatriat

expect *v* berharap; mengharapkan, menantikan; **expectancy** *n* harapan, pengharapan; *life* ~ harapan hidup; **expectant** *adj* menunggu; ~ *mother* ibu hamil; **expectation** *n* harapan

expedition *n* perjalanan, ekspedisi

expel *v* membuang; mengeluarkan

expend *v* mengeluarkan, membelanjakan, memakai; **expendable** *adj* dapat dipakai habis; **expense** *n* belanja, biaya, ongkos; **expensive** *adj* mahal

experience *n* pengalaman; *v* mengalami; ~*d* berpengalaman

experiment *n* percobaan, uji coba; *v* mengadakan percobaan, menguji coba; **experimental** *adj* bersifat percobaan; **experimentation** *n* percobaan, eksperimentasi

expert *n* ahli, pakar; *adj* ahli

expire *v* kedaluwarsa, jatuh tempo; mati; **expiry** ~ *date* tanggal kedaluwarsa

explain *v* menjelaskan, menerangkan, menyatakan; **explanation** *n* penjelasan; **explanatory** *adj* bersifat menerangkan, menjelaskan

expletive *n* [éksplitif] kata umpatan

explicit *adj* tegas, jelas, eksplisit; ~ *language* kata-kata jorok

explode *v* meletus, meledak

exploit *v* memanfaatkan, mengeksploitasi; **exploitation** *n* eksploitasi

exploration *n* penjelajahan, eksplorasi; **explore** *v* menjelajah; mengadakan penelitian; **explorer** *n* penjelajah

explosion *n* letusan, ledakan; **explosive** *adj* dapat meledak; **explosives** *n*, *pl* bahan peledak ← **explode**

export *n*, *adj* ekspor; *v* mengekspor; **exporter** *n* pengekspor, eksportir

expose *v* menyingkapkan, mempertunjukkan, memamerkan, membuka; **exposure** *n* pembukaan, pencahayaan

express *n* yang cepat, kilat, ekspres; *adj* cepat, kilat; *v* mengucapkan, mengungkapkan, menyatakan, mengutarakan;

expression *n* ucapan, peribahasa; raut muka; **expressive** *adj* ekspresif, menyatakan perasaan

expropriate *v* mengambil, merampas; **expropriation** *n* pengambilan, perampasan

expulsion *n* pengeluaran ← **expel**

exquisite *adj* [ékskuisit] sempurna, indah sekali

extend *v* merentangkan, membentangkan; memperluas; memperpanjang; **extension** *n* perpanjangan; **extensive** *adj* luas, panjang lebar; **extensively** *adv* secara besar-besaran, secara panjang lebar; **extent** *n* luas cakupan, derajat, tingkat; *to what* ~ sejauh mana

extenuating *adj* meringankan

exterior *n* luar, luarnya

exterminate *v* membasmi, memusnahkan; **extermination** *n* pembasmian, pemusnahan

external *adj* (di) luar

extinct *adj* punah; **extinction** *n* pemadaman; kepunahan

extinguish *v* [ékstinguisy] memadamkan; **extinguisher** *n* pemadam api

extol *v* memuji

extortion *n* pemerasan; **extortionate** *adj* sangat mahal

extra *adj* ekstra; *~-curricular* ekskul

extract *n* sari, ekstrak, petikan; *v* mencabut (gigi); mengambil; **extraction** *n* pencabutan; asal; *of Chinese* ~ berdarah Cina

extradite *v* menyerahkan ke negara lain; **extradition** *n* penyerahan, ekstradisi

extraordinary *adj* [ékstrodinari] luar biasa, istimewa

extravagant *adj* boros, berfoya-foya

extreme *adj* terlampau, ekstrem; **extremely** *adv* sangat, teramat; **extremist** *n* fanatik, ekstremis; **extremities** *n, pl* tangan dan kaki

extricate *v* mengeluarkan, membebaskan

exuberance *n* semangat, keriangan; **exuberant** *adj* riang gembira, bersemangat

exultant *adj* sangat bergembira

eye *n* [ai] mata; *black* ~ lebam biru di mata; *v* melirik; *to keep an* ~ *on* mengawasi, menjaga; **eyeball** *n* bola mata; **eyebrow** *n* alis; **eyelash** *n* bulu mata; **eyelid** *n* kelopak mata; **eyesight** *n* penglihatan; **eyesore** *n* yang merusak pemandangan; **eyewitness** *n* saksi mata

F

fable *n* dongeng, cerita rakyat; **fabled** *adj* terkenal, ternama; **fabulous** *adj* hebat

fabric *n* kain, bahan

fabricate *v* membuat, merekayasa, mengarang; ~ *a story* mengarang-ngarang; **fabrication** *n* pembuatan, fabrikasi

fabulous *adj* hebat, menakjubkan

façade [fasad] bagian muka gedung; muka, topeng

face *n* muka, paras, wajah; ~ *value* harga nominal; pada permukaan; *lose* ~ kehilangan muka, malu; *v* menghadapi; ~ *up to it* hadapilah; **facial** *n* perawatan muka, perawatan wajah; *adj* berkaitan dengan muka; ~ *expression* raut wajah

facilitate *v* mempermudah, melaksanakan; **facilitator** *n* pelaksana, pengurus, pengajar; **facility** *n* sarana, fasilitas; kemudahan

facsimile *n* salinan, kopi; ~ *machine* mesin faks → **fax**

fact *n* kenyataan, fakta; *in* ~ sesungguhnya; **factual** *adj* berdasarkan kenyataan

faction *n* fraksi

factor *n* unsur, faktor, elemen

factory *n* pabrik

faculty *n* daya, kemampuan; fakultas; ~ *of Engineering* Fakultas Teknik; ~ *of Medicine* Fakultas Kedokteran

fad *n* tren, mode

fade *v* luntur, pudar; mengecil (suara); **faded** *adj* luntur, pudar, redam

faeces → **feces**

fail *v* gagal; tidak jadi; jatuh; tidak lulus; *without* ~ pasti; **failure** *n* kegagalan, gagalnya

faint *n* pingsan; *v* (jatuh) pingsan; *adj* lemah, kecil; ~*-hearted* cepat takut

fair *n* pameran, pekan raya, pasar malam; *trade* ~ pameran; *adj* adil, berimbang; berkulit atau berambut terang; **fairly** *adv* cukup, agak; dengan adil

fairy *n* peri; *sl* bencong; ~ *floss* kembang gula; ~ *godmother* ibu peri; ~ *tale* dongeng, cerita rakyat; *away with the fairies* melamun; tidak waras

faith *n* iman, kepercayaan; *in good* ~ dengan itikad baik; **faithful** *adj* beriman, setia; **faithfully** *yours* ~ hormat kami

fake *n* tipuan; *v* menirukan, memalsukan; *adj* palsu; ~ *ID* identitas palsu

falcon *n* burung elang

fall *n* kejatuhan, keruntuhan, keguguran; musim gugur, musim rontok; *v* **fell, fallen** jatuh, runtuh, gugur; ~ *ill* jatuh sakit; ~ *apart* pecah; ~ *for* jatuh cinta pada; ~ *under* termasuk; ~ *in love* jatuh cinta

fallacious *adj* salah, keliru, sesat, menyesatkan; **fallacy** *n* kesalahan, kekeliruan

fallen *v, pf* → **fall**

fallible *adj* dapat bersalah

falls *n, pl* air terjun

false *adj* palsu; ~*hood* bohong, dusta; **falsification** *n* pemalsuan; **falsify** *v* memalsukan

falter *v* bergoyang, terputus-putus

fame *n* ketenaran, nama harum; **famed** *adj* tenar, kenamaan, termasyhur, ternama, tersohor

familiar *adj* dikenal; akrab; **family** *n* keluarga; rumah tangga; ~ *planning* keluarga berencana

(KB); ~ *besar* family

famine *n* kelaparan

famous *adj* terkenal, ternama ← **fame**

fan *n* kipas; penggemar, fans; *electric* ~ kipas angin; *v* mengipasi, mengembusi

fanatic *adj* fanatic; **fanaticism** *n* aliran fanatik

fancy *n* khayal, kesukaan, anganangan; *v* menginginkan; *adj* rumit, megah

fang *n* taring

fantastic *adj* ajaib, fantastis, tidak masuk akal; **fantasy** *n* fantasi, khayalan

FAQ *abbrev frequently-asked questions* pertanyaan biasa

far *adj* jauh; ~*sighted* bijaksana; *as* ~ *as* sejauh, sepanjang; *so* ~ sejauh ini, selama ini

farce *n* lelucon; **farcical** *adj* lucu

fare *n* ongkos perjalanan; makanan

farewell *n* perpisahan; *ejac* selamat tinggal, selamat jalan

farm *n* pertanian, peternakan; *v* bercocok tanam, menanami; **farmer** *n* petani; **farming** *n* pertanian

fart *n, coll* bunyi kentut; *v* kentut, membuang angin

farther, further *adj, adv* lebih jauh; **farthermost, farthest** *adj, adv* terjauh, paling jauh

fascinate *v* memesonakan, menarik hati; ~*d* terpesona; **fascination** *n* pesona

fascism *n* [fasyisem] fasisme,

sayap kanan; **fascist** *adj* fasis, sayap kanan

fashion *n* mode; cara; *v* membentuk; **fashionable** *adj* bergaya, gaya

fast *n* puasa; *v* berpuasa; ~*ing month* bulan puasa

fast *adj* cepat, laju; kokoh; ~*-track,* ~ *lane* jalur cepat; ~ *train* kereta api cepat

fasten *v* [fasen] mengikatkan, menambatkan; **fastener** *n* ritsleting; kait

fastidious *adj* rewel, rapi sekali

fat *n* lemak; *adj* gemuk, tambun

fatal *adj* mematikan; **fatality** *n* korban jiwa

fate *n* nasib; **fateful** *adj* yang menentukan nasib

father *n* ayah, bapak; *adopted* ~ ayah angkat; *founding* ~*s* bapak-bapak bangsa; *Our* ~ *Chr* Bapa kami; **fatherhood** *n* pengalaman menjadi ayah; **father-in-law** *n* mertua (lelaki); **fatherly** *adj* kebapakan

fathom *n* depa, ukuran kedalaman air; *v* menduga; **fathomless** *adj* dalam sekali; tidak terduga

fatigue [fatig] *army* ~*s* seragam tentara; *n* kelelahan, kecapekan; kerusakan; *v* capek

fatten ~ *up* membuat gemuk, memberi makanan banyak; **fatty** *n, sl* si gendut; *adj* lemak ← **fat**

faucet *n* keran

fault *n* kesalahan, salah; cacat; pemukulan awal yang meleset (tenis); *to find* ~ mencari kesalahan; **faultless** adj tanpa kesalahan, tanpa cela, sempurna; **faulty** adj cacat, rusak, kurang sempurna

favor n pertolongan; karunia, anugerah; ampun; in our ~ menguntungkan kita; in ~ of mendukung; v lebih suka; **favorable** adj baik, menguntungkan

favorite n kesukaan, anak emas; adj kesukaan, yang paling disukai, favorit

fax n ~ (machine) mesin faks; v (me)ngefaks, mengirim lewat faks ← **facsimile**

FBI abbrev Federal Bureau of Investigation Biro Nasional Penyelidikan (Amerika Serikat)

fear n ketakutan, rasa takut; v takut akan; ~ed menakutkan; **fearful** adj takut akan; **fearless** adj tidak takut, berani

feast n pesta, perjamuan, perayaan; ~ of the Sacrifice Idul Adha; v ~ on melahap, makan

feat n prestasi

feather n bulu; ~ed, ~y berbulu

feature n ciri (khas); pertunjukan utama; ~s pl wajah, paras; pertunjukan utama; v mempertunjukkan, memperlihatkan

February n bulan Februari

feces n, pl [fisiz] tinja

fed v, pf → **feed**

federal adj federal, berserikat; **federalism** n federalisme; **federation** n federasi, perserikatan

fee n upah, gaji, biaya

feeble adj lemah

feed n pakan, makanan hewan; v **fed fed** memberi makan; ~ on makan (dari); ~ up bosan, jenuh; **feedback** n tanggapan

feel n rasa; v **felt felt** berasa, merasa; meraba; **feeler** n sungut; peraba; **feeling** n perasaan; hurt ~s tersinggung

feet n, pl → **foot**

feign v berpura-pura

feint n perbuatan atau gerakan pura-pura; v pura-pura bergerak

feline n (binatang dari keluarga) kucing; adj berkaitan dengan kucing

fell v menebang, memotong (pohon); v → **fall**; **felling** n penebangan

fellow n lelaki; ~ worker teman sekerja; adj sesama; ~ man sesama manusia; **fellowship** n persahabatan, persaudaraan, peranggotaan; beasiswa

felt n bulu kempa; v, pf → **feel**

female n, adj perempuan, wanita; betina (animals)

feminine adj feminin; yang berkaitan dengan kewanitaan; **feminism** n feminisme, gerakan menuju persamaan hak perempuan; **feminist** adj, n orang feminis

fence n pagar; barbed-wire ~ pagar kawat berduri; v memagari; bermain anggar; **fencer** n pembuat pagar; pemain anggar; **fencing** n anggar

fend ~ *for yourself* mencari makanan sendiri, menjaga diri sendiri

fennel *n* adas

ferment *v* meragi, merendam; **fermentation** *n* fermentasi, peragian

fern *n* paku; **ferny** *adj* dengan banyak paku

ferocious *adj* ganas, buas; **ferocity** *n* keganasan, kebuasan

ferret *n* semacam musang; *v* mencari-cari, menguber

ferry *n* feri; *v* membawa penumpang bolak-balik, menyeberangkan; **ferryman** *n* pengemudi feri

fertile *adj* subur; **fertilizer** *n* pupuk; **fertility** *n* kesuburan

fervent *adj* bersemangat, bernafsu, bergairah; **fervor** *n* semangat, nafsu, gairah

fester *v* **festerin** nah

festival *n* pesta, perayaan, hari raya, festival; **festive** *adj* perayaan, pesta; ~ *season* masa Natal; **festivity** *n* pesta, perayaan, acara

fetch *v* menjemput (orang), mengambilkan; **fetching** *adj* menarik

fete *v* [féit] pekan raya, pasar malam

fetid *adj* berbau busuk

fetus *n* [fitus] janin

feud *n* [fyuud] permusuhan, perseteruan; *v* bertengkar, berkelahi

feudal *adj* feodal; **feudalism** *n* feodalisme

fever *n* demam; *dengue* ~ demam berdarah; **feverish** *adj* demam, panas

few *adj* sedikit, beberapa

fiancé *n* [fiansé] tunangan (laki-laki); **fiancée** *n* tunangan (perempuan)

fiasco *n* kegagalan, kesalahan besar

fiber *n* [faiber] serabut, serat; **fiberglass** *n, adj* kaca serat; **fibrous** *adj* berserabut

fiction *n* fiksi; **fictional** *adj* fiksi; **fictitious** *adj* palsu, tidak benar, fiktif

fiddle *n, arch* biola; **fiddler** *n* pemain biola

fiddlesticks *ejac* omong kosong

fidelity *n* kesetiaan; kemurnian; *high-~ (hi-fi)* kualitas tinggi (suara)

fidget *n* orang yang tidak bisa duduk diam; *v* bergerak terus karena gelisah; **fidgety** *adj* gelisah

field *n* bidang, daerah; padang, medan, ladang; ~ *marshal* panglima tertinggi; *rice~* sawah; *v* mengambil bola (olahraga)

fiend *n* hantu jahat, setan; **fiendish** *adj* jahat

fierce *adj* buas, galak, ganas; **fierceness** *n* keganasan

fiery *adj* berapi-api ← **fire**

fifteen *adj, n* lima belas; **fifteenth** *adj* kelima belas ← **five**

fifth *adj* kelima; *one-~* seperlima ← **five**

fiftieth adj kelima puluh; **fifty** adj, n lima puluh ← **fifty**

fig n buah ara; ~ tree pohon ara; I don't give a ~ saya sama sekali tidak peduli

fight n [fait] pertengkaran; perkelahian; pertempuran, perjuangan; v **fought fought** bertengkar; berkelahi; bertempur, berperang, berjuang; **fighter** n pejuang; pesawat tempur

figurative adj kiasan; **figure** n rupa, bentuk; bagan, gambar; angka; harga; ~-skating main sepatu es; v menghitung, berpikir; ~ out mencari solusi, memahami

Fiji n Fiji; **Fijian** n bahasa Fiji; orang Fiji; adj berasal dari Fiji

filch v mengutil, mencuri sedikit demi sedikit

file n berkas, arsip, dokumentasi; single ~ antri satu per satu; v menyimpan; mengikir; ~ a suit against menuntut, mendaftar di pengadilan; **filings** iron ~ serbuk besi

filigree n cara menempa logam sehingga menjadi benang halus

fill n jatah; v mengisi, menempati, memenuhi

fillet n filet, potongan daging tanpa tulang

filly n kuda betina yang belum beranak

film n film

film n selaput; **filmy** adj berselaput

filter n saringan, filter; v menyaring, menyeleksi; ~ paper kertas saring

filth n kotoran, sampah; **filthy** adj kotor sekali; ~ language kata-kata jorok

filtrate n (air) saringan; **filtration** n penyaringan ← **filter**

fin n sirip; shark ~ soup sup sirip ikan hiu

final n (pertandingan) final; adj final, penghabisan, terakhir; **finally** adv akhirnya

finance n keuangan; v membiayai, mendanai; **financial** adj keuangan; **financier** n pemilik modal

find n [faind] (hasil) temuan; v **found found** menemukan; menyimpulkan

fine n denda, tilang; v mendenda, menilang

fine adj bagus, baik; halus; **finery** n hiasan, perhiasan, kemewahan

finger n jari; ~ bowl tempat cuci tangan, kobokan; ~ food makanan kecil; index ~ telunjuk; little ~ kelingking; middle ~ jari tengah; ring ~ jari manis; **fingernail** n kuku jari; **fingerprint** n sidik jari

finish n (garis) akhir; penghabisan, penyelesaian; v berhenti; mengakhiri, menghentikan; menyelesaikan; menghabiskan; ~ off menghabiskan; ~ up menyelesaikan

Finland n Finlandia; **Finn** n orang Finlandia; **Finnish** n bahasa Finlandia; adj berasal dari Finlandia

fire n api; kebakaran; ~ brigade, ~ department pasukan

pemadam kebakaran; ~ *engine* mobil pemadam kebakaran; ~ *escape* tangga darurat; ~ *extinguisher* alat pemadam kebakaran; *on* ~ sedang terbakar; *v* melepaskan tembakan, menembak; ~ *up* memberi semangat; *to catch* ~ terbakar; *to set* ~ *to* membakar; **firearm** *n* senjata api; **firefighter, fireman** *n* anggota pasukan pemadam kebakaran; **firefly** *n* kunang-kunang; **fireplace** *n* perapian; **fireproof** *adj* tahan api; **fireworks** *n* kembang api, petasan, mercon

firm *n* perusahaan; *adj* tetap, pasti, tegas

first *adj* pertama; ~-*born* anak sulung, anak pertama; ~ *cousin* (saudara) sepupu; ~ *name* nama depan; ~-*rate* terbaik, nomor satu; ~ *prize* hadiah utama; *at* ~ pada awalnya, semula; **firstly** *adv* pertama-tama

fish *n* ikan; *v* memancing; **fishbone** *n* duri ikan; **fisherman** *n* nelayan; **fisheries** *n* perikanan; **fishing** *n* memancing; ~ *rod* joran; **fishy** *adj* berbau amis atau anyir; mencurigakan

fission *n* pembelahan, fisi; **fissure** *n* celah

fist *n* tinju, kepalan tangan; **fistful** *n* segenggam, sekepal

fit *adj* pas, tepat, layak, patut; fit, sehat; *v* menyesuaikan; **fitness** *n* kebugaran, kesehatan; ~ *center* pusat kebugaran, tempat fitnes

five *adj* lima; ~-*star hotel* hotel bintang lima; ~ *ways* simpang lima; **fiver** *n* uang kertas lima pon

fix *n* masalah; *v* memperbaiki; menetapkan, memasang; **fixation** *n* obsesi; **fixed** *adj* tetap; ~ *price* harga pas

fizz *n* busa; **fizzle** *v* berbusa, berdesar, mendesis; ~ *out* lama-lama mati

flab *n* lemak; **flabby** *adj* gemuk, tidak berotot

flag *n* bendera; *v* menjadi capek; ~ *down* memberhentikan kendaraan di pinggir jalan

flake *n* serpih, lapis, keping; *v* hancur; **flaky** *adj* berlapis-lapis

flame *n* (kobaran) api; *eternal* ~ api abadi; **flaming** *adj*, *sl* gila; **flammable** *adj* dapat terbakar

flank *n* sisi; *v* mendampingi, mengiringi

flannel *n* kain panas, flanel; handuk kecil untuk menyabuni

flap *n* tutup, penutup; *in a* ~ dalam kesulitan; *v* mengepak

flapjack *n* semacam panekuk

flare *n* nyala api; *v* bernyala, menyala; ~ *up* bangkit marahnya

flash *n* kilau; blits; *a* ~ *of lightning* halilintar, kilat; *in a* ~ dalam sekejap mata; *v* berkilat-kilat; **flashcard** *n* kartu (pengingat) untuk menghafalkan kosa kata; **flashlight** *n* (lampu) senter

flask *n* botol minuman

flat *n* apartemen; *adj* rata, datar;

~ *tire* ban kempes; **flatten** *v*
meratakan

flatter *v* membujuk, merayu,
menyanjung; **flattery** *n* rayuan
gombal, kata-kata manis

flautist *n* pemain suling, pesuling
← **flute**

flavor *n* rasa; *v* membumbui

flaw *n* **flawed** *adj* cacat, cela;
flawless *adj* sempurna, tanpa
cacat

flax *n* rami; **flaxen** ~-*haired*
berambut pirang

flea *n* kutu (binatang); ~ *market*
pasar loak

fled *v, pf* → **flee**

fledgling, fledgeling *n* [flejling]
anak burung; *adj* muda, belum
berpengalaman

flee *v* **fled fled** melarikan diri,
kabur, minggat

fleet *n* armada (angkatan laut); ~
of foot, ~-*footed* cepat; **fleeting**
adj sepintas lalu, sekejap

flesh *n* daging

flexible *adj* lentur; fleksibel;
flexi-time *n* jam kerja yang
mudah disesuaikan

flick *n* sentilan; *v* menyentil;
flicker *v* berkedip-kedip

flight *n* [flait] penerbangan; ~ *of
stairs* tangga; ~ *deck* geladak
pesawat terbang; **flighty** *adj*
ringan, tidak bisa diandalkan,
mudah terpengaruh

flimsy *adj* lemah, tidak kuat;
halus

flinch *v* bereaksi terhadap sesuatu yang mengagetkan; *Jane
didn't even* ~ Jane tidak

bereaksi sama sekali

fling *n* lemparan; *sl* perselingkuhan; *highland* ~ tari adat
Skotlandia; *v* **flung flung**
melemparkan

flip *n* salto; *v* membalik, memutar-
balikkan

flippant *adj* enteng, sembrono

flirt *n* orang genit; *v* bermain
mata; **flirtatious** *adj* genit

flit *v* melayang, terbang

float *n* pelampung; semacam
minuman es; *v* mengapung,
terapung

flock *n* kawanan, gerombolan,
kumpulan; *a* ~ *of sheep*
segerombolan domba; *v* datang
berbondong-bondong,
berkumpul, berhimpun

flog *v* memukuli, mencambuk; *sl*
menjual

flood *n* banjir, air bah; *v* banjir;
membanjiri; **flooded** *adj* banjir;
floodgate *n* pintu air; **flood-
light** *n* lampu sorot

floor *n* lantai, tingkat; ~ *cleaner*
obat pel, obat pembersih lantai;
~ *plan* denah

flop *n, sl* kegagalan; *v* gagal;
jatuh, tidak berdiri; **floppy** *adj*
tidak tegak, lembut

floral *adj* berkaitan dengan
bunga; **florist** *n* (pemilik) toko
bunga; **floristry** *n* seni
merangkai bunga

floss *dental* ~ benang pembersih
gigi

flounder *n* semacam ikan laut; *v*
bersusah-susah

flour *n* tepung (terigu); *corn*~

tepung maizena; **floury** *adj*
cepat hancur, seperti tepung

flourish *n* [flarisy] gerakan yang
lincah; *v* mekar, tumbuh subur;
melambai-lambaikan

flow *n* aliran; *v* mengalir; **flowing**
adj mengalir

flower *n* bunga, kembang;
~-*seller* penjual bunga; **flowery**
adj berbunga-bunga, mewah

flown *v, pf* → **fly**

flu *n* flu, selesma; *bird* ~ flu
burung ← **influenza**

fluctuate *v* naik turun, bergejolak;
fluctuation *n* naik turunnya,
gejolak, fluktuasi

fluency *n* kelancaran, kefasihan;
fluent *adj* lancar, fasih

fluff *n* bulu (kain), debu; isi yang
tidak berarti; **fluffy** *adj* berbulu

fluid *n* cairan; *adj* cair, tidak tentu

fluke *n* kebetulan, untung

flung *v, pf* → **fling**

flurry *n* kesibukan; hujan salju
yang tiba-tiba

flush *n* serangkaian kartu; *v*
memerah (muka); ~ *the toilet*
menyiram WC

flute *n* suling

flutter *n* kepakan sayap; *v*
berkibar-kibar; mengepakkan

fly *n* lalat; **flyswat, flyswatter** *n*
pemukul lalat

fly *v* **flew flown** [flon] terbang;
berkibar-kibar; mengibarkan;
~ *ball* bola yang dipukul tinggi;
frequent ~*er* orang yang sering
naik pesawat; ~ *a kite* main layang-layang; ~ *into a rage* naik
darah; **flywheel** *n* roda gila

flyer, flier *n* selebaran, brosur

foal *n* anak kuda atau zebra

foam *n* buih, busa; *v* berbuih,
berbusa

focus *n* titik perhatian, pusat
perhatian, fokus; *v* memfokuskan, memusatkan perhatian; **focused** *adj* terarah

fodder *n* makanan ternak

foe *n* musuh

foetid → **fetid**

foetus → **fetus**

fog *n* kabut; ~ *up* berembun;
foggy *adj* berkabut; *I haven't
the foggiest (idea)* saya sama
sekali tidak tahu

foil *n* kertas perak; *v* menggagalkan

fold *n* lipatan; *v* melipat

folk *n* orang; ~ *tale* cerita rakyat;
my ~*s* keluarga saya; **folksy**
adj kampungan

follow *v* mengikuti, menuruti;
follower *n* pengikut, anggota;
following *adj, n* yang berikut;
para pengikut

fond *adj* suka, gemar; ~ *of* suka
akan, menggemari; **fondness**
n kesukaan

fondle *v* membelai, mengusap

font *n* jenis huruf (cetakan)

food *n* makanan, pangan, pakan
(hewan); *World* ~ *Organization*
Organisasi Pangan Sedunia

fool *n* orang bodoh; *to make a*
~ *of* memperolok-olokkan;
foolhardy *adj* terlalu berani,
tidak aman; **foolish** *adj* bodoh

foot *n* **feet** kaki; *athlete's* ~
jamur (di kaki); **footage** *n*
rekaman; **football** *n* sepak bola;

footballer n pemain sepak bola; **foothill** n kaki gunung, bukit; **footing** on equal ~ sederajat; **footpath** n jalan setapak, trotoar; **footprint** n tapak kaki; **footwear** n sepatu

for prep bagi, untuk; selama; ~ hours berjam-jam; ~ my mother untuk ibuku; Kelvin was sick ~ two days Kelvin sakit selama dua hari; ~ all I know sepengetahuan saya; conj karena

forbid v **forbade forbidden** melarang; **forbidden** adj terlarang, dilarang

force n kekuatan, tenaga, daya; armed ~s angkatan bersenjata; by ~ dengan paksa; v memaksa

fore to the ~ muncul (ke depan)

forecast n ramalan; weather ~ ramalan cuaca; v meramalkan; **forecaster** n peramal, analis

forefather n nenek moyang, leluhur

forefinger n jari telunjuk

forefront n paling depan

forego v **foregone forewent** menolak, meninggalkan; **foregone** a ~ conclusion sudah ditentukan

forehead n dahi, kening

foreign adj [foren] asing, luar negeri; ~ exchange, ~ currency mata uang asing, devisa; **foreigner** n orang asing

foreman n **foremen** mandor

foremost first and ~ terutama

foresee v **foresaw foreseen** meramal, memprediksi

forest n hutan; **forestry** n perhutanan

forestall v mencegah, menghambat

foretell v **foretold foretold** v meramalkan

forever, forevermore adv untuk selamanya

forewent v, pf → **forego**

forgave v, pf → **forgive**

forge v memalsukan; menempa, membuat; **forger** n pemalsu; **forgery** n pemalsuan, tiruan

forget v **forgot forgotten** lupa, melupakan, terlupa; **forgetful** adj pelupa

forgive v **forgave forgiven** memaafkan, mengampuni; ~ and forget memaafkan dan melupakan; **forgiveness** n ampun, maaf

forgot, forgotten v, pf → **forget**

fork n garpu; belokan, pertigaan; pitch~ trisula; v bercabang

forlorn adj memelas

form n bentuk, rupa; formulir, blangko; true to ~ seperti biasa; v merupakan, membentuk

formal adj formal, resmi; **formality** n formalitas

format n bentuk, format; **formation** n pembentukan, formasi ← **form**

former adj dahulu, bekas, mantan (orang), lama; **formerly** adj dahulu, sebelumnya

formidable adj disegani; berat

formula n rumus, formula; milk ~ susu bubuk, susu formula; **formulate** v merumuskan, menyusun fort *n* benteng ← **fortress**

forth *adj* ke depan; *and so* ~ dan seterusnya (dst)

forthcoming *adj* yang akan datang, mendatang; memberi informasi, terbuka

forthright *adj* terus terang, blak-blakan, ceplas-ceplos

forthwith *adj* serta merta, pada saat ini juga

fortieth *adj* (ulang tahun yang) keempat puluh ← **forty**

fortification *n* benteng, kubu; **fortify** *v* memperkuat

fortitude *n* ketabahan, kekuatan

fortnight *n* dua minggu; **fortnightly** *adj, adv* tiap dua minggu

fortress *n* benteng

fortuitous *adj* kebetulan

fortunate *adj* beruntung; **fortunately** *adv* secara beruntung; **fortune** *n* rezeki; harta karun; *to seek your* ~ merantau; ~-*teller* peramal, dukun

forty *adj, n* empat puluh ← **four**

forward *adj, adv* ke depan, maju; *from this day* ~ mulai hari ini; *v* mengirimkan; **forwarding** ~ *agent* agen pengiriman barang, ekspedisi

fossil *n* fosil; **fossilized** *adj* telah menjadi fosil; tidak dapat berubah lagi

foster *v* memelihara; ~ *child* anak angkat, anak pungut; ~ *mother* ibu angkat

foul *adj* jorok, kotor, najis, jijik; *v* melanggar peraturan (olahraga); mengotori

found *v* mendirikan; *v, pf* →

find; **foundation** *n* yayasan; fondasi, alas; bedak dasar; **founder** *n* pendiri

fountain *n* air mancur, pancuran air; ~ *pen* pulpen; ~ *of knowledge* sumber pengetahuan

four *adj, n* empat; **fourteen** *adj, n* empat belas; **fourteenth** *adj* keempat belas; **fourth** *adj* keempat

fowl *n* unggas; ayam

fox *n* rubah; *v* menipu; **foxy** *adj* seksi; licik

fraction *n* pecahan; *a* ~ *of the cost* jauh lebih murah

fracture *n* keretakan, patah; *v* patah, retak; mematahkan, meretakkan

fragile *adj* mudah pecah atau patah

fragment *n* potong, pecahan, keping; **fragmentary** *adj* terpotong-potong

fragrance *n* [frégrant] **fragrant** *adj* harum, wangi

frail *adj* lemah, rapuh

frame *n* rangka, kerangka; bingkai, lis (gambar); kusen (pintu); tubuh, badan; *v* membingkai; menjebak

France *n* Perancis

franchise *n* waralaba

frangipani *n* bunga kamboja

frank *adj* terus terang, ceplas-ceplos; **frankly** *adv* terus terang saja

frankfurter *n* semacam sosis

frantic *adj* kalang kabut

fraternal *adj* persaudaraan (terutama yang laki-laki); ~

twins kembar lelaki dan perempuan; **fraternity** *n* persatuan, persaudaraan; *college* ~ perkumpulan mahasiswa laki-laki

fraud *n* penipuan, penipu; **fraudulent** *adj* palsu

fray *v* mulai robek; ~ed compang-camping

freak *n* orang dengan cacat yang luar biasa; *adj* luar biasa, kebetulan; **freakish, freaky** *adj* luar biasa, kebetulan

freckle *n* bintik-bintik; ~d berbintik-bintik

free *v* membebaskan, melepaskan; *adj* bebas, merdeka; cuma-cuma, gratis; ~ *sex* bersanggama di luar ikatan perkawinan; ~ *trade* perdagangan bebas; **freestyle** *n* gaya bebas; **freedom** *n* kemerdekaan, kebebasan, keleluasaan; **freeway** *n* jalan bebas hambatan, jalan tol

freeze *v* **froze frozen** membeku; **freezer** *n* lemari es; **freezing** *adj* membekukan, sangat dingin

freight *n* [frét] muatan, kargo; *v* mengirim; **freighter** *n* kapal barang, kapal pengangkut

French *n* bahasa Perancis; *adj* berasal dari Perancis; ~ *kiss* mencium dengan lidah; **Frenchman** *n* lelaki Perancis; **Frenchwoman** *n* perempuan Perancis

frequency *n* gelombang, frekuensi; **frequent** *adj* berulang kali, sering; *v* sering mengunjungi

fresh *adj* segar; baru; sejuk; ~ *graduate* orang yang baru tamat; **freshness** *n* kesegaran; **freshwater** *adj* air tawar

fret *v* kuatir, resah

friar *n* biarawan

friction *n* gesekan

Friday *n* hari Jum'at; *Good* ~ Jum'at Agung

fried *adj* goreng → **fry**

friend *n* [frénd] kawan, sahabat, teman; **friendly** *adj* ramah, bersahabat; **friendship** *n* persahabatan

fright *n* [frait] rasa takut; **frighten** *v* menakut-nakuti, menakutkan; **frightful** *adj* dahsyat, menakutkan

frigid *adj* [frijid] dingin, tidak suka bercinta

frill *n* embel-embel; *no* ~s sederhana, polos

fringe *n* pinggir; poni

frisk *v* menggeledah

frisky *adj* berlompat-lompat

frivolity *n* hura-hura, foya-foya; **frivolous** *adj* sepele, sembrono

frizz *v* mengeriting; **frizzy** *adj* keriting, kribo

frock *n, arch* rok

frog *n* kodok, katak; **frogman** *n* penyelam; **frogkick** *n* gaya kodok

from *prep* dari

front *n* bagian muka; hadapan; *adj* muka; ~ *door* pintu depan, pintu masuk; *in* ~ *of* di depan, di muka; **frontage** *n* bagian yang hadap ke depan; **frontier** *n* tapal batas, perbatasan

frost *n* embun beku; *~-bitten* radang dingin; **frostbite** *n* radang dingin; **frosty** *adj* dingin, tidak ramah

froth *n* busa, buih; *v* berbusa, berbuih

frown *n* [fraun] muka cemberut; *v* mengernyit dahi

froze, frozen *v, pf* → **freeze**

frugal *adj* pelit, sederhana, bersahaja

fruit *n* buah, buah-buahan; *~ salad* buah campur; **fruiterer** *n* penjual buah; **fruitful** *adj* berbuah; **fruitless** *adj* tidak berguna, percuma, sia-sia

frustrate *v* menghambat; **frustration** *n* frustasi

fry *small ~* ikan teri; *v* menggoreng; menjadi panas; *~ pan* penggorengan, kuali; *out of the ~ing pan, into the fire* lepas dari mulut harimau, jatuh ke mulut buaya

ft *foot* kaki

fudge *n* semacam gula-gula

fuel *n* bahan bakar

fugitive *n* buron

fulfill *v* memenuhi; **fulfillment** *n* terlaksananya, kepuasan, pemenuhan

full *adj* penuh; kenyang; lengkap; *~-blood* totok; *~-grown* akil balig, dewasa; *~ moon* bulan purnama, terang bulan; *~ stop* titik

fumble *v* meraba-raba, salah tangkap

fume *v* marah; *~s n, pl* asap, uap, emisi

fumigate *v* menyemprot; **fumigation** *n* penyemprotan, fumigasi

fun *n* keasyikan; *adj* asyik; *~ park* taman hiburan; *~ run* lomba lari jarak jauh; *to make ~ of* memperolok-olokkan

function *n* fungsi; *v* berfungsi, berjalan, bekerja; **functionary** *n* pejabat, fungsionaris

fund *n* dana

fundamental *n* dasar-dasar; *adj* dasar, asasi

funeral *n* (upacara) pemakaman; *~ parlor* pelayanan pemakaman

fungus *n* **fungi** [fanggai] jamur, cendawan

funky *adj* ngetren, gaya, gaul

funnel *n* corong

funny *adj* lucu, jenaka; aneh

fur *n* bulu (binatang); **furry** *adj* berbulu

furious *adj* marah sekali, geram, naik pitam ← **fury**

furnace *n* [fernes] oven, tungku

furnish *v* melengkapi; **furniture** *n* mebel, perabot rumah

further *adj* lebih jauh, lebih lanjut; **furthermore** *adv* lagipula; **furthermost** *adj* yang paling jauh

fury *n* kemarahan, berang

fuse *n* sumbu, sekering; *to have a short ~* cepat marah; *v* melebur, menyatu; **fusion** *n* fusi; santapan yang memadukan dua unsur regional

fuss *n* repot; kekacauan; *v* cerewet; **fussy** *adj* teliti, cerewet

futile *adj* sia-sia, percuma

future *n* in (the) ~ di masa depan; *adj* yang akan datang, mendatang, bakal, calon (orang)

fuzz *n* bulu; **fuzzy** *adj* berbulu

Fwy *Freeway* jalan bebas hambatan, jalan tol

FYI *abbrev for your information* agar diketahui

G

g *gram* g (gram)

gab *gift of the* ~ banyak bicara, pandai bicara

gabble *v* bicara terlalu cepat dan kurang jelas

gable *n* [gébel] dinding rumah berbentuk segi tiga di bawah ujung atap

Gabon *n* Gabon; **Gabonese** *n* orang Gabon; *adj* berasal dari Gabon

gad ~ *about* jalan-jalan, sering pergi

gadget *n* alat, perkakas

gag *n* ikat mulut; lelucon; *v* menyumbat mulut; nyaris muntah

gaiety *n* [géiti] kegirangan, keramaian ← **gay**

gain *n* untung, keuntungan, laba; *v* memperoleh, mendapat, mencapai; ~ *entrance* dapat masuk; ~ *weight* bertambah berat badan

gait *n* gaya berjalan

gale *n* angin besar, badai; ~ *force wind* badai

gall *n* empedu; keberanian; *David had the* ~ *to ask for my phone number* berani-beraninya David minta nomor teleponku; **galling** *adj* pahit

gallant *adj* berani, gagah perkasa; **gallantry** *n* keberanian, kekesatriaan

gallery *n* serambi, ruang pameran, galeri

galley *n* dapur (di kapal)

gallon *n* galon (4.54 liter)

gallop *v* mencongklang, lari congklang, berlari cepat

gallows *n, pl* tiang gantung; *to the* ~ digantung, dihukum mati

galore *adj* sesukanya; *there were cakes* ~ ada banyak sekali macam kue

galvanized ~ *iron* besi berlapiskan seng

Gambia *n* (the) ~ Gambia; **Gambian** *n* orang Gambia; *adj* berasal dari Gambia

gamble *v* berjudi, bertaruh; *it's a* ~ ada risiko; **gambler** *n* penjudi; **gambling** *n* judi, perjudian

game *n* permainan, pertandingan; satwa buruan; *to have a* ~ bermain; *adj* berani; **gaming** ~ *laws* undang-undang perjudian; ~ *machines* mesin judi

gander *n* angsa jantan

gang *n* kawanan, gerombolan, geng; **gangster** *n* preman, penjahat, perampok, garong

gangway *n* tangga naik kapal; jalanan sempit

gaol *n* [jéil] penjara; **gaoler** *n* penjaga penjara

gap *n* lubang, celah, jurang pemisah; ~-*toothed* bergigi celah; ~ *year* tahun sesudah tamat SMA sebelum kuliah

gape *v* menganga, memandang dengan mulut terbuka

garage *n* [garaj] garasi; bengkel

garden *n* kebun, taman; ~ *center* pusat perbelanjaan perlengkapan kebun; ~ *party* pesta taman; **gardener** *n* tukang kebun; **gardening** *n* berkebun

gargle *v* berkumur

garish *adj* [garisy] norak, ramai, berwarna mencolok

garland *n* karangan bunga

garlic *n* bawang putih

garment *n* garmen, pakaian; ~ *factory* pabrik garmen

garnish *n* hiasan; *v* menghiasi

garter *n* ikat stoking

gas *n* gas; bensin; ~ *bill* rekening gas; ~ *chamber* kamar gas; ~ *cooker* kompor gas; ~ *fitter* tukang gas

gash *n, v* luka

gasoline *n* [gasolin] bensin; ~ *station* pompa bensin ← **gas**

gasometer *n* tangki gas ← **gas**

gasp *n* embusan napas; *v* menarik nafas dengan cepat; *last* ~ mati-matian

gasworks *n* pabrik gas ← **gas**

gate *n* pintu (masuk), gerbang; **gatecrash** *v* datang tanpa diundang; **gatecrasher** *n* tamu tak diundang; **gatekeeper** *n* penjaga pintu, juru kunci;

gateway *n* pintu masuk

gather *v* berkumpul; mengumpulkan, memetik; **gathering** *n* perkumpulan

GATT *abbrev General Agreement on Tariffs and Trade* Persetujuan Umum tentang Tarif dan Perdagangan

gaudy *adj* norak, mencolok

gauge *n* [géj] ukuran, kadar; *v* mengukur, menaksir; *narrow* ~ *track* rel sempit

gaunt *adj* kurus, ceking

gauze *n* kain kasa

gay *n* orang homoseksual; *adj* homoseksual; senang hati, meriah; ~-*bashing* pemukulan terhadap orang homoseksual

gaze *n* pandangan; *v* menatap, memandangi

gazelle *n* semacam rusa

gazette *n* [gazét] surat berita, koran

GBH *abbrev grievous bodily harm* terluka berat (oleh penjahat)

gear *n* peralatan, perkakas, perabot; persneling, gigi; gir; *second* ~ gigi dua

gecko *n* cicak

gee *ejac* wah, aduh

geese *n, pl* → **goose**

gelatine *n* semacam agar-agar; **gelatinous** *adj* seperti agar-agar, lengket

gem *n* permata; yang gemilang; **gemstone** *n* permata

gender *n* jenis kelamin; jender; ~-*specific* khusus untuk laki-laki atau perempuan; ~ *studies* kajian jender gene *n* gen

general *n* jenderal; *adj* umum; *Attorney-~* Jaksa Agung; *director-~* direktur-jenderal (dirjen); *in ~* pada umumnya; **generalization** *n* pendapat yang terlalu luas, penyamarataan; **generalize** *v* menyamaratakan; **generally** *adv* biasanya, umumnya

generate *v* menghasilkan, membangkitkan

generation *n* angkatan, generasi; pembangkitan

generator *n* pembangkit listrik ← **generate**

generosity *n* kemurahan hati; **generous** *adj* murah hati, dermawan

genesis *n* asal; *Chr* Kejadian

genetic *adj* genetik; *~ engineering* rekayasa genetik; **genetics** *n, pl* genetika ← **gen**

genial *adj* [jinial] ramah

genital *n* kemaluan; *adj* berhubungan dengan kemaluan; **genitalia** *n* [jénitélia] kemaluan

genius *n* [jinius] kecerdasan; jenius, orang berotak cemerlang

genocide *n* pembunuhan massal

genre *n* [jonre] gaya, aliran

gentle *adj* (lemah) lembut, halus, jinak; **gentleman** *n* **gentlemen** tuan; orang pria; orang sopan; *ladies and gentlemen* bapak-bapak dan ibu-ibu; **gentlemanly** *adv* sopan; sportif; **gently** *adv* perlahan-lahan, lemah lembut

genuflect *v* berlutut; **genuflection** *n* tekuk lutut

genuine *adj* [jényuin] asli, sejati, tulen

geographic, geographical *adj* [jiografik, jiografikal] geografis, berkaitan dengan ilmu bumi; **geography** *n* ilmu bumi, geografi

geological *adj* [jiolojikal] geologis, berkaitan dengan geologi; **geologist** *n* geolog, ahli geologi; **geology** *n* geologi

geometric *adj* [jiométrik] geometris; **geometry** *n* ilmu ukur sudut, geometri

Georgia *n* [Jorjia] Georgia; **Georgian** *n* bahasa Georgia; orang Georgia; *adj* berasal dari Georgia

geothermal *adj* [jiotérmal] berhubungan dengan panas bumi; *~ springs* air panas (gunung)

geriatric *n* orang lanjut usia (lansia), manusia lanjut usia (manula); *adj* sangat tua

germ *n* kuman

German *n* bahasa Jerman; orang Jerman; *adj* berasal dari Jerman; **Germanic** *n* berkaitan dengan negara-negara dekat Jerman (Skandinavia, Belanda & Austria); **Germany** *n* Jerman; *East ~* Jerman Timur

germinate *v* berkecambah ← **germ**

gesture *n* isyarat, gerak-gerik tangan; *v* memberi isyarat get *v* **got gotten** mendapat, menerima; mengerti; menjadi; ~ *along,* ~ *on* maju; berangkat; bergaul; ~ *away* pergi; lari, kabur; ~ *away with* berhasil; ~ *back* (mendapat) kembali; ~ *better* sembuh; menjadi lebih baik; ~ *by* bertahan; ~ *down* turun; ~ *off* turun; ~ *out* pergi, keluar, turun; ~ *through* menempuh, melewati; ~ *up* bangun; ~ *into trouble* mendapat masalah; ~ *well soon* semoga lekas sembuh; ~ *your own way* menang sendiri

geyser *n* [giser] air mancur panas

Ghana *n* Gana; **Ghanaian** *n* [Ganéan] orang Gana; *adj* berasal dari Gana

ghastly *adj* pucat, mengerikan

gherkin *n* mentimun (yang diasamkan)

ghost *n* hantu; **ghostly** *adj* seperti hantu

GI *abbrev* government issue tentara Amerika Serikat

giant *n, adj* [jaiant] raksasa

gibbon *n* [gibon] siamang

giddiness *n* [gidines] rasa pusing; **giddy** *adj* pusing, pening

gift [gift] kado, hadiah, pemberian; bakat; ~ *voucher* kupon belanja; ~*ed* berbakat

gigantic *adj* [jaigantik] besar sekali, raksasa

giggle *n* [gigel] kikikan, *v* cekikik; *v* tertawa terkikik-kikik

gild *v* [gild] menyepuh,

menyadur dengas emas; menghiasi

gills *n, pl* [gils] insang

gilt *n* [gilt] sepuh ← **gild**

gin *n* [jin] jenewer, minuman keras; ~ *and tonic (G & T)* gin dan tonik

ginger *n* [jinjer] jahe; *adj* merah (rambut); kuning (bulu kucing); **gingerbread** *n* roti keras rasa jahe

gingerly *adv* dengan hati-hati, perlahan-lahan

gipsy → **gypsy**

giraffe *n* [jiraf] jerapah

girl *n* [gerl] anak perempuan, putri, gadis; ~ *Guide,* ~ *Scout* pramuka remaja putri; **girlhood** *n* masa gadis, masa kecil

gist *n* [jist] intisari, garis besar, pokok cerita

give *v* [giv] **gave given** memberi; ~ *away* membagikan; membuka rahasia; ~ *birth* bersalin, melahirkan; ~ *in* mengalah; ~ *off* mengeluarkan, menghasilkan; ~ *up* menyerah, menyerahkan; ~ *way* memberi jalan; ~ *and take* memberi dan menerima; ~ *your word* berjanji; **giveaway** *n* hadiah; **given** *adj* tertentu

glacial *adj* [glésyial] sangat dingin; **glacier** *n* gletser

glad *adj* gembira, senang; **gladden** *v* menggembirakan, menyenangkan; **gladly** *adv* dengan senang hati; **gladness** *n* kegembiraan

glamorous *adj* memesona,

menarik, menawan, glamor;
glamor *n* kemewahan, daya
tarik, pesona

glance *n* pandangan sekilas,
pandangan sekejap; *v* melirik,
memandang sekejap mata

gland *n* kelenjar; *~ular fever*
radang kelenjar

glare *n* cahaya yang menyilaukan;
v membelalak, melihat dengan
sikap marah; **glaring** *adj*
menyolok; *~ mistake* kesalahan
yang menyolok

glass *n* kaca; gelas; *looking-~*
cermin; **glasses** *n* kacamata;
dark ~ kacamata hitam;
glasshouse *n* rumah kaca;
glassy *adj* seperti kaca; **glazier**
n tukang kaca

gleam *n* sinar, cahaya, kilap; *v*
bersinar, bercahaya, mengkilap

glen *n* lembah

glib *adj* fasih, enteng

glide *v* meluncur; **glider** *n*
pesawat peluncur, pesawat
layang; *hang-~* gantole

glimmer *n* cahaya redup; *a ~ of
hope* ada sedikit harapan

glimpse *n* pandangan sekilas; *v*
melihat sekilas

glisten *v* [glisen] berkilau-kilauan

glitter *n* kegemilapan, kemegahan;
v gemilap

global *adj* seluruh dunia; *~
warming* pemanasan bumi;
globalization *n* globalisasi;
globe *n* bola dunia; bola
lampu, bohlam; **globetrotter** *n*
penjelajah dunia

gloom *n* remang-remang,

kesuraman; **gloomy** *adj* suram

glorification *n* pemujaan; **glorify**
v memujakan; **glorious** *adj*
megah, mulia, agung; **glory** *n*
kemuliaan; kemenangan

gloss *n* kilau, kilap; *~ over*
meremehkan, menyembunyikan

glossary *n* daftar istilah

glossy *adj* licin, mengkilap ←
gloss

glove *n* [glav] sarung tangan;
hand in ~ bekerja sama

glow *n* sinar, cahaya; *v* bersinar,
berseri; menyala; *~-worm* ulat
yang mengeluarkan cahaya;
glowing, glowingly *adj* sangat
memuja

glucose *n* glukosa

glue *n* [glu] lem, perekat; *v* me-
ngelem; *~d to the spot* terpaku
di tempat

glum *adj* murung

glut *n* kebanyakan; **glutton** *n* orang
rakus; **gluttonous** *adj* rakus

GMT *abbrev Greenwich Mean
Time* waktu GMT

gnarled *adj* [narld] berbonggol

gnash [nasy] *~ your teeth*
mengertakkan gigi

gnaw *v* [noa] menggerogoti

gnome *n* [nom] orang kerdil,
katai; *garden ~* patung kerdil
sebagai hiasan taman

go *v* **went gone** pergi, berjalan;
hilang; *~-ahead* izin; *~-between*
perantara, calo; *~-kart* gokar; *~
along* ikut serta; *~ back* kembali; *~ before* mendahului; *~
by* berlalu; *~ in* masuk; *~ on*
meneruskan; *~ out* keluar; *~*

under bangkrut; ~ *out with* berpacaran dengan; ~ *through with* menyelesaikan; ~ *through a lot* mengalami banyak kesulitan; *no* ~ tidak bisa; *to have a* ~ berusaha

goal *n* gawang, gol; tujuan; *v (to score a)* ~ mencetak gol; **goalie** *n, sl;* **goalkeeper** *n* penjaga gawang, kiper

goat *n* kambing

goatee *n* jenggot pendek

gobble *v* makan dengan cepat, melahap

goblet *n* piala

god *n* dewa; **God** *Isl, Chr* Allah, Tuhan; *Chr* Bapa; *~mother* ibu baptis, ibu permandian; ~ *speed* selamat jalan; ~ *willing Isl* insya Allah; *thank* ~ *Isl* alhamdulillah; *Chr* puji Tuhan; ~ *bless you* Tuhan memberkati; ~ *for* ~*'s sake* demi Tuhan; **goddess** *n, f* dewi

going ~ *to* mau, akan; naik; *~s-on* kejadian ← **go**

gold *n* emas; *~-digger* penambang emas; wanita yang mencari suami kaya; ~ *dust* serbuk emas; *~-leaf* emas prada; ~ *mine* tambang emas; **golden** *adj* terbuat dari emas; ~ *anniversary* hari ulang tahun perkawinan yang kelimapuluh; *the ~ years* tahun-tahun paling bahagia; **goldfish** *n* ikan emas

golf *n* golf; ~ *course* padang golf; **golfer** *n* pegolf, pemain golf

gone *v, pf* [gon] ← **go**

goo *n* cairan lengket, seperti lem

good *adj* baik, bagus; *~-natured* baik hati; ~ *at* pandai; ~ *evening* selamat malam; ~ *Friday* Jum'at Agung; ~ *lord* astaga; ~ *night* selamat tidur; *for* ~ untuk selama-lamanya; *no* ~ tidak ada gunanya, tidak ada baiknya; *for your own* ~ demi kebaikan sendiri; *what* ~ *is it* apa gunanya; **goodbye** *ejac* selamat tinggal, selamat jalan; **goodness** *n* kebaikan, kebajikan; ~ *me* ampun; *thank* ~ syukur; **goods** *n, pl* barang-barang; ~ *train* kereta (api) barang; **goodwill** *n* niat baik; **goody** *n* permen; *~-~* murid yang terlampau baik hingga terkesan menjilat

goose *n* **geese** [gis] angsa; **gooseberry** *n* semacam buah frambus; **goose-pimples** *n, pl* bulu roma berdiri

gorge *n* [gorj] jurang, ngarai; *v* melahap

gorgeous *adj* [gorjes] sangat menawan atau menarik, indah

gorilla *n* gorila

gosh *ejac* wah!

gospel *n* injil, ajaran; ~ *music* musik gospel; ~ *(truth)* kebenaran

gossip *n* gosip, isu, gunjingan, buah bibir, kabar burung; raja gosip (ragos); *v* bergosip; menggosipkan

got, gotten *v, pf* ← **get**

gout *n* asam urat

govern *v* [gavern] memerintah;

self-~ing swapraja; **governance** *n* pemerintahan; *good ~* pemerintahan yang baik

governess *n, f* [gavernés] guru pribadi yang mengajar di rumah zaman dahulu

government *n* [gaverment] pemerintah, pemerintahan; **governor** *n* gubernur; *sl* bos; *~-general* gubernur-jenderal ← **govern**

gown *n* gaun; jubah; *dressing ~* kimono

GPA *abbrev* grade point average IP (indeks prestasi)

GPO *abbrev* General Post Office Kantor Pos Besar

grab *n* rampasan; *v* merampas, menjambret, menyerobot, menangkap; *up for ~s* tersedia, tinggal diambil

grace *n* keanggunan; rahmat, anugerah, karunia; masa tenggang; *v* menyemarakkan; *to say ~ Chr* membaca doa bersyukur sebelum makan; **graceful** *adj* anggun, lemah gemulai; **gracious** *adj* ramah; murah hati; *(good) ~* astaga

grade *n* tingkat, pangkat, derajat; nilai (rapot); kelas; *first ~* kelas satu; *v* memberi angka atau nilai; memeriksa, menyortir; *~d* disortir menurut tingkat; **gradual** *adj* **gradually** *adv* lama-kelamaan, berangsur-angsur

graduate *n* [gradyuet] lulusan, tamatan; sarjana; *post-~* pascasarjana; *under~* sarjana muda; *v* [gradyuét] lulus, tamat;

wisuda; **graduation** *n* tamat sekolah, acara lulus-lulusan; wisuda

graft *n* [graft] korupsi, kolusi

graft *n* pencangkokan; *v* mencangkokkan

grain *n* butir; sereal, biji-bijian; urat kayu; *against the ~* melawan arus; **grainy** *adj* berserat, tidak mulus

gram *n* gram

grammar *n* tata bahasa, gramatika; *~ school* sekolah swasta; **grammatical** *adj* menurut tata bahasa, gramatikal; **grammatically** *adv* secara tata bahasa, secara gramatika

grand *n* besar, agung; bagus, mewah; *~ piano* piano besar

grandchild *n* cucu; **granddad** *n, sl* kakek; kek; **granddaughter** *n* cucu (perempuan); **grandfather** *n* kakek; *~ clock* jam dentang besar; **grandma** *n, sl* nenek; nek; **grandmother** *n* nenek; **grandpa** *n, sl* kakek; kek; **grandson** *n* cucu (lelaki)

granite *n, adj* granit

granny *n* nenek, perempuan tua ← **grandmother**

grant *n* (dana) pemberian, sumbangan, subsidi, beasiswa; *v* memberi, menganugerahkan; *~ a prayer, ~ a wish* mengabulkan doa, mengizinkan; *taken for ~ed* dianggap sudah begitu

granular *n* berupa butiran atau biji-bijian ← **grain**

grape *n* buah anggur; *adj* (rasa) anggur; **grapefruit** *n* semacam jeruk kuning yang besar; *pink* ~ jeruk Bali; **grapevine** *n* tanaman anggur; *to hear it on the* ~ mendengar kabar burung

grraphic *adj* grafik, bergambar, jelas; ~ *artist* pelukis grafis

grapple *v* bergulat

grasp *n* genggaman, pegangan; *v* memegang, menggenggam, menangkap, mengerti

grass *n* rumput; **grasshopper** *n* belalang

grate *n* tutup riol, kisi

grate *v* memarut; mengganggu; **grating** *n* riol, kisi; *adj* kasar, mengganggu

grateful *n* berterima kasih

grater *n* parut ← **grate**

gratitude *n* [gratityud] rasa terima kasih, rasa syukur

gratuitous *adj* [gratyuitus] tidak perlu; **gratuity** *n* persenan

grave *adj* berat, genting, gawat, serius

grave *n* kuburan, makam; ~ *digger* penggali kubur

gravel *n* [gravel] batu kerikil; **gravelly** ~ *voice* suara serak-serak

graveyard *n* kuburan ← **grave**

gravitate *v* condong, cenderung; mengendap; **gravitation** *n* gravitasi; kecenderungan; **gravitational** *adj* berkaitan dengan daya tarik bumi; **gravity** *n* daya tarik bumi, gaya berat; kegawatan, kegentingan; *specific* ~ berat jenis

gravy *n* [grévi] saus atau kuah daging

gray *adj* (warna) abu-abu, kelabu; suram; *a* ~ *day* hari yang sedih; ~ *matter* sel-sel otak; **grayhound** *n* anjing pacu; ~ *racing* pacuan anjing; **grayish** *adj* keabu-abuan

graze *n* goresan pada kulit; *v* mendapat goresan pada kulit

graze *v* makan rumput

grease *n* [gris] gemuk, minyak; *v* [griz] memberi gemuk, meminyaki; ~ *monkey* montir; *elbow* ~ kerja keras; **greasy** *adj* berlemak, berminyak; bermanis mulut

great *adj* [grét] besar, agung, mulia, raya; *--aunt* nenek; ~ *Britain* Inggris Raya, Britania Raya

great-grandchild *n* cicit; **great-granddaughter** *n* cicit (perempuan); **great-grandfather** *n* kakek buyut; **great-grandmother** *n* nenek buyut; **great-grandson** *n* cicit (lelaki); *--uncle* kakek ← **great**

greatness *n* kebesaran, keagungan, kemuliaan ← **great**

Greece *n* Yunani; *Ancient* ~ Yunani Kuno

greed *n* kerakusan, ketamakan; **greedy** *adj* rakus, tamak, loba

Greek *n* bahasa Yunani; orang Yunani; *adj* berasal dari Yunani ← **Greece**

green *adj* hijau; mentah; baru, muda; ramah lingkungan; ~ *finger* kemampuan berkebun atau memelihara tanaman; ~ *light* lampu hijau; izin; *the* ~

room ruang tunggu sebelum naik ke atas panggung; ~ *with envy* sangat iri; **greenback** *n* dolar AS; **green-eyed** *adj* bermata hijau; *the ~ monster* rasa cemburu, kecemburuan; **greengrocer** *n* tukang sayur; toko sayur; **greenhorn** *n* orang yang masih baru, pemula; **greenhouse** *n* rumah kaca; ~ *effect* efek rumah kaca, pemanasan bumi; ~ *gas* gas yang ikut memperparah efek rumah kaca; **greenish** *adj* kehijau-hijauan; **greens** *n, pl* sayuran, sayur-mayur; partai hijau, partai peduli lingkungan

greet *v* memberi salam, menegur, menyambut; *meet and ~* acara ramah tamah; **greeting** *n* salam, ucapan selamat; *season's ~s* Selamat (Hari Natal)

gregarious *adj* [gregérius] ramah, mempunyai banyak kawan

Grenada *n* [Grenéda] Grenada; **Grenadian** *n* [Grenédian] orang Grenada; *adj* berasal dari Grenada

grenade *n* granat

grew *v, pf* → **grow**

grey → **gray**

grid *n* jaringan; ~ *reference* rujukan (kisi); *electricity* ~ jaringan listrik

gridiron *n* sepak bola Amerika

grief *n* kesedihan, duka cita; **grieve** *v* menangisi, meratapi

grievous *adj* berat, menyakitkan; ~ *bodily harm (GBH)* terluka berat (oleh penjahat)

grill *n* pemanggangan, barbekiu; *v* memanggang; memeriksa; **griller** *n* pemanggangan (di kompor)

grim *adj* seram

grime *n* kotoran, daki; **grimy** *adj* kotor

grin *n* senyum, seringai; *v* tersenyum, menyeringai

grind *n* [graind] pengalaman yang susah, kesusahan; *v* **ground ground** menggerinda, menggiling, mengasah; ~ *your teeth* mengertakkan gigi; **grinder** *n* gerinda; **grindstone** *n* batu gerinda, batu pengasah; *keep your nose to the ~* bekerja keras, membanting tulang

grip *n* pegangan, genggaman; *v* memegang, menggenggam; *to come to ~s with* bergulat dengan, membiasakan diri dengan; **gripping** *adj* menegangkan, mengasyikkan

grisly *adj* berdarah, menjijikkan

gristle *n* [grissel] tulang muda

grit *n* kerikil, pasir; kenekatan; **gritty** *adj* berpasir; dengan unsur nekat

grizzle *v* mengadu, rewel, cengeng

grizzled *adj* beruban

grizzly ~ *bear* sejenis beruang

groan *n* keluh, erang; *v* berkeluh, mengeluh, mengerang

grocer *n* penjual bahan makanan; **grocery** *n* toko bahan makanan; **groceries** *n, pl* bahan makanan

groin *n* selangkangan, lipat paha

groom *n (bride)~* mempelai pria,

pengantin pria, calon suami;
groomsman *n* pendamping
mempelai pria

groom *n* pengasuh kuda; *v*
memelihara penampilan, merias;
grooming *n* penampilan

groove *n* alur; gaya; **groovy** *adj*
bergaya

grope *v* meraba-raba

gross *n* gros, 12 lusin, 144; *adj*
kotor; jorok; sangat gemuk; *~
salary* gaji kotor; *~ national
product (GNP)* pendapatan
(kotor) nasional

grotto *n* gua

ground *v, pf* → **grind**

ground *n* [graund] tanah, bumi;
v mendasarkan; melarang
(pergi); *home ~* lapangan
sendiri; *well ~ed* beralasan;
grounds *n, pl* pekarangan,
taman; alasan; *coffee ~* ampas
kopi; *on the ~ of* berdasarkan

group *n* kelompok, grup; *v*
mengelompokkan

grow *v* [gro] **grew grown**
tumbuh; bertambah; menjadi;
menanam; *~ up* jadi besar,
tumbuh; *~n-up* dewasa, sudah
besar

growl *n* [graul] geram; *v* menggeram

grown *v, pf* → **grow**

growth *n* pertumbuhan, pertambahan; benjolan ← **grow**

grub *n* tempayak; *sl* makanan;
grubby *adj* kotor

grudge *n* dendam; *to bear a ~,
have a ~* menaruh dendam;
grudgingly *adv* dengan segan-

segan, ogah-ogahan

gruesome *adj* [grusam]
mengerikan, berdarah

gruff *adj* kasar, pendek

grumble *n* keluhan; bersungut-
sungut, menggerutu

grumpy *adj* mengomel, marah-
marah

grunt *n* dengkur; *v* mengeluarkan
bunyi dengkur

guarantee *n* [garanti] jaminan; *v*
menjamin, menanggung

guard *n* [gard] jaga, pengawal;
kondektur; *v* menjaga, pengawal;
guardian *n* wali, orang tua
asuh; penjaga

Guatemala *n* [Gwatemala]
Guatemala; **Guatemalan** *n*
orang Guatemala; *adj* berasal
dari Guatemala

guava *n* jambu

guerilla, guerrilla *n, adj* gerilya,
gerilyawan

guess *n* [gés] tebakan, terkaan,
sangkaan; *v* menebak, menerka

guest *n* [gést] tamu; *~house*
losmen, hotel kecil; *~ room*
kamar (tidur untuk) tamu

guidance *n* [gaidans] pimpinan,
tuntunan, bimbingan; **guide** *n*
pemandu, pembimbing; *v* membimbing, memandu; **guide-
book** *n* buku petunjuk, buku
panduan; **guideline** *n* pedoman

guilder *n, arch* [gilder] gulden

guillotine *n* [gilotin] alat
pemenggal kepala

guilt *n* [gilt] kesalahan, rasa
bersalah; *~-free* tanpa rasa
bersalah; **guilty** *adj* bersalah

Guinea *n* [Gini] Guinea; ~-*Bissau* Guinea-Bissau; *Equatorial* ~ Guinea Katulistiwa; **Guinean** *n* orang Guinea; *adj* berasal dari Guinea

guinea ~ *fowl* ayam mutiara; ~ *pig* marmot

guitar *n* gitar; *bass* ~ gitar bas; *electric* ~ gitar listrik; **guitarist** *n* pemain gitar, gitaris

gulf *n* teluk besar; jurang

gull *n (sea)*~ burung camar

gullet *n* kerongkongan

gullible *adj* lekas percaya, mudah tertipu

gully *n* jurang

gulp *n* teguk; *v* meneguk, menelan

gum *n* getah; *chewing* ~ permen karet

gum *n* gusi; **gummy** *adj* ompong

gun *n* bedil, senapan, revolver, pistol; *v* menembak; **gunboat** *n* kapal meriam; **gunpowder** *n* mesiu

gurgle *v* berdeguk; mendeguk

gush *n* pancaran, semburan; *v* memancar, mengalir dengan deras; memuji-muji secara berlebihan

gust *n* hembusan angin

gusto *n* cita rasa; semangat, kesukaan

gusty *adj* berangin ← **gust**

gut *n* usus; **guts** *n, pl* nyali, keberanian; **gutsy** *adj* berani

gutter *n* parit, selokan

guy *n, sl* [gai] orang, lelaki, cowok; *good* ~ orang baik

Guyana *n* [Gaiyana] Guyana; *French* ~ Guyana Perancis;

Guyanese *n* orang Guyana; *adj* berasal dari Guyana

guzzle *v* makan dengan rakus; *gas* ~*r* mobil yang boros bensin

gym *n* [jim] aula, tempat senam; pusat kebugaran; **gymnasium** *n* aula, tempat senam, gimnasium; **gymnast** *n* pesenam; **gymnastics** *n* senam

gynecologist *n* [gainekolojist] ginekolog; **gynecology** *n* ginekologi

gypsy, gipsy *n* [jipsi] nomaden, gipsi; *Sea* ~ orang Bajau

H

haberdashery *n* [haberdasyeri] toko peralatan menjahit

habit *n* kebiasaan; *bad* ~ kebiasaan buruk; **habitat** *n* tempat tinggal, lingkungan; **habitual** *adj* biasa, sehari-hari; **habitually** *adv* biasanya

hack *v* memotong-motong, mencincang; memasuki jaringan komputer; **hacker** *n* orang yang memasuki jaringan komputer

had *v, pf* → **have**

hadn't (**had not**) ← **have**

haemorrhage → **hemorrhage**

haemorrhoid → **hemorrhoid**

haggard *adj* kurus, ceking; tidak terawat

haggle *v* tawar-menawar

Hague *the* ~ Den Haag

ail, hailstone *n* hujan es

ail *n* salam, hormat; *v* memberi salam

air *n* rambut, bulu; *~-raising* mengerikan, menakutkan; *~ pin* tusuk konde; *~ tie* ikat rambut; *blonde ~* rambut pirang; *black-~ed* berambut hitam; *body ~* bulu; **hairbrush** *n* sikat rambut; **haircut** *n* potong rambut; **hairdo** *n, sl* rias rambut, tata rambut; **hairdresser** *n* penata rambut, potong rambut; **hairdryer** *n* pengering rambut; **hairspray** *n* semprot rambut; **hairy** *adj* berbulu

Haiti *n* [Héti] Haiti; **Haitian** *n* [Hésyen] orang Haiti; *adj* berasal dari Haiti

alf *n* [haf] **halves** *adj* setengah, separuh; *~-baked* setengah matang, tidak masuk akal; *~-blood* berdarah campuran, peranakan; *~-hearted* setengah hati; *~ time* istirahat (dalam pertandingan); *~ a dozen* setengah lusin; *~ past three* (jam) setengah empat; **halfway** *adj* stengah jalan; *~ house* rumah singgah

all *n* [hol] aula, balai, ruang; lorong, koridor; *concert ~* gedung konser, gedung pertunjukan; **hallmark** *n* cap

allo → **hello**

Hallowe'en *n* malam 31 Oktober

allucinate *v* berhalusinasi; **hallucination** *n* khayal, halusinasi

allway *n* lorong, koridor

halo *n* [hélo] lingkaran cahaya di sekitar kepala

halt *n* [holt] pemberhentian; *v* berhenti; memberhentikan; **halting** *adj* terpatah-patah

halter *n* [holter] tali leher; *~-neck* baju dengan tali di leher

halve *v* [hav] membagi dua ← **half**

ham *n* irisan daging babi; *~-fisted* secara kasar, secara salah;

hamburger *n* burger

hamlet *n* dusun

hammer *n* palu; *~ and sickle* palu arit; *v* memalu, memukul

hammock *n* tempat tidur gantung

hamper *n* bakul, keranjang

hamper *v* menghambat

hamster *n* marmut

hand *n* tangan; jarum (jam); *~-in-glove* bekerja sama; *~-me-down* pakaian lungsuran; *~ out* membagi-bagikan; *~s off* jangan ikut campur, jangan disentuh; *~s up* angkat tangan; *~ towel* lap; *old ~* orang lama, orang berpengalaman; *on ~* hadir, tersedia; *on the other ~* di lain pihak; *to lend a ~* menolong, membantu; *v* memberi, menyampaikan; *~ in* menyerahkan; **handbag** *n* tas tangan; **handbook** *n* buku panduan, pedoman; **handcuff** *n* belenggu, borgol; *v* memborgol, membelenggu; **handful** *n* segenggam

handicap *n* rintangan, cacat; *~ped* cacat

handicraft *n* kerajinan tangan ← **hand**

handkerchief *n* sapu tangan

handle *n* pegangan; *v* menangani, memegang; **handlebar** *n* setang; **handling** *n* penanganan, perlakuan

handmade *adj* buatan tangan ← **hand**

handphone → **phone**

handsome *adj* [handsam] ganteng, tampan

handwriting *n* [handraiting] tulisan tangan ← **hand**

handy *adj* berguna, praktis; **handyman** *n* tukang ← **hand**

hang *v* bergantung; menggantung; ~ *on* menunggu; ~ *out* menonjol; nongkrong; ~ *up* memutuskan sambungan telepon; **hang-glider** *n* gantole; ~-*up* masalah; *to get the* ~ *of* mengerti

hangar *n* hanggar, bangsal

hangman *n* algojo

hangout *n* tempat tongkrongan

hangover *n* tidak enak badan setelah banyak minum

happen *v* terjadi; **happening** *n* kejadian, peristiwa

happily *adv* dengan senang hati; **happiness** *n* kebahagiaan; **happy** *adj* bahagia, berbahagia, senang

harass *v* mengganggu, mengusik; **harassment** *n* gangguan; *sexual* ~ pelecehan seksual

harbor *n* [harber] pelabuhan; **harbormaster** *n* syahbandar, kepala pelabuhan

hard *adj* keras; susah, sulit; *adv* dengan rajin; ~-*hearted* keras

hati; ~ *cash* uang tunai; ~ *currency* mata uang yang kuat; ~ *labor* kerja paksa; ~ *shoulder* bahu jalan; ~ *up* tidak punya uang banyak; ~ *work* kerja keras; ~ *of hearing* agak tuli; **harden** *v* mengeras; mengeraskan, menguatkan; **hardened** *adj* tegar

hardly *adv* nyaris tidak, hampir tidak

hardship *n* kesusahan, kekurangan, penderitaan ← **hard**

hardware *n* alat-alat pertukangan; peranti keras ← **hard**

hare *n* kelinci besar; ~-*brained idea* pikiran gila; **harelip** *n* bibir sumbing

harm *n* bahaya; kerugian, kerusakan, kejahatan; *v* merusak, mengganggu; *no* ~ *done* tidak apa-apa; **harmful** *adj* membahayakan, merusak, merugikan; **harmless** *adj* tidak jahat

harmonica *n* harmonika

harmonious *adj* selaras, serasi, sepadan, harmonis; **harmony** *n* keselarasan, kerukunan, kecocokan

harness *n* tali pengaman, tali keselamatan; pakaian kuda; *v* memasang; memanfaatkan

harp *n* harpa; **harpist** *n* pemain harpa

harsh *adj* kasar, keras hati; tidak ramah; **harshness** *n* kekasaran, kekerasan

harvest *n* (hasil) panen; *v* memanen, memotong (padi)

has → **have; has-been** *n* orang yang ketinggalan zaman, sudah tidak terkenal lagi

hash *n* pagar (#)

haste *n* [hést] perbuatan tergesa-gesa, kegopohan; *more ~ less speed* terlalu cepat jadi lambat; **hasten** *v* [hésen] cepat-cepat; mempercepat; **hasty** *adj* tergesa-gesa, tergopoh-gopoh

hat *n* topi; *to take your ~ off to* mengangkat topi terhadap; *to wear many ~s* merangkap

hatch *n* pintu kecil; *v* mengeram, menetas

hatchet *n* kapak; *to bury the ~* berdamai

hate *n* kebencian, rasa benci; *v* membenci; **hateful** *adj* membangkitkan benci; **hatred** *n* [hétred] kebencian, rasa benci

haughty *adj* [hoti] sombong, angkuh

haul *n* hasil tangkapan; muatan; *long-~ flight* penerbangan jarak jauh; *v* menarik, menghela

haunt *n* tempat yang sering dikunjungi; *v* menghantui; *~ed house* rumah hantu; **haunting** *adj* menghantui, sering teringat

have *v* [hav] **had had** mempunyai, memiliki; ada; mendapat; menyuruh; *~ a shower* mandi; *~ a tooth out* gigi dicabut (oleh dokter); *~ it* mengerti; *~ lunch* makan siang; *~ on* memakai, berpakaian; *~ to* harus, terpaksa, wajib; *~ your hair cut* potong rambut; *the ~s and the ~-nots*

si kaya dan si miskin; *Patricia will ~ a coffee* Patricia memesan kopi

haven *n* pelabuhan, tempat berlindung

havoc *n* [havek] kerusakan

hawk *n* burung elang

hawk *v* berjualan, menjajakan; **hawker** *n* penjaja, pedagang kaki lima; *~ center* pujasera, tempat pedagang kaki lima

hay *n* rumput kering, jerami; *~ fever* alergi rumput; *~ stack* tumpukan rumput kering

hazard *n* bahaya, risiko; **hazardous** *adj* berbahaya

haze *n* kabut, asap; **hazy** *adj* berkabut; tidak jelas

hazel *adj* warna mata yang hijau kecoklatan; **hazelnut** *n* semacam buah kemiri

he *pron, m* [hi] dia, ia (subyek); **He** *pron* Dia, Tuhan

head *n* [héd] kepala; pemimpin, direktur; puncak; *v* mengepalai; menyundul (bola); *~-dress* hiasan kepala; *~ for* menuju; *~-hunter* pengayau; pencari bakat; *~ office* kantor pusat; *~ start* mulai lebih awal; *~s or tails* permainan atas atau bawah dengan keping logam; *~ teacher* guru kepala; *~ over heels* tergila-gila; *Rp 60.000 a ~* Rp 60 000 rupiah per orang; *section ~* kepala bagian; *v* mengepalai, memimpin; **headache** *n* sakit kepala, pusing; **heading** *n* judul (karangan); **headlights** *n, pl* lampu depan (mobil); **headline** n kepala berita; **headlong** adj tunggang langgang; **headmaster** n, arch, m **headmistress** f kepala sekolah; **headquarters** n markas besar; **headstone** n batu nisan; **headstrong** adj keras kepala; **headway** n kemajuan; **heady** adj memabukkan, gegabah

heal v menyembuhkan, menyehatkan; **healer** n dukun, sinse; **health** n kesehatan; in good ~ sehat walafiat; **healthy** adj sehat

heap n timbunan, tumpukan, susunan; v menimbun; ~ praise on memuji

hear v heard heard [hérd] mendengar; ~ from mendapat kabar dari; ~ of mendengar tentang; mengetahui; ~ out mendengarkan sampai selesai; **hearing** n (indera) pendengaran, sidang; ~ aid alat bantu dengar

hearse n [hérs] mobil atau kereta mayat

heart n [hart] jantung; hati, inti; ~ attack serangan jantung; ~ disease sakit jantung; ~-rending yang mengiris hati; ~-shaped berbentuk hati; ~-throb idola; know by ~ hafal; to lose ~ putus asa; ~ of gold berhati baik; ~ of stone tidak berhati, tidak mempunyai hati; cross my ~ bersumpah; to take ~ mendapat semangat, mengambil hikmah; **heartbeat**

n denyut jantung; **heartbreak** n patah hati; **hearten** v membesarkan hati; **heartily** adv **hearty** adj sungguh-sungguh, dengan semangat

heat n panas, kepanasan, hangat; bagian dari balapan; dry ~ panas terik; v memanaskan, menghangatkan; ~ up memanas; memanaskan; **heater** n alat pemanas

heathen adj kafir, penyembah berhala

heave v mengangkat; ~ a sigh of relief menarik nafas karena lega

heaven n [héven] surga; **heavens** n, pl langit; ejac masya Allah; for ~'s sake demi Allah; **heavenly** adj sangat menyenangkan

heavy adj [hévi] berat, berbobot; ~ rain hujan lebat

Hebrew n [Hibru] bahasa Ibrani; arch orang Ibrani

hectic adj sibuk, ramai, hirukpikuk

hedge n pagar hidup; v mengelak dari memberi jawaban

hedgehog n landak

heed n perhatian; to pay ~ to, to take ~ mengindahkan

heel n tumit; hak; high ~s sepatu hak tinggi

height n [hait] ketinggian; tinggi badan; puncak; **heighten** v memuncak, menambah

heir n [ér] **heiress** f ahli waris; **heirloom** n harta pusaka

held v, pf → hold

helicopter n helikopter, heli;

helipad *n* landasan helikopter; **heliport** *n* lapangan helikopter

hell *n* neraka; **~-bent** nekat; *go to ~* masuk neraka; *a ~ of a match* pertandingan yang seru; *to ~ with it* persetan; **hellish** *adj* seperti neraka

hello, hallo *ejac* halo; apa kabar?

helm *n* kemudi

helmet *n* helm

helmsman *n* juru mudi ← **helm**

help *n* pertolongan, bantuan; *v* menolong, membantu; *it can't be ~ed* apa boleh buat; **helpful** *adj* suka menolong; berguna; **helpless** *adj* tidak berdaya

hem *n* kelim; *v* mengelim

hemisphere *n* [hémisfir] belahan (bumi); *Southern ~* belahan bumi Selatan

hemorrhage *n* [hémerej] perdarahan, pendarahan; *v* berdarah

hemorrhoid *n* [hémeroid] wasir, ambeien

hen *n, f* ayam betina; **~pecked** dikuasai isteri

hence *adv* maka; dari sini; **henceforth** *adv* mulai sekarang

henhouse *n* kandang ayam ← **hen**

hepatitis *n* [hépataitis] hepatitis, radang hati, sakit kuning

heptagon *n* segi tujuh

her *pron, f* -nya (kepunyaan); dia, ia (obyek)

herald *n* bentara, pelopor; *v* memberi tahu, memaklumkan

herb *n* jamu, bumbu; **~s** ramuan bumbu; **herbivore** *n* pemakan tumbuh-tumbuhan; **herbivorous** *adj* memakan tumbuh-tumbuhan

herd *n* kawanan; *v* menggembala

here *adv* di sini; *come ~* (ke) sini; *~ and there* di sana-sini; *~ she is* ini dia; *~ is my card* ini kartu nama saya; *Eileen lives ~* Eileen tinggal di sini; **hereafter** *the ~* dunia akhirat; **hereby** *adv* dengan ini, bersama ini

hereditary *adj* turun-temurun, genetik; **heredity** *n* keturunan

herewith *adv* dengan ini, bersama ini ← **here**

heritage *n* [héritej] warisan, harta pusaka

hermit *n* petapa; **hermitage** *n* pertapaan

hernia *n* burut

hero *n* [hiro] pahlawan; **heroic** *adj* seperti pahlawan, heroik, berani

heroin *n* [héroin] heroin, putau

heroine *n, f* [héroin] pahlawan (wanita); **heroism** *n* kepahlawanan ← **hero**

heron *n* burung bangau

herring *n* ikan haring

hers *pron, f* miliknya; **herself** *pron* dirinya, sendiri; *by ~* sendiri

hesitancy *n* keraguan; **hesitant** *adj* **hesitate** *v* ragu-ragu, bimbang; **hesitation** *n* keraguan, kebimbangan

heterosexual, hetero *n* heteroseksual, orang yang suka lawan jenis

hey *ejac* he, oi

heyday *n* zaman emas

hexagon *n* segi enam

hibernate *v* **hibernation** *n* tidur selama musim dingin

hiccup, hiccough *n* cegukan, sedu; *v* cegukan, bersedu

hid, hidden *v, pf* → **hide**

hide *n* kulit (binatang)

hide *v* **hid hidden** bersembunyi, berlindung, mengumpet; menyembunyikan; **~-and-seek** petak umpet, sembunyi-sembunyian; **hideaway** *n* tempat persembunyian

hideous *adj* [hidius] mengerikan

hiding *n* persembunyian; *in ~* bersembunyi; *~ place* tempat sembunyi, tempat berlindung ← **hide**

hierarchy *n* [haierarki] susunan, hirarki

hi-fi *n* [hai fai] radio kompo (dengan suara berkualitas tinggi) ← **high fidelity**

high *adj* [hai] tinggi, mulia; *~ chair* kursi bayi; *~-class* kelas satu; *~-handed* angkuh, otoriter; *~ heels* (sepatu) hak tinggi; *~ jump* loncat tinggi; *~ life* cara hidup kaum atas; *~ noon* tengah hari, jam 12 siang; *~-pitched* nyaring; *~-rise* bertingkat tinggi; *~ school* sekolah menengah (atas); *~-spirited* bersemangat; *~ tide* air pasang; *~ and low* di mana-mana; *on a ~* sedang bahagia; *on your ~ horse* sombong; *(the) ~ street* jalan utama; *the ~ seas* laut lepas; **highbrow** cendekiawan;

highlands *n* tanah tinggi, pegunungan; **highly** *adj* tinggi; sangat; **highness** *Your ~* Yang Mulia; **highway** *n* jalan raya, jalan besar

hijack *v* membajak; **hijacker** *n* membajak; **hijacking** *n* pembajakan

hike *n* perjalanan kaki; kenaikan (harga, gaji); *v* berjalan kaki, mendaki gunung; **hiker** *n* pendaki gunung, orang yang gemar berjalan kaki; **hiking** *n* mendaki gunung; berjalan kaki

hilarious *adj* [hilérius] lucu sekali, sangat menggelikan; **hilarity** *n* keriangan

hill *n* bukit; **hillside** *n* lereng bukit; **hilltop** *n* puncak bukit; **hilly** *adj* berbukit-bukit

hilt *n* pangkal (pedang), hulu (keris)

him *pron, m* dia, ia (obyek); **himself** *pron* dirinya, sendiri; *by ~* sendiri

hind [haind] *~ leg* kaki belakang (binatang)

hinder *v* merintangi, menyusahkan; **hindrance** *n* rintangan, gangguan

Hindi *n* bahasa Hindi

hindsight *n* [haindsait] peninjauan kembali, melihat ke belakang

Hindu *n* orang Hindu; *adj* Hindu; **Hinduism** *n* agama Hindu

hinge *n* [hinj] engsel; sendi; *v ~ on* bergantung pada

hint *n* tanda, isyarat, sindiran; *v* mengisyaratkan; *handy ~* tips

hip *adj* gaya, gaul, ngetrend;
hippie *n* orang berpenampilan
urak-urakan, hipi

hip *n* pangkal paha, pinggul;
hipsters *n* celana dengan
pinggang rendah

hire *n* sewa; *v* menyewa; mempekerjakan; ~ *car* mobil
sewaan; ~ *out* menyewakan; ~
purchase sewa beli

his *pron, m* -nya (kepunyaan)

hiss *n* desis; *v* berdesis, mendesis

historian *n* sejarahwan; **historic**
adj bersejarah; **historical** *adj*
historis, berkaitan dengan
sejarah; **history** *n* sejarah,
hikayat; *medical* ~ riwayat
medis

hit *n* pukulan; *v* **hit hit** memukul,
kena, mengenai; ~ *out* menyerang; ~-*and-run* tabrak lari; ~ *it*
off bergaul dengan baik

hit *n* (lagu) yang sedang naik
daun; *adj* laku, populer

hitch *n* rintangan, halangan; *v*
menambatkan, mengaitkan

hitchhike *v* menumpang mobil
orang yang lewat; **hitchhiker** *n*
orang yang menumpang mobil
yang lewat

hive *n* sarang lebah, sialang

hives *n, pl* penyakit gatal-gatal

HM *abbrev* Her Majesty, His
Majesty Yang Dipertuan Agung

hoard *n* timbunan; *v* menimbun,
mengumpulkan; **hoarder** *n*
penimbun

hoarse *adj* serak, parau

hoax *n* [hooks] tipuan, cerita
bohong; *v* menipu; **hoaxer** *n*
penipu

hobble *v* berjalan pincang

hobby *n* hobi, kegemaran,
kesukaan; ~ *farm* pertanian
sebagai tempat peristirahatan;
~-*horse* kuda-kudaan, kuda
mainan

hockey *n* hoki; ~ *stick* tongkat
hoki; *ice* ~ hoki es

hoe *n* [ho] pacul, cangkul; *v*
memacul, mencangkul

hog *n* babi; orang rakus; *v*
mengambil semua untuk diri
sendiri, memonopoli

hoist *clothes* ~ jemuran (baju); *v*
menaikkan

hold *n* pegangan, genggaman;
palka; *v* **held held** memegang,
menggenggam; bermuatan; ~
off menjauhkan, menahan; ~
fast bersikukuh; ~ *forth*
mengutarakan pendapat; berbicara lama; ~ *out* bertahan;
~ *up* tahan; menodong; ~-*up*
perampokan, penodongan; ~
with setuju, percaya; ~ *a posi-*
tion menjabat; ~*ing company*
perseroan induk; **holdings** *n,*
pl saham, sero

hole *n* lubang, liang; ~-*in-one*
memasukkan bola golf ke
dalam lubang dengan sekali
pukul saja

holiday *n* hari libur; *religious* ~
hari raya; *v* berlibur

holiness *n* kesucian; *His* ~ Yang
Mulia Sri Paus ← **holy**

Holland *n, sl* Belanda; propinsi
Holland di negeri Belanda

hollow *n* rongga, ruang; lembah kecil; *v* mengorok, membuat rongga; *adj* hampa, kosong

holly *n* tanaman dengan daun berbentuk tajam dan buah merah, digunakan sebagai hiasan Natal

holocaust *n* [holokost] bencana (pembakaran), pemusnahan; *nuclear* ~ bencana akibat perang nuklir; *The* ~ pembinasaan orang Yahudi di Eropa selama Perang Dunia Kedua

holster *n* sarung (senjata)

holy *adj* suci, kudus; *Cath* ~ *Father* Sri Paus; ~ *Ghost,* ~ *Spirit* Roh Kudus; ~ *water* air suci

homage *n* [hommej] hormat, sembah; *to pay* ~ *to* menghormati, menyembah

home *n* rumah; panti jompo; *adj* di rumah, di kandang sendiri; ~ *Counties* wilayah di sekitar kota London; ~ *economics* pendidikan kesejahteraan keluarga (PKK); ~ *ground* kandang sendiri, lapangan sendiri; ~ *Office* Departemen Dalam Negeri; ~ *Secretary* Menteri Dalam Negeri; ~ *sweet* ~ hujan emas di negeri orang, hujan batu di negeri awak, lebih senang di negeri sendiri; *at* ~ di rumah; betah, mapan; *to bring* ~ *to* membuat sadar; *to go* ~ *to the village* pulang kampung, mudik; *to see someone* ~ mengantarkan pulang; **hometown** *n* kampung

(halaman); **homely** *adj* sederhana, bersahaja; buruk rupa; **homemade** *adj* buatan sendiri; **homesick** *adj* **homesickness** *n* rindu pada rumah, kampung halaman atau negeri sendiri; **homestead** *n* rumah dan pekarangan, rumah pertanian; **homeward** *adv* pulang, ke (arah) rumah; ~ *bound* dalam perjalanan pulang; **homework** *n* pekerjaan rumah (PR); **homing** ~ *pigeon* merpati pos

homicide *n* [homisaid] pembunuhan; **homicidal** *adj* bersifat pembunuh

homo *n, sl* orang homo; **homoseksual** *n* orang homoseksual; *adj* homoseksual, suka sesama jenis

Honduran *n* orang Honduras; *adj* berasal dari Honduras

honest *adj* [onest] jujur; **honesty** *n* kejujuran

honey *n* [hani] madu; sayang, sayangku; ~*ed* manis; **honeybee** *n* lebah madu; **honeycomb** *n* sarang madu, sarang lebah; **honeymoon** *n* bulan madu; *v* berbulan madu; **honeymooners** *n, pl* orang yang berbulan madu

Hong Kong *n* Hong Kong; *adj* berasal dari Hong Kong

honk *n* bunyi klakson; *v* mengklakson, membunyikan klakson

honorable *adj* terhormat; ~ *discharge* pemberhentian dengan hormat; *The* ~ Yang Terhormat; **honorably** *adv* dengan hormat;

honorary *adj* kehormatan; ~ *member* anggota kehormatan; **honor** *n* hormat, kehormatan; *v* menghormati; *in* ~ *of* untuk menghormati; *on my* ~ sungguh mati

hoodwink *v* menipu, memperdayakan

hoof *n* **hooves** kuku (binatang)

hook *n* kait, kali; *v* mengait; ~ *up* memasang, menghubungkan; ~ *and eye* kancing cantel, kait; *off the* ~ lepas, selamat; *to swallow* ~, *line and sinker* percaya semua dari ceritanya; **hooked** *adj* keranjingan; ~ *nose* hidung bengkok

hooligan *n* pengacau; penggemar sepak bola yang brutal, bonek

hoop *n* gelindingan, simpai; *hula* ~ hulahup

hoot *n* suara burung hantu; bunyi klakson; suara tertawa; *v* bersuara (burung hantu); tertawa; *I don't give a* ~ saya tidak peduli; **hooter** *n* klakson

hop *n* lompat (pada satu kaki); *v* melompat-lompat, melonjak-lonjak; ~, *step and jump* tidak jauh; *arch* lompat tiga

hope *n* harapan; *v* berharap; mengharapkan; *no* ~ tidak ada harapan; **hopeful** *adj* penuh harapan; **hopeless** *adj* putus asa

horde *n* [hord] kelompok, kawanan

horizon *n* [horaizon] cakrawala, kaki langit, ufuk, horison; **horizontal** *adj* [horizontel] melintang, horisontal

hormone *n* hormon

horn *n* tanduk; terompet, klakson; **horned** *adj* bertanduk

hornbill *n* burung enggang

hornet *n* penyengat, langau

horoscope *n* horoskop; *your* ~ bintang anda

horrible, horrific *adj* mengerikan, dahsyat; **horrify** *v* mengerikan; **horror** *n* kengerian, ketakutan, horor; *house of* ~s rumah hantu

horse *n* kuda; ~ *around* bermain-main; *clothes* ~ jemuran (baju); *rocking-*~ kuda goyang, kuda mainan; *saw-*~ kuda-kuda; **horseback** *on* ~ berkuda; **horseplay** *n* permainan kasar; **horsepower** *n* daya kuda, PK *(paardekracht)*; **horseshoe** *n* ladam, tapal kuda

horticultural *adj* berkaitan dengan perkebunan, hortikultural; **horticulture** *n* perkebunan, hortikultura

hose *n* selang; *panty-*~ stoking

hospice *n* [hospis] panti (untuk orang sakit)

hospitable *adj* ramah

hospital *n* rumah sakit; *mental* ~ rumah sakit jiwa

hospitality *n* keramahtamahan

host *n, m* [hoost] tuan rumah

hostage *n* sandera, tawanan; *to take* ~ menyandera

hostel *n* asrama; *youth* ~ losmen

hostess *n, f* [hoostés] nyonya rumah; *arch air* ~ pramugari ← **host**

hostile *adj* bermusuhan; **hostility** *n* [hostiliti] permusuhan

hot *adj* panas, hangat; pedas; seksi, menggairahkan; *~-blooded* cepat marah; *~-cross-bun* roti Paskah; *~ dog* roti sosis; *~ plate* tungku; *~ spring* sumber air panas; *~ water bottle* botol karet; *in ~ water* dalam kesulitan

hotel *n* hotel; *four-star ~* hotel bintang empat

hothead *n* pemarah ← **hot**

hotline *n* sambungan langsung, nomor telepon langsung ← **hot**

hotshot *n* jagoan ← **hot**

hound *n* anjing pemburu; *v* memburu, mengejar

hour *n* [auer] jam; *~ hand* jarum pendek; *half-~, half an ~* setengah jam; *quarter of an ~* seperempat jam; **hourglass** *n* jam pasir; **hourly** *adj* per jam, setiap jam; **hours** *(for) ~* berjam-jam; *after ~ (ah)* setelah jam kerja

house *n* rumah; dewan; *~ of Representatives* Dewan Perwakilan Rakyat; *on the ~* gratis; **houseboat** *n* rumah perahu; **houseboy** *n, m* pembantu, pelayan rumah; **housecoat** *n* daster; **household** *n* rumah tangga; **housekeeper** *n* kepala pembantu; **housekeeping** *n* pengelolaan (rumah tangga); **housemaid** *n, f* pembantu, pramuwisma; **housemother** *n, f* ibu asrama, ibu kos; **housewarming** *n* pesta atau selamatan untuk rumah baru; **housewife** *n, f* ibu rumah tangga; **housework** *n* pekerjaan rumah; **housing** *n* perumahan; *~ estate* perumahan

hovel *n* gubuk (derita)

how *adv* bagaimana; betapa; *~ about* bagaimana kalau; *~ beautiful* betapa cantiknya; *~ do you do?* apa kabar?; *~ much?, ~ many?* berapa banyak?; *~ much is it?* berapa (harganya)?; **however** *adv* biarpun, akan tetapi, namun; bagaimanapun

howl *n* gonggong; teriak, tangis; *v* melolong; menangis (dengan keras); **howler** *n* kesalahan yang sangat lucu

HP *abbrev* horsepower GK (gaya kuda), PK *(paardekracht)*

HQ *abbrev* headquarters mabes (markas besar)

HR *abbrev* human resources SDM (sumber daya manusia)

HRH *abbrev* His/Her Royal Highness Yang Dipertuan Agung

HS *abbrev* high school sekolah menengah (umum, SMU)

hub *n* pusat (kota); **hubcap** *n* dop

huddle *n, v* berkumpul, berhimpitan

hue *n* [hiu] warna, rona; *~ and cry* keributan, tampik sorak

hug *n* pelukan; *v* berpelukan; memeluk; *~s and kisses* peluk cium; *bear-~* memeluk erat

huge *adj* besar sekali

hull *n* lambung kapal

hum *n* senandung; dengung; *v* bersenandung; mendengung

human *n, adj* manusia, orang; ~ *resources (HR)* sumber daya manusia (SDM); ~ *rights* hak azasi manusia (HAM); **humane** *adj* manusiawi, berperikemanusiaan; **humanitarian** *adj* berperikemanusiaan; ~ *aid* bantuan kemanusiaan; **humanity** *n* umat manusia; perikemanusiaan

humble *adj* rendah hati; *v* merendahkan

humbug *n* penipu; semacam permen

humdrum *adj* membosankan, menjemukan, biasa

humid *adj* lembab; **humidity** *n* kelembaban

humiliate *v* menghina, merendahkan; **humiliation** *n* penghinaan

humility *n* kerendahan hati

hummingbird *n* semacam burung kolibri

humorous *adj* lucu, kocak, menggelikan; **humor** *n* kelucuan; sifat; *sense of* ~ selera humor

hump *n* punuk (unta), bongkol; ~-*backed whale* ikan paus bongkok

hunch *n* perasaan, firasat, dugaan

hunchback *n, adj* bungkuk

hundred *n* ratusan; *adj* seratus; **hundredth** *n* perseratus; *adj* keseratus

Hungarian *n* [Hanggérian] bahasa Hongaria; orang Hongaria; *adj* berasal dari Hongaria; **Hungary** *n* Hongaria

hunger *n* [hangger] rasa lapar; ~ *for* rindu akan, merindukan; **hungry** *adj* lapar

hunt *n* perburuan, buruan; *v* berburu; memburu; **hunter** *n* pemburu; **hunting** *n* pemburuan, perburuan

hurdle *n* gawang; rintangan; *v* melompati; mengatasi; **hurdles** *n* lari gawang

hurl *v* melempar, melemparkan

hurrah, hurray *ejac* hore; *hip, hip* ~ hip hip hore

hurricane *n* angin topan

hurried *adj* terburu-buru, tergopoh-gopoh; **hurry** *n* ketergopoh-gopohan; *v* bergegas; menggegaskan; ~ *up* bergegaslah; *sl* cepatan, ayo cepat; *in a* ~ tergesa-gesa

hurt *n* sakit hati, luka; *v* melukai, menyakiti, mencederai, merusak; **hurtful** *adj* menyakitkan

husband *n* suami

hush *n* kesunyian (sejenak), keheningan; *v* diam; ~ *up* menutup-nutupi

husk *n* kulit (biji)

husky *n (Siberian)* ~ anjing Eskimo; *adj* serak, parau

hut *n* pondok, gubuk

HW *abbrev homework* PR (pekerjaan rumah)

Hwy *Highway* Jl Ry (Jalan Raya)

hydraulic *adj* [haidrolik] hidrolik, hidrolis; **hydraulics** *n, pl* hidrolika

hydrochloric ~ *acid* asam garam; **hydroelectric** ~ *power station* pembangkit listrik tenaga air; **hydrogen** *n* [haidrojen] hidrogen, zat air; **hydrology** *n* [haidroloji] hidrologi; **hydrophobia** *n* takut air

hygiene *n* [haijin] kebersihan; higiene; **hygienic** *adj* bersih; higienis

hyperactive *adj* sangat aktif, hiperaktif

hypertension *n* hipertensi, darah tinggi

hypnotism *n* [hipnotisem] hipnotisme; **hypnotist** *n* (ahli) hipnotis; **hypnotize** *v* menghipnosis

hypochondriac *n* orang yang selalu merasa dirinya sakit

hypocrite *n* [hipokrit] orang munafik; **hypocritical** *adj* munafik

hypodermic ~ *syringe* jarum suntik

hypothesis *n* [haipothesis] hipotesa, hipotesis

hysteria *n* penyakit histeria; **hysterical** *adj* histeris

I

I *pron* saya, aku
IBRA *abbrev Indonesian Bank Restructuring Agency* BPPN, Badan Penyehatan Perbankan Nasional

ice *n* es; ~ *block* es batu; ~ *hockey* hoki es; ~ *pack* kompres dingin; ~*d tea* es teh; ~*-skating* bermain sepatu (luncur) es; ~*-skating rink* gelanggang es; ~ *a cake* memberi lapisan manis pada kue; **ice cream** *n* es krim, es puter; **iceberg** *n* gunung es; **Iceland** *n* Eslandia; **Icelandic** *n* bahasa Eslandia; *adj* berasal dari Eslandia; **icing** *n* lapisan gula di atas kue; ~ *sugar* tepung gula; *the* ~ *on the cake* penutup yang indah

icon *n* orang ternama; *Chr* ikon, gambar orang suci

icy *adj* [aisi] dingin sekali, sedingin es ← **ice**

ID *abbrev identification* identitas, jati diri

IDD *abbrev international direct dialing* SLI (sambungan langsung internasional)

idea *n* [aidia] ide, gagasan; **ideal** *adj* [aidil] yang diinginkan atau diidamkan, ideal, yang terbaik

identical *adj* sama, serupa, identik

identification *n* pengenalan, identifikasi; **identify** *v* mengenal, mengidentifikasi; **identity** *n* identitas, jati diri; ~ *card* kartu pengenal, kartu tanda penduduk (KTP)

ideology *n* [aidioloji] paham, ideologi

idiom *n* ungkapan, idiom

idiot *n* orang dungu; **idiotic** *adj* dungu, idiot

idle *v* [aidel] menganggur, bermalas-malas; jalan tapi belum tarik (mesin); *adj* malas, tidak dipakai

idol *n* idola; berhala; **idolize** *v* mendewakan, memuji-muji

idyllic *adj* [aidilik] yang didambakan, asri

ie *id est = that is* yaitu, yakni

if *conj* kalau, jika; apabila, bila

ignite *v* menyala, membakar; menyalakan; **ignition** *n* starter, kontak; ~ *key* kunci kontak

ignorance *n* ketidaktahuan, kebodohan; **ignorant** *adj* tidak tahu; **ignore** *v* tidak menghiraukan, tidak mengindahkan

iguana *n* iguana, sejenis biawak

ill *n* penyakit; *adj* sakit; jahat, salah; ~ *at ease* tidak betah; ~-*advised* keliru; ~-*fated* (bernasib) sial, naas; ~-*gotten* didapat secara tidak halal; ~-*mannered* kurang ajar, tidak sopan; ~-*suited* tidak cocok; ~-*tempered* cepat marah; ~-*treat* menganiaya

illegal *adj* melanggar hukum, tidak sah, ilegal

illegible *adj* tidak terbaca

illegitimate *adj* lahir di luar nikah; ~ *child* anak yang lahir di luar nikah, anak haram

illicit *adj* gelap, tidak sah

illiteracy *n* kebutahurufan; **illiterate** *adj* buta huruf

illness *n* penyakit; *mental* ~ penyakit jiwa

illogical *adj* tidak logis

illuminate *v* menerangkan

illusion *n* ilusi, khayal; **illusionist** *n* tukang sulap

illustrate *v* menggambarkan, melukiskan; **illustration** *n* gambar, lukisan, ilustrasi; **illustrator** *n* pelukis

illustrious *adj* ternama

image *n* gambar; **imaginary** *adj* khayal; **imagination** *n* daya cipta, khayal, fantasi; **imagine** *v* membayang; membayangkan

imbalance *n* ketidakseimbangan, ketimpangan

imbecile *n* [imbesil] lemah pikiran

IMF *abbrev International Monetary Fund* Dana Moneter Internasional

imitate *v* meniru; **imitation** *n* tiruan, imitasi; ~ *leather* kulit palsu; **imitator** *n* peniru

immaculate *adj* rapi sekali, apik; *Chr* suci

immediate *adj* langsung; **immediately** *adv* serta merta

immense *adj* sangat besar; **immensely** *adv* sangat (besar)

immerse *v* mencelupkan, membenamkan; **immersion** *n* pencelupan

immigrant *n* pendatang, imigran; **immigrate** *v* datang dari daerah lain untuk menetap; **immigration** *n* imigrasi

imminent *adj* segera

immobile *adj* tidak bisa bergerak

immoral *adj* tuna susila, cabul; **immorality** *n* perbuatan cabul

immortal *adj* kekal, abadi, baka; **immortality** *n* keabadian, kekekalan; **immortalize** v mengabadikan

immovable adj [imuvabel] tidak bisa bergerak

immune adj kebal, imun; **immunity** n kekebalan; **immunization** n imunisasi, pengebalan

imp n sejenis roh jahat; anak nakal

impaired adj rusak, terganggu

impartial adj tidak memihak, adil, obyektif

impassable adj tidak dapat dilintasi atau dilalui; **impasse** n jalan buntu, impas

impassive adj tanpa perasaan, tenang

impatience n [impésyens] ketidaksabaran, rasa tidak sabar; **impatient** adj tidak sabar

impeach v menuduh, mendakwa, memanggil ke pengadilan; **impeachment** n dakwaan, tuduhan; pemanggilan

impede v menghalangi, merintangi; **impediment** n halangan, rintangan

impending adj mendatang

impenetrable adj tidak bisa dimasuki atau dilalui

imperative n bentuk perintah; adj harus

imperceptible adj nyaris tidak kelihatan

imperfect adj kurang sempurna, tercela

imperial adj [impirial] kaisar; **imperialism** n imperialisme; **imperialist** n orang penjajah, imperialis; adj imperialis,

penjajahan ← **empire**

impersonal adj bersikap dingin; tidak mengenai orang tertentu

impersonate v menyamar sebagai; **impersonation** n penyamaran

impertinence n tindakan kurang ajar; **impertinent** adj kurang ajar

imperturbable adj tenang

impervious adj tahan air; tak terpengaruh

impetuous adj tidak sabar, cepat bereaksi

impetus n pemicu; dorongan

implement n perkakas, perabot, alat; v menerapkan, melaksanakan; **implementation** n penerapan, implementasi

implicate v melibatkan; **implication** n implikasi, dampak

implicit adj secara tersirat, implisit

implore v memohon

imply v [implai] menyindir, menyiratkan

impolite adj kurang sopan

import n barang impor, pemasukan; v mengimpor, mendatangkan

importance n pentingnya; **important** adj penting

importer n pengimpor, importir

impose v membebankan; **imposing** adj mengagumkan, mengesankan; **imposition** n beban

impossible adj mustahil, tidak mungkin; **impossibility** n sesuatu yang mustahil

impostor *n* penipu, penyamar, gadungan

impotence *n* lemah syahwat, impotensi; **impotent** *adj* tidak berkuasa; lemah syahwat, impoten

impoverished *adj* miskin

impractical *adj* tidak praktis

impress *v* memberi kesan, mengesankan; **impression** *n* kesan; cetakan; **impressionable** *adj* mudah terpengaruh; **impressive** *adj* mengesankan, hebat, dahsyat

imprison *v* [imprizon] memenjarakan; **imprisonment** *n* hukuman penjara

improbable *adj* kemungkinan kecil

impromptu *adj* mendadak

improper *adj* tidak layak, tidak senonoh; **impropriety** *n* ketidakpantasan

improve *v* [impruv] memperbaiki; meningkatkan; menjadi sembuh, membaik; **improvement** *n* perbaikan, peningkatan, kemajuan

impudent *adj* kurang ajar, tidak sopan

impulse *n* kata hati, dorongan hati; **impulsive** *adj* menurut kata hati

impure *adj* kotor, cemar, najis, tidak murni, tidak suci; **impurity** *n* noda

in *prep* di (dalam), dalam, pada; *adj, coll* laku, populer; ~ *addition* lagipula; ~ *contrast* sebaliknya, di sisi lain; ~

Indonesian dalam Bahasa Indonesia; ~ *Semarang* di Semarang; ~ *spite of* walaupun, meskipun; *Rhonda's not* ~ Rhonda tidak ada; Rhonda tidak masuk; ~-*depth* secara mendalam; ~-*laws* keluarga suami/isteri, ipar; ~*s and outs* seluk-beluk; ~-*service* latihan dalam perusahaan; ~ *the pond* di dalam kolam

inability *n* ketidakmampuan

inaccessible *adj* [inaksésibel] tidak dapat diakses, terpencil

inaccuracy *n* kesalahan; **inaccurate** *adj* tidak teliti, tidak tepat

inactive *adj* tidak aktif, tidak bergerak

inadequacy *n* [inadekuasi] kekurangan; **inadequate** *adj* kurang, tidak cukup

inadmissible *adj* tidak dapat diterima

inadvertent *adj* lalai, tidak sengaja; **inadvertently** *adv* secara tidak sengaja

inappropriate *adj* tidak pantas

inarticulate *adj* tidak jelas

inaudible *adj* tidak kedengaran, tidak terdengar

inaugural *adj* [inogyural] perdana; **inaugurate** *v* melantik; membuka, memulai; **inauguration** *n* pelantikan; pembukaan

inborn *adj* asli, bawaan, naluriah

incalculable *adj* tidak terhitung

incarnation *n* penjelmaan

incendiary *n* pembakar; ~ *device* bom pembakar

incense *n* dupa, kemenyan

incessant *adj* tidak berhenti-henti, selalu; **incessantly** *adv* secara terus-menerus

inch *n* inci

incident *n* peristiwa, kejadian, insiden; **incidental** *n* soal kecil; *adj* kebetulan, tidak penting; **incidentally** *adv* ngomong-ngomong

incinerate *v* membakar; **incinerator** *n* tempat pembakaran sampah

incision *n* [insisyen] torehan, irisan; **incisive** *adj* tajam; **incisor** *n* gigi seri

incite *v* menghasut; **incitement** *n* hasutan

inclination *n* [inklinasyen] kecenderungan, kecondongan; **incline** *n* lerengan, tanjakan; *v* cenderung, condong

include *v* mengandung, meliputi; **including** *conj* termasuk; **inclusive** *adj* inklusif; sampai dengan

incognito *adj* [inkognito] dengan menyamar

incoherent *adj* tidak jelas

income *n* [incam] pendapatan, penghasilan, gaji; ~ *tax* pajak penghasilan; **incoming** *adj* yang masuk

incomparable *adj* tiada tanding, tiada banding

incompatible *adj* tidak cocok; **incompatibility** *n* ketidakcocokan

incompetence *n* ketidakmampuan; **incompetent** *adj* tidak mampu

incomplete *adj* kurang lengkap, tidak komplet

incomprehensible *adj* tidak masuk akal; tidak dapat dimengerti

inconceivable *adj* tak terbayangkan

incongruous *adj* tidak sesuai

inconsiderate *adj* tidak memperhatikan (perasaan orang lain)

inconsistent *adj* tidak konsisten

inconsolable *adj* tidak dapat dihibur

inconvenience *n* repot, gangguan, kesulitan; **inconvenient** *adj* merepotkan, mengganggu

incorporate *v* merangkum, menggabungkan; **incorporated** *adj* perseroan terbatas

incorrect *adj* tidak benar, salah

increase *n* pertambahan, kenaikan; *v* tambah, bertambah; menambah, menaikkan, meningkatkan

incredible *adj* luar biasa, tidak dapat dipercaya, hebat

incredulous *adj* kurang percaya

incriminate *v* melibatkan, memberatkan; **incriminating** *adj* yang melibatkan, yang memberatkan

incubate *v* mengeram; **incubation** *n* penetasan, pengeraman; ~ *period* masa perkembangan (penyakit)

incumbent *n* pemegang jabatan

incur *v* mendatangkan; ~ *expenses* memakan biaya

incurable *adj* [inkyurabel] tidak dapat diobati, tidak

dapat disembuhkan

indebted [indéted] ~ *to* berhutang (budi) kepada

indecency *n* perbuatan cabul; **indecent** *adj* tak senonoh, tidak sopan

indecision *n* kebimbangan, kebingungan; **indecisive** *adj* ragu-ragu, bimbang

indeed *adj, adv* betul, sebetulnya; *conj* memang; bahkan; *it is* ~ benar sekali

indefinite *adj* tidak tentu, tidak tetap; **indefinitely** *adv* untuk jangka waktu tidak terbatas; ~*ly* untuk jangka waktu tidak terbatas

indelible *adj* tidak bisa dihapus

indent *n* lekuk; *v* memasukkan ke dalam (alinea)

independence *n* kemerdekaan; kebebasan; ~ *Day* Hari Kemerdekaan; **independent** *adj* mandiri, merdeka, bebas, tidak tergantung

indescribable *adj* **indescribably** *adv* tidak dapat digambarkan

indestructible *adj* tidak dapat dibinasakan atau dimusnahkan

indeterminate *adj* tidak jelas

index *n* daftar, indeks; ~ *finger* telunjuk

India *n* India; *the Dutch East* ~ *Company* VOC; Kompeni; **Indian** *n* orang India; orang Indian; *adj* berasal dari India; ~ *file* berjalan satu per satu; ~ *ink* tinta hitam; ~ *Ocean* Samudera Hindia, Samudera Indonesia

indicate *v* menunjukkan; **indication** *n* tanda, petunjuk, alamat; **indicator** *n* penunjuk; indikator; lampu sein

indict *v* [indait] mendakwa; **indictment** *n* dakwaan

Indies *the East* ~ Hindia Belanda; *the West* ~ Hindia Barat

indifference *n* sikap acuh tak acuh, sikap masa bodoh; **indifferent** *adj* acuh tak acuh, masa bodoh

indigenous *adj* asli; ~ *people* penduduk asli

indigestion *n* salah cerna

indignant *adj* marah, jengkel

indigo *n* nila; *adj* biru tua

indirect *adj* tidak langsung

indiscreet *adj* tidak bijaksana; bocor mulut

indiscriminate *adj* tak pandang bulu, membabi buta, sembarangan

indispensable *adj* perlu, wajib

indisposed *adj* tidak enak badan

indisputable *adj* tidak dapat dibantah

indistinct *adj* kurang terang, kurang jelas, samar-samar

individual *n* pribadi, orang, oknum; *adj* perseorangan; ~*ly* masing-masing; **individuality** *n* kepribadian

indivisible *adj* tidak dapat dibagi

Indochina *n* [Indocaina] Indocina; **Indochinese** *adj* berasal dari Indocina

indolent *adj* malas

Indonesia *n* Indonesia; **Indonesian** *n* Bahasa Indonesia; orang

Indonesia; *adj* berasal dari Indonesia; ~ *Embassy* Kedutaan Besar Republik Indonesia (KBRI)

indoor *adj* di dalam rumah atau gedung; ~ *cricket* kriket yang dimainkan di dalam gedung; ~**s** *adv* di dalam rumah atau gedung

induce *v* mempercepat, menyebabkan; membujuk; **inducement** *n* dorongan, insentif, pancingan

induct *v* melantik; **induction** *n* pelantikan; induksi

indulge ~ *in* menikmati; **indulgent** *adj* terlalu baik, sabar

industrial *adj* berkaitan dengan industri atau pabrik; **industrious** *adj* rajin, telaten; **industry** *n* industri, perindustrian; kegiatan

inebriated *adj* [inibriéted] mabuk

inedible *adj* tidak dapat dimakan

inefficient *adj* tidak efisien, tidak jalan dengan baik

ineligible *adj* tidak dapat dipilih

inept *adj* tidak cekatan, kurang bisa

inequality *n* ketidaksamaan, kesenjangan

inert *adj* lembam, tidak bergerak; ~ *gas* gas lembam, gas mulia; **inertia** *n* kelembaman, inersia

inevitable *adj* tidak dapat dielakkan, mau tidak mau

inexact *adj* kurang tepat

inexcusable *adj* tidak dapat dimaafkan

inexhaustible *adj* [inexostabel] tidak habis-habisnya

inexpensive *adj* tidak mahal

inexplicable *adj* [inéksplikabel] tidak dapat dijelaskan, tidak masuk akal

infallible *adj* sempurna, bisa diandalkan, tidak pernah salah

infamous *adj* [infemus] punya reputasi buruk; **infamy** *n* nama buruk

infant *n, adj* bayi, balita, anak kecil; ~**s**, ~ *school* taman kanak-kanak (TK); **infantile** *adj* berkaitan dengan bayi; seperti anak kecil

infantry *n* infantri

infatuated *adj* tergila-gila pada

infect *v* menulari, menjangkiti; **infection** *n* penyakit, infeksi, ketularan; **infectious** *adj* menular

infer *v* mengambil kesimpulan; **inference** *n* kesimpulan, dugaan

inferior *adj* [infirior] kurang bagus atau baik, bermutu rendah; **inferiority** ~ *complex* perasaan minder

infernal *adj* dari neraka; **inferno** *n* kebakaran besar, api besar

infertile *adj* mandul, tidak subur; **infertility** *n* kemandulan

infidel *n* [infidél] kafir; **infidelity** *n* perselingkuhan; ketidaksetiaan

infiltrate *v* menyusup, (diam-diam) memasuki; **infiltration** *n* penyusupan, infiltrasi

infinite *adj* [infinit] tak terhitung; **infinitive** *n* bentuk dasar kata kerja; **infinity** n jumlah tak berakhir

infirm adj sakit(-sakitan); **infirmary** n rumah sakit

inflame v meradangkan; memperparah; **inflammable** adj dapat terbakar

inflate v membesar; **inflation** n inflasi; ~ rate laju inflasi

inflect v mengubah (suara, kata); **inflection** n perubahan suara

inflexible adj kaku

inflict v membebankan; memberikan, menimbulkan

influence n [influens] pengaruh, efek; v mempengaruhi; **influential** adj berpengaruh

influenza n flu, selesma

inform v memberitahu, mengabarkan, menginformasikan

informal adj santai, tidak resmi

informant n sumber, narasumber, pelapor; **informer** n pelapor, pengadu; **information** n informasi, keterangan, penerangan; Department of ~ Departemen Penerangan (Deppen); **informed** adj berpengetahuan luas ← **inform**

infra ~-red infra merah; **infrastructure** n prasarana

infrequent adj [infrikuent] jarang

infringe v melanggar, menyalahi; **infringement** n pelanggaran

infuriate v membuat marah

infusion blood ~ tambah darah

ingenious adj [injinius] sangat pandai

ingredient n [ingridient] bahan (mentah)

inhabit v mendiami, menghuni; **inhabitant** n penduduk, penghuni

inhale v menarik nafas, mengisap; **inhaler** n isapan, sedotan

inherent adj tersirat; berpautan

inherit v mewarisi; **inheritance** n warisan

inhuman adj tidak manusiawi, bengis, biadab

initial n huruf pertama, paraf; v teken, memaraf; adj pertama, perdana, permulaan; **initially** adv awalnya; **initiate** v memulai, memprakarsai; **initiation** n (upacara) pengenalan; **initiative** n prakarsa, inisiatif; **initiator** n pemrakarsa

inject v menyuntik, menyuntikkan; **injection** n suntik, suntikan; injeksi

injure v merugikan, melukai; **injury** n luka; kerugian; hinaan

injustice n ketidakadilan

ink n tinta; **inky** adj berwarna gelap

inlaid adj bertatahkan

inland n pedalaman; the ~ Revenue kantor pajak

inlet n teluk kecil

inmate n tahanan, penghuni

inn n penginapan; ~-keeper pengurus penginapan

innate adj bawaan, naluriah

inner adj (di) dalam; batin

innocence n keadaan tidak bersalah, keadaan tanpa dosa; **innocent** adj tidak bersalah, tanpa dosa

innovate v mencari atau menciptakan yang baru; **innovation** *n* ciptaan baru; **innovative** *adj* mampu menciptakan yang baru

input *n* masuknya; *v* memasukkan

inquest *n* pemeriksaan, penyelidikan; *coroner's* ~ pemeriksaan mayat

inquiry, enquiry *n* pertanyaan; penyelidikan, pemeriksaan; *to make inquiries* minta keterangan; **inquisitive** *adj* ingin tahu

insane *adj* gila, sakit jiwa; **insanity** *n* kegilaan

insatiable *adj* [insésyabel] tidak dapat dipuaskan

inscribe *v* menulis, memahat, menoreh; **inscription** *n* tulisan, suratan, prasasti

insect *n* serangga; **insecticide** *n* obat pembasmi serangga

insecure *adj* gelisah, tidak percaya diri; **insecurity** *n* rasa gelisah atau tidak percaya diri

insemination *n* pembuahan; *artificial* ~ inseminasi buatan

inseparable *adj* [inséparabel] tidak terpisahkan

insert *n* sisipan; *v* menyisipkan, menyelipkan, memasukkan

inside *prep, adj* (di) dalam; ~ *information* informasi dari orang dalam; ~ *out* terbalik; **insider** *n* orang dalam

insight *n* [insait] wawasan, pemahaman

insignificance *n* **insignificant** *adj* tidak berarti, sepele

insinuate *v* menyindir; **insinuation** *n* sindiran

insipid *adj* tawar; lemah

insist *v* mengotot, bersikeras, bersikukuh; mendesak; **insistence** *n* desakan

insolence *n* sikap tidak sopan atau kurang ajar; **insolent** *adj* tidak sopan, kurang ajar

insoluble *adj* tidak dapat larut

insolvent *adj* bangkrut, palit, tidak mampu membayar

insomnia *n* (keadaan) sulit tidur; **insomniac** *n* orang yang sulit tidur

inspect *v* memeriksa; **inspection** *n* pemeriksaan, inspeksi; **inspector** *n* pemeriksa

inspiration *n* ilham, inspirasi; **inspire** *v* mengilhami, memberi inspirasi; **inspiring** *adj* yang mengilhami atau memberi inspirasi

instability *n* ketidakstabilan

install, instal *v* melantik; memasang; **installation** *n* pelantikan; pemasangan; **instalment, installment** *n* angsuran; *to pay in* ~s mencicil, membayar dengan mengangsur

instance *for* ~ misalnya, seumpamanya

instant *n* saat; ~ *coffee* kopi instan; **instantaneous** *adj* [instanténius] **instantly** *adv* saat itu juga, serta-merta

instead *conj* [instéd] alih-alih, melainkan, malah; ~ *of* daripada, sebagai pengganti

institute *n* lembaga, institut; **institution** *n* adat (istiadat); lembaga, institusi instruct *v* mengajar; memerintahkan, menginstruksikan; **instruction** *n* pengajaran; perintah, instruksi; **instructor** *n* pengajar, guru, instruktur

instrument *n* alat, perkakas, pesawat; *string* ~ alat musik gesek

insubordinate *adj* membangkang; **insubordination** *n* pembangkangan

insufficient *adj* kurang cukup

insular *adj* berkaitan dengan pulau; berwawasan sempit

insulate *v* mengisolasikan; **insulation** *n* isolasi; **insulator** *n* isolator

insult *n* cemoohan, hinaan; *v* menghina, mencemoohkan

insurance *n* asuransi, pertanggungan; ~ *agent* agen asuransi; ~ *policy* polis asuransi; **insure** *v* mengasuransikan; memastikan; **insurer** *n* penanggung asuransi

insurgent *n, adj* pemberontak; **insurgency** *n* pemberontakan

insurrection *n* pemberontakan

intact *adj* utuh

intake *n* masukan, kiriman, asupan

integral *adj* perlu; pokok; **integrity** *n* ketulusan hati, kejujuran

intellect *n* akal budi, intelek; **intellectual** *n* cendekiawan; *adj* pandai

intelligence *n* kecerdasan; perintelan, intelijen; **intelligent** *adj* cerdas, pandai

intend *v* berniat, bermaksud;

intended *n* calon, tunangan

intense *adj* hebat, mendalam, kuat, intens; **intensify** *v* meningkatkan; **intensity** *n* intensitas, kekuatan; **intensive** *adj* intensif

intent, intention *n* maksud, niat, kehendak, tujuan; **intentional** *adj* sengaja ← **intend**

inter *v* menguburkan

interact *v* bergaul; **interaction** *n* pergaulan, interaksi

intercede *v* [intersid] menjadi perantara, mengetengahi; **intercession** *n* perantaraan

intercept *v* mencegat

interchange *n* simpang, belokan; *clover-leaf* ~ simpang susun semanggi; **interchangeable** *adj* dapat ditukar

intercom *n* radio antar ruangan

intercontinental *adj* antarbenua

intercourse *n* pergaulan, perhubungan; *(sexual)* ~ persetubuhan; *social* ~ pergaulan (sosial)

interest *n* kepentingan; perhatian, minat; daya tarik; bunga (uang); ~ *rates* suku bunga; *of* ~ menarik perhatian; *v* menarik perhatian; **interested** *adj* tertarik, berminat; **interesting** *adj* menarik (perhatian)

interfaith *adj* antar agama

interfere *v* [interfir] campur tangan; mencampuri, mengganggu; **interference** *n* campur tangan, gangguan

interim *n, adj* sementara

interior *n* [intirior] pedalaman,

dalamnya; *adj* (bagian) dalam;
Minister of the ~ Menteri
Dalam Negeri (Mendagri)

interject *v* berseru; menyeletuk,
menyisipkan; **interjection** *n*
kata seru

interlude *n* selingan, jeda

intermediary *n* perantara;
intermediate *adj* sedang

interminable *adj* [intérminabel]
lama sekali, tidak berkeputusan

intermission *n* waktu istirahat

intermittent *adj* selang-seling,
terkadang-kadang

intern *v* menawan, menginternir;
n orang magang

internal *adj* dalam (negeri);
international *adj* internasional,
antar bangsa

internee *n* tawanan; **internment**
n penawanan, penahanan; ~
camp kamp tawanan; **intern-
ship** *n* masa magang (di rumah
sakit) ← **intern**

interpret *v* menafsirkan; menerjemahkan, (secara lisan); **interpretation** *n* penafsiran;
interpreter *n* penerjemah, juru
bahasa; **interpreting** *n* penerjemahan

interrogate *v* [intérogét]
memeriksa, menginterogasi,
menanyai; **interrogation** *n*
pemeriksaan, interogasi; **inter-
rogator** *n* pemeriksa

interrupt *v* menyela, menyeletuk,
memotong pembicaraan; **interruption** *n* interupsi

intersect *v* memotong, menyilang; ~*ing* silang-menyilang;

intersection *n* perempatan,
simpang; persilangan

interval *n* antara, selang, jeda,
waktu istirahat

intervene *v* [intervin] campur
tangan, menghalangi; **interven-
tion** *n* halangan, campur tangan,
intervensi

interview *n* wawancara, tanya
jawab, interpiu; *v* mewawancarai;
interviewee *n* orang yang
diwawancarai; **interviewer** *n*
pewawancara

intestine *n* [intéstin] usus, isi
perut; *small* ~ usus kecil

intimacy *n* [intimesi] kemesraan;
intimate [intimet] *adj* mesra,
intim, karib; ~ *relations*
hubungan intim

intimidate *v* menakuti-nakuti,
mengintimidasi; **intimidation** *n*
intimidasi

into *prep* ke (dalam); menjadi;
menuju; *Amy went* ~ *the shop*
Amy masuk toko itu; *David's*
~ *Japanese girls* David suka
gadis-gadis Jepang; *that
company has gone* ~ *debt*
perusahaan itu sedang banyak
hutang

intolerable *adj* tidak tertahankan,
tidak dapat dibiarkan; **intolerant**
adj tidak tenggang rasa, tidak
bertoleransi

intoxicant *n* obat atau minuman
perangsang; **intoxicate** *v*
memabukkan; **intoxication** *n*
keadaan mabuk

intransitive *adj* tanpa pelengkap
atau obyek; ~ *verb* kata kerja

tanpa pelengkap

intravenous ~ *drip* infus

intrepid *adj* [intrépid] berani

intricacy *n* [intrikesi] keruwetan; **intricate** *adj* [intriket] berbelit-belit, ruwet

intrigue *n* [intrig] intrik; *v* membuat penasaran, menuntut berpikir

intrinsic *adj* hakiki; **intrinsically** *adv* secara hakiki

introduce *v* memperkenalkan; **introduction** *n* perkenalan; (kata) pengantar; **introductory** *adj* awal

introvert *n* orang yang suka menyendiri dan tidak bergaul; ~ed suka menyendiri

intrude *v* mengganggu; **intruder** *n* orang yang memasuki tempat tanpa izin; maling; **intrusive** *adj* yang mengganggu urusan pribadi

intuition *n* intuisi, gerak hati; **intuitive** *adj* naluriah

inundate *v* membanjiri, menggenangi; **inundation** *n* banjir, air bah

invade *v* menyerang, menyerbu; **invader** *n* penyerang

invalid *n* [invelid] orang sakit, orang cacat; *adj* [invalid] tidak berlaku, tidak sah; **invalidate** *v* membatalkan

invaluable *adj* tak ternilai

invariably *adv* [invériabli] selalu, senantiasa, setiap kali

invasion *n* serangan, serbuan ← **invade**

invent *v* menciptakan, menemu-kan; membuat-buat; **invention** *n* ciptaan; **inventor** *n* pencipta

inventory *n* inventaris

inverse *n* kebalikan; *adj* terbalik; **inversion** *n* pembalikan, inversi; **invert** *v* membalikkan; ~ed *commas* tanda kutip

invest *v* menanamkan (modal), menginvestasikan

investigate *v* menyelidiki; **investigation** *n* penyelidikan; **investigator** *n* penyelidik

investment *n* penanaman modal, investasi; **investor** *n* penanam modal ← **invest**

invincible *adj* tidak terkalahkan

invisible *adj* tak terlihat, gaib

invitation *n* undangan, ajakan; **invite** *v* mengundang, mengajak; mempersilakan; **invitee** *n* tamu, orang yang diundang

invoice *n* faktur, surat tagihan

involuntary *adj* tidak sengaja, secara tanpa sadar

involve *v* melibatkan; ~d terlibat, yang bersangkutan

invulnerable *adj* kebal

inward *adj* ke dalam; batin

IOC *abbrev* International Olympic Committee Komite Olimpiade Internasional

iodine *n* [aiodin] yodium

IOU *abbrev* I owe you saya berhutang kepada anda

Iran *n* Iran; **Iranian** *n* [Irénian] orang Iran; *adj* berasal dari Iran

Iraq *n* Irak; **Iraqi** *adj* orang Irak; *adj* berasal dari Irak

irate *adj* [airét] marah sekali, geram, berang

Ireland n Irlandia; *Northern ~* Irlandia Utara

iris n bunga iris; selaput pelangi, iris

Irish n [Airisy] orang Irlandia; *~ (Gaelic)* bahasa Irlandia; *~ Republican Army (IRA)* Tentara Republik Irlandia; *the ~ Sea* Laut Irlandia; *adj* berasal dari Irlandia; **Irishman** n lelaki Irlandia; **Irishwoman** n wanita Irlandia ← **Ireland**

irk v [érk] membuat jengkel, menjengkelkan, mengganggu; **irksome** adj menjengkelkan, menyusahkan

iron n besi; setrika; *~ filings* serbuk besi; *cast ~* besi tuang; *the ~ Curtain* Tirai Besi; v menyetrika; *~ out* menyelesaikan; **ironing** n setrikaan; kegiatan menyetrika; *~ board* papan setrika

ironic adj ironis; **irony** n ironi, ejekan

irrational adj tidak masuk akal

irreconcilable adj tidak dapat didamaikan

irredeemable adj tidak dapat lagi diterima atau diselamatkan

irregular adj tidak teratur, luar biasa; **irregularity** n ketidak-beresan, kekecualian

irrelevance n **irrelevant** adj tidak relevan

irreparable adj [iréperabel] tidak dapat diperbaiki

irrepressible adj tidak dapat dilawan atau ditahan

irresponsible adj tidak bertang-gung jawab

irreverence n [iréverens] **irreverent** adj kurang hormat

irrevocable adj [irévekebel] tidak dapat diubah atau ditarik lagi

irrigate v mengairi; **irrigation** n pengairan, irigasi

irritable adj cepat marah, marah-marah; **irritant** n yang meng-ganggu; **irritate** v mengganggu, membuat jengkel; **irritation** n rasa gatal, iritasi

Islam n agama Islam; **Islamic** adj berkaitan dengan Islam

Is. *island* P. (pulau)

island n [ailand] pulau; *the Andaman ~s* Kepulauan Andaman; **isle** n [ail] pulau kecil; *the ~ of Man* Pulau Man

isolate v mengasingkan, men-jauhkan; **isolation** n pengasi-ngan

Israel n [Isrél] Israel; **Israeli** n orang Israel; *adj* berasal dari Israel; **Israelite** n, arch orang Israel

issue n [isyu] masalah, isu; terbitan; v menerbitkan; mengeluarkan, memancarkan

isthmus n tanah genting; *the ~ of Kra* tanah genting Kra

it pron dia, ia (barang); -nya; itu; *who is ~?* siapa?; *~ is (it's) hot* hari ini panas

Italian n bahasa Italia; orang Italia; *adj* berasal dari Italia ← **Italy**

italic n [italik] tulisan miring; *adj* miring; **italicize** v membuat tulisan miring

Italy *n* Italia; *Little ~* kampung Italia

itch *n, v* **itchy** *adj* gatal

item *n* [aitem] barang; pasal, ayat; nomor; **itemize** *v* membukukan

itinerary *n* [aitinereri] rencana perjalanan

its *pron* -nya (barang); *the clock lost ~ hand* tangan jam hilang

it's → it

itself *pron* sendiri

IUD *abbrev intra-uterine device* IUD

ivory *n* [aivori] gading; *~ Coast* Pantai Gading

ivy *n* tanaman menjalar, tanaman merambat

J

jab *n* tusukan; pukulan pendek

jack *n* dongkrak, tuas, kuda-kuda; *~-rabbit* kelinci jantan; *~ up* mendongkrak

jackal *n* serigala

jacket *n* jaket; sampul buku; *potatoes in ~s* kentang yang dibakar dalam kulitnya

jackfruit *n* buah nangka

jackpot *n* hadiah utama

jade *n* batu giok; **jaded** *adj* sayu, lesu; jemu

jagged *adj* [jaged] bergerigi

jaguar *n* semacam macan di Amerika

jail, gaol *n* penjara; **jailer** *n* sipir

jam *n* selai; *~-packed* penuh

sesak; *~ session* latihan bermain musik; *traffic ~* kemacetan lalu lintas; *in a ~* dalam kesulitan; *v* macet; menyumbat, menjepit; berlatihan main musik

Jamaica *n* [Jaméka] Jamaika; **Jamaican** *n* orang Jamaika; *adj* berasal dari Jamaika

jamb [jam] *door ~* kusen pintu

jamboree *n* jambore

janitor *n* petugas pembersihan, penjaga

January *n* bulan Januari

Japan *n* Jepang; **Japanese** *n* bahasa Jepang; orang Jepang; *adj* berasal dari Jepang

jar *n* kendi, stoples, botol; *v* menggetarkan

jargon *n* bahasa khusus, istilah di bidang tertentu

jasmine *n* [jasmin] bunga melati

jaundice *n* [jondis] kuning

jaunty *adj* periang, bergaya

Java *n* pulau Jawa; *Central ~* Jawa Tengah (Jateng); *West ~* Jawa Barat (Jabar); **Javanese** *n* bahasa Jawa; orang Jawa; *adj* berasal dari Jawa Tengah atau Jawa Timur

javelin *n* lembing; *~ throw* lempar lembing

jaw *n* rahang

jay *n* semacam burung

jaywalk *v* menyeberang jalan tanpa melihat rambu lalu lintas; **jaywalker** *n* penyeberang jalan yang sembrono

jazz *n* musik jazz; **jazzy** *adj* bergaya, menyolok

jealous adj [jélus] cemburu;
jealousy n kecemburuan, rasa
cemburu

jeep n mobil jip

jeer n ejekan, cemoohan; v
mengolok-olok, mencemooh

jell v mengeras, membeku,
mengental; **jellied** adj yang
dibekukan; **jelly** n agar-agar;
jelly-bean n semacam gula-
gula agar; **jellyfish** n ubur-
ubur

jeopardize v [jépardaiz] membahayakan; **jeopardy** n bahaya

jerk n sentakan, renggutan; orang
bodoh; v menyentak,
merenggut

jerrycan n jerigen

jersey n [jérsi] switer, baju hangat

jest n kelucuan, senda gurau; v
bersenda gurau; **jester** n, arch
badut

Jesus n [Jisus] Yesus, Isa; ~
Christ Yesus Kristus

jet n semburan air; pancar gas;
jet; v, sl terbang; **jetset** n gaya
hidup yang sering terbang ke
luar negeri; ~-black hitam
legam; ~ fighter pesawat perang
jet

jetty n jeti, dermaga

Jew n orang Yahudi

jewel n [jul] (batu) permata;
jeweler n tukang emas; **jewel-
ry** n perhiasan

Jewish adj Yahudi ← **Jew**

jiffy in a ~ dalam sekejap mata

jigger n anu, barang kecil; v, sl
merusak

jigsaw n gergaji ukir; ~ puzzle

teka-teki menyusun potongan
kayu

jingle n lagu iklan; v bergeme-
rincing

jinx n nasib malang, sial

jitters to have the ~ gelisah,
kegugupan; **jittery** adj gelisah,
gugup

job n pekerjaan, tugas; ~-hunting
mencari pekerjaan; good ~
bagus; part-time ~ pekerjaan
paruh waktu; **jobless** adj
menganggur; the ~ kaum
penganggur

jockey n joki

jog n, v lari pagi, lari sore; ~
your memory membantu
mengingat; **jogging** n kegiatan
lari; ~ track jalan untuk lari

join v bergabung, ikut serta;
menghubungkan, menggabungkan; ~ the army masuk tentara

joiner n tukang kayu, tukang
kusen

joint n sendi, ruas; adj bersama;
~ venture usaha patungan

joke n senda gurau, lelucon,
guyonan; v bersenda gurau,
melucu, melawak; only joking
bercanda kok; **joker** n pelawak;
joker (kartu)

jolly adj riang, gembira

jolt n goyangan, guncangan; v
bergoyang

Jordan n Yordania; **Jordanian** n
orang Yordania; adj berasal dari
Yordania

jostle v [josel] berdesak-desakkan

jot v mencatat; ~ting pad kertas
catatan

journal *n* (buku) harian, majalah; **journalism** *n* kewartawanan, jurnalisme; **journalist** *n* wartawan, jurnalis

journey *n* [jurni] perjalanan

jovial *adj* riang, gembira

joy *n* kebahagiaan, kegembiraan; **joyful, joyous** *adj* berbahagia, gembira

JP *abbrev* Justice of the Peace hakim setempat

jubilant *adj* bergembira; **jubilation** *n* kegembiraan

jubilee *n* peringatan, hari ulang tahun; *silver* ~ peringatan 25 tahun

Judaism *n* [Judéizem] agama Yahudi

judge *n* hakim; *v* menghakimi, menilai; **judgment** *n* keputusan; **judicial** *adj* berkaitan dengan hakim dan kehakiman; **judiciary** *n* pengadilan, kehakiman; **judicious** *adj* bijaksana

judo *n* judo, yudo

jug *n* tempat untuk saus atau minuman; teko; *milk* ~ tempat susu

juggle *v* bermain sunglap; bermain sulap; **juggler** *n* tukang sunglap; tukang sulap; **juggling** *n* sunglapan; sulapan

juice *n* air (buah), sari buah, jus; *orange* ~ air jeruk; **juicy** *adj* berair banyak

jukebox *n* kotak musik, mesin pemutar lagu

July *n* bulan Juli; *the fourth of* ~ hari kemerdekaan Amerika

jumble *n* campuran; ~ *sale* pasar barang bekas; *v* mencampuradukkan

jumbo *adj* (berukuran) besar

jump *n* lompatan, loncatan; *v* melompat, meloncat; melompati; *high* ~ lompat tinggi

jumper *n* switer, baju hangat

jumpy *adj* gelisah

junction *n* simpang (jalan), perempatan; *T-*~ simpang tiga

June *n* bulan Juni

jungle *n* [janggel] hutan, rimba (raya)

junior *n* yunior; *adj* yunior, lebih muda, lebih rendah pangkatnya; ~ *high school* sekolah menengah pertama (SMP)

junk *n* barang bekas, barang loak, sampah

junkie *n, sl* pecandu

jurisdiction *n* yurisdiksi, wilayah kekuasaan; **jurisprudence** *n* ilmu hukum, yurisprudensi; **jury** *n* juri

just *adj, adv* hanya, saja; tepat, persis; ~ *now* baru saja

just *n* adil; **justice** *n* keadilan; **justify** *v* membenarkan

juvenile *adj* kekanak-kanakan; muda

K

kaleidoscope *n* [kalaidoskop] kaledoskop

kangaroo *n* kanguru, kangguru

kapok *n* [képok] kapuk

kayak *n* dayung; kayak, kano; sampan; **kayaker** *n* pedayung; **kayaking** *n* dayung kayak

Kazakh *n* bahasa Kazakh; orang Kazakh; **Kazakhstan** *n* Kazakhstan; **Kazakhstani** *n* orang Kazakh; *adj* berasal dari Kazakhstan

keel ~ *over* terjatuh, oleng

keen *adj* antusias; tajam; *to be ~ on* menyukai, menaksir

keep *v* **kept kept** menyimpan, memegang, menaruh, memelihara, menjaga; ~ *time* menghitung waktu; ~ *a promise* menepati janji; ~ *a secret* menyimpan rahasia; ~ *at it* meneruskan; ~ *on* terus melakukan; ~ *off* tidak mengganggu; ~ *out* dilarang masuk; ~ *up* melanjutkan, meneruskan; *for ~s* untuk selamanya; **keeper** *n* pemegang, penjaga, kurator; **keeping** *in ~ with* sesuai dengan, selaras dengan; **keepsake** *n* kenang-kenangan, oleh-oleh

keg *n* tong

kennel *n* kandang anjing; ~*s* tempat penitipan anjing

Kenya *n* Kenia; **Kenyan** *n* orang Kenia; *adj* berasal dari Kenia

kept *v*, *pf* → **keep**

kernel *n* biji, inti

kerosene *n* [kerosin] minyak tanah; ~ *lamp* lampu petromaks

kettle *n* teko; **kettledrum** *n* genderang kecil

key *n* [ki] (anak) kunci; tuts; nada; ~ *chain* rantai kunci; ~ *ring* gantungan kunci; *piano* ~ tuts (piano); *major* ~ nada mayor; *adj* pokok; *v* ~ *in* memasukkan, mengetik; **keyboard** *n* kibor; papan tuts; **keyhole** *n* lubang kunci; **keynote** ~ *speech* pidato pembukaan

kg *kilogram* kg (kilogram)

Khmer *n* bahasa Kamboja

kick *n* tendangan; perangsang; *v* menendang, menyepak; ~ *off* memulai; *just for ~s* iseng

kid *n* anak kambing; *sl* anak; **kiddie, kiddy, kids** *adj, coll* kanak-kanak

kidnap *v* menculik; **kidnapper** *n* penculik

kidney *n* [kidni] ginjal; ~*-bean* kacang merah

kill *v* membunuh; ~*ed in action* gugur, tewas; ~ *off* menghancurkan, membinasakan; ~ *time* menghabiskan waktu; **killer** *n* pembunuh; **killing** *n* pembunuhan; **killjoy** *n* orang yang merusak kesenangan orang lain

kiln *n* tempat pembakaran (genteng, keramik)

kilogram, kilo *n* kilo, kilogram

kilometer, kilo *n* kilo, kilometer

kilt *n* rok khas Skotlandia

kilter *out of* ~ tidak sesuai, rusak

kin *n* kerabat, kaum, keluarga

kind *n* [kaind] macam, jenis, ragam; *adj* baik hati, simpati; ~*-hearted* baik hati; ~ *of* agak; *of a ~* sejenis

kinder, kindergarten *n* taman kanak-kanak (TK)

kindle *v* menyalakan, mengobarkan; **kindling** *n* ranting-ranting kecil untuk perapian

kindly *adv* [kaindli] dengan baik hati; tolong; ~ *inform me* tolong diberitahu ← **kind**

kindness *n* [kaindness] kebaikan hati ← **kind**

kinetic *adj* kinetika

king *n* raja; **kingdom** *n* kerajaan

kink *n* kekusutan; **kinky** *adj* aneh

kinship *n* kekeluargaan ← **kin**

kiosk *n* kios, loket, warung

Kiribati *n, adj* [Kiribas] Kiribati

kiss *n* ciuman, sun, kecupan; *v* mencium, (memberi) sun; ~ *on the cheek* cium pipi, sun; memberi sun; *hugs and ~es* peluk cium

kit *n* peralatan, perlengkapan; *sports* ~ seragam olahraga

kitchen *n* dapur; ~ *sink* tempat cuci piring; ~ *stove* kompor

kite *n* layang-layang; *to fly a* ~ main layang-layang

kitten *n* anak kucing; **kitty** *n, coll* kucing (kecil); *n* celengan, dana

kiwi *n* burung kiwi; **kiwifruit** *n* (buah) kiwi

kleptomania *n* keinginan mengutil barang; **kleptomaniac** *n, adj* pengutil

km *kilometer* km (kilometer)

knack [nak] *to get the* ~, *to have the* ~ mampu, mengetahui caranya

knead *v* [nid] menguli; ~*able eraser* penghapus yang bentuknya bisa diubah

knee *n* [ni] lutut, dengkul; ~ *deep,* ~ *high* selutut; **kneecap** *n* tempurung lutut

kneel *v* [nil] **knelt knelt** berlutut

kneepad *n* pelindung lutut ← **knee**

knew *v, pf* → **know**

knickers *n, sl* [nikers] celana dalam; *n, arch* celana

knife *n* [naif] pisau; *v* menikam; *at* ~*point* ditodong

knight *n* [nait] kesatria; **knighthood** *n* gelar bangsawan Inggris

knit *v* [nit] merajut; ~ *your brow* mengernyitkan alis; **knitter** *n* orang yang merajut; **knitting** *n* rajutan; ~ *needle* jarum rajut; **knitwear** *n* baju rajutan, busana rajutan

knob *n* [nob] tombol, pegangan; **knobbly** ~ *knees* tulang lutut menonjol

knock *n* [nok] pukulan, ketok; *a* ~ *at the door* ketukan di pintu; *v* mengetuk; memukul; ~ *down* membongkar; memukul sampai jatuh; ~ *up sl* menghamili; ~*-kneed* berkaki pengkar keluar; **knockout** *n* (pukulan) yang sangat hebat

knot *n* [not] simpul; buku, mata kayu; mil laut; *v* menyimpulkan; **knotty** *adj* sulit

know *v* [no] **knew known** tahu, mengetahui; mengenal; mengerti; ~*-all* sok tahu; *in the* ~ tahu; **knowing** *adj* pengertian; **knowledge** *n* [nolej] pengetahuan; *to my* ~ setahu saya; **knowledgeable** *adj* banyak tahu; **known** *adj* dikenal

knuckle *n* [nakel] buku jari; ~ *down* bekerja dengan rajin

KO *abbrev* *knockout* pukulan yang sangat hebat

koala *n* koala

Koran *the* ~ al-Quran; **Koranic** *adj* dari al-Quran; ~ *recital* pengajian

Korea *n* [Koria] Korea (Selatan); *North* ~ Korea Utara; **Korean** *n* bahasa Korea; orang Korea; *adj* berasal dari Korea

kosher *adj* halal (menurut adat Yahudi)

kph *kilometers per hour* kilometer per jam

Kuwait *n* Kuwait; **Kuwaiti** *n* orang Kuwait; *adj* berasal dari Kuwait

Kyrgyz *n* bahasa Kirgistan; orang Kirgis; **Kyrgyzstan, Kirgistan** *n* Kirgistan; *adj* berasal dari Kirgistan; **Kyrgyzstani, Kirgistani** *n* orang Kirgistan

L

L *abbrev* *Lane* Gg (Gang)

L *abbrev* *liter* liter

label *n* merek; nama; *v* memberi nama, menulis nama pada barang

labial *adj* berkaitan dengan bibir

laboratory, lab *n* laboratorium; **laborious** *adj* berat; **labor** *n* pekerjaan (kasar); ~ *Day* Hari Buruh; *in* ~ sedang bersalin; *v* bekerja; ~ *Party* Partai Buruh; **laborer** *n* buruh, tukang, pekerja

labour → **labor**

labyrinth *n* susunan yang simpang siur, labirin

lace *n* renda

lack *n* kekurangan; *v* kurang, tidak memiliki, tidak mempunyai

lacklustre *adj* [laklaster] kurang semarak, biasa

laconic *adj* [lakonik] pendek (kata)

lacquer *n* [laker] lak, pernis; *v* memberi pernis

lacrosse *n* [lakros] permainan yang memakai tongkat dengan keranjangan kecil dan bola

lad *n* anak lelaki; *when I was a* ~ waktu aku kecil; **laddie** *n, sl* anak lelaki

ladder *n* tangga, jenjang

laden *adj* dimuat

ladle *n* [lédel] sendok besar

lady *n, f* [lédi] nyonya, wanita; gelar bangsawan; *ladies and gentlemen* bapak-bapak dan ibu-ibu; ~ *friend* teman wanita, pacar; **ladybird, ladybug** *n* kepik; **ladylike** *adj* seperti wanita yang sopan

lag *n* ketertinggalan, kelambatan; *v* tertinggal, ketinggalan

lagoon *n* laguna

laid *v, pf* → **lay**

lain *v, pf* → **lie**

lair *n* sarang binatang buas

lake *n* danau, telaga; **lakeside** *adj* di tepi danau

lamb *n* [lam] anak domba, anak biri-biri; ~ *chop* potongan daging (iga) domba

lame *adj* lumpuh, pincang; lemah

lament *n* [lamént] ratapan; *v* meratapi; **lamentation** *n* ratapan, tangisan, lamentasi

laminate *v* melaminasi, melapis dengan lembaran plastik, laminating

lamp *n* lampu, pelita; *kerosene* ~ lentera, lampu petromaks; **lamplight** *n* cahaya lampu; **lamppost** *n* tiang lampu, tiang lentera

lance *n* tombak lembing

land *n* tanah, bumi, darat; negeri, negara; ~ *tax* pajak tanah; *by* ~ jalan darat, lewat darat; *v* mendarat; **landing** *n* pendaratan; tempat beristirahat di tangga; **landlady** *n, f* induk semang; **landlocked** *adj* tidak berbatasan dengan laut; **landlord** *n, m* tuan tanah, pemilik rumah; **landmark** *n* patokan, petunjuk; peristiwa penting; **landmine** *n* ranjau (darat); **landowner** *n* tuan tanah; **landscape** *n* pemandangan, lanskap; ~ *architect* arsitek lanskap; **landslide** *n* tanah longsor

lane *n* gang, lorong; jalur; lajur; *slow* ~ jalur lambat; *to change* ~*s* pindah jalur

language *n* [languej] bahasa; *bad* ~ kata-kata jorok, makian

languish *v* merana

lanky *adj* tinggi, jangkung

lantern *n* lentera; *Chinese* ~ lampion

Lao *n* bahasa Laos; orang Laos; **Laos** *n* Laos; **Laotian** *n* orang Laos; *adj* berasal dari Laos

lap *n* haribaan, pangkuan; **lapdog** *n* anjing piaraan yang kecil; penjilat

Lapland *n, arch* Lapland, Samiland; **Lapp** *n* orang Sami

lapse *n* jatuh; kehilangan; selang; *v* kambuh, menjadi; habis

laptop *n* komputer laptop

lard *n* lemak babi; **larder** *n* tempat menyimpan makanan

large *adj* besar, luas; ~ *size* ukuran besar; *at* ~ bebas

lark *n* semacam burung; *sl* iseng

larva *n* **larvae** jentik-jentik

laryngitis *n* [larinjaitis] radang tenggorokan (sehingga suara hilang); **larynx** *n* pangkal tenggorokan

lascivious *adj* [lasivius] merangsang, menggairahkan

laser *n* (sinar) laser

lass, lassie *n, sl* anak perempuan

lasso *n* jerat; *v* menjerat

last *v* tahan, bertahan, berlangsung; awet; *it will* ~ *a year* setahun lamanya; *adj* terakhir, penghabisan; ~ *month* bulan lalu; ~ *night* semalam; *at* ~ akhirnya; **lasting** *adj* awet, abadi

latch *n* palang pintu, kunci, grendel; **latchkey** *n, adj* kunci pintu

late *adj* lambat, terlambat; almarhum, mendiang, *f*

almarhumah; **latecomer** n
pendatang baru; **lately** adv
belum lama, belakangan ini,
baru-baru ini; **lateness** n
keterlambatan

latent adj tersembunyi, terpendam

later adj, adv nanti; kemudian
← **late**

latest adj, adv terakhir, paling
akhir; ~ news berita terkini; at
the ~ paling lambat, selambat-
lambatnya

latex n getah

lathe n [léth] mesin bubut

lather n buih, busa (sabun); v
menyabun

Latin n bahasa Latin, bahasa
Romawi; ~ America Amerika
Latin; ~ script huruf Romawi

latitude n lintang; southern ~
lintang selatan

latter n, adj yang kemudian,
yang tersebut

lattice n kisi-kisi, ruji-ruji;
latticework n kisi-kisi

Latvia n Latvia; **Latvian** adj
berasal dari Latvia; n bahasa
Latvia; orang Latvia

laugh n, v [laf] tertawa, coll
ketawa; ~ at menertawakan,
menertawai; **laughable** adj
menggelikan; tidak masuk akal;
laughter n ketawa, tawa

launch n peluncuran; kapal
berkas; v meluncurkan; ~ into
memulai

launder v mencuci; **laundromat**
n tempat cuci pakai mesin
otomat; **laundry** n cucian, baju
kotor; binatu

lava n lahar, lava

lavatory n [lavetori] kamar kecil,
WC

lavender adj ungu muda; n
semacam bunga harum berwarna
ungu

lavish adj mewah, berlebihan; v
mencurahkan, menghamburkan

law n hukum, undang-undang;
peraturan; ~-abiding taat
hukum; against the ~ melanggar hukum; **lawful** adj sesuai
dengan hukum, sah; **lawless**
adj tanpa hukum; **lawmaker** n
pembuat undang-undang

lawn n lapangan rumput; ~
bowls boling taman; ~ mower
mesin potong rumput; ~ tennis
tenis

lawsuit n perkara, dakwaan; to
bring a ~ against menuntut ←
law

lawyer n pengacara, advokat,
praktisi hukum ← **law**

lax adj lemah, longgar, lalai

laxative n obat peluntur, pencahar

lay v laid laid meletakkan; ~ off
memberhentikan, mempehaka-
kan; membiarkan; ~ eggs
bertelur

layer n lapis, lapisan

layman n orang awam

layout n tata letak; rancangan,
rencana ← **lay**

laziness n kemalasan, **lazy** adj
malas; ~ river kolam renang
berbentuk aliran air; ~ susan
baki makanan yang berputar;
lazybones n pemalas

lb pound pon

lead *n* [léd] timbal, timah hitam, plumbum; ~ *pencil* pensil; **leaden** *v* terbuat dari timah hitam

lead *v* [lid] **led led** memimpin; ~ *role* peranan utama; ~ *the way* memelopori, merintis; **leader** *n* pemimpin; **leadership** *n* kepemimpinan; **leading** *adj* penting, utama, terkemuka

leaf *n* **leaves** daun

leaflet *n* selebaran

leafy *adj* rimbun, rindang ← **leaf**

league *n* [lig] liga, persatuan, perserikatan

leak *n, v* bocor, merembes; **leakage** *n* bocoran, rembesan; **leaky** *adj* bocor, rembes

lean *n* kurus; sedikit

lean *v* tidak lurus, condong, bersandar; **leaning** *n* kecenderungan

leap *n* lompatan; ~ *year* tahun kabisat; *v* melompat; **leapfrog** *n* permainan loncat katak; *v* melompati

leapt *v, pf* [lépt] → **leap**

learn *v* belajar; mendengar berita; **learned** *adj* [lérnéd] terpelajar; **learner** *n* pelajar; **learning** *n* pembelajaran

lease *n* sewa; *v* memyewakan; **leaseholder** *n* penyewa

leash *n* pengikat binatang; *on a* ~ dirantai

least *adj* terkecil, paling sedikit; *at* ~ setidak-tidaknya, sekurang-kurangnya; *not in the* ~ tidak sama sekali

leather *n* [léther] kulit

leave *n* cuti; *maternity* ~ cuti hamil; *paternity* ~ cuti untuk ayah baru; *on* ~ sedang cuti; *v* **left left** berangkat, pergi, bertolak; membiarkan; meninggalkan; ~ *me alone* biarkan saya sendiri; jangan ganggu saya; *to take* ~ pamit, mohon diri; cuti

Lebanese *adj* berasal dari Libanon; *n* orang Libanon; **Lebanon** *n* Libanon

lecture *n* kuliah, ceramah, pidato; *v* memberi kuliah, menguliahi; memberi teguran; **lecturer** *n* dosen, lektor; ~ *in economics* dosen ilmu ekonomi

led *v, pf* → **lead**

leech *n* lintah

leek *n* bawang perai

leer *n* pandangan yang tidak senonoh; *v* mengerling, melirik

leeward *adj* di bawah angin

leeway *n* waktu tambahan, tempat tambahan

left *adj* (sebelah) kiri; ~*-handed* kidal

left *adj, v, pf* tertinggal → **leave**; **leftover** *n, adj* sisa

leg *n* kaki; *you're pulling my* ~ kamu memperolok-olokkan saya

legacy *n* [légasi] warisan, harta pusaka

legal *adj* sah, legal, menurut undang-undang; **legalization** *n* pengesahan, legalisasi; **legalize** *v* mengesahkan, membolehkan

legend *n* legenda; kunci peta; **legendary** *adj* terkenal

leggings n, pl [légings] stoking tebal, celana ketat ← **leg**

leggy adj berkaki panjang ← **leg**

legible adj [léjibel] dapat dibaca

legion n [lijen] legiun, pasukan; banyak sekali

legislate v [léjislét] membuat undang-undang; **legislation** n perundang-undangan; **legislative** adj legislatif; **legislator** n pembuat undang-undang; **legislature** n badan pembuat undang-undang

legitimacy n hak kekuasaan; **legitimate** adj sah

legroom n ruang untuk kaki (selama duduk) ← **leg**

leisure n [lésyer] waktu luang, waktu senggang; at your ~ di waktu senggang

lemon n jeruk nipis, limun; **lemonade** n air jeruk nipis; Sprite

lend v meminjamkan; ~ a (helping) hand menolong; **lender** n pemberi pinjaman

length n panjang; jarak, lama; at ~ panjang lebar; at arm's ~ menjaga jarak; **lengthen** v memperpanjang; **lengthy** adj panjang lebar; panjang, lama; **lengthwise** adj menurut panjangnya

leniency n sikap lunak, toleransi; **lenient** adj lunak, toleran

lens n lensa; contact ~ lensa kontak

leopard n [lépard] macan kumbang

leper n [léper] penderita kusta;

leprosy n penyakit kusta

lesbian n lesbi

Lesotho n [Lesutu] Lesotho

less adj kurang, lebih kecil; **lessen** v mengurangi, mengecilkan; **lesser** adj lebih kecil; the ~ Sundas Nusa Tenggara

lesson n pelajaran; les; piano ~ les piano

lest conj agar tidak, supaya tidak; kalau-kalau; ~ we forget jangan dilupakan (jasa pahlawan perang)

let v let let membiarkan; menyewakan (rumah); ~ alone apalagi, jangankan; ~ down mengecewakan; menurunkan; ~ fly melepaskan; ~ go melepaskan; ~ up reda, berhenti; ~ us, let's marilah; to ~ disewakan; ~-down n kekecewaan

lethal adj [lithal] mematikan

lethargic adj malas, lesu; **lethargy** n rasa lesu, rasa letih

let's → **let us**

letter n surat; huruf, aksara; Chinese ~ huruf Cina; man of ~s sarjana; Faculty of ~s Fakultas Sastra; ~ box kotak surat; bis surat; **letterhead** n kop surat

lettuce n [létes] selada

leukaemia, leukemia n [lukimia] kanker darah, leukemia

levee n [lévi] tanggul; dermaga

level adj [lével] datar, rata; n tingkat; permukaan; v meratakan; ~-headed berkepala dingin; ~ off, ~ out mendatar;

on the ~ jujur

lever *n* pengungkit, tuas, tuil

levy *n* [lévi] pajak, retribusi

lewd *adj* cabul, jorok

lexical *adj* berkaitan dengan kata; **lexicon** *n* kosa kata

liability *n* [laiabiliti] tanggungan; **liable** *adj* tanggung; bertanggung jawab; ~ *to* cenderung

liaison *n* [liéson] hubungan; ~ *officer* pegawai hubungan masyarakat (humas)

liar *n* [laier] pembohong ← **lie**

liberal *adj* murah hati; liberal; **liberate** *v* membebaskan; **liberation** *n* pembebasan; **liberator** *n* pihak yang membebaskan; **liberty** *n* kemerdekaan, kebebasan

Liberia *n* [Laibiria] Liberia; **Liberian** *adj* berasal dari Liberia; *n* orang Liberia

libido *n* [libido] gairah seksual

librarian *n* [laibrérian] pustakawan, kepala perpustakaan; **library** *n* perpustakaan

Libya *n* Libia; **Libyan** *adj* berasal dari Libia; *n* orang Libia

license, licence *n* [laisens] izin, ijazah; ~ *plate* pelat polisi; *driving* ~ surat izin mengemudi (SIM); *off-*~ toko minuman keras; **license** *v* mengizinkan, membolehkan; **licensee** *n* pihak yang diizinkan

lichen *n* [laiken] sejenis lumut

lick *n* jilatan; *v* menjilat; mengalahkan dengan telak

lie *v* bohong; *v* berbohong, membohong

lie *v* **lay lain** terletak, berada; berbaring; ~ *down* merebahkan diri, berbaring, tiduran

Liechtenstein *adj* [Likhtenstain] berasal dari Liechtenstein; *n* Liechtenstein; **Liechtensteiner** *n* orang Liechtenstein

lieu [liu] *in* ~ *of* sebagai pengganti

lieutenant *n* letnan; ~-*Colonel* Letkol (Letnan Kolonel)

life *n* hidup, kehidupan; ~ *insurance* asuransi jiwa; ~-*size* berukuran yang sebenarnya; *for* ~ sepanjang hidup; *to save a* ~ menyelamatkan jiwa; **lifeboat** *n* sekoci (penyelamat); **lifebuoy** *n* pelampung; **lifeguard** *n* penjaga pantai, penjaga kolam renang; **lifejacket** *n* baju pelampung; **lifeless** *adj* tidak hidup lagi, mati; **lifelong** *adj* seumur hidup, sepanjang hidup; **lifesaver** *n* penjaga pantai; *sl* yang sangat menolong; **lifestyle** *n* gaya hidup; **lifetime** *n* seumur hidup ← **live**

lift *n* lift, pengangkat barang; *v* mengangkat; *to get a* ~ menumpang, *coll* tebeng

light *n* [lait] cahaya, sinar; lampu; *sl* korek api; *adj* terang; ringan, enteng; *v* **lit lit** menyalakan, memasang (lampu); ~-*fingered* tangan panjang; ~-*headed* pusing; ~-*hearted* enteng, menyenangkan; ~ *year* tahun cahaya; *to bring to* ~ membukakan; *to come to* ~ terbuka, terkuak; *to make* ~ *of* meremehkan; **lighten** *v* meringankan, menerangkan; **lighter** n korek api, geretan; **light-house** n mercu suar; **lightning** n kilat, halilintar, petir; ~ *rod* penangkal petir

like v suka, menyukai, gemar; *adj* sama, serupa, sepadan, setara; *conj* seperti, sama dengan; v suka, menyukai, gemar; *~-minded* sependapat; *I ~ fish* saya suka ikan; **likeable** *adj* ramah, menyenangkan; **likely** *adj* agaknya, kemungkinan; **likeness** n kesamaan, kemiripan; **likewise** *adv* begitu juga, demikian pula; **liking** n kesukaan

lilac *adj* ungu muda; n semacam tanaman yang berbunga ungu

lily n [lili] teratai; *~-white* tidak berdosa

limb n [lim] anggota badan

limbo *in* ~ telantar

lime n limau; kapur; ~ *green* hijau lumut

limelight n [laimlait] pusat perhatian; sorotan

limit n batas, limit; v membatasi; *that's the* ~ itu keterlaluan; **limitation** n pembatasan; **limited** *adj* terbatas; *Proprietary* ~ *(Pty Ltd)* perseroan terbatas (PT)

limousine n [limosin], **limo** *n, sl* limosin, limo

limp v berjalan pincang; *adj* lemah

line n garis, gores; tali; baris, deret; ~ *manager* atasan; *shipping* ~ perusahaan perkapalan; *in* ~ *with* sesuai dengan; *out of* ~ menyimpang; *to stand in* ~ antri; *to toe the* ~ mematuhi peraturan; v melapisi

linen n kain linan; ~ *cupboard* lemari seprei

liner n kapal penumpang yang besar

linger v [lingger] tidak mau pergi-pergi

lingerie n [lonjeri] pakaian dalam wanita

linguist n [lingguist] ahli bahasa, munsyi; **linguistics** n ilmu bahasa, ilmu linguistik; *applied* ~ linguistik terapan

lining n lapisan, furing ← **line**

link n mata rantai, hubungan; *golf* ~*s* padang golf; v menghubungkan

linoleum n [lainolium] **lino** *coll* linolium

lion n [laion] singa; *~-hearted* pemberani; ~*'s share* bagian terbesar; **lioness** n singa betina

lip n bibir; **lipread** v **lipread** **lipread** [lipréd] membaca gerakan bibir; **lipstick** n lipstik

liqueur n [likur] sopi manis, minuman keras yang manis

liquid *adj* cair; n cairan, zat cair; ~ *petroleum gas (LPG)* elpiji

liquidate v menghentikan, membubarkan, melikuidasi; **liquidation** n likuidasi, pembubaran

liquor n [liker] minuman keras

lisp n cadel, pelat; v berbicara cadel

list *n* daftar; *short* ~ daftar pendek; *v* mendaftar, menyebutkan

listen *v* [lisen] mendengarkan, menyimak; **listener** *n* pendengar; ~**s** para pendengar; **listening** *n* (pelajaran) menyimak

lit *v, pf* → **light**

liter *n* liter; *per* ~ seliter, per liter

literacy *n* [literasi] (angka) melek huruf; **literal** *adj* harfiah; **literally** *adv* secara harfiah; benar-benar; **literate** *adj* melek huruf; terpelajar; **literary** *adj* sastra; **literature** *n* kesusastraan

Lithuania *n* [Lithuénia] Lituania; **Lithuanian** *adj* berasal dari Lituania; *n* orang Lituania

litigate *v* [litigét] menuntut (secara hukum); **litigation** *n* proses pengadilan

litre → **liter**

litter *n* usungan, tandu

litter *n* seperindukan (anak binatang)

litter *n* sampah (di jalan); *v* membuang sampah sembarangan; **litterbug** *n* orang yang sering membuang sampah sembarangan

little *adj* kecil; sedikit; ~ *finger* kelingking; *n* sedikit; ~ *by* ~ lambat laun, sedikit demi sedikit

live *v* [liv] hidup, tinggal, berdiam; ~ *off* hidup dari; ~ *with* hidup dengan; kumpul kebo dengan; **live** *adj* [laiv] langsung; hidup; ~ *broadcast* siaran langsung; ~*wire* orang yang penuh semangat; kawat yang ada setrum; **livelihood** *n* rezeki, nafkah; *to seek a* ~ mencari nafkah, cari makan; **liven** ~ *up* memeriahkan

liver *n* [liver] hati, lever

livestock *n* hewan ternak

livid *adj* [livid] pucat; sangat marah

living *n* [living] mata pencarian; *to make a* ~ mencari nafkah; ~ *room* kamar keluarga ← **live**

lizard *n* [lizerd] kadal, biawak, cicak; *lounge* ~ orang yang banyak bermalas-malas

llama *n* sejenis binatang di Amerika Selatan seperti unta

LLB *abbrev Bachelor of Laws* SH (Sarjana Hukum)

load *n* muatan, beban; *v* memuat; memuati, mengisi; **loading** *n* pemuatan; ~ *bay* tempat bongkar muat

loaf *n* **loaves** roti; *v* bermalas-malas; **loafer** *n* pemalas; sejenis sepatu santai

loan *n* pinjaman; ~ *shark* lintah darat; *v* meminjamkan, meminjami → **lend**

loathe *v* membenci; **loathsome** *adj* memuakkan

lob *n* bola yang dipukul tinggi; *v* memukul tinggi-tinggi

lobby *n* lobi (hotel); gerakan; *the green* ~ gerakan pro lingkungan; *v* berusaha memengaruhi, memperjuangkan; **lobbyist** *n* aktivis, pejuang

lobe *ear* ~ cuping

lobster *n* udang karang, udang laut

local *adj* setempat, lokal; *n* orang setempat; **locality** *n* kawasan, tempat; **locate** *v* mencari; **location** *n* lokasi, tempat; penempatan

loch *n* [lokh] danau (di Skotlandia)

lock *n* kunci, gembok; pintu air; *~-up* sel tahanan; *steering ~* kunci stir; *~, stock and barrel* semuanya; *a ~ of hair* seikat rambut; *v* mengunci; **locker** *n* loker

locket *n* liontin (yang dapat dikunci atau dipasang foto kecil) ← **lock**

lockjaw *n* kejang mulut ← **lock**

locksmith *n* tukang kunci ← **lock**

locomotion *n* daya penggerak; **locomotive** *n* lokomotif, lok

locust *n* belalang

lodge *n* pondok, pemondokan; *v* mondok, menginap; *~ a complaint* mengajukan pengaduan; **lodger** *n* pemondok, anak kos; **lodging** *n* pemondokan; akomodasi

loft *n* loteng; **lofty** *adj* tinggi, mulia

log *n* catatan, buku harian; *ship's ~* buku harian di kapal; *v* mencatat; *~ in* memasukkan nama atau kata kunci; *~ off, ~ out* keluar dari program

log *n* batang kayu, kayu gelondongan; *~ cabin* pondok (dibuat dari balok kayu); *v* menebang (pohon); **logging** *n* penebangan; *illegal ~* penebang-

an liar, pembalakan liar

logarithm *n* [logarithem] logaritma

logbook *n* buku harian di kapal

logic *n* [lojik] logika, akal; **logical** *adj* logis, masuk akal; **logistics** *n, pl* logistik

loincloth *n* cawat; **loins** *n, pl* selangkangan

loiter *v* mondar-mandir, berlamalama di suatu tempat

lone *adj* tunggal, sendiri; **loneliness** *n* (rasa) kesepian; **lonely** *adj* sepi, kesepian, sunyi, sendirian; **loner** *n* penyendiri

long *~ for* rindu akan, merindukan, mengidamkan; **longing** *n* hasrat, kerinduan

long *adj* panjang; lama; *~-distance call* telepon interlokal; *~-haired* berambut panjang; *~-haired cat* kucing angora; *~-playing record (LP)* piringan hitam; *~-range* jarak jauh; *~-sighted* rabun dekat; *~-winded* bertele-tele; *~ jump* lompat jauh; *before ~* tidak lama kemudian; *so ~* sampai jumpa, sampai bertemu; *as ~ as* selama; *I won't be ~* saya tidak akan lama; **longhouse** *n* rumah panjang

longitude *n* [longgityud] bujur

look *n* penampilan, gaya; *v* melihat; *~ after* merawat, menjaga; *~ around* melihat-lihat; *~ at* melihat; *~ back* menoleh; *~ for* mencari; *~ forward to* menantikan; *~ on* menonton; *~ out!* awas!; *~ing glass* cermin;

lookout *n* tempat meninjau; pengintai; **looks** *n, pl* paras, wajah, penampilan

loom *n* perkakas tenun; *v* terbayang, timbul

loon *n* sejenis burung; *sl* orang gila; **loony** *adj, n* gila ← **lunatic**

loop *n* lingkaran, ikal, putaran; *v* menyimpulkan; ~ *the* ~ terbang jungkir balik; **loophole** *n* jalan keluar

loose *adj* longgar, kendur, terurai; lepas; ~ *living* kehidupan bebas; **loosen** *v* melonggarkan, mengendurkan

loot *n* rampasan, hasil jarahan; *v* merampas, menjarah; **looter** *n* penjarah; **looting** *n* penjarahan

lop *v* memenggal

loquacious *adj* [lokuésyius] berbicara banyak

lord *pron* tuan; ~ *(it) over* bertindak sombong; **Lord** *n, Chr* Tuhan

lorry *n* truk

lose *v* [luz] hilang, kehilangan; rugi, kalah; ~ *face* malu; ~ *weight* mengurangi berat badan; ~ *your way* tersesat; **loser** *n* yang kalah; **loss** *n* rugi, kerugian, kehilangan; *at a* ~ tidak mengerti; **lost** *adj* hilang; tersesat; tewas

lot *n* undi

lot *a* ~ banyak; **lots** *n, pl* banyak

lotion *n* salep

lottery *n* lotere, undian ← **lot**

lotus *n* bunga seroja, bunga teratai

loud *adj* berisik, riuh, gempar, bising; **loudspeaker** *n* pengeras suara

louse *n* **lice** kutu; **lousy** *adj* [lauzi] jelek

lout *n* orang yang berkelakuan tidak baik

love *adj* [lav] kosong (dalam permainan tenis); *forty* ~ empat puluh kosong (40-0)

love *n* [lav] cinta, asmara; kasih (sayang); *pron* kekasih, sayang; *v* mencintai, menyayangi; ~ *triangle* cinta segitiga; *in* ~ kasmaran; *for the* ~ *of* demi; *to fall in* ~ jatuh cinta; *to make* ~ bercinta; **lovely** *adj* manis, cantik, asri; **lover** *n* kekasih; penggemar

low *adj* rendah, hina; murah; *n* titik rendah, nadir; ~ *spirits* sedih hati; ~ *tide* air surut; **lower** *adj* lebih rendah; *v* menurunkan; **lowland** *n* tanah rendah; **lowly** *adj* hina

loyal *adj* setia, setiakawan; **loyalty** *n* kesetiaan, kesetiakawanan

LPG *abbrev liquid petroleum gas* elpiji

lubricant *n* [lubrikant] pelumas; **lubricate** *v* meminyaki, melumasi

lucid *adj* terang, jelas

luck *n* untung; *bad* ~ sial; *good* ~ untung; semoga; *down on your* ~ celaka, bernasib sial; *to push your* ~ mencari untung secara berlebihan; **lucky** *adj* beruntung lucrative *adj* [lukratif] menguntungkan; **lucre** *filthy ~* duit, uang

luggage *n* bagasi, barang-barang; *~ tag* tanda bagasi

lukewarm *adj* [lukworm] suam-suam kuku

Luxembourg *adj* berasal dari Luksemburg; *n* Luksemburg; **Luxembourger** *n* orang Luksemburg

lullaby *n* [lalabai] (kidung) ninabobo

lumbago *n* [lambégo] sakit pinggang

lumber *n* kayu; *v* berjalan dengan berat; **lumberjack** *n* penebang kayu

luminary *n* orang terkenal, tokoh; **luminous** *adj* terang, bercahaya

lump *n* gumpal, bongkah; benjolan; *v* menaruh tanpa banyak berpikir; menyatukan; *a ~ in my throat* ingin menangis; *like it or ~ it* walau tidak suka, harus terima; **lumpy** *adj* bergumpal, tidak encer

lunacy *n* sakit gila

lunar *adj* berkaitan dengan bulan; *~ eclipse* gerhana bulan

lunatic *adj* gila; *n* orang gila

lunch *n, v* makan siang; **luncheon** *n, arch* makan siang

lunge *n* sergapan, terjangan; *v* menyergap

lungs *n, pl* paru-paru; *to shout at the top of your ~* berteriak sekeras-kerasnya

lurch *v* bergerak secara mendadak; *to leave in the ~* mening-galkan dalam kesulitan

lure *n* iming-iming, bujukan; *v* memancing, mengiming-iming

lurid *adj* menyolok, berwarna terang; jorok

lurk *v* bersembunyi, menunggu diam-diam

luscious *adj* [lasyes] sangat enak

lush *adj* lebat, subur

lust *n* hawa nafsu, berahi; *~ after* menaksir

luster *n* kegemilangan; **lustrous** *adj* berseri

lusty *adj* kuat, bersemangat

lute *n* kecapi

luxurious *adj* [laksyurius] mewah, lux; **luxury** *n* kemewahan

lychee *n* buah leci

lymph *n* [limf] getah bening; *~ node* kelenjar getah bening; **lymphatic** *~ cancer* kanker getah bening

lyric *n* lirik, kata-kata yang dinyanyikan

M

m *meter* m (meter)

ma'am *pron* Nyonya, Nona ← **madam**

mac, mack → **mackintosh**

Macau *n* Makau; **Macanese** *n* orang Makau peranakan

macaroni *n* makaroni

Macedonia *n* [Masedonia] Makedonia; *Former Yugoslav Republic of ~ (FYROM)* Makedonia; **Macedonian** *adj* berasal dari Makedonia; *n* orang Makedonia

machine *n* [masyin] mesin, alat; ~ *gun* mitraliur, senapan mesin; *washing* ~ alat pencuci pakaian; **machinery** *n* mesin-mesin, alat-alat

mackerel *n* sejenis ikan air tawar

mackintosh, mac, mack *n* jas hujan

mad *adj* gila, tergila-gila; marah; *like* ~ cepat sekali; ~ *about cars* tergila-gila akan mobil; *as* ~ *as a hatter* gila betul

Madagascar *n* Madagaskar

madam *pron* Nyonya; *a little* ~ anak perempuan yang manja

madman *n* orang gila

madness *n* kegilaan, penyakit gila

maestro *n* [maistro] musisi ternama, maestro

magazine *n* majalah

maggot *n* belatung

magic *n* [majik] ilmu sihir, ilmu sulap; **magical** *adj* berkaitan dengan sihir; ajaib; **magician** *n* [majisyen] penyihir, penyulap

magistrate *n* [majistrét] hakim; ~*'s court* pengadilan negeri

magnate *n* pengusaha, konglomerat

magnesium *n* [magnisium] magnesium

magnet *n* magnet, maknit; **magnetic** *adj* magnetik

magnificent *adj* sangat bagus, mewah

magnify *v* memperbesar; ~*ing glass* kaca pembesar

magnitude *n* besar(nya); kebesaran

magpie *n* burung murai

mahogany *n* pohon mahoni, kayu mahoni

maid *n* pembantu; gadis; *old* ~ perawan tua; **maiden** *adj* perdana; ~ *voyage* pelayaran perdana; *n* perawan, gadis

mail *n* pos; surat email; *v* mengepos, mengirim lewat pos; ~ *order* pesanan lewat pos; **mailbox** *n* kotak surat; **mailman** *n* tukang pos

maim *v* memuntungkan, mencederai sehingga cacat

main *adj* utama; ~ *road* jalan utama, jalan raya; *in the* ~ umumnya; **mainland** *n* daratan; **mainly** *adv* terutama

maintain *v* memelihara, mempertahankan; **maintenance** *n* pemeliharaan

maize *n* jagung

majestic *adj* agung; **majesty** *n* keagungan; *Your* ~ Baginda, Sri Paduka

major *adj* utama, terbesar; *n* mayor; ~-*general* mayjen (mayor jenderal); **majority** *n* kebanyakan, mayoritas

make *n* jenis, macam; *v* membuat, membikin, mengadakan; ~-*believe* khayalan; ~ *do* puas; ~ *for* menuju; ~ *love* bercinta; ~ *off* lari, kabur; ~ *up* merias; mengarang, berdusta; mengganti; ~ *fun of* meledek; ~ *light of* menganggap enteng; ~ *up your mind* memutuskan, mengambil keputusan; **make-up** n rias wajah; ~ *artist* perias; **makeover** n perubahan gaya rambut atau rias; **maker** n pembuat, pencipta; **makeshift** adj sementara

malady n [maladi] penyakit

Malagasy adj berasal dari Madagaskar; n bahasa Malagasi; orang Malagasi; ~ *Republic* Madagaskar

malaria n [maléria] malaria

Malawi n Malawi; **Malawian** adj berasal dari Malawi; n orang Malawi

Malay adj Melayu; n Bahasa Melayu, Bahasa Malaysia; orang Melayu; *the ~ Annals* Sejarah Melayu; **Malaya** n, *arch* Semenanjung Melayu; **Malayan** adj berasal dari Semenanjung Melayu; **Malaysia** n Malaysia; *East ~* Sarawak dan Sabah; **Malaysian** n orang Malaysia

Maldives [Maldivs] *the ~* (Kepulauan) Maladewa; **Maldivian** adj berasal dari Maladewa; n orang Maladewa

male adj lelaki, pria; jantan; ~ *friend* teman lelaki

malfunction n kerusakan, kegagalan; v gagal

Mali n Mali; **Malian** adj berasal dari Mali; n orang Mali

malice n [malis] kebencian, niat jahat; **malicious** adj jahat; dengan sengaja

malign v [malain] memfitnah; **malignant** adj jahat; ganas

mallet n palu dari kayu

Malta n (pulau) Malta; **Maltese** adj berasal dari Malta; n orang Malta

mama, mamma n, *pron* ibu

mammal n mamalia, binatang menyusui

man n **men** orang laki-laki, pria; suami, pasangan, pacar; *arch* orang, manusia; ~*-made* buatan manusia; *men at work* awas ada penggalian; ~ *in the street* orang kebanyakan; v bertugas di; **manned** adj diawaki

manage v mengelola, memimpin; mengurus, menangani; **manageable** adj dapat ditangani, dapat diurus; **management** n pimpinan, direksi; pengelolaan, pemerintahan, pengurusan, manajemen; **manager** n manajer, pemimpin, pengurus; **managing** ~ *director* direktur pelaksana

mandate n mandat; **mandatory** adj wajib, keharusan

mane n surai; rambut yang lebat

maneuver, manoeuvre n [manuver] latihan perang-perangan; tipu daya; manuver

manganese n manggan

mange n [ménj] kudis

manger n [ménjer] palung

mango n mangga

mangosteen n manggis

mangrove n bakau

mangy adj kudisan → **mange**

manhood n, m kedewasaan; kejantanan

mania *n* [ménia] kegilaan, demam; **maniac** *n* orang gila, penggila

manicure *n* perawatan tangan, manikur

manifest *adj* nyata; *n* manifes; *v* menampakkan; **manifestation** *n* manifestasi, perwujudan

manikin, mannequin *n* orang-orangan, maneken

manipulate *v* memanipulasi; memainkan, mendalangi; **manipulation** *n* manipulasi, perbuatan curang; **manipulative** *adj* suka memanipulasi

mankind *n* [mankaind] umat manusia ← **man**

manly *adj* jantan, perkasa ← **man**

mannequin → **manikin**

manner *n* cara, jalan; macam; ~s sopan santun; **mannered** *adj* well-~ sopan, beradat

manservant *n, m, arch* pelayan, jongos

mansion *n* [mansyen] rumah besar

manslaughter *n* [mansloter] pembunuhan yang tidak disengaja

mantelpiece *n* rak di atas perapian

manual *adj* dengan tangan, tidak otomatis; *n* pedoman, buku panduan; ~ *labor* pekerjaan kasar

manufacture *n* pembuatan; *v* membuat, membikin; **manufacturer** *n* pabrik

manure *n* pupuk (kotoran)

manuscript *n* naskah

many *adj* [méni] banyak; ~ *a time* beberapa kali

map *n* peta; *v* memetakan

marauder *n* perampok, perusak

marble *n* marmer, pualam; kelereng

March *n* bulan Maret

march *n* perjalanan (militer); mars; *v* jalan kaki; ~ *fly* lalat besar

mare *n* kuda betina

margarine *n* [marjarin] mentega

margin *n* (garis) tepi, batas, pinggiran; **marginalized** *adj* terpinggirkan

marijuana *n* [marihuana] ganja

marina *n* dermaga; **marine** *adj* berhubungan dengan laut; **mariner** *n* pelaut; **maritime** *adj* berhubungan dengan laut

marinade *n* saus perendam; **marinate** *v* merendam

marital *adj* berhubungan dengan perkawinan

mark *n* tanda, alamat; cap; sasaran; bekas; nilai; *good* ~s nilai (rapot) yang baik; *to miss the* ~ meleset; *v* menandai, mengecap; mencatat, memperhatikan; mengoreksi; **marker** *n* penanda; spidol besar; penilai

market *n* pasar, pasaran; *black* ~ pasar gelap; **marketing** *n* pemasaran; **marketplace** *n* pasar

marksman *n* penembak jitu ← **mark**

marmalade *n* selai jeruk

maroon *adj* merah tua

marooned *adj* tertinggal, terdampar (di pulau pasir)

marriage *n* [marij] perkawinan, pernikahan; *related by* ~ berkerabat karena perkawinan; *to ask for her hand in* ~ meminang; ~ *certificate* surat kawin, akte pernikahan; **married** *adj* kawin, nikah; *m* beristri; *f* bersuami ← **marry**

marrow *n* sumsum

marry *v* menikah, kawin; menikahi; ~ *off* menikahkan, mengawinkan

marsh *n* rawa

marshal *n* marsekal; *field-*~ panglima; *v* memanggil

marshmallow *n* penganan manis yang putih dan empuk

marshy *adj* berawa ← **marsh**

Martinique *n* Martinik; **Martiniquais** *adj* [Martiniké] berasal dari Martinik; *n* orang Martinik

martyr *n* martir; **martyrdom** *n* mati syahid

marvel *n* keajaiban; **marvelous** *adj* ajaib, hebat, mengagumkan

mascara *n* perona mata, maskara

masculine *adj* [maskulin] laki-laki, lelaki, jantan; **masculinity** *n* kejantanan

mash *v* menghancurkan, mengaduk sampai halus; ~*ed potato* kentang rebus yang dihaluskan

mask *n* topeng; masker; *v* menyamarkan; ~*ed* bertopeng, berkedok

mason *n* tukang batu

masquerade *n* [maskeréd] pesta bertopeng; *v* menyamar

mass *n* massa; banyak sekali; misa; ~*es* banyak sekali; ~ *rally* demo, unjuk rasa

massacre *n* [masaker] pembunuhan atau pembantaian besar-besaran; *v* membunuh secara besar-besaran

massage *n* pijatan; *v* memijat, mengurut; **masseur, masseuse** *f* tukang pijat

massive *adj* raksasa, besar sekali ← **mass**

mast *n* tiang (kapal)

master *n* tuan (rumah); ahli, guru; *v* menguasai; ~ *bedroom* kamar tidur utama; ~*'s (degree)* S2, magister; **masterly** *adj* ulung; **mastermind** *n* dalang, otak; **masterpiece** *n* adikarya; **mastery** *n* penguasaan, keahlian

masturbate *v* beronani; **masturbation** *n* onani, masturbasi

mat *n* tikar; matras; *door* ~ keset

match *n* korek api; tara, jodoh; pertandingan; *v* menyesuaikan; menyamai, menandingi; **matchbox** *n* tempat korek api; **matchless** *adj* tiada taranya; **matchmaker** *n* mak jomblang

mate *n* kawan, sahabat; pasangan; *v* kawin (binatang)

material *n* bahan, perkakas, alat; materi; ~ *girl* cewek matre; **materialism** *n* materialisme; **materialistic** *adj* materialistis; **materialize** *v* mewujudkan

maternal *adj* keibuan; dari pihak ibu; **maternity** *adj* masa kehamilan; ~ *clothes* pakaian hamil

mathematician *n* ahli matematika; **mathematics, math, maths** *n* matematika

matrimony *n* perkawinan

matron *n* [métron] kepala perawat, suster; **matronly** *adj* berbadan keibuan

matter *n* perkara, hal, perihal; bahan; *as a ~ of fact* ngomong-ngomong; *~-of-fact* terus terang; *what's the ~?* ada apa?; *v* berarti; *it doesn't ~* tidak apa-apa; *no ~ what* bagaimanapun juga

matting *n* anyaman jerami, tikar ← **mat**

mattress *n* kasur

mature *adj* dewasa, tua, matang; *~-age student* mahasiswa dewasa

Maundy ~ *Thursday* hari Kamis Putih

Mauritania *n* [Morakténia] Mauritania; **Mauritanian** *adj* berasal dari Mauritania; *n* orang Mauritania

Mauritius *n* [Morisyes] Mauritius; **Mauritian** *adj* berasal dari Mauritius; *n* orang Mauritius

mausoleum *n* [mosolium] bangunan kuburan

mauve *adj* [mov] lembayung muda, merah tua

maximal *adj* maksimal, sebanyak-banyaknya; **maximum** *adj, n* maksimum, sebanyak-banyaknya

May *n* bulan Mei; ~ *Day* Hari Buruh

may *v, aux* boleh, dapat; **maybe** [mébi] *adv* mungkin, barang-kali, boleh jadi

mayor *n* [mér] walikota

maze *n* labirin, jalan yang ruwet atau simpang siur

MBA *abbrev Master of Business Administration* MBA

MD *abbrev medical doctor* dr, dokter

me *pron, obj* saya, aku, daku

meadow *n* [médo] padang rumput

meager *adj* sedikit

meal *n* makanan, santapan; *the evening ~* makan malam

mean *adj* sedang, rata-rata; kurang, hina

mean *adj* jahat, membuat sakit hati

mean *v* **meant meant** [mént] berarti, bermaksud; memaksud-kan, menghendaki; **meaning** *n* arti, maksud

means *n* harta, kekayaan; alat; cara; *of ~* kaya, berada; *by all ~* tentu, pasti

meant *v, pf* → **mean**

meantime *in the ~* sementara itu; **meanwhile** *adv* sementara itu

measles *n, pl* [mizels] penyakit campak

measure *n* [mésyer] ukuran, takaran; besarnya; tindakan; *v* mengukur; **measurement** *n* ukuran

meat *n* daging; **meatloaf** *n* perpaduan daging dan sayur berbentuk roti

mechanic *n* [mekanik] montir, ahli mesin; **mechanical** *adj* teknik; ~ *engineering* teknik mesin

medal *n* medali

meddle *v* campur tangan; **meddler** *n* orang yang campur tangan

media *n, pl* [midia] pers; perantara, bahan; *print* ~ media cetak

mediate *v* [midiét] menjadi perantara, menengahi; **mediation** *n* perantaraan; **mediator** *n* perantara

medical *adj* kedokteran, medis; ~ *school* jurusan kedokteran; **medicated** *adj* mengandung obat; **medicine** *n* [médisin] obat; jurusan kedokteran, ilmu kedokteran

medieval, mediaeval *adj* [médiivel] dari Abad Pertengahan

mediocre *adj* [midioker] cukupan, tidak istimewa

meditate *v* bermeditasi, bersemadi; **meditation** *n* meditasi, semadi

Mediterranean *the ~ (Sea)* Laut Tengah; ~ *countries* kawasan Laut Tengah

medium *adj* sedang; **media** *n* cenayang, dukun, perantara; bahan

medley *n* campuran (lagu); ~ *relay* nomor estafet gaya ganti (renang)

meet *n* perlombaan atletik atau renang; *v* **met met** bertemu, berjumpa; menemui; berkumpul; **meeting** *n* rapat, pertemuan

melancholic *adj* [mélankolik] **melancholy** *n* murung, sayu

mellow *adj* matang, empuk

melodious *adj* merdu; **melody** *n* lagu

melon *n* semangka

melt *v* meleleh, mencair, melebur; melelehkan, meleburkan; **melting pot** *n* tempat pertemuan berbagai budaya

member *n* anggota; **membership** *n* keanggotaan

membrane *n* selaput

memento *n* kenang-kenangan, cinderamata; **memoir** *n* (buku) kenangan; **memorandum, memo** *n* memorandum, surat peringatan; **memorial** *adj* peringatan; *n* tanda atau tugu peringatan; **memorize** *v* menghafalkan; **memory** *n* ingatan, memori

men *n, pl* → **man**

menace *n* [ménas] ancaman; *v* mengancam

mend *v* memperbaiki, membetulkan; menambal; ~ *your ways* mengubah kebiasaan buruk; *on the ~* mulai sembuh

menial *adj* [minial] kasar; ~ *work* pekerjaan kasar

menstrual *adj* berkaitan dengan datang bulan; ~ *cycle* siklus datang bulan; ~ *pain* sakit mens; **menstruate** *v* **menstruation** *n* datang bulan, mens mental *adj* jiwa; ~ *arithmetic* mencongak, berhitung di kepala; **mentality** *n* mentalitas, cara berpikir

mention *n* [ménsyen] sebutan; *v* menyebutkan; *don't ~ it* (terima kasih) kembali, sama-sama

mentor *n* penasihat

menu *n* daftar makanan, menu

meow *v* [miau] mengeong

mercantile *adj* perniagaan, perdagangan

mercenary *adj* demi uang; *n* tentara bayaran

merchandise *n* (barang) daga-ngan; **merchant** *n* pedagang, saudagar

merciful *adj* murah hati; **merci-less** *adj* tanpa belas kasih, tidak mengampuni

mercury *n* air raksa

mercy *n* belas kasih, kemurahan hati

mere *adj* [mir] hanya, saja, belaka

merge *v* menyatu; menggabung-kan; **merger** *n* pemersatuan, penggabungan

meridian *n* garis bujur

merit *n* jasa; manfaat; **meritori-ous** *adj* berjasa

mermaid *n* putri duyung

merriment *n* keramaian; **merry** *adj* ria; ~-*go-round* komedi putar, korsel

mesh *n* mata jala, lubang

mess *n* kekacauan, keadaan berantakan; *in a ~* dalam kesulitan, biro erasing; *v* mengacaukan; ~ *around* tidak

memperlakukan dengan jujur; ~ *up* mengacaukan

message *n* pesan; **messenger** *n* pesuruh, kurir

Messrs *messieurs* Tuan-Tuan, dkk

messy *adj* berantakan, tidak rapi ← **mess**

met *v, pf* → **meet**

metal *n* logam

metamorphosis *n* metamorfosis

metaphor [métafor] *n* kiasan, ibarat, perumpamaan; **meta-phorical** *adj* secara kiasan

meteor *n* [mitior] bintang jatuh; **meteorologist** *n* ahli cuaca; **meteorology** *n* [mitioroloji] ilmu cuaca, meteorologi

meter *n* meter; ~*ed taxi* taksi argo

method *n* metode, cara, jalan; **methodical** *adj* metodis

metre → **meter**

mew *v* mengeong (anak kucing)

Mexican *adj* berasal dari Meksiko; *n* orang Meksiko; **Mexico** *n* Meksiko

mezzanine *adj* [mézanin] lantai tengah (di antara lantai satu dan lantai dua)

mg *milligram* mg (miligram)

Mgr *Monsignor* Mgr, Uskup

MI5 Dinas Intelijen Inggris

mice *n, pl* ← **mouse**

Micronesia *n* [Maikronisia] Mikronesia; **Micronesian** *adj* berasal dari Mikronesia

microphone *n* [maikrofon] mikrofon, corong radio

microscope *n* [maikroskop] mikroskop

midday *n* tengah hari, jam 12 siang

middle *adj* tengah, menengah; *n* pertengahan, titik tengah; *~-aged* setengah baya; *~-class* kelas menengah; **middleman** *n* perantara, tengkulak

midget *n* katai, cebol

midnight *n* [midnait] tengah malam, jam 12 malam

midriff *n* daerah pinggang

mid-sized *adj* berukuran sedang

midst *n* tengah; *in the ~ of* di tengah

midway *adj* di pertengahan jalan, di tengah jalan

midwife *n* bidan

might *v, aux* [mait] mungkin, boleh jadi

might *n* [mait] kuasa, kekuasaan; **mighty** *adj* berkuasa; besar

migraine *n* [maigrén] migren, sakit kepala sebelah

migrant *n* [maigrant] pendatang; **migrate** *v* pindah, bermigrasi; **migration** *n* migrasi

mild *adj* [maild] lembut, ringan, enteng; *~ weather* cuaca yang tidak panas atau dingin

mile *n* mil; **milestone** *n* batu peringatan; tonggak bersejarah

militant *adj* militan, berhaluan keras; *n* orang militan; **military** *adj, n* militer, ketentaraan; **militia** *n* [milisya] milisi, wajib militer (wamil)

milk *n* susu; *v* memerah susu; *~ bar* warung (susu); *~ cow* sapi perah; **milkman** *n* tukang susu; **milkshake** *n* minuman susu

bercampur (coklat dsb); **milky** *adj* (mengandung) susu, tidak jernih; *the ~ Way* Bimasakti

mill *n* penggilingan, kilang; *v* bergerak dalam keramaian; **miller** *n* penggiling

millimeter *n* mili, milimeter

million *n* juta; **millionaire** *n* jutawan, milyuner

mimic *n* pemain mimik; *v* **mimicked mimicked** meniru

minaret *n* [minarét] menara (mesjid)

mince *n* (daging) cincang; *~ pie* kue Natal yang berisi buah cincang; *v* mencincang, mengiris

mind *n* [maind] akal (budi), pikiran, jiwa; *of one ~* sependapat; *to change your ~* berubah pikiran; *to keep in ~, to bear in ~* ingat akan, mempertimbangkan; *to lose your ~* menjadi gila; *v* ingat akan, memperhatikan, mengindahkan; merasa keberatan; *never ~* tidak apa-apa; *~ your own business* jangan ikut campur; *do you ~* apa anda keberatan; **mindless** *adj* tanpa alasan; **mindreader** *n* orang yang bisa membaca pikiran orang lain

mine *pron, poss* milikku, saya punya

mine *n* ranjau; **minefield** *n* daerah ranjau

mine *n* tambang; *tin ~* tambang timah; **miner** *n* buruh tambang; **mineral** *n* [mineral] barang tambang, barang galian; *~ water* air dari sumber gunung mini *adj, sl* kecil, mungil, mini; **miniature** *adj* kecil; *n* ukuran kecil; *in ~* berskala kecil, berukuran kecil

mingle *v* [minggel] campur, bergaul

minimum *adj, n* minimum, sedikit-sedikitnya, terendah

mining *n* [maining] pertambangan

minister *n* menteri; pendeta; *~ of Agriculture* Menteri Pertanian (Mentan); *~ of the Interior* Menteri Dalam Negeri (Mendagri); *Prime ~* Perdana Menteri; **ministry** *n* kementeri-an, departemen

minor *adj* [mainor] kecil; di bawah umur, belum dewasa; *n* anak; **minority** *n* golongan kecil, minoritas

mint *n* percetakan mata uang; *v* menempa uang; *~ condition* sempurna

mint *n* sejenis kemangi; permen penyegar mulut

minus *v* [mainus] kurang; tanpa; *six ~ one is five* enam kurang satu sama dengan lima

minute *adj* [mainyut] kecil sekali

minute *n* [minet] menit; *~s* notulen, laporan; *~ hand* jarum panjang

miracle *n* [mirakel] keajaiban, mukjizat; **miraculous** *adj* ajaib

mirage *n* [miraj] fatamorgana

mirror *n* cermin; *v* mencerminkan

misadventure *n* kemalangan, nasib buruk

misbehave *v* berkelakuan buruk; **misbehavior** *n* kelakuan buruk

miscalculate *v* **miscalculation** *n* salah hitung

miscarriage *n* [miskarej] **miscarry** *v* keguguran

miscellaneous *adj* [miselénius] beraneka ragam; lain-lain

mischief *n* [mischef] kenakalan, kejahilan; **mischievous** *adj* nakal, jahil

misconception *n* salah paham, salah pengertian

misconduct *n* kelakuan buruk

misdeed *n* perbuatan jahat

miser *n* orang kikir, orang pelit; **miserable** *adj* [mizerabel] sedih, murung; **miserly** *adj* kikir, pelit; **misery** *n* [mizeri] penderitaan, kesusahan

misfortune *n* kecelakaan, kesialan

misgovernment *n* pemerintahan yang buruk

mishmash *n* campuran

misinformation *n* salah informasi

misinterpret *v* **menyalahtafsir-kan; misinterpretation** *n* kes-alahtafsiran penyalahtafsiran

misjudge *v* salah sangka, salah menilai

mislead *v* **misled misled**; **misleading** *adj* menipu, menyesatkan

misprint *n* salah cetak

Miss *n, pron* Nona *(before a surname)*

miss *v* meleset; rindu akan, merindukan; *~ing* tidak hadir; hilang, kurang; *~ person* orang hilang misshapen *adj* salah bentuk, cacat

mission *n* zending; *Cath* misi; perutusan; **missionary** *n* misionaris

mist *n* kabut, halimun

mistake *n* kesalahan; by ~ tidak sengaja; *v* **mistook mistaken** keliru, salah mengerti

Mister *pron* Tuan (before a surname); **mistress** *n* kekasih, gundik

mistook *v*, *pf* → **mistake**

mistrust *v* tidak percaya

misty *adj* berkabut ← **mist**

misunderstand *v* **misunderstood misunderstood** salah mengerti, salah paham, salah tangkap; **misunderstanding** *n* kesalahpahaman

misuse *n* penyalahgunaan; *v* menyalahgunakan

mitten *n* sarung tangan, kaus tangan

mix *n* campuran; *v* mencampur(kan); ~ *up* mencampuradukkan; membingungkan; ~*ed marriage* perkawinan campuran; **mixture** *n* campuran, adonan

ml *milliliter* mili, mililiter

moan *n* erangan; keluhan; *v* mengerang, mengeluh

mob *n* orang banyak; *v* mengerumuni

mobile *adj* dapat bergerak, dapat dipindahkan; *n* hiasan gantung; ~ *phone* telepon genggam, ponsel; **mobilization** *n* mobilisasi, pengerahan

mock *adj* palsu, pura-pura, tiruan; ~ *exam* latihan ujian; *v* mengejek; **mockery** *n* penghinaan

mode *n* cara, jalan

model *adj* contoh; *n* contoh, macam, model; peragawati, peragawan; ~ *aircraft* model pesawat terbang; *v* memperagakan

moderate *adj* sedang, moderat; *n* orang moderat

modern *adj* modern, baru, kini; **modernize** *v* memperbarui

modest *adj* sederhana, rendah hati; sopan; **modesty** *n* kerendahan hati; kesopanan

modification *n* perubahan, modifikasi; **modify** *v* mengubah

moist *adj* basah, lembab; **moisten** *v* [moisen] membasahi; **moisture** *n* embun, kelembaban; **moisturizer** *n* pelembab

molar *n* gigi geraham

mold, mould *n* cetakan; jamur; *v* membentuk, mencetak

Moldova, Moldavia *n* Moldova; **Moldovan** *adj* berasal dari Moldova; *n* orang Moldova

moldy, mouldy *adj* berjamur, jamuran, apak ← **mold**

mole *n* sejenis tikus; spion, mata-mata; tahi lalat

molecule *n* molekul

molest *v* mengganggu (secara seksual), mencampuri

molt, moult *v* berganti bulu atau kulit

molten *adj* cair, leleh ← **melt**

Moluccan *adj* berasal dari Maluku; *n* orang Maluku; **Moluccas** the ~ Maluku

Mom, Mum *pron* Bu, Mak

moment *n* saat; *in a ~, just a ~* sebentar

mommy, mummy *pron* Ibu, Mama, Mami ← **mom**

Monaco *n* Monako; **Monegasque, Monacan** *adj* berasal dari Monaco; *n* orang Monaco

monarch *n* [monark] raja, ratu; **monarchy** *n* kerajaan

monastery *n* [monastri] biara

Monday *n* [Mandé] hari Senin; *Easter ~* hari Senin sesudah Paskah

monetary *adj* [manetéri] keuangan, moneter; ~ *crisis* krisis moneter (krismon); **money** *n* uang; ~ *changer* penukar uang asing; ~ *market* pasar uang; ~ *order* poswesel; *dirty ~* uang haram; **moneybox** *n* celengan

Mongolia *n* Mongolia; **Mongolian** *adj* berasal dari Mongolia; *n* bahasa Mongolia, orang Mongolia; **Mongoloid** *adj, n* orang Asia

mongrel *adj, derog* [manggrel] campuran; *n* anjing kampung

monitor *n* pengawas; layar (komputer); *v* mengawasi

monitor *n* biawak

monk *n* [mank] biarawan, rahib

monkey *n* [mangki] monyet; ~ *business* kenakalan; ~ *wrench* kunci Inggris

monopolize *v* memonopoli;

monopoly *n* monopoli

monorail *n* monorel, kereta api rel tunggal

monotone *n* nada tunggal; **monotonous** *adj* monoton, senada

Montenegro *n* Montenegro; **Montenegrin** *adj* berasal dari Montenegro; *n* orang Montenegro

Montserrat *n* Montserrat; **Montserratian** *adj* berasal dari Montserrat; *n* orang Montserrat

monsoon *n* musim hujan, muson

monster *adj* raksasa; *n* makhluk besar yang mengerikan; **monstrous** *adj* amat besar, mengerikan

month *n* [manth] bulan; *at the end of the ~* akhir bulan; **monthly** *adj, adv* bulanan; *n* majalah bulanan

monument *n* monumen, tanda peringatan, tugu peringatan; **monumental** *adj* sangat besar

mood *n* suasana hati; **moody** *adj* muram, murung

moon *n* bulan, rembulan; *crescent ~* bulan sabit; *full ~* terang bulan, bulan purnama; *new ~* bulan muda; **moonlight** *n* [munlait] sinar bulan; **moonshine** *n* minuman keras yang dibuat secara gelap

moor *n* tanah tinggi yang berumput

moor *v* bertambat; menambatkan

moose *n* rusa besar (di Amerika Utara)

mope *v* bermuram, mengasihani diri sendiri

moral n [morel] kesusilaan, etika; moral, moril; ~ *support* dukungan moral; *the ~ of the story* pelajarannya, pesannya; **morale** n [moral] semangat juang; **morality** n moralitas, kesusilaan

morbid adj yang banyak memikirkan kematian dan hal buruk

more adv lebih, lagi; ~ *and* ~ semakin; ~ *or less* kurang lebih; *one ~ glass* satu (gelas) lagi; *the ~ the merrier* makin banyak, semakin ramai; **moreover** adv lagipula

morgue n [morg] kamar mayat

morning n pagi (hari); ~ *paper* koran pagi; *good* ~ selamat pagi (diucapkan sampai jam 12 siang)

Moroccan adj berasal dari Maroko; n orang Maroko; **Morocco** n Maroko

moron n orang bodoh; **moronic** adj bodoh sekali

morose adj murung, muram

morsel n sesuap, secuil (makanan)

mortality n kematian; ~ *rate* tingkat kematian

mortar n adukan semen dan pasir; mortir; lumpang; *pestle and* ~ alu lumpang; **mortarboard** n topi mahasiswa

mortgage n [morgej] hipotek

mortify v membuat malu, menghina

mortuary n kamar mayat

mosaic n [moséik] mosaik

Moses n Nabi Musa

Moslem → **Muslim**

mosque n [mosk] mesjid

mosquito n [moskito] nyamuk; ~ *net* kelambu

moss n lumut; **mossy** adj berlumut

most adv paling, maha; *at (the)* ~ sebanyak-banyaknya, paling-paling; **mostly** adv kebanyakan

motel n hotel transit

moth n ngengat; ~ *ball* kapur barus; ~-*eaten* usang, lusuh, dimakan ngengat

mother n [mather] ibu; induk; *pron* Ibu, Mama, Mami; ~-*in-law* (ibu) mertua; ~-*of-pearl* kulit mutiara; ~ *ship* kapal induk; ~ *tongue* bahasa ibu; **motherhood** n keibuan; **motherless** adj piatu, tidak beribu

motion n gerak; mosi, usul; ~ *sickness* mabuk (jalan); **motionless** adj tidak bergerak, diam

motivate v memotivasi, menggerakkan hati; **motivation** n dorongan, dukungan, motivasi; **motive** n [motiv] alasan, dalil, motif

motor n motor, mesin; **motorboat** n perahu bermotor; **motorcar** n, arch mobil; **motorcycle** n **motorbike** sl sepeda motor; **motorcyclist** n pengendara motor; **motorist** n pengendara mobil; **motorway** n jalan bebas hambatan

mottled adj burik

motto n semboyan, slogan, moto

mould → **mold**

mount *n* (nama) gunung; ~ *Bromo* Gunung Bromo; *v* naik; menaiki, menaikkan; memasang; ~ *up* meningkat, menumpuk; **mountain** *n* [maunten] gunung; **mountaineer** *n* pendaki gunung; **mountainous** *adj* [mauntenes] bergunung-gunung; **mountainside** *n* lereng gunung, sisi gunung

mourn *v* [morn] berkabung; meratapi, menangisi; **mourner** *n* orang yang berkabung; **mournful** *adj* penuh kesedihan, memilukan; **mourning** *n* perkabungan

mouse *n* **mice** tikus; **mousehole** *n* lubang tikus; **mousetrap** *n* perangkap tikus

mouth *n* mulut; muara; ~ *organ* harmonika; **mouthful** *n* sesuap; **mouthy** *adj* bermulut besar; **mouthwash** *n* obat kumur

movable *adj* [muvabel] dapat digerakkan; **move** *n* perpindahan, gerakan; *v* bergerak; berpindah (rumah); menggerakkan, memindahkan; **movement** *n* gerak, gerakan, pergerakan; **movers** *n, pl* jasa pindah rumah

movie *n, sl* [muvi] film

mow *v* [mo] memotong rumput; ~ *down* menumbangkan; **mower** *n* mesin pemotong rumput

Mozambican *adj* berasal dari Mozambik; *n* orang Mozambik; **Mozambique** *n* Mozambik

MP *abbrev* Member of Parliament anggota DPR

mpg *miles per gallon* mil per galon

mph *miles per hour* mil per jam

Mr *Mister* Tn (Tuan) (harus dipakai dengan nama keluarga, mis. *Mr Brown*)

Mrs *Mistress, Missus* Ny (Nyonya) (harus dipakai dengan nama keluarga, mis. *Mrs Thatcher*)

Ms Ny, Ibu (status perkawinan tidak disebut. Harus dipakai dengan nama keluarga, mis. *Ms Smith*)

Mt *Mount* G, Gg (gunung)

much *adv, n* banyak; ~ *of a muchness* hampir sama semua; *how* ~ berapa banyak, berapa harganya; *so* ~ sekian; *as* ~ *as* sebanyak

muck *n, v* kotoran, sampah, lumpur; ~ *around* iseng, membuang waktu

mucus *n* lendir, ingus, dahak

mud *n* lumpur

muddle *n* kekacauan, kekusutan; *v* mengacaukan

muddy *adj* berlumpur ← **mud**

mudguard *n* [madgard] sepatbor ← **mud**

muffled *v* tidak jelas kedengaran; **muffler** *n* kenalpot; selendang

mufti *n, arch* pakaian sehari-hari, pakaian bebas

mug *n* cangkir besar; *v* menodong, merampok; **mugger** *n* penodong; **mugging** *n* penodongan

muggy *adj* lembab (cuaca)

mule *n* bagal; semacam selop wanita

multi- *pref* lebih dari satu, aneka; **multi-colored** *adj* warna-warni, beraneka warna; **multi-level** ~ *marketing (MLM)* pemasaran berpola piramida

multiple *adj* [maltipel] berlipat ganda; *n* kelipatan; **multiplication** *n* perkalian; **multiply** *v* berkembang biak; mengalikan

multitude *n* banyak

Mum → **Mom**

mumble *v* bergumam, berkomat-kamit

mummy *n* mumi → **mommy**

mumps *n* penyakit gondok; *to have the* ~ gondokan

munch *v* mengunyah; **munchies** *n, pl, sl* cemilan

municipality *n* [munisipaliti] kota (praja), kotamadya; **municipal** *adj* berkaitan dengan kotamadya

munitions *n, pl* mesiu, munisi

mural *n* lukisan pada tembok atau dinding

murder *n* pembunuhan; *v* membunuh; **murderer** *n* pembunuh

murky *adj* gelap, suram, keruh

murmur *n* bisikan; *v* berbisik; membisikkan

muscle *n* [masel] urat, otot; kekuatan; **muscular** *adj* berotot

muse *n* ilham, inspirasi; *v* termenung, melamun

museum *n* musium

mushroom *n* cendawan, jamur

music *n* musik, lagu; **musical** *adj* (berbakat) musik; **musician** *n* musikus, pemain musik

Muslim, Moslem *adj* Islam, Muslim; *n* orang Islam

muslin *n* kain kasa

mussel *n* kerang, remis, kepah

must *n* keharusan; *v, aux* harus, wajib, terpaksa

mustache, moustache *n* [mustasy] kumis, misai

mustard *n* mostar

musty *adj* lapuk

mutate *v* berubah, bermutasi; **mutation** *n* mutasi, perubahan

mute *adj* bisu; *deaf-~* bisu tuli

mutilate *v* memotong (anggota badan); **mutilation** *n* mutilasi, pemotongan

mutiny *n* [myutini] pemberontakan (di kapal); *v* memberontak

mutter *v* bergumam, berkomat-kamit

mutton *n* daging biri-biri, daging domba; ~ *bird* sejenis burung laut

mutual *adj* [myutyual] saling, dari kedua pihak, timbal balik; ~ *friend* saling berteman; *the feeling's* ~ dia pun merasa begitu

muzzle *n* moncong, mulut; *v* membredel, memberangus

my *pron, poss* saya, -ku

Myanmar *n* [Mianmar] Myanmar

mynah ~ *(bird)* burung béo

myopia *n* [maiopia] **myopic** *adj* rabun dekat

myriad *adj* [miriad] beribu-ribu, tidak terbilang

myrtle *n* [mertel] sejenis pohon kemunting

myself *pron* saya sendiri; sendirian

mysterious *adj* gaib, misterius;
mystery *n* kegaiban, misteri

mystic *n* mistik; *Isl* tasawuf;
mystical *adj* **mysticism** *n*
mistik, aliran kebatinan

mystify *v* membingungkan,
menakjubkan

myth *n* [mith] isapan jempol,
dongeng, mitos; **mythological**
adj berkaitan dengan mitologi;
mythology *n* mitologi

N

nag *v* mengomeli, mencereweti;
a ~ging feeling perasaan yang
tak kunjung hilang

nail *n* paku; kuku; ~ *file* kikir
kuku; ~ *polish,* ~ *varnish* cat
kuku, kuteks; ~ *scissors* gunting kuku; *to hit the ~ on the
head* benar sekali; *v* memaku;
nailbrush *n* sikat kuku

naked *adj* [néked] telanjang;
stark ~ telanjang bulat

name *n* nama; *v* menamai,
menamakan, memberi nama;
~-*dropping* menyebut orang
ternama sebagai kenalan; *to
call ~s* mengejek; **named** *adj*
bernama; *in the* ~ *of* atas nama,
demi; **nameless** *adj* tidak
bernama, anonim; **namely**
conj yakni, yaitu; **nameplate** *n*
papan nama

Namibia *n* Namibia; **Namibian**

adj berasal dari Namibia; *n*
orang Namibia

nanny *n* penjaga anak, pengasuh
anak

nap *n* tidur siang; *to take a* ~
tidur sebentar; *v* tidur sebentar

nape *n* tengkuk

napkin *n* serbet; popok; **nappy**
n popok; ~ *rash* ruam popok;
disposable ~ pampers, popok
plastik

narcotic *n* obat-obatan, narkotika

narrate *v* menceritakan; **narra-
tive** *n, adj* cerita; **narrator** *n*
orang yang bercerita

narrow *adj* sempit; ~ *escape*
nyaris celaka; *v* menyempitkan;
~ *down* memusatkan pada;
~-*minded* picik, berpikiran
sempit

NASA *abbrev National Aeronau-
tics and Space Administration*
Administrasi Angkasa dan
Aeronautika Nasional

nasal *adj* berhubungan dengan
hidung, sengau

nastiness *n* kejahatan, keburukan; **nasty** *adj* buruk, jahat; *a
~ cut* luka yang dalam

nation *n* [nésyen] negara, bangsa;
national *n, adj* [nasyonal]
nasional, kebangsaan; ~ *anthem*
lagu kebangsaan; **nationalism**
n nasionalisme; **nationalist**
adj nasionalis; **nationality** *n*
kebangsaan, kewarganegaraan;
nationalize *v* menasionalisasi

native *adj* [nétif] asli; ~ *speaker*
penutur asli; *n* orang asli,
pribumi

NATO *abbrev North Atlantic Treaty Organization* NATO, Pakta Pertahanan Atlantik Utara

natural *adj* [natyurel] alami, alamiah; **naturalize** *v* menjadikan warganegara; **naturally** *adj* tentu, memang; **nature** *n* alam (semesta); tabiat, kepribadian, sifat; *good-~d* berhati baik

naught → **nought**

naughty *adj* [noti] nakal, jahil

Nauru *n* pulau Nauru; **Nauruan** *adj* berasal dari Nauru; *n* bahasa Nauru; orang Nauru

nausea *n* [nozia] (rasa) mual, mabuk; **nauseous** *adj* [nosius] memualkan, memabukkan

nautical *adj* berkaitan dengan pelayaran, kelautan

naval *adj* perkapalan, berhubungan dengan angkatan laut ← **navy**

navel *n* pusar

navigate *v* [navigét] melayari, mengemudikan kapal; **navigation** *n* pelayaran, navigasi; **navigator** *n* mualim; **navy** *n* [névi] angkatan laut

nb. *nota bene = note well* catatan

near *adj* dekat; *~-sighted* rabun jauh; *a ~ thing, a ~ miss* hampir saja, nyaris; **nearby** *adv* [nirbai] dekat; **nearly** *adv* hampir

neat *adj* apik, rapi, bersih; *sl* hebat, bagus; **neatness** *n* kerapian

necessary *adj* [néseséri] perlu; **necessarily** *not ~* tidak selalu, tidak harus; **necessitate** *v* mengharuskan; **necessity** *n* kebutuhan, keperluan; *daily necessities* kebutuhan sehari-hari

neck *n* leher; *to break your ~* leher patah; *to stick your ~ out* mengambil risiko; **necklace** *n* kalung; **neckline** *n* garis leher; **necktie** *n* dasi

nee, née [ni, né] nama gadis

need *n* kebutuhan, keperluan; *in ~* perlu bantuan; *if ~ be* jika perlu; *no ~* tidak usah, tidak perlu; *v* membutuhkan, memerlukan

needle *n* jarum; *darning ~* jarum tisik; *v, sl* mengejek, menyindir; **needlepoint, needlework** *n* semacam sulaman

needless *~ to say* tidak usah dikatakan ← **need**

needy *adj, n* miskin, melarat ← **need**

negate *v* menyangkal, meniadakan; **negative** *adj* negatif, buruk; *n* klise

neglect *n* keadaan telantar; *v* mengabaikan; **neglectful** *adj* lalai, alpa

negligence *n* [néglijens] kelalaian, kealpaan, keteledoran; **negligent** *adj* lalai, alpa; **negligible** *adj* sedikit sekali, tidak usah diindahkan

negotiable *adj* [negosyabel] dapat ditawar; **negotiate** *v* bermusyawarah, berunding; merundingkan; **negotiation** *n* negosiasi, perundingan; **negotiator** *n* juru runding

neigh *v* [néi] meringkik

neighbor *n* [nébor] tetangga;
neighborhood *n* lingkungan
(dekat rumah); **neighboring**
adj bertetangga, berdekatan

neither *conj* [nither, naither]
kedua-duanya (tidak); ~ ... nor
bukan ... maupun

Nepal *n* Nepal; **Nepalese** *adj*
berasal dari Nepal; **Nepali** *n*
bahasa Nepal; orang Nepal

nephew *n, m* [néfyu] keponakan
(lelaki); *great*-~ anak (lelaki)
dari keponakan

nepotism *n* [népotizem] nepotisme

nerve *n* saraf; nyali, keberanian;
~-*racking* menggelisahkan;
nervous *adj* gelisah, gugup;
~ *system* jaringan saraf

nest *n* sarang; *v* bersarang; ~ *egg*
tabungan, persediaan; **nestle** *v*
[nésel] bersarang

net *adj* bersih, netto; *n* jala, jaring

Netherlands *the* ~ (negeri)
Belanda

nettle *n* jelatang; *v* mengganggu,
membuat sakit hati

network *n* jaringan; *v* menjalin
hubungan

neurologist *n* [nurolojist]
ahli saraf; **neurology** *n* ilmu
penyakit saraf; **neurotic** *adj*
berpenyakit saraf, menderita
gangguan jiwa

neutral *adj* [nutral] netral, tidak
memihak; **neutrality** *n* kene-
tralan; **neutralize** *v* mene-
tralkan

never *adv* [néver] tidak pernah;
~ *again* tidak pernah lagi; ~
before belum pernah; *well I* ~
astaga

nevertheless *conj* [néverthelés]
walaupun demikian, namun

new *adj* baru; ~ *Caledonia* kepulauan Kaledonia Baru; ~ *Cale-
donian* berasal dari Kaledonia
Baru; orang Kaledonia Baru; ~
moon bulan muda; ~ *Year*
tahun baru; ~ *Year's Eve* malam
tahun baru; ~ *Zealand* Selandia
Baru; berasal dari Selandia
Baru; ~ *Zealander* orang
Selandia Baru; *Papua* ~ *Guinea*
Papua Nugini; **newborn** *adj*
baru saja lahir; ~ *baby* orok;
newcomer *n* pendatang baru;
newly *adv* baru saja, belum
lama; ~-*weds* pengantin baru;
news *n, s* berita, warta, warta
berita; kabar; **newsletter** *n*
selebaran; **newspaper** *n* surat
kabar, koran

next *prep* berikut, sebelah,
samping; ~ *door* rumah sebelah;
~ *month* bulan depan; ~ *of kin*
keluarga terdekat; ~ *time* lain
kali

NGO *abbrev* non-governmental
organization LSM (lembaga
swadaya masyarakat)

NHK *abbrev* Nihon Housou
Kyoukai NHK, penyiaran
nasional Jepang

NHS *abbrev* National Health
Service Pelayanan Kesehatan
Nasional

nib *n* mata pena

nibble *v* [nibel] mengunggis

Nicaragua *n* Nikaragua;

Nicaraguan *adj* berasal dari Nikaragua; *n* orang Nikaragua

nice *adj* enak, sedap; manis, cantik, apik

nick *n* torehan; *sl* sel tahanan; *in the ~ of time* pas waktunya; *v, sl* mengutil

nickel *n* nikel

nickname *n* nama kecil, nama panggilan

nicotine *n* nikotin

niece *n, f* [nis] keponakan (perempuan); *great-~* anak perempuan dari keponakan

Niger *n* [Niger] Niger; **Nigerien** *adj* [Nijérien] berasal dari Niger; *n* orang Niger

Nigeria *n* [Naijiria] Nigeria; **Nigerian** *adj* berasal dari Nigeria; *n* orang Nigeria

niggle *v* [nigel] mengorek, mengganggu

night *n* [nait] malam; *~ club* kelab malam, kafe; *~ owl* orang yang suka bangun waktu malam; *~ school* kursus malam; *~ shift* jam kerja malam; *~ and day* siang malam; *at ~* pada waktu malam, malam hari; *good ~* selamat tidur; *last ~* tadi malam, semalam; *all through the ~* sepanjang malam; *in the dead of ~* tengah malam; **nightcap** *n* minumam keras (diminum sebelum tidur); **nightdress** *n, f*; **nightie** *sl* daster; **nightfall** *n* senja, magrib; **nightingale** *n* bulbul; **nightlife** *n* kehidupan malam; **nightly** *adv* tiap malam; **night-**

mare *n* mimpi buruk; **night-watchman** *n* jaga (malam)

nimble *adj* [nimbel] cekatan, tangkas, gesit

nine *n, adj* sembilan

nineteen *n, adj* sembilan belas; **nineteenth** *adj* kesembilan belas ← **nine**

ninetieth *adj* kesembilan puluh; **ninety** *adj. n* sembilan puluh ← **nine**

ninth *adj* [nainth] kesembilan ← **nine**

nip *n* gigitan kecil; *v* mencubit, menggigit

nipper *n, sl* anak kecil

nipple *n* [nipel] puting, pentil, dot

nitrogen *n* [naitrojen] nitrogen

no. *number* no. (nomor)

no tidak; bukan; *~ way, ~ chance* tidak mungkin; *~-nonsense* tidak main-main, serius

nobility *n* [nobiliti] kaum bangsawan, kaum ningrat; **noble** *adj* bangsawan, ningrat; **nobleman** *n* bangsawan

nobody *n* [nobodi] bukan siapa-siapa; *pron* tidak seorang pun

nocturnal *adj* (hidup pada waktu) malam

nod *n* anggukan, tanda setuju; *to get the ~* mendapat persetujuan; *v* mengangguk, terangguk-angguk

noise *n* bunyi, kegaduhan, keributan, suara bising; *~ pollution* polusi suara; **noiseless** *adj* tidak bersuara, tidak berbunyi; **noisy** *adj* gaduh, ribut, berisik, bising; **noisily** *adv* dengan berisik

nomad *n* pengembara, nomaden

nominal *adj* nominal, hanya atas nama saja; **nominate** *v* mencalonkan; **nomination** *n* pencalonan, nominasi; **nominative** *adj, n* subyek, nominatif

non- *pref* tidak, non-; ~-committal tidak berkomentar; ~-existent tidak ada; ~-party tidak berpartai; ~-profit nirlaba; ~-stop tanpa berhenti

nonchalant *adj* [nonsyalant] enteng, tanpa beban

none *n* [nan] seorang pun tidak, sesuatu pun tidak; tidak sama sekali; there's ~ left tidak ada sisanya

nonsense *n* omong kosong

nook *n* sudut, pojok

noon (at) ~ jam duabelas siang

noose *n* jerat

nor neither … ~ bukan … maupun; juga tidak

norm *n* norma; **normal** *adj* biasa, lazim, lumrah, umum; normal; **normally** *adv* biasanya, pada umumnya

north *adj, adv* utara; *n* (sebelah) utara; ~ Korea Korea Utara (Korut); ~ Korean orang Korea Utara; berasal dari Korea Utara; ~ Pole Kutub Utara; to the ~ of di sebelah utara; **northeast** *adj, n* timur laut; **northern** *adj* utara; the ~ Hemisphere belahan bumi utara; (the) ~ Territory (NT) Australia Utara; **northwest** *adj, n* barat laut

Norway *n* Norwegia; **Norwegian** *adj* [Norwijen] berasal dari Norwegia; *n* bahasa Norwegia; orang Norwegia

nose *n* hidung; to have a blood ~ mimisan; to look down your ~ at memandang rendah; to stick your ~ in ikut campur; **nostril** *n* lubang hidung; **nosy** *adj* ingin tahu

not *adv* tidak, tak; belum; bukan; ~ ready belum siap; ~ yet belum; ~ at all sama sekali tidak; ~ my type bukan selera saya

notable *adj* [notabel] istimewa, patut dicatat; *n* orang ternama

notary *n* notaris

notch *n* takik, torehan; *v* menakik; a ~ above lebih baik dari

note *n* catatan, peringatan; nada, not; nota; *v* mencatat, menulis; memperhatikan; to take ~ of memperhatikan; **notebook** *n* buku catatan, buku tulis, notes; **noted** *adj* masyhur, tersohor, kenamaan; **notepaper** *n* kertas tulis; **noteworthy** *adj* patut diperhatikan

nothing *n* [nathing] tidak sesuatu pun; ~ like tidak seperti; to come to ~ gagal

notice *n* [notis] perhatian; pemberitahuan, maklumat; at short ~ dengan mendadak, serta merta; *v* melihat; memerhatikan; to take ~ of mengindahkan, memerhatikan; **noticeable** *adj* [notisabel] nyata, tampak, kelihatan

ENGLISH–INDONESIAN

notification *n* [notifikésyen]
pemberitahuan, surat panggilan; **notify** *v* memberitahu;
memberitahukan

notion *n* pikiran, ide

notorious *adj* [notorius] mempunyai nama buruk

notwithstanding *conj* meskipun,
walaupun

nougat *n* [nuga] gula-gula keras
terbuat dari kacang

nought, naught *n, arch* [not]
nol, kosong; tanpa hasil

noun *n* [naun] kata benda

nourish *v* [narisy] memberi gizi,
memelihara; **nourishing** *adj*
bergizi; **nourishment** *n* gizi

November *n* bulan November

novice *adj, n* [novis] pemula,
orang baru

now *prep* [nau] sekarang, kini; ~
that sejak; *just* ~ baru saja,
tadi; *(every)* ~ *and then,* ~ *and
again* sekali-sekali, kadang-
kadang; *from* ~ *(on)* mulai
sekarang; *conj* nah; **nowadays**
prep sekarang (ini)

nowhere *adv, pron* [nowér] tidak
di mana-mana; *(going)* ~ tidak
ke mana-mana, tidak bergerak

nuclear *adj* nuklir; ~ *energy,* ~
power tenaga nuklir; **nucleus**
n [nuklius] inti

nude *adj* telanjang, bugil; *in the*
~ telanjang; **nudist** *n* orang
yang suka bertelanjang; **nudity**
n ketelanjangan

nudge *n* [naj] sentuhan; *v*
menyentuh, menyinggung

nuisance *n* [nusens] gangguan;
orang pengganggu; *what a* ~
mengganggu saja

null ~ *and void* tidak berlaku

numb *adj* [nam] mati rasa,
kesemutan

number *n* nomor; bilangan,
angka; banyaknya; *in great* ~s
berbondong-bondong; *v* memberi
nomor; **numeral** *n* angka;
Roman ~s angka Romawi;
numerous *adj* banyak sekali

nun *n* biarawati, suster

nuptial *adj* [naptyel] berkaitan
dengan perkawinan; ~s upacara
perkawinan

nurse *n* juru rawat, perawat; *v*
merawat; menyusui; **nursery** *n*
kamar anak; toko tanaman; ~
rhyme lagu anak-anak; **nursing** *adj* menyusui; ~ *home*
panti asuhan

nut *n* kacang; *sl* penggemar
berat, penggila; *cashew* ~
kacang mede; *to go* ~s menjadi
marah, menjadi gila; **nutmeg** *n*
pala

nutrient *n* [nutrient] gizi;
nutrition *n* [nutrisyen] ilmu
gizi; **nutritionist** *n* ahli gizi;
nutritious *adj* bergizi

nutshell *in a* ~ pendeknya,
intinya ← **nut**

nutty *adj* berasa kacang; *sl* gila
← **nut**

nylon *n* [nailon] nilon; **nylons**
n, pl stoking

nymph *n* [nimf] bidadari, peri; **nymphomaniac** *n, f* perempuan yang gila seks

NZ *abbrev New Zealand* Selandia Baru

O

o/s *overseas* LN (luar negeri)

oak *n* pohon ek

oar *n* dayung; **oarsman** *n* pendayung

oasis *n* [oésis] **oases** oase

oatmeal *n* havermut

oath *n* sumpah; umpatan; *under* ~ di bawah sumpah; ~ *of office* sumpah jabatan; *to take an ~, to swear an* ~ bersumpah

oats *n, pl* sejenis gandum; *to sow your wild* ~ berfoya-foya ketika masih muda

obedience *n* [obidiens] ketaatan, kepatuhan; **obedient** *adj* taat, patuh ← **obey**

obelisk *n* tugu

obese *adj* [obis] gemuk sekali; **obesity** *n* keadaan sangat gemuk

obey *v* [obé] taat, patuh

obituary *n* berita duka, berita kematian, obituari

object *n* benda, obyek; *v* berkeberatan; **objection** *n* keberatan; **objective** *adj* obyektif, tidak memihak; *n* tujuan

obligation *n* [obligésyen] kewajiban; **obligated** *adj* diharus-

kan; **obligatory** *adj* wajib; **oblige** *v* membantu, menolong; ~*d* diharuskan; tertolong

oblivious *adj* [oblivius] tidak sadar, tidak mengindahkan

oblong *adj, n* persegi panjang

oboe *n* obo

obscene *adj* [obsin] cabul, jorok

obscure *adj* tidak terkenal, terpencil; *v* mengaburkan; **obscurity** *n* [obskuriti] kesunyian, keadaan tidak dikenal

observant *adj* suka memperhatikan; taat; **observation** *n* pengamatan, peninjauan; **observatory** *n* observatorium, teropong; **observe** *v* mengamati, meninjau; menghormati; **observer** *n* pengamat, peninjau

obsessed *adj* berobsesi; **obsession** *n* obsesi; **obsessive** *adj* obsesif

obstacle *n* [obstakel] rintangan, hambatan

obstetrician *n* dokter kandungan; **obstetrics** *n* ilmu kebidanan

obstinate *adj* [obstinet] keras kepala

obstruct *v* merintangi, menghalangi; **obstruction** *n* rintangan, halangan

obtain *v* memperoleh, mendapatkan, menerima

obtrusive *adj* menonjol

obtuse ~ *angle* sudut tumpul

obvious *adj* [obvius] jelas, terang, nyata; **obviously** *adv* dengan jelas

occasion *n* [okésyen] kesempatan, peluang; peristiwa,

acara; **occasional** adj **occasionally** adv kadang-kadang

occult the ~ dunia gaib

occupant n penghuni; **occupation** n pekerjaan; pendudukan; **occupy** v [okupai] mengisi; menduduki

occur v terjadi; **occurrence** n kejadian, peristiwa

ocean n [osyan] samudera, lautan; the Indian ~ Samudera Hindia, Samudera Indonesia; the Pacific ~ Lautan Teduh; **Oceania** n Oseania, kawasan (Laut) Pasifik

o'clock jam, pukul; it's six ~ sekarang jam enam

octagon n segi delapan; **octagonal** adj bersegi delapan

October n bulan Oktober

octopus n ikan gurita

OD abbrev overdose overdosis

odd adj aneh, ganjil; **oddball** adj aneh; n orang aneh; **odds** n, pl kemungkinan; --on kemungkinan besar; against the ~ kemungkinan kecil; **oddity** n keanehan

odious adj menjijikkan, membangkitkan kebencian

odor n bau; body ~ (BO) bau badan

of prep [ov] milik; dari, daripada; a cup ~ tea secangkir teh

off prep jauh; adj mati, tidak hidup; basi (makanan); tidak jadi; ~ chance kemungkinan kecil; ~ duty tidak sedang dinas; --key bersuara sumbang; --license toko minuman keras;

~-limits tidak boleh; ~ the record (dikatakan) secara tidak resmi; ~ and on sekali-sekali; a day ~ hari libur; the milk is ~ susu sudah basi; turn ~ the light lampu tolong dimatikan

offbeat adj tidak biasa, antik

offend v menghina, membuat tersinggung; melanggar hukum; **offender** n yang bersalah, yang melakukan; repeat ~ residivis; **offense** n pelanggaran hukum, kesalahan; serangan (olahraga); **offensive** adj menghina, tidak sopan; serangan

offer n tawaran, penawaran; v menawarkan, menawari; mempersembahkan; **offering** n persembahan, sesajen

offhand adj begitu saja, enteng; ~ remark komentar iseng ← **off**

office n [ofis] kantor, ruangan, tempat kerja; jabatan; ~ hours (OH) jam kerja; at the ~ di kantor; **officer** n pegawai, petugas; perwira; police ~ polisi; **official** adj resmi; n pegawai, pejabat

offset v **offset offset** mengganti rugi ← **off**

offshoot n cabang ← **off**

offspring n anak, keturunan ← **off**

often adv sering; more ~ than not cukup sering

ogre n [oger] raksasa; makhluk yang menakutkan

oil n minyak; v meminyaki; ~ colors, ~ paint cat minyak; ~ palm kelapa sawit; ~ rig pengebor minyak; ~ tanker kapal minyak; **oilfield** *n* ladang minyak; **oilwell** *n* sumur minyak; **oily** *adj* berminyak

ointment *n* salep, balsem

OK, okay [oké] baik, oke, jadi; *v* menyetujui

old *adj* tua; sepuh, lanjut usia; *~-fashioned* kuno, kolot; *~ maid* perawan tua; *~ school* kuno; *~ Testament* Perjanjian Lama, Taurat; **olden** *~ days* masa lalu, tempo dulu, zaman baheula

olive *n* [oliv] (buah) zaitun; *~ green* berwarna hijau pudar

Olympiad *n* Olimpiade; **Olympic** *adj* Olimpiade; *~ Games* Pertandingan Olimpiade; **Olympics** *the ~* Olimpiade

Oman *n* Oman; **Omani** *adj* berasal dari Oman; *n* orang Oman

omelet, omelette *n* telur dadar

omen *n* tanda, pertanda, alamat; **ominous** *adj* [ominus] buruk kelihatannya

omission *n* kelupaan; **omit** *v* melupakan, menghilangkan

omnibus *n* kumpulan, antologi; *arch* bis → **bus**

omnipotent *adj* mahakuasa

omnivore *n* **omnivorous** *adj* pemakan segala, omnivora

on *adj* hidup; *~ and off* kadang-kadang; *prep* di (atas), pada; *~ the phone* sedang menelepon; *~ the way* sedang dalam perjalanan; *from that day ~* mulai hari itu; *adv* terus; sedang berjalan, sedang berlangsung; *~ and ~* terus-menerus

once *adv* [wans] sekali (waktu); dahulu kala; *all at ~* serentak; tiba-tiba; *at ~* pada saat itu juga, segera; *~ upon a time* sekali waktu; *just this ~* sekali ini saja; *the ~-over* pandangan sekilas ← **one**

oncoming *adj* [onkaming] yang mendekat

one *n, adj* [wan] satu, suatu; seorang; *pron* orang; *~ another* satu sama lain; *~ apple* sebuah apel; *~ day* kapan-kapan; suatu hari, sekali waktu; *~-eyed* bermata satu; *berat sebelah; *~ hundred* seratus; *~ thousand* seribu; *~ million* sejuta; *~ of* salah satu (dari); *~-sided* sepihak, berat sebelah; *~-way street* jalan satu arah; *as ~* serentak; *not (even) ~* tidak satu pun; *the ~* yang satu itu; *~ by ~* satu per satu; *I for ~* menurut pendapat saya; **oneself** *pron* diri sendiri

ongoing *adj* terus-menerus ← **on**

onion *n* [anien] bawang; *spring ~* daun bawang

onlooker *n* penonton ← **on**

only *adj* tunggal; *~ child* anak tunggal; *one and ~* satu-satunya; *adv* saja, hanya; *if ~* kalau saja; *not ~ ... but also* tidak hanya ... tetapi juga ← **one**

onset *n* awal, permulaan

onward *adv* ke depan, seterusnya ← **on**

onyx *n* [oniks] batu akik

ooze v [uz] mengalir, meleleh, melumer

opal n opal, baiduri; *white* ~ kalimaya

opaque adj [opék] tidak tembus pandang, buram

open adj buka, terbuka; terang-terangan; ~ *house* acara menerima tamu di rumah sepanjang hari; ~-*minded* berpandangan terbuka; ~ *secret* rahasia umum; *(out) in the* ~ (di alam) terbuka; v membuka; **opener** n pembuka; **opening** adj pembuka; n pembukaan; lubang, celah, lowongan; **openly** adv secara terbuka, dengan terus terang

opera n opera; ~ *house* gedung opera

operate v [operét] membedah, mengoperasi; beroperasi; menjalankan (mesin), mengoperasikan; **operation** n pembedahan, operasi; cara menjalankan; **operator** n penjaga mesin, penjaga telepon

opinion n [opinion] pendapat; *in my* ~ menurut pendapat saya

opium n candu

opossum, possum n semacam tupai

opponent n lawan

opportunity n kesempatan, peluang; *job* ~ lowongan kerja; ~ *shop* toko loak

oppose v menentang, melawan; **opposite** n, adj [opozet] berlawanan, bertentangan, lawan (kata); **opposition** n perlawanan, oposisi

oppress v menindas, menekan; **oppression** n penindasan, tekanan; **oppressive** adj bersifat menindas, menekan; menyesakkan napas; **oppressor** n penindas

optical adj optik; ~ *illusion* tipu mata; **optician** n ahli kaca mata

optimist n **optimistic** adj optimis

option n [opsyen] opsi, pilihan; **optional** adj bebas (memilih)

optometrist n dokter mata; ahli kacamata

opulence n kekayaan, kemewahan; **opulent** adj kaya, mewah

or conj atau; *either ...* ~ salah satu

oral adj lisan, berkaitan dengan mulut; ~ *sex* seks oral

orange adj [orenj] oranye, jingga; n jeruk; ~ *juice* air jeruk, jus jeruk

orangutan n orang hutan

orator n orator, ahli pidato

orbit n orbit, peredaran; v mengitari

orchard n [orced] kebun buah

orchestra n [orkestra] orkes

orchid n [orkid] (bunga) anggrek

ordeal n cobaan atau pengalaman berat

order n urutan; peraturan; perintah; pemesanan; *in* ~ teratur; beres; *in* ~ *to* supaya; *on his* ~s atas perintahnya; *out of* ~ rusak; v memerintahkan, menyuruh, mengatur, memesan; **orderly** adj rapi, tertib; n juru rawat

ordinary *adj* [ordineri] biasa, lazim

ore *n* bijih

organ *n* orgel, organ; **organist** *n* pemain orgel

organ *n* bagian badan; **organic** *adj* organik; **organism** *n* makhluk

organization *n* organisasi, persatuan; penyusunan, pengaturan; **organize** *v* menyusun, mengatur, mengurus; **organizer** *n* pengurus

orgasm *n* [orgazem] orgasme, puncak (nafsu)

Orient *the* ~ kawasan Timur; **oriental** *adj* timur, ketimuran

orientate *v* menentukan arah, mencari arah; **orientation** *n* orientasi, pencarian jalan

origin *n* asal, asal-usul; **original** *adj* orisinil, asli, semula; **originality** *n* keaslian; **originate** *v* berasal dari; memulai

ornament *n* hiasan; **ornamental** *adj* hiasan, hias

orphan *n* [orfan] anak yatim (piatu); **orphanage** *n* rumah yatim piatu; **orphaned** *adj* yatim (piatu)

orthodontist *n* dokter gigi

orthodox *adj* ortodoks, biasa; *Russian* ~ gereja Rusia (ortodoks)

ostentatious *adj* [ostentésyus] suka pamer

ostracize *v* [ostrasaiz] mengasingkan, mengucilkan

ostrich *n* burung unta

other *pron, adj* [ather] lain, berlainan; *every* ~ *day* selang sehari; *the* ~ *day* kemarin, belum lama ini; *the* ~ *woman* orang ketiga; **otherwise** *conj* kalau tidak, bila tidak

otter *n* berang-berang

ouch *excl* [auc] aduh, sakit

ought *aux, v* [out] seharusnya, semestinya, sebaiknya

ounce *n* [auns] ons

our *pron* kita, kami; **ours** *pron* milik kita, milik kami; **ourselves** *pron* kita sendiri, kami sendiri

out *prep* (di) luar; *adj* di luar, tidak ada; tidak berlaku lagi; ~ *and* ~ betul-betul, sungguh-sungguh; ~-*of-date* ketinggalan zaman, kolot; ~-*of-the-way* jauh, terpencil; ~-*of-work* menganggur; **outbreak** *n* pecahnya, meletusnya (perang); terjangkitnya (penyakit); **outbuilding** *n* bangunan tambahan, bangunan luar; **outburst** *n* letusan, ledakan; **outcast** *n* orang buangan; **outcome** *n* hasil, keputusan; **outdated** *adj* ketinggalan zaman, kuno; **outdo** *v* mengungguli, melebihi; **outdoor** *adj* **outdoors** *prep* (di) luar (rumah); **outer** *adj* bagian luar; ~ *space* angkasa luar; **outfit** *n* busana; perlengkapan; **outgoing** *adj* ramah; **outlandish** *adj* aneh; **outlaw** *n* (orang) buronan; **outlet** *n* jalan keluar, saluran pembuangan; toko, cabang; **outline** *n* garis besar; **outlive** *v* hidup lebih lama dari; **outlook** *n* wawasan; **outlying** *adj* jauh, terpencil; **outpatient** *n* rawat jalan; **outpost** *n* pos yang terpencil; **output** *n* hasil, produksi; keluaran; **outrageous** *adj* [autréjus] keterlaluan; **outright** *adj* langsung, terus terang, tulus; **outset** *from the* ~ sejak awal; **outside** *n, prep* (di) luar, ke luar, bagian luar; **outsider** *n* orang luar; **outskirts** *n* pinggir, daerah pinggiran; **outspoken** *adj* blak-blakan, terang-terangan; **outstanding** *adj* luar biasa; ~ *debts* hutang yang belum dilunasi; **outward** *adj* berpenampilan; *adv* keluar; **outwit** *v* menipu, memperdayakan

oval *adj* lonjong, oval; *n* (lapangan) bulat panjang

ovary *n* [overi] indung telur

oven *n* [aven] oven, kompor, tungku

over *adj* selesai, rampung; *prep* di atas; melalui; tentang, mengenai; lebih daripada; *all* ~ seluruh; selesai semua; ~ *and* ~ berulang kali; ~ *there* di sebelah sana, di seberang; **overact** *v* bertindak secara berlebihan; **overall** *adj* secara keseluruhan; **overalls** *n, pl* pakaian montir; **overarm** *adv* (melempar) dengan tangan dari atas; **overbearing** *adj* sombong; **overboard** *adj* ke dalam air (dari atas kapal); **overcast** *adj* mendung, berawan; **overcharge** *v* meminta bayaran terlalu tinggi;

overcome *adj* **overcame overcome** kewalahan; *v* mengalahkan, mengatasi; **overcrowded** *adj* penuh sesak; **overdo** *v* **overdid overdone** melakukan secara berlebihan; **overdose** *n* overdosis, OD; *v* OD; **overdue** *adj* kedaluwarsa, terlambat; **overeat** *v* **overate overeaten** terlalu banyak makan; **overflow** *v* banjir; **overgrown** *adj* penuh tetumbuhan; **overhaul** *n, v* menurunkan mesin untuk diperiksa; **overhead** *adj* di atas (kepala); *n* ongkos eksploitasi; **overhear** *v* **overheard overheard** menguping; terdengar; **overload** *v* kebanyakan (muatan); **overlook** *v* melupakan; **overnight** *adv, prep* bermalam, menginap, semalaman; **overpass** *n* jembatan penyeberangan; **overpower** *v* menguasai; **overrated** *adj* tidak sebagus rekomendasinya, dinilai terlalu tinggi; **overripe** *adj* busuk, kematangan; **overseas** *adv, adj* (di) luar negeri; **oversee** *v* **oversaw overseen** mengawasi; **overseer** *n* mandor, pengawas; **overshadow** *v* membayangi; **oversight** *n* kelupaan; **oversleep** *v* **overslept overslept** bangun kesiangan; **overtake** *v* **overtook overtaken** menyalip; **overthrow** *v* **overthrew overthrown** menjatuhkan, meruntuhkan; **overweight** *n* kelebihan berat (badan); **over-**

whelming *adj* besar sekali

oviduct *n* saluran indung telur

ovum *n* telur

owe *v* [o] berhutang; **owing** ~ *to* berkat, sebab, karena

owl *n* [aul] burung hantu

own *adj* [oun] sendiri; *my* ~ *house* rumahku sendiri; *v* memiliki, mempunyai; **owner** *n* pemilik; **ownership** *n* kepemilikan, hak milik

ox *n* **oxen** sapi, lembu

oxide *n* [oksaid] oksida; **oxidize** *v* mengoksidasi; **oxygen** *n* [oksijen] oksigen

oxtail ~ *soup* sop buntut ← **ox**

oyster *n* tiram

oz *ounce* ons

ozone *n*, *pl* ozon; ~ *layer* lapisan ozon

P

p *page*, **pp** (pages) halaman

pa *per annum* per tahun, setahun

PA *abbrev personal assistant* asisten pribadi

Pa *pron, sl* Pak, Yah

pace *n* langkah; kecepatan; *v* melangkah; mengukur kegiatan; **pacemaker** *n* alat pacu jantung

Pacific ~ *Ocean* Lautan Teduh, Samudera Pasifik; **pacifier** *n* dot; **pacify** *v* mendamaikan, menenteramkan, menenangkan

pack *n* bungkusan, pak; ~*ed* penuh (sesak); ~ *horse* kuda beban; *ice* ~ kompres dingin; *v* membungkus, mengepak, menyusun; **package** *n* bungkus; bingkisan, paket; ~ *deal* paket; **packaging** *n* pengemasan; **packer** *n* pembungkus; **packet** *n* paket, pak, bungkus; **packing** *n* pengepakan, pengemasan

pact *n* pakta, perjanjian

pad *n* bantalan; *sanitary* ~ pembalut (wanita); *writing* ~ bloknot; *v* ~ *out* mengisi

paddle *n* [padel] kayuh; *v* mengayuh; ~ *steamer* kapal kincir

paddy *n* ~ *(field)* sawah

padlock *n* gembok; *v* mengunci, menggembok

pagan *adj* [pégan] *n* penyembah berhala

page *n* halaman, lembar; *v* memanggil

pageant *n* [pajent] lomba; arak-arakan; *beauty* ~ lomba kecantikan

pagoda *n* kuil

paid *v*, *pf* → **pay**

pail *n* ember

pain *n* rasa sakit, rasa nyeri; *in* ~ kesakitan; **painful** *adj* sakit, pedih; **painstaking** *adj* teliti, cermat

paint *n* cat; *oil* ~ cat minyak; *wet* ~ cat basah; *v* mengecat; **painter** *n* tukang cat; pelukis; **painting** *n* lukisan; seni lukis

pair *n* pasang, rangkap; pasangan; ~ *of glasses* kacamata; *a* ~ *of shoes* (sepasang) sepatu;

~ *of trousers* celana; *v* ~ *off* berpasang-pasangan

pajamas → **pyjamas**

Pakistan *n* Pakistan; **Pakistani** *adj* berasal dari Pakistan; *n* orang Pakistan

pal *n, sl* kawan, sobat

palace *n* [pales] istana, puri

palatable *adj* dapat dimakan, enak; **palate** *n* [palet] langit-langit

pale *adj* pucat, lemah

Palestine *n* [Palestain] Palestina; **Palestinian** *adj* [Palestinian] berasal dari Palestina; *n* orang Palestina; ~ *Liberation Front (PLO)* Front Pembebasan Palestina

pall-bearer *n* pengusung jenazah

palm *n* [pam] palem; telapak tangan; ~-*reading* membaca garis tangan; ~ *oil* minyak kelapa sawit; ~ *sugar* gula aren

palsy *n* [polzi] kelumpuhan; *cerebral* ~ kelumpuhan akibat penyakit otak

pamper *v* memanjakan

pamphlet *n* brosur, selebaran, pamflet

pan *n* panci, wajan, kuali; **pancake** *n* panekuk

Panama *n* Panama; **Panamanian** *adj* berasal dari Panama; *n* orang Panama

pane *n* daun kaca (jendela)

panel *n* panel; sehelai papan; ~ *beating* ketok; **panelist** *n* anggota panel

panic *n* panik, ketakutan; *v* panik

panorama *n* pemandangan

pansy *n* sejenis bunga

pant *v* terengah-engah

panther *n* macan kumbang

pantomime *n* pertunjukan sandiwara

pantry *n* [pantri] gudang (dapur), lemari untuk menyimpan makanan kering

pants *n, pl* celana; **pantsuit** *n* setelan celana dan baju atas

panty ~ *hose* stoking; ~ *liner* pembalut (tipis); **panties** *n, pl* celana dalam wanita

papa *pron* pak, ayah

papal *adj* berkaitan dengan Sri Paus

papaya *n* pepaya

paper *n* kertas; koran, surat kabar; makalah; ~*back* buku bersampul tipis; ~*s* surat-surat, dokumen; ~ *clip* jepitan kertas; **paperboy** *n* tukang koran, loper koran; ~ *weight* penindih kertas; **paperwork** *n* pekerjaan tulis-menulis

Papua *n* Irian (Jaya); ~ *New Guinea (PNG)* Papua Nugini; ~ *New Guinean* berasal dari Papua Nugini; orang Papua Nugini; *Free* ~ *Organisation* Organisasi Papua Merdeka (OPM); **Papuan** *n* orang Papua

par *n* derajat, tingkat; *below* ~ lebih rendah, kurang baik

parachute *n* payung, parasut; *v* terjun payung; **parachuting** *n* terjun payung; **parachutist** *n* penerjun payung

parade *n* [paréid] pawai, arak-arakan; jalan; *v* berpawai, berbaris

paradise *n* surga

paraffin *n* parafin, malam

paragraph *n* paragraf, alinea

Paraguay *n* Paraguay; **Paraguayan** *adj* berasal dari Paraguay; *n* orang Paraguay

parakeet *n* burung bayan, burung parkit

parallel *adj* sejajar, paralel; *n* garis lintang; *without* ~ tanpa tanding, tanpa tara

paralysis *n* [paralisis] layuh, kelumpuhan; **paralyze** *v* melumpuhkan; **paralyzed** *adj* lumpuh

paramount *adj* terpenting, paling penting

paranoid *adj* takut sekali (sakit jiwa)

paraphrase *v* [parafréiz] menguraikan dengan kata-kata sendiri, memfrasakan

paraplegic *n* [paraplijik] orang yang separuh badannya lumpuh, orang cacat

parasite *n* [parasait] parasit, benalu

parasol *n* payung (hias)

paratrooper *n* pasukan payung

parcel *n* bingkisan, paket; parsel

pardon *n* ampun, maaf; grasi; *v* mengampuni, memaafkan; ~ *me* maaf

parent *n* [pérent] orang tua, ibu bapak, ayah bunda; **parental** *adj* orang tua; **parenthood** *n* masa orang tua, pengalaman menjadi orang tua

parentheses *n, pl in* ~ dalam kurung

Paris *n* Paris

parish *n* paroki

Parisian *adj* [Parizian] berasal dari Paris; *n* warga Paris ← **Paris**

park *n* taman; *car* ~ tempat parkir; *v* parkir; memarkirkan mobil; ~*ing lot* tempat parkir; *no* ~*ing* dilarang parkir; **parkway** *n* jalan raya dengan jalur hijau di tengah

parliament *n* Dewan Perwakilan Rakyat (DPR), parlemen; **parliamentary** *adj* berhubungan dengan dewan perwakilan rakyat

parlor *n, arch* kamar tamu, kamar duduk

parody *n* parodi, plesetan; *v* memarodikan, memelesetkan

parrot *n* burung nuri

parsley *n* [parsli] peterseli

parson *n* pendeta

part *n* bagian, potong; peranan; belahan; ~*-time* paruh waktu dipisahkan; *in* ~ sebagian; *side* ~ belahan samping; *a bit* ~ peranan kecil; *on my* ~ dari pihak saya; *to play a* ~ memainkan peranan, berperan; *to take* ~ *(in)* ikut serta, mengambil bagian; *v* membagi, memisahkan; ~ *with* melepaskan; **partial** *adj* sebagian; memihak; ~ *to* suka, menggemari

participant *n* peserta; **participate** *v* ikut serta, mengambil bagian; **participation** *n* keikutsertaan, partisipasi

particle *n* butir; unsur; partikel; **particular** *adj* istimewa, spesial, khusus; ~s keterangan, data; *in* ~ khususnya, terutama; *very* ~ berpilih-pilih; **particularly** *adv* terutama, khususnya

parting *n* perpisahan; belahan (rambut) ← **part**

partition *n* sekat, dinding pemisah; pembagian ← **part**

partly *adv* sebagian ← **part**

partner *n* pasangan, mitra; **partnership** *n* persekutuan, kemitram

partridge *n* sejenis burung puyuh

party *n* pesta, perayaan; partai, kelompok, pihak; rombongan; ~ *animal* orang yang suka berpesta; ~ *line* sambungan telepon bersama; *third* ~ pihak ketiga; *to follow the* ~ *line* mengikuti garis partai; *v* berpesta

pass *n* surat izin masuk, pas jalan; jalan kecil; *press* ~ kartu pers; *v* lulus ujian; lewat; melalui, melewati; mengesahkan; ~*er-by* orang lewat, orang di jalan; ~ *away* meninggal dunia, berpulang; ~ *for* dipandang sebagai, mirip; ~ *out* pingsan; ~ *time* iseng, mengisi waktu; ~ *up* melewatkan; ~ *sentence* menjatuhkan hukuman; ~ *wind* kentut; *to come to* ~ terjadi; **passable** *adj* dapat dilalui, dapat dilewati; boleh juga; **passage** *n* [pasej] jalan lintas, jalan tembus, lorong, terusan; bagian dari tulisan; pelayaran; **passenger** *n* [pasenjer] penumpang; **passing** *in* ~ sepintas lalu

passion *n* [pasyen] hawa nafsu, gairah; *a* ~ *for* kegilaan akan; **passionate** *adj* [pasyenet] bernafsu, bergairah, bersemangat; **passionately** *adv* sungguh-sungguh

passive *adj* pasif, terdiam; ~ *smoker* orang yang terpengaruh oleh asap rokok orang lain

Passover *n* perayaan Yahudi

passport *n* paspor

password *n* kata sandi

past *adj* lalu, lewat, lampau, silam; ~ *tense* bentuk lampau; *n* masa lalu

paste *n* [pést] adonan, pasta; *v* tempel

pastel *n* warna pastel; kapur berwarna

pastime *n* pengisi waktu

pastor *n* pastor, pendeta

pastry *n* [péstri] kue

pasture *n* padang rumput

pat *n* tepukan; *v* menepuk, mengelus

patch *n* tambal, tempelan; *v* menambal; **patchwork** *n* penjahitan kain perca; campur aduk; **patchy** *adj* tidak konsisten

patent *n* [pétent] paten; *v* mematenkan

paternal *adj* [patérnal] kebapakan; dari pihak bapak; ~ *grandmother* nenek dari pihak bapak

path *n* jalan (tapak), lorong

pathetic *adj* [pathétik] menyedihkan, memelas

patience *n* [pésyens] kesabaran;

soliter; **patient** *adj* sabar; *n* pasien

patio *n* teras, emper terbuka

patriot *n* [pétriot] patriot, pecinta tanah air; **patriotic** *adj* cinta tanah air; **patriotism** *n* patriotisme, kecintaan kepada tanah air

patrol *n* patroli, ronda; *v* berpatroli, meronda

patron *n* [pétron] pengasuh, pelindung; **patronize** *v* berlangganan; memperlakukan sebagai sesuatu yang rendah

pattern *n* pola, corak; patron, contoh

patty *n* perkedel; ~ *cake* kue mangkuk

pauper *n* [pouper] orang miskin, orang papa

pause *n* [pouz] jeda, waktu istirahat; *v* berhenti sebentar; menghentikan sementara

pave *v* mengaspal, memberi lapisan beton; **pavement** *n* trotoar

pavilion *n* [pavilion] anjungan; tenda besar; bangunan dekat taman atau lapangan

paw *n* kaki binatang; *cat's* ~ diperalat

pawn *n* gadai; pion; *v* menggadaikan; **pawnbroker** *n* penggadai; pegadaian; **pawnshop** *n* rumah gadai, pegadaian

pay *n* pembayaran; gaji, upah; *v* **paid paid** membayar; ~ *attention* memperhatikan; ~ *back* mengganti, membayar kembali; ~ *off* melunasi; berhasil; ~ *rise* kenaikan gaji; ~ *TV* TV kabel; ~ *a visit* berkunjung; mengunjungi; ~ *your respects* melayat; **payable** *adj* dapat dibayarkan, untuk dibayarkan; **payday** *n* (hari) gajian; **payee** *n* [péyi] orang yang dibayar; **payment** *n* pembayaran; **payoff** *n* imbalan; **payphone** *n* telepon umum

PC *abbrev* (personal computer) komputer

PC *abbrev police constable* polisi

Pde *Parade* Jl (Jalan)

pea *n* kacang polong

peace *n* perdamaian; ~ *of mind* ketentraman hati; *rest in* ~ *(RIP)* beristirahat dengan tenang; **peaceful** *adj* damai, tenteram, tenang

peach *adj* warna kuning kemerahan, warna persik; *n* buah persik

peacock *n, m* burung merak; **peahen** *n, f* burung merak

peak *n, adj* puncak; ~ *hour* jam-jam sibuk (di jalan); ~ *season* musim ramai; *v* memuncak

peanut *n* kacang tanah; ~ *butter* selai kacang, pindakas; ~ *sauce* bumbu kacang

pear *n* [pér] buah pir

pearl *n* mutiara; ~ *of wisdom* kata mutiara; ~*y whites* gigi

peasant *n* [pézent] petani; **peasantry** *n* kaum tani

pebble *n* [pébel] batu kerikil

pecan *n* semacam kemiri

peck *v* mematuk

peculiar *adj* [pekyulier] aneh, ganjil; ~ *to* khas; **peculiarity** *n* keganjilan, keanehan

pedal *n* [pédel] injakan kaki, pedal; *v* mengayuh (sepeda)

peddle *v* [pédel] menjajakan, mengedar; **peddler** *n* penjaja, pengedar

pedestrian *n* [pedéstrien] pejalan kaki; ~ *crossing* penyeberangan jalan

pediatrician *n* [pidiatrisyen] dokter anak-anak

pedicab *n* [pedikab] becak

pedicure *n* pedikur, perawatan kaki

pedigree *n* [pédigri] trah; silsilah

pedlar *n* penjaja, pedagang

pee *v, sl* kencing, pipis; *to have a* ~ kencing

peek *v* mengintip, menengok sejenak; **peekaboo** cilukba

peel *n* kulit (buah); *v* mengelupas; menguliti, mengupas; **peeler** *n* alat pengupas

peep *v* mengintip, mengintai; menengok; ~*ing Tom* orang yang mengintip; *not a* ~ diam, tidak bersuara; **peephole** *n* lubang pengintai

peer *n* kawan sebaya (sesama rekan kerja, pelajar dsb); ~ *pressure* tekanan dari teman-teman sekolah

peer *v* melihat dengan susah

peg *n* pasak; sangkutan; patokan; *v* mematok, memasak; ~ *doll* boneka pasak; *clothes* ~ jepitan (baju); ~ *leg* kaki kayu, kaki palsu

pelican *n* [pélikan] burung pelikan, burung undan

pelt *v* melemparkan, menghujani

pelvic *adj* daerah panggul; **pelvis** *n* panggul, tulang pinggul

pen *n* pena, kalam; bolpoin, pulpen; ~ *name* nama samaran

penal *adj* [pinal] berkaitan dengan hukuman atau hukum pidana; ~ *code* kitab undang-undang hukum pidana; **penalize** *v* menghukum; **penalty** *n* denda, hukuman, penalti

pencil *n* pensil; ~ *case* tempat pensil; ~ *sharpener* rautan pensil

pendant *n* liontin

pendulum *n* bandul

penetrate *v* tembus; menerobos, menembus; **penetrating** *adj* tajam, menusuk; **penetration** *n* penerobosan, penembusan, penetrasi

penguin *n* pinguin

penicillin *n* penisilin

peninsula *n* [peninsula] semenanjung

penis *n* [pinis] penis, zakar; ~ *sheath* koteka

penknife *n* [pén naif] pisau lipat ← **pen**

pennant *n* panji, umbul-umbul

penniless *adj* tak memiliki sepeser pun, papa; **penny** *n* **pence** *pl* sen Inggris

penpal *n* sahabat pena

pension *n* [pénsyen] pensiun; *v* ~ *off* memensiunkan; **pensioner** *n* orang pensiunan

penthouse *n* [pént haus] apartemen (mewah)

pent-up *adj* tertahan, terpendam

people *n, pl* [pipel] orang, bangsa, rakyat, kaum; *the ~'s Republic of China (PRC)* Republik Rakyat Cina (RRC)

pepper *n* merica, lada; *salt and ~* garam merica; beruban (rambut); **peppermint** *adj* mentol; *n* permen

per *prep* setiap, tiap, per; *two dollars ~ person* satu orang dua dolar

perceive *v* [persiv] menafsirkan; **perceptive** *adj* cepat mengerti, suka memperhatikan

percent *adj* persen; **percentage** *n* persentase

perception *n* persepsi, tanggapan ← **perceive**

perch *n* tempat bertengger di sangkar burung; sejenis ikan; *v* bertengger

percolate *v* menyaring, menapis; **percolator** *n* penyaring kopi

percussion *n* perkusi

perennial *adj, n* [perénial] tahunan, selalu, kekal

perfect *adj* [pérfekt] sempurna; *v* [perfékt] menyempurnakan; **perfection** *n* kesempurnaan

perforate *v* melubangi; **perforation** *n* lubang

perform *v* melakukan, menyelenggarakan, memainkan (peran); *~ the pilgrimage to Mecca* menunaikan ibadah haji; **performance** *n* pertunjukan; **performer** *n* pemain, pemeran; **performing** *~ arts* seni peran, musik dan tari

perfume *n* wewangian, minyak wangi, parfum; wangi

perhaps *n* mungkin, barangkali

peril *n* [péril] bahaya; **perilous** *adj* [périlus] berbahaya

period *n* [piried] zaman, masa, kala, waktu; titik; *coll* datang bulan, haid; **periodic** *adj* berkala, periodik; **periodical** *n* terbitan berkala, majalah

peripheral *adj* [periferal] **periphery** *n* tepi, pinggir

periscope *n* periskop

perish *v* hilang, tewas; molor (karet); **perishable** *n* makanan yang dapat menjadi busuk

perjury *n* [pérjeri] sumpah palsu

perk *n, sl* untung, sisi baik; *~ up* menjadi bersemangat

perm *n, coll* keriting rambut; **permanent** *adj* tetap, permanen; *~ residence (PR)* izin tinggal tetap; *~ resident* penghuni tetap; *~ wave (perm)* keriting rambut

permeate *v* [pérmiét] meresap

permissible *adj* boleh, diizinkan; **permission** *n* izin; **permissive** *adj* serba boleh; **permit** *n* surat izin; *v* mengizinkan, memperboleh

perpendicular *adj, n* tegak lurus

perpetual *adj* terus-menerus, abadi

perplex *v* membingungkan

persecute *v* menyiksa, mengejar-ngejar; **persecution** *n* penyiksaan, penganiayaan

perseverance *n* [persevirens] ketekunan, kegigihan; **persevere** *v* bertekun, gigih

Persia *n, arch* Persia, Iran; **Persian** *adj* berasal dari Persia; *n, arch* orang Persia; ~ *cat* kucing angora

persimmon *n* buah kesemak

persist *v* tetap (melakukan), bertekun, bertahan; **persistence** *n* ketekunan; **persistent** *adj* gigih, tekun

person *n* **people** [pipel] orang, pribadi; *in* ~ sendiri; **personal** *adj* pribadi; perorangan; **personality** *n* kepribadian; tokoh; **personalize** *v* menyesuaikan untuk orang tertentu; **personally** *adv* secara perorangan; secara pribadi; **personnel** *n* [pérsonél] personalia, para karyawan; ~ *department* bagian personalia

perspiration *n* [pérspirésyen] keringat, peluh; **perspire** *v* [pérspair] berkeringat

persuade *v* [pérsuéd] meyakinkan; **persuasion** *n* [pérsuésyen] keyakinan, persuasi; **persuasive** *adj* meyakinkan

Peru *n* Peru; **Peruvian** *adj* berasal dari Peru; *n* orang Peru

perverse *adj* menyimpang; **pervert** *n* orang yang mengidap kelainan seksual; orang yang suka mengintip

pessimist *n* orang pesimis; **pessimistic** *adj* pesimis, bersangka buruk

pest *n* hama; gangguan; **pester** *v* mengganggu, mengusik

pestle *n* alu; ~ *and mortar* alu lumpang

pesticide *n* [péstisaid] pestisida, obat pembasmi serangga

pet *adj* kesayangan; *n* hewan peliharaan; ~ *shop* toko yang menjual hewan peliharaan dan keperluannya; *teacher's* ~ murid kesayangan; *v* mengelus

petal *n* [pétel] daun bunga

petite *adj* [petit] (berukuran) kecil, mungil

petition *n* [petisyen] permohonan, petisi; *v* memohon

petrified *adj* [pétrifaid] membatu, sangat ketakutan

petrol *n* bensin; ~-*sniffing sl* ngelem; **petroleum** *n* [petrolium] minyak bumi olahan

petticoat *n* rok dalam

petting *n* cumbuan; *heavy* ~ bercinta, indehoi ← **pet**

petty *adj* kecil, remeh, sepele; ~ *cash* uang kecil, uang receh

petunia *n* semacam bunga

pew *n* bangku gereja

pewter *n* [pyuter] campuran timah

phantom *n* [fantom] hantu, momok

pharmacist *n* [farmasist] apoteker; **pharmaceutical** *n* [farmasutikel] farmasi, kefarmasian; **pharmacy** *n* apotik

phase *n* [féiz] tahap, masa; *v* ~ *out* menghapus secara bertahap

Ph.D. *abbrev Doctor of Philosophy* S3 (Strata Tiga)

pheasant *n* [fézant] burung kuau, burung pegar

phenomenal *adj* luar biasa, istimewa, menakjubkan; **phe-**

nomenon n **phenomena** pl fenomena

phew excl [fyu] aduh

philanthropist n [filantropist] dermawan; **philanthropy** n cinta kepada sesama manusia

Philippines [filipins] the ~ Filipina

philosopher n [filosofer] filsuf, ahli filsafat; **philosophical** adj berfilsafat, filosofis; **philosophy** n (ilmu) filsafat

phlegm n [flém] dahak

phobia n penyakit ketakutan, fobi

phone n, coll telepon; ~ book daftar nomor telepon; ~ box telepon umum; ~ tap sadapan telepon; on the ~ sedang telepon; v bertelepon; menelepon ← **telephone**

phonetic adj fonetik, sesuai dengan abjad

phoney, phony adj [foni] palsu

phosphorus n fosfor

photo n, sl foto; **photocopy** n fotokopi; ~ machine mesin fotokopi; v memfotokopi; **photograph** n foto, potret, gambar; v memotret; **photographer** n tukang foto, tukang potret, fotografer; **photography** n potret-memotret, fotografi

photosynthesis n fotosintesa

phrase n [fréz] frase, kelompok kata; **phrasebook** n buku ungkapan bahasa asing

physical adj (secara) fisik; jasmani; ~ sciences ilmu-ilmu eksakta

physician n [fizisyen] dokter

physics n, pl ilmu fisika

physiotherapist n ahli fisioterapi; **physiotherapy** n fisioterapi

pianist n [pienist] pemain piano; **piano** n piano; ~ key tuts piano

piccolo n [pikelo] pikolo, semacam suling kecil

pick n pilihan; beliung; first ~ pilihan pertama; v memilih; mencungkil; memetik; ~ flowers memetik bunga; ~ on mengganggu, mengusik; ~ up mengambil; menjemput; ~ your nose mengupil

picket n tiang pancang; ~ fence pagar kayu; ~ line barisan depan pemogok

pickle n [pikel] acar; v mengasinkan; in a ~ dalam kesulitan

pickpocket n copet, pencopet

pickup n pikap

picky adj memilih-milih

picnic n piknik

pictorial adj bergambar; **picture** n gambar, lukisan; v membayangkan; melukiskan; in the ~ sudah tahu; **picturesque** adj [piktyurésk] asri

pie n pai; sejenis kue

piece n [pis] potong, keping, bagian; a ~ of music sebuah lagu; v ~ together menyusun

pier n [pir] jeti, dermaga, pelabuhan

pierce v [pirs] menembus, menindik, menusuk; ~d ears telinga yang ditindik

pig n babi; orang yang bengis atau jorok; ~-headed keras kepala pigeon n [pijen] burung merpati, burung dara; **pigeonhole** n kotak pribadi

piggybank n [pigibank] celengan ← **pig**

pigment n pigmen, zat warna

pigsty n [pigstai] kandang babi; sl kamar yang berantakan ← **pig**

pigtail n kepang dua ← **pig**

pile n timbunan; v menimbun

pilgrim n haji; peziarah; **pilgrimage** n ziarah, peziarah; the lesser ~ umroh; to make a ~ berziarah; make the ~ naik haji

pill n pil, obat; the (contraceptive) ~ pil KB; **pillbox** n tempat obat

pillar n [piler] tiang, soko guru; ~ box bis surat

pillow n [pilo] bantal; ~ case, ~ slip sarung bantal

pilot adj percontohan; n pilot, penerbang, pandu; contoh

pimple n [pimpel] jerawat; **pimply** adj berjerawat, jerawatan

pin n peniti; ~-stripe garis-garis halus; ~-up girl gadis pujaan; v menyematkan

pinafore n [pinafor] sejenis rok anak

pincers n, pl sepit, capit

pinch n cubitan; sedikit; a ~ of salt sedikit garam; to feel the ~ merasa tertekan; v mencubit

pine n ~ (tree) pohon pinus

pineapple n nanas

pingpong n tenis meja, ping-pong

pink adj merah muda, merah jambu, pink; in the ~ sedang dalam keadaan sehat

pint n [paint] ukuran cairan sebesar seperdelapan galon (0,568 liter)

pioneer n [payonir] perintis, pelopor; v memelopori

pious adj [payus] soleh, saleh

pipe n pipa; ~ dream impian belaka; v menyalurkan; **pipeline** n saluran pipa; in the ~ sedang dikembangkan

pirate n [pairat] bajak laut, pembajak; **pirated** adj bajakan

pit n lubang, terowongan dalam tambang; biji (buah); v mengadu; the ~s (keadaan) yang terburuk; the ~ of your stomach ulu hati; **pitted** adj tanpa biji

pitch n pola titinada; lemparan (bisbol); usaha; to make a ~ for berusaha; v melemparkan; ~ in ikut membantu; ~-dark, ~ black gelap gulita; **pitcher** n pelempar; kendi, tempat air

pitchfork n trisula

pith n intisari

pitiful adj [pitiful] memelas, menyedihkan; **pitiless** adj kejam, bengis; **pity** n belas kasihan; v mengasihani; what a ~ sayang (sekali); to have ~ on, to take ~ on mengasihani; I ~ the woman saya prihatin dengan perempuan itu

pivot n [pivet] poros, pasak, sumbu; **pivotal** adj sangat penting

pixie n [piksi] peri, makhluk halus

placard *n* plakat

place *n* tempat; kedudukan; ~ *card* kartu nama tempat duduk; ~ *mat* tatakan piring; *first* ~ pemenang, juara; *my* ~ rumah (saya); ~ *of worship* rumah ibadah; *in* ~ *of* sebagai pengganti; *v* menempatkan, meletakkan; *to take* ~ terjadi, berlangsung

placenta *n* [plasénta] ari-ari, tembuni

plagiarize *v* [pléjeraiz] menjiplak, mencontek; **plagiarism** [pléjerizem] *n* plagiat

plague *n* [plég] penyakit sampar, wabah; *v* sangat mengganggu

plain *adj* polos; sederhana, bersahaja; nyata; ~ *sailing* lancar; ~-*spoken* ceplas-ceplos, terus terang; ~ *clothes police* polisi reserse; *n* medan, dataran; **plainly** *adv* terus terang

plaintive *adj* [plaintiv] sedih, sayu

plait *n* [plat] kepang; *v* mengepang

plan *n* rencana, rancangan, bagan, denah; ~*ned economy* ekonomi terencana, ekonomi sentral; *five-year* ~ rencana lima tahun (Repelita); *v* merancang, merencanakan

plane *n, sl* pesawat terbang ← **aeroplane**

planet *n* planet; ~ *Earth* Bumi

plank *n* papan

planner *n* perencana; *daily* ~ buku agenda; *town* ~ planolog; **planning** *n* perencanaan;

family ~ keluarga berencana ← **plan**

plant *n* tetumbuhan, tanaman; pabrik; *v* menanam, menanamkan; **plantation** *n* perkebunan; *tea* ~ kebun teh; **planter** *n* penanam; pemilik (pengusaha) perkebunan

plaster *n* kapur, gips, plester; ~ *cast* gips; *sticking* ~ plester; *v* memasang secara sembarangan

plastic *adj, n* plastik; ~ *bag* keresek, kantong plastik; ~ *surgery* bedah plastik

plate *n* piring; pelat; ~ *glass* sehelai kaca jendela; *number* ~ pelat polisi

plateau *n* [plato] dataran tinggi; *the Dieng* ~ dataran tinggi Dieng

platform *n* peron; panggung; ~ *heels* hak tinggi yang tebal

platinum *n* [platinum] platina, emas putih; *to go* ~ menjual jutaan keping (album musik)

platoon *n* [platun] peleton

platter *n* piring besar

plausible *adj* [plozibel] dapat diterima, masuk akal

play *n* pertunjukan, sandiwara; permainan; *v* main, bermain; memainkan; ~ *along* berpura-pura kerjasama; ~ *around* berfoya-foya; ~ *back* *v* memutar kembali; ~ *down* mengecilkan; ~ *equipment* tempat bermain anak-anak, ayunan; ~ *tag* main kejar-kejaran; ~ *truant* membolos dari sekolah; ~ *up* membesar-besarkan; menjadi nakal; ~

a part memainkan peran; ~ *a trick on* mempermainkan; **playboy** *n* lelaki yang suka mempermainkan perempuan; seorang Arjuna; **player** *n* pemain; **playground** *n* tempat bermain, tempat ayunan; **playmate** *n* teman sepermainan; **playpen** *n* boks (bayi); **plaything** *n* mainan; **playwright** *n* pengarang drama

plaza *n* alun-alun

plea *n* permohonan, permintaan; pembelaan, dalih; **plead** *v* memohon; mengaku

pleasant *adj* [plézant] menyenangkan, enak, nyaman, nikmat; sopan; **please** tolong; silahkan; coba; ~ *help me* tolong bantu saya; ~ *sit down* silahkan duduk; ~ *try* cobalah; *v* menyenangkan; ~d senang, puas; ~ *yourself* terserah; **pleasure** *n* [plézyur] kesukaan, kenikmatan

pledge *n* [pléj] janji, ikrar; ~ *of allegiance* janji setia; *v* berjanji, berikrar; menjanjikan

plenty *adj* banyak, cukup; *n* kemakmuran

pliers *n, pl* [players] tang

plight *n* [plait] keadaan buruk

plot *n* sebidang tanah; alur cerita; komplotan; *v* merencanakan; berkomplot, bersekongkol; **plotter** anggota komplotan

plow, plough *n* [plau] bajak; *v* membajak

plucky *adj* berani

plug *n* sumbat; steker, stopkontak; *v* menyumbat

plum *n* buah prem

plumber *n* [plamer] tukang ledeng; **plumbing** *n* ledeng

plump *adj* tambun, subur

plunder *n* hasil rampasan, hasil jarahan; *v* merampas, menjarah

plunge *n, v* terjun, cemplung

plural *adj* jamak; ~ *society* masyarakat yang heterogen

plus [plas] *n* nilai plus; *v* plus, ditambah

pm *post meridiem* siang, sore, malam (jam 12.00–24.00)

PM *abbrev Prime Minister* PM (Perdana Menteri)

pneumatic *adj* [nyumatik] berisi udara, berisi angin; ~ *tire* ban pompa

pneumonia *n* [nyumonia] radang paru-paru

PNG *abbrev Papua New Guinea* PNG (Papua Nugini)

pocket *n* saku, kantong, kocek; ~ *money* uang saku, uang jajan; *air* ~ kantong udara; *v* mengantungi; **pocketknife** *n* [poketnaif] pisau lipat

podiatrist *n* [podayatrist] ahli penyakit kaki

poem *n* [poem] syair, pantun; **poet** *n* penyair; **poetic** *adj* puitis; **poetry** *n* puisi

point *n* titik, noktah; tanjung; ~-*blank* langsung, terus terang; *compass* ~ mata angin; ~ *of view* (sudut) pandangan, pendapat; *beside the* ~ tidak penting; *that's not the* ~ bukan itu; *to the* ~ tepat, pendek; *v* menunjuk, menunjukkan; ~ *out*

menunjukkan; **pointed** *adj*
runcing, tajam; **pointer** *n* (jari)
penunjuk; **pointless** *adj* tiada
gunanya

poison *n* racun; bisa; *food ~ing*
keracunan makanan; *rat ~*
racun tikus; *v* meracuni;
poisonous *adj* beracun,
berbisa; *~ snake* ular berbisa

poke *v* menyodok, menusuk

Poland *n* Polandia ← **Pole**

polar *adj* berhubungan dengan
kutub; *~ bear* beruang kutub;
pole *n* kutub; *the South ~*
Kutub Selatan

pole *n* tiang; *~ vault* loncat galah

Pole *n* orang Polandia

police *n* [polis] polisi; *~ officer*
polisi; *~ station* kantor polisi,
pos polisi; **policeman** *n, m*
polisi; **policewoman** *n, f* polisi
wanita (polwan)

policy *n* kebijaksanaan; *insurance ~* polis (asuransi)

polio *n* penyakit lumpuh layuh,
penyakit polio

Polish *adj* berasal dari Polandia;
n bahasa Polandia

polish *n* pelitur, semir; *shoe ~*
semir sepatu; *v* menggosok,
menyemir

polite *adj* sopan (santun); **politeness** *n* kesopanan, kesopan-
santunan

political *adj* politik; **politician** *n*
[politisyen] politikus, politisi;
politics *n* [ilmu] politik

polka *~ dot* berbintik-bintik

poll *n* pemberian suara; *opinion
~* jajak pendapat; *the ~s* tempat

pemungutan suara (TPS)

pollen *n* tepung sari

pollute *v* mencemarkan; **polluted**
adj tercemar; **pollution** *n*
pencemaran, kecemaran, polusi; *air ~* polusi udara

polo *n* polo; *~ shirt* kaus berkerah; *water ~* polo air

polygamy *n* poligami, beristeri
lebih dari satu

Polynesia *n* Polinesia; *French ~*
Polinesia Perancis; **Polynesian**
adj berasal dari Polinesia; *n*
orang Polinesia

pompous *adj* [pompes] sombong

poncho *n* ponco, mantel besar

pond *n* kolam

ponder *v* memikirkan, menimbang, merenungkan

pony *n* kuda kerdil, kuda poni;
ponytail *n* ekor kuda

poo, pooh *n, sl* tahi; *v* berak;
pooh-pooh *v* meremehkan

pool *n* kolam (renang); bilyar;
pul; *swimming ~* kolam renang;
v menggabungkan, menyatukan

poor *adj* miskin, papa; hina,
malang; *the ~* kaum miskin,
orang papa; *a ~ excuse* alasan
yang lemah; *in ~ health* kurang
sehat

pop *n ~ (musik)* lagu pop, musik
populer ← **popular**

pop *v* meletup; *~-gun* pistol
mainan; *~ in, ~ over* mampir; *~
up* muncul; *~ the question*
meminang

Pope *the ~* Sri Paus

poppy *n* bunga opium, bunga
madat

popular *adj* populer, laku; **populate** *v* mendiami, menghuni; **population** *n* (jumlah) penduduk, populasi; **populous** *adj* banyak penduduk, padat penduduk

porcelain *adj, n* porselen, keramik

porch *n* serambi, beranda, teras

porcupine *n* [porkyupain] landak

pore *n* pori

pork *n* daging babi

pornographic *adj* jorok, cabul, pornografis; **pornography** *n* pornografi

porous *adj* [porus] berpori ← **pore**

porpoise *n* [porpus] lumba-lumba

porridge *n* [porij] bubur

port *adj* kiri (di kapal); *n* pelabuhan; lubang, colokan; anggur port; ~ *of call* pelabuhan persinggahan, pelabuhan transit

portable *adj* dapat dibawa ke mana-mana, jinjing

porter *n* kuli

portfolio *n* tas, map, sampul; koleksi

porthole *n* [port hol] tingkapan kapal

portion *n* porsi, bagian

portrait *n* potret, lukisan, gambar; **portray** *v* melukiskan, menggambarkan; **portrayal** *n* cara memerankan, pelukisan; lukisan

Portugal *n* Portugal; **Por-**

tuguese *adj* [Portugis] berasal dari Portugal; *n* bahasa Portugal; orang Portugal

pose *n* [poz] gaya, lagak; *v* bergaya

posh *adj, sl* mewah, berkelas tinggi

position *n* [posisyen] letak, kedudukan, pangkat, jabatan; keadaan

positive *adj, n* positif, pasti, tentu

possess *v* memiliki, mempunyai; **possession** *n* kepunyaan, (harta) milik; **possessive** *adj* ingin memiliki, posesif

possibility *n* kemungkinan; *a slight* ~ kemungkinan kecil; **possible** *adj* [posibel] mungkin; **possibly** *adv* barangkali, mungkin

possum, opossum *n* semacam binatang malam seperti tupai

post *adj* sesudah, pasca; *~-graduate* pascasarjana; *~-mortem* otopsi; *~-war* pascaperang

post *n* pos; jabatan; tiang; layanan pos; ~ *office* kantor pos; *v* mengeposkan; menempelkan; **postage** *n* [postej] perangko, ongkos kirim; ~ *stamp* perangko; **postal** *adj* berkaitan dengan pos; **postcard** *n* kartu pos; **poster** *n* plakat, gambar

posterior *adj* [postirior] belakang; *n* pantat

postman *n* tukang pos ← **post**

postmark *n* cap pos ← **post**

postmaster *n* kepala kantor pos ← **post**

postpone *v* menunda, mengundurkan

postscript, PS tambahan tulisan

posture *n* [postyur] sikap badan, postur

pot *n* pot, periuk, tempat bunga, tempat tanaman; ~ *belly* gendut; ~ *luck* bisa baik, bisa tidak; seadanya; ~ *scourer* penggosok panci

potassium *n* kalium, potasium

potato *n* [potéto] kentang; *(hot)* ~ *chips* kentang goreng; ~ *crisps* kripik kentang

potent *adj* kuat, manjur, mujarab; **potential** *adj* mungkin, berpeluang, calon; *n* kemungkinan, kekuatan, tenaga

pothole *n* [pot hol] lubang di jalan

potion *n* ramuan

potpourri *n* [potpuri, popuri] bunga rampai

potter *n* perajin tembikar; **pottery** *n* tembikar, pecah belah, keramik

poultry *n* [poltri] unggas

pounce *v* menerkam

pound *n* pon; tempat penerimaan barang yang hilang; ~ *sterling* pon sterling, pon Inggris; *v* menumbuk; memukul-mukul

pour *v* mengalir; menuangkan, mencurahkan; menyiram; ~ *out your heart* mencurahkan hati (curhat); ~ *with rain* hujan lebat

poverty *n* [poverti] kemiskinan

POW *abbrev prisoner-of-war* tawanan perang

powder *n* [pauder] bubuk, serbuk, puyer; bedak; ~ed milk susu bubuk; *talcum* ~ bedak; *v* membedaki; **powdery** *adj* seperti bubuk

power *n* kekuasaan, kekuatan, daya, tenaga; ~ *line* saluran listrik; ~ *station* pembangkit listrik; ~ *steering* setir daya; **powerful** *adj* berkuasa, kuat; **powerless** *adj* tak berkuasa, tak berdaya

PR *abbrev public relations* hubungan masyarakan (humas)

practical *n* praktis, berguna; ~ *lesson* praktek; **practically** *adv* hampir-hampir, benarbenar; **practice** *n* praktek, kebiasaan, adat; latihan; *doctor's* ~ praktek dokter; *piano* ~ latihan piano; *to put into* ~ mempraktekkan; *v* berlatih; mempraktekkan, melatih

Prague *n* [Prag] Praha

praise *n* [préiz] pujian; *v* memuji; ~ *the Lord* puji Tuhan

pram *n* kereta bayi, kereta anak-anak ← **perambulator**

prank *n* gurauan, permainan

prawn *n* udang

pray *v* berdoa, sholat, bersembahyang; **prayer** *n* [préir] doa, sembahyang; ~ *beads Isl* tasbih; *Cath* rosario; ~ *mat* sejadah; *the sunset* ~ sholat magrib, sembahyang magrib

pre- *pref* [pri] pra-, sebelum; ~-*school* taman kanak-kanak (TK); ~-*war* sebelum perang

preach *v* berkhotbah, mengajari; **preacher** *n* pemuka agama; *Isl* khotib, dai

precarious *adj* [prekérius] berbahaya

precaution *n* tindakan pencegahan; **precautionary** *adj* kalau-kalau, pencegahan

precede *v* [presid] mendahului; **precedence** *n* [présedens] prioritas; **precedent** *n* preseden

precinct *n* daerah

precious *adj* [présyus] berharga, mahal; mulia; ~ *metal* logam mulia

precipice *n* [présipis] ngarai, tebing tinggi

precipitate *n* endapan; *v* mempercepat, memicu; **precipitation** *n* hujan, salju

precise *adj* tepat, saksama; **precision** *n* kesaksamaan, ketelitian

predator *n* [prédater] pemangsa, pemakan hewan lain

predicate *n* sebutan (kalimat), predikat

predict *v* meramalkan; **prediction** *n* ramalan

preface *n* [préfas] pendahuluan, kata pengantar, prakata; *v* mengawali, memulai

prefer *v* lebih suka, memilih; **preferably** *adv* [préferabli] lebih baik; **preference** *n* kecenderungan, pilihan; **preferential** *adj* [préferénsyal] istimewa, diutamakan

prefix *n* awalan

pregnancy *n* (masa) kehamilan; **pregnant** *adj* hamil, mengandung

prehistoric *adj* prasejarah

prejudice *n* [préjudis] prasangka; **prejudiced** *adj* berprasangka

preliminary *adj* pendahuluan, persiapan, awal

premature *adj* prematur, sebelum waktunya, pradini

premier *adj* utama, terbaik; *n* pemimpin, perdana menteri, kepala negara bagian

premiere *n* [prémiér] pemutaran perdana, pertunjukan perdana

preoccupied *adj* [priokupaid] asyik memikirkan, termenung; **preoccupation** *n* keasyikan

prepaid *adj* prabayar; *v, pf* → **prepay**

preparation *n* [préparésyen] persiapan; **prepare** *v* menyiapkan, mempersiapkan; **prepared** *adj* siap, bersedia

prepay *v* **prepaid prepaid** membayar di muka

preposition *n* [préposisyen] kata depan

prerequisite *n* [prirekuisit] prasyarat, syarat

prescribe *v* menetapkan; *v* memberikan resep; **prescription** *n* resep

presence *n* [prézens] hadirat, hadapan; kehadiran; ~ *of mind* kesadaran, kecepatan berpikir; **present** *adj* [prézent] sekarang, kini; hadir; *n* hadiah, kado, pemberian; ~ *tense* (kata kerja) masa kini; *at* ~ sekarang ini; *v* [prezént] menyajikan, mempersembahkan; **presentation** *n* penyajian, presentasi; **presently** *adv* segera

preservation *n* [préservésyen] pelindungan, preservasi; **preservative** *n* [presérvativ] pengawet; **preserve** *n* [presérv] cagar; selai; *nature* ~ cagar alam; *v* mengawetkan, melindungi, memelihara

preside *v* [prezaid] mengetuai; **presidency** *n* masa jabatan presiden; **president** *n* presiden; ketua; **presidential** *adj* [prézidéntyal] untuk presiden

press *n* percetakan; pers; alat penekan; ~ *agency* kantor berita; ~ *clipping* guntingan koran; ~ *conference* jumpa pers; ~ *gallery* ruang wartawan; *in* ~ sedang dicetak; *v* menekan, menindih, mendesak; ~ *on* maju, menekan; **pressing** *adj* mendesak; **pressure** *n* [présyur] tekanan

prestige *n* [préstij] gengsi; **prestigious** *adj* bergengsi

presumably *adv* kiranya, agaknya; **presume** *v* menganggap; mengira; **presumption** *n* anggapan; **presumptuous** *adj* lancang, sombong

pretend *v* berpura-pura, berdalih; **pretense** *n* dalih, kepurapuraan; **pretentious** *adj* berpretensi, mengada-ada

pretext *n* dalih

pretty *adj* [priti] manis, cantik, molek; *adv* cukup

pretzel *n* cemilan kering yang asin

prevail *v* menang, bertahan;

prevalent *adj* [prévalent] umum, berlaku, lazim

prevent *v* [prevént] mencegah, menghalangi, menangkis; **preventative, preventive** *adj* pencegahan; **prevention** *n* pencegahan

preview *n* previu; prapertunjukan

previous *adj* yang dahulu, yang sebelumnya

prey *n* [pré] mangsa; *v* ~ *on* memburu

price *n* harga; ~ *list* daftar harga; **priceless** *adj* tidak ternilai

prick *n* tusukan; *v* menusuk; **prickly** *adj* tajam, berduri, menusuk

pride *n* kesombongan, kebanggaan, harga diri; ~ *yourself on* bangga pada

priest *n, Cath* [prist] pastor; *Hin* pedanda

primary *adj* pertama, terpenting, dasar; ~ *colors* warna dasar; ~ *school* sekolah dasar (SD); **prime** *adj* perdana, utama; ~ *minister (PM)* Perdana Menteri (PM); ~ *number* bilangan pokok; *in your* ~ pada masa keemasan

primitive *adj* sederhana, primitif

primrose *n* semacam bunga berwarna kuning muda

prince *n, m* pangeran; *crown* ~ putera mahkota; **princess** *n, f* putri, permaisuri

principal *adj* utama; *n* kepala sekolah; uang pokok

principle *n* [prinsipel] asas, prinsip; *in* ~ pada prinsipnya, pada dasarnya; *on* ~ karena keyakinan

print *n* tapak (kaki); gambar, reproduksi; tulisan, ketikan; ~ *media* media cetak; *fine* ~ tulisan kecil; *in* ~ masih dicetak; *out of* ~ sudah tidak dicetak lagi; *v* mencetak; menulis dengan huruf cetak; ~*ing press* mesin cetak; **printer** *n* printer, pencetak; ~**s** percetakan; **print-out** *n* hasil cetak

prior *adj* [praior] terlebih dahulu; **prioritize** *v* mengutamakan; **priority** *n* prioritas

prism *n* [prizem] prisma

prison *n* [prizon] penjara; *in* ~ dipenjara; **prisoner** *n* orang yang dipenjara, terpidana; *in* ~ dipenjara

private *adj* [praivet] pribadi; swasta; milik sendiri; *n* tamtama, prajurit biasa; ~**s** *sl* kemaluan; ~ *sector* (perusahaan) swasta; ~ *school* sekolah swasta; *in* ~ tidak di depan umum

privilege *n* [privilej] hak istimewa

prize *n* hadiah; *v* menilai tinggi

pro *adj* pro, setuju dengan; ~- *abortion* setuju dengan aborsi; (olahragawan) profesional

probable *adj* **probably** *adv* kemungkinan besar, mungkin

probe *n* pemeriksaan, penelitian; pesawat penjelajah; *v* menyelidiki

problem *n* masalah, soal

procedure *n* prosedur, tata cara; **proceed** *v* maju, jalan; meneruskan; **proceedings** *n*,

pl cara kerja, acara kerja; **proceeds** *n, pl* hasil dari jualan; penghasilan; **process** *n* cara, proses; *v* memproses, mengolah; ~*ed meat* daging olahan; **procession** *n* arak-arakan, prosesi; **processor** *n* alat pengolah, alat pemroses; *word* ~ semacam mesin tik elektronik

proclaim *v* menyatakan, memproklamasikan, mengumumkan; **proclamation** *n* proklamasi, pengumuman

prodigious *adj* [prodijus] sangat banyak; **prodigy** *n* anak ajaib

produce *n* hasil; *v* menghasilkan; **producer** *n* produsen; **product** *n* hasil, produk; **production** *n* produksi, pertunjukan; **productive** *adj* produktif, subur

profession *n* profesi, pekerjaan; pernyataan; **profess** *v* menyatakan; **professional** *adj* profesional

professor *n* guru besar; ~ *of Asian Languages* Guru Besar Bahasa-bahasa Asia

profile *n* profil

profit *n* untung, keuntungan, laba; ~ *and loss* laba rugi; *non-*~ nirlaba; *v* beruntung, memperoleh keuntungan; **profitable** *adj* menguntungkan

profound *adj* dalam, mendalam

program, programme *n* acara, program; *v* memprogram; **programmer** *n* pembuat program (komputer)

progress *n* kemajuan; *v* maju; *in* ~ sedang berlangsung; **pro-**

gressive *adj* berpikiran maju, progresif

prohibit *v* melarang; **prohibition** *n* [prohibisyen] larangan

project *n* proyek; *v* memproyeksikan; **projection** *n* proyeksi; **projector** *n* proyektor

prolific *adj* [prolifik] subur, banyak hasil

prolog, prologue *n* prolog, pendahuluan

prolong *v* memperpanjang

prominent *adj* terkemuka, menonjol

promise *n* [promis] janji; *v* berjanji; menjanjikan

promote *v* memajukan, menaikkan pangkat, mempromosikan; **promotion** *n* kenaikan pangkat; promosi

prompt *adj* cepat; *n* bisikan; *v* membisiki; mendorong

prong *n* gigi garpu; cabang tanduk

pronoun *n* kata ganti

pronounce *v* melafalkan; menyatakan; **pronunciation** *n* lafal

proof *n* bukti; *~-read* mengoreksi naskah

prop *n* penopang, sangga; alat-alat yang diperlukan di panggung; *v* menyangga, menopang

propagate *v* [propagét] mengembangbiakkan; menyebarkan

propeller *n* baling-baling

proper *adj* benar, betul, patut, layak; **properly** *adv* benar-benar, dengan betul

property *n* kepunyaan, (harta) milik; sifat

prophecy *n* [profesi] ramalan; **prophet** *n* nabi, rasul; *the ~ (Muhammad)* Nabi Mohammad (s.a.w.); *the ~s* Rasul-Rasul

proportion *n* perbandingan, proporsi; **proportional** *adj* proporsional, sebanding; **proportionate** *adj* [proporsyenét] yang sebanding

proposal *n* usul; lamaran; **propose** *v* mengusulkan; meminang; **proposition** *n* usul, rencana

proprietary [proprayetri] *~ limited (Pty Ltd)* persero, perseroan terbatas (PT); **proprietor** *n* [proprayetor] pemilik

prosecute *v* menuntut; **prosecution** *n* pihak penuntut; **prosecutor** *n* jaksa, penuntut; *public ~* jaksa umum

prosper *v* berhasil, menjadi makmur; **prosperity** *n* kemakmuran; **prosperous** *adj* makmur

prostate *n* (kelenjar) prostat

prostitute *n* [prostitut] pelacur, pekerja seks komersial (PSK), wanita tunasusila (WTS); **prostitution** *n* pelacuran, prostitusi

protect *v* melindungi; **protection** *n* perlindungan; **protective** *adj* [protéktif] bersifat melindungi; pencegah; **protector** *n* pelindung

protest *n* protes, pembangkangan, unjuk rasa; *v* memprotes, melawan, membangkang, berunjuk rasa; **Protestant** *adj* Kristen; *n* orang Kristen;

protester *n* pemrotes, pengunjuk rasa

protrude *v* menjorok, menonjol keluar; **protruding** *adj* yang menonjol

proud *adj* bangga; angkuh, sombong; ~ *of her son* bangga akan anaknya

prove *v* [pruv] membuktikan; **proven** *adj* ternyata, terbukti

proverb *n* peribahasa

provide *v* menyediakan, membekali, melengkapi; ~ *for* mengurus, memelihara; **provided, providing** ~ *(that)* asal, asalkan; **provider** *n* pemberi nafkah; pemberi jasa

province *n* propinsi; **provincial** *adj* berhubungan dengan provinsi; picik, kampungan

provision *n* [provisyen] persediaan; ketetapan; **provisional** *adj* sementara ← **provide**

provocation *n* provokasi, hasutan, pancingan; **provocative** *adj* provokatif, menghasut, memancing; **provoke** *v* menghasut, memancing

proxy *n* wakil, kuasa

prudent *adj* bijaksana, hati-hati

prune *n* buah prem kering

pry *v* mencampuri; ~ *open* mencongkel

PS *abbrev postscript* catatan tambahan pada akhir surat

PS *abbrev primary school* SD (sekolah dasar)

psalm *n* [sam] mazmur

pseudonym *n* [siudonim] nama samaran

psychiatric *adj* [saikiatrik] berhubungan dengan penyakit jiwa; ~ *hospital* rumah sakit jiwa; **psychiatrist** *n* [saikayetrist] psikiater, ahli jiwa; **psychiatry** *n* ilmu penyakit jiwa, psikiatri

psychic *adj, n* [saikik] mempunyai indera keenam, cenayang

psychological *adj* [saikolojikal] kejiwaan; **psychologist** *n* psikolog, ahli ilmu jiwa; **psychology** *n* ilmu jiwa, psikologi

PTO *abbrev please turn over* di halaman berikut

Pty Ltd, Pte *Proprietary Limited* PT (Perseroan Terbatas), CV, NV

puberty *n* masa puber, pubertas; **pubic** *adj* ~ *hair* bulu yang tumbuh di sekitar kemaluan

public *n* orang banyak, umum; ~ *administration* tata usaha negara; ~ *health* kesehatan masyarakat; ~ *relations (PR)* hubungan masyarakat (humas); ~ *servant* pegawai negeri; ~ *speaking* berpidato di depan umum; ~ *telephone* telepon umum; ~ *toilet* WC umum; ~ *transport* angkutan umum; *in* ~ di depan umum; **publication** *n* terbitan, keluaran; pengumuman; **publicity** *n* [pablisiti] hubungan masyarakat (humas); publisitas; ~ *stunt* kegiatan untuk membuat berita; **publicize** *v* mengumumkan, memasarkan

publish *v* menerbitkan, mengeluarkan, mengumumkan; **publisher** n penerbit

pudding n puding, pencuci mulut, podeng

puddle n [padel] genangan

Puerto Rican adj [Porto Rikan] berasal dari Puerto Rico; n orang Puerto Rico; **Puerto Rico** n Puerto Rico

puff n embusan; isapan; tiupan; v terengah-engah; mengepul; meniup; **puffy** adj bengkak

pug n sejenis anjing kecil

puke v, sl muntah

pull n tarikan, daya tarik; v [pul] menarik; ~ *back* menarik ke samping; mundur; ~ *down* menarik ke bawah; membongkar, merobohkan; ~ *out* batal; mencabut; ~ *over* minggir, menepi; ~ *through* sembuh; melewati; ~ *together* bekerja sama; ~ *a muscle* keseleo; **pulley** n [puli] katrol; **pullover** n switer, baju hangat

pulp n bubur; daging buah; ampas; ~ *fiction* fiksi murahan; *wood* ~ bubur kayu

pulpit n [pulpit] mimbar

pulsate v berdenyut; **pulse** n nadi

pumice n [pamis] batu apung

pump n pompa; v memompa

pumpkin n labu

punch n pukulan, tonjokan; minuman campuran; v menghantam, meninju, menonjok

punctual adj tepat waktu; **punctuality** n sikap selalu tepat waktu

punctuation n [pangktyuésyen] pemberian tanda-tanda baca; ~ *mark* tanda baca

puncture n [pangktyur] lubang kecil, kempes; *I had a* ~ ban mobil saya kempes

punish v [panisy] menghukum; **punishment** n hukuman

punk n kaum muda yang memakai baju robek, perhiasan logam serta rambutnya dicat

pupil n murid; anak mata, pupil

puppet n boneka; wayang; ~ *government* pemerintahan boneka; **puppeteer** n dalang

puppy n [papi] anak anjing

purchase n [perces] pembelian, pembelanjaan; v membeli

pure adj murni, bersih; **purification** n pembersihan, penyaringan; **purify** v membersihkan, menyaring, memurnikan; **purity** n kemurnian

purple adj ungu, lembayung; ~ *patch* keberhasilan secara mendadak

purpose n maksud, niat, tujuan; *on* ~ dengan sengaja

purr n dengkur (kucing); v mendengkur

purse n dompet

purser n penata usaha di kapal atau pesawat terbang

pursue v mengejar, mengikuti, memburu; **pursuit** n pengejaran, pencarian

purveyor n [pervéyer] pemasok

push n [pusy] dorongan; v mendorong; ~ *button* tombol; ~ *in* menyerobot, mendorong masuk; ~ *off* pergi; **pusher** *n* kereta anak; *sl* bandar narkoba; **pushover** *n* sesuatu yang mudah; **pushy** *adj* suka memaksa kehendak, lancang

puss, pussycat *n, sl* [pus, pusikat] kucing

put *v* **put put** [put] meletakkan, menaruh, menyimpan; menempatkan; ~ *down* memadamkan; meremehkan; menyuntik mati binatang; ~ *on* mengenakan (baju); ~ *on weight* menjadi lebih gemuk; ~ *off* menunda, mengundurkan; ~ *out* mengeluarkan; tersinggung; ~ *up* memasang; menginap; ~ *up with* tahan; ~ *upon* membebankan; *shot* ~ tolak peluru; ~-*down* hinaan

putrid *adj* [pyutrid] busuk

puzzle *n* [pazel] mainan, teka-teki; *crossword* ~ teka-teki silang (TTS); *jigsaw* ~ teka-teki menyusun; **puzzled** *adj* [pazeld] bingung

pygmy *n* [pigmi] orang kerdil; *adj* kerdil

pyjamas, pajamas *n, pl* piyama, baju tidur

pylon *n* [pailon] menara listrik, tiang listrik yang besar

pyramid *n* piramida

python *n* [paithon] ular sanca, piton

Q

Qatar *n* [Katar] Qatar; **Qatari** *adj* berasal dari Qatar; *n* orang Qatar

QC *abbrev Queen's Counsel* pengacara kerajaan

quack *n* suara bebek; *sl* dukun, tukang obat; *v* membebek

quad, quadrangle *n* [kuod-ranggel] (lapangan) segi empat

quadratic *adj* kuadrat; ~ *equation* persamaan kuadrat

quadrilateral *adj, n* segi empat

quadruped *n* [kuodrupéd] binatang berkaki empat

quadruple *v* [kuodrupel] berlipat empat

quadruplet *n* [kuodruplet] kembar empat

quail *n* burung puyuh

quaint *adj* kuno, aneh

quake *n* gempa; *v* gemetar

qualification *n* kualifikasi, ijazah; **qualified** *adj* berkualifikasi, berhak, berijazah; **qualify** *v* memenuhi syarat, lolos

qualitative *adj* [kuolitatif] kualitatif, menurut mutu; **quality** *n* mutu, kualitas; sifat

qualm *n* [kuam] *no* ~*s* tidak merasa cemas atau ragu

quantity *n* [kuontiti] banyaknya, kuantitas

quarantine *n* [kuorantin] karantina

quarrel *n* [kuorel] pertengkaran, percekcokan; *v* bertengkar, ribut

quarry *n* [kuori] tambang, penggalian batu

quart *n* [kuort] ukuran cairan (944 ml)

quarter *n* [kuorter] perempat; kampung, daerah; ~s tempat tinggal; *three ~s*, (¾) tiga perempat; **quarterly** *adv* tiap tiga bulan; *n* majalah triwulan

quartet *n* [kuortét] empat sekawan, kwartet

quasi- *pref* [kuazi] pura-pura, tidak benar

quay *n* [ki] dermaga

queasy *adj* [kuizi] mual, muak

queen *n* ratu; *the ~ Mother* Ibu Suri

queer *adj* aneh; *adj, n, sl* homoseksual

quell *v* memadamkan, mengatasi

query *n* [kuiri] pertanyaan; *v* menanyakan, meragukan

quest *n* pencarian; *in ~ of* mencari

question *n* pertanyaan; masalah, soal; *~ mark* tanda tanya; *out of the ~* tidak mungkin; *to beg the ~* menerima tanpa bukti; *without ~* tentu saja, niscaya; *v* bertanya; menanyai, menanyakan; meragukan; mempersoalkan; **questionable** *adj* patut dipertanyakan, dapat diragukan; **questionnaire** *n* [kuéstionér] angket

queue *n* [kyu] antre, antrean; *v* antri, berantri

quick *adj* cepat; *~ smart* sekarang juga; *~-witted* cepat berpikir; **quicksilver** *n* air raksa; **quicksand** *n* pasir hanyut; **quicken** *v* menjadi lebih cepat

quid *n, sl* pon sterling

quiet *adj* [kuayet] teduh, tenang; *to be ~* diam; *on the ~* diam-diam; *n* keteduhan, ketenangan; **quieten** *v* menenangkan, meredakan

quilt *n* selimut tebal

quinine *n* [kuinin] kina

quintuplet *n* kembar lima

quip *n* sindiran, ejekan; *v* menyindir, mengejek, melucu

quirk *n* kebiasaan yang lucu; **quirky** *adj* lucu, mempunyai kebiasaan yang aneh

quit *v* **quit quit** putus asa, berhenti, meninggalkan

quite *adv* cukup sama, rada, lumayan

quiver *n, v* gemetar

quiz *n* kuis, ulangan singkat, tanya jawab; *v* menanyai

quota *n* jatah, kuota

quotation *n* kutipan; penawaran; *~ marks* tanda kutip; **quote** *v* mengutip, menyebut, mencatat

quotient *n* [kuosyent] hasil bagi

R

R. *river* S. (sungai)

rabbi *n* [rabai] pendeta Yahudi

rabbit *n* kelinci

rabble *n* rakyat jelata

rabies *n* [rébis] penyakit anjing gila, rabies

raccoon *n* sejenis musang, rakun

race *n* lomba, balap, pacuan; *v*

berlomba, membalap; **race-course** n pacuan kuda; **race-horse** n kuda pacu, kuda balap; **racetrack** n sirkuit; pacuan kuda

race n (suku) bangsa, ras; ~ *relations* hubungan antar suku bangsa; ~ *riots* kerusuhan etnis; *the human* ~ umat manusia; **racial** adj rasial, berhubungan dengan suku bangsa; **racism** n [résizem] rasisme, pembedaan rasial; **racist** adj rasis; n orang yang membenci suku bangsa lain

rack n rak; *luggage* ~ tempat barang

racket, racquet n raket

radial ~ *tire* ban radial

radiant adj [rédient] bersinar; berseri-seri; **radiation** n radiasi, penyinaran; **radiator** n radiator; alat pemanas

radical adj [radikel] radikal, ekstrem; n orang radikal

radio n [rédio] radio

radioactive adj [rédioaktif] radioaktif; **radiology** n [rédioloji] radiologi

radish n [radisy] lobak

radius n [rédius] jari-jari, radius

RAF abbrev Royal Air Force Angkatan Udara Kerajaan Inggris

raffle n [rafel] undian; v mengundi

raft n rakit; *white water ~ing* arung jeram

rag n lap, kain jelek; ~ *doll* boneka dari potongan-potongan kain; *in ~s* compang-camping;

the ~ *trade* industri busana

rage n kemarahan, geram; *all the* ~ sangat digemari; v mengamuk, marah-marah; sl berpesta

ragged adj [raged] compang-camping, robek-robek ← **rag**

raid n razia, serangan, penggerebekan; *dawn* ~ serangan fajar; v merazia, menyerang, menyerbu; **raider** n perompak

rail n rel; *by* ~ dengan kereta api; *off the ~s* tergelincir; **railing** n susuran; **railroad, railway** n jalan kereta api; *railway station* stasiun kereta api; *railway yards* langsiran

rain n, v hujan; *heavy* ~ hujan deras; *light* ~ gerimis; **rainbow** n pelangi, bianglala; **raincoat** n jas hujan; **raindrop** n tetesan hujan; **rainfall** n curah hujan; **rainy** adj banyak hujan; ~ *season* musim hujan; *to save for a* ~ *day* menabung untuk masa depan

raise n kenaikan; v mengangkat, menaikkan, meninggikan; membesarkan (anak-anak); menimbulkan

raisin n kismis

rake n penggaruk; v menggaruk, menyapu

rally n reli; pertemuan; ~ *driver* pembalap reli; v berkumpul, berhimpun

ram n biri-biri jantan; v membenturkan

ramble n pengembaraan; v berjalan kaki, mengembara; berbicara bertele-tele ramification *n* dampak

ramp *n* jalur mendaki, jalur yang melandai

rampant *adj* merajalela

ran *v, pf* → **run**

ranch *n* peternakan, pertanian

rancid *adj* anyir

rancor *n* dendam, benci

random at ~ secara sembarangan, membabi buta

rang *v, pf* → **ring**

range *n* [rénj] jajaran, barisan; kisaran, jangkauan; lapangan, tempat; *mountain* ~ pegunungan; *rifle* ~ lapangan tembak; *v* berkisar; **ranger** *n* penjaga hutan; **rangy** *adj* tinggi (badan)

rank *n* pangkat, derajat; ~ *and file* militer bawahan; rakyat jelata; *v* menduduki; *Henin-Hardenne ~s no.1 in the world* Henin-Hardenne menduduki peringkat pertama di dunia; mengatur, menyusun; menggolongkan; **ranking** *n* urutan

ransack *v* menggeledah

ransom *n* (uang) tebusan, penebusan

rap *n* musik rap; ketukan; *to take the* ~ menerima hukuman; *v* mengetuk

rape *n* perkosaan, pemerkosaan; *v* memerkosa, menggagahi

rapid *adj* [rapid] cepat, lekas; **rapids** *n, pl* jeram

rapist *n* pemerkosa ← **rape**

rapt *adj* suka sekali

rare *adj* mentah; jarang; **rarely** *adv* jarang

rascal *n* bangsat

rash *n* gatal-gatal; *nappy* ~ ruam popok

raspberry *n* frambozen

rat *n* tikus (besar); ~ *poison* racun tikus; ~ *race* kehidupan kota yang amat sibuk; *to smell a* ~ menjadi curiga

rate *n* tarif, perbandingan, angka; kecepatan; *birth* ~ angka kelahiran; *exchange* ~ kurs; *interest* ~ suku bunga; *at any* ~ bagaimanapun; *v* menilai; **rated** *adj* dinilai, dianggap

rather *adv* agak, rada, cukup; melainkan; ~ *than* daripada

ratification *n* ratifikasi, pengesahan; **ratify** *v* mengesahkan, meratifikasi

rating *n* penilaian

ratio *n* [résyio] perbandingan

ration *n* rangsum, jatah; *v* merangsum

rational *adj* rasional, masuk akal

rationale *n* [rasional] alasan

rattan *n* rotan

rattle *n* mainan bayi yang berbunyi; *v* gemertak; membuat bingung

ravage *v* [ravej] membinasakan, merusakkan

rave *n* ~ *(party)* pesta dansa; *v* meraban; *sl* sangat memuji; *raving mad* sangat gila

raven *n* burung gagak; ~-*haired* berambut hitam

ravenous *adj* [ravenus] sangat lapar

ravine *n* [ravin] jurang

ravishing *adj* menggairahkan, sangat menarik

raw *adj* mentah; kasar; ~ *materials* bahan mentah; ~ *silk* sutera kasar

ray *n* sinar; ikan pari; *a ~ of hope* seberkas harapan

razor *n* pisau cukur

Rd *Road* Jl (Jalan), Jl Ry (Jalan Raya)

reach *n* jangkauan; *v* sampai, tiba, mencapai; menghubungi

react *v* [riakt] bereaksi; menanggapi; **reaction** *n* tanggapan, reaksi; **reactionary** *adj* konservatif; *n* orang konservatif; **reactive** *adj* reaktif

read *v* **read read** [réd] membaca; ~ *aloud* membaca dengan suara keras; ~ *to* membacakan; ~ *the Koran*, ~ *Arabic* mengaji; ~ *up on* mempelajari; ~ *someone's mind* membaca pikiran orang; *a good ~* buku yang menarik untuk dibaca; **reader** *n* pembaca; buku bacaan

readily *adv* [rédili] laku, laris, cepat; **ready** *adj* siap, sedia; selesai, sudah; ~ *to use* siap pakai

reading *n* membaca; bacaan ← **read**

real *adj* nyata, betul, sejati; *adv* sangat, benar-benar; ~-*life story* kisah sejati; **reality** *n* kenyataan, realitas; **realization** *n* kesadaran; perwujudan; **realize** *v* sadar; mewujudkan, melaksanakan; **realistic** *adj* realistis; **really** *adv* sangat, benar-benar

realm *n* [rélm] dunia; kerajaan

ream *n* rim; ~*s* banyak sekali

reap *v* menuai, memungut; **reaper** *n* penuai; *grim ~* malaikat maut

rear *adj, n* (bagian) belakang; pantat; ~ *view mirror* kaca spion; *at the ~* di belakang; *v* membesarkan

reason *n* sebab, alasan; akal (budi); *it stands to ~* sudah tentu, memang; *within ~* yang pantas, yang masuk akal; *without ~, no ~* tanpa sebab; *v* berunding; **reasonable** *adj* masuk akal

reassure *v* [riasyur] menenteramkan hati, menenangkan

rebel *n* [rébel] pemberontak; *v* [rebél] memberontak; **rebellion** *n* pemberontakan; **rebellious** *adj* bersifat melawan

rebuke *n* teguran; *v* menegur, memberi teguran

recalcitrant *adj* keras kepala, kurang ajar

recall *n* [rikol] ingatan; pemanggilan kembali; *v* ingat; memanggil kembali, menarik kembali

recapture *n* perebutan kembali; *v* merebut kembali

recede *v* surut, menyusut, mundur

receipt *n* [risit] kuitansi, tanda terima, struk; penerimaan; *on ~ of* setelah menerima; **receive** *v* menerima, mendapat, memperoleh; menyambut; **receiver** *n* (pesawat) penerima

recent *adj* baru; **recently** *adv* baru-baru ini

reception *n* resepsi; penyambutan; tangkapan ← **receive**

recess *n* istirahat; *in* ~ sedang istirahat, tidak bersidang

recession *n* resesi

recharge *v* mengecas, mengisi ulang

recipe *n* [résipi] resep

reciprocal *adj* saling, timbal balik; **reciprocate** *v* membalas

recital *n* pertunjukan, konser; **recite** *v* membaca dari luar kepala, mendeklamasikan

reckless *adj* nekat, ugal-ugalan, berani

reckon *v* menghitung; *sl* pikir; ~ *with* berurusan dengan; **reckoning** *n* perhitungan

reclaim *v* memperoleh kembali; menguruk pantai; **reclamation** *n* pengurukan pantai, reklamasi

recognition *n* pengenalan; penghargaan; **recognizable** *adj* dapat dikenal; **recognize** *v* mengenal, mengenali; mengakui, menghargai

recollect *v* ingat akan, mengingat; **recollection** *n* ingatan; *to the best of my* ~ seingat saya

recommend *v* menganjurkan; memuji; **recommendation** *n* rekomendasi, saran

reconciliation *n* rekonsiliasi, perdamaian

record *n* [rékord] catatan; daftar; rekor; piringan hitam; dokumen; ~*s* arsip; *off the* ~ tidak boleh disiarkan; *to break a* ~ memecahkan rekor; *v* [rekord] mencatat, mendaftar, merekam

recorder *n* semacam suling

recording *n* rekaman; ~ *artist*

penyanyi, artis ← **record**

recover *v* [rikaver] sembuh, pulih; menemukan kembali, menyelamatkan; **recovery** *n* kesembuhan; penemuan kembali

recreate *v* [rikriét] menciptakan ulang; **recreation** *n* [rékriésyen] hiburan, rekreasi

recruit *n* pegawai baru, orang baru; *v* merekrut; **recruitment** *n* penerimaan pegawai baru

rectangle *n* [rektanggel] empat persegi panjang; **rectangular** *adj* empat persegi panjang

rectify *v* [rektifai] membetulkan, meralat

rector *n* rektor

rectum *n* dubur

recur *v* (terjadi) kembali, terulang; **recurrence** *n* terjadinya kembali

recycle *v* [risaikel] didaur ulang; **recycling** *n* daur ulang

red *adj* merah; ~ *Cross* Palang Merah; ~ *tape* birokrasi; *in the* ~ berhutang; ~-*letter day* hari penting; *caught* ~-*handed* tertangkap basah; **redden** *v* memerah; **reddish** *adj* kemerah-merahan

redeem *v* menebus; **redemption** *n* penyelamatan; penebusan

redhead *n* [rédhéd] orang yang berambut merah

reduce *v* mengurangi, memperkecil; **reduction** *n* potongan, pengurangan, penurunan, reduksi

reef *n* (batu) karang

reek *n* bau; ~ *of* berbau

ref. *reference* rujukan

refer *v* mengacu; menunjukkan; mengenai; **referee** *n* wasit; **reference** *n* surat keterangan, referensi; **referral** *n* (surat) rujukan

refill *n* isi ulang; pengisian kembali

refine *v* menghaluskan, menyaring; ~d halus; **refinery** *n* kilang

reflect *v* membayang; mencerminkan, memantulkan; merenung, merenungkan; **reflection** *n* bayangan; renungan; **reflective** *adj* memantulkan sinar; termenung; **reflector** *n* reflektor, pemantul cahaya

reflex *adj*, *n* refleks

reforestation *n* reboisasi

reform *n* perubahan, reformasi; *v* berubah; mengubah; menyusun kembali; ~ *school* sekolah untuk anak-anak nakal; **reformation** *n* penyusunan kembali

refrain *n* bagian ulangan; refrein

refresh *v* menyegarkan; **refresher** ~ *course* kursus penyegaran; **refreshments** *n*, *pl* minuman, makanan

refrigerate *v* [refrijerét] mendinginkan; **refrigeration** *n* pendinginan; **refrigerator** *n* lemari es, kulkas

refuel *v* mengisi bensin

refuge *n* tempat suaka, perlindungan; *to take* ~ berlindung; **refugee** *n* pengungsi

refund *n* pembayaran kembali; *v* mengembalikan uang

refusal *n* penolakan; **refuse** *n* [réfyus] sampah; *v* [refyuz] menolak

regard *n* hormat; *in* ~ *to, with* ~ *to* sehubungan dengan, mengenai; *v* menganggap; *my* ~s salam saya; **regarding** *conj* mengenai, tentang; **regardless** *conj* tanpa menghiraukan

regency *n* kabupaten ← **regent**

regenerate *v* [rijénerét] hidup kembali, tumbuh kembali; menghidupkan kembali

regent *n* bupati

regiment *n* [réjiment] resimen

region *n* daerah, wilayah; **regional** *adj* daerah

register *n* [réjister] daftar; *v* daftar; mendaftarkan; mencatat; ~ed *mail* pos tercatat; **registrar** *n* pendaftar, pencatat; panitera; **registration** *n* pendaftaran, pencatatan; **registry** *n* (kantor) pendaftaran; ~ *office* kantor catatan sipil

regret *n* rasa sesal; *v* menyesal

regular *adj* biasa; teratur; tetap

regulate *v* mengatur; **regulation** *n* aturan, peraturan

rehabilitate *v* merehabilitasi; **rehabilitation** *n* rehabilitasi

rehearsal *n* [rihérsal] latihan; *dress* ~ gladi bersih, gladi resik; **rehearse** *v* berlatih; melatih

reign *n* [réin] pemerintahan, masa bertakhta; *v* memerintah, bertakhta

reimburse *v* [riimburs] membayar kembali, mengganti uang;

reimbursement *n* penggantian uang

reindeer *n* [reindir] **reindeer** rusa kutub

reinforce *v* [riinfors] memperkuat, memperkokoh; **reinforcement** *n* penguatan, pengokohan

reject *n* [rijékt] barang yang ditolak, apkiran; *v* [rejékt] menolak; **rejection** *n* penolakan

rejoice *v* bergembira, bersyukur

relapse *n* kambuh, sakit lagi

relate *v* menceritakan; mengaitkan, menghubungkan; ~ *to* memahami, bersimpati; **related** *adj* bersanak saudara; berkaitan, berhubungan; **relation** *n* saudara, keluarga; hubungan; *in* ~ *to* mengenai, tentang; **relationship** *n* hubungan; *in a* ~ pacaran; **relative** *adj* relatif; *n* saudara, keluarga

relax *v* bersantai-santai; mengendurkan; **relaxation** *n* relaksasi; **relaxing** *adj* santai

relay *n* (lari) estafet; *v* menyampaikan, meneruskan

release *n* pembebasan; rilis, keluaran; *v* melepaskan, membebaskan, memerdekakan

relegate *v* [rélegét] membuang; menurunkan

relentless *adj* terus-menerus

relevance *n* hubungan, sangkut paut, relevansi; **relevant** *adj* bersangkut paut, relevan

reliability *n* [rilayabiliti] keadaan yang dapat dipercaya; **reliable** *adj* andal, tepercaya; **reliance** *n* ketergantungan; **reliant** *adj* tergantung pada; *self-*~ mandiri ← **rely**

relic *n* [rélik] (barang) peninggalan

relief *n* [rilif] bantuan, pertolongan, sumbangan; rasa lega; *what a* ~ syukur; *Isl* alhamdulillah; *in* ~ timbul; **relieve** *v* membantu, menolong; ~ *yourself* buang air; **relieved** *adj* lega, plong

religion *n* [rilijen] agama; **religious** *adj* beragama, saleh, religius

relinquish *v* menyerahkan, meninggalkan, melepaskan

relish *n* [rélisy] acar, bumbu; *n* cita rasa, nikmat; *v* menikmati

reluctance *n* keengganan; **reluctant** *adj* enggan

rely *v* [relai] percaya

remain *v* tinggal, tetap; ~*s* sisa; **remainder** *n* sisa

remark *n* komentar; catatan; *v* berkomentar, mengomentari; berkata; **remarkable** *adj* pantas diperhatikan, luar biasa

remedy *n* [rémédi] obat, penawar; *home* ~ obat tradisional; **remedial** *adj* yang berhubungan dengan perbaikan

remember *v* ingat; ~ *me to* salam saya untuk; **remembrance** *n* kenangan; *in* ~ *of* mengenang

remind *v* [remaind] mengingatkan; **reminder** *n* surat peringatan

reminisce *v* [réminis] mengenang, bernostalgia; **reminiscence** *n* kenangan

remnant *n* sisa, bekas

remote *adj, n* terpencil; jarak jauh; ~ *control* remot

removal *n* [remuvel] pemindahan; **remove** *v* memindahkan; menjauhkan; *cousin once ~d* anak sepupu

render *v* membuat

rendezvous *n* [rondévu] (tempat) pertemuan

renew *v* memperbarui, memperpanjang; **renewable** *adj* dapat diperbarui; **renewal** *n* pembaruan

renovate *v* merenovasi, memperbaiki; **renovation** *n* perbaikan, renovasi

renowned *adj* masyhur, kenamaan, tersohor

rent *n* (uang) sewa; *v* menyewa; ~ *out* menyewakan; **rental** *adj* sewaan; ~ *car* mobil sewaan; *DVD ~* rental DVD

Rep. *Republic* Rep. (Republik)

repair *n* perbaikan, reparasi; *v* memperbaiki

repay *v* **repaid repaid** membayar kembali, mengganti

repeal *v* membatalkan, mencabut

repeat *n* pengulangan, tindakan yang diulang-ulang; tayangan ulang; *v* mengulangi; ~ *offender* residivis, bromocorah; **repeatedly** *adv* berulang kali; **repetition** *n* [répetisyen] perulangan; **repetitive** *adj* berulang

repel *v* menolak; **repellent** *n* obat (nyamuk, serangga)

replace *v* mengganti, menggantikan; **replacement** *n* pengganti; pergantian

reply *n* [replai] jawaban, sahutan, balasan; *v* menjawab, menyahut, membalas

report *n* laporan, pemberitaan; *v* melapor; melaporkan, memberitakan; **reporter** *n* wartawan

represent *v* mewakili; menggambarkan, melambangkan; **representation** *n* perwakilan; gambaran; **representative** *adj* terwakili; *n* wakil, utusan

repressive *adj* bersifat menekan, menindas

reprimand *n* [réprimand] teguran; *v* menegur

reprint *n* cetak ulang; *v* mencetak ulang

reproduce *v* mempunyai keturunan, berkembang biak; meniru; **reproduction** *n* reproduksi, perkembangbiakan; **reproductive** *adj* berkaitan dengan reproduksi manusia

reptile *n* binatang melata

republic *n* republik; *the ~ of Indonesia* Republik Indonesia; *the People's ~ of China (PRC)* Republik Rakyat Cina (RRC); *Union of Soviet Socialist ~s (USSR)* (Republik Sosialis) Uni Soviet (URSS); **republican** *adj* berkaitan dengan republik, republikan; pro-republik; *n* pendukung republik; **Republican** ~ *Party* Partai Republik

repulsive *adj* menjijikkan

reputable *adj* mempunyai nama baik; **reputation** *n* nama baik, reputasi; **repute** *ill ~* nama buruk request *n* permohonan, permintaan; *by* ~ atas permintaan; *v* memohon, minta

require *v* memerlukan; **requirement** *n* syarat; ~s kebutuhan

rescue *n* penyelamatan; *search and* ~ *(SAR)* (usaha) penyelamatan; *v* menolong, menyelamatkan

research *n* penelitian, riset; ~ *and development (R & D)* penelitian dan pengembangan (litbang); *v* meneliti, meriset

resemblance *n* kemiripan; **resemble** *v* menyerupai, mirip

resent *v* benci, marah; **resentment** *n* rasa marah, dendam

reservation *n* reservasi, pesanan, buking; **reserve** *n* cadangan, persediaan; *nature* ~ cagar alam; *v* memesan, menyediakan; ~d pendiam

reservoir *n* [résérvwar] waduk

reshuffle *n* perombakan; *v* merombak

reside *v* berdiam; **residence** *n* kediaman; *permanent* ~ *(PR)* hak tinggal secara tetap; **residency** *n, arch* karesidenan; **resident** *n* penduduk, penghuni; *arch* residen; **residential** *adj* berkaitan dengan perumahan

resign *v* [rizain] mundur, mengundurkan diri, berhenti bekerja; ~ed pasrah; **resignation** *n* [rézignésyen] pengunduran diri; kepasrahan

resin *n* [rézin] damar

resist *v* [rezist] melawan, menahan; **resistance** *n* perlawanan, pertahanan

resolution *n* keputusan, resolusi; **resolve** *v* memutuskan, bermaksud

resonance *n* gema, gaung

resort *n* tempat beristirahat, resor

resource *n* sumber daya; *human* ~ *(HR)* personalia; *natural* ~ sumber daya alam

respect *n* hormat; hal; *in that* ~ mengenai, berhubungan dengan hal itu; *with* ~ *to* dalam hal itu; *to pay your* ~s melayat; memberi hormat; *v* menghormati; **respectable** *adj* baik-baik, terhormat; **respectful** *adj* (penuh) hormat; **respectfully** *yours* ~ hormat kami

respective *adj* masing-masing

respiration *n* pernapasan, pernafasan; **respire** *v* bernapas

respond *v* membalas, menjawab, menanggapi; **response** *n* tanggapan, jawaban, respons; *in* ~ *to* sebagai tanggapan atas; **responsive** *adj* mau mendengarkan, menanggapi

responsibility *n* [responsibiliti] tanggung jawab; **responsible** *adj* bertanggung jawab

rest *n* (waktu) istirahat; sisa; *v* berhenti, beristirahat, mengaso; tinggal; ~ *in peace (RIP)* beristirahat dengan tenang; ~ *on* berdasarkan, bersandarkan; **restroom** *n* toilet, WC

restaurant *n* restoran, rumah makan

restless *adj* resah, gelisah

restoration *n* perbaikan, pemugaran; pengembalian; **restore** *v* memperbaiki, mengembalikan, memugar

restrain *v* menahan

restrict *v* membatasi; **restriction** *n* pembatasan

result *n* akibat, hasil; ~ *in* mengakibatkan, menyebabkan

resumé, resume *n* [rézumé] riwayat hidup, ikhtisar

resume *v* mulai lagi, meneruskan; **resumption** *n* penerusan

resurrect *v* menghidupkan kembali; **resurrection** *n* kebangkitan

ret. *retired* pensiunan, purnawirawan

retail *adj* [ritél] eceran, ritel; *n* perdagangan eceran; *v* berharga eceran; *recommended* ~ *price (RRP)* harga eceran yang disarankan; **retailer** *n* pengecer, pedagang eceran

retain *v* menyimpan, menahan, tetap; **retainer** *n* alat penahan (gigi)

retarded *adj* tunagrahita, terkebelakang

retch *v* muntah

retire *v* pensiun; *Klinsmann has ~d* Klinsmann telah menggantung sepatu; **retired** *adj* pensiunan; ~ *general* Jenderal (Purnawirawan); **retirement** *n* masa pensiun

retort *n* jawaban pedas; *v* menjawab dengan ketus

retract *v* mencabut, menarik kembali; **retraction** *n* pencabutan

retreat *n* [retrit] penarikan (diri); retret; *v* mundur, menarik diri

retrenched *adj* dipehakakan, diPHKkan, diberhentikan; **retrenchment** *n* pemutusan hubungan kerja (PHK)

retrieve *v* [retriv] mengambil, mendapat kembali; **retrieval** *n* pengambilan kembali

retrospective *n* pameran karya sepanjang masa, retrospektif

return *n* kembali, pemulangan, perjalanan pulang; ~ *address* alamat pengirim; ~ *ticket* karcis pulang pergi, tiket pulang pergi; ~ *to sender* dikembalikan kepada pengirim; *in* ~ *for* sebagai pengganti; *many happy* ~*s* selamat (ulang tahun); *on my* ~ sekembali saya; *v* pulang, kembali; mengembalikan, membalas; ~ *a good deed* membalas budi

reunification *n* [riunifikésyen] penyatuan kembali, reunifikasi

Rev. *Reverend* pendeta

reveal *v* [revil] membuka, menyingkapkan; menyatakan; **revelation** *n* wahyu

revenge *n* (rasa) dendam, pembalasan; *to take* ~ membalas dendam

revenue *n* [révenyu] penghasilan, pendapatan

reverence *n* hormat, takzim; **reverend** *n, Chr* pendeta

reversal *n* pembalikan; **reverse** *adj* terbalik; *n* sisi balik; *v* mundur, memundurkan kendaraan; membalikkan

review *n* [revyu] tinjauan; resensi; majalah; *v* meninjau kembali; menilai; **reviewer** *n* penulis resensi

revise *v* memperbaiki, memeriksa ulang, merevisi; **revision** *n* perbaikan, periksa ulang, revisi

revival *n* kebangkitan; **revive** *v* bangun kembali; menghidupkan lagi

revoke *v* mencabut, membatalkan

revolt *n* pemberontakan; *v* memberontak

revolution *n* revolusi; peredaran; **revolve** *v* berputar, berkisar; *revolving door* pintu putar

reward *n* [reword] hadiah, imbalan, ganjaran; *v* mengganjar; menghadiahi; **rewarding** *adj* menguntungkan, berguna

rheumatism *n* [rumatizem] encok, rematik, sengal

rhino *sl* **rhinoceros** *n* [rainoseres] **rhino** *sl* badak; *one-horned* ~ badak bercula satu

rhubarb *n* [rubarb] sejenis sayur

rhyme *n* [raim] sajak; *v* bersajak; **rhythm** *n* [rithem] irama, ritme; **rhythmic** *adj* berirama; ~ *gymnastics* senam irama

rib *n* tulang rusuk, iga; *spare* ~*s* iga panggang; **ribbed** *adj* bergerigi

ribbon *n* pita; *blue* ~ mutu terbaik

rice *n* padi; beras; nasi; ~ *cake* krupuk; lontong; ~ *field* sawah; ladang; ~ *straw* jerami, merang; *fried* ~ nasi goreng; *husked* ~ beras

rich *adj* kaya, subur; ~ *kid* anak kaya, anak gedongan; ~ *in protein* kaya akan protein; **riches** *n, pl* kekayaan

rickety *adj* goyah, tidak stabil

rickshaw *n* becak; langcia

rid *v* membersihkan, membebaskan; *to get* ~ *of* menyingkirkan, menghilangkan; **riddance** *good* ~ syukur (sudah dibuang)

ridden *v, pf* → **ride**

riddle *n* teka-teki

ride *n* perjalanan; *v* **rode ridden** mengendarai, naik; ~ *a horse* naik kuda; ~ *a motorbike* mengendarai sepeda motor; **rider** *n* penunggang; pengendara

ridge *n* punggung gunung

ridicule *n* [ridikyul] ejekan, olok-olok; *v* menertawakan, mengejek, memperolok; **ridiculous** *adj* menggelikan

rifle *n* [raifel] senapan, bedil; *air* ~ senapan angin

rift *n* celah; keretakan

rig *n* perlengkapan; *big* ~ truk besar; *oil* ~ alat pengebor minyak, alat pengeboran minyak; *v* melakukan dengan curang; ~*ged election* pemilu yang tidak jujur dan adil; **rigging** *n* perlengkapan, tali-temali

right *adj* [rait] (sebelah) kanan; betul, benar; patut, layak; ~ *angle* sudut siku-siku, tegak lurus; ~ *away* segera; ~ *now* sekarang juga; ~ *wing* sayap kanan; *all* ~ baiklah; *n* hak; *by* ~*s* sebetulnya, sebenarnya; *human* ~*s* hak azasi manusia

(HAM); *on the* ~ di sebelah kanan; **righteous** *adj* [raices] adil; **rightly** *adv* dengan benar, sepantasnya, selayaknya

rim *n* tepi (roda, piring); *wheel* ~ velg

rind *n* [raind] kulit (buah, keju)

ring *n* cincin; lingkaran; jaringan; gelanggang; dering; ~ *finger* jari manis; ~ *road* jalan lingkar; *boxing* ~ ring; *wedding* ~ cincin kawin; *v* **rang rung** berdering; *coll* telepon, menelepon; ~ *the bell* membunyikan bel, memukul lonceng; **ringleader** *n* dalang, biang keladi; **ringtone** *n* nada dering; **ringworm** *n* kurap

rink *ice (skating)* ~ gelanggang es

rinse *n* bilasan; *blue-~* (rambut) dicet agak kebiru-biruan; *v* membilas

riot *n* [raiot] kerusuhan; kegaduhan; *v* rusuh, memberontak

RIP *abbrev rest in peace* beristirahat dengan tenang

rip *n* robekan; *v* merobek

ripe *adj* masak, matang; **ripen** *v* menjadi matang

ripple *n* riak

rise *n* kenaikan; *pay* ~ kenaikan gaji; *v* **rose risen** [rizen] bangkit, terbit, berdiri

risk *n* risiko; *v* mengambil risiko; **risky** *adj* berisiko

rite *n* upacara, tata cara; **ritual** *n* upacara (agama)

rival *n* saingan, lawan; *v* menyaingi; **rivalry** *n* persaingan

river *n* [river] sungai, kali

RM *abbrev Malaysian ringgit* ringgit

road *n* jalan (raya); ~ *accident* kecelakaan lalu lintas; ~ *map* peta perjalanan; *to hit the* ~ jalan, berangkat; **roadhouse** *n* rumah makan di pinggir kota; **roadwork** *n* perbaikan jalan; **roadworthy** *adj* [rodwérthi] layak jalan

roar *n* aum; deru; *v* mengaum; menderu

roast *adj* panggang; ~ *beef* sapi panggang; *n* daging panggang; *v* memanggang, membakar

rob *v* merampok, merampas; **robber** *n* perampok; **robbery** *n* perampokan; *armed* ~ perampokan bersenjata

robe *n* jubah

robust *adj* kuat, kokoh

rock *n* batu, cadas; ~ *music* musik rock; *v* mengayunkan; menggoncang; ~*ing chair* kursi goyang; ~*ing horse* kuda goyang, kuda-kudaan

rocket *n* roket; *v* meroket

rocky *adj* berbatu-batu ← **rock**

rod *n* batang; *lightning* ~ penangkal petir

rode *v, pf* → **ride**

rodent *n* binatang pengerat

rodeo *n* pertunjukan ketrampilan menangani kuda dan hewan ternak

rogue *n* [roug] bangsat, bajingan

role *n* peran, peranan

roll *n* gulung, gulungan; roti bulat; daftar; ~*ing pin* gilingan

adonan; *toilet* ~ tisu gulung;
~ *call* apel; *v* bergulung, berputar; menggulung, menggulingkan, menggelindingkan; ~
over bergulung; **roller** *n* ombak
besar; ~ *blades,* ~ *skates* sepatu roda; *hair* ~ alat penggulung
rambut

Roman *adj* Romawi; *n* orang
Romawi; *the* ~ *Empire*
Kekaisaran Romawi

romance *n* cerita cinta

Romania, Rumania *n* Romania;
Romanian *adj* berasal dari
Romania; *n* orang Romania

romantic *adj* romantik; *n* orang
yang romantik ← **romance**

roof *n* atap

room *n* ruang, ruangan; kamar;
dining ~ ruang makan; *single* ~
kamar untuk satu orang; *v* kos;
roomy *adj* lapang

rooster *n* ayam jago

root *n* akar; *to take* ~ berakar; *v*
berakar

rope *n* tali; ~ *ladder* tangga tali

rosary *n, Isl* tasbih; *Cath* rosario

rose *n* bunga mawar, bunga ros;
v, pf → **rise**

roster *n* daftar nama

rosy *adj* berwarna merah; menyenangkan

rot *n* kebusukan; *v* membusuk

rotate *v* berputar, berkisar;
rotation *n* perputaran, per-
kisaran

rotten *adj* busuk ← **rot**

rouge *n* [ruj] perona pipi

rough *adj* [raf] kasar; mentah; ~
draft naskah pertama; **roughly**

adv kurang lebih, kira-kira;
secara kasar

round *adj* bulat, bundar; di sekitar; ~ *table* meja bundar; ~ *trip*
perjalanan pulang pergi; ~ *the*
world keliling dunia; *all year*
~ sepanjang tahun; *n* giliran,
putaran, ronde; *v* mengelilingi;
~ *off* membulatkan; **round-**
about *adj* keliling; *n* bundaran;
komidi putar

route *n* [rut] trayek, jalur, rute

routine *adj* biasa, sehari-hari,
rutin; *n* kebiasaan sehari-hari

row *n* [rau] pertengkaran;
keributan

row *n* [ro] baris, jajar, deretan

row *v* [ro] berkayuh; mendayung,
mengayuh; **rower** *n* pendayung,
pengayuh

rowdy *adj* [raudi] berisik ← **row**

royal *adj* kerajaan; *n* anggota
kerajaan; **royalty** *n* keluarga
raja; honorarium, honor

RRP *abbrev recommended*
retail price harga eceran

RSA *abbrev Republic of South*
Africa Afsel (Republik Afrika
Selatan)

RSVP *abbrev répondez s'il vous*
plaît tolong dikonfirmasi

Rt Hon. *Right Honorable* yang
terhormat

rub *v* menggosok, menggosok-
gosok; ~ *out* menghapus; **rub-**
ber *n* karet; penghapus

rubbish *n* sampah; omong
kosong

ruby *n* batu mirah

rucksack *n* ransel

rudder *n* kemudi

rude *adj* kasar, tidak sopan;
rudeness *n* ketidaksopanan

rug *n* permadani

ruin *n* reruntuhan, puing-puing;
in ~s jadi puing; *v* meruntuhkan, merobohkan, merusak

rule *n* aturan, peraturan; pemerintahan; *~ out* mengesampingkan; *as a ~* biasanya; *v*
memerintah; *~ a line* membuat
garis, menggaris; **ruler** *n*
kepala pemerintah; penggaris;
ruling *adj* yang sedang
berkuasa; *n* putusan

rum *n* room

Rumania → **Romania**

ruminant *n* pemamah biak,
pemakan rumput

rumor *n* kabar angin, kabar
burung, desas-desus

run *n* perjalanan, latihan berlari,
perlombaan; *~-down* lesu; tidak
terpelihara; *~-in* pertengkaran;
fun ~ lomba lari untuk amal;
on the ~ sedang melarikan diri;
in the long ~ lambat laun, lama-
lama, dalam jangka panjang; *v*
ran run lari; berlangsung; mengalir; memimpin; menjalankan;
~ amuck, ~ amok mengamuk;
~ away kabur, melarikan diri; *~
over* melindas; **runaway** *n*
pelarian; **runny** *adj* cair, berair;
~ nose pilek

rung *v, pf* → **ring**

runner *n* pelari; pesuruh, pengantar; *~-up* juara kedua ←
run

runway *n* landasan terbang

rural *adj* pedesaan, pedalaman

rush *n* ketergesa-gesaan; *~ hour*
jam padat; *~ job* pekerjaan
kilat; *v* terburu-buru; menyerbu

Russia *n* Rusia; **Russian** *adj*
berasal dari Rusia; *n* bahasa
Rusia; orang Rusia

rust *n* karat; *v* berkarat

rustle *n, v* [rasel] gersak, gersik,
gemersik

rusty *adj* berkarat, karatan ← **rust**

rut *n* bekas roda, lubang di jalan;
in a ~ tertahan di keadaan yang
membosankan

ruthless *adj* [ruthles] keji,
kejam, tanpa belas kasihan

Rwanda *n* Rwanda; **Rwandan**
adj berasal dari Rwanda; *n*
orang Rwanda

rye *n* [rai] gandum hitam

S

sabotage *n* [sabotaj] sabotase; *v*
menyabotase

sachet *n* [sasyé] kemasan
(kecil), sase (berisi saus, sampo
dll)

sack *n* karung, goni; *to get the
~* dipehakakan, dipecat

sacred *adj* [sékred] suci, kudus

sacrifice *n* [sakrifais] korban,
pengorbanan; *Isl* kurban,
qurban; *v* berkurban; mengorbankan

sad *adj* susah, sedih; **sadden** *v*
menyedihkan, membuat sedih

saddle *n* pelana, sadel, tempat duduk

sadness *n* kesedihan ← **sad**

safari *n* wisata melihat atau memburu binatang liar (terutama di Afrika); *on* ~ sedang mengikuti wisata tersebut

safe *adj* selamat; aman, dapat dipercaya; *~-keeping* penyimpanan yang aman; ~ *bet* pasti, tentu; ~ *and sound* selamat; ~ *as houses* aman sekali; *n* brankas; *~-deposit box* kotak tempat menyimpan barang berharga di bank; **safeguard** *v* melindungi; ~ *against* menjaga; **safely** *adv* dengan selamat; **safety** *n* keselamatan; keamanan; ~ *goggles* kacamata pelindung; ~ *net* jaringan pengaman; ~ *pin* peniti cantel; ~ *vest* baju pelampung

saffron *n* kunyit, kuning

sag *v* turun, mengendur, terkulai; **saggy** *adj* kendor, longgar

saga *n* [saga] hikayat, cerita yang panjang

sago *n* [ségo] sagu

said *v, pf* [séd] → **say**

sail *n* layar; *v* berlayar; **sailcloth** *n* kain layar; **sailing** *n* berlayar; **sailor** *n* pelaut, anak buah kapal (ABK)

saint (St) *n, Chr, m* santo; *f* santa; orang suci, orang kudus; ~ *Peter* Santo Peter

sake *for God's* ~ demi Allah; *for your own* ~ untuk (kebaikan) diri sendiri

salad *n* selada; ~ *dressing* bumbu selada; *fruit* ~ buah campur

salami *n* [salami] semacam sosis masak besar yang diiris

salary *n* [salari] gaji

sale *n* obral; *for* ~ dijual; *on* ~ diobral, didiskon; **sales** *n* penjualan; **salesperson** *n* agen; pelayan toko

saline *adj* [sélain] asin, mengandung garam; *n* salin, larutan garam, salin

saliva *n* [selaiva] air liur

sallow *adj* pucat, kekuning-kuningan (wajah)

salmon *n* [samen] ikan salmon; *adj* merah muda kekuningan

salt *n* garam; ~ *cellar,* ~ *shaker* tempat garam; ~ *and pepper* garam merica; **saltpeter** *n* sendawa; **salty** *adj* asin

salute *n* pemberian hormat; *v* memberi hormat

salvage *v* [salvej] menyelamatkan (barang)

salvation *n* keselamatan; ~ *Army* Bala Keselamatan

same *adj* sama; serupa; *all the* ~, *just the* ~ walaupun begitu; *adv* sama, seperti itu

sample *n* [sampel] contoh; *v* coba

sanction *n* [sangsyen] persetujuan; sanksi; *economic* ~*s* sanksi ekonomi; *v* menyetujui; memberi sanksi

sand *n* pasir; ~ *dune* bukit pasir

sandal *n* [sandel] sepatu sandal

sandalwood *n* kayu cendana

sandbag *n* karung pasir ← **sand**

sandbox *n* tempat pasir (untuk anak-anak) ← **sand**

sander *n* mesin penggosok

sandpaper *n* kertas gosok, ampelas; *v* mengampelas ← **sand**

sandstone *n* batu pasir ← **sand**

sandwich *n* [sandwij] roti lapis

sandy *adj* mengandung pasir ← **sand**

sane *adj* waras, berakal sehat

sang *v, pf* → **sing**

sanitary *adj* bersih, saniter; ~ *pad* pembalut (wanita); **sanitation** *n* kebersihan

sanity *n* [saniti] kesehatan mental ← **sane**

sank *v, pf* → **sink**

Sanskrit *n* bahasa Sansekerta

Santa *n* ~ *(Claus)* Sinterklas, Santa

sap *n* getah; *v* melemahkan

sapling *n* anak pohon

sapphire *n* [safair] batu nilam, batu safir

sarcasm *n* [sarkezem] sarkasme, sindiran tajam; **sarcastic** *adj* sarkastis, menyindir

sardine *n* [sardin] ikan sarden

sarong *n* sarung

sash *n* ikat pinggang; selempang

sassy *adj* lancang, berani

Satan *n* [séten] setan, iblis; **satanic** *adj* [setanik] berkaitan dengan setan

satchel *n* tas sekolah, tas buku

satellite *n* [satelait] satelit; bulan; ~ *dish* parabola

satire *n* sindiran; **satirical** *adj* bersifat menyindir; **satirize** *v* menyindirkan

satisfaction *n* kepuasan; **satis-factory** *adj* memuaskan, cukup; **satisfy** *v* [satisfai] memuaskan; memenuhi; *satisfied* puas

saturated *adj* penuh, jenuh; ~ *fat* lemak jenuh; **saturation** *n* kejenuhan; ~ *point* titik jenuh

Saturday *adj, n* [saterdé] hari Sabtu

sauce *n* kuah, saus; *tomato* ~ saus tomat

saucer *n* piring cawan; *flying* ~ piring terbang

Saudi Arabia *n* Arab Saudi; **Saudi, Saudi Arabian** *adj* berasal dari Arab Saudi; *n* orang Arab Saudi

saunter *v* berjalan-jalan (perlahan-lahan)

sausage *n* [sosej] sosis; ~ *roll* sejenis roti sosis

savage *adj* [savej] buas, liar, ganas; *n* orang biadab

savanna, savannah *n* sabana, padang rumput

save *n* penyelamatan, tangkapan; *prep* kecuali; *v* menyelamatkan; ~ *money* menghemat uang; menabung uang; ~ *up* menabung; **savings** *n, pl* (uang) tabungan, simpanan

Savior *n* Juru Selamat

savory *adj* tidak manis (asin, tawar); *n* makanan kecil

saw *n* gergaji; *v* menggergaji; ~-*horse* kuda-kuda; **sawdust** *n* serbuk kayu

saw *v, pf* ← **see**

sax, saxophone *n* saksofon

say *v* **said said** [séd] kata, berkata; mengatakan; *the final*

~ kata terakhir, hak memutus-kan; *never* ~ *die* jangan putus asa; **saying** *n* pepatah, periba-hasa

SC *abbrev secondary college* SMU (sekolah menengah)

scabies *n* kudis; *to have* ~ kudisan

scaffold, scaffolding *n* tangga-tangga, perancah

scald *n, v* [skold] luka kena air panas

scale *n* skala, ukuran; sisik, kulit; *large-*~ secara besar-besaran; **scales** *n, pl* timbangan, neraca

scallop *n* semacam kerang laut dalam

scalp *n* kulit kepala; *v* menguliti (kepala)

scalpel *n* pisau bedah

scalper *n* calo, tukang catut ← **scalp**

scan *n* peninjauan; *v* meninjau; pindai, memindai

scandal *n* skandal, keonaran; **scandalous** *adj* memalukan

Scandinavia *n* [Skandinévia] Skandinavia; Norwegia, Swedia, Finlandia, Denmark dan Eslandia; **Scandinavian** *adj* berasal dari Skandinavia; *n* orang Skandinavia

scanner *n* pemindai, scanner ← **scan**

scapegoat *n* kambing hitam; *v* mengambing-hitamkan

scar *n* bekas (luka); *v* mem-bekas, menggoresi; **scarred** *adj* terluka

scarce *adj* [skérs] jarang; kurang;

scarcely *adv* hampir tidak, nyaris

scare *n* [skér] peristiwa yang menakutkan; *v* menakut-nakuti, menakutkan; ~ *away* mengusir; **scarecrow** *n* orang-orangan untuk mengusir burung di ladang; **scared** *adj* takut

scarf *n* syal

scarlet *adj* merah tua

scary *adj* [skéri] menakutkan ← **scare**

scatter *v* menaburkan, menye-barkan

scavenge *v* [skavenj] memulung; **scavenger** *n* pemulung

scene *n* [siin] pemandangan; adegan; ~ *of the crime* tempat kejadian perkara (TKP); *not my* ~ bukan selera saya; *to make a* ~ membuat heboh; **scenery** *n* pemandangan alam; **scenic** *adj* asri, penuh peman-dangan

scent *n* [sént] (minyak) wangi, harum, bau

scepter *n* [sépter] tongkat lam-bang kekuasaan

sceptic, sceptical → **skeptic, skeptical**

schedule *n* [skédyul] jadwal, program, daftar acara; *behind* ~ terlambat; *v* merencanakan, mengatur

scheme *n* [skim] rencana; bagan, skema, rancangan; *color* ~ susunan warna; *v* merekayasa

schizophrenia *n* [skitsofrénia] skizofrenia

scholar *n* [skolar] pelajar; orang

terpelajar; **scholarship** *n* beasiswa; pengetahuan; **school** *n* sekolah; ~ *uniform* seragam sekolah; ~ *year* tahun ajaran; *elementary* ~, *primary* ~ sekolah dasar; *junior high* ~ sekolah menengah pertama (SMP); *medical* ~ fakultas kedokteran; *night* ~ kursus malam; *secondary* ~ sekolah menengah; **scholarly** *adj* ilmiah

science *n* ilmu (pengetahuan alam, IPA); sains; ~ *fiction* fiksi ilmiah; **scientific** *adj* ilmiah, keilmuan; **scientist** *n* ilmuwan

scissors *n, pl* [sizers] *pair of* ~ gunting

scold *v* menegur, menghardik; **scolding** *n* hardikan, teguran

scoop *n* sendok, ciduk, gayung; *v* menyendok, menciduk, menyekop

scooter *n* otopet, skuter

scope *n* ruang lingkup, jangkauan; bidang, lapangan

scorch *v* membakar (tidak sengaja)

score *n* skor, angka, nilai; *on that* ~ tentang hal itu; *v* mencetak gol, angka atau poin; memperoleh nilai; **scoreboard** *n* papan angka

scorn *n* cemoohan, caci-maki; *v* mencemoohkan, mencaci-maki; **scornful** *adj* mencemoohkan, menghinakan

scorpion *n* kalajengking

Scot *n* orang Skotlandia; **scotch** *n* wiski Skotlandia; **Scotland** *n* Skotlandia; **Scottish** *adj*

berasal dari Skotlandia

scoundrel *n* bangsat

scour *v* menggosok; menjelajahi; **scourer** *pot* ~ penggosok panci

scout *n* pandu, pramuka; pengintai; *girl* ~ pandu puteri; **scouting** kepanduan, kepramukaan

scramble *n* perebutan; *v* berebut; mengocok; ~*d eggs* telur kocok (goreng)

scrap *adj* bekas; ~ *metal* besi tua; ~ *paper* kertas bekas; *n* sisa, carik; *sl* perkelahian; **scrapbook** *n* buku tempel, album

scrape *n* goresan; *v* bergeseran; menggores, menggesekkan

scratch *n* goresan; *v* menggores, menggaruk, mencoret; *from* ~ dari nol, dari awal; *up to* ~ memenuhi syarat; bermutu baik

scrawl *n* tulisan cakar ayam; *v* menulis dengan tidak jelas

scrawny *adj* kurus

scream *n* jeritan; *what a* ~ lucu sekali; *v* berteriak, menjerit

screech *n* ciutan; jeritan; *v* menciut-ciut; menjerit

screen *n* tabir; layar putih; *v* menyaring; memutarkan (film); **screening** *n* pemutaran film; **screenplay** *n* skenario

screw *n* sekrup; *v* menyekrup; *vulg* bersetubuh; **screwdriver** *n* obeng

scribble *n* tulisan cakar ayam; *v* mencoret-coret

script *n* tulisan; naskah; *Latin* ~

huruf Romawi; **scriptwriter** *n* penulis skenario

scroll *n* surat gulungan; goresan berlekuk; *v* menggulung, naik

scrotum *n* kantong buah pelir, skrotum

scrub *n* semak, belukar

scrub *n* mandi, pencucian; sabun cair yang mengandung butir; *v* menggosok

scruffy *adj* berpenampilan tidak rapi

scuba ~ *diving* selam dengan tangki udara

scuffle *n* [skafel] perkelahian; *v* berkelahi, berebutan

sculpt *v* memahat patung, mematung; **sculptor** *n* perupa, pematung, pemahat patung; **sculpture** *n* (seni) patung

scum *n* buih kotoran (di atas cairan); *sl* sampah

SEA *abbrev South East Asia* Asia Tenggara

sea *n* laut; *at* ~ di laut; bingung; ~ *breeze* angin laut; ~ *captain* nakhoda kapal laut; ~ *cow* duyung; ~ *cucumber* teripang, timun laut; ~ *floor* dasar laut; ~ *front* tepi laut, pinggir laut; ~ *level* permukaan laut; ~ *urchin* bulu babi; *the Java* ~ Laut Jawa; **seaboard** *n* daerah pesisir; **seafarer** *n* pelaut; **seafood** *n* makanan laut; **seagull** *n* burung camar; **seahorse** *n* kuda laut

seal *n* anjing laut

seal *n* meterai, cap; *v* menutup; ~*ed road* jalan beraspal

sealion *n* [silayon] singa laut ← **sea**

seam *n* kelim, pelipit; *bursting at the ~s* penuh sesak

seaman *n* pelaut, kelasi

seamstress *n, arch* penjahit wanita ← **seam**

seance *n* [séans] pertemuan untuk mencoba menghubungi arwah orang

seaplane *n* pesawat terbang air ← **sea**

search *n* [sérc] pencarian, penggeledahan; ~ *party* rombongan pencari; ~ *warrant* surat kuasa untuk menggeledah; ~ *and rescue (SAR)* regu penyelamat; *v* mencari, memeriksa, menggeledah; **searchlight** *n* lampu sorot

seashell *n* kerang (laut) ← **sea**

seashore *n* pantai laut ← **sea**

seasick *adj* **seasickness** *n* mabuk laut ← **sea**

seaside *n* tepi laut ← **sea**

season *v* [sizen] membumbui

season *n* [sizen] musim; ~ *ticket* karcis terusan; ~*'s greetings* selamat (Natal); *the dry* ~ musim kemarau; **seasonal** *adj* musiman

seasoning *n* bumbu ← **season**

seat *n* tempat duduk, bangku, kursi; **seated** *adj* sedang duduk

seaweed *n* ganggang laut, rumput laut

secede *v* [sesid] memisahkan diri (negara); **secession** *n* pemisahan diri seclude *v* memingit; **secluded** *adj* sepi; **seclusion** *n* pingitan

second *n* [sékond] detik

second *adj* [sékond] kedua; ~ *gear* gigi dua; ~ *hand* jarum detik; ~-*hand* bekas; ~-*rate* bermutu rendah; *every* ~ *day* selang sehari, dua hari sekali; **secondary** *adj* sekunder; ~ *school* sekolah menengah; **secondly** *adv* yang kedua

secrecy *n* [sikresi] kerahasiaan; **secret** *adj, n* rahasia; *keep it a* ~ rahasiakanlah; **secretive** *adj* tidak terus terang

secretariat *n* [sékrétériet] sekretariat, kepaniteraan; **secretary** *n* sekretaris, panitera; ~ *of State* Menteri Luar Negeri

secrete *v* [sekrit] mengeluarkan; menyembunyikan; **secretion** *n* pengeluaran

secretly *adv* [sikretli] diam-diam, mencuri-curi ← **secret**

sect *n* sekte, aliran; **sectarian** ~ *violence* kekerasan berbau SARA

section *n* seksi, bagian, belahan; ~ *head* kepala bagian; **sector** *n* sektor, bidang

secular *adj* [sékuler] sekuler

secure *adj* [sekyur] kukuh; aman; *v* mengukuhkan; memperoleh; **security** *n* keamanan; ~ *police* polisi rahasia; *UN* ~ *Council* Dewan Keamanan PBB; **securities** *n, pl* surat-surat berharga

sedative *n* [sédatif] obat penenang

sediment *n* sedimen, endapan; **sedimentary** ~ *rock* batu endapan

seduce *v* menggoda, merayu; **seduction** *n* penggodaan, godaan; **seductive** *adj* menggodakan

see *v* **saw seen** melihat; mengunjungi; ~ *Paris* berkunjung ke Paris; *I* ~ saya mengerti; ~ *someone off,* ~ *someone out* mengantarkan; ~ *to* mengurus

seed *n* biji, benih; ~*less grapes* anggur tanpa biji; **seedling** *n* bibit

seek *v* **sought sought** [sot] mencari

seem *v* nampak; ternyata, kelihatannya; rupanya, rasanya; *so it* ~*s* begitulah

seen *v, pf* → **see**

seesaw *n* papan jungkat-jungkit

segment *n* bagian, golongan, pangsa, segmen

segregate *v* memisahkan (golongan); **segregation** *n* pemisahan; *racial* ~ pemisahan berdasarkan suku bangsa

seismic *adj* [saizmik] yang berkaitan dengan gempa bumi; **seismograph** *n* [saizmograf] seismograf

seize *v* [siz] menangkap; menyita; **seizure** *n* serangan (penyakit); penyitaan

seldom *adv* jarang

select *adj* [sélékt] terpilih, pilihan; *v* memilih, menyaring; **selection** *n* pilihan, pemilihan, seleksi

self *pron* sendiri, pribadi;
~-*centred* egois; -*confidence*
percaya diri (PD); ~-*control*
pengawasan diri sendiri;
~-*conscious* sadar akan
dirinya, canggung; ~-*defense*
bela diri; ~-*educated* otodidak;
~-*employed* swausaha;
~-*government* otonomi,
swapraja; ~-*interest* kepentingan
diri sendiri; ~-*portrait* potret
diri; ~-*reliant* mandiri; **selfish**
adj egois, suka mementingkan
diri sendiri

sell *v* **sold sold** menjual,
berjualan; ~ *off* menjual habis,
mengobral; ~ *out* habis terjual;
~ *like hot cakes* laku (seperti
pisang goreng); **seller** *n* penjual

semen *n* [simen] air mani

semester *n* semester, paruh
tahun

semi- *pref* tengah, separuh;
~-*colon* titik koma; ~-*detached*
sebagian bersambung, bersampingan (rumah); ~-*trailer* truk
gandeng

Semitic [Semitik] *anti*-~ anti
Yahudi

senate *n* [sénet] senat; **senator**
n anggota senat, senator

send *v* **sent sent** mengirim,
mengirimkan, mengirimi; ~-*off*
upacara pemberangkatan; ~ *for*
memanggil, minta datang; ~ *off*
mengantarkan; ~ *on* meneruskan; ~ *away for*, ~ *out for* memesan; ~ *my love* kirim salam;
sender *n* pengirim

Senegal *n* Senegal; **Senegalese**
adj berasal dari Senegal; *n* orang
Senegal

senile *adj* pikun

senior *adj* [sinior] lebih tua,
tertua, senior; *n* orang yang
lebih tua; ~ *high school*
sekolah menengah atas (SMA);
seniority *n* senioritas,
kedudukan yang lebih tinggi

sensation *n* kegemparan,
sensasi; **sensational** *adj*
menggemparkan, sensasional

sense *n* indera; perasaan; arti,
pengertian; *common* ~ akal
sehat; ~ *of humor* selera
humor; *the five* ~s pancaindera;
to make ~ masuk akal; **sensi-
ble** *adj* waras, berpikiran sehat,
berakal sehat; **sensitive** *adj*
peka, sensitif; **sensual** *adj* yang
berkaitan dengan hawa nafsu

sent *v, pf* → **send**

sentence *n* kalimat; keputusan,
hukuman; *death* ~ hukuman
mati; *v* menghukum

sentiment *n* perasaan, sentimen;
sentimental *adj* sentimentil

sentry *n* [séntri] penjaga; ~ *box*
gardu jaga, rumah (jaga) monyet

separate *adj* [séperet] terpisah;
v [séperét] berpisah; pisah
ranjang; memisahkan; **separation** *n* pemisahan

sepia *adj* (warna) coklat

September *n* bulan September

septic *adj* busuk, terinfeksi;
~ *tank* tangki septik

sequel *n* [sikuel] lanjutan, sambungan

sequence *n* [sikuens] urutan, rangkaian

Serb *n* orang Serbia; **Serbia** *n* Serbia; **Serbian** *adj* berasal dari Serbia; **Serbo-Croat** *n, arch* bahasa Serbia-Kroasia

sergeant *n* [sarjent] sersan

serial *n* [siriel] seri; film seri; cerita bersambung (cerber); ~ *killer* pembunuh berantai; ~ *number* nomor seri, nomor urutan; **series** *n* seri, rangkaian

serious *adj* sungguh-sungguh, serius; **seriously** *adv* sungguh-sungguh; berat

sermon *n* khotbah, ceramah

serpent *n* ular, naga

servant *n* pembantu, pelayan, pramuwisma, babu; **serve** *v* melayani, mengabdi; menghidangkan; **service** *n* pelayanan; pemeliharaan; kebaktian; masa bakti, jasa; ~ *station* pompa bensin; *v* memperbaiki (mobil)

serviette *n* [sérviét] serbet

sesame *n* [sésami] wijen

session *n* [sésyen] sidang; *in* ~ bersidang

set *adj* sudah ditentukan; siap; ~ *price* harga pas; *n* sepasang, seperangkat, perlengkapan; pesawat (radio/televisi); kelompok; *v* **set set** menaruh; memasang, menyetel; menetapkan; terbenam (matahari); ~ *(down)* meletakkan; ~ *aside* menyisihkan; ~ *off,* ~ *out* berangkat; ~*-up* susunan; **setback** *n* kemunduran, halangan; **setting** *n* penyetelan; lingkun-

gan, latar belakang

settle *v* [sétel] berdiam; menempati; menyelesaikan, menenangkan; mengatur, mengurus; ~ *for* bersedia menerima; **settlement** *n* perkampungan; penyelesaian; **settler** *n* pendatang, penghuni

seven *adj, n* [séven] tujuh; **seventeen** *adj, n* tujuh belas; **seventeenth** *adj* ketujuh belas; **seventh** *adj* ketujuh; **seventy** *adj, n* tujuh puluh; *the seventies* tahun 70an

sever *v* memutuskan, memotong

several *adj* [séveral] beberapa

severe *adj* [sévir] keras, ketat, parah; streng (guru)

sew *v* [so] menjahit; ~*ing machine* mesin jahit

sewage *n* [suej] tinja; **sewer** *n* selokan, saluran air kotor; **sewerage** *n* penyaluran tinja

sewn *v, pf* [son] → **sew**

sex *n* jenis kelamin; (hubungan) seks, persetubuhan, sanggama; ~ *appeal* daya tarik seksual; ~ *education* pendidikan seks; *to have* ~ bersetubuh, bersanggama; **sexual** *adj* seksual; ~ *harassment* pelecehan seksual; ~ *intercourse,* ~ *relations* hubungan badan; **sexuality** *n* seksualitas; **sexy** *adj* seksi

Seychelles *n* [Séisyéls] Kepulauan Seychelles; **Seychellois** *adj* [Séisyélwa] berasal dari Seychelles; *n* orang Seychelles

shabby *adj* lusuh, jelek

shack *n* gubuk, pondok
shade *n* naungan, tempat teduh; krei; warna
shadow *n* [syado] bayangan; *v* membayangi; membuntuti; **shadowy** *adj* remang-remang
shady *adj* teduh; tidak legal, curang ← **shade**
shaft *n* lubang, terowongan; batang; *mine ~* lubang tambang
shaggy *adj* tidak rata, kasar (rambut, bulu)
shake *n* goncangan, gelengan (kepala); jabat tangan; *v* **shook shaken** mengguncang, mengocok; *~ hands* berjabatan tangan; *~ off* melepaskan diri dari; *~ a leg* ayo cepat; **shaky** *adj* goyang, goyah, kurang kuat
shake *n* minuman bercampuran susu (coklat/biskuit/es)
shall *v, aux* akan; *~ not (shan't)* takkan, tidak akan
shallow *adj* dangkal; *the ~s* tempat dangkal
sham *adj, n* pura-pura; *v* berpura-pura
shame *n* malu; *what a ~* sayang sekali; *v* membuat malu; **shameful** *adj* memalukan; **shameless** *adj* tanpa malu
shampoo *n* [syampu] sampo; *v* berkeramas
shan't *v* takkan, tidak akan → **shall**
shanty *n* gubuk, pondok; *~ town* daerah kumuh
shape *n* bentuk; *v* membentuk
share *n* bagian, andil, saham; *the lion's ~* bagian paling

besar; *v* berbagi; membagi; **sharecropper** *n* petani bagi hasil; **shareholder** *n* pemegang saham
shark *n* ikan hiu; *~ fin soup* sup sirip ikan hiu, sup hisit
sharp *adj* tajam, runcing; cerdik; *C ~* Cis; *F ~* Fis; *ten o'clock ~* jam sepuluh tepat; **sharpen** *v* meruncingkan, mengasah, meraut; **sharpener** *n* raut pensil
shave *v* bercukur; mencukur; mengiris; *~n head* gundul; *a close ~* nyaris celaka; *to have a ~* bercukur; **shaving** *n* serutan; *~ cream* sabun cukur; **shaver** *n* alat cukur (listrik)
shawl *n* syal, selendang
she *pron, f* [syi] dia
shear *v* [syir] mencukur (domba), memotong; **shearer** *n* pencukur domba; **shears** *n, pl* gunting besar; *pinking ~* gunting bergerigi
sheath *n* [syith] sarung; pelapah; *penis ~* koteka
shed *n* gudang
shed *v* rontok; *~ blood* menumpahkan darah; *~ leaves* merontokkan daun; *~ light* memberi keterangan; *~ tears* mencucurkan air mata
sheep *n* **sheep** domba, biri-biri; *a flock of ~* sekawanan domba; **sheepdog** *n* anjing gembala; **sheepish** *adj* malu; **sheepskin** *n* kulit domba
sheer *adj* tipis; curam; belaka; *~ stockings* stoking tipis; *~ joy* kebahagiaan besar

sheet *n* helai, lembar; seprai; ~ *lightning* kilat; *a ~ of paper* sehelai kertas

shelf *n* papan, rak

shell *n* kulit, kerang; *coconut ~* tempurung kelapa; *v* mengupas

shell *n* bom kecil, peledak; ~ *shock* trauma (karena perang); **shelling, shellfire** *n* penembakan atau peledakan (dalam perang)

shellfish *n* kerang-kerangan

shelter *n* tempat berlindung, tempat teduh; *bus ~* halte bis; *v* berlindung, bernaung; melindungi

shepherd *n* [shéperd] gembala; *German ~* anjing herder

sheriff *n* [syérif] kepala polisi daerah (AS)

sherry *n* semacam anggur

shield *n* [syild] perisai, tameng; *v* melindungi

shift *n* perubahan, pergeseran; jam kerja; *night ~* jam kerja malam; *v* berpindah tempat, beralih; mengubah, menggeser; **shifty** *adj* licik, tidak dapat dipercaya

shilling *n, arch* mata uang Inggris

shin, shinbone *n* tulang kering

shine *n* cahaya, sinar; *v* **shone shone** [syon] bercahaya, bersinar; memancarkan; ~ *shoes* menggosok sepatu; *the sun's shining* matahari bersinar

shingles *n, pl* penyakit ruam syaraf

shiny *adj* berkilau, mengkilap ← **shine**

ship *n* kapal, perahu; *v* mengirim (lewat kapal); ~*'s log* buku harian di kapal; **shipment** *n* kiriman; pengiriman; **shipowner** *n* pemilik kapal; **shipping** *n* perkapalan, pengiriman dengan kapal; ~ *agent* perwakilan ekspedisi, ekspeditur; ~ *line* perusahaan perkapalan; **shipwreck** *n* [syiprék] peristiwa kapal karam; **shipyard** *n* galangan kapal

shirt *n* baju, kemeja; *polo ~* kaus berkerah; *T-~* kaus oblong

shiver *n* [syiver] getaran; *v* menggigil, gemetar

shock *n* guncangan; kejutan; ~ *absorber* sokbreker; *electric ~* kena setrum; **shocking** *adj* mengejutkan

shoe *n* [syu] sepatu; ~ *polish* semir sepatu; *horse~* ladam, tapal kuda; *running ~s, sports ~* sepatu olahraga; *v* **shod shod** ~ *a horse* meladami kuda; **shoelace** *n* tali sepatu; **shoemaker** *n* tukang sepatu; **shoeshine** ~ *boy* penggosok sepatu

shone *v, pf* → **shine**

shook *v, pf* → **shake**

shoot *n* tunas

shoot *v* **shot shot** menembak; merekam; ~ *by* lewat dengan cepat; ~ *up* tumbuh dengan cepat; ~ *a film* membuat film; ~ *a goal* mencetak gol; **shooting** *n* penembakan; menembak (olahraga); syuting, pengambilan gambar

shop n toko; ~ *assistant* pramu-niaga, pelayan toko; *to talk* ~ membicarakan soal pekerjaan; v berbelanja; ~ *around* melihat-lihat; **shopkeeper** n pemilik toko; **shoplift** v mengutil atau mencuri dari toko; **shopper** n orang yang berbelanja, pembeli; **shopping** n hasil belanja, belanjaan; ~ *center*, ~ *mall* (pusat) pertokoan, mal

shore n pantai, tepi

shorn v, pf → **shear**

short adj pendek, ringkas, singkat; kurang; kekurangan; ~-*changed* dapat uang kembali yang kurang; ~-*haul* jarak pendek; ~-*sighted* rabun jauh; ~-*tempered* cepat marah; ~-*term* jangka pendek; ~ *circuit* kortsleting; ~ *list* daftar pendek; ~ *story* cerita pendek (cerpen); ~ *wave* gelombang pendek; *caught* ~ tidak mempunyai uang yang cukup; *for* ~ singkatannya, nama pendeknya; *in* ~ singkatnya, pendek kata; ~ *of money* tidak mempunyai uang yang cukup; *to cut* ~ memperpendek, memotong; n film pendek; **shortage** n [shortej] kekurangan; **shorten** v memendekkan, memperpendek; **shortcoming** n kekurangan, kelemahan; **shortfall** n kekurangan; **shorthand** n tulisan steno; **shortly** adv tidak lama lagi; secara ketus; **shorts** n, pl celana pendek, kolor

shot n tembakan; suntikan; ~ *glass* seloki; ~ *put* (tolak) peluru; ~ *tower* menara mesiu; *big* ~ pembesar; v, pf → **shoot**

should v, aux [syud] seharusnya, sebaiknya, semestinya

shoulder n [syolder] bahu, pundak; *hard* ~ bahu jalan; ~ *blade* tulang belikat; v memikul, menanggung

shout n [syaut] teriakan; v berteriak; ~ *at the top of your lungs* berteriak sekeras-keras-nya

shout n [syaut] giliran membayar; *it's my* ~ giliran saya membayar; v traktir, membayarkan

shove n [shav] dorongan; v mendorong dengan kasar; ~ *off* derog pergi

shovel n [shavel] sekop; v menyekop

show n [sho] pertunjukan, tontonan; acara di televisi; pameran; ~-*off* orang yang berlagak; *no* ~ tidak jadi, tidak datang; *run the* ~ berkuasa, memerintah; v memperlihatkan, mempertunjukkan; menunjukkan, menampakkan; membuktikan; ~ *off* beraksi; berlagak, sok; memamerkan; ~ *up* muncul; mempermalukan; ~ *someone in* membawa orang masuk; ~ *someone out* mengantarkan orang (keluar); **show-business** n **showbiz** sl dunia hiburan; **showcase** n lemari kaca untuk pameran; contoh yang baik; **showdown** n [shodaun] bentrokan

shower n [syauer] pancuran

(mandi); hujan sebentar; ~ *cap* tutup kepala; *baby* ~ perayaan kelahiran anak; *v* mandi (di pancuran); menghujani, menaburi

shown *v, pf* → **show**

showroom *n* ruang pameran, ruang pajangan ← **show**

shrank *v, pf* → **shrink**

shrapnel *n* serpihan dari bahan peledak

shred *n* carik, sobekan; *v* mencarik, memarut

shrewd *adj* cerdik, lihai

shriek *n* [syrik] jeritan, pekikan; *v* menjerit

shrill *adj* nyaring, melengking

shrimp *n* udang

shrine *n* kuil, tempat keramat

shrink *v* **shrank shrunk** susut; menyusutkan; ~ *back* mundur, segan

shrink *n, coll* psikiater, dokter jiwa

shrivel [syrivel] *v* ~ *(up)* keriput, layu

shroud *n* kain kapan

shrub *n* tanaman kecil

shrug *n* angkat bahu; *v* mengangkat bahu; *to* ~ *off* mengganggap enteng

shrunk *v, pf* → **shrink**; **shrunken** *adj* berkerut, menyusut

shudder *n* gigil, getar; *v* menggigil, gemetaran

shuffle *v* mengocok; menyeret kaki; ~ *cards* mengocok kartu

shun *v* menghindarkan, mengelakkan

shush, ssh *ejac* [syusy] hus, sst

shut *v* **shut shut** tutup; menutup; ~ *down* mematikan; ~ *up* tutup mulut, diam; **shutter** *n* daun penutup jendela

shuttle *adj* [syatel] ulang-alik; ~ *bus* bis ulang-alik; *n* kendaraan ulang-alik; *space* ~ pesawat ulang-alik

shuttlecock *n* kok

shy *adj* [syai] malu, pemalu; **shyly** *adv* kemalu-maluan; **shyness** *n* rasa malu

Siam *n, arch* [Sayam] Thailand, Muang Thai; **Siamese** *adj* [Sayamiz] ~ *cat* kucing Siam

sibling *n* saudara (kandung); *John has three* ~s John bersaudara empat

sick *adj* sakit; ~ *bay* kamar untuk orang sakit; ~ *leave* cuti sakit; ~ *of* bosan, jenuh, jemu

sickle *n* [sikel] sabit; *hammer and* ~ palu arit

sickly *adj* sering sakit, sakit-sakitan ← **sick**

sickness *n* sakit, penyakit ← **sick**

side *n* sisi, segi; samping; ~ *effect* efek samping; ~ *by* ~ bersebelahan; *both* ~s kedua belah pihak; *on the* ~ diam-diam, sampingan; *to take* ~s berpihak, memihak; **sideboard** *n* laci besar yang panjang; **sideburns** *n* brewokan, cambang; **sidecar** *n* sespan; **sidelong** *adj* dari samping; ~ *glance* lirikan; **sidetrack** *v* melenceng; menggelincirkan; **sidewalk** *n* trotoar; **sideways**

adv miring, ke samping

siege *n* [sij] pengepungan

Sierra Leone *n* [Siéra Lion] Sierra Leone; **Sierra Leonean** *adj* berasal dari Sierra Leone; *n* orang Sierra Leone

sieve *n* [siv] ayakan, saringan

sift *v* mengayak; menyaring

sigh *n* [sai] keluh, nafas panjang; *a ~ of relief* bernafas lega; *v* menarik nafas panjang; mendesah

sight *n* [sait] pemandangan; penglihatan; *in ~* kelihatan; *long-~ed* rabun dekat; **sight-seer** *n* wisatawan, turis; **sight-seeing** *n* wisata, tamasya

sign *n* [sain] tanda, pertanda, isyarat; rambu; plang; papan merek; *~ language* bahasa isyarat; *v* menandatangani; teken, memberi paraf; *~ up* mendaftar; **signal** *n* [signal] tanda, isyarat; *v* memberi tanda; mengisyaratkan; **signature** *n* [signatyur] tanda tangan

significance *n* arti, makna; **significant** *adj* berarti, penting; **signify** *v* [signifai] berarti, bermakna; menandakan

signpost *n* [sainpost] rambu

silence *n* keheningan; *~ is golden* diam itu emas; *to observe a minute's ~* mengheningkan cipta; *v* mendiamkan; **silent** *adj* diam; *~ letter* huruf yang tidak diucapkan

silhouette *n* [siluét] bayangan hitam

silk *adj, n* sutera; **silky** *adj* terbuat dari sutera; *~-smooth* sehalus sutera

silliness *n* kelucuan; kebodohan; **silly** *adj* bodoh, tolol; lucu

silo *n* gudang (terigu, jagung dsb)

silver *adj, n* perak; *~ anniversary* ulang tahun perkawinan perak; *~ screen* layar perak; **silversmith** *n* pandai perak, perajin perak; **silverware** *n* sendok garpu; barang-barang perak

similar *adj* [similer] serupa, mirip; **similarity** *n* keserupaan, kemiripan

simmer *v* sedikit mendidih

simple *adj* [simpel] sederhana, bersahaja; **simplicity** *n* [simplisiti] kesederhanaan; **simplify** *v* menyederhanakan; **simply** *adv* dengan sederhana; hanya; benar-benar, sungguh-sungguh

simulation *n* simulasi

simultaneous *adj* [simulténius] serentak, serempak; *~ equation* persamaan berganda

sin *n* dosa; *to commit a ~* berdosa; *v* berdosa

since *conj* sejak, sedari; sebab, karena

sincere *adj* [sinsir] tulus (hati), ikhlas; bersungguh-sungguh; **sincerely** *yours ~* salam hormat; **sincerity** [sinsériti] ketulusan, keikhlasan

sing *v* **sang sung** bernyanyi, menyanyi; menyanyikan; *~-a-long, ~-song* menyanyi bersama; **singer** *n* penyanyi; *backing ~* penyanyi latar

Singapore *n* Singapura; **Singaporean** *adj* [Singaporian] berasal dari Singapura; *n* orang Singapura

singer *n* penyanyi

single *adj* [singgel] tunggal, sendiri; lajang, *m* bujangan; lagu; ~-*handed* sendirian; ~ *bed* tempat tidur untuk satu orang; ~ *file* antri satu per satu; ~ *ticket* karcis sekali jalan; *every* ~ *time* setiap kali; *women's* ~*s* pertandingan tunggal putri; *v* ~ *out* memilih satu

singlet *n* singlet

singular *adj, n* [singguler] tunggal

sinister *adj* [sinister] angker, seram

sink *n* tempat cuci (piring); *v* **sank sunk** tenggelam, mengendap; menenggelamkan; ~ *in* meresap, masuk ke dalam hati; ~*ing feeling* perasaan tertekan

sinner *n* orang yang berdosa ← **sin**

sinus *adj* berkaitan dengan lubang antara hidung dan mulut

sip *n* isapan; *v* mengisap, meminum sedikit

sir *pron* tuan

siren *n* sirene

sirloin *n* [sérloin] daging pinggang

sister *n* saudara perempuan, adik atau kakak perempuan; kepala perawat, suster; ~ *city* kota kembar; ~-*in-law* kakak/adik ipar (perempuan)

sit *v* **sat sat** duduk; bersidang; ~ *down* (pergi) duduk; ~ *nicely*, ~ *properly* duduk dengan manis; ~ *through* duduk sampai selesai

site *n* lokasi, situs; *archeological* ~ situs purbakala; *web*~ situs (di) internet

sitting *adj* ~ *room* kamar duduk; *n* sidang ← **sit**

situated *adj* [situyuéted] terletak; **situation** *n* keadaan, situasi

six *adj, n* enam; ~-*pack* kotak berisi enam botol minuman; ~ *of one, half a dozen of the other* setali tiga uang, sama saja; **sixteen** *adj, n* enam belas; **sixteenth** *adj* keenam belas; **sixth** *adj* keenam; ~ *sense* indera keenam; **sixtieth** *adj* keenam puluh; **sixty** *adj, n* enam puluh; *the nineteen-sixties* tahun enam puluhan

size *n* ukuran, nomor; besarnya; *one* ~ *fits all* satu ukuran

skate *n* sepatu luncur, sepatu es; *ice*-~ sepatu es; *roller*-~ sepatu roda; *v* bermain sepatu luncur atau sepatu roda; **skating** *n* bermain sepatu luncur

skeleton *n* [skéleton] kerangka; ~ *key* kunci induk

skeptical, sceptical *adj* raguragu, kurang percaya, skeptis

sketch *n* sketsa; gambar; *v* membuat sketsa; menggambar; **sketchy** *adj* kurang jelas

skewer *n* [skyuer] tusuk daging, tusuk sate

ski *n* (sepatu) ski; *v* main ski; **skier** *n* pemain ski; **skiing** *n* main ski

skid *n* bekas gelincir; *on the* ~*s*

sedang kesulitan; *v* gelincir, tergelincir, selip

skill *n* keterampilan, keahlian; *~ed craftsman* perajin; **skillful, skilful** *adj* terampil

skim *v* membaca secara pintas; *~ milk* susu tanpa kepala susu

skimpy *adj* kecil, sedikit

skin *n* kulit; *~ cancer* kanker kulit; *thick-~ed* berkulit badak; *v* menguliti

skinny *adj* [skini] kurus, ceking

skip *v* melompat-lompat; melewati; meloncati; *~ping rope* tali lompat; *hop, ~ and jump* sangat dekat

skipper *n* nakhoda; kapten

skirt *n* rok

skull *n* tengkorak, batok kepala; *~ and crossbones* bendera bajak laut; **skullcap** *n, Isl* kopiah

skunk *n* sigung; orang yang kurang ajar

sky *n* langit, angkasa, udara; *~-high* selangit, setinggi langit; **skydiver** *n* penerjun payung; **skydiving** *n* terjun payung; **skylight** *n* [skailait] atap tembus cahaya; **skyline** *n* kaki langit; **skyscraper** *n* pencakar langit; **skywriter** *n* pesawat yang meninggalkan tulisan asap

slab *n* papan, potong

slack *adj* kendur, lesu; tidak rajin; **slacken** *v* mengendur, berkurang

slacks *n, pl* celana panjang (perempuan)

slain *v, pf* → **slay**

slam *n* gerdam; *Grand ~* empat pertandingan tenis yang besar; *v* membanting, menggerdam, menutup dengan keras

slander *n* fitnah (secara lisan)

slang *n* bahasa percakapan, bahasa gaul

slant *n* kemiringan, sudut, pandangan; *~-eyed* bermata sipit

slap *n* tampar, tamparan; *v* menampar; **slapdash** *adj* sembrono, asal jadi

slate *n* batu tulis

slaughter *n* [sloter] pembantaian; penyembelihan; *v* membantai; memotong, menyembelih

Slav *n* orang Slavia; **Slavic** [Slavik] *~ language* bahasa Slavia

slave *n* budak; **slavery** *n* perbudakan

Slavonic *adj* [Slavonik] berasal dari daerah orang Slavia (Eropa Timur)

slay *v* **slew slain** membunuh

sleazy *adj* jorok, tidak senonoh, tidak sopan (pakaian)

sled, sledge *n* kereta luncur; **sledgehammer** *n* palu besar

sleek *adj* licin, mengkilap

sleep *v* **slept slept** tidur; *~ in* bangun siang; *~ together, ~ with* tidur bersama; bersetubuh; *~ well* selamat tidur; **sleeper** *n* orang yang tidur; balok rel kereta api; **sleepless** *adj* tanpa tidur; **sleepwalk** *v* mimpi jalan; **sleepy** *adj* mengantuk

sleet *n* hujan bercampur es dan salju

sleeve *n* lengan baju; sisipan kertas di CD; **sleeveless** *adj* tanpa lengan

sleigh *n* [slé] kereta luncur

slender *adj* ramping, langsing

slept *v, pf* → **sleep**

slew *v, pf* → **slay**

slice *n* irisan, sayatan; *a ~ of cake* sepotong kue; *v* mengiris, menyayat

slide *n* perosotan; *v* **slid slid** meluncur; tergelincir; *~ down* merosot

slight *adj* [slait] sedikit; mungil; **slightly** *adv* sedikit

slim *adj* ramping, langsing, lampai; *v ~ down* menjadi (lebih) langsing; *~ming tea* teh pelangsing

slime *n* kotoran, lumpur, lumut; **slimy** *adj* berlumpur, kotor

sling *n* ambin; *Singapore ~* sejenis koktail; **slingshot** *n* katapel

slip *n* kesalahan; longsor; rok dalam; *v* tergelincir; terlupa; *~ up* keliru, berbuat salah; *it ~ped my mind* saya terlupa akan hal itu

slipper *n* selop; sandal

slippery *adj* licin ← **slip**

slit *n* celah, belah; *v* membelah; *~ your wrists* memotong urat nadi; *~ your throat* menggorok

slob *n* orang yang sembrono

slogan *n* semboyan, slogan

slope *n* lereng; *v* melandai; **sloping** *adj* miring

sloppy *adj* tidak rapi; cengeng

slot *n* celah, lubang (kunci); tempat; *v ~ in* masuk (dengan pas)

Slovak *n* bahasa Slovakia; orang Slovakia; **Slovakia** *n* Slovakia

Slovene *n* [Slovin] orang Slovenia; **Slovenia** *n* Slovenia; **Slovenian** *adj* berasal dari Slovenia; *n* bahasa Slovenia

slovenly *adj* [slavenli] jorok, tidak rapi

slow *adj* perlahan-lahan, pelan-pelan; lambat, lamban; lama; *~ lane* jalur lambat; *~ motion (slo-mo)* gerak pelan; *v ~ down* mengurangi kecepatan; memperlambat; **slowly** *adv* pelan-pelan

sludge *n* lumpur

slug *n* semacam siput; **sluggish** *adj* malas

sluice *n* [slus] pintu air

slum *n* daerah kumuh

slumber *n, v* tidur

slump *n* kemerosotan; *v* merosot; terjatuh

sly *adj* cerdik; *on the ~* diam-diam, sembunyi-sembunyi

smack *n* tampar, tamparan, tempeleng; *sl* heroin; *v* menampar, menempeleng

small *adj* kecil; *~-minded* berpikiran sempit; *~ change* uang kecil, uang receh; *~ fry* ikan teri; *~ talk* basa-basi, obrolan ringan; *too ~* kekecilan; *~ is beautiful* kecil itu indah; **smallholder** *n* petani yang mengerjakan ladang kecil; **smallpox** *n* cacar

smart *adj* cerdas, pintar; cantik,

tampan; cepat; *quick* ~ sekarang juga; *v* pedih, sakit

smash *n* tabrakan, kecelakaan (mobil); smes; ~ *hit* laku keras; *v* memecahkan, menghancurkan; ~ *a record* memecahkan rekor

smell *n* bau; *delicious* ~ harum; *sense of* ~ indera penciuman; *v* bau; ~ *sweet* wangi; mencium; **smelly** *adj* berbau (tidak sedap)

smile *n* senyum, senyuman; *v* tersenyum

smith *n* pandai besi; **smithy** *n* tempat pandai besi

smog *n* asbut (asap kabut)

smoke *n* asap; *sl* rokok; *to have a* ~ merokok; *v* berasap; merokok; **smoker** *n* perokok; **smoking** *no* ~ dilarang merokok; **smoky** *adj* berasap

smolder, smoulder *v* membara

smooth *adj* licin; lancar; ~-*talking* pandai berbicara

smorgasbord *n* sajian prasmanan

smoulder → **smolder**

smuggle *n* [smagel] menyelundupkan; **smuggler** *n* penyelundup; **smuggling** *n* penyelundupan

snack *n* makanan kecil, camilan; ~ *bar* warung, tempat menjual makanan kecil

snail *n* keong, siput; ~ *shell* rumah siput, rumah keong; ~*'s pace* sangat lama, sangat lambat

snake *n* ular

snap *n* bunyi yang keras; *v* mematahkan; ~ *at* membentak;

~ *up* cepat membeli; ~ *your fingers* mengertak jari; **snapshot** *n* potret, foto

snarl *n* gertak; *v* menggeram; membentak

snatch *in* ~*es* sepotong-sepotong; *v* menjambret, merampas

sneak *n* orang yang melaporkan kawan; *v* menyelinap; ~ *off* pergi secara diam-diam, kabur; ~ *out* diam-diam keluar; **sneakers** *n* sepatu kets, sepatu olahraga; **sneaky** *adj* tidak terus terang

sneer *n* mimik wajah yang menyeringai; *v* menyeringai; ~ *at* menertawakan; memandang rendah

sneeze *n, v* bersin

snicker → **snigger**

sniff *n* hirupan; *v* mencium, mencium-cium; ~*er dog* anjing pencium

sniffle *n* [snifel] pilek; *v* tersedu-sedu

snigger, snicker *n, v* tertawa dengan nada menyindir

sniper *n* penembak jitu

snivel *v, derog* [snivel] tersedu-sedu; cengeng

snob *n* orang sombong; **snobbish, snobby** *adj* sombong

snooze *n, sl* tidur sebentar

snore *v* mendengkur; *sl* mengorok

snout *n* moncong

snow *n* salju; *v* hujan salju; ~ *line* garis salju; ~ *White* Putri Salju; ~-*white* seputih salju, seputih kapas; **snowball** *n* bola salju; **snowflake** *n* kepingan

salju; **snowman** *n* boneka salju;
snowy *adj* bersalju; putih

snug *adj* hangat, nyaman; pas

so *adv* begitu; sangat; demikian;
~~~ biasa saja; ~ *are we* kami
juga; *I think* ~ saya kira begitu;
conj jadi, maka, oleh sebab itu;
~ *that* supaya; sehingga; ~
what terus?; *sl* emang gue
pikirin (EGP); ~-*and*-~ (si) anu

soak *v* merendam; **soaked,
soaking** ~ *wet* basah kuyup

soap *n* sabun; ~ *opera* opera
sabun; ~ *powder* sabun cuci
baju; *liquid* ~ sabun cair;
soapdish *n* tempat sabun;
soapsuds *n* busa

soar *v* membubung tinggi,
melonjak

sob *n* sedu; *v* tersedu-sedu

sober *adj* tidak mabuk; waras;
serius

soccer *n* sepak bola; ~ *field*
lapangan sepak bola

social *adj* [sosyal] sosial,
kemasyarakatan; ramah; ~ *studies,* ~ *science* ilmu pengetahuan sosial (IPS); ~ *welfare*
kesejahteraan sosial; ~ *worker*
pekerja sosial; **socialize** *v*
bergaul

socialism *n* [sosyalizem] sosial-
isme; **socialist** *n* sosialis;
Union of Soviet ~ *Republics
(USSR)* Republik Sosialis Uni
Soviet (URSS)

society *n* [sosayeti] masyarakat;
perkumpulan, perhimpunan;
high ~ kalangan atas; **sociolo-
gist** *n* sosiolog; **sociology** *n*

sosiologi, ilmu masyarakat

sock *n* kaus kaki

socket *n* lubang, stopkontak

soda ~ *water* air soda; *whiskey
and* ~ wiski soda

sodium *n* sodium, natrium

sofa *n* dipan, sofa, kursi empuk

soft *adj* lunak, lembek, lembut;
~-*boiled egg* telur setengah
matang; ~ *drink* minuman
ringan, minuman tanpa alkohol;
~ *spot* titik lemah, kelemahan;
~ *toy* boneka; **softball** *n* sofbal;
soften *v* [sofen] melunak,
melembut; melunakkan,
melembutkan; **softener** *n*
[sofener] pelembut

soil *n* tanah; *v* mengotori; **soiled**
adj kotor

solar *adj* [soler] berhubungan
dengan matahari; ~ *eclipse*
gerhana matahari; ~ *energy,* ~
power tenaga surya; ~ *system*
tata surya

sold *v, pf* → **sell**

solder *v* patri, mematri

soldier *n* [soljer] tentara, laskar,
serdadu

sole *adj* satu-satunya, tunggal;
~ *parent* orang tua tunggal; *n*
telapak kaki, alas sepatu; ikan
lidah

solemn *n* [solem] khidmat, serius

solicitor *n* [solisiter] pengacara,
ahli hukum

solid *adj* padat; kuat, kokoh; *n*
zat padat; **solidarity** *n* solidari-
tas, kesetiakawanan

solitary *adj* sendiri; sepi; ~ *confinement* dikurung tersendiri

solo *adj, adv* sendiri, solo; ~ *concert* konser tunggal; **soloist** *n* solois, penyanyi atau pemain tunggal

Solomon ~ *Islander* [Solomon Ailander] orang dari Kepulauan Solomon; ~ *Islands* Kepulauan Solomon

soluble *adj* dapat larut atau dilarutkan, mudah larut; **solution** *n* larutan, solusi

solution *n* cara pemecahan, cara penyelesaian, solusi; **solve** *v* memecahkan; menyelesaikan

Somalia *n* Somalia; **Somali** *adj* berasal dari Somalia; *n* orang Somalia

some *adj* [sam] beberapa; kurang lebih; salah satu; sedikit; ~ *time*, ~ *day* kapan-kapan; **somebody** *pron* seseorang, ada orang; **somehow** *adv* bagaimanapun juga; **someone** *pron* [samwan] seseorang, ada orang

somersault *n* [samersolt] jungkir balik; *v* berjungkir balik

something *pron* [samthing] sesuatu ← **some**

sometimes *adv* [samtaimz] kadang-kadang ← **some**

somewhat *adv* [samwot] agak, sedikit ← **some**

somewhere *adv* [samwér] entah di mana ← **some**

son *n* [san] anak (lelaki), putera; ~-*in-law* menantu

song *n* nyanyian, lagu; **songwriter** *n* pencipta lagu

soon *adv* segera, lekas; *as* ~ *as*, *no* ~*er than* begitu; *the* ~*er,*

the better makin cepat makin baik

soothe *v* menghibur, menenangkan

sophisticated *adj* [sofistikéted] canggih, pintar, berpengalaman

soprano *n* sopran

sorcerer *n* penyihir; **sorcery** *n* ilmu sihir

sore *adj* sakit, pedih; *a* ~ *throat* sakit tenggorokan; *sl* marah; ~*ly missed* sangat dirindukan; *n* luka kecil

sorrow *n* kesedihan, duka cita; **sorry** *adj* menyesal; maaf

sort *n* macam, jenis; *v* menyortir, memilih, memilah-milah

SOS *abbrev save our souls* tolong, selamatkan jiwa kami

sought *v, pf* → **seek**

soul *n* sukma, nyawa, jiwa, semangat; ~ *(music)* musik khas orang hitam

sound *adj* sehat, kuat; ~ *asleep* tidur nyenyak, tidur pulas; *n* bunyi, suara; *v* berbunyi, kedengaran; ~ *barrier* tembok suara; **soundly** *adv* sungguh-sungguh; nyenyak, pulas; **soundproof** *adj* kedap suara; **soundtrack** *n* musik dari film

soup *n* [sup] sop, sup; ~ *kitchen* dapur umum

sour *adj* [saur] asam, kecut; ~ *grapes,* ~*puss* orang yang cengeng karena tidak dapat sesuatu; ~ *milk* susu basi; *sweet and* ~ asam manis

source *n* [sors] sumber, mata air; narasumber

south *adj, n* [sauth] selatan; ~

Africa Afrika Selatan (Afsel); ~ *Pole* Kutub Selatan; **southeast** *adj, n* [sauth ist] tenggara; **southern** *adj* [sathern] sebelah selatan; ~ *Cross* Bintang Pari; **southwest** *adj* barat laut

souvenir *n* [suvenir] oleh-oleh, kenang-kenangan, cenderamata; ~ *shop* toko cenderamata

sovereign *adj* [soveren] berdaulat; *n* raja, ratu; **sovereignty** *n* kedaulatan

sow *v* [so] menaburkan

soy ~ *milk* susu kedelai; ~ *sauce* kecap asin; *sweet* ~ *sauce* kecap manis; **soya** ~ *bean* kacang kedelai

space *n* ruang, tempat; spasi, jarak; angkasa; *outer* ~ angkasa luar; **spaceship** *n* kapal angkasa; **spacious** *adj* [spésyus] luas, lapang

spade *n* sekop

spaghetti *n* spageti

Spain *n* Spanyol

span *n* jangka; masa; rentang; *v* merentang

Spaniard *n* [Spanyard] orang Spanyol; **Spanish** *adj* [Spanisy] berasal dari Spanyol; *n* bahasa Spanyol ← **Spain**

spare *adj* cadangan; ~ *part* suku cadang, onderdil; ~ *ribs* iga panggang; ~ *time* waktu luang; ~ *tire* ban serep; *n* cadangan

spark *n* (percikan) api; ~ *plug* busi; **sparkle** *n* kilau; *v* berkilau-kilauan, bergemerlapan

sparrow *n* [sparo] burung gereja

spasm *n* [spazem] kejang-

kejang; **spastic** *adj* kejang; *n* orang yang mengalami kejang-kejang

spat *n* pertengkaran, pertikaian; *v, pf* → **spit**

spawn *n* telur ikan; *v* menimbulkan, menghasilkan

spay *v* mensterilkan (binatang betina)

speak *v* **spoke spoken** berbicara, berkata; ~ *Japanese* berbahasa Jepang; ~ *about,* ~ *on* membicarakan; ~ *up* berbicara dengan keras; ~ *well of* memuji; *so to* ~ boleh dikatakan; **speaker** *n* pembicara; Ketua Dewan; **speaking** *n* berpidato; *public* ~ berpidato di depan umum

spear *n* tombak, lembing

special *adj* [spésyal] istimewa, khusus, spesial; ~ *school* sekolah luar biasa; **specialist** *n* spesialis, ahli; **specialty** *n* bidang khusus

species *n* [spisyis] jenis, macam

specific *adj* khusus, tertentu, spesifik; **specification** *n* spesifikasi

specimen *n* [spésimen] contoh

specs *n, coll* kacamata; **spectacle** *n* [spéktakel] tontonan; **spectacles** *n, pl* kacamata; **spectacular** *adj* hebat, spektakuler; **spectator** *n* penonton

sped *v, pf* → **speed**

speech *n* pidato; cara bicara; ~ *writer* penulis pidato; **speechless** *adj* terdiam, kehabisan kata-kata ← **speak**

speed *n* laju, kecepatan; *top ~* secepat-cepatnya; *v* **sped sped** *~ up* mempercepat; *~ limit* batas kecepatan, kecepatan maksimum; *~ trap* polisi tidur; **speedboat** *n* perahu motor cepat; **speedy** *adj* lekas, cepat

spell *n* pesona; masa; *v* mengeja; **spelling** *n* ejaan; *~ bee* lomba mengeja

spend *v* **spent spent** membelanjakan, memakai; **spendthrift** *n* pemboros

sperm *n* sperma, air mani

sphere *n* [sfir] bulatan, bola; bidang; **spherical** *adj* [sférikal] bulat, berbentuk bola

spice *n* bumbu, rempah-rempah; **spicy** *adj* pedas

spider *n* laba-laba; *~ web* rumah laba-laba, jaring laba-laba

spike *n* paku; **spiky** *adj* berduri, tajam

spill *v* tumpah; menumpahkan

spin *v* **spun spun** berputar-putar; memintal; *~ning wheel* mesin pintal

spinach *n* [spinec] bayam

spinal *adj* berkaitan dengan tulang punggung; *~ cord* urat saraf tulang belakang; **spine** *n* tulang punggung; *~-chilling* mengerikan; **spineless** *adj* tak bertulang; lemah

spinster *n, f* perawan tua

spiral *adj* [spairal] spiral; *v* bergerak naik atau turun

spire *n* puncak menara (gereja)

spirit *n* [spirit] semangat; roh, hantu; **spirits** *n* minuman keras; *(methylated)* ~ spiritus; *in high ~s* bergembira; **spirited** *adj* bersemangat; **spiritual** *adj* batin, rohani; keagamaan; *n* lagu rohani

spit *n* air ludah; *v* **spat spat** meludah; *~ up* meludahkan

spite *n* dendam, dengki; *in ~ of* kendati, walaupun; **spiteful** *adj* pendendam

splash *n* bunyi ceburan atau cemplungan; *v* bepercikan; memercikkan

spleen *n* limpa

splendid *adj* bagus sekali; **splendor** *n* kemegahan

splinter *n* serpih; *v* memecah, menyerpih

split *adj* retak, sobek; *~ second* sekejap; *n* belahan, retakan; *v* **split split** retak, membelah; membagi; *~ up* pisah, berpisah; *~ting headache* sakit kepala yang parah

spoil *v* memanjakan; merusak; **spoilsport** *n* orang yang merusak suasana; **spoilt** *adj* manja

spoke *n* ruji, jari-jari roda

spoke, spoken *v, pf* → **speak**; **spokesperson** *n* juru bicara

sponge *n* [spanj] spons, bunga karang

sponsor *n* sponsor; *v* mendukung, mensponsori; **sponsorship** *n* dukungan

spontaneous *adj* [sponténius] spontan

spooky *adj* angker, ngeri

spool *~ of thread* kumparan,

segelendong benang

spoon *n* sendok; *~-feed*
menyuapi; *dessert ~* sendok
makan; *table~* sendok besar;
tea~ sendok teh

spore *n* spora

sport *n* olahraga; **sporting** *adj*
berhubungan dengan olahraga;
sportif; **sportsperson** *n*
olahragawan; **sporty** *adj* suka
berolahraga

spot *n* titik, noda; *sl* jerawat;
~ check sidak (inspeksi mendadak); *on the ~* di tempat, di
situ juga; *v* melihat; **spotlight**
n lampu sorot; **spotty** *adj*
berjerawat, jerawatan

spouse *n* pasangan; suami, isteri

spout *n* bibir, corot; *v* memancar

sprain *n, v* salah urat, keseleo

sprang *v, pf* → **spring**

spray *n* percikan, semprotan; *v*
menyemprot, memerciki

spread *n* [spréd] penyebaran;
sajian; mentega, selai; *v*
spread spread mengolesi;
menyiarkan, menyebarkan,
membentangkan

spree *n* pesta; *shopping ~* acara
berbelanja

spring *n* musim semi, musim
bunga; sumber (air); per, pegas;
~ bed kasur pegas; *~ chicken*
muda; *~ cleaning* pembersihan
(pada musim semi); *~ onion*
daun bawang; *hot ~* sumber air
panas, mata air panas; *v*
sprang sprung melompat,
meloncat; **springboard** *n*
papan loncat; **springtime** *n*

musim semi

sprinkle *v* [sprinkel] menaburkan,
membubuhi; **sprinkles** *n, pl*
chocolate ~ meses; **sprinkler** *n*
alat penyiram

sprint *n* lari cepat (jarak pendek);
v berlari dengan cepat; **sprinter**
n pelari cepat

sprout *n* tunas; *bean ~s* tauge;
brussel ~s kubis Brussel; *v*
bertunas, tumbuh

sprung *v, pf* → **spring**

spun *v, pf* → **spin**

spur *n* pacu, taji; *on the ~ of the
moment* tanpa berpikir terlebih
dahulu, secara mendadak

spurt *n* semburan; *v* berlari atau
bekerja dengan cepat; menyem-
bur; menyemburkan

spy *n* mata-mata, spion; *v* memata-
matai; **spyglass** *n* teropong,
keker

Sq *square* alun-alun

squabble *n* [skuobel] pertengkaran kecil; *v* bertengkar

squad *n* [skuod] regu, pasukan

square *adj* [skuér] persegi; *55 ~
meters* 55 meter persegi;
n persegi empat; alun-alun,
medan; hasil perkalian; *~ dance*
tarian rakyat Amerika; *~ meal*
makanan yang cukup; *~ root*
akar dua; *town ~* alun-alun; *v*
mengkuadratkan

squash *n* [skuosy] posisi yang
sempit atau penuh sesak;
semacam labu; olahraga squash;
v memasukkan dengan paksa

squat *v* [skuot] jongkok,
berjongkok

squeak *n* [skuik] ciutan; cicit;
a *narrow* ~ nyaris celaka; *v*
menciut-ciut; mencicit;
squeaky *adj* menciut-ciut; ~
clean bersih sekali, tak bernoda
squeeze *v* memeras; memeluk;
a *tight* ~ sempit
squid *n* cumi-cumi
squint *n* mata juling; *v* melihat
dengan susah
squirrel *n* bajing
Sri Lanka *n* Sri Lanka; **Sri
Lankan** *adj* berasal dari Sri
Lanka; *n* orang Sri Lanka
St *Saint* Santo, Santa
St *street* Jl (jalan)
stab *n* tikam, tikaman; *to have a*
~ *at* mencoba; ~ *wound* luka
tikam; *v* menikam
stability *n* [stabiliti] kemantapan,
stabilitas; **stabilize** *v* [stébilaiz]
menjadi stabil; **stable** *adj*
[stébel] mantap, stabil; kandang
kuda, istal
stadium *n* stadion, gelanggang,
arena
staff *n* staf, para karyawan, para
pegawai; para guru atau pengajar; tongkat; ~ *room* ruang
guru; *editorial* ~ (staf) redaksi
stag *n* rusa jantan; ~ *night* pesta
bujang
stage *n* tahap; panggung, pentas;
~ *fright* demam panggung; ~
show pertunjukan; tahap; *on* ~
di pentas, di panggung; *on the*
~ menjadi pemain di panggung;
v mengadakan, menyelenggarakan
stagger *v* tertatih-tatih; menga-

dakan secara bertahap
stagnant *adj* **stagnate** *v* tidak
bergerak atau berkembang
stain *n* noda; *v* menodai, mencemarkan; ~*ed glass* kaca patri;
stainless ~ *steel* baja anti
karat
stair *n* anak tangga; **stairs** *pl*
tangga; *down*~s turun tangga;
staircase, stairway *n* tangga
stake *n* pancang; taruhan; bagian;
v mematok, memancang
stale *adj* keras (roti); basi, pengap,
apak; membosankan
stalk *n* [stok] tangkai; *v* mengikuti,
mengejar; **stalker** *n* orang yang
mengikuti atau mengejar
stall *n* [stol] warung, kedai, kios;
kandang; *v* mogok, tidak langsung hidup
stallion *n* kuda jantan
stamina *n* daya tahan
stammer *n* kegagapan; *v* menggagap
stamp *n* perangko; meterai,
segel, tera, cap; *v* membubuhi
prangko, memberi meterai,
mengecap; ~ *out* memadamkan; membasmi; ~ *your foot*
mengentakkan kaki; **stampede**
n penyerbuan (gajah); perebutan; *v* lari berebutan
stand *n* *tribune*; pendirian,
sikap; kios; *to take a* ~, *to
make a* ~ bertahan; *v* **stood
stood** berdiri; tahan; ~-*by* siap
siaga; ~ *by* membela, menunggu; ~ *down* mundur, mengundurkan diri; ~ *for* berarti,
melambangkan; ~ *in line* antri

standard *adj* baku, standar, tolok; *n* patokan, ukuran, norma, standar; **standardize** *v* membakukan

standing *adj* tetap; *n* martabat, reputasi ← **stand**

standpoint *n* pendirian, sudur ← **stand**

stank *v, pf* → **stink**

staple *v* [stépel] menjepret (kertas); **stapler** *n* jepretan

staple *adj* [stépel] pokok; ~ *food* makanan pokok, sembako (sembilan makanan pokok); *n* makanan atau bahan pokok

star *n* bintang; *guest* ~ bintang tamu; *shooting* ~ bintang berekor; *the* ~*s and the Stripes* bendera AS

starboard *adj, n* [starbed] sebelah kanan kapal

starch *n* kanji; sari pati

stare *n* pandangan, tatapan; *v* memelototkan mata; memandang, menatap

starfish *n* bintang laut ← **star**

stark *n* ~ *naked* telanjang bulat

starling *n* burung jalak

start *n* awal, permulaan; *v* mulai, berangkat; memulai; menghidupkan mesin; **starter** *n* starter

startle *v* [startel] mengejutkan, mengagetkan; ~*d* kaget, terkejut

starvation *n* kelaparan; **starve** *v* (mati) kelaparan; **starving** *adj* sangat lapar, kelaparan

state *adj* kenegaraan; ~ *Department* Departemen Luar Negeri (Amerika Serikat); ~ *funeral* upacara pemakaman kenegaraan; *the (United)* ~*s* Amerika (Serikat); *n* negara (bagian); keadaan; suasana; *v* menyatakan, menyebutkan, memaparkan; **stateless** *adj* tanpa kewarganegaraan; **statesman** *n* negarawan; **statement** *n* pernyataan, pengumuman; *bank* ~ rekening koran

station *n* stasiun, pos; pangkalan; ~ *master* kepala stasiun

stationary *adj* tetap, tidak bergerak

stationery *n* alat tulis

statistics *n, pl* statistik, angka

statue *n* [statyu] patung

status *n* keadaan, kedudukan, status; pangkat, derajat; ~ *quo* keadaan tetap; *marital* ~ status

stay *n* (masa) tinggal; *v* tinggal, menginap; bertahan; ~ *away* menghindar; ~ *behind* tidak ikut, tetap tinggal; ~ *over* menginap

STD *abbrev sexually transmitted disease* PMS (penyakit menular seksual)

STD *abbrev subscriber trunk dialing* SLJJ (sambungan langsung jarak jauh)

steadfast *adj* [stédfast] tetap, teguh; **steady** *adj* [stédi] tetap, terus-menerus, teguh, mantap

steak *n* [sték] stek, bistek

steal *v* **stole stolen** mencuri; ~ *into* menyelinap

stealthy *adj* [stélthi] mencuri-curi, diam-diam

steam *n* uap; *v* beruap; mengukus; ~ *engine* (kereta api) mesin uap; **steamboat** *n* kapal uap; jenis masakan yang direbus di tempat; **steamer** *n* kapal uap; **steamroller** *n* penggiling jalan; **steamy** *adj* beruap, panas, lembab

steel *n* baja; *stainless* ~ baja anti tidak berkarat; **steelworks** *n* pabrik baja

steep *adj* curam, terjal; *sl* mahal

steeplechase *n* [stipelcés] lomba (kuda) berpalang

steer *v* mengemudikan; ~*ing wheel* roda stir

stem *n* batang; ~ *cell* sel induk

stench *n* bau busuk

stencil *n* stensil

stenographer *n* [sténografer] juru steno

step *n* langkah, jejak; anak tangga; tahap; ~*s* tangga; ~ *by* ~ selangkah demi selangkah; *in* ~ sejalan; *out of* ~ tidak sejalan, salah langkah; *v* melangkah; ~ *down* meletakkan jabatan, mengundurkan diri; ~ *on* menginjak; ~*ping stone* batu loncatan; **stepfather** *n* bapak tiri, ayah tiri; **stepmother** *n* ibu tiri

stereo *n* [stério] peralatan pemutaran musik

stereotype *n* [stériotaip] stereotip, klise

sterile *adj* [stéril] steril, suci-hama; mandul; **sterilize** *v* menyucihamakan, mensterilkan

stern *adj* keras, tidak senyum; *n* buritan (kapal)

stew *n* rebusan; *v* merebus

steward *n* pramugara; **stewardess** *n, arch* pramugari

stick *n* tongkat, batang; *walking* ~ tongkat; *in the* ~*s* daerah udik; *v* **stuck stuck** bertekun, bertahan; melekatkan; ~ *at* tetap (melakukan); ~ *it out* bertahan; **sticker** *n* stiker, tempelan; **sticky** *adj* lengket, lekat; ~ *tape* selotip, isolasi

stiff *adj* keras, kaku; pegal; *to keep a* ~ *upper lip* tidak menangis; *that's a bit* ~ itu sedikit keterlaluan

still *adj* tenang, teduh, sepi; ~ *life* lukisan benda mati; *adv* masih; *conj* bahkan, tetapi; **stillborn** *adj* lahir mati; **stillness** *n* keteduhan, ketenangan

stimulate *v* mendorong, merangsang

sting *n* sengat; *v* **stung stung** menyengat

stingy *adj* [stinji] kikir, pelit

stink *n* bau (busuk); *v* **stank stunk** berbau (busuk)

stipulation *n* ketentuan, syarat; **stipulate** *v* mensyaratkan, menetapkan

stir *n* [ster] keributan, kekacauan; *v* bergerak; mengaduk; mengacaukan; ~ *fry* oseng-oseng

stirrup *n* pemijak kaki, sanggurdi

stitch *n* jahitan; *v* menjahit

stock *n* persediaan; hewan ternak; ~ *exchange* bursa efek; *out of* ~ persediaan habis; **stockbroker** *n* pedagang saham

stocking *n* stoking

stockpile *n* persediaan, penimbunan; *v* menimbun ← **stock**

stocky *adj* berbadan pendek gemuk

stole, stolen *v, pf* → **steal**

stomach *n* [stamek] perut, lambung; ~ *ache* sakit perut

stone *n* batu; biji (buah); ~ *Age* Zaman Batu; ukuran timbang (14 pon); *v* merajam; ~-*deaf* tuli, pekak batu

stood *v, pf* → **stand**

stool *n* bangku, dingklik; tinja, kotoran

stoop *v* membungkuk, merendahkan diri

stop *n* perhentian, akhir; *bus* ~ halte (bis); *full* ~ titik; *v* berhenti, menahan; ~ *over* singgah; ~ *work* mogok kerja; **stopover** *n* tempat persinggahan; **stopper** *n* penyumbat, tutup

storage *n* penyimpanan; gudang; **store** *n* toko; persediaan, perbekalan, gudang; *v* menyimpan

storey → **story**

stork *n* (burung) bangau; *to have a visit from the* ~ kelahiran bayi

storm *n* angin badai; **stormy** *adj* (berangin) ribut

story, storey *n* lantai, tingkat; *two-*~ *house* rumah berlantai dua

story *n* cerita, riwayat, kisah, dongeng; *to tell stories* berdongeng; berdusta, berbohong

stout *adj* gemuk, tambun; ~-*hearted* berani

stove *n* kompor; *gas* ~ kompor gas

stowaway *n* [stowewé] penumpang gelap (di kapal)

straddle *v* [stradel] mengangkang

straight *adj* [strét] lurus, terus; *sl* heteroseksual; *adv* langsung; jujur, terus terang; ~ *ahead* terus, lurus; ~ *away* langsung, segera; **straighten** *v* meluruskan; ~ *hair* meluruskan rambut; **straightforward** *adj* terus terang

strain *n* ketegangan; *v* bersusah payah; mengejan; menyaring; memaksakan; mengejan; ~ *a muscle* salah urat, keseleo; **strainer** *n* saringan

strait *n* selat; *the* ~*s of Malacca* Selat Malaka

strand *n a* ~ *of hair* sehelai rambut; **stranded** *adj* terdampar

strange *adj* [strénj] aneh, ganjil, asing; **stranger** *n* orang asing, orang luar

strangle *v* [stranggel] mencekik

strap *n* tali; cambuk; **strapless** *adj* tanpa tali baju

strategic *adj* [stratijik] strategis; **strategy** *n* [strateji] strategi, siasat

straw *n* sedotan; jerami, merang

strawberry *n* stroberi, arbei

stray *adj* yang tersesat; tidak bertuan (binatang); *n* binatang yang tidak bertuan; *v* sesat, menyasar

streak *n* garis, coret, coreng; *blonde* ~*s in her hair* rambutnya bergaris pirang; *v* mencoreng

stream *n* sungai, kali; aliran; *v* mengalir; **streamer** *n* pita hiasan; **streamline** *v* merampingkan; **streamlined** *adj* ramping, efisien

street *n* jalan; ~ *children* anak-anak jalanan; ~ *sweeper* penyapu jalan; ~s *ahead* jauh ke depan; *one-way* ~ jalan satu arah; **streetcar** *n* trem

strength *n* kekuatan, tenaga, kekuasaan; **strengthen** *v* memperkuat, memperkokoh ← **strong**

strenuous *adj* [strényuus] berat, melelahkan; kuat

stress *n* tekanan; ketegangan, stres; *v* menekan, mementingkan, menitikberatkan; ~ *(out)* menjadi tegang atau stres; **stressful** *adj* menegangkan

stretch *n* bagian, ruas (jalan); jangkauan; *v* menegangkan; merentangkan

stretcher *n* usungan

strict *adj* keras; streng (guru); **strictly** *adv* dengan ketat, hanya

strike *n* pukulan; pemogokan, mogok kerja; serangan; *on* ~ mogok; *v* **struck struck** memukul; menyerang; mogok; ~ *down* menjatuhkan; ~ *up* memulai; **striker** *n* pemogok; pemain depan, ujung tombak (sepak bola); **striking** *adj* mengesankan, menyolok

string *n* tali; senar (raket, alat musik); untaian; ~ *instrument* alat musik gesek; *v* **strung strung** ~ *out* memperpanjang

strip *n* garis, jalur; *v* menghilangkan, membersihkan; membuka baju; menari telanjang; **stripper** *n* penari telanjang

stripe *n* garis, belang; **striped** *adj* bergaris, belang

striptease *n* tari telanjang ← **strip**

strive *v* **striven strove** ~ *after* menuntut, mengejar

stroke *n* pukulan; gaya (renang); serangan otak; *on the* ~ *of five* tepat pukul lima; *v* mengelus

stroll *n* jalan kaki yang santai; *v* berjalan kaki; **stroller** *n* kereta dorong anak

strong *adj* kuat, kokoh; keras (minuman); ~-*arm* tangan besi; ~ *tea* teh kental

strove *v. pf* → **strive**

struck *v. pf* → **strike**

structure *n* bangunan, susunan, struktur; *v* menyusun

struggle *n* [stragel] perjuangan; *Indonesian Democratic Party of* ~ Partai Demokrasi Indonesia (Perjuangan) (PDIP); *v* berjuang

strung *v, pf* → **string**

stubborn *adj* keras kepala

stuck *adj* terjebak, terjepit; ~-*up* congkak, sombong; ~ *on* suka, menaksir; ~ *in traffic* terjebak macet; *v, pf* → **stick**

stud *n* kancing; tempat pembiakan kuda

student *n* pelajar, murid, mahasiswa; **studies** *n, pl* pelajaran, penelitian

studio *n* studio; sanggar;

recording ~ dapur rekaman

studious *adj* [styudius] rajin belajar; **study** *n* [stadi] pelajaran, studi; penelitian, riset; ruang belajar; *v* belajar, mempelajari, mengkaji

stuff *n* bahan; barang-barang; *v* mengisi; ~ *this* persetan dengan ini; **stuffing** *n* isi, pengisi; busa; **stuffy** *adj* pengap

stumble *v* [stambel] tersandung; *stumbling block* batu sandungan, halangan

stump *n* puntung; bekas pohon; tiang (kriket); **stumped** *adj* bingung, habis pikiran

stun *v* membuat tertegun atau pingsan; mengagetkan; **stunning** *adj* memesonakan, cantik sekali

stung *v, pf* → **sting**

stunk *v, pf* → **stink**

stunt *n* perbuatan yang luar biasa; pertunjukan, akrobatik; *publicity* ~ kegiatan untuk membuat berita

stunt *v* menghalangi, memperlambat; **stunted** *adj* kerdil, terhalang

stuntman *n* pemeran pengganti ← **stunt**

stupid *adj* bodoh, dungu; **stupidity** *n* kebodohan, kedunguan

sturdy *adj* kokoh

stutter *n* bicara menggagap; *v* menggagap, berbicara dengan gagap

sty *n* kandang babi

sty, stye *n* bintitan

style *n* [stail] gaya, cara; *not my* ~ bukan selera saya; *v* ~ *yourself on* meniru; **stylish** *adj* bergaya

stylus *n* alat tajam untuk menulis di layar (plastik atau kaca)

sub- *pref* (di) bawah

subconscious *adj, n* bawah sadar

subcontinent *the (Indian)* ~ Asia Selatan

subcontract *v* mengontrakkan kepada orang lain; **subcontractor** *n* pemborong bawahan

subculture *n* cabang kebudayaan, aliran

subdistrict *n* kecamatan, wilayah; ~ *head* camat

subdue *v* menaklukkan; mengendalikan; **subdued** *adj* tertunduk

subject *n* soal, topik, subyek; mata pelajaran; ~ *to* kena, menjadi sasaran; *on the* ~ *of* tentang; *v* menaklukkan, menundukkan; **subjective** *adj* subyektif, berat sebelah

subjugate *v* menaklukkan, menundukkan; **subjugation** *n* penaklukan, penundukan

submarine *adj* [sabmarin] di bawah (permukaan) laut; *n* kapal selam

submerge *v* menyelam; merendamkan; **submerged** *adj* di bawah permukaan air

submission *n* penyerahan, pengajuan; ketundukan; **submit** *v* menyerahkan, menyampaikan; ~ *to* tunduk; mematuhi; **submissive** *adj* bersifat menyerah, bersikap tunduk

subordinate *adj, n* [sabordinet] bawahan

subscribe *v* berlangganan; menganut; **subscriber** *n* pelanggan; **subscription** *n* langganan

subsequent *adj* berikut; **subsequently** *adv* kemudian, setelah itu

subside *v* surut, turun, reda

subsidize *v* mensubsidi, memberi subsidi; **subsidy** *n* tunjangan, subsidi

subsistence ~ *agriculture* pertanian untuk bertahan hidup

substance *n* zat; bahan; isi pokok; hakikat; *of* ~ berbobot; **substantial** *adj* (cukup) besar, banyak, berbobot

substitute *adj, n* ganti, pengganti; wakil; *v* mengganti; **substitution** *n* penggantian

subtitler *n* [sabtaiteler] pemberi teks (pada film berbahasa asing); **subtitles** *n, pl* teks

subtle *adj* [satel] halus, tidak kentara

subtract *v* **subtraction** *n* mengurangi

subtropical *adj* subtropis

suburb *n* [sabérb] daerah perumahan, daerah perkotaan; *Kebayoran is a ~ of Jakarta* Kebayoran adalah daerah perumahan di Jakarta; **suburban** *adj* [sebérben] di daerah perumahan atau perkotaan; **suburbia** *n* daerah perumahan

subversive *adj* subversif, melawan tata sosial

subway *n* kereta api bawah tanah; terowongan penyeberangan

succeed *v* [saksid] berhasil, menjadi sukses; mengganti; **success** *n* keberhasilan, sukses; **successful** *adj* berhasil, sukses; **succession** *n* [saksésyen] penggantian, penerusan; *in* ~ berturut-turut; **successively** *adv* secara berturut-turut; **successor** *n* pengganti

such *adj* seperti itu, sedemikian; sungguh; *adv* demikian, begini, begitu; *pron* demikian, begitu; ~ *as* seperti misalnya, sebagaimana; *as* ~ sebagai

suck *v* mengisap, mengemut

Sudan *n* Sudan; **Sudanese** *adj* berasal dari Sudan; *n* orang Sudan

sudden *adj* tiba-tiba, mendadak; ~ *death* gol pertama mengakhiri pertandingan; *all of a* ~ tiba-tiba, tahu-tahu; **suddenly** *adv* tiba-tiba, secara mendadak

suds *n, pl* busa

sue *v* menggugat, menuntut

suede *n* [suéd] kulit halus

suffer *v* menderita; ~ *from* mengidap; **sufferer** *n* penderita, pasien; **suffering** *n* penderitaan

sufficient *adj* [safisyent] cukup

suffix *n* akhiran

suffocate *v* mati lemas; mencekik

sugar *n* [syuger] gula; ~ *cane* tebu; ~ *palm* aren; *brown* ~ gula aren; *castor* ~ gula; *icing* ~ tepung gula; **sugary** *adj* manis, mengandung gula

suggest v [sejést] menyarankan, mengusulkan, menganjurkan; **suggestion** n saran, usul, anjuran; **suggestive** adj sugesti

suicide n [suisaid] bunuh diri; to commit ~ bunuh diri

suit n [sut] setelan (pakaian); rupa (kartu); v cocok; berpadanan; **suitability** n kecocokan; **suitable** adj patut, layak, cocok; **suitcase** n koper

suite n [swit] setelan; sederetan (kamar); rangkaian (musik)

sulfate, sulphate n [salfét] sulfat; **sulfide** n sulfida; **sulfur** n belerang; ~ic acid asam sulfat, asam belerang

sullen adj cemberut, murung

sulphur → **sulfur**

sultan n [saltan] sultan; **sultanate** n kesultanan

Sumatra n (pulau) Sumatera; **Sumatran** adj berasal dari Sumatera; n orang Sumatera

summarize v meringkas; **summary** n ringkasan, ikhtisar

summer n musim panas; Indian ~ cuaca panas pada musim gugur

summit n (pertemuan) puncak

summon v memanggil; **summons** n (surat) panggilan

sun n matahari; v ~ yourself berjemur; ~-baked terjemur, kering; ~ lamp alat penyinar; **sunbathe** v [sanbéth] berjemur; **sunbeam** n sinar matahari; **sunburn** n, v terbakar sinar matahari; **sunny** adj cerah; riang

sundae n [sandé] es krim dengan sirop

Sundanese adj [Sundaniz] berasal dari daerah Jawa Barat atau Banten; n bahasa Sunda; orang Sunda

Sunday n hari Minggu ← **sun**

sundial n [sandail] jam matahari ← **sun**

sundown n matahari terbenam, matahari tenggelam, magrib ← **sun**

sunflower n bunga matahari; ~ seeds biji bunga matahari ← **sun**

sung v, pf → **sing**

sunglasses n, pl kacamata hitam ← **sun**

sunk adj tenggelam; v, pf → **sink**; **sunken** adj cekung; tenggelam; ~ treasure harta karun di dasar laut

sunlight n [sanlait] cahaya matahari ← **sun**

sunrise n matahari terbit ← **sun**

sunset n matahari terbenam, matahari tenggelam, magrib; ~ prayer (sholat) magrib ← **sun**

sunshine n sinar matahari, cahaya matahari ← **sun**

sunstroke n kelengar matahari ← **sun**

suntan n kulit berwarna coklat karena kena sinar matahari ← **sun**

super adj luar biasa, hebat

superb adj bagus sekali, istimewa

superficial adj [superfisyel] dangkal, enteng

superfluous adj [supérfluus]

berlebihan, tidak perlu
superintendent *n* pengawas, pemimpin, kepala instansi
superior *adj* [supirior] ulung, unggul, tinggi; sombong; *Mother* ~ kepala biarawati; *n* atasan; **superiority** *n* keunggulan
supermarket *n* (toko) swalayan
superstition *n* [superstisyen] takhayul; **superstitious** *adj* [superstisyes] sering percaya takhayul
supervise *v* mengawasi; **supervision** *n* [supervisyen] pengawasan; **supervisor** *n* [supervaizer] pengawas
supper *n* makan malam; *to have* ~ makan malam
supple *adj* [sapel] lentur, gemulai
supplement *n* [saplement] tambahan, pelengkap, suplemen; **supplementary** *adj* tambahan, pelengkap
supplier *n* [saplayer] pemasok; **supply** *n* pasokan, persediaan, suplai; ~ *and demand* persediaan dan permintaan; *v* memasok, menyediakan
support *n* dukungan, bantuan; *v* mendukung, membantu; **supporter** *n* pendukung
suppose *v* mengandaikan, menganggap, mengira; ~*d to* seharusnya; **supposing** *conj, v* andaikata
suppress *v* menekan, menindas; **suppression** *n* penekanan, penindasan
supremacy *n* [suprémasi] keunggulan; **supreme** *adj*

unggul, teratas; ~ *command* komando tertinggi, pimpinan tertinggi
surcharge *n* biaya tambahan, tunjangan
sure *adj* [syur] tentu, pasti; yakin; ~ *enough* ternyata benar; *for* ~ pasti; *a* ~ *thing* kepastian; **surely** *adv* tentu, tentu saja, pasti
surf *n* buih ombak; *v* berselancar; ~ *the Web* menjelajahi internet; **surfer** *n* peselancar; **surfing** *n* (main) selancar, berselancar; *wind-*~ selancar angin
surface *n* [sérfes] muka, permukaan; *v* naik ke permukaan, muncul
surfboard *n* papan selancar ← **surf**
surgeon *n* [serjen] ahli bedah; *plastic* ~ ahli bedah plastik; **surgery** *n* pembedahan, operasi; tempat praktek dokter
Surinam *n* Surinam; **Surinamer** *n* orang Surinam; **Surinamese** *adj* berasal dari Surinam
surname *n* nama keluarga, nama marga
surpass *v* melebihi, mengungguli
surplus *adj, n* kelebihan, sisa, surplus
surprise *n* kejutan; *v* membuat kejutan, mengejutkan
surrender *n* penyerahan; *v* menyerahkan
surround *v* mengelilingi, mengepung; **surrounding** *adj* yang di sekitar; **surroundings** *n* daerah sekitar, lingkungan

surveillance *n* [sérvélens] pengawasan, peninjauan; **survey** *n* angket; penelitian; peninjauan; *v* meneliti, meninjau; **surveyor** *n* juru ukur tanah

survival *n* kelangsungan hidup; **survive** *v* bertahan (hidup), tetap hidup, selamat; **survivor** *n* orang yang selamat

suspect *n* [saspekt] tersangka; *v* [saspékt] menyangka

suspend *v* menggantung; menangguhkan, menunda; **suspenders** *n, pl* tali selempang; **suspension** *n* penskorsan; suspensi; ~ *bridge* jembatan gantung

suspicion *n* [sespisyen] kecurigaan; **suspicious** *adj* curiga, mencurigakan

SUV *abbrev* sports utility vehicle mobil jip

swagger *n* cara berjalan yang angkuh; *v* berjalan dengan berlaga

swallow *v* [swolo] menelan

swallow *n* [swolo] burung layang-layang

swam *v, pf →* **swim**

swamp [swomp] paya, rawa; **swampy** *adj* berawa

swan *n* [swon] angsa, soang; ~ *song* karya terakhir

swap, swop *n* pertukaran; *v* bertukar; menukar; ~ *card* kartu koleksi yang bisa ditukar-menukar

swarm *n* [sworm] sekawanan; *v* berkerumun

swat *v* [swot] memukul (serang-

ga); *fly* ~ alat pemukul lalat

sway *n* goyangan; kekuasaan; *v* bergoyang; menggoncangkan; mempengaruhi

swear *v* [suér] **swore sworn** bersumpah; mengumpat

sweat *n* [swét] keringat, peluh; *v* berkeringat; **sweatband** *n* gelang penyerap keringat; **sweatshirt** *n* semacam baju hangat; **sweatshop** *n* pabrik dengan upah rendah; **sweaty** *adj* berkeringat, keringatan

Swede *n* [Swid] orang Swedia; **Sweden** *n* Swedia; **Swedish** *adj* berasal dari Swedia; *n* bahasa Swedia

sweep *v* **swept swept** menyapu; *chimney* ~ tukang pembersih cerobong; *clean* ~ sapu bersih; **sweeping** *adj* besar, meyakinkan

sweep, sweepstakes *n* taruhan, undian

sweet *adj* manis; *n* permen; ~ *and sour* asam manis; ~ *corn* jagung (manis); ~ *potato* ubi jalar; ~ *talk* kata-kata manis, rayuan gombal; ~ *tooth* penggemar makanan manis; **sweeten** *v* memaniskan, membuat manis; **sweetener** *artificial* ~ pemanis buatan; **sweetheart** *n* kekasih

swell *adj, sl* hebat; *n* gelombang; *v* membesar; ~ *up* bengkak; **swelling** *n* pembengkakan

swept *v, pf →* **sweep**

swift *adj* cepat, lancar

swim *v* **swam swum** berenang, mandi; *to go for a* ~, *to have* *a* ~ (pergi) berenang; mandi di laut; **swimmer** *n* perenang; **swimming** *n* renang; ~ *pool* kolam renang; *synchronized* ~ renang indah; **swimsuit, swimwear** *n* baju renang

swindle *n* [swindel] penipuan; *v* menipu

swine *n* babi; *sl* orang jahat

swing *n* **swung swung** ayunan; pergeseran; *v* bergoyang, berayun

swipe *v* menggesek; memukul; mencuri; ~ *card* kartu gesek

Swiss *adj* berasal dari Swis; *n* orang Swis ← **Switzerland**

switch *n* sakelar, penghubung; pertukaran; ~ *off* mematikan; *on* menghidupkan, memasang; **switchboard** *n* sentral telepon

Switzerland *n* (negeri) Swis

swollen *adj* bengkak, kembung ← **swell**

swoop *v* menyambar; *one fell* ~ dalam sekali kejadian

swop → **swap**

sword *n* [sord] pedang

swore, sworn *v, pf* → **swear**

swot *n, coll* orang yang rajin sekali belajar

swum *v, pf* → **swim**

swung *v, pf* → **swing**

syllable *n* [silabel] suku kata

syllabus *n* [silabus] rencana pelajaran, daftar pelajaran

symbol *n* lambang, simbol; **symbolic** *adj* **symbolize** *v* melambangkan

symmetrical *adj* [simétrikal] simetris, setimbal; **symmetry**

n [simetri] simetri

sympathize *v* [simpathaiz] ber-simpati, menyatakan simpati; **sympathy** *n* [simpathi] simpati

symphony *n* simfoni

symptom *n* gejala

synagogue *n* sinagoga, tempat ibadah orang Yahudi

synchronised ~ *swimming* renang indah

syncretic *adj* [sinkrétik] sinkretis, bersifat menyatukan

syndicate *n* sindikat, kongsi

syndrome *n* sindrom, sindroma; *Down's* ~ sindrom Down

synonym *n* padanan, sinonim; **synonymous** ~ *with* berarti sama dengan

synopsis *n* ringkasan, ikhtisar, sinopsis

synthesis *n* [sinthesis] sintesis, sintesa

synthetic *adj* sintetis; ~ *rubber* karet sintetis, karet buatan

Syria *n* Suriah; **Syrian** *adj* berasal dari Suriah; *n* orang Suriah

syringe *n* [sirinj] alat suntik, suntikan

syrup *n* sirop; **syrupy** *adj* ter-lalu manis

system *n* sistem, susunan, jaringan; **systematic** *adj* sistematis

T

T ~-*bone steak* sejenis steik; ~-*junction* pertigaan, simpang tiga; ~-*shirt* kaus (oblong)

tab *n* label; *to keep* ~s *on* mengawasi

tabby *n* kucing belang

table *n* [tébel] meja; daftar; ~ *napkin* serbet; ~ *tennis* tenis meja, pingpong; ~ *of contents* daftar isi; **tablecloth** *n* taplak meja; **tablespoon** *n* sendok besar

tablet *n* pil, tablet

tabloid *n* koran, tabloid

taboo *adj* tabu; *n* pantangan

tackle *n* serangan; rangkulan; perkakas, perabot; *v* mengganjal kaki; mengerjakan

tacky *adj, coll* norak

tact *n* kebijaksanaan, sikap diplomatis; **tactful** *adj* bijaksana, diplomatis

tactic *n* taktik, siasat, kiat; **tactical** *adj* taktis

tactless *adj* membuat sakit hati, tidak bijaksana ← **tact**

tadpole *n* kecebong

taffeta *adj, n* tafeta

tag *n* label, merek, nama, kartu; *luggage* ~ tanda bagasi; *v* memberi tanda; ~ *along* membuntuti, ikut; *to play* ~ main kejar-kejaran

tail *n* ekor, buntut; bagian belakang; *v* membuntuti, mengikuti secara diam-diam; ~ *wind* angin buritan; *heads or* ~s permainan atas atau bawah (dengan uang logam); **tailgate** *v* mengikuti mobil terlalu dekat; **taillight** *n* lampu belakang (kendaraan)

tailor *n* tukang jahit, modist; ~-*made* buatan tukang jahit; dibuat khusus

tainted *adj* tercemar, ternoda

Taiwan *n* Taiwan; **Taiwanese** *adj* berasal dari Taiwan; *n* orang Taiwan

Tajik *n* bahasa Tajik; orang Tajik; **Tajikistan** *n* Tajikistan; **Tajikistani** *adj* berasal dari Tajikistan; *n* orang Tajikistan

take *v* **took taken** mengambil, membawa (pergi); menganggap; menangkap, menerima; makan (waktu), memerlukan; ~-*over* pengambilan alih; ~ *after* mirip; ~ *for* mengira, menyangka; ~ *ill* jatuh sakit; ~ *in* mengerti; ~ *it* tahan; ~ *off* lepas landas; berangkat; membuka; ~ *on* menerima, menanggung; ~ *over* mengambil alih; ~ *part* ikut serta, ambil bagian; ~ *place* berlangsung, terjadi; ~ *to* suka; ~ *the bus* naik bis; *do you* ~ *tea or coffee?* ingin minum teh atau kopi? **takeaway** *adj, n* dibungkus, bawa pulang; **taking** ~s pendapatan selama masa tertentu

talc *n* bedak; **talcum** ~ *powder* bedak

tale *n* cerita, dongeng; *fairy*-~ (kisah) dongeng; *to tell* ~s melapor; membohong talent *n* [talent] bakat; **talented** *adj* berbakat

talk *n* [tok] percakapan, pembicaraan, ceramah; ~s perundingan; *small* ~ basa-basi, obrolan ringan; ~ *of the town* buah bibir; *v* berbicara, berunding, bertutur; ~ *of* membicarakan; **talkative** *adj* [tokatif] cerewet, banyak omong; **talkback** ~ *radio* acara kontak pendengar; **talking** ~ *point* topik pembicaraan, isu; ~-*to* teguran; **talkshow** *n* acara diskusi

tall *adj* [tol] tinggi, jangkung; *a* ~ *order* permintaan yang berat

tally *n* jumlah, perhitungan; *v* cocok

talon *n* [talon] cakar (burung)

tamarind *n* [tamarind] asam jawa

tambourine *n* [tamburin] rebana

tame *adj* jinak; *v* menjinakkan; *elephant* ~*r* pawang gajah

Tamil *adj* berasal dari kebudayaan Tamil atau Keling; *n* bahasa Tamil; orang Keling, orang Tamil

tamper *v* merusakkan, mengubah

tan *adj* coklat muda; *n* kulit berwarna coklat; *v* bermandi matahari; menyamak (kulit); *coll* mencambuk

tandem ~ *(bike)* sepeda untuk dua orang; *in* ~ bersama, berdua

tang *n* rasa, bau

tangerine *n* [tanjerin] jeruk garut, jeruk keprok

tangle *n* [tanggel] kekusutan, kekacauan

tango *n* [tanggo] (dansa) tango; *v* berdansa tango; *it takes two to* ~ kegiatan yang melibatkan dua orang

tank *n* tangki; panser; ~ *top* kaus tanpa lengan; **tanker** *n* kapal tangki

tanner *n* penyamak ← **tan**

Tanzania *n* Tanzania; **Tanzanian** *adj* berasal dari Tanzania; *n* orang Tanzania

tap *n* keran; ketukan; ~ *dance* dansa tep; *phone* ~ sadapan telepon; *v* mengetuk; menyadap

tape *n* pita; plester; kaset; ~ *measure* meteran; ~ *recorder*, ~ *deck* mesin pemutar kaset, tep; *masking* ~ lakban; *sticky* ~ isolasi, selotip; *v* memakai selotip; membalut; merekam; **tapeworm** *n* cacing pita

taper *v* meruncing

tapestry *n* [tapestri] sulaman, permadani hiasan dinding

tapioca *n* tepung ubi kayu, tapioka

tapir *n* babi alu

tapper *n* penyadap

tar *n* ter; aspal

tarantula *n* sejenis laba-laba besar

tardy *adj* terlambat, telat

target *n* sasaran, tujuan, target; *v* mengincar

tariff *n* tarif, ongkos

tarnish *v* menjadi buram atau hitam (logam)

taro *n* talas

tarpaulin *n* terpal

tart *adj* asam, kecut; *n* kue kecil yang bulat; *coll* perempuan murahan tartan *n* corak kotak-kotak khas Skotlandia

tartar *n* karang gigi

task *n* tugas, pekerjaan

taste *n* [tést] (cita) rasa; nuansa; selera; *in good ~* berselera tinggi; *v* mengecap, merasai; **tasteful** *adj* berselera (baik); **tasteless** *adj* tidak berselera, norak; **tasty** *adj* enak, sedap; *~ cheese* keju parut

tatter *~ed, in ~s* sobek-sobek, compang-camping; **tatty** *adj* dalam keadaan tidak terpelihara

tattoo *n* tato, rajah; *v* merajah, menato

taught *v, pf →* **teach**

tavern *n* [tavern] tempat minum, hotel yang merangkap sebagai bar

tax *n* pajak, bea; *~-free* bebas pajak; *~ evasion* penghindaran pajak; *goods and services ~ (GST)* pajak pelayanan dan barang (PPB); *v* mengenakan pajak atau bea; **taxable** *adj* yang wajib dikenakan pajak; **taxation** *n* pajak, perpajakan

taxi, taxicab *n* taksi; *metered ~* taksi argo

taxpayer *n* pembayar pajak ← **tax**

TB *abbrev* tuberculosis TBC, radang paru-paru

tea *n* [ti] teh; *~ bag* celup teh, kantong teh; *~ cosy* tutup teko; *~ plantation* kebun teh; *afternoon ~* makan sore; *strong ~* teh kental

teach *v* **taught taught** [tot]

mengajar; **teacher** *n* guru, pengajar; *~'s pet* murid kesayangan; **teaching** *n* pengajaran; *~ and learning* hal belajar-mengajar; **teachings** *n, pl* ajaran

teacup *n* cangkir teh, cawan teh ← **tea**

teak *n* (kayu) jati

team *n* regu, tim; *~ spirit* semangat tim; *v ~ up with* bekerja sama dengan; **teammate** *n* kawan (seregu); **teamwork** *n* kerjasama sekelompok

teapot *n* poci, teko

tear *n* [tér] sobekan, robekan; *v* **tore torn** menyobek, merobek, mengoyak

tear *n* [tir] air mata; **tearful, teary** *adj* (cenderung) menangis

tearooms *n, pl* restoran kecil tempat minum teh ← **tea**

tease *v* mengganggu, meledek, mengusik; *~ hair* menyasak rambut; **teaser** *n* teka-teki

teaspoon *n* sendok teh ← **tea**

technical *adj* [téknikel] teknis; **technician** *n* teknisi; **technicality** *n* alasan teknis

technique *n* [téknik] cara, teknik

technological *adj* [téknolojikel] berhubungan dengan teknologi; **technology** *n* teknologi; *science and ~* ilmu pengetahuan dan teknologi (iptek)

tedious *adj* [tidius] membosankan, menjemukan

teen *n* remaja, anak baru gede (ABG); **teenage** *adj* remaja, umur belasan tahun; **teenager** *n* (anak) remaja; **teens** *n, pl* umur belasan tahun

teeth *n, pl* ← **tooth**; **teethe** *v* tumbuh gigi; *Lastri is teething* gigi Lastri sedang tumbuh

teetotaler *n* orang yang tidak minum alkohol

tel. *telephone* tlp (telepon)

telecast *n* [télekast] tayangan (langsung); *v* menayangkan, menyiarkan

telecommunications *n, pl* telekomunikasi

telegram *n, arch* telegram, surat kawat; **telegraph** *n, arch* telegraf; *~ pole* tiang listrik

telepathic *adj* berhubungan dengan telepati; **telepathy** *n* telepati

telephone *n* (pesawat) telepon, telefon; *~ box, public ~* telepon umum; *v* menelepon

telescope *n* teropong (bintang), teleskop

televise *v* [télevaiz] menyiarkan lewat televisi, menayangkan; **television (TV)** *n* televisi (teve, tivi)

tell *v* **told told** bercerita; menceritakan, memberitahukan; menyuruh, memerintahkan; *~ off* menegur; *~ on* melaporkan, mengadukan; *~ stories* berdongeng; berdusta, berbohong; *~ tales* melapor, membuka rahasia; *~ the truth* mengatakan dengan jujur

teller *n* kasir

telltale *n* orang yang membuka rahasia; *~ sign* tanda jelas

temper *n* sifat, watak; *bad-~ed* pemarah; *to lose your ~* menjadi marah; **temperament** *n* tabiat, perangai; **temperamental** *adj* emosional

temperate *adj* sedang; *~ zone* daerah beriklim sedang

temperature *n* suhu; *Rifki has a ~* badan Rifki panas

temple *n* pelipis; candi, kuil; *Hind* pura, kuil

temporary *adj* untuk sementara

tempt *v* menggoda; *~ing* menggoda, menggodakan; **temptation** *n* godaan

ten *adj, n* sepuluh

tenant *n* [ténant] penyewa

tend *v* cenderung; merawat, memelihara; **tendency** *n* kecenderungan

tender *n* penawaran, pelelangan; *legal ~* alat pembayar yang sah

tender *adj* (berhati) lembut; lunak, halus; kurang matang (daging); **tenderizer** *meat ~* alat pemukul untuk melunakkan daging; **tenderness** *n* kelembutan (hati)

tendon *n* urat

tennis *n* tenis; *~ court* lapangan tenis; *~ player* petenis, pemain tenis

tenpin *~ bowling* boling

tense *n* masa; *past ~* bentuk lampau; *present ~* (kata kerja) masa kini

tense *adj* tegang; **tension** *n* ketegangan, tegangan; *high ~ wires* saluran udara tegangan ekstra tinggi (SUTET)

tent *n* kemah, tenda

tenth *adj* kesepuluh ← **ten**

term *n* istilah; jangka waktu, triwulan, caturwulan (cawu); ~
deposit deposito berjangka; *in*
~*s of* mengenai, dari segi;
terms *n, pl* syarat-syarat;
hubungan; *on good* ~ berhubungan baik; *to come to* ~*s*
with menerima, mencapai
kesepakatan

terminal *adj* penghabisan, terakhir; ~ *cancer* kanker stadium
lanjut; *n* terminal, pangkalan;
terminate *v* berakhir; mengakhiri; **termination** *n* pemutusan; pengguguran, aborsi;
terminus *n* terminal, tujuan
terakhir

terminology *n* [términoloji]
peristilahan

termite *n* rayap, anai-anai

terrace *n* teras

terrapin *n* [térapin] kura-kura

terrible *adj* [téribel] mengerikan,
menakutkan, buruk sekali

terrier *n* [térier] jenis anjing

terrific *adj* [terifik] hebat; **terrify**
v menakutkan, membuat ngeri

territorial *adj* [téritorial]
berhubungan dengan daerah;
territory *n* daerah, wilayah;
Northern ~ Australia Utara

terror *n* rasa takut, teror; **terror-
ism** *n* [térorizem] terorisme;
terrorist *n* teroris; **terrorize** *v*
meneror

tertiary *adj* [térsyeri] ketiga;
~ *education* pendidikan di perguruan tinggi; ~ *Period* Jaman
Tersier

test *n* ujian, pemeriksaan, tes;

percobaan, uji coba; *v* memeriksa, menguji; mengujicoba; ~
case batu ujian; ~ *tube* tabung
reaksi

testament *Old* ~ Perjanjian Lama;
last will and ~ surat wasiat

testicle *n* [téstikel] buah pelir

testify *v* [téstifai] bersaksi; **testimonial** *n* surat kesaksian; tanda
penghargaan; **testimony** *n*
kesaksian

testing *n* pengujian, percobaan

text *n* naskah, teks; ~ *message*
pesan singkat, SMS; *v* mengirim pesan singkat; **textbook** *n*
buku pelajaran

texta *n* spidol

textiles *n, pl* tekstil, barang
tenunan

texture *n* tekstur

Thai *adj* berasal dari Thailand;
n bahasa Thai; orang Thailand;
Thailand *n* Muang Thai, Thailand

than *conj* daripada, dari; *bigger* ~
lebih besar daripada

thank *v* mengucapkan terima
kasih; ~ *God Isl* alhamdulillah;
Chr puji Tuhan; ~ *goodness*
syukur; ~ *you* terima kasih;
thankful *adj* berterima kasih;
thanks *coll* terima kasih,
makasih; ~ *to* berkat; ~ *very*
much terima kasih banyak;
Thanksgiving *n* hari pernyataan terima kasih (di Amerika
Utara)

that *pron* **those** itu; ~ *way* begitu; ke arah sana; *conj* bahwa;
yang; supaya; ~*'s all* sekian; ~*'s*

~ habis perkara; *Bill said ~ he was coming* Bill mengatakan bahwa dia akan datang; *the house ~ Jack built* rumah yang dibangun Jack

thatch *n* jerami, rumbia; *~ed cottage* rumah beratap jerami

thaw *n* cair; *v* mencair, menjadi cair

the *art* itu, -nya

theater *n* (gedung) teater; *movie ~* (gedung) bioskop

thee *pron, Chr, arch* engkau, kamu

theft *n* pencurian ← **thief**

their *pron, poss, pl* [thér] **theirs** mereka (punya), milik mereka; **them** *pron, obj, pl* mereka; **themselves** *pron, pl* mereka sendiri

theme *n* tema, pokok

then *adv* pada waktu itu; *conj* sesudah itu, kemudian, lalu; maka; *n* waktu itu

theology *n* [thioloji] teologi

theoretical *adj* [thiorétikel] teoritis, menurut teori; **theory** *n* teori

therapeutic *adj* [thérapyutik] bersifat menyembuhkan atau mengobatkan; **therapist** *n* ahli; psikolog ← **psychotherapist**; **therapy** *n* terapi

there *adv* [thér] (di) situ; (di) sana; *~ and back* pulang pergi; *ejac* nah; *n* sana; itu; *~ is, ~ are* ada; *~ you are* silahkan, itu dia; **thereabouts** *adv* kira-kira, kurang lebih; **thereby** *adv* dengan (cara) demikian; **therefore** *conj* maka, oleh sebab itu

thermal *adj* berkaitan dengan panas

thermometer *n* termometer

thermos *n* [thérmes] termos

thermostat *n* alat pengatur panas, termostat

thesaurus *n* [tesorus] sejenis semacam kamus

these *pron, pl* ini ← **this**

thesis *n* **theses** [thisis] skripsi, disertasi, tesis; dalil

they *pron, pl* [thé] mereka

thick *adj* gemuk; tebal; kental; *coll* bodoh; *~-skinned* berkulit badak; *in the ~ of* ditengah-tengah; *through ~ and thin* dalam suka dan duka; **thickness** *n* ketebalan, kekentalan

thief *n* [thif] **thieves** pencuri, maling; **thieve** *v* mencuri

thigh *n* [thai] paha

thimble *n* [thimbel] bidal, sarung jari

thin *adj* kurus; tipis; encer; *through thick and ~* dalam suka dan duka

thine *pron, Chr, arch, poss* kepunyaan engkau

thing *n* barang, benda, alat; *just the ~* inilah dia; *the ~ is* soalnya

think *v* **thought thought** [thot] pikir, berpikir; berpendapat; *~ about* memikirkan; *~ over* menimbang, mempertimbangkan; *~ing of you* saya ingat kepada anda; *to have a good ~* berpikir baik-baik; **thinker** *n* pemikir

thinner *adj* lebih kurus, lebih tipis; *n* bahan pengencer, tener ← **thin**

third *adj, n* ketiga; pertiga; ~ *degree* penyiksaan; pemeriksaan yang melelahkan; ~ *party* pihak ketiga; ~ *person* orang ketiga; ~ *world* dunia ketiga; *two-~s* dua pertiga; **thirdly** *adv, conj* (yang) ketiga

thirst *n* kehausan, dahaga; *v* ~ *for* haus akan; **thirsty** *adj* haus

thirteen *adj, n* tiga belas; **thirteenth** *adj* ketiga belas; *Friday the* ~ Jumat tanggal tiga belas (dianggap angker)

thirtieth *adj* ketiga puluh; **thirty** *adj, n* tiga puluh

this *pron* **these** ini; ~ *evening* nanti malam; malam ini; ~ *morning* tadi pagi; pagi ini

thong *n* celana dalam berbentuk tali; **thongs** *n, pl* sandal jepit

thorax *n* dada, toraks

thorn *n* duri; **thorny** *adj* berduri; sulit

thorough *adj* [thoro] teliti, cermat; **thoroughly** *adv* dengan teliti

thoroughbred *n* [thorobréd] kuda trah

thoroughfare *n* [thorofér] jalan

those *pron, pl* itu ← **this**; ~ *who* mereka yang, barangsiapa yang

thou *pron, arch, Chr* kamu, engkau

though *adv* [tho] bagaimanapun; *conj* sungguhpun, meskipun, biarpun; *even* ~ walaupun

thought *n* [thot] pikiran, ide; *v,*

pf → **think**; *in my* ~*s* dalam doa saya; **thoughtful** *adj* penuh perhatian; **thoughtless** *adj* tidak ingat; lalai

thousand *adj, n* ribu; *one* ~, *a* ~ seribu; *the* ~ *Islands* Pulau Seribu

thrash *v* menggelepar-gelepar; mencambuk; **thrashing** *n* dicambuk

thread *n* [thréd] benang; urutan; *v* ~ *a needle* memasang benang

threat *n* [thrét] ancaman; **threaten** *v* mengancam; ~*ed* terancam

three *adj, n* tiga; ~ *quarters* tiga perempat; **threesome** *n* kelompok tiga orang

thresher *n* mesin pengirik

threshold *n* ambang, batas

threw *v, pf* → **throw**

thrift *n* penghematan; **thrifty** *adj* hemat, irit

thrill *n* getaran (jiwa); sensasi; *v* menggetarkan; ~*ed* berdebar hati; **thriller** *n* film atau buku yang menyeramkan; **thrilling** *adj* menggetarkan

thrive *v* tumbuh dengan subur, berkembang dengan cepat

throat *n* tenggorokan, kerongkongan; *ear, nose and* ~ *specialist* dokter THT (telinga, hidung dan tenggorokan); *at each other's* ~ selalu berkelahi; **throaty** *adj* parau

throb *n* debar, denyut; denyutan; *heart* ~ idola; *v* berdebar, berdenyut-denyut

throne *n* takhta, singgasana

through *adj* [thru] selesai; *adv* terus; *prep* melalui, melewati, oleh, karena, terus; ~ *and* ~ benar-benar; *no* ~ *road* jalan buntu; *to go* ~ *a lot* mengalami banyak kesulitan, banyak menderita; **throughout** *prep* di mana-mana; sepanjang

throw *v* **threw thrown** *n* lemparan; *a stone's* ~ sangat dekat; *v* membuang, melemparkan; ~ *on* memakai baju (dengan tergesa-gesa); ~ *out,* ~ *away* membuang (sampah); ~ *up* muntah; ~ *a party* mengadakan pesta; **throwaway** *adj* tidak berarti; **throwback** *adj* warisan ciri-ciri dari leluhur

thrush *n* keputihan; sejenis burung murai

thrust *n* daya dorong; serangan; tusukan; *v* mendorongkan; menyerang; menusuk

thud *n* gedebuk; *v* bergedebuk

thumb *n* [tham] jempol, ibu jari; ~ *tack* paku payung; ~*s-up* tanda setuju; *v* membaca sepintas lalu (buku); **thumbnail** *n* kuku jempol; ~ *sketch* gambar sederhana; **thumbprint** *n* cap jempol

thump *n* gebukan; bunyi gedebuk; *v* menggebuk; berdebar (hati, jantung)

thunder *n* gemuruh, geluduk; **thunderbolt, thunderclap** *n* petir; **thundercloud** *n* awan hujan; **thunderstorm** *n* gemuruh dan petir; **thunderstruck** *adj* seperti disambar petir, terheran-heran

Thursday *adj, n* (hari) Kamis

thus *conj, arch* maka; ~ *far* selama ini; sampai sekarang, hingga kini

thy *pron, poss, arch, Chr* mu, kepunyaan engkau

thyme *n* [taim] sejenis rempah

thyroid ~ *gland* kelenjar gondok

tiara *n* mahkota kecil, tiara

Tibet *n* Tibet; **Tibetan** *adj* berasal dari Tibet; orang Tibet

tick *n* tanda √; detik; kutu (binatang); *v* berdetik; ~ *off* mencoret satu per satu; menegur, memarahi

ticket *n* karcis, tiket; *plane* ~ tiket pesawat; *train* ~ karcis kereta api; ~ *collector* kondektur; ~ *office* loket; *speeding* ~ tilang; **ticketholder** *n* pemilik karcis (langganan)

tickle *v* [tikel] menggelitik; ~*d pink* senang sekali; **ticklish** *adj* geli

tidal *adj* berhubungan dengan air pasang dan surut; ~ *wave* gelombang pasang; **tide** *high* ~, ~*'s in* air pasang; *low* ~, ~*'s out* air surut; *to turn the* ~ mengubah arus

tidings *n* berita, kabar, salam

tidy *adj* apik, rapi; *n* tempat menyimpan barang; *v* merapikan; ~ *up* merapikan, memberes-beres

tie *n* tali, ikat; dasi; pertalian; seri; ~ *pin* tusuk dasi, jepitan dasi; ~*-dyed* jumputan; ~*-in* hubungan; *hair* ~ ikat rambut; ~*s of friendship* tali persahabatan; *v* mengikat; ~ *in* bersambung, menyambung

tiger *n* harimau, macan

tight *adj* [tait] erat, tegang, ketat; *coll* sukar, sulit; ~ *pants* celana ketat; ~ *squeeze* keadaan terjepit; ~-*fisted* pelit; ~-*lipped* terdiam; **tighten** *v* mengeratkan, mengetatkan; **tightrope** *n* tali akrobat; **tights** *n* stoking tebal

tile *n* ubin, tegel; genteng; *floor* ~ ubin; *roof* ~ genteng; *v* memasang ubin, genteng

till *conj, coll* sampai, sehingga

till *n* laci uang; *v* bercocok tanam

tiller *n* pasak kemudi

tilt *n* kemiringan; *full* ~ secepat-cepatnya; *v* miring; memiringkan

timber *n* kayu (bahan bangunan)

time *n* waktu, masa; kali; ~ *bomb* bom waktu; ~-*consuming* memakan waktu; ~ *limit* batas waktu; ~ *off* waktu cuti, istirahat; ~ *out* istirahat (olahraga); ~ *zone* zona waktu, wilayah waktu; *it's* ~ sudah waktunya; *for the* ~ *being* untuk sementara; *in* ~ sebelum waktunya; *on* ~ tepat waktu; *that* ~ waktu itu; ~ *after* ~ berkali-kali; *a good* ~ pengalaman yang menyenangkan; *all the* ~ selalu, senantiasa; sejak semula; *all this* ~ selama ini; *at a* ~ sekaligus; *to have* ~ sempat, ada waktu; *to pass* ~ iseng, mengisi waktu; *to serve* ~

dipenjara; *to take* ~ memakan waktu; *what* ~ *is it* pukul berapa; *v* mencatat waktu; **timekeeper** *n* pencatat waktu; **times** kali; *two* ~ *three equals six* dua kali tiga sama dengan enam; ~ *table* perkalian; **timeless** *adj* tidak kenal waktu, abadi; **timely** *adj* pada waktunya; **timepiece** *n* jam; **timer** *n* jam (pasir), pencatat waktu; **timesaving** *adj* menghemat waktu; **timetable** *n* jadwal

timid *adj* [timid] malu-malu, takut-takut

tin *n* timah; kaleng; ~ *opener* pembuka kaleng; *v* mengalengkan; **tinfoil** *n* kertas perak

tinker *n* tukang patri; *v* mengutak-atik, main-main

tinsel *n* kertas ermas

tint *n* warna; *v* memberi warna

tiny *adj* [taini] kecil sekali, mungil

tip *n* ujung; uang rokok, tip; saran, tips; tempat pembuangan akhir (TPA); *v* memberi tip; menumpahkan; memutar-balikkan; *no* ~*ping* dilarang memberi tip; ~-*off* informasi rahasia

tipsy *adj* sedikit mabuk

tiptoe *v* jalan berjinjit; *on* ~ berjinjit, berjingkat

tire, tyre *n* ban; *spare* ~ ban serep

tire *v* menjadi lelah; melelahkan; **tired** *adj* lelah, capek, letih; ~ *of* bosan, jenuh; **tireless** *adj* tidak tahu lelah; **tiresome** *adj* membosankan, mengganggu

tissue *n* tisu; jaringan

tit ~ *for tat* balas dendam, balas-membalas

title *n* [taitel] gelar; judul; **title-holder** *n* pemegang gelar, juara bertahan

T-junction *n* pertigaan, simpang tiga

to *prep* [tu] ke, kepada; untuk; lawan; ~ *and fro* bolak-balik; *five (minutes)* ~ *three* jam tiga kurang lima (menit)

toad *n* katak, kodok; **toadstool** *n* cendawan, jamur payung

toast *n* sulangan; *v* bersulang; ~ *of the town* dipuji semua orang

toast *n* roti panggang; *v* memanggang; **toaster** *n* alat pemanggang roti

tobacco *n* tembakau; **tobacconist** *n* toko tembakau

toboggan *n* kereta peluncur; *v* main kereta peluncur

today *adv, n* [tudé] hari ini; (masa) kini

toddler *n* (anak) batita (bawah tiga tahun)

toe *n* [to] jari kaki; ujung (kaus kaki); ~ *hold* tumpuan kaki; *baby* ~ kelingking kaki; *big* ~ jempol kaki; *v* ~ *the line* mematuhi, menurut; **toenail** *n* kuku jari kaki

toga *n* jubah

together *adv* [tugéther] bersama, bersama-sama; **togetherness** *n* rasa kebersamaan

Togo *n* Togo; **Togolese** *adj* berasal dari Togo; *n* orang Togo

toil *n* kerja keras; *v* bekerja keras, membanting tulang

toilet *n* kamar kecil, WC; kloset; ~ *paper* tisu gulung; ~ *training* anak kecil belajar menggunakan WC; ~ *water* wewangian; air kloset; *women's* ~ WC wanita; **toiletries** *n, pl* perlengkapan mandi, alat-alat kecantikan

token *n* tanda (penghargaan), tanda masuk; ~ *gesture* basa-basi; *by the same* ~ sama, begitu pula

tolerance *n* toleransi, kesabaran; **tolerant** *adj* tenggang rasa, toleran, sabar; **tolerate** *v* sabar menghadapi, tahan, menerima

toll *n* tol, bea; jumlah korban; bunyi lonceng; ~ *road* jalan tol; *road* ~ korban kecelakaan; **tollgate** *n* pintu tol, gerbang tol

tomato *n* **tomatoes** tomat; ~ *sauce* saus tomat

tomb *n* [tum] kuburan, makam

tomboy *n* gadis yang bersifat laki-laki

tombstone *n* [tumston] batu nisan ← **tomb**

tomcat *n* kucing jantan

tomorrow *adv, n* [tumoro] besok, esok (hari); masa depan; *the day after* ~ lusa

ton *n, arch* [tan] ton; *a* ~ *of* banyak; **tonne** *n* [ton] ton (1.000 kg)

tone *n* bunyi, nada; warna, rona; *ring* ~ nada dering; *v* ~ *down* mengurangi (sifat)

Tonga *n* Tonga; **Tongan** *adj* berasal dari Tonga; *n* bahasa Tonga; orang Tonga

tongs *n, pl* jepitan

tongue *n* [tang] lidah; bahasa; ~-*tied* kehabisan kata, membisu; ~ *twister* ucapan ketangkasan lidah; *mother* ~ bahasa ibu; *to hold your* ~ tutup mulut, diam

tonight *adv, n* [tunait] malam ini, nanti malam

tonsillitis *n* radang amandel; **tonsils** *n, pl* amandel

too *adv* terlalu, terlampau; sekali; juga; ~ *fast* terlalu cepat; ~ *late* terlambat; ~ *much* keterlaluan, kebanyakan

took *v, pf* → **take**

tool *n* alat, perkakas; **tools** *n, pl* peralatan; *gardening* ~ peralatan kebun; **toolbox** *n* tempat peralatan

toot *n* tet, bunyi klakson; *v* membunyikan klakson, mengklakson

tooth *n* **teeth** gigi; **toothache** *n* [tuthék] sakit gigi; **toothbrush** *n* sikat gigi; **toothless** *adj* ompong; **toothpaste** *n* pasta gigi; **toothpick** *n* tusuk gigi

top *adj* atas; teratas, terbaik, tertinggi; ~ *brass* perwira tinggi; ~ *hat* topi tinggi; ~ *secret* sangat rahasia; ~ *speed* kecepatan tertinggi, secepat-cepatnya; *n* puncak, (bagian) atas, ujung; tutup; gasing; ~-*heavy* berat di atas; *over the* ~ keterlaluan; *v* melebihi

topaz *n* ratna cempaka

topic *n* topik, isu; **topical** *adj* hangat

topless *adj* dengan dada terbuka ← **top**

topping *n* saus, lapisan atas ← **top**

topple *v* [topel] tumbang; menjatuhkan

topsoil *n* lapisan atas tanah

topsy-turvy *adj, adv* kacau-balau

torch *n* obor, suluh; senter; ~ *song* lagu cinta; *v* membakar

tore *v, pf* → **tear**

torment *n* siksaan, kesengsaraan; *v* menyiksa, menyengsarakan

torn *v, pf* → **tear**

torpedo *n* [torpido] torpedo; *v* menorpedo, menenggelamkan

torrent *n* aliran air yang deras, semburan; **torrential** *adj* lebat, deras

torso *n* batang tubuh

tortoise *n* [tortes] kura-kura; ~-*shell* (corak seperti) kulit kura-kura; ~-*shell cat* kucing tiga warna

torture *n* siksaan; *v* menyiksa

toss *n* lemparan; *to win the* ~ memenangkan undian (olahraga); *v* melemparkan, melontarkan, melambungkan; mengundi

total *adj* sama sekali, seluruh; *n* jumlah, total; **totalitarian** *adj* totaliter; **totally** *adv* sama sekali, secara total

touch *n* [tac] sentuhan, nuansa; ~ *football* semacam rugby tanpa kontak fisik; *finishing* ~ sentuhan terakhir; *in* ~ berhubungan; tahu; *a* ~ *of* sedikit; *to lose* ~ kehilangan hubungan; *v* menyentuh, menyinggung, mengenai; *--type* mengetik tanpa melihat papan tuts; *~ up* memperbaiki; menggerayangi; *--and-go* hampir-hampir; **touching** *adj* bersentuhan; mengharukan; **touchy** *adj* cepat marah

tough *adj* [taf] kasar; liat, alot, awet; *~ guy* orang kuat; *~ luck* sayang sekali; **toughen** *v* menguatkan, memperkuat

tour *n* tamasya, tur, perjalanan, pelayaran; *~ guide* pemandu wisata; *v* mengikuti tur, menjelajahi; **tourism** *n* wisata, pariwisata, turisme; **tourist** *n* wisatawan, turis; *~ brochure* brosur pariwisata; *domestic ~* wisnu (wisatawan nusantara); *foreign ~* wisman (wisatawan mancanegara)

tournament *n* kejuaraan, pertandingan, turnamen

tow *v* [to] menarik, menderek; *--truck* mobil derek

toward [tuwod] **towards** *prep* ke (arah); kepada, akan, untuk; terhadap; menjelang, menuju

towel *n* [taul] handuk; *~ rack* rak handuk; *hand ~* lap; *v ~ down* mengelap badan (sesudah berolahraga); *to throw in the ~* putus asa, berhenti

tower *n* [tauer] menara; *v* menjulang tinggi

town *n* kota; *~ hall* balai kota; *~ square* alun-alun; *country ~* kota kecil di pedalaman; *in ~* sedang di kota; *out of ~* keluar

kota; *to go into ~* pergi ke kota; *~ planner* planolog; *~ planning* planologi; **township** *n* kota

toxic *adj* beracun; **toxin** *n* racun, toksin

toy *n* mainan

trace *n* bekas, jejak; *v* merunut, mengikuti jejak, memetakan; meniru (di atas kertas)

track *n* jejak, tapak jalan; *~ event* olahraga lari; *~ and field* olahraga lari, lompat dan lempar; *athletics ~* lintasan lari; *on the right ~* di jalan yang benar; *v* mengikuti jejak; **tracker** *n* alat atau orang yang mengikuti jejak

tractor *n* traktor

trade *n* niaga, perniagaan, perdagangan; *~ fair* pameran (perdagangan); *~ secret* rahasia (yang hanya dikenal di lingkungan tertentu); *~ union* serikat kerja, serikat buruh; *the rag ~* industri busana; *v* berdagang, berbisnis; bertukar; tukar-menukar; *~ in* tukar tambah; *~ places* bertukaran tempat; **trademark** *n* merek dagang; **trader** *n* pedagang; **tradesman** *n* tukang

tradition *n* [tradisyen] adat (istiadat), tradisi; **traditional** *adj* menurut adat, tradisional; *~ dance* tari adat

traffic *n* lalu lintas; peredaran, perdagangan; *~ jam* kemacetan lalu lintas; *~ light* lampu merah, lampu lalu lintas; *v* mengedarkan; **trafficker** *n* pengedar narkoba; **trafficking** *n* pengedaran tragedy *n* [trajedi] cerita sedih; kecelakaan; **tragic** *adj* tragis, menyedihkan

trail *n* tapak jalan, bekas, jejak; ~ *bike* (sepeda) motor gunung; *v* mengikuti jejak; **trailblazer** *n* pelopor, perintis; **trailer** *n* kendaraan gandengan

train *n* kereta api; *by* ~ dengan kereta api, naik kereta api; ~ *of thought* jalan pikiran; *v* melatih; **trainee** *adj* calon; *n* orang yang ikut latihan, orang yang magang; **trainer** *n* pelatih; **training** *n* latihan, pelatihan, pendidikan; *education and* ~ pendidikan dan pelatihan (diklat)

traitor *n* pengkhianat

trajectory *n* jalan peluru

tram *n* trem

tramp *n* gelandangan, orang gila; *v* mendaki gunung, berjalan kaki di alam bebas

trample *v* [trampel] menginjak-injak

trance *n* kerasukan, keadaan tidak sadar diri

tranquil *adj* tenang, teduh; **tranquility** *n* ketenangan; **tranquilizer** *n* obat penenang

trans- *pref* lintas, melalui

transaction *n* transaksi

transcribe *v* menyalin; **transcription** *n* salinan

transfer *n* pemindahan, mutasi; *v* memindahkan

transform *v* berubah bentuk; **transformation** *n* perubahan bentuk, transformasi; **transformer** *n* travo

transfusion *n* transfusi; *blood* ~ transfusi darah

transit *in* ~ dalam perjalanan; ~ *lounge* ruang tunggu

transition *n* peralihan, transisi

transitive *adj* transitif, mempunyai obyek

translate *v* menerjemahkan; **translation** *n* terjemahan, penerjemahan; **translator** *n* penerjemah

translucent *adj* tembus cahaya

transmigration *n* transmigrasi

transmission *n* pengiriman, penyiaran, penyebaran, transmisi; **transmit** *v* mengirimkan, menyiarkan, memancarkan; **transmitter** *n* pemancar

transparency *overhead* ~ *(OHT)* transparensi; **transparent** *adj* bening, tembus cahaya

transplant *n* cangkok, pencangkokan; *v* mencangkokkan

transport *n* angkutan, pengangkutan, transportasi; *public* ~ angkutan umum; *v* mengangkut, membawa; **transportation** *n* transportasi

transvestite *n* bencong, banci

trap *n* perangkap, jerat, jebakan; *v* memerangkap, menjerat, menjebak; **trapdoor** *n* pintu di lantai atau plafon

trash *n* sampah; ~ *can* tempat sampah; **trashy** *adj* murahan

trauma *n* [troma] pengalaman buruk, trauma; **traumatic** *adj* traumatis

travel *v* jalan, berjalan, bepergian; ~ *agent* biro perjalanan;

~ *guide* buku panduan wisata; **travels** *n, pl* perjalanan-perjalanan; **traveler** *n* orang yang sedang dalam perjalanan, musafir; ~'*s checks* cek perjalanan

trawler *n* kapal pukat

tray *n* dulang; baki

treacherous *adj* [trécerus] bersifat pengkhianat; sangat berbahaya; **treachery** *n* [tréceri] pengkhianatan

tread *n* [tréd] alas sepatu, telapak (ban); *v* **trod trodden** menginjak, memijak; **treadle** *n* pedal, tempat injakan kaki; **treadmill** *n* mesin latihan jalan atau lari

treason *n* [trizon] pengkhianatan

treasure *n* [trésyur] barang berharga tinggi; *buried* ~ harta karun

treasurer *n* [trésyurer] bendahara; Menteri Keuangan; **treasury** *n* perbendaharaan; Departemen Keuangan

treat *n* [trit] sesuatu yang menyenangkan; *my* ~ saya yang traktir; *v* mengobati; memperlakukan; **treatment** *n* pengobatan, perawatan; perlakuan

treaty *n* [triti] pakta, perjanjian

tree *n* pohon; ~ *house* rumah di pohon, rumah mainan; ~-*lined* dipagari pohon; **treetops** *n, pl* puncak pohon

trek *n* perjalanan (yang jauh dan melelahkan); *v* berjalan jauh, mendaki gunung

trellis *n* terali, jari-jari

tremble *n* gemetar, getaran; *v* bergetar, gemetar

tremendous *adj* [treméndus] hebat, dahsyat

tremor *n* gemetaran; gempa bumi

trench *n* parit; ~ *coat* jas hujan (tentara)

trend *n* mode, gaya, tren; kecenderungan; **trendy** *adj* gaya, bergaya, modis

trepidation *n* [trépidésyen] rasa segan, ragu-ragu bercampur takut

trespass *v* memasuki tempat tanpa izin; *no* ~*ing* dilarang masuk; **trespasser** *n* orang yang masuk tanpa izin

trestle *n* [trésel] kuda-kuda; ~ *bridge* jembatan dari batang-batang besi atau kayu

trial *n* [trail] sidang pengadilan, proses; percobaan; ~ *period* masa percobaan; ~ *run* percobaan; *on* ~ sedang diadili; ~ *and error* mencoba-coba; *v* menguji

triangle *n* [trayanggel] segi tiga; kerincing; *right-angled* ~ segi tiga siku-siku; **triangular** *adj* berbentuk segi tiga

tribal *adj* suku (bangsa), kesukuan; **tribe** *n* suku (bangsa)

tribunal *n* [traibunal] dewan pengadilan

tributary *n* [tributeri] anak sungai

tribute *n* penghargaan; upeti

trick *n* tipu daya; permainan; *to play a* ~ *on* mempermainkan; *v* menipu; **trickster** *n* penipu; **tricky** *adj* sulit, rumit tricycle n [traisikel] sepeda roda tiga

trigger n [triger] pelatuk, picu, pemicu; ~-happy terlalu cepat bertindak; v memicu, menyebabkan

trigonometry n ilmu ukur segi tiga, trigonometri

trillion adj, n trilyun (1 000 000 000 000)

trilogy n [trileji] seri tiga serangkai, trilogi

trim adj langsing, rapi; n potong sedikit; garis hiasan; v menggunting; menghiasi

trinket n (barang) perhiasan kecil dan murah

trip n perjalanan; business ~ perjalanan dinas; v tersandung; menjebloskan

tripe n babat; sl omong kosong

triple adj [tripel] lipat tiga; n rangkap tiga; v berkembang tiga kali lipat; **triplet** n kembar tiga

tripod n [traipod] (tumpuan) kaki tiga, tripod

triumph n [trayemf] kemenangan, keberhasilan; v menang, berhasil; **triumphant** adj dengan jaya

trivial adj [triviel] sepele, tidak berarti

trod, trodden v, pf → **tread**

trolley n kereta dorong, troli; ~ bus bis listrik

trombone n trombon

troop n pasukan; v jalan ramai-ramai; **trooper** n polisi

trophy n [trofi] piala

tropic the ~s daerah khatulistiwa, daerah tropis; ~ of Capricorn garis balik selatan; **tropical** adj tropis

trot n lari derap, lari kecil; v berderap, menderap

trouble n [trabel] kesusahan, kesulitan; gangguan; kerusakan; repot; kidney ~ sakit ginjal; ~-shooting mencari dan memecahkan kesulitan; v membuat kuatir; menyusahkan; **troublemaker** n pengacau; **troublesome** adj menyusahkan

trough n [trof] palung; titik rendah

troupe n [trup] rombongan (pemain); **trouper** n anggota rombongan, pemain

trousers n, pl [trauzerz] celana panjang

trousseau n [truso] pakaian dan perlengkapan lain milik pengantin wanita

trout n semacam ikan air tawar

truant to play ~ membolos sekolah

truce n gencatan senjata

truck n truk; dump ~ truk sampah; **trucker** n supir truk

true adj [tru] benar, betul, sungguh; setia; ~ blue setia, tulus; ~-life story kisah nyata; ~ to his word setia pada janjinya; **truly** adv sesungguhnya, sungguh-sungguh; yours ~ salam hormat

trumpet n trompet; ~ player pemain trompet

trunk n belalai; batang (tubuh); arch koper; swimming ~s baju renang

trust n kepercayaan; in ~ sebagai

titipan; *v* percaya akan, mempercayai; **trustee** *n* wakil, wali; **trustworthy** *adj* andal, terpercaya; **trusty** *adj* setia

truth *n* [truth] kebenaran; *in* ~ sebenarnya; *some* ~ ada benarnya; *to tell the* ~ mengatakan dengan jujur; **truthful** *adj* jujur

try *n* usaha, percobaan; *v* mencoba, berusaha; ~ *on* coba memakai baju; ~ *out* ikut seleksi; orang yang terlalu ingin diterima oleh kalangan tertentu; **tryout** *n* seleksi, percobaan

T-shirt *n* kaus (oblong) ← **T**

tub *n* bak mandi

tubby *adj* gendut, tambun

tube *n* tabung; pipa, pembuluh; *inner* ~ ban dalam; *the* ~ *sl* kereta api bawah tanah di London

tuber *n* akar umbi, ubi

tuberculosis *n* radang paru-paru, tebese, TBC

tuck *n* lipatan; *tummy* ~ bedah untuk melangsingkan perut; *v* melipat, menyimpan, memasukkan; ~ *in* memasukkan baju ke dalam celana

Tuesday *adj, n* [Tyusdé] (hari) Selasa

tug *n* sentakan, tarikan; *v* menarik, menyentak; ~-*of-war* tarik tambang; **tugboat** *n* kapal penarik

tuition *n* [tuwisyen] pengajaran; uang belajar

tulip *n* bunga tulip, tulpen

tumble *n, v* [tambel] jatuh terguling-guling

tumbler *n* gelas minum

tummy *n, coll* perut

tumor *n* benjolan, tumbuhan, tumor; *benign* ~ tumor jinak; ~ tumor ganas

tuna *n* ikan tongkol

tune *n* bunyi, lagu; melodi; *out of* ~ tidak selaras; *v* menyetel; menala; ~ *in* ikut mendengar; ~ *out* berhenti mendengar; ~ *up* menyetel (mesin), memperbaiki; **tuning** ~ *fork* garpu tala, penala

Tunisia *n* Tunisia; **Tunisian** *adj* berasal dari Tunisia; *n* orang Tunisia

tunnel *n* terowongan; *v* menggali terowongan atau lubang

turban *n* serban

turbine *n* [terbain] turbin

turbulence *n* pergolakan; cuaca buruk; **turbulent** *adj* bergolak

turf *n* tanah berumput

Turk *n* orang Turki; *young* ~ pemuda, orang muda yang bersemangat; **Turkey** *n* Turki

turkey *n* kalkun

Turkish *adj* berasal dari Turki; ~ *delight* sejenis agar-agar; *n* bahasa Turki; orang Turki

Turkmen *adj* berasal dari Turkmenistan; *n* bahasa Turkmen; orang Turkmenistan; **Turkmenistan** *n* Turkmenistan

turn *n* putaran; giliran; belok; *a good* ~ perbuatan baik; *v* berputar, membelok, menoleh; memutar, membalikkan; ~ *away* menolak; ~ *down* menolak; mengecilkan; ~ *into* berubah menjadi; ~ *off* mematikan; ~ *on* menghidupkan; ~ *heads* membuat pusing, menarik perhatian; ~ *up* muncul; menemukan; ~ *the tide* mengubah arus; ~ *your stomach* memuakkan; ~ *of the century* pergantian abad; **turncoat** *n* pembelot, pengkhianat

turnip *n* lobak cina

turnoff *n* pintu keluar (jalan tol) ← **turn**

turnout *n* jumlah hadirin ← **turn**

turnover *n* penjualan, omzet; pergantian ← **turn**

turnstile *n* pagar putar ← **turn**

turpentine *n* [térpentain] **turps** *coll* terpentin

turquoise *adj* [térkoiz] biru toska; *n* (batu) pirus

turtle *n* kura-kura, penyu; ~*-neck* berleher tinggi; **turtledove** *n* perkutut

tusk *n* gading

tutor *n* guru pribadi; wali kelas; *v* memberi les privat kepada; **tutorial** *n* kelas diskusi

Tuvalu *n* Tuvalu; **Tuvaluan** *adj* berasal dari Tuvalu; *n* bahasa Tuvalu; orang Tuvalu

tux *n, coll* **tuxedo** *n* [taksido] setelan pakaian malam pria

TV *abbrev* *television* teve, tivi, TV (televisi)

tweezers *n, pl* pinset, penyepit

twelfth *adj* kedua belas; **twelve** *adj, n* dua belas

twentieth *adj* kedua puluh; **twenty** *adj, n* dua puluh

twice *adv* dua kali; *to think* ~ berpikir baik-baik

twig *n* ranting

twilight *adj, n* [twailait] senjakala

twin *n* kembar; ~ *sister* saudara kembar

twine *n* benang ikat

twinkle *n* kelip; *v* berkedipkedip, berbinar-binar; *in the twinkling of an eye* dalam sekejap mata

twist *n* tikungan; pelintir; putaran; *v* memutar, memintal, menganyam; **twisted** *adj* terpelintir; sinting; **twister** *n* angin puyuh

two *adj, n* [tu] dua; ~*-edged* bermata dua; ~*-faced* munafik; ~*-legged* berkaki dua; ~*-timer* orang dengan lebih dari satu pacar; ~*-tone* berwarna dua; ~*-way* dua arah

tycoon *n* [taikun] hartawan, taipan

type *n* macam, jenis, bentuk, tipe; golongan; huruf cetak; *bold* ~ huruf tebal; *v* mengetik; *to touch-*~ mengetik tanpa melihat; **typecast typecast** *adj* **typecast** menetapkan sebagai tipe tertentu; **typewriter** *n, arch* mesin tik

typing *n* bahan untuk diketik; ~ *school* sekolah mengetik; **typist** *n* juru ketik ← **type**

typhoid *n* [taifoid] ~ *(fever)* tifus, tipus

typhoon *n* [taifun] (angin) topan

typist *n* juru ketik

typo *n* [taipo] kesalahan cetak

tyrannical *adj* [tiranikel] kejam; **tyranny** *n* kekejaman, tirani; **tyrant** *n* orang yang kejam

tyre → **tire**

U

UAE *abbrev United Arab Emirates* UEA (Uni Emirat Arab)

ubiquitous *adj* [yubikuitus] (ada) di mana-mana

udder *n* ambing

UFO *abbrev unidentified flying object* piring terbang

Uganda *n* [Yuganda] Uganda; **Ugandan** *adj* berasal dari Uganda; *n* orang Uganda

ugliness *n* [aglines] penampilan yang buruk; **ugly** *adj* buruk (rupa), jelek; ~ *as sin* sangat jelek

UHF *abbrev ultra-high frequency* UHF

UK *abbrev United Kingdom* Kerajaan Inggris

ukulele *n* [yukelélé] gitar kecil, ukulele

Ukraine *n* [Yukrén] *(the)* ~ Ukraina; **Ukrainian** *adj* berasal dari Ukraina; *n* bahasa Ukraina; orang Ukraina

ulcer *n* bisul, borok; *mouth* ~ sariawan; *peptic* ~ borok usus

ultimate *adj* [altimet] terakhir, penghabisan, mutakhir; paling (mewah); pokok; **ultimately** *adv* pada akhirnya

ultimatum *n* [altimétem] ultimatum

ultra- *pref* [altra] teramat sangat; **ultramarine** *adj, n* [altramarin] biru laut; **ultraviolet** *adj* [altravayolet] ~ *rays* sinar UV

um *interj* anu, er

umbilical ~ *cord* tali ari-ari, tali pusar

umbrella *n* payung; ~ *stand* tempat payung

umpire *n* wasit

UN *abbrev United Nations* PBB (Persatuan Bangsa-Bangsa)

un- *pref* tidak, tak

unable *adj* [anébel] tidak mampu, tidak dapat, tidak bisa ← **able**

unabridged [anabrijd] ~ *dictionary* kamus lengkap ← **abridge**

unacceptable *adj* [anakséptabel] tidak dapat diterima ← **accept**

unaffected *adj* [anafékted] tidak terpengaruh ← **affect**

unaided *adj* [anéded] tanpa bantuan ← **aid**

unanimous *adj* [yunanimus] **unanimously** *adv* dengan suara bulat, secara aklamasi

unappetizing *adj* [anapetaizing] (tampak) tidak enak, tidak membangkitkan selera

unappreciated *adj* [anaprisyiéted] tidak dihargai ← **appreciate**

unapproachable *adj* [anaproca-bel] tidak dapat didekati, tidak ramah ← **approach**

unarmed *adj* [anarmd] tidak bersenjata ← **arm**

unashamed *adj* [anasyémd] tanpa merasa malu; **unashamedly** *adv* [anasyémedli] dengan tidak merasa malu ← **ashamed**

unassuming *adj* [anasyuming] sederhana, bersahaja

unattached *adj* [anatacd] sendiri, belum kawin; tidak terikat ← **attach**

unattended *adj* [anaténded] tanpa pengawasan ← **attend**

unauthorized *adj* [anothoraizd] tanpa wewenang, tidak sah ← **authorize**

unavoidable *adj* [anavoidabel] tidak dapat dihindarkan, tidak dapat dielakkan ← **avoid**

unaware *adj* [anawér] tidak sadar, tidak menyadari; **unawares** *adv* tiba-tiba; secara tak terduga ← **aware**

unbalanced *adj* tidak waras

unbearable *adj* [anbérabel] tak tertahankan ← **bear**

unbeatable *adj* [anbitabel] tak terkalahkan, tidak dapat dikalahkan; **unbeaten** *adj* belum pernah dikalahkan ← **beat**

unbecoming *adj* [anbekaming] tidak pantas

unbeknownst *adj* [anbenonst] tanpa diketahui; ~ *to me* tanpa sepengetahuan saya ← **know**

unbelievable *adj* [anbelivabel] tidak dapat dipercaya, bukan main; **unbeliever** *n* kafir, orang yang tidak beriman; **unbelieving** *adj* tidak percaya ← **believe**

unbiased *adj* [anbayesd] tidak memihak, berimbang ← **biased**

unbleached *adj* [anblicd] tidak diputihkan ← **bleach**

unbolt *v* membuka (kunci selot) ← **bolt**

unborn *adj* belum lahir; ~ *baby,* ~ *child* janin ← **born**

unbreakable *adj* [anbrékabel] anti pecah, tahan banting; **unbroken** *adj* tidak terputus-putus, terus menerus ← **break**

uncalled [angkold] ~ *for* tidak beralasan, tanpa alasan

uncanny *adj* aneh, gaib, luar biasa

unceasing *adj* [ansising] tidak berkeputusan, selalu, senantiasa ← **cease**

uncertain *adj* [ansérten] tidak yakin ← **certain**

unchain *v* melepaskan ← **chain**

uncivilized *adj* [ansivilaizd] biadab ← **civilized**

uncle *n* [angkel] paman, om; ~ *Sam* Paman Sam, Abang Sam (Amerika Serikat); *great-*~ kakek

unclean *adj* tidak bersih, kotor ← **clean**

unclear *adj* kurang jelas ← **clear**

uncomfortable *adj* [ankamftabel] tidak enak, kurang nyaman ← **comfortable**

unconditional *adj* [ankondisyenel] mutlak, tidak bersyarat ← **conditional**

unconscious *adj* [ankonsyus] pingsan, tidak sadar; **uncon-**

sciously *adv* tanpa disadari ←
conscious

unconstitutional *adj* [ankonsti-
tyusyenel] tidak berdasarkan
undang-undang dasar, inkonsti-
tusional ← **constitutional**

uncontrollable *adj* [ankontrola-
bel] tidak terkendali ←
control

unconventional *adj* [ankonvén-
syenel] tidak biasa, di luar
kebiasaaan ← **conventional**

uncoordinated *adj* [anko
ordinéted] canggung, tanpa
koordinasi ← **coordinate**

uncover *adj* [ankaver] membuka
← **cover**

undated *adj* tak bertanggal ←
dated

undecided *adj* ragu-ragu, bimbang ← **decide**

undefeated *adj* tak pernah
terkalahkan ← **defeat**

under *conj* menurut; *prep* (di)
bawah; ~ *oath* di bawah
sumpah; ~ *repair* sedang diperbaiki; **underage** *adj* di bawah
umur; **underclothes** *n, pl*
pakaian dalam; **undercoat** *n*
lapisan dasar (cat); **undercover**
adj rahasia, menyamar; **under-
dog** *n* pihak yang lemah;
underdone *adj* masih mentah;
underestimate *v* meremehkan;
underfed *adj* kurang mendapat
makanan; **undergo** *v* **under-
went undergone** menempuh,
mengalami; **undergraduate**
adj, n sarjana muda; **under-
ground** *adj* (di) bawah tanah; *n*

the ~ kereta api bawah tanah
(di London); **undergrowth** *n*
semak-semak; di bawah pepo-
honan; **underline** *v* menggarisbawahi; **undermine** *v* merusak,
merongrong; **underneath** *adv,
prep* (di) bawah; **underpaid**
adj dibayar tidak selayaknya;
underpants *n, pl* celana
dalam; **underpass** *n* terowongan (di bawah jalan); **under-
privileged** *adj, n* kurang
mampu; **underscore** *n* tanda
_; *v* menggarisbawahi; **under-
secretary** *n* menteri muda;
undersigned *the* ~ yang tertanda tangan (ytt)

understand *v* **understood
understood** mengerti, paham;
memahami; **understanding**
adj pengertian; *n* pengertian,
pemahaman; *to come to an* ~
mencapai persetujuan; **under-
standable** *adj* dapat dimengerti, dapat dimaklumi

undertake *v* **undertook
undertaken** menjalankan,
melakukan

undertaker *n* pengurus jenazah

undertaking *n* usaha ← **undertake**

undertook *v, pf* → **undertake**

undertow *n* arus bawah ←
under

underwater *adj* [anderwoter]
(di) dalam air ← **under**

underway *adv* sedang berlangsung ← **under**

underwear *n* pakaian dalam ←
under

underworld *n* [anderwerld] dunia bawah tanah, dunia penjahat ← **under**

undesirable *adj* [andisairabel] tidak dikehendaki, tidak diinginkan ← **desirable**

undies *n, pl, coll* celana dalam ← **underwear**

undo *v* [andu] **undid undone** membuka ← **do**

undoubtedly [andautedli] tentu saja, tidak diragukan lagi ← **doubt**

undress *v* melepas pakaian ← **dress**

undying [andaying] ~ *love* cinta abadi ← **die**

unearth *v* [anérth] menggali; menemukan

uneasy *adj* [anizi] gelisah

uneducated *adj* [anédyukéted] tidak berpendidikan ← **educate**

unemployed *adj, n* [anemploid] pengangguran; **unemployment** *n* pengangguran ← **employ**

unenthusiastic *adj* [anenthuziastik] kurang antusias, tidak bersemangat ← **enthusiastic**

unequal *adj* [anikwel] tidak sama, tidak sederajat, tidak seimbang; **unequaled** *adj* tidak ada bandingnya, tiada tara ← **equal**

UNESCO *abbrev* United Nations Educational, Scientific and Cultural Organization UNESCO, Organisasi Persatuan Bangsa-Bangsa untuk Budaya, Ilmu Pengetahuan dan Pendidikan

uneven *adj* [aniven] tidak rata, bergelombang; tidak konsisten, tidak seimbang ← **even**

unexpected *adj* [anekspéked] tidak terduga; **unexpectedly** *adv* tiba-tiba ← **expect**

unexplained *adj* [aneksplénd] misterius, tidak diterangkan ← **explain**

unfair *adj* tidak adil, tidak jujur; **unfairness** *n* ketidakadilan, ketidakjujuran ← **fair**

unfaithful *adj* tidak setia, durhaka; menyeleweng ← **faithful**

unfasten *v* [anfasen] membuka (kancing, kait) ← **fasten**

unfit *adj* tidak sehat; tidak patut ← **fit**

unfold *v* menguraikan, membuka (lipatan) ← **fold**

unforgettable *adj* [anforgétabel] tak terlupakan ← **forget**

unforgivable *adj* [anforgivabel] tidak dapat dimaafkan ← **forgive**

unfortunate *adj* [anfortyunet] malang, sial; **unfortunately** *adv* sayang ← **fortunate**

unfounded *adj* tidak beralasan, tidak berdasar

ungracious *adj* [angrésyus] tidak sopan ← **gracious**

ungrammatical *adj* [angramatikel] tidak menurut tata bahasa, bukan bahasa yang baik dan benar ← **grammatical**

ungrateful *adj* [angrétful] tidak tahu berterima kasih ← **grateful**

unhappiness *n* [anhapines] kesedihan, rasa tidak bahagia; **unhappy** *adj* tidak bahagia, sedih; malang ← **happy**

unhealthy *adj* [anhélthi] tidak sehat ← **healthy**

UNICEF *abbrev United Nations International Children's Fund* Organisasi Persatuan Bangsa-Bangsa untuk Anak-anak, Organisasi Anak Sedunia

unidentified *adj* [anaidéntifaid] tidak dikenal; ~ *flying object (UFO)* piring terbang ← **identify**

unification *n* [yunifikésyen] pemersatuan, unifikasi ← **unify**

uniform *adj, n* [yuniform] (pakaian) seragam; *school* ~ seragam (sekolah)

unify *v* [yunifai] menyatukan, mempersatukan

uninhabitable *adj* [aninhabitabel] tidak dapat dihuni; **uninhabited** *adj* tidak dihuni ← **inhabit**

unintelligible *adj* [anintélijibel] tidak dapat dimengerti ← **intelligible**

uninterrupted *adj* [aninterupted] tidak terputus ← **interrupt**

uninvited *adj* [aninvaited] tak diundang ← **invite**

union *n* [yunien] persatuan, serikat, uni; ~ *Jack* bendera (Kerajaan) Inggris; *Soviet* ~ Uni Soviet; *trade* ~ serikat kerja

unique *adj* tunggal, unik, tiada duanya

unison [yunison] *in* ~ serentak, bersama

unit *n* [yunit] unit, satuan

unite *v* [yunait] bersatu, menyatu; menyatukan, mempersatukan; **united** *adj* bersatu, serikat; *(the)* ~ *Arab Emirates (UAE)* Uni Emirat Arab; *the* ~ *Kingdom (UK)* Kerajaan Inggris; *the* ~ *States (US), the* ~ *States of America (USA)* Amerika Serikat (AS)

universal *adj* [yunivérsel] umum, universal; **universe** *n* alam semesta

university *n* [yunivérsiti] universitas; ~ *student* mahasiswa

unjust *adj* tidak adil ← **just**

unkind *adj* [ankaind] kejam, bengis ← **kind**

unknowingly *adv* [an noingli] tanpa mengetahui; **unknown** *adj* tidak ketahuan, tidak dikenal ← **knowing**

unlace *v* membuka tali (sepatu) ← **lace**

unlawful *adj* tidak sah, terlarang ← **lawful**

unless *conj* (kecuali) kalau

unlike *adj* tidak seperti, tidak sama; ~ *me, Colin enjoys golf* tidak seperti saya, Colin suka main golf ← **like**

unlikely *adj* kemungkinan kecil; tidak dapat dipercaya; *an* ~ *story* cerita yang tidak dapat dipercaya ← **likely**

unlimited *adj* [anlimited] tak terhingga, tak terbatas ← **limited**

unlisted ~ *number* nomor telepon rahasia, nomor pribadi ← **list**

unload v membongkar (muatan), mencurahkan; **unloaded** adj kosong (senjata) ← **load**

unlock v membuka (kunci, gembok) ← **lock**

unlucky adj celaka, sial, malang ← **lucky**

unmade adj tidak diselesaikan, tidak dirapikan; ~ bed tempat tidur yang belum dirapikan; ~ road jalan yang belum diaspal ← **made, make**

unmarried adj [anmarid] belum kawin, tidak kawin, lajang ← **married**

unmask v membuka kedok, membuka topeng ← **mask**

unmentionable adj [anménsyenabel] tidak dapat disebut ← **mention**

unmistakable adj [anmistékabel] tidak dapat diragukan, jelas ← **mistake**

unmoved adj [anmuvd] tidak terpengaruh, tidak berubah ← **move**

unnamed adj [an némd] tidak dikenal, anonim ← **named**

unnatural adj [an natyurel] tidak wajar ← **natural**

unnecessary adj [an néseseri] tidak perlu, tidak usah ← **necessary**

unpack v membongkar ← **pack**

unpaid adj tidak dibayar, belum dibayar ← **pay, paid**

unpleasant adj [anplézent] kurang menyenangkan, tidak enak ← **pleasant**

unplug v mencabut ← **plug**

unprecedented adj [anprésedénted] belum pernah terjadi ← **precedent**

unpredictable adj [anprediktabel] tidak dapat diramalkan ← **predict**

unprepared adj [anprepérd] tidak siap, belum siap; tidak disiapkan, belum disiapkan ← **prepared**

unprintable adj [anprintabel] tidak patut ditulis (kata jorok) ← **print**

unprofessional adj [anprofesyenel] tidak profesional ← **professional**

unprofitable adj [anprofitabel] tidak menguntungkan ← **profitable**

unprotected adj tidak dilindungi; ~ sex hubungan seks tanpa alat kontrasepsi ← **protect**

unqualified adj [ankuolifaid] tidak berijazah, tidak memiliki kualifikasi ← **qualified**

unreal adj tidak nyata; **unrealistic** adj tidak realistis ← **real**

unreasonable adj [anriznabel] tidak masuk akal ← **reasonable**

unrelenting adj tak henti-hentinya ← **relent**

unreliable adj [anrelayabel] tidak dapat dipercayai, tidak dapat diandalkan ← **reliable**

unrest n kerusuhan

unripe adj mentah, kurang matang ← **ripe**

unroll *v* membuka gulungan ← **roll**

unsafe *adj* tidak aman, berbahaya ← **safe**

unsatisfactory *adj* [ansatisfaktori] tidak memuaskan ← **satisfactory**

unscrew *v* membuka sekrup, melepaskan sekrup ← **screw**

unsealed [ansild] ~ *road* jalan tanah ← **sealed**

unseeded *adj* [ansided] bukan unggulan ← **seed**

unseen *adj* tidak terlihat, tidak kelihatan ← **seen**

unselfish *adj* tidak egois, tidak mementingkan diri sendiri ← **selfish**

unskilled *adj* [anskild] tidak terampil, tidak mahir; ~ *labor* tenaga buruh ← **skilled**

unsolved *adj* [ansolvd] belum terbongkar ← **solve**

unspeakable *adj* [anspikabel] tidak terkatakan; sangat buruk ← **speak**

unstable *adj* [anstébel] goyah, tidak stabil; mudah tergoncang ← **stable**

unsteady *adj* [anstédi] tidak tegak, goyah ← **steady**

unsuccessful *adj* [ansaksésful] tidak berhasil, tidak lulus, gagal ← **successful**

unsuitable *adj* [ansutabel] tidak cocok ← **suitable**

unsuited *adj* [ansuted] tidak cocok ← **suit**

unsure *adj* [ansyur] tidak yakin, tidak pasti ← **sure**

unsuspecting *adj* tidak curiga ← **suspect**

unsweetened *adj* [answitend] tanpa gula, tanpa pemanis ← **sweeten**

untapped *adj* [antapd] belum dimanfaatkan ← **tap**

unthinkable *adj* [anthinkabel] tak terpikirkan, tak terbayangkan; **unthinking** *adj* tidak berpikir, membabi buta ← **think**

untidy *adj* [antaidi] tidak rapi, tidak teratur, jorok ← **tidy**

untie *v* [antai] membuka (tali), menguraikan ← **tie**

until *conj* sampai; *prep* hingga, sampai (dengan)

untimely ~ *death* meninggal sebelum waktunya ← **timely**

untouchable *n* [antacabel] paria, orang tanpa kasta, orang hina (di India); **untouched** *adj* tak tersentuh ← **touch**

untrained *adj* tidak terlatih, tanpa pendidikan ← **train**

untranslatable *adj* [antranslétabel] tidak dapat diterjemahkan ← **translate**

untrue *adj* [antru] tidak benar; **untruth** *n* [antruth] bohong, dusta; **untruthful** *adj* tidak benar, bohong ← **true, truth**

unusual *adj* [anyusyuel] tidak biasa, tidak lazim; **unusually** *adv* luar biasa, tidak seperti biasa ← **usual**

unveil *v* [anvél] membuka (selubung), memperkenalkan ← **veil**

unverified *adj* [anvérifaid]
belum diteliti kebenarannya ←
verify

unwanted *adj* [anwonted] tidak
diinginkan; ~ *pregnancy*
kehamilan (yang) tidak
diinginkan ← **wanted**

unwelcome *adj* [anwélkem]
tidak dikehendaki, tidak disam-
but ← **welcome**

unwell *adj* tidak enak badan ←
well

unwilling *adj* tidak mau, segan,
malas ← **willing**

unwind *v* [anwaind] **unwound**
unwound beristirahat;
melepaskan ← **wind**

unwise *adj* tidak bijaksana,
bodoh ← **wise**

unwitting *adj* dengan tidak
sengaja, tanpa disadari ← **wit**

unwound *v, pf* → **unwind**

unwrap *v* [anrap] membuka
(bungkus)

unwritten *adj* [anriten] tak tertulis,
tidak dituliskan ← **written**

unzip *v* membuka ritsleting ←
zip

up *adj* habis; bangun; naik; ~ *all*
night semalam tidak tidur;
what's ~? apa kabar? ada apa?;
~ *at dawn* dinihari sudah
bangun; *time is* ~ waktu sudah
habis; *adv* ke atas; naik; ~ *and*
down naik turun; mondar-
mandir; ~*s and downs* suka
(dan) duka; *prep* (di) atas; ke
atas; ~ *against* menghadapi; ~
front di muka; ~ *to* sampai;
sedang; ~ *to you* terserah

(anda); ~ *to no good* sedang
berbuat jahat; *what are you ~*
to? sedang apa?; ~-*to-date*
modern, terbaru, mutakhir;
~-*to-the-minute* terkini;
upbringing *n* asuhan, didikan;
upcoming *adj* [apkaming]
yang mendatang; **update** *n*
laporan terbaru; *v* memperbarui; **upfront** *adj* [apfrant]
terus terang, jujur; **upgrade** *n*
penataran; *v* menaikkan kelas;
uphill *adj* sulit, berat; *adv* ke
atas (bukit), menanjak; **uphold**
v **upheld upheld** menegakkan;
~ *the law* menegakkan hukum

upholster *v* melapisi (mebel)
dengan kain; **upholsterer** *n*
tukang pelapis mebel; **uphol-**
stery *n* kain pelapis atau bantal
di kursi, sofa dll

upkeep *n* perawatan, pemeliharaan ← **up**

upon *prep* [apon] (di) atas; *once*
~ *a time* sekali waktu → **on**

upper *adj* (tingkat) atas; tinggi;
~ *case* huruf besar; ~ *class,*
~ *crust* golongan atas; *to keep*
a stiff ~ *lip* tidak menangis ←
up

upright *adj* [aprait] tegak (lurus);
jujur ← **up**

uprising *n* pemberontakan ← **up**

uproar *n* kegaduhan, keributan
← **up**

uproot *v* menumbangkan, mencabut dari tanah ← **up**

upset *adj* tersinggung; tidak
tenang; terbalik; terganggu;
~ *stomach* sakit perut; *n* gang-

guan; *v* membuat tersinggung, mengganggu, merusak; ~*ting* membingungkan, menguatirkan

upside ~ *down* terbalik ← **up**

upstairs *adj* di (lantai) atas; *adv* ke (lantai) atas; *n* lantai atas ← **up**

upstream *adv* ke hulu ← **up**

uptake *quick on the* ~ cepat mengerti ← **up**

uptown *adv* ke kota bagian atas; *n* daerah perumahan, bukan di tengah kota

upturn *n* perbaikan, kemajuan; **upturned** *adj* terbalik; menengadah ← **up**

upward *adj* [apwerd] naik; *adv* (menuju) ke atas; ~*ly mobile* menuju tingkat sosial yang lebih tinggi ← **up**

uranium *n* [yurénium] uranium

urban *adj* [érben] perkotaan; ~ *renewal* peremajaan kota; ~ *sprawl* pertumbuhan (liar) perkotaan

urchin [ércin] *sea* ~ bulu babi

urethra *n* [yurithra] saluran kencing, saluran kemih

urge *n* [érj] dorongan; *v* mendorong, mendesak; **urgency** *n* urgensi, keadaan yang mendesak; **urgent** *adj* mendesak, penting, genting

urinal *n* tempat kencing (laki-laki); **urinary** *adj* [yurinari] berkaitan dengan air kencing; ~ *tract* saluran kemih; **urinate** *v* [yurinét] kencing, buang air kecil; **urine** *n* air kencing, air seni

urn *n* [érn] jambangan; perabuan; cerek

Uruguay *n* [Yuruguai] Uruguay; **Uruguayan** *adj* berasal dari Uruguay; *n* orang Uruguay

US *abbrev United States* AS (Amerika Serikat)

us *pron, obj* kita (termasuk lawan bicara); kami

USAF *abbrev United States Air Force* Angkatan Udara Amerika Serikat

usage *n* [yusej] pemakaian, penggunaan; **use** *n* [yus] pemakaian, penggunaan; *in* ~ masih dipakai, masih dipergunakan; *to make* ~ *of* memanfaatkan; *what's the* ~? apa gunanya? *it's (of) no* ~ tidak ada gunanya, percuma, sia-sia; *of* ~ berguna, bermanfaat; *v* [yuz] memakai, menggunakan; ~ *up* menghabiskan; **used** *adj* bekas (pakai); ~ *to* terbiasa; dulu; *Jane* ~ *to work in Nigeria* dulu Jane bekerja di Nigeria; *I'm* ~ *to children* saya biasa bergaul dengan anak-anak; **useful** *adj* [yusfel] berguna, bermanfaat; **useless** *adj* tidak berguna, sia-sia; tidak dapat dipakai; **user** *n* [yuzer] pemakai

USG *abbrev ultrasonogram* USG

usher *n* penjaga pintu (di teater atau bioskop), penerima tamu; *v* mengantarkan, memandu

USSR *abbrev Union of Soviet Socialist Republics* Republik Sosialis Uni Soviet usual *adj* [yusyual] biasa, lazim, lumrah; *as* ~ seperti biasa; *the* ~ yang biasa; **usually** *adv* biasanya ← **use**

usurer *n, arch* [yuserer] lintah darat; **usury** *n* riba

utensil *n* [yuténsil] alat (masak)

uterus *n* [yuterus] rahim, kandungan, peranakan

utility *n* [yutiliti] keperluan; *sport* ~ *vehicle (SUV)* mobil jip; **utilities** *n, pl* keperluan (air, listrik, gas); **utilize** *v* mempergunakan

utmost *adj* yang sepenuhnya; *n* sepenuhnya; *to the* ~, *to do your* ~ berusaha sekeras mungkin

utopia *n* [yutopia] negeri khayalan; **utopian** *adj* bersifat khayalan, tidak praktis

utter *v* mengucapkan, memanjatkan (doa)

utter *adj* **utterly** *adv* sama sekali

UV *abbrev ultra violet* ultraviolet

Uzbek *n* [Uzbék] bahasa Uzbek; orang Uzbek; **Uzbekistan** *n* Uzbekistan; **Uzbekistani** *adj* berasal dari Uzbekistan; *n* orang Uzbekistan

V

vacancy *n* lowongan; ada kamar; *no* ~ penuh; **vacant** *adj* kosong

vacate *v* mengosongkan

vacation *n* [vakésyen] liburan; *summer* ~ liburan musim panas

vaccinate *v* [vaksinét] memvaksinasi, menyuntik; **vaccination** *n* vaksinasi, pencacaran; **vaccine** *n* vaksin, benih cacar

vacuum *n* [vakyum] kedap udara, vakum; ~ *cleaner* pengisap debu, penyedot lantai; *v* mengisap debu, menyedot lantai

vagina *n* [vejaina] vagina, liang peranakan; ~ *discharge* keputihan

vague *adj* [vég] tidak jelas, samarsamar

vain *adj* bangga pada penampilan sendiri; *(in)* ~ sia-sia, percuma

valance *n* [valans] tirai pendek atau renda di bawah tempat tidur

valedictory [valediktori] ~ *dinner* makan malam sebagai acara perpisahan

Valentine [Valentain] ~*'s Day* Hari Kasih Sayang, Hari Valentin (tanggal 14 Februari)

valet *n, m* [valé] pelayan pria; ~ *parking* pelayanan parkir

valiant *adj* [valient] berani

valid *adj* [valid] berlaku, sah; ~ *reason* alasan yang kuat; **validate** *v* mengesahkan, memvalidasi; **validation** *n* pengesahan, validasi; **validity** *n* [validiti] masa berlaku; kebenaran

valley *n* [vali] lembah

valor *n* keberanian

valuable *adj* [valyuabel] berharga; mahal; *n, pl* barang-barang berharga; **value** *n* nilai; *good* ~ harga baik; *pl* norma, nilai; *of* ~ berharga; *v* menghargai, menilai

valve *n* [valv] klep, katup, pentil; *heart* ~ katup jantung

vampire *n* [vampair] vampir, drakula, pengisap darah; ~ *bat* sejenis kelelawar

van *n* mobil bagasi; gerbong; *luggage* ~ gerbong bagasi

vandal *n* perusak, orang iseng yang merusak sarana umum; **vandalism** *n* [vandelizem] kerusakan akibat orang iseng; **vandalize** *v* merusak sarana umum

vanilla *n* panili, vanili; ~ *essence* sari vanili

vanish *v* [vanisy] hilang, menghilang, lenyap; ~*ing cream* krim untuk menyamarkan noda

vanity *n* [vaniti] kebanggaan pada penampilan sendiri; ~ *set* wastafel yang dilengkapi kaca cermin dan lemari ← **vain**

vanquish *v* [vankuisy] mengalahkan

vantage [vantej] ~ *point* tempat peninjauan

Vanuatu *n* Vanuatu; *ni-*~ orang Vanuatu

vapor *n* uap; **vaporize** *v* menguap; **vaporizer** *n* alat penguap

variable *adj* [vériabel] berubah-ubah, tidak tetap; *n* variabel; **variation** *n* perubahan, variasi ← **vary**

varicose [varikos] ~ *veins* varises

varied *adj* [vérid] berbagai, berbeda-beda; **variety** *n* [varayeti] macam; keanekaragaman; ~ *show* acara dengan berbagai adegan atau pertunju-

kan; *a* ~ *of reasons* berbagai alasan; **various** *adj* [vérius] berjenis-jenis, bermacam-macam; ~ *things* berbagai hal ← **vary**

varnish *n* pernis; *nail* ~ cat kuku

vary *v* [véri] berubah-ubah, berbeda-beda; mengubah

vase *n* vas, jambangan

vasectomy *n* vasektomi

vaseline *n* vaselin

vast *adj* luas, besar sekali; **vastly** *adv* sangat, amat; **vastness** *n* keluasan

VAT *abbrev value added tax* PPN (pajak pertambahan nilai)

vat *n* tong

Vatican *the* ~ kediaman Sri Paus di Roma, Vatikan; ~ *City* Kota Vatikan

vaudeville *n* [vodevil] acara dengan berbagai adegan atau pertunjukan

vault *n* [volt] ruang bawah tanah

vault *n* kuda-kuda loncat; ~*ing horse* kuda-kuda pelana; *pole* ~ loncat galah; *v* meloncat (dengan galah)

veal *n* daging anak sapi

vegan *n* orang yang tidak makan atau memakai produk dari hewan

vegetable *adj* [véjtebel] nabati; ~ *oil* minyak sayur; *n* sayur; *pl* sayur-sayuran, sayur-mayur; **vegetarian** *n* [véjetérien] orang yang hanya makan sayur, orang vegetarian; **vegetation** *n* [véjetésyen] tetumbuhan, tumbuh-tumbuhan

vehement *adj* [viement] berapi-api, penuh semangat, dengan (suara) keras

vehicle *n* [viekel] kendaraan, wahana; *motor* ~ kendaraan bermotor

veil *n* [vél] kerudung, kudungan; jilbab; tudung; selubung; *to wear the* ~ berjilbab, berkerudung; *v* menyelubungi; **veiled** *adj* terselubung; berjilbab, berkerudung; ~ *threat* ancaman yang tersirat

vein *n* [vén] urat, pembuluh balik, vena

velocity *n* kecepatan, laju

velvet *adj, n* beludru, beledu

vendetta *n* dendam (secara turun-temurun)

vendor *n* penjaja, penjual; *street* ~ pedagang kaki lima

veneer *n* lapisan (tipis); *brick* ~ memberi lapisan batu bata pada rumah kayu

venerate *v* memuliakan

venereal *adj* [veniriel] ~ *disease (VD)* penyakit menular seksual (PMS)

Venezuela *n* Venezuela; **Venezuelan** *adj* berasal dari Venezuela; *n* orang Venezuela

vengeance *n* [vénjens] balas dendam ← **avenge**

venison *n* [vénison] daging rusa

venom *n* [vénem] bisa; **venomous** *adj* [vénemus] berbisa

vent *n* lubang angin; *v* melampiaskan; **ventilation** *n* ventilasi, peredaran udara, sirkulasi udara

ventricle *n* [véntrikel] kamar (jantung)

ventriloquist *n* [véntrilokuist] ahli bicara perut

venture *n* usaha; *joint* ~ usaha patungan; *v* mengambil risiko, memberanikan diri

venue *n* [vényu] tempat acara berlangsung

veranda, verandah *n* beranda

verb *n* kata kerja; **verbal** *adj* lisan

verdict *n* putusan

verge *n* pinggir; jalur hijau; *on the* ~ *of* di ambang

verification *n* verifikasi, pembuktian; **verify** *v* [vérifai] membuktikan, membenarkan

vermicelli *n* [vérmicéli] ~ *noodles* bihun, soun

versatile *adj* [vérsatail] berbakat dalam berbagai hal; serba guna

verse *n* [vérs] ayat; sajak, syair; pantun; bagian (dari sajak); ~ *from the Koran* ayat suci dari Alquran

version *n* [vérsyen] versi

versus (vs) *conj* lawan, melawan

vertebra *n* **vertebrae** [vértebré] tulang belakang, tulang punggung; **vertebrate** *n* binatang bertulang belakang

vertical *adj* tegak lurus, vertikal

vertigo *n* [vértigo] rasa takut pada ketinggian

very *adv* [véri] amat, sangat, sekali; benar, betul; *that* ~ *woman* perempuan itu juga

vessel *n* perahu, kapal; bejana; *blood* ~ pembuluh darah

vest *n* rompi; singlet

vet *n, coll* dokter hewan (drh) ← **veterinarian**

vet *n, coll* veteran; **veteran** *adj* [vétran] kawakan; *n* veteran

veterinarian *n* [véterinérian] dokter hewan; **veterinary** ~ *surgeon* dokter hewan

veto *n* (hak) veto; *v* memveto

VHF *abbrev very high frequency* VHF

via *prep* [vaya] lewat, via; melalui; *to Melbourne* ~ *Sydney* ke Melbourne lewat Sydney

viaduct *n* [vayadakt] viaduk; jembatan

vial *n* [vail] botol kecil

vibrant *adj* [vaibrent] berwarna terang; bersemangat; **vibrate** *v* bergetar; **vibration** *n* getaran, vibrasi; **vibrator** *n* alat penggetar, vibrator

vicar *n, Chr* [viker] pendeta; **vicarage** *n* [vikerej] rumah pendeta

vice *n* sifat buruk atau jahat; ~ *squad* polisi kesusilaan

vice- *pref* wakil, muda; ~-*consul* konsul muda; ~-*president* wakil presiden

vice ~ *versa* sebaliknya

vicinity *n* [visiniti] sekitar, dekat; *in the* ~ di sekitar

vicious *adj* [visyes] kejam, jahat; ~ *circle* lingkaran setan

victim *n* korban

victor *n* pemenang; **victorious** *adj* jaya, yang menang; **victory** *n* kemenangan

video [vidio] alat perekam kaset video; ~-*conference* konperensi jarak jauh; ~ *cassette recorder (VCR)* alat perekam kaset video; **videotape** *n* kaset video; *v* merekam pada kaset video

vie [vai] ~ *for* bersaingan

Vietnam *n* Vietnam; *South* ~ Vietnam Selatan; **Vietnamese** *adj* berasal dari Vietnam; *n* bahasa Vietnam; orang Vietnam

view *n* [vyu] pemandangan; pandangan, pendapat; *in* ~ kelihatan, tampak; *in* ~ *of* mengingat; *on* ~ dipertontonkan; *scenic* ~ pemandangan yang asri; *point of* ~ sudut pandangan; *v* melihat, meninjau; *with a* ~ *to* dengan maksud; **viewer** *n* pemirsa; **viewfinder** *n* lubang kecil untuk mengukur ruang di kamera; **viewpoint** *n* sudut pandangan

vigil *n* [vijil] berjaga; **vigilant** *adj* waspada, berjaga-jaga

vigor *n* [viger] tenaga, kekuatan; **vigorous** *adj* kuat, bersemangat

vile *adj* jorok, menjijikkan; buruk; keji, hina

villa *n* vila

village *n* [vilej] desa, kampung, dusun; ~ *chief* lurah, kepala desa; *my* ~ kampung (halaman); **villager** *n* orang desa

villain *n* [vilen] penjahat, orang jahat, bangsat

vine *n* tanaman anggur; tanaman merambat

vinegar *n* [vineger] cuka

vineyard *n* [vinyerd] kebun anggur

vintage *adj* [vintej] tulen; *n* kuno; tahun (anggur); *a 1934 ~* anggur hasil panen tahun 1934

vinyl *n* [vainel] plastik tebal

viola *n* biola alto

violate *v* [vayolét] melanggar; **violation** *n* pelanggaran

violence *n* [vayolens] kekerasan; *domestic ~* kekerasan di dalam rumah tangga; **violent** *adj* kasar; suka memukul; keras, hebat

violet *adj* [vayolet] ungu muda; *n* sejenis bunga berwarna ungu

violin *n* [vayolin] biola; **violinist** *n* pemain biola

VIP *abbrev very important person* orang yang sangat penting

viper *n* ular biludak, ular berbisa

viral *adj* *~ infection* infeksi akibat virus ← **virus**

virgin *n* [vérjin] perawan, gadis; *~ Islander* orang dari Kepulauan Virgin; *~ Islands* Kepulauan Virgin; *~ Mary* Perawan Suci; **virginity** *n* [vérjiniti] kegadisan, keperawanan

virtual *adj* [vértyuel] nyaris; maya; *~ reality* dunia maya; **virtually** *adv* nyaris

virtue *n* [vértyu] kebaikan, kebajikan; *by ~ of* berdasarkan, atas dasar; **virtuous** *adj* [vértyues] berbudi luhur

virus *n* [vairus] virus; *the AIDS ~* (virus) AIDS

visa *n* [viza] visa; *~ application* surat lamaran untuk visa,

aplikasi untuk visa

visibility *n* [vizibiliti] jarak penglihatan; **visible** *adj* [vizibel] kelihatan, tampak; **vision** *n* [visyen] penglihatan; visi; **visionary** *adj* [visyeneri] bisa melihat ke masa depan; *n* orang yang memiliki visi

visit *n* [vizit] kunjungan; *v* berkunjung; mengunjungi; *~ing hours* jam besuk; **visitor** *n* tamu, pengunjung; *~s book* buku tamu

visor *n* kaca penutup (di helm); *sun ~* pelindung (terik matahari)

visual *adj* [visyuel] berkaitan dengan mata atau penglihatan; *~ arts* seni rupa; **visualize** *v* membayangkan

vital *adj* penting sekali; **vitally** *adv* sangat, amat

vitamin *n* vitamin

vivacious *adj* [vivésyes] bersemangat, periang, gembira

vivid *adj* [vivid] hidup, jelas, terang

viz. yaitu, yakni

VJ *abbrev video jockey* VJ

VOA *abbrev Voice of America* VOA, siaran radio Suara Amerika

vocabulary *n* **vocab** *coll* [vokabuleri] kosa kata

vocal *adj* bersuara; berkaitan dengan suara; *~ cords* pita suara; *n* pembawaan lagu; *~s* pembawaan lagu; **vocalist** *n* penyanyi, vokalis

vocation *n* panggilan, pekerjaan; **vocational** *adj* kejuruan

vogue [vog] *in ~* sedang digemari

voice *n* [vois] suara; *in a loud ~* dengan suara keras; *~-over* pembacaan (dalam iklan); *to lose your ~* kehabisan suara; *v* menyuarakan, mengatakan

void *adj* tidak berlaku lagi; *null and ~* tidak berlaku; *n* kekosongan, kehampaan

volatile *adj* [volatail] tidak stabil, mudah menguap

volcanic *adj* [volkanik] berkaitan dengan gunung api; *~ ash* abu gunung berapi; **volcano** *n* [volkéno] gunung api, gunung berapi

volley *n* pukulan bola saat belum mulai jatuh; **volleyball** *n* bola voli; **volleyballer** *n* pemain (bola) voli

volt *n* volt; **voltage** *n* [voltej] tegangan listrik, voltase

volume *n* [volyum] isi, muatan, volume; jilid; *to turn down the ~* mengecilkan suara

voluntary *adj* [volentri] sukarela; **volunteer** *adj* sukarelawan; *v* menawarkan (jasa); menjadi sukarelawan

vomit *n* muntah; *v* muntah; *~ up* memuntahkan

voodoo *n* guna-guna; *~ doll* boneka yang ditusuki peniti dengan harapan seseorang akan menderita

vote *n* (pemungutan) suara; hak memilih; *~ of no confidence* mosi tidak percaya; *v* memberikan suara; memutuskan; memilih; **voter** *n* pemilih;

voting *n* pemungutan suara

vouch [vauc] *~ for* menjamin

voucher *n* [vaucer] vocer, bon

vow *n* janji; *marriage ~s* janji kawin; *Isl* ijab kabul; *to take a ~, to swear a ~* mengangkat sumpah; *v* bersumpah

vowel *n* [vaul] huruf hidup, vokal

voyage *n* [voyej] pelayaran, perjalanan lewat laut

vulcanologist *n* [valkanolojist] vulkanolog; ahli gunung api, ahli vulkanologi; **vulcanology** *n* ilmu gunung api, vulkanologi

vulgar *adj* [valger] kasar; tidak sopan; jorok

vulnerable *adj* [valnerabel] mudah diserang, rentan

vulture *n* [vultyur] burung nasar

W

wacky *adj, coll* nyentrik

wad *n* [wod] gumpal; *a ~ of gum* permen karet

waddle *n* [wodel] cara berjalan terseok-seok (seperti bebek), cara berjalan tergoyang-goyang; *v* berjalan terseok-seok

wade *v* berjalan dalam air; mengarungi; **waders** *n, pl* setelan celana plastik yang menyatu dengan sepatu

wafer *n* biskuit tipis; *~-thin* tipis sekali

waffle *n* [wofel] wafel; *~ iron* cetakan kue wafel; *v* cerocos, berbicara tanpa tujuan

wag *v* mengibas, mengibas-ibas; mengibaskan

wage *n* upah; *v* ~ *war* berperang

wager *n* taruhan; *v* bertaruh

wagon *n* [wagon] gerbong, kereta; *station* ~ mobil barang berpenumpang

waif *n* [wéf] anak terlantar; orang yang kurus kerempeng

wail *n* ratapan; *v* meratap

waist *n* pinggang; *--high* sepinggang, setinggi pinggang; *low-~ed* berpinggang rendah; **waistband** *n* karet pinggang; **waistcoat** *n* rompi; **waistline** *n* ukuran pinggang

wait *n* masa menunggu; penantian; *v* menunggu, menanti; ~ *for* menunggui, menantikan; ~ *on* melayani; *--list* memasukkan sebagai cadangan; *~ing list* daftar cadangan; *~ing room* ruang tunggu; ~ *and see* lihat dulu; **waiter** *n, m* pelayan; **waitress** *f* pelayan

wake *n* air alur kapal; selamatan sesudah upacara pemakaman; *v* **woke woken** membangunkan; ~ *up* bangun; membangunkan; **waken** *v* bangun; membangkitkan

walk *n* [wok] jalan-jalan, jarak yang dijalani; *the* ~ jalan cepat; *to go for a* ~ jalan-jalan; *v* jalan (kaki), berjalan (kaki); ~ *away*, ~ *out* meninggalkan tempat; ~ *the dog* membawa anjing jalan; ~ *someone home* berjalan kaki mengantarkan orang sampai di rumahnya; *~ing stick* tongkat; **walkabout** *on* ~, *to go* ~ mengembara, merantau; **walker** *n* pejalan kaki; **walkie-talkie** *n* woki-toki, HT; **walking** *adj* berjalan; ~ *stick* tongkat; **walkout** *n* aksi mogok; **walkover** *n* kemenangan mudah, w.o., menang telak

wall [wol] *n* tembok, dinding; *outer* ~ tembok; ~ *up* menutup dengan tembok, menembok; *--to-~ carpet* karpet yang menutupi seluruh lantai

wallet *n* [wolet] dompet

wallop *n, coll* [wolop] pukulan keras; *v* melabrak

wallow *v* [wolo] berkubang; ~ *in self-pity* mengasihani diri sendiri

wallpaper *n* [wolpéper] kertas dinding; *v* melapisi dinding dengan kertas

walnut *n* [wolnat] sejenis kenari

walrus *n* [wolras] singa laut

waltz *n* [woltz] vals; *v* berdansa vals; ~ *into* jalan dengan enteng

wan *adj* [won] pucat, lesu; pudar

wand *n* [wond] tongkat sihir

wander *n* jalan-jalan; *v* mengembara, berkelana, berputar-putar; ~ *off* pergi ke tempat lain; *her thoughts ~ed* pikirannya melayang

wane *on the* ~ sedang berkurang

want *n* [wont] keinginan; *v* ingin, menginginkan, menghendaki; membutuhkan, memerlukan; ~ *out* tidak mau bergabung; *for* ~ *of* karena tidak ada; **wanted** *adj* dicari; **wanting** *adj* kurang;

wants *n, pl* kebutuhan, keperluan; kekurangan

war *n* [wor] perang; ~ *correspondent* wartawan perang; ~ *crimes* kejahatan perang; ~ *cry* seruan perang; ~ *games* latihan perang; ~*-torn* hancur akibat perang; *to wage* ~ *on* berperang melawan, memerangi; *World* ~ *II* Perang Dunia Kedua; *the First World* ~ Perang Dunia Pertama

ward *n* [word] bangsal, ruang; wilayah

warden *n* [worden] pengawas, penjaga; sipir, juru kunci

wardrobe *n* [wordrob] lemari baju, lemari pakaian; koleksi busana

ware *n* [wér] barang; **warehouse** *n* [wérhaus] gudang

warfare *n* [worfér] peperangan, pertempuran, perjuangan; *guerrilla* ~ perang gerilya

warlike *adj* [worlaik] suka berperang

warm *adj* [worm] hangat, panas; ~*-up* pemanasan; *a* ~ *welcome* sambutan yang hangat; *v* memanaskan, menghangatkan; ~ *to* menjadi tertarik atau bersemangat; ~ *up* menjadi panas; menghangatkan (makanan); memanaskan (badan); **warmly** *adv* dengan hangat; **warmth** *n* panas, kehangatan

warn *v* [worn] memperingatkan; **warning** *n* peringatan

warp *n* [worp] *time* ~ percepatan waktu (ke masa lain); *v* membengkokkan, melengkungkan;

warped *adj* melengkung; kacau

warrant *n* [worant] surat kuasa

warranty *n* [woranti] jaminan, garansi

warren [woren] *rabbit* ~ sarang kelinci, lubang kelinci

warring *adj* sedang berperang ← **war**

warrior *n* [worier] pejuang, prajurit, kesatria

warship *n* [worsyip] kapal perang

wart *n* [wort] kutil

wartime *n* [wortaim] masa perang

wary *adj* [wéri] hati-hati, waspada

was *v, pf* [woz] → **be**

wash *n* [wosy] cucian; mandi; *car* ~ cuci mobil; *to have a* ~ mandi; *v* mencuci, membasuh; memandikan (orang); ~ *clothes* mencuci pakaian; ~ *dishes* mencuci piring; ~ *your hands* mencuci tangan; ~ *up* terhanyut; ~ *your hair* keramas, mencuci rambut; ~*ed up* habis, selesai; **washbasin** *n* tempat cuci muka, wastafel; **washcloth** *n* lap; **washer** *n* cincin karet, gelang karet; **washing** *n* cucian; ~ *machine* mesin cuci; **washout** *n* pertandingan ditunda atau dibatalkan karena hujan; kegagalan; **washroom** *n* kamar kecil, WC

WASP *abbrev* White Anglo-Saxon Protestant orang putih keturunan Inggris, beragama Kristen

wasp *n* [wosp] tawon

waste *n* [wést] sampah; keborosan; ~ *paper* kertas

bekas; *a ~ of time* membuang waktu; *v* memboroskan; membuang; **wasteful** *adj* boros; **wastepaper** *~ basket* tempat sampah

watch *n* [woc] jam tangan; jaga; *by my ~* menurut jam saya

watch *v* [woc] menonton; menjaga; *~ out* hati-hati, waspada; *~ over* menjaga, melindungi; **watchdog** *n* (anjing) penjaga; **watchman** *n* jaga, penjaga

water *n* [woter] air; *v* berliur; menyirami, mengairi; *~ bed* kasur air; *~ buffalo* kerbau; *~ heater* alat pemanas air; *~ level* permukaan air; *~ lily* (bunga) teratai; *~ polo* polo air; *~ pump* pompa air; *~-resistant* tahan air; *~ supply* pengadaan air, persediaan air; *~ table* permukaan air di bawah tanah; *~ wheel* kincir air; *~ wings* pelampung; *reticulated ~* air ledeng; *in hot ~* dalam kesulitan; *~ under the bridge* nasi sudah menjadi bubur; **watercolors** *n, pl* cat air; **waterfall** *n* air terjun; **waterfront** *n* tepi laut, tepi sungai, tepi danau; **watering** *~ can* cerek; **watermark** *n* cap air; **watermelon** *n* semangka; **waterproof** *adj* kedap air; **waters** *n, pl* perairan; *to break your ~* air ketuban pecah; **watershed** *n* daerah aliran sungai (DAS); **waterski** *n* [woterski] ski air; *v* bermain ski air; **watertight** *adj* kedap air, rapat; **waterway** *n*

jalan air; **watery** *adj* berair

wave *n* ombak, gelombang; *permanent ~ (perm)* keriting rambut; *sound ~* gelombang suara; *v* berkibar; melambaikan; *~ at* melambaikan tangan; **wavelength** *n* panjang gelombang; **wavy** *adj* bergelombang, berombak

wax *n* lilin; malam (untuk batik); **waxen** *adj* terbuat dari lilin

way *n* jalan; arah; cara; *~ out* (jalan) keluar; *one ~ (street)* (jalan) satu arah; *that ~* ke (arah) sana; *all the ~* sepanjang jalan; *on the ~* di perjalanan, sedang dalam perjalanan; *to give ~* memberi jalan; *to get your (own) ~, to have your (own) ~* menang sendiri

we *pron, pl* kami; kita

weak *adj* [wik] lemah; *~ tea* teh encer; **weaken** *v* melemahkan; **weakness** *n* kelemahan

wealth *adj* [wélth] kekayaan; **wealthy** *adj* kaya

wean *v* menyapih

weapon *n* [wépen] senjata

wear *n* [wér] **wore worn** pakaian; perlengkapan; *evening ~* busana malam; *v* memakai; *~ away* menjadi aus, tersusut; *~ out* menjadi usang; menjadi capek; *~ the veil* berjilbab, berkerudung

weary *adj* [wiri] letih, capek

weasel *n* [wizel] semacam musang

weather *n* [wéther] cuaca; *bad ~* cuaca buruk; *fine ~, good ~*

cuaca baik; ~ *forecast* prakiraan cuaca; *under the* ~ kurang sehat

weave *v* [wiv] **wove woven** bertenun; menenun; **weaver** *n* penenun, tukang tenun; ~ *bird* burung manyar

web *n* jaringan; rumah laba-laba; **website** *n* situs (di) internet

wed *v* nikah, kawin; **wedding** *n* (acara) perkawinan, pernika-han; ~ *cake* kue pengantin; ~ *dress* gaun pengantin; ~ *ring* cincin kawin

wedge *n* ganjalan; *v* mengganjal

Wednesday *adj, n* [Wénsdé] (hari) Rabu

weed *n* tanaman liar; gulma; *v* mencabut tanaman liar; menyiangi; **weedkiller** *n* obat pembasmi tanaman liar; **weedy** *adj* kurus dan kecil

week *n* minggu; **weekday** *n* hari kerja; **weekend** *n* akhir minggu, akhir pekan; *long* ~ libur tiga hari, libur empat hari; **weekly** *adj, adv* tiap minggu; mingguan; *n* (majalah) ming-guan

weep *v* **wept wept** menangis

weigh *v* [wé] menimbang; ~ *anchor* membongkar sauh; ~ *down* membebani; **weight** *n* berat, bobot; *to lose* ~ mengu-rangi berat badan; **weightlifter** *n* atlet angkat besi; **weightlift-ing** *n* angkat besi

weird *adj* [wird] aneh, ganjil

welcome *n* [wélkem] sambutan; *v* (mengucapkan) selamat datang

weld *v* mengelas; **welder** *n* tukang las

welfare *n* [wélfér] kesejahteraan; *on* ~ menerima tunjangan sosial dari pemerintah

well *adv* baik; sehat; *as* ~ (begitu) juga, demikian juga; ~-*behaved* berkelakuan baik; ~-*bred* tahu adat, sopan; ~-*built* kokoh; ~-*loved* tercinta; ~-*meaning* bermaksud baik, berniat baik; ~-*off* kaya, berada; ~-*preserved* awet muda; ~-*read* berpengetahuan luas; ~-*to-do* kaya, berada, mampu

well *n* (sumber) mata air, sumur

Welsh *adj* berasal dari Wales; *n* bahasa Wales; *pl the* ~ bangsa Wales

went *v, pf* → **go**

wept *v, pf* → **weep**

west *adj, n* barat; *south-*~ barat laut; *the* ~ (negeri-negeri) Barat; *the* ~ *Indies* Hindia Barat; **western** *adj* barat; **westerner** *n* orang Barat; **westernized** *adj* kebarat-baratan

wet *adj* basah, berair; ~ *nurse* ibu susu; *the* ~ *(season)* musim hujan; *v* **wet wet** membasahi

whack *n* [wak] pukulan hebat; *v* memukul dengan kasar

whale *n* [wél] ikan paus; **whal-ing** *n* pemburuan ikan paus

wharf *n* [worf] **wharves** dermaga

what *adj* [wot] apa; alangkah; ~ *a nice view* alangkah indahnya pemandangan ini; *interrog* [wot] apa; ~ *about* bagaimana den-gan, bagaimana kalau; ~ *for* untuk apa, mengapa; ~'s your name? siapa nama anda?; so ~ emang gue pikirin (sl); **whatever** adj apa saja, apa pun; **whatsisname** n [wotzisném] si anu; **whatsoever** adj apa saja, apa pun

wheat n [wit] gandum

wheel n [wil] roda; **wheelbarrow** n [wilbaro] kereta dorong, gerobak; **wheelchair** n kursi roda

wheeze v [wiz] mendesah, bernafas dengan susah

when conj [wén] ketika; bila, kalau; interrog kapan; **whenever** adv, conj [wénéver] kapan saja

where adv, conj, pron [wér] di mana; interrog di mana; **whereabouts** interrog [wérabauts] tempat berada, di mana; n tempat, lokasi

whereas conj [wéraz] sedangkan, padahal

wherever adv, conj [wéréver] di mana saja, di mana pun

whether conj [wéther] apakah

which conj, pron [wic] mana; **whichever** pron [wicéver] mana saja

while, whilst conj [wail] selama; saat, ketika; sedangkan; n waktu; once in a ~ sekali-sekali

whine n [wain] rengekan; v merengek

whinny n [wini] ringkikan; v meringkik

whip n [wip] cambuk, cemeti; v mencambuk, mencemeti; ~ped cream krim kocok

whir n [wér] deru, desing; v menderu, mendesing

whirl v [wérl] berputar, berpusar; **whirlpool** n pusaran air; **whirlwind** adj sangat cepat, kilat; n angin puyuh, angin beliung

whisk n alat kocok

whisker n [wisker] kumis; **whiskers** n, pl cambang, berewok

whiskey, whisky n wiski

whisper n [wisper] bisikan; v berbisik; membisikkan

whistle n [wisel] peluit; v bersiul

white adj [wait] (berkulit) putih; ~ bread roti tawar; ~ goods barang elektronik (yang besar); ~ lie dusta; ~ Russia arch Belarus; ~ trash orang kulit putih yang miskin; ~ wine anggur putih; egg ~ putih telur; ~-collar worker orang kantoran; ~ water rafting arung jeram; n (orang kulit) putih; **whiten** v memutihkan; **whitewash** n kapur; v mengapur

WHO abbrev World Health Organization Organisasi Kesehatan Dunia

who conj [hu] yang; interrog, pron siapa; **whoever** pron [huéver] barang siapa

whole adj [hol] seantero, seluruh, semua; lengkap, utuh; n semua, keseluruhan; **wholemeal** adj tepung terigu yang masih mengandung biji-biji; **wholesale** adj grosir, rabat; **wholly** adv sama sekali

whom pron, obj [hum] siapa

whooping [huping] ~ *cough* batuk rejan

whoops *ejac* [wups] aduh

whoopee *ejac* [wupi] hore

whopper *n, sl* [woper] sesuatu yang sangat besar

whore *n, derog* [hor] pelacur

whose *conj* yang; *pron, poss* [huz] milik siapa; ~ *coat is that?* Mantel siapa itu?; *the friend ~ car I bought* teman yang mobilnya saya beli

why *conj, interrog* [wai] mengapa; *ejac* nah; *he didn't know ~ it failed* dia tidak tahu mengapa gagal

WI *abbrev West Indies* Hindia Barat

wicked *adj* [wiked] jahat

wicker *adj* anyaman; ~ *chair* kursi (anyaman) rotan

wide *adj* lebar, longgar, luas; *adv* jauh, lebar; ~ *awake* sudah bangun (dan tidak mengantuk lagi); ~-*eyed* mata terbelalak; **widely** *adv* secara luas; **widen** *v* melebarkan, memperluas; **widespread** *adj* [waidspréd] tersebar luas

widow *n, f* [wido] janda (mati); **widower** *n, m* duda (mati)

width *n* lebar(nya) ← **wide**

wife *n* **wives** isteri; *coll* bini

wig *n* rambut palsu, wig

wiggle *v* [wigel] bergeliat, bergoyang; menggoyangkan

wild *adj* [waild] liar, ganas, buas; gila; ~ *animal* binatang buas; **wilderness** *n* [wildernes] hutan (belantara), gurun; **wildfire** *n* [waildfair] kebakaran hutan; **wildflower** *n* bunga liar; **wildlife** *n* [waidlaif] margasatwa, fauna; ~ *sanctuary* cagar alam

will *n* kehendak, kemauan; wasiat; *at* ~ sesuka hati; *political* ~ kemauan politik; *of your own free* ~ dengan sukarela; *where there's a* ~, *there's a way* kalau ada kemauan, ada jalan; *v* **would would** [wud] akan, mau, pasti, hendak; ~ *not (won't)* tidak akan, takkan; **willful** *adj* disengaja; **willing** *adj* rela, bersedia, sudi; *God* ~ insya Allah; **willingness** *n* kesediaan; **willpower** *n* kehendak

win *v* **won won** [wan] menang; memenangkan; memperoleh, mendapat; ~ *your heart* memikat hati

winch *n* derek, katrol, kerekan

wind *n* [waind] belok, belokan, belitan; *v* **wound wound** memutar, menggulung; membelit, membalutkan; ~ *up* berakhir; mengakhiri; *coll* meledek; ~ *a clock* memutar jam

wind *n* [wind] (mata) angin; ~ *power* tenaga bayu; *north* ~ angin dari utara; **windbreak** *n* penahan angin; **windbreaker** *n* jaket ringan; **windcheater** *n* sejenis switer yang terbuat dari katun

winding *adj* [wainding] berliku-liku, berputar-putar ← **wind**

windmill *n* kincir angin ← **wind**

window *n* [windo] jendela; ~ *box* pot kembang di jendela; ~ *frame* kusen jendela; *shop* ~ etalase; ~-*shopping* cuci mata; **windowpane** *n* kaca jendela

windpipe *n* batang tenggorokan ← **wind**

windscreen, windshield *n* [windsyild] kaca depan mobil; ~ *wiper* kipas kaca mobil ← **wind**

windsurfer *n* peselancar angin; **windsurfing** *n* selancar angin; *to go* ~ berselancar angin

windward *adj* di atas angin, arah dari mana angin bertiup; *the* ~ *Islands* Kepulauan Windward ← **wind**

windy *adj* banyak angin, berangin ← **wind**

windy *adj* [waindi] berliku-liku, berputar-putar ← **wind**

wine *n* (minuman) anggur; *white* ~ anggur putih; ~ *bar* tempat minum anggur; ~ *list* daftar minuman; **winery** *n* [waineri] kilang anggur, tempat pembuatan anggur

wing *n* sayap; sisi (panggung); *left*-~ bersayap kiri; **wingspan** *n* panjang sayap pesawat terbang

wink *n* kedip, kedipan; *forty* ~*s* tidur siang, tidur sebentar; *Dini didn't sleep a* ~ Dini sama sekali tidak tidur; *v* kedip, berkedip; mengedipkan mata

winner *n* pemenang; **winnings** *n* hasil kemenangan ← **win**

winnow *n* [wino] penampi; *v* menampi

winter *adj, n* musim dingin; *in* ~ pada musim dingin; *the* ~ *Olympics* Olimpiade Musim Dingin; **wintertime** *n* musim dingin

wipe *n* tisu basah; sapuan; *v* menyapu, menyeka, menghapus; ~ *out* menyapu bersih; menghapuskan; ~ *the board* menghapus papan; **wiper** *(windscreen)* ~ kipas kaca depan mobil

wire *n* [wair] kawat; *arch* telegram, surat kawat; ~ *cutters* tang potong kawat; ~ *netting* kawat kasa; **wireless** *n, arch* radio; ~ *operator* markonis; **wiring** *n* penggelaran kabel listrik; **wiry** *adj* [wairi] bersifat seperti kawat

wisdom *n* kearifan, kebijaksanaan; ~ *teeth* gigi geraham bungsu; **wise** *adj* arif, bijaksana; ~ *guy* orang yang sok tahu; **wisecrack** *n* lelucon

wish *n* keinginan; *best* ~*es* salam; *v* ingin, menginginkan; mengharapkan; **wishbone** *n* tulang garpu; **wishful** ~ *thinking* mengkhayal

wit *n* kejenakaan; orang jenaka; **wits** *n, pl* akal (budi); *at your* ~*'s end* kehilangan akal

witch *n, f* penyihir, tukang sihir; ~-*hunt* pemfitnahan atau pemburuan orang; **witchcraft** *n* ilmu sihir; **witchdoctor** *n* dukun

with *prep* dengan, bersama, serta; pakai; ~ *that* maka; *tea* ~

milk teh pakai susu; **withdraw** *v* **withdrew withdrawn** mundur, mengundurkan diri; menarik, mencabut; ~ *money* menarik uang, mengambil uang; **withdrawal** *n* pengunduran; penarikan (uang); **withdrawn** *adj* pendiam, suka menyendiri

wither *v* layu, kurus

withhold *v* **withheld withheld** menahan, menyembunyikan ← **with**

within *adv, prep* (di) dalam; ~ *a week* dalam waktu seminggu; ~ *this room* di dalam kamar ini ← **with**

without *prep* tanpa, dengan tidak ← **with**

withstand *v* **withstood withstood** *v* tahan; menahan, melawan ← **with**

witness *n* saksi; *to bear* ~ bersaksi; *v* menyaksikan

witty *adj* jenaka, lucu, bersifat menyindir ← **wit**

wives *n, pl* → **wife**

wizard *n, m* [wizerd] penyihir, tukang sihir; **wizardry** *n* ilmu sihir

wobble *n* [wobel] goyang, goyangan; *v* goyang, goyah; **wobbly** *adj* goyang

woke, woken *v, pf* → **wake**

wolf *n* [wulf] serigala; ~ *whistle* suitan; *to cry* ~ pura-pura memberitakan bahaya

woman *n* [wumen] **women** [wimen] perempuan, wanita; ~ *doctor* dokter wanita; *women's rights* hak-hak perempuan; *women's toilet* WC wanita

womb *n* [wum] kandungan, rahim, peranakan

won *v, pf* → **win**

wonder *n* [wander] keajaiban; ~ *drug* obat manjur; *no* ~ tidak mengherankan, pantas; *v* berpikir, berpikir-pikir; **wonderful** *adj* ajaib, mengherankan

won't *v, aux* takkan → **will**

wood *n* kayu; hutan; ~ *carving* ukiran kayu; ~ *pulp* bubur kayu; *touch* ~ semoga terkabul; **woodcut** *n* (lukisan dari) ukiran kayu; **woodcutter** *n* penebang kayu; **wooden** *adj* terbuat dari kayu; **woodland** *n* daerah hutan; **woodpecker** *n* burung pelatuk; **woods** *n, pl* hutan; **woodwind** ~ *instrument* alat musik tiup yang terbuat dari kayu; **woodwork** *n* prakarya, pelajaran memotong dan mengolah kayu

wool *n* wol, bulu domba; **woolen** *adj* terbuat dari wol; **woolly** *adj* terbuat dari wol, berbulu; tidak jelas

word *n* [wérd] kata; ~ *search* teka-teki mencari kata; ~ *for* ~ kata demi kata; ~ *of mouth* secara lisan; *lost for* ~s kehilangan kata; *in a* ~ secara singkat; *in other* ~s dalam perkataan lain; *not a* ~ tidak sepatah kata pun; *to eat your* ~s menarik kembali apa yang diucapkan; *to give your* ~ berjanji; *what's the Indonesian* ~? Apa Bahasa Indonesianya?;

wording *n* cara mengungkapkan, cara bertutur (spoken);
wordy *adj* panjang lebar
wore *v, pf* → **wear**
work *n* [wérk] pekerjaan, karya, kerja; kantor, tempat kerja; *at ~* sedang bekerja; di kantor; *hard ~* kerja keras; *out of ~* tidak bekerja, menganggur; *v* bekerja, berjalan, jalan; *~ at, ~ on* mengerjakan; *~ off* mengurangi; *~ out* menyusun, memecahkan; berolahraga; *~ up* menimbulkan; meningkatkan; *that old camera still ~s* kamera lama itu masih jalan; **workaholic** *n* orang yang gila bekerja; **workbook** *n* buku tulis; **worker** *n* pekerja, buruh; **workforce** *n* tenaga kerja; **working** *adj, n* bekerja; *~ class* kaum buruh, rakyat jelata; *~ holiday* bekerja sambil berlibur; *~ woman* karyawati; **workload** *n* beban kerja; **workman** *n* pekerja, tukang; **workmanship** *n* hasil kerja; **workout** *n* latihan; **works** *n, pl* pabrik; mesin; *Department of Public ~* Departemen Pekerjaan Umum (PU); **worksheet** *n* kertas tugas belajar; **workshop** *n* bengkel; **workstation** *n* meja kerja
world *n* [wérld] dunia, alam; planet; *~ record* rekor dunia; *~-class* berkelas dunia; *~-famous* terkenal di seluruh dunia; *~ Food Organization* Organisasi Pangan Sedunia; *~ War II*

(WWII) Perang Dunia Kedua; *to go around the ~* mengelilingi dunia; *it's a small ~* dunia ini kecil; **worldly** *adj* duniawi; berpengalaman; **worldwide** *adj* yang meliputi seluruh dunia
worm *n* [wérm] cacing, ulat; *how the ~ turns* betapa keadaan sudah berubah
worn *v, pf* → **wear**
worry *n* [wari] kekhawatiran, beban pikiran, urusan, kesusahan; *v* khawatir, merasa cemas; *~ about* mencemaskan; *don't ~* jangan khawatir; *no worries* tidak masalah
worse *adj, adv* [wérs] lebih buruk, lebih jelek ← **bad**; **worsen** *v* menjadi lebih buruk
worship *n* ibadah, pujaan, pemujaan; *v* memuja, menyembah; *place of ~* rumah ibadah
worst *adj, adv* [wérst] paling buruk, paling jelek, terburuk ← **bad**
worth *adj* bernilai, bermanfaat, berharga; *n* [wérth] nilai, harga, guna; *~ your while* berguna, bermanfaat; *it was ~ it* ada manfaatnya, ada hikmahnya; *not ~ mentioning* tidak pantas disebutkan; **worthless** *adj* tidak berguna; **worthwhile** *adj* berguna, bermanfaat; **worthy** *adj* layak; berguna
would *v, aux, pf* [wud] akan → **will**; *~-be* gadungan; calon, bakal; **wouldn't** *v aux, neg* [wudent] tidak akan, takkan
wound *n* [wund] luka; *stab ~* luka tikam; *v* melukai; **wound-**

ed *adj* terluka; *n* korban (luka)

wound *v, pf* [waund] → **wind**

wove, woven *v, pf* → **weave**

wow *ejac* [wau] wah

wrangle *n* [ranggel] pertengkaran, percekcokan; *v* bertengkar

wrap *n* [rap] semacam roti isi yang digulung; *cling* ~ plastik pembungkus makanan; *v* membungkus; ~*ped in* asyik dengan; ~*ping paper* kertas bungkus, kertas kado; **wrapper** *n* bungkus, pembungkus

wrath *n* [roth] murka

wreath *n* [rith] karangan (bunga); *olive* ~ karangan daun zaitun

wreck *n* [rék] rongsokan kapal karam; ~*ed* karam, tenggelam; *a nervous* ~ gila ketakutan; *v* merusak, menghancurkan; **wreckage** *n* [rékej] rongsokan, rosokan; **wrecker** *n* perusak; tukang bongkar

wren *n* [rén] semacam burung kecil

wrench *n* [rénc] *(monkey)* ~ kunci Inggris; renggutan; *v* merenggut; keseleo, terkilir; ~ *your ankle* pergelangan kaki keseleo

wrestle *n* [résel] pergumulan, pergulatan; *v* bergumul, bergulat; **wrestler** *n* [résler] pegulat; **wrestling** *n* [résling] gulat

wretched *adj* [réced] celaka, sial, buruk

wriggle *n, v* [rigel] geliat-geliut

wring *v* **wrung wrought** *v*

memeras; ~ *someone's hand* berjabat tangan dengan keras; ~ *someone's neck* mencekik; **wringer** *n, arch* [ringer] alat pemeras baju basah

wrinkle *n* [ringkel] (garis) keriput, kerut

wrist *n* [rist] pergelangan tangan; **wristwatch** *n* jam tangan

write *v* **wrote written** [rait] menulis, mengarang; ~ *down* mencatat, menuliskan; ~ *off* mencoret, menghapuskan; menghancurkan (mobil); ~ *to* menyurati; ~ *a letter* menulis surat; ~ *an essay* membuat karangan; **writer** *n* penulis, pengarang; **writing** *n* tulisan, karangan; ~ *desk* meja tulis; ~ *materials* alat tulis; ~ *pad* bloknot; ~ *paper* kertas tulis, kertas surat; *in* ~ secara tertulis; **written** *adj* tertulis

wrong *adj* [rong] salah, keliru; *n* kesalahan; *what's* ~? ada apa?

wrote *v, pf* → **write**

wrought *v, pf* → **wring**; ~ *iron* besi tempa

wrung *v, pf* → **wring**

WWI *abbrev World War One* PD I (Perang Dunia Pertama)

WWII *abbrev World War Two* PD II, PD ke2 (Perang Dunia Kedua)

X

xenophobia *n* [zénofobia] kebencian atau ketakutan pada orang asing

X-ray *n* [éksré] rontgen, sinar X; *v* merontgen, menyinar

xylophone *n* [zailofon] xilofon

Y

yacht *n* [yot] kapal layar, kapal pesiar; **yachting** *n* berlayar

yank *n* renggutan, sentakan; *v* merenggut, menyentak

Yank, Yankee *n, coll* orang Amerika (Serikat, terutama dari bagian utara)

yap *v* menyalak (anak anjing)

yard *n* ukuran panjang sebesar 0.9144 m; *back* ~ halaman belakang; *railway* ~s langsiran; **yardstick** *n* ukuran

yarn *n* benang (rajutan); *coll* cerita

yawn *v* menguap; terbuka lebar

ye *pron, arch, Chr* engkau

yea *arch, Chr* [yé] ya

yeah *sl* [yéa] ya, iya ← **yes**

year *n* [yir] tahun; *financial* ~ tahun buku; *last* ~ tahun lalu; *next* ~ tahun depan; *school* ~ tahun ajaran; *for* ~s bertahun-tahun; *Chinese New* ~ (Tahun Baru) Imlek; *New* ~'s *Eve* Malam Tahun Baru; **yearbook** *n* buku tahunan; **yearly** *adj* tahunan

yearn *v* [yérn] sangat ingin; rindu; ~ *for* merindukan; **yearning** *n* kerinduan, hasrat

yeast *n* ragi

yell *n* pekik, pekikan; *v* memekik

yellow *adj* [yélo] kuning; *sl* takut; ~ *Pages* buku (telepon) kuning; **yellowish** *adj* kekuning-kuningan

yelp *n* salak; *v* menyalak

yen *n* yen (mata uang Jepang)

yep *sl* ya ← **yes**

yes ya

yesterday *adv, n* kemarin; ~ *evening* tadi malam, kemarin malam; *the day before* ~ kemarin dulu

yet *adv* masih (belum); *as* ~ sampai sekarang, sehingga kini; *not* ~ belum; *conj* namun

Yiddish *n* bahasa Yahudi (dari Eropa Timur)

yield *n* [yild] hasil, produksi; *v* mengalah; menghasilkan

YMCA *abbrev Young Men's Christian Association* Asosiasi Pemuda Kristen

yodel *v* bernyanyi yodel; **yodeler** *n* penyanyi yodel

yoga *n* yoga

yogurt, yoghurt *n* yogurt

yoke *n* kuk, pasang; beban, penindasan; *v* memasang kuk

yolk *n* [yok] kuning telur

yonder *adv* di sana, di sebelah sana

you *pron* [yu] kamu, engkau; *form* Anda; *pl* kalian; ~ *all* kalian, anda sekalian; **you'd** anda akan ← **you would**; **you'll** anda akan ← **you will**

young *adj* [yang] muda; ~ *girl* anak gadis; ~ *man* pemuda; ~ *people* remaja, kaum pemuda; *coll* anak baru gede (ABG); ~ *woman* pemudi; *n* anak (binatang); **youngster** *n* yang muda

your *pron* -mu, kamu punya, milik anda, kepunyaan anda; **you're** kamu adalah ← **you are**; **yours** *pron, poss* milikmu, milik anda; ~ *truly,* ~ *sincerely,* ~ *faithfully* hormat kami; **yourself** *pron* **yourselves** engkau sendiri, kamu sendiri, Anda sendiri; *do it* ~ *(DIY)* kerjakan sendiri ← **you**

youth *n* [yuth] masa muda; kaum muda; ~ *center* gelanggang remaja; ~ *hostel* losmen; *in my* ~ waktu masih muda; **youthful** *adj* muda, belia

you've [yuv] kamu sudah ← **you have**

yowl *n* [yaul] meong, raung; *v* memeong, meraung

Yugoslav *n, arch* orang Yugo, orang Yugoslavia; **Yugoslavia** *n* Yugoslavia

Yule ~ *log* kayu yang dibakar saat Natal; **Yuletide** *n* masa Natal

yum *ejac* sedap, enak; **yummy** *adj* enak, sedap; *ejac* enak, nyam-nyam

Z

zany *adj* jenaka, lucu

zeal *n* semangat; **zealous** *adj* [zélus] bersemangat, giat

zebra *n* kuda zebra, kuda belang

zenith *n* [zénith] puncak, titik tertinggi

zephyr *n* [zéfir] angin sepoi-sepoi

zero *adj, n* [ziro] nol, kosong

zest *n* semangat, gairah, animo

zigzag *adj, v* berkelok-kelok, berliku-liku

zinc *n* seng

zip ~ *code* kode pos; **zipper, zip** *n* ritsleting, kancing tarik; ~ *up* menutup ritsleting

zither *n* semacam kecapi

zodiac *n* bintang, zodiak

zone *n* zona, daerah; *war* ~ daerah perang

zoo *n, coll* kebun binatang (bonbin); **zoological** [zuolojikel] ~ *gardens* kebun binatang; **zoology** *n* zoologi, ilmu hewan; **zoologist** *n* zoolog, ahli ilmu hewan

zoom *v* meningkat, meluncur; ~ *in* memfokuskan lebih dekat pada